Pedir info solve LAN_

The
Automated Factory Handbook

Technology and Management

The
Automated Factory Handbook
Technology and Management

David I. Cleland
Bopaya Bidanda

TAB Professional and Reference Books

Division of TAB BOOKS
Blue Ridge Summit, PA

Notices
MOST®   H. B. Maynard and Company Inc.

TPR books are published by TAB Professional and Reference Books, an imprint of TAB BOOKS. The TPR logo, consisting of the letters ''TPR'' within a large ''T,'' is a registered trademark of TAB BOOKS.

FIRST EDITION
FIRST PRINTING

Library of Congress Cataloging-in-Publication Data

Cleland, David I.
   The automated factory handbook : technology and management / by
David I. Cleland, Bopaya Bidanda.
     p.   cm.
   Includes bibliographical references.
   ISBN 0-8306-9296-7
   1. Production management—Data processing. 2. Manufacturing
processes—Automation. 3. Computer integrated manufacturing
systems. I. Bidanda, Bopaya. II. Title.
TS176.C54 1990
670.42'7—dc20   90-30673
                                          CIP

TAB BOOKS offers software for sale. For information and a catalog, please contact
TAB Software Department, Blue Ridge Summit, PA 17294-0850.

Questions regarding the content of this book should be addressed to:

   Reader Inquiry Branch
   TAB BOOKS
   Blue Ridge Summit, PA 17294-0214

Vice President & Editorial Director: Larry Hager
Book Editor: Barbara Ann Ettinger
Production: Katherine G. Brown
Cover Design: Lori E. Schlosser

Contents

Part III Controlling and Operating the Automated Factory

Acknowledgments

Many people helped in putting this handbook together. The review of these authors' credentials given on the first page of each chapter should convince the reader that truly a panel of experts have contributed their knowledge and time toward making this book a reality. We thank these chapter contributors.

We thank our graduate students at the University of Pittsburgh for their development of a bibliography on the automated factory and for the many discussions that we had with them on the strategy for the design and development of the book.

We especially thank Mr. Shriram Dharwadkar for his outstanding support in developing the book.

We are deeply indebted to Claire Zubritzky, who managed the administration in the design, development, and production of this handbook. As usual, her professionalism is unparalleled—she kept all of us on schedule and on quality—another example of her sustained outstanding performance in the School of Engineering at the University of Pittsburgh.

We also thank Dr. Harvey W. Wolfe, the Chairman of the Industrial Engineering Department, and Dr. Charles A. Sorber, Dean of the School of Engineering, who continue to provide us with the appropriate resources and environment to pursue our publication objectives.

David I. Cleland
Bopaya Bidanda
Pittsburgh, Pennsylvania

Introduction

U.S. manufacturers are currently facing their greatest challenge—to survive in an intensely competitive world market. Quality, productivity, cost, manufacturing efficiency, service, strategic planning, and implementation for the automated factory have become prime concerns of corporate management today. Concentrating on design, engineering, manufacturing, service, and meeting customer demands are just a few of the competitive conditions that contemporary manufacturers must face to survive and grow in the global marketplace. Corporate managers are finding that all of the systems involved in the conceptualization, design, manufacturing, delivery, and service of today's products require a change in their traditional methods of designing and implementing manufacturing strategy. Time has become one of the key performance parameters in meeting global competition. Hardware, software, organizational design, information technology, cultural factors, and the changing roles of both management and workers are posing challenges for corporate management that are unparalleled in our manufacturing legacy.

Over the past few years, there has been a tidal wave of interest in strategic planning for manufacturing, particularly in the context of the automated factory. The automated factory has to be planned, just as a company needs a business plan for its overall operations, a marketing plan for its customers' satisfaction, a research and development plan for the choices it faces in selecting and implementing the needed increments of technology into its factory, and a technology plan for the products and services it provides to its customers.

The sobering recognition is that all too many U.S. firms are being consistently beaten in both the domestic and world marketplace in the areas of process development and manufacturing implementation. Survival as a substantial manufacturing organization, both as an individual company, and collectively as an entire nation, requires the acquisition and use of new knowledge, skills, and attitudes by manufacturing managers, professionals, and workers.

Manufacturing strategies now require development from the systems perspective, starting with a definition and acceptance of the firm's manufacturing purpose followed by supporting plans and strategies for integrating the drivers of success in manufacturing: economy, quality, delivery, and responsiveness to change. Computer Integrated Manufacturing (CIM), MRP, JIT, TQM, Computer-Aided Design (CAD), CAM, CAE, and Flexible Manufacturing Systems (FMS) are all individual pieces of a medley that ties the automated factory together into an efficient and effective system capable of producing the products and services to sustain a competitive presence in the formidable world class manufacturing environment today.

New technologies have outdated some time-proven manufacturing management strategies. Product design teams, production teams, quality circles, union-management cooperative teams, project management teams—a few of the alternative organizational designs in use today—have altered the traditional authority and responsibility patterns found in the modern factory. The first-line supervisor's role has changed to a facilitator, rather than the classical "command and control" function. Workers are contributing to the management functions of planning, organizing, motivation, and control in a fashion and degree unheard of even a few years ago. Computer technology has had an awesome impact on the modern factory.

The motivation for the design and development of this handbook came from our disappointment in not finding a suitable text to reach a graduate course in manufacturing technology and management at the University of Pittsburgh. Many excellent articles and papers that described the individual elements of the modern factory existed, but a book that described these elements in a synergistic mode simply could not be found. This problem quickly became an opportunity for us to pull together the excellent articles and papers into a reference source for practical how-to-do-it information.

We believe that a manufacturing manager or professional who has a problem or opportunity with manufacturing management and technology can find the needed help in this handbook to make a substantial gain in improving the enterprise's manufacturing strategies. Even experienced manufacturing people who are faced with the challenge of keeping up with what is happening in their field by reviewing the current developments, and selecting those concepts and techniques that are most appropriate, will find this handbook useful. For the newcomer to the field of the automated factory, this handbook will provide a valuable source for self-study, and as a reference text for learning about different aspects of the factory of the future.

General managers, marketing managers, and other functional managers of the enterprise will also find this handbook a suitable reference. It will help them gain an appreciation of the technical and managerial considerations facing the enterprise that elects to use the automated factory in the design and execution of its strategies.

This handbook presents practical explanations and descriptions by leading authors and experts in the field of the concepts, tools, and techniques of operating the automated factory. The most useful approaches have been filtered from the abundance of the literature that has dominated the manufacturing discipline in the last several years. The authors of select literature in this field were asked to prepare their chapters by drawing on their previous writings and experiences yet still remain within the overall framework of the handbook. The handbook thus has become a practical guide to factory and manufacturing planners, managers, professionals, and other people in the enterprise who have a stake in the automated factory.

Management of the automated factory lies with senior managers as well as the traditional factory managers and professionals. The strategic implications of investing in an automated factory are awesome considering the capital, people, and supporting systems required. To not invest in automated factory technology and management is to run the inevitable long-term risk of being replaced by a competitor who has made strategic investments in the factory of the future. The processes and techniques of the automated factory are no longer esoteric methodologies that are the sole province of an elitist group of specialists. Rather the concepts, processes, and techniques of the automated factory will become part of the work-a-day world of those contemporary managers who require competitive manufacturing to survive in the global marketplace. Thus, real-world people, trying to survive in a competitive manufacturing market, will find that this book satisfies their needs for a reference handbook in the field. This book is for practitioners and all ''students'' of the automated factory who need an integrated reference source that will provide access to the latest thinking in the field.

The topic content of the handbook is broadly designed to be germane to the context in which the automated factory exists. The basic dichotomy of *Management and Technology* of the handbook provides for a further breakdown of the relevant topics: ''Part I, Automated Manufacturing: A Managerial Perspective'' presents the major management considerations involved in successfully managing the automated factory. Part II, ''Planning and Design Issues in the Automated Factory,'' discusses the key considerations in planning for the automated factory. Part III, ''Controlling and Operating the Automated Factory,'' is devoted to methods of monitoring, evaluating, and controlling the automated factory.

[Handwritten notes:]

"MANUFACTURING SYSTEMS" STRATEGY, TECHNOLOGY, ENGINEERING & MANAGEMENT" (THE AUTOMATED FACTORY) 1991

Estrategia, Tecnología, Ingeniería y Dirección de Sistemas de Manufactura"

DIAGNOSTICS
STRATEGY ✓
MANAGEMENT
TECHNOLOGY ✓

TECNOLOGÍA DISPONIBLE

Tecnología existente (Estrategia a adoptar) Requerimiento de producción

Project Mgmt,
ENGINEERING ✓ (the project)
(Project Mgmt).

Ingeniería de diseño, implementación y puesta en marcha

STEM

MANAGEMENT ✓
(Planning, Operation, Control)

Dirección

T
S E m

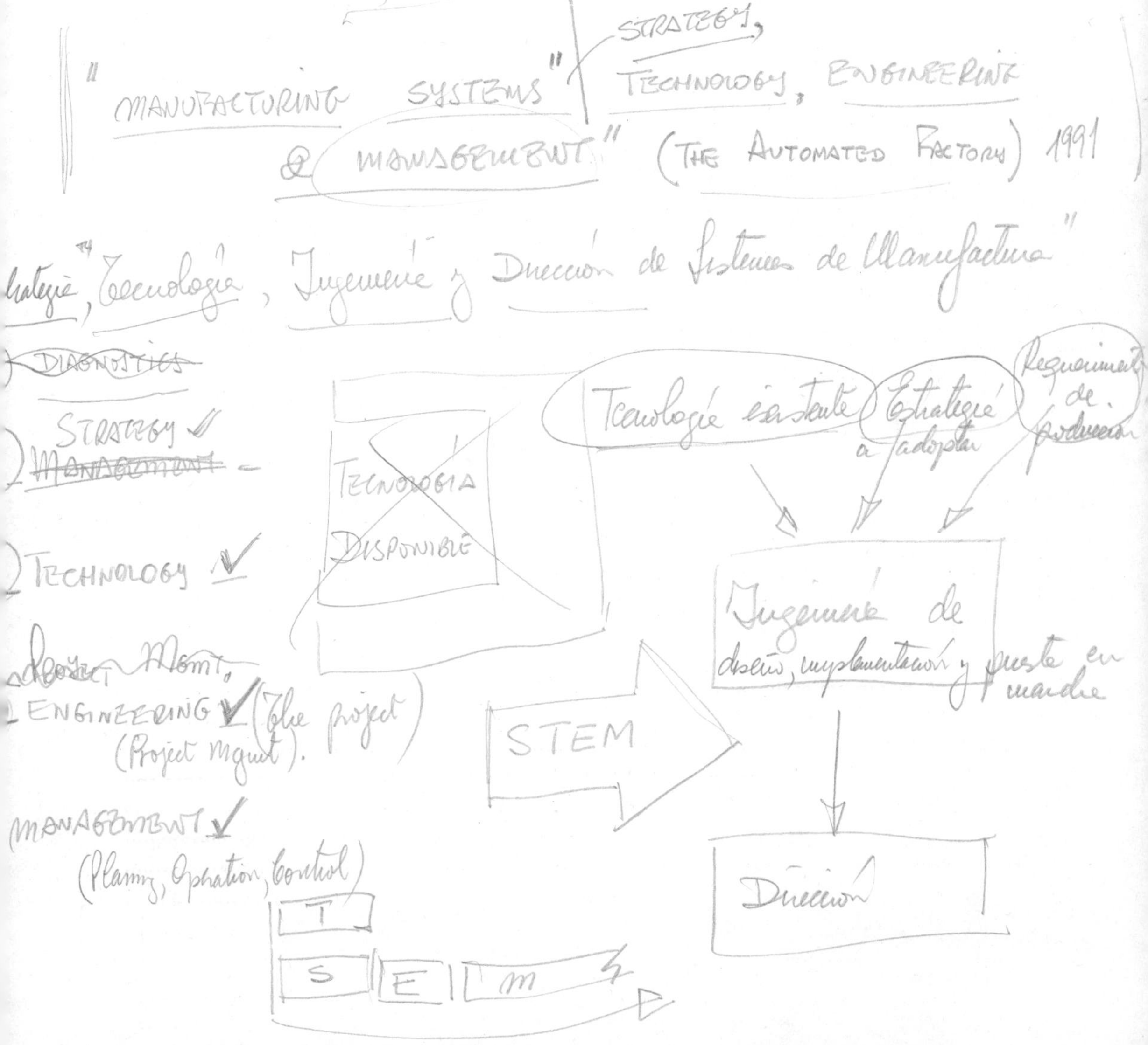

Part I

Automated Manufacturing
A Managerial Perspective

IN CHAPTER 1, HOMER J. HAGEDORN DISCUSSES THE MANAGEMENT AND ORGANIZATION OF people in the automated factory. He opines that computerized factory automation lags far behind its potential because of a set of human and organizational hang-ups. Where these problems are confronted openly and objectively, progress is made. The author presents the salient features of the management and organization of people within a cultural vision for the automated, integrated factory.

No one doubts that the automated factory requires significant changes in both management and technology. The production supervisor's role has undergone a remarkable change in the last decade. These changes will accelerate as we near the twenty-first century. The supervisory function will change from that of being ''in charge'' to that of a ''facilitator'' who provides the people with the resources required to do the job, and who works with the production people in coordinating, communicating, and resolving the conflict in the use of resources to accomplish the production objectives and goals. In chapter 2, Joel C. Polakoff gives an informed overview of the present and the future role of the new production supervisor-facilitator.

In chapter 3, Jerry Banks takes you into the world of quality management, an increasingly important aspect of world class manufacturing. The author warns that the achievement of quality involves humans and has proven to be one of the most difficult managerial tasks in the automated factory. After this warning, he provides a meaningful definition of the management of quality and then analyzes three important aspects of this activity: quality engineering, strategic management of quality, and management programs for quality.

Quality circles have found many uses in today's business organizations. The results have been mixed. As a participative process that integrates sociotechnical factors, a quality circle can facilitate the implementation of major technological changes such as automated manufacturing. In chapter 4, Larry R. Smeltzer and Karen J. Gritzmacher provide meaningful insight into the advantages and disadvantages of quality circles, as well as a prescription on how to best use such organizational mechanisms to improve the efficiency and effectiveness of the automated factory.

In chapter 5, Hans J. Thamhain, a noted project management expert, explains the use of proven project management techniques from other fields in the manufacturing environment. He describes the organizational alternatives for project management, methods of organizing the team, and the application of project management tools and methods. He concludes by discussing the organizational interfaces brought about by using the project approach and the role of leadership in making such teams effective.

In chapter 6, Karen M. Bursic explores the use of production teams composed of 5 to 15 works who have a high degree of responsibility and authority in dealing with manufacturing problems and opportunities. Her analysis includes an assessment of the extent of use of such teams in American industry and some of the benefits and problems to be considered in the use of such teams. She concludes that the team structure in manufacturing has had a tremendous impact on the policies, practices, and procedures within the manufacturing organization.

James V. Jones provides, in chapter 7, insight into the emerging use of integrated logistics support concepts and processes in the modern factory. An expert in this field, he draws from his vast experience in logistics systems to present an explanation and suggested strategy on how the manufacturing manager can improve effectiveness and efficiency through the use of such concepts and processes. A careful perusal of Jones' chapter will provide manufacturing managers and professionals with an exciting insight into an important field of innovation in modern manufacturing.

The introduction of automated technologies into the factory usually raises some strategic issues for the enterprise. In chapter 8, Jack Byrd, Jr., looks at the role of strategic issues and strategic planning in the automated factory. He provides guidelines on how automation can be incorporated into the strategic plan. His chapter outlines the strategic questions that should be asked in considering automation issues. He concludes that the impact of automated technologies on the strategic direction of a business must be carefully considered.

Gary N. Chaison's chapter 9 provides penetrating insight into the influence of collective bargaining and unionism on the automated factory. He presents an overview of the trends in unionism and assesses their importance in general and in manufacturing concerns undergoing major technological change. He sees a role for unions and collective bargaining in the automated factory, and that joint union and management collaboration in dealing with introduction and impact of new technology can be a major step toward a new system of industrial relations.

In chapter 10, Klaus Weiermair states that the first factor that determines the level of automation and consequences for work organization is found in a firm's general strategy. Each strategy then, according to the author, has different implications for work organization. From this perspective he provides a description of worker incentives and automation in manufacturing.

In chapter 11, Daniel E. Whitney describes the use of product design teams as one element in the strategic approach in manufacturing. By drawing on the strategies already in use in some U.S. and many Japanese companies, he presents their approach in raising productivity both by integrating their design and manufacturing functions and modifying their manufacturing institutions. In his conclusions he states, "...the advantages of applying advanced technology can be achieved only through this integrated approach."

John H. Manley, in chapter 12 on managing software in the automated factory, focuses on one category of software: that contained in information systems. Manley believes that information systems represent the largest software cost in any enterprise, especially the automated factory. In addition, this class of software is one of the most difficult to manage. He concludes that all managers—from the CEO down to the lowest supervisor in the automated factory—must learn to use this important asset of information systems software.

In chapter 13 on maintenance management, Andrew K.S. Jardine deals with four primary issues: organization structure, component/system replacement, machine inspection, and information systems as related to maintenance. He describes various replacement policies within the context of component and capital equipment replacement. The model of manpower planning for maintenance will prove especially useful, since there is often a tendency to understaff maintenance departments. A broadbased methodology for developing an information system for maintenance is also detailed.

The Management and Organization of People in the Automated Factory

Dr. Homer J. Hagedorn*

WHATEVER THE RELATIVE SUCCESS IN GERMANY OR Japan of integrated computerized factory automation, we in the United States are having our problems. The glimmerings we had in the early 1980s, that informated automation was just our kind of technology fix, have not yet quite come true.

Maybe the difficulty lies entirely in the technologies—complex, cranky, and costly. But there is at least one other possibility: people problems. I, for one, am convinced that computerized factory automation lags far behind its potential because of a set of human and organizational hang-ups. Where these management problems are being confronted, progress—sometimes spectacular—has been made. Elsewhere, progress is sooner or later stalled, or not even attempted; such is the power of these management obstacles.

This time around, it is not machine wrecking that is in the way; it is managerial resistance. When managers begin to learn what is actually involved in informated automation, they intuitively recognize a basic problem with it for themselves. Computer integrated manufacturing does not seem practical to them, they say. I think what they are sensing—and quite accurately as far as their vision takes them—is an abyss of fundamental, wrenching change so deep it seems to threaten the very basis of control, orderliness, and even managerial legitimacy.

Understandably, the prospect of such fundamental change is not very alluring. It is probably even less attractive because it is still so vaguely understood. The prospect of vaguely understood but fundamental change is particularly unwelcome in manufacturing. Even incremental changes in a manufacturing process can be maddening to manage when they cross functional or departmental lines. What is in prospect here is something much more basic and transformational, and not at all limited and incremental.

PROSPECTIVE AUTOMATED INTEGRATION: The Managerial Bind

For middle managers in manufacturing companies, the prospect of informated automation creates a dilemma. If automated integration turns out to be workable and they have not embraced it, they

---

*Homer Hagedorn is an organization development specialist with over 24 years experience at Arthur D. Little, Inc., the international consulting and research firm. He is an editor of the *Journal of Management Consulting*. He received his Ph.D. at Harvard University in 1955.

risk potential obsolescence, both for themselves and their companies. If they do embrace the new technologies, they risk opening Pandora's box. They risk an apparently endless unraveling and respinning of the threads that have held their organizations together and have made those organizations work. Threads that run deep and far. Threads that run far beyond the territory of any one middle manager—and actually beyond the scope of middle management as a whole because some of the threads run upward into higher management. Either aspect of the dilemma—obsolescence or pandemonium—forces responsibilities on middle managers they cannot handle. It is altogether too easy to understand why many middle managers are simply shrugging their shoulders. The dilemma is too much for them.

At higher levels, the dilemma is a different one. Senior managers cannot openly oppose automated integration. I have been told by dozens of such managers, "Computer integration is inevitable." There has been too much hype, and the case for integration is too strong for them to deny it. Senior managers may claim not to know when, how, or where to implement automated integration in manufacturing, but they know integration must come. So the dilemma for senior managers is not the choice between yes and no; but the choice between the whole hog or a few bites at a time.

If upper management forges ahead with the integrating technologies, despite middle management's reluctance, lack of confidence in success, and lack of know-how, there are enormous risks. To begin with, upper management must assume responsibility for changes in the managerial environment that are sure to accompany the decision to integrate. These changes carry major risks, including immense amounts of senior management time to establish new work flows, politics, boundary settlements, career paths, and maybe a basic rearrangement in pecking order. If middle management is resistant and not able to guarantee to upper management the success of the transformation, the risks are all the higher. (In all too many cases, of course, trust levels between senior and middle

management are so low and the press of current business so great, that the prospect of integrated manufacturing has not yet been explored much beyond the exchange of superficialities and biases.)

The prospect of breaking into integration a few bites at a time is no more pleasant to senior managers than the whole hog approach. Installing the new technologies piecemeal either creates isolated islands of automation hard to hook up with anything else (which does not make much of a case for the feasibility of integration), or yields results so slowly that benefits are scarcely discernible. In fact, there might be no results apparent by the time the senior manager's next job transfer is normally scheduled.

Let's sum up the situation. The prospects of making it to the promised land of Integration by direct confrontation are not very promising. It is no wonder integration is being pursued no more wholeheartedly than it is. Pilot projects are still being enthusiastically undertaken, but somehow do not lead to the speedy replication and extension that was expected.

This chapter is part of the adventure of figuring out what to do under the circumstances. Those who have tried integration or have thought about it know that: (1) the pathway to automated integration is a rocky one, and (2) no good model exists to indicate what full integration will be like when we get there.

People hang back a little under such conditions. It took a whole generation for the pioneers emerging from the woodlands north of the Ohio River to become willing (or really able) to move out bravely and settle the rich lands under the bright sun of the Grand Prairie of Illinois. We may not have that much time.

This chapter is devoted to understanding what we already know about manufacturing integration, organizationally and managerially speaking. It is an attempt to interpret the meaning of the clues we have so far, so that those beginning on the pathway toward automated integration will be better able to figure out where they are going and better able to profit from what they see others doing.

Interestingly enough, the best clues probably

do not come from the thousands of computer-integrated manufacturing (CIM) pilot projects that were established during the mid-1980s. Large as many of these projects were, they were still not big enough (expenditures of tens of millions of dollars per project have not been uncommon). They did not often affect enough different elements of manufacturing operations. They have not penetrated deeply enough into the lives and workings of their companies.

The few companies that have really learned by doing are not talking about automated integration. Instead, they attribute their restored success to a new generation in top management, or to massive redesign of their products—improvements that can be accomplished only by people of very unusual talents. Media reports make little or no mention of how these companies have actually spent the hundreds of millions of dollars they have invested since the early 1980s. They have, in fact, put a lot of money into making the new manufacturing technologies work in an integrated way. These improvements in technology integration are also hard to come by, but they require genius and inspiration only in the management of large-scale sociotechnical change. Without taking anything away from the astuteness of their executives or their product engineers, successful companies still would not be winning out over world-class competition if their manufacturing capabilities had not also been sharply upgraded.

GRADUAL STEPS TOWARD INTEGRATION

Managers may no longer need to directly confront the issue of overall integration, for another route now exists. This new route somewhat reduces the risks. It makes it possible to tackle some of the people problems first, thereby deferring massive investments in computers and communications, materials handling, and robots and manufacturing cells. Real integration naturally flows from intense work in implementing such methods as *total quality, statistical process control, just in time, design for manufacturability,* and *concept to customer.*

Different Methods: Similar Characteristics

These and other methods shift the consciousness of people in manufacturing industries, instill necessary new skills, and provide a set of powerful new goals toward which to work. Different as these methods are in origins, applications, and intentions, they do share similarities. Each of these systems inculcates managers and working level people to do the following:

- Embrace common purposes, attitudes, philosophies, terminologies, and productivity-related goals
- Take a highly organized approach built around team spirit and teamwork skills
- Rethink the work process; simplify by identifying what the work elements are, how each step relates to all others, and what can be eliminated
- Analyze the work process for root causes of quality, cost, or lead time problems
- Apply quantitative techniques to ascertain how much improvement is available and whether or not it is achieved
- Develop the new communications paths necessary for overcoming barriers to cost, lead time, and quality improvement
- Soft-pedal organizational, cultural, staffing, and other people-related problems until their causal significance is clear and until many of the necessary new working patterns become obvious
- Allow interaction between managers and working level people to lead to decisions about how and when to convert growing organizational pressures into processes or organizational change

Benefits of Gradual Change

The kinds of change processes implied by the common factors listed above are more workable than a head-on confrontation with the need to integrate. Gradual changes through these processes put initial emphasis on what needs to be improved and why, which in turn makes things simple enough to become manageable. In contrast, integration pursued directly is all too often perceived to be integration for its own sake.

These change processes create common understanding, enthusiasm, and commitment around specific and concrete goals, the accomplishment of which are inherently manageable. In contrast, a direct onslaught on integration often seems very abstract.

Furthermore, these processes start with what exists as the point of departure, an approach that fits the instincts of manufacturing people better than starting with an abstraction about the future. In contrast, integration as an idea comes across somehow as ignoring existing reality.

When management employs these processes literally everyone comes to understand the productive process from a similar perspective and uses the same terms. This in turn leads to creating a natural common vision of the future. In contrast, the effort needed to bring people to common understandings around the concept of integration seems to fuel any and all existing organizational paranoia, and for awhile actually delays the development of a workable vision.

All these change processes lead to *organizational integration*. This is a condition in which most members of an organization are deeply and specifically aware of how the whole affects the parts and how the parts affect one another, and in which the key information flows needed to control organizational activities are firmly established. Successful installation of one or more of the process-improving approaches to manufacturing and materials handling creates a perfectly lovely environment in which to begin large-scale computerized automation!

ORGANIZATION CONCEPT AND STRUCTURE

We are at a point where we know in a conceptual and intellectual sense much of what we need to know in order to take full advantage of the new technologies. We just are not using all we know. We have not got it all together. There is no orthodoxy. We know that taking full advantage of the new technologies requires rethinking and revising structure,

culture, and staffing. Those few who have gone through it know that it is possible to move a long way in one large leap—but your heart will be in your mouth while you are airborne. Those who are trying to tackle quality and productivity problems by installing comprehensive productivity and quality-oriented management systems seem to be on a promising pathway toward integrated manufacturing. Once they arrive at a sharply upgraded level of organizational integration, they will find using the new manufacturing technologies much easier.

We do not yet have a very good picture of what organizational integration will be like. The rest of this chapter lays out some of that picture.

Loosening the Framework

Even in early stages of implementation, the new manufacturing technologies require loosening up the organization. While extensive use of product and other multifunctional teams sometimes is enough to overcome the handicaps inherent in functional boundaries, it often turns out to be necessary to dissolve or combine previously distinct groups, such as:

- Product engineering and manufacturing engineering, to make such systems as computer-aided design and manufacturing (CAD/CAM) truly productive in enabling product and process to fit one another
- Manufacturing engineering and information systems, to enable confrontation of standardization, prioritization, and the issue of who is in charge of reality
- Shop floor maintenance organizations based on individual trades such as electricians and mechanics, to adapt to the integrated nature of the equipment embodying the new manufacturing technologies
- Shop floor workers and first line supervisors, to reduce costs and improve operational decision making

Until there is a shared and credible integration vision, putting together any of these combinations is a tough sell. Combining some or many of the elements of manufacturing engineering and of the manufacturing-oriented parts of information systems is probably the toughest and most crucial of all because each side all too often feels it cannot lose in this conflict without risking the eventual loss of its ability to carry out its vital functions.

The point is that the functional principle for organizing simply has to be toned down as integration proceeds. Functional or disciplinary groups may still need to exist in order to ensure professional integrity, standards, and access to new developments in the outside world. If they do remain, they will be heavily overlaid by matrixing, product/project teams, or extensive staff rotation schemes. In those cases where functional organization can completely disappear, it will be replaced by off-line professional practice groups and highly developed programs for periodic retraining or restaffing to ensure up-to-date professional input. Bureaucratically defined occupations and functions—autonomously organized to carry out successive steps on a production treadmill, such as polishing departments and packaging departments—will almost certainly become rarities.

Automated information is the driver that diminishes the utility of the functional organizational principle. Integrated manufacturing ultimately implies the capability to collect or to deliver only the information needed at precisely the right time and place to enable the right things to happen next in the production process. Information so intimately geared to perfectly sequenced production steps is inherently not packaged in disciplinary or functional bundles. Furthermore, this information produces a type of overall integrated control that intermediary levels of functional (or other) controls will only diminish. Intermediary levels do, however, need to be able to halt the process when emergencies occur.

Another dimension of the change away from functional organization involves access to information. Previously, anybody in a particular function was a specialist in the information that was the stock and trade of that function. Middle managers were specialists in collecting, transmitting, and sometimes, as in the case of foremen or supervi-

sors, acting on that information. Now, nearly everyone in the plant has broad access and is becoming an information specialist, but in a more generalized fashion. For example, nearly everyone on the floor of an integrated plant will know quite a lot about the kinds of data flowing in many different and significant channels, and may be able to obtain access to those data, even though not normally needing to know the specifics.

Broader access to information is allowing some plants to do away with first line supervisors: "A foreman is a person with a shirt pocket full of notes. Now that all the information in those notes is available to all of us on the tube, what do we need the foreman for?''

Flattening the Framework

The new availability of information enables a flattening of the organization by eliminating some middle layers of management and some of the least skilled layers of workers, as well. We have already mentioned eliminating some foreman positions, the first line of supervision. Cost reduction is the driving force. In the actual incident referred to, management pressed shop floor employees to come up with additional savings following the installation of expensive new technologies. The workers responded by doing away with the foreman's slot.

Cost reduction is not the only driver. Speeding up the decision process can be important. Fewer management layers means less delay while analyses, recommendations, and implementation plans flow uphill or decisions and implementation constraints flow back downhill.

The ultimate appears to be a three layer plant hierarchy, composed of a plant manager, a few middle managers, and everybody else. At least a few plants in the 500 to 1000 staffing bracket have already achieved what they describe as a three level hierarchy. In plants with more than 1500 employees on board, five or six layers seems to be the flattest they can get.

When 500 to 2000 people are formally related in such a flat structure, the structure can still be charted as a hierarchy, but overlapping circles or wheels within wheels really make it function. The organization works because teams interact horizontally and not as branching limbs of authority.

Once a plant is structured in a flat hierarchy, even the fiction that operational decisions are made at the top level tends to disappear. In fact, almost all decisions needed to ensure current production decisions are made and implemented at the lowest level. People at the base level increasingly formulate operational and contingency plans, ensure preventive maintenance, and conduct operational decision making. In integrated automated manufacturing, people no longer make things, The automated systems make things, and the people keep the automated systems in balance.

Management Functions

The handful of middle managers remaining after an organization flattens its framework will have several functions. First, they must see to it that the right combinations of people are brought together from within and without the plant to do the detailed planning required for future operations to succeed. In so doing, they incorporate product and process improvements already underway.

Managers also translate and expand upon the strategic insights, business vision, and directives of the topmost level of plant management and higher levels of corporate management. The middle managers must keep the plant "integrated" in human terms. They must provide the intellectual context and the sense of emotional wholeness that everybody else needs to function synergystically. The middle managers continue to be devoted to communications but at more creative, conceptual, and contextual levels, rather than in issuing directives and detailed instructions.

Personnel management remains the special venue of middle management in a streamlined organization. While the working people will make most of the detailed staffing and other personnel decisions, they can do so only because of training and counseling provided by middle managers. The middle managers must ensure adequate training status,

staffing processes, performance appraisals, and career management. Their backup will be a small, highly competent, specialized human resources staff, too few in number to do the work, but sufficient in number to form policy and provide guidance both to necessary specialized resources and to problem solving on the part of middle managers.

The plant manager creates or translates business strategy, depending on whether or not his plant functions in the company as the autonomous executor of a business unit. He exercises major management intervention at the plant's external and internal interfaces, through the mostly base level employees who manage those interfaces. The implication is important: while the handful of middle managers remain an important constituency of the plant manager, communication between plant manager and middle managers takes relatively little time.

Base level people are regarded as professionals; that is, people with appropriately focused educations, special occupational training, and something of a vocation for doing skilled work in a relatively autonomous way. Whether they require two years of postsecondary education or 20 years of college, graduate school, and professional experience, their lives at the base level will be in many respects similar. They may be *entrants*—people in training for a productive job or role, with a mix of characteristics of importance to profession, company, and industry. When qualified, they become *cadre*—potentially permanent employees, depending on the personnel policy of the company, economics, and other circumstances of the industry. Some of the cadre will be singled out for tracking into line management or to become senior knowledge workers (fundamentally planners) at plant or corporate levels.

Do any plants exist that demonstrate this model? Not completely. Many midwestern appliance manufacturing plants seem to be moving in this direction, as are some of the newer and larger electronics fabrication and assembly plants located throughout the country.

Staff Functions

A different set of organization design issues stems from the extraordinary planning complexities that accompany the informed automation of factories. Somebody has to figure out how to trade off the projected benefits against the undoubted disruptions and costs associated with each transition to the next phase of automation. Somebody has to write down a foolproof plan to get through the transition without major catastrophe. Plant-level engineers, technicians, and managers are involved. Many of the people doing this work will, however, be in corporate knowledge worker roles, or will be the employees of contractors, and not be thought of as managers.

That this function will absorb the attention of a large number of people is vaguely discernible from the current behavior of the telecommunications services industry in the United States (U.S.). As this postdivestiture industry works ever further into the digital revolution, the long-time AT&T preoccupations with operational integration, system reliability, and intergenerational compatibility have become the shared concerns of all the independents as well as the seven Bell operating companies. At this point all the operating companies devote much of their own planners' time to system planning and transitional problems, but that is not all. The Bell companies also support some 7000 people at Bell Communications Research doing some of the crucial circuit, system, and network design—and associated standards and implementation planning—for the next generation telephone system, the one perpetually in the future.

The manufacturing industry will be facing something analogous as it pursues its own digital revolution. Will large numbers of people be needed to do the design, standard setting, and planning? Even in absolute terms, the staff now involved in systems architecture, analysis, design, and testing will have to greatly increase to accommodate a breathtaking increase in computer applications and an equally phenomenal increase in planning required for a wide range of digitally driven manufacturing-related technologies.

In relative terms, the increase will probably be even more startling. Bear in mind that by the early part of the twenty-first century, only two major activities in automated manufacturing industry will require significant numbers of people:

- Change management including all of technology development, product development, process development, and systems planning, as well as changes in structure, culture, and staffing
- Customer relations including all of marketing and sales as well as plant base level professionals engaged at the customer interface, mentioned earlier in this chapter

It is too early to say with certainty how large the planning complement is going to have to be. I believe it will be shockingly large, by current standards. If in-plant, in-company, and contractor resources are combined I think the numbers engaged in change management (design, planning, implementation, training, testing, and maintenance-level changes) will rise to 20 to 30 percent of total employees in the U.S. manufacturing industry. The percentages will depend in part on whether computer-associated technologies continue to evolve at their current rate, slow down some, or speed up. At a rough guess, one third of the planning people will be plant level, one third staff level, and one third contractors.

This distribution of planners reflects three important considerations. First, essentially continuous analysis of production flows and sensitivities will lead to frequent revelations of how and where major gains are to be had. These high leverage opportunities will immediately be matched to technological capabilities. Taking advantage of these opportunities for continuous improvement will be at the heart of competitive strategy in manufacturing industry.

Second, planning will have to be done in almost infinite detail, and checked out very carefully. Anything less than complete understanding of what is to be done and why will surely result in catastrophe. The new technologies are not forgiving.

Finally, implementation planning, and implementation itself, will require meeting transition schedules now unthinkable. The alternative to what today would seem improperly speedy is either prolonged periods of maintaining incredibly expensive systems in dual operation or unbearable periods of down time.

The planning staffs will work in multidisciplinary teams, mobilized to carry out projects of varying lengths. In fact, their organizational structure will be so fluid as to deserve the name Alvin Toffler coined to describe the National Aeronautics and Space Administration (NASA) in the 1960s—adhocracy. Little or none of the traditional functional staff structure will remain, and planners will be perpetually on temporary assignment. They will likely be without a professional home base within the firm that employs them, but they will have access to intensive retraining sessions in academia and in their professional societies, to help them uphold professional integrity and achieve necessary upgrading and updating.

JOB DESIGN CHANGES AND THEIR HUMAN IMPLICATIONS

The current round of informed automation leads consistently to changes in the roles of those touched by it. Some of the changes are the direct result of the automation itself. New technologies demand new skills on the part of those still working on the plant floor. This can happen sometimes because the new equipment is unfamiliar, sometimes because of a wider range of equipment and processes to work with, or sometimes because someone has to take over functions of formerly existing management layers above him. In addition to these obvious and anticipatable changes in scope, there often are actual changes in role. These arise because of improved information, faster information flow, and much wider access to information. Changes occur in manual skills, conceptual and intellectual skills, and what have in the past been regarded as management skills.

Most integrated approaches to manufacturing result in a significant net reduction in manpower requirements. Most workforce savings occur fairly close to the shop floor: direct labor, production schedulers and expediters, production planners, supervisors, equipment maintenance tradespeople, and line managers. Many of the more routine and repetitive activities previously done by all of these people may literally be automated. Remaining activities are likely to be much more intellectually demanding and probably require a lot more initiative. Automated integration requires many people to understand more of what is going on—in a more thoroughly conceptual way—and to do more about it!

Initiative

Very few people can be allowed to remain simply as square pegs in square holes during or after the transition into automated integration. In fact, virtually everyone has to forget the four little words, "That's not my job." While plenty of job differentiation and specialization continues to be necessary, nobody can be "just a specialist," and nobody can be tolerated who is other than purposefully and broadly initiating. Why is this so? Well, for starters, there are fewer people around. All available eyes, ears, and noses are needed for troubleshooting and problem fixing. In addition, the economic penalties of downtime are worse than before integration, and the practical likelihood of eliminating downtime is much higher but only if everybody pitches in.

Causes and consequences may be no further removed from one another in time or space than before integration but now many people in the integrated environment have the data needed to allow them to notice conditions needing attention. Those with the data may or may not be physically or organizationally close to the problem location, may or may not have the same organizational relation to the current problem and to others recently encountered, and may or may not have primary responsibilities for troubleshooting.

The overriding demand is not who notices first but that problems be noticed and acted on as soon as possible. The fundamental principle is different now for economizing organizational resources and keeping control. It is no longer the assignment of unique accountability for particular elements of the production process. The fundamental principle instead is teamwork. The design encourages a human network of alert and thoughtful attentiveness, presupposing the necessary information redundancy exists to underlie collaboration. They all have to share enough to have something to talk about together.

Except where computer systems can monitor what individuals do down to individual keystrokes, it is extraordinarily difficult in the automated and integrated environment to ascertain exactly what anybody knows or is doing. Performance testing will help but having people who are up-front initiators in jobs where they are entitled to initiate is about the best way available to "know where people are coming from." It is a hallmark of effective, high-trust teams that the members know one another in this respect.

Responsibility for a Bigger Picture

In the past, the reluctance to allow—let alone to encourage—undirected initiative within manufacturing organizations has been well founded. Now that more initiating behavior is desirable in typical factory jobs something other than narrowly defined roles and close supervision must provide motivation and discipline. Peer pressure, a generally supportive organizational culture, and better selected staff and necessary supplements to the required discipline. Its foundation, however, is intellectual mastery of the factory operations flow chart at the appropriate level of detail.

While few people will have the same need for the same amount of detailed understanding uniformly throughout the operation, neither will many people be able to get along without considerable in-depth understanding for selected parts. What makes for discipline, and constitutes a major break with the past, is that everybody has to have the same flow chart literally in mind, the same perception of the following:

- Structure
- Flows and other patterns
- Operational concepts
- System dynamics

Conceptual and Logical Skills Requirements

People cannot respond to the requirement for understanding the bigger picture unless they are capable conceptualizers and logical thinkers. Demanding these qualities of individuals is one thing; understanding that they are role requirements and what that entails is another.

Those engaged directly in factory operations or their planning will be buying into a continuing obligation somewhat analogous to the classic responsibility of the old-time postal clerk to learn and keep up to date on a number of route schemes. General familiarity and approximate accuracy will not be good enough. Knowing how it was last year is not good enough. Knowing only your own neighborhood is not good enough. The difference is that in integrated manufacturing, unlike postal clerking, the logical thinking required is even more important than the sheer memory for abstract or arbitrary facts and labels.

Everyone a Planner

Another quite consistent role change that comes with integrated manufacturing is the consistent requirement on people at all levels to be good planners. People generally have to be able to figure out how long it is likely to take to make particular changes, adjustments, or calibrations and to be able to figure out when in the operational cycle it makes most sense to carry out such planned activities. They have to be able to anticipate and express something of the impact of what they intend to do on operations and on other people. They have to be able to put together schedules and planning rationales that make sense. They need to know how and when to involve other people in both planning and implementation—and to be able to express effectively what they need from other people.

Summary of Generic Role Changes

Although not everyone on the floor of an integrated manufacturing operation has to have a truly formidable intellect, their required roles take a lot of sharp, literate, energetic, psychologically active people capable of a high order of teamwork and with the ability to carry out intricate plans. These are some of the personal attributes required in order to carry out roles that are for the most part neither routine nor unskilled jobs. What most of these jobs require is acute observation, sharpened by detailed awareness of what is going on; quick and well studied reactions to things that are out of the ordinary; endless anticipation of contingencies and possibilities for improvements; and an above average ability to interact assertively with other people.

IMPLICATIONS FOR JOB DESIGN PHILOSOPHY

Roles demanding initiative, teamwork, and accountability for in-depth understanding of a bigger picture do not fit the tradition of manufacturing job design. Two old definitions no longer hold: (1) jobs used to be assemblages of tasks for which the incumbent had narrowly specified fixed responsibilities; and (2) each job was assumed to fit up against the next, rather like bricks in a wall, so that there was little space between, and what space there was between jobs had supposedly standard thickness and consistency.

We are now forced to abandon these assumptions. Rather than being rigid lists of tasks surrounded by a firm boundary, most jobs in integrated

manufacturing have a living core surrounded by a permeable boundary. The core contains three layers of activities and obligations, as a result of the need to adapt job design to the fact that everyone must demonstrate initiative:

- Central areas in which, if the incumbent does not initiate and carry out tasks, they probably will not get done—except contingently or because somebody comes in to help
- Areas in which the incumbent shares the initiative with a clearly identified individual or group, so each has a significant responsibility to collaborate with the other(s)
- Areas in which the incumbent must initiate communication; his only additional responsibility is to be sure that someone with core responsibility in that area acknowledges his communications and plans to take appropriate action where needed

As we apply this new job design philosophy, we see that the employee who notices a need bears the responsibility to keep after it until the right person responds appropriately. When a job design philosophy embraces the need for universally initiated behavior, there need be no assumption of job completeness. All the jobs taken together look more like a flexible network than a brick wall. The nodes in such a network move around quite freely as needed. In an operation where "downsizing" has occurred, people are already accustomed to a similar phenomenon, although with different causes.

This design philosophy creates an environment in which traditional direct supervision is obsolete. Managers must actively seek reliable ways to collect data for performance appraisals, goal setting, and rewards. Managers must be far more subtle, and must rely on collective input, and not just their own observations.

IMPLICATIONS FOR TRAINING AND SKILL BUILDING

Automated integration of manufacturing leads to a need for both reskilling and deskilling. Although requirements for skills upgrading will probably be in the overwhelming majority, for those left out, or downgraded in the process, it is little consolation that someone else may be winning.

Most jobs targeted for deskilling are in those areas of the production routine that cannot be done as well by machines as by human beings. Total cost, physical task variability, or complicated sensing requirements may be the distinguishing factors. Automated material handling systems already do a better job of order picking in many typical warehouse situations than do people, but when odd lot orders (of, for example, electronic components) have been picked and assembled into "baskets" ready for checking and packing, people may still be better capable of verifying the contents and competently packaging the order for mailing.

These routine kinds of jobs are often surrounded by computer automation so job performance of incumbents can be very easy to monitor. Detailed, continuous, inexpensive measurements of speed, accuracy, variability, or other job performance parameters tend to be available—and highly satisfying to the industrial engineering mentality. Second by second surveillance, however, is not usually to the liking of the initiating, conceptualizing, problem-solvers who will be needed in most of the other jobs in an automated and integrated factory setting.

Therefore, at least some need for a multitrack staff selection and training capability will persist. The most important point in common to both classes of jobs (the deskilled and the reskilled) is the enlarged significance of aptitude testing and vestibule training in advance of job selection. At least for a few years, both classes of jobs are going to be somewhat unfamiliar. Giving prospective employees a really good opportunity to confront the nature of the job (in a realistic testing or training setting) is going to be crucial to selection, both on the part of employers and employees. When much of the new labor force draws from among existing employees, people need to try one of the new jobs for themselves in a realistic training setting. In doing so, they can deselect themselves voluntarily from untenable situations with minimum public exposure.

Training Dos and Don'ts

We are still at an early stage in the transition towards manufacturing integration in the U.S. There are as yet no standardized methods for establishing selection and training programs for new jobs. Some principles are, however, beginning to emerge.

Do not simply transfer batches of people wholesale into automated integrated settings. Look for volunteers. Major efforts to learn new skills will likely be required. Strongly motivated people are a must, to do the hard work entailed in learning, especially during the start-up, and while getting the new culture going in the right direction.

Do not transfer people wholesale even into training programs, especially not in situations in which continued employment depends on successful transition to the new job via successful retraining. Remember, most of the people needed are going to have to be initiators. People previously valued for reliably getting the job done may be initiators, but many are not. People who are in their own view arbitrarily transferred have an excuse to become more passive rather than more initiating.

Do recognize that middle managers will have to assume direct responsibility for managing training. It cannot be shuffled off to personnel or training staff. Nobody but the middle managers can know or care enough about the unique requirements of their own customized systems and interfaces to manage the training closely enough. Nor will they really want someone else to manage a resource that will vary from between 5 to 15 percent of total payroll. Training requirements are becoming very costly and very important to satisfy.

Do support the use of a variety of training vendors, both in house and on contract. System vendors and resellers are not necessarily oriented or equipped properly to train people who are going to be working on super systems built up out of components supplied by many different vendors.

Will training be a permanent condition of employment? I think it will. The growing homogeneity of international competition in the manufacturing industries forces efforts at continuous improvement, which will in turn inevitably lead to new training requirements.

Continuous Improvement

There is little to suggest basic changes in current worldwide industrial dynamics. New industrializing areas open up almost before the last generation of new factories is well developed and stable. This trend will continue to put heavy pressure on the prices of many if not most industrial products, unless protectionism is able to counter with new tools and with a political clout greater than it can now muster in most countries. If pressure on prices continues, the current revival of the fad for continuous improvement in cost and quality will become a reality.

How can we obtain continuous improvement? One source will surely still be reduction of labor costs, although the time is coming when labor inputs will be so trivial as to no longer have high leverage on total costs. Technology innovations in product design, manufacturing process, and materials will become proportionally more important sources of improvement as labor costs are squeezed out.

Technology based improvements, however, are likely to result in continuing heavy needs for upgraded and revised training for staff at all levels. Whether the improvements are based on continuing integration of new technologies, rapid development, or growth in core technologies or on digesting incremental changes learned by doing, continuous improvement is coming to imply continuous training, as well as a higher level of continuous restaffing by hiring in new employees trained elsewhere.

MOTIVATIONAL PROBLEMS AND INFORMATED INTEGRATION

We asserted at the beginning of this chapter that it is the managerial levels rather than the workers who seem to be having the worst problems with computer integrated manufacturing. Should management quickly begin to get its act together, this will change. Workers will then begin regularly and much more frequently to confront job pressures, work rules pressures, training pressures, and plant closings.

Management will have reasonably potent economic tools available to deal constructively with some of the subjective aspects of these problems and many of the material effects as well. However, retraining, relocation, outplacement, and favorable early retirement packages are not likely to be easily affordable. Management will be constrained in its use of these tools—far from cost free—by all the usual business causes plus the combined effects of heavy competitive pressures and the continuing high costs of investment in the new manufacturing technologies. Do not be misled by financial analysts working for stock brokers who prophesy that some of our bellwether companies in the smokestack industries are about finished with their reinvestment in manufacturing equipment and facilities. These companies may be up to date—so far as concerns current versions of Manufacturing Resources Planning (MRP), automated materials handling, shop floor process control, robotics, and the like. Hardly any are more than just beginning down the road toward true integration, or even have any workable plans for getting there. So, the required additional investments do not show up in long-term financial plans, let alone capital budgeting.

This speculative analysis leads to the conclusion that in the early 1990s, U.S. industry in the process of informating and integrating will have to deal with increasing resistance from workers. This resistance will probably take the form of renewed union activity and legislative pressure based on coalitions of union leaders and local political leadership determined not to lose manufacturing jobs from their communities.

The major available mitigating factor will be a cure worse than the disease. If chronic structural employment rises as we get deeper into the renewal of the manufacturing industry, and that trend coincides with economic stagnation or recession, jobs will be in such short supply that resistance to automation and integration will be attenuated.

In that kind of unfavorable economic environment, industrial reinvestment will also slow down somewhat. However, regaining and maintaining competitiveness in the U.S. manufacturing industry will become an even stronger driver than it has been for the past decade. The consequences of crushing national indebtedness are catching up with us in a world inhabited with a rising number of countries better able than we to invest in their own future economic viability. We will mobilize, finally to face the problem. This national effort to dig ourselves out before it is beyond our strength to do so will also help management in dealing with worker resistance to informated integration in manufacturing industry.

It is a curious irony that management will almost surely have to become very imaginative in figuring out how to surmount worker resistance just as soon as it overcomes its own ambivalence and uncertainty. Management will need more psychological tools and more genuine leadership assets than at anytime in the twentieth century.

When the internal basis for understanding and acceptance is slight, managers will have to become genuine adult educators. They must not be like authoritative and patronizing teachers in ghetto-like school settings, but rather they must be like people who have received a generous vision and are driven by it.

When the organizational culture is too inhospitable to support changes, management will have to quit debating whether culture change can be managed, and get on with managing it constructively. When the pressures are too great, management will have to learn how to sit down with itself, its employees, and other constituencies, and negotiate intelligently and nondefensively. When management becomes isolated from or polarized with some of its constituencies, the executive cadres will have to learn and practice the skills of conflict management.

CULTURAL AND ATTITUDINAL PRECONDITIONS FOR SUCCESS

It would be in the fine American tradition of managerial oversimplification to prescribe an ideal culture for getting to integration in manufacturing. It is more useful to list some essential values that are often deficient or lacking in manufacturing cultures in the U.S. These values by themselves do not, however, define the culture. In most cases, they are values that simply need to be built into the existing culture as their opposites are eliminated, repositioned, or repatterned.

A Bias for Strategic Gains

It is essential but it is not enough to convert people to the doctrine of continuous improvement. Everyone has also to develop a strong bias for seeking and finding strategic gains. If these two values are twined, so that large numbers of people start actively looking out for competitive advantage, continuous improvement will not so easily revert to the urge to achieve old-fashioned cost reduction.

While there is nothing inherently wrong with cost reduction, it is too narrow in the circumstances under discussion. Integrated manufacturing will not develop if management confines itself just to doing things right; it must also do the right things.

Faith in Technology

Americans have been notoriously enthusiastic about new technologies for 150 years. So it is no wonder that plenty of hard-bitten people—often those with sad experience with immature, oversold, or inappropriate technologies—have developed an almost pathological suspicion of new technologies. A good many of these people are to be found in almost any U.S. factory. Where the skeptics have things all their way, integrated manufacturing will begin to founder when it reaches the point at which it depends on new technologies.

The point is to preserve the healthy skepticism but combine it with some equally healthy enthusiasm for new technology. The culture needs to have some protechnology values embedded in it.

Respect for Planning

Planning is surely one of the seven deadly virtues. Planning is such a cliché that nearly everyone except bulls of the woods give it lip service. It is so boring it has to be good for you. However, planning is also something that truly results-oriented hard hats will point to as getting in the way of practical action. Powerful forces exist in most manufacturing cultures that tend to denigrate planning more than is consistent with smooth implementation of integrated manufacturing projects and concepts. Planning has to become macho. Planning cannot continue to be limited to production scheduling and preparing for equipment relocation by moving little three-dimensional models around on a grid representing the shop floor. Planning has to become something that everyone is or wants to be good at. Planning has to be valued. If not, integrated manufacturing is not going to be valued either.

Acceptance of Participative Management

Obtaining consistently the necessary levels of initiating behavior and overcoming bureaucratic tendency towards passivity on the job also generally require significant culture change. The culture can preserve adequate respect for rank, expertise, seniority, and other valued attributes but it must also give strong support to people who speak up and regularize their involvement in decision making processes.

In fact, the values that underlie participation have to be carried far enough that people in the factory feel more or less on the same plane. If they think of themselves as beings of subordinate rank, they are less likely to speak up when they need to. If they do not speak up, they deny themselves one of the most potent stimuli and symbols for maintaining the initiating mode in their jobs.

SUMMARY

The rocky road to integrated manufacturing is paved with people and organization problems. The worst of these problems deals with the vague and threatening nature of changes facing middle and senior managers as they contemplate enacting computerized integrated factory automation. The threatening nature of these changes is made worse

by the lack of a clear vision about what the outcome will be, organizationally speaking, when a factory ultimately integrates and automates. Let us review the salient features of an organizational, staffing, and cultural vision for the automated integrated factory.

Organizational units will largely be composed of multidisciplinary teams, rather than of functional departments. The first step toward such team organizations is to loosen existing functional boundaries. Next, the plant hierarchy must flatten out by removing layers from the middle and the bottom, thus leaving as few as three to five organizational layers even in plants with 1000 employees or more.

The "base level" people will run the plant's current operations and participate in planning and implementing major changes.

The middle level will maintain the staff's capability to perform, carry the brunt of responsibility for implementing major changes, and participate in planning those changes. The major communications responsibility of the middle level will shift dramatically from routine operating instructions to translations, interpretations, and applications of the strategic vision of the company, needed to provide key motivational leadership.

The plant manager will stimulate and control communications at all major external and internal interfaces, take a significant leadership role in bringing business strategy to the plant, and as always set the tone.

Many people, including contractors and staff specialists outside the plant as well as plant-level people, will be primarily engaged in detailed planning and implementation of major ongoing technology and systems changes. These people, too, will be organized in ad hoc teams of varying degrees of permanence, rather than in functional staff units.

The nature or basic structure of jobs will change. The central implication of Teamwork will mean that everyone is initiating; nobody can be allowed the luxury of saying, "That's not my job." Everyone will also be obliged to help develop and to use a well informed, deeply shared road map or big picture of how the factory works. This logical flow diagram is neither *as designed* nor *as built* but *as works*. All this is considerably beyond what engineers can develop by themselves and put into manuals and primers.

Everyone must now be good at making, interpreting, and executing plans. The management of change in the interest of continuous improvement will be a fundamental value, policy, and working requirement in a setting that has little tolerance for casual or underplanned change.

All these changes in skill and role requirements at both base and managerial levels imply a significant revision in philosophy about what jobs consist of and how they are related. Jobs can no longer be thought of as nonduplicative (or alternatively, as precisely identical and parallel) sets of rigidly defined accountabilities. Nor can they be thought of as interfacing smoothly and cleanly with adjacent jobs. Instead, jobs will have permeable boundaries, allowing people to be initiative about whatever requires initiation. In the automated integrated factory discipline and control over behavior will arise more from the precisely and accurately shared view of the big picture and from high mutual trust teamwork than from a rationalized and rigid system of job definitions.

Training requirements and responsibilities will be major and continuing. More and more international competition will force ever greater emphasis on continuous improvement that will come primarily from technological changes. These in turn lead to needs for continuous training.

Once management overcomes its own ambivalence toward integrated manufacturing, labor will begin to resist it. Plant closings and other disruptions will make it look as though the costs of integration are being borne by labor. Management will then truly be put to the test of wisdom and inspirational leadership.

One of the novel managerial requirements that will be explicit in carrying out the management's leadership role is the ability to create—swiftly and deftly—a plant culture in which integrated manufacturing can effectively flourish. While the new culture must be based on whatever its predecessors were like, it will also have to emphasize certain values that are by no means now universal in the U.S. manufacturing industry, including:

- a bias for strategic gains
- faith in technology
- respect for planning
- acceptance of participative management
- egalitarianism

2

The Changing Role of the Production Supervisor in the "Factory of the Future"

Joel C. Polakoff[*]

MANUFACTURING TODAY IS AT THE CROSSROADS. AS companies attempt to rekindle the spark that once ignited the industrial revolution, with new techniques such as computer integrated manufacturing, computer aided design, and flexible manufacturing systems, the role of the production supervisor has been neglected and much maligned. All too often, entrepreneurs aggressively attempt to solve their lack of innovation through technological means, yet never fully understand that a successful implementation of flexible automation comes through the synthesis of both machines and people. Unfortunately, human relations aspects of incorporating the "factory of the future," are more often than not an afterthought to a flexible automation project.

As we incorporate advanced manufacturing technology (AMT) in our factories, the role of the first-level supervisor on the production floor will change significantly as we near the twenty-first century. The standard operating functions such as supervising, investigating, coordinating, planning, scheduling, staffing, training, and evaluating employees will still exist in some form. What will change are the methods used and the scope by which each first level supervisor manages these activities. These areas will be structured quite differently from today. Peter Drucker noted that "no job is going to change more in the future than that of the first level supervisor." These changes will include:

- The increase in the education level of the work force
- The increase in the level of expectations about work outcomes
- Computer automation of the work place and the resultant impact on job design
- Growing governmental intervention in the work place
- Other influences such as union and staff involvement with first line supervisor[1]

Human relations and administrative consequences of the factory of the future are necessary now more than ever before and should be accounted for in factory planning today. Improved

*Mr. Polakoff is the National Director of Manufacturing and Logistics Consulting Services for BDO Seidman, headquartered in the firm's Chicago office. Previously, Mr. Polakoff was Director of Inventory Management Systems at Premier Industrial Corporation, and at Abbott Laboratories he was involved with the design and implementation of their integrated manufacturing and distribution systems. He is the author of numerous articles in various business, industrial, and management journals. Mr. Polakoff holds a B.S. and M.B.A. degree in Production/Operations Management. He is professionally certified as a CMC, CPIM, and CPM.

human relations on the factory floor will help improve productivity in the future. Growing global competition and pressures to raise efficiency mean that day-to-day operations management can no longer be a routine matter. It now involves the continuous search for improved methods of performing manufacturing tasks. The growing emphasis in manufacturing is on gaining the total commitment of workers. Numerous writers have argued that it is no longer satisfactory for firms to have their workers performing narrowly defined tasks and merely following the basic rules. What are now sought are an active pursuit of the firm's goals and the willing deployment of the workers' abilities. The ability to generate consent is a major issue in which first-level supervisors need to be continually involved.[2]

Thus, as organizations scurry to find the latest machines capable of performing with unsurpassed efficiency and unequaled effectiveness on the shop floor, first-level supervisors (foremen) will need to be part of this decision-making process. Flexible factory automation today is becoming a multibillion dollar business. Each year we see American manufacturers increase their plant and equipment budgets for state-of-the-art computer-based hardware and software. The size of these expenditures is indeed one measure of industry's commitment to automation.

The commitment of a corporate entity is one thing, but the commitment of the work force is another.[3] All too often we witness complex manufacturing systems being installed in an organization and never fully attaining the profit potential originally anticipated. Consequently, management faults the workers for lack of commitment, and workers blame management for their unrealistic expectations of performance. In reality the key issue is the lack of understanding of what is necessary to fully automate an integrated production facility.

Ironically, this lack of understanding is the fault of *both* top level management and the management of the production floor. Like most everything in industry, the yield of automated production systems is determined far more by the people than by invested capital—and it is not just a matter of individuals either.

Successful implementation of advanced manufacturing technology involves the cooperative efforts of numerous employees who have a diversity of responsibilities. Each professional involved in the job has a dual role. First, he must address his own responsibilities. Then he must see to it that his work is coordinated with that of his colleagues who are involved in the process. This latter role, and problems encountered in fulfilling it, requires interaction—something that the first-level supervisor has never been properly trained to do.[4]

How do we simultaneously coordinate the introduction of new technology and the required human relations and administrative tasks needed to make technology work? How will first-level supervisors' jobs now be defined? Which additional tasks will be asked of our first-level supervisors? How do we train the first-level supervisor on using machines that are highly sophisticated and require the use of precision tools and parts, as opposed to the traditional jolt with a hammer? How do we overcome factory resistance on the shop floor from first-level supervisors who see the upcoming educated generation of factory foremen as a potential job threat?

These are issues that will be dealt with throughout this chapter, as we attempt to sort out the changing role of the first-level supervisor in the factory of the future. As we will document, the supervisor's role is evolving throughout all types of manufacturing industries. Some research to date shows that in some manufacturing industries the function of a first-level supervisor will be eliminated as other production workers begin to take on additional responsibilities. Yet, the majority of evidence to date clearly shows that first-level supervisors will sustain their jobs. However, these jobs will be dramatically different in scope.

Due to better information on the factory floor through integrated manufacturing systems, and flexible automated machinery, first-level supervisors will maintain an equal level of responsibility but will have increased time to better manage specific duties which support their responsibilities. These changes in job duties and design include a decreased need to monitor and direct subordinates' work, increased time for coordinating with other personnel, more time spent investigating complex production problems, and a decreased ability to use previous methods to motivate and judge worker performance.

With conventional manufacturing equipment, most of a first-level supervisor's time is spent in monitoring and directing activities. However, when the machinery and systems are upgraded with AMT, first-level supervisors have more time for other production activities. This additional time can now be administered in more constructive ways, such as better coordination of worker and machine, group facilitation, change initiation and implementation, and improved employee training. In order to accomplish these new duties, first level supervisors will themselves need to learn more about the new technology, how it will integrate into the overall production system, and what effect it will have on organizational changes and boundaries on the shop floor.

Have first-level supervisors to date been effective in managing this metamorphosis of the production floor? To some degree the answer is yes. As a rule, the overwhelming majority of union members (e.g., 85 percent in Switzerland) accept technological change as a necessity for enterprises to survive in a highly competitive environment. Union members who welcome the new technology also see the improved benefits it brings: shorter hours, better work conditions, and higher pay through collective bargaining. On the other hand, they fear redundancies and job losses as well as a deskilling of occupations and subsequent income losses for members.[5]

Has industry to date been responsive to the needs of factory supervision with the new technology? At the new General Motors (GM) assembly plant in Detroit, the company has responded to the need of its workers, 5000 in all, by putting them through 200 to 2000 hours of technical and human resource training to help them adapt to working under GM's most advanced production system and dealing with the plant's 2000 programmable devices. The transition has been especially difficult because the new plant's workers are being recruited from two of the company's oldest plants. Says Fred Bullard, a 38-year-old worker at the new GM plant, who transferred from an aging assembly plant, "You didn't have to be a very smart guy to do most of the jobs at my old plant." At the old plant, Mr. Bullard repaired flaws in seats, carpeting, and other trim. Now as an electrical technician he is part of a team that uses a computer to test interior electrical and electronic hookups such as those in the instrument panels of the front-wheel-drive luxury cars built at the new plant. To qualify for the job he had to cram into six months a two-year college program in electronics that required everything from brushing up on reading, spelling, and algebra to learning trigonometry and understanding solid state circuitry.[6]

We will focus in this chapter on what has happened, what is happening, and what will happen with first-level supervisors and their roles on the production floor in the future. While these changes in factory supervision directly result from the implementation of AMT, they are nevertheless a necessary prerequisite for manufacturing if we are to enter a second industrial revolution. "Only people," says Japanese labor expert Harvo Shimada, "can give wisdom to the machines." It is an important lesson that leading edge U.S. manufacturing companies are now beginning to learn. By integrating multiskilled, highly trained workers, coupled with computer-driven technology, manufacturers are beginning to see remarkable gains. This synthesis may well represent the wave of the future in manufacturing—but only if management and labor discard obsolete practices and collaborate on innovative production systems.[7]

The ultimate cornerstone in this entire process is the first-level production supervisor. This position will more than anyone else in the factory require the greatest flexibility for change that results from the adoption of AMT.

TRACING THE ROOTS OF THE FIRST-LEVEL SUPERVISOR

Factory supervision at the foreman level will continue to evolve as technology moves onto the shop floor. Although the technical skills of first-level supervision differ based upon the type of industry, size of the organization, experience of the organization's work force, and educational background of the supervisor, a number of fundamental activities are a part of the first-level supervisor's function. The job duties usually include:

- Planning, scheduling, and rescheduling
- Fully documenting work and its respective workers
- Counseling employees
- Managing performance and rewarding employees
- Ensuring the quality of the product and the efficiency of how it is produced
- Maintaining a safe and clean work environment and ensuring good housekeeping is a part of each worker's duties
- Recruiting, selecting, and training workers
- Maintaining union management relations on the production floor, and encouraging employee suggestions
- Ensuring that the machinery and equipment are safe and fully operational

Yet this is not how the first-line supervisor—or, in the early days, the "foreman"—was always looked at. Back in the early days of the industrial revolution, the foreman was in fact an independent contractor, who was used to the extent needed by the owner of the manufacturing plant. It was the foreman's responsibility, not the company's, to hire a crew of workers, train them in what was expected relative to performance, supervise their efforts, and reward them with wages if he was satisfied with the work performed. If not satisfied with their work, he discharged them. The *foreman* had complete control over how the work was to be performed and who was going to do it. There was no interference from the government, the union—if one existed—or the management. The foreman had absolute control. However, over time this dominant role began to change as a result of the following circumstances.

Scientific Management Movement

In the early part of the twentieth century, Frederick Taylor introduced the concept of scientific management. As part of this overall doctrine, the term *functional foremanship* evolved and began to gain acceptance. Under this philosophy of management, the planning aspect of production was separated from the execution aspect. In addition, production workers could report to any number of foremen, contingent upon what the aspect of the task was. This thinking, coupled with other management concepts of the time, began to change the foreman's role.

The scope of the foreman's responsibility became limited to primary shop floor execution. Many, if not all, planning activities were now being assumed by upper management. The foreman himself—as well as such activities as selecting and training factory workers—was now being controlled by the organization. Hence, the foreman's role on the factory floor began to evolve to more of a liaison between factory workers and factory management.

The Union Movement

As the industrial revolution accelerated, there was a stronger need for factory workers to unite to ensure fair wages and fair working conditions. The formation of unions for factory workers also stripped much of the authority from the factory foreman. Now, negotiations between workers and foreman escalated a step higher to upper management, who now controlled what was previously within the worker/foreman relationship. Negotiations were now more formalized, and much more technical in nature, something the typical foreman was not trained for and therefore not capable of executing.

Thus with unions an integral part of the production environment, the once discretionary power of the foreman began to wane. Now, all job hirings needed to come off the prescribed union list. Now, all dismissals, suspensions, or firings needed to follow the letter of the law as indicated in the union contract. Now, company layoffs were controlled not by productivity standards but by union seniority. Equally disheartening for the first-level supervisor was that the union was now beginning to win major concessions in wage increases, job security, and working conditions—something the first-level supervisor had tried to do for years but never successfully did. These increased limitations on the first-level supervisor—once a prestigious person in the factory—further refined and narrowed his job scope and responsibilities.

Organization Structure

As organizations grew, the need to specialize different skills within the factory environment also grew. Many of these specialized skills had been the original job duties of the factory foreman, for he had been the chief "cook and bottle washer" within his department or the plant. Growing personnel staffs gradually began to assume much of the responsibility for hiring and training workers. New industrial engineers, brought into the organization to help track and monitor worker efficiency, started assuming a majority of the daily worker technology interface between man and machine. Again, the first-level supervisor was stripped of much of the responsibilities he had in early years.

The diminishing lack of power on the factory floor tended to distance the relationship between first-level supervisors and upper management. This distance in turn has led to status and role conflicts—something now intuitively obvious to factory workers.

Technological Change

The rate of growth via technological change on the production floor has also transformed the role of the first-level supervisor. In many automated factories, AMT performs tasks and monitors production status in much the same way as the first-level supervisor does. Moreover, many first-level supervisors are just not able to cope with the advancing technology and thus are finding it difficult to adjust to their new roles.

With extensive amount of training and education required to manage in an advanced technology environment, coupled with other factors mentioned, it has become exceedingly difficult for first-level supervisors to maintain a predominant role on the factory floor. Again, this direct blow to supervisor job status enhances the role conflicts among worker, supervisor, and upper management.

Government Intervention

What was once typically the judgment of the first-level supervisor with regard to working conditions has now been assumed by the federal government in an attempt to further protect the factory worker from unfair management practices. Now the first-level supervisor must conform to rules placed on him/her relative to specific government regulations. The impact of Occupational Safety and Health Act (OSHA), specific labor laws, detailed formal reporting relationships, and the makeup of the work force on the factory floor has again diluted much of the first-level supervisor's authority and power.

The government's affirmative action program has in fact made the biggest impact on the first-level supervisor. No longer does he hire workers of the same sex, color, or national origin. The government mandates a more heterogeneous work force, one more in line with the demographics of the country. Because of this, the first-level supervisor, who no longer selects or hires factory workers, has seen a further decrease in his power as a supervisor. Again we witness the widening rift between the status and roles the first-level supervisor had initially, and the new role being prescribed through the evolutionary process.

American Demographics

The change in the American work force in recent years has effected the role of the first-level supervisor. Factory workers now coming out of school are better educated and have taken specific courses in school which target their skills to maintain and operate the new machines. These workers often are as educated, if not more educated, than the supervisors who employ them. With the factory workers' increased awareness, they begin to demand and expect to receive work that will enhance the quality of their own work lives. Their increased exposure to leisure activities, a desire for a decreased work week that gives them more hours free, and a reluctant attitude toward autocratic leadership on the shop floor have revised the dominant role that the first-level supervisor once had.

Thus, supervision on the factory floor and prestige and status that were originally considered part of the position have been realigned and restructured. Whatever advantage the first-level supervisor once had relative to skills and education level has been now lost, as has the edge over the composition of the production work force. The factory floor is now much more heterogeneous than in prior years as a result the disparity in ages of workers has significantly widened. Women and minorities have also added to an increasing percentage of the work force. The first-level supervisor, once the dominant position on the production floor, now has to satisfy workers with stronger education backgrounds, different ethnic backgrounds, widening age spans, and varied social interests. It is no wonder this position is now at the crossroads.

The End of an Era

The era of the traditional factory foreman is now coming to an end. Management evolution and the need to perform a function on the factory floor more in step with the events of the day have taken hold. The ability to adapt to this change and develop the appropriate management attitude will be the key to this transformation effort.

Most first-level supervisors were originally employed at the present level they are now supervising. In fact, some first-level supervisors were actually members of a specific peer group they are now responsible for, and had enjoyed the company of these people as friends and equals. Therefore, now more than ever before, it is important for first-level supervisors to prevent subordinate perceptions of politics, favoritism, and diluted authority by creating social differentiation from erstwhile colleagues.[8] This ability to work with employees and adapt under a changing production environment will best position the first-level supervisor for his role in the factory of the future.

THE FIRST-LEVEL SUPERVISOR IN TODAY'S FACTORY

The events of the past mandate a change in the role of the first-level supervisor. The predominant position on the factory floor has to evolve past traditional roles in order to meet up with today's contemporary manufacturing practices. Experts generally agree that the change in today's first-level supervisor will occur somewhat radically. Barry A. Stein, President of Goodmeasure, Inc., a Cambridge, Mass., consulting firm, states "They (foremen) aren't going to control people anymore. They have to coach them, help do the planning, approve organizational direction, and make sure the directions are clear. It will be an enabling function, rather than a control function."[9]

What then are some of the major changes, and the implications of these changes on first-level supervision? In a 1965 study conducted by Mahoney, Jerdee, and Carroll, 452 supervisors were asked how they spent their workdays. This study showed that supervisors normally divide their workdays into six specific functions.[10]

- *Supervision*: The ability to monitor and facilitate technical processing and subordinate behavior
- *Investigation*: The ability to analyze problems in the production process
- *Coordination*: The ability to solve problems with other workers as a member of a team
- *Scheduling*: The ability to match both human and machine resources to the ultimate needs of the customer
- *Staffing and training*: The ability to have the right person in the correct function, adequately trained.
- *Evaluation*: The ability to monitor performance of their subordinates and award appropriate compensation for the work performed.

Based on this classic study, how do we visualize these activities changing as flexible factory automation moves onto the shop floor in today's manufacturing organization?

Supervising the Production Process

Advanced manufacturing technology makes it possible for various machines on the floor to regulate and monitor their own activities. Therefore, the need for workers to closely supervise each machine is moot; the need for first-level supervisors to monitor the workers who monitor machines becomes less as well. Therefore, those organizations that implement AMT will notice that their first-level supervisors can now be given a greater span of control and increased responsibility for more machines and a larger percentage of the production process.

Flexible automation is more technical in nature than traditional equipment. With the consequences of machine downtime, there is a greater need to develop an ongoing preventative maintenance program. Thus, the first-level supervisor will now become actively involved in the company's preventative maintenance program. This function will then no longer be just a maintenance engineering project. First-level supervisors will be actively involved.

Supervising the Human Process

The increase in AMT will cause the production worker to be less machine operator and more machine tender.[11] Since the machines require less monitoring, the production worker will have to increase his responsibilities as to how, what, and when specific functions are completed. Production workers will now become more self-disciplined and more self-directed. Consequently, the first-level supervisors who now manage these people will need to change the way they supervise. Examples of these changes are as follows:

- First-level supervisors will now need to heavily depend on operating staff. Production workers will now have to make the proper decision with the supervisor's direct input into the problem.

- First-level supervisors need to foster and maintain a stream of upward communication. The supervisor must encourage the staff to communicate effectively with other workers.
- First-level supervisors will now need to motivate their production workers based upon a different set of criteria. Rather than rewarding employees based upon obedience and physical activity, AMT supervisors will reward and motivate production workers based upon innovation, knowledge, product quality judgment, and initiative.
- First-level supervisors with AMT will monitor fewer people per specific machine. Thus, while a first-level supervisor's span of control in the production process may increase, the actual number of production workers involved in the process may decrease.

Investigation of Problems

All first-level supervisors investigate problems in production on a daily basis. Many of these problems can be easily solved while other problems require the first-level supervisor to obtain information from one or several sources prior to an answer. In the past, the supervisor was able to track down a specific problem with minimal assistance from others. This was because the supervisor was a master of his own area, and thus there tended to be a lack of integration between the machinery and the production process. With AMT, however, first-level supervisors are no longer responsible for a single type of machine or specific functioning area. Rather, supervision is now carried out in an area that is much more sophisticated and complex. A problem such as poor production quality can no longer be solved solely by a supervisor. Today, the first-level supervisor has to work jointly with different departments in order to determine what in the production process is causing sub-par product quality.

The integrated complexity of AMT requires all first-level supervisors to approach and investigate problems from a total systems perspective. However, once the problem has been thoroughly investigated, the first-level supervisor cannot walk away.

He can no longer simply correct the symptom. He now needs to correct the underlying cause of the problem. First-level supervisors need to roll up their sleeves and determine if a problem encountered and corrected will have an impact on future product coming downstream.

This type of internal investigation requires first-level supervisors to reevaluate the many uses of computer information. More time must be spent integrating streams of information and testing alternative hypotheses. In short, the first-level supervisor with AMT will have to be more an information broker and less a hands-on manager.

At Ford Motor Company's Edison, New Jersey, plant, this change has already taken place. Each first-level supervisor at this plant was once referred to as a "hard-nosed, loudmouth disciplinarian." Yet today things are different.

> He chats with the workers, solicits their ideas, and even encourages them to use recently installed buttons to stop the line if a defect prevents them from correctly doing their job. The thought of an hourly worker stopping the line here would make old Henry Ford apoplectic, but the stop concept is one aspect of a worker participation program that has inspired quality, reduced absenteeism, and lessened hostility between supervisors and workers. Its unique success depends on first-level supervisors. They must listen to what workers have to say, use the workers' ideas, and then focus on problem solving rather than meting out discipline.[12]

Coordination

The advances of AMT on the production floor create the need for first-level supervisors to be less independent and more dependent on the workers or other supervisors. This need for interdependence results in the supervisor now being responsible for a much larger segment of the production process. First-level supervisors today become involved with different people with varying types of expertise in order to function properly and to solve operating problems. The first-level supervisor, in essence, now becomes the central figure on the plant floor to coordinate and facilitate communications among groups.

Since AMT reduces the need for direct supervision of workers, the first-level supervisor now has time to coordinate meetings between different production areas, resolve problems, and promote active synergism. In the factory of the future, the need to coordinate activities across functional lines is imperative. The first-level supervisor is in the ideal position now to coordinate meetings, resolve operating dilemmas, facilitate change, and take a fresh look at problems that overlap several departments.

Scheduling

Every first-level supervisor schedules on a continual basis. This is compulsory in order to organize the production process to match the immediate demand requirements of the business. Scheduling in the past took up a considerable amount of the supervisor's time. Thus, less time was available to spend in the other functional areas. However, with AMT, the ability to schedule production more efficiently and in less time is a valuable benefit.

Since the machines on the production floor in a semiautomated plant are self-regulated and adjusting, they provide the supervisor with valuable input on production rates and status of orders. This information which was once obtained manually by walking through the plant and collecting data, is now aggregated and reported back to the first-level supervisor via video display terminals on the shop floor. Hence, less time is used collecting data for scheduling, and more time can be spent by each supervisor in planning future production loads. Advanced technology provides increased efficiency and management effectiveness for production schedulers.

Staffing and Training

Staffing and training have long been primary responsibilities for the first-level supervisor. The way individuals are selected for employment differs from company to company. Within some companies, the first-level supervisor takes an active part in the selection—and termination—process, while in others this function is relinquished to another staffing area in the company. Thus, the role the supervisor plays today in staffing a department depends more on specific management preference and less on AMT.[13]

However, AMT does substantially change the way supervisors train production workers. Training under the auspices of AMT increases significantly, as first-level supervisors require better trained production workers as flexible automation increases. Moreover, training becomes an important motivator as other more conventional motivators are eliminated from the factory floor.

First-level supervisors will now have to be actively involved in the training programs in their own organizations. They might be consulted with about the kinds of training required for workers under flexible automation. They might be actively involved in preparing documentation or user manuals. They might even conduct the training sessions themselves. Whatever the case, it is clear that training increases in importance for the first-level supervisor under AMT; the way each supervisor is involved in the training program varies with each organization.

Evaluation

The evaluation of production workers has always been the prime responsibility of the first-level supervisor. Who else is better equipped to understand how each employee performs than the individual who is in control of both the people and the process? While first-level supervisors continue to evaluate employees in an AMT environment, there is a significant twist. Flexible automation on the production floor gives the first-level supervisor more time to get involved with individual employees. Since AMT does not require the supervisor to closely monitor the employee, more time will be made available to actively review an employee's overall performance on a job and evaluate subsequent performance.

THE IMPACT OF AMT ON TODAY'S FIRST-LEVEL SUPERVISOR

As the factory of the future takes hold and the functions we described begin to evolve, the role of the first-level supervisor needs to be reviewed. What are the implications for a first-level supervisor's job design under AMT? What types of first-level supervisors should we be looking for in our factory? What will we need to do to train the first-level supervisor? Let us discuss these important questions.

The Impact on Job Design

Under AMT the first-level supervisor becomes increasingly dependent upon machine operators, support personnel, and other supervisors. Due to the need to coordinate communication among a myriad of shop floor supervisors, each supervisor must develop his own network for discussing mutual problems and opportunities with peers on the production floor.

Advanced manufacturing gives the first-level supervisor additional time for nonproduction activities. This time was not available before AMT. Consequently, each organization cannot let factory supervisors revert to their traditional responsibilities of foreman, but rather identify and match new tasks for the supervisor with activities that now best address the organization's needs.

Management must now specify to the organization what the new role responsibilities of the first-level supervisor are. AMT changes the role of the supervisor on the factory floor, but unless management specifically details and communicates what tasks are now expected from the first-level supervisor, AMT cannot be successful.

A large percentage of a first-level supervisor's position description will now include training and group facilitation. The first-level supervisor must spend increased time on employee development—even, if necessary, conducting training sessions himself. Moreover, the factory foremen will need to encourage group problem solving. Since AMT requires a "systems" approach to problem solving, the first-level supervisor must help his team members work together and solve problems as a group.

The most important effect of AMT on supervisor job design is that the supervisor now becomes a major facilitator of change in the factory. Since AMT will proceed in the future as a continuous project, factory workers will need to look to an individual on the shop floor who represents both stability and management's desire to improve productivity on the shop floor. The first-level supervisor, with his new role responsibilities, is the ideal candidate to act as this catalyst for change.

The Impact on Supervisor Selection and Training

What is the most important aspect in the selection of a first-level supervisor under AMT? Are the technical skills more important than the human relations skills? Or does the ability to manage a cohesive team of workers who understand their functions and are geared to a group effort outweigh the knowledge of the technical aspects of a job?

The evidence today suggests that the effective first-level supervisor needs to be taught the technical skills of a job so that he knows at least as much about the job as the worker. These skills would include, yet not be limited to:

- Fault finding
- Basic machine repair
- Data input
- Adjusting computer programs
- Problem solving

In addition, training for first-level supervisors could go one step further to include Numerical Control (NC) programming, maintenance, and a basic overview of manufacturing planning.

Yet, the technical skills cannot stand alone. First-level supervisors need to balance the technical aspects of their job with their interpersonal skills. These skills include but are not limited to:

- Team building
- Facilitating group meetings
- Communications between cross-functional departments
- Conflict resolution
- Motivating for good as well as sub-par performance

Can our first-level supervisor respond to today's challenge brought forth by AMT? Can we motivate a factory foreman to learn these skills and not be resistant to change? These questions must be resolved. Says Lyman Ketchum, who helped design the first sociotechnical plant in Topeka, Kansas, in 1971:

Teamwork requires a drastic change in management style and methods. The old idea that a supervisor's main function is to control workers is replaced with the concept that a supervisor should encourage employees to use initiative. This goes against the grain of everything supervisors have been taught since the early years of the century. To accept the commitment model of work, managers have to go through a personal paradigm shift, which is a deep psychological process.[14]

Thus, in order to make AMT survive on the production floor, management needs to understand any resistance to change and take steps to overcome this potential barrier.

Resistance to Change on the Factory Floor

In her study of twelve companies implementing AMT, Barbara Fossum asked managers from each company to list in specific terms what they felt were the nontechnical barriers to AMT. She found that the barriers most commonly mentioned were manifestations of managerial resistance to change, production managers' attitudes ("if it's not broken, don't fix it"), fear of the unknown, managerial caution, and a preference for traditional rather than systems thinking.[15]

In all industries implementing or considering the benefits of flexible automation on the shop floor, it must be understood upfront that not all first-level supervisors will accept this new technology with open arms. There will be some obvious resistance. In order to fully understand how to deal with this resistance, we must first determine its source. Once we have identified the root cause of the problem, we will be better able to actively pursue the solution.

Sources of Resistance to AMT   A truism in the workplace holds that any time a job gets redesigned via automation, there is always a lack of communication between the employee and management. This lack of communication leads directly to job ambiguity—the first source of resistance to AMT on the shop floor. As the factory of the future takes shape and facets of AMT are being implemented, management unfortunately fails to think through the first-level supervisors' roles clearly enough. This lack of role definition leaves the first-level supervisor wondering if his job will still be there after implementation of AMT, and if so, how it will now be structured. This lack of clear job definition tends to lead to the fear that the first-level supervisor's status will be eroded as production workers now take on responsibilities that for many years belonged to the first-level supervisor.

The possibility of losing status and power is another point of resistance to AMT. It is very difficult for shop floor management to relinquish power after having worked so hard to acquire it. Since power is based upon the ability to make decisions on the floor, if production workers or computers now exercise this authority to make decisions, there is a status of power loss. States Richard Mortell, research engineer at Boeing Aerospace, "The installation of a flexible manufacturing system to make parts for air launched cruise missiles was fought by supervisors afraid of relinquishing authority."[16]

Resistance to the implementation of AMT by first-level supervisors is a problem that will have to be dealt with today. Unless organizations work together to help install and implement flexible automation, from both the human relations aspect and the technical side, many more problems than nec-

essary will be created, all of which inhibit successful AMT implementation.

A third source of resistance is the matter of education. First-level supervisors who have been ingrained with the old methods of production have a tendency to not want to move out of their "comfort zone." Moreover, they are concerned about their need to learn both technical and nontechnical skills.

Overcoming First-Level Supervisor Resistance

Top management can pursue several avenues to effectively manage and overcome this potential resistance to AMT.

Increased Education   Education of all individuals involved with a flexible automation project will help counteract shop floor resistance. The more each factory foreman knows, the more likely he is to become enthusiastic about the project and offer assistance on how implementation could be successful. We need to educate both first-level supervisors and production workers about AMT, and its impact on them personally.

Supervisor Participation   Nothing makes a project succeed like active participation on the part of the users. If first-level supervisors become involved with an AMT project from the outset, they then have the opportunity to work through their concerns about the new system prior to its implementation.

Information Sharing   Keeping first level supervisors actively informed about the project on a daily basis enhances user involvement. Constant information allows supervisors to see that various options were considered in making any one decision and why the alternatives were rejected. The best way to communicate this type of information to first-level supervisors is via a weekly status memorandum.

Role Clarification   Management must respond to job anxieties before any AMT project begins. This helps define and clarify the role of the first-level supervisor upfront, before the lack of role clarity creates an attitude that is difficult to change.

Resistance will occur as AMT on the factory floor becomes more of a reality. Management must understand why it exists and more importantly, how to resolve this resistance before it becomes a major operational problem. Yet all resistance may not be necessarily negative. Many first-level supervisors may have compelling arguments against AMT as the future direction for the company. If their argument is strong enough and they cannot be convinced that AMT is a viable approach, it may be beneficial to sit down and listen to their ideas. They may know something intuitively that management may have overlooked.

THE FUTURE ROLE OF THE FIRST-LEVEL SUPERVISOR

Technology on the manufacturing floor will have an enormous impact on a first-level supervisor's job responsibilities in the future. In one way or another it has already changed the job functions of 40 to 50 million production workers, about half of the U.S. work force.[17] This trend will continue as the manufacturing community strives to remain competitive by reducing the components of product costs while simultaneously improving product quality.

Advanced technology will require radical changes in traditional work practices in the future. Frederick Taylor's techniques of "scientific management"—dividing work into discrete operating tasks that require little skill or training—are already passé. With flexible automation on the factory floor, where computers integrate a myriad of functions such as shipping, receiving, inventory control, and assembly, it will be impossible to define jobs or measure performance individually. Rather, manufacturing organizations of the future will require a collection of skilled people to manage a segment of technology and perform collectively as a team.

Flexible automation is here to stay. First-level supervisors, in order to be successful in their newly defined positions need to embrace the marriage of man and machine. The first-level supervisor of the future will be actively involved in activities quite unlike those of his predecessor. The following paragraphs describe some of these newly acquired work skills.

The first characteristic of the supervisor of the future is an increased emphasis on management by participation. Production workers in the future will be better trained and more highly educated than ever before. Flexible automation will require that these individuals are capable of making decisions on the production floor, decisions which at one time were solely made by the first-level supervisor. The first-level supervisor must in the future help develop his workers' decision skills, while at the same time provide synergism to the overall system's shared goals.

Second, the foreman of the future must recognize autonomous work groups. With the increase of automation on the factory floor and better skilled production workers, the first-level supervisor needs to see his work force as being more autonomous. Since each production worker will be held directly accountable for actions taken, the first-level supervisor will monitor results. The intent is to make each work group responsible for its actions, yet still overseen to ensure direct accountability by their first-level supervisor. Will this change the way the first-level supervisor performs his job? According to Cummings, the following will remain key supervisory responsibilities:

- Helping develop group members
- Helping the group maintain its boundaries

While these skills were not normally relegated to the first-level supervisor in the past, they will be in the future.

Third, supervisors must come to terms with increased computer information on the factory floor. Computers will entirely take over certain functions previously performed by first-level supervisors. Therefore, the degree of sophistication of the equipment will increase and so will the skills necessary for the first-level supervisor.

All over the factory, computer information systems will make it possible for all levels of management to obtain information about workers, production schedules, and problems on the shop floor. Supervisors will still be responsible for analyzing the data and reporting to management. However, the labor composition of the first-level supervisor on the shop floor will change. Factors contributing to this change include readily accessible product information, a declining need to supervise machines that are highly mechanized, and an increasingly skilled work force that needs less direction. Automation will eventually decrease the number of first-level supervisors, but those remaining supervisors will have greater operating influence then ever before.

Fourth, supervisors will be expected to work with more specialized staff members. As the need to be more competitive as a basic means of survival increases, each manufacturing organization will acquire specialized staff to work with first-level supervisors. In the areas of government intervention, union influence, and technological innovations specialists will be brought in to solve problems in conjunction with first-level supervisors—problems that may be beyond the scope of the supervisor's current skills. Because of this influx of specialists, the first-level supervisor will spend more time away from his specific work area, and will require increased training in functions such as ''brainstorming'' and alternative methods of influence. The presence of specialists will tend to reduce the supervisor's authority further, since he will now be required to implement programs created by others.

CONCLUSION

As flexible automation becomes a way of life on the production floor, the skill sets of the first-level supervisor will dramatically change. Human relations skills will take on a much higher value than in the past. The human factor will clearly be the key element in the implementation of AMT. Indeed, management commitment to motivating people through job enrichment and training is mandatory if the expected return on investment with AMT is ever to be realized. Yet success on the production floor must start with the first-level supervisor. For

in this position, more than with anyone else, will we immediately begin to witness the impact of AMT.

We have described the role of the first-level supervisor from past to present to future in order to demonstrate how flexible automation will impact supervisory performance on the production floor. Will there be a first level supervisor in our factory of the future, or will this position eventually be phased out due to AMT? The evidence is clear: contrary to the engineer's vision of factories run by robots, the workplace will depend more than ever on the skills of the first-level supervisor.

However, because of the declining need for direct worker supervision the number of first-level supervisors will be far fewer than today. More importantly, the tasks and activities associated with these positions will no longer resemble the activities of their predecessors; hence, the term first-level supervisor may no longer be appropriate. Tomorrow's supervisors will perform fewer activities than they do now. These tasks will be centered primarily around cultivating human relations at the workplace and being a liaison between upper management and the production workers on the floor.

The impact these changes will have on manufacturing organizations will be tantamount to culture shock. With AMT, companies will have to revise their selection practice for new supervisors and update their training methods as well. The first-level supervisor in tomorrow's factory will need to be more technically knowledgeable and possess superior human relations skills in order to deal with highly trained production workers, much more so than their predecessors. Also, organizations will have to realize that these increased required skill levels for first-level supervisors will mandate the need to increased compensation levels that match these skills. This hopefully will position the first-level supervisor closer to the position of lower management, and farther away from the production workers. This may have a positive effect of reducing the role and status conflicts that inadvertently occur when AMT is introduced.

The future of the first-level supervisor is a healthy one. This position will remain viable in tomorrow's factories. Yet, even after careful training and selection of tomorrow's factory leaders, the job will not come easy. The first-level supervisor will still have to deal with the conflicts between working staff and management. These problems have been with this position since inception, and have evolved over time as a result of changes in the organizational power relationships. As we see the job designs of the first-level supervisor changing in the future, we can develop action plans such as retraining the role restructuring to help combat and improve the supervisor's lot. Yet, without a systematic approach by upper management to resolve problems previously mentioned, the supervisor of the future will still be viewed as "the man in the middle," caught between the often conflicting expectations of upper management and the work force.

Manufacturing management must start today to plan for the role of AMT on the production floor. The first-level supervisor must be at least a part of the change process, if not the catalyst in his depart-ment. With AMT there are no limits to the progress that can be made. But as impressive as the statistics are, they have not come about solely because flexible automation is cheaper or robots have entered another generation. The technology is a part of the story, yet it is the second biggest part. Reevaluating the role of the first-level supervisor on the shop floor is obviously our biggest challenge.

If a company plans on hitching its future to machines that can perform with great speed and efficiency, then it must begin to revamp the social structure of the organization so that the appropriate skills of its people are as efficient as well. The first-level supervisor position will endure in the future, in a form which now is in an evolutionary process. The burden now lies with top management in each and every organization to facilitate the process so that the results of AMT implementation may benefit all members of society.

ENDNOTES

1. S. Kerr, "The First Level Supervisor: Phasing Out or Here to Stay," *Academy of Management Review*, 11: 1 (1986): 103-107.

2. P. Edwards, "Factory Managers: Their Role in Personal Management and Their Place in the Company," *Journal of Management Studies* 24:5 (September 1987): 479-499.

3. "Closing the Gap," *Duns Business Month* 125 (April 1985): Special Report.

4. *Ibid*.

5. K. Ebel, "Some Workplace Effects of CAD and CAM," *International Labor Review* 120 (May/June 1987): 306-361.

6. "Winners and Losers: On the Factory Floor, Technology Brings Challenge for Some, Dredging for Others," *Wall Street Journal* (September 16, 1985): 1.

7. "Getting Man and Machine to Live Happily Ever After," *Business Week* (April 20, 1987): 61.

8. S. Kerr, K. Hill, and L. Broedling, "The First Level Supervisor Phasing Out or Here to Stay?," *Academy of Management Review* 11:1 (1986): 109-110.

9. "The Old Foreman is on the Way Out and the New One Will Be More Important," *Business Week* (April 25, 1983): 97-110.

10. T. A. Mahoney, T. H. Jerdee, and S. I. Carrol, "The Jobs of Management," *Industrial Relations* 4 (1965): 97-110.

11. N. Napier, R. Peterson, "Putting Human Resource Management at the Management Level," Reprinted from *Business Horizons* (Jan-Feb 1984): 72. Copyright by the Foundation for the School of Business at Indiana University. Used with permission.

12. "The Old Foreman is on the Way Out and the New One Will Be More Important," 7.

13. Manufacturing Studies Board, Committee on the Effective Implementation of Advanced Manufacturing Technology, National Research Council National Academy of Sciences, *Human Resource Practices for Implementing Advanced Manufacturing Technology* (Washington, DC: National Academy Press, 1986).

14. J. Hoerr, M. Pollock, and D. Whiteside, "Management Discovers the Human Side of Automation," *Business Week* (September 29, 1986): 72.

15. B. Fossum, "A Survey of CIM Plants," Paper presented at the American Institute of Decision Services Meeting, Las Vegas, Nevada, November 1985, 5-6.

16. H. Brody, "Overcoming Barriers to Automation," *High Technology* (May 1985): 42-43.

17. Hoerr, et.al., "Human Side of Automation," 71.

18. T. G. Cummings, "Self-Regulating Work Groups: A Sociotechnical Synthesis," *Academy of Management Review* 3: 624-634.

3

Management of Quality

Jerry Banks[*]

THE ACHIEVEMENT OF QUALITY INVOLVES HUMANS and has proven to be one of the most difficult managerial tasks in the modern factory. Various effective statistical procedures have been developed, yet they only solve a portion of the problem. The statistical methods especially related to controlling the automated factory are discussed in chapter 34.

This chapter starts with the definition of the management of quality and then analyzes three important aspects of this activity: quality engineering, strategic management of quality, and management programs for quality. Each aspect is further divided into component sections. Under quality engineering, are the quality engineering function, quality engineering technology, and the activities of the quality engineer. Strategic management of quality includes appraisals, failure analysis, quality education and training, consumer affairs, product safety, and product liability. Described in management programs for quality are programs such as motivation, organization, zero defects, and quality information systems. Quality circles are briefly described, but chapter 4 is devoted entirely to this very effective technique. This chapter closes with two short sections on quality control in the 1990s and the concept of manufacturing excellence.

This chapter presents, in condensed form, a vast amount of knowledge and information published by various prominent authors. The goal is to familiarize you with the various concepts pertaining to management of quality.

THE MEANING OF THE MANAGEMENT OF QUALITY

Management of quality is the organizational function responsible for defect prevention. Activities that are accountable to quality management, as discussed in Feigenbaum (1983), include the following:

1. Accumulation, compilation, and reporting of quality costs
2. Establishment of quality cost reduction goals and programs
3. Development of systems for measuring the true outgoing quality level of the product
4. Establishment of product-quality improvement goals and programs
5. Establishment of product-quality improvement goals and programs by product line
6. Establishment of objectives, goals, and programs for the quality-control organizational component and the publication of these for use by appropriate personnel
7. Classification of quality-control activity as to generic kinds of work

*Much of this chapter is adapted with permission from J. Banks, "Management of Quality," Chapter 2 in *Principles of Quality Control* (New York: John Wiley & Sons, 1989). Jerry Banks is Associate Professor of Industrial and Systems Engineering at the Georgia Institute of Technology in Atlanta, Georgia. He teaches in the areas of discrete-event simulation and quality control. He is the author and coauthor of numerous books and many technical articles. One of his recent books was *Principles of Quality Control* published by John Wiley & Sons in 1989. He conducts research in on-line simulation and in the validation and verification of large-scale simulation models. Dr. Banks is the Institute of Industrial Engineer's representative to the Board of the Winter Simulation Conference and currently serves as Board Chairman.

8. Organization to do the quality-control work and staff the organization
9. Issuance of procedures for doing the quality-control work
10. Acceptance of the quality-control work assignments by individuals
11. Integration of all individuals into the quality-control organizational component and development of measures of effectiveness to determine the contribution of the quality-control function to the profitability and progress of the company[1]

The purpose of quality management is to manufacture a product whose quality is designed, produced, and maintained at the least possible cost, while still providing full customer satisfaction. This aim can be converted into the following list of tasks presented by Kivenko (1984):

1. Participate in design reviews, reliability analyses, environmental testing, and other defect-prevention tasks
2. Help create an environment and culture of quality
3. Keep within the operating costs established by budgets and estimates
4. Acquire adequate personnel, equipment, and facilities to perform professional quality control
5. Establish accurate, adequate, and economical measuring techniques and obtain equipment for control of product quality
6. Control the quality of purchased material as specified in engineering drawings, documents, and purchase orders
7. Measure product quality through process evaluation, product inspection, packaging inspection, and audit
8. Diagnose quality-inhibiting situations and conditions and identify the underlying causes
9. Return quality information to organizational groups and vendors requiring this knowledge
10. Initiate corrective action to eliminate poor design, material, processes, and worker skills
11. Collect quality data to assist in analysis and prevention activity
12. Respond promptly to customer complaints and queries[2]

FIGURE 3-1 summarizes the functions of management in the quality system. The *Plan* section can be considered the origin. The arrows pointing clockwise signify the direction to the next proper course of action. Once the *Control* section is reached, the cycle continues to the plan section. The inner circle represents the phases, the middle cycle represents the actions, and the outer circle represents the functions. The entire process, therefore, denotes the never-ending cycle of the quality system.

QUALITY ENGINEERING

This section describes three important constituents of quality engineering: the quality engineering function, quality engineering technology, and the activities of the quality engineer. Although this section does not cover all the aspects of quality engineering, it does review the general functions and applications.

The Quality Engineering Function

An important element of the quality management function is quality engineering. Quality engineering has a role in the activity of every department of the firm; establishment of quality control programs is the most important activity. By establishing acceptance methods and procedures, conducting failure analysis, reporting the results, and stressing the need for corrective action, quality engineering also assists the appraisal operation. This operation consists of the inspection and test functions, a topic discussed more fully later in this chapter in the section, "Product Appraisals."

Other roles of quality engineering, as discussed by Crosby (1986), include:

1. Assisting the purchasing department in
   (a) selecting a vendor

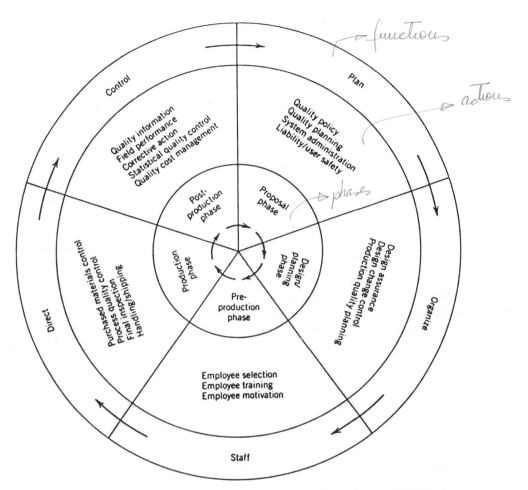

Source: Schilling, E.G., "The Role of Statistics in the Management of Quality", *Quality Progress*, Vol. 17, No. 8, pp. 33, © 1984 American Society for quality Control. Reprinted by permission.)

Fig. 3-1. Functions of management in the quality system.

(b) preparing the buyer rating results

(c) training supplier personnel

(d) determining the need for source control or inspection

(e) setting up the appraisal plan

2. Assisting the engineering department in

(a) arranging design reviews, product qualification, life testing, and other measurements oriented to prevention

(b) providing data concerning manufacturing and customer experience with products

3. Assisting the marketing and sales department in

(a) providing product performance data

(b) conducting quality seminars for customers

(c) handling customer affairs

(d) providing experience data to assist in developing new specifications

4. Assisting the comptroller in

(a) determining the cost of quality

(b) devising quality control programs to evaluate clerical accuracy

5. Assisting the manufacturing department in

(a) determining appraisal activities for each product and process

(b) selecting test equipment

(c) devising sampling techniques

(d) conducting quality orientation for manufacturing personnel

6. Assisting the administration department in

(a) setting up new employee orientation programs

(b) conducting companywide quality awareness activities

(c) providing measurement guidance for internal programs[3]

Quality Engineering Technology

Quality engineering technology is defined by Feigenbaum (1983) as the body of technical knowledge for formulating policy and for analyzing and planning product quality in order to implement and support the quality system that will yield full customer satisfaction at a minimum cost. There are three major techniques used in quality engineering: preparation of quality policy, product-quality analysis, and quality operations planning. Each of these will now be discussed in more detail.

Preparation of quality policy includes techniques for identifying the quality objectives of a firm. It is important that these quality objectives be clearly defined. Otherwise, no foundation is provided upon which to build functional quality plans. Policy provides the limits for all quality-related decisions needed to meet the quality objectives. This policy is the pattern that guides and governs all management decisions in product-quality areas, including reliability, safety, and inspection.

It is also important that the quality objectives be clearly understood by every employee. This process begins with the preparation of a formal policy statement. In this statement, management can identify the objective of quality leadership; point out the key role that quality plays in the company's acceptance by its customers; stress quality considerations that are of primary importance; and emphasize the importance of each employee's knowing and understanding individual and organizational responsibilities in achieving the company's quality goal.

Product-quality analysis includes techniques for isolating and identifying the factors that affect the quality of products. The act of analyzing involves decomposing a problematic quality situation and then synthesizing the segments to form the whole. Feigenbaum (1983) gives the following examples of segments found in a product-quality situation: customer-use needs and wants, the function to be performed by the product, environments encountered by the product, life and reliability requirements, safety requirements, requirements of regulatory agencies and government industry standards, attractiveness of appearance, product design, manufacturing process, shipping conditions, traceability of the product, liability loss control, installation, maintenance and services, characteristics of the market, and competitive offerings.

Quality operations planning includes techniques for emphasizing the development of a proposed course of action and methods for accomplishing the desired result. The proposed plan is prepared with the necessary diagrams, formulas, and tables in order to communicate the plan to the person or persons expected to execute it.

The primary purpose of planning is to deliver a product of satisfactory quality to the customer at the minimum quality cost. This objective is accomplished by carefully planning the necessary quality procedures that will later become part of the manufacturing process. The final output of the planning process is a set of detailed instructions specifying prescribed courses of action needed to meet the company's quality objective.

Activities of the Quality Engineer

Several or all of the following tasks, given by Simmons (1970), make up an important part of the quality engineer's job:

1. *Training*—prepare educational material for conducting training programs in all aspects of quality control, including statistical quality con-

trol (SQC); train employees at all levels of the organization and keep abreast of new developments for the purposes of training and application

2. *Quality standards*—develop and implement quality standards where needed in the organization; train members of the organization in their use

3. *Measurement and analytical facilities*—determine, recommend, and/or design measurement and analytical facilities required to evaluate product quality and reliability; develop and maintain an economical program for periodic precision and accuracy checks, for calibration, and for maintenance of all jigs, fixtures, physical testing, measurements, and analytical facilities

4. *Methods and procedures*—develop forms and instructions to be used for collecting, analyzing, and reporting quality and reliability data; institute procedures for identifying responsibilities and for implementing corrective action

5. *Nonconforming material*—establish and implement clear concise procedures for the disposition of nonconforming material; determine the responsibility and proper allocation of the extra costs involved

6. *Audit of the quality program*—provide methods and arrange for auditing and reporting the progress of the implementation stage, as well as the effectiveness, cost, and savings of the quality program[4]

STRATEGIC MANAGEMENT OF QUALITY

The modern corporation, as described by Hansen and Ghare (1987), is a complex system in which decisions are made, communicated, and implemented. The comments in this introductory portion describe the role of production-line workers, even though the automated factory may not have people in this category. However, the philosophy is so important to the management of quality that it requires discussion. The components of production, including quality, depend on the manner in which decisions are reached, the structure of the communication network, and the implementation system. Persons at all levels within the corporation, from chief executive officer to line supervisors in the automated factory, eventually have some influence on the final quality.

The production-line worker's influence is significant. Management systems, quality control techniques, and management goals do not produce high-quality products. Only motivated, well-trained workers using proper equipment and materials do so. If the worker is overlooked, any effort to improve quality is bound to fail.

Junior managers, such as line supervisors, are the last link in the communication of the decisions and the first link in their implementation. If junior managers feel apprehensive about or do not understand decisions, the implementation of those decisions will probably be inadequate or inappropriate. Therefore, for the purposes of quality control, it is very important that the goal and objective of the decisions be understood by junior managers.

Middle managers, from section supervisors to plant and division managers, are the persons who make all the decisions on the manufacturing floor. Motivation, training, equipment, and materials are four key elements in the production of high-quality products, and all depend on the decisions of middle managers.

Top managers, from vice presidents to the chief executive officer, usually are not involved in the day-to-day operational decisions. Any involvement in such decisions would greatly diminish the time these top managers spend on their principal function, which is strategic decision and policy making for the entire corporation. Their role in quality improvement includes setting the policy guidelines, creating an atmosphere within the corporation that encourages better decision making by the middle managers, and structuring the corporation so that the communication and implementation of decisions is facilitated.

The failure of management to plan for the future and to foresee problems causes waste of personnel, materials, and manufacturing resources—all of which raise the manufacturer's cost and the price that the purchaser must pay. Management cannot learn by gaining experience on the job. Doing one's best is not the answer. Productivity increases with improvement of quality. Low quality means high cost.

Managing Quality Control

Measures of productivity do not lead to improvement of productivity. Measures tell management how things are proceeding but they do not point the way to improvement. Best efforts are essential, but everyone is already doing his or her best. To be effective, best efforts require guidance to move in the proper direction. It is important that managers know what is required from them. Quality is everybody's job, but quality must be led by management. In order to help management improve quality, Deming (1983) suggested 14 points. These points are elucidated by Gitlow and Gitlow (1987).[5]

Point 1: Improve the Product or Service and Plan for the Future Create constancy of purpose toward improvement of the product and service, with a plan to become competitive and to stay in business.

There are, or should be, two management concerns. One deals with running the business on a day-to-day basis. The other deals with the future of the business. Problems of the future demand, first and foremost, constancy of purpose and dedication to improvement. To stay in business requires that top management spend time to innovate; put resources into research and education; constantly improve the design of the product and service; and put resources into maintenance of equipment, furniture, and fixtures.

Point 2: Adopt the New Philosophy We are in a new economic age. We can no longer live with commonly accepted levels of delays, mistakes, defective materials, and defective workmanship. The new philosophy is simple. We cannot accept today the levels of error that could be tolerated yesterday. Only management is in the position to do something about the vast majority of errors. It is management's task to remove the obstacles that prevent the worker from doing the job correctly.

Defective items are not free. The total cost to produce and dispose of a defective item exceeds the cost of produce a good one.

Point 3: Cease Dependence on Mass Inspection Require, statistical evidence that quality is built in to eliminate the need for inspection on a mass basis. Mass inspection is only 60 to 80 percent reliable. The problem with mass inspection is that it is an attempt to control the product, rather than the process. Routine 100 percent inspection is the same as planning for defects, or acknowledging that the process is not correct or that the specifications made no sense in the first place.

Inspection is too late, as well as ineffective and costly. Scrap, downgrading, and rework are not corrective actions. Quality does not come from inspection, but from improvement of the process.

Point 4: Improve the Quality of Incoming Materials End the practice of awarding business on the basis of a price tag. Instead, depend on meaningful measures of quality, along with price. Eliminate suppliers that cannot qualify with statistical evidence of quality.

One can no longer leave quality, service, and price to the forces of competition. Price has no meaning without a measure of the quality purchased. Without adequate measures of quality, business drifts to the lowest bidder; therefore, the result is low quality and high cost.

Many of the problems of poor quality and low productivity are due to poor quality of incoming materials and low quality of tools and machines. A buyer's job today is to be on the alert for lower prices. The buyer is not at fault. Management is at fault. Purchasing managers have a new job. They must now judge quality as well as price. The ability to judge quality requires education in statistical evidence of quality, supplemented by experience, which means trial and error. A supplier must qualify. There is a necessity for mutual confidence and aid between the purchaser and the vendor. There should be a reduction in the number of suppliers. It is necessary to find the few that show statistical evidence of quality.

Point 5: Find the Problems   It is management's job to work continually on the system (design, incoming materials, composition of material, maintenance, improvement of machines, training, supervision, retraining). Improvement of the system or process requires that it be under control. One should constantly improve the system of production and service. There should be continual reduction of waste and continual improvement of quality in every activity. This will yield a continual rise in productivity. A study of the defects and faults produced by a process under statistical control is ineffective. This situation can be improved only by studying the process itself.

Point 6: Institute Modern Methods of Training   Current methods of on-the-job training use control charts to determine if a worker has been properly trained and is able to perform the job correctly. Training must be totally reconstructed. Statistical methods must be used to learn when training is finished. A big problem in training and supervision is the determination of what is acceptable work and what is not.

Point 7: Institute Modern Methods of Supervision   The emphasis of production supervisors must be changed from sheer numbers to quality. Improvement of quality will automatically improve productivity. Management must prepare to take immediate action on reports from supervisors concerning problems such as inherited defects, lack of maintenance of machines, poor tools, or fuzzy operational definitions.

The basic principle is that it is the supervisor's job to coach the workers he controls. Supervision belongs to the system and is the responsibility of management. Management must take action on corrections so indicated.

Point 8: Drive Out Fear   Eliminate fear so that everyone may work effectively for the company. To achieve better quality people must feel secure. There is often fear of change, fear of the knowledge that one might have to learn a better way. Workers are afraid to inquire about a job. So they push along as best they can. One common result of fear is seen in inspection. An inspector may record the result of an inspection incorrectly for fear of exceeding the quota of allowable defectives.

Fear is a symptom of failures in hiring, training, supervision, and of bewilderment due to hard-to-follow company aims. Fear will disappear as management improves and as employees develop confidence in management.

Point 9: Break Down Barriers   People in the research, design, sales, and production departments must work as a team to foresee problems of production that may be encountered with various materials and specifications. Unless staff areas have an incentive to work jointly in a spirit of cooperation, each area will try to do what is best for itself rather than what is good for the firm. This results in losses in production due to the need to rework caused by attempts to use materials unsuited to the purpose.

Point 10: Eliminate Numerical Goals Get Rid of Posters and Slogans for the Work Force that Ask for New Levels of Productivity without Providing Methods   What is needed is not slogans but a road map to improvement. You cannot encourage workers to have zero defects or be proud of their work when many of the materials that they use are defective. Posters and standards never help workers do a better job; they fail to improve the potential of worker and machine. Instead, there should be posters explaining what management is doing to improve the system in order to make it possible to improve quality and productivity, not by working harder but by working smarter. Workers should understand that management is taking responsibility for problems and defects.

Goals are necessary, but numerical goals set for others, without a road map on how to reach the goals, have effects opposite to those sought. They generate frustration and resentment.

Point 11: Eliminate Work Standards That Prescribe Numerical Quotas   A work standard is a fortress against improvement of quality and productivity. Usually it does not include any trace of a system to help the worker do a better job.

Work standards guarantee inefficiency and high cost. At one extreme, during the last few hours of the day, workers usually stand around waiting for the whistle to blow because their daily quotas have been met. At the other extreme, to weed out those who cannot meet work standards, management may set the standards too high.

Point 12: Remove Barriers to Pride Tear down walls between hourly workers and their right to take pride in their performance. A common barrier occurs when organizations do not treat their employees properly. Often workers and managers are regarded as commodities and are treated as such. As a result, they lose not only pride in their work but also the motivation to achieve high quality. Organizations should do everything possible to restore the employees' pride in their work. By doing this, the organization will not only reap the benefits of maximizing the potential of its work force, but will also create loyalty, excitement, interest, and team spirit.

Some steps that can assist management in removing barriers include:

1. Let employees know what their job is and how it should be performed
2. Involve employees, at all levels, in the process of improvement
3. Supply workers with the proper tools, materials, and methods
4. Stress the workers' understanding of their importance in the extended process
5. Meet basic work-related needs of employees

Point 13: Institute a Vigorous Program of Education and Retraining The purpose of education and training is to fit people into new jobs and new responsibilities. Training and retraining prepare employees for changes in their current jobs with respect to procedures, materials, machines, and techniques. An educated worker is easily trained for new job duties.

Education and training can also prevent employee burnout by supplying employees with new information and job opportunities. This can be very valuable to the firm because it stimulates

interest in the job and encourages participation and involvement on the part of employees.

Point 14: Create Appropriate Structure Create a structure in management that will emphasize the preceding 13 points. To accomplish this objective, top management will require guidance from an experienced consultant. It is important to note that without such a structure, no viable long-term benefits will be achieved. Top managers must take an active part by leading the management of quality.

It is clear what Deming is referring to when he speaks of managing quality control in his 14-point plan. The problem today does not lie in the statistical quality control processes but rather in the administration of a quality program. Management needs to be retrained to realize that quality is not expensive. Quality, in turn, will increase profits. As Deming has repeatedly stated, quality does not come from inspection or a study of nonconforming items, but from an improvement of the process. It is management's job to improve this process.

Concepts with which quality-conscious managers must concern themselves include product appraisals, failure analysis, education and training, consumer affairs, product safety, and product liability. These concerns are discussed in the following sections.

Product Appraisals

An appraisal, in relation to quality, can be defined as the set of inspection and test functions that determine the value or quality of a product. The quality department is responsible for the appraisal functions relating to the acceptance of the company's products (Crosby, 1986). The data generated by performing appraisals are the quality department's most significant products. The company uses these data to form its prevention strategy and to run a continuous check on the status of the output.

An appraisal program should include plans for inspection points, instrumentation, methods, instructions, special requirements, procedures, and records. The inspection points are the physical locations in the production cycle where products or materials are appraised. Inspection usually starts in a receiving inspection station, continues to in-process inspection points, includes an end product inspection station, and concludes with a packaging and shipping inspection station. Inspections can be performed at inspection stations by using operators, process sampling, process control, or material analysis. The necessary instrumentation and method of inspection should be determined at an early stage in the planning process because of the lead time required to design or procure equipment, set physical area requirements, establish utility considerations, and train personnel.

The quality engineer should also establish an audit system to determine periodically how well the instructions are being followed and how effective the program is in realizing its goals (Simmons, 1970). Once the cycle has begun, follow-up plans should be made to include revision of instructions, modification of equipment when needed, and periodic evaluation to strengthen the weak points. The quality engineer should also serve as a communication link, forwarding inspection results to the design engineering groups. This information allows the design groups to make modifications in present or future projects.

Failure Analysis

In most instances, failures can be traced to the root causes by simple line troubleshooting or physical observation. Sometimes, however, the problem can be traced to a particular component but the method of failure and its cause remain unknown. In this instance, a failure analysis is used to pinpoint the problem. Involving a detailed, strict evaluation of the failed part, failure analysis includes elements such as stripping with an abrasive or other means to permit visual examination, microscopic or scanning electron microscopic examination to magnify defects for better understanding of failure mechanisms, and many others mentioned by Kivenko (1984).

Halpern (1978) discusses the situation that occurs when the equipment necessary to perform the failure analysis is not available within the firm. Instead, the failed parts are sent to external laboratories. When the failure report is completed, it is usually sent to the reliability department for analysis and corrective action recommendations. The reliability department investigates any previous occurrences and evaluates the possibility that a bad lot may have been responsible for several failures. If this condition is validated, the units involved are removed from the equipment and from stock.

Quality Education and Training

Quality is considered to be vital in improving productivity and is a key to economic survival in a competitive environment. As they strive to improve productivity, many firms are faced with the challenge of making their employees conscious of quality-related subjects. Quality improvement depends upon environment, system, education and training, roles and responsibilities, and cost of quality.

J. M. Juran, W. Edwards Deming, and Philip B. Crosby, well-known authors on the subject of the management of quality, emphasize training and education in quality improvement. They also stress massive training of management and employees. To maintain an acceptable skill level, more than on-the-job training is needed. A formal training program is recommended to supplement traditional types of training and to sustain highly skilled and knowledgeable employees. The training program should include top executives, exempt employees, hourly employees, and suppliers. Dedhia (1985) suggests that employee education programs be designed to eliminate functional illiteracy, develop career skills, satisfy individual goals, help employees to acquire basic knowledge and to understand their contributions to the company, improve communication, encourage technical vitality, and enable employees to achieve error-free performance.

Three basic questions about the quality-education process are asked by Feigenbaum (1983):

First, what is the scope, magnitude, and effectiveness of the company's training for plant personnel in the specific job knowledge and skills that are required for designing, building, and maintaining good quality? This question concerns the state of formalized training in the company. It raises other questions, including the following: How much emphasis is technical training placing on quality knowledge and skills? How much time is actually being spent in teaching plant personnel the skills related to quality? To what extent have development and design engineers become acquainted with modern requirements and analytical techniques?

Second, what is the net effect on the quality thinking of company personnel because of the informal, on-the-job, day-by-day influences of experience, contacts, and exposure that are so basic to the process of quality education in a company? This question is meant to explore the degree of *quality-mindedness* that exists throughout the company. This term is used to sum up a person's attitude toward quality. Quality attitudes of plant personnel are shaped by a process of quality education involving not only formal quality-control courses but also many informal quality influences. These influences, formed by actions and deeds that occur daily while on the job, become significant factors in shaping the attitudes of the individual. There are a number of ways to promote quality-mindedness. Some of the most common ones are short articles and cartoons in the company's newsletter, poster displays in the work area, quality slogans, and awards for quality-improvement suggestions.

Third, what is the scope, magnitude, and effectiveness of the company's efforts to train plant personnel in the modern concepts of quality and the programs and methods of quality control?[6]

According to Feigenbaum (1983), there are four basic principles in building a quality-control training program:

1. Keep the program simple and centered on real company quality problems. The emphasis should be on practical, meaningful quality material and case studies.
2. When developing quality-control training programs, the quality engineer and training staff should consult with the line organization, especially with respect to the scope and kinds of material to be used in the programs.

3. Since solutions to quality problems are always changing, education in quality-control methods and techniques can never be considered completed. Participants in quality-control courses should be strongly encouraged to continue their education on a self-training basis.
4. Training programs should include and involve all levels of personnel. Since interests and objectives differ among the organizational levels, courses in the quality-control training program should be tailored to fit these needs.[7]

Crosby (1984) separates the educational aspect of quality into the following:

1. *Executive education*, wherein senior managers learn their role in improving the quality process. Executives need to understand what other personnel will be taught, how to react in nonconformance situations, and what to do to encourage the improvement process.
2. *Management education*, wherein those who implement the process learn how to conduct it. In management education, all the topics from the executive education classes are covered, along with several others. The ability to make presentations is imperative, since managers will have to present quality improvement cases on a continuous basis.
3. *Employee education*, wherein all employees comprehend their roles. Employees can receive quality education using different media, such as reading material, video tapes, discussions, workshops, and work assignments.[8]

Apart from this kind of education, Mandel (1985) reports that executives, managers, and other decision makers miss potential gains in quality and productivity unless they learn to interrelate and understand basic principles, concepts, and techniques of statistics. Statistics offers powerful tools of fact finding and analysis leading to better decision making.

There appear to be two main obstacles to the more extensive use of statistics by management to improve quality. The first obstacle is the lack of sufficient publicity concerning the advantages that statistical knowledge offers to management. The second obstacle is the difficult nature of statistics courses. Such courses, when designed for management, need to be made more palatable, interesting, practical, and simple. They should cover only the basic principles, concepts, and techniques that are relevant to management.

Seminars describing the benefits of statistical tools applied to management problems are one possible solution to the publicity problem. These seminars, however, must be reinforced with statistical training. Even though present managers can gain much from this kind of training, the real potential for improved management lies in colleges and universities, where the students, our future managers, obtain their statistical education. Of particular importance are the introductory courses in statistics. These courses should concentrate not only on mathematics, but should also give equal importance to expanding the students' ability to formulate problems; increasing their exposure to logic, philosophy, and concepts of statistics; and enhancing their appreciation of the practical utility of statistical theory and methods. If statistics is taught in this manner, our future managers will be more able to accept it, appreciate it, and use it.

Since 1966, the American Society for Quality Control (ASQC) has offered formal certification programs for the quality engineer. As of the beginning of 1990, approximately 22,000 quality professionals from academia, industry, and government have been certified by ASQC. The certification program offers benefits such as potential for increased income, motivation for upgrading skills and knowledge through courses and study, college credit toward a completed degree in a relevant field, and specialization and greater expertise in the quality profession.

Today, a number of universities and technical colleges offer similar certificate programs in quality control and the quality sciences. These programs include courses in such subjects as manufacturing concepts and techniques, quality assurance, statistical process control, inspection, sampling, reliability, nondestructive testing, and computer inte-grated manufacturing (CIM).

Case Study: Final Inspection   The following case study, given by Burr (1984) illustrates how statistical techniques have helped managers help themselves.

A plant manufacturing trucks was concerned about the number of nonconformities found at final inspection. Nearly all trucks were affected. An attributes control chart was prepared on the average number of nonconformities per truck over the shift for each station. This procedure would permit management to determine which station was generating the most nonconformities. The chart created much interest, as it was plotted on a large scale and was prominently placed so that everyone could see it. At one station, the nonconformities ran about two per truck. It cost about $10 to correct each nonconformity, but the expense varied a great deal from this average. For a production of 225 trucks at one station, the cost would be 225(2)($10), or $4500 per shift. A record was kept on the kinds of nonconformities that occurred, and repeaters aroused great concern. Control limits were placed on the chart to indicate when a nonchance factor was at work. A point above the upper limit indicated an *assignable cause*, which should be sought out and corrected. Points between the control limits were, in general, attributed to chance, and no action was taken. All the workers took an interest in the chart and were proud when the nonconformities decreased. Savings through this approach amounted to hundreds of thousands of dollars.

Control charts were also used on the various machines and operators. The workers showed much interest in the charts, which were posted near their machine. They asked the plant manager to come and see their charts while touring the plant. The plant manager stated that the quality-mindedness in the plant was more important than the large number of dollars saved.[9]

As a summary of the entire education process, Crosby (1984) lists what he calls the "six C's": comprehension, commitment, competence, communication, correction, and continuance.[10]

Comprehension   This is the understanding of the entire scope of an organization's quality efforts. Management needs to abandon the conventional wisdom. Instead, management should focus on producing a "cultural change" for improvement, defined as a complete change in the way of thinking, acting, and communicating.

Commitment This is the expression of dedication on the part of management and workers. Everyone must understand the quality concepts, agree with the goals, and do his or her best to participate. Achieving widespread commitment to quality involves a broad range of actions throughout the quality program. Clear specifications, adequate process equipment, good tooling, careful screening of vendors and suppliers, routine feedback, evaluation of quality information, and other factors contribute to the achievement of quality commitment.

Quality systems thus involve a wide range of programs to emphasize positive quality motivation and strong quality achievement. Quality motivation is the act of furnishing employees with an incentive to manufacture high-quality items. This subject is discussed in more detail in the section, "Motivation" later in this chapter. Feigenbaum (1983) describes three fundamental areas that these programs emphasize:

1. *Quality attitudes*. It is essential that employees believe in the importance of good quality, excellent workmanship, well-conceived designs, and service-centered selling.
2. *Quality knowledge*. It is imperative that employees understand the kinds of quality problems facing the company and themselves. They should also appreciate the existing methods for solving their quality problems and accept the principles, facts, and practices of building, maintaining, and controlling quality.
3. *Quality skills*. The abilities, physical and mental, of plant personnel become important, since they actually perform the operations essential to quality. A range of programs are available for the improvement of personnel quality skills, such as quality education, training, planned activities, and employee participation in quality problem solving and troubleshooting.[11]

Competence This is the implementation of the improvement process. Management has a sig-

nificant responsibility in leading the quality improvement program to motivate employees to work harder than anyone else in doing the job properly the first time. The performance standard of the quality department has to be zero defects.

Competition among sellers has many aspects, including price, service, and quality. The quality of a product therefore becomes a weapon of competition. Juran and Gryna (1970) mention various opportunities to exploit quality. These include: clear knowledge of the user's service conditions and of the costs incurred due to service interruptions, as well as the costs incurred due to the use of the products; knowledge of "market quality" and use of this knowledge in redesigning and pricing; design of the product for high customer appeal through function, appearance, and life; development of a reputation for quality through invariable delivery of a conforming product; guarantee of the quality of the product in a way that minimizes any losses to the customer because of defectives; advertising the foregoing performance through public information campaigns; and avoidance of any notorious failure that can deal a serious or fatal blow to the company's reputation for quality.

In the marketplace, competition usually acts as a powerful incentive, according to Juran and Gryna (1980), for reducing users' costs and improving quality. Companies like to buy products that will avoid quality complaints and returns from their customers. Industrial buyers ask for competitive bids that include quality when making large purchases.

Correction This is the elimination of the chances for error by identifying current problems and tracking them to their root cause. *Corrective action* is defined as the permanent resolution of a quality problem. It is designed to review discrepancies, determine their cause, and ensure that a solution to the problem is implemented. An important function of corrective action is avoiding repetition of mistakes, which represent an unnecessary loss of production dollars. The effectiveness of a company's corrective action is, therefore, one of the key indicators of its strength, realism, and practicality.

Communication This is the complete understanding and support of all people in the corporation. It begins with management. Management must set its goals and relay them effectively to those involved in the production process. Goal setting is an area that can lead to many breakdowns in communication. In a production process, managers must convey their desired goals for quality to both process and quality control engineers. If these goals are not communicated effectively, they may not be met.

In order to meet these goals, the engineer must convey to management any quality-related needs he or she may have (Gehrke, 1987). The engineer must relay information that may affect the process, including improvements or problems that may be encountered. The engineer must also communicate with many others involved. Depending on the process, an engineer may have to communicate in many different ways, using many different media.

Many problems occur in the communication of information among those involved in the production process. Often there is a discrepancy between the idea that is being expressed and the information that is being transferred. There can be many reasons for this lapse in communication.

In the production process, one of the main reasons for the breakdown of communication among management, engineers, and personnel operating the factory is simply that each group usually uses a different vocabulary (Soderholm, 1982). Managers who do not have hands-on experience with technical processes may not use terms that engineers can understand. Conversely, engineers often use language that others cannot understand, especially if it is extremely technical. Managers and others who must communicate with engineers often complain that engineers do not take the time to relay information in an understandable manner. Another cause of communication breakdowns in the production process is that ideas and information are not expressed using the correct media. Using the proper medium in the proper manner is vital to effective communication.

Another major cause of breakdowns in communication in a production process is the lack of feedback by those who need it (Dalton, 1970). A manager who has expressed quality desires or needs to an engineer must receive feedback to ascertain that the message has been understood. This is also true of engineers and operators. In fact, it is true of everyone involved in a process. Much too often there is a shortage of feedback because the proper channels for this type of communication do not exist.

Continuance   This is the recollection of how the quality function was managed in the past and how it will be managed in the future. Someone has to be responsible for maintaining the ongoing quality activities.

Consumer Affairs

Customers are the ultimate source of income. As a consequence, there has been much investigation under the heading of *consumer affairs*. A company sells its products to a customer. The customer may be a manufacturer who, in turn, performs further processing on the product. A customer may also be a merchant who buys in order to resell. A *user* is one who receives the ultimate benefit of the product, such as a secretary operating a typewriter or a soldier firing a rifle. The user may also be a consumer. A *consumer* is the individual who purchases a product for personal consumption or use, such as a student who buys a computer or an angler who buys a fishing rod.

Because today's consumers are more conscious of value, and perhaps better educated, than their predecessors were, they are more vocal and demanding. They insist that product quality and safety functions be appropriately performed. They demand to be heard if, in their opinion, product quality and safety are not satisfactory. This has established the groundwork for a new major force in the economy, a force known as *consumerism*.

Consumerism may be thought of as one of the steps marking the rising expectations of consumers for what they receive in the marketplace. In consumer marketplaces, a key to business success has been the ability to understand the character of these consumer expectations, including those related to quality. It is important to respond effectively and rapidly to consumers, and possibly to anticipate their expectations and act on them before they are even verbalized. When consumers cannot find anyone to listen, they may complain to whoever will listen with attention and concern. If a considerable number of consumers report complaints, the firm's reputation for quality will begin to suffer. This can also be the beginning of the firm's loss of quality initiative and perhaps of business leadership status.

Consumer product failure data are recognized as an extremely valuable source of information. Failures, which are not always detectable during the manufacturing process, provide a basis for corrective action and product improvement. Manufacturers have always been concerned with failures because of their associated costs and their threat to sales. This concern has started a procession of product improvements aimed at increasing marketability and reducing failure losses. For these reasons, strong emphasis should be placed on an organized approach to complaint investigations. Two actions, prescribed by Kivenko (1984), that a customer's complaint should trigger are correction of the product condition that caused the complaint and correction of the basic cause of recurring problems. Beyond these, other necessary actions include investigation to determine if the incident is an isolated or a general problem, analysis of the problem for cause, elimination of the cause, and regular attention to chronic problems by reporting them and the status of their correction to the responsible management.

Warranty claims, product audits, and formal service failure forms provide a reliable source of data related to failures. These reports should contain information such as the customer location, customer complaint, description of the problem, part number and serial number, repairs necessary, and estimated repair cost. When completed properly, these reports can be used to pinpoint the products or components of products that are failing and the reasons for the failure.

Product Safety

In 1966 Congress enacted the National Traffic and Motor Vehicle Safety Act, concerning automo-

bile vehicle safety. The legislation was directed at the vehicle, the motorist, and the driving environment. Subsequent work by the National Highway Traffic Safety Administration (NHTSA) resulted in increased standards of safety.

The Consumer Product Safety Act of 1972 was the second major law concerning product safety. This law applied to various kinds of consumer projects, excluding those covered by other legislation. The act grants power to a Consumer Product Safety Commission to establish data sources, conduct investigations, publicize findings, promulgate safety standards, test products for conformance, ban dangerous products, and so forth.

The Pure Food and Drug Act of 1906 and the Food and Drug Administration (FDA) are the legal forces that regulate the food and drug industry. Recently, the FDA proclaimed standards of good manufacturing practice (GMP). These standards go into great detail with respect to material controls, material storage, processing facilities, quality control procedures, laboratory controls, and documentation.

Product Liability

Product liability is increasingly becoming a major concern of industry. The number of product liability suits filed in federal district courts alone increased 500 percent in the eight-year period ending in 1984 (Settle and Spigelmyer, 1984). In addition, the size of the awards is skyrocketing.

Product defects are still discussed by the courts but are reviewed under new theories of liability. A product may be found defective in one of four ways: its design, its construction, its failure to give an "adequate warning," or its failure to conform to an express warranty.

An injured party may sue the manufacturer or seller for these four types of defects under three different theories: negligence, breach of implied warranty, and strict liability. Under negligence, a manufacturer/seller is liable for an injury that was foreseeable at the time and that resulted from a lack of due care. In contrast, a manufacturer is liable under a breach of implied warranty if harm occurs due to the use of a product that is not fit for its intended purpose. Under strict liability, the focus shifts from the care taken by the manufacturer to the product itself. Strict liability laws vary from state to state but, in general, any person who sells a defective product that is unreasonably dangerous to the user or consumer, or to the consumer's property, will be strictly liable for any harm that occurs.

Product liability law is complicated by the fact that in most states a single claim can be brought on the basis of both tort theories—such as negligence, strict liability, or fraud—and contract theories such as breach of warranty. Different statutes of limitations, different remedies, and different levels of proof are required under tort and contract law. Since different states have used different rationales in passing strict liability laws, there is a wide divergence among the states in terms of defenses, definitions of design defects, who can recover, potential defendant liability, punitive damages, and the kind of evidence that can be offered as proof against the manufacturer/seller.

MANAGEMENT PROGRAMS FOR QUALITY

This section describes several quality improvement programs used by many companies in the United States. Although each of these programs is different, they are all effective. When joined together, these programs can supply an unlimited measure of quality improvement.

Motivation

Just as theory is essential to scientific disciplines, it is fundamental to an understanding of motivation. The most commonly quoted theory of human motivation is Abraham Maslow's hierarchy of needs developed in 1954 by Maslow and popularized by Douglas McGregor (1960) (Juran and Gryna, 1980). Under this theory, human needs fall into five fundamental categories, beginning with the physiological bases of motivation, like food and shelter, and continuing to higher orders such as self-respect and self-expression. TABLE 3-1 shows a hierarchy of human needs together with the associated motivations for quality.

An important function of the quality manager is to act as a motivator. The manager can assist employees by helping them set goals, helping them to attain these goals, and providing an atmosphere conducive to productive work. Other attempts to motivate include selecting and placing people in appropriate jobs, redesigning the work to include more motivating factors, and actually changing the behavior of others. Chapter 10, ''Worker Incen-

Table 3-1. Hierarchy of Human Needs and Forms of Quality Motivation.

McGregor's List of Human Needs	Usual Forms of Quality Motivation
Physiological needs (i.e., food, shelter, basic survival). In an industrial economy, this involves minimum subsistence needs.	Opportunity to increase earnings by a bonus for good work.
Safety needs (i.e., once a subsistence level is achieved, the need to remain employed at that level).	Job security (e.g., quality makes sales; sales make jobs).
Social needs (i.e., the need to belong to a group and to be accepted).	Appeal to the employee as a member of the team—he or she must not let the team down.
Ego needs (i.e., the need for self-respect and for the respect of others).	Appeal to pride of workmanship, to achieving a good score. Recognition through awards, publicity, etc.
Self-fulfillment needs (i.e., the urge for creativity and self-expression).	Opportunity to propose creative ideas and participate in creative planning.

Source: Juran, J. M. and F. M. Gryna, Jr., *Quality Planning and Analysis*, © 1980, pp. 150. With permission of McGraw-Hill, New York.

tives and Automation in Manufacturing,'' discusses motivational and related topics.

The following basic principles, discussed by Cash (1986), can provide managers with knowledge that will help them initiate motivation programs.

1. Motivation is internal. A person must decide what factors create motivation.
2. Most goals are self-defined and often self-limiting. Encouragement cannot motivate an employee unless the goal is desired by that person.
3. Motivation and behavior are learned. Employees can learn new behavior or can be shown new ways of doing things.
4. Because behavior is learned, it can be changed.
5. Motivation is specific to the individual; therefore, the selection of goals and the need to accomplish them may vary from employee to employee.
6. The strength or desire to achieve a goal depends on whether the employee sees the goal as achievable.
7. One way of making a goal more achievable is to break it into smaller, easier steps.
8. Motivation can be influenced by positive and negative reinforcement and feedback.
9. Reinforcement and feedback should be given as soon as possible.
10. To be effective, positive reinforcement, especially when attempting to change behavior, must be continuous.[12]

Case Study: AT&T Atlanta Works—Motivating Employees through Involvement Programs In 1985, customer satisfaction became the focus of all the production of AT&T Atlanta Works (Hatala, 1987). In order to achieve customer satisfaction, the quality of products and services provided had to be the number one priority. Management recognized that an important step toward this goal was to involve all employees in this effort. This included participation in quality forums.

Quality forums are the successful joint effort of the plant's quality and training organizations and are designed for informal discussions of quality, its importance to manufacturing, to employees' jobs, and to the customer. Attendees are encouraged to stand up, talk, and become involved. This type of forum, quite different from previous meetings, has had excellent results. Employees actually become excited about the forums. Every day more and more people commit themselves to quality improvement.

Another employee involvement program that has had exceptional results has been the use of line workers as plant tour guides. In the past, only managers and supervisors were allowed to ''show and tell'' plant processes to their numerous visitors. This program begins by providing training and guidance to the line workers. After its completion, the workers explain to the visitors the tasks they perform and the result achieved.

This program has created pride of workmanship in the line workers. These workers became very enthusiastic when they learned that they would have an opportunity to show visitors the high-quality production and low number of nonconformities for which they were responsible. Recently this program was put to the test when a group of high-ranking executives arrived at Atlanta Works for a plant tour. Management decided to allow the workers to direct half of the tour. It was not an easy decision, but it proved to be the correct one. The executives wrote back to Atlanta Works complimenting the dedication and motivation to quality that the line workers had demonstrated.

Organization

Organization can be defined as a style of authority, responsibility, and communication relationships with provisions for structural coordination, both vertically and horizontally, facilitating the accomplishment of work and objectives (Kivenko, 1984). Improved organization of the quality control function has the following benefits:

1. Improved company return on investment through better quality, less scrap and rework, and improved sales

2. Enhanced customer satisfaction
3. Greater emphasis and concentration on quality cost-reduction opportunities
4. Identification and resolution of conflicts among management objectives
5. Development of better production plans
6. Improved operating controls
7. Reduction of costs associated with supporting redundant quality control procedures and systems[13]

The responsibilities of a plant's quality control personnel, as prescribed by Mikelonis (1986) include:

1. Quality control manager
   (a) Establishes and monitors process control procedures
   (b) Initiates scrap reduction projects
   (c) Maintains quality records and customer specifications
   (d) Maintains a plant quality control manual
   (e) Establishes and maintains incoming materials control
   (f) Maintains instrument surveillance for accuracy and calibration
2. Process control supervisor
   (a) Aids line supervisors in writing process control procedures
   (b) Supervises process control observers
3. Process engineer
   (a) Defines process procedures in conjunction with line supervisors
   (b) Documents process procedures
4. Process control observer
   (a) Observes and audits compliance of process procedures with documented procedures
   (b) Aids line supervisors in detecting process deviations
   (c) Aids in associating production defects with process deviations
5. Chief inspector
   (a) Supervises all sensory inspection procedures
   (b) Supervises all nondestructive evaluations of products

   (c) Aids in defining and documenting defects for correction
   (d) Acts as product-customer liaison on production problems
6. Audit inspector audits production quality beyond line inspection[14]

Aulds (1988) argues that placing quality control in a position subsidiary to the plant manager is inadequate in a computer integrated environment. Rather, quality control, along with manufacturing engineering, management information systems and computer aided engineering should be placed in a computer integrated manufacturing (CIM) group. The CIM manager should be a "computer jock" who is knowledgeable in manufacturing, total quality control (TQC), and statistical process control (SPC). The CIM manager is a real member of the team. The team concept allows quality control to relate directly with its other counterparts rather than going through the plant manager.

Managers use many devices to control the operations of the firm. These devices are actually instruments of organization, which serve to illustrate the scope of the organization function and can lead to the identification of basic organizational problems. The following sections discuss some of the instruments of organization described by Kivenko (1984).[15]

The Organization Chart   The organization chart shows the formal structure of the organization; defines the hierarchy of positions; and identifies the flow of authority, responsibility, and accountability from the top of the organization to the bottom.

The type of organization chart used depends on the type of company. Examples include the multiproduct plant chart, the chart of a basic production line, the chart of a plant with different manufacturing sections, the small-company chart, the large-company chart, the chart of a highly automated plant, the chart of a multiplant company, and a multinational company chart. Chapter 1, "The Management and Organization of People in the Automated Factory," provides a general introduction to this topic.

Policy The policies of an organization establish guidelines and constraints, impose responsibilities on the functions of the firm, and assist in providing structural coordination by orchestrating the work of individuals in the achievement of objectives.

Procedures Procedures establish a standard methodology among elements of an organization; define authorities, responsibilities, accountabilities, and communication relationships; and provide for vertical and horizontal coordination of the organization.

Audit Audits help determine if control systems are working as desired, and aid in uncovering duplication of effort and communication blockages.

Committees Committees can provide a forum for airing different points of view. They can also confer, deliberate on questions, and coordinate the activities of multiple functions.

Job Descriptions Job descriptions define the tasks involved in a job. They perform the organizational function of specializing labor and defining responsibilities.

Quality Circles

Quality circles consist of individuals from different levels of the plant who meet regularly to define, select, and solve quality problems. Usually the individuals join the program on a voluntary basis and are trained prior to their actual participation in a quality circle. The groups usually consist of 5 to 15 individuals. The philosophy behind the quality circle concept is that the people on the production floor know their jobs better than anyone else and should be involved in cutting waste and proposing solutions.

To the quality control engineer, *quality* usually refers to improving the quality of a product. However, quality circles are used for many other reasons, such as improving productivity and the work environment. However, no matter how the term *quality* is defined, quality circles help people to feel that they are an important part of the company.

Chapter 4 describes the origin of quality circles, the quality circle process, and the manner in which quality circles are implemented. The chapter also describes pitfalls in the quality circle process.

Zero Defects

Implementing a zero defects (ZD) program is a complex task involving not only the application of theory but also the use of sensitivity analysis. Since the variables and parameters needed to construct a space shuttle are somewhat different from those used to produce potato chips, a program planner must be able to utilize certain basic concepts and then adapt the program to fit the situation at hand. Nevertheless, it is through the main ZD philosophy of addressing and changing employee attitudes that management is able to achieve the rare miracle of cutting costs while gaining better production quality.

The idea of implementing a program that would allow production with no defects came into being around the beginning of 1962. According to Halpin (1966), at Martin Marietta Corporation's Martin Company in Orlando, Florida, construction of the Pershing missile system for the U.S. Army had a quality assurance problem. Due to the extremely high costs (in terms of both money and security) associated with missile failure, Martin and the Army teamed up in an effort to decrease and perhaps completely eliminate defects. Finally, on December 21, 1961, Martin was able to deliver a missile system that had no defects. By employing the techniques and experiences learned in its construction, Martin was able to begin to produce a missile system with zero discrepancies in hardware and documentation. The ZD program was born.

The purpose of a ZD program is to eliminate defects caused by inattention. What is this attitude that can have such a dramatic effect on quality results? It is what Halpin (1966) calls "the acceptance of a standard requiring a few mistakes each day in order to be certified as human beings."[16] Where does it come from? It comes from the attitude communicated by management. It is not uncommon for five percent to be an acceptable level for scrap. Almost all processes have an acceptable quality level that Crosby (1979) calls "a commitment before we start that we will produce imperfect material.''[17] The purpose of the ZD program is to convince individuals that it is worth the effort to try to perform error-free work. It is easier to do this if workers can see how their work affects the final product. This is not easy if the worker is far removed from the final product as in the automated factory. Yet, by educating the worker on the importance of the job in the overall picture, management is communicating that the job is important to them. When management notices that the worker's performance is error free, it begins to affect the worker personally.

Once workers are convinced of the virtues of a ZD program, the question arises of how to go about implementing it. One of the basic strategies that is essential to the success of all ZD programs is the backing of top management. They must realize, or be made to realize, that savings can be obtained by cutting defect costs. The importance of having their backing cannot be overstressed; any resistance or lack of conviction will be perceived as just that by subordinates and subsequently passed on down the line to the individual worker. Crosby's conclusion: If management is not sold on this new attitude, the worker will not be either. Management must understand the concepts of the ZD program and be prepared to do the following:

1. Study its own organization in light of new techniques
2. Establish general goals that can be met by engendering ZD consciousness in groups
3. Be supportive of the ZD program and demonstrate this support
4. Recognize outstanding effort wherever it occurs

At this point the go-ahead has been given, but it may prove wise to inform certain groups before announcing the program. Informing the local union beforehand, and even allowing it to participate in the setup stages, can give the program added support. Another group to be considered is the media. Adverse publicity that can adversely affect the impact and understanding of your program can be avoided by making sure that the media are given accurate information. Halpin (1966) suggests a kickoff rally complete with pledge cards, posters, banners, and slogans. However one chooses to do it, the startup day must be recognized as special, the beginning of a new way of thinking and doing.

Finally, the program is up and running. Management must now determine if the program is producing the desired results. Data must be gathered and compared with formal measurement criteria. These data must be accurate and applicable to the particular operation. After evaluating the results, management must decide if the goals were realistic for the time interval and adjust them accordingly. Also, in keeping with their commitments, management must ensure continuation of the program's ideals. Positive reinforcement elicits repetition of behavior.

Since quality is a concept we wish to encourage, there should be rewards for outstanding individual and group efforts. Halpin (1966) suggests that this recognition need not be monetary, but perhaps commendation in a company publication. However this is done, it is once again up to management to continue to reinforce the concepts that make the program successful.

Case Study: IBM Corporation's ZD Program The following case was reported by Cloer (1984). Another participant in the ZD program is the outside supplier. Making high-quality products from inferior components is not possible. Therefore, a major part of any ZD program is to qualify vendors that can supply acceptable conforming parts. This is a departure from the traditional point of view, whereby vendors often expect customers to discover and weed out nonconforming parts. One company that has put much time and effort into the supplier side of the ZD program is IBM. IBM called in their suppliers' chief executive officers and quality managers to seminars in order to stress IBM's top-level commitment to ZD and to their dependence on suppliers' improvements in quality. In the seminar, the suppliers saw firsthand how their products were used, as well as the difficulty, expense, and loss of productivity incurred by IBM as a result of nonconformities in the suppliers' parts.

parts. Since the implementation of their supplier awareness program, IBM has seen a significant drop in the number of shipments rejected by the inspection department for failing to conform to their requirements. IBM has also developed a commodity-based list used to select potential suppliers. This list considers the total quality performance of the supplier. IBM's objective is to work with fewer and fewer high-quality suppliers. IBM works constantly to improve a supplier's record of conformance to IBM standards. If a supplier fails to meet the requirements of a plan set forth by IBM to bring the supplier's acceptance rating to a satisfactory level, the supplier will have to conduct its business elsewhere.

Case Study: Parts per Million Control for Electronic Parts A procedure that resembles the ZD program is the parts per million (PPM) program. This program is generally used in processes that require great precision and high reliability, where products are measured in terms of nonconforming PPM (Feigenbaum, 1983). The manufacture of microcomputer components and other electronic parts are examples of this type of process.

The following case was reported by Murakami *et al* (1984). A common problem encountered in the manufacture of electronic instruments is the unreliability of electronic parts. In order to supply quality products, the manufacturers of electronic equipment must demand reliable parts.

Since the number of nonconforming electronic parts must be measured in PPM terms, common inspection methods such as receiving inspection become too difficult and costly. Instead, these manufacturers must resort to *original source control* as a prerequisite for reducing the problems caused by nonconforming electronic parts. In other words, the manufacturer becomes involved in seeking the reasons why nonconforming parts were made by the supplier in the first place. In addition, it has become common for electronic instrument manufacturers to use double and triple inspections as another means to eliminate nonconforming parts and obtain PPM quality levels.

Quality Information Systems

A *quality information system*, as defined by Juran and Gryna (1980), is an organized method of collecting, storing, analyzing, and reporting information on quality to assist decision makers at all levels. Since products are more complex than in the past, programs for controlling quality now emphasize fitness for use rather than conformance to specifications. This new viewpoint recognizes that information consists not only of data but also of other knowledge needed for decision making.

Information needed by a quality information system includes:

1. Market research information on quality, such as customers' opinions on the product and service provided, and results of customers' experience
2. Product design test data, such as development test data and data on parts and components being considered from suppliers
3. Information on design evaluation for quality, such as reliability predictions and failure mode and effect analysis
4. Information on purchased parts and materials, such as receiving inspection data or vendor survey information
5. Process data, such as manufacturing and inspection data
6. Field inspection data, such as warranty and complaint information
7. Results of audits, such as product and system audits[18]

Some fundamental factors, given by Kivenko (1984), that must be considered when developing a quality information system are:

1. Clearly delineate the purpose, functions, and objectives of the system
2. Secure solid approval and backing of top management
3. Contact all prospective users, such as general management and the purchasing, manufacturing, and engineering departments

4. Determine system input and output data requirements to satisfy users
5. Identify the scope of the proposed system, including altered and unaltered interfaces
6. Consider the use of tabular, graphic, and histogram presentations
7. Provide for management summaries, such as detail reports and exception reports
8. Define the information system's constraints, such as development and operating costs
9. Determine how often reports are needed and who needs them
10. Ensure adequate training of appraisal personnel to familiarize them with the new codes, definitions, and input forms[19]

An automated factory includes computerized numerical control (CNC) machines or the higher level distributed numerical control (DNC) machines, both of which allow the collection of data through an efficient shop floor data collection (SFDC) system. The advanced SFDC system controls, monitors, and coordinates diverse types of production equipment. It checks tolerances, makes adjustments to processes, downloads programs for CNC or DNC and monitors trends. The SFDC systems provide management with accurate and timely information that leads to quality improvement. Standard quality reports can be generated, or they may be customized; ad hoc queries of current or historical information are available in on-line or batch modes.

QC IN THE 1990s

There are several trends in quality control management for the 1990s. The first of these is a strong concentration on the process rather than the product. Quality control managers are realizing that quality cannot be inspected into a product but quality can be built into the product. The implications are extremely important to the automated factory as it is extremely expensive to rework nonconforming products. It is usually more cost effective to scrap nonconforming product.

When the process is in control, the quality of the product can be predicted and there is no added cost for inspection. This is the key to managing quality (Green, 1988).

The second major trend is an application of expert systems technology. The expertise of the quality control staff can be replaced by a number of rules of operation as described in the following case.

Case Study: Expert Systems at E. I. DuPont de Nemours and Company, Inc. The following case was reported by Karnofsky and Shipman (1988). Cusum charts are commonly used throughout E. I. DuPont de Nemours and Company to statistically detect process drift. In one of DuPont's textile fiber plants, a chemical engineer formerly made process correction decisions based on Cusum analyses of data from inline sensors, as well as more extensive tests in the quality control lab. With years of experience, the engineer knew just how to respond to each of the dozen or so conditions that could arise. But the judgements made when the engineer was not available were wrong 20 to 25 percent of the time.

The engineer built an expert system in about two months of part-time effort. The expert system interprets the results of the Cusum and lab analyses, then advises the operator on the appropriate corrective machine. The system even draws a diagram of the control panel to specify the knobs to adjust. Since the system became operational in early 1987, the operators have handled the corrections on their own without a single error or intervention from the engineer.

TOWARD MANUFACTURING EXCELLENCE

Manufacturing excellence concepts and methodologies include *total quality control, just-in-time manufacturing* and *employee involvement.* These methodologies are conducted in an interdependent fashion. In the pursuit of the automated factory, these issues must not be overlooked if the rejection rate is to be reduced from single-digit percents to single-digit or low double-digit parts per million. Love (1988) reports typical improvements from two percent rejected items to ten parts per million. Johnston and Collins (1988) report the experience of a General Motors plant—a 90 percent reduction in rejects. More on this subject can be obtained from chapter 34, "Quality Control Issues in Automated Manufacturing." Further readings on manufacturing excellence are provided by Huge and Anderson (1988) and Hall (1987).

ENDNOTES

1. A. V. Feigenbaum, *Total Quality Control*, 3rd ed. (New York: McGraw-Hill, 1983), 102. Reprinted with permission.

2. K. Kivenko, *Quality Control for Management* © 1984, Prentice-Hall (Englewood Cliffs, New Jersey: Prentice-Hall, 1984) 13-14. Used by permission of the publisher.

3. Reprinted from P. B. Crosby, "Management and Policy," *Quality Management Handbook*, L. Walsh, R. Wurster, and R. J. Kimber, eds. (New York: Marcel Dekker, 1986), 2-3. By courtesy of Marcel Dekker, Inc.

4. D. A. Simmons, *Practical Quality Control* (Reading, Massachusetts: Addison-Wesley Publishing Co., Inc., 1970), 15. Reprinted with permission.

5. Howard Gitlow/Shelly Gitlow, *The Deming Guide to Quality and Competitive Position* © 1987, p. 20. Reprinted by permission of Prentice-Hall, Inc. (Englewood Cliffs, New Jersey: Prentice-Hall, Inc., 1987), 20.

6. A. V. Feigenbaum, *Total Quality Control*, 3rd ed. (New York: McGraw-Hill, 1983), 203-204. Reprinted with permission.

7. Feigenbaum, *Total Quality Control*, 215.

8. P. B. Crosby, *Quality Without Tears* (New York: McGraw-Hill, 1984), 89-90. Reprinted with permission.

9. I. W. Burr, "Management Needs to Know Statistics," *Quality Process* 17:7 (American Society for Quality Control, 1984): 29-30.

10. Crosby, *Quality Without Tears*, 92-93.

11. Feigenbaum, *Total Quality Control*, 201.

12. Reprinted from W. Cash, "Motivation," *Quality Management Handbook*, ed. L. Walsh, R. Wurster, and R. J. Kimber (New York: Marcel Dekker, 1986), 79-81. Reprinted by courtesy of Marcel Dekker, Inc.

13. K. Kivenko, *Quality Control for Management* (Englewood Cliffs, New Jersey: Prentice-Hall, 1984), 17. Reprinted with permission.

14. Kivenko, *Quality Control for Management*, 18-20.

15. Reprinted from P. J. Mikelonis, "Foundry Technology," *Quality Management Handbook*, ed. Walsh et al., 757-758.

16. J. F. Halpin, *Zero Defects* (New York: McGraw-Hill, 1966), 4.

17. P. B. Crosby, *Quality is Free* (New York: McGraw-Hill, 1979), 171.

18. M. M. Juran and F. M. Gryna, Jr., *Quality Planning and Analysis*, 2nd ed. (New York: McGraw-Hill, 1980), 577-578. Reprinted with permission.

19. Kivenko, *Quality Control for Management*, 218.

BIBLIOGRAPHY

Aulds, S. D. "Organizing for Integration." *Autofact 88 Conference Proceedings*. Dearborn, Michigan: Society of Manufacturing Engineers, 1988. 1-57 – 1-70.

Burr, I. W. "Management Needs to Know Statistics." *Quality Progress* 17:7 (1984): 26-30.

Cash, W. "Motivation." In *Quality Management Handbook*, edited by L. Walsh, R. Wurster, and R. J. Kimber. New York: Marcel Dekker, 1986.

Cloer, W. C. "Objective: Zero Defects Suppliers." *Quality Progress* 17:11 (1984): 20-22.

Crosby, P. B. *Quality Is Free*. New York: McGraw-Hill, 1979.

_____. *Quality without Tears*. New York: McGraw-Hill, 1984.

_____. "Management and Policy." In *Quality Management Handbook*, edited by L. Walsh, R. Wurster, and R. J. Kimber. New York: Marcel Dekker, 1986.

Dalton, G. W. *Organizational Structure and Design*. Homewood, Illinois: Irwin, 1970.

Dedhia, N. S. "Education and Training for Quality." *Quality Progress* 18:1 (1985): 14-15.

Deming, W. E. *Quality, Productivity, and Competitive Position*. Cambridge, Massachusetts: Massachusetts Institute of Technology, 1983.

Feigenbaum, A. V. *Total Quality Control*, 3rd ed. New York: McGraw-Hill, 1983.

Gehrke, T. "Communication for Component Design." *Quality* 26:5 (1987): 20-23.

Gitlow, H. S., and Gitlow, S. J. *The Deming Guide to Quality and Competitive Position*. Englewood Cliffs, New Jersey: Prentice-Hall, 1987.

Green, M. "Approaches to the Issue of Quality Control." *Autofact 88 Conference Proceedings*. Dearborn, Michigan: Society of Manufacturing Engineers, 1988. 8-1 – 8-4.

Hall, R. H. *Attaining Manufacturing Excellence*. Homewood, Illinois: Dow-Jones-Irwin, 1987.

Halpern, S. *The Assurance Sciences: An Introduction to Quality Control and Reliability*. Englewood Cliffs, New Jersey: Prentice-Hall, 1978.

Halpin, J. F. *Zero Defects*. New York: McGraw-Hill, 1966.

Hansen, B. L., and Ghare, P. M. *Quality Control and Application*. Englewood Cliffs, New Jersey: Prentice-Hall, 1987.

Hatala, L. Personal interview with quality engineering manager, AT&T Atlanta Works, Atlanta, Georgia, August 26, 1987.

Huge, E. C., and Anderson, A. D. *The Spirit of Manufacturing Excellence*. Homewood, Illinois: Dow-Jones-Irwin, 1988.

Johnston, R. C. and Collins, M. R. "Improving Plant Productivity Through Synchronous Manufacturing." *Autofact 88 Conference Proceedings*. Dearborn, Michigan: Society of Manufacturing Engineers, 1988. 9-19 – 9-26.

Juran, J. M., and Gryna, F. M., Jr. *Quality Planning and Analysis*. New York: McGraw-Hill, 1970.

———. *Quality Planning and Analysis*. 2nd ed. New York: McGraw-Hill, 1980.

Karnofsky, K. E. and Shipman, L. L. "Demystifying Expert Systems: Into the Mainstream." *Autofact 88 Conference Proceedings*. Dearborn, Michigan: Society of Manufacturing Engineers, 1988. 5-1 – 5-14.

Kivenko, K. *Quality Control for Management*. Englewood Cliffs, New Jersey: Prentice-Hall, 1984.

Love, R. K. "Competitive Advantage Achieved Through Mastering the Art of JIT in South Korea." *Autofact 88 Conference Proceedings*. Dearborn, Michigan: Society of Manufacturing Engineers, 1988. 9-7 – 9-18.

Mandel, B. J. "What to Teach Management About Statistics—and How." *Quality Progress*. 28:1 (1985): 16-18.

Maslow, A. H. *Motivation and Personality*. New York: Harper & Brothers, 1954.

McGregor, D. *The Human Side of Enterprise*. New York: McGraw-Hill, 1960.

Mikelonis, P. J. "Foundry Technology." In *Quality Management Handbook*, edited by L. Walsh, R. Wurster, and R. J. Kimber. New York: Marcel Dekker, 1986.

Murakami, Kishii, and Inamura. "PPM Control for Electronic Parts." *Quality Progress* 27:11 (1984): 24-27.

Settle, S. M., and Spigelmyer, S. *Product Liability—A Multibillion Dollar Dilemma*. New York: American Management Association, 1984.

Simmons, D. A. *Practical Quality Control*. Reading, Massachusetts: Addison-Wesley, 1970.

Soderholm, L. G. "Breaking Through the Productivity Bottleneck." *Design News* 38 (1982): 7.

4

The Use of Quality Circles for Implementing Automated Manufacturing

Larry R. Smeltzer*
Karen J. Gritzmacher**

QUALITY CIRCLES HAVE FOUND MANY USES IN today's competitive business environment. Their traditional uses have emphasized quality control and productivity improvements, labor-management communication, the enhancement of job satisfaction, effective teamwork, and overall improvement of the quality of work life for employees. However, the effective use of quality circles can also facilitate the implementation of major technological changes, such as automated manufacturing. The reason is that quality circles are participatory; they integrate sociotechnical decision making for groups of employees with different kinds of job knowledge. An effective group can achieve far greater results in identifying alternatives and potential problems than one person working alone. Groups are especially valuable for a very complex and multifaceted project such as implementing automated manufacturing.

Automation at any level is a major decision. However, once a decision has been made to auto-mate a manufacturing facility, another question emerges: how shall automation best be accomplished? Many decisions must be made. What processes are to be automated? What will be the design of the work environment and plant layout? What automation systems must be purchased? How will the automated system be integrated with other functions of the organization? How will personnel be affected by the change?

An implementation plan that takes these and other issues into consideration can be accomplished more effectively by using a group of people, rather than by relying on the knowledge of just one or two individuals. This is true when choosing software programs, designing training sessions, determining the effect of automation on quality control and production planning, and identifying machines that need to be purchased.

Research on group dynamics indicates that correctly organized groups make better decisions than the same individuals working alone. The participa-

*Larry R. Smeltzer is Professor in the College of Business at Arizona State University. He has worked with a number of manufacturing firms at various stages of the quality circle process. He has also conducted research and written articles on different aspects of quality circles. Karen J. Gritzmacher is also affiliated with the College of Business at Arizona State University. Prior to her recent move to the academic setting, she was an executive with General Motors Corporation. She presently teaches and conducts research in the areas of productivity, quality, and operations.

tive process of groups is also considered to be the most effective technique for overcoming resistance to change, particularly technological change. Employees who participate in planning and implementing a change are better able to understand the reasons for the change. Uncertainty is reduced. Individual interests and social relationships are less threatened. With an opportunity to express their own ideas and to assume the perspectives of others, employees are more likely to accept the change gracefully and enthusiastically. A participative effort is important for changing a manufacturing environment.

Employees who are directly involved with planning the change to automation are in a good position to communicate the plan to other employees. Also, a sense of ownership evolves through the group process, and participants become advocates of the new ideas and approaches. Change is more effective if it is an evolution through group participation and planning, rather than a revolution through intimidation and fear. People become more committed if they are involved in the change process. In addition, through group discussions new employee interests and skills can be identified.

Another advantage to groups is that greater creativity can result when more people are involved in a decision-making process. Ideas that are generated often enable group members to identify untapped resources within themselves that are applicable to the new situation. For instance, some manufacturing engineers seem to have a knack for solving problems on how best to integrate the automated system with the production planning system. Other engineers, however, might consistently generate valuable ideas for linking machines with a new computer-aided design program. Automation of a manufacturing facility necessarily requires crucial insights. Acknowledging sociotechnical implications of automation through group decisions is paramount for successful implementation.

CONSIDERATIONS FOR ESTABLISHING EFFECTIVE GROUPS

The quality circle provides opportunities for quality, productivity, and implementation of automation. A typical quality circle consists of a small group of employees and their supervisor supported by a coordinator or facilitator. This group voluntarily meets on a regular basis with the intent of quality and productivity improvement. The type of group we describe here, however, is a combination of a quality circle and a task group.

Quality circles focus on quality problems and use quality control techniques to solve problems. *Task groups* are generally concerned with nonroutine organizational activities such as the implementation of automated manufacturing. Once the task group creates the implementation plan, it disbands. Quality circle groups and task groups are alike in that they lack the authority to implement proposals. The groups present their findings to management for approval.

The following section describes the steps to take and issues to consider when attempting to establish an effective group.

Group Composition

The types of employees who make up a group are obviously an important factor in the effectiveness of that group. The mission of quality improvement must be understood by all those involved. An employee who does not care about quality will probably not produce as good an implementation plan as another individual, regardless of what the problem or issue may be. At the same time, groups with very competent, task-oriented members may be expected to produce better decisions than groups without such members. What is the first thing to consider when establishing a group that will be analyzing the effects of the issues relating to automating a manufacturing facility? The first consideration is the identification of potential members that clearly have expertise, skills, experiences, and interest in areas of that plant that will be directly and indirectly affected by the change.

Although expertise, skill, and experience are all crucial, the most important criterion may be interest. Members who are not interested in quality improvement and automation, regardless of their expertise, will be of little assistance. In one plant it was rather prestigious to belong to the automation implementation teams; consequently, many uninterested employees volunteered. Not until this problem was identified and rectified did those teams become effective.

The characteristics of the particular members of a group do not tell the whole story. Just as individuals have unique personalities, the group tends to separate personalities or identities. Groups continually adapt and assume their own unique problem-solving behaviors; consequently, no two groups will respond to a problem in the same way.

Differences among groups arise from dynamics within the group as well as from the characteristics of the individual members. For example, one quality group never accomplished any project because the entire group defeated itself. Members were often late for meetings, argued over trivial items, and seemed to frequently diverge from the main topic. A different group was able to change a work environment because the group members agreed, worked as a team, and accepted further challenges for improvement. An interesting point is that some members from the first group were also members of the second group. However, different group personalities emerged.

The manner in which a group evolves as it attempts to solve problems is affected by the extent of member similarity. An example of a group composed of very similar members is a group of manufacturing engineers who are all at the same level in the organization. On the other hand, a group of dissimilar members would include the materials manager, manufacturing line supervisor, machinist, quality control inspector, manufacturing engineer-

ing manager, and secretary in the personnel department. In the latter situation, members are different with respect to skills, experiences, and organizational levels. All have different experience levels but their goal is the same—solve the problem in the immediate area. Although the composition of the two groups is entirely different, each might be appropriate in different situations.

The degree of member similarity can have positive and negative effects on the group's ability to perform. On the positive side, a highly differentiated group can often offer unique insights. An accountant, for instance, has a much different perspective than an engineer. However, their differences could also significantly impede the group process; their varying achievement levels, and willingness to learn and participate could be roadblocks to group progress. This is true simply because one professional group may have much more professional interest in a particular problem than another group. For instance, a manufacturing engineer may be more interested in an automation project than a product engineer.

Groups with a very similar composition may also become a problem. The required differences in knowledge may not be available for a multifaceted problem. Implementing automation in a manufacturing facility is a prime example. Both manufacturing engineers and line operators should be involved even though they are quite dissimilar. Each could have valuable insights.

The research available on group composition generally indicates that mixed groups tend to perform better than matched groups. This is logical when considering that the basic purpose of the group is to coordinate and motivate people with different insights. However, groups that are extremely different may not be able to develop a common perspective. When group members have extremely different perspectives, the leader should schedule time for participants to share their experience and background. This helps to develop a common perspective and language.

When the group is mixed, the status of the members will influence the interactions and decision-making process. Status operates as a filter in the communication process. Group members may filter or omit certain information they believe higher status members may not want to hear. Some members may also present select information that is not pertinent in order to appear knowledgeable or influential. A high status participant can subtly direct an entire discussion in a particular direction as lower status individuals attempt to please.

Status may also be used as a scapegoat mechanism within a group. A low status group member may provide key information. The high status member, meanwhile, may take a risk with the final decision because a scapegoat is available. That is, if the decision proves incorrect, simply blame it on the person who provided the information. This can easily be an unconscious process. As a result, the status of potential group members and the manner in which they view their status should be considered when members are chosen. An effective quality circle will acknowledge status but the rule is to remove status as a potential barrier. Employees who focus entirely on status should not be selected because their adjustment to an egalitarian situation will be difficult. An effectively mixed group acknowledges differences, ignores status, and commits to quality improvement.

Another point to consider when choosing employees for a group is how well potential group members can handle conflicts. Since the purpose of making a group decision is to allow different perspectives to be presented, open constructive conflict is often essential for the best decision to emerge from a group. Many employees have a strong dislike for confrontation or conflict and would rather participate in a group that is always agreeable. Although conformity may lead to a higher level of member satisfaction, it is also more likely to result in a poor decision. When you select employees for an automation project, remember the high incidence of ambiguous information and inevitable conflict associated with change. Group members must be comfortable with negative feedback and confrontation.

Group members should be chosen for their confidence and willingness to disagree on issues. They cannot be sensitive to having their ideas rejected and must be willing to express controversial viewpoints. After group members have worked together, they seem to be attracted to each other, have a high level of self confidence, and be more likely to express their opinions. Every group member must be committed to the concept of a team; this is inherent for survival and successful implementation.

Size of the Group

A vast number of relationships can develop in a group. Larger groups mean potentially more complex interactions and usually more time consumed. Smaller groups must have enough members to provide the necessary resources and expertise. The challenge is to have a sufficient number of members but to keep the number as low as possible.

Once a group exceeds approximately seven members, additional individuals will probably detract from the overall process. Three negative outcomes may result when groups are too large: (1) opportunities for each member of the group to share knowledge or insight decrease, (2) one or two members of the group may dominate the communication, and (3) subgroups may develop within the larger group.

What is an ideal size? Of course, this depends on the experience and skills of the people involved and the precise goals of the group. The optimum size of a problem-solving group is generally around five. A group of this size is large enough to take advantage of diverse skills, enable members to express good and bad feelings, and aggressively solve problems. It is also small enough to permit members to be an intimate part of the group and to serve everyone's needs. If 10 or 12 employees are needed to provide the required expertise, then the large group should be divided into subgroups based on logical subdivision of the tasks. A rule of thumb is five plus or minus two; that is, a good group size is from three to seven with five being the desirable average.

When the group must have more than nine members, it will need some special attention. One option is to divide the entire group into two small subgroups to analyze certain parts of a problem. Each subgroup would then report to the group as a whole. A second option is to establish special guidelines for—and to train group members in—problem solving in large groups.

Member Roles

The structural elements of a traditional quality circle program include three roles: facilitator, group leader, and group member. The facilitator is a link between the larger organization and the quality circle members. The facilitator: (1) promotes and helps implement the quality circle program, (2) trains the group members and leader in statistical and industrial engineering techniques and in group processes, (3) guides the initial meetings, (4) solves problems with the group's functioning, and (5) serves as liaison between the group and staff personnel controlling resources needed by the group.

The group leader is frequently the foreman; the group members are employees working under his supervision. However, the quality circle can also select a group leader other than the foreman. This often occurs in a well-trained and committed quality circle. Also, status barriers are removed when the foreman is not the group leader.

While an established structure exists for traditional quality circles, the member roles in a task group implementing automation can be much more flexible. For instance, a facilitator should train all the quality circle members in statistical techniques for good decision making. However, the members of an automation task group are generally chosen for their expertise; therefore, a facilitator probably would not be required to train members in specific statistical techniques. In addition, members chosen for an automation team should represent several different departments; consequently, it generally is not appropriate to have a foreman serve as a leader. Rather, an employee from one of the departments should be the leader.

Whether or not he is officially appointed, a leader will emerge in each group. Even if all members of the group are engineers at the same level of the organization, a leader will emerge. Whenever a group of more than three individuals gathers to solve problems, a person will emerge to coordinate activities.

Because a leader will emerge if not appointed, there must be a decision made as to whether or not a leader should be formally named for the group. Such a person should have adequate knowledge to coordinate the group, be an effective communicator, and have the respect of others in the group. The leader must be able to influence the other members to: stay on the topic without becoming distracted, remain objective, and strive for the groups' appointed goals.

The leader should not try to influence the decision or problem solving one way or another. Leaders have a different status from others in the group because of the very nature of the position. The results of the group discussion should not reflect the preferred solution of the leader but rather the solution of the group. Therefore, the leader must be especially careful to separate his discussion-leading function from the functions of contributing and evaluating ideas.

This problem of leader domination becomes more pronounced when the group leader also has higher status than other members. When this is the case, skillful communication is essential. Steps must be taken to encourage the free expression of ideas and airing of minority viewpoints; premature evaluation of ideas must be discouraged. As a group forms its own personality, the role of the leader varies and status becomes secondary to achieving the group's goal. Automation means commitment to a changed work environment; the leader and the group merge ideas to resolve problems and to demonstrate a philosophy of total work quality.

MANAGING GROUPS

Once a group has been established, steps must be taken to ensure that it reaches its potential. Group decision making is different than individual decision making. A tendency exists for groups to skip steps. For instance, while one person is discussing alternatives, another may want to talk about implementation. It is difficult to coordinate different individuals' problem-solving processes.

Another problem which must be considered is the dominance of the group by one or a few individuals. Consideration must also be given to whether or not the group is interacting cohesively, and to the consistency between the group's goal and the goals of management. This section describes the issues that can influence group performance. Specific group techniques that have been developed to manage or structure the group decision-making process are also presented.

Group Norms

A *group norm* is a standard of conduct that is shared by group members and guides their behavior. For instance, in one company it may be the norm to start all meetings precisely at the scheduled time. However, in another company meetings may casually begin five or ten minutes late. Norms are informal. They are not written down as are rules and procedures. Norms are valuable because they define boundaries of acceptable behavior. They make life easier for group members by providing a frame of reference for what is right and wrong. Norms identify key group values, clarify role expectations, and facilitate group survival.

Group norms can set standards that are either in concert with or conflict with the goals of management. For example, a group may develop a norm of only providing reasons against manufacturing automation. Group members might do this because they do not trust management's motives and fear that they may lose their jobs. Sometimes a group may develop the norm of continual improvement. It may develop a strong competitive norm and challenge management to do likewise.

The first behaviors that occur in a group often set a norm for later group activities. Consequently, a leader who is not prepared on the first meeting

and conducts an unorganized, haphazard meeting sends a signal to the group: this is the way all group meetings will be conducted. This is a major reason for group failures. At the first meeting, group members will decide not to take the group seriously and will not exert much effort. A norm has been established. If, on the other hand, top managers attend the first meeting and discuss the importance of the group's efforts, different norms may be established.

The experiences of a large multidivision corporation demonstrate the importance of norms. Two large divisions were simultaneously embarking on manufacturing automation projects. In the division that produced paper products, the project received extensive attention from top management. The vice-president wrote a long letter to all personnel explaining the project and described how problem-solving groups would be used. The VP and plant manager attended the initial meeting as well as extensive follow-up meetings of group volunteers. Also, top management listened to all final recommendations. A norm of professionalism and importance was established.

Meanwhile, a much different approach was taken in the pulp division. The plant manager wrote a memo explaining the program. The personnel manager named group leaders. Some of the leaders gave weak reasons why they could not participate and were quickly excused. Several meetings were cancelled at the last minute. A norm was established that stated the process was not important.

With explicit statements, leaders or group members can initiate norms by articulating them to the group. Leaders may state they expect all group members to attend every group meeting, to arrive on time, and to participate in group discussions. Such explicit statements make a big difference in member behavior and define norms for the group. Explicit statements are also probably the most effective way for a leader to change existing norms in a group that has already been established. Research indicates that the most successful groups have the mission and objectives clearly stated by the leader and understood by all members.

Group Cohesiveness

While the use of explicit statements can be useful for establishing norms, consideration must also be given to methods that will make members want to abide by the group's norms. Groups get their power from their members' willingness to be influenced. Members are willing to be influenced to the extent that they value and are attracted to the group.

Group cohesiveness is defined as the extent to which group members are attracted to the group and motivated to remain in it. Members of highly cohesive groups are committed to group activities, attend meetings, and are happy when the group succeeds. Members of less cohesive groups are less concerned about the group's welfare and success. Important initial training of all members yields more cohesiveness and commitment. It is common to train a rebellious employee, and then have him or her turn around and become a significant member. The employee develops a sense of achievement or success and wants to share it with other group members. This individual strengthens cohesion.

While high cohesiveness is normally considered an attractive feature of groups, it can only improve the group's contribution to the organization if it exists along with high performance norms. Therefore, it is important to establish high performance norms for the group. Once these norms are established, ever-improving group cohesion can enhance the group's ability to achieve high performance goals.

Cohesion generally can be affected by the extent of contact among group members. The greater the amount of contact and the more time spent together, the more cohesive the group. Several strategies are available for spending time together to improve cohesiveness. One approach is for quality groups to visit other departments or locations together. The common experience and opportunity for interaction during travel time encourages cohesion. Some companies have even rewarded quality circle groups with a trip to Japan. Through frequent interaction, members get to know one another and become more devoted to the group.

Sharing of goals can improve group cohesion also. If group members agree on goals, they will be more cohesive. While agreeing on purpose and direction binds the group, disagreement disrupts potential cohesiveness. Agreement on goals is necessary from the very first meeting. If agreement is not reached during the first meeting, additional sessions should be conducted until a mutual understanding of goals is achieved.

Factors external to the group can also influence group cohesiveness. When a group is in direct competition with other groups, its cohesiveness increases as it strives to win. Competition could be established among different groups striving to provide the best ideas for automated manufacturing.

Group success and favorable evaluation of the group by outsiders also adds to cohesiveness. When a group succeeds in its task and others in the organization recognize the success, members feel good and their commitment to the group grows. One way to promote group cohesiveness through outside evaluation is to ask the group to present its findings to top management. Knowledge that the group will receive attention from top management will encourage the group to unite to make a good impression. Members struggle to arrive at the best plan, but then the group naturally bonds together as the goal is completed and recognized. Also, many company presidents meet with groups to listen to their cost savings successes and listen to other ideas as well. The cohesiveness that results is valuable to other activities in the company beyond those targeted in the groups' goals.

Managing Conflict

When people work together in groups, some conflict is inevitable. Conflict can arise among members within a group or between one group and another. Conflict can be healthy when it results in constructive disagreement and open discussion. However, poorly managed conflict may result in bitterness and may ultimately destroy the group.

Competition should not be confused with conflict. Competition, which is rivalry between individuals or groups, can have a healthy impact because it energizes people toward higher performance. But too much competition can result in destructive conflict. Too much conflict can tear relationships apart and interfere with the healthy exchange of ideas and information.

What does a team leader do when a conflict erupts within a group or among groups? There are several helpful techniques for confronting and resolving conflicts. Ultimately, the leader and group must talk facts and use statistical techniques to reduce conflict.

If a team leader can focus group members on the group goals (a fact), the conflict will decrease because members will see the big picture and realize they must work together to achieve it. A plan for implementing automated manufacturing may generate numerous conflicts because of unknown factors. Thus, all facts must be addressed to resolve any conflict.

Bargaining and negotiation can also eliminate conflicts. The parties engage one another in an attempt to systematically reach a solution through facts. They attempt logical problem solving using simple pareto charts and fishbone diagrams to identify and correct the conflict.

Sometimes the use of a mediator to solve conflicts is helpful. This involves a third party, often a higher-level manager or someone from the personnel department. The mediator can discuss the conflict with each party and work toward a solution. If a solution satisfactory to both sides cannot be reached, the parties may be willing to turn the conflict over to the mediator and abide by his or her solution.

Often it is a good idea to ascertain whether or not there is actually a basis for conflict between the two parties. The conflicting parties may not hold accurate perceptions or facts. Providing opportunities for the disputants to get together and exchange factual information reduces conflict. Efforts can be made to increase the dialogue among parties. As they learn more about one another, suspicions diminish and improved teamwork becomes possible.

GROUP PROCESS TECHNIQUES

A number of techniques have been developed to manage or structure the group process. Three that are briefly discussed here are postproblem and consensus, nominal group technique, and the CEDAC technique.

Postproblem and Consensus

The group leader using this technique posts the stage of the problem-solving process on a chalkboard or flip chart. The stage might be diagnosing the problem, finding alternative solutions, analyzing and comparing alternatives, making a decision, or implementing a decision. Once the participants finish discussing a stage of the process, the leader posts a statement of consensus. If the participants agree with this statement, the group moves on to the next stage. The advantage is that the discussion remains on target; everyone is aware of the progress being made and the agreements that have been reached.

Nominal Group Technique

The nominal group technique or NGT is another valuable method for managing group decision making. Nominal groups are used most often to generate creative and innovative alternatives or ideas. In some ways, nominal groups are similar to brainstorming. To begin, the group leader outlines the problem to the group members. The group members then write down as many as possible alternatives, ideas, options, or solutions privately without discussing them with others. The members then take turns stating their ideas, which are recorded on a flip chart or chalkboard at the front of the room. There is no discussion. After all ideas are listed, questions may be asked to clarify an idea or proposal. However, at this point, there is no evaluation, no discussion, and no debate. Each person then privately ranks the various proposals. The results are tallied to determine the relative support for each idea. The proposal with the most tallies is then discussed for possible adoption.

When these steps are followed, NGT has been found to be effective. It integrates the advantages of both group and individual creativity. The primary advantage is that it identifies a large number of alternatives while minimizing individual inhibitions about expressing unusual or novel ideas. In many situations it also saves a great deal of time.

CEDAC Technique

The CEDAC technique is a graphic participation concept using the fishbone diagram. Employees offer ideas and see the progress of different ideas as they are implemented. The problem is displayed on a fishbone to offer solutions and results of solution attempts. It is a continuous process open for participation until the problem is solved. This positive feedback mechanism motivates workers for more ideas. Problem solving is out in the open. It develops a commitment to eliminate wasted time, to improve quality, and to work as a group.

Studies have shown that the quality of decisions is generally higher with NGT and CEDAC than with traditional group discussion procedures. However, group members prefer the contact and interactions that occur during group discussions.

POTENTIAL PROBLEMS WITH THE GROUP PROCESS

Perhaps the biggest drawbacks of the group process, compared with individual decision making, are the additional time and the greater expenses involved. Meetings take so much time because the number of interactions increases dramatically as the number of participants increases. Each person needs time to share his ideas. Since time is money, this can become a costly effort.

In addition to the time they spend in the meetings, group members must also spend time coordinating the activities of a group that enable it to perform its task. Schedules must be checked, telephone calls made, and meeting times arranged in order to get down to business. Time is consumed simply moving to and from a meeting and settling into the procedure. Although the "time and cost factor" is a disadvantage, the end results are worth it: increased knowledge regarding a new automated facility, greater commitment for the eventual decision, and increased coordination among employees.

Free Riding

The term *free rider* refers to a group member who attains benefits from group membership but does not do a proportionate share of the work. In large groups, some people are likely to work less. The team leader must be on the lookout for such members and must take steps to eliminate the problem. However, if the entire company is committed to teamwork and team successes, the free rider will not exist.

Diffusion of Responsibility and Risky Shift

Diffusion of responsibility means that a single individual cannot be assigned responsibility for group outcomes. Because each person may be expected to do a part of the group tasks, no one is at fault if the group fails and no one gets the credit if it succeeds. Two types of situations emerge as a result of the diffusion of responsibility. First, group members may believe that other members will perform an undesirable task. In short, nobody wants to take on the dirty work. This type of diffusion of responsibility can be resolved if group members are assigned specific responsibility for undesirable tasks. These tasks can be passed around in a logical way as long as everyone knows who is responsible.

The second situation is referred to as the risky-shift phenomenon. Studies have shown that, when confronting problems involving uncertainty, groups tend to choose riskier solutions than individuals. Since no one person can be ultimately responsible for a group decision, decisions tend to be more controversial or risky. This is not to say that the decisions will be better or worse, just that they will be at a higher risk level when made by a group. The issues evolving from the implementation of automation are complicated. The risk can vary; thus, groups tend to become more committed and share the risk because they know the total implications affect everyone.

Groupthink

Another potential problem that may arise during the group process is *groupthink*. This refers to the situation in which all members of the group tend to think alike. This condition is especially likely when the group members' desire for consensus or harmony becomes stronger than their desire for accuracy. Under such conditions, critical thinking and the independent and objective analysis of ideas is sacrificed to ensure a smooth running group. The likelihood of groupthink increases if the group becomes insulated from outside influences and the fresh flow of information.

Groupthink can be detected by watching for the symptoms:

- Illusion of unanimity on the viewpoint held by the majority and an emphasis on team play
- A view of the opposition as generally inept, incompetent, and incapable of countering effectively any action by the group, no matter how risky the decision or how high the odds are against success
- Self-censorship of group members in which overt disagreements are avoided, facts that might reduce support for the emerging majority view are suppressed, faulty assumptions are not questioned, and personal doubts are suppressed in the interests of group harmony
- Collective rationalization to comfort one another in the face of warnings that the agreed-upon plan is either unworkable or highly unlikely to succeed
- Self-censorship within the group that prevents anyone from undermining its apparent unanimity and protects its members from unwelcome ideas

and adverse information that may threaten consensus
- Reinforcement of consensus and direct pressure on any dissenting group member who expresses strong reservations or challenges, or argues against the apparent unanimity of the group
- An expression of self righteousness that leads members to believe their actions are moral and ethical, thus inclining them to disregard any ethical or moral objections to their behavior
- A shared feeling of unassailability, marked by a high degree of esprit de corps, by implicit faith in the wisdom of the group, and by an inordinate optimism that disposes members to take excessive risks

Any one of these symptoms could damage the group problem-solving and decision-making process. Take the following precautions to prevent groupthink.

- Assign one member to be a "devil's advocate" or critical evaluator to allow disagreement and criticism of the leader; criticism can be helpful
- As stated earlier in this chapter, leaders should not reveal their preferences to the group at the beginning of the discussion
- Several subgroups with different leaders can work independently on common problems to offer different perspectives
- Group members should discuss the group's process with trusted friends and report the friends' reactions to the group
- Outside experts should be called in periodically as resource persons; they should be encouraged to disagree with the group's assumptions
- After preliminary decisions have been reached, the group should adjourn and hold a "second chance" meeting at a later date to let their ideas incubate

Although these suggestions may not always be applicable, they do offer a constructive alternative set of procedures to reduce the dangers of groupthink. Specific group techniques such as the ones described above—postproblem and consensus, NGT, and CEDAC—are also designed to minimize the presence of groupthink.

MANAGEMENT SUPPORT

While groups may work effectively to prepare an excellent plan for implementing automation, the plan will not be worth much if it is not considered seriously by management. The support must be present from the very beginning of the group process. If group members sense that they will not be taken seriously by management or that their proposals will necessarily be rejected, they will have very little motivation to work effectively in the group. Since problem solving through the group process is a timely and costly matter, the group should be given multiple signs of management support.

First, management should address the group and stress the value and importance of the group's contribution. As noted earlier in the plant producing paper products, the top executives attended several meetings. Support was implied by the attention given to the groups.

Second, training and resources must be made available to all members. This is particularly true for those plants where groups have not been used extensively. Group members should be given adequate time to attend all meetings and to spend time outside of the meeting to accomplish their assigned tasks. Too frequently group members may be torn between their regular responsibilities and the additional burden associated with the automated manufacturing groups. Management must recognize the additional burden to re-establish priorities if necessary. In one case, all team members were given a special bonus upon completion of the project. Furthermore, management should be ready to provide information and resources that are not readily available to group members if they request it.

Once the group has finished its task of preparing a proposal, management should respond with timely feedback. Many managers regularly meet with employees in their work environment to provide frequent feedback. The presence of a manager who shows enthusiasm and dedication to groups offers positive feedback and motivation.

The most successful groups have been given autonomy and trust by top management. A group that has been adequately trained and has the ability to use appropriate techniques for solving problems can be depended upon to do a good job. Groups require employee time and effort; management must support this effort.

SUMMARY

Implementation of automated manufacturing requires consideration of the sociotechnical environment. This chapter has discussed a technique for involving the social system—the use of quality circles. Quality circles are particularly valuable because they provide the opportunity to use the expertise from a number of employees. Concurrently, teamwork is developed and commitment to automation strengthened.

For groups to fulfill their potential, however, they must include employees with the correct mix of expertise, skills, experience, and interest. Also, groups should not be too large and member roles must be clearly established. Group norms, cohesiveness, and conflict are also important considerations when managing the groups. Problem solving or decision making can generally be improved by using the postproblem and consensus technique, nominal groups, or the CEDAC process. However, it is important to be aware of the potential problems of free riding, risky shift, and groupthink when working with groups.

Regardless of the composition of the group or the specific techniques involved, support from top management is critical for group success. Large and small manufacturing firms—from international firms like General Motors, General Electric, and Weyerhouser to small, little-known companies—have used quality circle groups to help implement automated manufacturing. The correct procedures must be used and management support is required.

5

Project Management in the Factory

Hans J. Thamhain[*]

MANAGING TODAY'S FACTORY OPERATIONS INVOLVES enormous challenges far beyond the reliable manufacturing of complex products to predefined cost and performance measures. It involves running a sophisticated multilayered organizational system with complex interfaces as an integrated part of the total company and its business plans. Factory management must include flexibility toward operational changes and upgrades. New, powerful tools and techniques such as JIT, MRPII, and TQC evolved to provide better resource utilization and product quality. All these provisions add up to an operational environment that is too multidisciplinary to be structured strictly along functional lines. In essence, factory management is project management.

The project management approach that emerged in the 1960s responds to the need for effective integration and execution of the many operations coming into play during modern production operations. Companies that use the project approach find it effective, especially for planning, organizing, and controlling multifunctional activities within the factory and with interfacing organizations.

THE TASK TEAM CONCEPT

Within the global structure of the company, the factory has a wide range of options for organizing its operations. Although these structures take many forms, the factory typically retains most of its basic functional characteristics. That is, hierarchical relations exist within the organization with clearly established lines of command, responsibility, and authority. Each of the functional subunits is headed by a department manager responsible for its operation and for the implementation of the various projects and tasks that run through the unit, including the maintenance of personnel, facilities, and technological advancement.

If a functional unit is assigned the responsibility for a particular project, the unit manager appoints a task leader, who plans and organizes the resources needed and then manages the project toward its integration and completion. Such a project could be a simple maintenance task, requiring resources primarily under the control of the unit manager. Or, it could be a new product setup that involves the whole factory plus engineering, field services, and marketing. In either case, the project leader might

*Dr. Hans J. Thamhain has 20 years of experience in project and engineering management with such firms as Westinghouse, General Electric, and GTE. He has earned a Ph.D. in Management, an MBA, and Master and Bachelor degrees in Electrical Engineering. He has taught engineering/technology management and project management at management training programs and various universities. Dr. Thamhain is a frequent speaker at major conferences. He has written over 60 articles and research papers, as well as four books on these subjects. Dr. Thamhain is currently Associate Professor of Management at Bentley College and consults in all phases of technology and project management.

have to reach across functional lines and deal with others over whom he or she has no direct authority.

When a project leader must reach across functional lines, he or she must respect the two *axes of responsibility* that exist in the matrix organization and divide operational responsibility as shown in FIG. 5-1. One axis is concerned with managing the task integration, while the other is responsible for managing the resources. In short, the matrix is built around a cooperative relationship between the project manager, who is responsible for *what* needs to be done, and the resource managers, who are accountable for *how* it is being implemented.[1]

ORGANIZATIONAL ALTERNATIVES

The traditional organizational structure of a factory is along functional lines. However, when interdisciplinary tasks are performed, this functional structure turns into a matrix-type organization with various overlays. These overlays may projectize certain production resources or establish miniature matrices within production (FIG. 5-2). All these ''in-between'' choices must be carefully designed to accommodate the needed intrafunctional integration, while maintaining effective utilization of production resources and overall operational control.

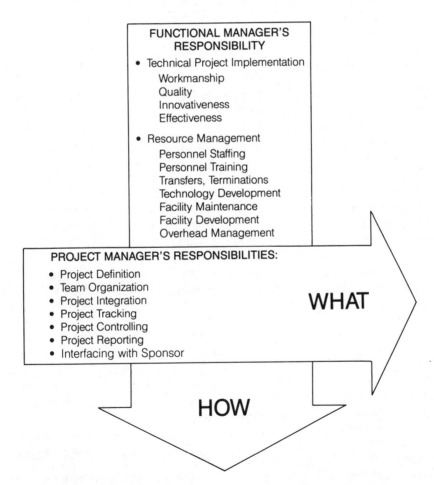

Fig. 5-1. Operating responsibilities within a matrix organization are divided along two axes.

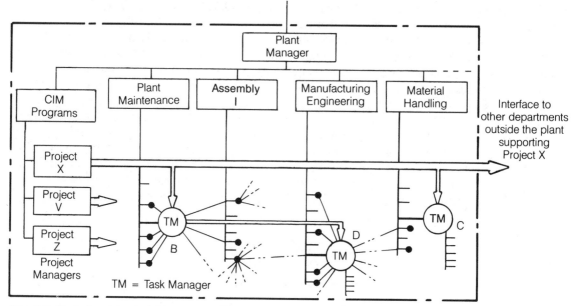

Fig. 5-2. Project matrix. Activities are coordinated and directed locally by task managers, while overall project integration is directed by "autonomous" project managers.

Four principal organizational forms are commonly found: functional structure, matrix, projectized structure, and individual project structure. In a modern factory, rarely is one form used alone; more likely, it is used in combination with other forms or is modified to meet the specific organization needs. However, the matrix has become one of the most common constructs, accommodating the widest span of project management requirements with the most flexibility, while retaining organizational stability and resource effectiveness.

Projects Managed within a Functional Structure

In the first organizational form, the factory retains its traditional functional characteristics. A clear chain of command exists for all organizational components within the production function. Department managers direct the functional production groups. Task managers or project engineers perform the internal coordination and interface with external operating groups.

Although weak in control and high on organiza-

tional conflict, this is still one of the most commonly used organizational structures of a factory. It provides a high concentration of specialization and production capabilities and ensures their economical use. However, limitations of this organizational substructure are its weak control of multifunctional resources resulting in poor planning, weak resource commitments, shifting priorities, limited ability to control the activities according to plan, and very poor interface with organizations outside the factory. Especially if the operations require considerable coordination of intraproduction activities, a subordinate matrix structure often evolves and provides the necessary interdisciplinary task integration, control, and initial organization buildup. As a result, an increasing number of production units are introducing an additional matrix layer within their organization.

Projects Managed within a Matrix

The second organizational form is essentially an overlay of temporary project organizations on the functional production unit. As shown in FIG. 5-2, task managers B and C are accountable to the project office for managing their tasks through all phases. This includes the planning, organizing, and control of all activities necessary to produce the agreed-on results. The integration of tasks B and C into project X is being managed by the Program Office (left side of FIG. 5-2). If the program is large enough, task manager B manages the work through other task leaders, such as D, who report to B regarding the job requirements, budget, and schedule. The program or project manager specifies the work for a new product start-up, including: what the product specifications are, what schedules and budgets must be met, and what the targets are for unit production costs.

The task managers essentially have two bosses: they are accountable to the project manager for the implementation of the requirements, and to the functional manager for the quality of the work, the availability of resources, and the utility of these resources in accomplishing the desired results.

In describing these multidimensional matrices, executives mostly resort to verbal tools such as charters, directives, and policies. They stay away from conventional charts or graphics, such as FIG. 5-2, which focus on the primary command channels but often confuse the issues of dual accountability and multidimensional controls.

The advantages of the matrix structure over functional organizations are a more rapid reaction time, better control, and more efficient integration of multidisciplinary activities. The program or project office also provides an effective interface with production-external organizations, while reducing the span of control through the task management hierarchy. On the other hand, the additional organizational overlay is likely to increase cost overheads, and requires a more sophisticated management style to operate smoothly and efficiently within an environment characterized by extensive sharing of resources, power, and responsibility, which often results in considerable interdepartmental conflict. The matrix may not be the panacea for all production organizations, but it can provide a powerful option to the sophisticated executive.

Project Management within a Projectized Structure

The third organizational form is a division within the production unit in which a production project manager directs a complete line organization. The manager exercises full authority over the personnel, facilities, and equipment with the charter to manage one specific project from start to finish. This organizational form offers the strongest project authority; encourages performance, schedule, and cost trade-offs; usually represents the best interfaces to production-external organizations; and has the best reaction time. However, by comparison with matrix, the projectized organization usually requires considerable start-up and phase-out efforts, and offers less opportunity to share production elements, utilize economics of scale, and balance work loads.[2]

Because of these limitations, companies seldom projectize their production units unless the project is large enough to fully utilize the dedicated resources. What is more common is a partially projectized organization where the project manager fully controls certain resources that are particularly critical to the project, or resources that can be fully utilized over the project life cycle. Other resources remain under the control of functional managers who allocate them to specific projects as needed, based on negotiated agreements with the project managers.

Project Management within an Individual Project Structure

The fourth organizational form offers a very effective method of coordinating smaller multidisciplinary tasks within the factory: charter one individual part time or full time with the task integration. This integration usually includes (1) coordination with the program office and the resource personnel, (2) front-end planning, (3) progress measurement and reporting, and (4) directing and controlling the activities toward the agreed-on results. This one-man project organization can be very quickly installed without disturbing other ongoing operations or establishing organization structures. The individual project organization is a scaled-down derivative of the matrix. It can be viewed as a miniature matrix within the larger construct of the factory.

Multilayer Matrices

Real-world project organizations are complex, both on paper and in practice; they do not necessarily lead to a single-layer matrix. In fact, so-called multidimensional matrices are quite common for complex businesses. In addition to the project matrix with its various levels of integration for each project, there may be overlays of other matrix axes with totally different and unrelated missions, such as a product-function matrix or product-region matrix. Furthermore, the production function may host many minor matrix and projectized structures within its functional framework. These organizations could be responsible for a production-internal project such as a new facility development or a quality-control procedure.

The Charter:
Defining the Organization

To work effectively, people must understand where they fit into the corporate structure and what their responsibilities are. Given the internally complex workings of the matrix, it is especially important to define the management process, responsibilities, and reporting relations for all organizational components within production and its organizational interfaces. Organization charters, job descriptions, policy directives, and management guidelines provide the management tools for clarifying the organizational network and directing the business activities coherently.[3]

Challenges for the
Production/Matrix Manager

To be effective, the new breed of production manager that evolved with the matrix must consider a broad range of issues. They must understand the people, the task, the tools, and the organization. The day of the manager who gets by with technical expertise alone or pure administrative skills is gone. Today, managers in a production matrix must relate socially as well as technically. They must understand the culture and value system of the total organization.

Many of the challenges faced by the matrix manager also arise in more conventional organizations, but they seem to have a stronger impact on operating efficiency within a matrix environment. The production manager in a matrix organization typically encounters seven specific challenges. The following paragraphs analyze the impact of these challenges and suggest ways to increase managerial effectiveness.

Dual Accountability Unconventional superior-subordinate relationships are common in the matrix environment. Both managerial and other work-related responsibilities are often divided along intricate horizontal and vertical organization lines. In order to direct and control activities in such a multiboss environment effectively, the organization must clearly define the two-matrix axis in terms of responsibilities, powers, and control. The organizational charter, management directives, policies, and procedures are management tools that can be used effectively. Moreover, the employee performance evaluation and reward system must be consistent with the shared managerial power system. That is, those who distribute the rewards must elicit feedback from all organizations that receive services, and the production managers themselves must be evaluated for the effectiveness with which they provide resources to the many components of their matrix organization.

Power Sharing No organization has managerial power equally distributed, but the matrix almost encourages managers to jockey for power. Managerial power is tested in ability to control resources, which can be done in many ways. Both project managers and functional resource managers may try to gain access to resources by (1) influencing the priorities, (2) controlling the budgets, (3) interfacing with the sponsor or top management, (4) creating more interest and visibility for their project among the performing personnel, (5) changing reporting relations, or (6) developing a more credible image as sound business managers.

For the matrix to work properly, a certain balance of power, or matrix parity, must be established via procedures or management guidelines. These guidelines should (1) delineate the basic responsibilities and authorities of each matrix axis and (2) define the basic process for initiating and executing a project so that one or a few individuals cannot accomplish their activities at the expense of others.

Matrix parity is based on induced cooperation; the matrix offers a strong incentive for the resource managers to cooperate with the project managers, and vice versa. This is usually accomplished by tying management performance to both functional and project performance. Proper planning early in the project life cycle will further help to establish cooperative relationships. Proper planning defines the specific work—and the division of responsibilities and controls—in a mutually agreed-on arrangement that encourages involvement and commitment by all project parties.

Product Quality The quality of a product must be both specified and designed into it. In a matrix environment, many individuals share the responsibility for defining product specifications. Conflict often arises over the technical feasibility and economics of these quality requirements; conflict resolution should be worked out in concert with all functions that must specify, implement, and live with outcome of the product design. Typically, these functions include (1) research and development, (2) design, (3) manufacturing, (4) field services, (5) product assurance, (6) marketing and sales, and (7) finance.

During project execution, the functional resource manager directs the project toward its proper implementation, ensuring technical excellence and quality, while the task or project manager directs the overall integration of the multidisciplinary activities in keeping with established requirements, schedules, and budgets. These operating responsibilities must be clearly defined to key personnel in the various matrix axes to ensure quality implementation. This is done orally, but for larger organizations the only consistently effective means are procedural documents, charters, and management directives.

Cost In a factory environment, cost challenges usually exist in three areas: (1) designing toward a given unit-production-cost target within an established design budget and schedule; (2) setting up the facilities and personnel for production within an established budget and schedule; and (3) actually producing and delivering the product at the target cost. Since produceability must be designed into the product from its very conception, key personnel from all product development phases must participate throughout product planning and implementation. Phased management approaches with specific review points, checks, and sign-offs may help to fine-tune the product design toward its lowest possible unit-production cost.

Conflict Conflict is inevitable in managing any complex production task. It is even more pronounced in a matrix environment, with its sharing of power and resources. Conflict can develop over many issues. Project personnel experience particularly intense conflicts over schedules, priorities, resource allocations (especially manpower), and technical issues. Project managers should not only be cognizant of the potential sources of conflict, but also should know when in the life cycle of a project they are most likely to occur. Such knowledge can help the project manager avoid the detrimental aspects of conflict and maximize its beneficial aspects. Conflict can be beneficial when disagreements result in the development of new information that enhances the decision-making process—a topic that is discussed in more detail below.

Resource Loading Matching resource requirements with available resources and defining future development needs is a challenge, because of inevitable contingencies that demand deviations from the original plan and also because of fluctuating work loads of the various projects. The impact of both overloads and underloads is usually higher overhead cost, with the obvious additional impact on project schedules for overload situations.

Dynamic project planning with a minimum of quarterly reviews may provide a realistic up-to-date picture of resource requirements for each project. In this process the best possible timing for resource requirements should be continuously negotiated between the project manager and production resource managers. However, contingencies will happen regardless of how carefully projects are reviewed, resulting in an unfavorable impact on resource loading. Dynamic resource scheduling may help offset some of these problems. Such scheduling prompts the production manager to anticipate a certain percentage of sudden work fluctuation on the basis of past experience, and to build these contingencies into the load model. In addition, the resource manager should develop resource alternatives such as relief labor pools, cross-trained employees, temporary employees, additional shifts, and subcontracting.

Developing Future Capabilities Production capabilities need to be continuously upgraded to ensure optimum product quality, cost, and features—all necessary prerequisites for unique positioning within the competitive field of the firm. These upgrades require a combination of foresight, creativity, funding, and properly timed actions. It is usually the chartered responsibility of the functional resource manager to identify the needs and develop the plans, including budgets and schedules. Although there is no easy formula, resource managers must think in terms of integrating the long-range requirements for all anticipated projects. To establish meaningful, cost-effective requirements, the manager needs to understand: (1) the technologies involved in future products; (2) the production techniques employed; (3) the specific markets, customers, and requirements; (4) the technological trends for both the products and the production means; (5) the relationship among supporting technologies; and last but not least, (6) the production personnel, their skills, needs, and desires.

ORGANIZING THE PROJECT TEAM WITHIN A FACTORY

Building the project team is one of the prime responsibilities of the project/program manager.

Team building involves a whole spectrum of management skills required to identify, commit, and integrate various task groups from traditional functional organizations into a single program management system. This process has been known for centuries, but it becomes more complex and requires more specialized management skills as bureaucratic hierarchies decline and multidisciplinary teams evolve.

An Effective Team Environment

Project managers who are successfully performing their roles in a team environment usually provide an atmosphere that fulfills the needs and leadership expectations of their team members, as shown in TABLE 5-1. They also recognize the barriers to effective team performance, as summarized in TABLE 5-2, so that preventative actions can be taken. The effective team builder is usually a social architect who understands the interaction of organizational and behavioral variables and can foster a climate of active participation and minimal conflict. He or she also has carefully developed skills in leadership, administration, organization, and technical expertise on the project. The combination of all of these skillful efforts may develop an effective and productive team with the following characteristics:

- Team members committed to the program
- Good interpersonal relations and team spirit
- Available resources
- Goals and program objectives clearly defined
- Top management involved and supportive
- Good program leadership
- Open communication among team members and the support organization
- A low degree of detrimental interpersonal and intergroup conflict

Organizing the New Production Team

Too often the program manager, under pressure to start producing, rushes into organizing the project team without establishing the proper organizational framework. While initially the prime focus

Table 5-1. The Needs of Project Team Members.

Team Members Have Needs	Team Members Expect from Project Manager
• Sense of belonging	• Direction and leadership
• Interest in work itself	• Assistance in problem solving
• Professional achievement	• Creation of stimulating environment
• Encouragement; pride	• Adaptation of new members
• Recognition for accomplishment	• Capacity to handle conflict
• Protection from infighting	• Resistance to change
• Job security/continuity	• Representation at higher management
• Potential for career growth	• Facilitation of career growth

Table 5-2. Barriers of Effective Team Building and Suggested Handling Approaches.

Barrier	Suggestions for Effectively Managing Barriers (How to Minimize or Eliminate Barriers)
Differing outlooks, priorities, interests, and judgments of team members	Make effort early in the project life cycle to discover these conflicting differences. Fully explain the scope of the project and the rewards which may be forthcoming upon successful project completion. Sell "team" concept and explain responsibilities. Try to blend individual interests with the overall project objectives.
Role conflicts	As early in a project as feasible, ask team members where they see themselves fitting into the project. Determine how the overall project can best be divided into subsystems and subtasks (e.g., the work breakdown structure). Assign/negotiate roles. Conduct regular status-review meetings to keep team informed on progress and watch for unanticipated role conflicts over the project's life.
Project objectives/outcomes not clear	Ensure that all parties understand the overall and interdisciplinary project objectives. Clear and frequent communication with senior management and the client becomes critically important. Status-review meetings can be used for feedback. Finally a proper team name can help to reinforce the project objectives.
Dynamic project environments	The major challenge is to stabilize external influences. First, key project personnel must work out an agreement on the principal project direction and "sell" this direction to the total team. Also educate senior management and the customer on the detrimental consequences of unwarranted change. It is critically important to forecast the "environment" within which the project will be developed. Develop contingency plans.
Competition over team leadership	Senior management must help establish the project manager's leadership role. On the other hand, the project manager needs to fulfill the leadership expectations of team members. Clear role and responsibility definition often minimizes competition over leadership.

Table 5-2. Cont.

Barrier	Suggestions for Effectively Managing Barriers (How to Minimize or Eliminate Barriers)
Lack of team definition and structure	Project leaders need to sell the team concept to senior management as well as to their team members. Regular meetings with the team will reinforce the team notion, as will clearly defined tasks, roles, and responsibilities. Also, visibility in memos and other forms of written media, as well as senior management and client participation, can unify the team.
Project personnel selection	Attempt to negotiate the project assignments with potential team members. Clearly discuss with potential team members the importance of the project, their role in it, what rewards might result upon completion, and the general "rules-of-the-road" of project management. Finally, if team members remain uninterested in the project, then consider replacing them.
Credibility of project leader	Credibility of the project leader among team members is crucial. It grows with the image of a sound decision maker in both general management and relevant technical expertise. Credibility can be enhanced by the project leader's relationship to other key managers who support the team's efforts.
Lack of team member commitment	Try to determine lack of team member commitment early in the life of the project and attempt to change possible negative views toward the project. Often insecurity is a major reason for the lack of commitment; try to determine why insecurity exists, then work on reducing the team members' fears. Conflicts with other team members may be another reason for lack of commitment. It is important for the project leader to intervene and mediate the conflict quickly. Finally, if a team member's professional interests lie elsewhere, the project leader should examine ways to satisfy part of the team member's interests or consider replacement.
Communications problems	The project leader should devote considerable time to communicating with individual team members about their needs and concerns. In addition, the leader should provide a vehicle for timely sessions to encourage communications among the individual team contributors. Tools for enhancing communications are status meetings, reviews, schedules, reporting system, and collocation. Similarly, the project leader should establish regular and thorough communications with the client and senior management. Emphasis is placed on written and oral communications with key issues and agreements in writing.
Lack of senior management support	Senior management support is an absolute necessity for dealing effectively with interface groups and proper resource commitment. Therefore a major goal for project leaders is to maintain the continued interest and commitment of senior management in their projects. We suggest that senior management become an integral part of project reviews. Equally important, it is critical for senior management to provide the proper environment for the project to function effectively. Here the project leader needs to tell management at the onset of the program what resources are needed. The project manager's relationship with senior management and ability to develop senior management support is critically affected by his own credibility and the visibility and priority of his project.

Source: H. J. Thamhain and D. L. Wilemon.

is on staffing, the program manager cannot effectively attract and hold quality people until certain organizational pillars are in place. At a minimum, the basic project organization and various tasks must be defined before the recruiting effort can start.

These pillars are necessary not only to communicate the project requirements, responsibilities, and relationships to new or prospective team members, but also to manage the anxiety that usually develops during the team formation.

Make Functional Ties Work for You It is a mistaken belief that strong ties of team members to the functional organization are bad for effective program management and therefore should be eliminated. To the contrary, loyalty to both the project and the functional organization is natural, desirable, and often very necessary for project success. While the program office gives operational directions to the program personnel and is normally responsible for the budget and schedule, the functional organization provides technical guidance and is usually responsible for personnel administration. Both the program manager and the functional managers must understand this process and perform accordingly, or severe jurisdictional conflicts can develop.

Structure Your Organization The key to successfully building a new project organization lies in clearly defined and communicated responsibilities and organizational relationships. The tools for systematically describing the project organization come, in fact, from conventional management practices.

The *charter of the program/project organization* clearly describes the business mission and scope, broad responsibilities, authorities, organizational structure, interfaces, and reporting relationship of the program organization. The *project organization chart*, a simple, conventional chart, defines the major reporting and authority relationships. These relationships should further be clarified in a *policy directive*.

A *responsibility matrix* defines the interdisciplinary task responsibilities—who is responsible for what. The responsibility matrix covers not only activities within the project organization but also functional support units, subcontractors, and committees.

Job descriptions are modular building blocks that form the framework for staffing a project organization. A job description includes (1) reporting relationships, (2) responsibilities, (3) duties, and (4) typical qualifications.

Define Your Project Both the project organization and the work itself must be defined before staffing can begin. The basic elements typically include:

- Work breakdown structure
- Statement of work for all first-level project components
- Overall specifications
- Master schedule
- Cost model and budget

Regardless how vague and preliminary these project components are at the beginning, the initial description will help in recruiting the appropriate personnel and eliciting commitment to the preestablished parameters of technical performance, schedule, and budget. Hopefully, the core production team will be formed prior to finalizing the overall program plan, thus giving it the opportunity to participate in the trade-off discussions and up-front development decisions that will affect produceability and cost during the production phase.

Staff Your Project After he defines the project organization and tasks, the project leader can start to interview candidates for the key project positions. The interview process normally has five facets that are often interrelated: (1) informing the candidate about the assignment, (2) determining skills and expertise, (3) determining interests and team capability, (4) persuading, or selling the assignment, and (5) negotiating terms and commitment.

Handling the Newly Formed Team

A major problem faced by many project leaders is managing the anxiety that usually develops when a new team is first formed. This anxiety experienced by team members is normal and predictable.

It is a barrier, however, to getting the team quickly focused on the task.

This anxiety may come from several sources. For example, if the team members have never worked with the project leader, the team members may be concerned about his or her leadership style and its effect on them. In a different vein, some team members may be concerned about the nature of the project and whether it will match their professional interests and capabilities. Other team members may be concerned about whether the project will help or hinder their career aspirations. Further, team members can be highly anxious about job expectations, work load and life-style disruptions.

Certain steps taken early in the project life cycle can be effective in terms of handling the above problems. First, at the start of the project the project leader should talk with each team member on a one-to-one basis about the following:

- What objectives the project has and its importance to the overall organization
- Who will be involved and what the team structure will be
- What the specific task requirements, schedules, budgets, and challenges are
- Why the team member was selected; what role the team member will perform, including reporting relationships
- What rewards might be forthcoming, including recognition
- What problems and challenges are likely to be encountered
- How the project will be managed and controlled; how team members will communicate, such as reports and status-review meetings
- What suggestions the team members have for achieving success
- What the team member's professional interests are
- What challenge the project will present to individual members and the entire team
- How other organizations will support and interface with the project
- What suggestions the team members have on how to work effectively as a project team

A frank open discussion with each team member on the above is likely to reduce his or her initial anxiety or identify its source, so that the underlying issues can be dealt with quickly.

The greater the feeling of team membership and the better the information exchange among team members, the more likely it is that the team will be able to develop commitment and effective problem-solving approaches. Such a team is likely to develop more effective project control procedures.

Project control procedures can be divided into two basic areas. The first includes the quantitative control procedures traditionally used to monitor project performance, such as PERT/CMP, networking, and work breakdown structures. The second is the willingness and ability of project team members to give feedback to one another regarding performance. Again, trust among the project team members makes the feedback process easier and more effective.

PROJECT MANAGEMENT TOOLS AND METHODS

Program managers today have available a set of powerful tools with proven capability to plan and control multidisciplinary activities effectively. Most of these tools were originally developed in the aerospace and construction industry. They are, however, equally effective and find increasing applications in other areas, ranging from new product introduction to political campaign management and social programs.

Make Planning Work for You

Effective planning and control techniques are helpful for any undertaking. They are absolutely essential, however, for successful management of large, complex engineering programs. Quality of planning means more than just the generation of paperwork. It requires the participation of the entire project team, including support departments, subcontractors, and top management. It leads to a realistic project plan plus involvement, commitment, and interest in the project itself. Proper planning fosters an environment conducive to the project goals. Such planning makes everyone's job easier and more effective, because it:

- Provides a comprehensive road map of your program
- Pervades and integrates the program and provides perspective
- Provides a basis for setting objectives and goals
- Defines tasks and responsibilities
- Provides a basis for directing, measuring, and controlling the program
- Builds teams
- Minimizes paperwork
- Minimizes confusion and conflict
- Indicates where you are and where you are heading
- Leads to satisfactory program performance
- Helps managers at all levels to achieve optimum results within the limits of available resources, capabilities, environment, and changing conditions

If done properly, the process of project planning must involve all the performing organizations and the sponsors. This involvement creates new insight into the intricacies of a project and its management methods. It also leads to visibility of the project at various organizational levels, and induces management involvement and support. This involvement at all organizational levels stimulates interest in the project and desire for success, and fosters a pervasive reach for excellence that unifies the project team. It leads to a commitment to establish and attain the desired project objectives, and to a self-forcing management system where people want to work toward these established objectives.

Managing the Project through Its Life Cycle

Managing the project from start to finish clearly involves all the functions of traditional business management throughout the project life cycle. To reduce complexity, most project managers use a phased approach for organizing their projects. These phases can follow functional lines such as system phase, development phase, and prototype phase; or business cycles such as preproposal phase, proposal phase, prototype phase, and production phase; or they can follow any other typology that divides the overall project into logical sets of activities with specific outputs.

The following approach divides the overall project into five managerial phases:

- Phase 1, Conceptual
- Phase 2, Project definition
- Phase 3, Project organization and startup
- Phase 4, Main phase execution
- Phase 5, Project phase-out

In each phase, certain managerial actions seem to precede others, as shown in FIG. 5-3. This approach permits the development of a framework for planning and controlling projects in a disciplined, systematic way, regardless of size and complexity of the project.

As the project moves through its life cycle, the focus of managerial activities shifts from planning to controlling. However, many of the activities are interrelated and cannot be confined to only one particular project phase. Plans are managerial tools; they are seldom final and should not be rigged. The purpose of the plan is to provide the basis for organizing the project, defining resource requirements, setting up controls, and eventually guiding the activities. As the various elements of the plan integrate and actual operations begin, modifications of the original program plan may become necessary. Continuous reviews and updates of all components of the program plan are needed throughout the project life cycle if the plan is to remain a useful reference and guidance document.

Planning for Measurability and Control

Every program manager takes a different approach to establishing measurable milestones and has a reason for following that particular approach. However, the common theme among those who

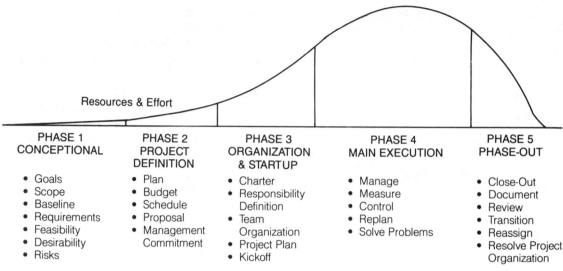

PHASE 1 CONCEPTIONAL	PHASE 2 PROJECT DEFINITION	PHASE 3 ORGANIZATION & STARTUP	PHASE 4 MAIN EXECUTION	PHASE 5 PHASE-OUT
• Goals	• Plan	• Charter	• Manage	• Close-Out
• Scope	• Budget	• Responsibility	• Measure	• Document
• Baseline	• Schedule	Definition	• Control	• Review
• Requirements	• Proposal	• Team	• Replan	• Transition
• Feasibility	• Management	Organization	• Solve Problems	• Reassign
• Desirability	Commitment	• Project Plan		• Resolve Project
• Risks		• Kickoff		Organization

Fig. 5-3. The project life cycle.

manage projects successfully is the ability to measure *technical status* at preestablished review points.

While at the time of the review milestones must be clearly defined down to specific measurable parameters, it is not necessary and is often impractical to establish these details at the outset of the program. What is required is a process that predefines the major milestones at the beginning of the program, and allows for incremental detailed development of the measurable parameters as the program progresses.

The process of establishing measurable milestones has two key features: (1) it provides the discipline for establishing detailed, measurable milestones, and (2) it creates involvement at all organizational levels, pervades project planning, and leads to improved communications and commitment.

The five-step procedure summarized in FIG. 5-3 relies on conventional project planning and control documents that constitute the program management plan. Project performance data usually evolve from the work breakdown structure and the statement of work into budgets, schedules, and specifications; these in turn form the basis for describing the deliverable items at various points in the project life cycle.

One of the key criteria for establishing measurable milestones is the ability to define deliverable items, not only for the termination point of the program, but also for all critical milestones throughout the project life cycle, including reviews and tests. Deliverables could also be defined first for various project phases and then be coupled with those task elements necessary to produce them. In either case, the ability to measure the status of the deliverables depends on the ability to determine the underlying task elements and their performance in accordance with the established project specifications, schedules, and budgets.

Criteria for Effective Project Control

The ability to measure and control project performance requires more than just another plan. It requires the total commitment of the performing organization. Successful companies stress the importance of carefully designing the project planning and control system and the structural and authority relationships that are critical for the implementation of the measurement system.

Other organization and management issues—such as leadership style, personnel appraisal and compensation, and intraproject communication—must be carefully considered to make the system *self-forcing.* That is, project team members work toward the established project objectives in an effective and self-disciplined way. The team members are involved and professionally interested in the project and have the desire for success. The team is unified and committed toward reaching each critical milestone. These are the characteristics of self-forcing control.

A number of specific recommendations are stated below. They summarize the criteria that are important for controlling projects according to plan. The recommendation sequence follows the life cycle of a typical project, wherever possible.

Detailed Project Planning Develop a detailed project plan, involving all key personnel, defining the specific work to be performed, the timing, the resources, and the responsibilities.

Break the Overall Program into Phases and Subsystems Use work breakdown structure as a planning tool.

Results and Deliverables Define the program objectives and requirements in terms of specifications, schedule, resources, and deliverable items for the total program and its subsystems.

Measurable Milestones Define measurable milestones and checkpoints throughout the program. Measurability can be enhanced by defining specific results, deliverables, and technical performance measures against schedule and budget.

Commitment Obtain commitment from all key personnel regarding the program plan, its measures, and results. This commitment can be enhanced and maintained by involving the team members early in the project planning, including the definition of results, measurable milestones, schedules, and budgets. It is through this involvement that the team members gain a detailed understanding of the work to be performed, develop professional interests in the project and desires to succeed, and eventually make a firm commitment toward the specific task and the overall project objectives.

Intraprogram Involvement Ensure that the interfacing project teams, such as engineering and manufacturing, work together, not only during the task transfer, but throughout the life of the project. Such involvement is necessary to ensure effective implementation and to simply ensure "doability" and responsiveness to the realities of the various functions supporting the project. Enhance cooperation among project teams by clearly defining the results and deliverables for each interphase point, agreed upon by both parties. In addition, a simple sign-off procedure, which defines who has to sign off on what items, is useful in establishing clear checkpoints for completion and to enhance involvement and cooperation of the interphasing team members.

Project Tracking Define and implement a proper project tracking system that captures and processes project performance data and conveniently summarizes those data for reviews and management actions.

Measurability Ensure accurate measurements of project performance data, especially technical progress against schedule and budget.

Regular Reviews Projects should be reviewed regularly, both on a work package—or subsystem—level and total project level.

Signing On The process of signing on project personnel during the initial phases of the project or each task is very important to proper understanding of the project objectives, the specific tasks, and personal commitment. The sign-on process that is so well described in Tracy Kidder's book, *The Soul of a New Machine*, is greatly facilitated by sitting down with each team member and discussing the specific assignments and overall project objectives, as well as professional interests and support needs.

Interesting Work The project leader should try to accommodate the professional interests and desires of supporting personnel when negotiating their tasks. Project effectiveness depends on the manager's ability to provide professionally stimulating and interesting work. This leads to increased project involvement, better communications, lower conflict, and stronger commitment. In such an environment, people work toward established objectives in a self-enforcing mode and require a minimum of managerial controls. Although the scope of a project may be fixed, the project manager usually has a degree of flexibility in allocating task assignments among various contributors.

Communication Good communication is essential for effective project work. It is the responsibility of the task leaders and ultimately the project manager to provide the appropriate communication tools, techniques, and systems. These tools are not only the status meetings, reviews, schedules, and reporting systems, but also the objective statements, specifications, list of deliverables, the sign-off procedure, and critical path analysis. The project leaders must orchestrate the various tools and systems and use them effectively.

Leadership Ensure proper program direction and leadership throughout the project life cycle. This includes project definition, team organization, task coordination, problem identification, and a search for solutions.

Minimize Threats Project managers must foster a work environment that is low on personal conflict, power struggles, surprises, and unrealistic demands. An atmosphere of mutual trust is necessary for project personnel to communicate problems and concerns candidly and quickly.

Design a Personnel Appraisal and Reward System This should be consistent with the responsibilities of the team members.

Ensure Continuous Senior Management Involvement, Endorsement, and Support of the Project Senior management involvement surrounds the project with a priority image, enhances its visibility, and refuels overall commitment to the project and its objectives.

MANAGING ORGANIZATIONAL INTERFACES

The factory must operate as an integrated part of the total business. Organizational interfaces with other parts of the company are critical for transfer of technology, bid proposal activities, strategic planning, factory upgrades, and many other processes that require effective flow of information, materials, and expertise. The most difficult of these interfaces involve intense joint activities such as during a new product development. Managing these interfacing activities among organizations within the factory—such as for a material handling improvement project—poses already considerable challenges. Each unit involved has its own objectives, language, culture, and operational problems. Misunderstandings and conflict can easily occur at these unit interfaces. These challenges are elevated if the activities involve interfaces with organizations outside the factory. Not only are the cultural and operational differences much greater, but one most likely also deals with different management styles, organizational structures, procedures, and people mentalities.

Types of Interface Problems

Understanding the types of interface problems, their sources, and occurrence in the project life cycle can help in managing these organizational interfaces more effectively and in avoiding the problems through proper project planning and team-oriented leadership.

Operational Focus Many interface problems occur because organizational units focus their activities too intensely on their particular expertise and discipline. For example, engineering may design a product for optimum performance without regard to produceability and field service.

Policies and Procedures Operating guidelines, policies, and procedures differ among organizational units. A test procedure or safety guideline may be very different for the factory than for an engineering lab.

Organizational Flexibility Flexibility may differ considerably throughout the company. Obviously facilities and people can be changed to accommodate a separate need much more quickly in a laboratory than on the factory floor.

Decision Making Methods of decision making differ with the managerial style, culture, and policies of various organizations. Joint decision making involving several departments—such as needed for new product developments and bid proposal activities—presents an especially difficult challenge.

Power Plays Struggles for project leadership or just organizational dominance can cause major interface problems.

Inadequate Plans Interface problems will invariably occur if the activities of the interfacing parties are not clearly defined. Plans must specify clear objectives, deliverables, schedules, resources, and responsible individuals.

Poor Communication Channels Information may not get properly communicated among interfacing organizations. The problem could lie with the medium, the channel, or the feedback mechanism. Some specific examples include: insufficient number of meetings, the wrong people in meetings, insufficient documentation, too much reporting, reports too cumbersome, no time to read reports or go to meetings, environment too threatening or uncomfortable to participate.

Schedule Slips Unless they can be synchronized throughout the project, schedule slips always cause interface problems. Delays in one organization affect the flow of information and activities among interfacing units, and destroy the operational integrity that had been built among these units.

Interface Process It is often unclear what is specifically required from interfacing organizations, when it is due, and how it is supposed to get transferred.

Conflict Open disagreement or quiet conflict among interfacing individuals and organizations contribute to many subtle problems, ranging from low levels of interest and participation to outright sabotage.

Poor Management Direction People often do not know what to look for and how to prepare for effectively interfacing with another organization. Task leaders must be given proper management direction.

Contingencies Unexpected problems and technical difficulties in one organization usually change the established interface process and prior agreements on timing, data, and deliverables.

Criteria for Effective Interfacing

The above problems are predictable for most interface situations. They are also natural and intensify with the complexity of the organization and its technology. The more massive the required integration of activities and the more differentiated the cultures of the interfacing organizations, the more difficulties should be expected in integrating project activities among various organizations. The following paragraphs offer guidelines for managing organizational interfaces effectively.

Recognize Potential Problems Managers must understand the various problem areas and barriers to effective interfacing, and focus on problem avoidance. Experience and organizational safeguards such as joint reviews can help in identifying problems early in their development and solving them effectively.

Plan the Total Project Jointly Multifunctional projects should be planned jointly, involving key members from interfacing organizations. The plan should cover the total project life cycle. While details may not be known for activities late in the project, the overall task structure and principal phases should be clearly defined and agreed on by the project team. The agreement should include major deliverable items for each phase, timing, budgets, and responsible individuals.

Define the Interface Process All individuals involved in this interfunctional transfer or integration should be able to describe how the interface is supposed to work, and what is expected when, and from whom. Their knowledge base should include data, hardware, software, decisions, meetings, verifications, and the transfer process itself.

Cultivate Management Involvement and Commitment Project leaders must continuously update and involve management to refuel the interest and commitment to the project and its integration across functional lines. Showing partial results and making progress visible are effective drivers toward management commitment and support.

Build Favorable Image A favorable image stimulates the desire for success, minimizes dysfunctional conflict, and helps to unify the multifunctional team. Emphasize positive aspects of the project: its importance to the company, interesting work, priority, high visibility, and potential for professional recognition and rewards.

Define Clear Project Objectives Clarify the relationship between project objectives and common organizational goals. This clear definition will enhance the favorable image of the project and will foster a climate of active participation, a lower impedance between interfacing organizations, and a strong desire to make the interfacing process work.

Provoke Interface Accountability Task leaders of interfacing activities should be jointly accountable for results. For example, the engineering design activity for a new product must be signed off by task leaders from engineering and manufacturing. Since both task leaders know of this condition, they will involve each other more intensely in the design phase. Engineering knows that their job is not complete under manufacturing is supposed to guide and validate the design on an ongoing basis. If the joint assignment is made properly, it will foster interfunctional cooperation and also establish an early warning system for detecting future interface problems.

Prepare for the Interface Effort With all good intentions and the willingness of the project team to cooperate, successful integration across functional lines requires careful preparation. For example, consider the transition of a new design into manufacturing. A produceability study should be conducted together with engineering. Guidelines should be given to the designers for production cost targets, testability, reliability, and adherence to manufacturing standards. The design efforts should be regularly monitored and fine-tuned to meet the produceability criteria. Design reviews, feasibility studies, produceability plans, test plans, project reviews and validations, simulations, and prototyping are some of the management tools available for preparing a successful project integration across organizational lines.

Establish an Organizational Support System Management can aid the efforts toward successful interfacing by establishing an effective support system. This might include some written guidelines, policies, and procedures; computer-aided tracking, monitoring and early warnings; oversight or steering committees; internal consultants; seminars and workshops; and changes in the organizational design to lower the interdepartmental impedance. One such organizational change would be some form of projectizing the activities across organizational lines by establishing clearly defined and recognized project management positions.

Manage and Lead Both functional and project managers can influence the organizational climate and facilitate cooperation across functional lines through their own actions. By providing effective leadership, these managers can move the organization in the desired direction. Also, through this experience and vision they should be able to see problems early on and facilitate their resolution.

PROJECT LEADERSHIP

With the evolution of modern project organizations and their complex environments, a new management style has gradually developed. This style complements the traditional, organizationally derived power bases—such as authority and reward and punishment—with bases developed by the individual manager. Examples of managerial power for this so-called Style II management include expertise, credibility, friendship, work challenge, promotional ability, fund allocations, charisma, project goal identification, recognition, and visibility. Style II management evolved particularly with the matrix, where managers have to elicit support from various organizational units, and where the frequently ambiguous authority definition of the project manager, and the temporary nature of projects, contribute to an intricately complex operating environment.

Leadership Style Effectiveness

The following paragraphs describe how the project manager can increase effectiveness and ultimately improve overall program performance.

Project managers must develop their skills in leading the task team within a relatively unstructured work environment. This involves the ability to:

- Provide clear project direction
- Assist in problem solving
- Facilitate group decisions
- Plan for and elicit commitment
- Communicate clearly and effectively
- Facilitate the integration of new team members
- Understand the organization and its interfaces

Project managers must foster an environment that is professionally stimulating and challenging, leading to recognition of professional accomplishments. To create such a work environment, the project managers must:

- Understand the needs, wants, and interests of their personnel
- Accommodate the interests of their personnel by discussing the assignments at the outset and distributing the work optimally
- Create visibility and management involvement for their projects via all available means such as meetings, planning, announcements, and news and information channels

Project managers must develop a credible image as experienced, effective task managers. Therefore, they should seek out progressively more responsible task management assignments, rather than take on a project that is over their heads. Moreover, an understanding of the technologies involved in managing the project is essential for building a credible image, for integrating technical solutions, and for communicating effectively with the team members.

Project managers should build a personnel appraisal and award system that is consistent with the demands on their personnel. The ingredients of such a system include:

- Clearly defined job objectives, rewards, and negotiated commitment to the established project plans
- Clearly defined roles and accountabilities among all project team members
- Shared responsibility for personnel appraisal between functional and project manager
- A nonthreatening work environment
- A minimum of one personnel appraisal per year
- Fair, integrated overall assessment of performance
- Strong reliance on nonmonetary rewards such as recognition for accomplishments, visibility, opportunity for professional growth, interesting work, and freedom to act
- Fair monetary rewards, consistent with the level of responsibility and performance

Project managers must develop a communication network that facilitates the flow of information and management directions both vertically and horizontally. The characteristics of such an effective communication network are:

- Proper up-front project planning involving all key personnel from all disciplines needed during the project life cycle
- Clear reporting relationships among project team members
- Proper project reviews and reports
- Top management involvement, interest, and participation
- Clear project management guidelines, directives, policies, and procedures

Suggestions for Effective Management of Factory Projects

A number of suggestions may be helpful in increasing the project manager's effectiveness and overall program performance.

Culture and Value System Project managers need to understand the interaction of organizational and behavioral elements in order to build an environment conducive to their team's motivational needs. This healthy environment will enhance active participation and minimize dysfunctional conflict.

The effective flow of communication is one of the major factors determining the quality of the organizational environment. Since the project manager must build support teams at various organizational layers, he or she must clearly communicate key decisions to all project-related personnel. By openly communicating the project objectives, managers minimize unproductive conflict. Regularly scheduled status review meetings can be an important vehicle for communicating project related issues and dealing with problems early in their development.

Leadership　Because their environment is often temporary, project managers should seek a leadership style that allows them to adapt to the changing requirements of their project organizations. They must learn to test the expectations of others by observation and experimentation. Although they may find it difficult, they must be ready to alter their leadership style as demanded by both the status of the project and its participants.

Conflict　The ability to manage conflict is affected by many situation variables. A project manager should recognize the primary determinants of conflict and when they are most likely to occur in the life of the project, and should consider the effectiveness of conflict-handling approaches. Proper planning involving all key project participants leads to sufficient work detail and measurability, and in the end to commitment by all project personnel. Planning seems to be one key element in minimizing dysfunctional conflict. Another element is a professionally stimulating work environment.

Interesting Work　The project manager should try to accommodate the professional interests and desires of supporting personnel. Project effectiveness often depends upon the project's ability to provide a professionally stimulating work environment. Work challenge can be a catalyst in matching individual goals with objectives of the project and the overall organization. Although the

scope of a project may be fixed, the project manager usually has a degree of flexibility in allocating task assignments among various contributors.

Technical Expertise　Project managers should develop and maintain technical expertise in their fields. Without an understanding of the technology, project managers are unable to participate effectively in the search for integrated solutions, or to win the confidence of team members, or to build credibility with customers.

Planning　Effective planning early in the life cycle of a project favorably influences the organizational climate and overall project performance. Insufficient planning may eventually lead to an unprepared work team, confusion, inability to measure and control progress, interdepartmental conflict, and discontinuity in the work flow.

Personal Drive　Finally, project managers can influence the climate of their work environment by their own actions. Concern for project team members, ability to integrate personal goals and needs of project personnel with project goals, and ability to create personal enthusiasm for the project itself—all these can foster a climate high in motivation, work involvement, open communication, and resulting project performance.

Situational Effectiveness of Project Managers

A situational approach to project management effectiveness is presented in FIG. 5-4. Summarizing the effects of managerial influence style on motivation and position power, the figure indicates that the intrinsic motivation of project personnel increases with the project managers' emphasis on work challenge, their own expertise, and their ability to establish friendship ties. On the other hand, emphasis on penalty measures, authority, and the inability to manage conflict effectively lowers personnel motivation.[4]

The figure further illustrates that the project manager's position power is determined by such variables as formal position within the organization, the scope and nature of the project, earned authority, and the ability to influence promotion and future work assignments. All factors appear to be important for sustained high work effort and organizational commitments over the project life cycle. Moreover, field research shows that project managers who foster a climate of highly motivated personnel not only to obtain higher project support from their project personnel, but also achieve high overall project performance as perceived by their superiors.

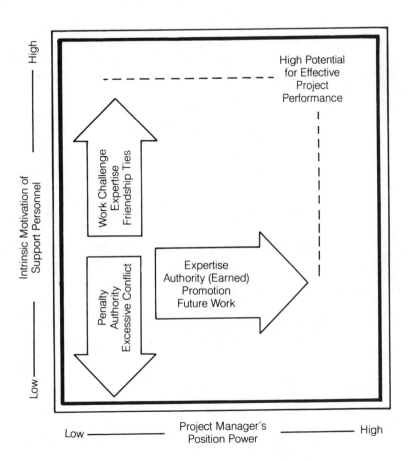

Fig. 5-4. Key variables that increase the situational effectiveness of project managers.

ENDNOTES

1. Various terms are used to define the title and task responsibility of managers in a matrix environment. Project management titles are often used interchangeably, although a certain hierarchy of responsibility is implied, for instance program manager refers to the highest responsibility, followed by task manager, and project administrator. In this discussion the term *project manager* is used in a general context to describe a matrix manager with multidisciplinary task responsibilities.

2. *See* H. J. Thamhain, "Conflict in Project Life Cycles," Chapter 42: Engineering Management in *Mechanical Engineers' Handbook*, New York: John Wiley and Sons, 1986 and Wiley, *Engineering Project Management* (New York: 1984).

3. For specific examples of project management charters, policies, procedures, and management guidelines see Harold Kerzner and Hans Thamhain, *Project Management Operating Guidelines* (New York: Van Nostrand Reinhold, 1986).

4. For a detailed discussion of the research leading to the situational leadership approach in project management, see G. R. Gemmill and H. J. Thamhain, "Influence Styles of Project Managers: Some Project Performance Correlates," *Academy of Management Journal* 17:2 (June 1974): 216-24, Hans Thamhain, "Managing Engineers Effectively," *IEEE Transactions on Engineering Management* (May 1983), and Hans Thamhain and David Wilemon, "Leadership, Conflict, and Project Management Effectiveness," *Executive Bookshelf on Generating Technological Innovation, Sloan Management Review*, 1987.

BIBLIOGRAPHY

Adler, P. S. and Helleloid, D. A. "Effective Implementation of Integrated CAD/CAM: A Model." *IEEE Transactions on Engineering Management* EM-34: 2 (May 1987): 101-107.

Allen, L. A. *Making Managerial Planning More Effective.* New York: McGraw-Hill, 1982.

Badiru, A. "Expert Systems and Industrial Engineers: A Practical Guide to a Successful Partnership." *Computers and Industrial Engineering* 14: 1 (1988): 1-13.

Barba, J. J., Grosman, L., Smith, R. "Plant Life Cycle Through Material Management and Computer-Aided Engineering." *AACE Transactions* (1986): K.4.1-K.4.7.

Barrett, T. H. "Research and Manufacturing Share a Common World." *European Journal of Operational Research* (Netherlands) 24: 3 (March/April 1988): 346-359.

Boudette, N. E. "Manufacturing Warms to Project Management Tool." *Industry Weekly* 237:5 (September 5, 1988): 124.

Clawson, R. T. "Controlling the Manufacturing Start-up." *Harvard Business Review* 63:3 (May/June 1985): 6-20.

Cleland, D. I. "A Kaleidoscope of Matrix Management Systems." *AMA Management Review* (December 1981).

Cook, R. *London Motivation and Job Design.* London: Institute of Personnel Management, 1976.

Devore, T., McCollum, J. K., and Ledbetter, W. N. "Project Engineering in a Plant Environment." *Project Management Quarterly* (September 1982): 25-30.

Elmes, M., and Wilemon, D. "Organizational Culture and Project Leader Effectiveness." *Project Management Journal* (September 1988).

"FMS for High-Volume Manufacturers—Economies of Scale/Planning and Designing for a Flexible Manufacturing System." *Production* 98: 2 (August 1986): 87-94.

Gemmill, G. R., and Thamhain, H. J. "The Effectiveness of Different Power Styles of Project Managers in Gaining Project Support." *IEEE Transactions on Engineering Management* 20: 2 (May 1973): 38-43.

"The General Electric Experience—Gaining Marketshare in a Declining Market." *Production* 97: 3 (March 1986): 66-69.

Graham, M. B. W. and Rosenthal, S. R. "Flexible Manufacturing Systems Require

Flexible People." *Human Systems Management* (Netherlands) 6: 3 (1986): 211-222.

Handbook of Industrial Engineering. New York: Wiley, 1982.

Harter, James A., and Mueller, Carl J. "FMS at Remington." *Manufacturing Engineering* 100: 3 (March 1988): 91-95.

Hopeman, R. J., *Production and Operations Management.* Columbus, Ohio: Merrill, 1980.

Huber, Laurence E. "Using Project Management Techniques in Manufacturing Systems." *Industrial Management* 30: 2 (March/April 1988): 19-22.

Janger, A. R., *Matrix Organizations of Complex Businesses* New York: The Conference Board, 1979.

Katz, Mayer, ed. *Mechanical Engineers' Handbook.* Wiley, 1986.

Kidder, Tracy, *The Soul of a New Machine*, Boston, Massachusetts: Little, Brown and Company, 1981.

Lockman, Michael. "A PM Approach to Production Improvement." *Manufacturing Systems* 6: 7 (July 1988): 42-43.

McAfee, R. B., and Poffenberger, W. *Productivity Studies.* Englewood Cliffs, New Jersey: Prentice-Hall, 1982.

Meredith, Jack. "Project Planning for Factory Automation." *Project Management Journal* 17: 5 (December 1986): 51-55.

Mize, Joe H., Seifert, Deborah J., and Berry, Gayle. "Strategic Planning for Factory Modernization: A Case Study." *National Productivity Review* 4: 1 (Winter 1984-1985): 33-44.

Monks, J. A. *Operations Management.* New York: McGraw-Hill, 1982.

Moore, F. G., and Hendrick, T. *Production-Operations Management.* Homewood, Illinois: Richard D. Irwin, 1980.

Morello, Carmine D. "Successful MRP Needs Full-Time Project Leader." *Computerworld* 18: 13 (March 26, 1984): p. Special Report 30.

Nelson, Craig A. "How to Develop a Competitive Manufacturing Strategy." *Production* 97: 3 (March 1986): 37-50.

Nordin, John R., Jr. "Managing Project Management." *Manufacturing Systems* 5: 11 (November 1987): 20-24.

Rao, Ashok. "Manufacturing Systems Implementation: Agenda for Top Management." *Production & Inventory Management* 26: 1 (First Quarter 1985): 88-102.

Schmidt, M. J. "Schedule Monitoring of Engineering Projects." *IEEE Transactions on Engineering Management* 35: 2 (May 1988): 108-114.

Schroder, R. G. *Operations Management.* New York: McGraw-Hill, 1981.

Szakonyi, Robert. "Tips for Improving the Management of Manufacturing Technology." *Industrial Engineering* 19: 11 (November 1987): 18-20.

Thamhain, H. J. "Developing Engineering Management Skills." *Management of Research, Development and Engineering* (D. Kocaoglu Editor), New York: Elsevier-North Holland, 1990.

_____. "Managing Technologically Innovative Team Efforts toward New Product Success." *Journal of Product Innovation Management* 7: 1 (March 1990).

_____. *Engineering Program Management.* New York: Wiley, 1985.

_____. *Engineering Management.* New York: Wiley, 1990.

_____. *Team-Building in Technology-based Organizations* Reading, Massachusetts: Addison-Wesley, 1990.

_____. ''Building High-Performing Engineering Project Teams.'' *IEEE Transactions on Engineering Management* (August 1987).

_____. ''Production.'' In *Matrix Management Systems Handbook*. New York: Van Nostrand Reinhold, 1983.

Thamhain, H. J., and Wilemon, D. L. ''Conflict Management in Project Life Cycles.'' Chapter 42: Engineering Management in *Mechanical Engineers' Handbook* (M. Kutz, Editor), New York: John Wiley and Sons, 1986.

Walsh, John J., and Kanter, Jerome. ''Toward More Successful Project Management.'' *Journal of Systems Management* 39: 1 (January 1988): 16-21.

6

Production Teams in Manufacturing

Karen M. Bursic*

TEAMWORK IN INDUSTRY HAS EXISTED IN MANY forms for a number of years. Consider, for example, operations research teams in the 1940s and project management teams in the 1960s. In addition, the study of behavior in small groups has been a social science issue for quite some time. However, the idea of teamwork, at least in the United States, became a central issue for manufacturing industries in the early 1970s with the introduction of Japanese-style quality circles into American companies.

The team concept has expanded and evolved into the use of production teams similar to those used at Volvo in the late 1960s and General Foods, Topeka in the early 1970s. Companies such as General Motors, Digital Equipment Corporation, Westinghouse Electric Corporation, and a host of others are currently altering traditional manufacturing management practices and organizational designs through the use of these kinds of teams. Teams are sometimes referred to as autonomous, semiautonomous, self-regulating, or self-managing; in this chapter, they will be referred to as *production teams*.

WHAT IS A PRODUCTION TEAM?

Production teams are usually made up of 5 to 15 operations workers from the same work area or cell. The workers have broad responsibilities beyond those commonly given to quality circle or task force team members and are normally not voluntary. Production teams have a high degree of responsibility and authority for making day-to-day decisions in areas such as task assignments, work scheduling, training, work methods, quality control, maintenance, and problem solving. More autonomous teams may work without a supervisor and even get involved in hiring and purchasing. In general, the employees become responsible for various planning, organizing, and control activities that affect operations within their work area. Usually team members rotate job assignments, are paid for the skills they master, and are evaluated based on group rather than individual performance.

While quality circles or task forces are primarily an overlay on the existing organizational structure, production teams become part of the overall organizational design and replace the traditional

*Karen Bursic is currently a senior consultant with Ernst & Young in Pittsburgh. She received a BS in Industrial Engineering in 1984 and worked as an Industrial Engineer and a Production Supervisor at General Motors Corporation. She earned an MS in Engineering Management in 1987 and a Ph.D. in Industrial Engineering in 1990 from the University of Pittsburgh. Her primary interest is in the use of alternative organizational designs, including production and other kinds of teams, in manufacturing. She received the Gilbreth Memorial Fellowship from the Institute of Industrial Engineers for the 1988-89 academic year.

organizational structure. Extensive education and training in team building and problem solving is usually required for implementing this type of structure. Various systems and processes—such as communications, information, and control—may be modified and altered. The production team organizational design allows for shared responsibility, accountability, and authority for decisions and, ultimately, results. This phenomenon is discussed by Cleland and Kerzner in the introductory chapter of their recent book, *Engineering Team Management*.[1]

WHAT A PRODUCTION TEAM IS NOT

To further clarify what a production team is, a discussion of other kinds of teams is needed. Organizations use a variety of teams in manufacturing operations including quality circles, product design teams, task forces, project teams, and management teams. Each of these is described below.

Quality Circles First introduced in the early 1970s, quality circles continue to be used in many organizations today. The quality circle concept has expanded to include more than solving quality problems. Many organizations use other names for these groups such as employee involvement groups, productivity teams, participation teams, performance circles, and employee participation circles.

Quality circles are most often defined as small groups of employees (usually including a supervisor) from the same work area who voluntarily meet regularly to study quality and productivity improvement techniques. The groups apply these techniques to solving work-related problems for increasing organizational efficiency and effectiveness. These teams select which problems they can address from a wide range of possibilities. Once a solution is reached and implemented the quality circle moves on to another problem. In addition, the groups often present their ideas to management and participate in their implementation. The teams are often rewarded for the creation of cost savings projects.

Product Design Teams These teams usually consist of design, engineering, manufacturing, marketing, purchasing, and other personnel who are assigned to the development of a specific product. The use of product design teams is based on the need to decrease the time from the inception of a product idea to the product's introduction in the market. It is a simultaneous rather than sequential approach to product design. The Ford Motor Company used this approach (often called simultaneous engineering) in designing its Taurus and Sable models. The approach reduces the number of design changes needed during development stages since representatives from all relevant departments are involved in product design from start-up. Many companies are adopting product design teams in order to decrease the time between development and introduction of new products and thus to gain a competitive edge in the market.

Task Forces Task forces are interdisciplinary teams primarily used as an ad hoc tool for problem solving. These teams address a variety of unique organizational problems including crisis management, organizational restructuring, competitive analysis, hiring of new top management personnel, or a specific quality problem. Task force team members are usually appointed by management based on the knowledge and skills that they possess. The teams meet regularly until a particular objective is met; then they disband.

Project Teams These are the traditional interdisciplinary teams used in project management. They primarily consist of engineers and other professionals who work on specific, ad hoc, complex projects that must meet time, cost, and technical performance objectives. Project teams are often used on major automation projects in manufacturing companies. The advantages of using project management scheduling and other techniques on projects for the automated factory have been described in the literature.

Management Teams Some firms have found a need to involve all levels of management in various decision-making tasks such as resource allocation, funds distribution, facility design, budgeting, and hiring. Honeywell's Systems and Research Center uses teams of managers to make decisions by consensus in areas that might affect the entire operation. IBM uses a program called Process Quality Management as a planning tool for various tasks including strategy formulation, funding, human resource management, and marketing. Teams of managers identify goals and activities critical to the attainment of those goals and provide a way to measure success.

The remainder of this chapter will focus on production teams as previously defined; however, some of the strategies and management suggestions to be described can apply to the introduction and use of other kinds of teams as well. For example, training in problem solving is critical to the introduction of quality circles and task forces while top management support is essential to all team programs.

WHY USE PRODUCTION TEAMS?

Business and technical journals, as well as the popular press, devote much attention to the decline in American manufacturing competitiveness. This attention focuses not only on quality and productivity but also on the increasingly global market in which many industries must compete and on the tremendous advancements in manufacturing and computer technologies. In attempting to increase competitiveness in automated factories, organizations have introduced a variety of changes in job designs, work methods, plant layouts, equipment, and accounting practices. A common thread runs through all of the changes occurring in manufacturing industries today: people. Managers have begun to recognize that an organization's most abundant and useful resource is its people.

The importance of people is emphasized in a report from the Manufacturing Advisory Board of the National Research Council entitled, *Toward a New Era in U.S. Manufacturing*. The report devotes an entire chapter to the subject of people and organization in the factory of the future. The board stated:

> The changes needed in people and organizations will be a difficult aspect of the revolution in manufacturing. They require a dramatic refocus of the traditional culture in the factory, away from hierarchical, adversarial relations and toward cooperative sharing of responsibilities.[2]

In addition, the report focuses on participation and ownership:

> Employees at all levels should be given an opportunity to contribute ideas, make decisions, and implement them in areas that may affect operations beyond the individual's formal responsibilities. The principle involved is intellectual ownership: if all employees can feel a degree of ownership in decisions that affect them and the company, they are likely to support those decisions more enthusiastically, resulting in a highly motivated work force and a more responsive, effective company.[3]

The use of production and other kinds of teams in manufacturing has been fueled by the recognition that involving the worker in decision making and problem solving in areas related to his or her job has tremendous potential for improving quality and productivity as well as employee morale and job satisfaction. Through teamwork, the potential exists for employees to make valuable contributions to organizational efficiency and effectiveness. Many organizations have recognized this and have attempted to harness the energy and knowledge of their workers.

This recognition is evidenced by the extensive use of teams in industry. FIGURE 6-1 lists 43 companies that use team management concepts. The use of problem solving teams (such as quality circles), production teams, engineering or project teams, management teams, and team development techniques is evident throughout the literature. Many larger companies, such as General Motors, take advantage of a variety of these kinds of teams in some form within their organizations. Smaller companies, such as Crane Plastics, have also recognized and taken advantage of the benefits of teamwork for enhancing the effectiveness of their organizations.

Although they do not always refer to them as quality circles, many companies use problem solving and decision making teams, as column 1 in FIG. 6-1 shows. In addition, most of these organizations understand the importance of training employees in problem solving and other team development skills. Production and other kinds of teams have emerged, in part, due to the recognition of the contributions that workers can make to organizational efficiency and effectiveness.

At Rohm and Haas Bayport, Inc. (a specialty chemical plant in La Porte, Texas), for example, all 67 employees belong to teams that play an active role in the management of the plant. Technicians routinely perform a variety of tasks without supervision and workers even evaluate one another and interview job applicants. There are only four executives on the management team. Two teams—engineers and chemists—work each shift, and mem-

bers rotate jobs. Although the plant had a difficult beginning characterized by a high employee turnover rate, they now have a well established work force that is overwhelmingly satisfied with the team concept.

Much talk in the organization development literature concerns the use of a sociotechnical approach to organizational design. Denison describes this approach as centering on the "joint optimization of the social and technical systems in an organization; the responsible autonomy of the individual worker; and the application of principles of group behavior to achieve these ideals."[4] The sociotechnical model advocates the use of production teams to achieve this joint optimization of

Company	Technique					Company	Technique				
	1	2	3	4	5		1	2	3	4	5
Acme Steel	★				★	IBM				★	
Alcoa		★			★	International Packings	★				★
Allen-Bradley			★			Kellogg	★				★
Amana			★			Kiethley Instruments		★			★
Burlington Industries	★					Lincoln Electric	★				★
Chrysler			★			Litton	★				★
Congoleum	★					Lockheed	★				★
Corning					★	Marietta	★				★
Crane Plastics	★	★				Ohio Edison				★	★
Deere			★	★	★	Paul Revere Insurance	★				
DEC			★			J.C. Penney	★			★	★
1st National Bank - Chicago	★					Rohm and Haas		★			
Ford	★		★		★	Saab		★			
Frito-Lay			★		★	Shell Oil		★			
General Dynamics					★	Sherwin Williams	★				
General Electric	★	★			★	Texas Instruments			★		
General Foods		★				TRW					★
General Motors	★	★	★	★	★	Union Carbide	★				★
Haworth	★				★	Volvo		★			
HP	★					Warner Lambert	★				
Honeywell	★	★	★	★	★	Westinghouse	★			★	★
						Xerox	★		★		★

*Indicates company is using the technique.

Techniques:
1 - Problem Solving / Decision Making Teams
2 - Production Teams, Autonomous or Semi-Autonomous Work Groups
3 - Engineering, Technical or Project Teams
4 - Management Teams
5 - Team Development Techniques

(Although team development is often included in many team efforts, unless the concept was specifically mentioned in the literature, it is not indicated here. Team Development might include team building, goal setting, interpersonal skills development, and learning problem solving techniques.)

Fig. 6-1. Survey of companies using team management concepts.

human and technical resources. Various organizational development research studies have been done in order to determine the benefits of this approach.

Digital Equipment Corporation took the sociotechnical approach in designing its Enfield, Connecticut, Plant. The plant was built at a greenfield site with the intention of adopting the concepts of teamwork at start-up. The organization is made up of several business units each with four operating teams who control and perform every activity that goes into building a product. The plant has a minimal number of managers who do more facilitating than decision making. The Enfield site is one of Digital's most successful operations.

Joint optimization has been advocated by Ettlie who describes a systems approach to the introduction and implementation of advanced technologies that emphasizes the simultaneous adoption of technological and organizational innovations. In his study of domestic manufacturing plants in the process of purchasing advanced automation for their factories, Ettlie found that:

> The most frequently used type of administrative innovation for synchronous deployment of advanced manufacturing technology in domestic plants today is integration of the hierarchy of the firm. The most commonly used method of hierarchical integration is the creation of an engineering-shop floor team.[5]

Ettlie has found significant evidence that the approach, known as *synchronous innovation*, is effective in increasing the chances of successful implementation of new technologies.

The emergence of production teams can also be attributed in part to the need for more innovative ways to structure the automated factory. Many recent reports on the automated factory of the future emphasize the need to consider altering organizational designs. For example, *American Machinist and Automated Manufacturing* recently reported:

> If a company is to make effective use of major advances in manufacturing technology, a critical mass of interrelated changes is required in plant culture; *job and organization design* [emphasis added]; selection; training

and compensation systems; and labor/management relations . . . . the interdependence of automated tasks requires more teamwork and therefore makes a formal team structure more appropriate.[6]

Hagedorn, in writing about people in the factory of the future, also recognizes the need for teamwork.[7] Although he disagrees with the need for permanent production teams on the shop floor, he does state that ad hoc problem-solving teams, and the "interpersonal and intellectual skills required to make such teams effective" will be prominent in automated factories of the future. He notes that most everyone employed in factories will be affected by job changes of some sort and is convinced that the overall impact of these changes will be favorable.

Other authors also offer their predictions for the future of manufacturing organizations. Goddard discusses the trend away from the traditional assembly line toward independent and interrelated work teams—production teams—that make their own decisions regarding work related tasks as well as task assignments. He also notes the increasing use of management-worker committees, product design teams, and task forces.[8]

In a recent *Harvard Business Review* article, Hayes and Jaikumar stated their belief that the use of a variety of traditional managerial practices including top-down decision making is incompatible with the requirements of advanced manufacturing systems.[9] Companies who continue to use these types of practices will run the risk of failure in the automated factory. The use of production teams is certainly one way to avoid traditional pure top-down decision making and to assign responsibility for some decision-making tasks to the shop floor.

Increasing the chances of successful introduction of advanced manufacturing technologies into the automated factory is one reason for advocating the use of production teams. Another important reason lies in the ability to create innovative organizations that can survive in an increasingly competitive market. Hewlett-Packard's Signal Analysis Division, for example, was facing stiff competition from foreign manufacturers, including the Japanese, in the early 1980s. Part of their solution to the problems of increasing competition and declining productivity was to generate employee awareness through communications. This was aided by the introduction of quality circles and small work groups—production teams—organized on a project basis. The program was intended to create a corporate culture that emphasizes the involvement of workers. The approach was designed to underscore the importance of each worker in the productivity improvement process and was successful at creating a more competitive division for Hewlett-Packard.

FIGURE 6-2 summarizes the primary reasons for advocating the use of production teams. First and foremost is the recognition that people are a company's most valuable resource. People can make significant contributions to organizational efficiency and effectiveness.

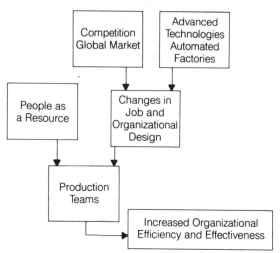

Fig. 6-2. Why use production teams?

The increasingly competitive, world-wide market has led to a need to make significant changes in the way a plant operates in order to improve productivity and, ultimately, lower operating costs. As the figure shows, these changes often occur in the areas of job and organizational design. The introduction of advanced manufacturing technologies and the advent of the automated factory have also

forced companies to make considerable changes in job and organizational design.

One way to address the needed changes in job and organizational design and to take advantage of the ideas and contributions that workers can make is to introduce production teams into the automated factory. Production teams are growing in popularity because organizations have begun to recognize the concepts depicted in FIG. 6-2.

STRATEGIES FOR THE USE OF PRODUCTION TEAMS

General Motors has introduced team concepts into a variety of its divisions including its Van Nuys, California, plant. The team approach, modeled after the successful NUMMI (New United Motors Manufacturing Incorporated, a joint venture between GM and Toyota) operation, was implemented as a last-ditch effort to keep the plant open. Every employee received extensive training in team building, problem solving, and statistical quality control. The introduction of production teams at the plant has had its problems, however, including lack of total union support.

If companies are to make successful use of production teams in automated factories, they must remember several important strategies. FIGURE 6-3 emphasizes the key strategies for the introduction of production teams. These steps are described in this section.

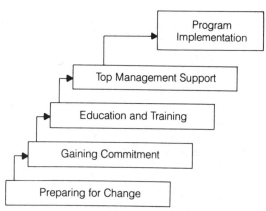

Fig. 6-3. Strategies for implementation.

Preparing for Change Although changes in the automated factory are inevitable and constant, resistance cannot be avoided. Management must take steps to prepare the organization and its members for the changes that will occur as a result of the introduction of production teams. Resistance nearly always occurs when a major organizational design change is to be introduced into a firm. Change threatens the traditional procedures and practices—the status quo within an organization. Most employees will fear a loss of status or power and may express uncertainty about job security.

People nearly always resist changes they do not understand or that run counter to the traditional way that things have been done. The need to expand job skills, common with the introduction of production teams, also causes concern. Employees may not be immediately willing to be retrained or reeducated. Resistance will be particularly prevalent in organizations whose members believe that the current system is effective and who do not believe that change is necessary.

Management can take a variety of steps to prepare the organization for change and uncertainty. First, top management must reduce the anxiety of employees regarding job security and learning new skills. Management must stress that the company does not intend to displace employees who do not currently possess the job skills needed in the new organizational structure. Emphasis should be placed on education and training of employees as well. Organizations should also reassure employees that the transition can be made without great personal cost to them. Managers must be consistent and clear in communications regarding the new organizational structure and their intentions for making the needed organizational changes. Inconsistency can lead to a loss of trust among organization members and will only enhance resistance.

The remaining key strategies for implementation—gaining commitment, education and training, and top management support—also contribute to the preparation for change. These strategies are listed as separate steps since they must continue throughout the implementation of the production teams as well as after changes are in place.

Gaining Commitment The purposes, objectives, and goals of the production teams must be clearly defined and stated to everyone that will be involved with or affected by them. Organization members must have a clear understanding of why the teams are being formed, how the teams will be used, and what is expected of team members. In addition, it is important to include a cross section of organization members in the planning and organization stages of the implementation process. Teams cannot be expected to have a positive effect on productivity and quality if management and labor do not cooperate in their formation and use. In a unionized plant, union support for the use of teams is particularly important and union members must have a say in how the program will be structured. Remember: involvement enhances commitment.

Education and Training Production teams require organization members to broaden their knowledge and skills in a variety of areas. Managers must recognize education and training as a key part of the introduction of teams into the structure of an organization. Education and training can ease employees' fears about job security. The following areas should be included as part of the educational process.

Team Building Team building creates a climate conducive to teamwork by establishing good interpersonal relationships among team members. Essentially this process helps to lay the groundwork for the operation of the teams and helps team members to understand group dynamics. The process involves answering questions:

- What is our mission?
- How will we get started?
- How does each individual fit in and contribute?
- What are our objectives and goals?
- Who has ultimate authority, accountability, and responsibility for decisions and results?
- By what standards will we operate?
- What policies and procedures are important?
- How do we judge performance?
- How do we handle conflicts?

Problem Solving If organization members are expected to make a variety of task-related decisions, they must have the ability to effectively solve problems. Organizations must teach the various steps in the problem-solving process—problem identification, data collection, evaluating alternatives—and the techniques used in each step—brainstorming, pareto analysis, cause and effect analysis, cost/benefit ratios.

Job Skills Production team members are usually required to rotate jobs and work assignments. Team members should possess the ability to perform a broad range of job related tasks. This may require that team members be trained to operate a variety of production machines and perform unfamiliar tasks. Training in job skills is especially important in the automated factory because of the tremendous variety of manufacturing and computer technology that is often used. This step not only involves extensive training but also requires supervisors to understand each individual's current capabilities and training needs.

Interpersonal Skills People can easily become uncomfortable when new job requirements, technologies, and management expectations are introduced. Therefore, it is vitally important to develop leadership and communication abilities in individual team members. There are a variety of methods that can be used in workshops and seminars for increasing these skills. Enhancing communication skills requires an understanding of the communication process and a recognition of the barriers that can impede it. Leadership training might focus on the traits that make an effective leader and the leadership styles that are useful in particular situations.

All these areas of education and training should be part of an ongoing, continual process so that new members can enter the system with ease and so that the education process is constantly reinforced. In addition, advanced computer and manufacturing technologies are likely to be continually updated in the automated factory, thus it is important that production team members understand changes and maintain their skills in operating various equipment.

Top Management Support The importance of top management support for any new program cannot be overemphasized. This support must not merely be displayed in words or memos but must be evidenced by such explicit actions as attendance at education sessions or "management by walking around." Management also demonstrates support by committing the necessary resources and providing the required information to the teams. Top management support is important for removing the belief that the introduction of production teams is "just another program" or a "fad" that management won't support for very long. In addition, top management plays an active and important role in shaping organizational culture through its established (as well as unwritten) policies and procedures. An organizational culture that is supportive of the team concept and is characterized by openness and trust eases the transition from a traditional structure to a team structure.

The changes introduced by the use of production teams should be built into the structure of the manufacturing organization to ensure that the program is continued throughout any management turnovers. Organization charts should clearly reflect the new structure.

The entire organization must be aware that the introduction of production teams will take time. Although early results are important and should be recognized, team members and managers cannot expect an immediate or easy turnaround in culture and behaviors. The benefits of using production teams may not be immediately evident but it should be clear to employees what long-term advantages are expected from the use of the team structure.

MANAGING PRODUCTION TEAMS

The management of a team-structured organization involves much more than gaining commitment, educating and training workers, and providing top management support. Although these strategies ease the implementation process, they do not guarantee the successful use of production teams. Managing the continuous development of the teams involves the creation of an organizational culture that fully accepts the new structure and is characterized by teamwork throughout its written and unwritten policies, practices, and procedures.

Communications and Information

Many organizational systems and processes may need modification. Communications, for example, must be developed as a two way, up and down process rather than simply a top-down approach. If workers, as team members, are expected to take on additional responsibilities, information must be widely shared. Team members cannot effectively solve problems if the information needed to make decisions is not made available to them.

When General Motors formed its NUMMI joint venture with Toyota in Fremont, California, they made the horizontal flow of information across all departments a priority. Management at the plant continues to make sure that information flows, not only horizontally, but also from the bottom to the top of the organizational hierarchy and back down again. *Kaisen*, or continuous improvement, also enhances the communication concept. Under this concept, any idea that the workers feel will improve the production process is considered important and is usually implemented. Workers are encouraged to make suggestions about how to improve the production process.

This communications and information process is important to the worker's effective involvement in the quality process as well. In the past, production workers at auto plants were never allowed to stop the production line. In the automated factory, it becomes vital that workers be aware of the quality of the products being produced. At NUMMI, which makes use of production teams, team members have access to a stop button, or *Andon*, that they may use to stop the production line if a problem arises. In this way, team members are taking the responsibility for sending a quality product to the next "customer" down the line. It is important to note that, unless supervisors and other managers take team members' quality concerns seriously, involvement in the quality process will not take place. The use of an Andon is one way to ensure that team members believe that management wants to hear about their concerns. However, management must take steps to follow up on the quality problems that team members bring to their attention.

One of the most effective and often-used ways of keeping the communications and information process going within the work groups is the team meeting. Most production teams meet once or twice a week for approximately one hour in order to discuss work related problems and opportunities. These meetings give the workers an opportunity to continue the team development process, which started during the implementation of the production team structure. It is important that team members continue to regard themselves as a team and work together to solve problems and make decisions. This cannot be done without a constant sharing of information; regularly scheduled team meetings facilitate this sharing.

Shared Responsibility

Sharing of responsibility is also important in managing the team process. Authority, accountability, and responsibility procedures must be altered to make effective use of production teams. For example, in order for team members to take full responsibility for making decisions regarding task assignments or work methods, they must have the authority to implement those decisions. Although managers and supervisors will still be held accountable for results, team members need to accept much responsibility for those results. This responsibility can be built by removing external regulators from the team's work environment, such as inspectors and production schedulers. In addition, workers must be given the authority to make adjustments in production goals and schedules when breakdowns, raw material shortages, or other factory interruptions occur.

First-Line Supervisor: Role Changes

The production worker's job is not the only one that is drastically altered with the introduction of production teams into a factory. The first-line supervisor's role changes more than any other managerial position. The increased use of production teams in the automated factory is likely to have a profound effect on this organization position. The role is also altered when a firm introduces complex manufacturing and computing technologies that may perform some of the tasks previously handled by the supervisor.

If teams are to become fully effective, the first-line supervisor must give up some of his or her authority for making various decisions. Due to the increased level of sophistication and education of the workforce as a result of the gradual implementation of production teams and the automated factory, workers will make many of the decisions previously made by management. However, the supervisor will likely maintain the power to prevent certain team decisions from being implemented. The difficulty with this often lies in the fact that responsibility and accountability for decisions remains with the supervisor and he or she can easily become caught between maintaining the self-management of the teams and maintaining control of the work area. This tradeoff poses a dilemma for a first-line supervisor since production teams require a consultative style of management if autonomy of the work groups is to be maintained.[10]

Another problem for the first-line supervisor in a production team structure involves recognition of performance. In some cases, while the supervisor is not rewarded for improved production team performance, he or she is often blamed for poor performance. These difficulties can cause tremendous stress for a first-line supervisor who is trying to adjust to the new organizational structure. It is vitally important for higher levels of management to understand the confusion in the first-line supervisor's role and to be sure that everyone agrees on clear practices and procedures.

The first-line supervisor's attitude directly reflects the top management support that is so important to the effective use of production teams. Therefore, it is vitally important for first-line supervisors to understand and support the sharing of authority, responsibility, and accountability for decisions and results with team members. Supervisors can help to build the knowledge and skills of the team members in their respective areas by encouraging this sharing. It is likely that first-line supervisors' responsibilities will shift away from traditional day-to-day operational decision making, such as work assignments and scheduling, and toward other tasks. These tasks will center on the development of production team members and the maintenance of team boundaries.

In some instances, a team leader position is created in lieu of the first-line supervisor. This person, also a team member, takes the responsibility for facilitating team development, problem solving, and decision making. Many organizations chose to eliminate the position of the first-line supervisor when production teams are introduced. The advantage of this approach is that a supervisor no longer has the potential to undermine the autonomy of the production teams. The effectiveness of fully self-managed production teams has not been proven in all instances. This approach requires a sophisticated, intelligent, and ambitious work force.

Feedback and Rewards

A discussion of the effective management of production teams would not be complete without a mention of the importance of performance feedback and rewards. Performance feedback is vital to the motivation and satisfaction of production team members as well as the organization as a whole. Managers should take early steps to demonstrate the effectiveness of the teams in order to generate support and commitment for the team program. This is important not only to team members but to administrative, professional, and other management personnel whose work tasks, procedures, and policies might be altered by the use of teams. If organization members do not see early results, they probably will not support the program and the organizational culture will not accept teamwork.

Most companies' performance evaluation and reward systems are based on individual achievements. A production team structure requires that an organization consider implementing some type of group reward system such as gainsharing or profit sharing. A discussion of group incentive systems is beyond the scope of this chapter, but suffice it to say that rewards are an important consideration in the effective management of production teams.

BENEFITS AND RESULTS OF PRODUCTION TEAMS

Production teams in manufacturing and the automated factory yield a variety of advantages and benefits that have been demonstrated in many firms. A team structure is not without some disadvantages, as well.

Case studies in the literature reveal many benefits: productivity improvements, increased worker morale, better union-management relations, improved product quality, a more flexible organization, reduced absenteeism, and more effective decision making and execution. Although less well documented, disadvantages might include the initial increase in operating costs (although, in the long run, operating costs are usually lower in a team structured plant), training and education expenses, high employee turnover (as employees try to adjust to the new environment), and implementation difficulties.

One of the earliest extensively studied uses of production teams was at the General Food's plant in Topeka, Kansas. Self-managing teams immediately assumed responsibility for much of the production process at this plant. Various studies of the Topeka experiment indicated positive results in both human and economic terms, including high levels of worker participation, positive work attitudes, and economic superiority.[11] However, some evidence indicates that the structure and results of the experimental plant had hurt rather than advanced the careers of a number of the pioneering

managers. This trade-off between benefits and disadvantages is typical in a factory that makes use of production teams.

A case study at an optical division of a national corporation indicated a substantial increase in productivity, reductions in operating costs, and improved worker morale. These were achieved primarily by revising the operating structure of the organization using production teams and by allowing employees to have greater control of their job situations. The division stressed the importance of feedback and supportive leadership as contributors to the success of the new work structure.[12]

When Frito-Lay introduced production teams at its then new operation in Kern County, California, the plant reached full production a week after start-up, compared with the usual six to thirteen weeks. The teams continue to meet weekly to address problems. One production worker stated, "we address problems, not people" and "so we decide what's right, not who's right."[13] One drawback of the new organizational structure was the initial high turnover caused by the difficulty of working in such an unusual environment. Despite its disadvantages, managers are confident that the Kern County plant will be one of the best operating plants at Frito-Lay.

The General Motors/Toyota NUMMI plant discussed earlier is considered to be one of the most efficient auto plants in the United States. The use of production teams at this automated factory is one of the characteristics that has earned the plant its reputation. The benefits of its innovative operating style include an absenteeism rate of less than five percent and the production of a car—the Nova—that has received some of the highest quality ratings in the industry. Union leaders at the plant are confident that management is supportive of the union and that the plant is producing the best car in the United States. In addition, they understand the advantages of each worker being more skilled. One long-time labor leader stated, "We want to learn more and better our conditions. Now if we are laid off, we have a lot more skills. We have more input into the job, more responsibility."[14]

The Digital plant in Enfield, also discussed previously, has been a tremendous success from a cost accounting perspective. The plant uses fewer people than the average for a plant of its type, yet accomplishes the same amount of work.

Several organizational development studies have attempted to scientifically determine the long-term outcomes of the use of production teams. The findings in a number of these studies indicate that employees do realize an increase in job satisfaction but that the use of production teams per se does not necessarily increase worker performance or productivity. In a study conducted in a British confectionery factory, Wall, Kemp, Jackson, and Clegg found that there was an increase in worker's job satisfaction when production teams were used. However, they could not demonstrate that the teams had any effect on actual worker performance.[15] In another study at a greenfield site using production teams, Kemp, Wall, Clegg, and Cordery again showed that the use of production teams did result in significantly higher levels of job satisfaction. The teams did not have a significant effect on employee motivation, organizational commitment, trust, or mental health.[16] A study by Denison found that workers as well as supervisors in sociotechnical plants using production teams had higher levels of perceived control than workers and supervisors in traditional plants.[17]

Manufacturing organizations that are interested in implementing a team structure into their automated factories should consider the disadvantages and drawbacks of such a structure before expecting to realize the many benefits. It is evident, however, that if managed properly and carefully introduced, the benefits of such a structure can far outweigh the disadvantages. TABLE 6-1 outlines the advantages and disadvantages of production teams.

SUMMARY

This chapter has discussed the use of production teams in manufacturing organizations and automated factories. Production teams consist of operations workers from a specific area of a plant who work together to perform various work-related tasks, make and execute work-related decisions, and solve production problems. When a team structure is introduced into a company, the entire organizational design including policies, procedures, and practices is effected. Responsibility is pushed down the organizational hierarchy.

The use of teams in manufacturing can help an organization address the increasingly competitive world-wide market and the introduction of advanced manufacturing and computer technologies. In addition, the organization will be better able to harness the energy and talent of its workers once it recognizes that people are a company's most valuable resource and that the worker can make significant contributions to organizational efficiency and effectiveness.

When implementing a team structure, managers must take steps to prepare the organization for change; gain commitment from the entire organization; prepare to educate and train workers in

Table 6-1. Potential Advantages and Disadvantages of Production Teams.

Potential Advantages/Benefits	Potential Disadvantages
Productivity improvements	Restructuring costs
Increased worker morale	Training and education expenses
Improved labor-management relations	Initially high employee turnover
Higher quality	Resistance to change
Flexibility	Loss of hierarchical control
Reduced absenteeism	Other implementation difficulties
Improved decision making	Complicated administration
Reduced operating costs (in the long run)	
Increase in employee skill levels	
Increased worker control of job tasks	

team building, problem solving, job skills, and interpersonal skills; and provide top management support. Managing the ongoing process requires attention to communication and information systems; the worker's contribution to the quality process; authority, accountability, and responsibility relationships; the role of the first-line supervisor; and feedback and rewards.

Although some drawbacks do exist, the use of production teams can provide a company with a variety of advantages and benefits. Many examples of the successful implementation of production teams can be found throughout industry.

Current manufacturing organizational designs may not be adequate for the automated factory of the future. To implement advanced technologies and to take advantage of human resources, manufacturing organizations need to consider changes in job and organizational designs. One way to address this need is to structure the organization using production teams. This type of structure has a tremendous impact on the policies, practices, and procedures within a firm.

A trend toward the use of teamwork in the automated factory is apparent and worth noting. This trend will not only occur on the factory floor but in engineering, design, and management groups as well. Teamwork has a number of implications for the management of manufacturing organizations. Top-down decision making will no longer be a strategy and all organization members will have some say in decisions that affect them and their jobs. The horizontal as well as vertical flow of communications will be emphasized. Education and training will become top priorities and organizations will begin to value employees at all hierarchical levels. Finally, labor-management relations will improve once union and management leaders recognize that they are working toward a common goal: the competitiveness of American manufacturing.

ENDNOTES

1. David I. Cleland and Harold Kerzner, *Engineering Team Management* (New York: Van Nostrand Reinhold Company, 1986.)

2. *Toward a New Era in U.S. Manufacturing: The Need for a National Vision*, Report from the National Research Council (Washington, D.C.: National Academy Press, 1986), 49. Copyright 1986 by the National Academy of Sciences.

3. *Toward a New Era*, 52.

4. Daniel Roland Denison, "Sociotechnical Design and Self-Managing Work Groups: The Impact on Control," *Journal of Occupational Behavior* 3 (1982): 298.

5. John E. Ettlie, *Taking Charge of Manufacturing* (San Francisco: Jossey-Bass Publishers, 1988).

6. Anderson Ashburn, "People and Automation," *American Machinist and Automated Manufacturing* (June 1986): 97-102.

7. Homer J. Hagedorn, "The Factory of the Future: What About the People?," *The Journal of Business Strategy* 5: 1 (Summer 1984): 38-45.

8. R. W. Goddard, "The Rise of the New Organization," *Management World* 14: 1 (January 1985): 7-11.

9. Robert H. Hayes and Ramchandran Jaikumar, "Manufacturing's Crisis: New Technologies, Obsolete Organizations," *Harvard Business Review* (September-October 1988): 77-85.

10. Thomas G. Cummings, "Self-Regulating Work Groups: A Socio-Technical Synthesis," *Academy of Management Review* (July 1978): 632.

11. Richard E. Walton, "Work Innovations at Topeka: After Six Years," *The Journal of Applied Behavioral Science* 13: 3 (1977): 423.

12. M. Scott Fisher, "Work Teams: A Case Study," *Personnel Journal* (January 1981): 42-45.

13. Thomas M. Rohan, "Bosses—Who Needs 'em?," *Industry Week* (February 23, 1987): 15.

14. Lee Branst and Agnes Dubberly, "Labor/Management Participation: The NUMMI Experience," *Quality Progress* (April 1988): 34.

15. Toby D. Wall, Nigel J. Kemp, Paul R. Jackson, and Chris W. Clegg, "Outcomes of Autonomous Workgroups: A Long-term Field Experiment," *Academy of Management Journal* 29: 2 (June 1986): 280-304.

16. Nigel J. Kemp, Toby D. Wall, Chris W. Clegg, and John L. Cordery, "Autonomous Work Groups in a Greenfield Site: A Comparative Study," *Journal of Occupation Psychology* 56 (1983): 271-288.

17. Denison, "Sociotechnical Design," 297-314.

BIBLIOGRAPHY

Aubrey II, Charles A. and Felkins, Patricia K. *Teamwork: Involving People in Quality and Productivity Improvement*. New York: American Society for Quality Control, 1988.
Geber, Beverly. "Teaming Up With Unions." *Training* (August 1987): 24-30.
Huse, Edgar F., and Cummings, Thomas G. *Organization Development and Change*. 3rd ed. New York: West Publishing Company, 1985.
Kerr, Steven, Hill, Kenneth D., and Broedling, Laurie. "The First-Line Supervisor: Phasing Out or Here to Stay?" *Academy of Management Review* 11: 1 (1986): 103-115.
McElroy, John. "Back to Basics at NUMMI: Quality Through Teamwork." *Automotive Industries* (November 1985): 63-64.
Nichols, Don. "Taking Participative Management to the Limit." *Management Review* (August 1987): 28-32.
Senia, Al. "Hewlett-Packard's Team Approach Beats Back the Competition." *Production* (May 1986): 89-91.
Solomon, Barbara. "A Plant That Proves Team Management Works." *Personnel* (June 1985): 6-8.

7

Integrated Logistics Support for the Automated Factory

James V. Jones[*]

LOGISTICS IS THE SCIENCE OF PLANNING, DEVELOP-ing, and acquiring the resources necessary to sustain the operation of any organization, system, or entity. These resources may include trained personnel, maintenance and repair capabilities, facilities, support and test equipment, technical documentation, spare and repair parts, and consumable supplies. Without these resources the organization, system, or entity cannot be relied upon to continually perform its intended purpose.

Integrated logistics support is the process of combining the planning for resources with the planning, design, and development of the organization, system, or entity. By combining these two processes, the resulting logistics support package required to sustain operations will be the most efficient and economical possible. The goal of the integrated logistics support planning process is to develop a resource package that provides the best support for the least cost.

The application of the principles of integrated logistics support planning to the automated factory will result in an installation that achieves a balance among performance, support, and cost factors. Without the necessary logistics support package, the automated factory cannot sustain a required

production capability and will, therefore, not provide the optimum return on investment.

INTEGRATED LOGISTICS SUPPORT PROGRAM

The integrated logistics support (ILS) program has a definitive set of goals:

- Require support to influence design
- Develop resource requirements
- Acquire resources
- Provide support for a minimum cost

These goals achieve a balance among factory performance, support resource requirements, and overall factory costs. The ILS program should participate in the development of the factory by coordinating and monitoring the activities of many disciplines that contribute to meeting these goals.

The goal of having support influence design is the most complex and difficult to achieve. This requires logistics engineers to interface with design engineers who are planning the factory throughout the design process to recommend changes to the design that enhance support. To develop resource

*James V. Jones is recognized as a pioneer in the field of computer-aided logistics and has participated in the development of many of the current applications of computer technology in the areas of logistics and reliability and maintainability. He has functioned as ILS program manager on major Department of Defense contracts and has routinely acted as a consultant within DoD and industry on ILS, logistics support analysis and LSA recording, and provisioning. Jones is president of Logistics Management Associates, a professional services company that provides logistics consulting and training services to DoD and industry clients.

requirements, one must systematically analyze the design to identify each resource that will be required to support the factory once it becomes operational. This includes resources to support both operation and maintenance of factory equipment. Not included in these resources are overhead items of a solely business-related nature.

Acquiring support resources is an extension of the identification process. This activity is concerned with the physical aspects of getting the resources to the right place at the right time to support operations or maintenance. To provide support for a minimum cost, one must continually analyze and trade off options to identify changes in design, processes, or procedures that result in the best balance among performance, support, and cost.

Factory Life Cycle

To understand how the ILS planning process works to meet its goals, one must first understand the typical life cycle of a factory. There are seven distinct phases in the typical life cycle of a factory:

• Pre-concept phase
• Concept development phase
• Concept validation phase
• Design development phase
• Construction and investment phase
• Operation phase
• Planned improvement or disposal phase

Each of these phases has a definitive purpose and support implications that must be considered by the ILS planning process.

Pre-concept Phase   The first phase in the life cycle of a factory is the pre-concept phase. This phase identifies and defines the need for and purpose of the factory. Basically, the pre-concept phase is the process of determining why a factory is to be built, what it is to produce, and what parameters must be met to yield a profitable enterprise. The result of the pre-concept phase is a clearly defined set of objectives for the future factory. Logistics support considerations should be included in these objectives. The objectives should include, at a minimum, product definition, cost objectives,

production rates, technology applications, long term support cost parameters, future expansion requirements, known limitations, and any other pertinent information available to be used in developing the factory.

Concept Development Phase   The concept development phase identifies through analysis and studies, all the possible alternatives that could be used to meet the objectives developed during the pre-concept phase. This phase answers the question of what type of physical plant could possibly meet the established factory objectives. Included in the studies would be equipment available to produce the products, production techniques, technologies, locations, and any other available information for each concept alternative. This is an information gathering phase, not necessarily a decision phase—except to decide on all the alternatives that are feasible to meet the established objectives.

Concept Validation Phase   The concept validation phase analyzes each alternative developed in the concept development phase to determine which concept, or concepts, best achieve the established factory objectives. Trade-off analyses may be conducted to evaluate each concept to see which best fits the overall factory requirements with regard to performance, support, and cost. Combinations and permutations of concepts may also be studied to optimize the final factory concept. At the conclusion of this phase, the most appropriate concept is chosen for development and detailed definition.

Design Development Phase   The design development phase takes the alternative that was selected during the design validation phase and with it creates a detailed factory design. The detailed factory design includes the selection and integration of equipment to be used in the factory, the physical plant layout, and the support requirements needed to sustain operations. This phase results in a comprehensive plan, including detailed facility and equipment specifications and blueprints for construction, set-up, testing, staffing, and opening of the factory. Detailed logistics support resource requirements are also identified during this phase.

Construction and Investment Phase
The plan developed during the design development phase is implemented during the construction and investment phase. Actual construction and set-up of the factory occurs during this phase. Up until the start of this phase, relatively few investments have been required; however, this phase represents a major commitment of resources to keep the project going. Included in this phase are construction of the new facility or renovation of an existing suitable facility; purchase or manufacture of equipment for the factory; installation, integration and testing of equipment; initial staffing; operator and maintenance training; and acquisition of support resources needed to start production. During this phase the ILS program emphasis changes from influencing the design and identification of support resources to acquiring these resources.

Operation Phase The operation phase, obvious from the name, is the period when the factory is in operation. This phase normally continues for many years of production. ILS during this phase maintains the factory by acquiring and managing the logistics support resources. As will be shown later in this chapter, the operation phase generates a significant portion of the ownership costs that will be realized over the life of the factory, a fact that is often overlooked or ignored when planning the design and support of the factory.

Planned Improvement or Disposal Phase The last phase in the life cycle of the factory is the planned improvement or disposal phase. Equipment wears out and, many times, the original products manufactured in the factory are no longer marketable. Therefore, the factory must either be upgraded to meet new manufacturing requirements or it must be disposed of to stop production. This phase must be planned in advance in order to eliminate any unnecessary costs. While it is impossible to predict the future when initially planning for the life of the factory, allowances and projections must be made to prepare for this phase. Activities that occur in this phase include renovation or replacement of equipment, physical plant changes, disposal of support resources, and sale of other assets connected with the operation of the factory. In some cases, disposal of a factory can be an expensive proposition that can impact the long term profitability of ownership.

Integrated Logistics Support Program Disciplines

As stated previously, the ILS program is actually a composite of several interrelated disciplines. Each of these disciplines, listed in FIG. 7-1, has a specific purpose and contribution to meeting the goals of the ILS program. The charter of the ILS program is to integrate, coordinate, and manage the efforts of each of these disciplines to achieve a factory design that provides the best balance among performance, support, and cost. The remainder of this chapter addresses the activities of each discipline that work together to make up the final logistics support requirements for the factory.

- Reliability Engineering
- Maintainability Engineering
- Testability Engineering
- Safety Engineering
- Human Engineering
- Maintenance Planning
- Personnel
- Training Development
- Supply Support
- Support and Test Equipment
- Support Documentation
- Life Cycle Cost

Fig. 7-1. Integrated logistics support program disciplines.

RELIABILITY ENGINEERING

A factory can only be productive when all the installed equipment is functional. Equipment failures cause the factory to lose profit due to reduced or stopped capability to manufacture products. The reliability of equipment also has a direct impact on the amount of logistics support resources required to maintain that equipment. The more often equipment breaks, the more maintenance resources will be required. Reliability engineering is charged with the responsibility of working with design engineers to develop or select equipment that has the lowest failure potential possible. A reliable factory where all equipment is available for use provides the highest return on investment and requires the least amount of maintenance support resources. To influence the design, reliability engineers conduct a series of analyses and studies to identify ways of increasing the reliability of factory equipment. These analyses and studies, when properly conducted and integrated into the factory design process, result in the most reliable factory possible.

Inherent Reliability

The basic goal of reliability engineering is to achieve the highest factory inherent reliability under a stated set of performance and operating characteristics. The basic measure of the potential for failure of an item of equipment is its inherent reliability. Inherent reliability is calculated, as shown in FIG. 7-2, as the number of failures that occur during a specific period of time divided by the period of time. The period of time is normally stated in hours of operation. This calculation gives a statistical indication of the theoretical number of failures that will occur for one increment of operating time: the *equipment failure rate*. The reciprocal of the equipment failure rate gives the amount of time, on the average, that an item of equipment will operate before experiencing a failure. This reciprocal is commonly termed the *mean time between failure* (MTBF). Reliability engineering uses the inherent failure rate and MTBF as guides for identifying ways to improve the inherent reliability of the equipment installed in the factory.

Reliability Prediction

The best way to predict the reliability of equipment is to study actual historical data on like equipment or to obtain reliability data from the equipment manufacturer. When such information is not available, reliability engineers use statistical methods to prepare a mathematical prediction of the equipment reliability. Two methods can be used to predict equipment reliability: the parts count method and the part stress analysis method.

$$\text{Failure rate (FR)} = \frac{\text{failure occurrences}}{\text{operating hours}}$$

$$\text{Inherent reliability} = 1 - \text{FR}$$

$$\text{Mean time between failure (MTBF)} = \frac{1}{\text{FR}}$$

Example: Where two failures occurred during 100 hours of operation

$$\text{FR} = \frac{2}{100} = 0.02$$

$$\text{Inherent reliability} = 1 - 0.02 = 98.0\%$$

$$\text{MTBF} = \frac{1}{0.02} = 50 \text{ hours}$$

Fig. 7-2. Inherent reliability calculation.

Parts Count Reliability Prediction The parts count method of predicting equipment reliability uses a rather simple formula. The formula, illustrated in FIG. 7-3, uses generic failure rates of the parts to be used in equipment and anticipated types and quantities of parts to derive a baseline equipment failure rate. Included in the calculations is the quality factor of the parts to be used; this factor indicates the level of testing and quality control the parts manufacturer uses when making parts. The parts count reliability prediction method is an early indicator of the reliability that can be expected for the equipment in the factory. This early prediction can then be used to compare alternatives in design or equipment selection to increase factory reliability.

Part Stress Analysis Reliability Prediction Several complex formulas are used to obtain a part stress analysis reliability prediction. There is a different formula tailored to each type of part, and each formula considers the electrical stress, heat, environment, and frequency of use of each part type. Through the use of the part stress analysis prediction method, reliability engineers produce detailed failure rates for all parts, assemblies, and the total equipment. It must be pointed out that these predictions are just that—statistical predictions. Actual failure rates are not developed until

Formula:

$$\lambda_{EQUIP} = \sum_{i = 1}^{i = n} N_i \, (\lambda_G \pi_Q)$$

Where:

λ_{EQUIP} = Total equipment failure rate (failures/10^6 hr.)
λ_G = Generic failure rate for the ith generic part (failures/10^6 hr.)
π_Q = Quality factor for the ith generic part
N_i = Quantity of ith generic part
n = Number of different generic part categories

Part Type	Failure Rate[1,2]	Quality[2]	Adjusted	Quantity	Total
Transistors (NPN)	0.86	2	1.72	8	13.76
Resistors (comp)	0.038	1.5	0.057	2	0.114
Resistors (vari)	0.34	1.5	0.51	6	3.06
Capacitors (cer)	0.17	1.5	0.255	10	2.55
Diodes (gen)	0.14	2	0.28	4	1.12
IC (MOS)	0.41	3	1.23	12	14.76
Connector	0.15	2.5	0.375	1	0.375
Printed board	0.01	3	0.03	1	0.03

Total predicted failure rate ($\times 10^{-6}$) = 35.769

Predicted MTBF ($1/(35.769)^{10^{-6}}$) = 27,957.16

---

1. Failure rates expressed $\times 10^{-6}$.
2. Failure rates and quality factors from MIL-HDBK 217D.

Fig. 7-3. Parts count reliability prediction formula.

the equipment is built and then used long enough to produce operation or test data on actual equipment usage.

Reliability Analysis

The equipment reliability prediction is used as a basis for analyzing the factory design to determine ways of improving overall reliability. The reliability analysis focuses on identification of design changes that raise the confidence in equipment reliability and thereby increase the long-term performance capabilities of the factory. Many factors that affect reliability are subject to detailed analysis. These factors include environmental conditions, quality, and equipment stress. Each factor can have a significant effect on factory reliability, and is, therefore, a candidate for in-depth analysis.

Environmental Conditions With few exceptions, equipment is sensitive to its environment. Factors such as ambient temperature, humidity, dust, and vibration can have a significant effect on the reliability of equipment. For example, computers are normally designed to operate in temperatures in the range of $+68°F$. When the equipment is continually operated at temperatures that exceed this range, it is far more prone to failure. Likewise, high humidity levels can have a detrimental effect on not only electronic equipment but mechanical equipment. The abrasive effect of dust on moving hardware will cause failures, in some cases in a relatively short period of time. Vibration can cause equipment to exceed operating tolerances or induce failures and damage components. Each of these factors must be analyzed to determine if changes in the selection of equipment design or the factory environmental control system can improve reliability.

Quality The quality of the equipment in the automated factory is a major factor in determining the reliability and resulting productivity that will be experienced. A trade-off analysis may be required to determine the most cost effective balance between quality, reliability, and performance. Normally, higher quality equipment is more expensive than that of lesser quality. However, low quality equipment, while less expensive, is also usually less reliable. A compromise in quality and reliability to reduce initial investment costs for factory equipment may prove to be far more expensive in the long run due to lower efficiency and unreliability. On the other hand, investment in high quality equipment may not be justified when a lower quality will fulfill production requirements even at the risk of lower reliability. This is a good example of how each alternative considered during the early life cycle phases of the factory must be analyzed to determine the best balance between performance and cost.

Equipment Stress Another factor that can have a significant impact on the long-term reliability of a factory is the operating stress placed on the equipment. Each item of equipment selected or designed for the factory should be reviewed to determine production ratings. These ratings are normally stated in terms of operating efficiency levels, peak load capacity, or maximum capacity. Whenever the factory requirements exceed individual equipment ratings, the induced stresses can be expected to cause a rise in failure occurrences and a corresponding decrease in productivity. Therefore, it is important to consider the long-term effect of equipment stress on reliability when planning the initial factory or future equipment replacement or upgrades.

Failure Trend Analysis

As stated previously, reliability engineering is a statistical projection of the future performance of the factory. Since predicting the future can never be done with certainty, the best aid to eliminating some of the uncertainty is to have very accurate historical data as a starting point. While these data may not be readily available when the factory is being built, a tremendous amount of data will be generated as the factory is in operation. These data can be very important in identifying areas where poor factory reliability is hurting performance, and can prove extremely useful when planning for future upgrades or modification of the factory. Failure trend data can pinpoint equipment that is hurting factory performance due to excessive downtime. This is a task that reliability engineers should continually perform throughout the life of the factory.

MAINTAINABILITY ENGINEERING

Maintainability engineering also participates in the design process; its efforts focus on making equipment as easy and inexpensive to fix as possible when it fails. Maintainability engineering's input to the design process results in an equipment design that: (1) makes faults easy to identify, (2) requires minimum manpower and other logistic support resources to perform maintenance, and (3) has the lowest life cycle cost possible.

The initial task of maintainability engineering is to develop predictions of how long it will take to repair equipment when it fails. Using these predictions, engineers can analyze the design to identify possible changes that would reduce the time required to perform maintenance. As the design matures, the maintainability aspects of the equipment can be determined through actual testing and demonstration of maintenance actions. The combination of equipment reliability—how often it will fail—and equipment maintainability—how long it takes to repair a failure—holds a direct correlation to the amount of time the factory will be capable of production. Fewer failures require less time for maintenance, and so yield more time for the equipment to operate.

Inherent Maintainability

The terms *maintainability* and *maintenance* are many times confused. *Maintainability* is the study of a design to make it easier to maintain. *Maintenance* is the actual performance of tasks to maintain the equipment. Strictly speaking, the measure of maintainability is a statistical prediction of the probability that a failed item can be repaired in a specified amount of time using a specified set of resources. The design characteristics of an item of equipment and its reliability drive its inherent maintainability. The basic measure of the maintainability of an item is the *mean time to repair* (MTTR), which is the predicted average time required to perform maintenance over a specified operating period.

When planning and designing a factory, one must consider the amount of time that equipment will not be available for production. A design goal should be established to state the maximum allowable time that will be allocated to perform maintenance when equipment fails. A typical goal would be that all failure should be capable of being repaired within thirty minutes of occurrence. This gives designers and maintainability engineers a parameter for planning for maintenance.

Maintainability Prediction

Maintainability prediction determines, using mathematical calculations, if an equipment design will meet the established maintainability goals. The prediction process also identifies designs that will not meet the goals. During the concept phase, there is not enough information available to perform detailed prediction calculations. Therefore, predictions are based on the performance of previous equipment, using design changes to modify the result to closely relate to the new design.

In order to perform detailed calculations, maintainability engineers need information such as the maintenance concept, functional block diagrams, identification of replaceable units, and reliability estimates. Using this information, maintainability engineers can develop predictions for the equipment. As the design matures, the quantity and quality of information increases, which allows further refinement of early predictions. This prediction process is updated throughout the design process to continually assess the maintainability status of the equipment and to provide information for the decision-making process. The results of this task feed into other analyses and the activities of other logistics disciplines.

Maintainability Analysis

The maintainability analysis is one of the key tasks of the maintainability program. The purposes of this task are to identify equipment maintainability design features that will enable the equipment to meet maintainability goals, evaluate design alternatives, provide detailed input to the maintenance planning process, and continually evaluate the design to ensure that goals are met. This task has a significant overlap with analyses being conducted simultaneously by other disciplines, so close coordination is required to avoid duplication of effort. To accomplish their analysis, maintainability engineers require detailed information on the equipment design and other information such as the maintenance concept and plan, anticipated test and fault isolation capabilities, maintenance skills, operational information, and reliability predictions.

The maintainability analysis process develops detailed design criteria that are necessary to meet established goals. These criteria include requirements for accessibility, tool usage, test points, standardization of tools and procedures, connectors and fasteners, and modularization. These criteria serve as guidelines for engineers as the equipment is designed. As the design evolves, engineers identify and evaluate alternatives and select the approach that provides the best maintenance capabilities. These alternatives must be evaluated as early as possible so as to allow implementation without unnecessary redesign that would occur later in the program phases.

TESTABILITY ENGINEERING

Adequacy and efficiency in equipment testability are vital to the maintainability of equipment. The easier it is to find a failure, the quicker it can be fixed. The clock starts for downtime when the failure occurs and does not stop until the equipment is repaired. Excessive time requirements for testing increase overall equipment downtime and degrade equipment maintainability.

Inherent Testability

The design characteristics of an item of factory equipment determine if testing can be accomplished in a manner that is timely and cost effective. Basically, this means that equipment designers must continually address testing of the equipment as it is being designed. If the features that are applicable to a specific design are incorporated by design engineers, the equipment will be testable. Several basic design considerations can significantly improve the inherent testability of equipment:

- Functional partitioning
- Isolation of complex circuitry
- Standardized parts
- Built-in test application
- Fault detection
- Observability for fault isolation
- Controllability for testing

Testability Analysis

Testability engineers work closely with design engineers to improve the inherent testability of a design. A testability analysis is oriented toward making the equipment design compatible with appropriate testing methods.

Testing methods can be divided into three categories: built-in testing, testing using additional automatic test equipment, and manual testing.

Built-in testing is the capability of an item to test itself. Additional circuitry is required to include built-in testing in equipment, but since it provides a significant improvement in testability, it can accurately detect and isolate equipment failures. Use of automatic test equipment is necessary when failures cannot be identified by built-in testing or when built-in testing is not capable of providing the required stimulus for running a test. Manual testing is the least desirable method of testing because of the labor that it requires. In some cases, manual testing remains the best alternative, as when the fault is easy to see or is obvious in some other way.

SAFETY ENGINEERING

No matter how good the design, if a piece of equipment cannot be operated and maintained safely, it is unacceptable. Safety engineering is charged with the responsibility of developing and implementing a safety program that continually evaluates the evolving factory design to identify potential safety hazards. As hazards are identified, they are analyzed to determine how they might be reduced or eliminated through design or procedure changes. Safety objectives influence the design or selection of equipment by using a systematic analysis and evaluation that results in a factory that is as safe as possible to operate and maintain. FIGURE 7-4 lists the general objectives of safety engineering. Safety engineers achieve these objectives by implementing the design criteria listed in FIG. 7-5.

Safety Hazards

A hazard is a situation that, if not corrected, might result in death, injury, or occupational illness to personnel, or damage to or loss of equipment. Safety engineers analyze and evaluate the proposed factory design to identify hazards. These hazards are then classified in terms of severity and probability of occurrence. TABLE 7-1 shows the four categories of hazards, and TABLE 7-2 provides an example of how the probability of occurrence can be assigned. The combination of severity and probability can be used to develop a hazard assessment matrix, as shown in TABLE 7-3. The matrix can help prioritize the effort of safety engineering by identifying the hazards that threaten safe factory operation.

Design Hazard Analysis

Safety engineers analyze the factory design for hazards throughout the life cycle. The first analysis identifies potential hazards. This potential hazard list then serves as a basis for in-depth analysis to

---

1. Stress safety consistent with performance and use requirements.
2. Identify and evaluate hazards associated with the design; eliminate or reduce them to an acceptable level.
3. Consider historical safety data gathered from other systems.
4. Minimize risk through use of new design, materials, and production and test equipment.
5. Minimize retrofit by addressing safety concerns in the early phases of acquisition.
6. Accomplish recommended design in a manner that does not increase risk of hazards.

Fig. 7-4. Safety engineering objectives.

---

1. Eliminate hazards through design.
2. Isolate hazardous substances, components, and operations.
3. Locate equipment in a manner that reduces hazards to personnel during operation and maintenance.
4. Minimize risks caused by environmental conditions.
5. Design to eliminate or minimize risk created by human error.
6. Consider alternate approaches to eliminate hazards.
7. Provide adequate protection from power sources.
8. Provide warnings and cautions when risks cannot be eliminated.

Fig. 7-5. Safety engineering design criteria.

Table 7-1. Hazard Categories.

Category	Description	Mishap Definition
I	Catastrophic	Death or system loss
II	Critical	Severe injury, major occupational illness, or major system damage
III	Marginal	Minor injury, minor occupational illness, or minor system damage
IV	Negligible	Less than minor injury, occupational illness, or system damage

Table 7-2. Hazard Occurrence Probability.

Level	Description	Predictability
A	Frequent	Likely to occur frequently
B	Probable	Will occur several times in life of an item
C	Occasional	Likely to occur sometime in life of an item
D	Remote	Unlikely but possible to occur in life of an item
E	Improbable	So unlikely, it can be assumed that occurrence may not be experienced

Table 7-3. Hazard Assessment Matrix.

| | HAZARD CATEGORIES | | | |
| | I | II | III | IV |
Frequency of Occurrence	Catastrophic	Critical	Marginal	Negligible
A. Frequent	1	3	7	13
B. Probable	2	5	9	16
C. Occasional	4	6	11	18
D. Remote	8	10	14	19
E. Improbable	12	15	17	20

Hazard Risk Index	Criteria
1-5	Unacceptable
6-9	Undesirable
10-17	Acceptable with review
18-20	Acceptable without review

either eliminate the hazards or develop ways of reducing risks. Hazard analyses can be categorized as: (1) subsystem hazards that can be identified by individual items of equipment, (2) system hazards that are created when equipment is integrated into the factory, (3) operation and support hazards that occur when the factory is either in operation or being maintained, or (4) materials hazards caused by materials in the factory or used in production. Safety engineers analyze potential hazards to determine the overall level of hazard in a proposed factory design. This analysis is used in trade-off studies that evaluate alternative design and deploy-

ment approaches during early acquisition cycle phases.

Design efforts that integrate major subsystems may require hazard analyses of each segment of the design to determine the potential subsystem hazards. A subsystem hazard analysis is applicable where several pieces of equipment integrate to complete the system design.

The system hazard analysis evaluates the total system operation and failure modes to determine the effect of these activities on the overall system. Special emphasis is placed on the effect of integrating subsystems and the results of failures in one subsystem that could cause a hazard to other subsystems or degrade the performance of the total system.

Safety engineers identify and evaluate operating and support hazards associated with the factory environment, personnel, procedures, and equipment. They evaluate operation, testing, installation, maintenance, storage, and training. Their analysis identifies needed design changes to eliminate potential hazards. The analysis of operation and support hazards is intimately related to the human engineering effort described later in this chapter. The occupational health hazard assessment identifies design characteristics that pose health hazards to operator and maintenance personnel.

Finally, safety engineers also identify the presence of hazardous materials and physical environments, such as noise, vibration, and extreme atmospheric conditions. This analysis also relates to the human engineering effort and provides input to design changes to correct or reduce inherent risks to personnel.

HUMAN ENGINEERING

All items of equipment, with few exceptions, require human interaction for operation, maintenance, or both. The goal of human engineering is to optimize this man-to-machine interface. The design of a factory must consider the limitations caused by having to use humans as part of the system. The human engineering process consists of analysis of human function requirements, participation in the design process to ensure that human factors are adequately addressed, and test and evaluation of the final factory equipment design to validate the operability.

Human Engineering Analysis

The first step in a human engineering program is to identify and analyze the functions and operations that factory equipment must perform. Particular interest is paid to the equipment operation and maintenance requirements and to the environment where the equipment will be used. The functions are assimilated in a logical flow and processing sequence to identify exactly how factory equipment must perform. Once the functional requirements have been identified, the man-to-machine interfaces that must be accomplished to meet the functional requirements are quantified. (The man-to-machine interfaces are the human tasks necessary to operate and maintain the equipment.)

Once the human tasks have been identified, they are analyzed to determine which ones are essential in terms of human engineering. Essential tasks are those that if not accomplished as needed to meet a functional requirement, would result in equipment failure, create a safety hazard, or significantly reduce factory productivity. Human engineering analyzes essential tasks to identify key human factors data about each task. TABLE 7-4 lists typical human factors data that are pertinent to the analysis of essential tasks. The results of the human engineering analysis are added to the design process to ensure that man-to-machine interfaces are optimized.

Design and Development

Human engineering provides input during the design phase based on the results of human engineering analyses. The design is continually evaluated and changes are recommended to enhance the man-to-machine interface. Through the use of mock-ups, models, and dynamic simulation, human engineering develops solutions to interface problems and evaluates design alternatives to achieve the best possible human interface situations. Human engineering adds quantitative requirements to the design process and the detailed design of work environments. Human engineering areas of concern in the design of work environments include:

- Physical man-to-machine interface (physical, aural, visual)

- Physical man-to-man interface (physical, aural, visual)
- Physical comfort of operator and maintenance personnel
- Equipment handling requirements (weight, cube)
- Temperature, humidity, environment to be encountered
- Inclement conditions anticipated
- Equipment environment (vibration, noise)
- Usable space available
- Effects of special clothing (gloves, coat, glasses)
- Safety and hazard protection

Human Engineering Design Criteria

Integration of the human aspect into the overall factory is necessary to achieve a productive and safe working environment. The goal of this integration is to optimize the effectiveness, efficiency, safety, and reliability of the operation and maintenance of the factory. Human engineering design criteria provide quantitative aids to analyzing and evaluating the human engineering aspects of the factory design.

Controls and Displays Most operational man-to-machine interfaces are done through controls and displays. Controls are devices that the operator uses to regulate or give commands to the equipment. Displays give the operator information for decision making and monitoring of the results of manipulation of controls. Controls should be grouped and arranged to reduce excessive operator movements. Design methods for coding and labeling and identifying controls should prevent accidental activation.

Displays can be either visual or audio depending on the type of information being provided to the operator. Visual displays range from simple indicator and warning lights to cathode-ray tube (CRT) displays. They also include mechanical scales, counters, meters, printers, and plotters. The type of visual display used is commensurate with the content and format of the information available and the precision of display required. The use of audio displays is limited to warnings and voice communications. Warnings are short, go/no go messages that require immediate or time critical responses. They are used to inform the operator of critical situations or indicators of impending danger to personnel, equipment, or both.

The integration and compatibility of controls and displays is critical. Co-location of controls with

Item	Description
Environment	Location and condition of work environment
Space	Amount of space required to perform tasks Amount of space available Body movements required to perform task
Information	Amount of information available to operator Amount of information required to perform task
Time	Amount of time allocated for task completion Frequency of task performance Maximum allowable time for task completion
Resources	Number of persons required to perform task Tools and other equipment required Instructions, training, and manuals required
Other	Safety hazards Interaction required between personnel Personnel performance limitations Equipment performance limitations

Table 7-4. Human Engineering Factors.

```
            W A L D E N B O O K S


SALE          0525   103  6828  11/01/90
              REL    2.3   29  19:31:31


01 0830692967                      69.95
            SUBTOTAL               69.95
CONNECTICUT 8.0% TAX                5.60
            TOTAL                  75.55
            CASH                   80.00
            CHANGE                  4.45-
            PV# 0036828


      AMERICA FINDS IT AT WALDENBOOKS
```

corresponding displays should be a basic design goal. The controls and displays selected should be complementary. The information provided by the display should be sufficient to allow the operator to effectively use the control, and the control should provide sufficient range to receive maximum benefit from operation.

Environment   The environment where equipment will be operated and maintained must be considered in the design process. The basic physical comfort of personnel directly relates to the productivity of the factory. Environmental considerations can be grouped into two categories: (1) factors that design can control—interior lighting, heating, ventilation, air conditioning, humidity, dust—and (2) inherent design factors—hazardous and nonhazardous noise and vibration. Human engineering analyzes the design in both environmental categories to identify deficiencies and propose solutions in both areas. Human engineering must also consider alternatives for coping with and minimizing the environmental problems that cannot be directly controlled by the design.

Anthropometry   *Anthropometry* is the study of measurements of the human body. Human engineering uses comparative human body measurements to determine the minimum acceptable sizing and dimensioning for man-to-machine interfaces. Anthropometry obtains data by actually measuring representative population samples. There are many sources available for this type of information.

The data are normally organized into limits of 5 to 95 percent of personnel measured, and theoretically provide design limits to accommodate 90 percent of the potential equipment users. For example, one data source shows that only 5 percent of the persons (male and female) measured were less than 152.4 centimeters (60.0 inches) tall, and that 95 percent were 185.6 centimeters (73.1 inches) tall, or less. Therefore, for human engineering purposes, factory designs should be able to accommodate personnel that are between the height of 152.4 and 185.6 centimeters. FIGURE 7-6 illustrates typical anthropometrical data for a standing person.

Work Space   The physical dimensions of work space must be adequate for personnel to operate and maintain factory equipment. Human engineering uses the anthropometric data discussed above to evaluate the proposed design of the factory to ensure that the provisions for work space do not impose unacceptable restrictions or hazards to personnel. Specific areas analyzed include: space required for standing and seated operations; standard and special console designs; crew compartments; stairs, ladders, and ramps; entrance and exit through doors and hatches; and surface colors.

The key to optimizing work space is to design the space around the person, rather than designing the space and then putting the person in it. By designing around the person, costly redesign efforts due to insufficient work space can normally be avoided. FIGURE 7-7 on pp. 122 – 123 shows how work space dimension requirements are determined.

Maintainability   Human engineering can have a tremendous impact on the maintainability of an item of equipment. Specific areas of maintainability interest are: accessibility of items to be removed and replaced; accessibility of lubrication points and test points; standardization of fasteners, connectors, and other hardware; design of covers and cases; design for efficient handling; and ease of using tools and test equipment. Significant improvements in the overall equipment repair time (MTTR) can be achieved through the application of human engineering criteria during equipment design.

Labeling   An area often overlooked is labeling of equipment. Labels are used to identify levels of equipment, state standard procedures, and identify hazards. Labels must be visible and legible, and they must also be durable. The contents, quality, and location of labels that provide directions for operation or maintenance increase the effectiveness of persons using the equipment.

MAINTENANCE PLANNING

Eventually all the equipment in a factory, regardless of how reliable it is, will require maintenance. *Maintenance* is any action taken to keep

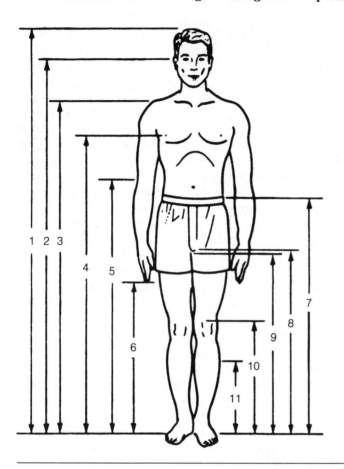

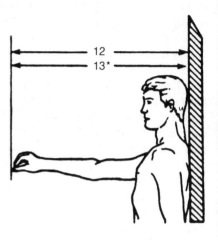

*Same as 12; however, right shoulder is extended as far forward as possible while keeping the back of the left shoulder firmly against the back wall.

| | Percentile Values in Centimeters | | | |
| | Percentile | | 95th Percentile | |
	Men	Women	Men	Women
Weight (Kg)	55.5	46.4	91.6	74.5
Standing Body Dimensions				
1. Stature	162.8	152.4	185.6	174.1
2. Eye height (standing)	151.1	140.9	173.3	162.2
3. Shoulder (acromiale) height	133.6	123.0	154.2	143.7
4. Chest (nipple) height*	117.9	109.3	136.5	127.8
5. Elbow (radiale) height	101.0	94.9	117.8	110.7
6. Fingertip (dactylion) height				
7. Waist height	96.6	93.1	115.2	110.3
8. Crotch height	76.3	68.1	91.8	83.9
9. Gluteal furrow height	73.3	66.4	87.7	81.0
10. Kneecap height	47.5	43.8	58.6	52.5
11. Calf height	31.1	29.0	40.6	36.6
12. Functional reach	72.6	64.0	90.9	80.4
13. Functional reach, extended	84.2	73.5	101.2	92.7

*Bustpoint height for women.

Fig. 7-6. Anthropometrical data— standing person.

equipment in a serviceable condition or to fix it when it fails. Maintenance planning is the process that develops the anticipated maintenance requirements for the factory and proposes solutions as to who will do required maintenance tasks and where they will be done.

This section will deal with the general concepts of maintenance planning, types of maintenance actions, and typical organizations that perform maintenance. The majority of the activities that will be discussed deal with a generic factory and make the broad assumption that all factories are maintained in the same manner; however, in reality, the maintenance for each factory is unique due to different types of equipment, facilities, environments, and products. The maintenance plan for a factory must be tailored to fit needs and unique requirements to optimize profitability and productivity.

Maintenance Concept

The way maintenance is performed on equipment does not just happen. It is the result of extensive planning and preparation that starts during the pre-concept phase and continues through full scale development. The maintenance planning process begins with the *maintenance concept*. The maintenance concept is a statement of general guidelines to be used in developing the maintenance plan for an item of equipment. The guidelines established by the maintenance concept are the foundation for maintenance planning. Areas addressed by the maintenance concept include: a strategy for allocation of maintenance tasks to the different sources of maintenance; the repair policy with regard to similar types of items contained in the factory; the criteria for scheduling maintenance tasks; and the anticipated availability of resources, in gross terms, to support maintenance.

Maintenance Sources

There are three basic sources of maintenance for a factory: (1) company maintenance personnel, (2) equipment manufacturer, or (3) service maintenance. Each of these sources has advantages and disadvantages that must be evaluated. Normally, factory maintenance planning includes some maintenance being performed by each of these sources.

Company Maintenance Personnel Maintenance of factory equipment by company employees is an alternative that provides a company with control over maintenance assets; however, it can be expensive in terms of salaries, training, support and test equipment, and maintaining a stock of spares and repair parts. Larger companies tend to choose this alternative since it provides the capability to direct maintenance activities and give priority to keeping the factory operational.

Equipment Manufacturer Maintenance Normally, manufacturers provide maintenance services as an extension of an equipment purchase. This type of maintenance support gives the company the most up-to-date capability for keeping an item of equipment operational. In addition, the company does not have to pay to maintain its own repair resources—mentioned above—to support maintenance. This type of maintenance has its drawbacks as well: it can be expensive in the long run, and the company does not have the capability to set the priorities of maintenance. If the equipment breaks, the company must rely on the manufacturer to get it back in working order.

Service Maintenance. An alternative to equipment manufacturer maintenance is maintenance performed by a service contractor. This is a third party organization that provides maintenance support on a contractual basis. The advantages with this type of maintenance support are the same as for equipment manufacturer maintenance; a plus is that service contractors may be less expensive than equipment manufacturers. On the other hand, such services may not be as versatile since the service contractor does not have access to the equipment manufacturer's resources to expedite spare parts or keep current on changing maintenance requirements.

PERSONNEL

As a factory is being developed and designed, management must identify the number and types of

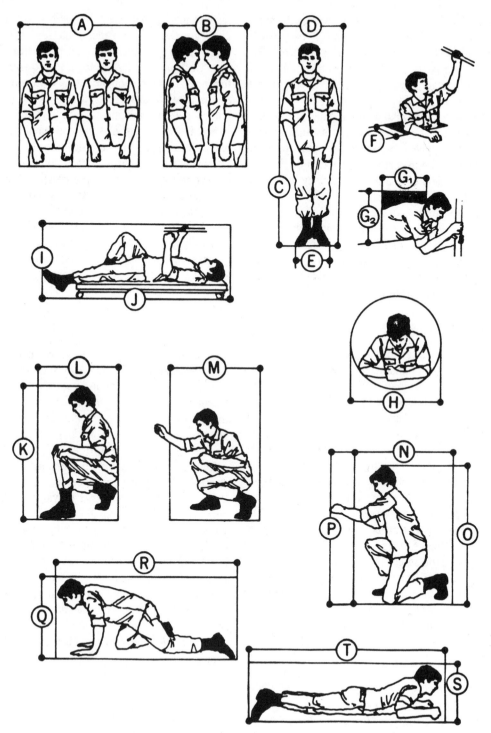

Fig. 7-7. Work space dimension requirements.

Work Space	Dimensions (mm)	
	Minimum	Preferred
A. Two men passing abreast	1.06m	1.37m
B. Two men passing facing	760	910
Catwalk dimensions		
C. Height	1.60m	1.86m
D. Shoulder width	560	610
E. Walking width	305	380
F. Vertical entry hatch		
Square	459	560
Round	560	610
G. Horizontal entry hatch		
1. Shoulder width	535	610
2. Height	380	510
H. Crawl through pipe		
Round or square	635	760
Supine work space		
I. Height	510	610
J. Length	1.86m	1.91m
Squatting work space		
K. Height	1.22m	–
L. Width	685	910
Optimum display area	685	1.09m
Optimum control area	485	865
Stooping work space		
M. Width	660	1.02m
Optimum display area	810	1.22m
Optimum control area	610	990
Kneeling work space		
N. Width	1.06m	1.22m
O. Height	1.42m	–
P. Optimum work point		685
Optimum display area	510	890
Optimum control area	510	890
Kneeling crawl space		
Q. Height	785	910
R. Length	1.50m	–
Prone work or crawl space		
S. Height	430	510
T. Length	2.86m	–

Fig. 7-7. Cont.

personnel needed to operate and maintain the factory. This planning must allow sufficient time for hiring and training prior to the plant's opening. Labor costs represent a significant expense for both plant start-up and continued operations. Therefore, management must carefully quantify personnel resource requirements as they plan for initial personnel costs, training costs, and long-term labor costs for the factory. Factory personnel can be placed into two categories: (1) personnel required to actually operate factory equipment, and (2) personnel required to maintain and support equipment operation.

Operating Personnel

The number of personnel required to operate factory equipment is usually fairly easy to determine. Each item of factory equipment has a definite number of operator personnel. By combining the number of operators required for each item of equipment, the minimum number of operators can be identified. This number must then be expanded to account for employee absences—such as medical and vacation—and attrition and training.

Support Personnel

The number of people required to support equipment maintenance is not as easily determined, but a working estimate can be developed by first determining how many hours the factory can expect to spend on maintenance. To develop an estimate of the actual time required for maintenance each year, personnel managers must combine the predicted mean time between failure and the mean time to repair an item, with the number of hours an item will be in operation on an annual basis. FIGURE 7-8 shows how to calculate support personnel requirements in hours. The predicted time for each item of factory equipment is then combined to show the total requirements for maintenance hours in a year.

For total maintenance personnel requirements, a factor can be applied to account for time required to support actual maintenance operations. This calculation produces an estimate of the manpower required to support the equipment in the factory.

$$\text{Annual support personnel requirement (hours)} = \frac{\text{AOH}}{\text{MTBF}} \times \text{MTTR}$$

Where:

AOH = Annual operating hours
MTBF = Mean time between failure
MTTR = Mean time to repair

Fig. 7-8. Support personnel requirements calculation.

This information can be extremely useful when developing the maintenance concept for factory equipment and choosing which alternative for maintenance support will be used.

TRAINING DEVELOPMENT

Operator and maintenance support personnel must be properly trained in order for the factory to be productive. Training must begin early enough in the development of the factory so that personnel are adequately trained when the factory is ready to begin production. The training program for the factory must consider the tasks that are required to operate and maintain factory equipment.

To identify training requirements, planners conduct an analysis that is an extension of operation and maintenance planning and the human engineering programs. The planners must document each operation or maintenance task in a procedural manner, and then use the information to develop the training curriculum for employee training courses. This analysis should be done in conjunction with other support related tasks to ensure that the final training program meets the requirements of a productive factory.

Basic operator training includes those functions that the equipment user is required to perform in order to operate and maintain the equipment. The word *user* is the key to this category. The training is comprehensive to the point that it provides the operator with everything that must be done to place the equipment into operation, perform scheduled and unscheduled operator maintenance, and identify equipment failures.

Basic maintenance training consists of training personnel who will staff the maintenance organizations responsible for performing maintenance on the new equipment. The training of maintenance personnel must reflect the maintenance concept and planning developed by the ILS disciplines. Each level of maintenance training becomes progressively more comprehensive since each level of maintenance is authorized to perform more detailed maintenance. Training for each level would also include instructions on how to operate test equipment and other support items required to perform maintenance. Equipment operation could also be included at each level if required for troubleshooting, fault verification, or repair checkout.

Once training requirements have been identified, training methods can be selected. These methods might include lectures, demonstrations, performance, on-the-job training, and self study.

SUPPLY SUPPORT

Spare parts are required to support both scheduled and unscheduled maintenance. Without spare parts, very little maintenance can be done, and without maintenance, you will soon have an inoperable factory. The objective of supply support is to have the parts available when and where required in the quantities necessary to support maintenance. For ease of understanding, the term *spare parts* will be used to refer to all parts required for maintenance whether the parts are indeed *spares* (repairable items), *repair parts* (items that are nonrepairable and are discarded when they fail), or *consumable parts* (items that are consumed when used such as gasket material or adhesives).

Spare Parts Identification

Determining the range or number of different items, and the depth or quantity of each item of spares to be procured and stocked in support of maintenance is a major factor in achieving an acceptable equipment availability. No magic formula identifies requirements for spares because no method of spare parts forecasting can accurately

predict the future. The only methods available use past experience to project the anticipated number of spares that will be required in the future.

If it is assumed that all factors that contribute to spares requirements, such as equipment usage, maintenance capabilities, and other resources, remain constant, then these spare parts forecasting methods have a degree of merit. The problem is that these factors do not remain constant. For example, there is always a fluctuation in equipment usage, environmental conditions, and equipment age. Therefore, no method is without error. The goal is to be as accurate as possible. The best way to determine the number of spares required is to use the most recent actual usage information as a basis for estimating future requirements.

Spare Parts Procurement

The range and depth of spares that are procured to support factory maintenance depends on several factors. The first and most important factor is the maintenance concept. As discussed previously, who performs maintenance influences how spare parts are procured. If the company maintenance staff is to perform all maintenance, they will require a significant quantity of spares. If the equipment manufacturer or a service contractor is to perform maintenance, then the company's own requirements for spares will be significantly less. In either case, spares requirements can be significant cost drivers, especially when the company first stocks up on spares. The cost of spares may steer the company in the selection of an alternative for performing maintenance.

SUPPORT AND TEST EQUIPMENT

An automated factory requires a wide range of support and test equipment to augment the installed factory equipment, either for actual production or for maintenance. The cost of these items must not be overlooked when planning the factory. The cost for initial procurement of support and test equipment can be a significant investment. Each item required must be identified and justified early in the factory development so that appropriate consideration can be given to additional resource requirements.

Operation Support Equipment

Equipment needed to support operation of the factory should be easy to identify. Planners analyze each operation function to identify which support equipment they will need to augment installed equipment. The types of items required can range from small hand tools to carts and dolleys. Some rather large and expensive items, such as portable test stations, can also be necessary. Each item identified in the analysis must be completely documented so that planners procure the proper number and type of each item. Planned replacement of these items due to loss, pilferage, or deterioration must also be addressed.

Maintenance Support and Test Equipment

The procurement of maintenance support and test equipment depends on the maintenance concept. If a company chooses to have staff employees perform all maintenance, then they must analyze each maintenance task to identify each required item. When a company chooses other alternatives for maintenance support, maintenance support and test equipment requirements should be significantly less. An automated factory normally contains many different types of state of the art equipment. Therefore, the investment for maintenance support and test equipment represents a cost that must be considered when choosing a maintenance concept for the factory or when choosing selected items of installed equipment.

SUPPORT DOCUMENTATION

An area that is often overlooked is the requirement for documentation to support the factory. This documentation consists of three basic categories: equipment documentation, operator procedures and manuals, and maintenance procedures and manuals. Each category of documentation sup-

ports the factory throughout the life cycle. Documentation is not cheap, so its preparation, control, and use must be planned and coordinated to ensure that the required documentation is available when needed.

Equipment Documentation

The company should obtain and control a complete engineering documentation package for each item of equipment installed in the factory. This documentation supports initial installation, development of upgrades or changes, and preparation of operator and maintenance procedures and manuals. It is also used as a primary input to planning for support resources, such as spare parts and support and test equipment, and facilities and environmental requirements.

The equipment documentation should consist of engineering assembly and installation drawings, parts lists, schematics and wiring diagrams, specifications, calibration requirements, and manufacturer data packages. A complete package should be retained for each item of equipment. As changes to equipment are implemented, the documentation package must be updated to show the current factory configuration.

Operator Procedures and Manuals

A complete set of operator procedures and manuals should be prepared for each item of equipment in the factory. This standardizes operations. The operator procedures and manuals are the basis for all training programs. Accurate and detailed documentation increases long-term factory productivity by providing operators with specific instructions on all required tasks. The ability for new operators to have ready access to instructions increases training capabilities and reduces the learning curve.

Maintenance Procedures and Manuals

The maintenance concept determines the type of maintenance procedures and manuals that will be required. The maintenance documentation describes all maintenance tasks, including: fault detection and isolation, repair, testing, calibration, preventative maintenance, spare parts, and support and test equipment. Standard maintenance procedures and manuals give a company the flexibility to train its own maintenance personnel to perform all maintenance. Detailed maintenance documentation can be expensive and requires a lengthy development process; however, if a company chooses to have staff employees perform maintenance, it is a mandatory requirement for adequate support.

LIFE CYCLE COST

The cost of ownership for an automated factory includes many elements. Some of the cost elements are obvious. Other elements are subtle but can have a significant effect on total cost of ownership. The purpose of *life cycle cost* is to develop a projection of the total cost of ownership, realized over the life of the automated factory. This projection is a very useful tool in evaluating alternatives for equipment selection, maintenance concept, and support parameters. Life cycle cost prediction early in the development of the factory can improve profitability.

Life Cycle Cost Elements

The four basic cost elements for the life cycle of an automated factory are development costs, factory set-up costs, operation and support costs, and costs due to factory changes or closure. Each cost element must be considered when planning the factory in order to minimize the total life cycle costs.

Development costs are all costs that occur during the pre-concept, concept development, concept validation, and design development phases.

The costs of factory set-up occur during the construction and investment phase. These include facility construction, factory equipment, support equipment, personnel recruitment and training, and documentation.

Operation and support costs occur during the operation phase but do not include the cost of materials consumed by the manufacturing process. They

do include costs for labor, equipment maintenance, factory maintenance, training, replacement support equipment, and utilities.

The costs of upgrading or closing the factory result from plant changes or closure during the planned improvement or disposal phase. These costs cover facility changes, equipment changes, new training, and new documentation.

Life Cycle Cost Modeling

Computerized models containing all parameters of each cost element help predict total life cycle costs. Keep in mind that the total life cycle cost is simply the sum of its parts: factory development costs, plus investment costs, plus operation costs, plus costs of changes or closures equals total life cycle costs. FIGURE 7-9 expresses this simple fact in a life cycle cost model that addresses a typical automated factory.

$$C_T = C_D + C_I + C_O + C_C$$

Where:

C_T = Total life cycle cost
C_D = Cost of factory development
C_I = Cost of investment
C_O = Cost of operation
C_C = Cost of changes or closure

Fig. 7-9. Typical life cycle cost model.

Because of the differences between each application for life cycle costing, models are tailored to fit specific requirements, based on information available and the aspects being considered. Remember that the life cycle cost model should include each cost element that can impact total ownership costs. Some costs elements, such as the cost of land or overhead costs, have little impact on choosing equipment or determining the support costs of a factory, but these elements must be accounted for as well.

Life Cycle Cost Prediction Example

I have included a basic life cycle cost prediction model to show how cost elements impact total ownership costs. TABLE 7-5 lists the input parameters and assumptions used in the prediction model. The life cycle cost prediction using these inputs appears in TABLE 7-6. Note that bottom line costs are presented in both current and future dollars.

Cost Sensitivity Analysis Example

It is impossible to accurately predict the future, so a life cycle cost prediction should not be used as the final word in determining the ultimate profitability of a company. However, a prediction does provide a useful tool in evaluating alternatives that impact long term costs. A cost sensitivity analysis of the life cycle cost prediction gives management

Table 7-5. Model Input Parameters and Assumptions.

Model Input Parameter/Assumption	Factor or Cost
Cost of concept studies	$ 200,000
Cost of factory design	$ 450,000
Cost of factory construction	$ 1,500,000
Cost of factory equipment	$ 4,000,000
Cost of operation and support equipment	$ 200,000
Cost of training	$ 2,000/per employee
Cost of support documentation	$ 50,000
Average cost of direct labor	$15/hour
Cost of equipment maintenance	5% of initial cost/year
Cost of factory maintenance	2% of initial cost/year
Number of employees to be trained each year due to terminations/new hires	10% per year
Cost of replacement operation and support equipment	15% of initial cost/year
Annual cost of utilities	$ 240,000
Planned cost of facility upgrades in 7th year	10% of initial Facility cost
Planned cost of equipment upgrades in 7th year	$ 1,500,000
Cost of additional training required due to upgrades	25% of initial training costs
Cost of upgrading support documentation	$ 25,000
Number of operation and support employees	150
Number of factory operating hours per year	2,016
Annual cost inflation rate	6%

Table 7-6. Life Cycle Cost Prediction ($ × 1000).

Cost Element	Year 1	Year 2	Year 3	Year 4	Year 5	Year 6	Year 7	Year 8	Year 9	Year 10	Year 11	Year 12	TOTAL
Development Costs													
Concept Studies	200.0												200.0
Factory Design	450.0												450.0
Sub-total	650.0												650.0
Construction & Investment													
Facility		1500.0											1500.0
Factory Equipment		4000.0											4000.0
Support Equipment		200.0											200.0
Training		300.0											300.0
Documentation		50.0											50.0
Sub-total		6050.0											6050.0
Operation													
Labor			4536.0	4536.0	4536.0	4536.0	4536.0	4536.0	4536.0	4536.0	4536.0	4536.0	45360.0
Equipment Maintenance			200.0	200.0	200.0	200.0	200.0	200.0	200.0	200.0	200.0	200.0	2000.0
Facility Maintenance			30.0	30.0	30.0	30.0	30.0	30.0	30.0	30.0	30.0	30.0	300.0
Training			30.0	30.0	30.0	30.0	30.0	30.0	30.0	30.0	30.0	30.0	300.0
Support Equipment			30.0	30.0	30.0	30.0	30.0	30.0	30.0	30.0	30.0	30.0	300.0
Utilities			240.0	240.0	240.0	240.0	240.0	240.0	240.0	240.0	240.0	240.0	2400.0
Sub-total			5066.0	5066.0	5066.0	5066.0	5066.0	5066.0	5066.0	5066.0	5066.0	5066.0	50660.0
Planned Factory Upgrades													
Facility							150.0						150.0
Equipment							1500.0						1500.0
Training							75.0						75.0
Documentation							25.0						25.0
Sub-total							1750.0						1750.0
TOTALS (CURRENT $)	650.0	6050.0	5066.0	5066.0	5066.0	5066.0	6816.0	5066.0	5066.0	5066.0	5066.0	5066.0	59110.0
TOTALS (FUTURE $)	650.0	6413.0	5692.2	6033.7	6395.7	6779.5	9668.6	7617.4	8074.4	8558.9	9072.4	9616.8	84572.6

the opportunity to do "what if" trade-off comparisons of different alternatives to see which provides the best long-term profitability for the company.

As an example, consider the data in TABLE 7-7. Management has to choose between two different alternatives, Alternative 1 described in TABLES 7-5 and 7-6, and Alternative 2, which differs from Alternative 1 as shown in TABLE 7-7.

Initially, it appears that Alternative 2 requires a sizable increase in up-front expense and yearly utilities expense while providing only a limited decrease in the number of employees, factory equipment maintenance, and planned upgrades. However, TABLE 7-8, a revised life cycle cost predic-

tion using the new input parameters for Alternative 2, shows significant long-term savings with Alternative 2. TABLE 7-9 is a cost sensitivity analysis using life cycle cost prediction. This table indicates that Alternative 2 would require an additional $2,240,000 expense up front, but should reduce total factory costs for the first ten years of operation by over $10 million—more than $1 million dollars for each year of production.

Life cycle costing is not an exact process; it is dependent on the accuracy and validity of input parameters and assumptions. However, it does provide a helpful tool for conducting trade-off analyses of many different alternatives that are considered during the design and development of any factory.

Table 7-7. Comparison of Alternatives.

Cost Element	Alternative 1	Alternative 2
Factory design	$450,000	$500,000
Facility construction	$1,500,000	$1,750,000
Factory equipment	$4,000,000	$6,000,000
Factory equipment maintenance	5% per year	4% per year
Utilities cost	$240,000/year	$300,000/year
Planned equipment upgrades	$1,500,000	$1,000,000
Number of O&S employees	150	120

Table 7-9. Life Cycle Cost Sensitivity Comparison.

Cost by Phase		Alternative 1	Alternative 2	Change
Development	(current $)	$650,000	$700,000	+ 8%
Construction and investment	(current $)	$6,050,000	$8,240,000	+ 36%
Operation	(current $)	$50,660,000	$42,578,000	− 16%
Planned upgrade	(current $)	$1,750,000	$1,260,000	− 28%
Total costs	(current $)	$59,110,000	$52,778,000	− 11%
	(future $)	$84,572,600	$74,279,500	− 12%

Analysis: Additional Up-front Costs for Alternative 2: $2,240,000
Predicted Life Cycle Cost Savings (current $): $8,332,000
Predicted Life Cycle Cost Savings (future $): $10,293,100

Table 7-8. Life Cycle Cost Prediction for Alternative Z.

Cost Element	Year 1	Year 2	Year 3	Year 4	Year 5	Year 6	Year 7	Year 8	Year 9	Year 10	Year 11	Year 12	TOTAL
Development Costs													
Concept Studies	200.0												200.0
Factory Design	500.0												500.0
Sub-total	700.0												700.0
Construction & Investment													
Facility		1750.0											1750.0
Factory Equipment		6000.0											6000.0
Support Equipment		200.0											200.0
Training		240.0											240.0
Documentation		50.0											50.0
Sub-total		8240.0											8240.0
Operation													
Labor			3628.8	3628.8	3628.8	3628.8	3628.8	3628.8	3628.8	3628.8	3628.8	3628.8	36288.0
Equipment Maintenance			240.0	240.0	240.0	240.0	240.0	240.0	240.0	240.0	240.0	240.0	2400.0
Facility Maintenance			35.0	35.0	35.0	35.0	35.0	35.0	35.0	35.0	35.0	35.0	350.0
Training			24.0	24.0	24.0	24.0	24.0	24.0	24.0	24.0	24.0	24.0	240.0
Support Equipment			30.0	30.0	30.0	30.0	30.0	30.0	30.0	30.0	30.0	30.0	300.0
Utilities			300.0	300.0	300.0	300.0	300.0	300.0	300.0	300.0	300.0	300.0	3000.0
Sub-total			4257.8	4257.8	4257.8	4257.8	4257.8	4257.8	4257.8	4257.8	4257.8	4257.8	42578.0
Planned Factory Upgrades													
Facility							175.0						175.0
Equipment							1000.0						1000.0
Training							60.0						60.0
Documentation							25.0						25.0
Sub-total							1260.0						1260.0
TOTALS (CURRENT $)	700.0	8240.0	4257.8	4257.8	4257.8	4257.8	5517.8	4257.8	4257.8	4257.8	4257.8	4257.8	52778.0
TOTALS (FUTURE $)	700.0	8734.4	4784.1	5071.1	5375.4	5697.9	7827.1	6402.2	6786.3	7193.5	7625.1	8082.6	74279.5

8

Automated Technologies
The Strategic Issues

Jack Byrd, Jr.*

STRATEGIC PLANNING IS BASICALLY THE DEVELOP-
ment of an action plan for competitive success.
Until recently, strategic plans were largely financial
and marketing plans. If manufacturing was considered at all, it was from a macro-level perspective;
for example, "Where should we place new capacity? Where do we consolidate operations?"

Strategic planning became the buzz-word of the
early eighties as consulting companies thrived from
the strategy business. Every business had to have a
strategic plan. From this concern for strategy came
an increased sensitivity for market share, acquisi-
tions, and other macro-level corporate competitive
options. Generally lost in the strategic planning
framework was a real concern for manufacturing.

As the economic realities of the eighties
unfolded, American businesses suddenly realized
that they were losing the competitive race to other
businesses in other countries. The irony was that
American businesses were following their strategic
plans: the plans themselves were deficient. American businesses were losing out in manufacturing.
The very same issues that Americans left out of the
strategic plans were the competitive tools of businesses in other countries. Quality control, manu-

facturing flexibility, and employee involvement were
some of the deciding forces in competitive success.

With the increased concern for manufacturing
came a realization that manufacturing "nuts-and-
bolts" issues deserved a place in the corporate
strategic plans. While manufacturing was creeping
back into the limelight of the corporate board-
rooms, automation technologies suddenly captured
the imagination of executives. Automation became
the savior just as marketing strategies and acquisition plans had been before automation. In jumping
from one fad to another, managers lost track of the
central competitive message: manufacturing is an
integral part of competitive success. How the product is made is just as critical to competitive survival
as is the marketing plan. Automation may be appropriate in some cases but not in others. The development of a successful strategic plan must examine
the role of automation as a strategic force in the
same way as other strategic options are examined.

This chapter will examine how automation can
be incorporated into the strategic plan. Automation
is not for every business, and it is critical that businesses understand the strategic implications of
automation. This chapter does not provide answers

*Dr. Jack Byrd, Jr. is a Professor of Industrial Engineering at West Virginia University (WVU). He also is the Executive Director of
the Center for Entrepreneurial Studies and Development, Inc., a nonprofit corporation affiliated with WVU established to support
innovation and change in West Virginia's economy. Dr. Byrd was recognized in 1985 as the Outstanding Professor of West Virginia.
He also was selected in 1986 as one of fifty faculty in the United States to be recognized by the American Association for Higher
Education and the Carnegie Commission in its Faculty Salute award program. Dr. Byrd is the author of three textbooks and numerous scholarly papers. He has served as an advisor to over 100 organizations in areas such as production operations, strategic planning, and innovation management.

as to the impact of automation on strategic planning. Rather, the chapter outlines the strategic questions that should be asked in considering automation systems.

THE STRATEGIC PLANNING PROCESS

There are many different approaches to strategic planning, but all of them have similarities. Essentially the strategic plan examines four questions:

- What are our missions?
- What is the environment in which we compete?
- How can we develop a competitive strategy?
- How do we assure ourselves that the strategic plan is properly executed?

Define Missions

The business missions reflect the essence of what the business is all about. The missions should respond to questions such as:

- What products do we provide to the public?
- Who are our customers?
- What segment of the industry do we serve (commodity, specialty)?
- Do we want to compete on price? Quality? Service?
- Do we want to be a product development leader or follower?
- Are we a regional, national, or international competitor?
- What are our corporate values?

Study Environment

The environment of the business reflects both the issues in the industry in which the business competes and the societal issues that are likely to affect the business. The environmental analysis should examine such questions as:

- Who are our competitors? What are their strengths and weaknesses?

- What forces are likely to affect our industry in the next five years? Customer changes? Product changes? Technology changes?
- What societal requirements are likely to impact our industry? Environmental impact, safety, other regulations?
- How are our competitors likely to change? New ownership? New directions? New competitive thrusts?
- Who are our likely competitors in the future?
- What societal changes are likely to occur in the near future? Population changes? Work force changes?

Establish Competitive Strategy

The development of a competitive strategy reflects the management's sense of how the business can develop distinctive competitiveness. The competitive strategy is generally developed from asking such questions as:

- Why do customers buy our product over other products? What customer preference factors do we want to establish?
- How do we compare with our competition on price, quality, and service? What do we want this comparison to be?
- How will the customer learn about out product?
- How will we finance our plans?
- Do we have the right people to be competitive?
- How are we going to respond to anticipated future events?
- What changes need to be made in manufacturing in order to be competitive?
- What is the competition likely to do in the next five years?

Implement Strategic Plan

The strategic plan is only a document unless it is acted upon by management on all levels. In order for the strategic plan to be implemented properly, management should answer questions such as:

- How can we communicate the strategic plan to others without endangering our competitive position?

- How can everyone in management reflect the strategic plan in his decision making?
- How can specific actions outlined in the strategic plan be tracked to ensure they are implemented?
- How can the success of the strategic plan be evaluated?
- How often should the strategic plan be reviewed?

There are no formulae or formal steps that guide a strategic plan. The process for developing a strategic plan involves considerable interaction and tentative development from top management. In order to appreciate the strategic planning process, a case study is presented next.

VALVETECH, INC: A Strategic Planning Case Study

Valvetech, Inc. was formed in 1945 by three World War II veterans who obtained experience in hydraulics in the U.S. Navy. They had an idea for new valve technology and got into the business of providing valves to the chemical and mining industries of the eastern United States.

The business succeeded better than any of the founders' expectations, and by 1962 Valvetech was manufacturing $135 million in valves per year. Valvetech had over 50 percent of the market for the big four chemical companies and virtually all of the original equipment market for the mining industry.

The oil boycott of the 1970s impacted Valvetech in different ways. Chemical markets, which depended on cheap sources of petroleum supplies, were faced with serious competitive problems. Companies that had formerly replaced valves when they failed adopted a program of contract maintenance. Valve business within the chemical industry declined significantly. At the same time, mining markets increased in response to the use of coal in traditional oil markets.

The 1980s were disastrous for Valvetech. Mining markets were adversely impacted by the decline of the energy industry. Chemical markets never recovered as the chemical industry continued to perform valve rebuilds. In 1986, the bottom fell out of Valvetech as one of the major remaining chemical clients decided to shift its business to Valvetech's major competitor.

Valvetech ultimately went from 1,100 employees to 270 by the end of 1986. Attempts were made to sell the business, but the only interested buyers were liquidators. Faced with no buyers, the senior management of Valvetech decided to develop a comprehensive plan to revitalize the business.

After many heated discussions, the management team evolved a strategy for the future. The essential elements of that plan are outlined in TABLE 8-1.

In the two years following the introduction of the strategic plan, the Valvetech fortunes began to revive. Business from new markets added $22 million to annual sales. Personnel costs declined by $8 million. Quality complaints were reduced to one complaint per $1.5 million in sales. The cost per unit declined to 12 percent. Research funds of $2.2 million were obtained to develop new valves for clean coal technologies. New business subsidiaries were created to serve remanufacturing and export markets. While Valvetech had not yet turned the corner, it was clearly on the road to recovery. A new challenge faced Valvetech in 1988. To what extent should automated technologies factor into the future of Valvetech?

AUTOMATION IN STRATEGIC PLANNING

The role of automation in Valvetech's strategic plan represents the issues that many businesses face today in reviewing the level of automation in their own facilities. The decision to employ automation is not simply an economic issue. Automation can affect the strategy of the business in many different ways other than economic. Outlined below are the types of questions that any business might ask when looking at a substantial automation program.

Automation and Missions

Automation might affect the missions of an organization in a number of ways as outlined below:

- Increased capability: Will automation allow us to manufacture new products that could not be

Table 8-1. The Valvetech Resurrection Strategy.

Manufacturing Strategies

1. Develop valve technology which extends the current operating life by 25 percent.

2. Develop quality programs which lead to the elimination of all customer complaints.

3. Develop the flexibility to complete a customer's order in two days or less.

4. Reduce production costs by 20 percent.

Human Resource Strategies

1. Develop the work force through continuous educational programs.

2. Implement a gain-sharing program coupled with cost reduction idea program to reward improvements in manufacturing.

3. Revise the pay system to a pay-for-knowledge system.

4. Reduce non-production staff by 40 percent.

5. Recruit a team of young engineers to staff new production and research programs.

Organizational Strategies

1. Create an entrepreneurial organization structure to stimulate new markets and products.

2. Develop organizational performance measures for every unit.

Product Development Strategies

1. Develop valve research function and secure research funding for valves to serve clean coal technology markets.

2. Develop specialized valves to serve the biotechnology markets.

3. Develop a valve rebuild capability to serve remanufacturing needs.

4. Develop international markets in the orient and middle east.

---

made with existing processes? Will automation improve quality and allow us to seek more value-oriented markets?

- Market responsiveness: Will automation give us more flexibility to serve a greater variety of customers?
- Price structure: How will automation change the basic economics of the product?

Automation may expand the production capabilities of the business. Tolerances that could not be maintained by manual or semiautomated technologies may be achieved through automation. Quality improvements may also be achieved through automation. If so, the business may be able to seek more value-oriented markets.

Automation may provide more flexibility. By reducing set-up times and other start-up activities, automation technologies may allow businesses to respond to smaller specialized orders. Automation may also eliminate many of the time consuming activities associated with getting an order through the plant.

While automation may expand customer responsiveness and production capabilities, automation may also affect the basic economic structure of the business. Manual or semiautomated technologies tend to generate lower fixed costs and higher variable costs than automation. Many of the costs of automation continue in periods of low demand, while businesses can reduce the costs of manual or semiautomated technologies in periods of low demand through layoffs. Automation raises the risk of businesses in cyclical industries.

The particular impact of automation on the missions of a business can only be determined by asking questions as outlined above. The failure to consider these issues may result in serious misdirection of the business.

Automation and the Business Environment

There are many environmental factors that are likely to affect the use of automated technologies. Perhaps the most significant environmental factor is the impending labor shortage facing the United States. By the year 2000, many businesses will find it difficult to hire skilled employees. The work force is also becoming more demanding in terms of what it expects from a job. The boredom and unsafe work environments of the past will be challenged by employees and governmental agencies. As labor shortages increase, quality-of-work-life issues will become more important determinants of where employees choose to work.

Competitive factors are likely to continue to emphasize quality, price, and service. The major competitive force of the future is likely to be innovation and responsiveness to market needs. The ability of a business to develop innovative new products quicker than the competition is likely to be the main determinant of competitive success.

The critical strategic questions to ask about new technologies in terms of environment are:

- How does the new technology fit into our human resource plans? How will the new technology affect our hiring needs?
- How does the technology fit into our quality-of-work-life? How are we affecting work in terms of safety and challenge?
- What competitive advantages do we gain from the new technology?
- What future governmental actions is our industry likely to see? How will the automated technology be affected by or be impacted by governmental action?
- How does the automated technology impact our ability to be innovative?

- How much quicker can we get into the market with new products as a result of the automated technology?

Automation and Competitive Strategy

The impact of automated technologies on competitive position must be viewed in terms of price, quality, and service. The history of automation with respect to these three factors is contradictory. In theory, automation should improve all three factors. Actual practice, however, has not always shown that automated technologies are better on price, quality, and service. Outlined below are some of the strategic issues that should be considered in testing the most likely effect of automated technologies on price, quality, and service:

- What costs are actually reduced as a result of the automated technology?
- What effect will the automated technology have on product prices? Will volume considerations impact product price?
- What are the quality risks associated with the new technology? What are the quality gains?
- How will the automated technology affect our economic adjustment to fluctuations in market demand?
- How will the automated technology respond to new product needs?
- What effect will the automated technology have on our ability to decrease the time from order entry to customer delivery?
- How will the automated technology change our overall competitive position?
- Have we adequately protected ourselves if the technology experiences lengthy downtime?

There is no single strategic impact of automated technologies. The impact of technology will obviously have a different effect on a small specialty products business than it will on a large, commodity business. But even in businesses with roughly the same market, the strategic impact of automated technologies will be different. There are no mathematical formulae to guide the understanding of the strategic impact of automated technologies on competitive position.

Automation and Implementing the Strategic Plan

The execution of the strategic plan is often the weakest link in the overall process. What sounds nice on paper is often resisted by others. The strategic plan may also be subverted by those who simply do not understand the implications of their decisions and actions on the chosen strategy of the business.

The impact of automated technologies on the strategic direction of the business may be less than desired unless the actual technology is carefully monitored. Representative issues that most often represent failures in the strategic plan implementation with respect to automated technologies are:

- The cost savings associated with the automated technology never materialize. Unexpected new costs are incurred or planned savings are not actually achieved.
- The expected flexibility of the new technology is not achieved. The traditional mentality of long runs and dedicated technologies is not changed. The automated technology is only used for part of its original mission.
- The automated technology does not prove to be as reliable as expected. Redundancies are added to increase the reliability of the system. The redundancies limit the strategic impact of the automated system by making it more costly and less flexible.
- The automated technology creates a capacity imbalance that is not resolved. As a result, the utilization of the automated technology is not as expected.
- Other system changes are not made to be compatible with the automated technology. For example, incoming materials to the automated technology may not meet the quality requirements of the automated system.

These issues are merely representative of the many issues that can limit the intended impact of a new system technology on the strategy of the business. These implementation issues do point to the need for a systematic strategic review of all new initiatives of the business. In the case of an automated technology, there should be a regular audit of the technology. Has it achieved the expected results? Audits such as this can provide useful midcourse corrections for automated technologies but can also serve as guides for future technology decisions.

VALVETECH REVISITED: A Strategic Plan for Automated Technologies

Valvetech represents a fairly typical American company in the 1980s. Faced with eroding market share, Valvetech is trying to reposition itself. Automated technologies are a part of the revival plan. Outlined below are brief summaries of Valvetech's strategic thinking with regard to automated technologies.

Evaluating Automation and Valvetech's Future

In Valvetech's case, the demands of new markets stimulated a search for automated technologies to provide the high quality valves demanded. While these technologies required significant capital investments, Valvetech management felt that the future customers of Valvetech would increasingly require tolerances not now available through existing process technology. A computer controlled machining center was proposed as the key technology in meeting new market requirements.

In Valvetech's case, the major environmental factors were governmental requirements, work force issues, and the demands of new customer segments. Valvetech found itself in tune with a developing environmental concern. Public demands for a clean environment placed Valvetech in the middle of a national effort to develop new technologies for cleaner burning of coal.

As new challenges were facing Valvetech, many of the skilled work force with 35 to 40 years of experience were beginning to retire. New employees who could perform the intricate machining requirements of the new valve technologies were hard to find.

In the past, Valvetech had relied upon standard designs to serve the majority of its customer requirements. With entry into new markets, Valvetech found itself faced with an ever changing product. Production runs that had averaged 25 units in the past were shifting to runs of five or less.

The general direction of environmental factors facing Valvetech indicated the development of new process technologies that would require less labor skill, be economic with small runs, and be adaptable to a variety of new products.

The selection of any new technology must examine the environmental forces that are likely to be impacted by the automated technology. The factors outlined above are representative of those that might be considered in the evaluation of automated technologies.

Competitive Strategy

As Valvetech thought through its competitive future, it realized that future markets would require sophisticated valves that were not possible with existing technologies. The competitor that provided high reliability and fast turnaround on valves would be the winner.

The computer controlled machining center provided the increased product capability, but Valvetech management was concerned about the reliability of the system. Reliability issues were thoroughly researched, and management decided to increase the system's reliability through plant environment improvements. The system also mandated changes in capacity balances.

The most important aspect of the automated technology was changing the traditional thinking of the production floor. Educational programs were introduced to make every employee and supervisor aware of the new manufacturing realities facing Valvetech.

From these discussions, a strategic plan for automated technologies evolved. TABLE 8-2 lists the five goals of the plan.

SUMMARY

The incorporation of manufacturing into the strategic planning process is a recent phenomenon. As automated technologies become more powerful, the impact of such technologies on the strategic direction of a business must be carefully considered. This chapter outlined the strategic issues associated with automated technologies. There are no models for testing the impact of automated technologies on the strategic direction of a business. Rather, the management of the business must consider fully the strategic issues associated with the new technology in terms of the missions, the environment, the competitive position, and the implementation plan.

Table 8-2. The Valvetech Automated Technology Strategic Plan.

1. We will invest in automated technologies that allow us to maintain the tolerances required of our new markets.

2. We will invest in automated technologies that make limited run sizes economical.

3. We will invest in automated technologies that reduce our skilled labor needs even though we realize that such technologies often require staffing additions of technicians and engineering support.

4. We will integrate automated technologies into our current manufacturing environment in order to fully utilize the capital investment in the technology.

5. We will invest in the education of our people to ensure that they know how to use the power of the automated technology.

9

Collective Bargaining and Unionism

Gary N. Chaison[*]

DURING THE PAST DECADE, THE AMERICAN LABOR movement has undergone a transition of historical significance. The size and influence of labor unions have declined, the conduct and outcomes of bargaining have changed dramatically, the employee participation programs have become widespread in unionized companies. In this chapter, I present an overview of these trends, and assess their importance in general and for manufacturing concerns undergoing major technological change.

In the opening section, I examine the present state of the labor movement. This includes a review of the decreases in union membership, the inability of unions to recruit new members, and the widespread practice of concession bargaining during and after the recent recession. Following this review are discussions of collective bargaining and quality of work life programs—the two approaches used by unions to respond to new technology and work processes. The section on collective bargaining deals primarily with collective agreement clauses that cushion the impact of technological change. The review of quality of work life programs covers the various types of employee participation programs in unionized firms, the barriers to their introduction, and their coexistence with collective bargaining.

THE STATE OF THE UNIONS

Since the beginning of the 1980s, American unions have faced problems of a severity and scope seldom encountered in their long history. Membership decline and the difficulty of recruiting new members, combined with the increasingly proactive stance of employers in negotiations, have greatly weakened the labor movement and have prompted many unions to reconsider their traditional ways of representing workers.

Declining Union Membership

TABLE 9-1 shows union membership and union density from 1960 to 1987. *Union density*, calculated as the percentage of nonagricultural wage earners who are union members, is a measure of the extent to which unions have recruited among potential members. The two time series in TABLE 9-1 clearly indicate the continuing decline of the labor movement. Since 1975, labor unions lost more than

*Gary N. Chaison is a professor of industrial relations at the Graduate School of Management, Clark University, Worcester, Massachusetts. He received his Ph.D. from the State University of New York at Buffalo and taught industrial relations and human resource management in the United States and Canada. His principal research interests are in the areas of collective bargaining and union structure, government, and growth. He is presently engaged in comparative studies of union organizing and collective bargaining in Canada and the United States. He is the author of *When Unions Merge* (Lexington Books, 1986). The author thanks Edward Ottensmeyer for his helpful comments on an earlier draft of this chapter.

Table 9-1. Union Membership[1] and Union Density [2] in the United States.

Year	TROY AND SHEFLIN SERIES[3]		CPS SERIES[4]	
	Membership	Density	Membership	Density
1960	15,516	28.6%		
1965	16,949	30.1%		
1970	20,990	29.6%		
1975	22,207	28.9%		
1976	22,153	27.9%		
1977	21,632	26.2%		
1978	21,757	25.1%		
1979	22,025	24.5%		
1980	20,968	23.2%		
1981	20,647	22.6%		
1982	19,571	21.9%		
1983	18,634	20.7%	17,717	20.4%
1984	18,306	19.4%	17,340	19.1%
1985			16,996	18.3%
1986			16,975	17.5%
1987			16,913	17.0%

1. Union members expressed in thousands.
2. Union membership as a percent of nonagricultural wage earners.
3., 4. Source: Troy and Sheflin series: Leo Troy and Neil Sheflin, *Union Sourcebook: Membership, Structure, Finance, Directory* (Industrial Relations Data and Information Services, West Orange, N.J., 1985), p.3.10 for 1960, 1970, 1975-1984 : George S. Bain and R. J. Price, *Profiles of Union Growth* (Blackwell, Oxford, 1980), p. 89 for 1965.

Note: The Troy and Sheflin series is a continuation of an earlier series developed for the National Bureau of Economic Research. The data is derived primarily from union financial reports and represents annual averages of full-time dues-paying union members.

five million members and density declined by about 12 percentage points. In 1965, unions had organized almost one third of their potential members. The present proportion is close to one sixth and some observers believe that it could fall to as low as one tenth in the private sector in the next decade.[1,2]

The 1980s show the greatest decline in union membership and density; from 1980 to 1987 membership dropped by four million and density fell by more than six percentage points. This has been largely attributed to the deteriorating competitive position of unionized employers. Competition from foreign and domestic nonunion companies has intensified, and higher wages and restrictive work rules have placed unionized companies at a disadvantage. Under these conditions, partially unionized companies often shifted production and employment to their nonunion operations. Unionized companies frequently resorted to layoffs and plant closings, or the creation of new nonunion facilities. In addition, when faced by deregulation, many employers in trucking, airlines, and communications sharply reduced their work forces in order to become competitive with the new nonunion entrants in their industries.[5,6,7,8,9]

TABLE 9-2 shows the 1987 union membership figures for various worker characteristics and industries. Membership levels were highest among

Table 9-2. Union Membership[1] and Union Density[2] by Employee Characteristics and Industries, 1987.

Characteristics and Industries	Membership[1]	Density[2]
Full-time workers	15,670	19.4%
Part-time workers	1,243	6.7%
Men	11,071	20.9%
Women	5,842	12.6%
Age		
16 to 24 years	1,299	6.6%
25 to 34 years	4,752	15.7%
35 to 44 years	5,080	21.7%
45 to 54 years	3,442	23.4%
55 to 64 years	2,142	22.9%
65 years and over	198	9.7%
Industry		
Agriculture	33	2.2%
Mining	143	18.3%
Construction	1,060	21.0%
Manufacturing	4,691	23.2%
Durable goods	2,969	24.7%
Nondurable goods	1,722	20.9%
Transportation, Communications and Public Utilities	1,947	33.5%
Transportation	1,051	32.1%
Communications and public utilities	897	35.2%
Wholesale and retail trade	1,440	7.1%
Wholesale trade	330	8.4%
Retail trade	1,110	6.7%
Finance, Insurance, and Real Estate	158	2.3%
Services	1,387	6.3%
Government	6,055	36.0%

1. Union members expressed in thousands.
2. Union membership as a percent of wage and salary employees.

Source: CPS figures from Larry T. Adams, "Union Membership of Wage and Salary Employees in 1987," *Current Wage Developments*, (February 1988), pp. 6-7.

full-time and male workers, and transportation, communications and public utilities, and government workers. Unions have been unable to make major organizing inroads in the expanding service and wholesale and retail sectors. In manufacturing and construction, often thought of as unionized industries, union members now comprise less than one quarter of the wage earners. Even in the most heavily unionized sectors—transportation, communications and the government—the majority of employees are not union members. Finally, membership levels remain low for two growing sectors of the labor force: the younger workers (those under 35 years of age) and female workers.

Union Organizing

In the private sector, unions achieve *certification*, the right to represent groups of employees, by petitioning for and winning secret ballot elections. These certification elections are conducted by the National Labor Relations Board (NLRB) under the Wagner Act of 1935 (National Labor Relations Act) and subsequent legislation. A union petitions for an election by producing the signatures on membership cards of at least 30 percent—and preferably 50 percent—of the employees in the group it wishes to represent. The NLRB determines the group of workers eligible to vote, called the *bargaining unit*, and supervises the election. If a majority of the votes are cast for the union, the NLRB will certify the union as a bargaining agent. The employer is required to bargain in good faith with the certified bargaining agent.

The union success rate in certification elections fell from 65 percent in 1956 to 46 percent in 1985. During the past recession there was also a significant decline in organizing activity. The number of annual elections fell from 6,443 in 1980 to 5,786 in 1981, and to 3,275 in 1982. From 1983 to 1985, an average of only 3,235 elections were held each year.[10]

Recent studies have concluded that unions no longer seem able or willing to use the certification process to recruit new members. An analysis by Chaison and Rose revealed that the net outcome of all NLRB election activity in 1985 was the right of unions to represent only 50,000 workers.[11] The actual membership gains were even less. About one third of certified unions are unable to negotiate their first agreements and establish ongoing bargaining relationships with employers. Furthermore, 11 percent of employees covered by collective agreements do not join the unions that represent them.[12]

In another study, Rose and Chaison analyzed union organizing effectiveness by creating indices of union organizing effort, success, and the selection of organizing targets. They concluded that "between 1976 and 1985 union organizing efforts and success fell dramatically . . . and there has not been a major effort to expand the frontiers of collective bargaining.[13]

The declining number of certification elections and the low union success rates have been blamed on increased employer opposition during election contests.[14,15] It has been shown that both legal conduct, such as procedural delays at NLRB hearings, and illegal conduct, primarily the discrimination against or discharge of union supporters, have increased in the past decade and significantly lowered the chances of union victory.[16] Employer resistance to unionization is at its highest level since the 1920s;[17] this is attributed to the increased wage differential between union and nonunion workers. Employers now devote greater effort and resources to opposing unions because they believe that unions are more costly in the face of increased domestic and foreign competition.[18,19]

Unions have also lost members through decertification elections. Workers or employers in unionized firms call for these contests with the objective of having unions lose their bargaining status. The annual number of decertification elections increased from 300 in the 1960s, to about 500 in the mid-1970s, to over 900 by the mid-1980s. Unions lost more than three-quarters of recent decertification elections.[20] From 1976 to 1985, about a quarter of a million employees were in the bargaining units lost to unions through decertification elections.*

Concession Bargaining

American unions have faced significant changes in the conduct and subject matter of collective bargaining. During the past recession, concession bargaining became widespread, particularly in industries facing slackened demand, increased foreign and domestic competition, or deregulation.

All collective bargaining requires concessions

---

*This figure is derived by the author from election data provided by the Data Systems Branch of the NLRB.

from the participants if they are to move from their initial positions and reach an agreement. However, in concession bargaining, the union relinquishes compensation or terms and conditions of employment, or forgoes gains that it could expect to receive under normal economic conditions. This approach to bargaining is a pragmatic reaction to atypical economic forces that threaten the job security of the employees in the bargaining unit.[21]

Between 1980 and 1984, an estimated half of the union workers in major establishments (those with 1,000 or more employees) were covered by collective agreements with wage freezes or cuts. When wage increases were granted, they tended to be very small and were determined primarily by the employers' ability to pay rather than changes in the cost of living, productivity, or comparable wages elsewhere. The average annual increases in compensation over the life of collective agreements fell from 7.1 percent in 1980 and 8.3 percent in 1981 to 2.8 percent in 1982. In the following years it never exceeded 3.0 percent.[22]

Cost of living allowances (COLAs), clauses that automatically increased wages in relation to changes in the cost of living, often had their payments deferred or were eliminated entirely. In 1981, COLA payments constituted about one third of wage adjustments in major collective bargaining agreements; two years later they accounted for only 15 percent of these wage adjustments.[23]

During concession bargaining many unions agreed to profit sharing as a means to recoup wages that were lost through concessions, or as a substitute for COLA payments or increases in benefits.[24,25,26] Annual bonus plans were also introduced to make compensation more responsive to the changing economic position of the firm. Finally, some unions, particularly those in the airlines and retail industries, agreed to two-tiered wage systems under which newly hired workers received substantially lower pay, often 20 to 40 percent less that those employed at the time the agreement was negotiated.[27,28] In its survey of employer bargaining objectives for 1988, the Bureau of National Affairs found that 43 percent of sampled employers had two-tiered wage provisions in their collective agree-

ments and about 90 percent of these employers intended to keep them in the next round of negotiations.[29]

A survey of employer bargaining objectives for 1988 conducted by the Bureau of National Affairs (BNA), suggests that employers have become resigned to lower wage levels:

> Employers seem determined to keep union wage levels from turning the corner next year and beginning an upward trend....Competitiveness is the buzzword of employers today and they seem poised to convince unions that labor costs must remain moderate to enable them to compete in a nonunion and worldwide marketplace.[30]

Ninety-nine percent of the surveyed employers intended to negotiate first year wage gains of four percent or less, and 29 percent of these employers planned increases of less than two percent. Employers were also attempting to reduce labor costs through health care cost containment, often by increasing employees' contributions, reducing benefits, or increasing deductibles.[31, 32]

During the recession, unions frequently demanded and attained quid pro quos in return for their concessions. Sometimes these took the form of "equality of sacrifice" provisions calling for cuts or freezes in management salaries or benefits, or reductions in management staff.[33] More often, unions were able to trade off wage and benefit concessions for greater roles in management decision making and access to information about company conditions and plans.[34] While forms of employee participation have a long history and concession bargaining has occurred in troubled industries from time to time, the two become closely linked during the past recession as companies had to introduce or expand participative programs in return for union acceptance of concessions.[35, 36, 37]

Concession bargaining seems to have changed some unions' attitudes about their roles as representatives. Mitchell observed:

> After World War II, a sharp distinction developed between the appropriate roles for union and management. Firms were to worry about such matters as market shares, product development, and investments.

The union role was simply to demand improved compensation and conditions, and leave it to management to deal with the resulting costs. But when faced with concessions and declining membership in the 1980s, unions began to take a more "managerial" perspective with regard to such matters.[38]

Mitchell believed that this change in perspective is a healthy sign and "the only path to union survival as a significant voice at the workplace and in society."[39]

Several observers claim that a new collective bargaining emerged from the pressures of the recession. This bargaining places a greater emphasis on job security, flexible work rules, and worker and union participation in management decision making. There appears to be a greater reciprocity between the parties and a willingness to accept collaborative arrangements that can coexist with traditional collective bargaining agreements and structures.[40]

The recent trends in bargaining may be best understood when we view collective bargaining as a complex process composed of several subsystems. In their landmark study, Walton and McKersie identified four processes in labor negotiations.[41] *Distributive bargaining* is the historically dominant form of bargaining in which the attainment of one party's goals conflicts with those of the other party. Such negotiations are usually over the distribution of financial resources and are often called zero-sum situations because one party's losses are equal to the other party's gains.

In a second process, *integrative bargaining*, objectives do not conflict and the parties adopt problem solving approaches as they reach negotiated settlements. A solution may benefit one party without causing a loss for the other. A frequently used example of integrative bargaining is negotiations to introduce new technology while protecting against job losses.

A third process, *attitudinal structuring*, is the attempt to influence the relationship between the parties. For example, when the parties are involved in integrative bargaining, attitudinal structuring is used to create a climate of trust, respect, and reciprocity. Finally, *intraorganizational bargaining* is

the process of building consensus among the constituencies within the union and company.

The new collective bargaining retains elements of distributive bargaining while expanding the role of integrative bargaining. This change calls for attitudinal structuring to build the levels of trust and reciprocity needed to propose, evaluate, and eventually agree upon satisfactory solutions to shared problems. Union officers are engaged in intra-organizational bargaining as they devise bargaining proposals and present tentative agreements to the membership for their approval.

The new approach to collective bargaining, combined with the severity of recent membership losses, have shaped union reactions to technological change in manufacturing. Few unions attempt to block the introduction of new technology: "The Luddite mentality is not characteristic of American unions."[42] The typical union approach is one of willing rather than reluctant acceptance.[43, 44] Technology itself is considered to be a neutral force and the union's objective is to protect the workforce from any negative consequences while maximizing the desirable ones.[45, 46]

This reaction to technology is largely the result of the presence of industrial rather than craft unions in manufacturing. Industrial unions such as the Automobile Workers or the Steelworkers recruit workers in an industry or set of related industries regardless of the work they perform. On the other hand craft unions such as many of the unions in the railroad, construction, and newspaper industries, organize workers primarily on the basis of their trade or craft. If manufacturing had been organized by craft unions, new technologies and work processes could erode the boundaries of traditional crafts, reduce the status and compensation of union members relative to other workers in the same companies, and diminish the pool of future union members. Technological change would pose an immediate threat to the craft unions' survival and would have to be rigorously controlled if not blocked entirely.[47]

In practice, however, the industrial unions, and not craft unions, usually represent all production and maintenance workers at plants. Their major concerns are that: technology improves rather than worsens working conditions, jobs and pay rates are protected, workers receive a share of the profits and other benefits of the technology, the union is consulted in the introduction of the technology, and that the technology does not undermine the representative position of the union.[48] While these concerns are certainly not new, they are now frequently addressed through both collective bargaining and programs that promote employee participation.

COLLECTIVE BARGAINING

While unions do engage in political and social activities, their primary objective is to serve as bargaining agents for employees in negotiations with employers. The results of these negotiations are legally binding collective bargaining agreements that enumerate the rights and responsibilities of the union and employer, the work rules, the system of wages and benefits, and the provisions for job and income security.

The collective bargaining process is basically adversarial because of the conflicting interests of the employer in managing the enterprise and the union in representing the workforce. However, as we noted in the preceding section, bargaining can also have an integrative or problem solving side. In automated factories, this side is prominent when negotiators balance the employer's goals of introducing new technologies and eliminating restrictive work rules, and the unions' concerns with job and income security.

Protection against the Impact of Technological Change

Employers are required by the National Labor Relations Act to negotiate in good faith with certified unions over wages, hours, and conditions of employment. In regard to technological change, the NLRB and the courts have generally found that this duty to bargain is limited to the effects of technology rather than the decision to introduce it.[49, 50, 51, 52] As a result, unions tend to respond to management decisions on a case by case basis, rather than by

establishing and enforcing any broad set of rules or principles on future implementation.[53] While some unions have issued policy statements on the introduction and implications of new technologies, these serve as local union guidelines in negotiations rather than as legally binding labor-management accords.

For example, the International Association of Machinists published a "Workers' Bill of Rights" that states that technology shall be used to create jobs; labor costs and productivity gains shall be shared with workers at the local enterprise level; new technologies will improve the conditions of work and enhance and expand the opportunities for knowledge, skills and compensation of workers; new technology will be evaluated in terms of worker health and safety; and workers shall have the right to participate in all phases of management deliberations and decisions that could lead to new technology.[54] The policy statement on robots of the International Union of Electrical, Radio and Machine Workers states that the use of robots shall be restricted to dangerous work, the union shall receive advanced notice of installation, the work force will be adjusted only through attrition, and the company shall provide for retraining of displaced workers.[55]

A 1983 survey conducted by the BNA found that technological change was specifically restricted in 21 percent of the sampled collective agreements.[56] These clauses dealt with two major issues: notification or consultation with the union, and the treatment of displaced workers. Some employers were required to provide periodic briefings to unions, or to serve advanced notice of technological change. Joint labor-management committees were often created for consultation or notification. In the rarest and strongest clauses, the employer cannot introduce new technology without the union's approval.[57]

The unions' principal concern is the impact of technological change on the income and job security of employees. Various plans have been negotiated to provide for continuing income. Displaced workers are frequently given retraining and broad transfer rights.

For example, the 1987 agreement between Ford and the United Automobile Workers (UAW) created a job security program, called "Guaranteed Employment Numbers," for the purpose of maintaining "current job levels at all units in all locations . . . and prevent[ing] layoffs for virtually any reason except carefully defined volume reductions linked to market conditions."[58] Backed by a $500 million Ford commitment, the clause specifies a certain number of protected employees, a number which can be reduced when employees retire, quit, or die. At each plant there is a pool of employees who would have been laid off if they had not been protected by the plan. Members of this pool receive the same rate of pay and benefits they would have received prior to entering the pool. They may be placed in training programs or given assignments outside of the bargaining unit. Employees can lose their protected status if they decline new jobs in the company.[59]

In many firms it may be necessary for unions to accept retraining programs instead of guarantees of continuous employment. In a recent Delphi study, a panel of experts were asked to name the incentives that would be necessary to gain union acceptance for the installation of robots.[60] While the most powerful incentive was a guarantee of continued employment for all workers, the panel believed that this was economically unfeasible. The second strongest incentive, the retraining of displaced workers, was judged to have the strongest likelihood of implementation.

Technological change often creates opportunities for employers to subcontract or *outsource*—to transfer production to other firms or to its employees outside the bargaining unit. In response to this possibility, unions frequently negotiate clauses that restrict or even prohibit this practice. The 1983 BNA study found that about half of the surveyed collective agreements contained outsourcing clauses.[61] Some clauses only required that unions be notified of outsourcing or subcontracting and be provided with an opportunity to consult with management and suggest possible alternatives. A stronger, more typical clause stipulated that the subcontracting of work normally performed by unit members is prohibited if it eliminates jobs, or results in layoffs or the failure to recall qualified employees on layoff. Very few clauses, only about two percent of those uncovered by the BNA, prohibit employers from subcontracting under any conditions.

Related to subcontracting clauses are those provisions that protect the integrity of the bargaining unit. These clauses generally require that jobs previously in the unit will stay in the unit when new technologies are introduced. For example, if an operator in the unit is replaced by a robot, then the robot's operator will be in the bargaining unit and covered by the collective bargaining agreement.[62]

Changing Work Rules and Job Classifications

Critics of collective bargaining claim that the process codifies inflexible work rules and large numbers of narrowly defined jobs. The jobs and skills called for by new technologies are difficult to introduce if they require the extensive revision of long-standing jobs and work rules. Under these conditions, technological change would not realize its fullest potential to reduce costs and increase productivity and quality.

Faced with severe competitive pressures in the past decade, management has begun to initiate proposals for fewer job classifications, the reduction in the size of work crews, and greater flexibility in employee transfers, training, and the assignment of overtime. Probably the most dramatic proposals replace complex sets of job classifications with a few jobs that have very broad skills and responsibilities.

In return for these changes, unions often ask for guarantees of continuous employment. There is an understandable rationale for this trade-off. When the traditional job classifications found in a plant are linked to the external labor market, workers who are laid off might find alternative employment. However, broadened job classifications often result in jobs that are unique to the firm. Workers fear that when they are trained for such positions they will become ill equipped for the job search in the external labor market. Consequently, when jobs are created specifically for the firm, unions demand that workers have long-term attachments to the firm.[63]

At the National Steel Corporation, the 1986 collective agreement with the United Steelworkers of America reduced job classifications from 66 to 16 at one plant. Some new classifications combined only two previous classifications: the crane millwright and the crane inspector were combined into the position of the crane repairman. On the other hand, a single mechanics' classification replaced 17 classifications, and three helper classifications—the electrical, mechanical, and service helpers—were created from 22 classifications.[64] This reduction in classifications, along with the elimination of restrictive work rules, enabled the company to reduce the number of man-hours needed to produce a ton of steel to about four by the end of 1987 from the more than five it took in 1986.[65]*

Perhaps the most sweeping and innovative work rules changes have occurred in the automobile industry.[67] Automobile plants had become notorious for their narrowly defined jobs; a typical plant had over 100 classifications. For example, in 1984, the Cadillac plant in Detroit had 182 job classifications—118 classifications for skilled workers and 64 for unskilled workers.[68]

The need to increase productivity and reduce labor costs in the face of foreign competition prompted a widespread restructuring of job classification systems. The recent agreement between Chrysler and the UAW calls for only ten skilled and nonskilled classifications at some facilities.[69] The New United Motor Manufacturing Inc., the General Motors and Toyota joint venture, has only four job classifications.[70] At the Saturn facility of General Motors, expected to open in the Fall of 1990, there will be one job classification for all nonskilled

trades, called the operating technician, and three to five additional classifications for the skilled workers.[71]

The consolidation of job classifications frequently coincides with the introduction of operating teams, also called production teams. In a typical operating team there is a single production classification and individual workers are not explicitly linked to a set of job tasks. For example, at the Buick Reatta plant, each team is given a set of operations to perform and team members decide individual work assignments. The workers perform a far broader range of operations than they would in a conventional plant. Under the collective agreement, workers cannot be laid off as a result of their increased productivity.[72]

At the Saturn facility, the operating teams, called *work units*, will consist of six to fifteen members. Their responsibilities will include:

. . . producing to schedule, producing a quality product, performing to budget, housekeeping, safety and health, maintenance of equipment, material and inventory control, training, job assignment, repairs, scrap control and absenteeism. They will hold meetings, obtain supplies, keep records, seek resources as needed, and be responsible for their job preparation . . . The Work Units will also be responsible for selection decisions for acceptance into the Work Units, the planning of work, and for the scheduling of work and communications within and outside the group.[73]

Obviously, radical departures from the traditional assembly line production and its narrowly defined jobs and skills may call for major modifications in compensation. At the Saturn facility, all production workers will receive an annual salary and a profit sharing adjustment rather than an hourly wage. Only 80 percent of the salary will be guaranteed; the remainder will be adjusted in relation to profitability and can exceed one hundred percent of the base salary.[74]

Another innovative form of compensation is the pay-for-knowledge system under which workers are paid their skill rate regardless of whether they are actually assigned to the job that requires the

---

*The concession bargaining and participation programs at the National Steel Corporation are described in a case study prepared by the Bureau of Labor-Management Programs and Cooperative Programs by the U.S. Department of Labor.[66]

use of that skill.[75] Rankin and Mansell described the pay-for-knowledge system at the Shell plant in Sarnia, Ontario:

> Process operators are paid on the basis of demonstrated knowledge and skills in both the process and support skill areas. The more operators learn, the more they are paid. Team members play a central role in assessing peer competence. Although there is no limit to the number who can reach the top pay rank, it takes a minimum of six years to do so. Currently, 80 percent of the plant's process operators are at the top.[76]

In a recent survey sponsored by the U.S. Department of Labor, eight percent of the responding corporate personnel officers had implemented pay-for-knowledge. Three quarters of the systems were introduced with the start-up of new operations. It is frequently assumed that unions resist pay-for-knowledge because it conflicts with the traditional wage systems and job classifications established under collective bargaining. This was not confirmed by the survey results. Most respondents from unionized firms reported that unions generally supported pay-for-knowledge. The respondents did not believe that pay-for-knowledge would change union influence or that it was more effective in non-union rather than unionized settings. In general, the personnel officers gave a favorable evaluation to pay-for-knowledge and believed that it contributed not only to greater flexibility but to improved employee satisfaction, commitment, and productivity.[77]

QUALITY OF WORK LIFE PROGRAMS IN UNIONIZED COMPANIES

Quality of work life (QWL) programs entail a:

> structured, systematic approach to the involvement of employees in group decisions affecting work and the work environment with goals that include reducing product costs, improving product quality, facilitating communication, raising morale, and reducing conflict.[78]

QWL programs may call for work redesign, pay restructuring, time rescheduling, problem solving,

and information sharing. They often are called employee participation or employee involvement programs. In 1985, about one third of all companies, and 58 percent of those with one thousand or more employees, had some type of QWL program. More than a third of these firms had quality circles and about one quarter had autonomous work groups.[79,80]

Kochan and Katz described three levels of QWL programs.[81] On the first level are the narrowly based programs, such as quality circles, that are specifically designed to increase individual and group problem solving around task related issues. If there is sufficient trust among the parties, first level programs can broaden and become second level work reforms. The operating teams described in the preceding section are typical of second level QWL efforts.

In some cases, participation spreads to the level of strategic decision making. At this third level, unions attempt to influence management decisions before they are made. These activities range from joint consultation and information sharing, to the inclusion of union officers in the plant manager's administrative staff, or the designation of union positions on boards of directors. In its strongest form, third level participation entails extensive union involvement in planning and strategy committees.

If QWL efforts are successful at lower levels, the union and management may be encouraged to expand them and experiment with higher level programs. The evolving QWL program at Xerox is a frequently cited example of spreading participation. In 1980, employee problem solving groups at the shop floor level, a variant of quality circles, were established under the collective agreement between Xerox and the Amalgamated Clothing and Textile Workers Union. In 1981, Xerox reacted to mounting competitive pressures by threatening to subcontract the production of wiring harnesses, a labor intensive process. Faced with strong opposition from the union and already accustomed to employee participation programs, the company decided to subject the process to a study by a team of union and management representatives. The team's recommendation identified several areas of potential savings and the company was persuaded not to subcontract the process. The next time the company and union negotiated the collective agreement, they mandated the use of problem solving teams in all potential subcontracting situations.

Participation spread even further in the following years. In one instance, worker representatives participated in the planning of a new facility and showed management that a plant could operate in the local area with employees transferred from the company's other operations. At the shop floor level, the union and the employer created an extensive network of "business area work groups," temporary problem solving teams composed of supervisors, workers, engineers, and management support staff. Over a period of seven years, the shop floor QWL effort at Xerox was intensified at the lowest levels and spread to the highest level of strategic decision making.[82, 83] The combination of collective bargaining and union-management committees developed into a system of collective governance of the employment relationship and was capable of addressing both the competing and common interests of management and the employees.[84]

It must be emphasized that successful QWL programs at any level are introduced as an addition to, rather than as a substitute for employee representation through collective bargaining. As Bluestone observed:

In essence the QWL process represents an outgrowth of the collective bargaining process in unionized settings. It is fashioned by the negotiating parties, molded into an ongoing process by them, nurtured as a joint activity.[85]

Labor-management cooperation requires that both parties perceive that their interests are being served. Initially QWL is not overwhelmingly accepted by union officers and members.[86] They will want to know the answers to several important questions. Will economic benefits accrue only to management? If productivity does increase, will employees lose jobs or job opportunities? Will employee involvement programs co-opt union members? Is QWL a ploy to legitimatize management decisions without granting any real power to unions? Will union committee members begin to identify with management rather than their own constituencies? If management interprets cooperation as a sign of union weakness, will it reduce the union's ability to seek economic gains at the bargaining table? Will union involvement in QWL undermine the role of the grievance procedure in enforcing the collective agreement and in resolving disputes about its interpretation or application? Can disagreements about participation in QWL programs divide the union's membership and create political problems for its officers?[87, 88, 89, 90]

Management may also question the philosophy and effectiveness of QWL programs. Will participation mean a loss of management prestige and authority? Are workers sufficiently knowledgeable to contribute to management decision making? Will participation bypass middle management and inhibit its development, or result in a loss of authority or power for frontline supervisors? Will employee participation and labor-management cooperation slow decision making and diffuse management accountability and responsibility? Will the union really be willing to give up restrictive work rules?[91, 92]

Because of these concerns, the services of a neutral consultant are often needed to aid in the start-up of QWL programs. At the earliest stages, the consultant usually holds separate meetings with labor and management to explore feelings about the new processes and structures. Later, intensive off-site joint meetings will be used to develop a climate of trust. The parties may be asked to participate in team building exercises and to prepare a statement of philosophy that defines their intentions and will guide their actions. A steering committee of an equal number union and management representatives will be established to plan and execute programs and to continuously monitor and expand them.[93]

The success of the QWL program depends on union and management consensus about the relative status of the QWL program and the collective bargaining agreement and process. In some organizations, the parties may decide to exclude the terms of the collective agreement from the jurisdiction of QWL programs. For example, Whatly and Hoffman report that the QWL program at the White Sands Missile Range excludes from discussions of participation teams such topics as pay, fringe benefits, job classifications, and other items contained in the collective agreement or subject to collective bargaining.[94]

On the other hand, there are some experts who believe that such guidelines could trivialize QWL by permitting only minor issues to be examined. They argue that the parties must be willing to allow the proposals and suggestions from joint committees to result in modifications to the collective bargaining agreement, either when negotiations are reopened or as memorandums of understanding attached to the present agreement.[95] For example, Rankin, and Rankin and Mansell believe that QWL and collective bargaining should be integrated because it is not possible to keep them apart.[96, 97] They propose that collective agreements be made sufficiently flexible to permit changes when the need arises, rather than only during the periods of renegotiations.

In their studies of labor-management cooperation and concession bargaining, Chaison and Plovnick found several successful uses of dual channels for collective bargaining and QWL.[98, 99, 100] The collective bargaining channel, made up of negotiating and grievance committees and staffed by union officers, was used for such distributive bargaining issues such as wages and benefits. A second, parallel channel of joint committees dealt with productivity improvement and joint decision making. The committees in this channel were staffed by employee representatives who might or might not have been union officers or members. In order to avoid conflict between the bargaining and the participation channels, managers and union officers had to respect the legitimacy of the two approaches.

Quality of work life must not be seen as a threat to the collective bargaining process or the status of the union as the representative of the employees. On the other hand, the parties should realize that QWL programs can change the bargaining process because, in these programs, parties share more information and deal with each other with greater trust. The union and management may find that they are adopting longer term and less combative perspectives when discussing issues. They may be willing to reopen negotiations in midterm if economic conditions demand it. Local unions may be more capable of settling issues without reliance on national union guidance. The parties may also be more willing to start negotiations early without the pressures of imminent contract expiration.[101]

CONCLUSIONS

Can major technological change occur in unionized companies? Is there a role for unions and collective bargaining in the automated factory? Based on recent trends described in this chapter, my answer would have to be yes.

The competitive pressures brought on by past recession, along with the continuing union membership declines and widespread concession bargaining, have made unions and employers more receptive to innovations in collective bargaining. This is most apparent in the accommodation of technological change through integrative bargaining. Many unions have demonstrated an acceptance of technologies and the relaxation of restrictive work rules, but with the critical proviso that job and income security is not threatened. There also appears to be a new openness to QWL programs in unionized enterprises. It is worth emphasizing once more that the successful introduction and diffusion of these programs occurs when they serve as supplements to, rather than substitutes for, the collective bargaining process.

The industrial relations system in the United States is in a period of great experimentation. Collective bargaining often coexists with forms of employee participation, and new work rules and work processes. QWL programs are becoming more widespread in unionized companies and are reaching higher levels of decision making. A new collective bargaining, with a greater emphasis on problem solving, is spreading from larger companies to smaller ones, and from firms in difficult economic condition to those experiencing growth and profits.

Union and management collaboration in dealing with the introduction and impact of new technology can be a major step toward a new system of industrial relations. The new approach could be based on parallel collective bargaining and QWL structures, and should involve extensive information sharing, flexible work rules, and union participation from the shop floor to strategic decision making committees. Those employers who are willing to be innovative in the design and operation of their factories should also be open to new approaches in their relationships with their unions and unionized workers.

ENDNOTES

1. D. E. Blum, "New Bargaining Units in 1987 Comprised Only Part-Time Professors and Assistant," *The Chronicles of Higher Education* (May 11, 1988):A18.

2. G. C. Rowan, "Canada's Unions Outpace U.S. Locals," *Boston Globe* (November 1, 1987):96-97.

3. L. Troy and N. Sheflin, *Union Sourcebook: Membership, Structure, Finance, Directory* (West Orange, New Jersey: Industrial Relations Data and Information Services, 1985). Data from 1960, 1970, and 1975-1984 found on page 3.10. Data for 1965 from G. S. Bain and R. J. Price, *Profiles of Union Growth* (Oxford: Blackwell, 1980):89. Note: The Troy and Sheflin series is a continuation of an earlier series developed for the National Bureau of Economic Research. The data are derived primarily from union financial reports and represent annual averages of full-time dues-paying union members.

4. United States Bureau of the Census, *Statistical Abstracts of the United States, 1987* (Washington, D.C.: United States Government Printing Office, 1987), 409 for data from 1983 to 1985. Data from 1986 and 1987 found in L. T. Adams, "Union Membership of Wage and Salary Employees in 1987," *Current Wage Developments* 39 (February 1988):6. Note: The CPS series is derived from a survey of households conducted by the Census Bureau for the Bureau of Labor Statistics. It covers employed wage and salary workers but excludes union members who are retired, self-employed, unemployed, or laid-off. Data were not collected for 1982 and an earlier series is not comparable with the post-1982 series.

5. G. N. Chaison, *When Unions Merge* (Lexington, Massachusetts: Lexington Books, 1986).

6. G. N. Chaison and J. B. Rose, "The State of the Unions Revisited: The United States and Canada," in H. M. Jain, ed., *Emerging Trends in Canadian Industrial Relations: Proceedings of the Twenty-fourth Annual Meeting of the Canadian Industrial Relations Association* (Hamilton, Ontario: Canadian Industrial Relations Association, 1988), 575-596.

7. T. C. Kochan and H. C. Katz, *Collective Bargaining and Industrial Relations*, Second Edition (Homewood, Illinois: Irwin, 1988).

8. T. C. Kochan, H. C. Katz, and R. B. McKersie, *The Transformation of American Industrial Relations* (New York: Basic Books, 1986).

9. D. J. B. Mitchell, "Alternative Explanations of Union Wage Concessions," *California Management Review* (Fall, 1986): 95-108.

10. G. N. Chaison and J. B. Rose, "Continental Divide: The Direction and Fate of North American Unions," *Advances in Industrial and Labor Relations* (forthcoming).

11. Chaison, "Continental Divide," *Advances in Industrial and Labor Relations*.

12. L. T. Adams, "Union Membership of Wage and Salary Employees in 1987," *Current Wage Developments* 39 (February 1988): 4-9.

13. J. B. Rose and G. N. Chaison, "New Measures of Union Organizing Effectiveness," *Industrial Relations* (forthcoming).

14. Chaison, "Continental Divide," *Advances in Industrial and Labor Relations*.

15. R. B. Freeman, "Contraction and Expansion: The Divergence of Private Sector and Public Sector Unionism in the United States," *Journal of Economic Perspectives* 2 (Spring 1988): 63-88.

16. Freeman, "Contraction and Expansion," *Journal of Economic Perspectives*, 63-88.

17. Kochan, *Transformation of Industrial Relations*.

18. H. S. Farber, "The Recent Decline of Unionization in the United States," *Science* 238 (November 13, 1987): 915-920.

19. Freeman, "Contraction and Expansion," 63-88.

20. S. M. Lipset, "Comparing Canadian and American Unions," *Society* 24 (January/February 1987): 60-70.

21. S. Rubenfeld, "Today's Contract Concessions: Tomorrow's Impact," Working Paper No. 83-6, Bureau of Business and Economic Research (Duluth, Minnesota: University of Minnesota, March 1983).

22. U.S. Bureau of Census, *Statistical Abstracts, 1987*.

23. Kochan, *Transformation of Industrial Relations*.

24. International Metalworkers Federation, *Changing Patterns of Collective Bargaining* (Geneva: International Metalworkers Federation, 1986).

25. D. H. Kruger, "Profit Sharing Arrangements and Collective Bargaining," in *Proceedings of the Thirty-Ninth Annual Meeting of the Industrial Relations Research Association* (Madison, Wisconsin: Industrial Relations Research Association, 1986) 152-158.

26. J. L. Zalusky, "Gainsharing, Profitsharing: Labor's Mixed Experience," *Work in America* 12 (March 1987): 2-4.

27. A. R. Karr, "Striking Out: Labor Unions' Chance for Gains in '88 Hits a Wall of Resistance," *Wall Street Journal* (June 29, 1988): 1, 17.

28. Mitchell, "Union Wage Concessions," 95-108.

29. Bureau of National Affairs, *1988 Employer Bargaining Objectives* (Washington, D.C.: Bureau of National Affairs, 1987).

30. Bureau of National Affairs, *1988 Objectives*, 1.

31. Bureau of National Affairs, *1988 Objectives*.

32. G. N. Chaison and R. C. Bradbury, "Local Union Support for Health Care Cost Containment: A Cooperative Strategy to Promote Competition and Choice," *New England Journal of Human Services* VII (1987): 27-28.

33. M. S. Plovnick and G. N. Chaison, "An Analysis of Concession Bargaining and Labor-Management Cooperation," *Academy of Management Journal* 28 (September 1985): 697-704.

34. B. E. Becker, "Concession Bargaining: The Meaning of Union Gains," *Academy of Management Journal* 31 (June 1988): 377-386.

35. M. Schuster, *Union-Management Cooperation: Structure, Process, Impact* (Kalamazoo, Michigan: Upjohn, 1984).

36. D. J. B. Mitchell, "Recent Union Contract Concessions," *Brookings Papers on Economic Activity* (1982): 163-204.

37. Rubenfield, "Today's Concessions: Tomorrow's Impact." University of Minnesota.

38. Mitchell, "Alternative Explanations of Union Wage Concessions," 105.

39. Mitchell, "Alternative Explanations," 105.

40. G. N. Chaison and M. S. Plovnick, "Is There a New Collective Bargaining," *California Management Review* 28 (Summer 1986): 54-61.

41. R. E. Walton and R. B. McKersie, *A Behavioral Theory of Labor Negotiations* (New York: McGraw-Hill, 1965).

42. S. Early and M. Witt, "How European Unions Cope With New Technology," *Monthly Labor Review* 105 (September 1982): 36-38.

43. J. Cutcher-Gershenfeld, "The Collective Governance of Industrial Relations," in *Proceedings of the Fortieth Annual Meeting of the Industrial Relations Research Association* (Madison, Wisconsin: Industrial Relations Research Association, 1987), 533-543.

44. C. Sims, "Unions Offer Labor Help on Automation" *New York Times* (October 21, 1987): D10.

45. A. Majchrzak, *The Human Side of Factory Automation* (San Francisco: Jossey-Bass, 1988).

46. P. Willman, "Industrial Relations Issues in Advanced Manufacturing Technology," in T. D. Wall, C. W. Clegg, and N. J. Kemp, eds., *The Human Side of Advanced Manufacturing Technology* (Chichester, U.K.: Wiley, 1987), 135-152.

47. Karl-H. Ebel, "The Impact of Industrial Robots on the World of Work," *International Labor Review* 125 (January-February 1986): 39-52.

48. Early, "European Unions Cope with New Technology," 36-38.

49. R. Ayres and S. Miller, "Industrial Robots on the Line," *Technology Review* 85 (May/June 1982): 34-47.

50. T. R. Knight and D. C. McPhillips, "Public Policy and Collective Bargaining Responses to New Technology," in *Proceedings of the Thirty-Ninth Annual Meeting of the Industrial Relations Research Association* (Madison, Wisconsin: Industrial Relations Research Association, 1986), 455-462.

51. R. S. Parks, "Bargaining Over the Introduction of Robots in The Workplace," *San Diego Law Review* 21 (September/October 1984): 1135-1150.

52. A. G. Rosenberg, "Automation and the Work Preservation Doctrine: Accommodating Productivity and Job Security Interests," *UCLA Law Review* 32 (1984) 135-176.

53. Knight, "Public Policy and Collective Bargaining," 455-462.

54. United States Congress, Office of Technology Assessment, *Computerized Manufacturing Automation: Employment, Education and the Workplace* (Washington, D.C.: United States Government Printing Office, 1984).

55. R. D. Weikle and H. N. Wheeler, "Unions and Technological Change: Attitudes of Local Union Leaders," in *Proceedings of the Thirty-Sixth Annual Meeting of the Industrial Relations Research Association* (Madison, Wisconsin: Industrial Relations Research Association, 1984), 100-106.

56. Bureau of National Affairs, *Basic Patterns in Union Contracts*, Tenth Edition (Washington, D.C.: Bureau of National Affairs, 1983).

57. Bureau of National Affairs, *Collective Bargaining Negotiations and Contracts* (Washington, D.C.: Bureau of National Affairs, 1988), 65.121-124.

58. "Wage Highlights," *Current Wage Developments* 39 (March 1987): 1-3.

59. "Wage Highlights," 1-3.

60. D. N. Smith and P. Heyter, Jr., *Industrial Robots: Forecasts and Trends* (Dearborn, Michigan: Society of Manufacturing Engineers, 1985).

61. Bureau of National Affairs, *Basic Patterns in Union Contracts*.

62. Ayres, "Industrial Robots on the Line," 34-37.

63. Kochan, *Transformation of Industrial Relations*.

64. Kochan, *Collective Bargaining*, 383.

65. J. Holusha, "A New Spirit at U.S. Auto Plants," *New York Times* (December 29, 1987): D1, D5.

66. United States Department of Labor, Bureau of Labor-Management Relations and Cooperative Programs, *Cooperative Partnership: A New Beginning for National Steel Corporation and the United Steelworkers of America*, Report BLMR 114, (Washington, D.C.: United States Government Printing Office, 1987).

67. D. D. Luria, "New Labor-Management Models from Detroit," *Harvard Business Review* 64 (September-October 1986): 22-23, 26, 28, 30.

68. International Metalworkers Federation, *Changing Patterns of Collective Bargaining*.

69. International Metalworkers Federation, *Changing Patterns*.

70. R. D. Sibbernsen, "What Arbitrators Think About Technology Facing Labor," *Harvard Business Review* 64 (March/April 1986): 8-10,12,14,16.

71. *Memorandum of Agreement Between Saturn Corporation and the United Automobile Workers* (Unpublished, 1985), p. 16.

72. Holusha, "A New Spirit at U.S. Auto Plants."

73. *Memorandum of Agreement Between Saturn Corporation and the UAW*, p. 9.

74. A. Taylor, "Back to the Future at Saturn," *Fortune* (August 1, 1988): 63-64, 68, 72.

75. Kochan, *Collective Bargaining*.

76. T. Rankin and J. Mansell, "Integrating Collective Bargaining and New Forms of Work Organization," *National Productivity Review* 5 (Autumn 1986): 342.

77. "Pay for Knowledge Study Challenges Some Myths," *Work in America* 12 (May 1987): 6-7.

78. W. J. Gershenfeld, "Employee Participation in Firm Decisions," in M. M. Kleiner, R. N. Block, and M. Roomkin, and S. Salsburg, eds., *Human Resources and the Performance of the Firm* (Madison, Wisconsin: Industrial Relations Research Association, 1987), 124.

79. W. C. Freund and E. Epstein, *People and Productivity: The New York Stock Exchange Guide to Financial Incentives and the Quality of Worklife* (Homewood, Illinois: Dow Jones-Irwin, 1984).

80. Y. Reshef, "Changing Environments and Management IR Practices," *Relations Industrielles* 43 (1988): 43-61.

81. Kochan, *Collective Bargaining*.

82. Cutcher-Gershenfeld, "The Collective Governance of Industrial Relations," 533-543.

83. Kochan, *Collective Bargaining*.

84. Cutcher-Gershenfeld, "Collective Governance," 533-543.

85. I. Bluestone, "Job Action and Collective Bargaining—and Vice Versa," in J. M. Rosow, ed., *Teamwork: Joint Labor-Management Programs in America* (New York: Pergamon, 1986), 47.

86. T. C. Kochan, H. C. Katz, and N. C. Mower, *Worker Participation and American Unions* (Kalamazoo, Michigan: Upjohn, 1984), 158.

87. J. G. Belcher, "The Role of Unions in Productivity Management," *Personnel* 65 (January 1988): 54-58.

88. C. Gold, *Labor-Management Committees: Confrontation, Cooptation, or Cooperation?*, Key Issues Number 29, (Ithaca, New York: Cornell University, ILR Press, 1986).

89. Kochan, *Worker Participation and American Unions*.

90. R. A. Oswald, "Joint Labor-Management Programs: A Labor Viewpoint," in J. M. Rosow, ed., *Teamwork: Joint Labor-Management Programs in America* (New York: Pergamon, 1986), 26-40.

91. Gold, *Labor-Management Committees*.

92. M. Schuster, "Cooperation and Change in Union Settings: Problems and Opportunities," *Human Resource Management* 23 (Summer 1984): 145-160.

93. Belcher, "Role of Unions in Productivity Management," 54-58.

94. A. A. Whatly and W. Hoffman, "Quality Circles Earn Union Respect," *Personnel Journal* 66 (December 1987): 89-93.

95. Gold, *Labor-Management Committees*.

96. T. Rankin, "Integrating QWL and Collective Bargaining," *The World of Work Review* 5 (July 1986): 22-27.

97. Rankin and Marshall, "Integrating Collective Bargaining and New Forms of Work Organization," 338-347.

98. G. N. Chaison and M. S. Plovnick, "How Concessions and Cooperation Affect Labor-Management Relations," *Personnel* 61 (November-December 1984): 57-59.

99. Chaison and Plovnick, "Is There a New Collective Bargaining," 54-61.

100. Chaison and Plovnick, "An Analysis of Concession Bargaining and Labor-Management Cooperation," 697-704.

101. T. D. Jick, R. McKersie, and L. Greenhalgh, "A Process Analysis of Labor-Management Committee Problem Solving," in *Proceedings of the Thirty-Fifth Annual Meeting of the Industrial Relations Research Association* (Madison, Wisconsin: Industrial Relations Research Association, 1982), 182-188.

BIBLIOGRAPHY

Bain, G. S. and R. J. Price. *Profiles of Union Growth* Oxford: Blackwell, 1980.

Bernstein, A., and W. Zellner. "Detroit vs. the UAW: At Odds Over Teamwork." *Business Week* (August 24, 1987): 54-55.

Bluestone, I. "QWL Warms Up the Climate for Negotiating." *The Pulse Report* 2 (June 1983): 3.

Chaison, G. N. and J. B. Rose. "The State of the Unions: United States and Canada." *Journal of Labor Research* VI (Winter 1985): 97-111.

Chamot, D. "Integrated Manufacturing—The Partners: Employees, Indispensable Elements." *Production Engineering* 31 (September 1984): 106-109.

Donn, C. B. and D. B. Lipsky. "Collective Bargaining in American Industry." In D. B. Lipsky and C. B. Donn eds. *Collective Bargaining in American Industry*. Lexington, Massachusetts: Lexington Books, 1988, 307-332.

Kochan, T. C. and H. C. Katz. "Collective Bargaining, Work Organization and Worker Participation: The Return to Plant Level Bargaining." *Labor Law Journal* 34 (August 1983): 524-530.

United States Department of Labor, Bureau of Labor-Management Relations and Cooperative Programs. *U.S. Labor Law and the Future of Labor-Management Cooperation.* Washington, D.C.: United States Government Printing Office, 1986.

10

Worker Incentives and Automation in Manufacturing

Klaus Weiermair*

FACTORY AUTOMATION IS, OF COURSE, NOT A RECENT phenomenon. Throughout the 1950s and 1960s, factories in many industrialized countries in various sectors—particularly those producing steel, machinery, chemical products and transportation equipment—introduced new mechanical production processes that could mass-produce large quantities of a single or a few materials with less manpower. These processes were automated in the sense that production could proceed automatically without much human intervention, provided no problems arose. Automation was typically used for single, repetitive, and sequential operations requiring low levels of information transfer. More complex operations with heavy information transfer could not be automated and hence, for the time being, remained under direct control of workers.

Spurred by a variety of demand factors—including high prices for labor and energy, demand for specialized products with smaller production runs, and intensified international competition—and by a forthcoming advance in computer technology, a new phase of automation started in the 1970s based on integrated circuits, the combination of machines and electronics. Electronic technology made it possible to produce a wide range of products in smaller quantities using the same technology. This type of automation soon became labeled as *factory automa-*tion or the *fully automated factory*. Sometimes it was also called computer integrated manufacturing (CIM).

When we examine factory automation more closely, however, we discover many different forms having varied effects on work organization and organization design, and thus on worker incentives. The general categories into which these forms fall include: numerically controlled machine tools; machining centers; computer aided design, manufacturing and inspection; and flexible manufacturing systems.

Numerically Controlled Machine Tools (NCMT) These NCMTs can be operated by a central computer or a person and are programmable for different uses. As a rule they have no feedback mechanism. Robots are programmable maaipulators, which, depending on their capability, can be divided into the following subcategories:

- *Fixed sequence robots*: manipulators that perform a series of actions in a set sequence, under set conditions, and at set positions, none of which can easily be changed
- *Variable sequence robots*: manipulators where sequence, position, and conditions can all be easily changed

---

*Klaus Weiermair is Professor of Economics, Faculty of Administrative Studies, at York University, Toronto and a Visiting Professor at Chuo University, Tokyo.

- *Play back robots*: manipulators that play back a series of actions that have been first performed manually
- *Numerically controlled robots*: robots that perform various actions as directed by a computer
- *Intelligent robots*: robots that decide their actions on the basis of sensory and recognition functions

Machining Centers   Machining centers are sets of flexible and complementary NCMTs, often with attached automatic handling and conveyer systems. These centers perform a large variety of interrelated operations.

Computer Aided Design, Manufacturing, and Inspection (CAD/CAM)   CAD/CAM consists of a series of computers, information transmission systems, and machines. Usually an engineer constructs a computer design in which the computer selects the machinery, methods, and parts needed to produce the designed product, calculates the time and costs, and subsequently transmits the information to the NCMT and robots that perform the manufacturing. Finally, the computer inspects the finished product for errors.

Flexible Manufacturing Systems   These are integrated systems of industrial robots, NCMTs, machining centers, automatic measuring instruments, and unmanned handling and transport systems under computer control that allow the manufacturing of a great variety of products.

Different emerging manufacturing systems and philosophies such as Just-in-Time (JIT), statistical process control (SPC), material requirement planning (MRP), and total quality control (TQC), while of considerable importance and concern to management (Aggarwal 1985), should be viewed and understood as subsets or combinations of the aforementioned categories of factory automation. As of today, few fully automated factories exist. Also, the types and extent of automation vary widely across firms, industries, and countries.

The first factor that determines the level of automation and consequences for work organization can be found in a firm's general strategy. Choice of technology appears to be closely linked to firms' explicit or implicit decisions regarding their manufacturing strategies and missions (Richardson, Taylor, and Gordon 1985). Thus, a new product-centered strategy is likely to involve a very different technological configuration than a strategy centered solely around minimizing cost.

Each strategy, in turn, has different implications for work organization. For example, highly integrated complex technologies based on a new product-centered manufacturing strategy (such as may be the case with communication systems), will require much more from the company's software and humanware systems in terms of technical skills than would be the case with a simple labor cost minimization manufacturing strategy. Variances in work organization are, therefore, not only determined by differences in technological configuration, but also by manufacturing strategies that predetermine the mix of hardware, software, and humanware. FIGURE 10-1 expresses this concept schematically. When making intraindustry, interindustry, or even international comparisons on the consequences of automation for such things as

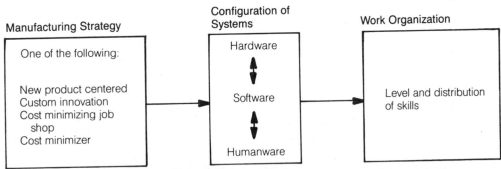

Fig. 10-1. Manufacturing strategy, configuration of systems, and work organization.

work configuration, skill levels, and worker satisfaction, analysts must take utmost care to use similar situations with respect to manufacturing technology and strategy.

After the firm's general strategy, socio-cultural forces are the next important determinant in the level and diffusion of automation and its consequences for work organization. These forces will be discussed in detail in the section on international differences. Socio-cultural forces are often cited as important in discussions of countries such as Japan, where a mushrooming literature describes the specifics of the country's employment and production system (Cole 1979). On the other hand, there have been relatively few attempts at integrating socio-cultural variables into a general theory of employment relations. Exceptions can be found in the Marxian-tradition Braverman (1974) and in the works of Shalev (1980) and Weiermair (1985).

In earlier work, I have shown how social and political dimensions affect labor market characteristics, evolving forms of employment relations, forms and levels of worker participation, and personnel strategies of companies. These effects, in turn, feed back into labor market and societal values through output characteristics such as labor productivity and labor quality (Weiermair 1985, 558). I take a somewhat similar approach here with respect to the adoption and implementation of new technology.

Schematically, the relationship between cultural determinants and employment is shown in FIG. 10-2. As is shown in the diagram, socio-cultural factors exercise both a direct and indirect (through

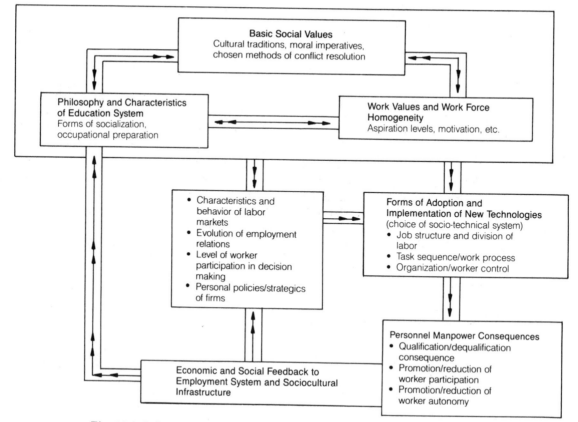

Fig. 10-2. Influence of sociocultural factors upon the level and form of technology.

labor market and employment system) influence upon the level and form of technology adopted. Socio-cultural determinants that directly influence the ways and forms of automation include: varying social views, expectations and evaluations regarding the benefits of automation among different countries, differences in the way a society handles the resolution of conflict among rivaling interest groups (capital, labor, and management), and time horizon of problem analysis and solution. These factors can also exert a secondary influence through the employment system, such as through alternate patterns of employment and composition of worker qualifications (Maurice et al. 1980; Sorge et al. 1983), differences in the distribution of power and control in the work place (Francis et al. 1983) and the evolution and prevalence of different organization cultures (Ouchi 1980).

This introduction has shown the embeddedness of the "humanware" dimension in the process of technological change and automation. Let us now turn to discussing the rise in the importance of humanware within manufacturing and manufacturing automation.

WORKER MOTIVATION: A New Production Factor in Today's Manufacturing

This section advances the hypothesis that motivation, effort, and quality of work have reemerged as new and important factors in production. Closely related to this is my second contention that, today, work incentives and work organization matter more than they ever have before. Supporting evidence comes from observations on global restructuring and competition, as well as from theoretical and empirical research on the subject matter.

Restructuring Industrialized Nation Manufacturing

Leading national and international economic agencies and data gathering institutions have gathered evidence that suggests that most industrialized countries, including the United States, are currently in a process of massive industrial restructuring toward higher value added and service intensive products (Porter et al. 1986; OECD, 1985). In turn, this has led to new forms of work organization and altered systems of motivation resulting in processes of organizational adaptation and change. Restructuring has met with considerable and varying difficulties across industries and countries. Several key factors have contributed to recent restructuring and the changed economic context of organizational functioning:

- The development of a global economy
- An acceleration of technological change and its diffusion across the market place, particularly in such fields as information technologies
- The transformation of industrial output and changes through the new service economy

Thus, it has become commonplace to speak of the evolution of a global economy. For example, in manufacturing, raw materials are being sourced in one part of the globe, manufactured in a second, and assembled in a third. Liberalized international trade and investment has led to an "internalization of the market for production location" (Braendgaard 1983, 174). This liberalization in turn enables multinational companies to invest capital so as to maximize their comparative advantage at each stage of the production cycle.

As a result, third world sources now threaten the production of mass-volume, unsophisticated products. As has been pointed out by Reich and others, "Whatever the final product, those parts of its production requiring high volume machinery and unsophisticated workers can now be accomplished more cheaply in developing nations" (Reich 1983). Earlier and lower cost technology transfers across firms, industries, and jurisdictions combined with shortened product cycles have made these changes more rapid and more uncertain.

In turn, industrialized jurisdictions, notably North America, now need new, sophisticated products in line with their changing comparative advantage: human capital intensive products and production processes. Indeed, one might argue that skilled labor remains the only production dimension where developed economies can retain a competitive advantage. However, high technology production is based on innovation and cooperation. Innovation identifies new needs; cooperation designs the products and brings them to the market. The new and successful product markets such as computers, precision casting, specialty steel, and specialty chemicals of bio-engineering (Piore and Sabel 1984) all rely ''on the development function within teams of sophisticated employee skills, merging the traditionally separate business functions of design, engineering, production and marketing into new flexible systems of production (Reich 1983, 46). Cooperative approaches are necessary when solving new problems rather than routinizing old ones and when highly integrated systems must respond quickly to new opportunities (Davis 1979). They rest on people working together closely; both innovation and cooperation are people skills requiring new forms of work organization and reward systems (Hackman and Oldham 1980).

The Changing World of Information Processing

The second major change in the manufacturing environment revolves around the rapid diffusion of information processing technologies. CAD/CAM technologies in manufacturing and computerization in office work both change the occupational composition of employment (OECD 1985) and the design of organizations. In fact, a recent issue of *Interfaces* (Ettlie 1987; Meredith 1987) devoted its entire volume to a comprehensive discussion of changes in the design and architecture of work and jobs resulting from automation in manufacturing systems.

In spite of these changes, some controversy remains over the relative importance of technology in determining the design of work organizations. A good and frequently cited example is that of maintenance skills in manufacturing. The introduction of automatic diagnostics routines to electronic controls could either lead to a stronger division of labor

and polarization of skills by de-skilling maintenance workers, or, alternatively, a flatter organization due to augmenting and upgrading the skills of operators and maintenance workers (Senker and Swords-Isherwood 1980). Many researchers have therefore concluded that the extent of technological change and the associated alterations in work organization and skill structure mainly result from varying policies and strategies of firms (Senker and Beesley 1986; Brady 1986; Gunn 1987).

Research particularly discusses, on the one hand, the relationship between the firm's desired type of worker control and associated options of organizational structuring (Francis 1986, 104-130), and, on the other hand, the firms' varying perceptions of short and long run competitive advantages in manufacturing (Porter 1985; Hayes and Wheelwright 1979; Frohman 1985). Transaction cost arguments in favor of tighter worker control, reduced worker skills, more standardization, and more hierarchy as advanced by Williamson and followers (Williamson 1980 and 1985) often tend to focus on the past. As such, these arguments serve as ex-post rationalizations of efficient decision making by management.

Against this stand are the strategic management theoretical perspectives, which are forward-looking and which consider differing manufacturing options, including the design of work organization, as strategic alternatives. The majority of disciples in this camp have concluded that new technologies must be accompanied by improvements in the software and humanware systems of organizations. As Jelinek and Goldhar have pointed out,

Manufacturing is no longer simply responsible for delivering what marketing demands or engineering designs; manufacturing and its capabilities have become increasingly central to the strategic positioning of the firm. Manufacturing now involves the management of:

- Enormous amounts of information about products and their underlying engineering and design characteristics, about production processes, and about the ever-increasing science base of manufacturing

- Important interfaces with other areas of the firm, with customers, and with suppliers
- The strategic capabilities of the firm

Fewer people will be needed for operations, but they must be better trained and more highly skilled. Many more better trained and highly skilled people will be needed for operations management, analysis, engineering design, and support activities—positions that are now typically thought of as staff jobs or even as luxuries. Software management will be crucial. (Jelinek and Goldham 1984, 35).

We concur that managers will have to provide workers with broader training if they want to receive the greatest benefits of automation. Undoubtedly, this is likely to cause greater problems in countries with long traditions of controlling the work force through de-skilling, such as may have been the case in the United States and the United Kingdom. The American car industry learned recent and bitter lessons with its skill problems on account of past de-skilling. These problems, however, have served as a useful first lesson. Even if the issue of international competitiveness could be discounted, there are a number of other factors, particularly regarding changes in social values, that equally call for work designs congruent with worker demands. They will be discussed next.

CHANGING SOCIAL VALUES, CHANGING TECHNOLOGIES, AND IMPLICATIONS FOR STRUCTURING INCENTIVES

A good starting point for discussing the impact of varying social values, forces, and characteristics is provided by Hackman and Oldham's conceptualization of interrelationships among job characteristics, critical psychological states of job incumbents, and motivational outcomes or performance. FIGURE 10-3 shows their job characteristics model.

Based on empirical results, Hackman and Oldham show in their book, *Work Redesign*, how appropriate designs in the organization of work and jobs create high levels of motivation. They are particularly concerned with factors that lead to workers wanting to do jobs well because of intrinsic satisfac-

tion from doing the work. They relate this internal or intrinsic motivation—as opposed to extrinsic motivation based on monetary rewards—to the amount of variety in work, the amount of interaction required in carrying out task activities, the level of knowledge and skill required, and the amount of responsibility entrusted to the jobholder. High intrinsic motivation in turn affects other correlates such as high degree of job satisfaction, low levels of absenteeism, and low turnover. Important to the earlier discussion of social values is the role of moderators; these moderators, as depicted in FIG. 10-3, can influence both job characteristics and job outcomes, most notably motivation.

As to the first moderator, *variable knowledge and skill level*, we can observe a steady, long-term increase in education and qualification levels among all workers, but especially younger workers, throughout the industrialized world. Educated people, furthermore, have a higher demand for intrinsically rewarding jobs, such as jobs that have the characteristics shown in FIG. 10-3. Thus, there has been considerable pressure on employers to restructure jobs on account of changing job expectations among younger and more educated employees. The model should, at the same time, also remind us of the considerable difficulties in providing adequate jobs for and motivating older and less educated workers.

The second moderator, *growth need strength*, is closely interrelated with the rise in levels of educational attainment among workers. It displays, however, additional variability on account of individual worker characteristics and organizational context. Emphasis on self-actualization and individual growth are positive correlates of socialization at school and educational exposure. The latter dimensions of worker characteristics and organizational contexts are considered as the third moderator of motivation. In addition, they depend on the whole process of setting individual levels of aspiration (Maslow 1970). Behavioral scientists agree that, throughout the postwar period, values changed in the direction of greater demands for individual growth and self-actualization (Mitchell and MacNulty 1981). Viewed from a broad perspective it

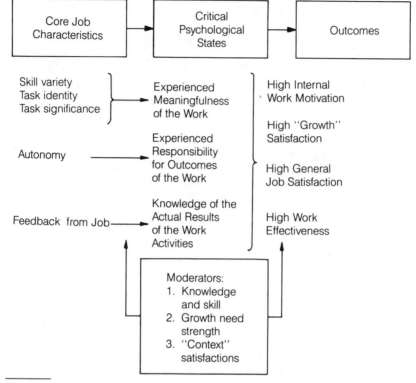

Source: Hackman & Oldham, *Work Redesign* (Reading, Massachusetts: Addison-Wesley, 1980) 90.

Fig. 10-3. The job characteristics model.

appears then that workers have shown an increasing interest in more motivating jobs.

In the previous section of this chapter, I showed that motivation has become an important factor in production and a competitive element in manufacturing strategy. Why then have organizations been so slow in applying sound principles of job design particularly when engaged in major technical or organizational restructuring on account of automation? To answer this question, one has to raise the issue of conflicting interests with different forms of work organization among capital and labor. Put differently, one has to consider work organization from the vantage of conflicting perspectives regarding organizational and managerial control. This will be undertaken in the next section, where I discuss organizational control alternatives under varying environmental constraints.

NEW TECHNOLOGY, WORK DESIGN, AND WORKER PARTICIPATION

Previous sections of this chapter have shown that in order to remain competitive, manufacturing organizations not only need strategies that keep them on the technological edge requiring the latest form of automated equipment, but they also require a highly committed, skilled, and motivated work force. Employees are generally willing to make these kinds of job and work commitments provided they are offered properly designed jobs. Organizations have to weigh the costs and benefits of varying degrees of worker participation with the economic benefits stemming from alternate forms of information processing and organizational control (Galbraith 1977). In addition, they have to contend with union interests and pressures. It would go far beyond the scope of this chapter to describe all the competing and often contradictory research on the interrelationship between changing technology and work organization. For a more thorough treatment see Francis (1986). Rather, I limit myself to those statements about work organization effects of technological change for which there is a relatively wide consensus. In so doing I include reported results from research on automation in manufacturing, leaving out the widely researched field of office automation.

Work Organization Changes

The research reports three major changes in work organization: changes in managerial tasks, changes in professional and technical work, and changes in clerical and secretarial work. Managerial work is being affected in three different ways. First, as the amount of routine to nonroutine work declines with the amount of automated equipment, a number of management jobs at the lower echelons cease to exist. These are usually jobs concerned with checking through figures or securing data on the control of people or functions. Second, managers are seeing an increase in the amount of capital and the diversity of people they control while the total number of workers supervised—the control span—has somewhat declined (Zink 1983; Hackstein 1985; Senker and Beesley 1986). Third, the level of qualifications among those to be supervised by the average manager has increased as a consequence of technical changes (Senker and Beesley 1986).

The change in the nature of managerial work stemming from successive waves of automation is most aptly described in the account of a British electronics factory manager, provided in Francis (1986, 133-134). The manager's account reads as follows:

Fifteen years ago, he remarked, he was in charge of several hundred women making electronic valves. His main concern was to ensure high productivity from each operator and his obsessions were with turnover, absenteeism, and the bonus system. The product technology changed and the women then made transistors. This involved the use of some capital equipment

and his concerns then had to include the maintenance of this. Now the transistors are produced by almost wholly automated machinery. There is only a handful of production operators within the production manager's responsibility, but he now also has large groups of technical people responsible for the operation of the automated equipment. Turnover and absenteeism are no longer the big issues, and the bonus system is virtually irrelevant to the productivity of the machines. His task is now that of managing this complex production process and its relations with other departments in the factory, such as materials supply, sales, and the finance department.

The prescriptive perspectives of both organization and industrial relations theory suggest that there has to be a change in the style and substance of supervision following the change in technology. The new demands described above call for an abandonment of direct controls and the *Tayloristic* methods of management, to be replaced by a strategy of *responsible autonomy*. With responsible autonomy, subordinates carry out more complex tasks not directly paced by the assembly line, and that require more autonomy and more trust between manager and subordinate (Walton 1985).

Professional and technical work demonstrate changes in job structures and work organization in three different ways as well. First, new technologies and automation frequently increase the complexity of production (CAD/CAM and CMTs in engineering firms), so different technical groups have to work more closely together. This requires some new form of organizational linkage. Second, automation may create a new division of labor when new technical jobs are added to the job structure—such as the introduction of parts programmers with the advent of CMTs. Third, there is the possibility of increased skill polarization and the associated de-skilling for certain types of jobs—like welding, which is being replaced by welding robots.

In the office the most pronounced change in clerical and secretarial work is the tremendous rise in productivity associated with computerization. Work organization changes often result in renegotiating the division of labor among management, clerical, and technical workers. Clerical workers might become semi-skilled operatives working in typing pools with limited access to the computer. Or, they might handle more complex tasks using software and more extensive computer applications associated with word processing, such as lower level accounting and statistical work, which can be done through computer access.

Changes in Management Control and Worker Participation

While behavioral scientists may agree on how new technologies ought to be implemented with respect to work organization, encouragement of worker participation, or boosting of worker motivation, real changes in the workplace ultimately depend on the way management wants to use new technologies. Traditional economic and efficiency analyses failed, in the past, to incorporate behavioral performance measures. This failure may help explain why firms were slow in shedding Tayloristic management control principles and practices. Leibenstein's path breaking contributions of X-efficiency theory—which incorporates concepts of work effort and motivation (Leibenstein 1976)—and its implications for comparative analyses of organizational advantage and management (Tomer 1987, Leibenstein and Weiermair 1988), eventually may help replace the orthodox analyses of efficiency that are closely linked to orthodox theories of management (Weiermair 1985).

Union interests in the introduction and use of new technologies, including automation, vary in attitudes and behaviors across different union jurisdictions and different countries. Again, it would go far beyond the scope of this chapter to describe all such differences. I will only report on major joint research efforts and findings from a few industrialized countries. First of all, massive evidence from Canada, the United States, Japan, and many European countries suggests that unions are not, per se, opposed to the introduction of new technologies. On average, only two to four percent of all unions are opposed to the introduction of new technologies. Unions are more concerned with the ways in which technologies are introduced, particularly

regarding consultation, negotiation, and specification of technology provisions in collective agreements. This is where international differences become more marked. Japan and some European countries (notably the Scandinavian countries and West Germany) show much more elaborate, at times legally prescribed, procedures for joint consultation and conflict resolution regarding the introduction of new technologies (Japan Institute of Labor 1985; Takahashi 1988; Sorge et al. 1983; TUC 1979; Economic Council of Canada 1987; Rothwell and Zegveld 1979).

One major implication of the analysis above, on the face of it, is that Taylorism as a form of management control will eventually die. Effective control will instead depend on management's ability to devise more systems which can generate more complex, high-trust forms of organizational arrangements suitable to fulfill both worker demands and organizational objectives. In the next two sections, I discuss major differences in managerial strategies and tactics toward new technology. In so doing I employ stereotype comparisons between X and Z—American and Japanese types of management systems.

AUTOMATION AND REWARD AND INCENTIVE SYSTEMS UNDER ALTERNATE ORGANIZATION DESIGN: Two Polar Cases

Two management system design prototypes to be discussed below are well known in both the behavioral science literature and the popular business press. Ouchi (1981) has labeled them X and Z or J-type organizations. Industrial psychologists often speak of mechanistic or X-type versus organic or dynamic (Z-type) organizations (Walton 1985). Peters and Waterman's description of corporate excellence essentially covers Z-type organizations to be found in the United States (Peters and Waterman 1982). Given the much greater prevalence of Z-style management among large Japanese companies, this form of management and organization is often being used synonymously with the Japanese form of management (Tomer 1985). We are confronted with accounts of Japanese companies who combine advance technology with thorough training participative management, lean organizations with respect to number of hierarchies and decision making pushed as close as possible to the assembly line.

The two extremes where a company is either managed like an asset (X-type) or an organization of people (Z-variety) can also be characterized in terms of management's ability to strike a psychological contract with its employees. An implicit psychological contract or interpersonal contract "relates a set of mutual expectations concerning performance, roles, trust and influence" and it specifies "what each should contribute to a relationship

tionship and what each should get out of it" (Gabarro 1979, 10). Tomer (1987) has portrayed implicit psychological contracts and their organizational correlates along a spectrum, with X and Z management styles forming the two extreme polar cases, as shown in FIG. 10-4.

On the left side of FIG. 10-4 we find the tightly controlled organization. Here, workers only display short term attachment to their jobs and management equally has a short term attachment to their workers. Employees perform according to tightly specified work contracts, which are explicit and only specify extrinsic economic rewards. The management style is autocratic. At the other extreme we find a supportive, participatory management

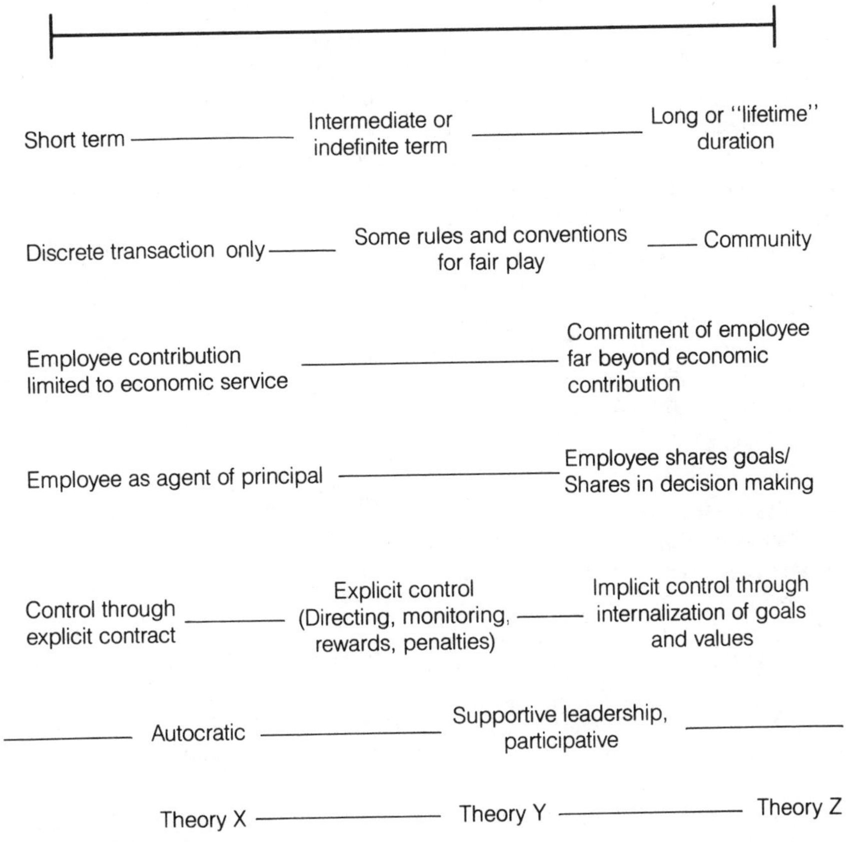

Fig. 10-4. Implicit psychological contract spectrum.

Short term ———— Intermediate or indefinite term ———— Long or "lifetime" duration

Discrete transaction only ——— Some rules and conventions for fair play ——— Community

Employee contribution limited to economic service ——— Commitment of employee far beyond economic contribution

Employee as agent of principal ——— Employee shares goals/ Shares in decision making

Control through explicit contract ——— Explicit control (Directing, monitoring, rewards, penalties) ——— Implicit control through internalization of goals and values

———— Autocratic ———— Supportive leadership, participative ————

Theory X ———— Theory Y ———— Theory Z

Source: Tomer, *Organizational Capital* (New York: Praeger, 1987), 75.

style coupled with a strong corporate culture and/or philosophy providing for implicit controls of employees who internalize these values. Relations at the workplace are wholistic and community-like rather than being uniquely determined by economic relations. Careers are characterized by nonspecialization (frequent job rotation and general training) and slow evaluation and promotion. Decision making and responsibility are more collective in nature, and are based on consensus.*

Japan has gone through two major waves of rationalization without any obvious negative consequences: one following the oil crisis in 1973 that involved most of its heavy industries, and the other the present automation and robotization of most of its manufacturing sectors. This success certainly would not have been possible in an environment of adversarial industrial relations and autocratic management. Let me offer further empirical proof that worker participation lowers opportunistic behavior of workers and management, increases productivity, and thus, in Williamson's terminology, lowers transaction cost—or in Leibenstein's terminology increases X-efficiency. Studies in West Germany show that, in certain firms, participation has become codified (Cable and FitzRoy 1980a and 1980b). American evidence has been mainly gathered by behavioral scientists who were the first to point at the superiority of participatory management (Likert 1961). Much of this research is qualitative in nature and has been deeply embedded in specialized disciplines such as industrial, applied, and social psychology. This may help explain the small impact it has had upon mainstream North American thought and practice in management. The situation appears to be changing rapidly, however, as the need for more flexible manufacturing is increasing globally. In the last and concluding section I will briefly describe the role Z-type organizations will play in the future.

---

*In so far as this describes the large Japanese organization a number of authors have reported similar results; see Ouchi (1981), Aoki (1986), Okumura (1984), Trevor (1987) and Cole (1979).

CONCLUSIONS

Over the past 15 years, a number of leading social scientists have predicted the transition from the second to the third industrial revolution (Toffler 1980; Naisbitt 1982; Bell 1973; Piore and Sabel 1984; Reich 1983). As of 1988 in at least some of the most advanced industrial countries, many of their forecasts have already come true. Toffler, for example, describes the quantum leap involved in moving from the second to the third wave of industrialization as follows:

> The second wave system was one of mass produced, mechanistic technology, mechanistic thinking and the idea of progressing through the exploitation of nature, involving as typical behavior standardization, synchronization, centralization, specialization and concentration of energy, power and money. On the other hand third wave civilization will emphasize flexible production which at the same time will be more decentralized and use renewable, less centralized energy . . . . the most representative organizations of the second wave were "classical industrial bureaucracy" a giant hierarchical, permanent, top-down, mechanistic organization, well-designed for making repetitive products or repetitive decisions in a comparatively stable industrial environment . . . . Third wave organizations have flatter hierarchies. They are less top-heavy. They consist of small components linked together in temporary configuration . . . [and are] capable of assuming two or more distinct structural shapes as conditions warrant. (Toffler 1980, 263).

Toffler continues his observations:

> In the smaller decentralized and self-managed third wave corporation, workers will have higher morale and will be able to satisfy their needs for belonging, self-actualization and participation. (Toffler 1980, 367-369).

Typically, third wave workers demand that their work be socially responsible.

> Third wave corporations accordingly will need to set goals responsive to the bio-sphere, the social environment, the infosystem, the power sphere and the moral sphere. (Toffler 1980, 235-243).

Using a somewhat different language Naisbitt's *Megatrends* (1982) expresses similar ideas when he forecast trends to:

- Move from an industrial to an information society
- Move toward a participatory democracy
- Move from hierarchies toward networking
- Shift toward a long-term orientation in business
- Increase in entrepreneurial behavior and self employment
- Move toward decentralization
- Along with high technology, a counterbalancing move to *high-touch* (very human) personal non-technical responses (Naisbitt 1982, 211-229)

Many large Japanese manufacturing organizations have already incorporated the seven principles outlined above. This, among other things, explains their great recent success in penetrating world markets in an unstable environment, for unstable environments require flexibility both with respect to manufacturing capacity (hardware) and the associated systems and people (soft and humanware). The phenomenal growth of Japanese foreign direct investment in the United States and Europe through joint-ventures and multinational corporations has equally demonstrated the viability of Japanese management systems in differing jurisdictions (Shimada 1987; Yoshida 1987; Trevor 1987).

Even if Japanese direct foreign investment were restricted, as has happened in the French automobile industry for example, strong tendencies exist to *Japanize* domestic production in order to remain internationally competitive (Ikeda 1988). What this seems to suggest is not only a goodbye to the old-fashioned personnel department, as P. Drucker put it (Drucker 1986) but also an odd twist in the long-standing debate on convergency versus divergency in industrial relations. Convergency once more appears as a more plausible explanation of comparative industrial relations developments. However, we are not observing a convergency toward standards set by the West as the original proponents of the convergency thesis foresaw but, rather, a convergency toward the East. The sooner we understand the causes and consequences of these developments the easier it will be to adjust and restructure our own organizations.

REFERENCES

Abegglen, James C. and George Stalk, Jr. *Kaisha: The Japanese Corporation*. New York: Basic Books, 1985.

Aggarwal, Sumer C. ''MRP, JIT, OPT, FMS?'' *Harvard Business Review* 63:5 (1985): 8-16.

Aoki, M. ''Horizontal versus Vertical Information Structures of the Firm.'' *American Economic Review* (December 1986).

Bell, Daniel. *The Coming of Post-Industrial Society: A Venture in Social Forecasting*. New York: Basic Books, 1973.

Boisot, M. ''The Shaping of Technological Strategy.'' *Management International* 23:3 (1983): 16-35.

Brady, T. M. ''Research on the Implications of New Technology for Manpower and Skills: Some Methodological Considerations.'' *New Technology, Work and Employment* 1:1 (1986): 77-83.

Braendgaard, A. ''Market, Hierarchy and Technology: Some Implications of Economic Internationalism for Labor'' in Francis et al., eds. *Power, Efficiency and Institutions*. London: Heinemann, 1983.

Braverman, H. *Labor and Monopoly Capital: The Degradation of Work in the Twentieth Century*. New York: Monthly Review Press, 1974.

Buchanan, D. A. and D. Boddy. *Organizations in the Computer Age: Technological Imperatives and Strategic Choice*. Aldershot: Gower, 1983.

Cable, John and Felix FitzRoy. "Productivity, Efficiency, Incentives and Employee Participation: Some Preliminary Results for West Germany." *Kyklos* 33:1 (1980a): 100-121.

_____. "Cooperation and Productivity: Some Evidence from West German Experience." *Economic Analysis and Worker's Management* 14:2 (1980b): 163-180.

Cieplik, Ulrich. "Die Personalplanung fuer den Robotereinsatz ist anders!" *Management Zeitschrift* 6 (1985): 274-279.

Cole, Robert E. *Work, Mobility and Participation: A Comparative Study of American and Japanese Industry*. Berkeley: University of California Press, 1979.

David, Louis E. "Optimizing Organization - Plant Design: A Complementary Structure for Technical and Social Systems." *Organizational Dynamics* 8:2 (Autumn 1979): 3-15.

Drucker, Peter F. "Goodbye to the Old Personnel Department." *Wall Street Journal* (May 22, 1986).

Economic Council of Canada. *Innovation and Jobs*. Ottawa: Minister of Supply and Services, 1987.

Ettlie, John E. and Stacy A. Reifeis. "Integrating Design and Manufacturing to Deploy Advanced Manufacturing Technology." *Interfaces* 17:6 (1987): 63-74.

Fox, A. *Beyond Contract: Work, Power and Trust Relations*. London: Faber & Faber, 1974.

Francis, Arthur. *New Technology at Work*. Oxford: Clarendon Press, 1986.

Francis, A., J. Turk, and P. Willman. *Power, Efficiency and Institutions*. London: Heinemann, 1983.

Frohman, Alan L. "Putting Technology into Strategy." *The Journal of Business Strategy* 5:4 (1985): 54-65.

Gabarro, John. "Socialization at the Top - How CEOs and Subordinates Evolve Interpersonal Contracts." *Organizational Dynamics* (Winter 1979): 3-23.

Galbraith, J. R. *Organizational Design*. Reading, Massachusetts: Addison Wesley, 1977.

Gallie, D. *In Search of the New Working Class: Automation and Social Integration within the Capitalist Enterprise*. Cambridge: Cambridge University Press, 1978.

Goodman, P. S. *Assessing Organizational Change: The Rushton Quality of Work Experiment*. New York: Wiley, 1979.

Gunn, Thomas G. *Manufacturing for Competitive Advantage*. Cambridge: Ballinger Publishing Company, 1979.

Hackman, J. R. and G. R. Oldham. *Work Redesign*. Reading, Massachusetts: Addison Wesley, 1980.

Hackstein, R. "Personaleinsatz an NC-Ma schinen." *Management Zeitschrift* 4 (1985): 190-193.

Hagerdorn, Homer J. "The Factory of the Future: What About the People?" *The Journal of Business Strategy* 5:1 (1985): 38-45.

Hayes, Robert H. and Steven C. Wheelwright. "Link Manufacturing Process and Product Life Cycles." *Harvard Business Review* 57:1 (1979): 133-140.

Ikeda, Masayoshi. "Japanification of the French Automobile Industry." Paper presented at the third meeting of the French/Japanese Economic Seminar, Waseda, Tokyo, 1988.

Japan Institute of Labor. *Technological Innovation and Industrial Relations*. Tokyo: Japan Institute of Labor, 1985.

Jelinek, Mariann and Joel D. Goldham. "The Strategic Implications of the Factory of the Future." *Sloan Management Review* 25:4 (1984): 29-37.

Leibenstein, Harvey and Klaus Weiermair. "X-efficiency, Managerial Discretion and the Nature of Employment Relations: A Game-theoretical Approach." in Dlugos and Weiermair, eds. *Management Under Differing Employment and Labor Market Systems*. Berlin: de Gruyter, 1988.

Leibenstein, Harvey. *Beyond Economic Men: A New Foundation for Microeconomics*. Cambridge: Harvard University Press, 1976.

Liker, Jeffrey K., David B. Roitman, and Ethel Roskies. "Changing Everything All at Once: Work Life and Technological Change." *Sloan Management Review* 28:4:(1987): 29-47

Likert, Rensis. *New Patterns of Management*. New York: McGraw-Hill, 1961.

Maidique, Modesto and Robert H. Hayes. "The Art of High-Technology Management." *Sloan Management Review* (Winter 1984): 17-31.

Maslow, Abraham. *Motivation and Personality*. New York: Harper & Row, 1970.

Maurice, M., A. Sorge, and M. Warner. "Societal Differences in Organizing Manufacturing Units: A Comparison of France, West Germany and Britain." *Organization Studies* 1:1 (1980) 59-86.

Meredith, Jack R. "Implementing New Manufacturing Technologies: Managerial Lessons over the FMS Life Cycle." *Interfaces* 17:6 (1987): 51-62.

Mitchell, A. and Ch. MacNulty. "Changing Values and Life Styles." *Long Range Planning* 4 (1981): 37-41.

Mueller, Clegg, Wall, Kerys, and Davies. "Pluralist Beliefs about New Technology Within a Manufacturing Organization." *New Technology, Work and Employment* 1:2 (1986): 127-139.

Mumford, E. *Values, Technology and Work*. The Hague: Martinius Nijhoff, 1981.

Naisbitt, John. *Megatrends: Ten New Directions Transforming our Lives*. New York: Warner Books, 1982.

Noble, D. F. "Social Choice in Machine Design: The Case of Automatically Controlled Machine Tools." in: A. Zimbalist, ed. *Case Studies on the Labour Process*. New York: Monthly Review Press, 1979.

OECD. *Employment Growth and Structural Change*. Paris: OECD, 1985.

Okumura, A. "Japanese and U.S. Management Methods Compared." *Economic Eye* 5:3 (1984).

Ouchi, William G. *Theory Z: How American Business Can Meet the Japanese Challenge*. Reading, Massachusetts: Addison Wesley, 1981.

_____. "Markets, Bureaucracies and Clans." *Administrative Science Quarterly* 25 (1980): 129-141.

Peters, Thomas J. and Robert H. Waterman, Jr. *In Search of Excellence: Lessons from*

America's Best Run Companies. New York: Harper & Row, 1982.

Piore, Michael J. and Charles F. Sabel. *The Second Industrial Divide: Possibilities for Prosperity*. New York: Basic Books, 1984.

Porter, Michael, et al. *Competition in Global Industries*. Boston: Harvard Business School Press, 1986.

Porter, Michael E. "Technology and Competitive Advantage." *The Journal of Business Strategy* 5:3 (1985): 60-78.

Reich, Robert R. "The Next American Frontier." *The Atlantic Monthly* (March 1983): 43-58.

Richardson, Peter R., R. Taylor, and P. Gordon. "A Strategic Approach to Evaluating Manufacturing Performance." *Interface* 15:6 (1985): 15-27.

Ross, Malcom H. "Automated Manufacturing - Why is it Taking so Long?" *Long Range Planning* 14:3 (1981): 28-35.

Rothwell, R. and W. Zegveld. *Technical Change and Employment*. New York: St. Martin's Press, 1979.

Schonberger, R. *World Class Manufacturing*. New York: The Free Press, 1986.

Senker, P. and M. Beesley. "The Need for Skills in the Factory of the Future." *New Technology, Work and Employment* 1:1 (1986): 9-17.

Senker, P. and N. Swords-Isherwood, eds. *Microelectronics and the Engineering Industry: The Need for Skills*. London: Frances Pinter.

Shalev, M. "Industrial Relations Theory and the Comparative Study of Industrial Relations and Industrial Conflict." *British Journal of Industrial Relations* 18:1 (1980): 26-43.

Shimada, Haruo and John Paul MacDuffie. "Industrial Relations and 'Humanware' Japanese Investments in Automobile Manufacturing in the United States." International Motor Vehicle Program, Cambridge: Massachusetts Institute of Technology, 1987.

Sorge, A., G. Hartmann, M. Warner, and I. Nicholas. *Microeconomics and Manpower in Manufacturing*. London: Gower, 1983.

Takahashi, Yoshiaki. "Job Organization and Labour Unions' Response to the Utilization of New Technology." Paper presented at the International Industrial Relations Association Meeting, Jerusalem, 1988.

Toffler, Alvin. *The Third Wave*. New York: Bantam Books, 1980.

Tomer, John F. "Working Smarter the Japanese Way: The X-efficiency of Theory Z Management" in Paul Kleindorfer, ed. *The Management of Productivity and Technology in Manufacturing*. Philadelphia: Plenum, 1985.

_____. *Organizational Capital: The Path to Higher Productivity and Well-Being*. New York: Praeger, 1987.

Trevor, M., ed. *The Internationalization of Japanese Business: European and Japanese Perspectives*. Frankfurt: Campus, 1987.

Trist, E., J. W. Higgin, H. Murray, and A. B. Pallock. *Organizational Choice: Capabilities of Groups at the Coal Face Under Changing Technologies-The Loss, Rediscovery and Transformation of a Work Tradition*. London: Tavistock, 1963.

TUC. *Employment and Technology*. London: Trades Union Congress, 1979.

Wall, T. D., B. Burns, C. W. Clegg, and N. J. Kemp. "New Technology, Old Jobs." *Work and People* 10:2 (1984): 15-21.

Walton, Richard E. "Challenges in the Management of Technology and Labour Relations." In Richard Walton and Paul Lawrence, eds. *Human Resource Management Trends and Challenges*. Boston: Harvard Business School Press, 1985.

Weiermair, K. "Worker Incentives and Worker Participation: On the Changing Nature of the Employment Relationship." *Journal of Management Studies*. 22:5 (1985): 547-570.

Weiss, Andrew. "Simple Truths of Japanese Manufacturing." *Harvard Business Review*. 62:4 (1984): 119-125.

Williamson, O. "The Organization of Work: A Comparative Institutional Assessment." *Journal of Economic Behavior and Organization*. 1 (1980): 5-38.

_____. *The Economic Institutions of Capitalism: Firms, Markets, Relational Contracting*. New York: Free Press, 1985.

Winch, G., ed. *Information Technology in Manufacturing*. London: Heinemann, 1983.

Wobbe-Ohlenburg, W. "The Influence of Robots on Qualification and Strain." *Proceedings of Conference on Robotics in the Automotive Industry*. Birmingham, 1982.

Woodward, J. *Industrial Organization: Theory and Practice*. London: Oxford University Press, 1965.

Yoshida, M. *Japanese Direct Manufacturing Investment in the United States*. New York: Praeger, 1987.

Zink, Klaus J. "Ergonomic Aspects of New Technologies in West Germany." (in German) *Zeitschrift fuer arbeitswissenschaft* 3 (1983): 134-137.

11

The Strategic Approach to Product Design: Use of Product Design Teams in Manufacturing

Daniel E. Whitney[*]

WITH GROWING EVIDENCE THAT U.S. MANUFACTURING is no longer competitive, we need an integrated approach to manufacturing systems supported by new technologies. This chapter discusses a strategic approach being used by some U.S. and many Japanese companies to raise their productivity by both integrating their design and manufacturing functions and modifying their manufacturing institutions.

According to General Motors executives, 70 percent of the cost of manufacturing truck transmissions is determined in the design stage. A study at Rolls-Royce reveals that design determines 80 percent of the final production costs of 2,000 components. Obviously, establishing a product's design calls for crucial choices, in materials being made or bought or how parts will be assembled. When senior managers put most of their efforts into analyzing current production rather than product design,

they are monitoring what accounts for only about a third of total manufacturing costs.

The first generation of advanced manufacturing technology is already firmly in place. It is called the flexible manufacturing system (FMS). The impact of the application of FMS has been enormous. Particularly important is the manner in which product design, carried out with computer aided design (CAD) systems, connects directly to these new manufacturing systems. Automatic inventory control and automatic tool operations are now closely coupled operations. However, the impact on the functional way in which companies operate is quite minimal.

This is not the case when companies consider the second generation of advanced manufacturing, automated flexible assembly. On the contrary, there is a growing awareness that automation for assembly cannot be treated in an isolated manner.

*Many of the ideas in this chapter appeared in "What Progressive Companies are Doing to Raise Productivity," by J. L. Nevins and D. E. Whitney, prepared for the Defense Manufacturing Forum: Rethinking DoD Manufacturing Improvement Strategies, at the Institute of Defense Analyses, October 29, 1986. Hay Wun Wain of the University of Pittsburgh assisted in organizing the concepts on which this chapter is founded in the present form.

Dr. Whitney received his Ph.D. in Mechanical Engineering from MIT in 1968. He taught there from 1968 until 1974 when he moved to the Charles Stark Draper Laboratory. His research and consulting interests include automation, robotics, CAD/CAM, design for assembly, controls, and use of computers in manufacturing. He has published over 50 technical papers and is coauthor of the book *Concurrent Design of Products and Processes: A Strategy for the Next Generation in Manufacturing*.

Assembly is closely coupled not only to manufacturing, but also to design, vendor control, and quality control. Thus assembly requires a new, more highly integrated approach to manufacturing that promises to attack the other 70 to 80 percent of manufacturing costs.

Assembly is the first time that parts are put together and must work together. Before assembly, they are designed, made, handled, and inspected separately. During and after assembly, they are joined together, handled together, and tested together. Thus assembly is inherently integrative. It focuses attention on pairs, then groups, of parts. It is thus a natural forum for launching an integrated attack on all the phases of a product, from conception and fabrication to quality and life cycle. Decisions that affect assembly affect nearly every other aspect of production and use of a product.

This integrative approach is a new activity called the strategic approach to product design (SAPD). Strategic product design treats the entire product design and manufacturing system in an integrated manner. This integrated approach allows the entire system to be rationalized. Further, it helps to identify the need for computer aided engineering databases and computerized design tools to support this tightly integrated activity and give it a scientific base in the future. Today this activity can be accomplished only with teams of highly trained people.

The recent interest in design for assembly (DFA) is an outgrowth of the realization that assembly is an important phase in the product's life cycle. Design for assembly cannot be done in isolation like design for fabrication because there are too many interactions and trade-offs. The SAPD deals with these trade-offs at the best time, when the product is being designed. While DFA usually deals with single parts, SAPD deals with groups of parts, subassemblies, and the whole product.

The interest in DFA also coincides with the advent of assembly robots. People can assemble almost anything, but robots will not be successful assemblers unless the product and its parts are designed correctly and manufactured according to the drawings. However, it is important to realize that SAPD is independent of any particular assembly technology. It deals with many nonassembly issues and provides rationally designed products. This rationality benefits assembly by any technique, including manual, and benefits other phases of production, such as inspection, plus the product's life cycle.

The recent realization that firms have to reduce their operating costs in order to survive has heightened the importance of SAPD. For instance, if managers used to think a five percent improvement was good, they now face competition that is drastically reducing the number of components and subassemblies for products and achieving a 50 percent or more reduction in direct cost of manufacture. Even greater reductions are coming, owing to new materials and materials processing techniques. Direct labor, even lower cost labor, accounts for so little of the total picture that companies still focusing on this factor are misleading themselves not only about improving products but also about how foreign competitors have gained so much advantage.

In short, design is a strategic activity, whether by intention or by default. It influences flexibility of sales strategies, speed of field repair, and efficiency of manufacturing. It may well be responsible for the company's future viability.

While many companies recognize the advantages of an integrated approach, the Japanese are the most proficient, since the best of Japanese companies have been using this approach for 20 to 30 years. Advanced U.S. companies have recently embraced the approach. The remainder of this chapter focuses on three aspects of SAPD. First, I will discuss the evolution in manufacturing leading to SAPD. Next, I will outline the steps of the SAPD approach in detail. Finally, I will discuss some of the educational and technology transfer implications.

DRIVERS OF CHANGE IN MANUFACTURING

Part fabrication is essentially a series of independent steps, with minimum interconnections between operations performed on individual piece parts. These operations attempt to enforce a particular geometric configuration on formable materials. The ideal geometry exists in the design, possibly in a CAD system. The output of the fabrication system is an approximation of that ideal geometry perturbed by the statistics of both the process and the materials.

The technology of part fabrication has advanced considerably in the last 30 years. In the early days, single numerically controlled machines took their instructions from hand delivered paper tapes. Today, systems of 10 or 20 such machines work together to make groups of parts that were designed on computers. The tapes have been replaced by direct data links. Once designers had to design parts via a cumbersome tool-steering language. Now design is supported by 3D geometric modeling programs. Design computers hold information on materials, stress analysis, and machining methods. Today, engineers and researchers face a problem of logistics and scheduling, finding the right mix of parts to keep the machines busy. Tools to aid this process are few.

The production capacity of these part fabrication systems is impressive, and so is the speed with which parts can be designed and made. Based on the performance of these design-fabrication systems, most manufacturers are convinced of the benefits of close integration between design and fabrication. However, too few recognize the fact that design for fabrication is not the same as design for overall productivity. Design for fabrication (sometimes mistakenly called design for manufacturing) considers parts as individuals in isolation rather than in groups that must function together. The SAPD seeks to correct this shortcoming.

Beyond this shortcoming is another, deeper problem: that of finding the right mix of parts to keep the machines running at optimum. This logistics problem forces manufacturers to integrate scheduling and system operation into their strategies, and to design parts and families of parts to best utilize these systems.

A second problem, that of improving and automating assembly, has proven more difficult to solve. Before the DFA became popular, almost no one in industry wanted to hear about redesign of products to make their assembly easier. The "correct" attitude of automation engineers was to take the product as it was designed and do their best to assemble it. Manufacturers wanted to make or buy parts cheaply, and push them through assembly and shipping as fast as possible. The result was that all the problems introduced during fabrication or logistics, including parts out of tolerance, or late, or damaged, had to be solved by the ingenuity of the assemblers, usually in undocumented and unappreciated ways. This was the social structuring of manufacturing, a sort of hidden agenda.

This hidden agenda made the introduction of robots and other advanced assembly technology either difficult or impossible. Manufacturers were unhappy with the cost of extra equipment that robots needed which people did not, such as part feeders, palletized parts, control computers, and lockouts. They were also unhappy with the fact that the robots could not use the ingenuity of people to work around problems like out-of-tolerance parts. Instead, feeders jammed, robots stopped, and high technology seemed inadequate. Few companies wanted to spend the extra money for higher quality parts just so robots could put them together. Instead they demanded better and more intelligent robots that could adapt and solve these problems.

In the last few years these attitudes have begun to change. Manufacturers are realizing that better quality parts do not just benefit assembly robots; they also create a better quality product. For the first time, too, manufacturers are getting a true picture of the quality of their parts and products based on the information obtained from sensors on assembly machines, and on the rate at which jams occur. They are realizing that using the assembly system as a filter to detect bad parts is not a good way to run a factory. Bit by bit, new technology is stripping away the hidden agenda.

But even this is an oversimplified view of what is happening. A deeper understanding of the role of technology in products and processes is developing. A number of forces are converging that demand new approaches. Three of these forces are described in detail below.

Complexity of Products and the Disappearance of the Learning Curve

Modern products can contain thousands of parts and many technologies. A new automobile can take five years from initial specifications to first production item. Many skills and disciplines from psychology and marketing to composite materials and inventory control contribute. A new surface combat ship can take up to ten years to cover the same process, and is probably the most complex item built today. Modern products are characterized by combinations of energy and information storage and transformation. They may be made of materials that, unlike past ones, are not merely transformed from mined ores or feedstocks but are created anew from basic atoms especially to serve the needs of the product. New products are tailored to specific market niches, so production volumes are small and product lives are short. Thus there is a need for rapid advances in a product line, fast design updating, and quick changes in production schedules. The learning curve that allowed design error or production glitches to be worked out over a long period of time is compressed or eliminated altogether. Instead, learning must be spread over a series of products. To be valuable, this learning must comprise generic issues rather than product-specific ones so that the lessons can be passed on to the next product.

The disappearance of the learning curve necessitates that manufacturers take two actions. First, manufacturers must respond directly to the resulting time compression by doing things faster. Products and systems need to be designed more rapidly so that there will be time to find the mistakes and eliminate them. Better planning and more effective computer tools are recognized methods of increasing speed. Better planning means organizing the design process so that more factors are taken into account early, reducing the chance of damaging surprises later. Planning also involves identifying a good sequence in which to make design decisions. Better sequencing retains some room for maneuver in the later design stages and also permits decisions

to be made in a one-way sequence, minimizing the need to iterate (Akagi et al. 1984). Without iteration, a decision can be made and can stand unaffected by later decisions. Better and more comprehensive computer tools allow calculations to be made more rapidly and to cover more cases. Well known efforts in computer aided design, computer aided engineering, and computer aided manufacturing are examples of this approach to the challenge of time compression.

Second, manufacturers must think more deeply about what they do and be able to use lessons from previous design activities to aid the current one. That is, the learning may still take longer than the time available to design one new product or system, but one may learn on a continuous basis. Although anyone with an active and open mind does this anyway, the process can be systemized. The basis for the systemization is the recognition of generic or repeating elements in the product, the processes, or the design steps themselves.

An analogous approach may be found in group technology (Opitz 1967). While the application of the approach differs from case to case, the concept is to recognize major similarities or differences between nonidentical items so that they can be grouped. For example, within a group, the similarities are used to advantage by means of sharing a machine or a measuring method. The items sharing the facility need not be identical; rather, they need only be similar enough that the differences between them do not matter to that particular facility. When facilities can be shared by a large number of items, time and cost are usually saved. Had the similarities not been recognized and the groups not formed, the facilities would have dealt with the items piecemeal, and no quantity savings could have been made.

To apply this idea in design, planners need a systematic, step-by-step approach, which asks the same kinds of questions and requires the same kinds of analyses again and again. As these design steps are performed repeatedly, the similarities are recognized quicker, even though each product or system is outwardly different.

Complexity of Processes and the Changing Nature of Competition

The production process is more complex as well, and not just because the product is changing more rapidly. Timing is more critical; processes require more care and attention, needing more data to determine how a manufacturing system is performing. New production technology requires new skills and attitudes from both workers and managers. It is becoming increasingly difficult to select the right type and right mix of technology and people to suit the product and its market.

Product and process complexity arise from the appearance of new kinds of products, mostly those characterized as *mechatronics*. Such products contain a true mix or integration of mechanical and electronic functions and thus require more broadly educated product and process designers. An example of this type of product is the precision product typified by computer disk drives. These items depend on careful design, precise tolerances, extreme cleanliness, fine timing and balance, and the skill and attention of dedicated people.

With the emergence of new products, the traditional basis of competition disappears. In older industries or in those that have reached maturity, the basis of competition is usually production efficiency. The managers in such industries focus on asset management and make most of their decisions based on incremental economic criteria. In newer industries, as well as older industries facing new competitors, the bases of competition are more likely to be product innovation, advanced technology, and quality. While mature products probably differ little in technology and are distinguished by price, newer products may command a price premium based on quality or novelty. Manufacturing decisions in such industries are less likely to be dominated by incremental economics. Rather, they are dominated more by the ability of the product and factory designs to support the competitive strategy behind the product, such as the ability to evolve rapidly or be responsive to a changing market without loss of quality.

Disappearance of the Manual Assembly Option

Until recently it was thought that manual assembly was always an option, and for many products it still is. Manual metal removal was never an option, so metal removal machinery developed early in the industrial revolution. Manual assembly is rapidly disappearing as an option in high technology products because people have too much difficulty providing the required quality, uniformity, care, documentation, and cleanliness. This is not to say that remarkable human performance is impossible. Consider that in Japan it is usual for a person to make only one assembly error in 25,000 to 100,000 operations. And this is considered not good enough. The Japanese use these numbers to justify automation.

Yet direct substitution of robots for people will not solve the problem. Such technology requires a carefully designed environment comprising a properly designed product, well trained operators, and well scheduled operations. Exactly the same kind of requirements that FMS need are needed for assembly. Design for assembly, too, is not enough by itself. Since many parts or subassemblies will be purchased, the same kinds of problems must be solved by vendors as well.

Techniques of economic analysis must also improve. Traditional manufacturers use economic analysis to decide on a case-by-case basis whether or not to replace a person with a piece of machinery. The usual labor or equipment replacement calculation is based on a fundamental assumption that the candidate substitute is equivalent and interchangeable with the current method in every way except cost. This assumption is too simple for most of today's needs. Failure rates, repair costs, and testing strategies, for example, must be considered. These in turn are affected by product design. In high technology products, materials cost much more than time or labor, so the ability of an assembly-test system to deliver a good yield is crucial to maintaining production volume and profit. Thus economically justifiable manufacturing systems can contain both machines and people if they can deliver superior quality or can make the company competitive.

The assembly process should be understood as deeply as a traditional manufacturing process—metal cutting, for example. All the processes in manufacturing such as material handling, stocking, inspecting, judgment of suitability, and granting of exceptions that are now routinely handled by people in an intuitive, judgemental, and often undocumented way, will have to be brought to a higher level of understanding, even if they are not executed by machines. Otherwise there is no way to overcome the complexity of manufacturing. Similarly, the decision making processes now accomplished with routine economic analyses such as return on investment and machine replacement must be supplanted by more sophisticated criteria, computer tools, assumptions, and priorities.

THE STRATEGIC APPROACH TO PRODUCT DESIGN

A product's life cycle is established at the time of product design. The effectiveness, efficiency, and cost of the various stages of the life cycle are all determined by design decisions, both product and process design. The product design involves strategic issues, strategic for the manufacturer and the user. It requires team participation from all departments of a manufacturer, plus good communication with potential users because no one person, department, or professional discipline alone can define a product or how it is made, or how best to couple it to a market or user. Design decisions should be integrated, informed, and balanced involving manufacturing engineers, repair engineers, purchasing agents, and other knowledgeable people early in the process.

Background

The team approach to design is rarely taught in engineering schools. Engineering schools usually teach a fairly straightforward version of how something is designed. FIGURE 11-1 illustrates this conventional approach to design. Engineers are given a technically oriented view that emphasizes determining the need, preparing product specifications, making trial designs, prototyping for bench test, making final designs, and writing a manufacturing process plan. There is a good deal of feedback as problems are uncovered and resolved. As a whole the process is self-contained from need to final design, with little outside interference.

Several things are wrong with this method. It has too much linearity, need-design-make-sell, and is too technical. Worst of all, it is too compartmentalized and assumes that design is the domain of the designer, manufacturing the domain of the manufacturing engineer, purchasing the domain of the purchasing manager, and so on.

The methods used by competitive companies share attributes with the procedure shown in FIG. 11-2. This method emphasizes the degree to which decisions made by the different parties affect each other's activities and alter the product's character (National Research Council 1986, 102-112). Consider, for example, the role of purchasing. A particular weapon depended for its function on an infrared detector. To save money, the purchasing department switched to a lower-cost detector, which caused an increase in final test failures. Subtle differences between detectors could not be found until the product was partially assembled with optics and power supplies. Since the construction was glue and solder, bad units had to be scrapped. Naturally, the product could have been redesigned to make detector replacement easier. But this would have actually increased the weapon's cost and served no purpose other than to facilitate factory rework. Disassembly would not have been advisable because the unit was too complex for field repair. It was a single-use weapon with a shelf life of five years and a useful life of ten seconds. It simply had to work the first time.

The point of this example is that a seemingly minor decision, made to minimize materials costs,

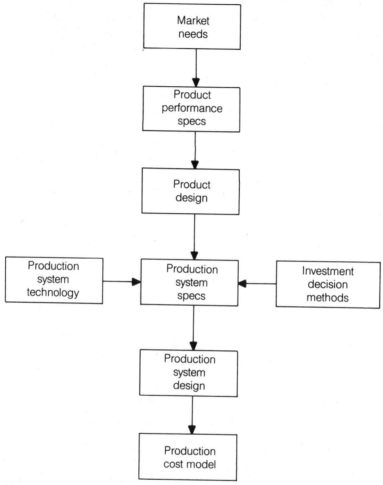

Fig. 11-1. The conventional product design—production system design process.

can have a pervasive effect on how a product is made or used, with severe consequences for operating costs or the customer's perception of the company. These decisions can completely defeat the intentions of the design. The design team has to work together to make a product successful.

Levels of Product Design Strategies

Product design can be divided up into levels of activities. At the bottom level is the functional design; manufacturing considerations come next, and then life cycle considerations at the top. Most companies use one of two basic types of design strategies, the bottom-up and top-down.

The bottom-up strategy, used by the more traditional product design organizations, starts with the functional design. Functional design is what product designers traditionally do. They choose materials, dimensions, and tolerances in such a way that the item will do the job it was intended to do. Then for manufacturing considerations, the functional design is given to manufacturing engineers who decide how to make it. The manufacturing engineers determine the processes for fabricating each part, including choice of machines, methods

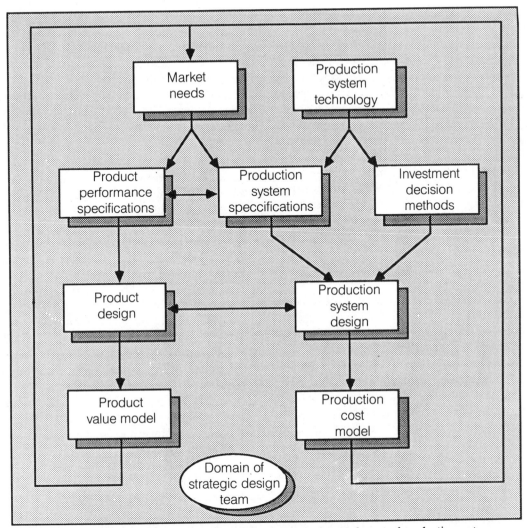

Fig. 11-2. The emerging concurrency method of designing products and production systems.

for maintaining tolerances, and make/buy decisions. These make/buy decisions essentially export to vendors some of the manufacturing engineers' problems. For this export to be successful, the engineers or the purchasing departments must monitor the vendors very carefully.

Next, the manufacturing engineers must design the assembly system or method for the product. This is usually done by straightforward economic analyses in which the choice is between manual and automatic assembly. The latter is typically chosen in cases where the product is small,

has less than twelve parts, and is made for several years in quantities of about a million or more per year.

In more competitive and productive companies, the approach is more complex and covers the entire life cycle of the product. It integrates the life cycle issues such as product use, repair, and upgrading with the functional design. Next, decisions affecting manufacturing issues such as the assembly system, assembly operations, tolerances, vendor control, make/buy, and fabrication methods are made in light of the higher level decisions. In this approach the manufacturing engineers are involved earlier in the design process.

In reality, neither the pure bottom-up nor pure top-down approaches are used. Usually, the process designers become involved late in the design process. This approach causes problems because the process of converting a concept into a product is an involved procedure consisting of many steps of refinement. The initial idea never quite works as intended, or does not perform as well as desired. The designers usually make many modifications to the original concept. Considerable study, experimentation, and investigation of basic physical processes are required. Along the way, designers make choices of materials, fasteners, coatings, adhesives, electronic adjustments, and other subtle changes that may have major impacts on the assembly process.

In many cases, these design choices become more interdependent and take on the character of a historical chain. Close choices could have been made differently, depending on the criteria used. Expensive analyses and experiments may have been carried out to verify portions of the design. Imagine that a production engineer comes into this increasingly detailed debate late in the process and begins asking for changes. It is likely that, if the product designers accede to the requests, a large portion of the design will simply unravel, and force difficult choices to be made all over again. Close choices may be made to go the other way, requiring new analyses and experiments.

On the other hand, if the production engineer had been a participant in the design debate from the start, his criteria could have been given weight as the difficult choices were being made and the design process would have turned out differently. Similarly, if repair engineers, purchasing agents, and other knowledgeable people had been represented, a better, more integrated design would have resulted. In each case, the design would represent an interconnected web of decisions.

The SAPD gives a structure to this integrated design process. It uses multifunctional teams to cut through barriers to good design. Teams can be surprisingly small, as small as four members, or up to twenty members for large projects. They should include every specialty in the company. Top executives should make their support and interest clear. Different companies emphasize different strengths within the team. The team's charter should be broad. Its chief functions are the following:

- Determining the character of the product, to see what kind of product it is and thus what design and production methods are appropriate
- Carrying out a design for producibility and usability study
- Subjecting the product to a product function analysis to determine if its producibility and usability can be improved without impairing functioning
- Designing an assembly process appropriate to the product's particular character; this involves creating a suitable assembly sequence, identifying subassemblies, integrating quality control, and designing each part so that its tolerances are compatible with the assembly method and sequence
- Designing a factory system that fully involves workers in the production strategy, operates on minimum inventory, and is integrated with vendors' methods and capabilities

The SAPD team should be formed early and maintained in position until the product is test-marketed. FIGURE 11-3 outlines the SAPD with an emphasis on assembly. The figure shows the activities of the SAPD team and how the activities interact. The next several sections expand on the major functions outlined above.

The Product's Character

Character defines the criteria by which designers judge, develop, or revamp product features. The product's character must be determined early and recognized by everyone involved in designing and making it. An essential by-product of involving

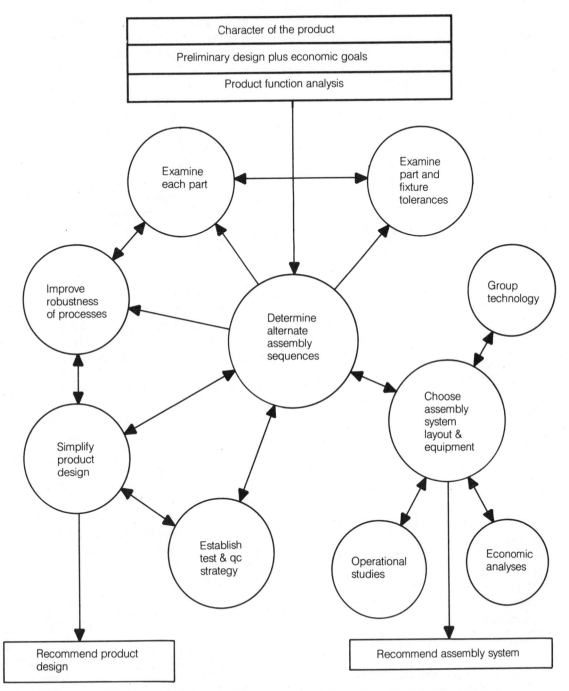

Fig. 11-3. Outline of the strategic approach to product design with emphasis on assembly issues.

manufacturing, marketing, purchasing, and other constituencies in product conception is that diverse team members become familiar enough with the product early in order to be able to incorporate the designer's goals and constraints in their own approaches. Here are two possible characters, together with their consequences for product design and production method:

- *Character*: Complex item, no model mix, used by untrained people, must have 100 percent reliability, used once, thrown away
  Consequence: Make high quality parts, glue them together, don't try to fix it after manufacture
- *Character*: Complex item, model mix and options, used by untrained people, lasts for years
  Consequence: Make high quality parts, screw them together, provide replacement parts and field repair service

Design for Producibility and Usability

Once the product's character has been defined, true product design can begin. Decisions about detailed design, materials, fasteners, and production methods must be made with full knowledge of their impact on the overall product. The main goals of the design team in this step are as follows.

- Convert product concept into a manufacturable, saleable, usable product design
- Anticipate fabrication and assembly methods and problems
- Simplify the design, fabrication, use, and repair by, for example:
  —Reducing the number of parts
  —Identifying and increasing the number of parts common to different models

- Improve the robustness of product and process by, for example:
  —Breaking the product and process into self-contained modules
  —Adjusting tolerances to eliminate chance failures
  —Identifying places where tests can be made

Recently, a company proudly told a business news weekly about saving a mere $250,000 by designing its bottles for a new line of cosmetics to fit existing machines for filling, labeling, and capping. This plan seems so obvious, and the savings were so small as compared with what is possible, that the celebration seemed misplaced. However, it is a better outcome than the experiences of many companies. A drug company spent a fortune to have a famous industrial designer create new bottles and caps for its line. They were triangular in cross section and teardrop shaped, and they did not fit either existing machines or any new ones the company designed. The company eventually abandoned the bottles, along with the associated marketing campaign.

Obviously, nothing is more important to manufacturing strategy than designing for the production process. In the past, this has meant designing for manufacturing and assembly, and value engineering, which both strive to reduce costs. Design for producibility is different from value engineering, an activity aimed chiefly at reducing manufacturing costs through astute choices of materials and methods for making parts. Value engineering occurs after the design is finished and thus is neither concurrent nor very thorough. The required thoroughness can be achieved only when decisions are made early. More importantly, design for producibility examines the entire life cycle of the product when considering cost reductions.

Design for producibility is also different from design for assembly. This activity, like value engineering, usually begins after the product is designed. It considers parts one by one, simplifying them, combining some to reduce the parts count, or adding features to make assembly easier. Valuable as it is, this process cannot achieve the most fundamental improvements because it considers the product as a collection of parts instead of having the objective of reducing costs over the product's entire life cycle.

Design for producibility and usability is a top-down process. It is guided by the product and helps in formulation of the manufacturing strategy. The distinction can be seen in many so-called examples of design for assembly, which are in fact just good re-engineering of the product itself without regard to an overall strategy. Innovative engineers can always come up with improvements. Without a guiding strategy, there is no way to tell which improvements really support the strategy and which merely look like improvements when considered in isolation.

Engineers are taught early on that design is an iterative process, but rarely are they taught about the iterations between design and production, or between production and marketing. Perhaps this is the cause of the traditional time separation between product design and manufacturing system design. It is not too early to begin this step before there are engineering prototypes. Below are two examples of an excellent implementation of design for producibility and usability.

Design for Producibility and Usability: Example One A complex electro-optical-mechanical product must be made in moderate quantities for a very low price. Yet it contains several precision parts and will not work unless some very close tolerances are achieved. Normally this would be impossible at low prices, but an ingenious approach succeeded. The mechanical parts were made to medium tolerances and the whole unit was such that the mechanical errors could be removed after assembly by means of totally electronic adjustments.

Example Two The Japanese revolutionized ship-building. Their philosophy is that "design is a subset of production." The need for increased ship production efficiency made the new approach necessary, and the welded structure of modern ships made it possible. Since welded joints are just as strong as the surrounding metal, it does not matter what shape the pieces are that become welded or where the joints are. The Japanese carefully choose the subassembly and module shapes to utilize efficient group-technology methodologies. The Japanese shipbuilders have introduced levels of planning and production in parallel with their new designs. They also cultivate their vendors, especially steel mills, to deliver on short notice the desired shape plates with the necessary uniform quality that permits carefully developed low distortion welding methods to be used.

The full potential of design for producibility cannot be realized until the team members fully understand how the product is supposed to work and be used. They achieve this understanding through product function analysis.

Product Function Analysis

In product function analysis, designers and engineers seek ways to simplify or rationalize a product's design. They start with what the product should do, rather than how it does it now, or did it in previous designs. This analysis used to be the exclusive province of product designers. Now it is understood that to improve a product's robustness a thorough understanding of a product's function in relation to production methods is essential. Product designers and manufacturing engineers used to try to understand these relations by experience and intuition. Now they have software packages for modeling and designing components to guide them through process choices.

Another important goal of product function analysis is to reduce the number of parts in a product. The benefits extend to purchasing, manufacturing, and field service since fewer parts have to be managed.

When a company first brings discipline to its design process, reductions in parts count are usually easy to make because the old designs are so inefficient. One company saved several million dollars a year by eliminating one part from a subassembly. The product has three operating states: low, medium, and high. Analysis showed that the actions of one part in the original design always followed or imitated the actions of two other parts. The redundant part was eliminated by slightly altering the shapes of the other two parts. Although a mechanical engineer came up with the new design, an electrical engineer performed the analysis that revealed the extra part. The electrical engineer recognized the similarity between this product and typical electric logic circuits. This change could never have been conceived, much less executed, if the designers had not had deep knowledge of the product and had not paid attention to the actions underlying its engineering.

Another example is of a company whose product was put together entirely with screws. Screws are among the most troublesome kinds of parts, and replacing screws with other kinds of fasteners such as glue, rivets, bent tabs, and force fits can often save money. The design team color coded the screws as follows:

- Red—any screw tightened by an assembler that is never loosened again
- Orange—any screw that is tightened by an assembler but may be loosened and retightened during final adjustment
- Yellow—any screw that a repair person may have to loosen
- Green—any screw that the customer may have to loosen

Since most of the screws in the product fell in the red or orange category, these were the subject of intense redesign activity. The red ones were replaced by rivets, a permanent part. The orange screws were eliminated and replaced by another method that enabled adjustments to be made.

The decisions regarding fabrication or assembly method can affect users as well as factory personnel and field as well as factory costs. They are design, not manufacturing, decisions. Because they affect the character of the product, they are strategic in their impact. No one department should make these decisions alone, nor can the decisions be distributed for decentralized action.

Assembly Processes

Assembly-related product design activities with strategic implications include the following: division of the product into subassemblies; establishment of an assembly sequence; selection of an assembly method for each step; and integration of a quality control strategy.

Subassemblies and Assembly Sequence Usually, assembly sequence is considered late in the design process when manufacturing

engineers are trying to balance the assembly line. But the choice of assembly sequence and the identification of potential subassemblies can affect or be affected by, among other factors, product-testing options, market responsiveness, and factory-floor layout. Assembly sequence studies require identification of potential jigging and gripping surfaces, grip and assembly forces, clearances and tolerances, and other issues that must be accounted for in piece part design.

These issues were not considered important when manual assembly was used; however, they are most relevant to machine assembly. For example, grip and jig surfaces must be adequately toleranced with respect to mating surfaces. Tolerance adequacy can be determined by using the part mating theory that has emerged in the last ten years (CSDL Reports: R-800, R-850, R-921, R-996, R-1111, R-1276, R-1407, R-1537, Whitney, 1982). In addition, sequence issues highlight assembly machine and tooling design problems, such as part approach directions, tolerance buildup due to prior assembly steps, access for grippers, stability of subassemblies, number of tools needed, and tool change requirements. Thus, choice of sequence, normally considered very late in the process design, really belongs in the early stages of piecepart design, where each can heavily affect the other.

Imagine a product with six parts. It can be built many ways, such as bottom up, top down, or from three subassemblies of two parts each. What determines the best way? A balance of many considerations: construction needs, like access to fasteners or lubrication points; ease of assembly (some sequences may include difficult part matings that risk damage to parts); quality control matters, such as the operator's ability to make crucial tests or easily replace a faulty part; process reasons, such as the ability to hold pieces accurately for machine assembly; and, finally, production strategy advantages, like making subassemblies to stock that will be common to many models, or that permit assembly from commonly available parts.

Software now exists to help the designer with the formidable problem of listing all the possible assembly sequences—and there can be a lot, as many as 500 for an item as simple as an automobile rear axle. It would be impossible for a team to attack so complex a series of choices without a computer design aid. Another use of the software is that it forces the team to specify choices systematically and reproducibly, for team members' own edification, but also in a way that helps justify design and manufacturing choices to top management.

Consider automatic transmissions, complex devices made up of gears, pistons, clutches, hydraulic valves, and electronic controls. Large transmission parts can scrape metal off smaller parts during assembly, and shavings can get into the control valves, causing the transmission to fail the final test or, worse, fail in the customer's car. Either failure is unacceptable and expensive. It is essential to design assembly methods and test sequences to preempt them.

Assembly Methods With respect to assembly machines and tooling, the design team should consider the following questions:

- Can the product be made by adding parts from one direction, or must it be turned over one or more times? Turnovers are wasted motion and costly in fixtures.
- As the parts are added in a stack, will the location for each subsequent part drift unpredictably? If so, automatic assembly machines will need expensive sensors to find the parts, or assembly will randomly fail, or parts will scrape on each other.
- Is there space for tools and grippers? If not, automatic assembly or testing are not options.
- If a manufacturing strategy based on subassemblies seems warranted, are the subassemblies designed so they do not fall apart during reorientation, handling, or transport?

Quality Control Strategy It is often easier to consider choice of an assembly method for each step and integration of a quality control strategy together rather than separately. The greatest influences on choice of method are anticipated production volume and the need for flexibility in model mix, part count, options, and method of treating units that fail tests. Integrating a quality control strategy into product and process design involves designing better subassemblies to meet functional specifications, ones that will be invaluable when the time comes to decide whether to take bids from outside vendors or make the part on the company's own lines, specifications that will determine how to test the subassembly before adding it to the final product. At this time, the availability of models for selection of assembly methods while integrating a quality control strategy is limited to just a few specialized cases of assembly machines, so most of the decision making is based on informed estimates by experienced individuals.

There exist, however, some computer-based tools for designing and analyzing assembly systems (CSDL Reports R-1284, R-1406, 1978-1980: Graves, 1983). Given adequate data, these tools permit the following issues to be addressed:

- What is the best economic mix of machines and people to assemble a given model-mix of parts for a product, given each machine's or person's cost and time to do each operation, plus production rate and economic return targets?
- How much can one afford to spend on an assembly system given an anticipated revenue stream?
- How much extra time, machinery, money, or product inventory are required to meet a production rate if a certain mix of failures and repair steps can be anticipated during production?
- How can one make the trade-off between the cost of higher quality parts and the cost of downtime of machines due to low quality parts?
- What is the best way to distribute work among workstations in an assembly system?
- Where in the assembly process should testing take place? Considerations include how costly and definitive the test is, whether later stages would hide flaws detectable earlier, and how much repaired or discarded assemblies would cost.

These are generic problems and they are stimulating the development of new software packages.

This new software enhances the ability of manufacturing people to press their points during the design process.

Factory System Design

Many features of good product design presuppose that machines will do the assembly. However, automation is not a prerequisite to reaping the benefits of strategic design. Indeed, sometimes good design makes automatic assembly unnecessary or uneconomical by making manual assembly so easy and reliable. Regardless of the level of automation, some people will still be involved in production processes, and their role is important to the success of manufacturing.

Kosuke Ikebuchi, general manager of the General Motors-Toyota joint venture, New United Motors Manufacturing Inc. (NUMMI), believes that success came to his plant only after careful analysis of the failures of the GM operation that had preceded it: low-quality parts from suppliers, an attitude that repair and rework were to be expected, high absenteeism resulting in poor workmanship, and damage to parts and vehicles caused by transport mechanisms. The assembly line suffered from low efficiency because work methods were not standardized, people could not repair their own equipment, and equipment was underutilized. Excess inventory, caused by ineffective controls, was another problem. Work areas were crowded. Employees took too much time to respond to problems.

NUMMI's solutions focused on the *Jidoka principle* that quality comes first. According to NUMMI's factory system today, workers can stop the line if they spot a problem; the machinery itself can sense and warn of problems. Two well-known just-in-time methods of eliminating waste are important to NUMMI's manufacturing operation: the kanban system of production control and reductions in jig and fixture change times.

Many other things also contribute to this plant's effectiveness: simplified job classifications, displays and signs showing just how to do each job and what to avoid, self-monitoring machines.

NUMMI has obtained high-spirited involvement of the employees, first by choosing new hires for their willingness to cooperate, then by training them thoroughly and involving them in decisions about how to improve the operations.

Recent Design Strategy Examples

Household Appliance: A Failure A particular manufacturer based its last hopes on a new version of its complex consumer product. The product depended on close tolerances for proper operation. Edicts from the styling department prevented designs from achieving required tolerances; the designers wanted a particular shape and appearance and would not change when they were apprised of the problems they caused to manufacturing. The entire product was built from single parts on one long line without any subassemblies or intermediate tests. Each finished product had to be adjusted into operation or taken apart after assembly to find out why it did not work. No one who understood the problem had enough authority to solve it, and no one with enough authority understood the problem until it was too late. This company is no longer in business.

Perfecting a New Process: A Failure One research scientist at a large chemical company spent a year perfecting a new process, involving, among other things, gases at laboratory scale. In the lab the process operated at atmospheric pressure. However, when a production engineer was finally called in to scale up the process, he immediately asked for higher pressures. Atmospheric pressure is never used in production when gases are in play because maintaining it requires huge pipes, pumps, and tanks. Higher pressure reduces the volume of gases and permits the use of smaller equipment. Unfortunately, the researcher's process failed at elevated pressures, and he had to start over.

People Mover Systems Factory: A Failure A division of a multinational company made transportation systems for subways and airports. Each system was unique and was designed and built to a customer's specifications. The systems consisted of control equipment or assembled cars and were sold to transit and airport authorities.

Communication among departments, especially between engineering and manufacturing, had always been poor for this division. Manufacturing engineers were rarely involved with design. Few design engineers even visited the manufacturing floor. In many cases when a completed design went to the shop floor, manufacturing engineers found that the product could not be built. They requested a myriad of changes to be incorporated. Once the changes were approved and properly documented this often meant panic buys, obsolete materials, and rework. The incredible part to this was that when a similar design had to be made for another contract, in most cases, none of these previously requested changes by manufacturing engineers were incorporated. There was no systematic method in place for incorporating the changes permanently. Manufacturing kept making change requests and engineering kept approving them. This process was extremely costly.

The top management realized that a better tool was needed for enhancing the communications between the two departments. Around this time the division initiated a major undertaking of modernizing its factory. Pallet racks and wooden shelves were replaced by automated carousels and part retrieval systems. An outdated computer system was replaced by a state-of-the-art computer system with an integrated database. The management thought that utilizing a common database would certainly improve the communications between the engineering and manufacturing departments. However, after several million dollars and several years of modernization, the division realized that it did not reap the benefits it expected. There were many problems. Because of the tediousness of the computer system design, engineers started to "go around the system." Many expensive computer programs were installed that were not used. Design engineers did not understand the manufacturing people and vice versa. Designs were still constantly changed. It was still common for a design to be changed on a product that was well into manufacturing. Nothing changed.

This is a typical case of a company that thinks that automation will correct all its problems. It completely ignored the reasons for its poor internal communications. It did nothing to improve the relationship between the departments, but kept pouring money into fancy computers and tools. No amount of automation will solve poor internal communications. The operating costs and investment levels of this division were so high that it became uncompetitive. Unfortunately, the division could not recover from its situation in time to prevent the parent company from selling it.

Automobile Factory: A Success Based on Technology and Product Redesign   Volkswagen recently violated conventional ease-of-assembly rules to capture an advantage the company would not otherwise have had. In the company's remarkable Hall 54 facility in Wolfsburg, Germany, where Golfs and Jettas go through final assembly, robots or special machines perform about 25 percent of the final-stage steps. Five percent had been Volkswagen's best in the past.

To appreciate the full impact of the story, one needs to be familiar with product cycles in automobile companies. Many products are proposed, but only a few are approved. Competition is fierce in an underfunded environment, but once a product is approved, money becomes available. Once the funds are approved, the product introduction date (PID) is established, usually only 24 or 36 months ahead. There is little time available for rationalizing the design; purchase orders for machinery are released immediately. The PID is the primary concern, and everything else is secondary.

To make Hall 54 a success, Volkswagen production management decided to examine every part (Hartwich 1985). It won from the board of directors a year-long delay in introducing the new models. Several significant departures from conventional automotive design practices resulted, the first involving front-end configuration. Usually, designers try to reduce the number of parts. Volkswagen engineers determined that, at a cost of one extra frame part, the front of the car could be temporarily left open for installation of the engine by hydraulic arms in one straight, upward push. Installing the engine used to take a minute or longer involving several workers. Volkswagen now does it unmanned in 26 seconds.

Another important decision concerned the lowly screw. Volkswagen engineers convinced its purchasing department to pay an additional 18 percent for screws with cone-shaped tips that go more easily into holes, even if the sheet metal or plastic parts were misaligned. Machine and robot insertion of screws thus became practical. Just two years later, so many German companies had adopted cone-pointed screws that their price had dropped to that of ordinary flat-tipped screws. For once, everyone from manufacturing to purchasing was happy.

Radiator Factory: Success Based on Integrated Design The Delco of Japan, Nippon Denso builds such car products as generators, alternators, voltage regulators, and antiskid brake systems. Toyota is its chief customer. Nippon Denso has learned to live with daily orders for thousands of items in arbitrary model mixes and quantities.

To meet this challenge, the company employed several strategies:

- The combinatory method of meeting model-mix production requirements
- In-house development of manufacturing technology
- Wherever possible, jigless manufacturing methods

The combinatory method, carried out by marketing and engineering team members, divides a product into generic parts or subassemblies and identifies the necessary variations of each. The product is then designed to permit any combination of variations of these basic parts to go together physically and functionally. If there are six basic parts and three varieties of each, for example, the company can build 3^6 or 729 different models. The in-house manufacturing team cooperates in designing the parts, so the manufacturing system can easily handle and make each variety of each part and product.

Jigless production is an important goal at this point. Materials handling, fabrication, and assembly processes usually employ jigs, fixtures, and tools to hold parts during processing and transport; the jigs and fixtures are usually designed specifically to fit each kind of part, to hold them securely. When production shifts to a different batch or model, old jigs and tools are removed and new ones installed. In mass-production environments, this changeover occurs about once a year.

In dynamic markets, however, or with just-in-time, batches are small, and shifts in production may occur hourly or even continually. It may be impossible to achieve a timely and economical batch-size-of-one production process if separate jigs are necessary for each model. Nippon Denso's in-house manufacturing team responds to this problem by showing how to design the parts with common jigging features, so that one jig can hold all varieties, or by working with designers to make the product snap or otherwise hold itself together so that no clamping jigs are needed.

By cultivating an in-house team, Nippon Denso also solves three difficult institutional problems. First, the company eliminates proprietary secrecy problems. Its own people are the only ones working on the design or with strategically crucial components. Second, equipment can be delivered without payment of a vendor's markup, thus reducing costs and making financial justification easier. Third, over the years the team has learned to accommodate itself intuitively to the company's design philosophy, and individual team members have learned how to contribute to it. Designers get to know each other too, creating many informal communication networks that greatly shorten the design process. Shorter design periods mean less lead time, a clear competitive advantage.

Nippon Denso used combinatory design and jigless manufacturing for making radiators. FIGURE 11-4 illustrates the radiators' jigless, batch-size-of-one manufacture. Tubes, fins, and end plates comprise the core of the radiator. These three snap together, which obviates the need for jigs, and the complete core is oven soldered. The plastic tanks are crimped on. The crimp die can be adjusted to

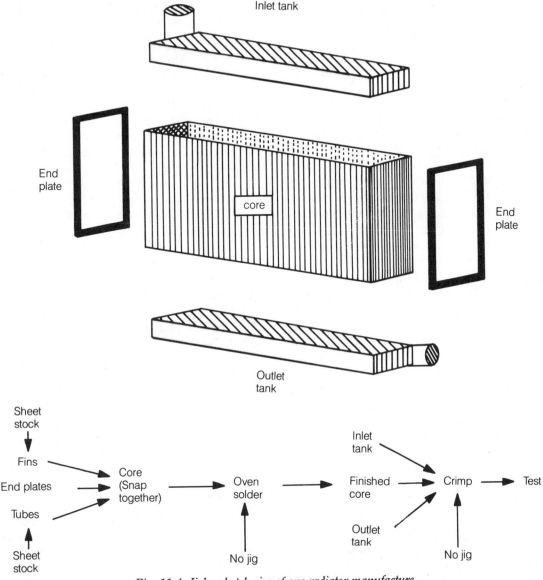

Fig. 11-4. Jigless batch-size-of-one radiator manufacture.

take any tank size while the next radiator is being put in the crimper, so radiators can be processed in any model order and in any quantity. When asked how much the factory cost, the project's chief engineer replied, "Strictly speaking, you have to include the cost of designing the product." A factory is not just a factory, he implied. It is a carefully

crafted fusion of a strategically designed product and the methods for making it.

A Robot That Assembles Precision Instruments: Success Based on Process Analysis   One laboratory successfully built and tested a robot-clean room combination that assembles precision instruments involving gas bearings with clearances of about 1 micron. Prior to this combination, it was widely believed that only skilled technicians could assemble these instruments.

The process analysis consisted of four elements: a basic strategy that integrated a number of mechanized steps that could be totally isolated from people, economic analysis of rework, determination of the sources of particulate contamination, and application of automated part mating. Rework is a major contributor to the high cost of precision instruments. Two major reasons for failures, particulate contamination and inadvertent damage, are both caused by the assemblers. The system that was designed recirculates the air through filters so many times that a Class 1 environment is maintained. Such recirculation would be impossible if assemblers had to be accommodated. The robot's wrist contains patented spring-loaded tooling and measuring instruments that permit a more delicate touch than people are capable of, and can monitor the machine for any errors. The result is a reproducible self-documenting process that duplicates or exceeds the care of the best technician (Stepien, et al, 1988).

To implement this system, the designers of the instruments had to be convinced that the changes in the assembly methods in no way affected the instruments' function or quality.

ROADBLOCKS TO IMPLEMENTATION

There are so many advantages in implementing a strong product-process link. Then why is it not done more often? Manufacturing is probably the most complex peacetime activity in which people engage. A natural response to complexity is specialization. Organizations grow up around specialization boundaries, and people must subscribe to one species or another in order to have a place. Implementing the product-process link requires boundary-crossing. Perhaps this is threatening.

Sometimes ideas that link product and process are simply too new to be acceptable to established organizations. If the processes are not well understood and seem to require certain ''experts'' or particular conditions for their success, then conservatism against change may be a quite rational response. This is certainly true in ship building, where welded structures often bulge or warp out of shape unpredictably due to the heat of welding. The Japanese ship builders' response was not to develop a quick method such as new shapes to eliminate the distortion, but rather to conduct years of experiments to make the bulges smaller and more predictable. The Japanese did not resist change that was necessary to make ship building a success.

The changes needed in people and organizations to carry out these integrated efforts are very difficult to accomplish. But as the NUMMI example cited earlier indicates, these changes must be made if the desired competitiveness is to be achieved. Companies have used various artifacts, short of terminating people, to rationalize the need for an integrated approach.

Some solutions to this problem are less enlightened. A home appliance maker refused to modularize its diverse product line so that some of the modules could be used in several products. The fact that its main competitor did so carried no weight. Later when a vice president of the competitor was asked how he was able to accomplish the modularity of his products, his response was ''we had to fire about a third of management.'' Sometimes this is what it takes.

NEW KNOWLEDGE NEEDED

The SAPD is based on using the assembly process as the focal point and integrator of all the complex decisions required to create a producible product. Simply trying harder is not enough to verify, improve, extend, and implement this strategy. Deeper understanding of fundamental problems is needed. Research to identify new information is essential. FIGURES 11-5 and 11-6 show the organization of these issues with respect to design of products and design of manufacturing systems.

Integrated synthesis, design, and evaluation tools and supporting databases are needed at each level to help designers and engineers seek alternatives and evaluate them technically and economi-

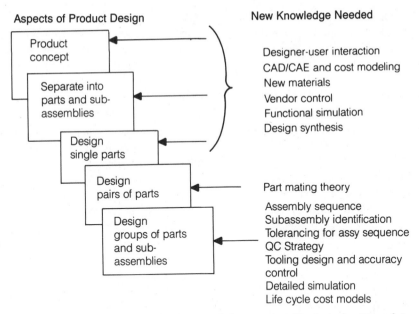

Fig. 11-5. Activities and knowledge needed to support the strategic approach to product design. Part One—product design itself.

cally. Fabrication by traditional methods is the most advanced, while assembly and concurrent design operate with few or no tools at all. Since the usefulness of assembly analysis in forming the total product design has been recognized only recently, there is a significant lack of effective strategies and tools. The lack of formal manufacturing design tools and computer implementations of them seriously sets back manufacturing engineers in comparison to product designers. The latter have a huge array of computer and analytical tools at their disposal, giving them a scientific as well as a psychological advantage over manufacturing engineers. The result is often overpriced and uncompetitive products.

If future products are to be designed by teams of product and manufacturing engineers, research on the group dynamics of complex design projects is needed. Matters of concern include sharing of data, moderating the dominance of one constituency over another, defining an effective sequence for making major decisions, and managing the process of negotiating decisions in the presence of conflicting aims. Accompanying the design tools and

methodologies used by manufacturing engineers must be a large array of databases. There exist many such bases suitable to the design of products, but more will be needed as new products are created using new materials and processes. Finally, the system design methodology itself needs databases. These include the following areas where progress is being made or where near-term results can be expected.

- Methods of generating alternate assembly sequences for products
- Algorithms for assessing the tolerances assigned to parts to see if they support a particular assembly sequence
- Procedures for predicting failure modes for a product so that opportunities to test for those failures can be integrated into each assembly sequence to create a test strategy
- Economic analysis methods for assessing:
  The basic assembly cost by various methods, including people and machines
  The cost of providing part, tool, and fixture tolerances of varying accuracies

The cost of doing texts at various points in an assembly sequence, including the cost of uncovering the fault by disassembly as well as fixing it

FIGURE 11-7 shows some of the interactions among these areas.

An important knowledge gap is performance, including performance models of both the product and the production systems and broad aspects of performance such as normal and abnormal operating modes, downtimes, repair scenarios, and the supporting logistics. In many cases, the lack of ade-

quate product performance models results in over-designed products. In manufacturing systems, performance models are often narrowly drawn with respect to local economic criteria. Too little is known about the cost-benefit relationships with respect to flexibility, or how to achieve flexibility by appropriately balancing product design, manufacturing system design, use of new technology, scheduling and resource allocation, and human effort.

Also missing is a strategy for educating engineering students to be effective team players in such activities. Interestingly, the Japanese universi-

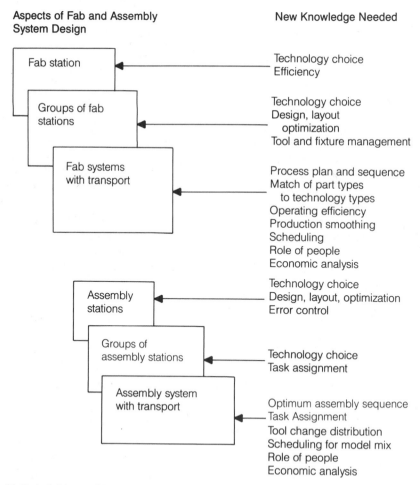

Fig. 11-6. Activities and knowledge needed to support the strategic approach to product design. Part Two—design of fab and assembly systems.

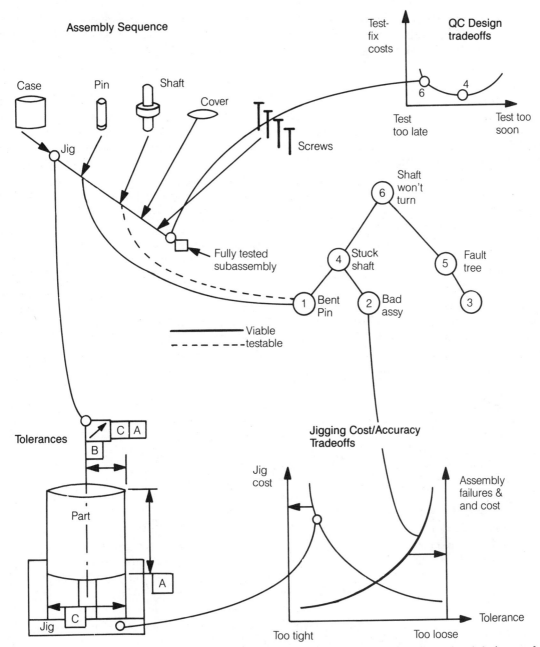

Fig. 11-7. The connection between the assembly sequence and detailed part design, jig and tool design, and QC strategy.

ties are no better off than American ones in this regard. Japanese companies typically give new hires three years of training, rotating them through the company, before they are ready to contribute meaningfully. In order to prepare students for the essential integrative nature of the design activities, they should be convinced that a systems approach is the unifying principle. Once they are aware of the importance of considering many diverse factors before making a design decision, they then can concentrate on becoming knowledgeable in one area of expertise.

SUMMARY

Productive manufacturing systems can be achieved by an integrated approach to manufacturing independent of technology. In fact, the advantages of applying advanced technology can be achieved only through this integrated approach. The integrated approach is more important than any specific technology. This approach, the SAPD, can act as the catalyst to rationalize product and process design.

The SAPD is not just a product design method, but is also a vehicle of systematizing the way people and manufacturing functions interact. It provides a basis for these new concurrency teams to exist. The method is not an end in itself. The application of the method provides insight into manufacturing systems and their interactions not presently analyzed or understood by any other method.

Individuals with the necessary skills for these concurrency teams are small in number. In some industries their average age is quite high. The U.S. has a vested interest in capturing their knowledge, creating new knowledge, and developing methods that will eventually allow a few individuals with the aid of a computer to explore new designs with the same range of sensitivities that concurrency teams have.

The U.S. needs to help generate a science base to replace the highly skilled, but principally experience-based, content of present concurrency teams. Much of the federal government research funding has been focused on advanced technology, technology demonstration, or new materials. Not much has been done to establish the science base of knowledge necessary for these advanced design and manufacturing systems. Support from industry to universities has also been limited. All researchers need to work on generating a broader pool of information so that the SAPD can be more fully integrated into U.S. manufacturing systems.

REFERENCES

Akagi, S., R. Yokoyama, and K. Ito. "Optimal Design of Semisubmersible's Form Based on Systems Analysis." ASME Paper 84-DET-87. *ASME Journal of Mechanisms, Transmissions, and Automation in Design* (1984).

Bourjault, A. "Contribution a Une Approche Methodologique de 1'Assemblage Automatise: Elaboration Automatique des Sequences Operatoires." Ph.D. diss., Universite de Franche-Comte, 1984.

Charles Stark Draper Laboratory, Inc. Reports: R-1407, R-1537; R-800, R-850, R-921, R-996, R-1111, R-1276; R-1284, R-1406. Cambridge, Massachusetts: Edited and reprinted by permission of The Charles Stark Draper Laboratory, Inc.

Chirillo, L. D. Product Work Breakdown Structure. U.S. Department of Transportation Maritime Administration: National Shipbuilding Research Program, 1982.

De Fazio, T. L. Uncertainty in Unit Costs Occurring During Low Throughput Operation of Process Systems That Include Testing and Rework. MAT Memo 1299. Cambridge, Massachusetts: Charles Stark Draper Laboratory, 1986.

Graves, S. C. and B. W. Lamar. An Integer Programming Procedure for Assembly System Design Problems: *Operations Research*. 31:3:522-545, 1983.

Gustavson, R. E. "Choosing Manufacturing Systems Based on Unit Cost." In *Proceedings, 13th International Symposium on Industrial Robots*. Chicago, 1983.

_____. A Statistical Analysis of Recycling, Rework, Yield, and Cost Reduction. MAT Memo 1300. Cambridge, Massachusetts: Charles Stark Draper Laboratory, 1986.

Hartwich, E. H. "Possibilities and Trends for the Application of Automated Handling and Assembly Systems in the Automotive Industry." In *International Congress for Metalworking and Automation, ICMA, Sixth EMC*, 126-131. Hannover: ICMA, 1985.

Ikebuchi, K. VP Mfg. New United Motor Manufacturing, Inc. (NUMMI): Unpublished Speech. New York University: Future Role of Automated Manufacturing Conference, 1986.

Klein, C. J. "Generation and Evaluation of Assembly Sequence Alternatives." SM thesis, Massachusetts Institute of Technology, ME Department, 1986.

Nag, Amal. "Tricky Technology; Auto Makers Discover Factory of the Future is Headache Just Now." *Wall Street Journal* (May 13, 1986):1.

National Research Council Commission on Engineering and Technical Systems. *Toward a New Era in U.S. Manufacturing: The Need for a National Vision*. Washington, D.C.: National Academy Press, 1986: IX 9-11, 102-112.

Ohta, K. and M. Hanai. Flexible Automated Production System for Automotive Radiators. In *Proceedings of First Japan-USA Symposium on Flexible Automation*, 553-558. Osaka, Japan, 1986.

Olmer, L. *U.S. Manufacturing at a Cross Road: Surviving and Prospering in a More Competitive Global Economy*. International Trade Administration: U.S. Department of Commerce, 1985: 4.

Opitz, H. *A Classification System to Describe Workpieces*. Oxford: Pergamon Press, 1967.

Porter, M. "Why U.S. Business is Falling Behind." *Fortune* 113 (1986) 155-262.

Taylor, F. W. *The Principles of Scientific Management*. New York and London: Harper and Brothers, 1911.

Todd, Daniel. *The World Shipbuilding Industry*. London: Croom Helm., 1985.

Wheelwright, S. C. and R. H. Hayes. "Competing Through Manufacturing." *Harvard Business Review* (1985): 99-109, Vol. 63 #1.

Whitney, D. E. "Manufacturing by Design." *Harvard Business Review* (July-August 1988): 83-91.

_____. "Quasi-static Assembly of Compliantly Supported Rigid Parts." *ASME Journal of Dynamic Systems, Measurement and Control* 104 (1982): 65-77.

Whitney, D. E. et al. *Implementation Plan for Flexible Automation in U.S. Shipyards*. CSDL report prepared for Todd Pacific Shipyard, Los Angeles Division, and the SNAME Ship Production Committee Panel sp-10, Flexible Automation, 1986.

Whitney, D. E., R. E. Gustavson, and M. P. Hennessey. "Designing Chamfers." *International Journal of Robotics Research* 2 (1983): 3-18.

12

Managing Software in the Automated Factory

John H. Manley[*]

FROM AN ENTERPRISE MANAGEMENT PERSPECTIVE, factory automation includes a wide variety of computing system assets, from automated machines to business information systems. Every automated system includes computing machinery, people, and software as basic component parts. Of these three, software is often regarded by management as the most troublesome to plan, develop, implement, and maintain. As a result, it is most often turned over to "software people" to handle, thus putting it out of sight, and out of mind. Consequently, when software begins to cost too much, is delivered late, will not work properly, or otherwise does not meet user expectations, management is often powerless to take effective corrective action.

The upside is that software can be effectively managed using a systematic approach that draws heavily from hardware engineering and project management principles. This chapter describes a software life cycle process model, software process measurements, and other essential elements that can place automated factory software under effective management control.

Managers are accustomed to thinking about software in terms of what the data processing (DP) or management information system (MIS) depart-

ments produce for them. In the 1980s, personal computer (PC) software has taken center stage for many managers, either by choice, or by company edict. Other categories of software rarely come to mind, such as the software embedded in consumer products, the software that makes robots perform on the shop floor, and especially the "throw away" code written by engineers and others in the course of their daily work. From an enterprise perspective, all categories of software should be of concern to managers, especially that which is essential to operating the automated factory.

In spite of the wide variety of software in use, this chapter focuses on only one category of software, that contained in information systems (IS). The reason for the emphasis is twofold. First, information systems represent the largest software cost to any enterprise, especially the automated factory. Second, this class of software is one of the most difficult to manage. Other categories, such as software embedded in machine tools, package software for computer aided design (CAD), personal computer software, and specialized project management support software are also important, but do not represent the difficulties to management that accompany factory information systems. This

*Dr. Manley is Professor of Industrial Engineering and Director, Manufacturing Systems Engineering Program, University of Pittsburgh. He is also President, Computing Technology Transition, Inc., an educational services and consulting company. Prior to joining the University of Pittsburgh, he served as Director, Carnegie Mellon University Software Engineering Institute; Vice President, Nastec Corporation; Director of Programming Applied Technology, ITT Corporation; and Assistant to the Director of The Johns Hopkins University Applied Physics Laboratory. Dr. Manley holds a B.Met.E. from Cornell University, an M.S. in Industrial Engineering, and a Ph.D. in Operations Research and Systems Management Engineering, both from the University of Pittsburgh.

choice is also appropriate since the principles to be discussed apply to all types of software and should be treated accordingly. Let us begin by looking briefly at some of the reasons why software must be taken seriously.

MANUFACTURING INDUSTRY SOFTWARE INVESTMENT

An 84-page special supplement to *Computerworld* in September 1988 reported the results of an extensive evaluation of United States commercial company investments in information systems.[1] According to their editorial, "the Premier 100 represents the most comprehensive attempt at quantifying and qualifying the prodigious investments in information systems made by America's leading firms." The report split up the world of information into vertical markets as follows:

- Utilities
- Equipment and materials manufacturing
- Aerospace, automotive, and industrial
- Insurance and financial services
- Food and consumer products
- Transportation and other services
- Chemicals
- Banking
- Petroleum products
- Retailing

From the above list, one can identify representative investments for information systems made by both discrete and process manufacturing companies that were included in the list of Premier 100 firms. The top rankings were based upon formulas that used data collected according to the following important categories of investment:

- Market value of installed equipment
- Estimated annual MIS/DP budget for the firm
- Corporation's average profit growth over the period 1983-87
- Percentage of current MIS/DP budget spent on staff

- Percentage of current MIS/DP budget spent on training and education
- Total number of personal computers and terminals

Computerworld's rationale for using the above data types was that they felt it important to look at where investments in information systems are being made, not just at the amount. Thus, amounts spent are only relevant in the context of a company's revenue and its competitors', as well as its profitability.

With this in mind, the following extracts from the *Computerworld* report are of significance to manufacturing in general, and the automated factory in particular.

1. Manufacturing companies scored well in information technology investment with four ranked in the top ten (Polaroid Corporation, Northrop Corporation, Gillette Company, and McDonnell Douglas Corporation).
2. General Motors Corporation, Ford Motor Company, and Chrysler Corporation (ranked 96th, 86th and 139th respectively) did not do well within the manufacturing sector.
3. Polaroid's $75 million estimated IS budget represents approximately four percent of revenue, and is significantly higher than the 1.4 percent average for its industry. IS supports a top-level corporate objective of producing more products with fewer employees. They have pioneered advanced distribution, and forecasting and tracking systems, as well as broadened their networking and work group computing functions.
4. Northrop's $300 million estimated IS budget includes much more than traditional data processing. According to W. Richard Howard, Vice President of Information Resource Management, "Information resource management in this world is not DP or MIS; it really focuses on what we are doing with technology throughout the company." They spend 55 percent of their IS budget on people, and have invested $2.5 billion in facilities and equipment since 1980.

Their most innovative goal is to move even further into three-dimensional design by performing all engineering design strictly in a three-dimensional database.* They also are acutely aware of the integration of heterogeneous systems problems and are actively trying to solve them by working with vendors, as well as by participating on the Open Systems Interconnect, Manufacturing Automation Protocol/Technical and Office Protocol, and other standards committees. They invest heavily in computing due to the nature of their business. One example is a $43 million Integrated Simulation Systems Laboratory for helping their engineers evaluate design options for building advanced aircraft.

5. Major investments are being made in automating production and engineering functions in aerospace, automotive, and other industrial manufacturing companies. The leaders such as McDonnell Douglas Corporation, The Lockheed Corporation, and Deere & Company are investing from 3.3 to 4 percent of their revenues in information systems to be competitive.

6. Information services is a crucial and high-profile group in heavy manufacturing for automating processes. Information systems are being used for shortening lead times and schedules, identifying and solving quality problems quickly, keeping track of parts and subassemblies, and costing the entire production process.

7. MIS answers cost questions somewhat differently depending upon the type of industry. In the automotive industry, data are collected that pertain to unit costs. In aerospace, questions are asked that relate to collecting data to comply with government reporting requirements. The government requirements, especially on defense contracts, are increasingly more complicated and place a heavier burden on the information system resource.

8. The automotive industry is using the "islands of automation" approach to increasing their efficiency. Here they work on areas such as computer-aided design for engineering, bills of materials, parts procurement, manufacturing automation, and corporate accounting systems. Ford Motor Company's investment in IS is estimated at $836 million per year. This budget will undoubtedly go up over time in order to accomplish longer-term goals to integrate these "islands" into an enterprise-wide system.

Information systems originated in the clerical and financial side of companies. It is clear that the terminology has changed over time to broaden its focus, based upon what industry perceives as the strategic purpose of IS. In general, IS includes computing support for improving process and product quality, increasing productivity, lowering costs, enhancing management activities, differentiating products; as well as keeping the books and maintaining corporate databases.

A Second Survey

According to another 1988 survey of 92 chief executive officers and 92 chief information officers in the same companies, both IS producers and IS users generally agree on the value of such systems but disagree somewhat on whether reducing overhead and resources are among the benefits.[2] Both sides generally agreed that the success of their companies were closely linked to their ability to gain competitive advantage using information systems. They were also very close on agreeing that their resource allocations for IS are generally based on promises of benefits or service that are seldom achieved. The disagreement over IS value stems from differing perceptions of whether investments in management information systems have reduced or increased company resource requirements and overhead.

What We Can Conclude

Both of the above survey results provide tangible examples to support the thesis that the IS area

---

*The B-2 Stealth bomber, rolled out on November 23, 1988, is the first aircraft in history completely designed in 3-D.

needs better quantitative goal setting and measurement of outcomes. Everyone agrees that information systems are necessary for survival in today's highly competitive global marketplace, but the question remains: Are we placing too little or too much of our total corporate resources into developing and maintaining such systems?

Evaluating software's values to the automated factory also applies to the other categories of software. However, it is already common practice to determine the value of an automated machine tool using standard engineering economic analyses. What comes with these answers is the value of the bundled, embedded software. Packaged software can also be evaluated in a relatively straightforward manner. In other areas, however, important questions remain. For example, how should management determine the value of company-developed software for a large-scale flexible manufacturing system?

A systematic, engineering-based, economic, analytical approach to answering these questions about software is needed.

PRESCRIPTION FOR SOFTWARE SUCCESS

The key to software success in the automated factory is the ability of both managers and software engineers to follow a consistent software development life cycle process. This requires managers to not only understand software fundamentals, but also actively participate in the software development process itself.

With a thorough mutual understanding of how the software process works, the next step is to develop and implement a system of measures, in the same manner that every hardware process is measured. With quantitative data in hand, management knowledge increases to the point that realistic cost and benefit analyses can be carried out.

Over time, tighter management control and quantitative analyses will systematically identify certain activities, methods, tools, and techniques that should be standardized. In particular, there

exist "best" programming design methods, computer-aided software engineering (CASE) tools, programming languages and test procedures that should be institutionalized for any given software development environment.

Once there is a standardized, measurable, and effective process in place, optimization programs can be instituted. These would include a productivity program that will refine the existing process in controlled steps, and will identify and install more efficient methods, tools, and techniques. This process refinement program should then be implemented on an annual review and improvement cycle.

In the next stage of the improvement program, software is placed under the same level of control as hardware. This includes traditional quality control and quality assurance systems that use comprehensive measurements and statistical analysis. By this time, management should have gained an honest appreciation for the tangible nature of software as a product. That is, software is an important asset to be managed, and it has great potential to be exploited in three very important ways:

- To differentiate company products from competitor's
- To improve all automated factory processes
- To simplify and aid human activity

After everyone understands that software is important to the success of the entire enterprise, the focus should be shifted from getting manager's arms and minds around software, to that of making it superior to their competitor's software. This takes an additional investment in time and resources that must be carefully traded off against other commitments and opportunities.

At a minimum, the software quality programmatic activities should be extended beyond reliance on after-the-fact measurements. A total software quality program should be fostered that makes quality a human experience of mind and heart. This includes continuous improvement, not just meeting statistical quality control two-sigma levels. Everyone should be trying to find sources of errors to

TSd

eliminate them, not just finding bugs and fixing them. To accomplish this final objective, managers must hire people that really care about quality software, just as they do when employing top-notch hardware people.

This suggested approach to bringing the software in an automated manufacturing enterprise under effective management control has an extremely important side effect. The enterprise will discover that managers and software people have many things in common and can actually work together effectively as a team. Software problems are no longer thrown over the wall. Instead, managers and software engineers will carry the software over the wall together!

MANAGEMENT INVOLVEMENT WITH SOFTWARE

It is important that the enterprise's chief executive officer (CEO) takes a personal interest in software and accepts the above prescription for bringing software under effective management control. He should begin treating software as an important asset that can be exploited to the benefit of the manufacturing enterprise as a whole.

The CEO's direction-setting interest in software should be transmitted to the rest of the enterprise through a written corporate policy statement that encourages all managers to increase their understanding of software, and become actively involved with it wherever appropriate. Specifically, the top-level policy document should emphasize that software must be carefully planned, and then managed throughout its entire life cycle. In this way, all automated factory software can be exploited to the fullest, thus maximizing its benefits and minimizing its cost to the enterprise.

Required Educational Objectives

The following list of educational objectives will help satisfy this recommended corporate need for thorough software understanding. The list can be transformed into an education and training program tailored to the specific needs of the enterprise.

- All managers should have a thorough understanding of software as a tangible product in order to successfully exploit its potential.
- Managers should understand that effective software management practices depend on a documented software development process.
- Managers should be able to evaluate software development status by effectively communicating with software personnel and by learning software jargon.
- Management must learn how to quantitatively assess the effectiveness of every software development activity and maintain a penetrating view of ongoing projects.
- Management must learn to make business demands that are consistent with good software development practices, demands that are feasible and reasonable.
- Management must learn how to make staffing and investment plans that will improve software quality and productivity.
- Management must understand how to improve software productivity through proper coupling of software development tools with modern programming methods.

Software Knowledge Can Never Be Complete

There is an insidious problem with software in that it can never be completely understood. This is not unique to software, but the problem is that many people think they know a lot about it, but really do not. It is important that managers understand why this is so.

It has been said that in any field of human endeavor "a little knowledge can be a dangerous thing." This is true today with respect to software, especially in the automated factory context. Engineers that routinely program complex mathematical routines in FORTRAN cannot understand why the data processing people take so long doing a "simple" update to the payroll system. A growing number of senior managers have become personal computer (PC) literate. They are able to write programs in Basic, use spreadsheet macros, and are comfortable using world-wide electronic mail systems on a routine basis. Many of these managers do not understand why there is a huge backlog of work in the information systems department, when the software tasks seem so simple to them.

The answer is that software is simply not simple. In fact, the Japanese have a target technology objective for the year 2002 to be able to write bug-free, large-scale software, in short order.[3] My belief is that the problem has to do with system size and knowledge requirements for understanding.

The amount of knowledge required by any individual to perform an assigned task is related not only to the technical and qualitative content of the job, but also to its physical size or scope as shown in FIG. 12-1. My hypothesis is that a distribution of specialized knowledge or "know how" versus system size exists in every field of science and engineering.

It seems reasonable that the majority of workers in any field have a knowledge base for their profession that encompasses systems of "normal size." Systems considered "large scale" are beyond the capabilities of most workers to define, design, and construct since they require greater

amounts of specialized knowledge. Similarly, systems that are "very small" as defined by terms such as "micro" or "miniature" also require more specialized knowledge.

Examples from Some Fields of Engineering In electrical engineering, for example, leading edge research and applications in microelectronics at the very small size system end of the scale definitely requires highly specialized knowledge. At the other end of the electrical engineering spectrum, large scale factory power generation and distribution systems such as in the metals industry, also require highly specialized knowledge, but of a very different kind. At the center of the system size scale are large numbers of electricians, for example, that know how to safely wire automated factory production lines and materials handling systems.

Specialized knowledge requirements in the field of mechanical engineering are similar. When one leaves the common center of designing and developing normal machine tools and begins to consider micro machining and assembly operations, highly specialized knowledge is required. Similarly, the design and construction of ocean-going ship unloaders, and heavy industry equipment such as

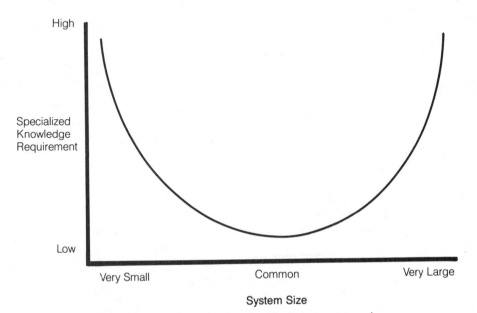

Fig. 12-1. Specialized knowledge required versus system size.

massive presses and rolling mills, require vastly different knowledge than that required of a person designing tools for microsurgery.

In the area of industrial engineering, the knowledge versus system size relationship also exists. The detailed ergonomics investigations concerning how individual human beings can best operate in a workplace is far different than organizing the layout for a new factory that will employ 5,000 workers.

In short, my thesis is that people working at different points along the system size scale must receive different education and training programs to be able to effectively perform their assigned tasks. The farther apart they are on this scale, the more disparate is their educational requirement.

Software Knowledge Requirements Are Similar to Engineering   The relationships described above in some of the traditional engineering fields also apply to software and information systems in the automated factory. Managers and software engineers also possess individual knowledge bases that help them perform work within one particular slice of the system size spectrum. As they move away from what is familiar, in either direction from that point, they become less and less competent, unless new training and education is provided.

To communicate with computer hardware, whether it be an IS mainframe or controllers on the factory floor, workers must write computer programs, or software. The majority of programmers are professionals who write application programs for others in COBOL, FORTRAN, or a similar higher order language. At the small scale end of the programming spectrum, hardware engineers and systems programmers write in microcode to communicate directly with computing hardware. At the large scale end of the programming spectrum, nonsoftware people or "users" write in application program command languages to make computers solve problems for them directly, without the aid of professional programmers.

Developing information systems requires the same diversity of knowledge. In the center, we generally have off-the-shelf computers programmed in common higher order languages that make up an information system. At the small system end of the

scale, we find special-purpose processors embedded in automated products. These are usually programmed in so-called "real-time" languages such as CMS, JOVIAL, or Ada, together with portions of code programmed in various assemblers. This is especially true in the aerospace and defense system industry.

At the other end of the size scale, we find automated factory systems made up of large numbers of heterogeneous computers that require not only different languages to make them operate, but also a new dimension of communication protocols and languages that tie them together as integrated systems. The integration of an automobile assembly plant is a typical example where local area networks (LANS) and perhaps the Manufacturing Automation Protocol (MAP) are used to tie dissimilar automated systems together into an integrated whole. Some of the most complex software development problems involve large-scale factory-floor information systems of this type, which tie together different systems into an integrated whole.

Most software people are educated and trained in computer basics and the programming of small to medium sized, commonly understood, software systems. They are not trained to cope with large-scale factory systems. Others work their way into the software field from a nonsoftware education base such as electrical engineering. These "software engineers" have learned for the most part how to program specialized small-scale application systems. Very few software professionals are formally trained in the development of large-scale systems, or even have experience in working with them.

Implications for Large-Scale Factory Software Systems

The implication of this knowledge-requirement hypothesis for large-scale software systems for the automated factory is far reaching. In short, there is no education or training program in computer science, software engineering, computer engineering, or computer programming that can provide a comprehensive set of knowledge for any individual in today's automated factory. The reason is that the field of software engineering is not only new,[*] but it has become as diverse as any other field of engineering. This fact must be recognized and taken into account by management.

For example, a straight-A graduate hired from one of the best universities in the country will still have a long way to go to be able to become functionally literate when placed at a point in the system size spectrum that is too far from his or her starting point knowledge base. Just as in the other scientific and technical fields, individuals must specialize with regard to information system size in order to become proficient in their day-to-day work.

The biggest problem facing the software industry today is not at the middle or small-scale end of the system size range, but at the very large size end. Three of the many reasons for this problem follow below.

First, graduate-level science and engineering programs tend to focus on adding knowledge at the micro end of the system scale since that is generally where science and engineering meet. For example, microelectronics engineers must take into account problems of physics and chemistry when dealing with submicron technology. Software design is concerned with timing considerations in the increasingly faster microcircuitry.

Second, large-scale information system planning, design, development, and operational support represent major problems for management. For this reason, large-scale system problems are of interest to professionals in the softer sciences of sociology and psychology—in the areas of organizational design and human behavior for example—since considerations of teaming, coordination theory, and human communication are major factors that impact the life cycle of large-scale information systems.

Third, too little attention is paid to large-scale computing and software from the computer science academic community. As a result, commercial and government organizations look primarily to vendors and consultants to help them solve their large-scale automated system problems. While in many cases this help is excellent, large-scale information system problems have not been dealt with in a rigorous manner by academe. In the factory, management's solution has been all too often to simply throw the problem over the wall to the experts. Remember, we should be carrying it over the wall together.

Fundamentals for Software Success

To successfully manage software in the automated factory, two fundamentals must be mastered. First, managers must understand their relationship to the software life cycle process, and especially the communication linkages between software professionals and themselves. Second, managers must take personal responsibility for software work product definition and control by extending their "command control" or "project management" rigor to all types of software product developments, especially the more difficult large-scale information systems.

Therefore, let me continue with a discussion of the first fundamental regarding relationships between management and software people. I will then follow with how to add rigor to software management practice.

THE DUAL LIFE CYCLE MODEL

A 1989 research paper I authored reports on an enterprise-wide concept of a large-scale information system birth-to-death life cycle.[4] This new integrated, layered, life cycle conceptual model has been named the "Dual Life Cycle Model (DLCM)." What is new is that the DLCM is composed of parallel management and engineering life cycles, connected by a well defined communications protocol.

Since software engineering is still a new field, practitioners have not yet decided on a standard way to develop software. For example, a recent journal article includes supporting arguments for yet another in a very long series of candidate life cycle models intended to improve the software

---

[*]The terminology *software engineering* was coined in 1968 at a NATO conference.

process.[5] The primary reason for this improved "spiral" model, according to the author, Dr. Barry Boehm, is that it is risk-driven, rather than document or code-driven. The latter types have been criticized for years, most recently in a major Department of Defense study published in 1986.[6] Boehm supports his case by providing an excellent chronology of software life cycle development history, together with reasons why each model has been found to be inadequate in some way.

The life cycle definition problem has also been troublesome to me, for over two decades. As a metallurgical and industrial engineer by formal training, and a software engineer and manager by practice, I have been trying to understand why managers who are responsible for major software development projects frequently have enormous difficulty defining software work packages that can be executed in an orderly manner over the life of a major system development effort. The reason for my frustration is that I have observed that work is planned and executed for large-scale physical systems than for software systems of equivalent complexity. When problems arise during a traditional hardware engineering life cycle, responsible managers and engineers can almost always locate the source of trouble and take prompt corrective action to fix whatever is wrong. Why do we seem to have so much trouble coping with similar software problems, especially those involved with large-scale factory information systems?

The conceptual model that evolved from this research has become known by the research team as the *Dual Life Cycle Model*. The new model portrays the conceptual differences between management and software engineering perspectives, and the content of communication work products needed to effectively connect management with engineering in general. A simplified version of the DLCM is shown in FIG. 12-2.

A More Detailed Look at the DLCM

The conceptual Dual Life Cycle Model in FIG. 12-2 draws attention to the communication paths that transfer project information back and forth between the two parallel (dual) life cycles.

FIGURE 12-3 represents a more detailed view of the DLCM and illustrates the interrelatedness of the sequence of specific products produced by software engineers and managers over the complete life of a generic information system. Furthermore, all processes within the dual life cycle are initiated by either a user need, called *technology pull*, or a product idea, called *technology push*.

The DLCM begins when a user need or product idea becomes a system concept document or product specification. This document is used to trigger a series of management actions, which in turn culminate in a formal project approval or rejection to construct and deliver the specified factory information system product. In addition to approval actions, planning activities that delineate project goals, define supporting work packages, and allocate personnel, equipment, and facilities for use on the project take place.

While management is busy planning, engineers are busy performing technical feasibility studies and conferring with their counterparts in the user's organization to determine more precisely what will satisfy user needs. At some point early in this dual life cycle, the software engineering organization receives formal work authorizations to proceed, along with allocations of resources to carry out their work. These activities are prerequisites for initiating a subsequent and subordinate software engineering life cycle that will be mentioned later.

Dual Life Cycle Artifacts or Work Products

The most important perspective that can be gained from the DLCM concept is the relationship between management and software engineering labor and resulting work products. In the management layer the primary concern is for project plans and status representations, whereas engineers are primarily concerned with software transformation representations. This valuable insight, which is obvious from an enterprise perspective, distinguishes the DLCM from the traditional *waterfall*

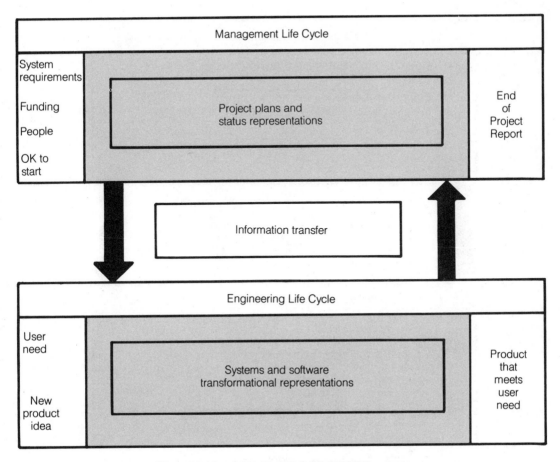

Fig. 12-2. Dual Life Cycle Model (DLCM) concept.

and *acquisition management* models, and variations such as the *spiral* model.

The Dual Life Cycle Model distinguishes and interrelates four categories of work products that can be represented by an orderly progression of artifacts over the life cycle of any information system product of interest: (1) communication work products or artifacts produced by managers for engineers, (2) communication artifacts produced by engineers for managers, (3) management artifacts produced by managers for their own use, and (4) technical artifacts produced by engineers for their own use. In the following paragraphs examples of typical artifacts in each of the above categories are identified with italic type.

Artifacts Produced by Managers for Engineers Managers are responsible for planning, organizing, staffing, directing, and controlling software engineering activities, just as they manage other engineering activities in the manufacturing enterprise. They manage engineers by providing them with *authorizations* to begin work and to use specified resources. As projects progress, they monitor and evaluate technical progress by analyzing technical *plans* and *reports*. Managers control work by redirecting specific activities and issuing new *approvals*. Finally, they terminate work by issuing new *task orders* to replace *current orders*. Note that these same types of activities are carried out by the higher layers of program, enterprise,

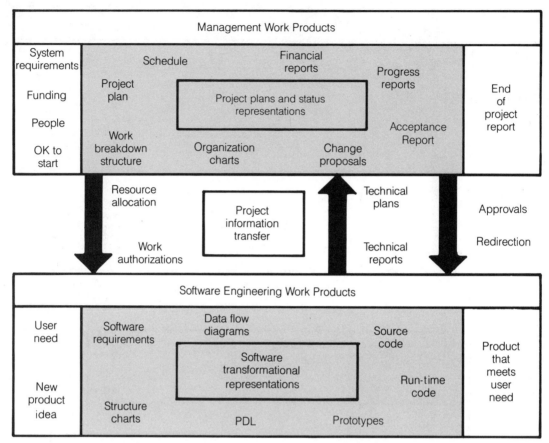

Fig. 12-3. Typical sequence of DLCM work products.

and customer management but in lesser detail the higher the management level.

Artifacts Produced by Engineers for Managers Software engineers are responsible for planning, organizing, and carrying out all types of software development activities, including software embedded in engine control processors, logic for machine tools, and shop-floor information systems. They communicate with management by providing *work plans* for approval, and *progress reports* on their accomplishments.

The project information transfer products described above, which are exchanged between the two DLCM layers, are difficult to prepare, since they involve communication between two quite different cultures. Thus, they are often not the work products of primary interest to the players in either

layer who prepare them. Work products of primary interest to most individuals are those pertaining to their own fields of expertise, such as those described below.

Artifacts Produced by Management for Management Work products created by management for its own use include *resource allocation and control documents* such as work breakdown structures, organization charts, project schedules, financial reports, and change proposals. These work products are the primary concern of management. This is the only category of products observed in traditional management life cycles.

Artifacts Produced by Engineers for Engineers Systems and software engineers are primarily concerned with producing *technical specifications*, software *design representations*, working *prototypes, source code,* and ultimately a *run-time code* product of high quality that satisfies user needs. These work products are the primary concern of software engineers. This is the only category of products observed in traditional software engineering life cycles.

DLCM Work Product Summary

In summary, there are four categories of work products or artifacts that have been identified using the DLCM conceptual model. These are highlighted in FIG. 12-4.

It is interesting to note that an enormous literature exists concerning the best ways to produce management and engineering work products that are useful to managers for hardware development in the automated factory. A smaller but growing literature is available concerning how software engineers should create work products for their own use during the process of developing information systems.

Missing from the current literature is a description of the minimum, yet essential, life cycle information artifacts that should be produced by managers and engineers for each other, whether they are engaged in software or hardware activities. This missing dimension can be provided by using a rigorous management approach to large-scale software life cycle functions. Properly produced and utilized, these essential communication work products can reduce complexity and improve the effectiveness of both the management and engineering life cycles.

ADDING MANAGEMENT RIGOR TO THE DUAL LIFE CYCLE MODEL

Fundamental to implementing the DLCM is a mutual understanding by line managers and software engineers of how to make effective use of the total automated factory objectives and goals developed for them by enterprise management. In other words, the personnel in all management and software development layers of the DLCM must clearly understand organizational objectives, and know the specific goals they are trying to achieve as individual members of the team. Without this mutual understanding of each other's roles, complex undertakings face an unnecessary risk of failure.

Software Work Product Definition and Control

Management communication to software engineers in the form of management information work products for engineers are vital for success. An organization's statement of vision or mission, "the business we are in;" timeless purposes or organizational objectives; measurable and scheduled goals

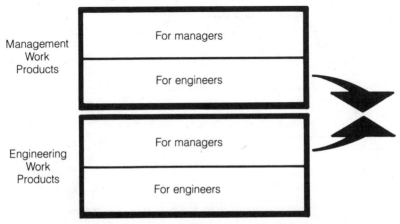

Fig. 12-4. Management engineering work product relationships.

or milestones; supporting action plans or building-block projects; and specific work packages or well-defined supporting activities constitute a hierarchical, linked set of information work products. Taken together, they communicate actions to be taken by subordinates for making things happen in a proactive, constructive, and efficient manner. The model in FIG. 12-5 shows how these management information products conceptually fit together.

Competent managers usually follow an orderly path to achieve positive results using a goal-setting approach. They seldom succumb to the pressure of unexpected, high-priority interruptions. They stick to the basics. The approach to management communication shown in FIG. 12-5 incorporates these fundamentals and is highly recommended. To help with its implementation and use, I define the communication work products in more detail below.

- *Mission*: a statement describing the well-defined business(es) the organization is currently in; or alternatively, a visionary statement of what business(es) the organization would like to be in; in other words, the organization's fundamental reason for existence.

- *Objective*: a timeless, broad-based, generalized statement of intent that supports the organizational mission

- *Goal*: a statement of specific intent that is quantitatively measurable and bounded by a specific period of time

- *Action plan*: a work plan detailing measurable steps that focus on achieving a specific goal; or alternatively, one of several work plans required to accomplish a single goal

- *Work package*: a description of how to perform a supporting activity or task. This can include how to set up a workplace, the major steps involved to accomplish the task, supporting method and tool descriptions, and the criteria or tests required to determine when the task has been satisfactorily completed

From an enterprise viewpoint, there is an obvious importance in employing these common-sense management tools to achieve organizational success in an engineering-oriented domain such as the auto-

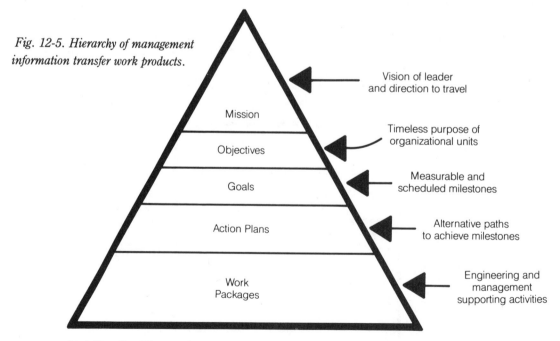

Fig. 12-5. Hierarchy of management information transfer work products.

Mission — Vision of leader and direction to travel

Objectives — Timeless purpose of organizational units

Goals — Measurable and scheduled milestones

Action Plans — Alternative paths to achieve milestones

Work Packages — Engineering and management supporting activities

Adapted From: King, W.R. and D.I. Cleland, Strategic Planning and Policy, Van Nostrand and Reinhold Company, New York 1981, pp. 133-138

mated factory. They ensure that everyone in an organization shares a common vision of the future and a common understanding of how their day-to-day tasks help move the organization toward its goal.

When we combine these communication work products with information products produced by software engineers for managers, we have all of the building blocks necessary for effective communications between the DLCM layers. In short, they support a closed-loop process that permits management to define broad objectives, translate them into specific work packages, and obtain quantitative feedback on the results.

The Management Process as a System of Tools—An Example

FIGURE 12-5 further implies that once top management decides on the precise "business we are in" statement (statement of mission or organizational purpose), and further declares such things as "we will constantly strive to improve our manufacturing process quality" (an objective statement), a transformation must be made to implement defined objectives in a concrete manner. This begins with goal-setting.

To set a goal we must transform an objective statement into a more tangible format. As we continue with the top-management-directed product quality improvement theme, we notice that the rather fuzzy statement of timeless purpose must be quantified before actual work can be defined and assigned for accomplishment. Thus, to improve a specific process in a manufacturing environment, the next step might be to define a goal such as "we will reduce our scrap loss on Machining Center 24B in Department A by at least 10 percent during the next fiscal year." Note that this statement is not only specific, but it requires a measurement (of scrap loss) and also must be completed within a specific period of time (next fiscal year).

To implement this goal, an action plan must next be defined and set into motion. One of the most important prerequisites for developing any detailed low-level plan is at least one metric to help

gauge whether or not all defined work succeeded. In our example, this is a measure of scrap loss rate (a surrogate negative measure of manufacturing process quality). In a simple case, this metric could be defined as "the actual number of parts produced by Machining Center 24B that do not pass inspection and are rejected over a specific period of time (e.g., daily or weekly), divided by the total number of parts produced in the same period."

Once we have defined the specific measure or criterion for success, we examine how we can achieve success within the scheduled time permitted for carrying out the work plan. As simple as this example is, a goal-supporting action plan is not always easy to define. In this case, the manager faces numerous options on how he could change the current metric and thereby improve quality in this highly focused dimension.

One possible way would be to first assign someone to observe the operator of Machining Center 24B to identify any errors he makes that result in scrap loss. Then, a retraining program could be instituted to help change the operator's behavior with the expectation that this will reduce the number of mistakes being made. If all goes well, the redirected operator will perform better work, and the metric of interest (percent of scrap loss per unit time) will decline. Another approach to the problem would be to inspect materials going into the machining center for their quality, since scrap could originate at this external source, rather than being generated by operator error alone.

Regardless of the specific alternative action plan chosen, at the end of the first one-year period, the work results are summed up in a final single measure of scrap loss rate, compared to the starting scrap loss rate. If the scrap loss rate has been reduced by at least 10 percent, the defined goal has been successfully achieved, and the timeless organizational objective of improving manufacturing process quality has been supported in a positive manner. At the bottom line, one specific goal has been reached, and the organization has benefited from the effort expended.

To implement the above sequence of actions, the factory needs an information system. This, in turn, requires software, if the press is to be a part of the automated factory.

FACTORY SOFTWARE ENGINEERING PROJECT CONTROL

Once a new information system development project is planned for the automated factory, the question of management control of the system development project must be addressed. The minimum essential elements of such a control system include the plan itself, a project monitoring system, and a reporting system. Each of these three elements must be present for the project manager to obtain information upon which to base corrective action decisions.

It was mentioned earlier that there are several other categories of software besides factory information systems. Both mainframe and PC-level software can be used to support project management and should therefore be considered by enterprise management as another software asset to be managed. This leads to one more important question: How well are factory managers utilizing this type of off-the-shelf packaged software?

PC-Based Project Management Software

According to an August 1988 personal computer trade press article,[7] large corporations are increasing their purchases of project management software. Two surveys polled approximately 30,000 public and private sector sites having personal computers installed in numbers ranging from less than 10 to over 500.

Of significance in this report was the trend in project management software tools among the approximately 4,800 sites that have 500 or more personal computers installed. Only 16 percent owned any project management packages in October 1986, whereas 31 percent had installed such software by December 1987. By comparison, the increases in project management software use by sites owning 100 or less personal computers were in the range of three percent or less. One can infer that the education of large-scale users in the bene-

fits of project management is significantly increasing. Given the increasing use of software to support project management, let us return to the main theme and see how project management should be used to control information system software.

Software Project Plans Are One Key to Success

The project plan is one key to large-scale factory software system success, since a detailed plan is necessary for effective management control. The project plan must identify the specific work packages involved, which collectively define the total scope of the project, as well as define the cost allowances and schedule requirements. The work packages are logically linked upward through the organizational hierarchy to support the direction of top level management and overall mission statement.

Monitoring a carefully prepared project plan is a matter of quantitatively measuring expected performance against the plan. Thus, measures of human and machine output, expenditures of funds, and times required for work accomplishment are the essential data to be collected on a continuing basis. In addition to raw data, the reporting system from the engineering layer of the dual life cycle model to the management layer must include analysis and interpretation. The most common examples of this type of reporting involve the identification of deviations from forecasted trends, and in some cases, standards.

When engineering reports on project plan deviations to management, management takes a variety of corrective actions. Such actions could include revising the project plan, retraining or replacing personnel, or modifying or changing equipment. In short, redirection is communicated back to the engineering layer of the DLCM; that closes the control process communication loop.

Software Project Control Documents— One Example

Documents that support a project control system are also critical elements for success in large-scale software engineering. There is a distinct parallel between the large-scale software project and the engineering and construction industry. Both areas need rigorous software requirements analysis, system architectural planning and design, and system development or "construction" control. Let us look at how one of the world's largest engineering and construction firms, Bechtel Corporation, defines its project control documentation. Their example serves as a model for large-scale software development projects. They have defined their control documents as follows.

Scope of Services Manual   This manual establishes a baseline for identifying changes in services and a definition of engineering, home office support, and field nonmanual services that will be performed by the company in executing the contract.

Division of Responsibility Document This document describes the responsibilities of the company, the client, and the major suppliers.

Project Procedures Manual   This defines the procedures involved in interface activities among the company, the client, and the major suppliers with respect to engineering, procurement, construction, preoperational services, quality assurance, quality control, project control, and communication.

Technical Scope Document   This describes the project's physical plant, establishes the design basis, and provides input to the civil and structural, architectural, plant design, mechanical, electrical, and control systems disciplines.

Project Activity Control Guide   This aids the administration of project activities by identifying and time phasing the development and execution of project plans, programs, procedures, controls, and other significant activities required for effective operation of the project.[8]

Project and Planning Documents— A Second Example

For very large-scale information system planning and development projects the basic control documents used by Bechtel are also appropriate

with minor modification. I base this assertion on my experience with another major engineering and construction company, and with a multicountry development of a digital public switching system by a major telecommunications manufacturer. In the telecommunications case, the switching system development project employed approximately 450 programmers at peak manloading, and had software development teams on both sides of the Atlantic located in five different countries. The key to the ultimate success of this project, just as in Bechtel's projects, involved detailed project and system engineering planning documents that covered the following five essential elements:

- Definition of the work breakdown structure to include specific responsibilities for every organization and individual involved in the project
- Definition of communication interface procedures among all of the organizations having project responsibilities
- Definition of the total system architecture and its relationship to the greater environmental system within which it will ultimately operate
- Definition of all required supporting disciplines and the specific roles they play in the project
- Definition of how the project is administered and controlled

I believe there is another major lesson that can be learned from the large-scale engineering and construction industry that applies to large-scale information system projects. This is their deliberate separation of engineering from construction.

SEPARATING ENGINEERING FROM CONSTRUCTION

It is easy for anyone to understand why the engineering of a skyscraper, subway system, or hydroelectric dam must be executed by carefully designing the system and documenting the results through thousands of blueprints, prior to breaking ground for physical construction. Why should the development of a large-scale information system be any different? The short answer to this rhetorical question is that there should not be any difference. The problem is that we can too easily jump ahead into coding software long before our "blueprints" are completed.

One possible solution to the problem of getting ahead of ourselves may be to separate *information system engineering* from *information system construction*, just as it is done in the engineering and construction industry. Conceptually, engineers should be able to design a system in sufficient detail that tradesmen can construct it under supervision of field engineers. What this means is that there are basically three classifications of jobs, not including managers and supervisors: (1) design engineers, (2) field engineers, and (3) construction workers.

If we treat large-scale information system planning and development projects in the same way, what key people will design the system? Who are the technical workers that will construct it? Who are the "field engineers" that supervise the construction process? We certainly do not need advanced degree software "gurus" to do all three of these jobs, just as high school trained programmers are not capable of performing some of the highly skilled architecture and design tasks. Thus, we can learn from the experienced engineering and construction industry when it comes to the planning and control of large-scale software development projects for the automated factory.

INFORMATION SYSTEM COST ESTIMATING AND CONTROL

One of the most important two-way communication processes between information system managers and engineers, as depicted by the DLCM in FIGS. 12-2 AND 12-3, involves cost estimating and control. Prior to launching a new project, and periodically during the system life cycle, management must constantly strive to obtain accurate estimates of projected costs for information system planning, development, and support activities.

Unfortunately, cost estimation and control of systems with large-scale software content is another area requiring additional research. This is true because no specific formulas or estimating

relationships are yet available off-the-shelf that are totally satisfactory. Therefore, let us look once again at methods used in traditional engineering to instruct us in how to deal more effectively with software. According to a leading textbook on engineering economic analysis a cost estimate is defined as follows:

> A cost estimate is an opinion based upon analysis and judgment of the cost of a product, system, or service. This opinion may be arrived at in either a formal or an informal manner by several methods, all of which assume that experience is a good basis for predicting the future. In many cases the relationship between past experience and future outcome is fairly direct and obvious; in other cases it is unclear, because the proposed product, system, or service differs in some significant way from its predecessors. The challenge is to project from the known to the unknown by using experience with existing items. The techniques used for cost estimating range from intuition at one extreme to detailed mathematical analysis at the other.[9]

The problem with large-scale information systems is that we have a very limited experience base. Furthermore, they more often than not differ considerably from any prior system due to rapid changes in computing technology. Not only that, it is rare that the team of individual software engineers building a new large-scale system have been involved with a similar project in the past due to the high mobility of software people within the industry, both upward and laterally. For these reasons, current techniques for estimating the costs of large-scale information systems tend to be based more on intuition, than on mathematics.

On the positive side, there are three fundamental cost estimating methods used in traditional engineering fields that should be reviewed for application to the world of automated factory information systems: (1) estimating by engineering procedures, (2) estimating by analogy, and (3) statistical estimating.

Estimating by Engineering Procedures

Estimating by engineering procedures can be best described as examining in detail large numbers of separate system segments. Each element is analyzed and costs assigned separately. The collection of individual results are synthesized into a total for a project, or system, or both. For large-scale systems, this method is very costly and time-consuming. More importantly, although it appears to be the most rigorous of all approaches, it is subject to error when thousands of individual estimates are combined into a total that can turn out to be much greater or less than the sum of its parts.

Estimating by Analogy

Estimating by analogy can be useful as a check on other methods, or can be used by itself when developing a new system or venturing into a new area. This method can be used at both the macro level and micro level. In the 1950s, aircraft manufacturers that bid on new missile systems performed macro estimating by analogy by drawing analogies between aircraft and missiles. At the micro level, analogies between direct labor hours and equipment hours required to complete Project A can be used to help estimate the cost of a different Project B that uses similar types of labor and machines. The biggest disadvantage of this method is the high degree of judgment required by those doing the estimating. According to Thuesen and Fabrycky, "considerable experience and expertise are required to identify and deal with appropriate analogies and to make adjustments for perceived differences."[9] On the positive side, estimating by analogy is fast and relatively inexpensive.

Statistical Estimating

The objective of statistical estimating is to discover a functional relationship between changes in costs and the factors on which the cost depends. This method is preferred in most situations, but depends upon a historical database to be able to make accurate predictions of the future. If historical records are unavailable then, estimating by analogy and/or by engineering analysis must be undertaken. This method uses statistical techniques that range from simple graphical curve fitting to complex multiple correlation analysis and varies according to

both the purpose of the analysis, and the information available.

All three of the above methods are used to one degree or another in estimating life cycle costs for large-scale information systems. The fundamental problem with obtaining accurate results, however, is the general lack of a solid historical database of quantitative information upon which to support accurate software estimates. All fields of traditional engineering foster the collection and analysis of data as a necessary function. Unfortunately, these activities have not yet been given a very high priority in the world of software engineering. Thus, estimating costs of software-intensive systems is still primitive and in need of further research.

FACTORY SOFTWARE REQUIREMENTS

The last major point to be made about managing software in the automated factory relates once again to the communication disconnect between managers and software people. In order to correct this deficiency, we must begin at the beginning. This means getting the requirements for software right in the first place, so we do not build the wrong systems efficiently.

Information for Getting Started

Factory information system software engineers normally begin their work on a large-scale system by analyzing software requirements documentation. This requirements information can be represented as an information input vector, I_r, which will be transformed over time into the runtime code embedded in the system to be developed. The significance of I_r is that it constitutes the generally accepted starting basis for a software engineering life cycle. This is also the point in the system life cycle where managers tend to throw their software management responsibilities over the wall to software people.

I_r most often takes the tangible form of a lengthy requirements document that spells out user technical needs to be satisfied with software. Since such software requirements documents for large-scale information systems are often developed by committees that focus primarily on system rather than software issues, they require further work to reduce their ambiguity and complete missing elements before they are useful to software engineering.

This generally accepted practice of analyzing software requirements documentation leads to a common end result. Most software engineering life cycles begin with a "requirements analysis phase" that is based upon a software-only perspective of information systems engineering.

Management Constraints on the Software Engineering Life Cycle

When we take a larger systems perspective of information system development life cycles, we find many other and often more complex activities involved in the development of the software requirements input vector, I_r, that should be taken into account. Of most importance is the fact that many critical software technical constraints are often included in the requirements documentation. For example, hardware memory size limitations, programming language preferences, required software development tool chains, and similar elements are often specified in the I_r information vector.

Therefore, in the context of the DLCM, the relationship of an IS management life cycle layer to the IS engineering life cycle is more complex than is generally discussed in software engineering literature. In fact we must rely on systems engineering concepts to properly orient ourselves. FIGURE 12-6 below provides this perspective by illustrating how software (and also hardware) engineering activities are sandwiched between both front-end and back-end system engineering activities, and are really subsets of the overall system engineering life cycle.

Although not shown explicitly in FIG. 12-6, it should be clear that there also exists a parallel information vector that provides requirements for the displayed hardware engineering life cycle. How we handle the inputs to hardware engineering can also be highly instructive for what we do for software.

VIEW OF THE FUTURE

The Computer and Automated Systems Association of the Society of Manufacturing Engineers (CASA/SME) has a charter objective to "provide comprehensive and integrated coverage of the field of computers and automation for the advancement of manufacturing." CASA/SME is applications ori-

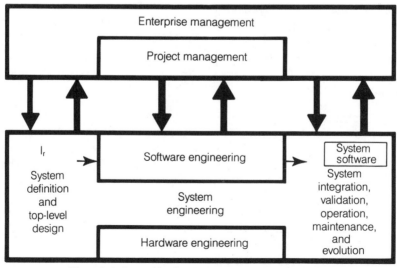

Fig. 12-6. System and software life cycle relationships.

ented rather than theoretical, yet is overtly trying to encourage the development of the totally integrated manufacturing facility. In pursuit of this futuristic objective, CASA/SME published the results of a "Round Table on Fifth Generation Management (FGM)," which contains several very special insights into computing and software from the total enterprise perspective.[10]

The round table participants derived the name Fifth Generation Management by drawing an analogy to the five generations of computer technology that they defined as follows:

- First: Electronic vacuum tube
- Second: Transistor
- Third: Integrated circuit
- Fourth: Very large scale integration
- Fifth: Parallel networked process units and symbolic processing

This sequence was compared to the following defined list of five generations of manufacturing enterprises:

- First: Small/entrepreneurial
- Second: Hierarchical/functional/divisional
- Third: Matrix
- Fourth: "Computer Interfaced Manufacturing (CIM I)"
- Fifth: "Computer Integrative Management of the Manufacturing Enterprise (CIM II)"

What is interesting in this CASA/SME analogy is the difference between the first four stages and the fifth in both of the above sequences. In essence, the first four generations of the computer are all sequential processors, or *von Neumann machines*. A totally different approach has been made with respect to so called *fifth generation computers*, such as parallel processors, and even multidimensional computers like the Hypercube.

The panel looked at management in the same way. In the first four generations of enterprise management, the enterprise structure is geared to supporting sequential flows of materials through hierarchical organizations as discussed throughout this chapter. Even the matrix organization does not fundamentally alter the primary organizational hierarchy.

When computers are applied to the enterprise management system in the form of computer-integrated manufacturing (CIM), they are only converting paper products to bits and speeding up information transfers in existing first, second, or third generation structures. However, fifth generation management is different, just as fifth generation computers are different than von Neumann machines. CASA/SME has chosen to use the word "integrative" to make their point.

Fifth generation management or FGM involves nodal networking and a total enterprise perspective. This permits a type of parallel processing in the management structure. The key is that each departmental function and subfunction becomes an independent knowledge center node, or decision point, on an interactive network. According to CASA/SME, "each node is capable of bringing their accumulated knowledge to bear in an interactive mode as the functions work in parallel."

FGM and Enterprise Objectives and Goals

FGM knowledge center nodes must be related through a common reference context. This reference point is in the form of the enterprise mission statement and top management objectives. In this way, the nodes will all be in tune with each other as they apply their individual accumulated knowledge and expertise to problems at hand.

The reference context, or top management direction, is not always made known to everyone in an enterprise. Thus, total integration will suffer due to noise in the information transfer network or internal communication channels. In addition to noise, we must recognize that FGM is not a von Neumann machine in that every employee only acts when he or she is told to, and in the exact manner prescribed by his job description or standard (strict command control structure).

FGM and Human Attitudes

FGM presupposes that personnel in each node can use their own initiative to solve problems in new and exciting ways, as long as they are supporting the enterprise mission, objectives, and goals. Thus we are talking about a major cultural change in moving from a fourth to fifth generation of management. The enterprise infrastructure is not only physically connected by computers and other information channels, but it is based on a new set of human attitudes. People must exhibit openness, trust, and intellectual honesty in pursuing the enterprise visions of success.

Needless to say, we have not yet reached the state of Fifth Generation Management, but it should be our goal. With that in mind, effective software management in the automated factory is not only desired, but to support FGM in the factory of the future, it is mandatory!

SUMMARY AND CONCLUSIONS

We began with an assertion that from an enterprise management perspective, factory automation includes the totality of computing system assets. This includes software, which is often regarded by management as the most troublesome to plan, develop, implement, and maintain.

Software can be effectively managed by using a systematic approach that draws heavily from hard-ware engineering and project management principles. In particular, a special software life cycle process model, the DLCM, should be used to better understand relationships, responsibilities, and communications between managers and software people. When the DLCM concepts are combined with careful attention to getting the initial software requirements right, and installing and using software quantitative controls, management has gone a long way toward placing their factory automation systems under effective management control.

I also caution management to be aware of the fact that we have a long long way to go to be able to fully understand software, especially how it can be most effectively developed quickly, without bugs. Recall that with focused effort, the Japanese do not expect to reach this goal before the year 2002!

Thus, managers from the CEO down to the lowest level supervisor in the automated factory must take time to learn about this most important asset, and most importantly, how to manage it effectively. Software may be troublesome, but it is absolutely necessary to the automated factory setting.

In short, to achieve success in the present, and attain the visions of the future, managers must learn to manage their software assets effectively. This challenge simply cannot be ignored!

ENDNOTES

1. "The Premier 100," supplement to *Computerworld* (September 12, 1988).

2. David A. Ludlum, "What do execs really want (from MIS)?," *Computerworld* (August 22, 1988):59-61.

3. "Charting the Future," in Special Section on Technology, *The Wall Street Journal* (November 14, 1988):R12.

4. John H. Manley, "The Dual Life Cycle Model," in *IEEE Tutorial: Systems and Software Requirements Engineering*, edited by R. H. Thayer and M. Dorfman (Silver Spring, Maryland: IEEE Computer Society Press, 1989).

5. Barry W. Boehm, "A Spiral Model of Software Development and Enhancement," *Computer* (May 1988):61-72.

6. F. P. Brooks, et al., *Defense Science Board Task Force Report on Military Software* (Washington, D.C.: Office of the Under Secretary of Defense for Acquisition, September 1987).

7. Lisa Day-Copeland, ''Project-Management Software Market Shows Indications of Growth,'' *PC Week* (August 22, 1988):102.

8. F. A. Hollenbach, ''Project Control in Bechtel Power Corporation,'' in *Project Management Handbook* (New York: Van Nostrand Reinhold Company, 1983), 458-459.

9. G. J. Thuesen and W. J. Fabrycky, *Engineering Economy*, 6th edition (Prentice-Hall, Inc., 1984), 408.

10. ''Fifth Generation Management for Fifth Generation Technology (A Round Table Discussion),'' in *SME Blue Book Series* (Dearborn, Michigan: Society for Manufacturing Engineers, 1987).

13

Maintenance Management

Andrew K.S. Jardine[*]

THIS CHAPTER DEALS WITH FOUR ISSUES OF IMPOR-
tance to maintenance within the automated factory:
component and system replacement, machine
inspection, organizational structure for maintenance, and an information system for maintenance.

The replacement section deals with identifying
which equipment components are candidates for
preventive replacement and then determining the
best time to make the preventive replacements.
The overall purpose of preventive replacement is to
enhance the reliability of manufacturing equipment.
Also discussed are complete system replacement
decisions, focusing on the life-cycle costing concept
before discussing how the economic life of capital
equipment can be identified.

The inspection section deals with setting the
frequency of inspection for equipment that is in
continuous operation but subject to failure. Inspection of equipment through health monitoring, such
as vibration or oil analysis, with the purpose of
improving overall system reliability is also discussed. In particular the procedure of proportional
hazards modeling as a method of improving decisions resulting from a health monitoring program is
identified.

The section dealing with problems of organizational structure focuses on requirements for maintenance in terms of manpower, equipment, and
spares.

In the final section of the chapter, a methodology is presented that enables identification of data
that should be collected as part of a Maintenance
Management Information System, thus ensuring
that an efficient decision-making system is in place.

COMPONENT AND SYSTEM REPLACEMENT

In the literature on maintenance, statements
appear such as: "We even change major parts like
starters and alternators before needed, to avoid
costly breakdowns . . . ," and "Nearly all current
planned maintenance systems prescribe work
which is unnecessary and which often achieves little
for the organization in terms of improved reliability
and performance of plant and equipment." This
section demonstrates how quickly it is possible to
objectively identify just which components are candidates for preventive replacement and what are
the best preventive replacement times.

The first requirement is to identify how a component fails. To do this, reliance is usually placed on
fitting a probability distribution to component failure
data (see chapter 32 in this book, "Reliability Engineering" by T. A. Mazzuchi and R. Soyer). As indicated in that chapter, the failure distribution, which
is usually Weibull, is given by:

$$f(t) = (\beta/\alpha) \, (t/\alpha)^{\beta-1} \exp\left[-(t/\alpha)^\beta\right] \, t > 0$$

*Andrew Jardine is Professor and Chairman of the Department of Industrial Engineering at the University of Toronto. Prior to joining
the University of Toronto in 1986 he was head of the Department of Engineering Management at the Royal Military College of
Canada. Dr. Jardine's interests lie in the general area of engineering management with a special interest in maintenance. He has had
practical experience in devising equipment maintenance and replacement procedures for a number of national and international
organizations.

where beta (β) is referred to as the shape parameter, and alpha (α) the scale parameter defined at the time at which the cumulative probability is 63.2 percent.

The reason that the Weibull is so attractive in preventive replacement analysis is because of the variety of failure patterns that can be represented by the distribution through modification of the value taken by the shape parameter, β. FIGURE 13-1 illustrates forms of the Weibull distribution for four alternative beta values. FIGURE 13-2 demonstrates that the beta value identifies whether or not the component has an increasing failure rate, decreasing failure rate, or constant failure rate. (See Mazzuchi and Soyer, chapter 32 for additional details.) As far as preventive replacement is concerned, it is necessary for a component's hazard function to be increasing, which is the case if $\beta > 1$. When this is the case the next question is: "Where on this increasing hazard curve is it economically justifiable to make a preventive replacement?" Before discussing that aspect, it is first necessary to discuss how, in practice, it is possible to identify the appropriate beta value given a history of component failures, and possibly also times at which components previously have been replaced on a preventive basis.

In 1967, Nelson had a paper published in *Industrial Quality Control*, in which he demonstrated how the Weibull parameters could be estimated through the use of specially prepared graph paper.[1] FIGURE 13-3 is an example of Weibull probability paper. Observe from the graph paper that the cumulative probability of failure is plotted on the Y-axis with time on the X-axis. To see how the paper is used, consider the data of TABLE 13-1 relating to the interval between failures for a sample of five bearings ordered by increasing interval. These data have been plotted on FIG. 13-3.

Plotting these data on Weibull probability paper and eyeballing a best fitting straight line (see FIG. 13-3) gives $\beta = 2.5$ and α (denoted η on the graph sheet) as 17.8 weeks. Since $\beta > 1.0$, the bearings are exhibiting an increasing risk of failure as they age, and, therefore, from a statistical point of view are candidates for preventive replacement.

Fig. 13-1. Weibull probability densities.

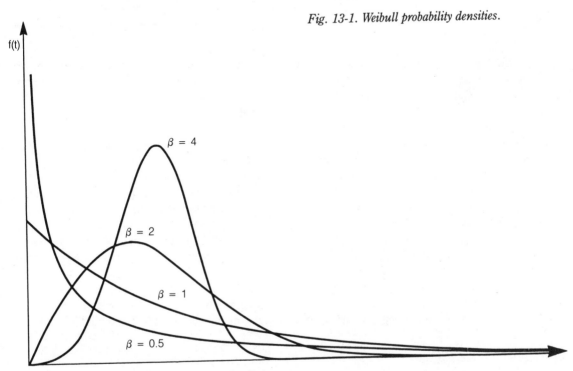

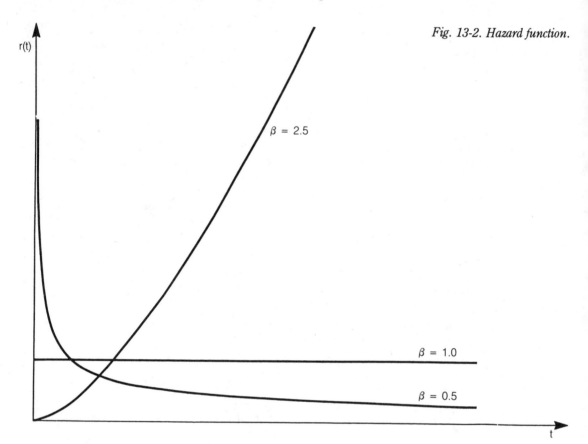

Fig. 13-2. Hazard function.

Of course rather than estimate the parameters of the Weibull distribution graphically, it is possible to use formal analytical estimation procedures. A useful reference to these procedures is given in Kapur and Lamberson, including the setting of confidence intervals on these estimates.[2]

Before a component is preventively replaced, two conditions must be met:

1. The total cost of a failure replacement is greater than the total cost of a preventive replacement. Of course, when identifying these costs, care has to be taken to ensure that all relevant costs are taken into account, such as materials, labor, and other costs associated with equipment being out of service.
2. There must be an increasing risk of failure occurring. In other words, if failure data are being analyzed by fitting a Weibull distribution, then the shape parameter beta must be estimated at greater than one.

Given that these two requirements are met, the objective frequently is to minimize the total cost associated with making preventive replacements and suffering the cost consequences of failure. These conflicting cost features are illustrated in FIG. 13-4.

The mathematical model used for total cost per week depends on the policy that is to be implemented. Two very common policies adopted for component preventive replacement are the block—sometimes also termed the constant interval, or group—model and the age-based model.

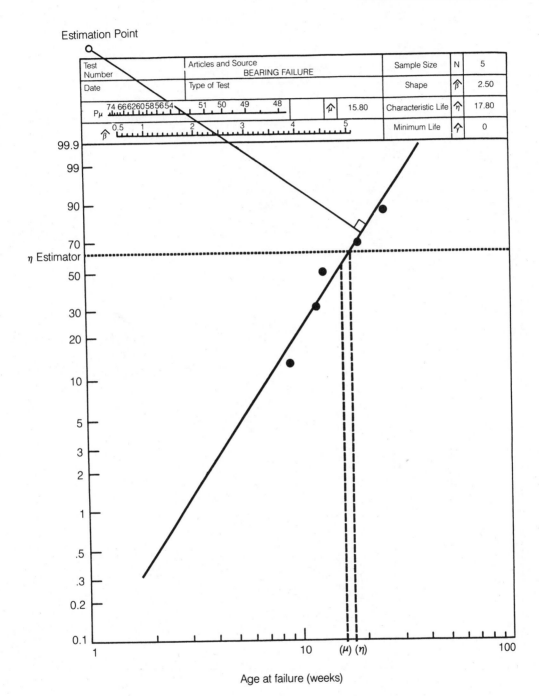

Estimation Point

Test Number	Articles and Source BEARING FAILURE	Sample Size	N	5
Date	Type of Test	Shape	$\hat{\beta}$	2.50
		15.80	Characteristic Life	$\hat{\eta}$	17.80
			Minimum Life	$\hat{\gamma}$	0

η Estimator

Age at failure (weeks)

Fig. 13-3. Weibull plot of bearing failure data.

Order Number	Ordered Failure Interval (Weeks)	Plotting Cum. (%)[1]
1	9	13.0
2	12	31.5
3	13	50.0
4	19	68.8
5	25	87.1

Table 13-1. Ordered Failure Times for Bearings.

1. Plotting cumulative obtained from median rank tables. See Kapur and Lamberson (1977) for median rank tables for samples of up to size 50.

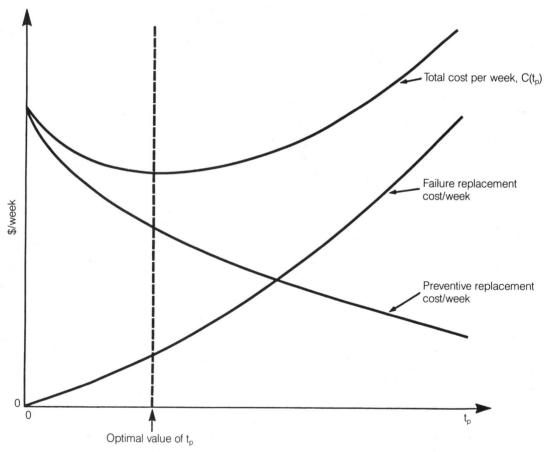

Fig. 13-4. Preventive replacement cost conflicts.

The Block Policy

The block policy assumes that a component is replaced at fixed intervals of length t_p with failure replacements occurring when required. This is illustrated in FIG. 13-5. The optimal replacement interval is then identified by solving the following model.

$$\text{Total Cost} = C(t_p) = [C_p + C_f H(t_p)]/t_p$$

where $H(t_p)$ is the expected number of failure replacements in interval $(0, t_p)$, and C_p and C_f are the total costs associated with preventive and failure replacement respectively.

The Age-Based Policy

The age-based policy assumes that a component is only replaced under preventive conditions once it reaches a specified age. If it fails before that age, then it is replaced under failure conditions. The model for the age-based policy is:

$$C(t_p) = [C_p R(t_p) + C_f (1 - R(t_p))]/[t_p R(t_p) + M(t_p)(1 - R(t_p))]$$

where $R(t_p)$ is the value of the reliability function at $t = t_p$ and is

$$\int_{t_p}^{\infty} f(t)\, dt$$

with $f(t)$ being the probability density function of the component failure times. $M(t_p)$ is the mean time to failure given that the system failed before t_p. It is the truncated mean life, and is:

$$\int_0^{t_p} t f(t)\, dt/[1 - R(t_p)]$$

Rather than solve the above models analytically, a very convenient graphical procedure was developed by Glasser in 1969.[3] Glasser's graphs require two assumptions: (1) the component's failure distribution is Weibull and (2) the ratio of the cost of the failure replacement to the cost of the preventive replacement can be obtained. Given these facts, it is a relatively easy process to identify the optimal preventive replacement age. Furthermore, the graph developed by Glasser enables cost saving to be identified that will accrue by replacing a component under preventive conditions at the best time, compared to replacing the component only on failure. Additionally, it is possible to write computer software to identify best preventive replacement times for components. One such package is REL-CODE,[4] which also establishes the economic benefit of replacing a component at its optimal time compared to any alternative time.

Let me give an example of the use of the age-based model. When cost data were combined with the result of the Weibull analysis of the bearing failure data in FIG. 13-3, then FIG. 13-6 was obtained, showing that the optimal replacement age is 14 weeks. The attraction of using the mathematical model is that the effect of deviating from the optimal can be clearly identified from the graph. Thus in practice, it would seem that a good preventive replacement age for these parts is anywhere from

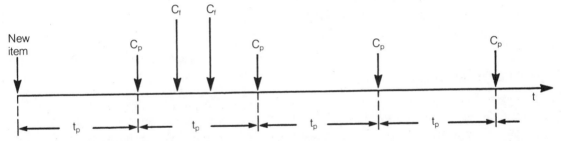

Fig. 13-5. The constant interval preventive replacement policy.

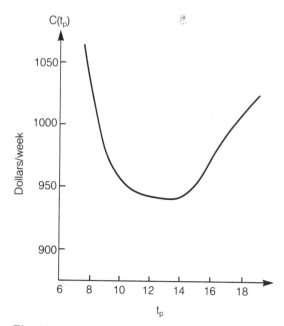

Fig. 13-6. Optimal preventive replacement of bearings.

about 10 to 14 weeks. Possibly in practice, preventive replacements would be scheduled to take place at an age of 12 weeks, but if at that time demand on the work force was such that it was impossible to carry out the preventive replacement without additional expense, then it would not be unreasonable to delay the replacement until week 13 or even week 14.

Similarly, if at week 11 or week 10 there was excess capacity in the work force, then it would be quite acceptable to advance the preventive replacement of the component to week 10 or 11. The graph demonstrates that the component should not be replaced before week 10, since it would mean that the component was being prematurely replaced. Neither should replacement be delayed past week 14, since in this case, the cost is building up quite rapidly.

Capital Equipment Replacement

FIGURE 13-7 illustrates the essential conflicts that need to be considered for the classical capital equipment replacement decision. The standard

economic life model (see for example Jardine[5]) is:

$$C(n) = \frac{[A + \sum_{i=1}^{n} C_i \, r^i - S_n r^n]}{1 - r^n}$$

In practice, the above model is often modified to take into account tax considerations. In addition, it is very important when undertaking such analysis, that a life cycle costing approach is considered. If this is done, then it certainly enhances the possibility that all relevant costs are incorporated into the model.

FIGURE 13-8, taken from Blanchard and Fabrycky,[6] depicts very nicely the iceberg effect; if care is not taken, then decisions may be made about capital equipment replacement based on certain clearly visible costs, but a large number of significant other costs may be omitted. Many text books dealing with engineering economics include the important aspect of the economic life of capital equipment, and indicate how it is possible to monitor capital equipment throughout its life and identify the point at which it is more economical to replace it rather than continue operating it.

As was the case with component replacement decisions, software can be acquired that enables analysis of a variety of capital equipment replacement problems. One such package is PERDEC that is used for plant, machinery and equipment replacement problems.[7] To use PERDEC, data on the purchase price of a new machine, trends in operations and maintenance costs, along with cost estimates of resale prices or scrap values and an appropriate interest rate for discounting are required. Many issues associated with asset replacement are covered in the standard engineering economic textbooks.

INSPECTION DECISIONS

Large complex systems in manufacturing are subject to failure, and since these system failures are undesirable, major components of the system are inspected at varying frequencies. Of course, as the frequency of inspection increases, a reduction is expected in the system failure rate. Just what the

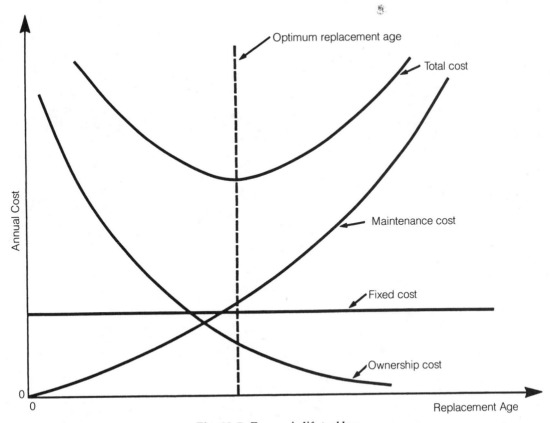

Fig. 13-7. Economic life problem.

best interval is, is our concern. A basic mathematical model relating different inspection frequencies to system unavailability is the following:

$$D(n) = \lambda(n)/\mu + n/i$$

where $\lambda(n)$ = arrival rate of system failure given an inspection frequency of n

$1/\mu$ = mean time to effect a repair
$1/i$ = mean time to inspect

$D(n)$ = total downtime of system for an inspection frequency of n

The optimal inspection frequency is that value of n that minimizes the right-hand side of the above equation.

While the equation seems relatively straightforward, in practice it is often quite difficult to identify the relationship between the system failure rate, and varying inspection frequencies. The reason for this difficulty is that organizations have in place a particular maintenance program (perhaps specified by the equipment manufacturer) and the outcome of that specified program is that there will be a particular system failure rate in place.

In order to identify the optimal inspection frequency, one must be able to identify the effect of different inspection intervals on the system failure rate. A possible way of obtaining this relationship is to experiment, and try different inspection intervals. In practice, this may be difficult. Perhaps a better alternative would be to cooperate with another organization that operates somewhat similar equipment but uses a different inspection fre-

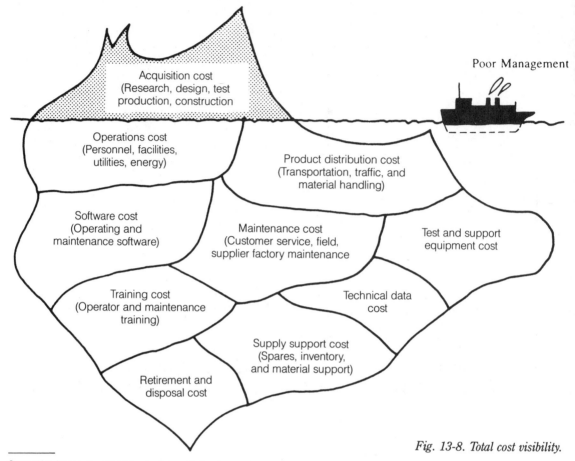

Poor Management

Acquisition cost
(Research, design, test
production, construction

Operations cost
(Personnel, facilities,
utilities, energy)

Product distribution cost
(Transportation, traffic, and
material handling)

Software cost
(Operating and
maintenance software)

Maintenance cost
(Customer service, field,
supplier factory maintenance

Test and support
equipment cost

Training cost
(Operator and maintenance
training)

Technical data
cost

Supply support cost
(Spares, inventory,
and material support)

Retirement and
disposal cost

Fig. 13-8. Total cost visibility.

Source: B. S. Blanchard and W.J. Fabrycky, *Systems Engineering and Analysis* (Prentice Hall, 1990).

quency. If neither of these two alternatives is possible, then a third possibility would be to simulate the system for varying inspection frequencies. This third alternative requires a large amount of detailed data on how constituent parts of the system fail.

Inspecting equipment through health monitoring is a procedure commonly used in industry. Two common forms of health monitoring are vibration and oil analysis. Health monitoring procedures do seem to prevent equipment failures, but there may be a significant proportion of time when, on examination, the equipment is found to have been removed prematurely. The proportion of time in which this occurs may range from 20 to 40 percent.

In fact, a quote by Pottinger and Sutton makes the point: ''Much condition monitoring information tells us something is not quite right, but does not necessarily inform us what margins remain for exploitation before real risk, and particularly real commercial risk occurs.''[8]

While this statement is undoubtedly true, the procedure of proportional hazards modeling that was developed in the context of human health monitoring seems to have scope for assisting maintenance management in interpreting efficiently the results of a health monitoring procedure. References to this procedure in the context of equipment reliability are Anderson et al.,[9] Ansell and Phillips,[10] and Bendell.[9, 11]

ORGANIZATIONAL STRUCTURE DECISIONS

This section focuses attention on the fact that maintenance requires available resources in terms of manpower and equipment. Clearly, if there are not sufficient resources available for undertaking required maintenance work, there will be unacceptable levels of production downtime.

A branch of mathematics entitled *queueing theory* (waiting line theory) can assist in the evaluation of alternative levels of resource requirements for maintenance, provided the problem is not too complicated. For example, if the problem is to determine how many similar machines there should be in a workshop, then queueing theory would enable management to identify the benefits, in terms of quality of service being provided to production, of different numbers of machines in the workshop.

The following example, taken from Jardine (1973), illustrates the application of queueing theory in assisting management in their determination of required installed machine capacity.

Statement of Problem

From time to time jobs requiring the use of workshop machines, say lathes, are sent from various production facilities within an organization to the maintenance workshop. Depending on the workload of the workshop, these jobs will be returned to production after some time has elapsed. The problem is to determine the optimal number of machines that minimizes the total cost of the system. This cost has two components: the cost of the workshop facilities, and the cost of downtime incurred due to jobs waiting in the workshop queue and then being repaired.

Construction of Model

1. The arrival rate of jobs to the workshop requiring work on a lathe is Poisson distributed with arrival rate λ.
2. The service time a job requires on a lathe is negative exponentially distributed with mean $1/\mu$.

3. The downtime cost per unit time for a job waiting in the system, being served or in the queue is C_d.
4. The cost of operation per unit time for one lathe either operating or idle is C_1.
5. The objective is to determine the optimal number of lathes n to minimize the total cost per unit time $C(n)$ of the system.

$C(n) = $ Cost per unit time of the lathes.
   + Dowtime cost per unit time due to jobs being in the system.

Cost per unit time of the lathes	= Number of lathes × Cost per unit time per lathe
	= nC_1
Downtime cost per unit time due to jobs being in the system	= Average wait in the systems per job × Arrival rate of jobs in the system per unit time × Downtime cost per unit time/ job
	= $W_s \lambda C_d$

where W_s = mean wait of a job in the system. Hence

$$C(n) = nC_1 + W_s \lambda C_d \qquad (13\text{-}1)$$

This is a model of the problem relating number of machines n to total cost $C(n)$.

Numerical Example

Letting λ = 30 jobs/week, μ = 5.5 jobs/week (for one lathe), C_d = \$500/week, and C_1 = \$200/ week, equation (13-1) can be evaluated for different numbers of lathes to give the results shown in TABLE 13-2. The optimal number of lathes to minimize total cost per week is eight. FIGURE 13-9 illustrates the underlying pattern of downtime and lathe costs, which, when added together, give the total costs shown in TABLE 13-2.

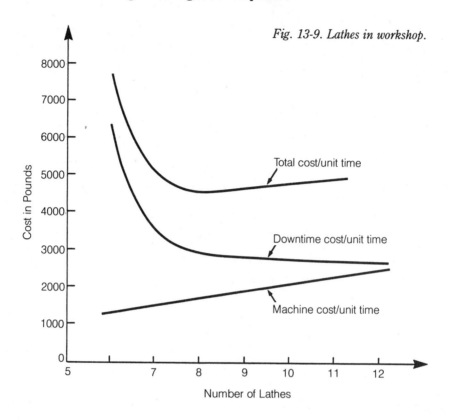

Fig. 13-9. Lathes in workshop.

Table 13-2. Illustration of the Underlying Pattern of Total Cost.

Number of Lathes (n)	Mean Wait of a Job in the System	Total Cost Per Week (C_n)
6	0.437	7755
7	0.237	4955
8	0.198	4570
9	0.189	4635
10	0.185	4775
11	0.183	4945
12	0.182	5130

In order to calculate W_s it is necessary to use a standard result available in most textbooks dealing with queueing theory for the mean waiting time in a queue at a multichannel queueing system. To that queueing time is added the mean processing time, which equals $1/\mu$, to give the overall system waiting time, which is equivalent to a turn-around time.

If the maintenance system is a complicated one, and an attempt is being made to identify resource requirements for maintenance, then a better procedure would be to use computer simulation and in particular, visual interactive simulation. There are many packages available to assist management in decision making in that area, such as SIMAN,[12] SIMFACTORY,[13] and GENETIC.[14]

MAINTENANCE INFORMATION SYSTEMS

Before quantitative decision making can take place, one must have appropriate data. Many organizations have information systems in place, but the question to be addressed is: "Are the right data being collected?" The following methodology consisting of seven steps, enables management to design a good information system for a facility. If an information system is already in place, then the methodology should enhance the system. Of course, it is possible that an alternative being considered is to acquire an off-the-peg information system. If that is the case, the methodology should assist management in evaluating alternative systems.

1. Determine Problems This first step enables management to focus attention on just what problems need answers. In this chapter, problems discussed have been in the areas of component preventive replacement, capital equipment replacement, inspection frequency, health monitoring, and organizational structure decisions.

There are many other problems of keen interest to maintenance management, such as inventory control. By identifying the problems, management obtains a clear picture of what data are required to solve the problems.

2. Determine Possible Objective In the context of the component replacement problems discussed, the objective was to minimize total cost. In the context of the inspection problem, the objective was to minimize machine downtime. It is important that the objective being sought is clear.

3. Construct Models Given a problem definition and an associated objective, a mathematical model can be constructed that attempts to capture the essential conflicts that need to be resolved.

Earlier in this chapter, models were presented for a variety of problem situations and associated objectives.

4. Determine Data Required to Solve Model By inspecting the models constructed in the previous step, management can now list the data that need to be acquired as input to these models.

5. Determine Data Currently Available If a maintenance information system is currently in place, then it will be possible to identify data currently in the database.

6. Determine Further Data Required Step (4.) of the methodology identifies necessary data, whereas step (5.) results in a specification of available data. The difference between these two sets will specify data that need to be gathered in the database in order to solve the specific problems specified by steps (1.) and (2.) of the methodology.

7. Determine Excess Data A comparison of the data specified in step (4.) with the data in step (5.) may identify certain data that are being gathered but that do not seem to be connected with the problems identified in step (1.). If this is the case, then perhaps this excess information should be collected less frequently, perhaps printed out less frequently, or perhaps not even collected at all. Of course care has to be taken about terminating data collection. It is possible that, in the future, a problem will be identified which in fact requires the now-excess data for its solution.

ENDNOTES

1. L. S. Nelson, "Weibull Probability Paper," *Industrial Quality Control* (March 1967):452.

2. K. C. Kapur and L. R. Lamberson, *Reliability in Engineering Design* (Wiley, 1977).

3. G. J. Glasser, "Planned Replacement: Some Theory and its Application," *Journal of Quality Technology* 1:2 (April 1969).

4. RELCODE: A Computer Software Package for Component Replacement Decisions, Specialized Software Division, OMI Inc., 1340 Williston Road, South Burlington, Vermont 95401, USA.

5. A. K. S. Jardine, *Maintenance, Replacement and Reliability* (Pitman/Wiley, 1973). A reprinted edition is available from Canadian Scholars' Press, 211 Grenadier Road,

Toronto, Ontario, Canada. Many of the models mentioned in this chapter are presented in this textbook.

6. B. S. Blanchard and W. J. Fabrycky, *Systems Engineering and Analysis* (Prentice-Hall, 1990).

7. PERDEC: A Computer Software Package for Capital Equipment Replacement Decisions, Specialized Software Division, OMI Inc., 1340 Williston Road, South Burlington, Vermont 05401, USA.

8. K. Pottinger and A. Sutton, "Maintenance Management—An Art or Science?," *Maintenance Management International* 3:4 (1983): 251-256.

9. A. K. S. Jardine, P. Ralston, N. Reid, and J. Stafford, "Proportional Hazards Analysis of Diesel Engine Failure Data," *Quality and Reliability Engineering International 5* (1989): 207-216.

10. J. I. Ansell and M. J. Phillips, "Practical Problems in the Statistical Analysis of Reliability Data," *JRSS* (1988).

11. A. Bendell, "Proportional Hazards Modelling in Reliability Assessment," *Reliability Engineering* 11 (1985):175-183.

12. SIMAN/CINEMA, Systems Modeling Corporation, Sewickley, Pennsylvania 15143, USA.

13. SIMFACTORY, CACI Products Company, 3344 North Torrey Pines Court, La Jolla, California 92037, USA.

14. GENETIC, Insight International Limited, 2 Robert Speck Parkway, Suite 750, Mississauga, Ontario, Canada L4Z 1H8.

Part II

Planning and Design Issues in the Automated Factory

THE KEY TO SUCCESSFUL IMPLEMENTATION OF AN AUTOMATED MANUFACTURING SYSTEM is effective planning. The focus of this section is on the philosophies and techniques needed for strategic and preproduction planning applicable to automated factories.

This section begins with chapter 14, in which Gregory L. Tonkay presents an overview and general taxonomy of manufacturing systems. He describes the driving forces behind automation and also the different parameters affecting the productivity of an automated factory. Tonkay includes a section on types of automation: fixed, programmable, and flexible. Manufacturing operations are characterized in terms of their volumes and these are related to how a factory can conceptually be laid out.

In chapter 15, Michael C. O'Guin discusses strategic and financial planning for automated environments. He develops the argument that traditional methods of financial justification do not support the automated factory. His liberal use of real life cases makes the chapter especially valuable. He explains how traditional cost justification procedures can often delude engineering managers into thinking that modern technologies are not affordable. Finally, he makes the case that benefits of automation have to be evaluated from a system-wide perspective and not on a piecemeal basis.

Bruce R. Dewey's chapter 16, on computer-aided design and drafting provides not only the theoretical basis for CAD systems, but also graphics standards in use today, and the hardware commonly associated with these systems. CAD systems are an important first step in the manufacturing process, and while using them increases productivity, the real power of these systems emerges when they are used to interface with other manufacturing software and systems.

Paul H. Cohen's chapter 17, focuses on the impact of product design on the production and manufacturing system. Specific emphasis is given to the effect of component and product design on the automation of assembly processes.

Value analysis is a helpful technique, not only during product design, but also during software design and product and process modifications. Vikram Cariapa, in chapter 18, introduces these concepts, details the methodology used in implementing these techniques, and finally demonstrates the application of these concepts in an automated manufacturing environment.

Group technology (GT) is a philosophy that can be applied throughout the life cycle of an automated factory. Chapter 19, by Ronald G. Askin and Asoo J. Vakharia describes the role of GT in both the planning and operative aspects of manufacturing. Since GT is an integrative philosophy, we decided to develop an integrated chapter applicable to both this section and the next section (Part III) of the handbook. Here in chapter 19, it can be seen that GT principles are interwoven into both the planning and control aspects of automation. This comprehensive chapter covers a range of topics from developing classification and coding systems for forming part families, to the formation of GT-based machine cells, to scheduling using GT principles.

Tien-Chien Chang and Sanjay Joshi describe the different approaches to computer-aided process planning (CAPP), in chapter 20. CAPP ties directly into the group technology concepts detailed in chapter 19. Chapter 20 also emphasizes a new research thrust in the area—CAD interfaces to CAPP. Industrial CAPP systems are surveyed; this feature will no doubt prove invaluable to users. The future of CAPP is discussed within the larger context of automated manufacturing software.

Thomas K. Joseph and Trevor Miles have drawn from their varied industrial experience in developing chapter 21, on the role of computer simulation in manufacturing systems. After providing an overview of discrete event simulation, the authors explain the process of simulating these systems. The authors discuss the applicability of simulation studies over the life cycle of an automated factory, from the design phase to operation and maintenance. Current trends in simulation like animation and the use of artificial intelligence are also detailed.

Chapter 22, by Michael P. Deisenroth and Hans Maurer, deals with physical simulation of automated manufacturing systems. It starts by reminding us that the design, implementation, and operation of a manufacturing system in today's environment involves the combined talents of many different disciplines and individuals. Physical simulation is offered as a powerful approach to visualization in the complex design task of the automated factory.

Tejpal S. Hundal and Harvey Wolfe detail the facility layout problem in an automated factory in chapter 23. They begin with an overview, then describe the constraints, and finally explain the different solution approaches. Heuristics comprising of computer-aided methods, the cluster analytic approach, and the graph theoretic approach are described.

The next logical planning step after facility layout is job design. A two-step approach was chosen in chapters 24 and 25 in this handbook. In these chapters, M. A. Ayoub and C. L. Smith describe general approaches to job design: Taylorism, work study, behaviorism, and the ergonomic approach are explained. These approaches are illustrated with a series of industrial cases. In the second of the two chapters, M. A. Ayoub and D. M. Scheltinga describe a predictive model for job design, using an aluminum smelting plant as the manufacturing environment. Five possible job design scenarios are discussed.

Adedeji B. Badiru, in chapter 26, on artificial intelligence (AI) as applied to automated manufacturing systems, traces the history of AI and details its emergence over the past three decades. The use of expert techniques in different manufacturing functions such as scheduling, system design, and process planning is discussed.

14

Taxonomy of Manufacturing Operations

Gregory L. Tonkay[*]

THIS CHAPTER INTRODUCES THE READER TO THE concepts and terminology of automated manufacturing systems and shows how they relate to traditional manufacturing. Exposure in this chapter is meant to provide the reader with the overall picture of factory automation, including an introduction to jargon and key concepts. Many of the principles mentioned in this chapter will be explained in greater detail in the following chapters.

Since I am discussing the taxonomy of manufacturing operations, it is fitting that my first area of exploration is an overview of the major types of manufacturing operations present in the United States. Next, I define key terms and concepts that readers are likely to encounter as they read further about factory automation. Next, I present the factors that affect the choice of manufacturing operations. Finally, I introduce the basic types of plant layouts. With the knowledge acquired in this chapter, the reader should be able to better understand the chapters that follow.

TYPES OF AMERICAN INDUSTRIES

In order to better understand the manufacturing operations used in industry, it is important to study the major types of industries in the United States and the great diversity that exists among them. There are many methods for classifying American industries. However, for this discussion, several of the larger industries will be presented in order to show how production strategies might differ among them. They are listed in alphabetical order instead of attempting to assign a rank of importance to each.

Aerospace Industry

The aerospace industry is well known as an innovator in the field of automation. Traditionally, aerospace firms have had to deal with complex three-dimensional shapes, exotic materials, and medium-volume to low-volume production quantities. A large part of the research budget of the federal government goes toward military aircraft and space applications. Much of the technology developed from this research is later implemented in industrial processes in other fields. Aerospace has pioneered work in numerical control machining, CAD/CAM applications, development and use of composites, and flexible manufacturing system applications.

*Gregory L. Tonkay is Assistant Professor at Lehigh University. He received his B.S. and Ph.D. in Industrial Engineering from The Pennsylvania State University. He is an active member in the Institute of Industrial Engineers, Society of Manufacturing Engineers, and American Welding Society. His teaching and research interests include manufacturing processes, manufacturing systems, automation, and artificial intelligence applications to manufacturing processes.

In general, the industry is concerned with design and construction of aircraft and space vehicles that are energy efficient and have a high power-to-weight ratio. A great deal of structural design and simulation is performed. Specialized metals and composites with a high strength-to-weight ratio are used in the designs, thus presenting new problems in the fabrication and assembly processes used to build aircraft and space vehicles.

Automotive Industry

A large portion of manufacturing in the United States centers around the automotive industry. One characteristic of this industry is its relatively large number of units produced each year. However, each unit can have multiple options, so it is difficult to automate the assembly processes. Traditionally, the industry has been heavily involved with metalworking operations. The primary metalworking operations are: machining the power train parts; forming and bending the sheet metal body panels; assembling, by spot welding and mechanical fasteners; and finishing, by spray painting and plating. In recent years, a greater emphasis has been placed on using new materials for outer body panels such as plastics, fiberglass, and galvanized steel.

In the past, cars were assembled on long assembly lines using mostly manual labor. More recently, robots have been added to replace the humans in spot welding and spray painting. As an alternative to assembly lines, several manufacturers are experimenting with another assembly layout. In this new scheme, a group of workers is responsible for assembling large portions of a car. With this method, errors can be corrected immediately, without stopping the entire production line. Furthermore, it is easier to hold the workers accountable for their work; this, in turn, has resulted in an increase in quality.

Chemical Industry

The chemical industry plays a much bigger part in American industry than many people realize. Most of the man-made fibers and virtually all plastics are manufactured through chemical processes.

Two other chemical processing industries that touch the lives of most consumers are the oil distillation and pharmaceutical industries.

Some of the chemicals are produced in a continuous fashion. Raw materials enter at one end of the process. Heat and pressure are applied. The process variables such as temperature, pressure, concentration of various compounds, and pH are controlled very closely. Additives and catalysts are added at appropriate times. The result is a continuous flow of product and byproducts.

Other chemicals are produced in batches. Large pressure vessels, called reactors, are loaded with base chemicals. Energy is applied and the process variables are closely controlled. When the process is finished, the new compound is removed from the reactor and a new batch is started.

Food Industry

Everyone is familiar with the foods packaged for consumers and found in grocery stores. Many of the products must be mixed, cooked, and packaged. This is a large volume industry with standard products and operations, so it has been reasonably easy to automate. Many of the products are produced using continuous processes. Examples include grinding flour, cooking spaghetti sauce, and mixing carbonated beverages. The packaging operations tend to be discrete processes, such as bagging, bottling, or canning.

Semiconductor Industry

The semiconductor industry is a large volume industry with an emphasis on design and production of low-cost integrated circuits. The unique aspect of this industry is that as the circuits have become smaller and denser, the cleanliness standards have become more stringent. Most VLSI (Very Large Scale Integrated) devices are now manufactured in an environment with very little human interaction. The process requirements have made it easier to justify automation and have forced the industry to invest the necessary capital to automate.

The semiconductor industry's processes of

primary concern include growing and processing silicon into thin wafers to be used as the base for the integrated circuits; building up the layers of materials on the silicon substrate to form electrical circuits; and packaging the silicon chips to provide connections to the outside world and adequate heat dissipation.

KEY CONCEPTS AND DEFINITIONS

This section introduces the reader to many of the general concepts that apply to automated manufacturing operations. Definitions for some of the jargon commonly used in the field are also presented.

Reasons for Automating

There can be many reasons for introducing automation to a manufacturing process. The optimal automation strategy could change based on which reasons are considered to be of primary importance. Some of the more common reasons to automate are discussed in the following paragraphs. Most of the time an automation strategy will affect more than one of these closely-related factors.

Increase Production Rate   This reason for automation is given in situations where the demand for the product has outstripped the supply. The primary goal is to reduce or eliminate segments of the manufacturing process that directly increase the production time. Examples of these segments include machine processing times, transfer times between operations, and setup times. Examples of automation strategies to increase the production rate include performing multiple operations simultaneously, reducing the setup time required by employing common fixtures and tooling, or employing an automated material handling system.

Remove Humans from Hazardous Environments   In many processes, the workers are at risk due to dangerous chemicals, fumes, temperatures, or radiation. Many of the first robotic applications displaced workers from operations such as loading and unloading furnaces, spray painting, and welding. Replacing humans in these situations is not always economically justifiable using conventional justification methods. Nevertheless, these processes are often automated because workers are willing to give the jobs up and companies do not wish to assume the increased liabilities associated with exposing workers to the hazardous environments.

Remove Humans from Processes That Require Extremely Clean Environments   Many products, such as semiconductors and drugs, must be produced in clean room environments. Humans are the primary source of the particles that disrupt these operations. A single hair or piece of lint could ruin many VLSI chips. By removing the humans from these operations, it is easier to maintain the clean environment and thus reduce the number of defective products.

Reduce Direct Labor   The direct labor and its associated cost can be reduced by automating some or all of the tasks performed by humans. For example, a worker who once operated a manual turret lathe could now tend several automatic machines. This worker could maintain the production rate of several manual workers and would require a lower skill level.

It is difficult to justify automation based solely on a reduction in direct labor because the direct labor savings will not support the substantial capital expenditure for new equipment. Furthermore, additional support and maintenance personnel are required to keep the systems running at peak efficiency.

Reduce Work-in-Process   If a snapshot were taken of a manufacturing facility, all of the unfinished products in the factory would be classified as WIP (Work-in-Process). WIP can be divided into two categories. The first category is parts that are actually being processed on a machine. The second category is parts waiting for machines to become available. It is counterproductive to reduce the number of parts in the first category. However, it is often easy to reduce the number of parts in the second category. In many plants, a significant part of the life of a product is spent waiting for busy machines to become idle.

A large volume of WIP can be detrimental in

several ways. First, it takes longer to fill customer orders, which can result in dissatisfied customers and lost sales. Second, it requires more storage space for the parts to wait for processing. Third, the value of the unfinished goods sitting idly on the floor is money that could be invested in other areas of the company.

In order to reduce WIP, automation strategies have concentrated on the reduction in waiting time. In some manufacturing operations, waiting time is estimated to be as high as 95 percent of the life of a product.[1] Better control and scheduling in the factory is the key to reduce WIP. Priority jobs often preempt the current jobs, thus forcing changes in all the schedules. A reduction in batch size can also reduce WIP. With large batches, all parts must be completed at the current operation before the whole batch can move to the next operation. The current trend among batch manufacturers is to minimize the batch size, although there are practical limits in most situations.

Reduce Manufacturing Lead Time Manufacturing lead time is the time it takes to make a product—from the time the order is released until the product is ready to be shipped out the door. The lead time can be divided into three categories: processing time, setup time, and waiting time. Lead time and WIP are closely related. As described above, the waiting time can be reduced by decreasing the WIP through smaller batch sizes and better control. The setup time can be reduced through the use of flexible automation, common fixtures, and common tooling. Common methods of reducing the processing time are combining, eliminating, or performing operations simultaneously; increasing the speed of the process; and applying classical industrial engineering work measurement principles.

Increase Quality Generally, one of the benefits of automation is an increase in quality and consistency. Automated processes perform repeatable operations through every cycle. This permits tighter control limits and makes it easier to detect when a process goes out of control. Often the computers used to control the operations can also monitor the performance of the operations. The instant

availability of the status of manufacturing operations provides additional input to the managers making production decisions.

Increase Productivity As a result of a reduction in labor and/or an increase in production rate, automated processes may provide an increase in productivity. Normally, an increase in productivity is not the primary objective for automation. However, it often occurs as a direct result of the capital that is invested in the operations.

Types of Automation

There are three types of automation commonly encountered in industry: fixed, programmable, and flexible. The selection of one type of automation generally depends on the volume of production and the flexibility required. FIGURE 14-1 shows the relationship of volume of production and flexibility to each type of automation.

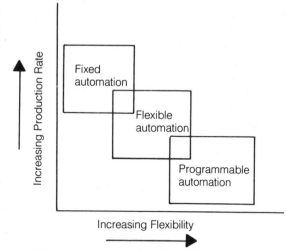

Fig. 14-1. Impact of flexibility and production rate on automation strategies.

Fixed Automation Fixed automation, also known as hard automation or automation for mass production, produces large numbers of nearly identical products. The cost of fixed automation is greater than programmable and flexible automation. Therefore, in order to justify the equipment, the cost must be spread over a large number of pieces. Since this equipment is very specialized, another requirement is that the product rarely changes over its life. Even minor engineering changes can require major equipment changes—if they are even possible to make.

However, there are several advantages to using hard automation. First, the equipment can be fine tuned to the application. This results in a decreased cycle time, and thus an increased production rate. Second, the equipment seldom requires setup. Third, an automated material handling device quickly and efficiently moves parts to the next operation. Finally, since parts proceed directly from one operation to the next, there is very little WIP.

Programmable Automation Programmable automation is normally applied in situations where smaller volumes of many different parts are produced. Therefore, this equipment has the advantage of being more flexible than hard automation equipment. Programmable automation is easy to modify and reprogram compared to hard automation. However, a period of setup is required to properly configure the machine for each new part. This period of setup is one of the major disadvantages of programmable automation.

As explained previously in the section on WIP, one goal is to minimize the batch size. Programmable automation does not tolerate small batch sizes. The batch size must be sufficiently large to spread out the setup time over all the pieces. Therefore, a trade-off exists between batch size and setup time. Another disadvantage of programmable automation is that it is slower than hard automation. Since the equipment must remain flexible, it cannot be fine tuned to a specific process. Thus, speed must be sacrificed to provide flexibility.

Flexible Automation Flexible automation is the most recently developed class of automated equipment. In theory, flexible automation provides a compromise between fixed and programmable automation in speed and flexibility. The primary advantage of flexible automation over programmable automation is that the programming and setup can be performed off-line. However, flexible automation machines are more expensive than those for programmable automation because of their physical size and their need to change tools during the machining operations. The capability to provide many types of preset tools substantially reduces the need for on-line setup and allows the batch sizes to be reduced. This in turn reduces both WIP and lead time.

In practice, however, flexible automation has been limited to specific types of production. The volume of parts must be sufficient to justify the expense of the equipment. The parts to be produced are normally diverse enough to preclude their production on hard automation equipment, but at the same time similar enough to utilize the same general tooling. Typically, the parts that are produced are expensive, large, and require some complex machining. Flexible automation can produce certain types of parts at a lower cost than either hard or programmable automation.

Group Technology

Group technology has taken on a new importance with the interest generated by flexible automation. Group technology is the science of grouping similar parts into families to enhance production. The families can be composed of parts which require similar types of manufacturing operations or are similar in appearance, shape, and size. In conjunction with flexible automation, group technology forms families which require similar fixtures and tooling. The automated equipment is then set up to produce one or more families of parts. From a discussion in my later section about plant layouts, you can see that group technology has given rise to a specific type of plant layout.

Classification and coding are essential to successful group technology. Code systems, for example, uniquely represent, with a code or series of digits, every part produced by a company. Parts with codes that are similar can then be grouped into families. The codes can have up to 30 or more digits to accurately represent the products. The design and implementation of a classification and coding system is usually a customized job. No single system can suit all users. Thus, a disadvantage of group technology is the expense and time required to generate a classification and coding system.

Numerical Control Systems

Numerical control (NC) is the backbone of programmable automation. The first NC machine was developed in the early 1950s at the Massachusetts Institute of Technology to perform machining on complex three-dimensional shapes found in the aerospace industry. Initially, NC machines were developed to read simple instructions from a tape and perform the resulting actions. The burden was on the programmer to calculate the coordinates of points along the complex surfaces. Next, hardware was developed to execute more sophisticated instructions such as circular and linear interpolation. Languages such as *Automatically Programmed Tool* (APT) and COMPACT II were developed to remove some of the calculation burden from the programmers and provide a standard interface to many types of machine tools.[2]

When computers became available, they were interfaced to the NC controllers and *Computer Numerical Control* (CNC) was born. CNC offered additional capabilities, such as the ability to offset a tool without changing the paper tape, on-line editing of programs, the use of subroutines, and communication with other devices. Programs could now be downloaded from a higher level computer and stored in memory instead of being read from a tape.

Initially, computers were very expensive so a single computer was configured to supply instructions to several machine tools. The computer was connected in such a way as to imitate the tape reader. Unlike a CNC system, the computer was not part of the control system. Since the computer was directly feeding instructions to the machine tool, this configuration became known as *Direct Numerical Control* (DNC).

Direct numerical control was never widely realized because of the phenomenal drop in computer prices. The additional cost of CNC was no longer a factor. However, there was still a need to connect the machine tools to higher level, more centrally located computers to transfer part programs, data, and machine status. Since the information was distributed throughout a network, the acronym DNC was modified to represent *Distributed Numerical Control*.

Information Processing

The following paragraphs discuss key concepts with respect to gathering and processing information vital to automated manufacturing systems. Each of the items discussed in this section can be implemented singly or in groups. The long-term goal of any manufacturing organization should be to have all of these information systems integrated so that data and effort are not duplicated in the manufacturing environment.

Materials Requirements Planning Materials Requirements Planning, or MRP, systems aid the plant management in determining what raw materials are required and when they are required. In order for the MRP system to function properly, it must have access to the master schedule of products to be produced and a list of the components required to produce each product. With the help of MRP, inventories of raw materials and in-process parts can be substantially reduced.

Capacity Requirements Planning Capacity Requirements Planning, or CRP, is similar in principle to MRP, but instead of materials, the system is concerned with the machine and resource capacities required to produce products. The CRP system can assist management in decisions about where to allocate capital to purchase new equipment, how to schedule existing machines, and whether a proposed master schedule is feasible given the current resources available.

Just-in-Time (JIT) Manufacturing Just-in-Time, or JIT, is an extreme example of reducing inventory levels to save storage costs. In this environment, suppliers are expected to deliver needed materials when they are required, possibly several times a day. Furthermore, no time is spent checking the supply for quality. Instead, a trust is developed between the supplier and the producer to have good parts delivered on time in exchange for continued orders. JIT requires a high level of information flow and real-time control within the manufacturing operations.

Computer Integrated Manufacturing Computer Integrated Manufacturing, or CIM, is a term given to computer systems which link all of the information flow within a company. CIM systems include the hardware and software required to store and pass information from design systems to manufacturing operations. For example, a part could be designed using a computer aided design system; the geometric data could then be passed to a design analysis program such as a finite element analysis to determine if the design would meet the functional specifications.

Next, a computer aided process planning (CAPP) system could determine what operations are required to produce the product. After the operations are known, the programs could be generated to guide the machine tools. At the same time, the MRP and CRP systems could determine whether the appropriate materials and capacities are available to produce the product. The CIM system can be thought of as traffic cop, routing the appropriate information to the users and systems that need it. It can also assist management in determining the utilization and status of the machines in the plant. It can locate bottlenecks and provide information to keep the plant running smoothly.

FACTORS THAT AFFECT THE CHOICE OF MANUFACTURING OPERATIONS

A manufacturing engineer must consider many factors when determining the best operation to make a specific product. In this section some of the more important factors will be discussed.

Discrete versus Continuous Operations

In the most general terms, every manufacturing operation can be classified as either a discrete or a continuous operation. A product can undergo both discrete and continuous operations while it is being formed.

Discrete Operations A discrete operation is one in which the operation is performed on a single unit, or on a group of units simultaneously. Examples of discrete processes including drilling a hole in a washer, assembling a computer, and painting an automobile.

Discrete operations can be broken down into the fundamental types of manufacturing operations show in FIG. 14-2. Most consumers are familiar with products produced from discrete operations. These products are sold as a unit or multiples of a unit. Examples include cars, books, and telephones.

Continuous Operations A continuous operation is one in which the operation does not produce distinct or discrete units. Examples of these operations include refining gasoline from crude oil, grinding flour, and producing chemicals for industrial applications.

The products produced by a continuous operation can be divided into any size lot or bundle by adjusting the size of the container. For instance, wine is sold in various sizes of bottles or casks; molten steel is poured into various sizes of molds and ingots; and liquid propane gas is sold by the pound or the gallon. Often, continuous operations are erroneously thought to be concerned only with liquids or gases; in fact, they can also operate on solids that can flow as liquids. For example, flour is ground in a mill and placed in various types of packaging and coal is crushed and shipped through pipelines in a slurry.

The production of an item often involves both continuous and discrete operations. When this occurs, the continuous operations usually precede the discrete operations and involve the conversion of natural resources or raw materials into useful components. The discrete operations occur later in the sequence where shaping, assembling, finishing, and packaging operations are performed.

Size of the Product

The size of a product can affect the selection of manufacturing operations, especially in the case of discrete products. Building a bridge or a nuclear-powered reactor is going to require all of the final

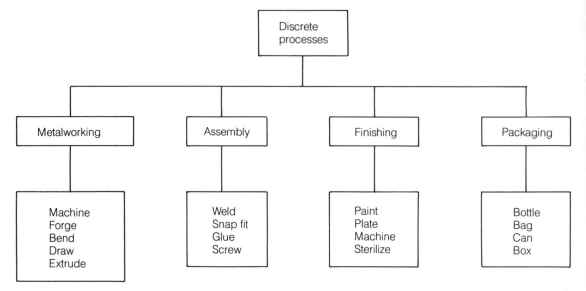

Fig. 14-2. Examples of discrete manufacturing operations.

assembly to take place at the site. On the other hand, assembling automobiles can take place at many different locations because automobiles are easily transported. Very large or very small products require specialized machines and fixtures to hold them. Often, the optimal method to produce a part will not be chosen because a machine is not available to perform the operation. Instead, an "acceptable" alternative will be chosen from the available machines.

Degree of Standardization

The number of options available on a given product can affect the manufacturing operations. The best example of a product with multiple options is an automobile. Other examples include mainframe computers and houses.

The product with the greatest consumer appeal would allow the consumer to mix and match any available options. The problem with this strategy is that it is difficult to apply hard automation principles because the equipment must be flexible. Since each unit must be individually made, it is difficult to schedule the operations and have the correct

parts on hand when they are required. Also, it is easy to make mistakes by installing the wrong options.

The other extreme is to manufacture only a single model with no options and apply hard automation principles. This is fine for some products such as staplers, coffee pots, or other products which primarily serve a functional purpose. However, most consumers demand some options to distinguish their model from others, even if it is only a choice of color.

For these reasons, a strategy is often chosen midway between the two extremes. Options are grouped together into packages. The consumer can choose one or more of these packages. Automobile manufacturers usually offer a substantial discount for purchasing these packages instead of the individual options. The Japanese have used this principle in their production strategies. A consulting firm determined that at one point in time the Chevrolet Citation came in 32,000 versions and the Ford Thunderbird came in 69,000 while the Honda Accord was sold in 32 versions in the United States.[3] Often it is cheaper to make an item a standard feature on all products, rather than provide the extra scheduling and control capability required to make it an option. Many domestic manufacturers have recognized this principle and have included it in their manufacturing strategies.

Volume of Parts

The volume of parts is a very important factor to consider when selecting manufacturing operations. Often this factor alone can prevent automation from being justified. As a rule of thumb, the direct labor cost decreases as the volume of parts increases because more automation can be justified. With respect to production strategies, the volume of parts can be divided into three distinct categories: mass production, job shop production, and batch production. A fourth category, flexible manufacturing system principles, is also addressed in this section.

Mass Production Principles   In mass production, the same product is made repetitively over long periods of time. Typically, automation is easily justified for mass production operations. Examples of products produced in large volumes are bottles, munitions, and many electronic devices.

Mass production has several objectives. The first is to reduce the operation cycle time. In mass production, a part spends a greater percentage of the time actually being processed than in the other strategies. Therefore, if the operation cycle time can be reduced, savings can be realized.

The second mass production objective is to increase the reliability of the system. Since in most highly automated systems the whole line can be stopped if a single station breaks down, it becomes very important for each station to be highly reliable. For example, if a mass production line has 10 stations, each with a reliability of 90 percent, the overall reliability of the line would be $(0.9)^{10} = 34$ percent. By increasing the reliability of each station to 95 percent, the reliability of the line would be increased to $(0.95)^{10} = 60$ percent. If two operations were removed from the original line, the reliability of the line would increase to $(0.90)^8 = 43$ percent. Note in this example that the system reliability can be increased by increasing the reliability of the individual operations or by reducing the number of operations in the production line.

Since the line is rarely changed, the time required to set up the line is not as important as it is with the other strategies. Minimizing the setup time is not an important objective.

Finally, it should be noted that mass production lines are not flexible. They require a great deal of time to change the line for a new model or feature. It is very difficult to produce a different product on an existing line without substantial engineering changes and cost. Therefore, products with many options or limited production runs are difficult to produce using mass production principles.

Job Shop Production Principles   Job shop production is at the opposite end of the spectrum from mass production because the products are produced in small volumes. In this strategy, only one or two parts are made at a time. Typically, the amount of direct labor and the associated costs are much higher than with mass production. Examples of job shop production are parts for the space shuttle, designer dresses, product prototypes, and heavy equipment repair. It is difficult to justify automation in this category unless the products are too complex to be produced manually.

Job shop production must meet several objectives in order to improve its efficiency, most of which are in direct opposition to those for mass production systems. The first objective is to reduce setup time. This was not important for mass production because the machine was seldom undergoing setup. However, in job shop production, parts spend the majority of their life waiting for other jobs to finish and waiting for the machines to be set up.

The second objective is to reduce the processing time. A reduction in processing time will reduce the overall time to produce the part. However, since a greater proportion of the time is spent in setup, the percentage decrease in total time will not be nearly as large as with mass production.

Another important objective of job shop production is to reduce WIP. This can be accomplished by scheduling the workload to maximize machine utilization, minimize waiting time, and minimize the number of preempted jobs.

One final and important aspect of job shop production is that this is the most flexible of all the production strategies. The same machine can produce many different types of parts. Anything that can be manufactured can be produced using this strategy as long as cost is not a factor. However, unlimited cost is rarely a practical assumption.

Batch Production Principles Products manufactured using batch production are produced in batches, lots, or groups. The manufacturing operations are set up, and a group of parts proceed through the operations. In traditional batch manufacturing, all of the parts must be completed at a given operation before they all move to the next. However, in special cases, the parts can be transferred to the next operation as they complete the current operation. The majority of parts produced in the United States are produced in batches. Examples of batch production are a refinery that produces different brands of gasoline, a compact disc manufacturing plant, or a heavy equipment manufacturing plant.

Batch production provides a trade-off between job shop and mass production principles. Since parts are produced in batches, the operations require a single setup for each batch. The setup time is distributed over all of the parts in the batch. Thus, there is a tendency to increase batch size at the expense of an increase in waiting time and WIP. The objectives of batch production are the same as job shop production: minimize setup time, minimize production time, and minimize work-in-process.

Scheduling and production control have a much greater importance in batch production. The batch size must justify the setup time required for the machine. However, if too many parts are produced in a batch, the extra parts must be stored in inventory at an increased inventory cost.

Flexible Manufacturing System Principles A flexible manufacturing system, or FMS, is a highly automated group of machines connected by an automated material handling system in such a way that a given part can access the machines in any order. All of the devices in the system are under computer control. Thus, the FMS overcomes the flexibility limitation of the fixed sequence in mass production. Almost any type of part can be made using an FMS, but because of the large capital expense, the parts are usually complex and expensive. Examples include systems to produce tractor parts, aircraft cylinder heads, and motor starters.[4,5]

In principle, the FMS greatly reduces the setup time for each operation over that of job shop or batch production. This is achieved by allowing the machines to access multiple tools and change them during the cycle. Each of the tools is carefully installed in a holder to eliminate the need for on-line tool setups. The programs to perform the operations are stored offline and can be downloaded to the machines virtually instantaneously. Since the setup time is minimized, complex parts can be produced with a minimum amount of lead time. This provides the capability for JIT manufacturing. Each part can be made to order and very little inventory is maintained in comparison to a batch production system. Therefore, FMS allows options to be selected for each part with minimal penalties for lead time and WIP.

The drawbacks to this production strategy are that all of the products have to be somewhat similar in nature. Typically, they all belong to a few group technology families. Each part may include different operations in its sequence, but the basic tooling is usually similar. The material handling system of an FMS is slower than mass production equipment, so the production rates will not be as high. The fixtures to hold the pieces during machining are precisely machined and expensive. Finally, the machines within the FMS are very expensive. They must be capable of communicating with the other components in the system, as well as performing many different operations and changing tools automatically. For these reasons, there must be a sufficient volume of parts projected over the planning horizon in order to justify the equipment.

Life Cycle

The final factor affecting the selection of a production strategy is the life cycle of the product and the expected number of engineering changes. If the projected life cycle is short or there are many engineering changes expected, equipment must be flexible so that it can adjust to future changes. On the other hand, if the life cycle is projected to be long, there will be sufficient justification to invest in more specialized equipment, which will last the life of the product line.

FACILITY LAYOUT

Plant layout is another factor affecting the production strategy. Which layout would maximize productivity? This question is particularly important when a new facility is being built or a major renovation is being planned. However, plant layout principles also apply to adjustments of existing production facilities.

Differences exist between plant layout for a discrete facility and for a continuous facility. Normally, in a continuous facility, all of the operations are connected through the use of pipes, conveyers, or other material handling devices. All materials move throughout the facility in these material handling systems. Most of the principles in a continuous facility are analogous to those in a discrete product flow layout.

In a discrete manufacturing facility, many different products can be produced in the same factory. Many different types of material handling systems connect the operations, some of which are automatic, others manual. Also, the sizes and types of products vary. For these reasons, several types of facility layouts have evolved. In this section four types of plant layouts are discussed: (1) fixed position, (2) process layout, (3) product flow layout, and (4) group technology layout. The discussions will not be concerned with how to lay out a manufacturing facility. Instead, these discussions will be concerned with the general principles, advantages, and disadvantages of each type of layout.

Fixed Position

The fixed position layout is selected whenever the product must remain stationary throughout the production sequence. Often, size is the limiting factor, although there could be other reasons, such as avoiding vibrations or shielding from unwanted environmental factors.

In this type of plant layout, the machines are brought to the product throughout the sequence of operations. An excellent example of fixed position layout is the vehicular assembly building at Kennedy Space Center. Other examples of products made using this type of layout would include bridges, railroad locomotives, and aircraft. In the case of aircraft or other large, movable objects, other types of layouts could be utilized. However, the cost of moving the object from operation to operation would be more expensive than bringing the machines to the product.

In general, the machines utilized in a fixed position layout are more expensive than those used in the other layouts because they must be movable. Often they must maintain a high degree of accuracy even when transported across the factory or even around the world.

Process Layout

A process layout, also known as a functional layout, is the traditional layout utilized for small, discrete-parts manufacturing. In this type of layout, the machines are grouped in departments according to the type of operations they perform. An example layout is shown in FIG. 14-3. Examples of process layouts can be found in many U.S. factories, especially in job shops where the annual production rates of most products are relatively small.

Advantages of a Process Layout One advantage of this type of layout is that the operators are more skilled on their particular machines. Since all of the machines in a department perform the same functions, the operators become accustomed to the type of jobs that are normally processed. Another advantage of the process layout is that the

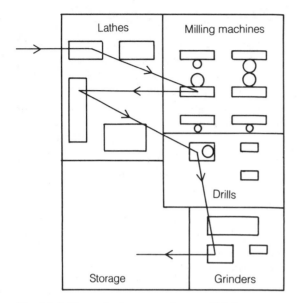

Fig. 14-3. Example of a process layout. This layout produces the same part made in the layouts shown in Figs. 14-4 and 14-5.

workloads can be more flexibly scheduled. For example, if a certain part needs a grinding operation, a quick check can tell management what machines are currently being utilized. One of the remaining machines can perform the operation. In the days before computerized shop floor control, status checks were completed visually. Thus, placing machines with the same function next to each other to assist with scheduling was a logical choice.

Disadvantages of a Process Layout   The process layout also has several disadvantages. The first and probably most important is that WIP is very large. If the next operation to be performed on a part is located at the other end of the factory, each part cannot be transported immediately after processing. Instead, all of the parts in a given batch are processed on the current machine first, and then moved to the next machine. Each part is being processed only a small proportion of the lead time. The rest of the time it is waiting for other parts to be processed. In a large factory, hundreds of thousands of parts can be waiting for processing, thus costing the company valuable storage space as well as inventory.

The second disadvantage is high material handling cost. Since the sequence of operations will usually cause the part to move from one department to the next, a large cost is incurred in moving the parts. The smaller the distance between sequential operations, the lower the material handling costs. Furthermore, it is much more difficult to automate material handling when the handlers must move throughout the factory in no specific pattern.

The third disadvantage of the process layout is that often, larger batches are made than are required. This is because the lead time to complete a batch of parts is too long. If a rush order is placed for a part, it is quicker and easier to have several stored in inventory than to make new ones. However, all of the parts stored in inventory cost the company money. Ideally, the lead time should be small so that a part can be made on demand. Therefore, the inventory and its associated costs can be reduced.

The fourth disadvantage of the process layout is the difficulty in maintaining control. For example, it is difficult to track a batch of parts throughout the plant. Often parts can be "lost" for periods of time, especially if rush jobs must preempt them on a particular machine. It is also difficult to determine how many parts should be made in each batch and how many parts should be kept in inventory, and to predict which machines should be available at a future time.

Product Flow Layout

A product flow layout, also known as a line layout, is particularly well-suited to high volume production. In this type of layout, the machines are arranged in the general sequence of operations required to produce the product. Raw materials enter at one end of the line, flow through all the operations, and emerge as completed products; hence the name "product flow layout." FIGURE 14-4 shows an example of a layout that would produce the same part made in the layout shown in FIG. 14-3. A nonmanufacturing example of a product flow layout is an automated car wash. Dirty cars enter one

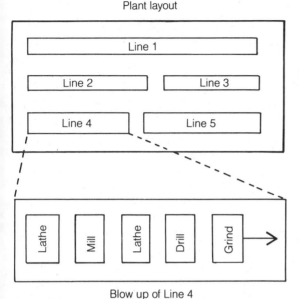

Plant layout

Blow up of Line 4

Fig. 14-4. Example of a product flow layout. This layout produces the same part as in the layouts in Figs. 14-3 and 14-5.

end of the line; they undergo a fixed sequence of operations; clean cars exit at the other end. In some car washes, you can select and pay for only the operations you wish to receive. Other examples of the product flow layout are automotive assembly lines and semiconductor fabrication lines.

Advantages of a Product Flow Layout A product flow layout has several advantages over the process layout, especially in higher production situations. First, since the machines are arranged in the general sequence required to make a part, the material handling time is minimized and a variety of automated material handling systems can be employed.

The second advantage is that since the machines are close to each other, a part can be transferred to the next machine as soon as it is finished on the current machine. Since the whole batch of parts does not have to be completed before moving on, there is less WIP on the line.

The final advantage of a product flow layout is that it is easier to control. It is easier to keep track of the parts in the factory and the sequence of the

machines is such that scheduling individual machines presents fewer problems.

Disadvantages of a Product Flow Layout There are several disadvantages with the product flow layout. The first is that all the products require the same general sequence of machines. The equipment is positioned in such a way that it becomes inefficient to alter the general sequence, especially if the product must flow backward to get to a machine that it has already passed.

The second disadvantage is that in highly automated production lines, a breakdown of one machine can often halt the whole line. If the material handling system fails, no parts can be transferred. If the final machine in the sequence is broken, no finished parts can be produced and eventually the machines upstream will be forced to shut down until the final machine is fixed.

The final disadvantage of the product flow layout is that the operators require a higher skill level than with the process layout. Each operator must be familiar with several types of machines in the sequence. If the machines are highly automated, a higher level of skill is required to program and maintain them.

Group Technology Layout

A group technology layout, also known as a cellular layout, is an attempt to combine the advantages of the process layout and the product flow layout. In this layout, several different types of machines are grouped together to form a cell as shown in FIG. 14-5. This cell could produce the same product as the layouts in FIGS. 14-3 and 14-4. There are many of these cells located throughout the plant. Each cell is designed to produce a group technology family of parts. For example, a cell might be designed to produce eight different crankshafts for small gasoline engines. A group technology layout is particularly useful for small to mid-volume production of parts where most of the parts are processed in batches and can be grouped into families.

Advantages of a Group Technology Layout There are many advantages to using the

Plant layout

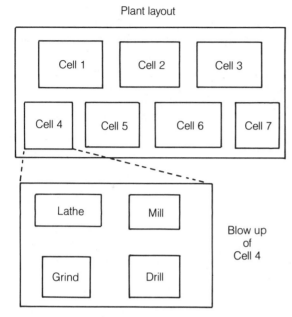

Fig. 14-5. Example of a group technology cell. This layout produces the same part as in the layouts in Figs. 14-3 and 14-4.

group technology layout. The first is that the setup time is greatly reduced. Since each cell is designed to produce a family of parts, the general tooling for that family of parts is already in place. Small modifications to the tooling or fixtures may be required, but in general the setup time is less than for the other layouts.

The second advantage is that the lead time is reduced. Since the setup time is small and the machines are located close together, the time to complete a batch is smaller than for the process layout. Also, the rigid requirements of a fixed sequence in a product flow layout are relaxed.

The third advantage of the group technology layout is that the WIP is reduced. Less time is spent waiting for processing on the machines and the setup time is less. Within the cell, parts can advance to the next machine as soon as they are ready. However, normally, parts do not leave the cell until the entire batch is complete.

The fourth advantage of this layout is that the finished inventory can be reduced. Since the lead

time to finish a batch is less, less advanced notice is required to produce a batch of parts. Thus, fewer parts are required in inventory.

The final advantage of the group technology layout is that often an increase in quality is achieved. Since a group of workers is responsible for all the work performed in a cell, they can be held accountable for the product they produce and are therefore more concerned with the quality.

Disadvantages of a Group Technology Layout   There are several disadvantages associated with the group technology layout. The first is that the parts must be grouped into families. Often vast amounts of time and money are spent classifying the parts. However, this classifying can positively affect other factors in the manufacturing process as well, such as standardization of tools, fixtures, components, and designs.

The second disadvantage is that since the machines are grouped into families, the layout is less flexible than a process layout. If a new part must be produced that does not fit into an existing family, a new cell must be created or several cells must be utilized in succession to produce the part. Slight changes in design could require new processes to produce the part, thus causing a change in the cell layout.

The third disadvantage of the group technology layout is that batches from the same family cannot be run simultaneously. This can cause a delay in the processing of one or more of the batches. Therefore, schedules to resolve these conflicts must be formulated well in advance.

The fourth and final disadvantage of this layout is that a higher skill level is required for the employees. Each employee in a cell must be familiar with all of the processes in the cell. Also, it is difficult to shift employees between cells because the cells contain different types of machines.

SUMMARY

This chapter started with an overview of the major types of manufacturing present in the United States. Details and principles of manufacturing were discussed for the aerospace, automotive, chemical, food, and semiconductor industries. Next, key concepts were presented for manufacturing systems. These included reasons for automating, types of automation, group technology, numerical control, and information processing. Next, several factors that affect the choice of manufacturing operations were discussed. These factors included the type of operation, size of product, degree of standardization, volume of parts, and life cycle. Finally, an overview of facility layout was presented. Four major types of layouts were discussed: fixed position, process layout, product flow layout, and group technology layout.

The understanding of the material in this chapter should allow the reader to proceed to the other chapters in this section with a solid background in the underlying principles of automation and manufacturing operations.

ENDNOTES

1. M. E. Merchant, ''The Inexorable Push for Automated Production,'' *Production Engineering* (January 1977): 45-46.

2. Y. Koren, *Computer Control of Manufacturing Systems* (New York: McGraw-Hill Book Company, 1983).

3. John Koten, ''Giving Buyers Wide Choices May be Hurting Auto Makers,'' *The Wall Street Journal* (December 15, 1983): 33.

4. T. J. Drozda and C. Wick, eds., *Machining*, Vol. 1 of *Tool and Manufacturing Engineers Handbook*, 4th ed. (Dearborn, Michigan: SME, 1983), 15.88-15.98.

5. M. P. Groover, *Automation, Production Systems, and Computer Integrated Manufacturing* (Englewood Cliffs: Prentice-Hall, 1987).

BIBLIOGRAPHY

DeGarmo, E. P., J. T. Black, and R. A. Kohser. *Materials and Processes in Manufacturing*, 7th ed. New York: Macmillan Publishing Company, 1988.

Monks, J. G. *Operations Management Theory and Problems*, 3rd ed. New York: McGraw-Hill Book Company, 1987.

15

Strategic and Financial Planning for the Automated Factory

Michael C. O'Guin*

TRADITIONAL METHODS OF FINANCIAL JUSTIFICA-
tion do not support the automated factory. They are
strongly biased toward capacity expansion and
incremental cost reduction, and away from revenue
enhancement and quality improvement; they ignore
a company's competitive position. This chapter
describes the criteria to be used when deciding
whether or not to invest in the automated factory,
and, specifically, how the automated factory can
support the business strategy. I explore *value* and
how it is incorporated in the justification process. In
addition, I describe and give examples of how to
develop the cost baseline for both a current and a
greenfield facility.

TRADITIONAL FINANCIAL JUSTIFICATION PROCEDURES

It is no coincidence that the U.S. has one of the
lowest capital investment rates as a percent of
gross national product (G.N.P.) in the world; most
American executives use conventional financial
analysis as their principle decision-making tool.
Conventional financial procedures rely on poor cost
accounting systems, exclude quality improvement

from the analysis, and disregard the company's
competitive position. Subsequently, these procedures understate a proposed investment's benefits
and ignore the penalties of failing to invest.

Conventional financial analysis dates from the
early part of this century, when work measurement
and standard costing were being developed. These
systems reflect Frederick Taylor's, and his scientific management's, orientation toward incremental
improvement of direct labor efficiency. At that time,
direct labor was a company's largest cost driver and
its mechanization resulted in vast improvements in
throughput, quality, and cost over manual labor.
Conventional financial analysis was quite adequate
for justifying a faster press, transfer machine, or
conveyor. Buying an overhead conveyor for an auto
plant could be easily justified by saving two minutes
per engine. Unfortunately, not only have cost drivers changed over the last fifty years, but so have
the sources of competitive advantage.

All rational decisions rely on accurate information, but our capital justification must rely on our
obsolete cost accounting systems, which generate
fallacious information. Current cost systems still
treat direct labor as a company's largest cost driver.

*Michael O'Guin is the President of Activity Costing Systems, Huntington Beach, CA. Activity Costing Systems specializes in
designing activity-based costing systems and developing manufacturing strategies and has worked with numerous clients developing
their manufacturing strategy and improving their capital planning process. Mr. O'Guin frequently lectures on financial justification
and has had numerous articles published in such magazines as *Managing Accounting, Managing Automation, Industrial Engineering, CIM Technology,* and *Production and Inventory Management Review.* Mr. O'Guin received the Outstanding Paper award at
CIMTECH in 1986 and holds a B.S. in Mechanical Engineering from University of California at Santa Barbara and M.S. in Systems
Management from University of Southern California.

The present systems track direct labor down to the seconds by part and process but aggregate overhead at the department level or above, in spite of the fact that overhead represents five to ten times as many dollars as direct labor. Because the tracking of overhead is made in such a gross fashion, it is very difficult, if not impossible, to relate overhead costs to their cause, which greatly hinders cost saving projects.

In present systems, overhead costs are allocated on direct labor hours, as if by automating and eliminating an hour of direct labor, 50 dollars of overhead cost are also eliminated. Not only do these obsolete cost systems misdirect cost saving efforts toward the machine operator and away from the forklift driver, but they also camouflage the relationships between a punch press department and its tooling support or numerically controlled (NC) machining and its data processing requirements. Therefore, one of the first and most important tasks in the financial justification process is a reallocation of the company's overhead. I will discuss reallocation in more detail later in this chapter.

Conventional financial analysis compares a capital project's investment to its cost savings. Generally, the conventional analysis does not incorporate any changes in revenue resulting from the capital investment or any decline in revenues if an investment is not made. This is in spite of common sense, which tells us if a company invests and improves a product's quality, it becomes more desirable and, therefore, more customers buy it. Also, if new investments are not made or products are not improved, competitors steal our customers away.

It is not uncommon to find a company with a minimum hurdle rate of 20 percent, while the company is running a return on investment of half that. Executives claim the higher hurdle rate protects them from an investment's uncertainty and from overly optimistic savings estimates, while providing a more challenging target for their subordinates. What many executives fail to incorporate into their financial analysis is the consequence of failing to invest. Capital equipment deteriorates over time, tolerances cannot be held, scrap increases, mainte-

nance costs go up, and downtime becomes more frequent.

Failing to invest also transmits a message to the organization about what is really important: quality or profits. It is very difficult to motivate workers when all they have to work with is old, obsolete, leaky equipment. On the other hand, non-American competitors rarely halt innovation, new product introduction, and capital investment, all of which result in a constantly improving competitive product. If a company fails to invest, it suffers market share erosion.

Company A and Company B are identical printed circuit board assemblers who compete against one and another, and both are evaluating an investment in a new vapor phase soldering system. Company A has a 14 percent hurdle rate, Company B a 16 percent hurdle rate, and the new process for both companies has an internal rate of return of 15 percent. Company A invests in the vapor phase soldering system and Company B does not. Over the next year, Company A picks up a few of Company B's customers with its new process. During the next budgeting cycle, Company B again fails to invest in the new process, because the project's return is even lower, as fewer customers are available for Company B and Company A has already proven itself. By failing to invest, Company B suffers permanent competitive loss from which conventional financial analysis would never permit a recovery.

MANUFACTURING STRATEGY AND THE AUTOMATED FACTORY

Typically, manufacturing generates 70 percent of a company's total cost and uses 75 percent of a company's assets. Therefore, configuring the automated factory is crucial to success. To successfully configure the factory, management must define how the factory will support the company's competitive strategy, which in turn guides the trade-offs on such issues as how many products will be produced, at what cost, providing what level of service, and possessing how much customer value.

The successful manufacturing strategy directly

supports the company's competitive position by providing the company with a competitive advantage. Manufacturing provides this competitive advantage by directly supplementing one of three highly profitable competitive positions: high market share, differentiation, and focus.

High Market Share

The high market share position is just what it says—the highest market share in its market. The firm has a broad scope and serves many industry segments. This position provides a company with the lowest cost structure, allowing a company to supply customers with products at the lowest price, while maintaining high margins. A high market share gives a company economies of scale in manufacturing, purchasing, research and development, and sales. Companies like I.B.M., Emerson Electric, and Du Pont are well known for successfully achieving this position.

The manufacturing mission which best supports developing and maintaining the high market position is to become the low cost supplier. In order to become the low cost supplier, a company pursues a manufacturing strategy that includes such elements as total quality control, standardized products, and low cost sourcing. The low cost supplier strategy guides trade-offs between such issues as building to stock or order, adding optional product features or sticking with no frill models, and distributing through retail channels or selling direct.

When designing the automated factory, the firm wishing to be the low cost supplier must control its costs without letting customer value slip. The firm should set policies to reinforce and exploit economies of scale. The firm must manage itself down the learning curve and attempt to level the factory throughput while keeping capacity utilization high. Keeping process yields high, providing short delivery times, and allowing customization on standardized products permits the low cost supplier to hold down costs while delivering high value to its customers.

General Electric's Erie, Pennsylvania, Locomotive Plant used manufacturing to become the high market share company. In the early 1980s, GE began a $300 million investment program in their Erie Plant to meet the expected 50 percent increase in locomotive demand, caused by the energy crisis. When it became apparent that the world recession would actually cause demand to decline, GE redirected its attention and investment at staying competitive. GE redesigned its products, cut its management structure, and installed a Flexible Manufacturing System. These efforts substantially reduced GE's product cost and improved customer value by reducing production lead times, cutting product defects, and raising locomotive reliability. Overall, GE's locomotive market share increased from 20 percent in 1980 to nearly 50 percent by the end of 1985, putting GE in the high market share position.[1]

Differentiation

Companies in the highly profitable differentiation position successfully distinguish their products from the competition, supporting a price premium over the low cost supplier. As an example, owner operators are willing to pay extra for Kenmore trucks with their carefully handcrafted interiors and wide range options. Michelin tires, Perdue chicken, and Cray Research are just some of the companies who have successfully achieved this competitive position. There are three different approaches to obtaining a differentiation position, each with its own manufacturing mission: product differentiation, service differentiation, and technology differentiation.

The manufacturing mission to support a product differentiation approach might include the flexible manufacture of customized products or precision production resulting in high product conformance, which is highly valued by the customer. Film in the movie industry is a good example; the failure of a single roll of film can be financially disastrous as it might require the reshooting of an epic scene on location. Consequently, movie studios are not only very reluctant to switch film suppliers, but are also willing to pay a premium for high conformance film.

The manufacturing mission to support service differentiation requires short product lead times or spare parts availability. Before Caterpillar Tractor Co. introduces a new product, it builds up a two-month supply of spare parts. Cat guarantees its parts will be delivered anywhere in the world within 48 hours or the customer gets them free. To support this strategy, Cat has been trying to become a leader in the operation of Flexible Manufacturing Systems.[2]

The last approach to differentiation is technology leadership. In some industries, like aerospace and semiconductors, possessing the most advanced technology is very attractive to certain customers. Lockheed's famous Skunk Works has provided the Air Force and Central Intelligence Agency with the latest photo reconnaissance aircraft for the past forty years. Manufacturing can support technology leadership by allowing rapid new product introductions, by providing an innovative working environment, or by developing proprietary processes.

Focus

Focus, the last highly profitable competitive position, depends on achieving either high relative market share or differentiation in only a segment or a few segments of the market. By concentrating on the needs of a particular segment, a company can customize its products and services, thus permitting the company to charge a premium price. Conversely, by voiding costly features unimportant to a particular market segment, the firm can successfully compete on price. By providing specialized features or services a firm can obtain an advantage with certain customers. For example, Hewlett-Packard caters to engineers with their calculators, and Next is trying to target the educational market for personal computers with high fidelity sound, a huge memory capacity, and an UNIX operating system.

A company may achieve the low cost focus position by excluding superfluous product features or geographically positioning itself for a lower cost structure. Charles Schwab & Co., the brokerage house, follows the low cost focus strategy by targeting the professional investor who requires little investment advice or service. Schwab is able to charge substantially lower fees than their larger competitors and still make a good profit. Manufacturing can pursue this strategy by assisting in the development of high quality products aimed at a particular segment, integrating production planning with customer systems to provide superior service, or locating production facilities for market proximity. As an example, auto component suppliers have traditionally located as close as possible to the Big Three's plants to differentiate themselves and maximize their cost advantage.

Many different competitive strategies exist in the same market. As an example, let us consider the contract printed circuit board (PCB) assembly business. Solectron differentiates itself by providing customers with a high degree of manufacturing flexibility at a low cost. Solectron cross trains its work force, practices statistical process control, and drives toward continuous improvements and rapid equipment changeovers. These characteristics make Solectron very attractive to companies with either high demand variability or frequent engineering changes. Flextronics, another contract PCB assembler, concentrates on worldwide and effective purchasing of PCB components. This allows Flextronics to leverage purchases and currency fluctuations for its customers. A third PCB business, Array Technology, differentiates itself by providing "design for manufacturability" services to their customers. They help their customers design the most cost effective PCB possible.[3]

Factory automation can yield a competitive edge, if factory planners understand the business strategy. Without that understanding, a business encounters many pitfalls. For example, some components included in low cost design, such as application specific integrated circuits (ASICs), cannot be found worldwide. In addition, procuring components from the far east could cause long delays in implementing a design change. Both examples demonstrate why a clear understanding of the business strategy is required before the factory configuration is selected. The automated factory can provide a competitive advantage, if it is consistent with the business strategy. If it is not, it can undermine a company's competitive position and can move the company out of its highly profitable position.

THE CONCEPT OF VALUE

Experience shows that customers select a particular product from a group of competing products, not necessarily because it has the lowest price, but because it has the highest *worth*, or ratio of *value* to *price*. *Value* is the relative customer-perceived quality, or all of the nonprice attributes the customer believes the product or service possesses. Value is not quality of conformance, the traditional manufacturing view, but a measure of relative customer desirability and satisfaction.

A television set's value might consist of picture resolution, portability, reliability, and exterior styling. Value is a set of attributes, with some attributes being more important than others, as defined by the market. While no two people may have the same desires, tastes, and perceptions, value represents the collective sum of the market's desires. For instance, consumers consistently rank picture resolution as more important than portability when choosing a television to buy.

Each attribute's value is also relative to the competitor's products and current technology. How well RCA's resolution compares to Sony's determines value. As technology changes, no matter how good RCA's resolution is, it will pall when compared to the new high definition televisions.

If a company improves value, it increases worth and, therefore, customer desirability and sales. The PIMS, or Profit Impact on Marketing Strategy, database of over 1500 business units has established a statistically proven relationship between value improvement (which they call customer-perceived quality) and market share increase for different types of businesses. This relationship allows value improvements to be incorporated into the financial justification of new capital investments.

Measuring Value

To incorporate value in the justification process, a company must first identify what its customers perceive as desirable about its product lines. How does the company's product satisfy the customer's needs and what about the product causes customers to buy it? Management should charter a multidisciplinary team to undertake the study of value. First, the team establishes a common vocabulary so customers, engineers, and marketeers can communicate about the product and its uses. The company team then documents how the product's nonprice attributes satisfy customer needs and expectations. To do this, the firm interviews and surveys the company's customers, potential customers, and distributors for their needs, expectations, and perceptions.

Once the attributes have been identified, each one is assigned a weight reflecting its relative importance to the customers. In the television example, the customers rank resolution as the most important characteristic; therefore, resolution would get a higher weight than portability. A technique called conjoint analysis used by marketing researchers establishes weights. In this analysis, consumers are first given a list of product attribute combinations and are asked which combination of attributes they find most desirable. Conjoint analysis then takes these results and converts them into relative attribute weightings.

After the attributes and their weights have been determined, the customers rate the company's product as vastly superior, superior, average, inferior, or vastly inferior relative to competing products for each product attribute. The responses are scaled so that vastly superior ratings are worth one point; superior one-half point; average, zero; inferior, negative one-half; and vastly inferior, negative one. Multiplying the resulting difference by the attribute's weight generates the attribute's score. The sum of the product's scores equals the product's relative value rating, which ranges from a high of $+100$ to a low of -100. This value rating represents the customer's perception of a product's desirability relative to the competition. The higher the value rating the greater the customer perceived gap between the product and its competition.

TABLE 15-1 shows value ratings of a Digitronics power supply. Digitronic's customers are instrument manufacturers. They identify their buying criteria as: percent of power supplies received as defective, the order lead time, average operating cycles, and power output variance. As TABLE 15-1 shows, Digitronic's power supplies are perceived as superior on shipping good product and controlling output variance, but inferior on reliability. After applying the appropriate attribute weight, Digitronic's value rating is 5.4 or average.

By relating a specific product, service or process performance measures to each attribute, Digitronics can monitor its value rating, and that of its competitors, over time. For example, measuring the average elapsed time between a customer order and delivery represents order lead time. TABLE 15-1 shows a quantification of this attribute's value: it is weighted at 40 percent. Digitronics can estimate the resulting value improvement of a modernization project by estimating the project's impact on the lead time performance measure.

Putting Value into a Justification

Justifying a value improvement project should include not only the project's cost savings, but also the increased market share and its resulting additional cash flow. As an example, Digitronics is considering installing a vapor phase soldering system, which will produce more consistent solder joints. Inconsistent soldering quality has been identified as the principal cause of poor power supply reliability and a contributor to power output variance. Therefore, this project results in a direct impact on customer value, and the project's justification includes the improved market share that the project will generate.

In TABLE 15-2, the Digitronics power supply sales are shown with and without the new soldering system. The system is expected to improve value by 12 points over two years. But within Digitronic's market, relative value drops by 3 points each year, if no product or process improvements are made. Therefore, in Year 1, the soldering system improves value 5 point, or 2 net points. Digitronic's 2 point value improvement is converted into a market share change by multiplying it by the PIMS Value/Market share coefficient for the components businesses listed in TABLE 15-3. In this case, Digitronics

Table 15-1. Survey Results on Digitronics Power Supply.

Attribute	CUSTOMER VALUE PERCEPTION					Weight	Score
	Vastly Superior	Superior	Average	Inferior	Vastly Inferior		
Percent Defective		x				40%	16
Order lead time			x			30%	1.5
Average operating cycles				x		25%	-13
Output variance			x			5%	0.9
Overall value rating			x			100%	5.4
	100	50	0	-50	-100		

Table 15-2. Digitronics Sales with and without Vapor Phase Soldering System.

DIGITRONICS WITH VAPOR PHASE SOLDER SYSTEM

Year	Market Size ($MIL)	Market Coefficient	Relative Value Rating Change	Market Share Change	Market Share	Sales ($MIL)
CURRENT	$21				32.0%	$6.7
1	$23	0.16	2	0.32%	32.3%	$7.4
2	$25	0.16	4	0.64%	33.0%	$8.2
3	$28	0.16	−3	−0.48%	32.5%	$9.1
4	$31	0.16	−3	−0.48%	32.0%	$9.9
5	$34	0.16	−3	−0.48%	31.5%	$10.7

DIGITRONICS WITHOUT VAPOR PHASE SOLDER SYSTEM

Year	Market Size ($MIL)	Market Coefficient	Relative Value Rating Change	Market Share Change	Market Share	Sales ($MIL)
CURRENT	$21				32.0%	$6.7
1	$23	0.16	−3	−0.48%	31.5%	$7.2
2	$25	0.16	−3	−0.48%	31.0%	$7.8
3	$28	0.16	−3	−0.48%	30.6%	$8.6
4	$31	0.16	−3	−0.48%	30.1%	$9.3
5	$34	0.16	−3	−0.48%	29.6%	$10.1

Table 15-3. Value/Market Share Coefficients.

Business Type	Consumer Durables	Consumer Nondurables	Capital Goods	Raw & Semi-finished Materials	Components	Supplies
Value/Market Share Coefficient[1]	.17	.38	.15	.30	.16	.38

1. From Phillips, L.W.; Cheng, D.R.; Buzzell, R.D., "Product Quality, Cost Position and Business Performance: A test of Some Key Hypothesis," *Journal of Marketing* (Spring 1983).

will gain 0.3 percent of market share in Year 1 and 0.6 percent in Year 2. Using market size, a $1.6 million sales increase is estimated with the new soldering system over sales without. This additional revenue will be incorporated in the project's financial justification.

The analysis includes a declining market share over time. Competitors rarely halt innovation and new product introductions and, therefore, if a company fails to invest it should assume a deteriorating competitive position. To estimate competitive loss over time, a company first identifies its most aggressive competitor and compares this competitor's products over the last five years to estimate the value improvement in their products. It must be assumed that at least one of Digitronics' competitors will improve its product at this rate and the project's analysis must consider this improvement.

Advantages of Using Value

Putting value into a cost justification overcomes one of the traditional financial procedures' greatest failings, the bias for inaction. For instance, at Ford Motor Company in the 1960s, management continually judged manufacturing investment and new products, like the Mustang, not against what the customers wanted or even against what its American competitors were doing, but against standard volume. Standard volume was simply the base sales from the previous year, or what Ford believed was its guaranteed share of the market without risk.[4] Ford management believed—or at least their financial systems evaluated all investments as if—doing nothing would mean no change in the status quo. However, if standard volume were true, and if, by taking no action competitive positions would not change, Ford would still be selling 1,870,000 Model T's a year, just as it did in 1922!

Because the automated factory's economics derive from integration or maximizing the whole system and not one part of it, the proper method for evaluating these projects is using the Du Pont Equation, a company wide return on assets (ROA) equation. Using the Du Pont Equation to evaluate the projects not only incorporates increased sales, but also evaluates higher asset utilization and faster inventory turns.

COST SAVINGS—
The Other Side of the
Justification Process

Most of today's capital investments are based strictly on cost savings: if $400,000 is spent on a new machining center, how many dollars will it save? For nonstrategic investments, this is a good evaluation approach, but it typically depends on the traditional cost accounting systems, which are obsolete. The traditional cost systems used today still rely on direct labor as their basis for allocating overhead, as if direct labor were manufacturing's largest variable cost and direct labor drove all overhead costs.

Cost Accounting:
Overhead Allocated to Direct Labor

Today's traditional cost accounting systems allocate costs through a two-step process. Labor and expenses are accrued in a given department and then all of the overhead department expenses are allocated back to the direct labor departments based on the number of standard direct labor hours earned. These overhead costs include production control, purchasing and manufacturing engineering, and supervision. Items such as tooling, utilities, and maintenance costs may be allocated on annual depreciation dollars in each manufacturing department.

While this procedure is the standard cost accounting practice, it provides a distorted picture of the manufacturing process and its interrelationships with the overhead costs. For example, on one recent assignment, a screw machine department was allocated the largest portion of tooling overhead, because it had the largest concentration of equipment depreciation in the company. However, screw machines required almost no tooling support. On the other hand, the punch press department consumed 40 percent of the tooling department's resources, but was allocated just over 9 percent of the tooling overhead, or $162,000.

Furthermore, the implied relationship of allocating overhead on direct labor should mean increasing labor hours results in a proportional increase in overhead or decreasing labor hours results in a subsequent reduction in tooling, maintenance, purchasing, receiving, and production control. But this is not the case. A reduction in direct labor does not necessarily mean a reduction in tooling or maintenance, especially if a process is being automated. If a process is being automated it is likely that more tooling and maintenance will be required.

At one company, an automated punch press

line's justification had an annual estimated savings of $215,000, which included $48,000 of direct labor. The rest of the savings were from the direct labor's allocated overhead. Tooling as part of the allocated overhead was slated to be reduced by $32,000, but the automated line was going to make the same parts and use the same dies as before. There was no reason for the tooling costs to go down. In addition, maintenance costs were also slated to go down by $22,000 but this did not reflect good planning; the automated line would require more maintenance since it had so many mechanical subsystems. On the other hand, the justification using the overhead allocation procedure understated the savings from the automated line's faster setup time and integrated material handling. Overall, this justification overstated the project's savings, and grossly misrepresented where the savings would come from. This misrepresentation would make any subsequent overhead budget changes very dangerous and a project post audit meaningless.

Cost Accounting: Zero Based Budget

The other common approach to estimating cost savings is the zero based budget approach. The zero based approach relies on identifying each activity and its cost, which is to be reduced or eliminated by the automation project. The cost of an activity includes only labor costs, fringe benefits, and identifiable expenses. If a new electronic component machine is being justified, the savings would come from faster insertions and reduced setup times resulting in less direct labor. No overhead savings would be assumed. There usually is one of two consequences of this approach: either not enough cost savings are found to justify the project or too many savings are found to be real.

At one very large corporate client, my management consulting firm came across the justification for a $100 million flexible manufacturing system. The project team had used a zero-based approach and had found more annual savings with their proposed flexible manufacturing system than the current facility's annual operating cost. After this

embarrassing discovery, the project team analyzed their justification and found numerous instances of overestimating present costs and double-counting savings. Therefore, the one good approach to generating the savings is to build a new cost database for your company.

BUILDING THE COST DATABASE

Since each direct labor department represents a manufacturing process or work center, one should attempt to allocate all manufacturing overhead to these groups. Starting with either last year's or the forecasted journal of accounts, obtain an accurate cost detail for each direct labor and overhead department. Typically, this leaves you with the substantial task or redistributing the overhead. When you undertake this recosting, remember that it is much better to be approximately right, then precisely wrong. Some of the cost allocations will be less than ideal and not extremely accurate; nevertheless it is more accurate to include these costs than ignore them.

The first step in the overhead distribution process is to interview each overhead department's manager or supervisor to gain an understanding of not only what each department does, but also what causes or drives its work. The maintenance supervisor should be asked, "What causes your work or increases its frequency?," "How is your work recorded or tracked?," and "Which direct labor departments consume most of your people's time?" Hopefully, you will discover an accurate and practical method to distribute the overhead costs, and in turn the piece parts, to the direct labor departments.

For example, at one company, my management consulting firm learned that the tooling and maintenance staff recorded which departments they supported on their time cards. Therefore, we used the time card distribution to allocate tooling and maintenance costs.

In purchasing at this same company, most of a buyer's time was spent identifying sources, coordinating with vendors, and writing purchase orders. All of these activities were driven by the number of purchase orders. Unfortunately, there was no purchase order information collected and accessible but purchased parts did have unique part numbers. So, we distributed the purchasing costs to the punch press department by the quantity of purchased part issues from the warehouse to the punch press department.

The work associated with the shop floor control, warehousing, receiving, and production control departments were not driven by the volume of parts made in a given department, but by the number of transactions or number of times a part number was processed through the department. When a planner scheduled a part number for manufacture it did not matter if it represented two parts or two thousand, the time to schedule the part was the same. The same was true for the other material functions as well; a purchase order for one part takes as long to write as a purchase order for a thousand. The quantity of work was proportional to the number of times the parts were issued to the floor, pulled from stock, received on the dock, or set up on a lathe, and not to how many parts were in a batch or how long the parts would take to be machined. Thus, we ratioed all of these material departments by the number of material issues from the warehouse to that direct labor department and distributed the costs by that proportion.

For most of the management and engineering departments no quantitative measure of work existed and we were forced to rely on management surveys for the cost distribution. The tool engineering manager and operations vice-president each estimated how much of his people's time was devoted to each department.

The entire overhead redistribution at this company did not take more than four man-weeks, maintaining an accuracy of plus or minus 5 percent. In most cases, the recosting increases the fabrication (punch press, machining, molding, and die casting) departments' overhead by adding more tooling and maintenance costs. This is followed by a corresponding decrease in the overhead assigned to labor intense assembly departments. Twenty percent swings in total overhead costs are not uncommon.

An additional benefit of this recosting is the traceable relationship between a production department and its overhead requirements. If the punch press department is outsourced, a very accurate budget cut for the tooling department can be calculated using this cost database.

PIECE PART COSTING

Present cost systems erroneously distribute overhead costs to parts passing through a department on the number of earned standard labor hours the part accumulates. This cost absorption method is flawed. The part standard is the sum of the theoretical time for each of the manufacturing operations required to produce the part. It may or may not include setup, but it certainly does not include receiving, stocking, and testing the part or any of the other overhead activities required to move the part through the factory. Those costs are added to the part when the overhead rate is multiplied by the part's earned standard hours. However, when a planner schedules a part, an operator sets up a machine or the dock receives a batch of material; it is irrelevant whether it will take two minutes or 20 hours to assemble the circuit board. Those costs are the constant. Presently, these activity costs are aggregated at the department level and spread across all of the parts based on earned labor hours.

For instance, a batch of one hundred screw machine parts with a standard of six minutes would be allocated just $4.50 of overhead. This fails to take into account that it would take a material handler 15 minutes to deliver the steel rod, an operator 40 minutes to set up the machine, and an inspector two minutes to check the batch. Therefore, dividing up the overhead strictly on labor hours understates a low volume part's cost, and conversely, overstates a high volume part's cost. Because the cost system does not justly discriminate against low volume products, a company's vice president of sales can always be found trying to introduce new specialized products and raise sales. Moreover, the vice president does not have to price these products outrageously high, reflecting their true cost. As a result, American factories are filled with odd-ball, one of a kind parts, which every plant manager knows is a loss leader.

A common problem with many automated production lines is trying to build too many product variations on the same equipment. One client, only after installing its flexible manufacturing system (F.M.S.), discovered its machining centers had inadequate tool capacity for the variety of parts to be manufactured. This resulted in high downtime and insufficient capacity utilization for the F.M.S. to be profitable. Those companies with successful installations not only make their F.M.S.'s flexible but standardize their product designs to support the production process. These companies have found it less expensive to restrict design freedom than to compensate for design permutations with production hardware.

At this point, we have developed a cost distribution matrix for each direct labor department. We have overhead pools for tooling, maintenance, indirect labor, utilities, and supervision. For some applications this is as far as the recosting must go. If one intends to use this cost database to identify key cost drivers and overhead relationships for project justification, then one is finished. However, if the proposed automation project is going to produce a wide variety of parts, the recosting should be extended to the piece part level.

Activity-Based Costing

Activity- or transaction-based costing provides vital insight into the costs and benefits of a diverse product mix on the proposed automated line. In many companies automated machines stand idle because setup times between changeovers is exorbitant or product changes lead to excess process variability and subsequent scrap. Frequently, changeover times are not analyzed during the project justification process because they are not part of the standard work measurement system and are thought to be insignificant. In fact, setup times average more than 25 percent of uptime in most fabrication shops.

A comparison of piece part costs under traditional and activity-based cost systems is shown in TABLE 15-4. An activity-based cost system allocates some overhead costs with every production changeover. By using such a system, one not only discriminates against low volume products in cost, but one also identifies the changeover costs for reduction.

Punch Press Quantity	Traditional Costing (per PC)	Activity-Based Costing (per PC)	% Change
3,732,360	$0.09106	$0.08705	−4.4%
3,465,048	$0.05417	$0.05422	0.1%
1,771,947	$0.02461	$0.02479	0.7%
1,683,513	$0.14196	$0.13550	−4.6%
762,869	$0.04437	$0.04492	1.2%
405,589	$0.02675	$0.03096	15.7%
360,960	$0.05145	$0.05418	5.3%
203,513	$0.03948	$0.04904	24.2%
170,406	$0.02565	$0.02846	11.0%
118,312	$0.01284	$0.01805	40.6%
96,662	$0.02323	$0.02906	25.1%
51,219	$0.07552	$0.08522	12.8%
13,872	$0.02461	$0.02739	11.3%
7,247	$0.01792	$0.03905	117.9%
3,098	$0.02319	$0.12815	452.6%
22	$0.02792	$13.87500	49595.6%

Table 15-4. Comparison of Unit Cost of Traditional vs. Activity-based Costing.

How to Develop an Activity-Based Cost System

With your cost matrix of overhead pools and direct labor departments firmly in hand, allocate overhead costs to each part that passes through a given department. First, the overhead pools must be grouped by allocation method.

Group Overhead Pools by Allocation Method The first group of overhead pools consists of those driven by direct labor such as fringe benefits, supervision, and janitorial services. These dollars are allocated to parts on their direct labor standard. The second group includes volume driven pools, which can be measured by machine time such as tooling, maintenance, and utilities. These dollars should be allocated on machine usage hours. The third group are those overhead pools which are driven by transactions such as purchasing, warehousing, and indirect labor. These dollars should be allocated on the number of transactions a part creates, where a transaction is defined as a production run of a single part number.

Typically, dividing up these pools into groups involves a great deal of debate over which measure—labor, machine hours, or transaction—most closely drives a given overhead department. In the end, transaction and machine hour groups usually receive 35 to 40 percent of the overhead dollars each, and the labor group about 20 to 25 percent.

Utilities, equipment depreciation, and maintenance are machine driven. The more machine time spent stamping or material punched in the punch press department, the more electricity used. The longer a part takes to be stamped the more capacity it requires and the greater the equipment depreciation it consumes. The greater the volume turned on a screw machine, the more maintenance needed.

Direct labor is not used for volume allocation because this would encourage automating direct labor activities on false economics. At a recent client, we investigated an automated punch press line's justification. The project's savings were mostly direct labor and overhead reductions, where the overhead reductions were calculated from the overhead rate being applied to the direct labor sav-

ings. By using this overhead rate calculation, reductions in tooling and maintenance were being assumed. In fact, if the manual punch press line were replaced with an automated one, tooling would remain unchanged and the maintenance costs would increase substantially. When the overhead was applied on material dollars and not labor hours a much more realistic project savings for the automated line was computed.

Purchasing, receiving, warehousing, shop floor control, and shipping are all transaction driven. It does not matter to a planner if one part or a thousand parts are in a batch—only that each must be bought, received, stored, tracked, and shipped. The workload is proportional to the number of batches processed and not part quantity, labor hours, machine time, or material weight.

Tooling is typically an area of debate. Some tooling activities are transaction driven and some are machine-time driven. When one builds a new die, it does not matter if 2 parts or 2,000 parts will be cast by the die, the cost is the same. But if 200,000 parts go across a tool, it needs maintenance and repair. Also, in many processes like injection molding, after shooting a batch of parts the die moves to the tooling department for cleaning, which is another transaction cost. Therefore, tooling costs should be split between the transaction group and the machine time pools. The tooling costs should be split between new tool fabrication and tool cleaning, from tool repair and maintenance.

Indirect labor costs are transaction driven. Indirect costs are direct labor costs not charged to production work; setup, supervision, material handling within a department, and training are some examples. The more the parts vary, the more indirect labor is required.

Another cost element included in this transaction group is *lost labor efficiency*, the difference between earned labor and actual labor expended. Typically, labor inefficiency results from the learning process. If an operator changes parts, the operator must figure out how to set up the new part, what speed to run the machine at, and when to change the cutting tools. Hence, the more transactions the more time lost to learning.

Quality control inspects batches of parts, not individual parts, thus it too is transaction driven. Scrap and rework can be both volume and transaction driven. The more the parts and the bigger the batches, the more scrap produced. However, the more different parts produced the less chance a company has to get all of the bugs out of each part, tooling, and process; so the more transactions, the more quality problems. Therefore, the scrap and rework dollars should be split between these two pools.

Calculate Allocation Rates Once the pools have been accumulated for each direct labor department, the next step is to calculate allocation rates for the pools. To do this, create a database of all of next year's component parts. On a company mainframe, explode next year's forecasted sales into quantities of end products, which are then multiplied by each product's bill of material. Then put these parts into each department, and process the parts by multiplying these components by the department routings. This gives you a listing of all of next year's components requirements and quantities by department. On this database, you can now allocate the overhead.

Use earned labor hours to allocate the labor overhead pool; use either machine time or material dollars, or even material pounds, to allocate the volume pool; and use transactions for the transaction pool. What exactly is a transaction depends on how the company schedules and runs the production departments.

At one client, the fabrication and finishing departments run a batch of parts every four weeks if it is a high volume part (*A part*), once every 12 weeks if it is a medium volume part (*B part*), and twice a year if it is a low volume part (*C part*). This production schedule from the Material Requirements Planning (MRP) system is based on a part's annual usage times its dollar value. In the MRP system each part receives an A, B, or C rating: A parts are given 13 transactions; B parts are given 4; and C parts, 2.

However, this client's assembly departments build to order. They build assemblies only when they have customer orders for it. Therefore, cus-

tomer orders are the transaction for the assembly departments. We give an assembly in the assembly departments a transaction for every different customer order which includes it.

On our component part database we add earned labor hours, machine hours, and transactions for the forecasted year. Dividing the transaction pool by the total number of forecasted transactions, we calculate a transaction rate for every direct labor department. In the fabrication departments, the transaction rate varies from a high of $722/transaction in the die cast department to a low of $28/transaction in power wash. Die cast's rate reflects the high cost of changing a die cast machine's setup, while power wash reflects little more than dumping parts on a conveyor.

For every department a part number passes through, the part number picks up a transaction cost. If a part is an *A part*, it picks up 13 transactions, times the department's transaction rate. So punch press part 18-5080-001 receives $2,158 (13 transactions, times $166/transaction) of transaction overhead. This $2,158 is then allocated over the forecast requirements of 1,334,245 for a transaction overhead cost of $.00161 per unit. A similar punch press part 18-5082-005 is a lower volume part. It has $166 allocated to its 51 parts for a unit transaction cost of $3.2549. Overall, this new cost system reflects the substantially higher cost of low volume parts over high volume parts.

Equally dramatic is the effect of rolling up the component costs into products. TABLE 15-5 illustrates this claim. Spare parts products once reported to be the most profitable are found to be losing money. Traditional cost systems make no allowance for volume, but the marketing department intuitively knows low volume products cost more to produce, so they price them at a premium. This results in low volume products, such as Product Line B, reporting the highest profitability. Conversely, the high volume products receive more than their fair share of overhead and have their profitability understated as Product Line A shows.

Additional Benefits of Activity-Based Costing This activity-based cost system not only helps justify the discontinuance of low volume prod-

PRODUCT LINE A

	Tradition	Activity-based	Change
Units	4,616,000		
Sales	$49,012	$49,012	
Cost	$47,596	$42,459	−11%
Profits	$1,416	$6,553	363%
ROS	2.9%	13.4%	

PRODUCT LINE B

	Tradition	Activity-based	Change
Units	11,700		
Sales	$279	$279	
Cost	$224	$285	27%
Profits	$55	($6)	−111%
ROS	19.7%	−2.2%	

SPARE PARTS

	Tradition	Activity-based	Change
Units	12,647,000		
Sales	$1,892	$1,892	
Cost	$1,539	$2,710	76%
Profits	$353	($818)	−332%
ROS	18.7%	−43.2%	

Table 15-5. Comparison of Traditional Activity-based Cost Systems on Company and Productline Profitability.

uct lines, but also provides an industrial engineer with excellent data on the trade-offs between flexibility and changeover costs. The industrial engineer can determine whether the additional costs of flexible setups are worth the marginal return of low volume products on a flexible manufacturing system, whether the products should be dropped, or whether a separate production line should be established for these products.

In two unpublished benchmark studies, one of chemical processing plants conducted by Harvard Business School and one of PCB assembly plants by A.T. Kearney, both the high and low cost factories turned out to be highly automated plants. The principle factors which differentiated the high cost from the low cost plants were production volume and product line width. The high cost plants had significantly lower production volumes with wider product lines. These factors caused the factories to have higher down times from product changeovers, lower yields from processing a variety of materials to different specifications, and higher support costs from the control and management of the large number of components flowing through the factory. The use of an activity-based cost system can guide a company around these problems.

PROFILING THE COST BASELINE AT AN EXISTING FACILITY

To profile an existing facility, all one has to do is extrapolate current costs with forecasted volumes to create cost profiles for the upcoming years. Remember to calculate the sales estimates from the market share/value analysis. From this cost baseline, cost changes resulting from the automation project will be estimated. Typically, automation reduces direct labor, production control, scheduling, and material handling costs, while improving production yields. Additional questions the justification should answer are: Will setup times increase or decrease? Will the proposed equipment require more or less maintenance? Will the tooling and utility costs go up or down? Unless a specific mechanism for each saving is identified, then no saving should be included in the justification.

Automation usually requires more tooling, programming, and maintenance support than manual methods. Since these are frequently significant costs, the project's justification should include data to support the recommended levels of expenditures. Data from the cost baseline should be compared to historical records, previous installation reports, and vendor projections.

Cost Savings Justification Example

In TABLES 15-6 and 15-7, the cost savings justification analysis for a mill-turn cell is shown. The mill-turn cell, in this case, is a distributed numerical controlled machining cell of lathes with milling capacity and robotic arms for machine loading and unloading. The mill-turn cell turns parts and then mills them without a new setup. This substantially reduces setup times, material handling, scrap, and some tooling. The new machine tool has higher spindle speeds to heighten productivity. Because it is a new machine, it will save on maintenance expense.

Look at TABLES 15-6 and 15-7 together to see the complete financial analysis. The financial analysis shows two scenarios: one without the mill-turn in TABLE 15-6, and one with it, in TABLE 15-7. The $1,145,000 investment on TABLE 15-7 has an estimated rate of return of 20.8 percent of five years. The current scenario, in TABLE 15-6, with no

Table 15-6. Mill-Turn Machining Cell Project Financial Analysis: No Changes in Lathe Department.

	Current	Year 1	Year 2	Year 3	Year 4	Year 5
Machine hours (000HRS)	26.6	27.4	28.3	29.1	30.0	30.9
Capacity-2 shifts (000HRS)	30.6	30.6	30.6	30.6	30.6	30.6
Transactions	2360	2360	2360	2515	2515	2515
COSTS ($000):						
Materials	$1,494.3	$1,539.1	$1,585.3	$1,632.9	$1,681.8	$1,732.3
Labor based:						
Earned labor	$349.0	$359.5	$370.3	$381.4	$392.8	$404.6
Fringe benefits	$316.8	$326.3	$342.6	$352.9	$363.5	$378.9
Volume based:						
Utilities	$120.2	$123.8	$127.5	$131.3	$135.3	$139.3
Scrap & rework	$458.1	$471.8	$486.0	$500.6	$515.6	$531.1
Supplies & other	$355.4	$366.1	$377.0	$388.4	$400.0	$412.0
Tooling	$25.7	$26.5	$27.3	$28.1	$28.9	$29.8
Maintenance	$143.7	$148.0	$152.5	$157.0	$161.7	$166.6
Transaction based:						
Lost labor eff.	$79.1	$79.1	$79.1	$84.3	$84.3	$84.3
Indirect labor	$272.2	$272.2	$272.2	$290.1	$290.1	$290.1
PC & shop floor	$38.1	$38.1	$38.1	$40.6	$40.6	$40.6
Warehousing	$27.1	$27.1	$27.1	$28.9	$28.9	$28.9
Q.C.	$45.0	$45.0	$45.0	$48.0	$48.0	$48.0
Other:						
Depreciation	$264.1	$224.5	$190.8	$162.2	$137.9	$117.2
Support eng.	$11.1	$11.1	$11.1	$11.1	$11.1	$11.1
TOTAL COST	$3,999.9	$4,058.2	$4,131.9	$4,237.6	$4,320.5	$4,414.7

Table 15-7. Financial Analysis with
Mill-Turn Center in Lathe Department.

	Current	Year 1	Year 2	Year 3	Year 4	Year 5
Machine hours (000HRS)	26.6	23.6	24.3	25.0	25.7	26.5
Capacity-2 shifts (000HRS)	30.6	35.2	35.2	35.2	35.2	35.2
Transactions	2360	1699	1699	1811	1811	1811
COSTS ($000):						
Materials	$1,494.3	$1,479.4	$1,523.7	$1,569.4	$1,616.5	$1,665.0
Labor based:						
Earned labor	$349.0	$309.1	$318.4	$328.0	$337.8	$347.9
Fringe benefits	$316.8	$216.8	$227.7	$234.5	$241.5	$248.8
Volume based:						
Utilities	$120.2	$106.5	$109.7	$113.0	$116.3	$119.8
Scrap & rework	$458.1	$284.0	$292.6	$301.3	$310.4	$319.7
Supplies & other	$355.4	$366.1	$377.0	$388.4	$400.0	$412.0
Tooling	$25.7	$20.5	$21.1	$21.7	$22.4	$23.1
Maintenance	$143.7	$95.5	$98.3	$101.3	$104.3	$107.4
Transaction based:						
Lost labor eff.	$79.1	$57.0	$57.0	$60.7	$60.7	$60.7
Indirect labor	$272.2	$117.6	$117.6	$125.3	$125.3	$125.3
PC & shop floor	$38.1	$27.4	$27.4	$29.2	$29.2	$29.2
Warehousing	$27.1	$19.5	$19.5	$20.8	$20.8	$20.8
Q.C.	$45.0	$32.4	$32.4	$34.5	$34.5	$34.5
Other:						
Depreciation	$264.1	$720.0	$540.0	$405.0	$303.8	$227.8
Support eng.	$11.1	$55.1	$19.0	$16.1	$14.0	$14.4
TOTAL COST	$3,999.9	$3,906.8	$3,781.4	$3,749.2	$3,737.6	$3,756.6
Cost Savings		$151.3	$350.5	$488.4	$582.8	$658.1
Taxes (@38%)		$57.5	$133.2	$185.6	$221.5	$250.1
TOTAL CASH FLOW		$93.8	$217.3	$302.8	$361.4	$408.0
Investment:	$1,145.0					
5 Year Internal Rate of Return:			20.8%			

changes, shows a lathe department with a three percent increasing workload over the next five years and a new product introduction in Year 3. The new product introduction results in little more than an increase in transactions. In addition, a fringe benefit hike is expected in Year 2. Materials, labor, and volume overhead costs are proportioned to machine hours. Support costs are expected to be constant and depreciation will decline as the department's lathes age.

Justifying the New Equipment: Benefits of Automation

The mill-turn scenario shows a 14 percent productivity improvement, from the mill-turn's higher spindle speeds. This is reflected in the lower machine hours, earned labor costs, and utilities costs. Since a substantial quantity of the lathe department's scrap has been traced to the machines to be replaced, it is estimated that scrap and rework will decline by 30 percent under this scenario. In addition, the mill-turn requires four percent less material, because excess material for milling fixtures is no longer needed. Cutting tools make up the majority of the supplies and no change in their requirements are foreseen. Tooling costs are reduced as milling fixtures are eliminated. Maintenance and calibration costs for the new machine are also expected to decline with the replacement of the troublesome old lathes.

The mill-turn reduces machine changeovers, resulting in 14 percent less transactions. This in turn leads to less lost labor efficiency, and lower costs for indirect labor, production control, shop floor control, warehousing, and quality control. Since the mill-turn also has tool change capability, the required setup is drastically reduced, cutting indirect labor by 40 percent.

The new machine's depreciation is included in the analysis along with support engineering needs. The engineers will need to change the routing sheets, program the machines, and train the operators, all of which is accounted for in the analysis.

This example demonstrates how a project's cost savings can be baselined. While all projects need not depend on just cost savings, this approach is just as applicable if the project is one with revenue enhancement. All the project's effects need to be included in the analysis, from engineering support to setup times or scrap to utilities. No significant costs should be ignored.

PROFILING THE GREENFIELD FACILITY

The greenfield facility, a new plant unencumbered by the past, is a much more difficult project to profile, since it is not just an improvement over a current method, but a completely new installation. It may or may not involve totally new products, processes, or methods. Generally, the approach to justifying a greenfield facility is to model the proposed facility under different levels of automation and production requirements. These models compare the facility's cost, capacity, product value, and payback under these different scenarios, and thus allow the trade-offs between investment and cost reduction or quality improvement to be evaluated.

Planning a Greenfield: Where to Start

Typically, the planning and construction of a greenfield results from one of two things. Either the company wants to introduce a new product—such as with Apple's Fremont MacIntosh plant—or, a company is trying to make a quantum competitive leap—like GE's Louisville dishwasher complex. In both of these cases, the companies sought a substantial competitive advantage from automated manufacture. These greenfield facilities allowed superior products to be produced at lower cost, which in GE's case, resulted in it's market share increasing from 31 percent to over 40 percent.[5]

If you evaluate the projects under various levels of production and automation, you not only determine the optimum factory configuration, but you also develop the transition plan. Initially, only a limited amount of automation is installed, although a fully automated factory is planned. As the production rate ramps up, more automation is added. In this way, the company maximizes its return on investment, and minimizes its investment risk. Most importantly, the company avoids overextending its engineering resources by not requiring engineers to debug many different types of equipment all at once.

Planning a Greenfield: A Case Study

TABLE 15-8 shows three alternative plant configurations for a greenfield oscilloscope plant. The three configurations reflect increasing levels of automation. The major manufacturing configuration decisions revolve around the oscilloscope's major components and processes: whether to make or

**Table 15-8. Alternate Plant Configurations for
Proposed Oscilloscope at Greenfield Manufacturing Plant.**

Major components/ Processes	ALTERNATIVE PLANT CONFIGURATIONS		
	#1	#2	#3
Tube	Purchased	Purchased	Automatic
I.C.	Off-the-Shelf	Semi-custom	Semi-custom
P.C.B.	Purchased	Purchased	Purchased
Assembly	Manual	Some robotic cells	Automated line
Test/calibration	Semi-automatic	Semi-automatic	Full cycle P.C. driven
Packaging	Semi-auto	Semi-auto	Automatic in-line

buy tubes; use off-the-shelf ICs or develop application specific ICs (ASICs); assemble by hand or automated line; have semiautomatic or full cycle test; and semiautomatic or automatic packaging. Each configuration has different costs, results in different product value, and requires different levels of investment.

After the approximate demand and the process flow of the new product are established, the team is ready to begin analyzing the different facility options. Only by laying out the conceptual design of each of the facility configurations can the design team analyze the different costs. The design team identifies for each production step what equipment is required, how many people will man each station, and how much overhead support will be required. TABLE 15-9 shows this analysis.

Based on the equipment being specified, the design team estimates the product performance effects of the equipment. How much more reliable is the product with automated versus manual assembly? How many more features can be added if ASICs are used instead of standard ICs? This allows changes in value to be estimated under different configurations as TABLE 15-10 shows. Finally, all the information together allows the team to establish market shares for each facility configuration, as shown in TABLE 15-11.

Once the production and yield rates have been established, the inventory levels are estimated. This allows the design team to draw a conceptual floor layout and calculate floor space. Occupancy costs are estimated from the floor space requirements. Based on the proposed equipment's value, depreciation is computed. The equipment specifications and local utility rates allow utility costs to be estimated. Using the headcounts and local labor and fringe rates, the factory's labor costs are computed. After estimating the factory expenses and supplies, the design team can now draw a fairly accurate picture of the different configuration costs.

The financial analysis in TABLE 15-12 shows the resulting profitability and financial ratios of the different configurations in Year 3. The analysis does not show the initial years, but Alternative #1 is an intermediate configuration prior to extensive automation. While Alternative #2 is the least risky of the two automated choices and has the highest return on assets, Alternative #3 best positions the firm for the long term. Alternative #3 has the highest product capacity, produces the product of the highest value, and will hinder the competition the most. Each of the configurations has its own strengths and weaknesses; management's job will be to decide which course of action best fits its strategic and financial goals.

Table 15-9. Cost of Sales Analysis.

	ALTERNATIVE PLANT CONFIGURATIONS		
	#1	#2	#3
Headcounts:			
Production labor			
Tube manufacture	0	0	5
Assembly	26	25	11
Test/calibration	6	7	3
Packaging	3	4	1
Indirect Labor			
Receiving/shipping	3	3	3
Maintenance	2	5	6
Materials	2	2	2
Quality assurance	7	4	4
Engineering	3	6	6
Management	3	3	3
Total headcount	55	59	44
Cost of Sales ($MIL):			
Salaries & benefits	$2.3	$2.6	$2.2
Materials	$2.6	$2.8	$2.6
Supplies & expenses	$0.5	$0.5	$0.6
Utilities	$0.1	$0.1	$0.1
Other	$0.2	$0.3	$0.3
Total	$5.5	$6.0	$5.5

Table 15-10. ACME M2000
Oscilloscope Customer Value Perception.

	CUSTOMER VALUE PERCEPTION					
Attribute	Vastly Superior	Superior	Average	Inferior	Vastly Inferior	Weight
Reliability ——— x —— • —— * ———————————————————						35%
Advanced Features ——————— x• ——— * —————————————						30%
Ease of use ————————— x • * —————————————————						20%
Ease of Maintenance ————————— x • —— * ————————						10%
Portability ——————— x • —— * —————————————————						5%
Overall value rating ——————— x —— • —— * ————————						100%
	100	50	0	−50	−100	

*   Facility configuration #1
•   Facility configuration #2
x   Facility configuration #3

Table 15-11. Alternate Facility
Sales Analysis—Year 3.

BASELINE	Value Rating	Market Size ($MIL)	Market Share	Sales ($MIL)
Facility #1	24	$64.0	15%	$9.60

Change From Baseline

	Value Rating	Change in Value	Market Share/ Value Coeff.	Change in Market Share	Increase in Sales ($MIL)	Total Sales ($MIL)
Facility #2	52.0	28.0	0.15	4.20%	$2.69	$12.29
Facility #3	61.1	37.1	0.15	5.57%	$3.56	$13.16

Table 15-12. Financial Analysis
of Alternative Plant Configurations.

	Configuration ($MIL)		
	#1	#2	#3
Investment	$10.0	$12.5	$15.5
Company Financials (Year 3):			
Sales	$9.6	$12.3	$13.2
Cost of sales	$5.5	$16.0	115.5
Net income	$4.1	$6.3	$7.6
G&A	$0.7	$0.7	$0.7
Sales expense	$0.7	$0.8	$0.8
Depreciation	$1.0	$1.6	$2.5
R&D	$0.4	$0.4	$0.4
Fixed cost	$2.7	$3.5	$4.4
Profit before taxes	$1.4	$2.8	$3.2
Taxes	$0.5	$1.0	$1.2
Profit after taxes	$0.9	$1.7	$2.0
Return on sales	9.1%	14.1%	15.5%
Inventory	$0.6	$0.5	$0.6
Accounts payable	$0.4	$0.4	$0.4
Cash	$0.2	$0.2	$0.2
Accounts receivable	$0.4	$0.5	$0.4
Current assets	$0.8	$0.6	$0.8
Plant	$7.0	$7.1	$6.5
Equipment	$1.8	$4.2	$7.8
Fixed assets	$8.8	$11.3	$14.3
Total assets	$9.6	$11.9	$15.1
Asset turnover	1.00	0.97	1.15
Return on assets	9.1%	14.6%	13.5%

Purpose of the
Greenfield Financial Analysis

No recommendation for the facility configuration is presented, nor does one solution stand out. This is because the objective of the financial analysis is to provide information that assists the decision maker in determining the best investment for his company. The financial analysis should never verify a decision that has already been made. If the analysis is to be used for verification, the result is always the same. The company is left with a solution in search of a problem. The financial analysis becomes a test of creating accounting capability; strategic investments are left unidentified.

SUMMARY

The financial analysis is a tool for identifying sound capital investment. Investments should target a company's cost drivers or value levers, with an eye on the company's strategic environment and direction. The analysis should begin before the project is conceived to identify where the best opportunities exist, and should end with a post audit of the project's results.

Strategic investments develop out of clear understanding of the company's strategic position, whether it is differentiation or low cost supplier. The project should directly support the company strategy. Customer value, and how the proposed project affects it must be addressed. If customers will perceive value as improved, more customers will buy the product; therefore, revenue enhancement should be incorporated into the justification. Additionally, the consequences of not investing must be evaluated and included in the justification. Companies which fail to invest concede market loss to their competitors and this has a very high cost.

Many strategic capital projects cannot be justified using today's obsolete cost systems. Present cost systems put too much attention on direct labor and not enough on the real overhead drivers, like part counts and defects. In most cases, a new look at a company's cost structure must be taken before a company's true cost drivers can be identified.

The capital project justification must profile the company's cost and value both before and after the project's implementation to ensure a high level of accuracy.

In the end, numbers and analysis should only support decision making; they are not a judgment. Numbers can be manipulated by a smart analyst, data can be wrong, and unforeseen markets and technology can appear; all of which make analysis subject to error. To paraphase Tracy O'Rouke, President of Allen-Bradley, when asked why he decided to invest in their very successful automated contractor facility, "It is what we had to do to be successful in the contractor business, and we did not base it on what the financial analysis said." Financial analysis should only support good judgment, not replace it.

ENDNOTES

1. "The General Electric Experience," *Production Magazine* (March 1986): 66-69.

2. *HBS Case Services* (Boston: Harvard Business School), 9-385-276.

3. "Manufacturing Strategy Can Beat a Bum Rap," *Electronic Packaging & Production* (September 1988): 56-61.

4. David Halberstam, *The Reckoning* (New York: Avon Books, 1986), 371.

5. "And the Bottom Line," *Industry Week* (May 26, 1986): 64, 81–82.

BIBLIOGRAPHY

Buzzell, Robert and Bradley Gale. *The PIMS Principles*. New York: Free Press, 1987.

Hayes, Robert, Steven Wheelwright, and Kim Clark. *Dynamic Manufacturing*. New York: Free Press, 1988.

O'Guin, Michael. "Information Age Calls for New Methods of Financial Analysis." *Industrial Engineering Magazine* (November 1987).

Porter, Michael E. *Competitive Advantage*. New York: Free Press, 1985.

16

Computer-Aided Design and Drafting

Bruce R. Dewey*

DIGITAL COMPUTERS HAVE BROUGHT CONSIDERABLE change to the engineering workplace. With the potential of doing work better at less cost, computers have a major place in practically all phases of modern industry. Production of engineering documentation, traditionally a very labor intensive process, is now largely done by specialized computing systems. Word processing is used for text, spreadsheets and database systems are used for tabular data, and specialized graphics systems are used for engineering drawings.

The acronym *CAD* probably best stands for ''Computer-Aided Drafting'' because that is exactly what most CAD systems do. Having the ''D'' mean ''Design'' is a misnomer because design encompasses much more—economics, product planning, testing, analysis, manufacturing planning, and so forth. Systems that do some design functions in addition to drafting are better called *CADD* for ''Computer-Aided Drafting and Design'' systems. Most engineers will have several specific design packages in addition to their CAD systems.

CAD systems are specialized according to the engineering function performed. For example, electrical CAD systems contain libraries of components such as diodes and integrated circuits. To produce drawings of structural components and machines, mechanical CAD systems have the ability to do dimensioning. Architectural CAD systems have building components in their libraries and do specialized drawing functions such as the double lines for walls. In what follows, the term *CAD* will be used for general-purpose mechanical CAD and CADD systems.

This chapter is intended to provide background material which will help in selecting such a system. Just as with any engineered product, there are trade-offs between features and cost. A common measure of cost of CAD systems is called *productivity*. Measurement of productivity is very elusive. Usually, a number (not always greater than 1) is determined that is the ratio of the amount of drawing done by CAD to that done the old way for the same cost. Variability in this number arises from many factors, such as the skill of drafters and how well the work being done matches the capability of the CAD system. In any measurement of productivity, CAD systems are much better at changing existing work than in the input of new work. Since most real engineering design involves modification of earlier work and other changes, CAD systems have by and large met wide acceptance.

In addition to cost savings, CAD systems facilitate coordinating the work of many people. Manag-

---

*Bruce R. Dewey is Professor of Mechanical Engineering and Assistant Dean of Engineering at the University of Wyoming, Laramie. He is a graduate of Iowa State University and the University of Illinois. Dr. Dewey is the author of many articles dealing with computer-aided engineering and the 1988 textbook, *Computer Graphics for Engineers*. As a consultant to industry for over twenty years, he has been involved in the development of finite element analysis and computer-aided design software.

ing the electronic storage of engineering documentation can guarantee that information is up-to-date and that only authorized persons can use or change the information. Sharing information electronically between various engineering groups has no geographical limitation. A company with offices in several cities can quickly muster a large force of drafters to work on a rush project.

CAD improves quality of work. Database features in professional CAD systems keep track of the effects of changes, such as changing a single component which is used in several different products. Legibility is always excellent. Checking functions can be built in, such as checking interference and tolerance. Animation of a mechanism can be used to check function and packaging.

In order to select a CAD system, information should be gathered in two areas: what is needed for the target applications and what is available in CAD systems. This chapter provides some theoretical background about CAD that will help the engineer understand more about what is actually going on in such systems. While CAD systems are all essentially similar, the extra effort in finding the best one for the given situation will be rewarded many times over.

HARDWARE FOR COMPUTER GRAPHICS

In setting up a new system it is far preferable to select software, and then use the software vendor's recommendations for the needed hardware. Usually there is some latitude in hardware platforms, where a balance will be struck between performance and cost. Workstations, hardcopy output devices, and networking will be included on a shopping list.

Workstations

A *graphics workstation* manages the interactive input, processing, storage, and output of graphics information. A *terminal* is an input-output device of limited capability which requires that most processing and data storage be done by a remote computer. When standing alone, a personal computer (PC)

system functions as a workstation; when communicating with a larger computer, the PC functions as a terminal.

Processing capability, memory size, and disk capacity set workstations apart from PCs. The microprocessors of first generation PCs (for example, Intel 8086 and Motorola 6502) are inadequate for all but the most rudimentary CAD system. Second generation PC microprocessors (for example, Intel 80286 and Motorola 68000) are adequate for many entry-level professional applications. Workstations utilize advanced microprocessors (for example, Intel 80386 and Motorola 68020, and proprietary RISC chip sets), which provide virtual memory and graphics-intensive computing. Workstations run multitasking operating systems such as Unix, while PCs run a single-tasking system such as DOS.

Graphics display technologies may be classified according to the support of interactive output, interactive input, and hardcopy output. The brief descriptions here illustrate important features. Detailed information is available in brochures and manuals available from manufacturers.

Practically all interactive output in computer graphics is on a cathode-ray tube (CRT) display. As shown schematically in FIG. 16-1, a stream of electrons strikes a layer of phosphors, selected to emit light of the proper colors, on the inside of the screen. Color systems have red, green, and blue phosphors; monochromatic systems have white, green, or amber phosphors.

Just like television, most systems use *raster scan*, a row-by-row system, to create pictures. The dot-by-dot description of such a display is called a *bit map*, which in its simplest form is a system where each dot or pixel (picture element) is assigned either 0 (black) or 1 (white). The resolution of the screen is given by the number of columns and rows of pixels that are displayed. The lowest satisfactory resolution for CAD is approximately 480×360, that of the so-called VGA on PC graphics systems. For professional use, large screens (19 inch) and high resolutions (approximately 1200×1000) are desirable. Some raster

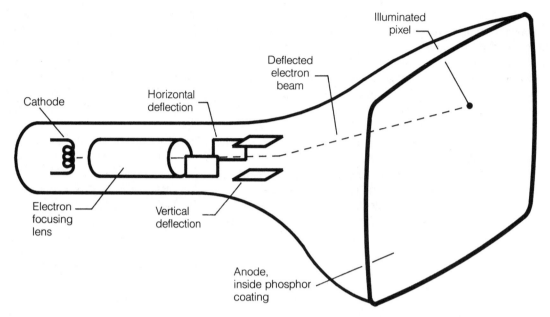

Fig. 16-1. Cathode-ray tube. Electrons from the heated cathode are attracted to the positively charged anode. The phosphor coating is selected for color and persistence characteristics. Elements within the CRT focus and steer the beam under processor control.

Fig. 16-2. Rasterized line segment or vector. Antialiasing circuitry, incorporated in some display systems, improves the appearance of an oblique line by partially illuminating the pixels.

scan displays have *antialiasing* circuitry which makes a line appear sharper by decreasing the illumination of the first and last pixels in each row as shown in FIG. 16-2.

In addition to the graphics display technology used in the workstation, consideration should be given to provisions for interactive input of information. Support of the various types of input devices depends on the software. A digitizing tablet can address screen locations in an absolute or relative mode and also hold printed menus from which commands can be picked. In contrast, the lower-cost mouse addresses screen locations only in a relative

mode, and cannot be used to pick items from a printed menu. Some software supports multi-button mice, where the buttons can be programmed to give certain commands. In contrast, CAD systems using arrow keys or a joystick as a pointing device will not be very productive. Valuator dials, often found in top-end, three-dimensional (3-D) systems, are convenient for twirling and moving the image for interactive viewing. A function keyboard, also found on top-end systems, is used for menu input of commands.

With the advent of stand-alone workstations, the trend is away from multiple input devices toward the use of a mouse and screen menus. Here menus are rapidly displayed on the screen as needed and the operator picks commands with the mouse buttons. The advantage is that the operator's eyes can stay on the screen, instead of looking at the tablet.

Hardcopy Output

Devices for recording graphics information on paper and film are line-drawing or bit-mapping devices. With the exception of the pen plotter, most output devices are based on reproducing bit maps.

The pen plotter is the earliest type of hardcopy graphic output device and is still very widely used. The line drawing process is accomplished by moving a pen on the paper under computer control. The pen is "down" to draw and "up" to be repositioned without drawing. FIGURE 16-3 shows that relative motion between pen and paper is accomplished two different ways. Pen plotters produce high quality line drawings and allow a choice of inks and papers to be used. Although pen plotters are relatively inexpensive, they are inherently slow devices and are unsatisfactory for shaded images.

A dot-matrix printer is the least expensive of all graphics output devices. Dot-matrix printers are very slow, and the resulting graphics are generally of inferior quality. While most dot-matrix printers have only black ribbons, there are some with multicolor ribbons which can do very limited color work. Jagged line work is frequently a problem with images from dot-matrix devices, particularly if the image is a screen dump (copy of bit map used for screen display).

While ink-jet and wax printers have resolution capabilities similar to those of dot-matrix printers, they are good choices for color work. Images must be printed on special paper. The better devices in this category have high resolution as well as the ability to do color shading. The glossy wax makes colors which appear more vivid than those from inks.

Laser printers and electrostatic printers typically are faster and work with much finer resolutions (typically 300 dots per inch) than other bit-mapping devices. Low-end laser printers compare in cost with small pen plotters. While such laser printers are limited to black lines, the speed far exceeds that of pen plotters and the quality is comparable. A cost effective combination that provides maximum versatility consists of a laser printer and an E-size (36-inch) pen plotter.

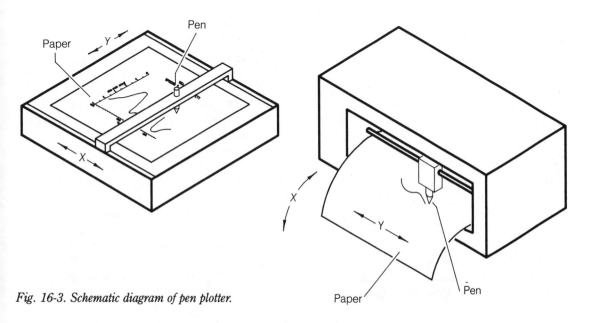

Fig. 16-3. Schematic diagram of pen plotter.

Computer graphics output film recorders are available to make microfilm or 35 mm slides. Microfilm conserves storage space and is more permanent than magnetic computer tape. Some firms produce all images on a microfilm output device, with paper prints being made photographically as needed.

Networking

Interconnection of computing equipment is vitally important in most engineering offices. One reason is that large capacity, high quality output devices should be readily available to all users. A more important reason is that files need to be shared and managed by engineers with different specialties. In setting up a CAD system where more than one engineer works on a project, the administrator needs to pay close attention to setting up the system to keep track of changes. This indicates that drawings will be kept centrally on a file server and that access will be over a network.

Networking has been progressing toward standards in hardware and software that make possible sharing of information between diverse platforms (Van Deusen 1985). Equipment and software choices should always be made with networking possibilities in mind.

GRAPHICS STANDARDS

Graphics standards make it possible to share computer graphics data, port software between different systems, and interconnect equipment. Historically, standards have evolved as manufacturers selectively use features found in existing systems. Now, most of the standards are set under the auspices of the American National Standards Institute (ANSI) and its international counterpart, the International Standards Organization (ISO). Graphics standards have also been developed by the Special Interest Group on Graphics (SIGGRAPH) of the Association of Computing Machinery, several aerospace companies, the National Bureau of Standards (NBS), the Canadian Standards Association (CSA), and American Telephone and Telegraph (AT&T).

Graphics standards fall into three categories:

- Protocols for storage and transmittal of graphics data (Van Deusen 1985). Initial Graphics Exchange Specification (IGES), Computer Graphics Metafile (CGM), and Drawing Exchange Format (DXF) deal with encoding images in such a way that the files can be shared among differing systems and applications.
- Application programming conventions (Brown 1985, Hopgood 1986). Here source programs incorporate subroutines structured according to Core, Graphical Kernel System (GKS) or Programmer's Hierarchical Interactive Graphics Standard (PHIGS) which produce graphical actions. These standards allow moving software between different computing platforms and are of interest only to programmers.
- Graphics device interfaces (Van Deusen 1985). North American Presentation-Level Protocol Syntax (NAPLPS) defines data transmission interfaces for hardware. Computer Graphics-Virtual Device Interface (CG-VDI) deals with the interface between software and device drivers.

The relationship among the categories is shown schematically in FIG. 16-4. The standard most widely applied to the transfer of CAD files is IGES.

Initial Graphics Exchange Standard

Files transferred under the IGES protocol are used to generate engineering drawings and part descriptions for numerically controlled machining. This graphics standard specifies the structure of the text files in ways appropriate to the features, or *entities*, found in engineering drawings. Entities in IGES are classified according to whether they are geometry, annotation, or structure and definition.

Geometry entities include categories such as arcs, lines, planes, spline curves, and ruled surfaces. Each geometry entity must be accompanied by specified parameters. For example, the parameters for a line are the coordinates of the starting and ending point.

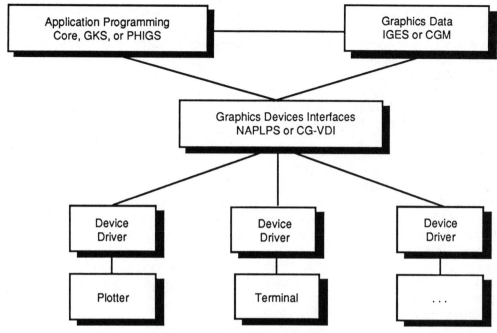

Fig. 16-4. Division of graphic standards.

Annotation entities include dimensions, notes, labels, witness lines, and other features pertinent to engineering drawings. Parameters associated with a linear dimension, for example, include the text, the leaders with arrowheads, and extension lines.

Structure and definition entities define relationships among the elements of the model. Typical capabilities include description of the interrelation of the parts of the drawing, properties associated with lines and regions, and definitions of text fonts.

In a sense, an IGES file is a "picture" because it contains all the information needed to generate an engineering drawing independent of any software or system. IGES is popular because software modules for IGES preprocessing and postprocessing can be added to existing systems, and the IGES primitives are similar to those used in existing CAD data structures. On the other hand, IGES files are so verbose, that they are only used when required for data transfer. In practice, discrepancies in IGES translation require careful review and possible editing of the transferred drawing.

TRANSFORMATIONS

This section introduces the algorithms used to manipulate graphical images. Of particular interest are the methods for making pictorials of 3-D images.

The locations of line ends, centers of circles, and other graphic entities are stored in CAD system databases as a *points matrix*. The 2-D systems need store only x and y coordinates, while 3-D systems store x, y, and z coordinates. For purposes of the subsequent discussion, the n points describing an entity will be assumed to be stored in the matrix:

$$[\mathbf{P}] = \begin{bmatrix} x_1 & y_1 & z_1 \\ x_2 & y_2 & z_2 \\ \cdot & \cdot & \cdot \\ \cdot & \cdot & \cdot \\ \cdot & \cdot & \cdot \\ x_n & y_n & z_n \end{bmatrix} \qquad (16\text{-}1)$$

Transformation is the mathematical operation which arranges the points, and hence changes the image. *Modeling transformations* change the actual geometry of object; for example, stretching a member to fit within a certain space. *Viewing transformations* alter the displayed image, as for example rotating the object to see it from a different location. In interactive CAD applications, a modeling transformation changes the database description of the object, while a viewing transformation does not.

There are five basic transformations that can be performed on points (Dewey 1988): (1) *translation*, where points move in such a way that all lines connecting points retain the same direction; (2) *scaling*, where the magnitudes of the coordinates change; (3) *shearing*, where the angles between lines change; (4) *rotation*, where points move in concentric circular arcs; and (5) *perspective*, where the x and y distances between points are made smaller the farther away they are from the viewer. (By convention, the x-y plane is the plane of the screen and the z axis is normal to the screen, directed outward toward the viewer.) Transformations (1), (2), and (4) are common menu items in CAD programs. Transformation (3) can be applied to 2-D data to make a pictorial view—a feature found in so-called 2 1/2-D systems. Transformations (1), (4), and (5) are used to make pictorials from true 3-D databases.

The transformation process can most conveniently be expressed in terms of matrix multiplication,

$$[P^*] = [P] [T] \qquad (16\text{-}2)$$

where $[P^*]$ is the new points matrix, $[P]$ is the old points matrix, and $[T]$ is the transformation matrix. In equation writing, the left-hand side contains the result, just as with statements in programming languages. In modeling transformations, the $[P^*]$ matrix overwrites the $[P]$ matrix, while in viewing transformations, the $[P^*]$ matrix is used to display the object while an unchanged copy of $[P]$ is retained.

A special convention, the homogeneous coordinate system, allows the matrices $[T]$ to have the same dimensions (3×3 for 2-D and 4×4 for 3-D systems) regardless of the transformation. For conformability in matrix multiplication, it follows that the points matrix must have an extra column. Thus the points matrix for 3-D, for equation 16-1 would be written as:

$$[P] = \begin{bmatrix} x_1 & y_1 & z_1 & 1 \\ x_2 & y_2 & z_2 & 1 \\ \cdot & \cdot & \cdot & \cdot \\ \cdot & \cdot & \cdot & \cdot \\ \cdot & \cdot & \cdot & \cdot \\ x_n & y_n & z_n & 1 \end{bmatrix} \qquad (16\text{-}3)$$

and the 2-D points matrix would have all *ones* in the third (last) column. Because it is inefficient to store all the extra *ones* in the database, software simply infers their presence when needed.

Translation

Adding Δx, Δy, and Δz to each value of x, y, and z respectively is accomplished by postmultiplying the points matrix by:

$$[T_t] = \begin{bmatrix} 1 & 0 & 0 & 0 \\ 0 & 1 & 0 & 0 \\ 0 & 0 & 1 & 0 \\ \Delta x & \Delta y & \Delta z & 1 \end{bmatrix} \qquad (16\text{-}4)$$

In CAD systems, this transformation is invoked by commands such as *move*, *copy*, and *pan*.

Scaling

To change the size of an entity, the points matrix is postmultiplied by:

$$[T_s] = \begin{bmatrix} s_x & 0 & 0 & 0 \\ 0 & s_y & 0 & 0 \\ 0 & 0 & s_z & 0 \\ 0 & 0 & 0 & 1 \end{bmatrix} \qquad (16\text{-}5)$$

where the scale factors s_x, s_y, and s_z may be sized to stretch or shrink the entity different amounts in the three coordinate directions or may be equal to each other to give uniform scaling. A scaling factor, s, greater than unity enlarges the image; less than unity shrinks the image. Use of -1 for one of the scaling factors produces the mirror reflection, a very useful modeling transformation for creating objects with symmetry. For example, setting $s_x = -1$, $s_y = 1$, and $s_z = 1$ produces a mirror reflection about the y-z plane, which would be the plane of symmetry. In addition to the CAD *mirror* command, the scaling transformation is invoked when the user encloses an entity in a box and pulls "handles" to stretch or shrink the selection.

Shearing

Shearing is the least used of the basic transformations, although some so-called $2^{1}/_{2}$-D CADD systems use a shearing transformation to make objects appear in pictorial views. To change the angles between lines parallel to the x, y, and z axes, the points matrix is postmultiplied by

$$\begin{bmatrix} 1 & T_{xy} & T_{xz} & 0 \\ T_{yx} & 1 & T_{yz} & 0 \\ T_{zx} & T_{zy} & 1 & 0 \\ 0 & 0 & 0 & 1 \end{bmatrix} \quad (16\text{-}6)$$

where the terms T_{xy}, T_{xz}, etc., are assigned values to produce the desired results. A special case of this transformation, the "oblique" projection (Gardan 1986), is accomplished with $T_{xy} = T_{xz} = T_{yx} = t_{yz} = 0$, $t_{zx} = k \cos \theta$, and $t_{zy} = k \sin \theta$, where k is commonly 0.5 (for the "cabinet" projection) and θ is roughly 30° to 60°.

Rotation

For the most part, pictorial views are produced with the use of rotation as a viewing transformation. The sign convention for the positive sense of rotation is according to the right hand rule—the thumb points along the axis of rotation while the curled fingers indicate the sense of rotation around the axis.

The transformation matrices for rotation around the x, y, and z axes are:

$$[\mathbf{T}_{rx}] = \begin{bmatrix} 1 & 0 & 0 & 0 \\ 0 & \cos \theta_x & \sin \theta_x & 0 \\ 0 & -\sin \theta_x & \cos \theta_x & 0 \\ 0 & 0 & 0 & 1 \end{bmatrix} \quad (16\text{-}7)$$

$$[\mathbf{T}_{ry}] = \begin{bmatrix} \cos \theta_y & 0 & -\sin \theta_y & 0 \\ 0 & 1 & 0 & 0 \\ \sin \theta_y & 0 & \cos \theta_y & 0 \\ 0 & 0 & 0 & 1 \end{bmatrix} \quad (16\text{-}8)$$

$$[\mathbf{T}_{rz}] = \begin{bmatrix} \cos \theta_z & \sin \theta_z & 0 & 0 \\ -\sin \theta_z & \cos \theta_x & 0 & 0 \\ 0 & 0 & 1 & 0 \\ 0 & 0 & 0 & 1 \end{bmatrix} \quad (16\text{-}9)$$

where θ_x, θ_y, and θ_z are the rotations around the x, y, and z axes respectively. Most pictorials are produced by rotations around two coordinate axes. It is important to note that the order of rotation affects the result, as is illustrated for one special case in FIG. 16-5.

Isometric pictorials, a common default in CADD systems, are produced by a first rotation of $\theta_y = -45°$, followed by the rotation $\theta_x = 35.264°$ (Dewey 1988). The isometric pictorial makes the angles between the original x, y, and z axes all equal to 120°. The popularity of the isometric is due to its showing equal detail on all three sides of a box-like object. It should be noted that rotating first around the y axis and then around the x axis keeps vertical lines vertical. Rotations other than the special one given above will produce *axonometric* projections, which can be adjusted to give a pictorial showing more of one side and less of others.

Instead of user input for rotation angles, some CAD systems allow the input of a *viewpoint*. The *view vector* runs from the viewsite, which usually defaults to the origin, to the viewpoint. With the

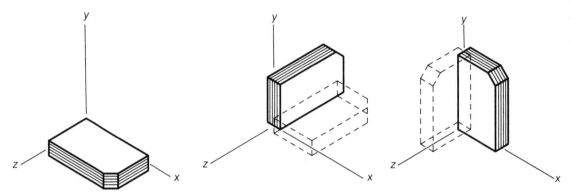

Fig. 16-5. Demonstration of two successive rotations around the y axis and z axis performed in opposite order.

designation of a unit vector coincident with the view vector as $[m_x \, m_y \, m_z]$, the rotations

$$\theta_y = -\tan^{-1} \frac{m_x}{m_y} \qquad (16\text{-}10)$$

and

$$\theta_x = \frac{m_y}{\sqrt{m_x^2 + m_y^2}} \qquad (16\text{-}11)$$

are used in two rotation transformations in the order given.

Perspective

The *perspective* transformation produces a realistic pictorial, because the length of displayed lines is decreased in proportion to the viewing distance. The result is affected by the location of the view vector, which is the only line remaining perpendicular to the viewing surface under perspective transformation, and by the distance between the viewsite and the viewpoint. With CAD systems, perspective pictorials may most conveniently be produced through user specification of the desired viewpoint, and optionally, the corresponding viewsite. The system first performs the necessary translations and rotations to line up the view vector with the screen z axis, with the viewsite at the origin. Next the points matrix is postmultiplied by

$$[\mathbf{T}_p] = \begin{bmatrix} 1 & 0 & 0 & 0 \\ 0 & 1 & 0 & 0 \\ 0 & 0 & 1 & -1/d \\ 0 & 0 & 0 & (z_{max}+d)/d \end{bmatrix} \qquad (16\text{-}12)$$

where z_{max} is the largest value of z in the points matrix and $(z_{max} + d)$ is the distance from the origin to the viewsite (length of the view vector). It is required that $d < (z_{max} + d)$. The choice of d determines the appearance of the perspective. As d becomes large compared to z_{max}, the perspective effect is deemphasized, approaching an axonometric pictorial as $d \to \infty$. Small values of d exaggerate the perspective effect. A good rule of thumb for a normal perspective is to select d approximately equal to the largest dimension in the object being pictured. This choice may be done automatically in some systems.

The technique for making one point, two point, or three point perspectives is a matter of selecting the viewpoint and viewsite. Examples of the three types are given in FIGS. 16-6 through 16-8, pictorials of the same "house" from three different perspectives.

Using perspective images is highly recommended, since the results are more realistic and the added computing is minimal. Because the control of perspective is difficult to understand, the options available to users in commercial systems are sometimes simplified to require only a view-

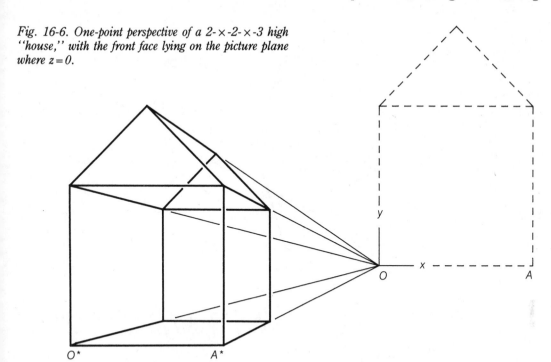

Fig. 16-6. One-point perspective of a 2-×-2-×-3 high "house," with the front face lying on the picture plane where z = 0.

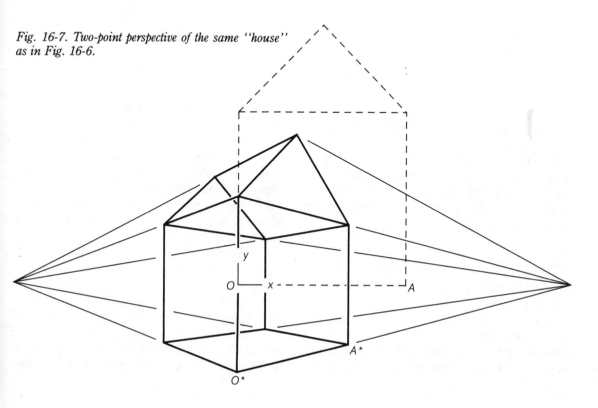

Fig. 16-7. Two-point perspective of the same "house" as in Fig. 16-6.

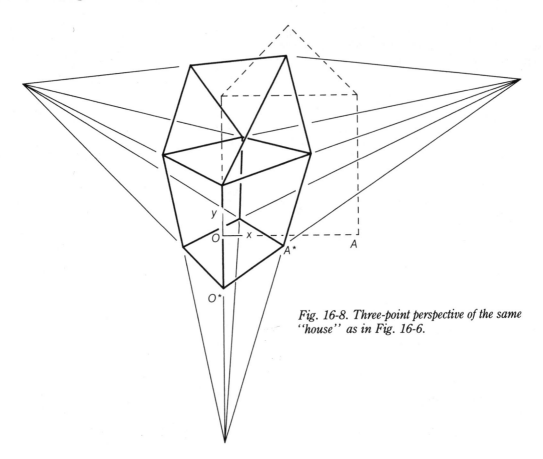

Fig. 16-8. Three-point perspective of the same "house" as in Fig. 16-6.

point as input. With the origin assumed as the viewsite, the transformations of equations 16-10 and 16-11 are used to determine the y and x axes rotations. The distance from the origin to the viewpoint is ($z_{max} + d$) in the perspective transformation. The result of such simplified user control is that it is usually not possible to get one- and two-point perspectives in such systems.

ENGINEERING GRAPHICS SYSTEMS

Graphic images can be stored and displayed either as *objects* or as *bit maps*. Most engineering work is done with graphics based on objects such as lines, polygons, and tetrahedra. Pen plotters and graphics terminals are based on *vector* graphics, where vectors are simple straight-line segments.

(Vectors received by raster graphics terminals are converted to bit maps to be displayed.) With no compromise in quality, an image based on vector graphics requires an order or two of magnitude less storage than a bit map. The difference in file size is important when transmitting images over data networks. Since rendered pictures are bit maps, advanced graphics systems are adept at handling both methods of description.

CAD and solid modeling systems are primarily object-oriented. The difference between the two systems is how and what objects are stored. In CAD, the database identifies an operation or entity type (e.g. draw a circle) followed by a list of parameters that describe the location, size, and other particulars (e.g. location of color and radius) about the operation. In solid modeling, the stored data describe the geometry of the stored object, according to the type of modeler used. A former distinction no longer valid is that CAD is 2-D and solid modeling is 3-D. Transfer of part descriptions between CAD systems and solid modeling systems is generally possible.

Certain features are generally expected of CAD and various solid modeling systems. Because there is no standardization in what should be in such systems, selection should be done with a good understanding of the requirements for the intended application. It is important to note that unneeded features may not only increase costs, but also may increase the complexity of achieving productive use of the system. Experienced evaluators of systems look for ease of learning, speed, compatibility with existing data files, and special features. A good choice will easily incorporate previous work and allow networking among other existing systems. Some groups who work together at different companies have found it advantageous to standardize on one system.

CAD

Few users have found their CAD systems to be more productive than manual drafting for the first-time input of a drawing. However, CAD systems excel at modifying drawings that are already in the computer. The real productivity of CAD systems is realized with the inevitable give and take, and the change and change again, as a project moves through design and production. With database management tied in with the CAD system, the work of all personnel may be coordinated. The database will be the repository of the up-to-date information, with records being automatically kept on the progress of the project.

Systems can be classified according to engineering field by having special libraries of symbols, special drawing features, and particular links to analysis and manufacturing. "Mechanical" CAD, for example, typically supports dimensioning; has library symbols for welding, screw threads, and

springs; and prepares data for numerically controlled machining and stress analysis.

For professional use, a CAD system should:

- Be fast and large enough that the system can be cost-justified by time and labor savings
- Possess the ability to make drawings of the accepted size, complexity, and quality
- Provide database management facilities for archiving and retrieving old drawings, standard symbols, and other existing work
- Be networked with other computer systems as needed to interchange information

Decisions on the platform and software should allow for flexible upgrading because the amount of work usually increases.

An essential peripheral at a CAD workstation is a pointing device for moving the graphics cursor around the screen. Pointing devices found in older systems include light pens, joy sticks, track balls, and arrow keys. The graphics tablet, while good as a pointing device, is losing ground to the simpler mouse. While the tablet is now in common use for digitizing old drawings, intelligent optical scanners are beginning to come into widespread use.

CAD systems are driven by commands that provide lines, circles, arcs, polygons, smooth curves, dimensions, text, and other elements expected on engineering drawings. The most versatile systems provide users with two or more ways to issue commands. Some of the available ways to communicate commands are described below.

Commands Typed on the Keyboard Surprisingly, this method of interaction is the choice of many "power" users. Professional systems provide macro languages, which allow building new commands by combining two or more low-level commands (Raker and Rice 1988). The new commands may be invoked with function keys or with typed abbreviations.

Commands Picked by the Mouse from Menus These menus either are always on the screen, or they pull down, or they pop up in windows. While such menu systems promote easy learning, there may be some sacrifice of speed for experienced users. For example, there may be a second or two lost if the user has to go through a hierarchy of menus to access the desired command. Although pull-down or pop-up menus are better because more screen area is available for the drawing, they do require more computing resource. When appropriate, CAD systems may stay armed with the same command, to permit the astute user to do the same operation over and over without taking the time to pick a new command.

Commands on Special Function Keyboards or on Paper Overlays on Graphics Tablets In earlier days, such systems were used to compensate for slow transmission from the host to the terminal—time would not be wasted writing menus on the screen. Special keyboards and tablet overlays are now less preferred because the user's hands and focus must move to a new location. Furthermore, the tablet menus often contain small icons, which fit the available space but which convey little meaning to novice users. Overlay menus, which flip over each other, can be a source of frustration because the user may forget to tell the computer which menu is up.

In addition to the usual operations of drawing lines, crosshatching selected areas, and applying dimensions, most professional CAD systems do much more. Many work with a 3-D database, so that pictorials may be displayed, perhaps as a wireframe drawing, or perhaps as a color-shaded rendering. Database "hooks" permit counting entities such as nuts and bolts to produce a property take-off, either as a part of the drawing or as an input file to a spreadsheet program. Routine calculations such as perimeter, area, measurement of an angle, and checking tolerances, are often accommodated in CAD programs.

The better CAD programs permit trading data to and from foreign systems through IGES translators, or other drawing exchange methods. Within the same system, the ability to transfer data and graphics to and from other applications is extremely useful.

Solid Modeling

Solid modeling systems generally produce high quality pictorials, with hidden surfaces removed and visible surfaces rendered with light source shading. Important for engineers is the fact that solid models convey numerical information. The better the solid model, the more accurately it represents the real world part, structure, or machine. In the context of design, solid models provide numerical information such as mass, surface area, and dynamic properties. Furthermore, information needed to prepare manufacturing plans for the part can be extracted from solid models. Solid modeling capabilities are found in some systems which are primarily for CAD. The solid models produced should be readable by finite element programs, CAD, CAM, and other systems in use.

In the order of increasing sophistication and complexity, solid modeling systems can be placed into the categories of wireframes, faceted surface models, curved surface models, constructive solid geometry models, and analytic solid models.

Wireframes Wireframe models have a simple database with two lists. The first lists the x, y, and z coordinates of all the nodes, or end points of the lines, which describe the model. The second lists the pairs of node numbers which are connected by straight lines. The list of nodes, or points matrix, is transformed by rotation, translation, and so forth, while the list of node numbers, or topology matrix, is invariant under transformation. Curved lines in elementary wireframe modeling are represented with a large number of straight line segments.

It is clear that much of the information expected of solid models cannot be conveyed by the simple wireframe. For example, FIG. 16-9 shows that a wireframe model of a simple box can represent several variations. Furthermore, since the surfaces are not actually described by the wireframe model, correct hidden line removal and surface rendition are not possible. On the other hand, wireframe models are relatively simple to create and manipulate, making them a good choice for use with less powerful computing systems.

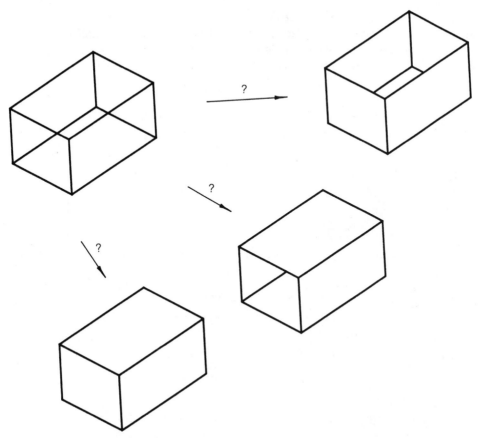

Fig. 16-9. The wireframe model on the left has more than one interpretation.

Faceted Surface Models Faceted surface models are composed of polygons such as triangles and quadrilaterals with shared edges. Surface models are called boundary representations, or B-reps. The databases for these models are similar to the databases for wireframe models, where the connectivity data are modified to show the list of vertices bounding the polygons which pave the surface. Accurate representation of a flat surface requires just one polygon, but a curved surface requires a large number. The simplest rendering of a faceted surface model looks exactly like that of a wireframe model, where only the edges of the polygons are displayed. Graphics workstations with special hardware processors fill polygons in order from back to front to remove hidden surfaces. Gouraud shading, a rendering algorithm that blends the shading between adjacent polygons to give the look of a continuously shaded surface, is also done in many graphics hardware processors.

Curved Surface Models Curved surface models provide much greater accuracy with significantly less data than faceted solid models. Curved B-reps use surfaces mathematically described by parametric cubic, Bezier, or B-spline functions (described in the next section). Rendering of such surfaces is better than with faceted solid models since the mathematical functions can be selected to describe the surface to any desired accuracy. In addition, such surfaces make it possible to describe the cutting tool paths precisely.

Constructive Solid Geometry Constructive solid geometry (CSG) is a popular scheme for making true solid models because of the intuitive user interface. Building CSG models involves combining primitives such as cylinders, spheres, and prisms by the use of the Boolean operators of union (∪), difference (−), and intersection (∩) (Requicha and Volker 1981). An example of use,

FIG. 16-10, shows how primitives are transformed and combined to form a useful part. One reason for the appeal of CSG is its close relationship to machining. For example, a hole is formed by differencing a cylinder with the part. Furthermore,

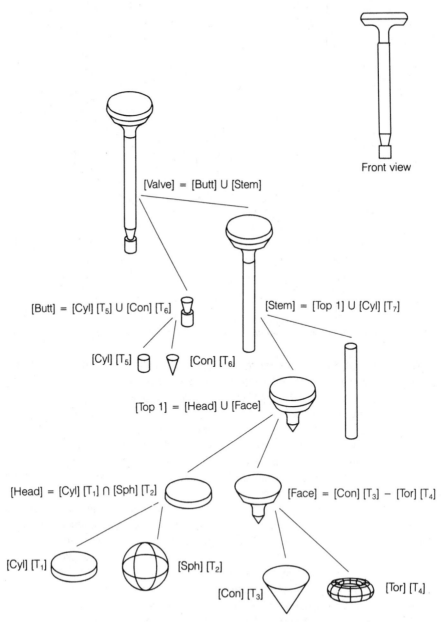

Fig. 16-10. A CSG representation of a small engine valve stem.

accurate computation of mass and dynamic properties is simplified with a true solid model (Dewey 1988, Mortenson 1985). While the construction of a model is not computationally intensive, the evaluation (extraction of the surface) is. Here, either a faceted or curved surface model is developed by the computer program to allow rendering and the preparation of cutting paths. One problem with CSG is the difficulty of describing models such as turbine buckets, which have arbitrarily sculptured surfaces. The solution may be using special primitives or bringing in a curved surface model.

Analytic Solid Modeling The newest approach to solid modeling, analytic solid modeling (ASM), is based on extension of the mathematics of curved surface models to solids (Casale and Stanton 1985, Dewey 1988). Advantages of ASM include the production of true solid models, the easy extraction of surfaces and lines, the ability to accurately model complex sculptured shapes, and a consistent mathematical basis for the entire modeling process. Disadvantages include computational complexity (which precludes using ASM on personal computers) and a more abstract user interface.

Many commercial modeling systems have grown into combinations of the types listed here. For example, one popular older system "skins" a faceted surface with a B-spline surface to take advantage of the true curved surface model. Advanced workstations with parallel graphics processors and menu-driven user interfaces are a good choice for solid modeling applications. Selection needs to balance complexity, performance requirements, cost, and ease of use.

GEOMETRY OF CURVES AND CURVED SURFACES

Most CAD and solid modeling systems provide splines and other curved line and surface representations of one of three types: Bezier, B-spline, and parametric cubic (or Hermite). The mathematics used in these systems is called *parametric geometry* which implies definition by parameters other than the usual *x-y-z* coordinates.

Confusion may exist with the term *parametric geometry*. In some CAD systems, this term means description of a part with selected dimensions given as algebraic quantities instead of numbers. Then, upon user input of numbers for these dimensions, the part is produced to the correct dimensions. The term "macro" may be used in this same context.

Coordinates on curves and surfaces described by parametric geometries can be extracted to any desired accuracy from far less data than that required by piece-by-piece linear representations (Dewey 1988, Mortenson 1985). The parameters can be considered as local coordinates, where a curve can be described by a single coordinate, a surface by two, and a solid by three. In what follows, the parametric variable u has the value of 0 at the beginning of a curve and 1 at the end. The two parametric variables u and v describe a surface patch where each has the range of 0 to 1. In a similar way, a parametric solid requires three parametric variables, u, v, and w, all three of which have the range 0 to 1.

Bezier

The earliest practical application of parametric geometry in computer-aided design is attributed to P. Bezier of France. Although the geometries developed by Bezier include higher order (Faux 1979, Mortenson 1985) curves and surfaces, most users are familiar with the cubic Beizer curve, FIG. 16-11, which is incorporated in many CAD programs. The equation of this curve is:

$$\mathbf{P}(u) = (1-u)^3\mathbf{P}_1 + 3u(1-u)^2\mathbf{P}_2 \\ + 3u^2(1-u)\mathbf{P}_3 + u^3\mathbf{P}_4 \tag{16-13}$$

where $0 \leq u \leq 1$. The four control points, $\mathbf{P}_1$ through $\mathbf{P}_4$ are stored as the matrix

$$\begin{bmatrix} x_1 & y_1 & z_1 \\ x_2 & y_2 & z_2 \\ x_3 & y_3 & z_3 \\ x_4 & y_4 & z_4 \end{bmatrix} \tag{16-14}$$

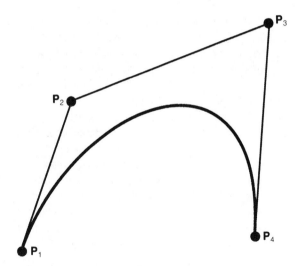

Fig. 16-11. A cubic Bezier curve is described by four control points.

Bezier curves have interpolating functions of any order, although the cubic (see equation 16-13) and quartic are in most common use. Blending two Bezier curves with first derivative continuity requires that the three control points be in a straight line—the one which is shared and the adjacent one from each of the two curves. For higher order continuity, higher order Bezier curves are required.

A more flexible curve can be constructed with the *rational* Bezier formulation,

$$\mathbf{P}(u) = \frac{(1-u)^3\mathbf{P}_1 + 3(1-u)^2\mathbf{P}_2 + 3u^2(1-u)\ \mathbf{P}_3 + u^3\mathbf{P}_4}{(1-u)^3 h_1 + 3(1-u)^2 h_2 + 3u^2(1-u)\ h_3 + u^3 h_4}$$

(16-15)

where h_1, h_2, h_3 and h_4 are weighting factors applied to each control point. If the four weighting factors are identically 1.0, the rational Bezier curve is exactly the same as the ordinary one, represented by equation 16-13. The control points with weighting factors can be stored in the same way as homogeneous coordinates (see equation 16-3), where

the stored points in equation 16-14 are modified to

$$\begin{bmatrix} x_1 & y_1 & z_1 & h_1 \\ x_2 & y_2 & z_2 & h_2 \\ x_3 & y_3 & z_3 & h_3 \\ x_4 & y_4 & z_4 & h_4 \end{bmatrix}$$

(16-16)

Bezier curve geometry can be extended into a surface patch, defined by a rectangular array of control points, such as shown in FIG. 16-12. Here the surface fits the corners exactly, the four edges are Bezier curves, and the shape of the surface is influenced by the four control points in the center. In a manner analogous to curves, Bezier patches may be blended to fit arbitrarily curved surfaces.

Viewing transformation of Bezier curves and patches is routinely done, since the data of equation 16-14 are only points in space. It happens that Bezier is a special case of the more general B-spline geometry, described next.

B-Spline

A *spline* is a curve made out of two or more simpler curve segments pieced together (Dewey 1988). In the case of B-spline curves, the *periodic* type uses the same equation over and over to form each segment. The *nonperiodic* B-spline type uses the same segment equations as the periodic type for the central part of the curve, but different equations are used for beginning and ending the curve. The periodic form for a cubic B-spline curve is

$$\mathbf{P}_i(u) = \frac{(1-u)^3}{6}\mathbf{P}_i + \frac{3u^3 - 6u^2 + 4}{6}\mathbf{P}_{i+1}$$
$$+ \frac{-3u^3 + 3u^2 + 3u + 1}{6}\mathbf{P}_{i+2}$$
$$+ \frac{u^3}{6}\mathbf{P}_{i+3}$$

(16-17)

where $0 \le u \le 1$. The indexed subscripts show how each succeeding segment is based on its four nearest control points.

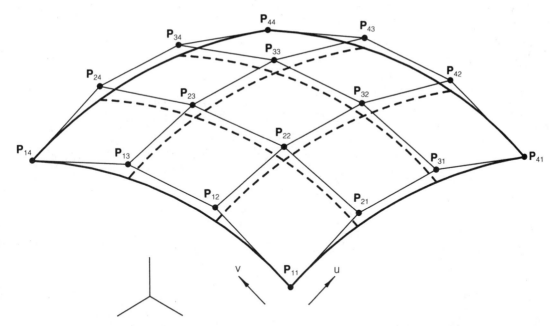

Fig. 16-12. A bicubic Bezier surface is defined by a 4- × -4 net of control points.

The relationship between one segment and its four control points is shown in FIG. 16-13. The segment shown blends with second order continuity with adjacent segments, which are not shown. The periodic cubic B-spline can have any number n (greater than 3) of control points, but there will be only $n-2$ segments joined with $n-3$ knots. The periodic B-spline is particularly useful for a closed curve, where there are n segments and n control points.

If, like a Bezier curve, a B-spline must begin and end at specified points, the nonperiodic formulation is used. Here, there are special segments for starting and ending the B-spline, which make the transition to the central segments formed from the periodic B-spline.

A *rational* B-spline curve, which has more flexibility, is based on assigning weights to the control points in the same way as the quotient shown in equation 16-15. In wide use is the so-called *NURB*, which stands for the Non-Uniform Rational B-spline curve. *Non-uniform* refers to the parametrization, which is the distribution of the u values

along the curve. The particular advantage in the use of NURBs is the ability to exactly describe a circular arc.

The use of B-spline geometry for curved surfaces works very well, finding use in commercial modeling systems where a grid of points describing a faceted surface can be "skinned" to make a smooth surface. Skinning the surface makes possible excellent rendering and more accurate description of the surface for machine tool paths.

The versatility of B-spline curves and surfaces justifies a mathematical formulation that is much more complex than that for Bezier curves and surfaces. With B-splines, the interior control points provide local control, which means that moving one control point only affects the curve or surface in the immediate vicinity.

The present preference in solid modeling systems is that the B-spline be used for surfaces, with solids begin described through CSG representations. A B-spline solid, which would be needed for analytic solid modeling, may be developed in the future.

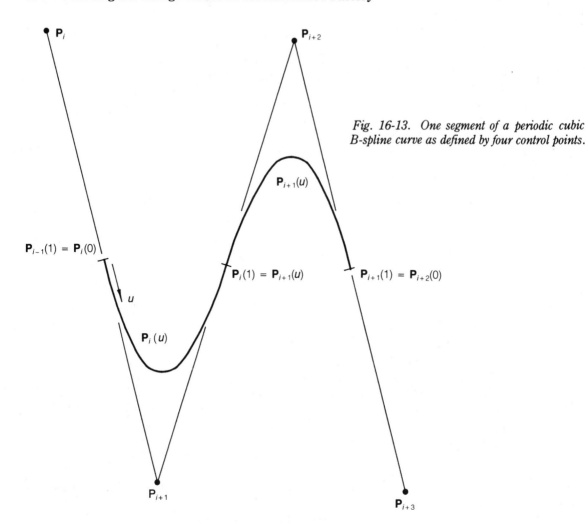

Fig. 16-13. One segment of a periodic cubic B-spline curve as defined by four control points.

Parametric Cubic

Hermite interpolation, named for the nineteenth century French mathematician, uses both the data point $y(x)$ and the slope $y'(x)$ to establish an interpolating curve. The natural cubic spline is a special case of Hermite interpolation where the first derivative vectors are chosen so that the second derivatives match as well.

A major disadvantage in working with the natural cubic spline $y = f(x)$ is that two values of y with one value of x and infinite slopes cannot be accommodated. This limitation makes construction of a closed contour very cumbersome at best. These are not limitations in parametric geometry where

$$x = x(u), \ y = y(u), \ z = z(u) \qquad (16\text{-}18)$$

with the parameter having the usual range $0 \leq u \leq 1$. The parametric cubic curve can be written in algebraic format as

$$\mathbf{P}(u) = \mathbf{a}_1 + \mathbf{a}_2 u + \mathbf{a}_3 u^2 + \mathbf{a}_4 u^3 \qquad (16\text{-}19)$$

where the coefficients are vector-valued (have x-y-z components) functions. The four coefficients are stored as 12 real numbers. The same curve can also be defined by four spatial points, called point format, because the four points are four vectors, which can convey the same information at 12 different real numbers. The point format, like the control points for Bezier and B-spline curves, are straight forward to transform by rotation or translation. The third format is the geometric format, where the data describe the two end points of the curve and the two parametric slopes at the ends of the curves, again four vectors or 12 real numbers. For conversion between a parametric cubic curve and a Bezier curve (see equation 16-13), the two parametric end slopes $P'(0)$ and $P'(1)$ are related to the Bezier control points $P_1...P_4$ by

$$P'(0) = 3 (P_2 - P_1)$$

and $\quad\quad\quad\quad\quad\quad\quad\quad\quad\quad\quad$ (16-20)

$$P'(1) = 3 (P_4 - P_3)$$

A particular advantage of the geometric form is that segments of parametric cubic curves can be blended with second-order continuity to form a spline.

As shown in FIG. 16-14, such a spline is composed of n parametric cubic curves, which pass through a set of n specified points (which are also the knots).

The scheme of describing curves with parametric cubic geometry is routinely extended to surfaces. The parametric cubic patch, FIG. 16-15, originally developed by S. Coons, is described in terms of 16 vector-valued functions, making a total of 48 real numbers. In a way analogous to the geometric format of curves, the patch has a geometric format which permits making a spline surface with second degree continuity.

It happens that most arbitrarily curved surfaces can be described with just a few patches, so that storage requirements will not be at all excessive considering the complexity of the surface.

A newer extension, the *parametric solid*, or *hyperpatch*, is described in terms of three parameters, usually $0 \le u \le 1$, $0 \le v \le 1$, and $0 \le w \le 1$. A surface may be extracted by holding any one of the three parameters constant; a curve, by holding any two parameters constant. If any one of the isoparametric values of u, v, or w is 0 or 1, the surface (or curve) will be on the outside surface of the hyperpatch.

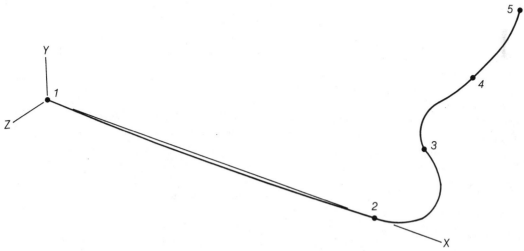

Fig. 16-14. A parametric cubic spline joins n knots with piecewise parametric cubic curves having continuity in the first and second parametric derivatives at the knots.

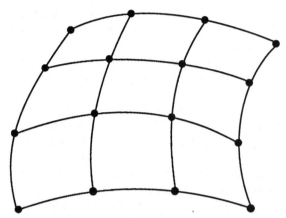

Fig. 16-15. A parametric cubic patch is described by 16 vector-valued functions which may be algebraic, geometric, or points.

An arbitrary point within the parametric solid is given by the vector-valued function

$$\mathbf{P}(u,v,w) = [x(u,v,w)\ y(u,v,w)\ z(u,v,w)] \quad (16\text{-}21)$$

In a manner analogous to curves and surfaces, the parametric cubic hyperpatch has the three formats, algebraic, point, and geometric (Dewey 1988). Defining a parametric cubic hyperpatch takes $4^3 = 64$ vector-valued functions, or $64 \times 3 = 192$ real numbers.

Parametric geometry provides a unified and systematic method for representation of curves, surfaces, and solids. Compared to tessellated surfaces, such curved surfaces have much higher accuracy with significantly less data storage. Furthermore, computation of rendering, cutting tool paths, geometric property calculation, and other applications can be done more efficiently.

OTHER DESIGN TOOLS

This chapter has concentrated on CAD and solid modeling. A discussion would not be complete without mentioning that there are many more computer software tools available to aid design. Sometimes handbooks, codes, and other references specify design procedures in the form of equations, graphs, and charts. Solution of such equations may be obtained by writing a program in FORTRAN or BASIC, or by building tables of data in a spreadsheet, or by using software especially for equation solving. Spreadsheets and solvers are now linked with presentation graphics to help visualize results.

For mechanism design and simulation, several specialized packages are available which solve kinematics and kinetics problems. This software especially permits simulating the proposed design on the computer before building any hardware. Product performance and durability, in many cases, still must be determined by testing production samples or prototypes. Software related to testing—such as packages that interface with instrumentation, reduce data, apply statistical tests, and plot results—also has a place in design. By automating the plotting of results, the engineer can rapidly see trends in data and adjust tests accordingly.

Finite element analysis is another valuable design tool. Here, stress and deflection analysis is done by breaking the part into blocks or elements. The elements in turn are combined into an entire structure. Because the deflection and stress relationships are known for the simple elements, they can routinely be combined and solved for the deflection and stress of the structure. Vibration modes, heat transfer, interaction with fluid, and other mechanical analyses can be made. A CAD or solid model system is a valuable adjunct to prepare meshes for finite element systems.

New and useful software systems for designers as well as faster and easier to use computer hardware continue to come out. Time the engineer spends in keeping up with trade publications, technical meetings, short courses, and even computer salesmen, will be well invested.

REFERENCES

Adams, J. Alan and Leon M. Billow. *Descriptive Geometry and Geometric Modeling*. New York: Holt, Rinehart and Winston, 1988.

Barr, Paul C., et al. *CAD: Principles and Applications*. Englewood Cliffs, New Jersey: Prentice-Hall, 1985.

Bartels, Richard H., et al. *An Introduction to Splines for use in Computer Graphics and Geometric Modeling*. Los Altos, California: Morgan Kaufmann Publishers, Inc., 1987.

Bertoline, Gary R. *Fundamentals of CAD*. Albany, New York: Delmar Publishers, 1988.

Besant, C. B. *Computer-Aided Design and Manufacture*. New York: Halsted, 1980.

Brown, Maxine D. *Understanding PHIGS*. San Diego: Megatek Corporation, 1985.

Casale, Malcomb S. and E. L. Stanton. "An Overview of Analytic Solid Modeling." *IEEE Computer Graphics and Applications* 5:2 (1985): 45-56.

Cook, Robert D. *Concepts and Applications of Finite Element Analysis*, 2nd ed. New York: Wiley, 1981.

Demel, John T. and Michael J. Miller. *Introduction to Computer Graphics*. Monterey, California: Brooks/Cole Engineering Division, 1984.

Dewey, Bruce R. *Computer Graphics for Engineers*. New York: Harper and Row, 1988.

Faux, I. D. and M. J. Pratt. *Computational Geometry for Design and Manufacture*. New York: Halsted, 1979.

Gardan, Yvon. *Numerical Methods for CAD, Mathematics and CAD*, Vol. 1. Cambridge, Massachusetts: MIT Press, 1986.

Goetsch, David L. *Computer-Aided Drafting*. Englewood Cliffs, New Jersey: Prentice-Hall, 1985.

Hopgood, F. R. A., et al. *Introduction to the Graphical Kernel System GKS*, 2nd ed. London: Academic Press, 1986.

Hordeski, Michael F. *CAD/CAM Techniques*. Reston, Virginia: Reston Publishing Co., 1986.

Mantyla, Martti. *An Introduction to Solid Modeling*. Rockville, Maryland: Computer Science Press, 1988.

Mortenson, Michael E. *Geometric Modeling*. New York: Wiley, 1985.

Raker, Daniel and Harbert Rice. *Inside AutoCAD*. Thousand Oaks, California: New Riders Publishing, 1988.

Requicha, A. A. G. and H. B. Volker. "An Introduction to Geometric Modeling and Its Applications." In *Advances in Information Science Systems*, edited by J. Tou, ed. New York: Plenum, 1981, 293-328.

Van Deusen, Edmund, ed. *Graphics Standards Handbook*. Laguna Beach, California: CC Exchange, 1985.

17

Design for Robotic Assembly

Paul H. Cohen*

A MAJOR AREA OF INTEREST IN MANUFACTURING industries today is product assembly. Statistics show that for most companies, assembly operations account for more than half the production cost for a product (Riley 1982). Because of factors such as overseas competition and the continually increasing cost of labor, many companies need to increase assembly productivity in order to remain competitive.

In recent years, because of the many advantages associated with automation and robotics, much work has been done in developing robotic systems for product assembly. Unfortunately, many products that are assembled manually cannot be easily assembled by robot. The human hand with 22 degrees of freedom is an ideal gripper and manipulator for assembly operations. With two hands and sensory capability (vision and tactile) to aid in the assembly process, the human assembler has exceptional adaptability and flexibility. A robot is much more limited in capability. A standard assembly robot typically has between three and six degrees of freedom, and limited sensory feedback capabilities. Therefore, it is necessary to design products that facilitate robotic assembly.

The use of robots for assembly will most likely continue to expand. Robotic assembly systems are gaining wider acceptance because of their repro-

grammability and ability to quickly respond to product design changes, style variations, fluctuations in demand and modest production volumes. In addition, robotic assembly systems with appropriate sensing can detect insertion problems and enhance productivity. Despite the many seemingly obvious advantages of products designed for assembly, designers typically have not given adequate consideration to assembly when determining product structure and component design. Reasons for this may include:

- A lack of understanding of the importance of assembly to the cost, quality, and production schedule of the product
- A lack of knowledge of design oriented assembly (Andreasen, et al. 1983)
- Organizational problems, which limit communication, interaction, and cooperation among design, manufacturing, and other departments (Andreasen, et al. 1983, Dean 1989)

In order to minimize the robot system requirements and cost, good product design for assembly is needed. This chapter seeks to convey an understanding of the importance of design and how product design can facilitate assembly. Although not addressed in detail, organizational barriers to the

*Paul H. Cohen is currently an Associate Professor of Industrial Engineering and an Associate Director of the Manufacturing Research Center at The Pennsylvania State University. Dr. Cohen received his B.S. degree in Industrial Engineering from the University of Rhode Island and M.S. and Ph.D. degrees in Industrial and Systems Engineering from The Ohio State University. He is an NSF Presidential Young Investigator and was the recipient of ASEE's Dow Outstanding Faculty Award, IIE's Outstanding Young IE Award, and SME's Outstanding Young Manufacturing Engineer Award.

integration of design and manufacturing are equally important.

PART DESIGN AND SELECTION

The design of components and products to facilitate assembly has become increasingly important over the last decade. Many researchers have developed working rules to guide designers with respect to component and product design that facilitates assembly. This section describes and illustrates these principles.

Minimize Number of Parts

One simple criterion espoused by many authors is to minimize the total number of parts in the product. This philosophy encourages the designer to clearly think about the function of the product and how that function may be achieved with the minimum number of parts and fasteners (Wood, et al. 1985; Bracken 1983; Andreasen, et al. 1983). Functionally separate parts are required for only a few simple reasons:

- Required differences in material properties
- Required relative motion between mating parts
- Required access for assembly
- Required disassembly of the product for maintenance or repair

Required differences in material properties may necessitate additional parts. For example, thermal or electrical insulation may require additional parts to meet this functional need. The need for relative motion also necessitates that additional parts be specified for a product. Again, it is product functionality that drives this requirement. The need to gain access to a product for purposes of assembly or inspection may also cause additional parts to be specified. These parts may include housings or covers, which may also be required for disassembly for maintenance and repair. Many case studies in the literature illustrate the need to minimize the total number of parts to improve design effectiveness (Wood, et al. 1985; Dewhurst and Boothroyd

1982; Boothroyd and Dewhurst 1982; Boothroyd and Dewhurst, "Assessment," 1983; Poli 1983).

Eliminate Nonrigid Parts

Nonrigid parts are inherently difficult to assemble due to difficulty in gripping and transport, inadequate knowledge of exactly where the entire part is during insertion, and the frequent need for special tooling to solve these problems (Wood, et al. 1985; Bracken 1983; Behjuniak 1983). Nonrigid parts may include belts, hoses, and wires.

In some products, it might be possible to replace belts with mechanisms and hoses with appropriate nonflexible conduit. The difficulty associated with wiring in electronic products can be extensive. FIGURE 17-1 illustrates a simple electromechanical device, a pencil sharpener, where a printed circuit board has replaced the previous loose wiring and the cord is packed rather than handled and installed. This design is far easier to assemble both automatically and manually.

Hole Design

Tolerancing and hole design can also influence the ease or difficulty of robotic assembly. A great deal of work over the past several years has investigated the effect of tolerancing and process capability on assembly. These studies conclude that the use of grooves or *chamfers* on the hole and/or part being inserted facilitates robotic assembly as shown in FIG. 17-2 (Andreasen 1983).

One should also avoid situations where more than one feature is placed simultaneously. As illustrated in FIG. 17-3, a multidiameter peg may have difficulty locating more than one chamfered diameter at the same time since tipping and subsequent misalignment may occur. Lengthening the larger diameter and shortening the smaller diameter enables the larger diameter to be inserted in its hole first. Once the larger diameter is inserted, the component will be properly oriented for the shortened portion of the smaller diameter shaft to be properly aligned with its hole. It is desirable to design parts to adequately guide a mating part.

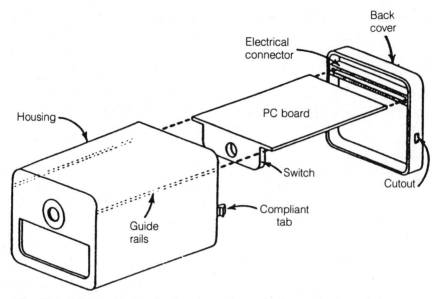

Fig. 17-1. PC board fastened to housing with part back cover in a pencil sharpener.

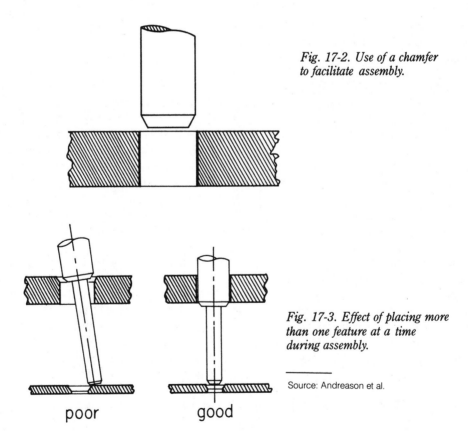

Fig. 17-2. Use of a chamfer to facilitate assembly.

Fig. 17-3. Effect of placing more than one feature at a time during assembly.

Source: Andreason et al.

Unidirectional Assembly

For many products, assembly requires access from more than one side. This may result in increased requirements for robot degrees of freedom. The need to flip the product for proper access can increase the payload requirements. Rotation of the product is also an expensive, nonproductive operation. Unidirectional assembly allows for the stacking of parts from the bottom up. This can decrease robot requirements as well as assembly time. This unidirectional configuration also allows the designer to take advantage of gravity for positive location and reduces the need for special fixturing. Many examples in the literature illustrate this concept (Wood 1985, Dewhurst and Boothroyd 1982, Boothroyd and Dewhurst 1982 and "Assessment" 1983, Poli 1983).

The use of a base component also facilitates bottom-up assembly. The base component is typically a larger part that can be transported from station to station; it allows adequate access both vertically and horizontally for parts to be added, and requires no flipping. In addition, the base component can self-fixture other components through the use of special features that hold other parts (Wood 1985, Andreasen 1983).

FIGURES 17-4 and 17-5 illustrate the original design of an electric pencil sharpener and its redesign for bottom-up assembly. The original design requires that new parts and fasteners be added from many directions. This product requires rotation of the part and enhanced robot capabilities to successfully assemble it. The redesigned product realizes the advantages of unidirectional assembly using a base component with self-fixturing capability. All new parts are added from one direction. Moreover, the housing self-locates and fixtures the parts added, thereby easing the robot requirements and decreasing assembly time.

Parts Feeding

The ability to feed and orient parts is critical in robotic assembly. The design of the part dictates how easily a part can be fed and the amount of addi-tional hardware or sensing needed to determine orientation. Parts with improper design can meet all functional requirements but may tangle, causing a stoppage in assembly.

For ease of feeding, a part should have adequate rigidity to withstand feeding forces and robot gripping force without bending or distortion. Components to be avoided include brittle ones and those with thin sections. Also, the number of surfaces with strict requirements on surface finish should be minimized to avoid damage during feeding (Andreasen 1983).

Parts which tangle should be avoided. FIGURE 17-6 illustrates several examples of simple design changes that do not influence part function but avoid tangling. As FIG. 17-6 shows, open retaining rings (FIG. 17-6a) and lock washers (FIG. 17-6b) have a high propensity to tangle. Closing the configuration will eliminate tangling. A similar idea may be applied to springs (FIG. 17-6c). An open-ended spring will tangle; a closed-end spring, where the ends are formed close to the coil, will only tangle under pressure (Boothroyd, et al. 1982; Andreasen 1983).

The nesting of parts may also present difficulty in feeding. Parts which nest, one inside the other, may jam and stop the assembly process. The inclusion of a nonfunctional rib as shown in FIG. 17-7 will prevent nesting.

Parts with thin or tapered edges have a tendency to climb and overlap each other, which then causes wedging of parts in the tracks on which they feed, and leads to subsequent jamming. Steeper angles or thicker edges will minimize overlap, as FIG. 17-8 shows. Overlapping in thin edge parts can be minimized by bending the edges upward, as shown in FIG. 17-9.

Part Orientation

Feeding of certain parts may also require that they be presented to the robot in a particular orientation. When possible, component symmetry decreases orientation requirements. The addition of nonfunctional features such as holes, illustrated in

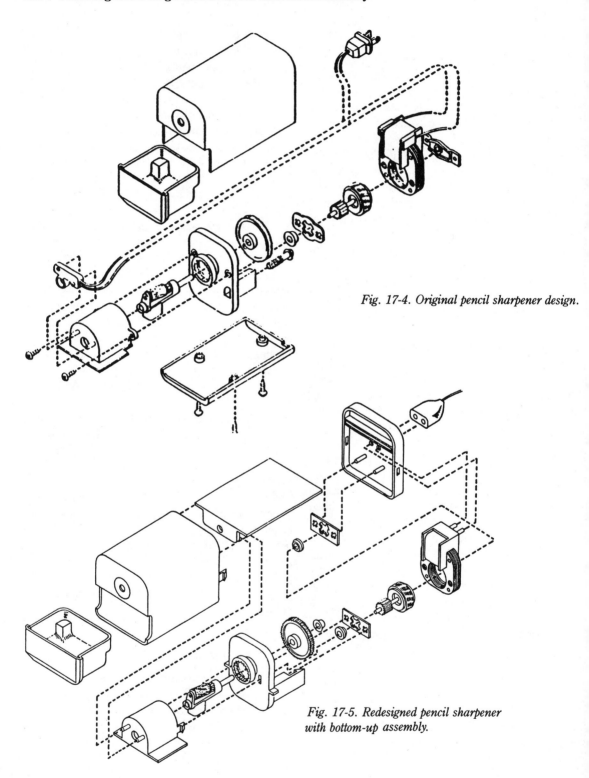

Fig. 17-4. Original pencil sharpener design.

Fig. 17-5. Redesigned pencil sharpener with bottom-up assembly.

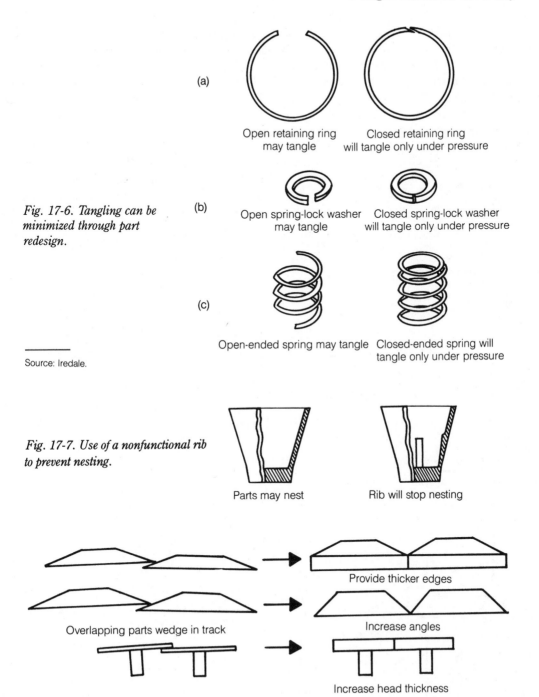

(a)

Open retaining ring
may tangle

Closed retaining ring
will tangle only under pressure

*Fig. 17-6. Tangling can be
minimized through part
redesign.*

(b)

Open spring-lock washer
may tangle

Closed spring-lock washer
will tangle only under pressure

(c)

Open-ended spring may tangle

Closed-ended spring will
tangle only under pressure

Source: Iredale.

*Fig. 17-7. Use of a nonfunctional rib
to prevent nesting.*

Parts may nest

Rib will stop nesting

Provide thicker edges

Overlapping parts wedge in track

Increase angles

Increase head thickness

*Fig. 17-8. Shingling or overlapping can be avoided by providing thicker contact edges, or increased angles, or
thicker heads.*

Source: Andreason et al.

FIG. 17-10, or extension of a slot, shown in FIG. 17-11, eliminates some of the difficulty in orientation. When this is not possible, then increased asymmetry may aid in orientation. FIGURE 17-12 illustrates this concept for several parts. In each case, adding a feature to add asymmetry to the component makes orientation easier and does not change the part's functionality.

Fastener Selection

The influence of fastener selection and design on the ease of robotic assembly has been cited by several authors, including Wood, et al.; Bracken; and Hoyle. The selection of the appropriate fastener should incorporate pre-installation, installation, and post-installation attributes. Pre-installation attributes are those attributes considered before installation. These attributes include cost of the fastener, ease of parts feeding, and special material preparation.

Fasteners that are easier to feed may be symmetric, or may be channel fed. Tangleprone fasteners like open circlips should be avoided. Fastening techniques such as adhesive bonding, soldering, and brazing may require surface preparation prior

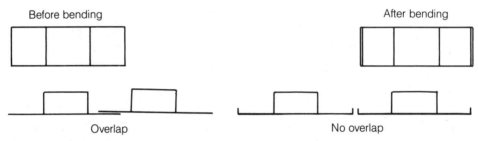

Fig. 17-9. *Overlapping, wedging, and jamming can be eliminated in thin edge parts by bending the edges upward.*

Source: Andreason et al.

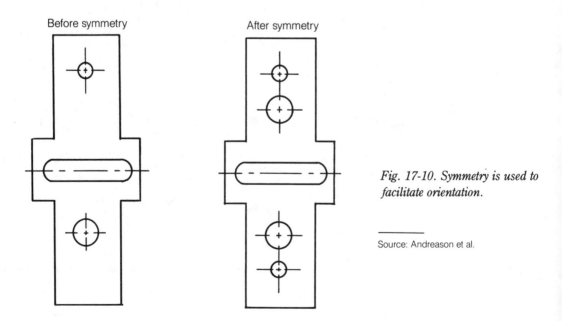

Fig. 17-10. *Symmetry is used to facilitate orientation.*

Source: Andreason et al.

to execution of the process. This adds additional cost and may also necessitate additional automation and the design of special tooling.

Installation attributes must also be considered.

The method and direction of assembly must be analyzed. Simple fasteners requiring quick, one-step procedures and unidirectional installation are preferred. For example, split and pop rivets are much

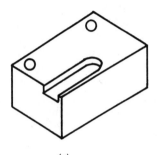 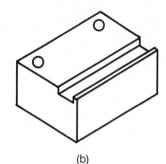

Fig. 17-11. Extension of a slot to facilitates orientation.

Source: Boothroyd and Poli.

(a)
Very difficult to orient

(b)
Possible to orient

Difficult to orient

Flats on the sides make it much easier to orient

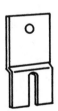 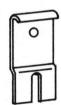

Fig. 17-12. Part asymmetry is used to facilitate orientation.

Source: Iredale.

No feature
significant for orientation

When correctly oriented
will hang from rail

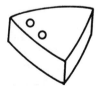 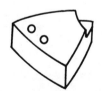

Shape of
part makes
hole orientation
difficult

Shoulder
permits orientation
to be established

preferred to solid rivets, which require insertion and the constraint of the head from one direction while the rivet is deformed from the other side. Fastening methods meeting these criteria will require less installation time, less special tooling, and cost less to insert. In addition, those fastening methods which generate high contact forces or torques, or require special tooling, are candidates for replacement.

Consideration of the criteria above must be tempered with the knowledge that an interface requires a certain strength and that disassembly may be required for maintenance and repair. In addition, reuse of a fastener may be desirable; it may be reinstalled after repair or maintenance. These post-installation attributes are also of vital importance and should be carefully considered during fastener selection.

In general, threaded fasteners provide some difficulty for robotic assembly. FIGURE 17-13 illustrates several shapes for fastener points. Oval and cone points provide very good location while dog and chamfer points provide only reasonable location (Boothroyd, et al. 1982). The header and rolled thread points provide poor location and are unable to centralize without positive control on the outside diameter of the screws.

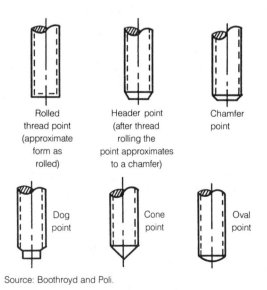

Source: Boothroyd and Poli.

Fig. 17-13. Various forms of screw point.

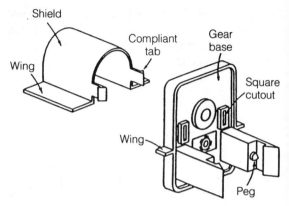

Fig. 17-14. Fastening features for parts shield and gear base featuring a compliant tab.

Compliant fasteners such as true circlips, retaining rings, spring clips, and compliant clips frequently make assembly easier. In addition, special compliant tabs or clips may be designed to fasten multiple parts or may even be designed into plastic or sheet metal parts. FIGURE 17-14 illustrates this concept.

SOFTWARE TO PROMOTE DESIGN FOR ASSEMBLY

The principles presented in the previous section offer a challenge for implementation. Several researchers have developed software which seeks to implement selected design rules in a structured manner and to create some measures of design adequacy.

Boothroyd and Dewhurst: Software to Redesign Products for Assembly

Boothroyd and Dewhurst have developed a handbook and a corresponding software package for personal computer systems to aid in the design of products for assembly (Boothroyd and Dewhurst, *Handbook*, 1983). In the words of the authors, "The techniques described in this handbook are concerned with minimizing the cost of assembly within the constraints imposed by the other design features of the product." This handbook contains two different sections dealing specifically with manual and automatic assembly, as well as a section to help determine which type of system is most practical for the product being considered.

Boothroyd's and Dewhurst's handbook and software aim to assist in the redesign of products to better facilitate assembly. Specific goals of their package include minimizing the total number of parts in a product and making all parts easy to feed and to assemble. Also, part geometries are considered and possible areas of redesign to improve part feeding ability are output.

Several technical papers written by the handbook authors have been published to illustrate these design techniques with specific examples. Products redesigned using the handbook or the corresponding software include a Sony Walkman Radio (Dewhurst and Boothroyd 1982), a water filter (Boothroyd and Dewhurst 1982), and a pneumatic piston (Boothroyd and Dewhurst, "Assessment," 1983). Another paper, by C. Poli, describes the redesign of a floppy disk drive using the handbook techniques. To its credit, this methodology synthesizes some of the previously mentioned principles but requires an existing design or product as input. It is essentially to help redesign products for assembly.

Jakiela:
Software to Identify Design Suggestions

Jakiela, et al. used data from Boothroyd and Dewhurst's *Handbook* to aid the design concept phase through the programming of optimal suggestions. Jakiela evaluated part geometry using the data from the *Handbook* with respect to part orienting efficiency, relative feeder cost, additional feeder cost, and relative workhead cost. He implemented the tabular information from the *Handbook* in a binary tree representation. Jakiela's program is capable of accessing the data and outputting design suggestions.

Wood:
Software to Design Robotic Assembly

Wood, et al. (1985), developed a methodology to aid in the design process either from the initial conceptual stage or for redesign. The only input required to this methodology is a conceptual idea of the product and its functional requirements.

Specifically, this package addresses design for robotic assembly, although many of the design principles can be extended to manual and "hard automation" assembly. This methodology consists of the following sections: (1) define major components, (2) analyze "floppy" parts, (3) structure a parts tree, (4) define interface components, and (5) list output.

The first step of the methodology is to define the major components necessary to achieve a product's functional requirements. Parts such as fasteners, whose only functions are to secure and orient the major components, are defined later in the methodology.

Since it is desirable to minimize the total number of parts for a product, major components are defined only when they are functionally necessary. The basic strategy for defining major components is to break off new components from previously defined components. Once major components are defined, the package then seeks to eliminate nonrigid or "floppy" parts.

The next section in the methodology determines which parts are to be used to hold and orient other components. Planners structure a parts tree. The objective is to determine the parts that can best serve as self-fixturing bases. A self-fixturing base is large, rigid, and strong enough to hold and orient other component parts in the proper position. Having a self-fixturing base is desirable because it facilitates bottom-up assembly. A self-fixturing base component can serve to fixture other parts as they are added, thus reducing auxiliary fixturing and/or tooling requirements. Initially, the methodology defines a major self-fixturing component for the entire product, and then determines self-fixturing components for groups of parts treated in subassemblies.

Next, the designer must determine the method of securing these parts. He must define interface components. The designer is encouraged to choose fastening methods that will best facilitate ease of assembly and minimize assembly costs. Interfaces are examined, one at a time. The first piece of information collected is whether or not the robotic gripper can access all necessary assembly points to interface parts in question. If there is an access problem, the designer must choose a solution from a set of alternatives. Finally, the designer obtains output containing a list of parts with interfaces, interface requirements, and assembly system requirements.

Zorowski:
PDM Design Tool

Product Design Merit (PDM) for Ease of Assembly, developed by C. Zorowski is another microcomputer based, menu driven program developed as a design tool. PDM was developed to address three critical issues in the integration of design and manufacturing:

- The development of a means to increase the sensitivity of designers to their impact on assembly
- The adoption of a design methodology based on the principles of design synthesis and assembly
- The development of a quantitative measure of ease of assembly, even though based on subjective values of assembly option priorities

PDM analyzes the product for three main assembly functions: part feeding, part insertion, and fastening. A designer can analyze each part in the design for all three criteria by using menus where the user selects the most appropriate description. A merit vector is calculated for each part. Each criterion is scaled from 0 to 100 with the combined merit proportioned and normalized on the same scale. This overall assembly merit can be useful in evaluating the effectiveness of redesign alternatives for a current product. After PDM has acquired the data required to establish the merit of a part, it queries the user to determine the potential for eliminating that part from the design.

SUMMARY

The last decade has seen advancement in the development of robotic assembly systems. Advances in robot hardware, control, sensing, and other areas have opened vast new areas of application. The development of design for assembly principles and software for their implementation is now being exploited and promises to encourage companies to take fuller advantage of new technologies for robotic assembly. New structures are needed to organize firms to design for manufacturability (Dean and Susman 1989). With this recognition of organizational needs and an increased understanding of how to design for assembly, the economic use of robotic assembly should continue to grow.

REFERENCES

Andreasen, M. M., S. Kahler, and T. Lund. *Design for Assembly*. U.K.: IFS Publications Ltd., 1983.

Behjuniak, J. A. "Product Design—The First Step in Assembly Automation." *Proceedings 15th CIRP International Seminar on Manufacturing Systems*. University of Massachusetts, 1983.

Boothroyd, G. and P. Dewhurst. "Computer-Aided Design for Automatic or Manual Assembly." *SME Technical Paper* AD82-151 (1982).

————. "Assessment of the Suitability of Product Designs for Robot Assembly." *Proceedings 15th CIRP International Seminar on Manufacturing Systems*. University of Massachusetts, 1983.

Boothroyd, G. and P. Dewhurst. *Design for Assembly Handbook*. University of Masschusetts: Department of Mechanical Engineering, 1983.

Boothroyd, G., C. Poli, and L. Murch. *Automatic Assembly*. New York: Marcel Decker, Inc., 1982.

Bracken, F. L. "Design of Electro-Mechanical Products for Flexible Manufacturing Line." *Proceedings 15th CIRP International Seminar on Manufacturing Systems.* University of Massachusetts, 1983.

Dean, J. W. and G. I. Susman. "Organizing for Manufacturable Design." *Harvard Business Review* 67:1 (1989): 28-37.

Dewhurst, P. and G. Boothroyd. "Computer Aided Design for Assembly—A Microcomputer System." *Proceedings 10th NAMRC* (1982): 468.

Hoyle, P. "The State of the Art of Automatic Fastener Feeding and Installation." Technical Report No. 6387, SPS Laboratories, December 1987.

Iredale, R. "Automatic Assembly—Components and Products." *Metalworking Production* (April 8, 1964).

Jakiela, M., P. Papalambros, and A.G. Ulsoy. "Programming Optimal Suggestions in the Design Concept Phase: Application of the Boothroyd Assembly Charts." ASME Paper 84-DET-77.

Poli, C. "A Design for Assembly Analysis of a Floppy Disk Drive." *Proceedings 15th CIRP International Seminar on Manufacturing Systems.* University of Massachusetts, 1983.

Riley, F. J. "The Look of Automatic Assembly." *Manufacturing Engineering* 89 (August 1982): 79-80.

Wood, B. O., P. H. Cohen, D. J. Medeiros, and J. G. Goodrich. "Design for Robotic Assembly." *Robotics and Manufacturing Automation* ASME PED-Vol. 15 (1985): 259-268.

Zorowski, C. "PDM - A Product Assemblability Merit Analysis Tool." ASME Paper 86-DET-124.

———. *PDM Usrr's Manual*, Report IMS/SR/88/I/743/02. North Carolina State University: Integrated Manufacturing Systems Engineering Institute, December 1987.

18

Value Analysis in Flexible Manufacturing Systems

Vikram Cariapa*

THIS CHAPTER DEMONSTRATES THE USE OF VALUE analysis in the design and implementation of a generic flexible manufacturing system. The first section of the chapter introduces concepts in value analysis, while the latter half demonstrates the application of these concepts to broad areas of a flexible manufacturing system.

CONCEPTS OF VALUE ANALYSIS

Value analysis is a systematic approach of continuously identifying unnecessary costs in products, processes, or systems (Miles 1972). This approach closely relates the costs of and expectations from the products, processes, and systems.

Value

Value is a customer's concept of how well a product performs with respect to its cost. It is a relative measure which normally increases with a decrease in product cost. Conversely, an increased performance accompanied by an increased cost is not perceived to be an increase in value, unless a customer needs it, desires it, or is willing to pay for

it. Value can be categorized into three components: use, esteem, and exchange. It is theorized that customers purchase items only when the exchange value is less than the anticipated use and esteem value. It is this mix of *use* and *esteem* that a product must satisfy before it can be sold. Hence, a manufacturer must understand a customer's use of or function for a product before embarking on its manufacture.

Function

Understanding the function of a product is a complex task. It is essentially the definition of what a product does to justify its existence as an independent entity or as part of an assembly. The function of an item is its use to a customer. An example would be a nail. Its basic or primary function could be described as, "to fasten two wooden items together." Ancient nailed artifacts do exist, attesting to the permanency of nailing. Modern material and tooling developments like staples, screws, and adhesives have made inroads into the "nailing" function. In addition, since the joining of dissimilar materials is common, the design of the common nail

*Dr. Vikram Cariapa is an Assistant Professor in the Department of Mechanical and Industrial Engineering at Marquette University. His primary responsibility has been the development of a Flexible Manufacturing Laboratory for the Industrial Engineering Program. Current research involves experimental work with wire brushes for applications on robotic deburring and surface finishing. Other projects involve the correlation of surface finish with machine tool vibrations in order to aid on-line quality control decisions. Dr. Cariapa has had extensive industrial experience in designing tooling and processes for high pressure boilers and boiler auxiliaries.

has radically changed. Its current function would now be, "to fasten dissimilar materials together." Fastening could be temporary or permanent, and materials range from carpeting to metal sheathing.

Functions may be subdivided into secondary functions, which support the primary function. In the case of assembling wooden furniture, either an iron nail or a brass nail could be used to fasten two pieces of wood together. The secondary function of the brass nail would be rust resistance and aesthetics. A third subdivision of function is the so-called *unnecessary* function. Considering the case of nails and galvanized nails in particular, the need for galvanizing the entire nail must be questioned. It is the head of the nail that is exposed to the rigors of nature; the remaining portion is embedded in the nailed-down parent material. Thus, from a functional point of view, galvanizing the entire nail is wasteful. The galvanizing of any part other than the head of a nail is an unnecessary function.

Let me stress that the function of the product—primary, secondary, or unnecessary—is a variable. It depends on the customer's intended *use* for it. Taking the nail as an example, potential customers may range from a weekend handyman who needs a nail—any nail, to a cabinet maker whose name rests on his product, to a housing contractor who uses a mechanized nailer. The primary function for each of the above users is the same: the fastening aspect. The secondary and unnecessary functions would vary. To the handyman, the nail has to be pounded in to complete a minor repair, requiring only his limited skills. The cabinet maker will demand more uniform nails with uniform heads to ensure that the aesthetic appeal is maintained. Mechanized nailing by the contractor may demand more uniform material properties, dimensional accuracy, and closer point geometry of the nails to ensure that the nails are fed smoothly and rapidly by the machine—properties that are totally irrelevant to the handyman. Thus, when determining the function of a part the need of the customer must be understood.

The *primary* function is that which answers the question "Does something fulfill the need?" *Sec-*

ondary functions are validated by identifying a sector of customers who have a more focused level of needs. *Unnecessary* functions are necessary or unnecessary relative to the current customer's needs. Manufacturers will have to identify their mix of the three types of functions in a product before they can sell it, and hence, profit from it.

Value Analysis— The Procedure

Value analysis can be applied to any activity to which a cost can be attributed. Value analysis follows the steps shown below:

- Identification of the product
- Validation of the functional requirements
- Creation of alternatives which satisfy the function
- Evaluation of alternatives
- Selection of the best alternative
- Implementing the changes required and following up

Identification of the Product Let me start by mentioning that the term *product* has two different connotations. The first is a physical product with a certain form and function. The second may be a service that a firm or department offers. The product offered by a consulting firm is expertise. A company like Ford offers a product with a physical form, a car or truck.

In value analysis, two criteria help identify a product. The first is the profit criteria; the second is the time factor. To use the profit criteria, identify the total profit from a product (volume into profit per unit). If a selection is to be made between products with the same total profit factor, the precedence would be given to a high-volume low-profit unit instead of a low-volume high-profit unit.

The time factor is essentially a question of when the value analysis should be undertaken. The life of the product is not clearly predictable, and it affects the cost of implementing changes. A "young" product will cost less to change than a "mature" product. The greater part of the value analysis activity (around 50 percent) should be done when a product is in the design stage. This value analysis must be executed on the overall product concept before such attempts are made on individual components. The next major concentration of the value analysis activity (around 40 percent) must be planned during the production and planning stage.

In the production and planning stage, the product is scheduled and planned for manufacture. Resources are mobilized and make or buy decisions are considered. Schedules are generated for available facilities. Support tooling and fixtures are created before production starts. Thus, at this stage a tremendous amount of resources and manpower has been committed. The product is now sent to the shop floor for manufacture. Since so much has been invested so far, attempting a value analysis at the shop floor stage should be restricted to around 10 percent of the total value analysis effort. At this stage, only a fine tuning could be expected from any value analysis activity as the majority of the investment for the system has been completed. Now, the cost of changing usually outweighs potential savings. In addition, if a product has a short life cycle, it is most likely to be made obsolete before the new changes are implemented.

Validation of Functional Requirements
As explained earlier, the concept of a product's function is of critical importance to a value analyst. A series of steps shown below aids the understanding of the function for which the product has been designed.

Step 1 Clearly identify what the product does for the end user. A verb and a noun in a simple sentence must unambiguously define the function. Typical examples are "prevents rust," "joins wood," and "ignites gas." The simple verb/noun combination demands extremely clear visualizations of the product's utility to the customer. It also anticipates that the customer needs this utility, and more importantly, is willing to pay for it.

Step 2 Identify aesthetic functions as separate entities from the use function. This is a crucial step as a customer's concept of aesthetics must be projected. Aesthetics are difficult to quantify using

objective parameters because they include such aspects as appearance, shape, color, features, and convenience. However, a clear definition must be made so that the use function is differentiated from the aesthetic function. In this manner, the costs associated with the aesthetics can be isolated from the costs associated with the use function, enabling a criterion for establishing the worth of the function.

Step 3 Segregate the use function into a primary and a secondary function. As the analysis is done for the whole product, a segregation into the two subgroups will give an idea of the product content that satisfies each grouping.

Step 4 Quantify functions, wherever possible, into measurable entities. This enables a reference to be created against which an improvement could be compared. For example, an electric conductor's function would be quantified as "carries 10 amps," and not simply, "carries current."

Step 5 Establish a monetary value against which the function can be compared. For example, take the case of fastening two pieces of wood together. Methods of fastening that could be compared include nailing, screwing, gluing, or clamping. The worth of the fastening method is obviously the cheapest one which satisfies the purpose. In this case, it is probably the nail. So stapling or gluing are of greater value only if their cost is cheaper than that of the nail.

Step 6 Consolidate all the functions identified so far into: (1) *use* functions (primary and secondary); (2) *aesthetic* functions; and (3) unnecessary function.

The first decision that could be made is the elimination of these unnecessary functions. "Tools for the Value Analyst" later in this chapter describes methods for evaluating functions.

Creation of Alternatives which Satisfy the Function This is the most challenging phase of the value analysis. It mandates a very open and aggressive look at the product being analyzed. The suggested strategy is to use a team with a company-wide representation. The team members should be from the same hierarchy in order to minimize the fear of ridicule or reprimand. Management should allocate time away from the normal routine followed by the team members. A database of materials, designs, processes, and appropriate costing methodologies should be made available. Creative thinking is stimulated using "no barrier" brainstorming sessions. In addition, specialized vendors and professional organizations may be consulted for their unique expertise. Such an atmosphere will be conducive to the generation of creative alternatives.

Evaluation of Alternatives This is explained under the section titled "Tools for the Value Analyst."

Selection of the Best Alternative The best alternative is closely related to the *time period* of the value analysis. Criteria for this selection may be the lowest cost, lowest process time, longest life, or highest strength to weight ratio. These criteria are unique to the situation at that time period. Hence, they should be developed based on the problem that necessitated the value analysis.

Implementing the Changes and Following Up The value analysis process creates change. These changes may be in systems or processes, or both. People affected by these changes must be kept informed at all times. Training, if necessary, should be part of the implementation phase. New procedures must be followed closely during the early stages of the implementation for it is normal to expect old habits to die hard. Finally, because there are always some problems when implementing new products, close follow-up ensures that start-up problems are solved expeditiously.

Tools for the Value Analyst

The following list shows some of the more advanced tools for a value analyst:

- FAST diagram
- MATRIX evaluation
- Simulation

FAST Diagram The term *FAST* means Function Analysis System Technique and the FAST diagram is a graphical-cum-analytical technique. Its objective is to validate the existence of a part by questioning its interrelationship with the function that is served. The FAST diagram is created according to the following steps.

The initial step is the definition of the scope of the analysis. *Scope* means the boundaries within which the analysis must be carried out. The upper boundary is the *need* that the part must satisfy or the objective that it satisfies. The lower boundary is usually an interface that falls beyond the manufacturer's control. For example, a lamp satisfies a basic objective of providing light. The interface beyond the lamp manufacturer's scope of control is the electric power supply. Hence, the lamp manufacturer must supply a plug and wire that satisfies a national standard.

In the second step, the part is split up into its individual components. FIGURE 18-1 depicts how an assembly is broken up into its individual components.

In step three, a well-defined list of functions satisfied by every part, assembly, or subassembly is created. This list must start with a function that satisfies the basic objective and end with one that satisfies the interface defined by the scope. Each function should be described by a noun/verb combination that clearly defines it.

In step four, the list of functions must now be serialized and organized according to the following procedure:

- The topmost function must be that which satisfies the question "How is the main objective or need accomplished?"
- All other functions are serialized based on how they satisfy the following questions:

"How is this function achieved?"
(A "how?" query)

"Why is this function performed?"
(A "why?" query)

"When is this function performed?"
(A "when?" query)

A lower level function will satisfy the "how" query put to a higher level function, and will also satisfy a "when" query put to it. A higher level

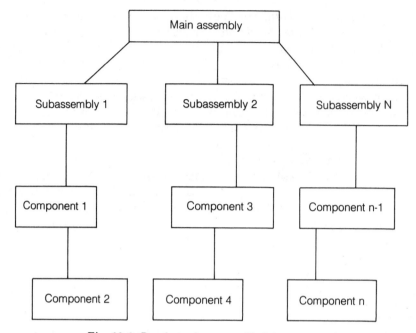

Fig. 18-1. Breakup of an assembly into components.

function will satisfy a ''why'' query put to the function just below it. Please see FIG. 18-2.

- The process continues until all functions are placed in the list.

In step five, a FAST diagram is now created using the list of functions as a reference. A graphical layout is created starting with the upper boundary on the left and the lower boundary on the right. FIGURE 18-3 shows an example of a FAST diagram. The highest level function is inserted in a box next to the left boundary. A ''how'' query put to this boundary (the objective) will be answered by this function from the box. The next function is then placed in a box to the right of the first one, if it satisfies a ''how'' query. A ''why'' query put to the

second box must be satisfied by the function in the first box. Hence a cross dependence between the functions is established.

Boxes are created and filled up in a similar manner until a ''how'' query is satisfied by the lower boundary or interface defined by the scope. In case more than one answer is given to the ''how'' query, parallel rows of boxes are created, emanating from this box. Similarly, answers to a ''why'' query may necessitate parallel rows of boxes merging into one box, the ''why'' query box.

In step six, it is time to determine the critical path of functions. The critical path depicts all functions, from the highest priority or basic function to the lowest level function, that are required to fulfill the objective. Hence, the critical path is essentially

Fig. 18-2. Functions at different levels and the queries that they satisfy.

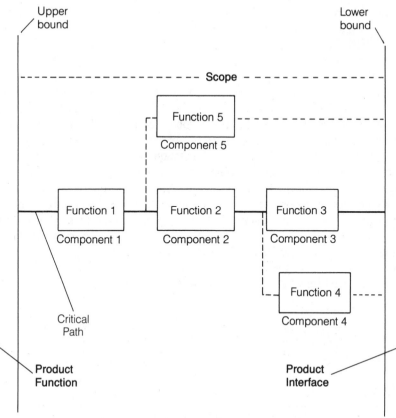

Fig. 18-3. A FAST diagram showing components and their respective interrelated functions.

a connection of all the cross-referenced functions in the FAST diagram.

Step seven refers back to the original list of functions created in step three. Functions on this list that are not on the newly created FAST diagram become secondary functions. These are placed on the FAST diagram by their answer to the "when" query. Dotted lines drawn from the critical path to these functions identify their secondary status.

By step eight, all functions on the original list are now expected to be on the FAST diagram. Critical path functions form the backbone of the diagram and secondary functions form the offshoots. At this stage, every function has been placed in the diagram after answering a "how," "why," and "when" question. A function still remaining on the list is automatically determined to be an unnecessary function.

In step nine, components used for particular functions are allotted to their respective positions on the FAST diagram.

Step ten completes the FAST diagram such as the one in FIG. 18-3. The diagram depicts all functions and associated components. Various types of cost data may also be included.

The FAST diagram creates a reference by which an analyst can validate a component's function. Thus, a first decision would be to focus on critical path components and try to minimize the number of components that satisfy a certain function. Succeeding steps would focus on rearranging or redrawing the diagram until the barest minimum number of parts serve the intended functions. At this stage, the value analyst has attained the desired objective satisfied by the product at the lowest possible cost.

MATRIX Evaluation The MATRIX evaluation tool evaluates alternatives generated to meet a desired objective. The first step in a MATRIX evaluation defines the functions required of a component or product. Then, different alternatives are generated that satisfy this function and achieve the desired objective. The MATRIX evaluation costs out and evaluates these alternatives, enabling the most satisfactory alternative to be chosen. A step-by-step procedure for this evaluation follows.

Step one lists all functions required to attain the product's desired objective, i.e., F1......FN.

Step two creates a relative importance matrix. Functions are arranged in rows and columns as shown in FIG. 18-4.

Step three fills in the relative importance matrix, as shown in FIG. 18-4. Begin in Row 1. Check if F1 is more important than F2. If it is, put a 1 in the matrix box. If it is not, put a 0 in the box. Continue until all rows and columns are filled up with 1's and 0's.

Step four sums up all the rows.

Step five assigns relative ranks to the functions. The row with the highest sum is the most important function, and so on. Arrange the functions accordingly. This is their relative rank.

Step six generates a weight factor for each function. This factor assesses the impact that this function has for the overall product.

Step seven generates different alternatives that satisfy the overall objective, and includes costs required to produce these alternatives. Alternatives may include in-house manufactured or purchased items.

Step eight creates the main evaluation matrix, as shown in FIG. 18-5.

	F1	F2	F3	F4	F5· · · · · · FN		SUM
F1	1	0	1	0	0	· 0	2
F2	1	1	0	1	0	· 0	3
F3	0	1	1	0	1	· 1	4
·	·	·	·	·	·	· ·	·
FN	1	1	0	1	1	· 1	5

Fig. 18-4. A relative importance matrix.

	Ranked Functions					C	G
	FN	F3	F2	F4· · · ·	F1		
Weight	W1	W2	W3	W4· · · · ·	WN		
Alt. 1	f11	·	·	·	f1N	C1	G1
Alt. 2	f21	·	·	·	f2N	C2	G2
·	·	·	·	·	·	·	·
Alt. m	fm1	·	·	·	fmN	Cm	Gm

Key

F1-FN:	Functions arranged in order of relative importance.
W1-WN:	Weight factors.
Alt. 1-Alt. m:	Different alternatives under evaluation.
C1-Cm:	Costs of each alternative.
f11-fmN:	Evaluation factors. For each alternative, an evaluation factor fii (between 0 and 10) is allocated based on its attainment of the desired function Fi. If fii = 0, the alternative must be rejected.
G1-Gm:	The product of the weight factor Wi and the evaluation factor fii.

Fig. 18-5. Main evaluation matrix.

In step nine, the following decisions may now be made from the completed matrix:

- If the objective is to obtain the best product, the alternative with the highest G factor is selected
- If the objective is to get the best product per unit cost, the alternative with the highest G/C factor is selected
- If the objective is to select the lowest cost alternative, then the lowest C value determines the most inexpensive alternative

Simulation Computerized simulation is probably the most versatile tool for a value analyst. Two types of simulation are suggested. First is the graphic simulation; an entire product could be created on the screen and engineered to suit the required parameters. This product could be subjected to varying end conditions in order to project its use in the field. After certain ideas have been crystallized, the accessing of production and cost databases would enable a quantifying of cost data for proposed product configurations. This could be the numeric simulation. Thus, the full benefit of the value analysis would be obtained while the product is in the design stage—well before it is sent down the processing pipeline. Computer simulation will be the most powerful tool for the value analyst of the future.

VALUE ANALYSIS AND FLEXIBLE MANUFACTURING SYSTEMS

The scope of this chapter is to introduce concepts of value analysis to broad areas of flexible manufacturing systems (FMS). Application of the concepts to a detailed area like a machine tool would be too voluminous for this chapter. In addition, no two flexible manufacturing systems are alike. Hence, this chapter focuses on those areas which have a high degree of commonality with various types of systems. This section identifies different stages in the development of an FMS and appropriate value analysis techniques associated with each stage. The stages include:

- Definition of a computer integrated manufacturing strategy
- Definition of FMS design parameters
- Implementation of FMS

Definition of a Computer Integrated Manufacturing Strategy

Computer integrated manufacturing (CIM) is an alluring concept. It implies the existence of a manufacturing system where all activities like marketing, design, processing, manufacturing, and shipping are tied together or integrated by a computer. In order to operate at this integrated level, companies usually phase in their networking plan for the entire operation (Ranky 1983). At the basic level of integrated operations are computer controlled work cells with automated raw materials and finished parts handling. A higher level is the integration of different cells or various subsystems into a major system. This could include creating a computer oriented engineering database, which drives computer controlled equipment; or interfacing various cells; or connecting various databases. The key here is that the variety is enormous and the need to standardize interface protocols is mandatory.

The highest level of operation is the fully integrated facility. All information is accessible for instant real time decisions at appropriate levels. This demands a breakdown of all departmental boundaries, both horizontally and vertically. All equipment and data protocols are totally compatible with each other. This is, unfortunately, not viable now, but is expected to be so in the 1990s. However, as companies attempt to move from each level to the next higher one, they accrue tremendous benefits (Savage 1985), as shown in TABLE 18-1. In order to achieve this computer integration in manufacturing, a broad strategy must be defined. This encompasses five areas (Appleton 1985):

- Planning
- Finance
- Project selection
- Project management
- Standards

Reduction in engineering design cost	15 – 30%
Increased capability of engineers as measured by extent and depth of analysis in same or less time than previously	3 – 35 ×
Increased productivity of production operations (complete operation)	40 – 70%
Increased operating time of capital equipment	2 – 3 ×
Increased product quality as measured by acceptable yield	2 – 5 ×
Reduced work in progress	30 – 60%
Reduction in overall lead time	30 – 60%

Table 18-1. Benefits Achieved by Interfacing and Integration.

Planning CIM planning organizes a rapid reaction of an enterprise to real world demands made on that enterprise. This is possible only if a precise relationship is generated between various possible product configurations and corresponding equipment and activities required to produce them. This is a dynamic relationship, for the time frame of a CIM facility has no bounds. As the real world situation is continuously changing, product selection boils down to those items that can be produced by the available facilities at that time.

The value analysis technique that would aid the planning function most is computer simulation. This simulation would identify desirable facilities for different product runs. A MATRIX evaluation would aid in selection of the most suitable alternative from those identified in the simulation. Plans could then be made for installing these facilities at the required time.

Finance Unlike conventional enterprises, finance for CIM is planned around bought out assets like machines and software, and developed assets like databases and in-house software utilities. Unlike normal operations where assets like machines belong to certain departments, these developed assets belong to the whole plant. The best value analysis techniques for controlling finance would be simulation and MATRIX evaluation. These two tools would also allow for a judicious allocation of funds across the whole enterprise.

Project Selection Under a CIM strategy, every project will have to be analyzed with respect to its impact on the whole enterprise. Typical project criteria include short runs, low costs, and relative impact on improving an asset's impact or leverage on the system. The ideal value analysis technique would be a FAST diagram. A definite relationship between the project and the enterprise would be validated, thus allowing for subsequent evaluation.

Project Management These projects are managed by the whole enterprise because everyone has a vested interest in their successful completion. Value analysis is not suggested here as it has already validated the project in the selection stage.

Standards Data, or terminology, standards and technical standards for equipment are critical for CIM. Technical standards control the flow of data from machines. Data standards are those which give real life meanings to the numbers that are stored. Value analysis will play a critical part in selection of the necessary standards. The FAST diagram and simulation would allow the wide variety of standards to be evaluated for adoption in the plant. This is the most important area; prediction of standards for the future have to be made early, even though no fully acceptable standards exist during the planning stages.

Definition of FMS Design Parameters

Flexible manufacturing systems may be defined as systems dealing with high-level distributed data processing and automated material flow using computer controlled production machines, assembly cells, industrial robots, inspection machines, and material handling machines (Ranky 1983). An FMS design must be an offshoot of the entire CIM strategy. This is the only way that a company can move toward total integration. Two distinct areas in an FMS are the hardware and data processing sections.

Hardware for Flexible Manufacturing Systems Major design criteria used in developing the hardware and data processing sections of generic FMS will now be considered; appropriate value analysis tools will be suggested for each case. Electronic and mechanical hardware have related criteria (Ranky 1983):

- Both types of hardware must be modular with provisions for upgrades. This includes machine tools and all electronic hardware.
- Tool storage and change, part location, and part inspection must be computerized.
- Material handling and storage must be computerized and have provisions for upgrades so that they remain compatible with machines and electronics. Material handling includes part transportation and handling.

Both mechanical and electronic hardware are constrained by physical limits. A machine tool has a limited range of movement. Electronic circuit boards have fixed dimensions to suit various standards. Hence, the best value analysis tools will be those that evaluate current viability of the design and possible future configurations. The best tool is the FAST diagram. This diagram will interrelate and validate the functions of each hardware unit with its interconnected member. In addition, a graphical simulation on a computer will depict planar relationships for both the present and the future. Mechanical items are easier to project into the future, as the shapes are more or less standardized.

Electronic hardware is more difficult to analyze. Drastic reductions in the cost of computing power, miniaturization of electronic circuits, and lack of widely accepted standards are major reasons for these difficulties. Electronic hardware includes motor controls, signal conditioners, computing, and networking equipment. Rapid changes in the electronics makes for early obsolescence of hardware. The highest cost, however, is not the hardware (though it is not insignificant) but the software that drives the system. Hence, value analysis must keep software compatibility and the probability of upgrade as key criteria. Electronic components could be identified by specifying overall operating parameters. In this manner, a functional interrelationship can be validated, without the need for knowing the innards of the components. Upgrading is ensured because operating parameters define the interfaces, and software changes can be made for performance upgrades.

Computer graphic simulation is the most viable tool for the value analysis of FMS hardware. This allows placement of sensory and control entities on mechanical components. Once all electronic and mechanical components are positioned on the computer screen, real time simulation of the entire system can be executed. This will test software and hardware interrelationships, appropriateness of components, and whether the system meets the required criteria. In order to ensure that a system can be upgraded, planners should develop the FMS on a modular basis. A mechanical/electronic module having known inputs, outputs, and operating parameters will allow for relatively easier upgrades.

Data Processing for Flexible Manufacturing Systems The magnitude of data processing depends greatly on the size of the FMS and its conceptualization with respect to the overall CIM plan. An FMS system created independently of the

CIM plan will have different data processing requirements than one conceived as a stage towards CIM. Nevertheless, major design criteria for FMS data processing include the following (Ranky 1983):

- A link to the company's CAD/CAM database must provide real time processing
- Control software for machine tools, sensors, material handling, and database management must be modular and have built-in provisions for upgrades
- Real time control must be available between the material storage, handling, and movement systems
- Intelligent software must continuously provide diagnostics and corrections to cell machine tools
- Production planning must ensure alternate routes for products in order to minimize scheduling bottlenecks

The value analysis tools suggested for this area are the FAST diagram and computer simulation. All software must have a clear objective. A FAST diagram clearly interrelates subobjectives with the overall objective. Hence, a FAST diagram created at the conceptualization stage of the FMS will ensure that all software modules fit into the overall framework. Computer simulation allows for the evaluation of each of the modules before they actually drive the system. In this manner, the entire system can be created and tested independently of the mechanical hardware—allowing for a quicker commissioning and testing of the actual FMS.

Implementation of FMS

As mentioned earlier, the implementation phase or shop floor phase of any product must not consume more than 10 percent of a value analysis effort. An FMS demands a different outlook, as it forms a small part of the entire long range CIM strategy. Hence, a value analysis can be executed at this stage also. Performance criteria from the FMS would be reviewed against designed expectations. Projected expectations would be revalued accordingly. Hence, the ideal value analysis tool at this stage would be a computer simulation.

CONCLUSION

This chapter suggests suitable value analysis tools for use in assessing a flexible manufacturing system. It must be emphasized that only concepts have been suggested. Detailed FAST diagrams for each machine tool or software design would be beyond the scope of the chapter, mainly because FMS are extremely complex entities. Hence, you may wish to peruse the references at the end of this chapter if you need more information on this concept.

REFERENCES

Ahuja, H. N. and M. A. Walsh. *Successful Methods in Cost Engineering*. Canada: John Wiley & Sons, Inc., 1983.

Appleton, D. S. "Building a CIM Program." In *A Program Guide to CIM Implementation*. Dearborn: CASA, SME Publications Development Department, 1985: 5-10.

Fasal, John H. *Practical Value Analysis Methods*. New York: Hayden Book Co. Inc., 1972.

Gage, W. L. *Value Analysis*. London: McGraw-Hill Publishing Co., 1967.

Greve, John W. *Value Engineering in Manufacturing*. ASTM Publications, 1967.

Miles, Lawrence D. *Techniques of Value Analysis and Engineering*. New York: McGraw-Hill Book Co., 1972.

Ranky, Paul. *The Design and Operation of FMS*. IFS (Publishing) Ltd., U.K.: North Holland Publishing Co., 1983.

Savage, Charles M. *A Program Guide for CIM Implementation*. Dearborn: CASA, SME Publications Development Department, 1985.

19

Group Technology Planning and Operation

Ronald G. Askin[*]
Asoo J. Vakharia[**]

GROUP TECHNOLOGY IS BECOMING A WIDELY
accepted strategy for organization and operation of
manufacturing systems. In the first section of this
chapter, we define group technology and indicate
the advantages it offers. Next, we describe part
coding and classification systems that underlie the
group approach to design and manufacturing. Then,
we discuss the formation of part and machine
groups in a manufacturing facility. The last two sections cover implementation aspects and operational
aspects of group technology.

DEFINITIONS OF GROUP TECHNOLOGY

Throughout most of the twentieth century,
mass production has been glorified for its achievements in production efficiency, placing a plethora of
consumer goods within the economic reach of the
masses. In recent years consumer expectations

have evolved toward customized goods, moving
production in the direction of high variety, low quantity products. Small batch production has always
constituted a major portion of manufacturing, but
new customer demands along with increased world
competition have created a need for more efficient
and timely production management in these environments. Group technology is one approach for
meeting the need for efficient design of a variety of
products and their production in small lots.

Group technology, or GT, is a philosophical
approach to system design and operation. The basic
philosophical tenet of GT states that similar tasks
should be performed in a similar manner. This holds
equally for design and manufacturing. The GT philosophy promotes standardization in part design,
process planning, tooling, and work elements. GT
simplifies as it standardizes. Learning curve effects
accrue, improving efficiency and quality. A simple

*Ronald G. Askin is an Associate Professor of Systems and Industrial Engineering at the University of Arizona, Tucson, AZ. Prior
to this appointment, he served on the faculty of The University of Iowa. Dr. Askin received a B.S. in Industrial Engineering from
Lehigh University, and an M.S. in Operations Research and Ph.D. in Industrial & Systems Engineering from Georgia Institute of
Technology. Dr. Askin is an active member of IIE, ORSA, ASQC, ASA, and CASA/SME. He has published in various professional
journals, predominantly in the areas of production system design and analysis and engineering statistics. Dr. Askin has received
several awards, including the IIE Transactions Development and Applications Award (coauthor), the ASEE/IIE Eugene L. Grant
Award (coauthor), and a National Science Foundation Presidential Young Investigator Award.

**Asoo J. Vakharia is an Assistant Professor in the Decision Sciences Group of the Department of Management Information Systems
at the University of Arizona. He has a Ph.D. in Operations Management from the University of Wisconsin-Madison and his current
research focuses on the design and operation of cellular manufacturing and group technology systems. Dr. Vakharia is an active
member of IIE, the American Production and Inventory Control Society, the Institute of Management Sciences, and the Decision
Sciences Institute and has published in the *Journal of Operations Management*, *IIE Transactions*, and *Naval Research Logistics*.

yet informative definition of group technology is, "The logical arrangement and sequence of all facets of company operation in order to bring the benefits of mass production to high variety, mixed quantity production" (Ranson 1972).

More specifically, GT is a methodology for organizing the design and operation of a wide class of manufacturing systems. By manufacturing system we mean all the activities required to plan and execute the conversion of raw materials into finished products, particularly the steps of product design, process planning, scheduling, parts fabrication, and assembly. Necessarily included in this system are the support functions such as information systems and human resources management.

The GT philosophy implies organization based on final product, component, or major task similarities instead of on manufacturing processes. The typical GT environment is one with a wide variety of production parts, but many of the parts have certain features in common. Experience has shown GT to be successful in many diverse environments. These include make-to-stock and make-to-order inventory planning; facilities with small machines, and facilities with large machining processes; job-shops and facilities with flowlines; small and large plants of small and large companies; and in fabrication, assembly, and process environments.

The basic steps in implementing group technology are:

- Developing a parts coding scheme
- Assigning part families and machines to groups
- Arranging machine layout within groups

Product characteristics such as material, shape, size, operations, and tooling are examined to determine the salient features which distinguish parts. The coding scheme is constructed such that parts with similarities in design and manufacturing can be identified by their assigned code. Families of parts are identified as those parts which are alike enough to be similarly designed and manufactured with the same basic plan and equipment. Part families are then grouped with the required production machines in an economic arrangement. Groups are laid out to facilitate the basic production sequence of their assigned parts. Efficient flow systems can often be achieved when design and manufacturing work together. FIGURE 19-1 illustrates how recognition of distinctive part families and subsequent organization along family lines can assist rational facility design and operation.

System Advantages

GT impacts product design, process planning, scheduling, and facilities planning. To the design engineer, GT is an attempt to standardize part numbers. A part coding scheme allows the designer to determine whether or not a part already exists to perform a particular function. The ability to efficiently search a database to answer this question can save considerable time and cost and reduce part proliferation. In addition to the cost directly attributable to the activity of product design, every new part incurs costs of tooling, data processing, inventory, and setup throughout its life. In a facility with thousands of part numbers, it is virtually impossible to expect designers to check for suitable existing parts before designing new parts. The standard coding schemes of GT make this a relatively painless process. Even if only similar parts are found, it is easier to modify existing drawings of similar parts to perform the new functions than to design from scratch. This is particularly true with CAD systems.

The process planner sees GT as an attempt to standardize processing methods, including sequencing, machining parameters, tooling, and fixturing. When new parts are being planned, the required manufacturing operations generate a part code. The part code is used to extract plans for existing similar parts from the database or to automatically generate a new optimal plan in a fashion similar to that used for the existing parts. Changes are kept to a minimum with an eye toward allowing common machine setups.

The manufacturing engineer views GT as an attempt to obtain the blessings of mass production

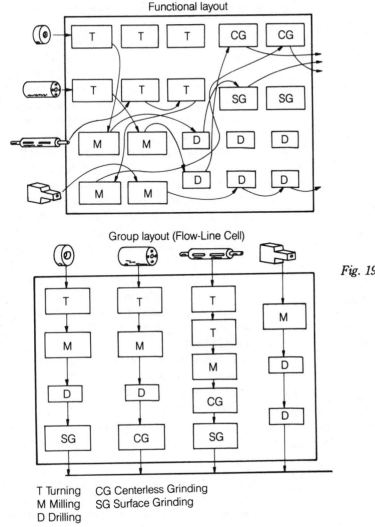

Fig. 19-1. Functional vs. group layout.

T Turning   CG Centerless Grinding
M Milling   SG Surface Grinding
D Drilling

Source: Hyer and Wemmerlov (1982) *Decision Sciences,* published with permission from Decision Sciences Institute.

flowline systems for medium variety, medium volume shops. Fewer part numbers translate into longer production runs. At the same time, common family setups reduce changeover times and lead to an increase in output. Moreover, parts can be rationally sequenced through work cells to further minimize setups. Well defined and independent machine groups facilitate material control and scheduling.

Manufacturing engineering sees many advantages to GT, including:

• Lower WIP levels
• Lower finished goods inventory
• Faster throughput
• Enhanced quality
• Enhanced worker productivity in design and manufacturing

- Reduced material handling cost
- Reduced space requirements
- Reduced tooling
- Simplified scheduling
- Reduced setup time and cost
- Reduced job tardiness
- Increased job satisfaction

Several studies of firms implementing GT have been conducted. TABLE 19-1 indicates the range of savings observed in these studies.

Table 19-1. Expected Savings with Group Technology.

Category	Percent Savings
WIP Cost	20 – 85%
Throughput Time	20 – 97%
Rework/Scrap	15 – 75%
Labor	15 – 50%
Tooling	20 – 30%
Machine Tools	15 – 25%
Setup	20 – 60%

Perhaps the most significant effect of GT is the reduction in throughput time. Component parts can now be scheduled dynamically to meet demand. Parts are more likely to be made to order than stock, reducing inventory costs and space requirements. Customers can be offered short delivery times. Parts do not become obsolete; hence, scrap is reduced. By converting from a job shop environment where parts traditionally spend 95 percent of their time in queue to a flowline layout, some practitioners have noted order of magnitude reductions in flow time. It can be shown that WIP levels are directly proportional to throughput time; hence, reductions in WIP costs are proportional to throughput time reductions.

A simple illustration can be used to indicate the tremendous potential of GT for throughput time reduction. First consider a traditional process layout. A particular part requires 10 operations. Each operation requires 5 minutes per part and the batch size is 100. Considering just time during process-ing, batch throughput time without lot-splitting is 5000 minutes (5 min/part/operation × 100 parts/batch × 10 operations).

If a group cell with a flowline is used instead, throughput time is 545 minutes. The assumption here is that the first part is transferred to machine two immediately upon completion of the first machine. The first machine then begins work on the second part. The process continues in this fashion with the first part being completed 50 min-utes (5 min/part/operation × 10 operations) after it enters the system and another part finishing every 5 minutes thereafter (99 parts × 5 min = 495 min-utes). Savings potential is already apparent, even without accounting for transit, queueing, and setup time at each workstation. Experience shows that these are major elements of throughput time in process shops. For the group cell, setup is virtually eliminated due to sequencing of intrafamily items. Transit is considerably reduced due to the auto-mated or simple transfer required. Queueing is eliminated due to the nature of scheduling the cell as a single resource.

In addition to WIP cost, we can formalize other savings as functions of system parameters. Con-sider setup time and cost. The basic economic order quantity is

$$Q = \left(\frac{2AD}{h}\right)^{1/2}$$

where A is setup cost, D is demand rate, and h is holding cost rate. Let subscripts g and f indicate group and functional systems respectively. Using the basic lot size formula, the ratio of GT setup costs per time to those for a functional layout is

$$\frac{(A_g D)/Q_g}{(A_f D)/Q_f} = \left(\frac{A_g}{A_f}\right)^{1/2}$$

The basic GT assumption is that groups can yield $A_g \leq A_f$; hence, setup costs are reduced. Setup labor should be reduced accordingly as well. Also note that the following relation holds:

$$\frac{Q_g}{Q_f} = \left[\frac{A_g}{A_f}\right]^{1/2}$$

As finished goods cycle stock is proportional to lot size, we obtain a similar reduction. Safety stock is proportional to the standard deviation of lead time demand. If demands are independent, this translates into safety stock reductions proportional to the square root of throughput time reductions—at least for continuous review inventory policies. The use of group tooling, which aids setup reduction, is of central importance in GT. The group tooling concept is discussed further in the section entitled "Group Tooling." Boucher and Muckstadt (1985) and Askin and Subramanian (1987) discuss economic justification of GT in more detail.

Houtzeel and Brown (1984) describe one case where GT was implemented. Before GT, 150 parts visited 51 different machines using 87 routings. After GT, the family of parts was produced on 8 dedicated machines. FIGURES 19-2 and 19-3 illustrate the change in the system. The increased simplicity is obvious. The reduction in material handling and improved scheduling and machine loading can readily be surmised from the figures.

Approaches to Group Technology

To many professionals, the term group connotes a department of machines and workers. The machines are typically single or limited purpose. Parts are routed to a number of machines in the group during their production plan. *Cellular manufacturing* is another term used to refer to small groups of machines. In fact, GT and cellular manufacturing are often used interchangeably. Except where otherwise noted, we use the terms *cell* and *group* interchangeably.

However, *cellular manufacturing* is also used to describe the work area about a modern CNC multipurpose machining center. This work area may contain several such machines, but usually includes a robot or other automated handling device, possible on or off-line inspection equipment, and equipment controllers. While groups are normally manned, such cells may be fully automated. Technological advances in the availability of CNC machining centers, coupled with the time and expense of implementing automation, have fueled a move toward cellular manufacturing in recent years. Although in many ways machining centers can be considered groups, this chapter is concerned with the traditional group. Operational issues for traditional groups revolve around organizational problems such as machine grouping, human resource management, and scheduling. Automated cells are more concerned with activity sequencing to minimize the common cycle time for all machines.

There are three basic approaches to GT in manufacturing. The first approach, the *GT flowline*, resembles a high volume product layout with items passing one at a time from machine to machine. At the conclusion of the batch, the system is emptied and a new, similar part type is loaded. Such systems are very efficient but require the highest degree of similarity between part types. In addition to size, shape, and material similarities, part types must share a common operation sequence. In the second approach, a *GT cell*, all the machines needed to process a set of parts are located close together, but parts may travel from any machine to any other machine in the cell. Part types still exhibit similar size, shape, and machining requirements but parts need not follow the same machine sequence. This is the traditional cell usually envisioned when GT is mentioned. Cross training of workers is common in GT cells. Workers operate all the machines required to complete a batch. Job enrichment is an added benefit.

The third approach is a logical cell or *GT center*. Machines need not be located in close proximity. Within the process layout, however, similar parts are directed to the same machine. Potential advantages in setup and simplified scheduling are exploited. Logical configurations are used when an existing layout cannot be changed, groups change with time, or where common operations between parts exist but the parts are not fully similar. The differences between the approaches are apparent in the layout and material handling methods. However, it is the processing requirements and life expectancy of the groups that should determine the approach adopted.

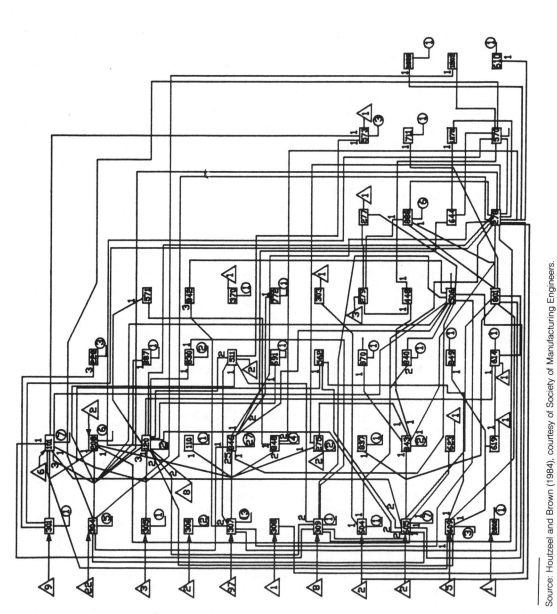

Fig. 19-2. Before group technology: current routings 150 very similar parts.

Source: Houtzeel and Brown (1984), courtesy of Society of Manufacturing Engineers.

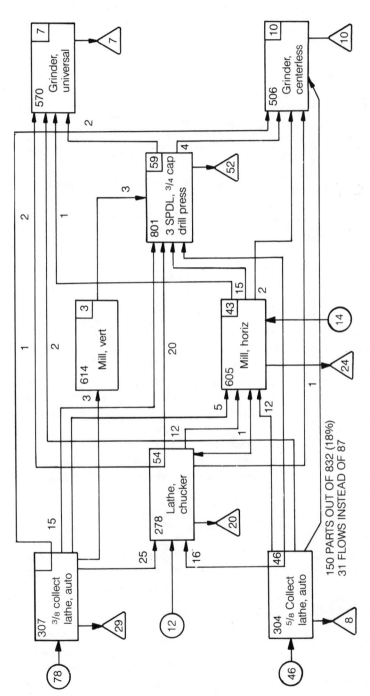

Fig. 19-3. After group technology: routings after standardization of 150 very similar parts.

Principles of Groups

Experience with formation and operation of groups has led to the development of basic principles for successful group formation and operation. After considerable experience at designing, implementing, and operating groups, Burbidge (1975) devised a basic set of principles for groups. These principles are characteristics found in successful groups. Burbidge's seven characteristics of groups are summarized in TABLE 19-2 and should be maintained in designing and operating GT systems.

A study by Pullen (1984) revealed that practicing cells adhere to many of these principles. In the study, cells tended to be physically disjointed from other work centers and required tooling was stored locally. An average cell consisted of 11 workers utilizing 14 machines. Group throughput time for an average batch of 330 parts was 2.4 weeks. Workers were granted greater autonomy to determine work practices than in other systems, but management retained the right to staff groups and discipline workers. Parts occasionally would have to leave the group for special processes but ordinarily all operations and inspections were performed within the group. Contrary to the principles, workers were occasionally reassigned by management or extra parts were routed to the group to meet overall production goals.

Of course, safety must be paramount in designing groups. Machines with conflicting environmental requirements may not be located in the same cell. Economics may be another reason why parts must occasionally leave the cell, perhaps to visit an expensive process shared by many parts. Heat treating is a common example of a process performed outside the cell. Cells should also be constructed to level workload across the machines in the group. With unbalanced workloads, management is strongly tempted to add additional work to the cell, for traditional beliefs are difficult to overcome.

Numerous GT and organizational behavior experts espouse the advantage of groups of six to ten workers for enhancing positive social interaction. Such groups can pull together without excessive organizational overhead or internal factions. This is an organizational behavior constraint, not a technological problem. Instances of successful groups with up to 35 workers have been reported. Normally, it is preferable to have one foreman per group. This individual acts as a facilitator and administrator, encouraging and assisting all workers to contribute toward group goals.

Group Tooling

The concept of group tooling is essential to understanding the implementation of GT in manufacturing facilities. An extensive discussion of the design and use of group tooling is given in Ivanov (1968). Expected reductions in tooling cost, both design and hardware, were listed in an earlier section of this chapter. Tooling is based on component

Table 19-2. Characteristics of Successful Groups.

Characteristics	Explanation
Team	Specific team of workers dedicated to the cell
Part types	Specific set of similar part types only
Facilities	Specific set of dedication machines/equipment
Group layout	Dedicated, contiguous floor space for group
Target	Common goal for group, set once each period
Independence	Between group buffers allow independent goal achievement
Size	Preferably 6 – 15 workers for positive social interaction

families. Each family may be described by the composite part, which includes all the features present on any component in the family and lists ranges for parameter values such as size and tolerance.

Traditional systems design unique tooling for each component. In GT, a group tool is designed with appropriate attachments for each component. The attachments must be designed for easy setup changeover. For instance, a precision groove can be placed in the group tool. Component attachments need merely to be slid into place and locked with a single screw. Such approaches are used for group chucks for lathes and milling machine fixtures. For drilling, a group jig with interchangeable strips for components can be designed. The limited range of component size permits such design. Restricting a group to similar tolerance and finishing requirements allows all components in the group to be machined on the same machine. Accordingly, all required tooling is stored permanently at the machine.

A simple model explains the savings in tooling hardware cost. Let c_t be the cost of tooling, a die or jig for instance, for each part in a conventional machine shop. With GT, we require a group tool at a cost of c_{gt} plus a possible part-specific adapter, c_a. If there are n parts in the group, cost per part is $(c_{gt}/n) + c_a$. We will assume $c_a < c_t < c_{gt}$. Tooling cost savings with GT is $nc_t - c_{gt} - nc_a$. Savings are positive provided $n \geq (c_{gt}/c_t - c_a)$.

Machine tools such as capstan lathes can be set up to produce an entire part family. Common tools and production sequences yield substantial reductions in setup time. FIGURE 19-4 gives an example of such a machine setup. Only minor adjustments are required to change over between parts within the family, as tools are already in position. It is not necessary that all tools or operations be required for all parts, but only that the majority of operations can be performed with the specified set of tools.

The reduction in setup time has far-reaching implications. Machine effectiveness increases due to increased productive usage. Lower setup times mean smaller batch sizes. Accordingly, decreases follow in work-in-process, throughput time, lead time, space requirements, and obsolescence.

CODING AND CLASSIFICATION

Coding and classification of parts has several potential uses and can make a significant contribution to improving the operating efficiency of a group technology manufacturing system. Over the past two decades, a number of U.S. manufacturers have taken advantage of GT based coding and classification systems (see Hyer 1984 for a list of industries identified as GT users). In a generic sense, a coding and classification scheme is used to record, retrieve, and sort relevant information about a set of objects. In manufacturing systems, the intent of a part code is to describe those characteristics which will facilitate the retrieval and identification of similar parts in terms of design, shape, materials used, and/or machining requirements. Subsequently, based on appropriate classification schemes, the part codes can be used to identify part families, a set of parts which are similar in terms of the characteristics used in the classification scheme.

Several examples in the literature on GT attest to the importance of using coding and classification systems in creating a cellular manufacturing process. For example, in their survey on GT, Ham and Shunk (1979) report that several applications are facilitated by using a coding and classification system. These are:

- Easier design data retrieval and a minimized design effort
- Machine grouping so that most processes required by a part family are localized and inter-process movements are minimized
- Design of a composite part prototype; if tooling is developed for a composite part then any part in the family can be processed with the same tooling
- Operational benefits from group jigs, fixtures, and tooling setups when a single composite part design is not possible

- Flexibility and efficiency in numerical control of equipment
- Easier computer-aided process planning and production control.

The remainder of this section discusses coding and classification in further detail. We first discuss the major issues in developing a coding system. This is followed by a description of classification

Ferrous, 2 or more 0/Dias (successively increasing)
1 or more 1/Dia

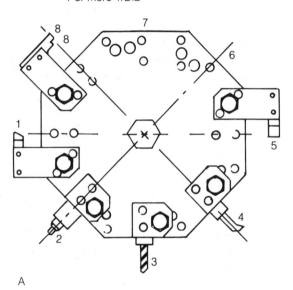

Turret Posn	Tool Description
1	Face & Rgt Turn (use as stop)
2	Centre
*3	Drill
*4	Boring
5	Finish turn
6	Free
7	Free
8	Part Off

* Change to suit requirements

Notes —Additional tools should be placed in a free position where possible thus preserving the basic settings

A

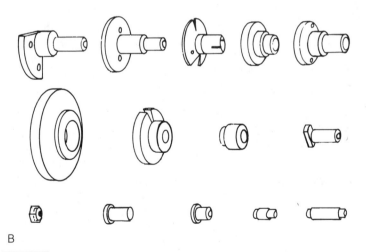

B

Source: Reproduced with permission from *Group Technology Production Methods in Manufacture* by Gallagher/Knight, published by Ellis Horwood LImited, Chichester, England, 1986.

Fig. 19-4. Group setup for turning: A: Turret setup; B: Member setup.

methods. Next, we discuss the composite parts concept and describe and evaluate the characteristics and key features of some of the coding systems that are currently available.

Major Considerations in Selecting and/or Designing a Coding System

As discussed above, a part coding scheme forms the basis of GT. In general, a part code is a string of numeric, alphabetical, or alphanumeric characters that represent much of the information relevant to the manufacturing system planning decision. This information can be characterized as relating to the part (size, shape, and material) and the processing operations or machining requirements. In developing a part code, emphasis should be placed on information that relates to how things should or could be done rather than on how things are currently done. The latter simply institutionalizes existing practices, missing opportunities for standardization and improvement. Hence, for example, the code should indicate operations required to manufacture a part and should not focus on the specific machines or processes currently used to perform the operations. In this manner, we can eliminate any of the shortcomings of current management practice.

The major considerations that guide the selection and design of a coding system are part population, code detail, code structure, and code representation. Each of these are discussed in more detail below.

Part Population The coding system designed and/or selected should cover the entire population of part types to be coded. Further, the code development team should know the classes of part types in the population (e.g., rotational, prismatic, sheet metal parts, etc.). Additionally, codes must specify those characteristics which may differ between parts within a class. Thus, codes should identify such differences as the specific part characteristics (e.g., materials required or geometric shapes) as well as the differences in operations required within a class of parts (e.g., some parts need threading and turning operations while others do not). Finally, the coding system selected and/or designed should be such that it captures all the relevant characteristics for all the parts to be classified. Relevant characteristics are those that make it desirable to treat the parts differently in design or manufacturing.

Code Detail The amount of detail maintained in the part codes is a function of several factors. The part family identification process would be greatly simplified if a short compact code describing all the relevant design and manufacturing details of every part in the population could be created. However, this would require a code which is inherently complex and hence, impractical to use. A preferred alternative is to ensure that the coding scheme chosen helps to create families of similar parts.

The level of detail desired in the code structure varies with the user. For manufacturing engineers involved in process planning and production control, all parts with identical routings and comparable machine utilizations may have a common code. This would facilitate the development and retrieval of such plans. On the other hand, design engineers would prefer to assign a unique code to identify all parts which include features useful as starting points in developing future designs. Thus, features such as outside shape, end shape, internal shape, protusions, and holes, in addition to the internal shaft, typically may be included in the code structure. Attributes that change over time (e.g., specific demand forecasts) should not be included in the code structure. However, an indicator for a standard, high volume production item justifying specific tooling might be appropriate. Finally, the code design and/or selection process must also consider the trade-off between the costs of collecting the relevant part information (in terms of time) versus the benefits of having a code structure that reflects all such information.

Existing codes vary from as few as five to more than 30 characters. Long codes which completely and uniquely identify each part are usually not cost effective. Development and maintenance time and cost is prohibitive. Likewise, such codes are cumbersome to learn and use. In summary, the level of detail in the coding system is a function of the use of the system as well as the cost/benefit trade-off of developing a system with complete information.

Code Structure   The process of assigning symbols to a set of code fields is referred to as coding. As pointed out earlier, coding schemes differ in terms of the symbols they employ: numeric, alphabetic, or alphanumeric. Further, variations in the way symbols are assigned produce three distinct types of codes: *monocodes* or hierarchical codes, *polycodes* or chain codes, and *hybrid codes* or mixed-mode codes.

Hyde defines a monocode as (Hyde 1981) ''an integrated code of fewest characters which describes a population of data in a reasonable balanced, logical and systematic order, where each code character qualifies a succeeding code.'' In a monocode, each symbol amplifies the information provided in the previous digit and hence, these are often referred to as hierarchical codes.

An example of a coding scheme which generates monocodes is shown in FIG. 19-5. In this case, the first digit signifies the division of the part population into sheet metal parts, rotational machined parts, nonrotational machined parts, and castings.

The second digit divides the sheet metal parts into three categories: those having 12 or more holes, between 6 and 12 holes, and having less than 6 holes. Finally, the third digit indicates if bends do or do not exist in the part. Based on this relatively simple example, a sheet metal part with 8 holes and no bends would have a code of 010. Note that the 1 in the second position would not be the same as a 1 in the second position in a code of 110. For example, the latter 1 may indicate the length to width ratio of a nonrotational machined part to be between 1 and 4. Thus digits in a monocode cannot be interpreted by themselves, but are dependent on the meaning contained in the preceding digit. This interrelationship of symbols in a monocode makes this type of coding scheme somewhat difficult to construct and learn. However, an advantage of this type of coding scheme is that it does allow the capture of a significant amount of information in a relatively short code.

In contrast to monocodes, polycodes are designed such that each digit of a code has a distinct meaning across all parts. Thus, all the code symbols in a polycode are independent of each other.

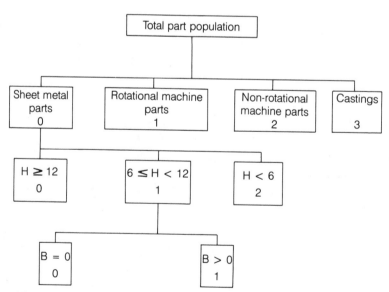

Fig. 19-5. An illustration of a hypothetical monocode generation scheme.

For example, a 2 in the sixth field for a given poly-code always indicates the same part attribute regardless of the digits in the other fields for the code. Hence, the coding schemes which generate polycodes are easier to develop and apply than monocode schemes. The major drawback of poly-codes is that they can be quite long. The differences between the information storage capacity of the monocodes and polycodes can be illustrated using the following example (Hyer and Wemmerlov, "Coding Systems," 1985). Assume that the code is to consist of two symbols and that in each of the code fields the digits 0 and 9 are to be used. With a monocode, 110 ($10^1 + 10^2$) unique characteristics can be potentially stored while with a polycode, only 20 ($10^1 + 10^1$) can be stored.

Since both monocodes and polycodes have advantages, a large number of commercial systems have features of both. Typically, frequently accessed characteristics where the number of options are low are included in a polycode to facilitate the retrieval process. Uncommon characteristics with a larger variety are captured by the monocode section of the coding scheme. Hence, a hybrid (or mixed-mode) code will typically utilize a section of the code, which is set up as a polycode, and then switch to several hierarchical digits. One example of a hybrid code system is the OPITZ system (Opitz 1970).

Code Representation The symbolic form for implementing the code must be selected. Since computerization of the coded information is essential, it is important to develop a coding system that facilitates quick retrieval of information, minimum storage, and a reliable, complete analysis. Thus, although a computer scientist would prefer to have information stored in binary digits so as to minimize storage and facilitate retrieval, the design and manufacturing engineers would prefer to use alphanumeric digits so as to facilitate understanding. Consequently, the code representation should be arrived at with these personnel working together as a team.

This discussion has highlighted several major considerations in selecting or designing an appropriate coding system. We conclude this section with the following four general principles of industrial coding (Hyde 1981):

- No code should exceed five characters without a break in the code string. COROLLARY: The shorter the code, the fewer errors.
- Identify codes of fixed length and pattern. COROLLARY: Varying-length codes within a given class of materials proliferate error rates and require justification in handling (right or left) to the longest code in use.
- All-numeric codes produce fewest errors. COROLLARY: A fixed-length, all-numeric code of five or fewer digits is best.
- Alphanumeric combination rules are acceptable if the alpha field is fixed and used to break a string of numbers. COROLLARY: Alphabetic and numeric codes intermixed in the same code position cause excessive transaction errors.

Classification:
The Key to Simplification

Once an appropriate part coding scheme has been developed, the next step is to identify part families using some type of classification system. In the context of GT manufacturing, such a system focuses on organizing part coded data in a hierarchical manner to enable quick identification of groups of similar parts. Gombinski (1969) identified the following different types of classification systems that are used in GT.

Product Oriented System The product oriented type of classification system creates part families based on the product the parts are used to manufacture. The part groups identified in this case might not be mutually exclusive since parts could be used in multiple products. Although this may help to identify product oriented manufacturing cells (i.e., cells in which a product is completely manufactured), it is unlikely that this would simplify the flow of materials in the complete plant. Further, such a classification of part families will probably lead to the creation of a large number of cells, since, typically, several products are manufactured in one organization.

Function Oriented System　A function oriented classification system identifies part families based on the names. The system assumes that these part names are indicative of their function; for example, gear boxes and input shafts. Although such a grouping of parts might be appropriate to identify cells within which similar "name" parts are processed, it is not clear how such cells will simplify the manufacturing process. The implication is that functionally grouped parts will share common requirements and methods.

Design Oriented System　The purpose of a design oriented classification system is to create part families such that the parts within a group have similar designs in terms of their overall shape and/or materials usage. Such systems provide a basis for standardization since they can be used by design personnel to retrieve existing designs and incorporate these designs in new products. This can also lead to an elimination of past design errors as well as the reduction of unnecessary variety in the part designs. Such classification systems have been used with some success in identifying manufacturing cells.

Process Oriented System　The process oriented classification system creates part families consisting of parts processed on similar technological processes, such as drills, mills, and lathes; or families in which all parts require similar operations to be manufactured, such as a turning, drilling, and grinding operation. Such a classification scheme not only creates part families requiring similar processes and/or operations, but also identifies groups of processes and/or operations which can be combined to set up a manufacturing cell. This classification scheme has been used as a basis in developing several methods of GT cell formation, a process we discuss later in the chapter.

Design/Process Oriented System　Most of the commercially available software systems developed by consultants and practitioners for implementing GT seem to have adopted a combined design and process orientation classification scheme. Such schemes help identify part families based on design and processing similarities and thus are useful for both design and manufacturing engineers.

Although several classification schemes exist to develop part families, in the context of GT, it appears that the design/process oriented classification system approach is preferable. An example of a part classification scheme using such a system is shown in FIG. 19-6. This example has been adapted from Ivanov (1968) and shows a design and process oriented classification scheme that can be used to identify part families in a machine shop.

The parts in a family should have similar codes. It would be helpful to maintain a table of possible code values for each part family. To construct the table for a family, form an empty array with a column for each code digit and a row for each defined digit value. Then, for each digit in the code (column), place an "x" in each row which is a possible value for a part in the family. The table then summarizes the range of features for the family. When a new part is coded, it can be compared to the family tables. To belong to a family, each digit value in the new part's code must correspond to an "x" in the family table.

The Composite Part Concept

The application of a coding and classification system to the entire part population results in the identification of part families. Once part families have been created, the next step is to identify a hypothetical or actual part within each part family to represent all the materials, design, and manufacturing attributes for the individual parts included in the family. Such a part is referred to as a *composite* part and the identification of such a part for each part family is useful for several reasons:

- The composite part for each family aids the part design process since it can be used as a basis for designing new parts are designed. This would also facilitate the standardization of parts and a simplification of the design process. Design engi-

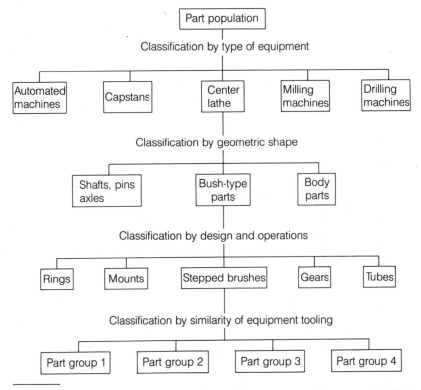

Source: E.K. Ivanov, *Group Production Organization and Technology* (Business Publications Limited, London, (1963), 4.

Fig. 19-6. A suggested design-process oriented classification scheme for a machine shop.

neers store a generic design for the composite part and create new part numbers by assigning specific parameter values to this generic design.
- The planning and design of tooling setups so as to process all the parts within a family is also made much easier with the identification of the composite part. For example, if a capstan lathe is set up to manufacture the composite part of a family, the same tooling setup can be utilized to process all the parts in the same family. Thus, the composite part can help to identify and plan for the tooling setups on the equipment required to process a part family.
- Since the composite part can be used to identify groups of machines required to process all the parts in a family, it is also useful in developing process plans for new parts that may need to be manufactured. Further, such a part should also facilitate the standardization of process plans for the current part mix.
- Grouping can be performed on the set of composite parts. In so doing, planners maintain confidence in the feasibility of the outcome while significantly reducing the size of the grouping problem. This is a significant advantage because of the computationally complex nature of the grouping problem.

FIGURE 19-7 is an example of a composite part for a set of parts included in a part family. The composite part is made of the material used to manufacture all the other parts and represents the design features for every part in the family.

Major Coding Systems Currently Available

Several commercial and nonproprietary coding and classification systems have been developed since the inception of GT. A selected listing of such

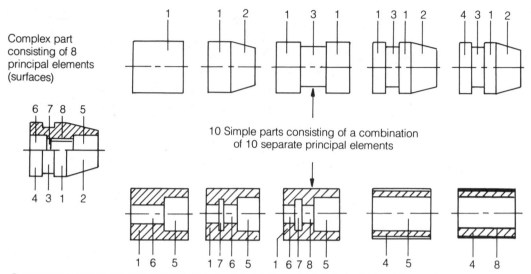

Fig. 19-7. Composite part example.

systems and the country in which they were developed is shown in TABLE 19-3. Although the majority of such systems have been designed for part coding, they can also be used to code and classify other items. In recent years, the trend seems to be toward the development of integrated systems that not only code and classify parts, but also help develop systems for implementing GT. Hence, some newer systems also include modules which focus on the facility layout, process planning, and scheduling aspects of GT. TABLE 19-4 describes the major features of some of the currently available systems.

The MULTITREEVE II (MICLASS/MULTI-CLASS) system is probably the most popular commercial coding system in use today (see Hyer and Wemmerlov, "Group Technology," 1988 and Wemmerlov and Hyer, "Cellular Manufacturing," 1988). MULTITREEVE II's software capabilities and the recent relational database developments within the system make it extremely easy to integrate with current systems, such as MRP. Other widely accepted schemes include OPITZ and KK-1. The method for generating a part code using the OPITZ

and the KK-1 system is illustrated in FIGS. 19-8 and 19-9, respectively. FIGURE 19-10 shows a part code developed using three of the four systems discussed in TABLE 19-4.

GROUP FORMATION

Once coding and classification are established, the second major activity in designing a GT system is to select the part and machine groups. The set of parts assigned to the group are normally referred to as a family. In this section we present several approaches for forming groups. Although coding and classification may be considered an alternative grouping method, we prefer to view it as a convenient preprocessor of the data. Indeed, coding and classification is also important as a product design and process planning tool, inducing standardization and planning efficiency.

The use of composite parts provides an effective mechanism for simplifying and improving the group formation process. Instead of forming groups from review of the entire part set, form groups or families looking only at composite parts. To achieve

Table 19-3. Selected Listing of Coding and Classification Systems.

System	Organization and Country
OPITZ	Aachen Technical University (W. Germany)
OPITZ's SHEET METAL	Aachen Technical University (W. Germany)
STUTTGART	University of Stuttgart (W. Germany)
PITTLER	Pittler Machine Tool Company (W. Germany)
GILDEMEISTER	Gildemeister Company (W. Germany)
ZAFO	(W. Germany)
SPIES	(W. Germany)
PUSCHMAN	(W. Germany)
DDR	DDR Standard (E. Germany)
WALTER	(E. Germany)
AUERSWALD	(E. Germany)
MITROFANOV	(U.S.S.R.)
LITMO	Leningrad Institute for Pre & Optics (U.S.S.R.)
NIITMASH	(U.S.S.R.)
VPTI	(U.S.S.R.)
GUREVICH	(U.S.S.R.)
VUOSO	Prague Machine Tool Res. Institute (Czechoslovakia)
VUSTE	Research Inst. of Eng. Tech. & Econ. (Czechoslovakia)
MALEK	(Czechoslovakia)
IAMA	IAMA (Yugoslavia)
PERA	Production Engineering Research Association (U.K.)
SALFORD	(U.K.)
PGM	PGM, Ltd. (Sweden)
KC-1	(Japan)
KC-2	(Japan)
KK-1	(Japan)
KK-2	(Japan)
KK-3	(Japan)
SHEET METAL SYSTEM	(Japan)
CASTING SYSTEM	(Japan)
HITACHI	Hitachi Company (Japan)
TOYODA	Toyoda, Ltd. (Japan)
TOSHIBA	Toshiba Machine Company, Ltd. (Japan)
BRISCH BIRN	Brisch Birn, Inc. (U.K. and U.S.A.)
MULTICLASS	TNO (Holland) and OIR (U.S.A.)
PARTS ANALOG	Lovelace, Lawrence and Co., Inc. (U.S.A.)
ALLIS CHALMERS	Allis Chalmers (U.S.A.)
SAGT	Purdue University (U.S.A.)
BUCCS	Boeing Company (U.S.A.)
ASSEMBLY PART CODE	University of Massachusets (U.S.A.)
HOLE CODE	Purdue University (U.S.A.)
CINCLASS	Cincinnati Milacron Co. (U.S.A.)

Source: Ham, I., K. Hitomi and T. Yoshida (1985), *Group Technology*, Kluwer—Nijhoff Publishing, Boston, 101 Philip Drive, Norwell, Massachusetts 02061-Reprinted with permission.

Table 19-4. Overview of Major Coding and Classification Systems.

System	Code Structure	Classification Orientation	Number of Digits	Part Types Covered	General Comments
OPITZ	Hybrid code	Design-oriented system	5 + 4 + 3 First 5 digits focus on design features Next 4 digits focus on manufacturing features Last 4 digits are optional	Purchased, machined, nonmachined and sheet metal parts	Nonproprietary system Software support not available Substantial literature on applications can guide potential users Freely available system making it attractive for small companies
BRISCH BIRN	Hybrid code	Design-oriented system using a polar logic tree	(4 – 6) + (1 – N) First 4 to 6 digits focus on design features Next 1 to N (value of N is flexible) digits focus on any other company specific features	Any Part types	Available from Brisch Birn and Partner, Ft. Lauderdale, FL Each system is tailored to company needs Complemented by The Alpha Graphics System (TAGS), which can facilitate storage and retrieval of data for part design
MULTI-TREEVE	Hybrid code Using MICLASS/ MULTICLASS	Design and proces oriented system	12 + (1 – 20) First 12 digits focus on design & materials features Next 1 to 20 digits can include company specific features	Up to nine different part types	Available from Organization for Industrial Research (OIR), Bedfrod, MA Marketed as part of a CIM/GT package which includes several other systems Includes a relational data base capability which helps to integrate the OIR systems with currently used system

Table 19-4. Cont.

System	Code Structure	Classification Orientation	Number of Digits	Part Types Covered	General Comments
KK-1	Hybrid code	Design-oriented system	2 + 7 + 2 First 2 digits focus on the functional part name	Rotational and non-rotational machined parts machined	Nonproprietary system Has not been used extensively in the U.S.
			Next 7 digits describe the materials used and the part featues		
			Last 2 digits focus on machining and tooling		

economic utilization levels of machines, it may be necessary to assign multiple composite parts to a group. Without composite parts, each part must be individually studied and assigned. A major advantage of groups is setup reduction. For some of the methods examined below, such as the similarity coefficient methods, the advantages of family setup can be lost if composite parts are not used and grouping decisions are made solely on the basis of machine requirements.

The first section below describes the production flow analysis approach popularized in England by J. L. Burbidge. The next section shows how product flows can be conveniently summarized in matrix form and used as a basis for other grouping methods. This is followed by overviews of the use of similarity coefficients, and graphical and mathematical approaches to grouping. Lastly, pattern matching for determining families of similar parts is addressed.

Factory and Production Flow Analysis

The production flow analysis approach of Burbidge (1971) has been widely used for group formation. The approach has the advantage of permitting manual solution of medium-sized problems and relies primarily on available data. Route sheets are the major data requirement. In this section we describe production flow analysis and the factory flow analysis step which precedes it.

Factory Flow Analysis Many plants are designed for one basic type of product such as valves. Such facilities may already be thought of as one large main group. Other facilities produce totally unrelated types of products such as components from castings and sheet metal. Factory Flow Analysis (FFA) is intended as a preliminary step for large plants with a wide variety of products and processes. FFA can help determine a set of main groups. Main groups have the characteristics of groups, except they are much larger in scale and must be subsequently subdivided.

FFA assumes the factory is already divided into large departments, presumably based on processes. Each department has an assigned number. The objective is to show flows between existing process departments and then to combine related departments or processes which should eventually be included in a single group. The combined departments will then be split into smaller groups via production flow analysis. The plant is represented by a network of nodes and arcs. A node represents a department or several combined departments. Arcs indicate material flow between departments. FIGURES 19-11a, 11b, AND 11c illustrate FFA. The steps are as follows:

1. Find current process routes. For each component, assign a process route number (PRN) indicating the sequence of departments currently visited by the component.

2. Form PRN frequency chart. For each unique PRN, count the number of components with this PRN. Order the PRNs by nonincreasing frequency.

3. Graph current system. Construct a network diagram showing all routes among current departments. Include all PRNs.
4. Find primary network. Begin to construct a network of primary flows as follows: Iteratively add the next PRN to the network until either all departments are included with flows in and out, or until a pair of departments are connected by flow in both directions.
5. List joining infeasibilities. Determine the set of department pairs which cannot be combined due to safety or other incompatibility.
6. Simplify primary network. Join together highly connected departments for which no constraint is given in step 5. The joined departments become a single node. The simplified network will likely integrate many minor PRNs as well.
7. Eliminate exceptions. Exceptional parts not falling totally within a simplified node must be individually examined. Where a significant number of parts can be accommodated by the addition of a small number of machines to a move, add those machines. Remaining exceptional components are candidates for redesign, rerouting, or subcontracting out (buy).
8. Check loads. Allocate sufficient machines of each type used in each department to handle the component induced loads.
9. Specify interdepartmental flow system. Produce an interdepartmental from-to flow chart along with a list of machines and components assigned to each department.

Production Flow Analysis Each main group in FFA must be subdivided adhering to the seven characteristics listed in TABLE 19-2 and discussed earlier in "Principles of Groups." Production Flow Analysis (PFA) is one such approach. Process route cards for each component guide the decision. PFA is generally a manual activity, consisting of three steps: data collection and verification, consolidation into atomic subgroups, and combination of subgroups into groups. We will outline each of these steps. Succeeding sections of this chapter describe other approaches for the entire grouping process or for specific steps described here.

Data Preparation We list this activity as a separate step to underscore the importance of accurate data. For PFA to be successful, accurate facts are required on existing machines, component routes, standard times for operations, and bills of material. Machines are classified by type. Two machines of the same type are assumed to be interchangeable with respect to the set of manufacturing operations they can perform.

Subgroup Identification One approach to finding subgroups is to focus on *key machines*. A key machine is one used by only a few part types. These part types and all their required machines constitute a subgroup. Burbidge calls this approach Group Analysis and it can by summarized in the following steps:

- For each machine type, list all components which require it. Identify the key machine with the fewest associated components. All components using this key machine, along with the other machines used by these parts, form a subgroup.
- Consider a subgroup. If except for the key machine, the machines fall into two or more disjoint sets (no component visits more than one set), the subgroup is divided into two or more subgroups, respectively. If any machine is included due to use by only one component, remove this machine and component.
- Return to the first step until all components and machines are assigned to subgroups.

Subgroups may also be determined by combination methods. Combination methods attempt to form subgroups from components with common routings. Many of the techniques described earlier in this chapter, in the section titled "Coding and Classification," follow this approach, using more formal mechanisms for combining subgroups. Thus, we will not discuss this further here.

Form Groups Subgroups are now combined to form groups of the desired size. Subgroups with the greatest overlap in common machine types are

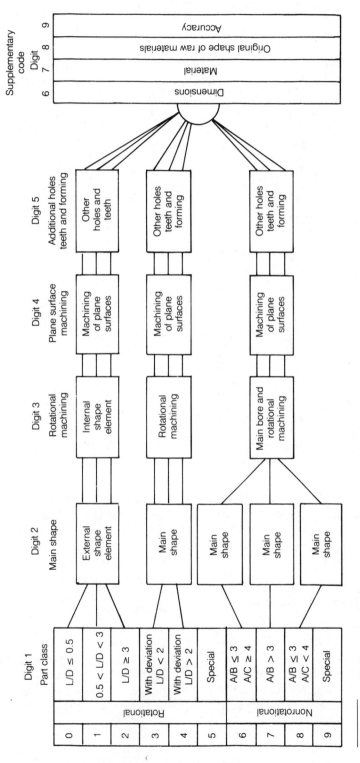

Fig. 19-8. Basic structure of the OPITZ system.

Source: Groover, M. and E.W. Zimmers, Jr. (1984)— *CAD/CAM: Computer Aided Design and Manufacturing*, Prentice-Hall, Inc., Englewood Cliffs, N.J. (Mikell P. Groover, Automation, Production Systems, and Computer-Integrated Manufacturing, copyright 1987, p. 440. Reprinted by permission of Prentice-Hall, Inc.)

COLUMN	I	II	III	IV	V	VI	VII	VIII	IX	X	XI	XII	XIII
POSITIONS	PARTS NAME (FUNCTION)		MATERIALS		MAIN DIMENSIONS		PRIMAL SHAPES, RATIO OF MAIN DIMENSIONS	GEOMETRICAL SHAPES AND MACHINING				ACCURACY	MAIN MACHINING TOOLS AT PRIMARY STAGE
	GENERAL CLASSIFICATION	DETAIL CLASSIFICATION	GENERAL CLASSIFICATION	DETAIL CLASSIFICATION	(R) L / (N) A	(R) D / (N) B		(R) EXTERNAL SHAPE / (N) PLANE SURFACE	(R) INTERNAL SHAPE / (N) PRINCIPAL BORES	(R) PLANE SURFACE MACHINING / (N) SPECIAL MACHINING	(R) AUXILIARY HOLES / (N) DITTO		
0													
1													
2													
3													
4	MATRIX	DITTO	MATRIX	DITTO	SEPARATE TABLES FOR ROTATIONAL (R) AND NON-ROTATIONAL (N) COMPONENTS		DITTO	DITTO	DITTO	DITTO	DITTO	COMMON TABLE FOR R AND N	DITTO
5													
6													
7													
8													
9													

Source: Ham, I., K. Hotomi and T. Yoshida (1985), *Group Technology: Applications to Production Management,* Kluwer-Nijhoff Publishing, Boston, p. 157. 101 Philip Drive, Norwell, Massachusetts, 02061. Reprinted with permission.

Fig. 19-9. Basic structure of the KK-1 system.

combined. This approach helps reduce the need for additional machines and simplifies load balancing. Each group should have sufficient machines and staff assigned to complete the part families associated with the group.

Machine/Component Matrix Ordering

A basic decision aid in group formation is the machine/component matrix (MCM). The matrix indicates the set of machines used for each component, and is compiled from the same route sheets used in PFA. TABLE 19-5 shows the MCM for a simple 9-machine, 12-component problem. For real problems with many machines and components the sparse matrix would be stored implicitly, only indicating the nonzero elements. The manipulation algorithms discussed below would also be implemented with efficient computer science constructs.

At first glance the MCM appears uninformative. However, King (1980) provides a useful method for ordering the MCM. Each row and column of the MCM is a binary string. Blanks are zeros. Similar row strings indicate machines with many common components; similar column strings indicate components with similar routes. The underlying similarity structure can be made more apparent by ordering or sorting the rows and

Sample Part

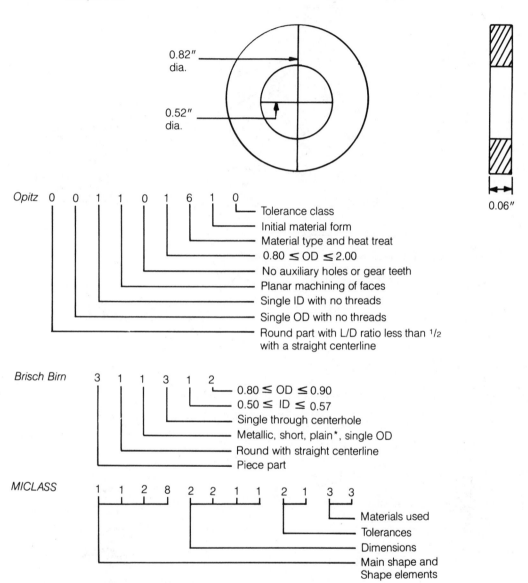

Round Part with single OD and ID without faces, threads, slots, grooves, splines, or additional holes. OD and length are within certain size ranges.

Source: Schalfer, G.H. (1981), "Implementing CIM", *American Machinist*, August, 152-174.

    * No threads, splits, keyways, flats, grooves, slots, or knurls

Fig. 19-10. Part code developed using the OPITZ, BRISCH BIRN, and MICLASS systems.

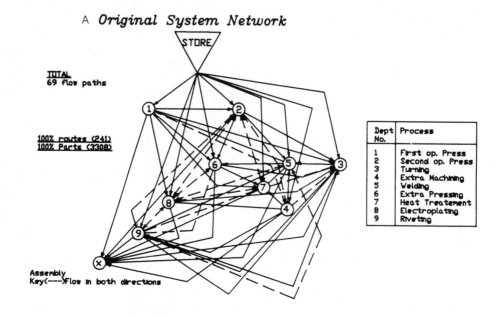

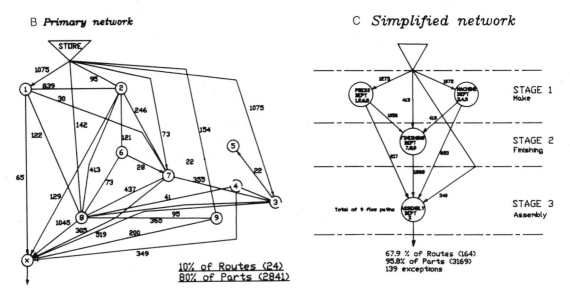

Fig. 19-11. Factory flow analysis.

columns based on their binary string value. The basic ordering algorithm is as follows:

MCM Ordering Algorithm

Step 1. Arrange machine rows in order of nonincreasing binary value. If step 1 has been previously executed and row order is unchanged, stop; otherwise go to 2.

Step 2. Arrange component columns in order of nonincreasing binary value. If no columns are moved, stop; otherwise go to 1.

Any sorting algorithm may be employed at each step. For instance, rows (columns) can be assigned their decimal equivalents and then sorted. Alternatively, iteratively compare adjacent row (column) pairs. The row (column) with the first "1" is placed on top (front). Ties are broken by proceeding until the next "1" is found. Starting with the second row (column) each row (column) is moved up (forward) through a sequence of comparisons until it fails a comparison test.

While the algorithm will converge, it is not guaranteed to converge to a unique solution. Nonetheless, the convergent solution should be considerably more informative than the arbitrary starting order, and nearly block diagonal. Each diagonal block indicates a natural machine group or part family. If implemented, this group will have no interaction with other groups. We will illustrate the technique in an example problem in the following paragraphs.

Reexamine TABLE 19-5. Column values for the kth component are 2^{12-k}, i.e. a "1" in the component 1 column receives value $2^{11} = 2048$. Machine A uses components (columns) 3, 4, and 8 for a value of $V_A = 2^9 + 2^8 + 2^4 = 784$. Reordering machines based on binary values produces the updated MCM shown in TABLE 19-6. A diagonal structure from upper left to lower right has begun to emerge. Continuing, we reorder columns, then rows then finally columns again. At this point no further order changes are found. The final matrix is shown in TABLE 19-7.

With the exception of component 3 requiring machine A, we have three natural groups. The groups are machines (E, H, A), (D, F, C, I), and (G, B). The exceptional component 3 can be handled manually. The component may either be routed to both groups or an additional machine A can be added. In later sections we address the issue of automatic group formation. In addition to exceptional parts, we will consider machine utilizations.

Similarity Coefficients

Similarity coefficients offer an alternative approach to exploiting the information in the machine/component matrix. Similarity coefficients are measures of the degree of commonality between pairs of machines or components. Large values indicate that the pair should be in the same group. We will describe several measures that have

Table 19-5. Example Machine/ Component Matrix.

	Component											
Machine	1	2	3	4	5	6	7	8	9	10	11	12
A			1	1				1				
B						1			1			1
C		1	1							1	1	
D		1	1				1			1		
E	1			1				1				
F		1	1				1				1	
G					1	1						
H	1			1								
I		1					1			1	1	

Table 19-6. Machine/Component Matrix with Machines Reordered.

Machine	1	2	3	4	5	6	7	8	9	10	11	12
E	1			1				1				
H	1			1								
D		1	1				1			1		
F		1	1				1				1	
C		1	1							1	1	
I		1					1			1	1	
A			1	1				1				
G					1	1						
B						1			1			1

Table 19-7. Final Ordered Machine/Component Matrix.

Machine	4	1	8	3	2	7	10	11	6	5	9	12
E	1	1	1									
H	1	1										
A	1		1	1								
D				1	1	1	1					
F				1	1	1		1				
C				1	1		1	1				
I					1	1	1	1				
G									1	1		
B									1		1	1

been proposed for both machine pairs and component pairs and then describe a hierarchical clustering approach for forming groups from the coefficients.

Machine Pair Measures Let x_i be the number of components using machine i, and x_{ij} the number of components using both machine i and j. McAuley (1972) proposed use of the Jacard coefficient. For similarity between machines i and j the coefficient is

$$s_{ij} = \frac{x_{ij}}{x_i + x_j - x_{ij}} \qquad (19\text{-}1)$$

Values close to 1.0 indicate strong commonality between the machines. For instance, if machine 1 receives 10 part types and machine 2 receives 20 part types, 8 of which are the same, then $s_{12} = 8/(10 + 20 - 8) = 0.364$. This measure has one serious drawback. Suppose machine 2 receives 100 parts instead of 20. Refiguring, $s_{12} = 8/(10 + 100 - 8) = 0.078$. Machine 1 still sees 80 percent of its component types go to machine 2; from its perspective it is highly linked to machine 1 in both cases. This problem occurs when machines receive very different numbers of components. In PFA we made a point of saying that machines with few part types were influential in describing groups; the current result is antithetic to that belief. An alternative coefficient which overcomes this problem is

$$s_{ij} = \max\left\{ \frac{x_{ij}}{x_i}, \frac{x_{ij}}{x_j} \right\} \qquad (19\text{-}2)$$

	Machines							
Machine	**B**	**C**	**D**	**E**	**F**	**G**	**H**	**I**
A	0	1/3	1/3	2/3	1/3	0	1/2	0
B	-	0	0	0	0	1/2	0	0
C	-	-	3/4	0	3/4	0	0	3/4
D	-	-	-	0	3/4	0	0	3/4
E	-	-	-	-	0	0	2/3	0
F	-	-	-	-	-	0	0	3/4
G	-	-	-	-	-	-	0	0
H	-	-	-	-	-	-	-	0

Table 19-8. Maximum Relationship Similarity Coefficient.

With this measure $s_{12} = 0.8$ in both cases. TABLE 19-8 contains the s_{ij} values of equation 19-2 for the nine-machine example of TABLE 19-5.

Component Based Measures The above measures could be computed for component pairs. Instead of the number of components visiting the machines, we use the number of machines visited by the components, and the number of common machine types. Grouping is then performed on components.

The similarity measures introduced thus far ignore processing sequence. In order to construct flowlines, components must share a common processing sequence. Moreover, components may use machines in different fashions, obviating the desirability of grouping them. Different setup or tooling requirements may be needed. Choobineh (1988) proposes a measure which takes these factors into account. A component's sequence is made up of an ordered set of manufacturing operations. Operations are defined such that components having operations in common should ideally be grouped together. N is the number of operations in the shortest component sequence. Then for $l \leq N$, define $c_{ij}(l)$ as the number of identical operation sequences of l operations in the routings of parts i and j. A measure of similarity based on sequences of L common operations is

$$s_{ij}(L) = L^{-1}\left[s_{ij}(1) + \sum_{l=2}^{L}\frac{c_{ij}(l)}{N - l + 1} \right] \qquad (19\text{-}3)$$

where $s_{ij}(1)$ is the Jacard measure given by common

operations, divided by total number of operations used by either component.

As an example of $s_{ij}(l)$, consider the two component sequences $O_1 = \{b,a,e,c,d,f\}$ and $O_2 = \{a,b,e,c,d,a,e\}$. First, using equation 19-1, compute $s_{12}(1)$. Five operations (a,b,c,d,e), are common to both components. The union of operations contains six operations, (a,b,c,d,e,f). Accordingly, $s_{12}(1) = 5/6$. This is an indication of high similarity despite the fact that the two parts are incompatible for a flowline.

To compute $s_{12}(2)$ we must determine $c_{12}(2)$. Pairs of common operation sequences are $\{(a,e), (e,c), (c,d)\}$ for $c_{12}(2) = 3$. Note that $c_{12}(3) = 1$ for the triplet (e,c,d). Our measure is

$$s_{12}(2) = \frac{1}{2}\left[\frac{5}{6} + \frac{3}{6 - 2 + 1} \right] = 0.717 \qquad (19\text{-}4)$$

While this measure overcomes the lack of sequence consideration inherent in other similarity measures, as L increases, computation of all $c_{ij}(l)$ becomes time consuming. To facilitate this process, compute $s_{ij}(L)$ only for component pairs with large $s_{ij}(L-1)$ values, as these are the only candidates for strong L level similarity.

An alternative part operation similarity measure was proposed by Vakharia and Wemmerlov (1988). Let

$$s_{ij} = 0.5\left[\frac{y_{ij}}{y_i} \right] + 0.5\left[\frac{y_{ij}}{y_j} \right] \qquad (19\text{-}5)$$

In this case, y_i is the total number of operations

required to process part i and y_{ij} is the maximum number of operations included in the same sequence in O_i and O_j (operation deletions are allowed). For the example above, the number of operations included in the same sequence in O_1 and O_2 are (a,e,c,d) or (b,e,c,d). Thus, $y_{12} = 4$ and the computed similarity value is

$$s_{12} = 0.5\left[\frac{4}{6}\right] + 0.5\left[\frac{4}{7}\right] = 0.62 \qquad (19\text{-}6)$$

Hierarchical Clustering Having found similarity measures, the next step involves forming clusters of machines or components. Each object forms an initial cluster. Hierarchical clustering then attempts to gradually combine clusters with the highest similarity. We continue until only one cluster remains. We may select final groups from any stage in the clustering tree that provides the desired group sizes.

We now describe the general hierarchical clustering procedure. We start with an NxN matrix of machines or components. Matrix values are the s_{ij}.

Step 0. Form N initial clusters.
Step 1. Select the max s_{ij}. Merge clusters i and j into cluster k. If more than one cluster remains, go to 2.
Step 2. Replace row and columns i and j with k. Compute s_{nk} for all clusters n. Go to 1.

A number of methods can be used to update s_{nk} values. Proposed methods include single linkage with $s_{nk} = \max(s_{ni}, s_{nj})$; complete linkage $s_{nk} = \min(s_{ni}, s_{nj})$; and average linkage

$$s_{nk} = \frac{\sum_i s_{ni} + \sum_j s_{nj}}{p(k)*p(n)} \qquad (19\text{-}7)$$

where $p(i)$ is the number of objects in cluster i.

Another method is set merging (Vakharia and Wemmerlov 1988). In set merging, the new cluster of machines or components is used to recompute the corresponding similarity coefficient from scratch. If the Jacard measure is being used on machines, for instance, and machines i and j now form cluster k, then s_{nk} gives the number of components using both machines n and at least one of i or j divided by the number of components using any of the three machines.

The outcome of clustering can be shown in a dendrogram. The dendrogram indicates how clusters are combined as we reduce the required threshold for the similarity coefficient. The result of applying single linkage on our nine-machine example is shown in FIG. 19-12. We begin with nine groups, one per machine. At a similarity coefficient value of 0.75 we combine machines C, D, F, and I. Employing single linkage, the updated coefficients for other clusters with this new cluster is set to the maximum of the values between the other cluster and any of the four machines. Machine A accordingly has a coefficient of (1/3) with the cluster (I, F, C, D). Descending to (2/3), we combine clusters A and E. The coefficient between this cluster and H is also (2/3). The cluster (A, E, H) results. The combination process continues until only one group exists. Horizontal slices of the dendrogram offer potential solutions with 9, 6, 4, 3, 2, or 1 groups. The probable 3 group solution—(E, A, H), (I, F, C, D), and (B, G)—found from ordering the MCM is seen to exist here for the coefficient range $(1/3) < s_{ij} \le (1/2)$.

Graph Theory Applications

Several graph theoretic approaches to group formation have been proposed. Graph theoretic models have the advantage of providing a visual interpretation of the problem. A graph $G = (N,A)$, is composed of a set of nodes N and arcs A. Each arc connects two nodes; for our purposes arcs are undirected. The arc connecting nodes i and j may have an associated cost, c_{ij}.

The simplest graph uses a node for each machine and arcs representing relationships between machines. This graph is called, simply, a *machine-machine graph*. (Machine types may be used instead of machines when operations are not yet assigned to individual machines. It is then

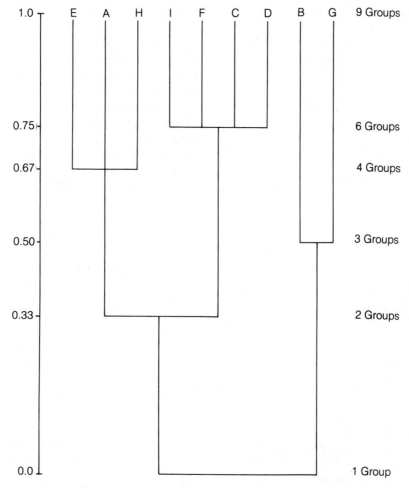

Fig. 19-12. A dendogram for the clustering example.

assumed that each machine type should only appear in one group.) Relationships are measured by intermachine similarity coefficients or actual material flows between the machines. The latter choice is preferable when ordered production sequences are known. The flow or coefficient value is called the arc "cost." Arcs are excluded if the cost is 0, or in some cases, if below an arbitrarily selected threshold T. The rationale for exclusion of small values centers on the GT belief that such links represent exceptional components, which are candidates for redesign or rerouting. We assume the resulting graph is "connected" in that there exists a path of arcs from every node to every other

node. If not, the procedure described below is applied separately to each disjoint subgraph.

A similarity graph for our example problem is shown in FIG. 19-13. Our objective then is to partition the graph into a set of subgraphs where each subgraph represents a machine group. The subgraphs are obtained by cutting (removing) arcs to disconnect the graph. The removed arcs represent interactions between groups. The weight of a cut is the sum of the costs of all arcs removed. Finding the minimum cost cuts that form disjoint subgraphs (groups), is, thus, analogous to forming groups based on minimum intergroup material flow or loss of similarity. We would also like to restrict the size

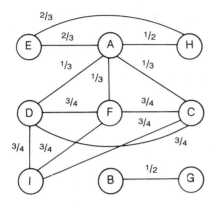

Fig. 19-13. Machine similarity graph for example problem.

of groups; this corresponds to limiting the number of nodes in each subgraph.

The problem of finding the minimum cost partitions to a graph is not easily solved. Nevertheless, an effective heuristic has been proposed by Kernighan and Lin (1970). The heuristic requires initial groups. Fortunately, the ordered MCM presents a convenient method for finding such groups. Let m_l and m_u be lower and upper bounds on the number of machines permitted in a cell.

Initial Group Formation

Step 0. Order machines by ordering the MCM.

Step 1. If less than m_u machines remain, remaining machines are a group and go to 2. Otherwise, assign the next m_l machines as a new group. Iteratively add the next unassigned machine to the new group until m_u machines are reached or the next machine has fewer components in common with the set of machines in the current group than with the next unassigned machine. Go to 1.

Step 2. Add dummy machines to each group to bring its machine level to m_u. Dummy machines have no incident arcs.

The overall procedure tends to be insensitive to the initial cutoff between m_l and m_u machines in the cell. The Kernighan and Lin improvement step which follows will compensate. The heuristic

selects a pair of groups and exchanges machine sets between the groups to reduce intergroup relationships (arc costs). The procedure must be used to compare all pairs of groups that are connected by arcs with positive cost. The heuristic's value lies in its ability to quickly find good machine sets to exchange. Let M_1 be the machines in group 1 and M_2 the machines in group 2. We seek the best, same-sized subsets of these groups to exchange: take the subset m_1 from M_1 and add it to M_2 while adding subset m_2 to M_1.

For nodes $i \epsilon M_1$ define external cost

$$E_i = \sum_{j \epsilon M_2} c_{ij}$$

and internal cost

$$I_i = \sum_{j \epsilon M_1} c_{ij}$$

E_i and I_i are interaction costs for i with nodes outside and inside its current group respectively. Values are similarly defined for machines in M_2. Switching nodes i and j yields cost savings $G_{ij} = G_i + G_j - 2c_{ij}$ where $G_i = E_i - I_i$. The best single node switch is that which maximizes G_{ij}. The procedure proceeds by temporarily making this switch then updating values. We then contemplate switching another node from each group. This process continues until we find the best switch of any size to make (t will denote the size of the switch). This switch is made official and the process restarts. Continue until no positive savings switches exist. The steps are as follows.

Partitioning Heuristic

Step 0. Initialize. $m_1 = m_2 = \phi$, $t = 0$. Compute all G_i, G_j.

Step 1. Find Best Next Exchange Pair. $t = t+1$. Compute all G^t_{ij}. Select i', j' such that $G^t_{i'j'} = \max \{G^t_{ij}\}$. Set $m_1 = m_1+i'$, m_2+j'. $G^t = G^t_{i'j'}$.

Step 2. Update Exchange Costs. $G^t_i = G^t_i = G^{t-1}_i + 2c_{ii'} - 2c_{ij'}$ for $i\epsilon M_1 - m_1$ and $G^t_j = G^{t-1}_j + 2c_{jj'} - 2c_{ji'}$ for $j\epsilon M_2 - m_2$. If $t = m - 1$, go to 3, otherwise go to 1.

Step 3. Make Best Exchange. Find

$$t^* = \underset{t=1}{argmax} \sum_{t=1}^{t^*} G^t. \; If \sum_{t=1}^{*} G^t > 0,$$

make corresponding switch and go to 0, otherwise stop.

To illustrate, reconsider the problem shown in TABLE 19-7. Let $m_l = 2$ and $m_u = 4$. We begin by assigning the first $m_l = 2$ machines, namely E and H to group 1. Machine A is added to the first group since it has two operations in common with the existing (E, H) group and only one in common with machine D. Continuing, our rule for constructing initial groups will generate the three groups (E, H, A), (D, F, C, I), and (G, B). Fortunately, these are the groups inferred by the matrix indicating our initial construction performed well. However, suppose instead we had initially formed the groups with three machines each and obtained (E, H, A), (D, F, C), and (I, G, B). Each group would also have a "Dummy" node to bring its total to m_u.

We will apply the heuristic to the latter two groups. These groups and their flows are shown in FIG. 19-14 where it is assumed each component has ten handling loads per period. Thus machine pairs sharing three components have an arc cost of $3x \; 10 = 30$. TABLES 19-9a and 19-9b summarize all computations. At $t = 1$ a savings of 90 is found by switching the Dummy in group 1 with machine I. We set $i' = Dummy$ and $j' = I$ and update the G_i^2 and G_{ij}^2 values. All potential 2 machines/group switches which contain this switch show a negative gain. Nevertheless, switching D with $Dummy$ is no worse (gain is -90) than any other so we update $m_1 = (Dummy, D)$ and $m_2 = (I, Dummy)$. Updating, we see adding any third machines to the exchange cannot help. This is the largest switch size that must be considered since groups contain 4 machines. Thus, we stop searching and switch only machines Dummy and I. The final groups (D, F, C, I) and (G, B) are once more obtained. We restart the process; no switch looks profitable, and we stop.

Having obtained the machine groups, components must be allocated. Rajagopalan and Batra (1975) suggest allocating components to the smallest group containing all required machine types. If no group satisfies this condition, then select the

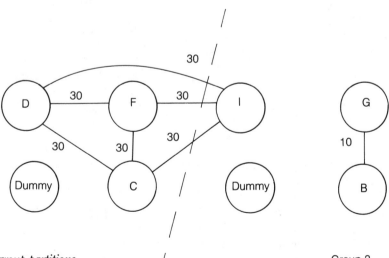

Fig. 19-14. Initial group partitions.   Group 1   Group 2

Table 19-9A. Gains for Node Switches.

Node i	E_i	I_i	G_i^1	G_i^2	G_i^3
D	30	60	−30	−90	-
F	30	60	−30	−90	−30
C	30	60	−30	−90	−30
Dummy	0	0	0	-	-
I	90	0	90	-	-
G	0	10	−10	−10	−10
B	0	10	−10	−10	−10
Dummy	0	0	0	0	-

Table 19-9B. Calculated Gains for Switches.

i	j	G_{ij}^1	G_{ij}^2	G_{ij}^3
	I	0	-	-
	G	−40	−100	-
D	B	−40	−100	-
	Dummy	−30	−90	-
	I	0	-	-
	G	−40	−100	−40
F	B	−40	−100	−40
	Dummy	−30	−90	-
	I	0	-	-
	G	−40	−100	−40
C	B	−40	−100	−40
	Dummy	−30	−90	-
	I	−90	-	-
	G	−10	-	-
Dummy	B	−10	-	-
	Dummy	0	-	-

group which maximizes the number of initial operations which can be performed on the part. The part is then routed to the group which can perform the largest number of consecutive operations beginning with the first unassigned operation. Continue until you have accounted for all operations. After routing all components, the loads on each type of machine in each cell can be computed to determine the num-

ber of machines required of each type in each cell.

We are left with two problems. First, cell size constraints now apply to machine types and not machines. Second, if we used machine types in the graph then we have overlooked the possibility of using a machine type in several groups to reduce part movement between groups. Askin and Chiu (1990) propose a two-stage partitioning scheme, which first assigns components to specific machines of the required type and then partitions the graph of all machines instead of the graph of machine types.

Rajagopalan and Batra (1975) propose first finding the maximal complete subgraphs or *cliques* of the machine-machine similarity graph. A clique is a set of nodes with an arc cost of at least threshold T between every pair of nodes in the clique. Maximal implies that no clique is contained in another clique. Cliques can be thought of as natural machine groups. Note that a machine type could appear in more than one clique. Using cliques as initial cells, components are assigned to initial cells as discussed above. Each cell is then treated as a node in a new graph. Arc costs represent material flows between cells. One then applies graph partitioning to this new graph to obtain final machine cells.

Integer Programming Approaches

Several integer programming models have been proposed for group formation. A simple formulation can be given for the graph partitioning problem. Let the binary indicator variables x_{jg} have value 1 if machine j is assigned to group g, and be 0 otherwise. Formally, the machine graph partitioning problem is

$$Maximize \sum_{i=1}^{N-1} \sum_{j=i+1}^{N} \sum_{g=1}^{G} c_{ij} x_{ig} x_{jg} \qquad (19\text{-}8)$$

subject to:

$$\sum_{g=1}^{G} x_{jg} = 1; \text{ for } all \text{ } j \qquad (19\text{-}9)$$

$$m_l \leq \sum_{j=1}^{N} x_{jg} \leq m_u \; ; \text{ for } all \; g$$

$$x_{jg} \; 0 \; or \; 1 \qquad (19\text{-}10)$$

The objective function (19-8) attempts to maximize within group interaction. Constraint set (19-9) ensures that each machine is assigned to a single group. Constraint set (19-10) restricts group size.

The quadratic nature of the objective combined with the integer variables make this a hard problem to solve. Nonetheless, Kumar et al. (1986) discuss approximations for a similar problem. The authors use a bipartite graph with nodes for each machine and component. Arcs connect components to the machines they visit. Arc costs are the volumes of the component processed on that machine. The formulation is as above, except now, the number of nodes N is the sum of the number of machines and the number of components. This is a much larger problem. The advantage is that components are automatically assigned to groups. The disadvantage is the increased problem size and the use of group size limits on machines plus components. In practice, we are generally concerned only with the number of machines or workers. While the formulation is easily modified to only include machine nodes in group size constraints, the heuristic solution procedure no longer directly applies.

Kusiak (1987) suggested a formulation that permits selection of the best process plan as well as groups when several alternative routings are possible. The modeler selects the desired number of groups, G. The model can be solved with various G values to determine the proper number of groups. The objective is then to find the allocation of components to the G groups which maximizes the sum of similarity coefficients, s_{ij}, between components in the same group. Each component is assigned to a unique group. Let N now represent the total number of process plans for all parts. Thus, if we have 1000 components with three plans each, $N = 3000$. P_k is the set of process plans for component k. Our decision variable is the binary indicator x_{ij}. We set $x_{ij} = 1$ if and only if process plan i is assigned to family group j. We will select G defining

plans and form groups around these plans. The objective function maximizes the sum of similarity values between the defining plans and all other plans assigned to their group. Interactions between nondefining elements are not counted. The formulation is as follows:

$$Maximize \sum_{i=1}^{N} \sum_{j=1}^{N} s_{ij} x_{ij} \qquad (19\text{-}11)$$

subject to:

$$\sum_{i \in P_k} \sum_{j=1}^{N} x_{ij} = 1; \text{ for } all \; k \qquad (19\text{-}12)$$

$$\sum_{j=1}^{N} x_{ij} = G \qquad (19\text{-}13)$$

$$x_{ij} \leq x_{jj} \; ; \text{ for } all \; i, j \qquad (19\text{-}14)$$
$$x_{ij} = 0 \; or \; 1$$

Constraints (19-12) select a plan for each component. Constraints (19-13) select exactly G plans to define groups. In (19-14), components can only be assigned to selected defining plans.

As with most integer programming formulations, problem size can be prohibitive, especially if several plans are considered for each component. Moreover, group size is not considered. A component with large similarity coefficients with many other components could normally be placed in any of several groups. This formation will tend to make such a component the base of a group, possibly combining otherwise dissimilar components.

Ignoring computational considerations, we can develop a comprehensive integer programming formulation for groups of desired size. Within the stated cell size limits, supervisory cost per group and material handling cost per intracell move are assumed constant. Knowledge of setup times and lot sizes is also assumed. In practice these might vary with the selected configuration. Lastly, it is assumed that each operation requires a specified machine type.

We add the following notation. Subscript f indicates component family with regard to setup and tooling requirements, possibly the composite part. Parts in the same family may share setup. i ranges over operations on components, g ranges over groups, and h over machine types.

c_h = fixed period cost per machine type h required (dollars/period)

C_g = fixed period cost per group (dollars/period)

D_i = period demand for product associated with operation i (units/period)

F_{fg} = binary indicator of group g containing family f components

L_i = number of unit material handling loads following operation i (loads/period)

m = intergroup material handling cost per load (dollars/load)

q_f = fixed period cost of tooling to assign one or more family f components to a group (dollars/period)

R_h = available productive time per period for a type h machine (hours/machine-period)

Θ_f = set of components (and associated operations) comprising family f

t_{ih} = processing time per operation i on machine type h (hours/unit)

X_{ig} = binary indicator of operation i being assigned to group g

Y_{hg} = integer number of machines type h assigned to group g (machines)

Z_g = binary indicator of use of potential group g

With the above notations, we formulate the economic group configuration problem with relevant costs as follows:

$$P : Min\ cost = \sum_{g=1}^{G} c_h Y_{hg} + \sum_{g=1}^{G} C_g Z_g + \sum_{g=1}^{G}\sum_{f=1}^{F} q_f F_{fg}$$

$$+ \ m\sum_{i=1}^{I} v_{ig}^{+} L_i \qquad (19\text{-}15)$$

Subject to:

$$m_l \le \sum_{h=1}^{H} Y_{hg} \le m_u \ \text{for all } g \qquad (19\text{-}16)$$

$$\sum_{i=1}^{I} D_i t_{ih} X_{ig} \le Y_{hg} R_h \ \text{for all } h, g \qquad (19\text{-}17)$$

$$X_{ig} - X_{i+1,g} = v_{ig}^{+} - v_{ig}^{-} \ \text{for } nonterminal\ i \quad (19\text{-}18)$$

$$\sum_{g=1}^{G} X_{ig} = 1 \ \text{for all } i \qquad (19\text{-}19)$$

$$\sum_{i=1}^{I} X_{ig} \le I\, Z_g \ \text{for all } g \qquad (19\text{-}20)$$

$$\sum_{i \in \Theta_f} X_{ig} \le I\, F_{fg} \ \text{for all } f, g \qquad (19\text{-}21)$$

Y_{hg} *integer*; X_{ig} 0 *or* 1; Z_g 0 *or* 1; F_{fg} 0 *or* 1

The four terms in the objective function represent costs of machine overhead, group overhead, family tooling, and intergroup material handling respectively. The family tooling term $(q_f F_{fg})$ is intended for use only if at least one or two conditions holds. If significant costs are associated with family setups, or if family tooling cost is incurred for each group containing at least one family part, then the term is required. The intergroup load handling cost m is difficult to estimate precisely. A lower bound could be obtained from the material handling cost per unit distance multiplied by the trip distance between adjacent groups. Additional actual contributions include cost of potentially longer trips as well as scheduling and shop floor control complications.

Constraints (19-16) restrict the number of machines allotted to a group. Alternatively, the constraint could be based on the number of workers required by including demand and standard times. Constraints (19-17) ensure sufficient machine capacity in each group. Constraints (19-18) force charging for intergroup material handling if consecutive operations are assigned to separate groups. Constraints (19-18) require the v_{ig}^+ to be 1 if and only if the component changes groups between operations i and $i+1$. *Nonterminal i* refers to all operations i except those which represent the last operation in a component production sequence. Constraints (19-19) assign each operation to a unique group. Constraints (19-20) determine if group g is used and constraints (19-21) account for the groups to which component families are assigned.

The large number of integer and binary variables makes problem P difficult to solve directly. Askin and Chiu (1990) decompose the formulation into two stages. Stage one is a formulation for selecting the specific machine within each type for each component. This problem must be solved for each machine type requiring more than one machine. Stage two then assigns machines to groups. Since component operations were assigned to specific machines in stage one, machine groups infer part groups, or routings, as well.

Pattern-based Formation Techniques

In computing the sequence-dependent similarity coefficient earlier in this chapter (in the section titled "Similarity Coefficients"), we indirectly examined the degree of similarity between strings of symbols. The symbols were the processing operations. Wu et al. (1986) formally describe the relationship between group formation and language theory. A language grammar describes how patterns such as sentences can be made from primitives such as syllables. In manufacturing, components can be made from primitive operations. Defining the unique grammar for each group indicates its range of components.

Describe each component by its sequence of machine types. Alternatively, specific operations which include tooling requirements can be used instead of machine types. For constructing flowlines, sequences are considered to be ordered. For constructing GT cells, the sequences are unordered.

The process begins by finding a distance measure between all component pairs. A sequence, or string, which is a subset of another string, is said to be dominated and the pair is given a weight zero. For the remaining pairs we determine the minimum number of deletions, insertions, and substitutions required to generate one string from the other. A fixed value is assigned for each type of transformation. The weight for the component pair is derived from the sum of the three transformation types. Each transformation type is equal to the product of the number of required transformations of that type and the transformation value. Letting q_d, q_i, q_s, w_d, w_i, w_s be the required number and weights for deletions, insertions, and substitutions respectively, we find the value for component pair i, j by

$$v_{ij} = q_d w_d + q_i w_i + q_s w_s$$

As an example, assume ordered sequences are used. Sequence i is (a, b, c, d, e) and sequence j is (b, g, e, f). Conversion of string i to j requires two deletions (a, c), one substitution (g for d), and one insertion (f). Thus, $v_{ij} = 2w_d + w_s + w_i$. A third component k with sequence (b, d, e) would be assigned value $v_{ik} = 0$ as it is dominated by i. This suggests setting $w_d \approx 0$. Likewise, it is reasonable to set $v_s \approx v_d + v_i$.

As with similarity coefficients, standard clustering techniques can be applied to component-pair values. Smaller values are now desired for clustering.

GROUP IMPLEMENTATION AND ORGANIZATION STRUCTURE

The initial GT implementation projects (in U.S.S.R. and U.K.) were motivated by a desire to reduce setup times and simplify flow patterns. More recently, in the U.S., a desire to reduce throughput times and thereby improve the performance of the shop in meeting delivery schedules has been a major factor for the implementation of GT. Further, in some cases, GT systems have also been implemented to increase worker satisfaction and improve labor productivity. Regardless of the initial reasons, GT has typically created an environment in which many operational and strategic benefits can be realized.

Implementation Objectives and General Approaches

In implementing GT, two major approaches can be taken. The approach adopted by many users focuses on identifying a small set of similar parts and subsequently creating a cell by grouping all machines required to process such parts. In this manner, a *pilot* cell is implemented and used as a basis of illustrating the advantages of GT as a whole. This approach minimizes the time and cost required to assess the potential impact of GT.

Although quick and inexpensive, the pilot cell approach has several drawbacks. First, the benefits of implementing a pilot cell may have been realized at the expense of the remaining system. This is likely since certain machines included in the pilot cell may no longer be available to process parts that are manufactured in the remaining system. Second, such a part grouping based on a restricted sampling of parts may overlook the fact that better groups may be possible if the complete part population is studied. Third, a natural resentment against the "privileged" workers assigned to this cell may develop among the other employees. This sidetracks the project from the primary mission of implementing and evaluating GT. Fourth, simply because the pilot cell was found to be beneficial, there is no guarantee that creating cells to process the remaining part population would also result in comparable benefits.

Finally, the success of the pilot cell could be jeopardized by the overt message created by its very existence. The pilot cell announces the lack of top-level commitment and confidence. Lacking evidence of organizational commitment, workers may hesitate to take the initiative required to make the cell successful. Moreover, management will find it easier to drop the project at the first sign of minor obstacles.

Since the pilot cell approach seems to be an incomplete method in several respects, researchers have recommended that management should consider the complete part population when implementing a GT system. This second approach calls for an all-out effort to restructure the manufacturing facility and its operation. This does not imply that all the parts will necessarily be processed within a cell or that the complete part population will be organized into families. In fact, if a job shop operation is reorganized into a cellular system, many new cells may process a portion of the part population, but the other parts will still be processed in a *remainder cell*—a small cell which is organized as a job shop. However, by considering the complete part population, we are focusing on the global problem and making the decision to implement GT at the strategic level. As with any change in organizational structure, policy, or philosophy, a sincere commitment from the top is essential.

In sum, regardless of the implementation objectives or the approach adopted, GT cannot be instantaneously implemented. A GT installation will typically require several years to be completely operational and will have far-reaching ramifications inside the organization, particularly if cells are created and implemented. We now proceed to discuss the impact of implementing GT on several specific organizational systems.

Implementation Considerations

The implementation of GT is likely to lead to changes in the manner in which the current organization operates. The planning, execution, control, and updating systems that are in place will require major modifications and new organizational structure. The key implementation considerations can be classified as those focusing on the design systems, the planning and execution systems, the human resources systems, and the control and information systems. Each of these considerations is discussed below.

Design Systems The coding and classification system allows design engineers to track part families within each cell. This can lead to a standardization of part designs. Further, such a design system can be used to develop and modify part process plans to achieve a flowline layout in many cells.

A related design consideration weighs whether to retain existing methods and machines, or to allocate resources into redesigning products and processes. Any reduction in part and process variety will facilitate group formation but it still may be preferable to carry this out after families and cells have been identified. Exceptional parts, which merit design consideration, can be identified more easily after groups are formed. Further, at this stage, inventory reduction resulting from the implementation of GT may provide the necessary capital to invest in new technology. Thus, although major improvements can be made initially by modifying parts and processes, it is for the reasons just discussed that Burbidge (1979) recommends first instituting groups with existing processes.

Lessons learned during GT implementation provide an opportunity for improving the design and coding systems. For example, a common problem companies face regarding coding and classification systems is the inability of the codes to adequately describe the materials used to make parts (Hyer and Wemmerlov 1954). Hence, when GT systems are implemented, the coding and classification systems are typically modified to suit the organizations' needs.

Planning and Execution Systems The functions of master production scheduling, materials requirements planning, and job scheduling may

need to be modified when GT is implemented. The potential changes in each of these functions are described below.

Master Production Scheduling Instead of preparing a separate MPS for each product, with the implementation of GT, schedulers can prepare an aggregate MPS for each major family of parts. Further, since family setup times are shared for a set of parts, such times can be incorporated in the rough cut capacity checks carried out to ensure that a capacity feasible schedule has been prepared. The capacity checks may also be carried out at key bottleneck machines for each cell, rather than every machine in a cell. Hence, the process of preparing a capacity feasible MPS for a GT system is considerably simplified.

Materials Requirements Planning GT leads to shorter, more predictable lead times by reducing queueing, setup, and processing time. Along with the simplified capacity check in the MPS, this yields more reliable time-phased demands. Since major setups are family dependent, an argument can be made for lot sizing by families rather than parts. In terms of capacity checks, capacity requirements planning (CRP) is typically used in conjunction with an MRP system. As with the MPS, the use of a key machine concept would greatly simplify the preparation of these capacity plans and make finite loading a possibility. If loads on the key machines are feasible, the MRP plan can be finalized.

Job Scheduling JS is one of the most complex functions in a job shop. With the implementation of GT, the JS function is greatly simplified for several reasons. First, GT tends to introduce more rigid, flow-oriented systems. Hence, the JS function is greatly simplified and focuses on developing schedules for small flowlines rather than a complex job shop. Second, creating part families that require a major setup when a change between families takes place, leads to the creation of a two-level scheduling problem. Initially, we need to develop a sequence for part families, and subsequently for jobs within each family. This also reduces the size of the scheduling problem considerably. Finally, the implementation of GT will create a more transparent and highly visible manufacturing process, which can be monitored easily. This should also lead to easier scheduling and processing of jobs within a GT system. A more technical approach to JS is given below in the section titled, "Group Operation."

The changes in the planning and execution systems required on implementation of GT are substantial. In general, each function will be greatly simplified. However, changes will have to be made in the way each of the systems is managed as well as in the methods by which tasks are carried out.

Human Resources Systems   The implementation of GT has several implications for the human resource and personnel systems. There are social benefits—increased worker satisfaction, autonomy and job enrichment, increased output quantity and quality—but they can be difficult to achieve. Resistance to change, lack of top management commitment, trade union opposition, and continued use of traditional performance measures and incentive wage schemes can all restrict improvements. To avoid these pitfalls, focus on education and training, introduce new performance evaluation systems, and develop appropriate wage incentive plans.

The implementation of GT must be simultaneously accompanied by an education and retraining of workers in the shop. The education aspect focuses on showing the commitment of top management to the new system. Education also informs the workers and design engineers that GT will not lead to an elimination of jobs; rather, it has the potential to increase worker satisfaction and reduce frustration. This education could decrease the resistance to change present at many levels and even inspire workers to help lead the change. Retraining of the workers is also necessary since each worker will normally be required to operate more than one machine. Union opposition may decrease as top management shows the willingness to expend resources to increase worker skills. Finally, the

education and retraining may also be necessary at middle management levels (e.g., planning staff), since duties and responsibilities will also change for personnel in these positions.

GT represents a different way of planning manufacturing and hence, traditional performance evaluation systems may be inappropriate. A new performance evaluation system may be required. The following two examples illustrate the necessity of introducing new evaluation systems when GT is implemented.

In the first case, we examine the corporate infatuation with equipment utilization. Typically, foremen stockpile orders to accomplish their assigned goal of "keeping machines busy." Thus, there is an incentive to import work from other groups so as to increase loads. The true objective is, however, to meet customer due dates. With GT, total workload should decrease due to a reduction in setup times, and workload imbalances could result due to the assignment of certain machine types in multiple groups. This should not constitute a problem as long as additional machines are not required. Hence, the foremen evaluation system should be changed from one based on equipment utilization for a cell to how well due dates are met with quality parts. A second criterion should be that of minimizing resource usage, the relevant resources being labor, machine time, and work-in-process.

A second example is in the area of designers' performance evaluations. Before GT was implemented, the performance evaluation of designers was most likely based on the number of new drawings produced. However, this is contradictory to the basic design objective in GT, where we want to enhance design standardization and thus reduce the number of distinct part drawings. Thus, the evaluation mechanism for such personnel needs to be changed so as to make a success of the GT implementation.

In summary, the performance evaluation systems for the organization need to be restructured to reflect the GT system objectives, since use of traditional, suboptimal objectives may be self-defeating.

Incentive wage schemes are affected by GT. Such systems normally include a base wage plus a bonus share. The bonus share is based on a combination of quantity and quality. Quantity may be measured by a *Time Utilization Factor*, TUF, where

$$TUF = \frac{standard\ time(hours)\ +\ day\ work(hours)}{paid\ time\ (hours)}$$

Standard time is obtained by dividing period production by standard time per unit. Day work corresponds to time spent on activities without standards. Quality can be obtained by sampling units produced. Units can be rated as *Corresponding* for good items, *Minor Defect* for items which, while not of desired quality are functionally acceptable, and *Major Defect* for rejected items. More than three levels may be used where appropriate. A weighting factor scheme such as four points for Corresponding, two for Minor Defect, and zero for Major Defect is then applied to each item. Averaging the factor over the units sampled yields a *Quality Value* (QV) for the period. A table or graph should then be provided for determining a bonus share rate as a function of TUF and QV. It is important that the group be provided with the training and responsibility to control and constantly improve processes. The bonus share rate table should remain fixed as quality improves. This provides continual motivation for quality improvement and positive feedback in the form of increased wages.

Technically, the above scheme may be applied on either an individual or group basis. Application on a group basis is strongly advised. Setting of group goals is an essential feature of successful GT. Group level application promotes sharing of knowledge and group decision making. It is especially important when more than one worker touches the part while in the group. If workers carry parts through the entire cell, or demand fluctuations force worker movement in and out of the group, analysis may be performed on an individual basis.

Based on this discussion it is clear that several changes in the human resource systems are required when GT is implemented. Education and retraining programs, new performance evaluation systems, and more appropriate incentive wage schemes all need to be developed to ensure that the implementation of GT is successful.

Control and Information Systems The implementation of GT also has an impact on the control and information systems that monitor and update all the activities in manufacturing. The quality control system should be designed to measure quality on an individual cell basis. While individual processes or machines will still be monitored, quality is a cell responsibility. This approach helps avoid propagation of errors. Appropriate checks and procedures can be developed for each part family. Poor quality items can simply be reworked in the same cell.

It is possible that the implementation of GT may lead to an initial decrease in overall quality since workers are expected to operate more than one machine type. However, once the workers familiarize themselves with the new equipment, there should be an increase in quality of output for each cell.

The information systems that will contribute to a successful implementation of GT focus on more than just a coding and classification system. Parts previously identified with processes now need to be oriented with groups. Machines also are no longer organized functionally, and thus, they should also be associated with manufacturing cells. In flow-line GT cells, shop loading is based on total cell utilization, not on individual processes. The most heavily utilized machine represents the relevant load factor for the cell. Within other cells, loading on individual processes is important, but all the processes must be simultaneously considered. Finally, group lead times are more important than process and individual part lead times. Thus, the shop information systems should be modified to reflect the new orientation on part groups and machine cells, rather than individual jobs and processes.

In this section we have outlined the impact of GT implementation on the important functions of product and process design, human resource management, control, and information management. As noted, major changes in each of these functions ensure that the implementation of GT is successful. We now proceed to discuss changes in organizational structure that are required when GT is implemented.

Organizational Structure and GT

The implementation of GT requires a substantial change in the organizational structure of the manufacturing function. Essentially, this involves changing the organization structure to reflect group-based responsibility rather than functional responsibility. The GT implementation may also require a reconfiguring of the organizational structure based on the type of objectives (i.e., short term versus long term) that are to be focused on by different functional areas. In this section, we discuss the types of modifications in structure that took place in two companies due to an implementation of GT. In the first case, the reorganization was in the manufacturing organization as a whole and especially middle level management, while in the second case, the restructuring focused on the operational organization and especially supervisors and foremen.

The first case focuses on an English company manufacturing friction linings (Connolly and Sabberwal 1971). The previous manufacturing organizational structure for this company was organized along functional lines (see Panel A; FIG. 19-15). Essentially, the functions of work study, materials control, production planning, manufacturing, quality control, and maintenance were all separately supervised. Although conflicts between these areas existed before GT, they intensified when GT was implemented. For example, although the production planning department was responsible for quoting due dates, it had no control over the manufacturing and maintenance functions; similarly, the production department supervisor had no control over the materials inputs needed. Hence, if the current structure is maintained, it is likely to lead to an unsuccessful GT implementation. However, the

company recognized this problem and a new structure was developed (see Panel B; FIG. 19-15). Consequently, all the direct manufacturing functions were coordinated better. This new structure for the organization has three distinct functional divisions with the following responsibilities:

- Works Administration—This department is responsible for preparing the operating budget, controlling labor and materials usage, planning plant capacity, liaison with the sales departments, and planning staff development programs.
- Quality Assurance—The responsibilities of this department include the control of raw materials and product quality, the investigation of customer complaints, as well as setting quality standards.
- Works Management—All the other functions (materials control, planning, manufacturing and equipment maintenance) are the responsibility of this department.

The second illustration focuses on the reorganization of the machining function of the Naval Avionics Center (NAC) at Indianapolis (Allison and Vapor 1979). The machining center at NAC processed a large number of different parts in small batches. The previous organization structure (see Panel A; FIG. 19-16) had seven foremen, each responsible for a group of similar machines. Once GT cells were established (five cells with approximately 16 workers each), one foreman was assigned to control each cell (see Panel B; FIG. 19-16). Hence, control at the operational level was completely decentralized and each cell was the responsibility of a different foreman who reported to the general foreman.

These two examples have outlined the restructuring of the organization that must take place at the middle management level as well as at the operational level when GT is implemented. In general, it is advisable to decentralize and assign as much responsibility as possible to the cell. Above these cells is an umbrella organization, which coordinates the timing and assignment of work to the cells and maintains an integrated information and planning system. The success of GT is also dependent on the type of organization structure that is in place.

facility. We then discuss operative issues, such as selecting batch sizes and sequencing.

GROUP OPERATION

After designing and installing cells, the system must be operated on a continuing basis. We begin with a brief discussion on the physical layout of the

Machine Layout

The location of machines within the manufacturing facility depends on the use of a GT flowline, GT cell, or logical GT center system. The three

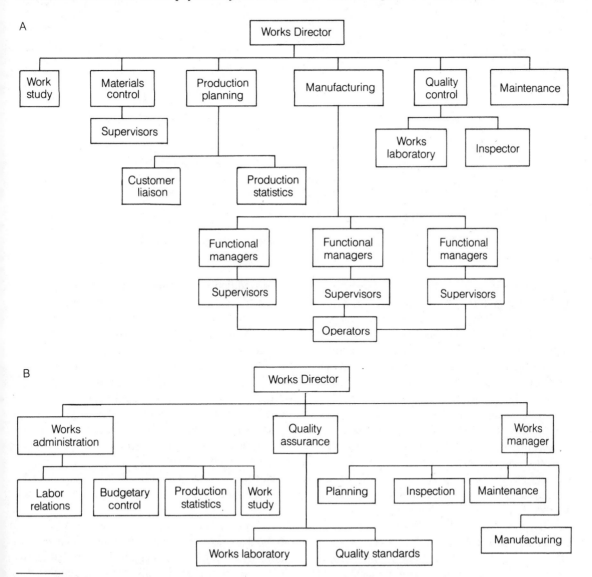

Source: Connolly, R. and A.J.P. Sabberwal, "Management structure for the Implementation of Group Technology," *CIRP Annals*, 19, 159-169.

Fig. 19-15. Old (A) and proposed (B) organization structures.

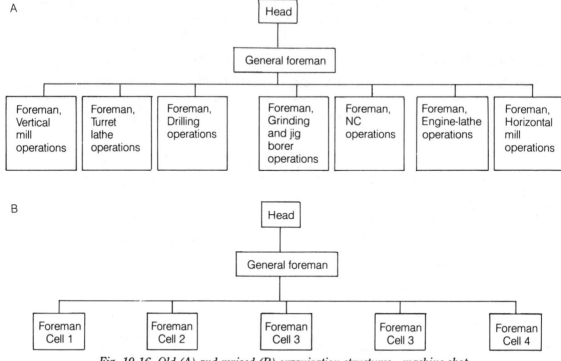

Fig. 19-16. Old (A) and revised (B) organization structures—machine shop.

systems are depicted in FIG. 19-17. The choice of system depends on the degree of commonality between the routings of components within the group. Flowlines are configured as in assembly or transfer line product layouts. They are used when family components share the same route and place relatively equal workloads on each machine. Flowlines have unidirectional flow.

When components require different routes or loops within a group, GT cell configurations are used. Most movement is within the group, but the material handling system must be able to connect all pairs of machines and not just adjacent machines. The layout of machines within each group should be handled as a separate facility layout problem using traditional approaches. The relative layout or positioning of groups can then be handled in a like fashion. In the within-group layout problem, the decision is based on flows between machines. The between-group problem uses only the flows of exceptional components that visit multiple groups.

The traditional-layout problem can be treated as a quadratic assignment problem or that of finding the rectangular dual of a maximally weighted planar graph. Both approaches have advantages and disadvantages.

No complete, optimal procedure exists for real sized problems. A popular approach treats each group in the between-group layout problem, or machine in the within-group problem, as a rectangular block. Rectangle size and shape are in accordance with the physical group. An initial block design is constructed arbitrarily. Pairwise exchanges of rectangles are made to reduce the sum of group interactions multiplied by intergroup distances.

The GT center is the weakest form of GT and resembles a process-based job shop. This system does differ from traditional job shops in that all the components within a family are assigned to the same machine in each center. Nonetheless, components travel to many centers. Standard layout tech-

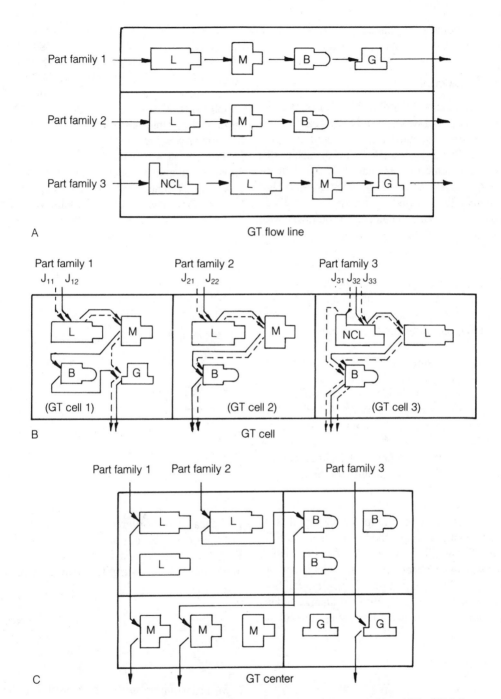

A   GT flow line

B   GT cell

C   GT center

Key L: Lathe; M: Milling machine; G: Grinding machine; B: Boring machine; NCL: NC lathe.

Source: Ham et al. (1979), courtesy of Kluwer-Nijhoff Publishing.

Fig. 19-17. Group technology layout alternatives.

niques can be applied in this case. Process groups constitute the departments to be located.

Batch Sequencing

The sequencing of orders in a GT system is structured to take advantage of family setups. The sequencing decision must interface with the production scheduling system. GT can be used with material requirements planning (MRP), Just-in-Time (JIT), OPT, or other scheduling system. Due to the longer time periods typically used in MRP, GT may offer greater scheduling advantages with MRP than with JIT. In either case, the process is similar. The production schedule determines the set of components to be produced during the next period. GT dictates the order in which the components will be run. Upon setting up for a family, all components in that family scheduled for the period will be run before switching to any components not in the family.

It is often advantageous to use a rotation cycle or base period system. The optimal family cycle (time between orders) is set for each family at T_f. The family is run every T_f periods. Actual production of each component in the family is set to cover demand for the next T_f time units. This process maximizes the savings effect from family setups. The selection of T_f is discussed in the next section of this chapter.

Given the set of component parts to be produced for each family in the upcoming period, several traditional job shop scheduling results can be modified to the GT environment. Assume that F families will be produced and family f has n_f components to run. Family setup time is S_f. Item i in family f has combined minor setup (to change tooling adaptor for instance) and processing time of p_{fi}. Family production time is then

$$P_f = \sum_{i=1}^{n_f} p_{fi}$$

Our objective is to minimize average flow time. Flow time for a job is the length of time from the start of the period to the completion of that job.

Consider first the case of a single machine, or the entire group is considered as a single processor with setup and production times computed accordingly. Let job fi have weight w_{fi}. Larger weights imply greater significance. Weights may be based on job value, due dates, customer importance, or other factor. Unless specific justification exists to the contrary, set all weights to 1. Mean (weighted) flow time is then minimized by ordering jobs within families by nondecreasing weighted machine utilization time. A similar ordering then applies to families. Algebraically, the result for jobs within families is

$$\frac{P_{f[1]}}{w_{f[1]}} \leq \ldots \leq \frac{P_{f[i]}}{w_{f[i]}} \leq \ldots \leq \frac{P_{f[n_f]}}{w_{f[n_f]}},$$

$$f = 1, \ldots, F \qquad (19\text{-}22)$$

and for families

$$\frac{S_{[1]} + P_{[1]}}{\displaystyle\sum_{j=1}^{n^{[1]}} w_{[1][j]}} \leq \ldots \leq \frac{S_{[f]} + P_{[f]}}{\displaystyle\sum_{j=1}^{n_{[f]}} w_{[f][j]}}$$

$$\leq \ldots \leq \frac{S_{[F]} + P_{[F]}}{\displaystyle\sum_{j=1}^{n_{[f]}} w_{[F][j]}}$$

[ ] indicates the ordered jobs and families. As an example consider the set of jobs in TABLE 19-10. Family 1 requires six units of time for family setup and family 2 requires eight. Family 2 will go first as

$$\frac{S_2 + P_2}{\displaystyle\sum_{j=1}^{3} w_{2j}} = \frac{8 + 44}{4} \leq \frac{S_1 + P_1}{\displaystyle\sum_{j=1}^{2} w_{1j}} = \frac{6 + 30}{2}$$

If we order within groups by weighted processing plus minor setup time, we obtain the schedule illustrated in the Gantt Chart shown in FIG. 19-18.

This discussion assumed that setup times were sequence independent. If this is not the case,

Table 19-10. Single Machine Scheduling in Group Technology.

Job	Family	Processing Time	Setup Time	Weight	Item Cost	Annual Demand
11	F1	10	1	1	-	-
12	F1	18	1	1	-	-
21	F2	15	1	1	100	1000
22	F2	5	2	2	50	1000
23	F2	20	1	1	70	500

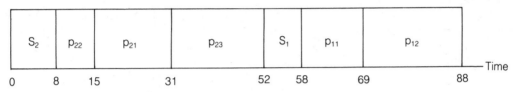

Fig. 19-18. Gantt chart for scheduling example.

changeovers become a traveling salesman problem and should be treated accordingly. In the traveling salesman problem a salesman must choose a sequence in which to visit n cities and return home. The objective is to minimize the sum of travel time (distance, cost) between adjacent cities. In our job scheduling minimizing total setup becomes the objective.

Ham et al. (1985) discuss extensions to k-machine flowlines. The extensions are based on Johnson's algorithm for two machine scheduling. The k-machine line is divided into two half lines with $(k/2)$ machines each. If $(k/2)$ is odd, the middle machine is assigned to the first half line. Total family setup and job processing times are computed treating the half line as a single machine: use the sum over all machines in the half line of setup plus processing time.

For F groups, we then apply Johnson's algorithm $F+1$ times; once to order families and once for each family to order jobs within the family. Johnson's algorithm assigns jobs iteratively. Selected jobs are added to one of two ordered lists. After all jobs are assigned, the *end* list is appended to the end of the *beginning* list to create the sequence. To construct the lists, at each iteration the unassigned job with the smallest processing time is selected. If this processing time is on

machine 1, the job is added to the rear of the *beginning* list; if the processing time is on machine 2, the job is assigned to the front of the *end* list. The first job selected is thus either permanently first or last in the sequence. The beginning and end lists move toward each other as jobs are sequentially placed.

In machining environments, processing time is determined by the cutting speed selected. Production engineering models can be used to determine the maximum production rate and minimum cost per piece cutting speeds. To select actual speeds, first determine if use of the maximum production rate speed will satisfy the demand schedule. If not, use these speeds, recognizing that the last parts will be late. If the maximum production rate speed yields slack time, the speeds may be uniformly reduced until the minimum cost speed, or a time capacity constraint, is reached for any machine stage. If all jobs can be completed on time using the minimum cost speed, then use this speed.

Batch Sizing

Reduced setup times have been noted as a major advantage of GT. Traditional batch sizing techniques are based on the assumption of a significant setup time. Static demand is often assumed and units are produced to stock. These methods may not apply in GT environments. In GT we would like to produce to exact, dynamic period demands, this being made possible in large part by the elimination of costly setups. As setup cost approaches zero, batch size approaches one.

We can develop modified batch sizing expressions for GT. Inferences on batch size strategies can then be drawn given relative sizes of parameters. A cell will be allowed to contain several families of part types. As in the previous section, a family has the advantage of being able to share a common setup, with perhaps an additional minor setup required for each operation of specific part types. We will determine the desired frequency for setting up product families. Individual part type i will be produced every z_i of its family's cycles. Our notation is as follows:

A_{fr} = cost of family f common setup on machine r (dollars)

a_{ij} = setup cost for part i operation j on machine

$$m \ (ij), \ a_i = \sum_{j=1}^{J_i} a_{ij} \ \text{(dollars)}$$

C_i = value of a finished part type i composed of raw materials M and value added V dollars

C_i' = average value of in-process part type i, $M + V/2$ (dollars)

D_i = demand for part type i (units/time)

h = inventory carrying cost rate (percent/time)

i = 1,..., N index for part types

j = 1,..., J_i index for operations on part type i

K_f = set of machines used by at least one family f part

m_{ij} = unit variable processing time for part i operation j,

$$m_i = \sum_{j=1}^{J_i} m_{ij}, \ \text{(time)}$$

Θ_f = set of parts in family f

Q_i = batch size for part type i, a decision variable (units)

S_{fr} = setup time for family f on machine r (time)

s_{ij} = setup time for part i operation j,

$$s_i = \sum_{j=1}^{J_i} s_{ij}, \ \text{(time)}$$

T_f = base period for family f, a decision variable (time)

W = factor for flow time as a multiple of setup + processing time. A value of 3 would indicate a system with one batch in operation, one batch in input queue, and one batch in output queue or being transferred to the next machine at arbitrary times

z_i = relative production frequency for part i, an integer decision variable

Consider one cell. Each family will be set up and run on a rotating basis. A basic economic batch sizing model for family f is

$$\textit{Minimize E (cost/time)} = T_f^{-1} \sum_{r \epsilon K_f} A_{fr} + T_f^{-1} \sum_{i \epsilon \Theta_f} \frac{a_i}{z_i}$$
$$(19\text{-}24)$$

$$+ \frac{h}{2} \sum_{i \epsilon \Theta_f} z_i D_i T_f C_i + h \sum_{i \epsilon \Theta_f} D_i C_i' \Big[s_i + m_i z_i D_i T_f \Big] W$$

Equation 19-24 includes terms for family setup, operation setup for individual part types, cycle inventory holding cost, and WIP holding cost. The assumption is for a GT cell in which parts are moved in batches between machines. In the case of GT flowlines the WIP holding cost is reduced and equation 19-25 should replace the last term in 19-24. The flowline adjustment acknowledges that parts move almost instantaneously between machines and do not wait for the entire batch.

$$h\sum_{i\epsilon\Theta_f} D_i C_i' m_i + h\sum_{i\epsilon\Theta_f} C_i' s_i \qquad (19\text{-}25)$$

Differentiating the above expressions we can show that the optimal cycle time for family f within the GT cell is

$$T_f = \left[\frac{\sum_{r\epsilon K_f} A_{fr} + \sum_{i\epsilon\Theta_f} \dfrac{a_i}{z_i}}{h\sum_{i\epsilon\Theta_f} z_i D_i \left(\dfrac{C_i}{2} + m_i D_i C_i W \right)} \right]^{1/2} \qquad (19\text{-}26)$$

and for flowlines we obtain

$$T_f = \left[\frac{\sum_{r\epsilon K_f} A_{fr} + \sum_{i\epsilon\Theta_f} \dfrac{a_i}{z_i}}{\dfrac{h}{2}\sum_{i\epsilon\Theta_f} z_i D_i C_i} \right]^{1/2} \qquad (19\text{-}27)$$

In either case, the *average* batch size is given by

$$Q_i = z_i T_f D_i$$

We emphasize that actual batch sizes will vary with the dynamics of demand. Each batch will be sized to cover expected usage during the next $z_i T_f$ time periods. In many cases products within a family have similar operation setup costs and demands. In this case all $z_i = 1$ and we can apply equations 19-26 and 19-27 directly. If this is not the case, we need z_i values prior to solving the above expressions. One approach is to use the natural relative frequencies. For all part types $i\epsilon\Theta_f$ compute $z_i' = (a_i/D_i C_i)^{1/2}$. Find the part type i^* with minimum z_i' and set $z_{i^*} = 1$ for this part. For all others,

$$z_i' = \left[\frac{z_i'}{z_i^*} \right]$$

where [ ] indicates rounding to the nearest integer.

As an example, reconsider family F2 of TABLE 19-10. We will assume jobs now represent part types and let setup costs be the labor rate of 10 dol-

lars/hour times the setup time. The holding cost rate is 40 percent/year. Natural item cycle times $(a_i/D_i C_i)^{1/2}$ are (0.01, 0.02, 0.017) respectively for the three family items. Setting the frequency (z_1) for the smallest relative cycle time to 1, this translates to relative production frequencies of (z_1, z_2, z_3) = (1, 2, 2). For a flowline process we obtain

$$T_f = \left[\frac{A_{fr} + \sum_i \dfrac{a_i}{z_i}}{\dfrac{h}{2}\sum_i z_i D_i C_i} \right]^{1/2}$$

$$= \left[\frac{80 + 10 + \dfrac{202010}{2\ 2\ 2}}{\dfrac{0.4}{2}\,[(1000^* \ 100) + (2^*1000^*50) + (2^*500^*70)]} \right]^{1/2}$$

$$= 0.044 \ years$$

Thus, part type 21 is produced every 0.044 years, and part types 22 and 23 every 0.088 years.

The above discussion implicitly assumes sufficient resources are available; groups may be scheduled to accommodate desired cycle times. Two relevant exceptions should be noted. First, capacity may be constraining. If available time on any machine is exceeded, T_f values must be increased. As processing time is fixed by demand, only setup time varies. Increasingly, T_f reduces the proportion of time spent in setup. If a bottleneck machine exists, a single constraint problem can be formulated to ensure that the proportion of time the bottleneck machine is required for setup and processing does not exceed one. The constraint includes family and item setup on the bottleneck machine. Let ϕ_r be the proportion of time available for setup on the bottleneck machine and $j(r)$ indicate an operation performed on machine r; then we require

$$\sum_{f=1}^{F} \frac{S_{fr} + \sum_{i\epsilon\Theta_f} \dfrac{S_{ij(r)}}{z_i}}{T_f} \le \phi_r \qquad (19\text{-}28)$$

The constraint (19-28) binds the T_f decisions together and can be solved by a Lagrangian multiplier approach. Second, once staffing levels are set, labor cost is fixed. It is prudent then to minimize inventory by using remaining time for setups. Let S^* be the time available during the period for setups. We will sequentially set up and run families $f = 1,\ldots, F$. Our policy will be to modify all T_f by $T_f^* = ZT_f$ such that total setup time required is S^*. This problem is easily solved. If S is the time required for setups using T_f family cycle times, then $Z = (S/S^*)$.

Equations 19-26 and 19-27 allow several observations. If the cell (or flowline) is assigned only one family of part types, then the family setup term (ΣA_{fk}) most likely is zero; no setup cost is incrementally incurred when the family is run. By assumption, the a_i terms are small or parts would not belong to the family. Thus, in this case, cycle time becomes very small. We basically have an economic justification for a dynamic make to order philosophy. The second observation compares the GT cell to the flowline setup. Unless batch sizes are one for both systems, the flowline approach of splitting lots instead of batch material movement results in strictly larger batch sizes. Throughput time in flowlines is independent of batch size. Lower WIP levels are obtained, allowing longer run lengths and less time spent in setup.

This entire section has thus far assumed demand is continuous. Suppose, on the other hand, demand is in the form of intermittent batch due dates. As before, the ideal situation occurs when setup time is minimal, as when there is only one family per group. In this case we can schedule to minimize inventory. Batch sizes are set equal to individual order requirements. Batches are released to the cell as near as possible to the due date minus cell lead time. Potential conflicts of batches requesting simultaneous processing are handled by issuing the prior batch earlier to maintain the integrity of all due dates.

REFERENCES

Allison, J. W. and J. Curt Vapor. "GT Approach Proves Out." *American Machinist* (February 1979): 86-89.

Askin, Ronald G. and Simon Chiu. "A Graph Partitioning Procedure for Machine Assignment and Cell Formation in Group Technology." *International Journal of Production Research*, to be published in 1990.

Askin, Ronald G. and Subramanian P. Subramanian. "A Cost-Based Heuristic for Group Technology Configuration." *International Journal of Production Research* 25 (1987): 101-113.

Boucher, T. O., "Lot Sizing in Group Technology Production Systems." *International Journal of Production Research* 22 (1984): 85.

Boucher, Thomas O. and John A. Muckstadt. "Cost Estimating Methods for Evaluating the Conversion from a Functional Manufacturing Layout to Group Technology." *IIIE Transactions* 17 (1985): 268-276.

Burbidge, J. L. *Group Technology in the Engineering Industry*. London: Mechanical Engineering Publications Ltd., 1979.

————. *Introduction to Group Technology* New York: Halsted Press, 1975.

————. "Production Flow Analysis." *The Production Engineer* (1971): 139-151.

Choobineh, F. "A Framework for the Design of Cellular Manufacturing Systems." *International Journal of Production Research* 26 (1988): 1161-1172.

Connolly, R. and A. J. P. Sabberwal. "Management Structure for the Implementation of Group Technology." *Annals of the CIRP* 19 (1971): 159-169.

Gallagher, C. C. and W. A. Knight. *Group Technology Production Methods in Manufacture*. New York: Halsted Press, John Wiley & Sons, Inc., 1986.

Gombinski, J. "The Brisch Classification and Group Technology." *Proceedings of the Conference on Group Technology*. Turin, Italy: Turin Center of the International Labor Organization, 1969.

Ham, Inyong, Katsundo Hitomi, and Teruhiko Yoshida. *Group Technology: Applications to Production Management*. Boston: Kluwer-Nijhoff Publishing, 1985.

Ham, I. and D. L. Shunk. "Group Technology Survey Results related to the I-CAM Program." SME Technical Paper MS79-348. Presented at the CASA conference, Dearborn, Michigan, 1979.

Houtzeel, A. and C. S. Brown. "A Management Overview of Group Technology." In *Group Technology At Work*, edited by N. L. Hyer. Dearborn, Michigan: Society of Manufacturing Engineers, 1984.

Hyde, W. F. *Improving Productivity by Classification, Coding and Data Base Standardization*. New York: Marcel Dekker, Inc., 1981.

Hyer, N. L. "The Potential of Group Technology for U.S. Manufacturing." *Journal of Operations Management* 4: 3 (1984): 183-202.

Hyer, N. L. and U. Wemmerlov. "Group Technology Oriented Coded Systems: Structures, Applications and Implementation." *Production and Inventory Management* 26: 2 (1985): 55-78.

_____. "Group Technology in U.S. Manufacturing Industry: A Survey of Current Practices." *International Journal of Production Research*, 1988.

_____. "MRP/GT: A Framework for Production Planning and Control of Cellular Manufacturing," *Decision Sciences*, 13 (1982): 681-701.

Ivanov, E. K. *Group Production Organization and Technology* translated by E. Bishop. London: Business Publications Limited, 1968.

Kernighan, B. W. and S. Lin. "An Efficient Heuristic Procedure for Partitioning Graphs." In *The Bell System Technical Journal* (1970): 291-307.

King, J. R. "Machine Component Grouping in Production Flow Analysis: An Approach Using a Rank Order Clustering Algorithm." *International Journal of Production Research* 18 (1980): 213-232.

Kumar, K. Ravi, Andrew Kusiak, and Anthony Vannelli. "Grouping of Parts and Components in Flexible Manufacturing Systems." *European Journal of Operational Research* 24 (1986): 387-397.

Kusiak, Andrew. "The Generalized Group Technology Concept." *International Journal of Production Research* 25 (1987): 561-569.

McAuley, J. "Machine Grouping for Efficient Production." *Production Engineer* 51 (1972): 53.

Opitz, H. *A Classification System to Describe Workpieces*. Oxford, U.K.: Permagon Press, 1970.

Pullen, R. D. "A Survey of Cellular Manufacturing Cells." In *Group Technology At Work*, edited by N. L. Hyer. Dearborn, Michigan: Society of Manufacturing Engineers, 1984.

Rajagapolan, R. and J. Batra. "Design of Cellular Production Systems—A Graph Theoretic Approach." *International Journal of Production Research* 24 (1975): 1255-1266.

Ranson, G. M. *Group Technology*. New York: McGraw-Hill, 1972.

Vakharia, A. J. "Methods of Cell Formation in Group Technology: A Framework for Evaluation," *Journal of Operations Management*, 6 (3) (1986): 257–272.

Vakharia, A. J. and Y. L. Chang. "A Simulated Annealing Approach to Scheduling a Manufacturing Cell." *Naval Research Logistics*, forthcoming.

Vakharia, A. J. and U. Wemmerlöv. "Designing a Cellular Manufacturing System: A Materials Flow Approach Based on Operation Sequences." *IIE Transactions*, 22 (1) (1990): 84–97.

Wemmerlöv, U. and N. L. Hyer. "Cellular Manufacturing in the U.S. Industry: A Survey of Users." *International Journal of Production Research*, 1988.

Wemmerlöv, U. and A. J. Vakharia. "Job and Family Scheduling of a Flow-Line Manufacturing Cell: A Simulation Study." *IIE Transactions, forthcoming.*

Wu, H. L., R. Venugopal, and M. M. Barash. "Design of a Cellular Manufacturing System: A Syntactic Pattern Recognition Approach." Journal of Manufacturing Systems 5 (1986): 81-87.

20

Computer-Aided Process Planning

Tien-Chien Chang[*]
Sanjay Joshi[**]

PROCESS PLANNING IS A VITAL FUNCTION IN MANU-
facturing. It can be defined in general terms as
"the act of preparing a detailed plan for production
of a piece part or assembly." The detailed plan contains the route, processes, process parameters,
machines, and tools required for production. It is
said that without a process plan, machining cannot
be performed; without machining, products cannot
be produced. Process planning is important in two
aspects. First, it is essential for production; and
second, it determines the efficiency of production.
A poor process plan may require excess labor and
resources and may produce unnecessary scrap.

INTRODUCTION TO PROCESS PLANNING

The process planning functions in an industry
involve several or all of the following activities:

- Selecting machining operations
- Sequencing machining operations
- Selecting machine tools
- Selecting cutting tools
- Determining setup requirements
- Calculating cutting parameters
- Planning tool path and generating Numerical
  Control (NC) part programs
- Designing jigs and fixtures

The degree of detail incorporated into a typical
process plan usually varies from industry to industry. It depends on the type of parts, production
methods, and documentation needs. A process plan
for a tool room type manufacturing environment
typically relies on the experience of the machinist
and does not have to be any great detail. In fact,
"make as per part print" may even suffice. In the

---

[*]Dr. Chang is an associate professor in the School of Industrial Engineering at Purdue University. He received his master's and
Ph.D. degrees from Virginia Polytechnic Institute and State University and his BSIE degree from Chung Yuan University. He had
several Summer appointments with Zenith Corporation, National Bureau of Standards, and General Motors. His research interests
are in the area of manufacturing automation. His current research activities include automated/intelligent process planning, manufacturing systems integration, and automated assembly planning. Dr. Chang has coauthored four books, seven book chapters, and
more than 40 technical papers published in refereed journals and conferences. He is a coauthor of the first book on automated
process planning.

[**]Dr. Joshi is an assistant professor in the Department of Industrial and Management Systems Engineering at The Pennsylvania
State University. He received his Ph.D. from Purdue University, MS from SUNY at Buffalo (both in Industrial Engineering), and BS
in Production Engineering from the University of Bombay, India. His research interests are in the area of Computer Integrated
Manufacturing. Current research activities include CAD integration with process planning, design and control of flexible manufacturing systems, and product design for manufacturability.

automobile industry and other typical mass production type industries, the process planning activity is embodied in the hard automation: transfer and flow lines used for manufacturing component parts and assembly. For metal forming type of manufacturing activities such as forging, stamping, die casting, sand casting, and injection molding, the process planning requirements are embedded directly into the design of the die/mold used, and most process planning activity is fairly simple. The job shop type of manufacturing environment usually requires the most detailed process plans since the design of tools, jigs and fixtures, and manufacturing sequence etc., are dictated directly by the process plan. FIGURE 20-1 shows an example of a process plan.

CIMTELLIGENCE

```
|=====================================================================|
|                CIMTELLIGENCE GROUP TECHNOLOGY SYSTEM                |
|=====================================================================|
| Part Number     | Part Description     | Dwg Rev | Pln Rev| Qty     |
| PC160           | SHAFT, ROTOR         |   A     |   A    | 30      |
|-----------------|----------------------|---------|--------|---------|
| Next Assembly   | Raw Material Type    | Material          | Cost    |
| PC960           | CASTING              | CARBON STEEL      | 165.00  |
|-----------------|-----------------------------|-------------------|---------|
| Diameter| Approval          Date. | Project           | Source  |
| 3.203   | Eng.  B. MALONE   06/01/86 | A-14 CONVERTOR    |   M     |
| Length  | Mfg.  K. PRENDERGAST 06/06/86 |-------------------------|
| 12.058  | Prod. C. BARRIER  06/12/86 | Document Location       |
| Width   | Q/A.  C. LOWE     06/30/86 | ON-LINE CADDS           |
|         |---------------------------|-------------------------------|
| Height  | Design Specifications/Remarks | Mfg. Specifications/Remarks|
|         | SHEAR SECTION             | PROTECT GROUND BEARING SURFACE|
| Thkness | 1416 IN. LBS MIN. 1572 MAX|                               |
|         |                           |                               |
|---------------------------------------------------------------------|
|=======================  CYLINDRICAL PARTS ATTRIBUTES ================
Group: POWER_COMPONENTS                    Family: SHAFT
View:                                      Features:
=====================================================================
Material: CARBON STEEL          Raw Material Type: CASTING

No. OD's:  4      Largest OD:  3.203    Length:  12.058   Best Finish: 32

No. ID's:  1               Largest ID: .5            Tightest Tol.:  .0005
=====================================================================
Taper/Cone/Profile (Y/N)  N           Off Center Turned Shape (Y/N)  N
Positional Tol. < or = .002" (Y/N) Y  Geometric Tol. < or = .001 (Y/N) Y
=====================================================================
No. Tool | Total | Para | Perp | Skewed | Surface Treatment   (Y/N)  Y
   Axes  |   2   |  1   |  1   |        | Heat Treatment      (Y/N)  Y
=====================================================================
Features |      | Slots | Grooves | Threads | Chamfers | Holes | Tapped | Flats
Y/N)     | OD   |   N   |    N    |    N    |    Y     |   Y   |   Y    |   N
         |------|-------|---------|---------|----------|---------------------
         | ID   |   N   |    N    |    N    |    N     |
         |------|-------|---------|---------|----------|---------------------
         |FACE  |   N   |    N    | Bolt Circle  Y     |   Y   |   N    |   N
         |---------------------------------------------------------------
```

Fig. 20-1. Example of a process plan

```
Part_number: PC160
```

```
Seq.| Dept. | Wrk Cent. | Operation Name                          |Set Up |Run Time
----  -----   ---------   -------------------------------------   -------  -------
0010  102A    STK-0000
```

RAW MATERIAL STORE

Operations Description

Issue Raw Casting Part Number PC-160-A per specified quantity

ENTER- DATA Shop order in to Mfg-Eng Computer

Operations Description

   PROCEDURE DTA: STORE-SO-DATA

```
Seq.| Dept. | Wrk Cent. | Operation Name                          |Set Up |Run Time
----  -----   ---------   -------------------------------------   -------  -------
0020  102B    BEN-0200
```

                    BENCH   .2   .08

Operations Description

Mark in area shown per sketch sheet.
   - Procedure *A33 Class *13 -

Sketch Sheet
----
*

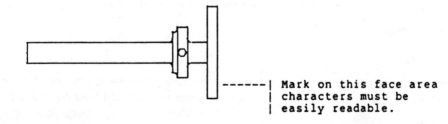

*

Fig. 20-1. Cont.

```
Part_number: PC160


Tool Number      | Qty  | Tool Description
---------------   -----   ----------------------------------------------------
STD                1      VIBRO PEN


Seq.| Dept. | Wrk Cent. | Operation Name                       |Set Up |Run Time
----  -----   --------    ----------------------------------    -------  -------
0030  312A    LTH-1000


                   LATHE                                          1.5     .3



                   Operations Description
-------------------------------------------------------------------------------
Rough turn cast 1.375 diameter to 1.235 + - .005 to flange shoulder allow
for .02 stock on shoulder face.  Face end of part to allow .02 stock overall
length.  Break Sharp Edges.


                   Sketch Sheet
-------------------------------------------------------------------------------
*


                 Rough Turn
            |--This Surface-----|
```

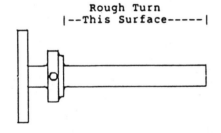

```
*

Seq.| Dept. | Wrk Cent. | Operation Name                       |Set Up |Run Time
----  -----   --------    ----------------------------------    -------  -------
                          COMMENTS

                   Operations Description
-------------------------------------------------------------------------------
         Parts must be handled with CARE during all operations
              Absolutely NO DAMAGE is permissible
```

(courtesy CIMTELLIGENCE).

Fig. 20-1. Cont.

In order to perform the process planning activities, a process planner must:

- Be able to understand and analyze part requirements

- Have extensive knowledge of machine tools and cutting tools and their capabilities
- Understand the interactions among the part, manufacturing, quality, and cost
- Possess analytical capabilities

The process planning activity has traditionally been experience-based and has been performed manually. According to a study (Houtzeel 1981), a typical process planner is a person 40 years of age, with long-term experience in the machine shop. This indicates that process planning is a job which requires a significant amount of experience. The study also points out that the U.S. needs about 200,000 to 300,000 process planners, but currently has only 150,000 to 200,000 available. A problem facing modern industry is the current lack of a skilled labor force to produce machined parts. Manual process planning also has other problems. Variability among the planner's judgment and experience can lead to differences in the perception of what constitutes the "optimal" or "best" method of production. This manifests itself in the fact that most industries have several different process plans for the same part, which leads to inconsistent plans and extra amounts of paperwork. Other problems in the manual process planning environment, such as introduction of new machine tools or temporary routing becoming permanent, and other changes in the environment make the process plans out of date.

The development of computer-aided process planning has been greatly influenced by the use of computers in manufacturing, and subsequent developments in NC and CAD. The development of NC machine tools in the 1950s and APT-like languages have eliminated some pressure on the machine operator requirement, and replaced the cumbersome cutter path instructions with computer generated NC codes. The process planner's task of creating the cutter programs was greatly reduced. However, the task of selecting processes and assigning machining parameters was still external to the NC program. The scope of NC has remained limited and does not incorporate the process planning functions. Automating process planning is an obvious way of eliminating this imbalance.

The developments of CAD since the mid 1960s have had a significant impact on the design activity. Since CAD systems provide the part geometry that could potentially be used to drive a process planning system, researchers have been trying to use process planning as a means to integrate the CAD and CAM functions. In fact, as we shall discuss later, process planning developments have kept pace with CAD technology, and are now beginning to dictate the requirements of a CAD system, since initial CAD systems were not designed for manufacturing in mind. The importance of computer-aided process planning as a means of integrating CAD and CAM, and the continued quest for an automated manufacturing environment has placed greater emphasis on automating the process planning function.

The idea of using computers in the process planning activity was discussed by Niebel (1965). Other early investigations on the feasibility of automated process planning were done at Purdue University (Scheck 1966, and Berra and Barash 1968). Many industries also started research efforts in this direction in the late 1960s and early 1970s. Early attempts to create automated planning systems consisted of building computer-assisted systems for report generation, storage, and retrieval. When used effectively, these systems saved up to 40 percent of a process planner's time. A typical example is Lockheed's CAP system (Tulkoff 1981). Such a system can by no means eliminate the process planning tasks; rather it helps to reduce the clerical work of the process planner.

However, recent developments in computer-aided process planning attempt to free the process planner from the planning process. Computer-aided process planning can eliminate many of the decisions required during planning. It has the following advantages:

- It reduces the demand on the skilled planner
- It reduces the process planning time
- It reduces both process planning and manufacturing cost
- It creates consistent plans
- It produces accurate plans
- It increases productivity

Several industries have benefited from computer-aided process planning systems (Vogel and Adlard 1981, Tulkoff 1981, Dunn and Mann 1978,

Kotler 1980). Such systems can reduce planning time from days to hours, and can result in large cost savings. The section in this chapter titled "Survey of Industrial Usage of CAPP Systems" discusses these benefits.

APPROACHES TO COMPUTER-AIDED PROCESS PLANNING

There are two basic approaches to computer-aided process planning: variant and generative. The variant approach as signified by the terminology uses the computer to retrieve plans for similar components using table look-up procedures, and the process planner then edits the plan to create a *variant* to suit the specific requirements of the component being planned. Creation and modification of standard plans are the process planner's responsibility.

The generative approach is based on generating a plan for each component without referring to existing plans. The generative approach is considered to be more advanced and difficult to develop. The terms *generative* and *automatic* have been used loosely and interchangeably. For the purpose of this chapter, we categorize generative process planning into two categories: semi-generative and automatic. *Semi-generative* type systems will be defined as systems which perform many of the functions in a generative manner, and the remaining functions are performed with the use of humans in the planning loop. Automatic systems on the other hand completely eliminate the human from the planning process. In this approach the computer is used all the way, from interpreting the design data to generating the final cutter path. The following sections discuss each of the two basic approaches to computer-aided process planning.

Variant Process Planning

The variant approach to process planning was the first approach used to computerize the planning techniques. It is based upon the concept that similar parts will have similar process plans, and the computer can be used as a tool to assist in the identification of similar plans, retrieving them and editing the plans to suit the requirements for specific parts.

In order to implement such a concept, group technology based part coding and classification is used as a foundation. Individual parts are coded based upon several characteristics and attributes. Part families are created of like parts having sufficiently common attributes to group them into a family. This family formation is determined by analyzing the codes of the part spectrum. A standard plan consisting of a process plan to manufacture the entire family is created and stored for each part family. The development of a variant process planning system has two stages: the preparatory stage and the production stage.

Preparatory Stage During the preparatory stage, existing components are coded, classified, and grouped into families. The part family formation can be performed in several ways. Families can be formed based on geometric shapes or process similarities. Several methods can be used to form these groupings. A simple approach would be to compare the similarity of the part's code with other part codes. Since similar parts have similar code characteristics, logic that compares part of code or an entire code can be used to determine similarity between parts.

Families can often be described by a set of family matrices. Each family has a binary matrix with a column for each digit in the code and a row for each value a code digit can have. A nonzero entry in the matrix indicates that the particular digit can have the value of that row. For example, entry *(3,2) equals one* implies that a code x3xxx can be a member of the family. Since the processes of all family members are similar, a standard plan can be assigned to the family.

The standard plan is structured and stored in a coded manner using operation codes (OP codes). An OP code represents a series of operations on one machine or workstation. For example, an OP code DRL10 may represent the sequence: center drill, change drill, drill hole, change to reamer, and ream hole. A series of OP codes constitute the representation of the standard process plan.

Before the system can be of any use, coding, classification, family formation, and standard plan preparation must be completed. FIGURE 20-2 illustrates some of the elements of the preparatory stage in variant process planning. The effectiveness and performance of the variant process planning system depends to a very large extent on the effort expended at this stage. The preparatory stage is a very time consuming process, and can take 18 to 24 man years (Planning Institute 1980).

Production Stage   This stage occurs when the system is ready for production. New components can be planned in this stage. An incoming component is first coded. The code is then sent to a part family search routine to find the family to which it belongs. Since the standard plan is indexed by family number, the standard plan can be re-

trieved from the database easily. The standard plan is designed for the entire family rather than for a specific component; thus, editing the plan is unavoidable. FIGURE 20-3 illustrates the various steps in the production stage.

Variant process planning systems are relatively easy to build. However, they have several problems associated with them. Some of these problems are:

- The components to be planned are limited to similar components previously planned
- Experienced process planners still must modify the standard plan for the specific component
- Details of the plan cannot be generated
- Variant planning cannot be used in an entirely automated manufacturing system without additional process planning

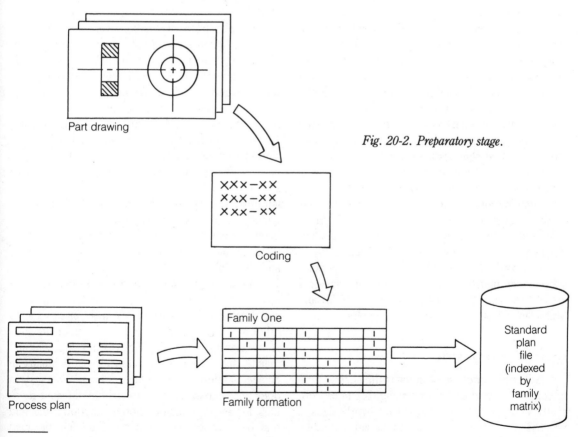

Part drawing

Coding

Process plan

Family formation

Standard plan file (indexed by family matrix)

Fig. 20-2. Preparatory stage.

Source: Chang (1983).

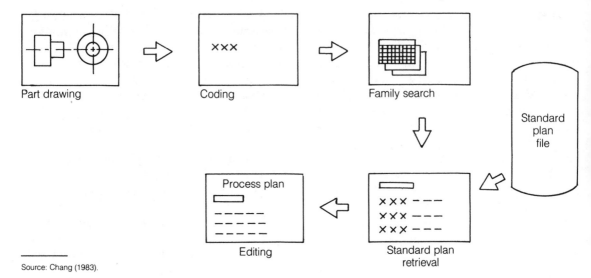

Part drawing

Coding

Family search

Standard plan file

Process plan

Editing

Standard plan retrieval

Source: Chang (1983).

Fig. 20-3. Production stage.

Despite these problems, the variant approach is still an effective method; especially when the primary objective is to improve the current practice of process planning. In most batch manufacturing industries, where similar components are produced repetitively, a variant system can improve the planning efficiency dramatically. Four other advantages of variant process planning are as follows. First, once a standard plan has been written, a variety of components can be planned. Second, implementing a planning system requires comparatively simple programming and installation (compared with generative systems). Third, the system is understandable, and the planner has control of the final plan. Finally, it is easy to learn, and easy to use.

The variant approach is the most popular approach in industry today. Most working systems are of this type, CAPP of CAM-I (Link 1976) and Multiplan of OIR (1983) are two examples.

Generative Approach

Generative process planning is the second type of computer-aided process planning. It can be concisely defined as a system which synthesizes a process plan for a new component automatically. The generative approach envisions the creation of a process plan from information available in a manufacturing database without human intervention. Upon receiving the design model, the system is able to generate the required operations and operation sequence for the component.

Knowledge of manufacturing has to be captured and encoded into computer programs. By applying decision logic, a process planner's decision-making process can be imitated. Other planning functions such as machine selection, tool selection, and process optimization can also be automated using generative planning techniques. A generative process planning system includes three main components: (1) part description, (2) manufacturing databases, and (3) decision-making logic and algorithms.

A typical system can be viewed as consisting of several modules, each with a well defined function, and input/output information, with interfaces to other modules and databases, as shown in FIG. 20-4. A modular approach simplifies the development and maintenance of software and increases flexibility in choice of different levels of automation. The system does not necessarily have to include different modules for every function. Some functions will and may be incorporated into a single module because of interdependence.

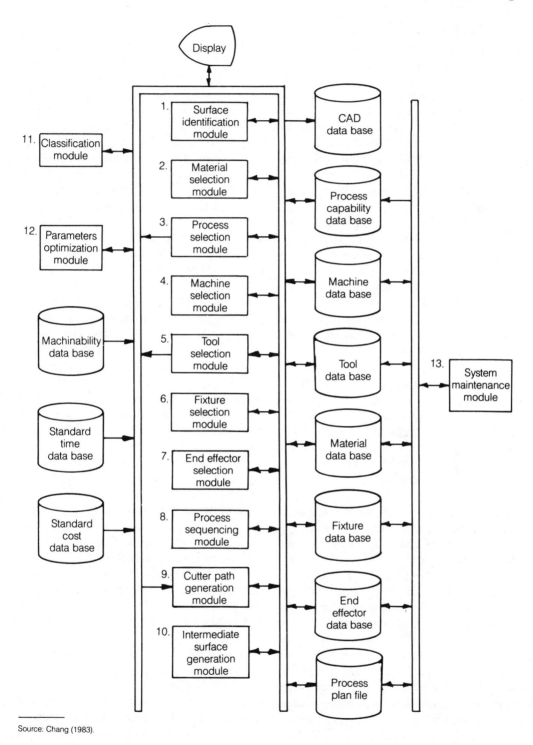

Source: Chang (1983).

Fig. 20-4. Process planning modules and databases.

The definition of generative process planning used in industry today is somewhat relaxed. Thus systems which contain some decision making capability on process selection are often also called generative systems. Generative process planning is regarded as more advanced than the variant process planning. Ideally, a generative process planning system is a turn-key system with all the decision logic built in. Since this is still far from being realized, generative systems currently developed provide a wide range of capabilities and can at best be only described as semi-generative.

The generative process planning approach has several advantages. It generates consistent process plans rapidly. In addition, new components can be planned as easily as existing components. Generative process planning also has potential for integrating with an automated manufacturing facility to provide detailed control information. Successful implementation of this approach requires the following key developments:

- The logic of process planning must be identified and captured
- The part to be produced must be clearly and precisely defined in a computer-compatible format
- The captured logic of process planning and the part description data must be incorporated into a unified manufacturing database

Part Description Methods for Generative Process Planning Systems

Part description forms a major part of the information needed for process planning. The way in which the part description is input to the process planning system has a direct effect on the degree of automation that can be achieved. Since the aim is to automate the system, the part description should be in a computer readable format. Traditionally engineering drawings have been used to convey part descriptions, and to communicate between design and manufacturing. Understanding the engineering drawing was a task suited for well trained human beings, and initially not suitable for direct input for process planning. The developments in CAD have provided some means for creating computerized storage of engineering drawings and increasing feasibility for their use as we shall see later. Several other methods have been used for representing parts for generative process planning.

Codes The first generation of generative process planning systems uses group technology codes or coding schemes based on other attributes to describe parts. The coding scheme consists of a sequence of symbols that identify a part's design characteristics and features, and/or its manufacturing attributes. Several commercial coding schemes are available, such as OPITZ (Opitz 1970), DCLASS (Allen 1979), and MICLASS (OIR 1983). Variant process planning systems have been based exclusively on coding schemes. Several generative process planning systems such as APPAS (Wysk 1977), GENPLAN (Tulkoff 1981), and COBAPP (Phillips 1978) have used coding schemes to describe parts for generative process planning systems. APPAS uses a 30-40 digit code to describe each machined surface, thus describing part details to assist in generation of detailed process plans.

Coding is typically a manual process; exact shape and size information, necessary for detailed planning, is lost when the part is described by a finite digit code. The degree of detail depends on the resolution allowed by the number and type of digits used. The code based representation is not suited for a completely automated process planning system, since the coding is a manual process, and a human interface is needed between the design and process planning function. Semi-generative process planning systems such as CORE-CAPP (Li et al. 1987) use coding schemes extensively.

Special Descriptive Languages The limitations in the use of group technology for a completely automated system led to the development of special descriptive languages to assist in describing the part. The format of these languages allows planning to be performed easily from the information provided.

The AUTAP system (Evershiem and Esch 1983) uses one such descriptive language. The part is described using both geometric and technological elements. FIGURE 20-5 shows an example of a part modeled using this approach. Besides using true

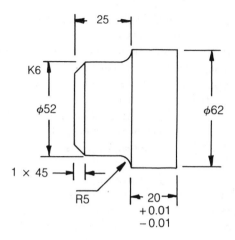

10 Cylinder/52,25/

11 Dfit/K,6/

12 Chamfer/1,45/

13 Radius/5/

20 Cylinder/62,20/

21 LTOL/ + 0.01, − 0.01/

Fig. 20-5. AUTAP part description.

geometrical elements such as cylinders and cones, it also uses subordinate elements such as patterns of holes. These elements are represented using key words and attributes. The geometrical elements characterize the main contour and the subordinate elements provide the details. Although reasonably complex elements can be modeled, this language lacks a complete set of Boolean operators and modeling a complex component may be difficult. Process planning is performed by analyzing the component description commands, and relating them to manufacturing.

The CIMS/DEC part description system (Kakino et al. 1977) forms the input to the CIMS/PRO system (Iwata et al. 1980). The part shape is described using volumetric elements obtained by revolving or parallel moving of the generating surfaces. The generating surface is composed of concatenation of profile elements which are given by directed line segments (FIG. 20-6). Technological information such as surface finish is associated and stored with each profile element. FIGURE 20-6

shows a CIMS/PRO part description. The goal of CIMS/PRO is to define a CAD/CAM oriented part description method to be used for process planning. The problem is the limitation of this method to a limited domain of parts.

Another similar approach based on syntactic methods was proposed by Jakubowski (1982) for describing parts. It uses the concept of basic primitives which are segments of straight lines or curves (see FIG. 20-7). A contour describing the part boundary is constructed from the set of primitives described by a character string, which is a left to right concatenation of primitives describing the part. This method is suited for part classification into families, by parsing the character strings describing the part. Since no technological elements are associated, it is not suitable for generative process planning.

GARI (Descotte and Latombe 1981) uses a part description based on a set of features, such as tapped holes, countersink holes, bores, grooves, notches, and faces, to describe the part (see FIG. 20-8). These features are described using system words such as diameter, surface finish, distance, perpendicularity, and tolerance. The relationship

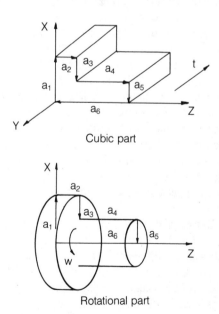

Fig. 20-6. CIMS/PRO part description.

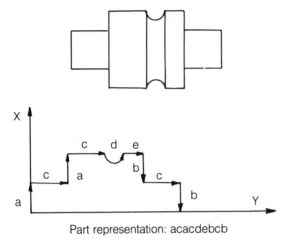

Part representation: acacdebcb

Fig. 20-7. Syntactic part description.

between features are also specified as attributes *starting from* and *opening into*. The part description as a set of features conveys some expertise about its manufacturing, when specified by this method. This representation is suited for planning tasks, but has to be manually prepared for input into the system. For complex components this can be tedious and difficult.

CAD Models   Although the previous methods can provide information for several process planning functions, the part design still needs to be manually converted into one of these representations. Since a part can be modeled effectively using a CAD system, and the internal representation provides another computer reachable and compatible format, using CAD models as input to the process planning module has potential of eliminating the human effort of translating a design into code or other descriptive form. Both 2-D and 3-D CAD models have been used and investigated for process planning applications (see section on CAD interface for details).

Representation of Process Planning Logic   Another major component of generative process planning systems is the process planning logic and knowledge. This includes the logic used by the process planner to make decisions on various aspects of planning such as machine selection, tool selection, and planning sequence. Several

methods have been used to represent this planning logic and data in formats and structures that facilitate program coding and documentation. The decision logic has to be synthesized and structured in a clear manner; it should be complete, unambiguous, nonredundant, and capable of expansion.

Decision Trees   A decision tree is a graph with a single root and branches emanating from the root. Each branch represents a possible course of action if the conditions specified to traverse the branch are true. Each branch can lead to another node or terminate in an action. The nodes provide further branching possibilities. When a branch is true it can be traversed to reach the next node, and so on until a terminal point on the tree is reached. An example of a decision tree is shown in FIG. 20-9.

Decision Tables   A decision table is partitioned in conditions and actions, and this is represented in a tabular form. Decision rules are identified by columns in the entry part of the decision table. When all conditions in a decision table column are met, the marked decision is taken. A more detailed discussion on decision trees and tables can be found in Montalbano (1974) and Metzner and Barnes (1977). The decision table has many advantages in structuring decision logic, and can provide a nice modular structure, thereby simplifying maintenance and modification. An example of a decision table is shown in FIG. 20-10.

Artificial Intelligence Based Approaches   Recent developments in Artificial Intelligence or AI/Expert systems have made them an important tool in the development of computer-aided process planning (CAPP) systems. The current use of AI in CAPP systems can be clearly divided into two parts: (1) use of AI for automated interpretation of the part description (see the section on CAD interface for Process Planning for details), and (2) expert systems for the development of the process plan itself.

Expert Systems   An *expert system* can be defined as a tool which has the capability to understand problem specific knowledge and use the domain knowledge intelligently to suggest alternative paths of action (Kumara et al. 1986). Several aspects of the process planning problem have made

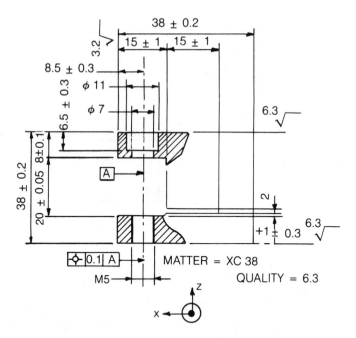

MATTER = XC 38
QUALITY = 6.3

Description of each feature:
FXP (type face) (direction xp) (quality 3.2)
FXM (type face) (direction xm) (quality rough)
FYM (type face) (direction ym) (quality rough)
FYP (type face) (direction yp) (quality rough)
FZP (type face) (direction zp)
FZM (type face) (direction zm)
H1 (type countersunk-hole) (diameter 7)
    (countersink-diameter 11)
    (starting-from FZP) (opening-into P1)
H2 (type trapped-hole) (diameter 6)
    (starting-from FZM) (opening-into P3)
N1 (type notch) (quality 3.2) (width 20)
    (starting-from FXP) (opening-into FYM FYP)
    (children [P1 (type face) (direction zm)]
             [P2 (type face) (direction xp)]
             [P3 (type face) (direction zp)])
N2 (type notch) (width 2)
    (starting-from P2) (opening-into FYM FYP)
    (children [Q1 (type face) (direction zm)]
             [Q2 (type face) (direction xp)]
             [Q3 (type face) (direction zp)])

Dimensions between features:
(distance FXM FXP 38 ± 200)
(distance P2 FXP 15 ± 1000)
(distance Q2 P2 15 ± 1000)
(distance (H1 H2) FXP 8.5 ± 300)
(distance FYM FYP 38 ± 200)
(distance (H1 H2) FYP 19 ± 100)
(distance FZM FZP 38 ± 200)
(countersink-depth FZP H1 6.5 ± 300)
(distance P1 FZP 8 ± 100)
(distance P3 Q3 1 ± 300)
(concentricity H1 H2 ± 100)

*Fig. 20-8. GARI part
description.*

Source: Descotte and Latombe, "GARI: An Expert System for Process Planning," in *Solid Modelling by Computers,* edited by Pickett and Boyse (Plenum Press, 1985): 329-346.

it amenable to solution by the expert systems approach. The problem has been traditionally experience based, and relies on large amounts of subjective and specialized knowledge acquired over long periods of time. Hence, systems attempting to automate process planning must place a high priority on the reproduction, representation, and manipulation of the subjective knowledge used by the

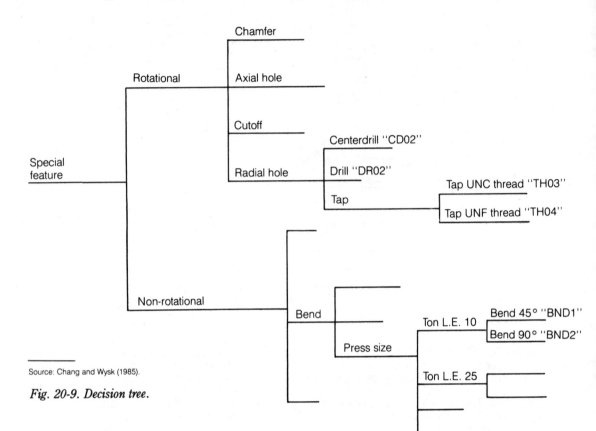

Source: Chang and Wysk (1985).

Fig. 20-9. Decision tree.

Fig. 20-10. Decision table.

			Machine tool selection			
		No.	1	2	3	4
Condition	300 < Length < 500	1	X	X		
	Dia < 200	2	X	X		
	Max speed < 3000	3		X		
	Tolerance < 0.01	4	X			X
	Lot size > 100	5		X	X	
	Fixture 123 exist	6		X	X	
	Fixture 125 exist	7			X	X
Conclusion	Machine 1001	1	X			X
	Machine 1002	2		X		
	Machine 1003				X	

Source: Chang and Wysk (1985).

by the process engineer. Expert systems provide an excellent framework to perform these tasks. A typical expert system consists of a knowledge base of domain-related facts; rules for drawing inferences; and an inference mechanism for triggering rules, enforcing consistency, and resolving con-

Knowledge Representation in AI/Expert Systems   Several schemes have been developed for representing knowledge and rules in expert systems, and these have been used extensively in the development of process planning systems:

- Predicate logic
- Production rules
- Semantic nets
- Frames
- Object oriented programming

Predicate Logic   The use of predicate logic or predicate calculus as a means of knowledge representation followed directly from propositional logic. Statements about individual items, both by themselves and in relationship to other items are called *predicates*. The description of the environment is given in terms of logic clauses and operators from propositional calculus. For example, the fact that all straight shank drills are a type of drilling tool can be represented as follows:

$$\forall \; x \; \text{straight shank drill} \; (x) \implies \text{drilling tool} \; (x)$$

Logic representation is useful in formal proof procedures. It offers clarity, is well defined, and is easily understood. Pure logic schemes have difficulty in representing procedural knowledge and rules. Predicate logic is used as the basis of representation in the Prolog programming language, which is often used to develop expert system applications for process planning.

Production Rules   This is one of the most commonly used knowledge representation schemes. Its basic concept is the notion of condition-action sets (or productions), and can be expressed simply in the form of IF-THEN rules:

IF {conditions} THEN {actions}.

This approach has been used by several process planning systems and its advantages and usefulness for encoding process planning knowledge is well documented. Those using this approach include: GARI (Descotte and Latombe 1981), TOM (Matsushima et al. 1982), PROPLAN (Mouleeswaran 1984), XCUT (Hummel and Brooks 1986), NBS's system (Brown and Ray 1987), and several others have used this approach. Rule based systems have been developed to perform several of the process planning tasks, machine selection (Nau and Chang 1983), tool selection (Giusti et al. 1986), fixture design and setup (Englert and Wright 1988), process sequencing and operation planning (Barkocy and Zdeblick 1984), machining data selection (Wang and Wysk 1986), and Computer Numerical Control milling (Preiss and Kaplansky 1984).

Semantic Nets   Semantic nets attempt to describe the world in terms of objects and binary relations. According to a semantic net representation, the knowledge is a collection of objects; associations are represented as a labelled directed arc. Semantic nets are easily understandable, but more difficult to implement. FIGURE 20-11 shows an example of a semantic net describing a hole.

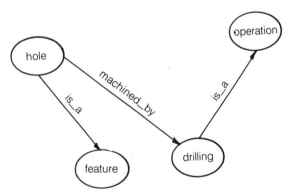

Fig. 20-11. Semantic net representation.

Frames   A frame structure is a more general representation scheme, and permits the representation of both procedural and declarative information in terms of attributes, hierarchical relations with other frames, constraints, default values, and procedures. Several systems have been developed which use the notion of a frame to represent both the part and manufacturing knowledge: SIPPS (Nau and Chang 1985), XCUT (Hummel and Brooks 1986), and Joshi, Vissa and Chang (1988). An example of a frame for representing an operation is shown in FIG. 20-12.

Object-oriented programming Object-oriented programming provides an excellent data structure for symbolic manipulation of conceptual information. With object-oriented programming, details about objects can be ignored, and common properties easily inherited through property inheritance. Each object is an entity combining both procedural and declarative knowledge associated with some particular concept. The properties of these objects can be considered as attributes, entities, relationships, or procedural code. The concept of object-oriented programming uses an idea similar to that of frames, but provides a more flexible programming environment due to its use of data abstraction, inheritance, and modularity. Object-oriented programming has been used by XCUT to represent the work piece description (Hummel and Brooks 1986).

Databases and Algorithms Databases and algorithms form the final major component of a generative process planning system. Several databases are required to provide the process planning system with the information required to make the decisions. Examples of the various databases required are shown in FIG. 20-4. In any given system not all databases are usually present; the few used depend on the final output desired from the system. The databases usually contain company specific information and have to be specifically tailored to each company.

Algorithms are used primarily to perform the computations and guide the system during the decision-making process. Typical applications of algorithms include determining optimum cutting conditions, such as machining and force requirements; tolerance distribution; process parameters such as speed, depth of cut, and feed; which are subject to solution by means of empirical formulas.

```
(
FACE_MILLING
(A_KIND_OF (VALUE SURF_BASIC_PROCESS))
(FRAME_LABEL (VALUE FACE_MILLING))
(TOOL_TYPE (VALUE (FACE_MILL)))
(REQUIRED_MACHINE (VALUE (VERT_MILLING_MC HORT_MILLING_MC 5AXIS_MC)))
(BATCH_QTY (VALUE 1))
(ORDER_QTY (VALUE 1))
(MACHINED_FEATURES (VALUE (FLAT_SURFACE STEP ISLAND)))
(HARDNESS (VALUE 369))
(WIDTH (VALUE (3.0 8.0)))
(SURFACE_FINISH (VALUE (126 249)))
(DIMENSION_TOL (VALUE .01))
(INDIVIDUAL_TOL (VALUE .005))
(RELATED_TOL (VALUE .005))
(PRE_MACHINED_FEATURE (VALUE FLAT_SURFACE))
(PRE_SURFACE_FINISH (VALUE 700))
(PRE_DIMENSION_TOL (VALUE .125))
(PRE_INDIVIDUAL_TOL (VALUE .05))
(PRE_RELATED_TOL (VALUE .05))
(PRE_HARDNESS (VALUE SAME))
(FINISH_ALLOWANCE (VALUE .08))
)
```

Fig. 20-12. Frame for FACE milling operation.

Examples of CAPP Systems

TABLE 20-1 presents a summary of some of the CAPP systems developed both in academia and industry and describes the approaches used in their development. Additional information on examples of CAPP systems can be found in Chang and Wysk (1985), and Weill et al. (1982).

CAD INTERFACE FOR PROCESS PLANNING

Although the specialized languages and codes provide adequate information to represent the part for process planning functions, manual input still extracts and converts the required information from the part drawing. CAD systems provide the computer readable part description (Requicha 1980). The potential for using the computer to extract the information from the part model automatically can eliminate the need for human effort in translating a design into a code or another descriptive form. The developments in CAD have had a significant effect on the evolution of different approaches used in harnessing the power of CAD for process planning. FIGURE 20-13 illustrates a few of the semi-generative and automatic planning approaches and their use of CAD.

The first approach is what most industries are currently using. In this approach the parts are designed using 2-D drafting systems (CADAM, AutoCAD, or CADkey) and CAD has replaced the paper drawings. Process planning systems used are based on variant type systems. The CAD representations are used only in the development of NC part programs which are created interactively by the process planner. The CAD/CAM function is not truly integrated and cannot be automated. The difficulty lies primarily in computer understanding and translating the 2-D engineering drawings into information suitable to drive a process planning system. Other problems with engineering drawings such as inconsistency, redundancy, and incompleteness of views (for better human understanding) make the process difficult. Some research has been done to automate the understanding of engineering draw-

ings (Markowsky and Wesley 1980, Haralick and Queeney 1982, Aldefeld 1983, Preiss 1984).

To develop integrated systems, some process planning systems utilize the part description directly from the 2-D CAD databases. Feature recognition is performed on the 2-D CAD description stored in the form of points and lines. The 2-D approach is limited and has been used primarily for axially symmetric rotational parts. Examples of such systems are PROPLAN (Mouleeswaran 1984), Turbo-CAPP (Wang and Wysk 1987), and Dong and Soom (1986).

As the CAD systems developed from being mere extensions of 2-D drafting systems into 3-D solid models, automated process planning moved its focus to using 3-D models to provide the input that would help automate the system. An early system using 3-D solid model was TIPPS (Chang 1982). In TIPPS the part is represented by its boundary model. The surfaces that require machining are identified interactively by the process planner using a cursor. The dimensional and technological information pertaining to the surfaces is obtained automatically from the database, and is used to drive the generative process planning system. This interactive approach of identifying machined faces reduces the tedious and error prone task of data translation. It is adequate for generating plans for single noninteracting machined features, and still requires the use of humans in the planning loop.

Direct Use of 3-D CAD Models

Two major approaches have been taken by most researchers in developing direct interface with 3-D CAD models: feature recognition and feature based design. Both these approaches are based on the view that planning can be performed efficiently if manufacturing features (such as holes, pockets, slots, and steps) are known. Features are considered elemental regions of the part and can be manufactured by one or a sequence of known manufacturing processes. For example, the feature hole can be manufactured by using a subset of the following sequence of operations {drilling, reaming,

Table 20-1. Summary of CAPP Systems.

SYSTEM NAME

Feature	CAPP [Link, 1976]	RPO [Tripnis, 1979]	ICAPP [Eskicioglu, 1983]	Horvath[a] [1979]	CAPP [Kyttner, 1979]	SIPPS [Nau & Chang, 1985]	APPAS [Wysk, 1977]	AUTAP [Evershiem, 1980]	CIMS/PRO [Iwata, et. al., 1980]	SAPT [Milacic, 1985]	Alder[a] [1986]	TOM [Matsushims, 1982]	EXCAP [Davies, 1984]	XPLANE [Kals, 1986]	PICAP [Pl, 1980]	Srinivasan[a] [1984]	XPS-1 [CAM-I, 1979]	CMPP [Sack, 1982]	CUTTECH [Barkocy, 1984]	Joshi[a] [1988]	CAPSY [Spur, 1983]	PROPLAN [Mouleeswaran, 1984]	TIPPS [Chang, 1982]	SIPS [Nau & Gray, 1986]	XCUT [Hummel & Brooks, 1986]	GARI [Descotte, 1981]	MICROPLAN [Phillips, 1986]	XMAPP [Inui, 1986]	MACHINIST [Hayes, 1986]	STOPP [Choi, 1982]	Turbo-CAPP [Wang, 1987]
1. Part Shape																															
Rotational	•	•		•	•	•		•		•		•	•				•	•			•	•					•	•		•	•
Prismatic	•		•	•		•	•			•	•						•					•		•	•	•	•		•	•	•
Sheet Metal	•							•																							
2. Plan Logic																															
Variant	•																														
Generative									•	•			•	•	•		•	•					•	•						•	•
Semigenerative			•	•	•	•																							•		
3. Decision Logic																															
(Exc. AI logic)																															
Decision tree					•			•				•									•										
Decision table	•	•	•	•				•											•			•					•	•	•		
Decision model																															
4. AI Logic																															
Production rule						•						•	•	•			•	•			•	•			•	•	•		•	•	•
Frame																								•							
Semantic net.																								•		•			•		
Object oriented																										•					
5. Feature Ext.																															
Specified	•	•	•	•	•		•	•			•						•	•								•	•		•	•	
Extracted					•					•	•		•	•	•	•				•									•		•
6. Automated Ft'n																															
Macro[b]	•	•	•	•	•	•	•	•	•			•	•				•	•	•	•	•	•	•		•		•	•	•	•	•
Macro[c]		•	•	•	•	•	•	•	•	•		•					•		•			•			•	•	•		•	•	•
7. Input Method																															
CAD data base						•		•	•			•	•	•				•	•				•	•			•		•	•	•
Code	•																														
Spec. input lang.			•	•		•	•										•	•			•				•			•			

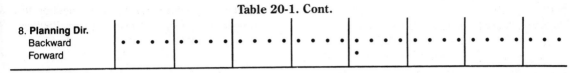

Table 20-1. Cont.

a. Author name
b. Machine tool and sequence selection
c. Cutting tool, cutting parameters, etc.

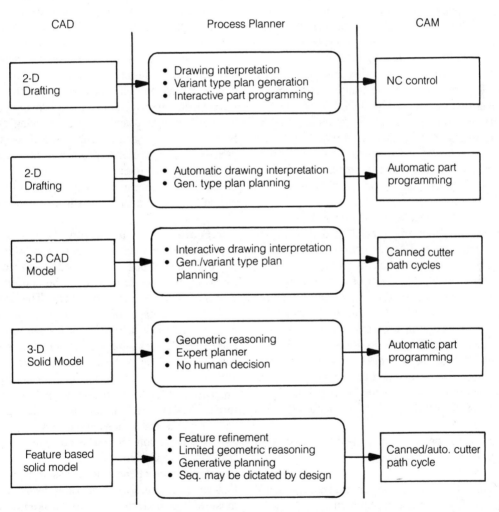

Fig. 20-13. Process planning and CAD/CAM.

boring, grinding}. The choice is made based upon the technological characteristics of the feature such as required accuracy or surface finish. As a matter of fact, nearly all process planning systems uses features in one respect or another. The coding systems use features to develop the group technology code to represent features, and the special languages developed essentially capture the feature information. Hence we can conclude that process planning is a feature based activity.

Feature Recognition For the purpose of process planning, features can be defined loosely as ''regions of a part having some manufacturing significance.'' Features reference part geometry and can be individually defined by referring to a collection of geometric entities, such that they exhibit some properties that can be translated into manufacturing requirements. The definition of a feature is dependent on the context. Features required for manufacturing may be quite different from those required for design. Also, within the manufacturing domain, the features required for planning machining operations may differ considerably from those required for forging.

The current generation of CAD systems places emphasis on geometric shapes, and designs are created primarily by Boolean operations on a set of primitive solids; the notion of features does not exist explicitly. The problem of feature extraction involves recognition of the higher level features from the set of lower level entities in the geometric model. Depending on the representation scheme used (CSG or BREP) the lower level entities are primitive solids, faces, edges, or vertices. This dependence on the representation scheme also has a bearing on the feature definitions, and the development of algorithms used to recognize the features.

The development of a feature recognizer entails the following problems:

- A representation scheme for the features that is suitable for automatic recognition
- Unique definition of the features based on the representation scheme

- Inference procedure capable of recognition in a complete and consistent manner (Hirschtick and Gossard 1986)

Several methods that have been used to develop feature recognizers can be classified as shown in TABLE 20-2. The problem of feature recognition is not an easy one, and several research issues still need to be addressed before this approach can be implemented in a generic system. One prototype system has implemented this approach using a limited part and feature domain (Joshi, Vissa, and Chang 1988). The features are recognized using a graph-based approach, and further geometric analysis is performed to determine tool approach directions and machining precedences based on local relationships between features (Joshi 1987). The feature information is then fed into a frame based process planning system. Since the technological data are not available in solid modelers, they are added to the frames manually along with the tolerance information. A frame based expert process planning system such as the one in FIG. 20-14 is then used to generate process plans.

Feature Based Design Feature recognition is essentially an *a posteriori* approach. Since the CAD model does not explicitly represent features, some procedures have to be applied to the model in order to recognize them. This approach has the advantage of continuing to allow the designer to work in traditional fashion, using the current CAD technology. However, this approach will only continue to be effective, if we see vast improvements in efficiency and performance in the procedures used to automatically extract the features. This is clearly a nontrivial task, as can be seen from the discussions in the previous sections, and the limited domain to which the current state of research is applicable.

Proponents of the feature based design argue that when the designer starts the design process, most of the features are already known to the designer, and in the process of converting them to the CAD system, the information is lost, and has to

Table 20-2. Summary of Feature Extraction Methods.

Recognition Approach	References	Domain of Use
Syntactic pattern recognition	Kyprianou [1980]	3-D depression & protrusions and rotational part families
	Jakubowski [1982]	Rotational part families
	Choi [1982]	Holes, pockets, slots
	Staley [1984]	Holes
	Srinivasan [1985]	Rotational part families
State transition diagrams and automata	Iwata et al [1980]	Step, slot, pocket
	Milacic [1985]	Rotational part families
Decomposition approach	Grayer [1976]	Milling 2-1/2 D parts
	Armstrong [1984]	Milling
	Woo [1982]	Volumetric decomposition
Expert system/logic	Henderson [1984]	Holes, pockets, and slots
	Henderson [1986]	Rotational part families
	Kung [1984]	Holes, slots, pockets, and planes
	Dong [1988]	2-D depressions such as steps and slots
CSG (set theoretic)	Woo [1977]	Cavity volumes for NC machining
	Lee and Fu [1987]	Features formed by subtraction and union of cylindrical primitives
Graph based	Joshi [1987]	Holes, pockets, slots, steps, blind steps, and blind slots

be recreated by feature recognizers. Why not capture this information at the design phase, when it is known? The push toward feature based systems also stems from the fact that the traditional CAD systems and representation schemes are not capable of providing the new information required for other analysis such as design for manufacturability and functional information about the part. These activities require information in the form of features—a lot more information than is currently provided by existing CAD systems.

The concept of feature based design is based on essentially providing the designer with a library of features—similar to primitives used in a CSG system—that can be used with a set of operators such as add, delete, and modify (Luby et al. 1986). The programs then create a features representation, which is also used to create a boundary representation of the object. The feature model maintains the additional information that is not kept in a conventional solid modeler, and eliminates the need for feature extraction.

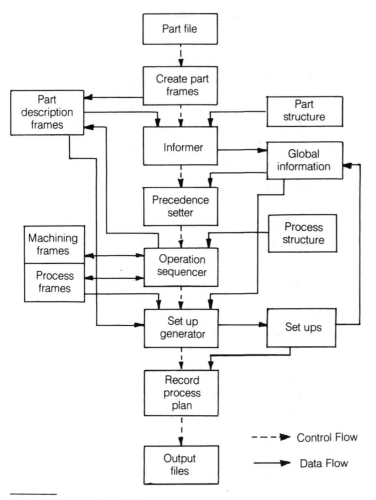

Fig. 20-14. Frame-based expert process planning module.

Source: Joshi, Vissa, and Chang (1988).

Process Planning Using Feature Based Design System

In process planning using a feature based design, a specially tailored feature based design system is used as the front end to a process planning system. A part is designed using the design features readily available to the designer. However, the design features cannot always be used directly for manufacturing purposes, and some kind of reasoning is necessary to recognize and extract manufacturing features. The size and location of a design feature could result in the feature being classified into different categories. In FIG. 20-15, for example, the feature could be classified as a through slot, blind slot, pocket and even a nonround hole depending on the size and location of the design feature. When feature based design is used, further reasoning still needs to be performed, or else the result can be erroneous.

An example of a system using this approach is the Quick Turnaround Cell (QTC) system (Kanumury, Shah, and Chang 1988). In this system a feature refinement module interfaces a feature based

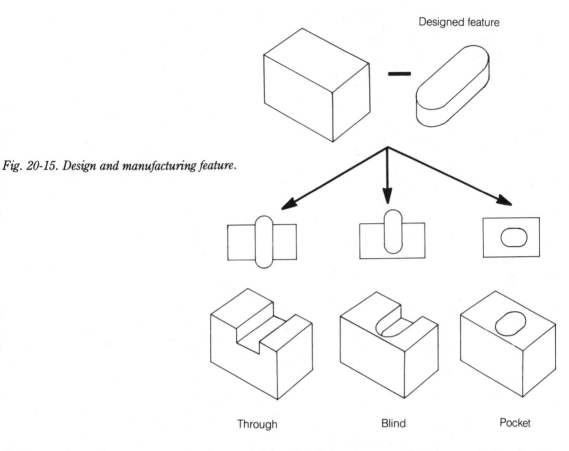

Designed feature

Fig. 20-15. Design and manufacturing feature.

Through   Blind   Pocket

design system with a process planning module. Feature intersection types and contained-in information are identified by the feature refinement module. This module uses a solid modeler TWIN (Mashburn 1987) to evaluate the feature model into a B-REP. The B-REP is then used for local region analysis. The system combines the global and local information and thus is able to generate good plans automatically.

Since it is difficult to attach technological information such as tolerances and surface finish on a B-REP, the QTC system keeps the technological information at the feature model level. Back pointers in B-REP are used to link back to the feature model as FIG. 20-16 shows. All the design and manufacturing information is available to the process planning system. Using this approach, the system not only completes the process selection, but

also determines the fixturing method and cutter path automatically. FIGURE 20-17 shows the results of a display of setups and intermediate part geometry generated by the system.

SURVEY OF INDUSTRIAL USAGE OF CAPP SYSTEMS

Haas and Chang (1988) undertook a survey of industrial use of CAPP systems as part of a project. The goal of the survey was to identify present trends in CAPP systems that both the CAPP developers and users are striving toward, and assess the status of industrial perspective on CAPP. The survey produced interesting results and clearly indicated a need for further research in CAPP systems. In this section the term *generative* is not used in its strictest sense; rather it takes on the broader

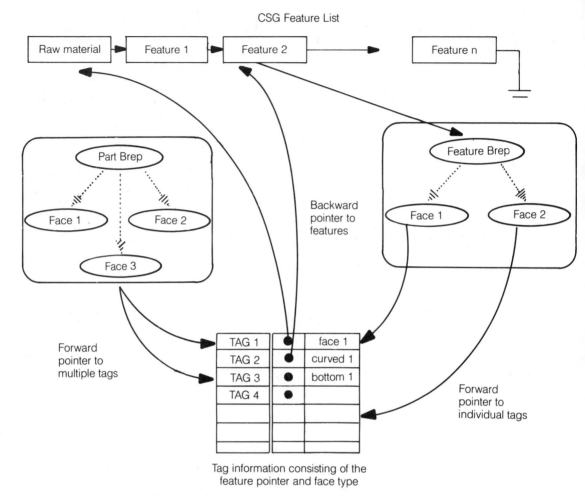

Fig. 20-16. Back pointers used to link B-Rep with features.

meaning used by the industry. Further, the claims made by the industrial users of CAPP on the capabilities of the systems have been stated as described by the individual users.

A total of 41 companies out of 196 to whom the survey was sent reported use of CAPP systems. The following presents a brief overview of the survey results.

Nature of Development

The results indicated that a majority of the CAPP systems in use (29/41) were developed in house. The other systems were either purchased from vendors (8/41) or co-developed with the vendor (4/41). The majority of the CAPP systems were developed in house due to the large amount of company specific data that is required. Companies also opted to develop their own due to other reasons such as lack of support from vendors, high price and monthly charges, and complexity and maintenance of systems developed by others. Developing their own systems has allowed them to create all the systems interfaces and production engineering needs. However, this should not create the impression that the systems must be developed

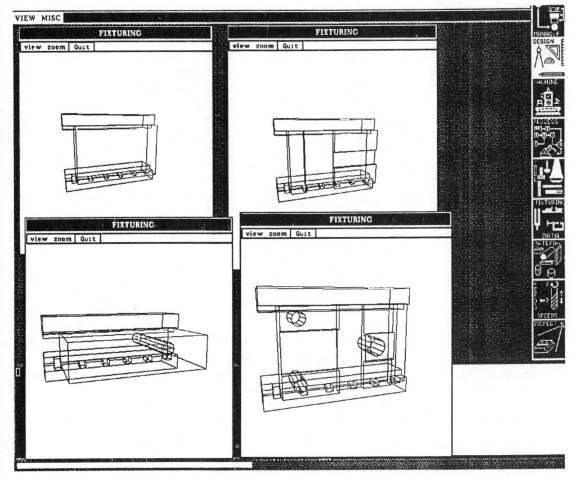

Fig. 20-17. Fixturing method display.

in house. Other developers of in house systems felt that it took a long time and effort, and it could be easier to maintain a system that was built around a commercially developed and maintained software.

System Generalities

Of the 41 companies using CAPP systems, there were 31 different CAPP systems in use. Eleven were described as generative in nature. Thirteen were described as variant. Seven were hybrid, a combination of both generative and variant (also called semi-generative).

The input information required for the CAPP systems was most often a code or special language that was local to the system. The part coding schemes for these systems varied. For those based on a group technology code, several were based on the DCLASS code developed at Brigham Young University, and several were developed in house. A majority used the MULTICLASS code developed by the Organization for Industrial Research (OIR). However, there were 12 systems that have been developed within the last five years that use some type of modified CAD database as input. Other information required by several systems was a part description through interactive dialogue; one system needed a relational database for input.

Fortran was by far the most frequently used language in the development of CAPP systems. Several of the systems were written in C and COBOL. The hardware needed to run these systems included a wide range of mainframes and super minicomputers, with the IBM 3000 and 4300 series being mentioned most often, followed by VAX 11/750. Others mentioned included the Prime 9955 and minicomputers and work stations from Data General, DEC, Apollo, and Sperry. From this we can easily infer that CAPP systems are not dependent to a large extent on the programming languages used and the types of computers. In fact, systems can be developed in any language to run on any computer. The future trend seems to be headed toward workstation based environments.

Some form of graphic capabilities were reported in 15 systems, and others noted the need for graphics and listed it as a goal they were striving toward. The type of graphics package used varied widely. Twenty-three of the 31 systems claimed that they were equipped with a CAD interface. The three CAD systems primarily used were CADAM (25 percent), ANVIL 4000 (15 percent), and other systems equipped with an IGES preprocessor (15 percent). It must be noted here that all the interfaces are typically to 2-D CAD systems. Twenty-two systems were equipped with a CAM interface, and the most widely recognized feature was NC programming capabilities. However several systems offered features such as graphic/instructional system, interface to MRP, production control and quality control systems, tolerance stacking, and automatic time standards.

Of the 31 CAPP systems in use, 13 were commercially available. All but three were priced above $50,000 and the others were in the $20,000 to $50,000 range.

System Usage and Benefits

Many of the systems have been recently installed, and with most of the systems, development is an ongoing process, as it typically should be. Systems are constantly being upgraded as new modules are developed. A great majority of the sys-

tems become a vital part of the process planning operation once they are installed. Sixty one percent of the users felt the system was vital, 13 percent said it was not, and 26 percent felt it was too early in the implementation to tell how important their system would become. Forty six percent said that at least three-quarters of their process planning was done using the CAPP system; 13 percent said at least half; 13 percent said at least one-quarter; and 29 percent said less than one-quarter of their process planning was done using the CAPP system. The extent to which the system was used depended to a large extent on the training and the number of people trained to use the system.

The typical types of products planned on CAPP systems, and the output generated by these systems is shown in TABLES 20-3 and 20-4. With the information generated by the system, 87 percent of the survey respondents said that the plan was directly ready for shop floor use. Of those systems that needed changes, several said that graphics were augmented, and others needed to provide tool selection and operation detailing.

Benefits of the CAPP system over those of

Table 20-3. Types of Products Planned on CAPP System.

Turned parts	25	(81%)
Prismatic parts	21	(68%)
Sheet metal	19	(61%)
Bulkforming	10	(32%)
Electronic assly.	13	(42%)
Others	12	(39%)

Table 20-4. Output Information Generated.

Processing sequence	30	(97%)
Material selection	16	(52%)
Machine selection	24	(77%)
Tool selection	21	(19%)
Machining parameters	20	(65%)
Cutter path	10	(32%)

manual process planning were quite significant. Twenty three percent said that they saved between 75 and 100 percent of the time it normally takes for manual process planning, while 38 percent said they saved between 50 and 74 percent; 39 percent estimated between 25 and 49 percent. The estimated money saved ranged anywhere from $10,000 to $250,000 annually.

A summary of the systems mentioned in the survey is presented in TABLE 20-5.

Table 20-5. Summary of Existing CAP Systems.

System Name	Developer	Commercially Available	Plannable Pieces	Variant (V) Generative (G) or Hybrid (H)	Output Info.	Graphics Interface	CAD Interface
GENPLAN	Lockheed		1,2,3 5,6,7	G	1,2,3 4,5,6	x	x
CMPP	UTRC	x	1	G	1,3,8	x	x
MASTERS PARTS LIST	General Dynamics		1,2,3,4 5,6,7	V	1,4,5		
DCLASS BASED SYSTEM	Eaton/ BYU		1	G	1,3,4, 5,6,7		x
CAP	Bell Helicopter		1,3,4, 5,6,7	V	1,2,3, 4,5,7		x
MULTICAPP	OIR	x	1	V	1,2,3, 4,5,6	x	x
APP	General Elec. & Logan Assoc.	x	1,2,3,4, 5,6,7	G	1,2,3,4, 5,6,7,8	x	x
CAPE	Garrett Turbine		1,2,3	V	1,3,4, 5,6,8		x
ZCAPPS	Zeus Data Systems	x	1,2,3,4, 5,6,7	H	1,2,3,4, 5,6,7,8		x
CAPP	Caterpillar		1,2,3	V	1,3,4		x
EMAPS	Tipnis Inc.	x	1,2,3,6	H	1,2,3,4, 5,6,7,8	x	x
POPS	Hughes Aircraft		6	V	1	x	x

Coding Scheme

Planable Pieces
1 – Turned part
2 – Prismatic
3 – Sheet metal
4 – Bulk forming
5 – Electronic assemblies
6 – Mechanical assemblies
7 – Others

Output Information
1 – Processing sequence
2 – Material selection
3 – Machine selection
4 – Tool selection
5 – Fixture selection
6 – Machining parameters
7 – Cutter path
8 – Others

Table 20-5. cont.

System Name	Developer	Commercially Available.	Plannable Pieces	Variant (V) Generative (G) or Hybrid (H)	Output Info.	Graphics Interface	CAD Interface
DAPP	NBS		1,2,5,6	H	1,3,4, 5,6,7	x	x
XPS-n	UTRC	x[1]	1,2,3	G	1,3		x
H-CLASS	Hughes Aircraft		5,6	G	1,8	x	x
STAR	Grumman		1,2,3, 4,5,6	V	1,2		
MSA	MSA	x	1,6	V	1,2,3, 4,5		
CRUNCH	Sperry		5	H	1		
ESTIMATE/ ROUTING	TRW		7	V	1,2,3,6		
CWOS-GPP	Texas Instrument		1,3,7	G	1,3,5, 6,8		
OMS	Cummins Engine		1,2,3, 6,7	V	1,3,4, 5,6	x	x
MIPLAN	OIR	x	1,2,3, 6,7,8	V	1,3,4, 5,6	x	x
ICAPP/ EXCAP/	University Manchester England		1,2	V	1,4,6,7	x	x
DISAP	Tech. U. of Aachen	x	1,2,3,4, 5,6,7	H	1,2,3, 4,5,6		
AUTAP	Tech. U. of Aachen		1	G	1,2,3,4, 6,8		x
AUTAP PRISMATIC	Tech U. of Aachen		2	G	1,2,3, 6,8		x
AUTAP NC PUNCHING	Tech. U. of Aachen		3	G	1,2,3,4, 5,6,7		x
INTELLICAPP	CIMTELLIGENCE	x	1,2,3,4, 5,6,7	H		x	x
CUTPLAN/ CUTTECH	METCUT	x	1,2	H	1,2,3, 4,5,6	x	
NO NAME YET	AVCO- LYCOMING	x	1,2,3,6	G	1,2,3,4, 5,6,7	x	x
GECAPP-PLUS	General Electric	x	1,2,3,4, 5,6,7,8	V	1,2,3,4, 5,6,7,8	x	x

1. To members of CAM-I only

FUTURE TRENDS IN CAPP SYSTEMS

FIGURE 20-18 illustrates the trends in development of process planning systems. In the figure we use the intelligence of the system to measure the capability of the system. The higher the intelligence measurement, the more sophisticated the system is and can generate better plans. Eventually, we will be able to build process planning systems with the same intelligence level as a human planner. However, this intelligence level is specific to the process planning task, which includes design interpretation, detailed process plan generation, fixture planning, process economic analysis, and NC cutter path generation.

As can be seen from the figure, before the 1960s, only manual process planning was used. In the 1960s database was introduced to store and to help formatting process plans on a computer system. Since those systems do not make decisions nor help in making decisions, there was no intelligence built in the system. The decisions are made by the user of the systems. In the mid-1970s, group technology was introduced in building variant process planning systems. Again, the plan creation and modification were done by the human user. However, as systems evolved, some intelligence was included. For example, some systems were able to find optimal cutting parameters, and estimate time and cost. Some decision tree and decision table based generative process planning systems were also developed.

In the 1980s, two major developments began. First, the application of AI and Expert Systems in building process planning systems enable us to model the process planning knowledge in a better manner. The second development is the geometric reasoning capabilities for process planning. This development stems from the advances in CAD modeling. Geometric reasoning (either feature recognition or feature refinement) allows the system to understand the design model, thus providing the capability to make more intelligence decisions.

The level of intelligence in process planning has

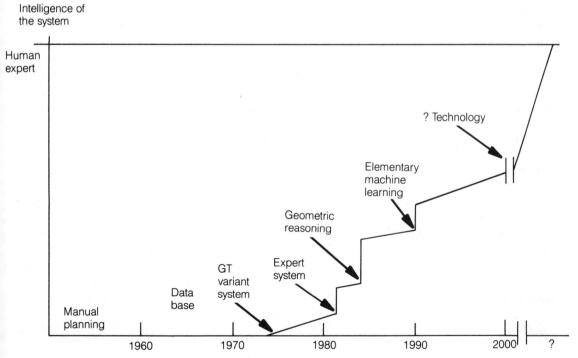

Fig. 20-18. Trends in the development of CAPP systems.

jumped to a much higher level due to these two technologies. However, process planning still needs much more development before it reaches the level of human intelligence. We believe that in the early 1990s the machine learning technology will have another major impact in the development of process planning systems. The methodology will continue to improve, thus increasing the intelligence of the system. In order to truly reach the level of a human process planner, CAPP needs a breakthrough in computer technology, in both hardware and software. Further study in the science of manufacturing processes and understanding how the human brain functions during decision making will also be necessary to make it happen. We do not know when this will happen, but it is a goal of many researchers in various fields.

In the next five to ten years, we believe that the major development will center around the integration of process planning systems with other design, manufacturing, and business functions. The availability of a common database fully shared among design, manufacturing, planning, scheduling and control, and purchasing will help in providing the completely integrated CAD/CAM environment capable of on-line generation of process plans. Process plans will also be generated based on shop floor scheduling and planning information, and will be globally optimized as opposed to the local optimization currently used.

To be more specific, a research and development agenda follows:

- Improve CAD interface—both feature recognition and feature refinement
- Perfect knowledge acquisition module—to help manufacturing engineer/knowledge engineer capture the ever changing shop and process knowledge
- Develop better CAD systems to provide better product models containing all technological information, instead of only geometric information
- Develop better understanding of the science of manufacturing processes

- Develop interface with shop floor control, scheduling, purchasing, marketing, and accounting systems
- Consider problems in other product domain, such as metal forming, composite manufacturing, and mechanical and electronic assembly

The future process planning systems will be used by the designer as a design evaluation tool, and by the marketing department as a quotation calculation tool. It will be sought by the production control department as an input to the master scheduling system, and by the shop floor control and scheduler for real time scheduling input. In order to do all of the above mentioned functions, it will need real time data from all related departments. Future process planning systems will be an integral part of the overall Computer Integrated Manufacturing (CIM) system, and will form the vital link between design and manufacturing systems.

CONCLUSIONS

Complete automation of process planning is a goal toward which industry strives. When and if it will be reachable are debatable issues. Nevertheless, it is quite clear that the results obtained during the path to this goal will help improve the CAPP activity, resulting in widespread use and great benefits. A major effort is needed both at the research level and the implementation level to transfer the research results into industrially usable systems.

A process planning system should never be a stand-alone system, nor should it be a static system. In order to fully utilize a computer-aided process planning system, integration of various system functions and constant maintenance of the system are extremely important. Cooperation of different manufacturing departments with engineering, marketing, and accounting departments is essential to the success of the development of a computer-aided process planning system.

In this chapter, we presented a complete picture of computer-aided process planning development and current implementation. Many concepts presented in this chapter are quite new. It is obvious that we were not able to go beyond the introduction level of details. For more details, readers are encouraged to refer to Chang and Wysk (1985) and Chang (1989),and to the specific references for different areas of reader interest.

REFERENCES

Aldefeld, B. "On Automatic Recognition of 3D Structures from 2D Representations." *Computer Aided Design* 15: 2 (1983): 59-64.

Alder, G. M. "Selection of Machining Process by Intelligent Knowledge Based Systems." In *International Conference on Computer Aided Production Engineering*, 61-66. Edinburgh: MEP Publication, 1986.

Allen, K. "Generative Process Planning System Using DCLASS Information System." Monograph 4, Computer Aided Manufacturing Laboratory, Brigham Young University, Utah, 1979.

Armstrong, G. T., G. C. Carey, and A. de Pennington. "Numerical Code Generation from a Geometric Modeling System." In *Solid Modeling by Computers*, edited by M. S. Picket and J. W. Boyse, 139-157. New York: Plenum Press, 1984.

Barkocy, B. E. and W. J. Zdeblick. "A Knowledge Based System for Machining Operations Planning." SME Technical Paper MS 84-716, 1984.

Berra, P. B. and M. M. Barash. "Investigation of Automated Process Planning and Optimization of Metal Working Processes." Report 14, Purdue Laboratory for Applied Industrial Control, West Lafayette, Indiana, July 1968.

Brown, P. F. and S. Ray. "Research Issues in Process Planning at the National Bureau of Standards." In *Proceedings of the 19th CIRP International Seminar on Manufacturing Systems*, 111-119. Pennsylvania State University, 1987.

CAM-I, "Functional Specification for an Experimental Planning System XPS-1." Computer Aided Manufacturing International, Arlington, Texas, 1979.

Chang, T. C. "TIPPS: A Totally Integrated Process Planning System." Ph.D. diss., Virginia Polytechnic Institute and State University, Blacksburg, Virginia, 1982.

_____. *Advances in Computer Aided Process Planning*. NBS-GCR-83-441. National Bureau of Standards, U.S. Dept. of Commerce, 1983.

_____. *Expert Process Planning Systems*. Addison Wesley (1989).

Chang, T. C. and R. A. Wysk. *An Introduction to Automated Process Planning Systems*. Englewood, New Jersey: Prentice-Hall, 1985.

Choi, B. K. "CAD/CAM Compatible Tool Oriented Process Planning for Machining Centers." Ph.D. diss., Purdue University, West Lafayette, Indiana, 1982.

Davies, B. J. and I. L. Darbyshire. "The Use of Expert Systems in Process Planning." *Annals of CIRP* 33/2/84 (1984): 303-306.

Descotte, Y. and J. C. Latombe. "GARI: A Problem Solver that Plans to Machine Mechanical Parts." In *Proceedings of IJCAI-7*, 766-772. 1981.

Dong, X. and M. Wozny. "FRAFES: A Frame Based Feature Extraction System." In *Proceedings of International Conference on Computer Integrated Manufacturing*. Rennselaer Polytechnic Institute, Troy, NY, May 23-25, 1988.

Dong, Z. and A. Soom. "Computer Interpretation of 2-D CAD Databases for Rotational Parts." In *Bound Volume of the Symposium on Integrated and Intelligence Manufacturing*, 181-192. ASME Winter Annual Meeting, Anaheim, California, Dec. 7-12, 1986.

Dunn, M. S. and S. Mann. "Computerized Production Process Planning." In *Proceedings of 15th Numerical Control Society Annual Meeting and Technical Conference*. Chicago, 1978.

Englert, P. J. and P. K. Wright. "Principles for Part Setup and Workholding in Automated Manufacturing." *Journal of Manufacturing Systems*. 7: 2 (1988): 147-161.

Erve, A. H. van't and H. J. J. Kals. "XPLANE: A Generative Computer Aided Process Planning System for Part Manufacturing." *Annals of CIRP*. 35/1/86 (1986): 325-329.

Eskicioglu, H. and B. J. Davies. "An Interactive Process Planning System for Prismatic Parts (ICAPP)." *Annals of CIRP*. 32: (1983): 365-370.

Eversheim, W., B. Holz, and K. H. Zons. "Application of Automatic Process Planning and NC Programming." In *Proceedings of AUTOFACT WEST*, 779-800. Society of Manufacturing Engineers, Anaheim, California, 1980.

Evershiem, W., and H. Esch. "Automated Generation of Process Plans or Prismatic Parts." *Annals of CIRP*. 32/1/83 (1983): 361-364.

Giusti, F., M. Santochi, and G. Dini. "COATS: An Expert System for Optimal Tool Selection." *Annals of CIRP*. 35/1/86 (1986): 337-340.

Grayer, A. R. "The Automatic Production of Machined Components Starting from a Stored Geometric Description." In *Advances in Computer Aided Manufacturing*, edited by D. McPherson, 137-151. Amsterdam: North-Holland Publishing Co., 1977.

Haralick, R. M. and D. Queeney. "Understanding Engineering Drawings." *Computer Graphics and Image Processing*. 20 (1982): 244-258.

Ham, I. and Y. C. Lu. "Computer Aided Process Planning: The Present and the Future." *Annals of CIRP*. 37: 2 (1988): 1-11.

Haas, M. and T. C. Chang. "Survey on Process Planning System Usage in Industry." School of Industrial Engineering, Purdue University, West Lafayette, Indiana, 1988.

Hayes, C. and P. Wright. "Automated Planning in the Machining Domain." In *Proceedings of the Symposium on Knowledge Based Expert Systems for Manufacturing*, 221-232. ASME Winter Annual Meeting, Anaheim, California, 1986.

Henderson, M. R. "Extraction of Feature Information from Three Dimensional CAD Data." Ph.D. diss., Purdue University, West Lafayette, Indiana, 1984.

Hirschtick, J. K. and D. C. Gossard. "Geometric Reasoning for Design Advisory Systems." In *Proceedings of the ASME International Computers in Engineering Conference*, vol. 1, 263-270. Chicago, July 20-24, 1986.

Horvath, M. "Semi-Generative Process Planning for Part Manufacturing." SME Technical Paper Series, MS79-153, 1979.

Houtzeel, A. "Computer Assisted Process Planning—A First Step towards Integration." In *Proceedings of the 18th Numerical Control Society Annual Meeting and Technical Conference*, 430-444. Dallas, Texas, 1981.

Hummel, K. E. and S. L. Brooks. "Symbolic Representation of Manufacturing Features for an Automated Process Planning System." In *Bound Volume of the Symposium on*

Knowledge Based Expert Systems for Manufacturing, 233-243. The Winter Annual Meeting of the ASME, Anaheim, California, Dec. 7-12, 1986.

Inui, M., H. Suzuki, and F. Kimura. "Generation and Verification of Process Plans using Dedicated Models of Products in Computers." ASME Winter Annual Meeting, Anaheim, California, Dec. 1986.

Iwata, K., Y. Kakino, F. Oba, and N. Sugimura. "Development of Non-Part Family Type Computer Aided Production Planning System CIMS/PRO." In *Advanced Manufacturing Technology*, edited by P. Blake, 171-184. Amsterdam: North-Holland Publishing Company, 1980.

Jakubowski, R. "Syntactic Characterization of Machine Parts Shapes." *Cybernetics and Systems: An International Journal*. 13 (1982): 1-24.

Joshi, S. "CAD Interface for Automated Process Planning." Ph.D. diss., School of Industrial Engineering, Purdue University, W. Lafayette, Indiana, 1987.

Joshi, S. and T. C. Chang. "Graph Based Heuristics for Recognition of Machined Features from a 3-D Solid Model." *Computer Aided Design*. 20:2 (1988): 58-66.

Joshi, S., N. N. Vissa, and T. C. Chang. "Expert Process Planning System with Solid Model Interface." *International Journal of Production Research*. 26: 5 (1988): 863-885.

Kakino, Y., F. Ohba, T. Moriwaki, and K. Iwata. "A New Method of Parts Description for Computer Aided Process Planning." In *Advances in Computer-Aided Manufacturing*, edited by D. McPherson, 197-213. Amsterdam: North-Holland Publishing Co., 1977.

Kanumury, M., J. Shah, and T. C. Chang. "An Automated Process Planning System for a Quick Turnaround Cell—An Integrated CAD and CAM System." In *Proceedings of USA-Japan Symposium on Flexible Automation*. Minneapolis, Minnesota, July 18, 1988.

Kotler, R. A. "Computerized Process Planning - Part 1." *Army Man Tech Journal* 4: 4 (1980): 28-36.

————. "Computerized Process Planning - Part 2." *Army Man Tech Journal* 4: 5 (1980): 20-29.

Kumara, S. R. T., S. Joshi, R. L. Kashyap, C. L. Moodie, and T. C. Chang. "Expert Systems in Industrial Engineering." *International Journal of Production Research* 24: 5 (1986): 1107-1125.

Kung, H. "An Investigation into Development of Process Plans from Solid Geometric Modeling Representation." Ph.D. diss., Oklahoma State University, 1984.

Kyprianou, L. K. "Shape Classification in Computer Aided Design." Ph.D. diss., Christ College, University of Cambridge, Cambridge, U.K., 1983.

Kyttner, R., Shtcheglov, and Kimmel, A. "A Complex Computer Aided Process Planning and Optimization for Machine Production." In *Advanced Manufacturing Technology* 185-198. Amsterdam: North Holland Publications, 1979.

Lee, Y. C. and K. S. Fu. "Machine Understanding of CSG: Extraction and Unification of Manufacturing Features." *IEEE Computer Graphics and Applications*. (1987): 20-32.

Li, J., C. Han, and I. Ham. "CORE-CAPP A Company-Oriented Semi-Generative Computer Automated Process Planning System." In *Proceedings of the 19th CIRP Inter-*

national Seminar On Manufacturing Systems, 219-225. Pennsylvania State University, June 1987.

Libardi, E. C., J. R. Dixon, and M. K. Simmons. "Designing with Features: Design and Analysis of Extrusions as an Example," ASME Paper No. 86-DE-4. Presented at the ASME Design and Engineering Conference, Chicago, March 1986.

Link, C. H. "CAPP-CAM-I Automated Process Planning System." In *Proceedings of 13th Numerical Control Society Annual Meeting and Technical Conference*. Cincinnati, Ohio, 1976.

Liu, C. R., and R. Srinivasan. "Generative Process Planning Using Syntactic Pattern Recognition." *Computers in Mechanical Engineering* 2: 5 (1984): 63-66.

Luby, S. C., J. R. Dixon, and M. K. Simmons. "Designing with Features: Creating and Using a Features Data Base for Evaluation of Manufacturability of Castings." In *Proceedings of the ASME International Computers in Engineering Conference*, Vol. 1, 285-292. Chicago, July 20-24, 1986.

Mashburn, T.A. "A Polygonal Solid Modeling Package." M.S. thesis, Department of Mechanical Engineering, Purdue University, 1987.

Markowsky, G. and M. A. Wesley. "Fleshing Out Wire Frames." *IBM Journal of Research and Development* 24: 5 (September 1980): 582-597.

Matsushima, K., N. Okada, and T. Sata. "The Integration of CAD and CAM by Application of Artificial Intelligence Techniques." *Annals of CIRP* 31/1/82 (1982).

Metzner, J.R., and B.H. Barnes. *Decision Table Language and Systems*. New York: Academic Press, 1977.

Milacic, V. R. "SAPT - Expert System for Manufacturing Planning." In *Computer Aided/Intelligent Process Planning*, edited by C. R. Liu, T. C. Chang, and R. Komanduri. Bound Volume of ASME Winter Annual Meeting, PED-Vol. 19, ASME, 1985.

Montalbano, M. *Decision Tables*. Science Research Associates, Chicago, 1974.

Mouleeswaran, C. B. "PROPLAN: A Knowledge Based Expert System for Manufacturing Process Planning." Master's thesis, University of Illinois at Chicago, 1984.

Nau, D. S. and T. C. Chang. "Prospects for Process Selection Using AI." *Computers in Industry* 4: 3 (1983): 253-263.

_____. "A Knowledge Based Approach to Process Planning." In *Bound Volume of the Symposium on Computer Aided/Intelligent Process Planning*, 65-72. The Winter Annual Meeting of the ASME, Miami Beach, Florida, November 17-22, 1985.

Nau, D.S. and M. Gray. "SIPS: An Approach of Hierarchical Knowledge Clustering to Process Planning." Paper presented at the ASME Winter Annual Meeting, Anaheim, California, Dec. 1986.

Niebel, B.W. "Mechanized Process Selection for Planning New Designs." ASTME Paper 737, 1965.

OIR, MULTIPLAN. Organization for Industrial Research, Inc. Waltham, Mass., 1983.

Opitz, H. *A Classification System to Describe Work Pieces*. Elmsford, New York: Pergamon Press, 1970.

Phillips, R. H. "A Computerized Process Planning System Based on Component Classification and Coding." Ph.D. diss., Purdue University, West Lafayette, Indiana, 1978.

_____. Arunthavanathan, and X. D. Zhan. "Microplan: A Microcomputer Based Expert System for Generative Process Planning." In *Proceedings of the Symposium on*

Knowledge Based Expert Systems for Manufacturing, 263-273. ASME Winter Annual Meeting, Anaheim, California, 1986.

Planning Institute Inc. "PICAPP," PII, Arlington, Texas, 1980.

Preiss, K. "Constructing the Solid Representations from Engineering Projections." *Computers and Graphics* 8: 4 (1984): 381-389.

Preiss, K. and E. Kaplansky. "Automated CNC Milling by Artificial Intelligence Methods." In *Proceedings of AUTOFACT 6*, 2.40-2.59, 1984.

Requicha, A. A. G. "Representations for Rigid Solids: Theory, Methods, and Systems." *Computing Surveys* 12: 4 (December 1980): 437-464.

Sack, C. F. "Computer Managed Process Planning—A Bridge Between CAD & CAM." *AUTOFACT4*, Nov. 1982.

Scheck, D. E. "Feasibility of Automated Process Planning." Ph.D. diss., Purdue University, West Lafayette, Indiana, 1966.

Spur, G., F. L. Krause, and H. M. Anger. "System for Computer Aided Process Planning including Quality Control." In Advanced Course on CIM (CIM83), 85-99. Karlsruhe, Germany, Sept. 1983.

Srinivasan, R., C. R. Liu, and K. S. Fu. "Extraction of Manufacturing Details from Geometric Models." *Computers and Industrial Engineering* 9: 2 (1985): 125-134.

Staley, S. M., M. R. Henderson, and D. C. Anderson. "Using Syntactic Pattern Recognition to Extract Feature Information from a Solid Modeling Database." *Computers in Mechanical Engineering* 2: 2 (Sept. 1983): 61-65.

Tipnis, V. A., S. A. Vogel, and C. E. Lamb. "Computer Aided Process Planning System for Aircraft Engine Rotating Parts." SME Technical Paper, Series MD79-155, 1979.

Tulkoff, J. "Lockheed's GENPLAN." In *Proceedings of 18th Numerical Control Society Annual Meeting and Technical Conference*, 417-421. Dallas, Texas, 1981.

Vogel, S. A. and E. J. Adlard. "The AUTOPLAN Process Planning System." In *Proceedings of the 18th Numerical Control Society Annual Meeting and Technical Conference*, 729-742. Dallas, Texas, 1981.

Wang, H-P. and R. A. Wysk. "An Expert System for Machining Data Selection." *Computers and Industrial Engineering* 10: 2 (1986): 99-107.

Wang, H. and R. Wysk. "Turbo-CAPP: A Knowledge Based Computer Aided Process Planning System." In *Proceedings of the 19th CIRP International Seminar on Manufacturing Systems*, 161-167. University Park, Pennsylvania, June, 1987.

Weill, R., G. Spur, and W. Eversheim. "Survey of Computer-Aided Process Planning Systems." *Annals of CIRP* 31: 2 (1982): 539-552.

Woo, T. C. "Computer Aided Recognition of Volumetric Designs." In *Advances in Computer-Aided Manufacturing*, edited by D. McPherson, 121-135. Amsterdam: North-Holland Publishing Co., 1977.

————. "Interfacing Solid Modeling to CAD and CAM: Data Structures and Algorithms for Decomposing a Solid." Technical Report 83-6, Department of Industrial and Operations Engineering, University of Michigan, Ann Arbor, 1983.

Wysk, R. A. "An Automated Process Planning and Selection Program: APPAS." Ph.D. diss., Purdue University, West Lafayette, Indiana, 1977.

21

Computer Simulation of Automated Manufacturing Systems

Thomas K. Joseph[*]
Trevor Miles[**]

DURING THE PAST TWO OR THREE DECADES, COM-
puter simulation has become a well established and
popular tool for planning, designing, and operating
manufacturing systems. With the emergence of
automated or integrated manufacturing systems,
computer simulation has proven to be invaluable.
The stiff global competition in recent years among
manufacturing companies to produce inexpensive
and better quality products more efficiently, has
further increased the need for such sophisticated,
automated manufacturing systems. However,
installing these systems can be complicated and it
involves risks and many factors of uncertainty.

Some of these factors include:

- Innovative concepts: The application of the latest
  technology often means that many of the concepts and designs are first-time applications,
  which may be untested or need to be uniquely
  customized.
- Costs: The initial investment in the development
  and use of sophisticated hardware and software
  can be very high.
- Ongoing adjustment: The complexity and essential integration of automated manufacturing sys-

The authors would like to thank Daniel J. Maas of National Center of Manufacturing Sciences, Ann Arbor, Michigan, and Jay Baron of
Volkswagen of America, Troy, Michigan, for their contributions and help in preparation of this chapter. The comments received from
staff members of Decision Technologies Division of EDS are also appreciated.

*Thomas K. Joseph is currently with the Consulting Division, at Electronic Data System (EDS) Corporation, Troy, Michigan. Prior
to joining EDS he was with Industrial Technology Institute, Ann Arbor, Michigan. He holds a B.Eng., from University of Madras,
India, and an M.S. from University of Windsor, Canada, in Industrial Engineering. He also holds an M.S. from Oakland University,
Rochester, Michigan, in Systems Engineering (Manufacturing Systems). He has several years experience in the application of simulation to automated manufacturing systems. He has also been involved with research projects in development of expert systems for
simulation, scheduling of automated manufacturing systems, and integration of control systems and simulation.

**Trevor Miles is a senior consultant with the Factory Automation Division of Hawker Siddeley in England. He previously worked for
Systems Modeling Corp., Sewickley, Pennsylvania. He holds a B.Sc. in Chemical Engineering from The University of Cape Town,
and an M.Sc. in Chemical Engineering from The University of the Witwatersrand. He is currently a Ph.D. candidate in Industrial
Engineering and Management Science at The Pennsylvania State University. His research interests include stochastic optimization, the integration of simulation with control systems and scheduling systems, and object-oriented model generation.

tems necessitates ongoing evaluation and fine tuning.

- Time: Planning, designing, implementing, and debugging an automated system typically takes longer than planned due to problems with interfacing, integration, and communication.
- Multidisciplinary: Designing and planning an automated manufacturing system requires close coordination among people with various backgrounds and experience (software, hardware, controls, manufacturing).

Because of these factors, manufacturers often need to systematically evaluate alternate system designs prior to implementation and to evaluate system performance during the operational phase. Computer simulation is a widely used tool because it serves these needs through its systematic approach. Computer simulation is also a dynamic field with regular advances in tools and techniques. These advances include:

- User friendly software: New simulation software packages, though more sophisticated, are easier to use and do not require extensive computer programming experience.
- Computing power: More efficient and cheaper hardware makes simulation accessible to even small companies.
- Graphic animations: Most simulation software packages enable users to animate color models of a system, making the simulations less abstract, and easier to understand and report on.
- Application specific software: Many simulation packages available today are industry-specific or support a specific application. Examples include scheduling, control systems, communications systems, and robotic simulation. Many of these occur in an almost program free environment. Such software encourages the widespread use and appreciation of computer simulation among nonsimulationists.

The major advantages of using computer simulation

for manufacturing systems are:

- It allows evaluation of alternative designs for proposed systems and prediction of their performance.
- It makes possible sensitivity or "what if" studies to verify design intent, and simulate changes prior to their actual implementation on existing systems, thus eliminating costly, unfeasible, or unsafe disruptions.
- It allows great flexibility by allowing manipulation of multiple factors to achieve a particular application. One is no longer limited by the need for oversimplified formulations as in the case of analytical modeling techniques.
- It provides the capability to study system dynamics accurately, examine the effects of time variations, and reduce the impact of uncertainty.
- It promotes a life cycle perspective and a more global view of the manufacturing system, and in so doing helps to identify areas that need further study.

As with any other decision making technique, simulation also has its shortcomings and limitations. It is important that users be aware of these in order to use simulation effectively and derive maximum benefit. This chapter covers some of the background of computer simulation and deals with applications to manufacturing systems. The primary emphasis in this chapter is on the simulation of *material flow*, the actual physical movement of parts in a system. The use and applications of simulation for issues such as computer communications, controls, or robotic simulations are not covered in detail. We refer you to other relevant chapters in this handbook for information in these areas.

BACKGROUND OF COMPUTER SIMULATION

Computer simulation is a process of designing a mathematical logical model of a real system and conducting experiments with this model. These experiments are for the purpose of understanding the behavior of the system and/or evaluating various strategies within the limits imposed by a criterion or set of criteria for the operation of the system (Shannon 1975, *Simulation: Art and Science*).

Types of Simulation Models

Discrete and Continuous Two types of simulation models are classified by changes which occur in the system over time. These are the discrete event models and continuous models.

In *discrete event* simulation, the changes in the system can occur only at specific points during a time period. The instances when change occurs are called the events. It is not necessary to track changes in the system between any two events. A typical example of this is when an operation or machining process is started on a part at a machine. The metal removal is not tracked by the model; the important events are: the start and finish times for the machining operation, and the machine breakdown, if one occurs during that time interval.

In *continuous simulation* changes occur between two points in time and are tracked by the model. These changes are represented by differential equations. A typical example of this in a manufacturing environment is tool wear. Changes in tool condition over time are represented with a differential equation as a function of the tool speed, depth of cut, coolant temperature, and material characteristics. Similarly, other changes in the system may occur on a continual basis over any period of time. These changes can be incorporated in the same simulation model.

These two types of simulation environments are not mutually exclusive and may be used concurrently in the same system model to describe various changes over time. Such representations are called *combined discrete and continuous* simulation models. Almost all automated manufacturing system applications, with the exception of the process industries (chemical plants, refinery), can be represented accurately with discrete event models.

Deterministic and Stochastic Simulation models are further classified as deterministic or stochastic, based on the characteristics of events which can occur in a given system. If the occur-

rence of all the events can be described at specific times with certainty, then this is called *deterministic* simulation. An example of such an event is the machining time of a part at an automated workstation. This time may be predicted accurately by the nature of the machining operation.

In *stochastic simulation* the occurrence and/or the duration of events may be uncertain and must be described by using a random number function. A typical example of such an event is machine breakdown, the occurrence of which is random and needs to be described by a probability distribution (such as exponential or uniform).

Static and Dynamic A *static* simulation model represents the system at a specific instant in time. System performance is estimated by quantitative measures derived from the system conditions, which are represented in the system at that instant in time. Measures obtained from spreadsheets or rough cut modeling and Monte Carlo simulation models are examples of static simulations.

Dynamic simulation models capture the various changes that occur as the system operates over a period of time. The simulation methods and applications described in this chapter are mainly of this type.

Discrete Event Simulation Terminologies

Manufacturing system simulations are typically represented using dynamic, discrete event models and may be stochastic or deterministic in nature, depending on each application. The terminologies frequently used for describing the discrete event simulation follow.

Entities: These are the physical components (such as machines, parts, and pallets) of a system that have to be defined in order to describe the system. There are mainly two types. Physical components, which enter the system, are operated upon and exit the system; these are called *temporary* entities. Physical components which exist in the system during the entire simulated period, such as the machines and transporters, are referred to as *permanent* entities.

Attributes: These are properties or information

that are attached to the entity and used to determine the status of the entity during the simulated period. Examples of this are the arrival time of a part into a system or the priority of a part waiting in a queue in front of a machine.

System variables: These are variables used to describe the state of the system. Changes in the system are recorded by the values of these variables and as a consequence of the occurrence of events in the model. Examples include queue length for parts waiting to commence a machining operation and number of busy transporters.

System state: This is the status or condition of the system at any given instant. It is described in the model by the value of all the variables in the system.

Events: These are any instances in the model in which a change occurs in the state of the system modeled. Examples include arrival of a part at a machine, or release of a transporter after the part is delivered at a station.

Queues: A queue is the position in the system of an entity that is waiting to be operated upon. Example of a queue is a part waiting in the input buffer area of a workstation.

Delay: This is a duration of time of unspecified length encountered by a part or entity as it flows through the system. An example of delay is the time spent by a part in the output buffer area of a workstation, waiting for an automated guided vehicle (AGV) to move it to its next location in its process sequence.

Activity: This is an operation over a finite duration of time (of known length described by a constant, function, or a random number distribution) that alters the property(s) of an entity, and thus the state of the system. Examples include tool change-over time and the process times at a machine.

Sets: A set is the collection of entities grouped either logically or physically to describe a state of the system. Examples include number of parts waiting in a workstation (a physical set) or those parts waiting at different locations in a system for an AGV to move it to its next location (logical set).

Model: The model is the abstract representation of a system using logical and/or mathematical relationships. It describes the states of the system on an event by event basis with the help of entities and attributes, system variables, delays, activities, and events.

Manufacturing System Modeling

Simply stated, a manufacturing system is modeled as a network of queues and activities. In general, a part (entity) in the model traverses this network from one queue to another (waiting for machines, AGVs, operator), as it gets serviced (activities). The queues are logically connected to approximately reflect the physical system. For material flow simulation in general, there is a one-to-one correspondence of the actual queues in the physical system to the queues used in the abstract model developed, making it easier to conceptualize. However, in order to control the flow of parts, one needs additional queues and entities describe the logical relationships. Using this notion of queues and activities, logical and physical, one can describe a manufacturing system to the desired level of detail. Incorporating issues such as the control system, scheduling rules, or computer communications involved in an integrated manufacturing system involves more logical network of queues, and thus tends to be more abstract.

Experience and creativity, coupled with the modeler's background or domain of expertise, play a major role in the modeling activity. Successful modeling requires not only capturing a sufficient level of detail in the system, but also identifying significant factors or variables, and interpretation of the results.

Modeling Uncertainty

It is very rare in any system modeled that all events are deterministic or known to occur without any uncertainty. Using a completely deterministic model may meet desired goals and objectives. However, in order to capture some realism in the system modeled, a certain level of uncertainty needs to be incorporated in the model. Typical events or activities which involve uncertainty in a manufacturing system include the arrival pattern of parts, repair time for machines, or the breakdown interval of machines. Such events can be incorporated by using random number distribution functions. Commonly used distributions for modeling manufacturing systems are uniform, exponential, Poisson, or normal. Most simulation packages provide the capability to incorporate such distributions. Computer generated random numbers provide the root of such functions.

Incorporating uncertainty in a model also requires an understanding of statistics, design of experiments, and analysis, for proper interpretation of the results. Some tips for this are described later in this section.

Computer Implementation of Discrete Event Simulation

Successful simulation and its widespread use are largely due to representation of queuing modeling concepts in a computer. This section defines some of the terms describing these representations, and how the representations of the discrete event modeling concepts are implemented in a computer program. An example illustrates the concepts.

The Event Calendar   Time does not progress smoothly in discrete event simulation; it advances in asynchronous steps, the sizes of which are determined by the completion time of the events. The events can be split into two categories: future and current events. The current events are all those events with an event time equal to the current simulation time, while the future events have a completion time later than the current simulation time.

The event calendar is the ordered list of all current and future events. Some discrete event simulation languages have two calendars—one for current events and one for future events—in order to minimize the central processing unit (CPU) time used for event calendar maintenance. The future events are ranked least value first based on event time.

Example   Let us take as an example a drive-through teller at a bank. Let us assume that there is only one teller and one line. The events that occur in this system are:

1. A new customer arrives at the bank
2. A customer enters the line
3. A customer enters service with the teller
4. A customer completes service with the teller
5. A customer leaves the bank

In the example, there is at least one event on the future events calendar; the arrival of the next customer. The other event in our example which affects the event calendar is event 3. The time the entities spend in the line—the time delay from event 2 to event 3—has an indirect effect on the event calendar, and hence on time. The effect these events have on time will be explained separately. Whenever a new customer arrives at the bank, another entity—representing the next arrival of a customer to the bank—is created and placed on the future events calendar. (Note that we will refer interchangeably to events and entities; entities are the computer's record of events.) Part of the information kept with this new entity is the time of arrival of the next customer. The time of arrival is used to rank the entities on the future events calendar.

When a customer enters service with the teller, an event is placed in the future events calendar. This event represents the completion of service. The time of completion of service is determined, by some mechanism unique to the simulation language, and is used to rank the entities on the future events calendar. When the simulation clock reaches the time for completion of service, the event is removed from the current events calendar and processed.

Other Ordered Lists   In the example, the only other event which caused time to progress is event 2, when customers enter the line. If we could predict the time at which the customers would enter service, then we could place this event on the future events calendar. However, the time that the customers spend in the line cannot be predicted.

The time spent in the line depends on how many customers are already in the line and the time they will spend in the line and at the teller. Consequently, these events cannot be placed in the future and current events calendars. The events representing customers waiting in a line are kept in separate ordered lists, queues.

A queue is maintained for every line in the model. The more advanced simulation languages allow the user to specify the ranking method of the queues separately. The queues are in effect separate event calendars for which the completion order is known but not the completion time. The completion time is based on some complex condition of the system and cannot be predicted. In terms of our example, whenever a customer completes service at the teller, the system state is set to reflect that the teller is now available. The customer at the front of the queue is then allowed to enter service at the teller.

In abstract terms, when the system enters a state that allows an event to proceed, the customer at the front of the queue is removed from the queue and the state of the system is changed to reflect this action. All the other events in the queue have to wait until the state of the system is such that others may proceed. Most simulation languages can enter several states which do not allow the events to exit the queues. These states range from the simple, such as gaining access to a server, to more complex states specified by the user.

Time Advance An explanation of how the simulation languages manipulate time is necessary. The simulation language will process the events on the current events calendar one at a time until the current events calendar is empty. The processing of the current events has no effect on time. When the current events calendar is emptied, the simulation language will look at the completion time of the event at the head of the future events calendar. The simulation clock is changed immediately to this time. Any other events on the future events calendar with the same event time as the current simulation clock will be removed and placed on the current events calendar.

The order of events on the current events calendar is specific to the simulation language. The most common are FIFO (First In, First Out) and LIFO (Last In, First Out). Each event on the current events calendar will be removed from the calendar and processed until the current events calendar is empty. The simulation clock is then updated again.

Statistics Collection and Analysis

One of the areas of computer simulation most overlooked is that of statistic collection and analysis. In this section we will not give detailed statistical techniques, but rather point out the most common errors and develop a methodology for "rough cut" analysis of simulation results. Before we discuss the problems and methodology, we will briefly discuss basic terms and definitions.

Definitions Two basic types of systems are simulated using discrete event simulation techniques. These are described below.

Terminating Systems As is indicated by the term, these systems have a finite period of operation. The most obvious example of such a system is a store. They are typified by an initial state which is the same at the beginning of each period of operation. The most common state is that of "empty and idle." That is, there are no customers in the store and all of the attendants in the store are available to assist a customer. Terminating systems are most amenable to statistical analysis but, unfortunately, they do not represent the majority of systems simulated.

Nonterminating System These systems do not have a finite period of production or, most importantly, no obvious initial state. For example, a system which operates for eight hours a day is not necessarily a terminating system. If the initial state of a period of operation is dependent on the ending state of the previous period, then the system must be classified as nonterminating. The most obvious example of a nonterminating system is a manufacturing facility which operates for three shifts a day. Unfortunately, the nonterminating systems are not as easy to analyze and usually require some manipulation of the data.

A store can be used to illustrate the difference between terminating and nonterminating systems. If the object of the simulation is to determine the number of store clerks required to adequately service the customers, then the system is best described as a terminating system. This classification results from the fact that there are no customers in the store at the beginning of each day of operation, and at the end of each day no customers remain in the store. If, however, the objective of the simulation is to determine the optimum reorder point for certain stock items in the store, then the nonterminating classification is more appropriate. The reason for this is that the items of interest do not vacate the store at the end of the period of operation. They are in the same state at the beginning of a particular period as they were at the end of the previous period.

To complicate matters further, there are two types of statistics collected. These are commonly referred to as observational and time-persistent and are discussed below.

Observational Statistics Observational statistics are characterized by taking on a value at the instance of observation but not at any other time. Classical statistics are developed around observational statistics. The most common observational statistic is the time taken to perform a particular task, such as running a race and serving a customer. Each observation is presumed to be independent and uncorrelated with the previous observations.

Time-persistent Statistics Time-persistent statistics are characterized by taking on a value at a particular time and retaining that value until some future time. Time-persistent statistics are usually collected on variables that describe the state of operation of the system. The number of customers waiting in a line to be serviced is a good example of a time-persistent statistic. When a new customer joins the line, the number of customers remains at that value until either a customer leaves the line to be serviced or a new customer joins the line.

Common Errors In the case of terminating systems, the most common error is to perform the analysis of the system based on the statistics gathered from a single run of the simulation. This form of analysis violates one of the most basic canons of classical statistics, namely the use of independent and uncorrelated data. However, much qualitative information can be garnered from single run analysis, while the model is still in the development stage. The qualitative information ranges from obvious capacity problems to incomplete control logic.

In the case of nonterminating systems, there are two common errors, namely ignoring the initialization bias and ignoring the correlation of the data. Often, because of cost constraints, the models are not run for a sufficiently long time to detect the initialization bias. Many complex systems have an extremely long start-up period, especially if started empty and idle. The data from discrete event simulation models are often strongly correlated. This correlation has to be removed before any of the statistical tests can be performed because of the requirement of independent data. This is normally performed by batching the data to form a single observation: the mean of the data in the batch.

"Rough-Cut" Analysis In the case of terminating systems, the initial state and the run length are usually fixed. Consequently, the only datum to be collected for analysis is the average value of the performance measures for each replication. By the Central Limit Theorem, these data values should be independent and normally distributed. At least ten replications are suggested, with 20 replications being preferred. Nonterminating systems are more difficult to analyze. A useful technique in dealing with them is to make a single run over a "long" period of simulated time, keeping a record of all the performance record information. The time at which the system reaches some form of steady performance must be determined. All the data collected during the initialization stage must be deleted from the performance measure data sets.

The remaining data must be batched by averaging the data values over a fixed period of time using the averages as the data values. For example, assume that data are collected over 480 hours of operation and that the initialization period is 80 hours. Ten data values could then be formed by averaging the remaining data over 40 hour periods. These new data values should be tested for significant correlation. If insignificant correlation exists, the number of batches must be reduced. At least ten batches should be formed. Once all correlation has been removed, the batch means can be analyzed by conventional statistical means, because, by the Central Limit Theorem, they should be independent and normally distributed.

Some of the tests which can be performed to distinguish between the performances of different systems are the paired t-test, analysis of variance, and ranking and selection. Consult statistics texts for details on how to perform these tests.

Animation

Animation can be defined as the dynamic visual depiction of the state of the system being simulated. As the state of the system changes, so does the graphic image.

Current animation capabilities range from simple images consisting of boxes which change color to reflect specific state changes, to sophisticated three dimensional images which can be zoomed and rotated. Simple animation systems do not show movement of entities, while sophisticated packages allow the user to specify different icons to reflect different levels of processing of the entities as they move through the system. Different icons may be used to show different states of resources—such as the bank teller in our earlier example, who can be busy or idle—or more complex system states as specified by the user.

Software ranges from systems in which the animation is the simulation—these usually lack the ability to simulate complex systems—to systems in which instructions to perform the animation are embedded in the simulation code. Other packages allow the user to build the animation separately so that the simulation can be run with or without the animation.

There are three major benefits of using anima-

tion over the lifetime of a simulation project. These are debugging, validation and verification, and presentation of results. The level of detail of the animation and the effort required usually increase in the same order.

The Debugging Benefit By *debugging* we mean the process of identification and correction of errors in the simulation code or logic. Debugging can be performed adequately by using very simple images to represent the system. Boxes and bars, with some system state variables displayed in numeric form, are usually sufficient to represent the different components of the simulation at this level.

The Validation and Verification Benefit By *validation and verification* we mean the process of ensuring that the simulation model accurately represents the system being modeled, and that the results obtained from the model are within the bounds of expectation. Obviously more complex and detailed animations are required at this stage.

The Presentation of Results Benefit By *presentation of results* we mean showing the simulation animation to an audience who has neither the time nor the knowledge to understand the details of the simulation. In this case, a very complex animation is required which depicts the system in as realistic terms as possible.

All three benefits of animation are of great importance to the simulation practitioner and should be accorded the same importance during the lifetime of a simulation project. As the project matures, the animation should become more detailed.

THE SIMULATION PROCESS

The process of conducting a successful simulation study can be a time consuming and painstaking process for automated manufacturing systems analysts. The diversity of the applications and the multidisciplinary nature of the knowledge domains involved in automated manufacturing system simulations dictate that the applications are seldom alike, with few hard and fast rules to follow.

The development of the model itself is an evolutionary process. Due to the flexible nature of the simulation technique, there are numerous approaches that can be followed to accomplish the same goals. A systematic step by step approach for conducting a successful study is presented here with some general guidelines and some of the typical pitfalls.

Modeling Process

The process of representing a manufacturing system with a simulation model requires that the system be described on an event-by-event basis to capture it in an abstract model. This forces the analyst to define and understand many of the interactions that are typically involved. Thus, with proper perspective and following a systematic approach, a simulation study can provide benefits beyond the tangible one of providing the quantifiable numbers required for decision making. One of the goals of any simulation study should be to gain, as much as possible, the intangible benefits, the experience gained from modeling and analyzing the system. These are benefits which can be gained irrespective of whether the objective of obtaining the quantifiable measures was satisfied.

Goals of Simulation Study

Goal setting is an important first step in any study. It is essential to establish a strategy for reaching the goals of the study. The overall goal of any study undertaken for automated manufacturing systems (AMS) is one or more of the following:

- Estimates of the performance of the system, based on quantifiable measures obtained from the simulation study, for evaluating alternative designs. Typical measures are given in TABLE 21-1 and include throughput times, machine utilization, and time spent by a part in the system.
- Comparative studies based on cost and performance criteria to evaluate alternative system designs, configuration, or a specific design feature.
- A tool for modeling a system to gain the intangible benefit of a better understanding of its dynamic characteristics and the sensitivities in-

volved. These intangible benefits gained from conducting a study include:

- Providing a system perspective of the manufacturing system under consideration, which leads to interaction among the various people involved.
- Increasing, through the exercise of the study, understanding of the complexities involved. These complexities may not be apparent or may be counter-intuitive, especially during the conceptual phase.
- Helping to reduce the learning time involved in the implementation and operation of the system installed.

Simulation Study Steps

A methodological approach in conducting the study is essential to maximize the benefits. We outline below a step-by-step procedure for conducting a simulation study. Since business and manufacturing objectives involve an evolutionary process, modeling a manufacturing system may involve several iterations or one or more of these steps.

1. Information Gathering Phase Analysts initiate this activity as the need for a simulation study becomes obvious. One of the major emphases during this step is to define the scope and requirements of the study to be conducted. In particular, the overall structure, objectives, and emphasis of the study, as well as the composition of the study team need to be defined. Visits to existing sites, or meetings with designers, vendors, or users will be necessary. Some of the quantitative information of the system under consideration, such as capacity requirements, process plans, and machines available, should be gathered during this phase. A list of the typical input parameters required for the development of a simulation model is given in TABLE 21-2.

2. Static Analysis This activity, equivalent to "back-of-the-envelope" calculation, is a necessary presimulation study. Calculation to obtain some of the aggregate values should be done now to help in setting the stage for the more detailed simulation model development and analysis.

Table 21-1. List of Performance Measures.

Typical statistics of measures to be obtained include, mean, standard deviation, minimum value, maximum values, and number of observations, where applicable.

SYSTEM MEASURES

Capacity per hour/shift/month
Throughput times of parts
Output rates (part/hr)
Scrap rate/rework rate
System uptime/downtime
System utiization
Setup/changeover/retooling times
Production time
WIP levels
Tardiness/lateness in schedules

MATERIAL HANDLING SYSTEMS

Part movements between stations
Number of parts in transit
Number pallets on conveyor
Pallets space used on conveyor
Total uptime/downtime
Utilization

AGV SPECIFIC

Travel times loaded
Travel times empty
Idle/ downtimes
Blocked times
Load/unload time
Battery charging time
Maintenance times
Frequency of moves between stations
Total number of moves
Total distances moved
AGV response times to request
AGV request frequency

RESOURCES

Machines:
Waiting times at each machine
Machine idle times
Machine production times
Machine nonproduction times
Machine setup times
Machine blocked times
Maintenance times
Downtimes

Manpower Requirements:
Manual load/unload
Setup crews
Maintenance crews

Miscellanious
Pallet requirements
Fixture requirements
Tool requirements
Waiting time for each resource
Queue length at each resource

BOTTLENECK AREAS

Percent utilization
Primary bottleneck operations
Potential bottlenecking operations
Material handling congestion
Capacity changes
Queue sizes
Waiting times

PRODUCT/PARTS

Total time spent in system
Material handling time
Waiting times
Inspection times
Actual machining times
Rework times

Besides providing some of the static characteristics for the system, the information generated at this stage will also help in the development of the model, in making realistic assumptions, and in the interpretation of the simulation results. A list of some of the measures that can be determined from such calculations are given in TABLE 21-3. Proper analysis of these measures can be invaluable for the subsequent steps. This step also helps to verify data consistency.

3. Objective Specification Detailed objectives and the scope of the study should be

Table 21-2. Input Data Required for Simulation Studies.

MATERIAL HANDLING SYSTEMS

From/to distances between stations
No. of pallet spaces in system
No. of AGVs available
Number of pallets available
Travel speeds of AGVs
    loaded
    unload
Maximum load of ACVs
Conveyor speeds
Capacity lengths

WORKSTATIONS

Number of workstations
Input buffer space capacity
Output buffer space capacity
Operation times
Setup information
    Frequency of setups
    Setup times matrix

EQUIPMENT RELIABILITY

Expected downtimes
Causes for breakdowns
Mean time between failures
Average downtimes
Average repair times
Distribution of data

QUALITY

Scrap rate at each macine
Scraps detected by inspection
Type of defects
Reworkable parts detected
Inspection frequency
Reject/rework rate
Rework times

MANPOWER REQUIREMENTS

Number of manual operations
Operation times
Skill level/efficiency levels

SCHEDULING & SEQUENCING

Part introduction policies
(fixed intervals, due-date)
Lot sizes
Priority at each queue
Bottleneck machines strategies
Process planning procedures
(Kanban, JIT, Push system)

PRODUCTION PLANNING

Production horizon
Shift schedules
Break times
Make-up schedules/overtime
Maintenance schedules
Shipping schedules
Production cycles

REPLENISHMENT POLICIES

Storage life
No. of perishable items
Finished goods storage capacity
Ordering cycles (criteria)

TOOLING REQUIREMENTS

Number of tools per station
Capacity at station
Redundant tools
GT classifications
Tool handling
Fixture requirements

SYSTEM REQUIREMENTS

Capacity needs
Acceptable utilization levels
Acceptable quality levels
Lead times
Response times

---

clearly defined during this stage. These are based on the information gained from the preceding two steps.

The capabilities of the simulation language to be used also plays a role in defining the scope. The study may need to be structured in multiple phases, with several iterations specifying the objectives and emphasis for each phase. The model parameters and all the assumptions should be clearly stated and understood at this time by all members of the team.

4. Simulation Model Development The actual simulation model development is undertaken during this step. It might prove worthwhile to build a quick prototype model, prior to developing a final model. It should be realized that in a study the model developed evolves with time and sometimes

**Table 21-3. Measures
from Presimulation Static Analysis.**

Measures to be determined for the desired part production requirements, where applicable.

Workstation Requirements
Machining/assembly time requirements at each machine
Setup time requirements at each machine
Number of setups required at each machine
Maximum utilized machines (potential bottlenecks)
Total tool changeover times
Slack time at each machine
Maximum buffer capacity

System Measures
Total production time for each part
Total travel times (minimum) required of each part in system
Batch sizes per part
Number of batches required for each part
Number of pallets per batch for each part
Manpower requirements

Material Handling
Minimum transfers of each AGV
Minimum moves for each AGV (from/to between stations)
Minimum distances moved by AGVs
From/to transfers of parts/pallets between stations
Density of part flow from/to stations
Number of transfers required for each spur

---

may tend to be unwieldy. The potential of initiating a new model should be considered if the initial model is too constraining.

5. Data Collection During this step accurate data necessary specifically for the model should be collected. It is very important to ensure that any data obtained are accurate. The value of the results obtained from a model is only as good as the input date used. The degree of accuracy required should be consistent with the objectives of the study, and should be realistically assessed prior to the collection of data.

6. Model Validation This step is undertaken concurrently with the preceding two steps, and continues with the subsequent step, the animation of the system. We encourage you to set aside time specifically for this verification effort. The logic of the model should be tested by monitoring various measures, such as the queue sizes, time taken between any two events, or the number of parts entering a station, and by varying certain parameter values individually. This process can be very valuable since it will help in determining the limitations of the model and in the interpretation of the results. It helps in gaining a better understanding of the system modeled and the sensitivities involved. No results should be distributed prior to the model validation.

7. Animation This powerful feature, provided with many simulation languages, is increasingly proving itself as an essential component of simulation. Animation helps a great deal in model building, debugging, and for communicating to personnel who may not be well versed with simulation concepts but who are very knowledgeable about the actual system modeled. The effort to be expended and the level of detail of the animation required should be determined by the audience, background of the other team members involved, and management reporting requirements.

8. Analysis and Verification of the Results This is a crucial step, initiated prior to the interpretation of the results; it is frequently categorized as a part of the next step. However, during this stage, the emphasis is primarily on designing the statistical experiments and collecting appropriate output data for the interpretations. The output measures obtained should be verified for statistical validity, especially if randomness has been incorporated in the model. Experiments to obtain information to help in determining some of the objectives of the study should be conducted during this step and the results analyzed.

9. Interpretation of the Results The activity involved here is a group effort by the team members to interpret the measures collected from the analysis. The results obtained from the simulation models should be examined with emphasis on implications. This may be done as part of an ongoing effort involving several iterations of the preceding two steps.

10. Recommendations and Documentation The documentation of the activities and the findings are an essential part of any study. All recommendations and suggestions for future work based on the information obtained from the study should be included. This is also an opportunity to document the intuitive knowledge gained from the study. In particular, all potential problem areas or issues identified as needing further study, either with continued simulation or other supportive studies, should be addressed.

General Guidelines

Appropriateness of the Tool Conducting a simulation study can be very time consuming and may involve considerable interaction and effort from various people. However, many of the questions may be answered through other, simpler methods, such as static analysis, with less effort than a simulation study. Prior to initiating a simulation study, you will find it worthwhile to consider its appropriateness. This can also help indirectly with defining some of the expectations for the study.

Clear Definition of the Objectives and Purpose of Study The objectives and purpose of the study should be clearly stated and understood by all concerned. Some of these may be general at the outset but must be made specific during the course of the study. Ownership of the manufacturing system must also be resolved, since the system integrator and the end user often switch as the prime owner during the course of the project. This may influence the goals and objectives.

A Team Approach As automated manufacturing systems involve multidisciplinary knowledge domains, the necessity to work as a team to achieve a successful study is of vital importance. Clearly define the responsibility and objectives of each member in the team, and especially those persons who will be closely involved with the simulation modeling effort. Interaction between the software model developer and the domain experts of the manufacturing system is required throughout the study.

Free and open communication among the team members is essential and should be encouraged very early in the study. Frequent presentations and discussions, both formal and informal, among the members should be encouraged.

Structure and Organization of the Overall Approach The simulation study should be organized and conducted in phases, especially if the level of effort is expected to be substantial. The objectives and the goals to be accomplished in each of these phases should be predefined. They may be weighted approximately at first and their values made more specific over time.

Studying Effect of Uncertainties Where uncertainties are represented in the model by the use of random numbers, care should be taken to avoid confounding the effects during analysis and interpretation of the results. Following a systematic approach in examining the effect of the uncertainties is recommended. Some guidelines follow.

- Phase in each uncertainty gradually, after its sensitivity is understood, in order to facilitate interpretation of the results.
- Make trial runs using different random number seeds and/or by replication, or validation of the model.

- Be sure that the system is in steady state prior to collecting output measures for interpretation.
- Be sure that results obtained by incorporating uncertainty are statistically valid. Care should be taken especially if the accuracy of a quantitative measure is very important and its value is critical in the decision making process.

Level of Detail of the Model   The golden rule here is "keep it simple." It should be realized that the intent of any simulation study is not to capture every event that could occur in a manufacturing system, but only those which are significant and have an impact on the particular issue being considered. The level of detail and accuracy required is, to a large extent, governed by the life cycle of the manufacturing system being considered and the specific issue under study.

Make realistic assumptions to keep the model simple. For instance, in modeling a closed loop conveyor system in an automated system, there may not be a need to model every specific movement of pallets on the conveyor and the spurs. For the given scope of the study only an estimate of the expected number of pallets in the system at any given time may be required. This can be accomplished by using unconstrained queues with infinite capacity and monitoring the queue sizes during the simulation period.

If the model becomes too large and unmanageable, with increasing time needed to get realistic numbers, steps should be taken to break up the model into separate modular components. The results of each study may be adequately interpreted, using a modular hierarchial design approach, with the output of one simulation feeding the input of the other. The validity of using this approach should be evaluated for a given application.

Potential Pitfalls

Listed below are a few inappropriate practices, which may be inadvertently followed during a simulation study, and some guidelines for avoiding them.

Haste to Provide Results   Emphasis on quick results from the simulation study should be avoided. This is almost a certain path to failure and may result in a loss of credibility and support from management or team members. A systematic methodology should be followed with a realistic time set for conducting the study.

Incorrect Assumptions   While some assumptions are almost always necessary to make a study manageable, making them overly specific may invalidate the results. Be sure that all assumptions are explicitly stated and that team members are aware of them.

Inaccurate Data   Any simulation model is only as good as the input data used. Verifying and updating all input data and logic is essential and should be done as an ongoing process.

Collection of Data   While all attempts should be made to verify the validity and accuracy of the data, one should avoid being over zealous. There is a tendency to get bogged down here and get diverted from the simulation modeling effort. The accuracy of the data to be collected should reflect the goals and objectives of the study.

Unrealistic Goals of Study   The benefits of a simulation study are, to a large extent, dependent on the expertise and background of the team members, especially of the model developer. The capability and background of all the team members should be carefully considered in planning and deciding on the scope of the study.

Over Specification of the Level of Detail   Over enthusiasm and the tendency to exploit the "nice" features available in the simulation language, may result in unnecessary details. Besides having minimal direct relevance to the study, they increase complexity and add to the time necessary for the study. The level of detail to be incorporated should be based largely on the scope of the study and also be influenced by the system life cycle of the manufacturing system.

Underspecifying the Level of Detail   This is typically caused by a shortage of necessary data or information and the tendency to overlook its significance. This also may result from the haste to provide quick results. Following a systematic methodology and setting realistic goals will prevent this from occurring.

Lack of Communication Between the User and the Modeler After the study begins, there is a tendency to shift all responsibilities to the modeler to complete the model development and then provide the results. This practice should be avoided, ensuring collective involvement and interaction of all responsible team members during the entire study period.

Overemphasis of Statistical Analysis of Data This is a trap into which many simulationists, especially the novices, easily fall. While statistical validity certainly is not to be overlooked, one should take care not to make the output analysis step into an academic exercise and get bogged down.

SIMULATION APPLICATIONS OVER SYSTEM LIFE CYCLE

Simulation is no longer restricted to the traditional areas of design and planning manufacturing systems. Its use has been expanded in the past few years to other phases of the system life cycle (SLC). A major reason for this is the availability of specialized software allowing the study of specific issues, such as the control system, scheduling, and robotic simulation. Some of these applications are addressed in greater detail elsewhere in this handbook. This section focuses primarily on the material flow in the manufacturing system and addresses the impact on related areas.

The applications of simulation can be classified over three distinct phases of the SLC of a manufacturing system:

- Strategic and conceptual design
- Detail design and planning
- Operation and maintenance

TABLE 21-4 shows the three SLC phases and some issues typically addressed in each.

Because of model limitations and the expertise required to use them, the scope of a study is generally confined to specific issues within one phase of the SLC. For studies with a scope beyond one phase of the SLC, it is better to structure the study in separate phases or stages. For instance, without major modifications, a model developed to study issues related to the strategic phase may not be adequate for studying the detail design phase, since the objectives and goals are different for each phase. However, a simulation study can be initiated at any time over the system life cycle. The essential difference distinguishing the simulation activity during each phase is governed by the following factors:

- Scope and objectives of the study
- Level of effort
- Level of detail in the model
- Accuracy of the data available
- Background of the people involved
- Capability and the availability of the tools

It is very difficult to generalize and categorize simulation languages that could be used during each phase of SLC. Factors such as the individual preference and familiarity with a language, as well as the factors brought out in the next section will have to be considered in order to help this classification. A general purpose simulation language such as GPSS (Henriksen and Crain 1983), SLAM II (Pritsker 1986), or SIMAN (Pegden 1982) can be used to address various issues over the entire SLC. There are also special purpose packages, which can be used to study specific issues, such as FACTOR (Grant 1987) for scheduling during the operational phase, or languages such as Xcell (Conway et al. 1987) for rapid modeling during the conceptual design stage. Let us now describe in greater detail areas of applications and some of the issues addressed.

Strategic and Concept Design Phase

Concept design is the first phase of the system life cycle of any manufacturing system. This phase addresses the issues of planning and design that have long-term implications. Studies undertaken

Table 21-4. Manufacturing System
Simulation and System Life Cycle Phases.

SLC PHASE	MAJOR AREAS	TYPICAL ISSUES
Strategy & Conceptual Planning	Business Strategy	Performance requirements Degree of automation/integration Make vs. buy decisions Product life Labor vs. capital intensity
	Manufacturing Strategy	Manufacturing flexibility Manufacturing system type Material handling methodology Operational philosophies System characteristics
Detail Design	System Design	Material handling specification Equipment selection Facility layout Capacity planning
	Operation Planning	Shift scheduling Production planning AGV scheduling Inventory/WIP levels
	Implementation	Control software fine-tuning Timing issues AGV/conveyor speeds AGV collision avoidance
Operation & Maintenance	System Operation	Bottlenecking problems Day to day scheduling & sequencing Preventive maintenance scheduling Equipment reliability Quality control/quality assurance Inventory control
	System Upgrade & Change	Addition of capacity Addition of new part types Expansion of facility Scheduling additional work load Reconfiguration of facility

during this phase should aid the design process before any commitments are made on hardware and operating philosophies. The major emphasis during this phase is to identify a few (typically three or less) alternative manufacturing approaches, each capable of achieving the required performance. It is essential that the key performance expectations be provided up front. Using these measures, alternatives are compared for technical feasibility, and to determine which ones make sense from a business point of view—namely, marketing and finance.

Since this phase is for identifying potentially viable options, significant operational detail need not be captured in the modeling activity. The more detailed modeling with simulation is reserved for the later phases of the selected alternatives, where appropriate. In fact, it is not uncommon to identify a single alternative at this point, which may then be studied in greater detail and depth for design and planning purposes. Use of rough cut modeling techniques such as MANUPLAN (Suri and Dean 1986) or simulation modeling systems such as Xcell are very efficient in rapidly evaluating various alternatives during this phase of SLC.

The simulation studies can be further divided during this phase into two major areas, business and manufacturing strategies. Some of the issues and approaches for the two areas involved in the simulation studies are elaborated on below.

Business Strategy   Business strategy is the driving force during the strategic design phase. Simulation studies conducted during this stage emphasize the market, competition, and technological developments in deriving the manufacturing performance requirements. These market-based performance goals provide the basis for later justifying technologies aimed at achieving better performances, such as targeted inventory levels, system reliability, and quality levels. These requirements are covered in concert with the manufacturing strategy evaluation. Thus, the criteria used to eliminate any alternative are market driven. Typical issues studied include:

- Overall system flexibility (for expansion or conversion)
- Operational performance requirements
- Degree of automation and integration
- Make versus buy decisions (subcomponent or subassembly level)
- Labor intensity versus capital intensity
- Financial measures of merit (pay-back period, cost/benefit ratio, return of investment)
- Expected life of the product
- Flexibility requirements for both product and processes
- Capacity planning

Manufacturing Strategies   Simulation studies conducted for evaluating manufacturing strategies are closely coupled with business strategies. With emphasis on the business criteria, simulation studies of manufacturing strategies eliminate technically unfeasible or less promising choices. Simulation must incorporate some of the dynamics of the manufacturing system in order to make effective comparisons. Comparison of alternatives are generally based on some of the global performance measures given in TABLE 21-1. Some of the strategic choices to be made are described below.

Flexibility Requirements   This important multidimensional issue has to be defined for any automated manufacturing system, and especially for new products or processes. Typically, the flexibility requirements concern such factors as part variety, volume requirement, type of process, and number of operations.

Type of Manufacturing System   The appropriateness of the type of system is largely dependent on performance characteristics and environment. Thus, flexibility and technology requirements heavily influence some of the options to be tested. Hardware specifications also influence these options. Typical alternatives include one or more of the following generic types: job shop, transfer lines, flow shops, flexible manufacturing systems (FMS), or a hybrid system.

Material Handling System   Choosing a concept is clearly a very important requirement for any automated manufacturing system. Simulation is ideally suited to evaluate material handling systems, since it can capture the dynamics of the system in order to make effective comparisons possible. Typical material handling systems studied include or involve AGV systems, conveyor systems, automated storage/retrieval systems (AS/RS), and hybrid systems.

System Evolution   Evaluation of the design and plans for future growth and expansion, for both short term and long term, take place as the system evolves and become fully functional. Anticipation of future technology capabilities is necessary here.

- Capacity planning: availability of the planned capacity against the needs to determine the system requirements
- Output rates: the number of parts produced over a time period; maximize this rate where possible
- Throughput time: the time required to produce a part starting from input to a finished part; minimize this time where possible
- Machine utilization: the actual productive time of the machines used during the available time; maximize this where possible
- Lead times: simulation studies can accurately predict this time, which should be added as *slack* to the actual operation time to ensure the part is produced by the due date
- Expected inventory levels: the amount of inventory in the form of raw materials, in-process, and finished parts that are accumulated during production; minimize the levels
- Equipment and resource requirements: supplies such as work pallets, fixtures, and tools needed obtain the ideal operating conditions

Detailed Design and Planning

During this phase, simulation evaluates the design to ensure that the system will perform as specified when implemented. Studies of the selected design therefore involve much greater detail, use more accurate data, and address some of the same issues from the previous phase in greater detail. This phase includes design evaluation activities through installation of the system. Three main stages are involved: system design, system planning, and implementation. These stages and some of the issues studied are described below.

System Design Simulation during the system design stage determines the system characteristics and hardware requirements of the design before placing procurement orders. This capability makes simulation more easily justified and thus more widely used during this phase than any other. Some of the issues addressed are as follows.

- Material handling system specifications: conveyor length, number of AGVs, and the speeds and expected response times to meet the desired or expected system requirements
- Equipment selection: purchase equipment from different vendors to meet the system requirements
- Manpower requirements: expected number of employees required in the system
- Facility layout: based on traffic, material handling, and safety to meet the ideal operating requirements
- Capacity planning: determines the number of machines, equipment, manpower production, and schedule with greater level of accuracy
- General operating philosophies: number of shifts, working hours, maintenance periods, rework orders, and handling hot orders

Operations Planning. Simulation studies conducted during the operations planning phase are carried over from the system design stage; they aid in planning the operation of the system. They determine actual operational procedures in order to obtain functional requirements from the design. Simulation assumes that the major hardware and equipment have been acquired or specified. Some typical issues examined are listed below.

- Buffer size requirement, such as the pallet spaces at various points in the system
- Scheduling material handling systems, specifically systems using AGVs
- Scheduling parts against available machines
- Expected inventory levels or work in progress (WIP)
- Pallets and fixtures requirements, which again relate to the buffer spaces requirements
- Shift scheduling the working hours or actual production times in meeting the planned requirements
- Maintenance scheduling to prevent breakdowns and avoid undue loss of productive time

- Replenishment policies of purchased and in-house manufactured parts to avoid starving or blocking and thereby idling machines

Implementation The implementation stage is an ongoing effort, carried on from the design and planning stages, to ensure that specifications are being met during the installation process. The applications of simulation during this stage are more diverse, with emphasis on control and integration issues. The extent to which simulation may be used in the implementation process is directly related to the complexity of the designed system, expertise of the model developer, and tools available. A successful study demands that the simulationist demonstrates a considerable amount of interaction and coordination with the control system engineers and other personnel involved in the implementation process.

Simulation models used during this stage require encompassing control system details. Simulation must be conducted as a parallel activity to verify and fine-tune the design and support the implementation process. By using special purpose packages, the applications of simulation to such processes as robotics, kinematics, and control systems may also be initiated. These applications may be used to aid the implementation process, without necessarily being tied in with the material flow simulation. Some of the issues includes the following.

- Collision avoidance, where applicable, for multiple AGV system
- Implementation of the designed control systems to determine timing
- Timing issues; specifically the response times from the various computers, control systems, and other hardware equipment
- Material handling requirements: conveyor lengths, AGV paths, conveyor speeds, and number of loops

Operation and Maintenance

The application of simulation during this phase, unlike all other phases of the SLC, is concerned

with an existing system. Thus a very accurate representation of the system is required. If a simulation model is maintained and is a good replica of the system, it can be used more extensively making simulation a better value. Alternatively, simulation may be initiated as required. For all studies initiated during this phase a very close interaction of the simulationist with those personnel involved in the actual operation is required in order for the study to be successful. The type of studies undertaken can be categorized in two ways: system operation and system upgrade or change. These are described in more detail below.

System operation. Simulation addresses issues related to day to day operation and maintenance of the system. These issues may also be related to improving the current system or addressing unexpected (crisis) problems. Typical applications include:

- Shift scheduling to meet the desired requirements
- Day to day production scheduling and control to meet daily or production horizon requirements
- Preventive maintenance scheduling
- Production planning and order review and release
- Inventory control and monitoring
- Equipment reliability
- Quality control and quality assurance

System Upgrade or Change Simulation studies may be used as a decision support tool in system upgrade and to study unanticipated changes. These studies are initiated as required and after the appropriateness of a simulation technique has been determined. Issues that are typically addressed with simulation include:

- Impact of automating an operation or material handling system
- Addition of more capacity by providing more machines or equipment
- Scheduling an additional part type through the system
- Scheduling an additional work shift
- Additional operations

- Expansion of facility
- Reconfiguration of facility

SIMULATION PACKAGES OVERVIEW

This section discusses the process of choosing a simulation/animation package. Some steps are listed below. This list should be modified and expanded to fit the needs of the individual company. The steps are in an approximate order of importance.

Important Features

- Availability and frequency of introductory and advanced training courses
- Modeling aids and language-specific editors
- General purpose language with features available to model complex situations and decisions
- Animation capability, ease of animation, and level of detail of animation
- Interactive debugging features which allow the user to change system variables without exiting the simulation
- Specific features appropriate to the industry such as conveyors, automatically guided vehicles, part routings, and scheduling
- Statistical data analysis features including comparison techniques and data plotting
- Interface to user-written code
- Availability on a large number of hardware platforms from PCs to mainframes
- Portability of model code across supported platforms
- Availability of language features across supported platforms

Selection Criteria

- Previous experience of manager or modeler with a specific language
- Required features from the important features list above
- In-house use:
  - Complexity of system to be simulated

- Design and planning phase of project
- Operational phase of project
- Frequency of use
- Features available for specific project needs

- Exposure of target audience to simulation: basis for decision on animation capability
- Length and detail of projects including management support and commitment
- In-house computer availability
- Purchase price of required additional hardware and software

Evaluation Procedures

Often the Management Information Systems division of a company, or its equivalent, will have specific criteria for selection of software. If such information is not available, rank the features listed above and any others your company needs. List the score of each of the packages being evaluated and determine the package with the best score. Because this method is very subjective, the scores determined should be used only as a guideline. Whenever possible, have the software demonstrated to as many of the members of the team as possible, especially if you are evaluating animation software.

Sources of Information

A complete list of requirements and evaluation criteria is beyond the scope of this section. Other sources of information will provide additional and more complete information as well as different opinions as to the importance of different features.

The magazine *Simulation*, a monthly publication of the Society of Computer Simulation (SCS), San Diego, California, publishes an exhaustive list of simulation software in its annual October issue. This list includes such valuable information as the address and telephone number of the software vendors.

The annual *Winter Simulation Conference* proceedings (sponsored by several professional societies, including SCS) include tutorials on popular simulation software products as well as many applications of these products to the manufacturing environment.

The magazine *Industrial Engineering* often has articles pertaining to simulation. This is the publication of Institute of Industrial Engineering (IIE), Atlanta, Georgia. IIE also sponsors several tutorials and seminars related to simulation.

The *Society of Manufacturing Engineers (SME)*, Dearborn, Michigan, sponsors several tutorials and seminars related to simulation of manufacturing systems.

Several references listed at the end of this chapter can provide additional information.

FUTURE TRENDS

Future trends in computer simulation hold great promise in several areas. These include computing power, animation, control, scheduling, and artificial intelligence.

Computing Power

In the last few years with the explosion of the personal computer market, we have experienced a rapid increase in the computing power available to the engineer. There has been a corresponding drop in the cost of the computing power. As a result, the focus of simulation has moved from the mainframe to the PC. However, the improved cost and convenience has been at the sacrifice of problem size and actual speed of simulation. The workstation market has offered many of the benefits of the PC without the drawbacks of the mainframe.

The improvements in hardware over the next decade are expected to be as dramatic as in the past decade. As in the past, however, hardware development is likely to move faster than the development of the operating system and application software needed to take advantage of these hardware improvements. If OS/2 becomes widely accepted, we can expect great improvements in the PC market software.

Networking is also an area which has great promise, especially with such tools as remote procedure calls (RPC) under UNIX. Using RPC, one machine can perform the computations while another can display the results. An operating environment which is being developed to exploit RPC is X.* X offers great promise in that a product developed under X should be able to be viewed on any hardware which supports X. Consequently, a simulation model which will not fit with the DOS 640k limitation can be run on a workstation and the results displayed on the PC.

Animation

The process of building the simulation model will become more simplified. The user will be able to place icons on the screen which represent whole areas of operation. The icon will include all the logic associated with the operations as well as the interaction with other areas of operation. By placing several icons on the screen and forming the connection between the icons, the user will be able to develop the model very quickly.

Modularity of code will be increased because the user will be able to collapse whole areas of operation into a single icon, which will change its appearance. The changes in appearance will be specified by the user. Furthermore, at any time the user will be able to *explode* the icon so that the image now visible on the screen will be the constituent parts of the icon.

Experienced users will be able to develop icon libraries specific to their needs. Less experienced users will be able to recall these libraries and develop sophisticated models that conform to company practices and terminology.

There are currently some packages available which have rudimentary forms of the capabilities described above. Unfortunately, they do not allow the user to tailor them to the user's needs and they are not flexible.

---

*O'Reilly et al. 1988.

Control

This area of the market is in its infancy, but should experience rapid growth in the next decade. There are two areas where simulation will be most useful. The first is in testing out control logic for large facilities. A simulation model of the facility, integrated with the control system simulator could be used in testing control strategies prior to their implementation. This could eventually help in reducing the upfront time in bringing a system on-line. Even in the case of existing facilities, alternative control strategies can be tested before they are implemented. The use of artificial intelligence (AI) techniques coupled with simulation for such applications also shows great promise.

Scheduling

While material requirement planning (MRP II) has contributed significantly to the improvement of scheduling practices, many of the assumptions, notably that of infinite capacity, are difficult to justify in the real world. By coupling the scheduling scheme to a simulation of the system, the throughput and order release sequence can be tested. The

simulation can feed back information to the MRPII system so that changes can be made to the schedule.

Artificial Intelligence and Simulation

A considerable amount of interest has been generated in the application of artificial intelligence (AI) techniques to simulation. The areas where AI shows promise of increased use in simulation are the following:

- Expert system *front ends* to simulation modeling
- Simulation model development and analysis in AI environment such as in KEE and SimKit (*SimKit System*, Intellicorp, 1985)
- Use of AI techniques tied with simulation to address specific issues such as controls and scheduling
- Expert systems for output analysis and interpretation of the simulation results

The availability of expert system shells shows promise by providing users with tools and the environment to support applications of AI and simulation.

SUGGESTED READING

Basics

Banks, J. and J. S. Carson II. *Discrete-Event System Simulation*. Englewood Cliffs, New Jersey: Prentice-Hall, 1984.

Bratley, P., B. L. Fox, and L. E. Schrage. *A Guide to Simulation*. 2d ed. New York: Springer-Verlag, 1987.

Fishman, G.S. *Principles of Discrete Event Simulation*. New York: Wiley, 1978.

Law, A. M. and W. D. Kelton. *Simulation Modeling and Analysis*. New York: McGraw-Hill, 1982.

Shannon, R. E. *Systems Simulation: The Art and the Science*. New York: Prentice-Hall, 1975.

Ziegler, B. P. *Theory of Modelling and Simulation*. New York: John Wiley and Sons, Inc., 1975.

Languages

Automod User's Manual. AutoSimulations, Inc., Bountiful, Utah, 1986.

Conway, R., W. Maxwell, J. McClain, and S. Worona. *User's Guide to the XCELL+ Factory Modeling System.* 2d ed. Redwood City, California: Scientific Press, 1987.

Haider, S. Wali and J. Banks. "Simulation Software Products for Analyzing Manufacturing Systems." Simulation Series Part 3. *Industrial Engineering* (July 1986).

Henriksen, J.D. and R.C. Crain. "GPSS/H User's Manual." Wolverine Software Corp., Annandale, Virginia, 1983.

Law, A. M. and C. S. Larney. "Introduction to Simulation Using SIMSCRIPT II.5." University of Arizona, Tempe, Arizona, 1984.

Lenz, J. "MAST and MAST Animation User Manuals." CMS Research Inc., Oshkosh, Wisconsin, 1985.

Pegden, C. D. "Introduction to SIMAN." Systems Modeling Corp., 1982.

Pritsker, A. A. B. *Introduction to Simulation and SLAM II.* 3d ed. Systems Publishing Corp., 1986.

Russell, E. C. "Building Simulation Models with SIMSCRIPT II.5." C.A.C.I. Inc., Los Angeles, California, 1983.

Grant, J. W. and S. A. Welner. "Factors to Consider In Choosing A Graphically Animated Simulation System." Simulation Series Part 4. *Industrial Engineering* (August 1986).

Tom, L. "See Why." *Simulation* 45: 2 (1985).

White, D. A. "PCModel—Personal Computer Screen Graphics Modeling System User's Guide." Simulation Software Systems, San Jose, California, 1985.

Statistical Analysis

Box, G. E. P., W. G. Hunter, and J. S. Hunter. *Statistics for Experimenters: An Introduction to Design, Data Analysis, and Model Building.* New York: Wiley, 1978.

Kleinjen, J. P. C. *Statistical Techniques in Simulation, Part I.* New York: Marcel Dekker, 1974.

————. *Statistical Techniques in Simulation, Part II.* New York: Marcel Dekker, 1975.

Kelton, D. W. "Statistical Analysis Methods Enhance Usefulness, Reliability of Simulation Models." Simulation Series Part 5. *Industrial Engineering* (September 1986).

General

Carrie, A. *Simulation of Manufacturing Systems.* New York: John Wiley and Sons, 1988.

Carson, John S. "Convincing Users of Model's Validity Is Challenging Aspect of Modeler's Job." Simulation Series Part 2. *Industrial Engineering* (June 1986).

Ingels, D. M. *What Every Engineer Should Know About: Computer Modeling and Simulation.* New York: Marcel Dekker, 1985.

O'Reilly, Tim. *X Window Systems User's Guide,* O'Reilly and Associates, 1988.

Suri, R., and R. Dean. "MANUPLAN User's Manual." Network Dynamics, Inc., Cambridge, Massachusetts, 1986.

Manufacturing

Grant, F. H. "Simulation in Manufacturing: Tools for Designing and Scheduling Production Systems." National Academy of Engineering. *Design and Analysis of Integrated Manufacturing Systems: Status, Issues and Opportunities*. (Feb. 25-27, 1987).

Joseph, T. K., S. K. Bhat, and D. Maas. "Evaluation of Three Material Handling Concepts for a High Volume Production Facility Using Simulation." In *Proceedings, Ultratech Conference* Vol. 2, pp. 2-31/32. Long Beach, California, 1986.

Law, Averill M. "Introduction to Simulation: A Powerful Tool for Analyzing Complex Manufacturing Systems." Simulation Series Part 1. *Industrial Engineering* (May 1986).

Lenz, J. "FMS: What Happens When You Don't Simulate." In *Simulation: Applications in Manufacturing*, R.D. Hurrion, ed. United Kingdom: IFS (Publications) Ltd., 1986.

Martin, D. L. and Kenneth J. Musselman. "Simulation in the Life Cycle of Flexible Manufacturing Systems." Paper presented at the ORSA/TIMS Special Interest Conference on FMS, Ann Arbor, Michigan, August 16, 1984.

Shannon, R. E. "Simulation Modeling in Manufacturing." In *Simulation and Artificial Intelligence in Manufacturing, SME Conference Proceedings*. Long Beach, California, Oct. 1987.

Simulation and AI

Doukidis, G. I. and R. J. Paul. "Research into Expert Systems to Aid Simulation Model Formulation." *Journal of Operations Research Society*, 36: 4 (1985), 319-325.

Joseph, T. K. "An Expert System to Aid Goal Definition for Manufacturing System Simulation." *Proceedings, Eastern MultiConference*. Tampa, Florida, March 1989.

Shannon, R. E. Phillips, and R. J. Mayer. "Knowledge Based Simulation for Manufacturing." *Proceedings of Ultratech-Artificial Conference*. SME Technical Paper MS86-966, September 1986.

Shannon, R. E., R. Mayer, and H. M. Adelsberger. "Expert Systems and Simulation." *Simulation* 44:6 (1985), 275-284.

"The SimKit System, Knowledge Based Siumulation Tools in KEE." Intellicorp, 1985.

22

Physical Simulation
of Automated
Manufacturing Systems

Michael P. Deisenroth[*]
Hans Maurer[**]

THE DESIGN, IMPLEMENTATION, AND OPERATION OF a manufacturing system in today's environment involves the combined talents of many different disciplines and individuals. The complexity of the system, both from a hardware and software standpoint, is enormous. Many different design systems and tools are necessary in order to ensure the adequacy and quality of the system under consideration. Physical stimulation is one of these tools. In physical simulation, scaled-down models of production facilities are operated under computer control to mimic the operations of the system under consideration. Physical simulation by itself is an inadequate tool for solving all problems encountered in the design and implementation of a complex manufacturing system; however, it does represent a powerful approach to visualization in this complex design task.

INTRODUCTION

To better understand the type of detail and scale often found in a physical simulation, consider the system shown in FIG. 22-1. This early-built, German model of a flexible manufacturing system contained an automatic storage and retrieval system (AS/RS), five machining workcells, and a material handling and delivery system. The model was controlled by an AEG 8020/4 minicomputer. It was developed to illustrate the applicability of using the PEARL computer language in manufacturing systems control. The model was first used in the development of the software support system for the 8020/4 computer.

There are a number of potential application areas for physical modeling. The educational community has adopted this technology as a means of

*Dr. Deisenroth is presently a professor of Industrial Engineering and Director of the Manufacturing, Automation, and Robotics Laboratory in the Department of Industrial and Systems Engineering at Virginia Polytechnic Institute and State University. He received his B.S., M.E., and Ph.D. from Georgia Institute of Technology. His research and teaching interests are primarily focused in various aspects of the planning, design, and control of manufacturing, automation, and computer aided manufacturing systems. Present topics include system modeling, automatic program generation for system control, and system integration issues. While at Virginia Tech, he has been primarily responsible for development of the Manufacturing Automation Laboratories and the Manufacturing, Automation, and Robotics Laboratory. He is a member of ASEE, ASME, IIE, and SME.

*Hans Maurer has degrees in both Business and Engineering. He is presently director of the Department of Modeling and Simulation for Fischerwerken, Tunliugen, West Germany.

Fig. 22-1. Early German built simulator of a flexible manufacturing system.

demonstrating fundamental concepts in manufacturing systems design and control. Industrial applications of physical simulation have been implemented in order to validate design concepts, test proposed control systems and structures, and demonstrate system feasibility. Additionally, physical simulation has been used as a training system in industrial applications both for general manufacturing systems control concepts and for training on the specific system being modeled. Marketing groups have used physical simulation to demonstrate specific features of the products as well as to show the interactions among components of complex systems.

Physical Simulation Defined

Most authors agree that physical simulation involves the use of scaled-down models of production systems that are fully functional and mimic the operations of the system being modeled. (Please see the following references: Aishton and Miller 1982, Diesch and Malstrom 1985, Falkner and Shanker 1984, Kimbler 1982, Mackuluk and Bedworth 1984, Nof, et al. 1979, Paidy and Reeves 1982, and Young, et al. 1984.) There is, however, a fine line between physical modeling and physical simulation. Physical modeling involves the design and implementation of the model. Specifically, there are benefits to be derived from the creation of a three dimensional model of a complex system. Individuals involved in the design of a new manufacturing facility have made use of such models for many years. But physical simulation extends beyond the static representation of the system and involves the dynamic manipulation of the system for the purpose of studying operational characteristics. To simulate, the model must be exercised.

Most authors agree that the models used in physical simulation are not necessarily built to a strict geometric scale or to strict criteria of physical similitude. Nevertheless, there have been cases where the physical simulators have been fully functional replicas which actually make parts (Wysk, et al., "Physical Machining System", 1982; Wysk et al. 1985; Young, et al. 1984). These models were used both for instructional purposes with the academic environment and for operational studies of manufacturing systems. The vast majority of the work in physical simulation, however, involves operational, but not fully functional models.

The control mechanisms used in physical simulation have been varied. Early simulators were controlled by minicomputers with microprocessor control implementations following as the technology became available. (Please see the following references: Bedworth and Sobczak 1976; Diesch 1982; Kimbler 1982; Nof, et al. 1979, "Using Physical Simulation"; Nof, et al. 1980, "Computerized Physical Simulators.") Presently, some physical simulators are controlled by industrial programmable logic controllers. Many academic systems are controlled by a combination of mechanisms. It is not unusual for an industrial model to be controlled by the same hardware system that is intended to control the actual system when it is installed.

A trend today associates physical simulation with models of complex manufacturing systems. While this in itself is not wrong, one should not exclude models of simplistic systems from the physical simulation area. Often models are created of basic system components for the purpose of control system testing. In such a case, the model will be used to test the actual control hardware (and possible software) that will be implemented on the real system. Additionally, such models are used for training purposes and within the academic community (Bassal, et al. 1986; Khoshnevis 1985; Leigh and Nazemetz 1985).

A Brief History of Physical Simulation

The use of physical modeling and simulation in manufacturing systems design and control is relatively new. There is, however, a long history of the use of models in other fields of engineering design. Aeronautical engineers have used wind tunnel models for many years to validate the results of analytical models. Chemical engineers build pilot plants

to test out systems design and to establish necessary operational parameters. One of the most massive physical models ever developed was done by the Corps of Engineers in the early 1930s. A scale model of the Mississippi River basin was constructed at the Vicksburg Waterways Experiment Station. Over the years, this model has been used to test and validate designs for dams, channel improvements, and diverters.

The earliest example of the use of physical modeling of a manufacturing system was reported by Bedworth in 1976. Bedworth describes a physical model of an AS/RS that was developed at Arizona State University for instruction on digital computer control. The model was built from scratch and used stepper motors to control the motion of the crane. A GE/PAC 4000 minicomputer was the control mechanism. The model provided a simple but realistic vehicle for teaching basic concepts in digital computer control and for demonstrating operational features of an automated storage system.

Pioneering work at Purdue University in the late 1970s by Deisenroth and Nof introduced the application of reusable, modular components for modeling more complex manufacturing systems (Nof, et al. 1979 and Nof, et al. 1980). Patterned after similar research at German universities, the research involved the use of Fischertechnik components as modeling tools. These components were used to build two basic systems—a sorting conveyor and a flexible manufacturing cell. A larger model was being constructed to replicate the installation of a flexible manufacturing system in a midwestern industrial plant, but the model was not completed. The models at Purdue were used primarily as instructional tools and were controlled by a Data General minicomputer or a single board microprocessor. Institutional applications of Fischertechnik modeling spread rapidly during the early 1980s and is now a common form of laboratory equipment in many industrial and mechanical engineering departments.

Two parallel efforts at Virginia Polytechnic Institute and State University (Wysk, et al. 1982, "Physical Machining") and Texas A & M University (Young, et al. 1984) developed physical simulators that were fully functional models capable of actually making parts. Young reports the development of models of individual system components that combined Fischertechnik components with other sensors and actuators for complete functionality (Young, et al. 1984). These components could then be combined to create models of complete manufacturing systems for experimentation and analysis. Wysk reported the development of miniature machine tools (Wysk, et al. 1985, ''Physical and Graphical Modeling''). Unlike most simulators, these machines were actual numerically controlled machine tools that were fully capable of cutting soft materials such as wax or plastic. The models were organized into a flexible machining system with three machine tools and a material handling robot.

Many applications of physical simulation have been research oriented and have primarily been associated with software development projects. (Please see the following references: Deisenroth 1985, ''Physical Model for Research;'' Deisenroth 1987, ''Physical Simulation;'' Feltner and Weirer 1985; Khoshnevis and Rogers 1983; O'Reilly, et al. 1984; Roberts and Deisenroth 1989; Young 1981.) Historically these applications have not received much publicity due to the ancillary nature of their

development. They have, however, proven to be a vital part of the research effort. Industrial applications of physical simulation were soon to follow. Most of these applications combined the resources of university laboratories within the context of an industrial problem. While not as commonplace as in the university setting, industrial applications of physical modeling have met with success in a number of instances, as will be shown below.

Types of Models

The design and implementation of an automated manufacturing system often involves the use of a number of different types of models. This is further complicated by the fact that many different individuals must be involved in the process and the types of tools to be used vary with the discipline of the individual. The models may be mathematical, graphical, or physical. Aishton and Miller identified a number of different types of modeling tools that might be associated with the design process (1982). As can be seen from TABLE 22-1, physical simulation is closely related to pilot models normally associated with the process industries. Additionally, physical simulation is often compared to mathematical modeling and digital simulation, due

Table 22-1. Comparison of Physical Modeling with Other Tools.

Tool	Form	Objective	Time	Variability of Behaviors	Level of Abstraction
Engineering drawing	Flat, 2-D, analog sometimes iconic	Descriptive or normative	Static	(d)	Moderate
Simulation model	State calculation device, symbolic	Descriptive	Dynamic	Nondeterministic or deterministic	Moderately high
Linear Programming	Mathematical variables and expressions	Normative (optimization)	Static or dynamic	Deterministic	High
Physical model	Solid, 3-D, analog, iconic	Descriptive	Dynamic	Deterministic or nondeterministic	Moderately low
Pilot scale hardware	Solid, 3-D, analog, iconic	Descriptive	Dynamic	Nondeterministic	Low

to the nature of the people associated with implementing the simulator.

Pilot systems models have found widespread use in chemical engineering, both as an instructional aid and as a design tool (Schmitz 1971, Schwartz 1976). These models are typically scaled down physical systems with a great deal of physical similitude to the actual system. They behave like the full scale system because they are governed by the same laws of physics and chemistry. Normally there is no time scaling associated with these models since they operate in the same time domain as the actual system. Functionally, these simulators are developed to study the physical and chemical behavior of the system in order to validate analytical studies and to identify any unforeseen operational problems. Physical simulation as applied to manufacturing systems design exists in a higher level of abstraction. While the models rarely represent the physical level of detail just mentioned, they do mimic the operational characteristics of the system in question.

Mathematical modeling and digital computer simulation are also used in manufacturing systems design. Mathematical modeling identifies a set of possible solutions from all of the alternatives that might be applicable to a specific problem. The mathematical models are normally associated with long-term, strategic issues and do not readily deal with tactical issues or real time control. While some mathematical models represent system behavior as nondeterministic, none are sufficiently robust to truly represent the dynamics of the system from an operational perspective. Computer simulation, on the other hand, provides an ability to model system dynamics. Computer simulation has found widespread acceptance in industrial systems design for both strategic and tactical decision analysis. Thus, computer simulation can be used to compare the systems identified through mathematical modeling in working toward a final system specification.

The level of detail present in a simulation model does not normally represent all of the potential physical interactions involved in an actual system. A number of potential operational problems associated with a specific system solution may still exist

even after a successful simulation run. Physical simulation identifies these problems by forcing the development and operation of a functional replica of the proposed system before the commitment is made to implement the solution in full scale. Thus, the three-dimensional nature and functionality of the simulators are important characteristics in physical simulation.

Typically, physical simulators have been designed and built from component sets consisting of a large variety of parts. The most popular method of developing models is with Fischertechnik components. Modeling elements are mostly plastic and include structural components (beams, building blocks, brackets, and braces), drive system components (motors, gears, sprockets, and chain), and control hardware (relays, switches, and photoresistors). There is a large variety of components from which to choose with over 450 different parts being available. FIGURE 22-2 provides a close up of a section of a model that was developed for industrial use. Three machining centers surround a turntable, which is fed from the conveyor shown in the background. A diverter transfers the parts from the conveyor to the turntable and then back to the conveyor. Each of the model machines has two axes of motion.

A logical extension to the use of Fischertechnik components for construction of the simulator, is to mix Fischertechnik parts with other mechanisms. Many universities have combined these components with small, educational robots and other benchtop mechanisms. Additionally, stepper motors and pneumatic cylinders have been used to supplement the parts provided by Fischer, Young, et al. (1984). have developed a set of standard manufacturing system components that consist of a mixture of Fischertechnik parts and other mechanisms. System components can then be used to model a complete manufacturing system in less time than it would take to design all of the machines from scratch.

In addition to Fischertechnik, there are four other widely used mechanical breadboarding parts sets: Automat, Proto, Fac, and Meccano. Unlike Fischertechnik, most of the parts included in these

Fig. 22-2. Close-up view of a Fischertechnik model with three machining systems, a turntable, and a conveying system in the background.

sets are made of metal. The selection of parts is heavily oriented toward gears and other drive train mechanisms since these breadboard sets had their origin in mechanical systems modeling. Additionally, gear component kits and supporting brackets are available from many small-gear manufacturing companies, including Winfred M. Berg or Stock Drive Products. These components can be combined with parts from other sets or used in scratch built models.

While the use of simulators that are capable of machining has been limited, there are one or two examples. Wysk documents the design, fabrication, instrumentation, and application of miniature machines for instruction in flexible automation (Wysk, et al. 1982). The miniature flexible manufacturing system developed consisted of two three-

axis machines and a material handling robot. The machines were totally designed and build within the laboratory at Virginia Tech and were individually controlled by separate controllers. A microcomputer served as the system controller and communicated with the individual machines through serial ports. Further development of these models has lead to the use of standard subsystems, such as a linear axis mechanism and drive system, for the major components of the machines. While the models are capable of machining soft materials, they are not to be considered as general purpose machine tools in that they are confined to working on parts of a limited geometric class. They do, however, provide an impressive demonstration of the operations of a flexible manufacturing system when operated as a totally integrated system.

This latter type of physical model—one capable of machining—is closely related to the set of bench-top machine tools on the market today. Fully functional, computer controlled machine tools such as lathes and milling machines are available from a variety of sources, such as Dyna Mechtronics, Emco Maier, or Light Machine. These machines can be combined with educational or downsized industrial robots, material delivery and storage systems, and computer control systems to create physical simulators that are definitely on the same level of functionality as a full scale manufacturing system. Some university laboratories have developed such systems by integrating the basic components with a computer control system while two or three companies offer these computer integrated manufacturing systems for instructional and research use. FIGURE 22-3 illustrates such a system that was developed by Technovate, Inc. It consists

of a loop conveyor system that transports carriers to their desired destinations. Four robots surround the system for parts handling. Two computer controlled machining centers serve as the material processors. The system is controlled by a single personal computer connected to the various mechanisms through a smart multiplexer. While the cost of these systems prohibits their use for modeling in the manufacturing systems design sense, they have significant potential for application in the research community for experimentation in general problems related to the design, implementation, and control of complex manufacturing systems.

PURPOSE AND OBJECTIVES FOR DEVELOPING A PHYSICAL SIMULATOR

There are many different reasons for developing a physical simulator. Most of the benefits for applying physical simulation in an industrial environ-

Fig. 22-3. Bench top physical simulator with XNC machines, industrial robots, and a loop conveyor.

ment can be grouped into one of five areas: conceptualization and communication, evaluation of system design, validation of computer simulation models, software testing and debugging, and training of operating personnel. Additionally, the educational community has made use of this technique for laboratory instruction and as a research mechanism.

Conceptualization and Communication

Two different problems often create the desire to use physical modeling in the design, implementation, and operation of a complex manufacturing system today. First, while management may be well aware of the basic concepts involved in many of today's complex, computer controlled manufacturing systems, most individual managers have not had the opportunity to observe and possibly interact with such systems from an operational standpoint. Physical modeling provides such an opportunity. Managers at all levels will easily understand the basic functionality of the system and be able to observe the interactions of the various system components. The tables and graphs that are normally presented at the end of a digital computer simulation, while very useful to the systems analysis, do not necessarily convey a high level of confidence to management. Primarily this is because the underlying simulator cannot be fully understood in the time available. This problem with understanding is further evidenced by the rapid increase in the use of animated computer graphics as a secondary output mechanism to computer simulation (Pope 1984). When the complex relationships of the system under evaluation are more fully understood through the application of physical simulation, the data created from other methods of analysis are more meaningful to the decision maker and can be integrated into the decision framework.

A second problem which may create the desire to use physical simulation is directly associated with the group of individuals involved in the design and implementation of the system. Normally these individuals come from a variety of backgrounds and disciplines. There are a variety of engineering fields involved: electrical, industrial, manufacturing, and mechanical. Additionally, operating personnel, management, equipment vendors, and suppliers will surely be involved. Differences between mental pictures of individuals, who must work together for a common design goal, can lead to inefficiencies in problem solving or disastrous results if an inappropriate solution is implemented. A common ground for conceptualization, analysis, and communication can greatly facilitate the teams' efforts. Physical simulation can supply the common ground. Unlike engineering drawings, simulation runs, mathematical models, and process diagrams, physical simulation is readily understood by most observers and can be used as the mechanism for further detailed descriptions of the system and its operational features.

Physical simulators can also be used, after the fact, as communication vehicles. Plant floor personnel can view the model as the system is being installed to better understand the overall design concepts and to see the interactions that will be required between human operators and the control system. Different operating scenarios can be presented and the effect on system requirements and performance can be observed. Physical simulation provides a more meaningful mechanism with which plant floor personnel can become involved in the design process due to its capabilities as a communication mechanism.

Evaluation of System Design

It would be a gross mistake to think that physical simulation can replace digital computer simulation. Nothing is farther from the truth. Digital computer simulation is a powerful analytical tool for evaluating manufacturing system designs. Yet physical simulation can be of value for analyzing, experimenting with, and evaluating system design. The strength of physical simulation again lies in the fact that it is a functional three-dimensional model of the system under study. The primary objective of applying physical simulation in this respect is to demonstrate design feasibility.

Falkner and Shanker liken physical simulation to an insurance policy (1984). Given that the system design was feasible, the model demonstrates that all is well and that the system will perform as desired; the expense of the model might be considered a burden in this case. On the other hand, the simulator may identify design problems and thus suggest the need for redesign in specific areas. Costly implementation errors can thus be reduced and hence, simulators provide savings that are greatly in excess of the cost of the simulator. Improving the confidence one has in the design can be of great benefit.

O'Reilly, Casey, and Weiner point out that the gap that exists between a system which adheres to a design specification and a fully operational, problem-free system can be enormous and that physical modeling can help to fill that gap (1984). Static engineering drawings and digital computer simulation are more abstract than physical modeling. Often, the interactions that will be realized between various system components are not fully understood or completely modeled with other forms of modeling. Physical simulation forces a more complete definition of the system in these important areas. The creation of the physical model may be of significant value from this standpoint alone. It will force a level of conceptualization and design that is not necessary in other analytical tools. Young, et al. (1984). observed that complex systems may exhibit behavior inconsistent with the modeler's perception of reality and that a computer simulation model may not always adequately represent the behavior of system components that interact dynamically. Physical simulation can help identify these problems and correct the design before it is implemented in the actual system.

Physical simulation can also be used to assist or support the people who generate solutions. The design and construction of the model may suggest system improvements that were not considered while the system was initially being designed. Since the physical model typically represents the lowest level of abstraction found during the design process, observation of the model, especially in a functional mode, may suggest further refinements to the system design. These design changes may take the form of additional system specifications or they might represent modifications in the original design. Without physical simulation, these system improvements may not have been considered until after the system was fully functional. In such a case, the changes could be either costly or economically unfeasible. If the model can be used to suggest the changes before the design is finalized, the improvements can be made before implementation of the physical system. Physical simulation of the design permits fine tuning of the system before the design is fully implemented in the actual plant.

Validate Output from Computer Simulation Models

A physical simulation can also be used as a means of validating the output obtained from a computer simulation. In many manufacturing applications of computer simulations, there is no prior existing system that can be used for model validation. Often, face validity must be obtained by ensuring that the system is a true representation of the modeler's understanding of the system to be modeled. If, however, the modeler's perceptions of system behavior and interactions are wrong, the model will reflect these inaccuracies. Physical simulation provides one means of obtaining a base line system for model validation. Young, et al. (1984) indicate that the link between physical simulation and computer simulation is much like the one that exists between mathematical modeling and computer simulation. When an analyst creates a mathematical model of a system, simplifying assumptions are often necessary that may make one doubt the validity of the model. A detailed computer simulation could then be used to demonstrate that the mathematical model behaved acceptably for some specific situations. Likewise, the computer simulation also has simplifying assumptions associated with its development. Physical simulation can be used to demonstrate the validity of the results obtained under these assumptions.

Physical simulation can be used to generate data that can be used in computer simulations. Typically the information obtained from a physical simulation is more than likely related to feasible operating scenarios than it is to the creation of some historic data record. Since many simulations run in near real time, there is no compression of the run time associated with the simulation execution; data collection is a long, involved process. To use the model to create a desired time distribution is probably not worth the effort. However, physical simulation can be used to investigate the feasibility of experiencing certain sequences of events or possible system interactions. Diesch and Malstrom provide detailed presentations of how a physical simulator can be used as an analysis tool (Diesch 1982; Diesch and Malstrom, 1984 and 1985). Specifically cited was the use of a physical model to evaluate machine interference conditions in a complex manufacturing situation. A detailed discussion on the time scaling mechanism is presented. The results of the physical model closely matched those obtained in a computer simulation and were representative of the outcomes expected in the actual system.

Software Testing and Debugging

Deisenroth (1987) and Feltner and Weiner (1985) indicate that one of the most promising areas for the application of physical modeling is in software development and testing. Two reasons given for this are the lack of other tools to aid in the development of real time system software and the desire to develop the software system while the hardware is being implemented. Physical models can be used as the test vehicle for the system control hardware and software that will be used on the target system.

The control system employed in a complex

Fig. 22-4. Fischertechnik model of an automated punch press line.

manufacturing system often utilizes a number of different mechanisms as controllers. This usually involves a mix of industrial computers and programmable logic controllers. These controllers must be integrated with intelligent device controllers (such as robot controllers or CNC controllers) and then linked to higher level computer systems. FIGURE 22-4 illustrates a section of a model of an automated punch press plant. The model and system were to be controlled by four programmable logic controllers and a computer. Trial runs with the model tested all functions of the software with respect to the specifications. Unlike computer simulation, this method of software development permits the actual computer systems that will be used in the factory to be used in the debugging process. Real time interaction between the various computing elements can be experienced. This is of particular importance when interaction is required between various components of a computing network.

Of significance is not only the fact that the model can be used for software development, but the realization that these procedures can be done in parallel with the installation of the actual system. Young observed in 1981 that the use of physical simulation can greatly reduce the design and implementation time for complex automated systems. During the development of a computer control system for a complex manufacturing system, the software development effort can only proceed to a certain point and then must wait for the completion of the manufacturing hardware. Physical simulation permits this debugging process to proceed one step further before the actual hardware system is complete. Furthermore, the size of the models often permit observation of the systems performance at a more macroscopic level than would be possible with the actual system.

Physical simulation can employ soft simulations on existing component controllers to generate desired interactions. For example, the interaction of a milling machine controller with a workcell controller might be simulated by using a microcomputer in the model. The computer could interact with the workcell controller according to the desired protocol while controlling the physical model. Zhaung (1989) demonstrated the use of such a simulation in the development of a shop floor software control system. His simulators could be manually driven to obtain some desired system interaction or they could be made to follow prescribed distribution functions.

Training of Operating Personnel

A number of authors have identified that physical simulators might be used in the training of operating personnel who will run the actual system (Maurer 1987, Nof, et al. 1979 and 1980, Paidy and Reeves 1982). There are, however, no reported applications in this area. Physical simulators do provide a realistic representation of the actual system; however, they may not contain the detail necessary to perform meaningful training. Additionally, the control system used in operating the model may have been moved to the actual system. The cost of creating a duplicate control system may exceed the benefits to be derived from the model as a functional training aid. Finally, physical simulators are, in many respects, as complex as the systems they model and the effort to keep them fully functional can be extensive. Industrial training experiences that have employed physical simulators are more educational in nature and not system specific as one might think. This application of physical simulators parallels efforts in the educational area.

Instruction and Research Applications

The educational community is one of the biggest users of physical simulation. (Please see the following references: Aishton and Miller 1982; Bassal, et al. 1986; Deisenroth 1985; Diesch 1982; Falkner and Shanker 1984; Foster and Durkin 1984; Kimbler 1982; Leigh and Nazemetz 1985; Mackuluk and Bedworth 1984; Nof, et al. 1979; Paidy and Reeves 1982; Verma 1985.) Not every college or university can afford to own and operate a flexible manufacturing system within the laboratory. Physical simulation, however, permits an institute to model a complex manufacturing system with only a small capital investment and at a significantly reduced space requirement. Some of the models used in the educational community are of simple systems, where some specific aspect of mechanism control can be stressed. Often, both the industrial and academic communities utilize physical simulators in laboratory exercises on programmable controllers or industrial computers. More elaborate *systems* models are often constructed to help students better visualize complex manufacturing systems and to provide facilities for them to experiment with changes in system design and control. Recently, the integration of benchtop machining systems has lead to installation of a few systems like the one illustrated in FIG. 22-3. While the growth of the use of physical modeling in this area has declined, the future will continue to see more educational applications.

Research applications of physical modeling are increasing in both the academic and industrial communities. Complex Fischertechnik models and fully functional benchtop systems provide excellent laboratory mechanisms for research and experimentation in a variety of aspects of manufacturing systems design and control. Never before has a research group had the ability to implement a fully functional computer integrated manufacturing system for observation and experimentation within a laboratory environment. Much of the work presently being done in this area is related to software issues in manufacturing systems integration and control. These facilities provide a real-world mechanism for implementing and testing control strategies that have been advanced through analytical studies. Without these laboratory models, these research efforts would be limited to purely mathematical analysis and/or computer simulation studies. Physical simulation permits the research to take an additional step toward the application of the proposed methodologies. Additionally, as soft simulation is further combined with physical simulation

and means for automatic data gathering are created, these laboratory models will be used to investigate hardware integration issues.

COSTS AND BENEFITS OF PHYSICAL SIMULATION

The major problems associated with the development and application of a physical simulator are capital investment, development time, and available expertise. While these problems are somewhat large, they are not insurmountable if the perceived benefits are acknowledged.

Many authors have identified the cost factor as a major issue in physical simulation. While it is true that the development and construction costs of the models are substantial, the costs are not significantly different from many other techniques. The materials used in the construction of a physical simulator may cost between $2,000 and $20,000 depending on the size and complexity of the model. Additionally, there is the cost of the control system hardware. For a "toy," this is definitely expensive. However, one should consider the complexity of the mechanism being developed.

The individual system components, sensors and actuators, and the power supply are only part of the cost. The control system hardware and interface must also be included. Since the model may only have a subset of the functionality of the target control system, it may not be necessary to have a comparable control system. Most physical models have been controlled by a combination of microcomputers, minicomputers, and programmable controllers. The costs of these items are usually much greater than the cost of the modeling components. The total component cost of some industrial models has been greater than $100,000 when the cost of the control system was included. In the academic environment, this is a large sum of money. If, on the other hand, this investment is being made by a company that is in the middle of a 3.4 million dollar expansion effort, the cost may easily be justifiable.

A second problem that is also identified with

physical modeling is the development time. Often this is seen as excessive and a possible source of delay in actual system implementation. This can be somewhat overcome if the commitment to modeling is made early enough so that model development can proceed in parallel with system design. Additionally, it should be remembered that application of the model to software system debugging can be done after final designs are established, while the actual hardware is under construction. Experience has indicated that model development does not necessarily have to exceed the time to develop a comparable computer simulation model if adequate personnel are available for the task.

This personnel problem is probably the key to successful model development. Who will build the model? The individual, or team of individuals, must understand the manufacturing system structure, be competent in electrical interfacing and control system technology, and be able to create the necessary system control software. Obviously, the project is not simply an exercise in playing with toys. Regretfully, there are not a lot of model builders around and those that have ventured into this area may be on the steep part of the learning curve. Regardless, a team with a reasonable mixture of electrical, industrial, manufacturing, and mechanical engineering talents can construct a good simulation model given adequate time.

The benefits of physical modeling are all design oriented. The most significant advantage found in applying physical modeling is in the increased confidence that one has in the design. As a communications mechanism, the model gives all members of the system design team a clearer perspective of the total system design concept. Additionally, the opportunity that the designers have to experiment with a functional model before actual implementation may increase the quality of the system as initially installed. A reduction in design and installation time is possible if some of the computer simulation analysis can be eliminated or if software development can be done with the physical simulator. These advantages equate to having a better design in a shorter time with less problems to fix after the fact.

PHYSICAL SIMULATION APPLICATIONS

In order to more fully develop the concepts of physical simulation, three actual applications are reviewed below. The first application details the use of a particular physical simulator in a number of software development efforts in both the academic and industrial communities. The second example is an application of physical simulation for performance analysis of a flexible manufacturing system. The final example details the use of a physical simulator during the design and installation of an automatic system in the automobile industry. More detailed descriptions of these three systems, and other applications of physical simulation, can be found in the appropriate references presented at the end of this chapter.

A Software Research Vehicle

Deisenroth presents a detailed description of a physical simulator that has been used both in the academic community and in an industrial research and development laboratory for software development applications ("Physical Model for Research," 1985). Originally, the model was developed by combining two of the first physical simulators that were created at Purdue University (Nof, et al., 1979 and 1980). That model was used as a marketing display to demonstrate the applicability of a specific computer system for manufacturing control applications. (This is a common use of such models today. See Foster and Durkin 1984, and Maurer 1987.) A second computer company saw the model and had one constructed which enhanced its functionality for use in a research and development laboratory. This company has also used a number of copies of the model for marketing purposes. Finally, Deisenroth has recreated the model within the university laboratory for use as a research vehicle in system control software development (Deisenroth and Galgocy 1986, Roberts and Deisenroth 1989).

The model is constructed of Fischertechnik components and represents a hypothetical manufacturing system. A schematic representation of the model is given in FIG. 22-5. The model has three loading stations, or loader rams, on the right that

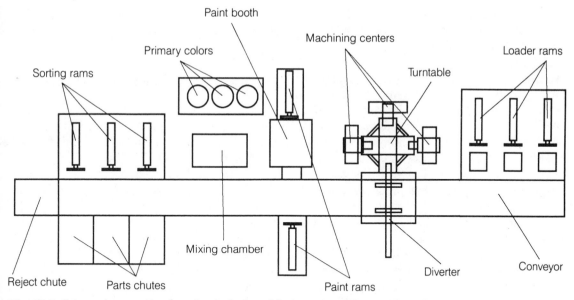

Fig. 22-5. Schematic representation of a physical model of an automatic manufacturing system.

place parts on a conveyor belt for further processing. Parts are then transported to machining centers, where a turntable carries the parts to three different machining stations. After machining, the parts are taken by the conveyor to a painting booth area and then to a sorting area. A close up picture of the paint booth area is shown in FIG. 22-6. It should be noted that in some of the copies of this model, the "paint" color is actually mixed under direction of the control system before the part is painted. Different versions of this model exist in the different organizations and facilities using it. The control system used with the model is greatly dependent on the software system being studied.

The first actual research application of the model involved the development of communication software to integrate programmable controllers into a factory network. The software was to function with a variety of different hardware systems that were involved in both discrete and process control applications. In order to test the functionality of the networking system, researchers wanted a "factory" to use as a pilot system. The model served as such a system. The control system interface was subdivided to permit the use of multiple controllers

to control the model. These controllers were then linked through the factory network to the higher level control system for total system control. The material delivery and machining system provided a framework to test discrete systems control operations while the painting system was used as a pilot process control system. All in all, programmable controllers from four different vendors were interfaced to the model. After development of the software system, additional copies of the model were constructed for use in demonstrating the software product to potential customers.

A slightly scaled down version of the model was constructed for laboratory use in the university setting. This model has been used in a number of research projects and continues to be used today. The model was first used in the development of tools for debugging control logic for discrete manufacturing system control. Specifically, the model assisted in demonstrations of the use of computer simulation as a tool for debugging control code for programmable controllers. The physical simulator functioned as the system that was to be controlled while the computer simulation model simulated the actions of the model.

A second university application of the model is in the development of techniques for applying knowledge based programming systems to the automatic generation of control logic (Roberts and Deisenroth 1989). This research combines the techniques of artificial intelligence with standard discrete control logic for manufacturing systems control. Finally, the model is being used for the development and testing of concepts in distributed systems control. Specifically addressed in this research is the use of distributed control function in a tightly coupled control system for real time system control. The model continues to serve as the sample factory for implementation of a variety of different concepts. Without physical simulation, these research efforts would either stop at the conceptualization stage or be implemented on systems of less complexity. We should note that a benchtop flexible manufacturing system is presently under development at Virginia Polytechnic Institute; this model system will serve as a more complex physical simulator for future research efforts. This system combines actual industrial robots with CNC machines and a material storage and delivery system to achieve an almost real factory environment.

Flexible Manufacturing System Model

Diesch and Malstrom reported the development and application of a physical simulator of a flexible manufacturing system that included a material delivery and storage subsystem, a machine center subsystem, and a turning center subsystem (Diesch 1982, Diesch and Malstrom 1984 and 1985). The simulation and analysis was conducted during the design and installation of a midwestern manufacturing facility. The objective of the application of the simulator was to analyze the effects of machine or component breakdowns in an actual flexible manufacturing system. The papers provide a detailed presentation of the model and its application in assessing downtime effects.

The flexible manufacturing system studied with the simulator is illustrated in FIG. 22-7. The backbone of the system is the material storage and

Fig. 22-6. Close-up view of painting booth area of physical simulator sketched in Fig. 22-5.

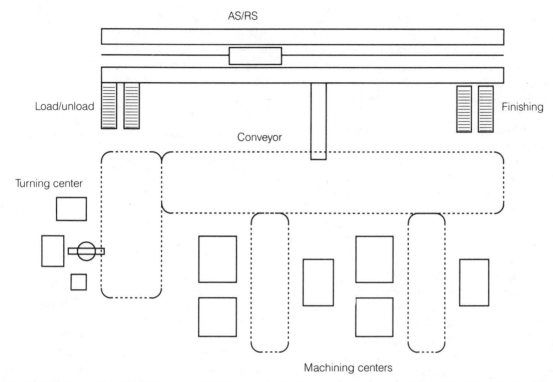

AS/RS

Load/unload

Finishing

Conveyor

Turning center

Machining centers

Fig. 22-7. Schematic model of the actual flexible manufacturing system that was modeled with a physical simulator.

delivery system. The AS/RS is used to store both raw materials and work-in-process. Materials are delivered to the processing areas by a programmable hoist which travels on an overhead monorail conveyor. The loading and unloading of parts at the turning center is done by a robot. Each of the six machines in the machining subsystem has a pallet changer for loading and unloading. Parts to be machined in the system are grouped into six part families. The system includes manual stations for loading the pallets for putting materials into the system, and an area for manual finishing operations on a subset of the products being manufactured.

The physical simulator consisted of components modeled from Fischertechnik modules and a Microbot Minimover robot. The system components included in the model were the AS/RS, the material delivery system, the machining subsystem, and the turning cell. System control was provided by a Radio Shack TRS-80 Model III and a Commodore PET Model 8032. Development of the

model and simulation analysis was conducted during the design stage of the facility.

Of primary significance in the development of the model was the realization that functionality was more important than form in representing various components of the system. It was noted that the material delivery system was designed to transport parts from device to device by elaborate mechanisms that precisely located each part. From a modeling perspective, the operational requirements were simply the automatic routing of the individual parts and the capability of moving the parts individually and automatically from machine to machine. The model utilized inclined ramps and motorized gates to move the simulated parts through the system. These parts were actually marbles which rolled down the ramps via gravity. The gates were computer controlled to stop, start, and divert the parts throughout the system.

As stated earlier, the purpose of the model was to study the effects of component breakdown on the performance of the flexible manufacturing system. Two significant aspects of this analysis should be noted. First, a classical simulation analysis technique was employed in this study. This technique consisted of the use of multiple runs of the model and the application of an appropriate statistical analysis tool. Physical simulation is simulation and should be treated as such. The researchers conducted 48 runs of the model. Each run took one hour and was run using preset values of the input variables. The results were analyzed using least-squares multiple linear regression to derive a multivariable linear estimation equation. Next, the analysis was time scaled to the component of the model with a fixed physical time. Often in physical simulation, some system activities, such as the retrieval of a part in an AS/RS, have processing times which are fixed by the physical layout of the model and the components used in model construction. Other operations, such as simulated machining, have processing times which are completely controlled by the modeler. The fixed time activities must be used to normalize the simulation time for analysis of the simulation data. Such was the case in this example.

Further enhancements to the model were expected to permit additional studies to be run on the system. Of significance was the desire to achieve better than real time in the simulation. A more detailed presentation on the model and the analysis can be found in the literature.

Automobile Assembly Plant Operations

O'Reilly, Casey, and Weiner (1984) presented the application of physical simulation in the automotive industry. The purpose of the study was to investigate the dynamic interaction among system components and to validate computer simulation model results. The system under study was the paint selectivity bank in an automobile assembly plant. Model development and analysis was done during the design stage of the facility with application of the model as a software development tool during system implementation.

Conceptually, relevant automobile assembly operations are organized as illustrated in FIG. 22-8. Automobile bodies move from the painting line, through the selectivity bank, to the trim line. The desired sequence of the car bodies in painting and

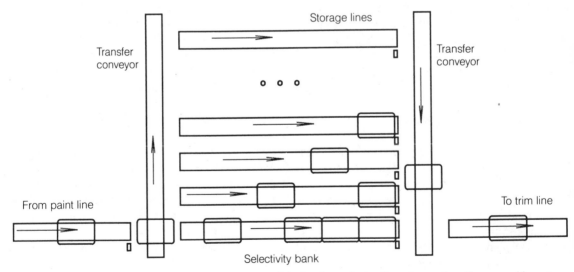

Fig. 22-8. Conceptual organization of paint line, selectivity bank, and trim line of an automotive assembly system.

trim are different and are dependent on the mix of cars being processed. The function of the selectivity bank is to permit a resequencing of the bodies between the two lines. The selectivity bank consists of a number of parallel holding lanes, a lateral transfer conveyor at the entrance to the lanes, and a lateral transfer conveyor at the exit from the lanes. Mechanically activated diverters at the inputs to the lanes and system controlled release gates at the outputs are used to control the motion of the bodies. Since bodies which enter the system can be routed to any desired lane, the output sequence can be a rearrangement of the input sequence.

Preceding the application of physical simulation, an intensive computer simulation was conducted to study various sequencing and body placement algorithms. Since such systems were then being controlled manually, the simulation studies were conducted to identify the limits imposed by manual operations and to investigate the gains that might be possible through implementing a computer controlled system. While the results of this phase of the project suggested that more advanced mechanization was in order, it was decided to perform a physical simulation to accomplish the following objectives:

- Demonstrate the feasibility of a totally automated selectivity bank
- Provide a realistic test environment for evaluation of the design options
- Provide a realistic environment for the development and testing of algorithms
- Provide an environment for the implementation of the actual in-plant system to minimize the impact of implementation problems on the plant

The model that was developed is believed to be one of the largest ever constructed in this country. It was approximately 1/35 scale and was controlled by a Data General minicomputer. It included ten storage lanes in the full model with a provision for "dropping out" individual lanes to simulate different capacity conditions. All conveying motors were driven as variable speed motors in order to be able to adjust the time scale of the model. The vast majority of the model was constructed with Fischertechnik modules with miniature brass air cylinders being used for some functions. The model used industrial bar code readers to read the identification tags of the simulated bodies. The model has 62 position sensors, 39 stops activated by solenoids, 31 pneumatically operated lift tables, and 46 motors. It took approximately ten weeks to design and assemble. All programming was done in Fortran and required approximately ten weeks as well.

The first phase of the application of the model consisted of running the model under computer control to demonstrate that the system could indeed function as desired. Next, the model was used to study a number of hardware and software design options. Finally, the model was used to evaluate various sequencing and placement algorithms that had been developed during the earlier phases of the project. The model identified several reductions in required hardware. Additionally, it was instrumental in improving the placement algorithms to accommodate problems that became apparent with the operation of the model. O'Reilly, Casey, and Weiner concluded their report on this model with a statement indicating that the model was to be used for pilot implementation studies of plant bound hardware and software.

CONCLUSION

The design, implementation, and operation of a manufacturing system in today's environment involves the combined talents of many different disciplines and individuals. The complexity of the tasks involved requires the application of many different tools. One of the latest tools to be applied in this area is physical simulation. By itself, physical simulation is an inadequate tool for solving all problems encountered in the design and implementation of a complex manufacturing system. However, it does represent a powerful approach to visualization in this complex design task. In physical simulation, scaled-down models of production facilities are operated under computer control to mimic the operations of the system under consideration.

There are many different reasons for developing a physical simulator. Most of the benefits for applying physical simulation within an industrial environment can be grouped into one of five areas: conceptualization and communication, evaluation of systems design, validation of computer simulation models, software testing and debugging, and training of operating personnel. Additionally, the educational community has made use of this technique for laboratory instruction and as a research mechanism.

The benefits of physical modeling are all design oriented. The most significant advantage found in applying physical modeling is in the increased confidence that one has in the design. As a communications mechanism, the model gives all members of the system design team a clearer perspective of the total system design concept. Additionally, the opportunity that the designers have to experiment with a functional model before actual implementation may increase the quality of the system as initially installed. A reduction in design and installation time is possible if some of the computer simulation analysis can be eliminated or if software development can be done with the physical simulator. These advantages equate to having a better design in a shorter time with less problems to fix after the fact.

REFERENCES

Aishton, T. H. and R. A. Miller. "Evaluation of Physical Modeling as a Tool for the Design and Implementation of Computerized Manufacturing Systems." In *Proceedings, 1982 Annual IIE Conference*, 411-418. New Orleans, May 23-27, 1982.

Bassal, F., L. Villeneuve, and D. Mercier. "Analysis of a Robotised Palletisation Workstation using Iconic-digital Simulation." In *Proceedings, 1986 IIE Conference*, 107-112. Dallas, May 11-15, 1986.

Bedworth, D. D. and J. E. Sobczak. "Students Learn on AS/RS Models." *Industrial Engineering* 8: 12 (December 1976): 30-39.

Deisenroth, M. P. "A Physical Model for Research in Manufacturing Systems Control." In *Preceedings, Manufacturing Engineering Education-Industry Conference*. Dearborn, November 1985.

Deisenroth, M. P. and C. B. Galgocy. "FMS Simulation for Software Development." SME Technical Paper MS86-166. 1986.

Deisenroth, M. P. "Physical Simulation of Software Development Systems." *CIM Review* 3: 3 (Spring 1987): 55-58.

Diesch, K. H. "Physical Modeling to Investigate the Effects of Machine/Component Breakdowns in an Automated Flexible Manufacturing System." Master's thesis, Department of Industrial Engineering, Iowa State University, Ames, Iowa, 1982.

Diesch, K. H. and E. M. Malstrom. "Physical Simulator Analyzes Performance of Flexible Manufacturing System." *Industrial Engineering* (June 1985): 67-77.

_____. "Physical Modeling of Flexible Manufacturing Systems." In *Proceedings, 1984 Fall Industrial Engineering Conference*, 3-9. Atlanta, October 1984.

Falkner, C. H. and N. Shanker. "Physical Simulation of Flexible Manufacturing Systems." In *Proceedings of the 1984 Winter Simulation Conference*, 397-404. 1984.

Feltner, C. E. and S. A. Weiner. "Models, Myths and Mysteries in Modeling." *Industrial Engineering* 17: 7 (July 1985): 66-76.

Foster, F. and J. Durkin. "Tabletop Technology: Comprehending the Factory of the Future." *Robotic Age* 6: 9 (September 1984): 14-16.

Khoshnevis, B. "Computer-aided Production Systems Laboratory at USC." In *Proceedings, 1985 Annual IIE Conference*, 488-494, Los Angeles, May 1985.

Khoshnevis, B. and R. V. Rogers. "An Automated Warehouse Physical Simulation Simulator." In *Proceedings, Fifth International Conference on Automation in Warehousing*, 67-74, 1983.

Kimbler, D. L. "Physical Simulation in Education: Critique and Alternatives." In *Proceedings, 1982 Annual IIE Conference*, 419-420. New Orleans, May 1982.

Leigh, D. J. and J. W. Nazemetz. "Laboratory Projects in Flexible Manufacturing and Robotics Education." In *Proceedings, 1985 Annual IIE Conference*, 479-487. Los Angeles, May 1985.

Mackuluk, G. T. and D. D. Bedworth. "Flexible Manufacturing Systems Planning (Physical/Digital Simulation Consideration)." *Computer-Integrated Manufacturing and Robotics*. ASME PED-Vol. 13 (December 1984): 161-176.

Maurer, H. "Innovations-marketing mit funktions- und simulationsmodellen." *Sonderdrunck aus Markforschung* (January 1987).

Nazemetz, J. W., D. Tabb, and D. Ashcraft. "Robotics Education." In *Proceedings, 1982 Annual IIE Conference*, 405-410, New Orleans, 1982.

Nof, S. Y., M. P. Deisenroth, and W. L. Meier. "Using Physical Simulation to Study Manufacturing Systems Design and Control." In *Proceedings, 1979 Annual IIE Conference*, 219-228. San Francisco, May 1979.

Nof, S. Y., W. L. Meier, and M. P. Deisenroth. "Computerized Physical Simulators are Developed to Solve IE Problems." *Industrial Engineering* (October 1980): 70-75.

O'Reilly, S. B., K. W. Casey, and S. A. Weiner. "On the Use of Physical Models to Simulate Assembly Plant Operations." In *Proceedings of the 1984 Winter Simulation Conference*, 385-388, 1984.

Paidy, S. R. "An AS/RS Physical Simulator for Education and Training." In *Proceedings, All About Simulation Conference*. Norfolk, April 1984.

Paidy, S. R. and R. Reeves. "The Use and Development of Physical Simulators." In *Proceedings, 15th Annual Simulation Symposium*, 197-209. Tampa, March 1982.

Paidy, S. R. and B. J. Brenner. "Physical Simulators for Work Sampling Studies." In *Proceedings, 1983 ASEE Annual Conference*. Rochester, June 1983.

Pope, D. N. "A Review of Graphics Animation of Manufacturing Systems." In *Proceedings, Autofact 1984*. 1984.

Reid, T. G. "The Kasper Wireworks Automated Wire Forming Machine." Report No. TR 81-5, Industrial Automation Laboratory, Department of Industrial Engineering, Texas A & M University, 1981.

Roberts, C. A. and M. P. Deisenroth. "Automatic Generation of Control Programs." *SME Technical Paper MS89-426*. May 1989.

Schmitz, R.A. "A Computerized Undergraduate Process Dynamics and Controls Laboratory." *Chemical Engineering Education* (Winter 1971): 136-141.

Schwartz, A. V. "Development of an On-line, Real-time Computer Experiment for an Undergraduate Laboratory." Master's thesis, Purdue University, May 1976.

Tsai, R. D., E. M. Malstrom, and H. D. Meeks. "Robotic Unitization of Warehouse Pallet Loads." In *Proceedings, 1985 Fall IIE Conference*, 222-227. Chicago, December 1985.

Verma, A. K. "Factory Automation and the Predicament of Educational Institutions—a Case Study." In *Proceedings, Robots 9*, pp. 21.139-21.150. June 1985.

Wysk, R. A., T. C. Chang, R. P. Davis, H. A. Scott, and C.E. Nunnally. "Physical Machining Systems at Virginia Polytechnic Institute and State University." In *Proceedings, 1982 Annual IIE Conference*, 398-404. May 1982.

Wysk, R. A., S. Y. Wu, B. K. Ghosh, and P. H. Cohen. "Physical and Graphical Modeling of Flexible Machining Systems." In *Proceedings, 1985 Annual IIE Conference*, 451-459. Los Angeles, May 1985.

Young, R. E. "Software Control Strategies for Use in Implementing Flexible Manufacturing Systems." *Industrial Engineering* (November 1981): 88-96.

Young, R. E., J. A. Campbell, and J. A. Morgan. "Physical Simulation: The Use of Scaledown Fully Functional Components to Analyze and Design Automated Production Systems." *Computers and Industrial Engineering* 8: 1 (1984): 73-85.

Zhang, Y. L. "An Integrated Intelligent Shop Control System." Master's thesis, Department of Industrial Engineering and Operations Research, Virginia Polytechnic Institute and State University, Blacksburg, Virginia, April 1989.

23

Facility Layout

Harvey Wolfe[*]
Tejpal S. Hundal[**]

THE *FACILITY LAYOUT PROBLEM* INVOLVES THE placement of work areas and equipment to optimize productivity. Poor layout may result in underutilization of equipment and space, increased material handling, and increased delay times, all of which raise manufacturing costs. A good layout aids in achieving overall integration of production facilities, efficiently utilizing people, effectively using equipment and space, providing the flexibility necessary to accommodate changes in technology, providing job satisfaction and safety for employees, and minimizing costs. The objective of this chapter is to provide an overview of the facility layout problem and to review those techniques available in the literature for achieving a solution. In addition, there will be a discussion of facility layout problems encountered in an automated manufacturing plant.

INTRODUCTION

Facility layout is a problem common in all organizations. Typically, significant expenditures are made for facilities planning every year. The major reason is that any change in the organization has impact on the layout. According to Tompkins and White (1984), eight percent of the Gross National Product (GNP) has been spent annually on new facilities in the United States since 1955. A significant percentage of this investment is spent modifying existing buildings. Tompkins and White claim that, on the average, 20 to 50 percent of the total operating expenses within manufacturing are due to materials handling. They also claim that these expenses can be reduced at least 10 to 30 percent by effective facilities planning.

Facilities are usually defined as specific areas or departments within the manufacturing environment and might include areas such as machining, finishing, packaging, storage, shipping, sales, and accounting. Given a floor space, facilities can be arranged in a fairly large number of ways even if the facilities are all the same size. If facilities are permitted to take different shapes and sizes, the number of possible layouts increases geometrically.

*Dr. Wolfe, Chairman and Professor of the Department of Industrial Engineering at the University of Pittsburgh, was an early researcher into the applications of Industrial Engineering and Operations Research to the Health Services. Dr. Wolfe earned his B.E.S. in Industrial Engineering and his M.S.E. and Ph.D. in Operations Research at the Johns Hopkins University. His current research involves the design of manufacturing facilities to produce new products, interfacing expert systems with facility layout algorithms, and development of simulation models for planning and evaluation of clinical and social programs to control AIDS.

**Tejpal S. Hundal is an Operations Research analyst in the Operations Research Group of United Parcel Service in Hunt Valley, Maryland. He is in the process of completing his Ph.D. in Industrial Engineering at the University of Pittsburgh. He received his B.Sc. (Honors) in mathematics from Hansraj College, Delhi University, India. He holds an MA in applied mathematics, and an MS in Industrial Engineering from the University of Pittsburgh. His professional affiliations include TIMS, ORSA, IIE, and Mathematical Programming Society.

Thus it is possible to find numerous layouts, but it is difficult to determine a good solution to the layout problem.

Finding a satisfactory solution is only a step in the facility layout planning process. Implementation plays a significant role in the selection of a final layout. In many situations a proposed layout achieved by available solution methods may not be considered practical, thereby requiring adjustments to the solution or starting the problem over. Clearly, the layout problem is very complex. In order to avoid mistakes and confusion, it can be approached using an organized, systematic procedure. A version of the systems approach consists of the following steps:

- Identify and define the problem
- Analyze the problem
- Generate and evaluate alternative layouts
- Select and implement the best solution

Layouts are generated based on some method of closeness measurement between facilities. These measurements can be defined in a number of ways; however, the difficulty involved in defining these values depends on the type of layout problem being analyzed. For example, a plant layout will have different requirements than an office layout or a school layout. Analysis includes the size of the various facilities, the distance requirements for the facilities, closeness measurements among facilities, and other constraints if applicable. In fact, this type of analysis is useful in distinguishing one layout problem from another. An analysis of this type, along with some standard techniques for generating layouts that are discussed later in the chapter, can provide alternative solutions to most layout problems.

In an automated manufacturing environment the type of material handling system used dictates the layout. This layout problem is difficult and different from many other facility layout problems because of different sizes of machines, the space required by the machines, the material handling system used, and the higher level of interaction between the machines. The layout problem for an automated manufacturing facility will be discussed later in the chapter.

OVERVIEW OF THE LAYOUT PROBLEM

Mathematically, the facility layout problem involves the placement of facilities on a constrained area subject to some constraints such that the costs involved—usually the material handling costs—are minimized. Clearly, the total area required by all the facilities must not exceed the total area available.

If it is assumed that there are n facilities that have the same area requirements and the area provided is divided into n equal blocks, and it is further assumed that the area available is considered to be square in shape, which will yield four similar layouts for a given layout problem by rotating in various directions, then the layout problem becomes a permutation problem with $n!/4$ different solutions. As n, the number of facilities increases, the number of possible layouts increases, making the problem more complex. The number of possible layouts increases drastically if there are no restrictions on the shapes and sizes of the facilities. Therefore some criteria are required to measure the effectiveness of different layouts so that the best solution can be selected for implementation.

Objective Functions

In most cases, it is difficult to find an optimal layout with respect to any given objective function. The facility layout problem for a large number of facilities becomes computationally intractable since it belongs to the family of NP-hard problems.

Most existing methods for solving the facility layout problem use a criterion of minimizing the material handling cost. Some methods try to maximize *closeness ratings*, some measure of how close facilities should be. Facilities which interact routinely with each other, if placed closer, will minimize material handling cost. However, many other criteria should be taken into account during selection of a good layout. Francis and White have summarized these criteria:

- Minimize capital investment in space and equipment
- Minimize overall production time and cost
- Utilize space effectively
- Minimize congestion and confusion
- Provide for employee convenience
- Flexibility in arrangement and operation
- Maintain easier and better supervision
- Minimize variation in types of material handling equipment
- Facilitate the manufacturing process
- Facilitate the organizational structure (Francis and White 1974)

Constraints

Prior to any analysis, it is important to recognize all of the factors that could influence the layout problem. Factors involved vary by application. All of the following may be important in a facility layout: physical and chemical properties of raw materials used; the type of machinery required, including its shape, size, weight, and height; distances required for the movement of machines, employees, and material; and space requirements for providing safety, convenience, and comfort to personnel. Also, space is required for inventory at various stages of production—raw materials, work in process inventory, and finished products. The type, shape, and number of stories of a building must also be considered.

Flexibility is a desirable factor in layout design. Companies must keep up with the rapid changes in production techniques and equipment if they want to retain their competitive position in the marketplace. Layouts should be planned such that new technology can be easily incorporated in the existing manufacturing system. The availability of financial resources often constrains layout flexibility.

Some of the objectives and constraints discussed above are quantitative and others are qualitative. Thus it is extremely difficult to formulate mathematically a layout problem with all its objectives and constraints. However, it is possible to subjectively define closeness ratings between facilities based on the various objectives and constraints applicable to the layout problem. These ratings can be defined quantitatively or qualitatively.

Closeness Ratings

Closeness ratings are measures of the interaction between facilities, defined subjectively. These ratings are given different names such as interaction costs and priorities. One way to define closeness ratings is to estimate the number of material handling trips for a fixed time period made between two facilities. Interaction cost is obtained by multiplying this estimate by the distance between the location of the facilities. More subjective constraints can be included by increasing the estimate of the number of trips if facilities need to be placed closer, or by decreasing the estimate if facilities should be distant. This method of computing closeness ratings was introduced by Cameron, who called this the *travel charting* method (1952). The estimates and distances are stored in $n \times n$ matrices called travel charts and from-to-charts, respectively, where n represents number of facilities.

Muther suggested a qualitative way of defining closeness ratings as A, E, I, O, U, and X (1961). These ratings are defined as:

- A = Absolutely necessary for two facilities to be located close together
- E = Essential for two facilities to be located close together
- I = Important for two facilities to be located close together
- O = Ordinary closeness of two facilities preferred
- U = Unimportant for two facilities to be located close together
- X = Undesirable for two facilities to be located close together

These ratings are usually displayed as an upper triangle of a $n \times n$ matrix and are called relationships charts, or *REL* charts. In a REL chart, all pairwise comparisons of relationships are evaluated and a closeness rating is assigned to each combination. Analogous to the costs in travel charts, these ratings are surrogates for subjective measurements of various objectives, constraints, communication between facilities, paper work, and other requirements, if any.

Some authors have defined penalties instead of closeness ratings as a measure by which to evaluate a plant layout. A *penalty* is defined as a loss if facilities are not placed together. Layouts are generated by minimizing these penalties. Again penalties are defined subjectively based on objectives and constraints of the layout problem.

SOLUTION APPROACHES

Although many approaches for solving the layout problem have been suggested, there is no best procedure. The layout problem for a large number of facilities is computationally infeasible, NP-hard; therefore, none of the proposed procedures ensures an optimal solution. Nevertheless, it is possible to achieve a good solution. Procedures discussed in the literature may be categorized into four methodologies: systematic procedures, exact procedures, heuristics, and computer assisted design (CAD) methods.

Systematic Procedures

Until forty years ago, layout problems were solved by understanding the facility requirements and using methods based on the intuition and the experience of the analyst. Promising layouts were constructed using flow diagrams and process charts. Templates and scale models were used to display the generated layouts. These layouts were evaluated with respect to the objective of minimizing material handling costs. These methods, known as schematic methods, were very time consuming mainly because of time it took to construct alternative layouts using templates and scale models. Each

change made to a layout typically required that a complete new schematic be constructed.

The *travel charting method*, suggested by Cameron in 1952, provided a better procedure for evaluating alternative layouts. As discussed earlier, this method used quantitative measures of closeness rating based on interaction between facilities.

In 1961, Muther suggested a method called *systematic layout planning* (SLP), which used REL charts to include various objectives and constraints in the analysis. As the name implies, the SLP method consists of first doing a systematic analysis of the sequence of operations, of the flow of materials, and of the relationships between the facilities. Then a check is made to ascertain whether space requirements are met before generating alternative layouts.

At about the same time that Muther introduced the concept of SLP, several other methods were proposed. Most of the methods were modifications of the travel charting method and systematic layout planning. It is clear from all of the methods suggested in that decade between 1952 and 1961 that the main emphasis was on the analysis phase because generating large numbers of alternative layouts was extremely difficult.

Exact Procedures

In 1957, Koopmans and Beckman formulated the layout problem as a quadratic assignment problem and called it the *economic activity location problem*. The quadratic assignment problem has the same form of constraints as the linear assignment problem; however, the objective function is quadratic. The quadratic assignment problem can be formulated as an assignment of equally sized facilities to prespecified locations, such that both the total fixed costs and the costs associated with transportation among facilities are minimized.

Suppose m facilities are to be assigned to n specified sites, where $n \geq m$, because $n < m$ implies that space available is not sufficient for all the facilities. If $n > m$, then $(n - m)$ dummy facilities can be added in the model with zero interaction costs with other facilities and it can be assumed that $n = m$. Sites represent blocks of equal areas on a two dimensional space. The distance between sites are measured as the distances between centroids of the blocks. If

a_{ij} = the fixed cost of locating facility i at site j

c_{ijkl} = the interaction cost between facilities i and k, when they are located at sites j and l, respectively

x_{ij} = 1 if facility i is located at site j, 0 otherwise

then the quadratic assignment formulation for the facility layout problem is

$$\text{Min} \sum_{i=1}^{n}\sum_{j=1}^{n}x_{ij} + \frac{1}{2}\sum_{i=1}^{n}\sum_{j=1}^{n}\sum_{k=1}^{n}\sum_{l=1}^{n}$$

$$C_{ijkl}X_{ij}X_{kl}$$

Subject to:

$$\sum_{j=1}^{n}x_{ij} = 1 \qquad i = 1,2,\ldots,n$$

$$\sum_{i=1}^{n}x_{ij} = 1 \qquad j = 1,2,\ldots,n$$

$$x_{ij} = \{0,1\}$$

The first term in the objective function gives the fixed cost of placing facility i at site j. The second term gives the interaction cost between facilities i and k if they are placed at sites j and l, respectively. The first set of constraints ensures that each facility is located at exactly one site. The second set of constraints ensures that at most one facility is assigned to each site.

A number of exact procedures have been proposed to solve the quadratic assignment problem. These procedures locate facilities optimally. Pierce and Crowston (1971) divided optimal procedures into three groups: the integer programming approach, the semienumerative procedures using single assignment problems, and the semienumerative approaches using the pair assignment problem.

The quadratic assignment problem may be reduced to an integer programming problem by lin-

earizing the objective function. This is achieved by adding many new integer variables and constraints, resulting in a more complicated problem. The new integer programming problem is then solved using a branch and bound procedure. The complexity of the new problem does not allow solution to layout problems with a large number of facilities. Lawler (1963) explains this procedure in detail.

The semienumerative procedures using the single assignment problem approach the optimal solution of the quadratic assignment problem by solving an assignment problem at each level of the branch and bound procedure. A feasible solution of the quadratic assignment problem can be arranged in an $n \times n$ matrix such that exactly one entry in each row and each column of the matrix has unit value and the rest are zeros. Here n is the number of facilities. Next, bounds in the branch and bound procedure can be obtained by fixing a facility and solving an assignment problem for the remaining facilities.

This approach was suggested by Lawler (1963), Gilmore (1972), and Bazaraa (1975). The differences among their approaches were in the methods they used to compute bounds. However, no layout problem with more than fifteen facilities has been solved by any of the variations of this approach.

The semienumerative approach using the pair assignment problem solves the quadratic assignment problem by assigning a pair of facilities at each level of the branch and bound procedure. Gavett and Plyter (1966) suggested this approach, but did not succeed in solving layout problems with a large number of facilities.

Many other researchers have tried exact procedures to solve the layout problem optimally and all have concluded that problems with $n > 15$ are computationally infeasible. Another criticism of the quadratic assignment problem is the assumption that facilities are of equal sizes. This problem could be overcome by considering facilities as integral numbers of equally sized area modules with large values of interaction costs between area modules of the same facility; this consideration would force these area modules to be neighbors in the final layout. However, this increases the number of variables in the formulation of the quadratic assignment problem, resulting in computational difficulties.

Heuristics

Heuristic procedures are more desirable for solving the layout problem than exact procedures because problems with a large number of facilities can be solved in relatively less computational time. Unfortunately, heuristics do not guarantee optimality. As discussed earlier, the facility layout problem is a combinatorial problem and none of the exact procedures solves it in real time for a number of facilities greater than 15. This section describes some popular heuristics used to solve the layout problem. Some heuristics are just computerized versions of the systematic methods; others use mathematical techniques and computer technology to construct good layouts.

In 1975, Scriabin and Vergin claimed that visual based methods generate layouts which are stochastically better than those produced by the *computer* programs. Buffa, in 1976, responded that this was true in layout problems with high flow dominance; i.e., a high coefficient of variation (mean/standard deviation) of the flow matrix. Layout problems with an assembly line have high flow dominance. Layouts are dictated by the sequence of operations or flows already established, and visual approaches can achieve a good layout without much difficulty. On the contrary, layout problems with low flow dominance—for example a job shop layout or an automated manufacturing plant—are much harder to solve using visual approaches. This justifies the need for procedures to generating alternative layouts.

Heuristics may be divided into the following categories.

- Computer aided methods: improvement techniques and construction techniques
- Cluster analytic approach
- Graph theoretic approach

Computer Aided Methods Over the last two decades a number of computer aided methods

have been proposed to solve the facility layout problem. With the advent of computer technology, computations have become less expensive; this makes it feasible to generate a large number of alternative layouts. The systematic methods discussed earlier can also be computerized to produce very good layouts.

Computerized techniques can be classified by the method used to record flows between facilities and by the method used to generate layouts. Flows among facilities are given either quantitatively, in the form of from-to charts or travel charts, or qualitatively as in the form of a REL chart. Some computer methods take an initial layout, and improve it by either heuristic or analytical operations to get the final layout. These methods are called improvement routines. On the other hand, some computer methods, so called construction routines, build a layout from scratch based on interactions between facilities.

Improvement Routines Computerized relative allocation of facilities technique, or *CRAFT*, developed by Armour and Buffa (1963), and later modified by Buffa, Armour, and Vollman (1964), is the most popular and successful technique to solve the facility layout problem. CRAFT requires an initial layout, which is then improved by using a Steepest Descent Pairwise Interchange or SDPIP. At each step, SDPIP swaps locations of two facilities and calculates value of the objective function of the quadratic assignment problem. Calculations are done for all possible exchanges and the exchange which minimizes the value of the objective function most is finally selected. This procedure continues until no improvement is possible or until the procedure has gone through the prespecified number of iterations.

CRAFT is a simple technique to implement; however, it does not guarantee optimality. Many variations have been developed that determine an initial solution using some analytical technique and then use SDPIP to improve it.

Computerized Facilities Design (COFAD), developed by Tompkins and Reed (1976), is a modification of CRAFT. It tries to optimize both the layout problem and material handling equipment alternatives. It includes costs due to material handling equipment as well as fixed costs and interactive costs. First it improves an initial layout using a procedure similar to CRAFT, and then it optimizes material handling equipment for the best layout found.

Construction Routines Construction routines, as explained earlier, build a new layout from scratch.

Biased sampling is a very simple and useful layout technique. It randomly generates a large set of layouts, which are evaluated relative to the total cost. The layout which minimizes the cost is taken as the solution. The computational experience of many researchers shows that biased sampling is a potential procedure to obtain a good layout. Obviously, the quality of the solution depends on the number of solutions generated. A good solution obtained from biased sampling can be used as an initial solution for an improvement technique, like CRAFT.

Computerized Relationship Layout Planning (CORELAP), developed by Lee and Moore (1967), requires a REL chart and maximizes total closeness ratings (TCR). Typically, the TCR of a facility is the sum of the numerical values assigned to the closeness relationships between the facility and other facilities. Numerical values can be subjectively assigned to the relationships in a REL chart, namely, A, E, I, O, U, and X. For example:

$$A = 16, E = 8, I = 4, O = 2, U = 0, \text{ and } X = -4$$

CORELAP attempts to construct the best layout. Unlike the other procedures discussed so far, CORELAP considers area requirements for facilities. The first step in CORELAP is to compute TCRs for all facilities. The facility with the highest TCR is selected and placed at the center of the layout. A tie is broken by the facility having largest area. Next a facility that has an *A* closeness rating (REL chart) with the facility selected at the first step is placed in the layout. A tie is broken by the higher TCR and then the larger area. If no *A* exists, then *E* is searched for, followed by *I, O,* and *U.* The procedure stops when all the facilities are placed. The layout obtained is measured by calculating the sum of the weighted closeness ratings between all facilities and their neighbors.

CORELAP is a good construction technique, but one major drawback is the placement of the selected facilities with respect to the assigned facilities. The choice of which sides are to be adjacent has great influence on the final layout. Obviously, optimality is not guaranteed. Moreover, the procedure becomes difficult when large number of As or Es are in the REL chart, when there is high flow between facilities.

Automated Layout Design Program (ALDEP) is a slight variation of CORELAP. The procedure for placing facilities is the same as CORELAP except that ties are broken randomly. It does not use TCR for selection of the first facility, but it chooses a facility at random. CORELAP tries to produce the best layout, where ALDEP produces many layouts and leaves to the facility designer the selection of a good one.

In 1974, Moore surveyed many other computer aided methods, including: CASS, COL, COLO1, COMP2, LAYOPT, LST, PLAN, PLANET, OFFICE, and others. Most of these methods are variations of CRAFT and CORELAP. In spite of all the computer aided methods suggested in 1960s and 1970s it is still unknown which is the best method for obtaining a solution closest to the optimal.

Good layouts can be obtained by using an improvement technique to improve a layout obtained from a construction technique. The choice of a method depends on the type of layout problem, availability of the method, computation time, input required, and accuracy.

Cluster Analytic Approach Carrie (1973) described the principles of numerical taxonomy applied to group technology and plant layout. This was the first attempt to implement the cluster analysis heuristic approach to the plant layout problem. Many researchers considered cluster analysis as a promising new direction to solve the layout problem, but it was not until the 1980s that Scriabin and Vergin proposed a method based on this heuristic approach.

In their method, Scriabin and Vergin use a REL chart to assign numerical values to flows or interaction between facilities. Facilities are then placed on an unconstrained map such that the euclidean distances between facilities are inversely proportional to the flows. Multidimensional scaling, a data reduction technique, is used to locate facilities on an unconstrained map, or two dimensional plane. Multidimensional scaling is a cluster analysis technique used for placing objects in groups according to similarities (Davison 1983).

In the next step of Scriabin and Vergin's procedure, facilities are forced to the *constrained map*—the space available where facilities are assumed to occupy equal areas—maintaining the positions attained in the unconstrained map based on the flows. This step is achieved by solving an assignment problem, where the cost (C_{ij}) is calculated as the distance facility i must move to be placed at site j, weighted by the sum of flows passing through the facility. Finally, the solution obtained in the second step is improved by the procedure similar to SDPIP.

The cluster analytic approach is useful in incorporating human judgement into a facilities layout model. It combines the best of both the visual based methods and the analytic tools to give a good solution. According to Scriabin and Vergin, their method provides better results than CRAFT and other known heuristics.

Graph Theoretic Approach Seppanen and Moore (1975) took a graph theoretic approach to solve the layout problem. Later, many other authors modified the idea, which is based on the relationship between maximal planar graphs and the corresponding dual graphs (Moore 1976, Foulds and Robinson 1978, Foulds 1983).

A graph $G(V,E)$ consists of a finite nonempty set V, of vertices or nodes, and E, a set of edges. Any graph $G(V,E)$ is called planar if it can be drawn on a plane such that no two edges intersect. A planar graph is maximal if, on adding a new edge, it will not remain planar.

The graph theoretic approach has three steps. In the first step, it constructs a maximal planar graph based on a REL chart. In the maximal planar graph each vertex represents a facility and edges represent closeness ratings. For n facilities there are $n(n-1)/2$ closeness ratings, but the maximum number of edges a maximal planar graph can have is $3n-6$. This implies that some of the relationships will be ignored.

The next step is to construct a dual graph from the maximal graph. A dummy vertex is introduced to represent the area outside of the final layout and it is joined with all possible vertices without violating maximality. Then a vertex is placed in each face—areas bounded by cycles of edges—and is joined to the new vertices whose faces have a common edge. Every face in the dual graph is a facility in the final layout. The last step is to square off the dual graph, taking into account the area requirements of the facilities.

If the three steps are carried optimally, then this becomes an exact procedure. However, for a large number of facilities, constructing the maximal planar graph is a difficult task. Squaring off can result in numerous layouts, which makes the decision making difficult unless there is a systematic approach of selecting a layout.

CAD Assisted Methods

Advanced computer technology has provided new directions for solving the layout problem. In 1950s and the early 1960s, emphasis was placed on the proper analysis of the layout problem. In the late 1960s and the 1970s, emphasis moved toward the generation of alternative layouts. Many computer methods were proposed during this time period that could provide faster computations and could generate large numbers of alternative layouts. In the 1980s computer methods assisted by CAD software became possible. Many methods proposed generated layouts using either systematic approaches or heuristics, which were displayed on computer screens using CAD systems.

A major advantage of a CAD system is that it allows the planner to view layout alternatives and make appropriate changes if required. The idea is the same as that used forty years ago when facility designers would build layouts using scale models and templates. The difference is that the layout alternatives are built on a CAD system, which not only takes less time, but also permits changes to be made without constructing an entirely new layout. Alternative layouts can also be generated easily and, in addition to analytical techniques, visual based methods can also be developed with the help of CAD systems.

LAYOUT OF AUTOMATED MANUFACTURING SYSTEMS

In this decade, automated manufacturing technology has received considerable attention. Automated manufacturing systems integrate computer-interfaced machine tools, robots, automated material-handling systems, and storage devices. These systems are capable of performing a wide variety of operations such as machining, welding, inspection, and assembly.

A typical automated manufacturing system links machines to an automated material handling system and a central computer. The computer provides control over the whole system including the sequence of operations, the schedule of various production stages, the tracking status of different jobs, downloading instructions to machine tools, and taking corrective actions. Thus, the very same attributes of an automated manufacturing system which permit integration of various stages of production using computer systems also create a very complex environment.

In an automated manufacturing system, many machines should be capable of performing different operations that require insignificant amounts of setup times. This flexibility increases the number of options of sequencing and routing jobs. The operations are controlled without interruption by the computer system until something unexpected happens, or maintenance is scheduled, or changes in the operating environment are required. High

interaction between machines add complexity to the design problem in an automated manufacturing system.

In contrast to the classical facility layout problem, the layout problem of an automated manufacturing system has received minimal attention in the literature. Major emphasis has been placed on the design of the physical aspects of an automated manufacturing system. The layout problem in an automated manufacturing environment is different and more complicated than the plant layout problem discussed in earlier sections. High interaction and flexibility make the problem difficult to solve.

A number of factors influence the design problem in an automated manufacturing environment, including types and numbers of machines, machine dimensions, robots, the material handling systems to be used, the characteristics of the central computer, the information processing capabilities, the movement of machines and personnel, and the method used to feed and locate parts at machines. In addition, there are other considerations such as size and locations of inventory, locations for maintenance tools, and locations for the various facilities required for employee convenience, comfort, and safety. Another major consideration is provision for incorporation of changes in the manufacturing environment and changes in the technology.

The solution to the layout problem for an automated manufacturing system must meet many objectives. The solution must minimize throughput time, minimize the total cost of operating the system including material handling cost, control work in process inventories, utilize storage space effectively, and operate the system smoothly and safely.

Heragu and Kusiak (1988) state that the layout problem of an automated manufacturing system cannot be formulated as a quadratic assignment problem because machines are of different sizes and the distances between sites vary and depend on the sequence of machines. These authors also mention that existing popular heuristics used for solving the facility layout problem, namely, CRAFT and CORELAP, cannot be used for an automated manufacturing system because shapes of some machines may be changed in the final layout. They discuss four basic types of layouts: circular machine layout, linear single row machine layout, linear double row machine layout, and cluster machine layout. Moreover, they state that layouts are generally dictated by the material handling system used in the automated manufacturing factory and suggest several alternatives such as material handling robots, automated guided vehicles, and gantry robots.

In a circular machine layout machines are placed in a semicircle and parts are moved by a materials handling robot. An automated guided vehicle is used to move parts in a linear single row machine layout, where machines are placed in a single row. It is also possible to place machines in two parallel rows called a linear double row machine layout. Parts are moved by an automated guided vehicle in between the two rows. Machines are clustered around gantry slides in a cluster machine layout. The arrangement of machines in each layout is determined by the frequency of trips to be made by the carrier. The frequency of trips are estimates computed in the same manner as travel charts.

Heragu and Kusiak discuss two algorithms in their article, one for solving a circular machine layout or a linear single row machine layout, and the other for solving a linear double row machine layout or a cluster machine layout. The first algorithm takes an adjusted flow matrix that has entries made up of the frequency of trips between two machines multiplied by the time required to move parts between them. Machines that are associated with the maximum entry in the adjusted flow matrix are selected first. Next, the machine that has the maximum interaction with any of the previously selected machines is chosen. This procedure is repeated until all the machines are selected and a solution is reached. The algorithm gives the order in which the machines should be placed and the authors show that the algorithm, which is similar to the maximum spanning tree algorithm, gives an optimal solution for systems that have up to four machines. Of course, this could be more easily accomplished through enumeration for problems of this size.

The second algorithm, called the triangle as-

signment algorithm, is recommended for the linear double row machine layout and the cluster machine layout. The algorithm has two phases. The first phase generates triangles of the maximum weight—the sum of the adjusted flows corresponding to edges which represent machines. Triangles are generated by constructing the maximum spanning tree based on the adjusted flow matrix and setting up its adjacency matrix. In the second phase, machines are placed on sites, which are assumed to have equal areas.

Afentakis, Millen, and Solomon (1986) use a simulation approach to solve the layout problem for an automated manufacturing system. They set up simulation experiments to study the total material handling cost for different layouts and material handling systems by varying the parameters in the system. These parameters include the number of parts in the system, the routing of parts in the system, the volume of each part to be produced in each period, the stability of volume over time, and the frequency of change in the part portfolio. In addition to comparing different layout strategies, the simulation approach helps to analyze the overall system.

Generating alternative layouts using CAD software is another approach to solving the layout problem of an automated manufacturing system. Software such as SIMAN and MANUPLAN can produce animated layouts, which can be improved by facility designers using visual based methods. Simulating a system for a given layout and a material handling system on a computer screen can help locate many problems which may not be obvious otherwise.

SUMMARY

We have reviewed the classical facility layout problem. Although layout problems vary in nature, many commonalities can be seen in the analysis and formulation of a particular plant layout problem and other layout problems.

The facility layout problem can be formulated as a quadratic assignment problem, but this formulation is difficult to solve when there are a large number of facilities. The quadratic assignment problem itself is NP hard, and therefore, is computationally infeasible. The exact procedures that have been proposed cannot be used for layout problems with more than fifteen facilities. As a result of the mathematical difficulties encountered in the quadratic assignment formulation, the focus has been shifted to heuristics. Although they do not guarantee optimality, heuristics can provide good solutions to layout problems with a large number of facilities at relatively less computation time.

We reviewed some widely used heuristics. All procedures provide the relative locations of facilities; however, solutions obtained may not be readily implementable. Since solutions obtained are generally in the shape of blocks, the facility designer still needs to make considerable modifications in order to get a final layout.

CAD software makes it possible to view layouts on a screen. In addition to permitting the improvement of the solution by visual methods, CAD allows the designer to add extra features as aisles, doors, windows, machines, and material handling systems, to complete the layout. This can help locate problems with the layout. By combining CAD and some existing heuristic, there is potential for obtaining a good procedure for generating layouts.

The layout problem for automated manufacturing systems is a different problem than the classical facility layout problem. High interaction between machines and greater flexibility make the problem more difficult. The type of material handling system used dictates the layouts. Simulation heuristics have been proposed to solve the layout problem in an automated manufacturing environment, but work in this area is at a very early stage.

REFERENCES

Afentakis, P., R. A. Millen, and M. M. Solomon. "Layout Design for Flexible Manufacturing Systems: Models and Strategies." In *Proceedings of the Second ORSA/TIMS Conference on Flexible Manufacturing Systems: Operations Research Models and Applications*, edited by K. E. Stecke and R. Suri. Amsterdam: Elsevier Science Publishers B. V., 1986.

Armour, G. C. and E. S. Buffa. "A Heuristic Algorithm and Simulation Approach to Relative Location of Facilities." *Management Science* 9: 2 (January 1963).

Bazaraa, M. S. "Computerized Layout Design: A Branch and Bound Approach." *AIIE Transactions* 7: 4 (December 1975).

Buffa, E. S. "On a Paper by Scriabin and Vergin." *Management Science* 23: 1 (September 1976).

Buffa, E. S., G. C. Armour, and T. E. Vollman. "Allocating Facilities with CRAFT." *Harvard Business Review* 42 (1964): 136-159.

Cameron, D. C. "Travel Charts—A Tool for Analysing Material Movement Problems." *Modern Material Handling* 8: 1 (1952).

Carrie, A. S. "Numerical Taxonomy Applied to Group Technology and Plant Layout." *International Journal of Production Research* 11 (1973): 399-416.

Davison. *Multidimensional Scaling*. New York: John Wiley, 1983.

Drezner, Z. "Heuristic Procedure for Layout of Large Number of Facilities." *Management Science* 33: 7 (1987).

Ettlie, J. E. and S. A. Reifeis. "Integrating Design and Manufacturing to Deploy Advanced Manufacturing Technology." *Interfaces* 17: (1987).

Foulds, L. R. "Techniques for Facilities Layout: Deciding which Pairs of Activities Should be Adjacent." *Management Science* 29: 12 (December 1983).

Foulds, L. R. and D. F. Robinson. "Graph Theoretic Heuristics for the Plant Layout Problem." *International Journal of Production Research* 16 (1978): 27-37.

Francis, R. L. and J. A. White. *Facility Layout and Location—an Analytic Approach.* Prentice Hall, 1974.

Gavet, J. W. and N. V. Plyter. "The Optimal Assignment of Facilities to Locations by Branch and Bound." *Operations Research* 14 (1966): 210-232.

Gilmore, P. C. "Optimal and Suboptimal Algorithms for the Quadratic Assignment Problem." *SIAM Journal on Applied Mathematics* 10: 2 (1972).

Heragu, S. S. and A. Kusiak. "Machine Layout Problem in Flexible Manufacturing Systems." *Operations Research* 36: 2 (1988).

Koopmans, T. C. and M. Beckman. "Assignment Problems and the Location of Economic Activities." *Econometrica* 25 (1957).

Lawler, E. L. "The Quadratic Assignment Problem." *Management Science* 9: 4 (1963).

Lee, R. and J. M. Moore. "CORELAP—Computerized Relationship Layout Planning." *The Journal of Industrial Engineering* 18 (1967).

Moore, J. M. "Computer Aided Facilities Design: An International Survey." *International Journal of Production Research* 12 (1974): 21-44.

_____. "Facilities Design with Graph Theory and Strings." *OMEGA* 4: 2 (1976): 193-203.

Muther. *Systematic Layout Planning* 1961.

Pierce, J. F. and W. B. Crowston. "Tree Search Algorithms for Quadratic Assignment Problem." *Naval Research Logistics Quarterly* 18 (1971): 172-181.

Scriabin, M. and R. C. Vergin. "Comparison of Computer Algorithms and Visual Methods for Plant Layout." *Management Science* 22: 2 (October 1975).

_____. "A Cluster Analytic Approach to Facility Layout." *Management Science* 31: 1 (January 1985).

Seehof, J. M. and W. O. Evans. "Automated Layout Design Program." *The Journal of Industrial Engineering* 18: 12 (1967).

Seppanen, J. and J. M. Moore. "Facilities Planning with Graph Theory." *Management Science* 17b (1975): 242-253.

Singhal, K., C. H. Fine, J. R. Meredith, and R. Suri. "Research and Models for Automated Manufacturing." *Interfaces* 17: 6 (1987).

Tompkins, J. A. and J. A. White. *Facilities Planning.* New York: John Wiley, 1984.

Tompkins, J. A. and R. Reed. "An Applied Model for the Facilities Design Problem." *International Journal of Production Research* 14 (1976): 583-596.

24

Job Design I: Approaches

Mahmoud A. Ayoub[*]
Clarence L. Smith[**]

SUCCESSFUL JOB DESIGN MEANS THAT A MATCH HAS been effected between human work capacity and job demands. If this match is not achieved, then there will be manufacturing inefficiency, poor product quality, and pain at work.

Based on applicable workplace and job laws and regulations, employers are expected to:

- Provide employees with a workplace free from all recognized safety and health hazards
- Train employees in how to handle known workplace hazards
- Structure the job to fit each employee and to ensure that the job will not be a source of physical or emotional burden for any person

Minimizing task performance time has traditionally been the hallmark of job design in industry. Minimum task time is generally equated with achieving high levels of productivity at the lowest product cost. However, this is often accomplished at a much greater expense: employee boredom, dissatisfaction, and outright health disorders.

In the discussion to follow, we will first define some basic concepts common to job design. Next, we review and evaluate several approaches typically used in connection with job design. Finally, a case study example for the optimum design of a physically demanding job is presented in chapter 25, ''Job Design II: Modeling.'' The case utilizes linear programming and multiattribute models to structure the job consistent with production goals as well as human criteria and constraints.

DEFINITIONS AND FUNDAMENTAL CONCEPTS

Job. A job is a set of structured activities performed over a finite period of time during the working day. These activities would be expected to reoccur on a routine basis.

Task. A task is the minimum set of activities that can be linked together to provide a meaningful and homogeneous utilization of human skill and performance. A job may contain only one task, or it may be a mix of several diverse tasks.

*Mahmoud A. Ayoub is a Professor of Industrial Engineering and Director of the Ergonomics Research Group (ERG) at North Carolina State University. He teaches and conducts research in ergonomics and occupational safety, areas in which he has published widely. He is a Fellow of the Institute of Industrial Engineers as well as a member of several professional societies. His consulting work has involved many companies, industrial concerns and government agencies throughout the U.S. and abroad. He is the recipient of many awards and citations.

**Clarence L. Smith is ERG Assistant Director and Assistant Director in Industrial Engineering at North Carolina State University. His industrial, consulting, and academic experience in work analysis and design includes both major U.S. and foreign corporations. He is a senior member of the Institute of Industrial Engineers and founding member of the International Foundation for Industrial Ergonomics and Safety Research.

Method. A method is a set of orderly motions that can be performed in a predictable and consistent manner. The method is optimal when it maximizes human efficiency without imposing undue stress on the human body.

Workplace. A workplace includes the specifications for workplace components, such as the seat and work surface; machines and tools; and the environment, such as lighting and color. An ergonomically correct environment will support task performance under the most favorable conditions.

Organization. Organization is the assignment, sequencing, and scheduling of various jobs and their corresponding tasks.

Job Assignment. A job, encompassing several distinct but related tasks, may be assigned to one or more persons. In the case of one person/one job, organization becomes centered around determining working hours, rest periods, and performance standards.

Multiple Assignments. When multiple persons are employed, organization takes on different perspectives; here the concern becomes one of determining the following:

- Sequencing of tasks. An optimum sequence is the order and schedule that minimizes delays and increases throughput
- Coupling among the tasks; in other words, how materials, products will move within and among workstations
- The level of coupling, or perhaps decoupling, among successive tasks or operators that would be necessary to maintain a steady performance; this magnifies the importance of issues related to line balancing and the performance of multiple operators
- The number of tasks to be assigned to each operator, from a minimum of one to a maximum that will ensure continuity of performance and minimum of interruptions; each job assignment will be balanced to confer the physiological and psychological benefits to be derived from task rotation and enrichment

- Formation of job teams or groups: composition of teams, degree of autonomy given to the teams, methods of evaluating team members performance, and role of management in the support given to the teams

Technology. Technology is the level of mechanization and automation employed in support of job performance. Mechanization means that machines will be used for aiding humans during processing and transportation of materials and resources. As machines start to exercise some degree of control over the process (manufacturing) automation becomes the operative label.

Technology Levels. Three levels of technology utilization can be recognized in the workplace (Ekkers 1984). The first is minimum, nothing beyond basic machines for processing and handling of materials. The jobs are totally under the control of the operator. The operator has to understand the information provided by the machine and integrate the provided information to decide on the next move. In this case, the operator has to have the necessary skills and training to command the machine throughout the entire process.

The second level of technology adds some degree of automation to the basic minimum-level scenario presented above. In this second case, many of the routine and repetitive activities will be performed by the machine. Upon command from the operator, the machine will carry out the desired task. The role of the operator will be that of monitoring and decision making. Another use of automation is that of freeing the operator from routine monitoring and data collection tasks. Computers can be used directly on the shop floor to gather, summarize, and display data on various attributes of the workplace. It is even conceivable to rely on the computer to make some routine decisions such as increasing or decreasing line speed to avoid material handling problems.

The third level of technology is full automation. The entire job is now handled by advanced machines, computers, and robots. The operator is in the workplace to monitor and observe the working of the system. The operator intervenes only in case of errors that cannot be corrected by the automatic systems, or, in cases of emergencies that were not anticipated when the total system was designed. The operator retains the option to override the automatic control system and basically make the necessary adjustments to restore the system to a proper operational level.

Job Planning Job planning or *architecture* is basically an allocation of resources—deciding on the job activities to be handled by human operators as well as the functions that will be handled by machines (robots, computers, decision support systems). All allocations will be made consistent with applicable job standards and regulations. These typically include specifications relative to safety and health in the workplace and employee selection and placement. Constraints or restrictions resulting from collective bargaining agreements have to be taken into consideration.

Job Design Steps A job is designed by following a sequence of steps ranging from method development to determining job content. The steps are:

- Specify job method, workplace, and working environment. All determinations must be based on sound ergonomics.
- Specify job content based on (1) physical/physiological requirements, and (2) behavioral consideration for the well-being of the workers.
- For a given job, demands are first estimated based on three parameters: force, posture, and frequency. Expected response for a range of operators are then predicted. Operator capacity profiles will reflect persons with varying degrees of fitness (low, average, high).

Starting with an acceptable task/job content, job assignments to operators or teams of operators are then made to maximize the behavioral considerations: variety, feedback, skill maintenance, interaction, self-worth, responsibility, and professional growth.

Anthropometry The study of anthropometry defines the workplace that will accommodate the potential work force. Arrangement of the workplace components to achieve optimum posture, minimum reach, and no static loading will be the primary consideration. Detailed anthropometric data are given in Woodson (1981) and Diffrient, et al. (1978).

Biomechanic/Work Physiology Physiology is used to determine job demands and the corresponding responses. Experimental methods can be used in lieu of models. There are several physiological methods that can be used to analyze the demands (stress) a job places on a worker. Astrand and Rodahl (1970) detail the basis for many of the methods of interest.

Mathematical Models The models are used in forming task clusters and work teams or groups. Linear and goal programming models are often used for this purpose. The models provide a logical and consistent means for determining the optimal job assignment for a given set of tasks. The objective is to minimize the total stress and strain on each worker subject to various production, physiological, and psychological constraints. Examples of using the modeling approach are given by Niehaus (1979). He provides a collection of useful models for manpower planning and assessment.

Simulation Simulation may be used to test the overall design of the jobs and the clustering of tasks. It is a powerful method for dealing with *What If* scenarios (Ayoub, 1987).

Expert Systems Expert systems may be utilized to support the applications of the various models utilized in job definition and structuring (Andriole 1985, Waterman 1986).

Measurements Measures of the appropriateness of job design and structure include cost, productivity, quality, safety and health of employees, absenteeism, and turnover.

Criteria An optimum job design should confer the following criteria: productivity, acceptable product and work quality, job accessibility for the available labor market, human well-being and satisfaction, and meeting regulatory requirements.

Job Rotation Rotation is used as a means to overcome stress concentration resulting from repetitive performance of a single task. By having the rotation among a mix of physical and monitoring (watching) tasks, the potential for muscle overloading, boredom, and reduction in vigilance will be minimized.

Job Enlargement. Enlargement expands the number of activities within a given task. As with rotation, enlargement is intended to minimize stress concentration. In contrast to rotation, this effect is achieved by expanding the activities within the task, rather than moving the worker among a mix of workplaces.

Job Enrichment. Enrichment gives the worker a degree of control and latitude in matters related to job performance, method, and scheduling of tasks.

Job Teams. Tasks can be arranged serially in the form of an assembly line, or in a cluster of workstations. Members of a job team can perform multiple tasks. Task rotation is used by the team. When applicable, group incentives are used.

Assembly Line. A product is made by sequentially moving it through a number of workstations—an assembly line. At each workstation, a specific task or operation is performed. The material is progressively changed until the final product is made. Balancing the line (number of tasks assigned to each operator) becomes an important design consideration. Specification of line speed (as in machine pacing) is another design consideration. A plant may utilize several types of assembly and transfer lines.

Work Clustering. To overcome line balancing problems and interdependence among line operations, the work force is divided into teams. Each team is capable of producing the final product. Therefore, disruption (due to absenteeism or turnover) within one team will have minimum impact on the overall production.

Job Evaluation. Evaluation is a formal procedure for hierarchically ordering a set of jobs or positions with respect to their value or worth. It is usually for the purpose of setting pay rates, with the basic tenet that the job, not the worker, is evaluated and rated. While many compensable factors may be used, they tend to fall into four categories: skill, effort, responsibility, and working conditions (Trieman 1979).

Value Added. If work is performed at a given point, the production process produces visible change or improvement of a product. Then, we may conclude that the work has a value added. On the other hand, if the work is simply that of inspection and verification of what has already been performed, the work will have no value added. Inventory, material handling, and auditing jobs for the most part can be viewed, in concert with our definition, to offer no additional value to the product.

APPROACHES TO JOB DESIGN

We now turn to a discussion of several approaches to job design. These include Taylorism, Work Study, Work Physiology, and Behaviorism.

Taylorism

In the late 1800s, issues related to job design and methods for increasing labor productivity became of prime interest to industry, in the U.S.A. as well as in Europe. Fredrick W. Taylor, a mechanical engineer from Pennsylvania, became interested in job methods and in defining skills for various jobs. His contributions and those of his contemporaries, namely Frank Gilbreth, founded a new approach for job design in industry. Their approach heralded the application of scientific management to industry, and subsequently formed the basis for today's industrial engineering. The approach encompasses the following (Parks and Collins 1976; Woolsey 1976):

- Training of workers for specific jobs. If deemed necessary, select workers who have the required skills to ensure effective job performance.
- Defining a standard method for each task. The method should produce efficient performance, eliminate waste of resources, and be compatible with human abilities. Train the workers to follow the standard method during job performance.

- Establishing a performance standard for each job. The standard is to reflect the degree of difficulty inherited in the task and the quality of the working environment. Workers will be expected to maintain a standard pace which is equated to 100 percent output or production. Those who exceed the stated production target get paid commensurate with the amount of increase. On the other hand, those who fail to meet the standard are kept on a watch list; their continued failure to be at or above the standard level may cause job transfer or loss. Workers are compensated for job difficulties arising from (attributed to) the nature of job motions, the environment in which the job is performed, and/or the specifics of the method devised for the job. The compensation is given in terms of fatigue allowance which, in turn, is accounted for in the job production standard.
- Organizing the job into maximum possible sets of basic motions (activities). Each of these sets is then assigned to one person; if the demands warrant, several persons may be assigned to perform the same set of activities. By severe fragmentation of the job into a set of stereotyped motions, it is reasoned that the workers will be efficient and productive. This is based on the fact that repeated performance of the same motion will be made habitually and almost subconsciously. In addition, by limiting each worker to a minimum number of motions, no waste or unnecessary delays typical of multiple and different activities will result.
- Monitoring performance of the workers by management (supervisors). Management makes all assignments relative to production requirements, job scheduling, and work hours. Workers are expected to do what is asked of them, for management knows better. Job methods and standards are continuously audited by management to claim back any improvements or gains resulting from changes in job motions or environment.

Scientific management means that management exercises total control over the workers from the time they walk into the plant until the end of the work day. Workers, in contrast, have very little say in what is happening to their bodies physically and emotionally. Although Taylor, in describing the elements of his scientific management, emphasized communication between management and their workers, industry at large conveniently ignored it (Woolsey 1976).

To sum up, Taylor's approach to job design is based on efficiency and control concepts: task specialization, time and motion standardization, and work simplification. The approach has strong advocates in industry for many obvious reasons:

- It is economical to hire workers for a specific level and type of skill.
- Job training time and staffing costs are minimized.
- At all levels, human performance is easily controlled and measured by management.
- Jobs can be staffed by most persons possessing minimal physical and mental skills.

Work Study

The steps of scientific management constitute the elements that are currently known as method study and work measurement. Both of these are grouped together under the work study label (International Labour Office 1979).

Method study is concerned with defining the best or optimum set of motions that can be efficiently used by a worker to perform a task. A method is typically the product of several variables: task, workplace, tools, machine, and working environment.

Work measurement, for a given method, is applied to develop the performance time to be expected from an average worker, the so called 100 percent person. Performance time may be estimated from existing data banks (also known as predetermined time systems) or through direct time study. In the latter case, workers performing the targeted job following the standard method are observed very closely. The time spent on each motion (e.g., getting material, positioning a work piece, etc.) is measured to a high degree of accuracy, normally within one one thousandth of a minute.

Simultaneously with the measurement of time, the observer also rates the performance of the worker. Here, it is assumed that the observer has been trained to recognize the characteristics of the 100 percent performance. The observed performance is judged relative to that reference and expressed as a percent change of the 100 percent value. The assigned rate can be either higher or lower than the standard 100 percent. The measured time value is prorated (adjusted up or down) to make it coincide with the 100 percent performance—the normal time.

Therefore, throughout the measurement process, two basic assumptions are made: (a) the observer is a rational observer (objective and consistent) and (b) the worker performs in a consistent and reproducible manner. Both of these assumptions are subject to serious criticisms.

Within work study, several methods and techniques are available to develop efficient job methods and the corresponding standards. Included among these are *work simplification* and *work sampling*. A variety of charting methods are used to describe both the workplace and job activities: *flowchart*, *process chart*, and *right/left hand chart*, to name a few. Simple descriptive statistics are often used in summarizing time measurements and performance data.

Currently, PCs and mainframe computers are routinely used at a large scale to develop job standards in industry. The Maynard Operation Sequence Technique system, or MOST, is an excellent example of using computer power and existing standard data for designing jobs and developing performance standards (Zandin 1980).

Work Physiology

At the same time Taylor and Gilbreth were making their marks on U.S. industry, the European literature started to show the results of some pio-

neering research on the functioning of the human body in the world of work. Amar (1920) in his classical book titled *Human Motor* details and reviews some pioneering studies relative to the biomechanic and physiologic basis of job design and tool design.

This approach to job design considers human capabilities, task demand, and workplace and equipment characteristics. It attempts to determine the optimum physical interface between man and his machine—the interface that will protect the human structure from excessive stresses and strains without compromising productivity and efficiency. This optimum interface can be realized if industrial tasks are designed so as to achieve maximum adjustments between human physiological capacity and job demands.

A body responds to job demands by exerting a muscular force. If the muscle is in shape, having sufficient strength, the force is delivered. When delivering this force over time, the body calls on the heart and the lungs to provide oxygen to the working muscle, and rid the muscle of waste products being produced. A complication of this scenario is the addition of a heat component to the job. When a body gains heat, it must face the problem of maintaining a constant core temperature. To accomplish this, the body must lose the heat gained from the environment; here sweating becomes a factor.

After more than 80 years, Amar's book remains in concert with the basis of current ergonomic principles and recommendations. In appraising Taylor's work, Amar raised serious concern about a job design approach that does not specifically deal with human characteristics and limitations. In fact, Amar was just one of many who felt that the Taylor/Gilbreth methodology was an improper method for job design (Schmidtke and Stier 1961; Bailey 1961; Sellie 1961; Taggart 1961; and Honeycutt 1962).

Behaviorism

Taylor's approach to job design was a natural recipe for development of the assembly line. Industrial labor was reduced to performing singular and repetitive motions for the duration of the workshift; people became an extension of their machines, and nothing more. In most cases, the lines were running at speeds in excess of tolerable levels for many of the workers.

In the 1940s and thereafter, behavioral scientists began to express their concerns about Taylorism and its premises for job design in industry. The approach has been severely criticized for the boredom and stress it creates for the worker. The behaviorists' quest has become centered around job *enlargement*, *enrichment*, and *teamwork*. In any event, the behaviorists rejected the assembly line as a way for productive and healthful utilization of human labor.

The Hawthorne study in 1920 brought the behavioral scientists, psychologists, and sociologists into head-on contact with Taylorism. At a Western Electric Hawthorne Plant in Chicago, a team of behavioral scientists undertook the task of studying the effect of several work factors such as rest breaks, illumination levels, and diet on job performance. The outcome of their studies was a surprise, for they found that productivity and satisfaction increased or decreased as a function of the attention given to the operators by management and the research team. In addition, the work factors under study did not influence the outcome significantly. The startling findings of the Hawthorne study heralded the behavioral assault on Taylorism and its approach of managing human labor in industry. The behaviorists argue strongly (and we might add persuasively) that, to a person, a job should be more than fulfilling an economic need.

The Hawthorne study ascertained that a Tayloristic job design is likely to result in lower job satisfaction, decreased motivation, higher absenteeism, and increased health disorders.

In contrast, the behaviorists accept a job design that contains five key characteristics (Hackman and Oldham 1975):

- Variety: maximize number and level of skills
- Identity: complete whole or specific part of job
- Significance: job has impact on other workers
- Autonomy: worker has decision-making power
- Feedback: worker is kept informed of job performance

Employing each of these concepts would increase participation by the worker and communication between co-workers and management. In addition, implementation of the concepts will yield an increase in job satisfaction, higher motivation, and more involvement by the workers. Indirectly, this will also result in lower absenteeism and higher productivity (Vaill 1967; Galbraith 1967; Sell and Shipley 1979; Davis and Taylor 1979; Wild 1975; Smith 1981).

WHICH APPROACH?

Each of the approaches presented above has its strengths and limitations. It would be naive to reject the Tayloristic approach outright, for a job has to exhibit a certain degree of efficiency and consistency. On the other hand, one cannot argue against the fact that extreme job fragmentation as practiced under Taylorism is not healthy for human well-being. In this context, the behavioral approach makes it strongest appeal—structuring a job to ensure human satisfaction and growth. A job regardless of its structure or demands has to be within human capabilities. This is the principle upon which the work physiology or biomechanics, approach is based.

Therefore, an acceptable job design approach is one that ensures the following (de Jong 1979; Corlett 1979):

- A sound efficient method supported by a proper workplace
- Job demands that do not tax the workers beyond acceptable physiological levels
- The job is structured (expanded) to ensure an acceptable behavioral content

Ergonomics offers an approach that satisfies all these prerequisites.

ERGONOMIC APPROACH

The pioneering work of Taylor and Gilbreth, and the contribution from behavioral and physiological sciences have evolved and matured into the ergonomic approach to job design. Ergonomics is simply the integration of the various facets of each approach into a comprehensive method for studying people and their working environment.

Ergonomics, as a discipline, is concerned with the design of jobs, workplace, and products as well as employee selection and training. In this context, ergonomics is closely allied with industrial engineering, for both seek efficiency and productivity. The point of departure between the two is in the consideration given to human capabilities and limitations. While seeking high levels of productivity, ergonomics attempts to assure that job stresses (physical, physiological, and psychological) can be tolerated by the human body and its systems.

The key to a successful ergonomic effort lies in the integration of people's abilities and the demands of their environment. The workplace is seen as a man-machine system, as shown in FIG. 24-1. Successful integration is achieved when people are not exposed to safety or health risks; when the job demands do not tax human work capacity, or can be met only by a select few individuals; when people are in control of their environment and machines; and when jobs promote the social interactions and well-being of those who perform them.

Ergonomics bases its principles and recommendations on knowledge and data taken from a wide cross-section of disciplines: engineering, physiology, anatomy, psychology, medicine, mathematics, and statistics. To this end, ergonomics offers a philosophy and approach for dealing with people's characteristics and limitations; it accepts people as they are, as individuals having various abilities that are neither constant nor completely measurable. It attempts to effect a match between people and their working environment, as well as their products. In so doing, it considers the whole of the person: behavioral, physical, and physiological attributes.

Sound jobs and workplaces can be achieved through the diligent application of well defined ergonomic principles and recommendations. There is a finite number of options to be considered in improving the ergonomic health of a job and workplace: (1) workplace redesign, (2) job restructure, (3) method improvement, (4) improvement of materials handling and flow within and among workstations, and (5) increasing employee fitness for work. A combination of several of these corrective measures is likely to ensure an effective and trustworthy solution.

JOB REDESIGN

In searching for ways to improve an existing job, the best approach is to critically examine the entire process, from start to finish, from receiving to shipping. As various workplaces and jobs are examined, the *what*, *why*, *how*, and *when* questions should be asked. At every point, detail and evaluate what is being done, by whom, and why it is being done.

Consider the overall sequence and scheduling of various activities, tasks, and operations. In every case, consider the effect of eliminating, combining, rearranging, and/or simplifying. Certainly, elimination is the greatest improvement of all and should be considered first. Only when elimination is impossible should we look at combining, rearranging, or simplifying some aspect of the work or workplace. Careful probing should help highlight the source of the observed deficiencies. This type of evaluation has its genesis in the methods engineering approach of study (Polk 1984, Konz 1979, or International Labour Office 1979).

Quite often, problems with the existing design may be attributed to one of three general classes of causes: (1) machine and tools, (2) materials handling within and among the workplaces, or (3) job method and tasks making up the job assignment.

We should always keep in mind that the causes may have their roots outside the workplace or job where most of the complaints occur. For example, changes in material or technology of the production process may translate into a difficult method at some workplace far removed from the point where the changes were first introduced. In this case, we may say that the observed deficiencies are referred from another area within the plant.

At times, the root cause may reside outside the plant and its environment altogether. Consider the case where components are supplied by outside sources. Typically such components have to meet certain manufacturing tolerances and specifications. Failure of the supplier to meet the established tolerances will make the assembly task

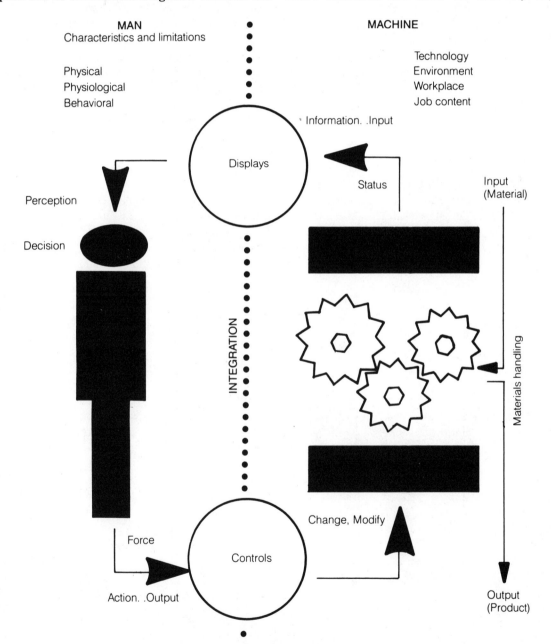

Fig. 24-1. Ergonomics produces a man-machine system.

difficult and may necessitate the application of excessive force and maintenance of extreme posture. Without recognizing that the problem lies with the component tolerances, any changes or improvements made at the workplace will not be the answer.

To this end, care and time should be spent on the analysis and evaluation of the triggering causes. Most often, the obvious deficiencies may be merely the symptom of a very fundamental flaw in the workplace and its components. The following example illustrates the point.

Example:
Islands of Automation

In an assembly plant, raw materials are converted into finished units through a set of serial progressive tasks, as shown in FIG. 24-2. As the material moves through the production line, it is continuously changed (form modified, components added) until the finished unit or product is made. At that point, the units are inspected for defects; 100 percent inspection is carried out.

The finished units are delivered to the inspection department in large trucks. From these trucks, operators retrieve and inspect each unit for defects in material and assembly. A defective unit is logged on a special form along with descriptions of the observed defects.

Inspection operators are paid on the basis of an incentive system. That is, they are paid a bonus in direct proportion to the number of units inspected above the established performance standard for the department. The inspection department as a whole maintains an average performance level of 130 percent. This high level means that the operators were earning, on the average, a bonus of 30 percent of their basic pay.

Workers in the assembly plant had a significant problem with cumulative trauma disorders (CTDs). Most of the department exhibited a high prevalence, except for inspection. Medical records showed that the inspection operators had very few

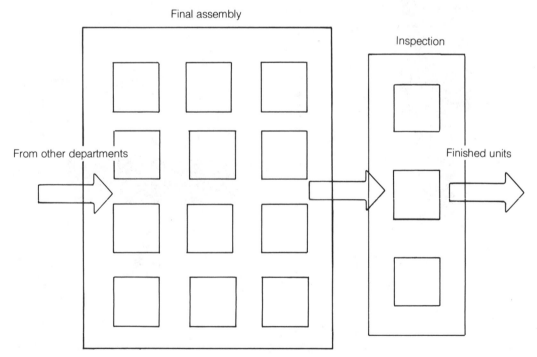

Fig. 24-2. The assembly process in the Islands of Automation example.

complaints relative to musculoskeletal pain, and for a period of three years, not a single case of CTD was reported for the department. In contrast, the CTD prevalence rate for the other departments varied from two to seven percent.

The department with the highest CTD prevalence assembled the finished units just prior to sending them to inspection. The work was highly repetitive and described as a series of rapid and short actions. In addition to the CTD problem, the same department was lagging behind in terms of productivity and efficiency. This translated into a higher production cost for the finished units. Concerned about the twin problems (CTD and productivity), management decided on a solution: automate the jobs within the troublesome department.

After a period of evaluation and testing, the department was equipped with new automatic assembly machines. They were the latest that available technology could offer. The machines were fast and required much skill for their operations and monitoring. The conversion from manual to automatic assembly was not a smooth one. It took some time before the production levels were stabilized and kept at steady state. Assembled units were moved up the line to inspection as had been done prior to automation.

As the automation efforts started to take hold, the inspection department became the focus of management attention as well as much concern. All of a sudden, many of the operators (in excess of 30 percent) went to the medical department complaining of CTD-like symptoms. A thorough review of the inspection department revealed very little: the job was the same; the target performance standard was not changed; no additional operators hired since the automation project started; overall management policies and practices remained unchanged. In light of all of this, the question asked by everybody was: *Why now?*

To find out, management initiated a review of the entire assembly process, including the major recent changes introduced at the plant. This led to the automatic assembly department. There two things were noticed: (1) production was dramatically increased and (2) the quality of assembly was not constant. It varied from day to day, and even from batch to batch. The variation was attributed to the complexity of the new machines.

Because of the occasionally high defective assemblies, productivity of the inspection operators declined sharply. The operators had to slow down considerably in order to handle the defects. This resulted in lower earnings for them. The drop in earnings compounded by aggravation and frustration sent the operators in large numbers to the medical department.

Having isolated the cause of the problem in the inspection departments, the solution was obvious as well as simple—improve the quality of the final assembly through machine modification and close monitoring of its working cycles. The recommendations were implemented, and the complaints from the inspectors subsided!

Lessons Learned:
No Automated Area is an Island

From all of this we can derive a critical point. When it comes to automation, we should always assess the impact of the change on the entire production system, not just where the changes are made. In a word, we should not make islands of automation! For an excellent collection of case studies on the impact of automation on jobs and workplaces, Butera and Thurman (1984) should be consulted.

CONCLUSION

Automation is inevitable, for better or worse. It is critical that we thoroughly understand the implication that automation may bring to us or to those who work for us. The growing integration of technology and human labor makes it both difficult and necessary to ensure that automation will be achieved without harming or degrading the quality of working life in and outside the workplace. This quest can be realized through sound job design. In the next chapter, we will examine specific methods for designing and structuring physically demanding jobs.

REFERENCES

Andriole, Steven J., ed. *Applications in Artificial Intelligence*. Princeton, New Jersey: Petrocelli Books, Inc., 1985.

Amar, J. *The Human Motor*. London: George Routledge & Sons, LTD., 1920.

Astrand, Per-Olof and Kaare Rodahl. *Textbook of Work Physiology*. New York: McGraw-Hill Book Company, 1970.

Ayoub, M. A. "How to Apply Simulation Modeling and Analysis to Occupational Safety and Health." In *Handbook of Occupational Safety and Health*, edited by L. Slote, 515-552. New York: John Wiley & Sons, 1987.

Bailey, G. "Comments on An Experimental Evaluation of the Validity of Predetermined Elemental Time Systems." *The Journal of Industrial Engineers 12*: 5 (1961): 328-330.

Butera, F. and J. Thurman, eds. *Automation and Work Design*. Amsterdam: North Holland, 1984.

Corlett, E. N. "Isolation and Curiosity as Sources of Work Attitudes." In *Satisfaction in Work Design*, 51-56. London: Tayler and Francis, 1979.

Davis, L. and J. Taylor, ed. *Design of Jobs*. Santa Monica, California: Goodyear Publishing Company, 1979.

Diffrient, N. et al. *Human Scale 1/2/3/, 4/5/6, 7/8/9*. Cambridge, Massachusetts: MIT Press, 1978.

Ekkers, C. L. "Job Design and Automation in the Netherlands." In *Automation and Work Design*, edited by F. Butera and J. E. Thurman, 407-430. New York: Elsevier Science Publishing, 1984.

Galbraith, J. "The Use of Subordinate Participation in Decision-Making." *The Journal of Industrial Engineering 18*: 9 (September 1967): 521.

Hackman, J. R. and G. R. Oldham. "Development of the Job Diagnostic Survey." *Journal of Applied Psychology 60*: 2 (1975): 159-170.

Honeycutt, J. "Comments on an Experimental Evaluation of the Validity of Predetermined Elemental Time Systems." *The Journal of Industrial Engineers 13*: 3 (1962): 171-179.

International Labour Office. *Introduction to Work Study*. 3rd ed. Geneva: International Labour Office, 1979.

de Jong, J. R. "Roles and Instruments in Work Design and Work Re-Design." *Satisfaction in Work Design* (1979): 41-50.

Konz, S. *Work Design: Industrial Ergonomics*. 2nd ed. Columbus, Ohio: Grid Publishing, Inc., 1979.

Niehaus, R. *Computer-Assisted Human Resources Planning*. New York: John Wiley & Sons, 1979.

Parks, G. M. and R. B. Collins. "Two Hundred Years of Industrial Engineering." *Industrial Engineering 8*: 7 (1976): 14-25.

Polk, E. *Methods Analysis and Work Measurement*. New York: McGraw-Hill, 1984.

Schmidtke, H. and F. Stier. "An Experimental Evaluation of the Validity of Predetermined Elemental Time Systems." *The Journal of Industrial Engineers 12*: 3 (1961): 182-204.

Sell, R. and P. Shipley, ed. *Satisfaction in Work Design: Ergonomics and Other Approaches*. London: Taylor & Francis LTD, 1979.

Sellie, C. "Comments on an Experimental Evaluation of the Validity of Predetermined Elemental Time Systems." *The Journal of Industrial Engineers* 12: 5 (1961): 330-333.

Smith, M. J. "Occupational Stress: An Overview of Psychosocial Factors." *Machine Pacing and Occupational Stress* (1981): 13-20.

Taggart, J. B. "Comments on an Experimental Evaluation of the Validity of Predetermined Elemental Time Systems." *The Journal of Industrial Engineers* 12: 6 (1961): 422-427.

Trieman, D. *Job Evaluation: An Analytic Review*. Washington, D.C.: National Academy of Sciences, 1979.

Vaill, P. "Industrial Engineering and Socio-Technical Systems." *The Journal of Industrial Engineering* 18: 9 (September 1967): 530.

Waterman, Donald A. *A Guide to Expert Systems*. Reading, Massachusetts: Addison-Wesley Publishing Company, 1986.

Wild, R. *Work Organization*. London: John Wiley & Sons, 1975.

Woodson, W. E. *Human Factors Design Handbook*. New York: McGraw-Hill, 1981.

Woolsey, G. "Reflections on the Past of Scientific Management and the Future of Management Science." *Interfaces* Institute of Management Sciences, 6: 3 (May 1976): 3-4.

Zandin, Kjell B. *MOST Work Measurement Systems*. New York: Marcel Dekker, 1980.

25

Job Design II:
Modeling

M. A. Ayoub[*]
D. M. Scheltinga[**]

VARIOUS WORK ENVIRONMENTS FOSTER A NEED TO develop a low-cost method for exploring job design changes. The pot-room jobs in an aluminum smelting plant are one example. The model explained here answers the need to explore job design changes. The model provides the means by which the impact of specific job changes—such as imposing rest periods and task reorganization—can be assessed. The model is extremely useful because it allows experimentation with various restructuring scenarios without the need to physically change existing jobs. It is intended to serve as a base from which design changes can be modeled to achieve more productive and less stressful jobs. To accomplish all this without expensive experimentation in the workplace is a plus!

The model is based on a series of equations designed to simulate the physiological responses to various types of physical tasks. It computes the energy expenditure rate for each of the tasks individually and for them collectively as a job. The model also determines an overall energy expenditure rate and the corresponding heart rate for a given job. This final step allows for testing the effect of job reoganization on the overall physiological responses.

JOB DEMANDS: A PREDICTIVE MODEL

The model was developed utilizing a comprehensive potroom database (see data below). It is composed of almost 300 equations and 600 variables that are combined to simulate specific tasks and jobs within the potroom. The equations or rules are modified versions of those reported in the literature (see Aberg, et al. 1968; Garg 1976). Specifically, the model has the following form:

$$\text{Total task energy} = [f(\text{posture}_i) \times \text{time}_i] + [f(\text{activity}_j) \times \text{time}_j]$$

$$\text{Energy expenditure (Kcal/min)} = \text{Total task energy} / \text{task time}$$

$$\text{Heart rate} = f(\text{energy expenditure, thermal stress})$$

*Mahmoud A. Ayoub is a Professor of Industrial Engineering and Director of the Ergonomics Research Group (ERG) at North Carolina State University. He teaches and conducts research in ergonomics and occupational safety, areas in which he has published widely. He is a Fellow of the Institute of Industrial Engineers as well as a member of several professional societies. His consulting work has involved many companies, industrial concerns and government agencies throughout the U.S. and abroad. Mahmoud is the recipient of many awards and citations.

**Donna M. Scheltinga works for IBM in the Research Triangle Park, where she is responsible for inventory management. She received her B.S. and M.S. degrees in Industrial Engineering with an emphasis on Ergonomics. While at North Carolina State University, Ms. Scheltinga was heavily involved with evaluation and redesign of jobs for several industrial clients.

Where:

$f(\text{posture}_i)$ = Kcalories associated with a given posture: sitting, standing, bending

time_i = duration of a given posture

$f(\text{activity}_j)$ = Kcalories associated with given task activities. A task can be described in terms of one or more of the following standardized classes of motions (general body motions): (a) lifting, carrying, pulling, and pushing; (b) arm motion—light, heavy; and (c) hand motions.

time_j = duration of a given activity (motion)

The Jobs

Smelters produce aluminum using the Hall-Heroult process. In this process, a large steel box called a *pot* or *cell* is lined with carbon and insulated to reduce heat loss. The electric current enters through carbon anodes suspended from a bridge and passes through the cryolite bath (954-999°C) to steel bars embedded in the carbon lining (cathode). Aluminum production is a continuous process; the pot must be tended 24 hours a day to achieve an efficient production rate. Servicing each pot encompasses several tasks with physical demands ranging from light, to moderate to heavy, to extreme. The four major jobs considered by the model are described in the following paragraphs.

Crane Operation   The operator remains seated while operating an overhead crane. The operator's cab is high and close to the ceiling of the pot room. The stress from the heat rising off the pot (maintained at about 1000°C) can be overwhelming even if the operator is sitting down. In addition, the crane operator must be mentally alert in the course of moving anodes (carbon blocks) and tools to and from the pot. The jerky motions of the crane make it difficult to accurately and quickly place the material and/or equipment in the correct position. Therefore, under extreme heat stress, the job can be physically and mentally demanding.

Pot Tending and Monitoring   Pot monitoring is a moderately demanding job that requires the worker to continuously tend the pots producing aluminum. The pot tender must walk from pot to pot checking the temperature, height of the anodes, and material content in the bath, and sweeping up the *butts* (hard cryolite bath) knocked off the anodes being removed for recycling. Although this job is moderately demanding under normal conditions, there is the potential for physiological overloading in emergency situations such as that of a *burn-off* where the pot is in danger of a complete shutdown.

Tapping or Siphoning   The tapping workers are responsible for siphoning or draining the aluminum out of the pot. A crucible is placed next to the pot with its spout dipping into the molten cryolite bath. The crucible is moved from pot to pot by a crane operated from the floor by the tapper. When full, the crucible is transferred to the casting department. The crucible must be cleaned periodically as the cryolite bath builds up on its inner surface. The inner lining is scraped manually with a jackhammer. The tapper helper performs most of the manual work related to placement and cleaning of the crucible.

Carbon Setting   Carbon (anode) setting is the most difficult and demanding job in the pot-room. Most of these job tasks require the use of heavy vibrating tools. For example, the carbon blocks are attached to rods that are bolted to the bridge (the pot super structure). As the carbon burns off into the cryolite bath, the rod must be lowered to maintain constant power load on the pot. Each carbon burns at a different rate; therefore, workers must manually adjust the rods' relative positions, one at a time. This involves handling of heavy power tools while maintaining extreme and difficult postures. Above average arm and back strength capabilities are prerequisite for performing this particular task. In another anode setting task, workers break up the crust that develops on top of the molten bath using jackhammers. Workers must have great back strength to move and guide the tool. Most of the carbon setting tasks are performed in the presence of high thermal load.

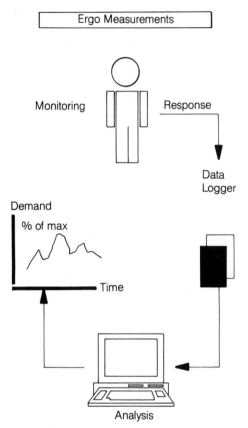

Fig. 25-1. Ergonomics data; collection and analysis.

Carbon setting includes several distinct and specific tasks: breaking crust (BC), setting anodes (SA), oreing up (OU), pulling arms (PA), getting up butts (GB), drilling butts (DB), stringing out anodes (SOA), and burn offs (BO).

Data

In order to define the model and later determine its accuracy and adequacy for supporting job redesign, a comprehensive database on the current jobs was established. This involved monitoring the physiological responses of several workers as they performed their respective jobs in the potroom. A total of 65 workers participated in some or all aspects of the data collection procedures.

The physiological demands of the potroom jobs were obtained by continuously monitoring the subjects' heart rates. Time studies were made of the same subjects throughout the performance of their respective jobs. The PC-based system shown in FIG. 25-1 monitored the subjects. Time studies were made both to document the length of the various tasks and to link work activities with the heart rates as recorded by the system. The association of tasks and their corresponding heart rates is a prerequisite for the determination of job demands. FIGURE 25-2 summarizes the overall heart rate profiles for

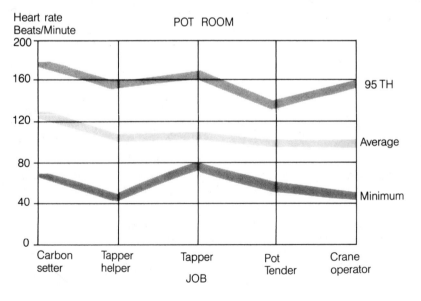

Fig. 25-2. Heart rate profiles for all jobs evaluated.

all the jobs evaluated. FIGURE 25-3 gives a summary of heart rates by each of the carbon setting tasks. The tasks tend to cluster into three groups based on their physiological demands, as shown in FIG. 25-4. Pulling arms, burn offs, getting up butts, setting carbon, oreing up, and drilling butts form the most demanding group with heart rates above 125 beats/min. Breaking crust and walking with tools

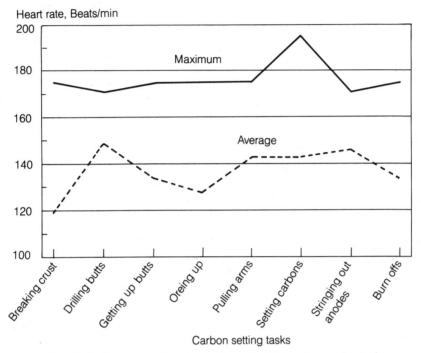

Fig. 25-3. Summary of heart rates by each of the carbon setting tasks.

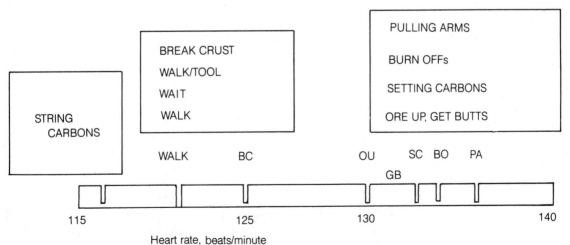

Fig. 25-4. Three task groups, based on physiological demands.

are in the second group with an average heart rate of 125. The least demanding set of carbon setting tasks include stringing out carbons.

For most workers, the general trend is for the average heart rate to rise and peak to a fairly consistent level throughout most of the shift. The minimum, however, steadily increases as work progresses through the shift. This indicates that the self-regulated work/rest schedule is ineffective at keeping maximum heart rates under control; the workers do not take enough rest to completely recover. Accordingly, they fail to avoid the cumulative effect of the physiological strain of their jobs.

In summary, the data indicate that the carbon setting job is significantly more taxing than all the other jobs in the potroom. The carbon setters spend a significant portion of their shift with a heart rate above 140 beats/min. This is well above the 110-120 values typically recommended for sustained work. The cumulative rise in heart rate over the shift, as exhibited by the rising minimum over time in FIG. 25-5, imposes a higher physiological strain on the carbon setters in contrast to all other potroom workers.

Model Prediction

The model was run to assess the current jobs, assuming an all male work force with an average weight of 205 pounds. The carbon setter and tapper helper tasks were modeled individually then

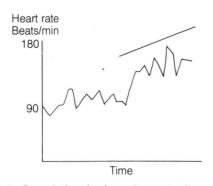

Fig. 25-5. Cumulative rise in carbon setter heart rate over the shift.

combined to produce an overall estimate of the demands for each of the two jobs. The tapper job as well as that of the crane operator and the pot tender were modeled to obtain only an overall demand level. These jobs involve fewer tasks and have much lower demand levels than carbon setting; therefore, a determination was made to model them in a more simplistic fashion. Finally, all potroom jobs were combined to determine an overall energy expenditure rate and corresponding heart rate for work involving any combination of the jobs included in the model. This final step allows for the restructuring of tasks within the model to determine the effect of job reorganization on the physiological demands.

For a number of tasks (breaking crust, setting anodes, oreing up, pulling arms, burn offs, and pot tending), there is a significant thermal load imposed on the workers by the heat generated in the smelting process. It was assumed that the heart rate increases in response to thermal stress by one beat per minute for every one degree Centigrade (C). This is applicable for temperature between 25 and 40 degrees C.

A comparison was made between the predicted and actual heart rates, shown in FIGS. 25-6 and 25-7. As is apparent from the data, in many cases, the predicted heart rate is within one beat per minute of the actual values measured in the potroom. In order to further test the validity of the model, a paired t-test was made to look for differences between the predicted and measured rates. The test ascertained that there is no difference.

A major contribution of the predictive model would be its ability to facilitate the reorganization of tasks within the potroom. Using the model, it has been shown that simply adding rest periods does not reduce job demands to an acceptable level. In order to create significant reductions in the physiological demands, the workers must alternate between difficult and less taxing jobs. We illustrated this by using the model to test 16 different scenarios of job restructuring. In most cases, we were able to bring the overall heart rate to an average of 110 beats/min. This was achieved through *job mixing*, a form of job rotation; two examples are given in TABLE 25-1.

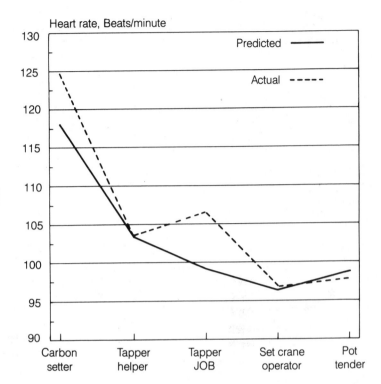

Fig. 25-6. Average actual vs. predicted heart rates for each job.

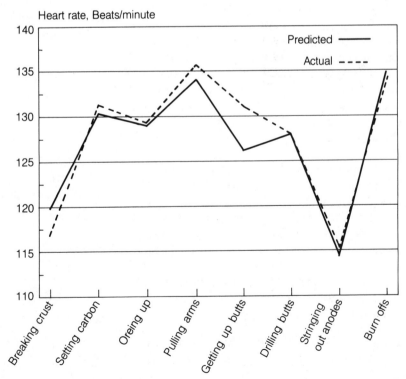

Fig. 25-7. Average actual vs. predicted heart rates for carbon setters.

SCENARIO # 1	Time (minutes)	Break (minutes)	% Rest	Heart rate (beats/min.)
Carbon setter	167	34	20	120
Tapper helper	124	24	20	105
Crane operator	70	14	20	96
Overall	361	72	20	108

SCENARIO # 2	Time (minutes)	Break (minutes)	% Rest	Heart rate (beats/min.)
Carbon setter	165	41	25	120
Tapper helper	122	22	20	101
Pot tender	80	16	20	98
Overall	367	82	22	107

Table 25-1. Job Restructuring to Control Worker Heart Rates

OPTIMUM JOB DESIGN

The job predictive model provides the means to assess the impact of imposed rest periods and/or task reorganization on physiological responses. Its greatest utility comes from determining the physiological impact of various job structuring scenarios. All the scenarios involve rotation of workers among a series of tasks that maximize the productive time while minimizing the physiological strain. However, each workable scenario is determined by trial and error. Therefore, a major weakness of the predictive model is its inability to produce an optimal job assignment for all workers in a shift. To overcome this limitation, optimization models offer an alternative.

Optimization modeling provides a consistent, logical, and efficient approach to restructuring the jobs in industry. To this end, linear programming is well suited for this purpose. As an illustration, we will reformulate the basic job predictive model to determine the optimum assignment of a number of workers to a set of potroom tasks consistent with physiological and production constraints. The basic structure of the linear programming (LP) model is as follows.

- *Objective*: Determine the time each worker spends on each task such that total energy expenditure (physiological strain) for the shift is minimized.
- *Constraints*:
  1. The average energy expenditure for each worker during the total task and break time must be less than 4 kcal per minute.
  2. Energy expenditure of each worker for the entire shift must fall in the range 2 to 6 kcal/min. A higher upper limit may be specified at will.
  3. The total energy expenditure of all the workers must be within 100 kcals of each other.
  4. A minimum level of production has to be met.
  5. Each worker is available for the full eight-hour shift. Work breaks are taken during that period.
  6. Each task has a minimum performance time during which it cannot be interrupted or divided.

Mathematically, the model is:

$$\text{MIN} \quad EER_{ij} \times JT_{ij} + BEER_{ij} \times RT_{ij}$$
$$\text{all } ij$$

Where:

EER: = task average energy expenditure rate
BEER: = rest average energy expenditure rate

JT: = work time for person i and task j
RT: = rest time for person i and task j
  i: = operator 1,2,...Ni
  j: = task 1,2,...Nj

Subject To

Energy Expenditure

$$\text{EER}ij \times (\text{JT}ij + \text{BEER}ij) \times \text{RT}ij \leq 4 \\ \times (\text{JT}ij + \text{RT}ij) \\ \text{for all } i,j \text{ with } \text{EER}ij \geq 4$$

$$2 \text{ kcal/min} \leq \frac{\sum_{i=1}^{N_j} (\text{JT}ij \times \text{EER}ij)}{\sum_{j=1}^{N_j}\text{JT}ij}$$

$$\leq 6 \text{ kcal/min} \quad \text{for each person } i$$

Balanced Workload

$$\sum_{j=1}^{N_j} \text{EER}1j \times \text{JT}1j - \text{EER}2j \times \text{JT}2j \leq 100 \text{ kcals}$$

for all possible pairs (1:2, 1:3, 1:4, etc.)

Total Standard Production

$$\sum_{i=1}^{N_i} \text{JT}ij = \text{P}j \quad \text{for all } js$$

where Pj: Production requirements for task j

Minimum Job Time

$$\sum_{j=1}^{N_j} \text{JT}ij + \text{RT}ij \geq 480 \text{ minutes} \quad \text{for all } is$$

Minimum Task Time

$\text{JT}ij \geq t$ minutes   for all i, j that are assigned. Minimum acceptable time per task is assumed to be t minutes.

Model Parameters

Production requirements and energy expenditure rates are needed to complete model formula-tion. These can be obtained as follows:

- Analyze each job and determine its basic motion elements and tasks
- Time study the elements to determine performance times
- Using the basic energy predictive model presented in the previous section, calculate the energy expenditure rate for each task. As a substitute for the model, the needed energy data can be obtained by direct measurement of representative samples of the jobs to be restructured. Again, standard ergonomic methods can be used for this purpose.

Using the available database (discussed above), the four potroom jobs (Carbon Setter, Crane Operator, Pot Tender, and Tapper) were regrouped into 17 specialized tasks plus rest periods. The energy predictive model was then used to obtain a basic energy rate (Kcal/min) for each of the tasks, as shown in TABLE 25-2. Here, the assumption is: any of the 17 tasks will be performed for at least one minute.

Applications

The utility of the above LP model will be demonstrated through structuring the potroom jobs for a crew of eight workers. Five possible job design scenarios will be examined. All the scenarios share the basic model. However, the constraints are modified to reflect specific job structure requirements or goals. The five scenarios and their specific additional constraints are discussed below.

Model 1: Traditional Approach with Modification The first model takes the traditional approach to job design one step further by ensuring a balance in energy expenditure. Each worker is assigned to the task that suits his or her particular skills. For example, the following initial task assignments could be made:

- Worker #1: break crust
- Worker #2: set anode
- Worker #3: tapping

Table 25-2. Energy Expenditure Rates (Kcal/min)

Task	Rate (Kcal/min)	Task	Rate (Kcal/min)
1. Breaking crust	3.77	10. Tapping	2.70
2. Setting carbon	4.70	11. Clean crucible	3.28
3. Oreing up	5.01	12. Head crucible	3.46
4. Pulling arm	5.09	13. Tighten bolts	3.84
5. Getting up butts	5.35	14. Shovel ore	4.54
6. Drilling butts	5.24	15. Tapper	2.67
7. String anodes	2.96	16. Crane operator	2.35
8. Burn offs	5.72	17. Pot tender	2.22
9. Reaming out siphon	6.59	REST BREAK	2.23

- Worker #4: clean crucible
- Worker #5: head up crucible
- Worker #6: pulling arms
- Worker #7: getting butts
- Worker #8: drilling butts

The remaining tasks are then assigned in accordance with the model production and physiological constraints. Therefore, this approach allows a worker to specialize in a skill and perform it with maximum efficiency. A summary of the tasks and time assigned to each worker is given in TABLE 25-3.

Model 2: Work Equally Shared The second model determines the optimal job mix for each worker on the basis that each person performs for an equal amount of time on each task.

$$JT1j = JT2j = JT3j = JT4j = JT5j = JT6j = JT7j$$
$$= JT8j \text{ for all tasks, } j = 1, .. 17$$

TABLE 25-4 gives the optimum assignment for the eight workers.

Model 3: Teamwork Teamwork is desired from both a physiological and psychological standpoint. A team acts as a support group that will ensure completion of the tasks and a safer work environment. The third scenario groups the workers into two teams of four persons each. Each team is responsible for the completion of servicing an equal number of pots. Within each team, pairs of workers equally share the tasks they are assigned to perform.

Team 1: $JT1j = JT2j$ Team 2: $JT5j = JT6j$
          $JT3j = JT4j$ $JT7j = JT8j$

for all the tasks, j, where Team 1 = Team 2

The optimum assignment is as shown in TABLE 25-5.

Model 4: Traditional/Teamwork Combination The fourth scenario is a combination of the traditional and teamwork approaches to job design. Pairs of individuals are responsible for the completion of one major task and its subtasks: carbon setting, tapper, tapper helper, crane operator, or pot tender. The model determines how much time each individual spends on each of the minor tasks such that the energy constraints are balanced. For example, the following may constitute the initial assignments:

Job	Worker Assigned
Carbon setting	#1 and/or #2
Tapper helper	#3 and/or #4
Tapper	#5 and/or #6
Crane operator	#7 and/or #8

The remaining job (Pot Tender) is arbitrarily assigned by the program to ensure an overall balance in the energy expenditure. A summary of the tasks and time assigned to each worker is presented in TABLE 25-6.

Model 5: Fitness Level Model (Marginal, Average, Superfit) The first four models assume an average energy expenditure rate for each of the workers, all of whom are considered to be of

Table 25-3. Optimal Task Assignment for Model 1: Traditional Approach (in minutes)

Worker	Task	1	2	3	4	5	6	7	8	9	10	11	12	13	14	15	16	17	Physical Work	Office Work	Total Shift
1	Task time Rest time	84 8														170			261 19	200	461 19
2	Task time Rest time		109 108					19 7		24 34									152 149	180	331 149
3	Task time Rest time			32 31					30 29		174			13				105	354 60	65	420 60
4	Task time Rest time											91				86		134	311 0	168	480 0
5	Task time Rest time												65				268		333 0	147	480 0
6	Task time Rest time				53 69													240	293 69	118	411 69
7	Task time Rest time					55 66										192			247 66	167	414 66
8	Task time Rest time						39 52								8 2		32	212	291 54	135	426 54
Total task time		84	109	32	53	55	39	19	30	31	174	91	65	13	8	480	480	480	2243	1180	3423

Table 25-4. Optimal Task Assignment for Model 2: Work Shared Equally (in minutes)

Worker		Task 1	2	3	4	5	6	7	8	9	10	11	12	13	14	15	16	17	Physical Work	Office Work	Total Shift
1	Task time	11	14	4	7	7	5		4	4	22	11	8			60	60	60	275	154	429
	Rest time	1	13	4	9	8	7		4	6									51		51
2	Task time	11	14	4	7	7	5	5	4	4	22	11	8			60	60	60	281	146	427
	Rest time	1	13	4	9	8	7	2	4	6									53		53
3	Task time	11	14	4	7	7	5		4	4	22	11	8	7		60	60	60	282	147	429
	Rest time	1	13	4	9	8	7		4	6									51		51
4	Task time	11	14	4	7	7	5	5	4	4	22	11	8			60	60	60	281	146	427
	Rest time	1	13	4	9	8	7	2	4	6									53		53
5	Task time	11	14	4	7	7	5		4	4	22	11	8		4	60	60	60	279	148	427
	Rest time	1	13	4	9	8	7		4	6					1				52		52
6	Task time	11	14	4	7	7	5	8	4	4	22	11	8	7		60	60	60	284	143	427
	Rest time	1	13	4	9	8	7	3	4	6									54		54
7	Task time	11	14	4	7	7	5		4	4	22	11	8			60	60	60	282	147	429
	Rest time	1	13	4	9	8	7		4	6									51		51
8	Task time	11	14	4	7	7	5		4	4	22	11	8		4	60	60	60	279	148	427
	Rest time	1	13	4	9	8	7		4	6					1				52		52
Total task time		84	109	32	53	55	39	19	30	31	174	91	65	13	8	480	480	480	2243	1179	3422

Table 25-5. Optimal Task Assignment for Model 3: Team Work (in minutes)

Worker	Task	1	2	3	4	5	6	7	8	9	10	11	12	13	14	15	16	17	Physical Work	Office Work	Total Shift
1	Task time		27	8	13				8				16			75		120	268	153	421
	Rest time		27	8	17				7										59		59
2	Task time		27	8	13				8				16			75		120	268	153	421
	Rest time		27	8	17				7										59		59
3	Task time	21				14	10	5		8	44	23		3	4	45	120		295	139	434
	Rest time	2				17	13	2		11					1				46		46
4	Task time	21				14	10	5		8	44	23		3		45	120		291	144	436
	Rest time	2				17	13	2		11									44		44
5	Task time		27	8		14	10	5	8	8	44		16				7	120	265	130	395
	Rest time		27	8		17	13	2	7	11							7		85		85
6	Task time		27	8		14	10	5	8	8	44		16				7	120	265	130	395
	Rest time		27	8		17	13	2	7	11							7		85		85
7	Task time	21			13							23		3	4	120	113		298	162	460
	Rest time	2			17										1				20		20
8	Task time	21			13							23		3		120	113		294	167	461
	Rest time	2			17														19		19
Total task time		84	109	32	53	55	39	19	30	31	174	91	65	13	8	480	480	480	2243	1180	3423

Table 25-6. Optimal Task Assignment for Model 4: Traditional Approach/Team Work Combination (in minutes)

Worker		Task	1	2	3	4	5	6	7	8	9	10	11	12	13	14	15	16	17	Physical Work	Office Work	Total Shift
1	Task time		84		32		55	33	19												223	101	324
	Rest time		8		31		66	44	7												156		156
2	Task time			109		53		6		30											198	69	267
	Rest time			108		69		8		29											213		213
3	Task time										5		91							317	413	60	473
	Rest time										7										7		7
4	Task time										26	174		65	13	8				153	439		439
	Rest time										39					2					41		41
5	Task time																	180			180	300	480
	Rest time																				0		0
6	Task time																	300			300	180	480
	Rest time																				0		0
7	Task time																		136		136	344	480
	Rest time																				0		0
8	Task time																		344	10	354	126	480
	Rest time																				0		0
Total task time			84	109	32	53	55	39	19	30	31	174	91	65	13	8	480	480	480	2243	1180	3423

equal fitness. Realistically, it would be more accurate to assume that a range of fitness will be exhibited on the job. The LP model can take this into account by preassigning each worker one of three fitness levels: marginal, average, and superfit. This determination can be based on a preemployment screening test.

The average worker would have an energy expenditure rate as determined for the first four models. The marginal worker is assumed to experience more strain while performing the same task. In other words, the task will be performed at a higher rate of energy expenditure. Similarly, the superfit worker will be expected to perform the task at a much lower energy rate than his average counterpart. The adjustment in the energy expenditure rate for each of the workers will be derived from the preemployment test results. As an example, the LP model can be formulated with the following fitness level assumptions:

- Worker #1: Average
- Worker #2: Superfit
- Worker #3: Superfit
- Worker #4: Average
- Worker #5: Marginal
- Worker #6: Average
- Worker #7: Marginal
- Worker #8: Average

The energy expenditure rates for all the tasks are adjusted by minus 20 percent, 0 percent, or plus 20 percent for each worker depending on the fitness level. The optimum job assignment in this case is as shown in TABLE 25-7.

MULTIPLE CRITERIA DECISION MODEL

In the previous section, four models emerged as feasible design alternatives to the current job structure. The models were evaluated on the basis of a sole criterion; minimization of energy expenditure while satisfying production requirements. However, there are other factors that should be taken into consideration prior to developing a practical and total solution. These include factors re-

lated to job satisfaction, communication, safety, efficient use of resources, and work simplification.

Thomas Saaty (1982) developed and documented the Analytic Hierarchy Process (AHP) as a means to structure a complex, multiperson, multiattribute, and multiperiod problem hierarchically. Pairwise comparisons of the alternatives and attributes with respect to each alternative are made using an established dominance scale. The scaling process is used to logically and systematically compare the alternatives so that an informed decision can be made (Canada and Sullivan 1989).

We will reexamine the potroom job restructuring problem previously presented through the use of the AHP process. In the formulation below, only four of the five optimum models will be considered.

Method

The AHP methodology includes the following three stages: (1) hierarchic structuring, (2) priority setting, and (3) consistency check.

Hierarchic Structuring At the first stage the problem is stated in three separate elements: focus, attributes, and alternatives.

- Focus: The objective is to determine the best overall job assignment approach
- Attributes: Energy expenditure, job satisfaction, training, safety, work/rest cycle, enforcement, and scheduling feasibility
- Alternatives: Four optimum models—traditional approach, work all tasks equally, teamwork, and traditional/teamwork combination

The *attributes* of the problem are defined as follows:

- Energy expenditure—the alternative that minimizes the total energy expenditure (Kcals) of all the workers is most desirable.
- Job satisfaction—the alternative that maximizes job satisfaction of each worker is preferred. Criteria positively related to worker satisfaction consist of: variety, social interaction, participa-

Table 25-7. Optimal Task Assignment for Model 5: Marginal, Average, and Superfit Fitness Levels (in minutes)

Worker		Task	1	2	3	4	5	6	7	8	9	10	11	12	13	14	15	16	17	Physical Work	Office Work	Total Shift
1	Task time													65				258		323	157	480
	Rest time																			0		0
2	Task time			11	16		55	39			31									152	262	414
	Rest time			3	4		22	19			18									66		66
3	Task time			98		53									13					164	265	429
	Rest time			26		25														51		51
4	Task time				16				19				91						149	275	182	457
	Rest time				16				7											23		23
5	Task time											174					175	55		404	76	480
	Rest time																			0		0
6	Task time		26																331	357	121	478
	Rest time		2																	2		2
7	Task time																305			305	175	480
	Rest time																			0		0
8	Task time		59							30						8		167		264	179	443
	Rest time		5							29						2				36		36
Total task time			85	109	32	53	55	39	19	30	31	174	91	65	13	8	480	480	480	2244	1417	3661

tion, recognition, communication, knowledge, skill, and responsibility.

- Training—the alternative that minimizes the training time and cost is favored. The less time and material needed for training the workers, the more desirable the job design approach.
- Safety—the alternative that minimizes accident potential by increasing the safety awareness of each worker is preferred.
- Enforcement—each potroom worker is required to alternate work and rest for the time (in minutes) determined by the job assignment model. The alternative that has a higher probability of enforcing the work/rest cycle is favored.
- Scheduling—the scheduling feasibility of the task assignment for each job design approach will vary. The alternative with the most efficient job flow process is preferred.

The *alternatives* for solving the problem are the four optimum job designs developed by the LP model. These designs constitute all the alternatives under consideration. A summary of the basis of each alternative is briefly restated below.

Model 1 (M1): Traditional Approach. Each worker is assigned to the task that suits his or her particular skills. The remaining tasks are assigned in accordance with the model constraints.

Model 2 (M2): Work Shared Equally. The second model determines the optimal job mix for each worker on the basis that equal amount of time is spent on each task. This assumes that each worker has been trained in all aspects of the job; therefore, there may be a higher initial implementation cost due to training. Furthermore, it may be difficult to develop a feasible and efficient job schedule. On the other hand, the added responsibility, increased social interaction, and broadened knowledge will increase job satisfaction. However, given the mixed and diverse nature of the jobs, the potential for stress and mental overload is high.

Model 3 (M3): Teamwork. Workers are divided into two teams of four persons each. Each team is responsible for the completion of all services for a predefined number of pots. This approach has the following advantages: (1) work/rest cycle is more

likely to be enforced since the pairs must alternate work, and (2) greater responsibility, growth in competence, and social interaction will increase job satisfaction. However, these potential benefits will be at a cost—strong need for employee selection and extensive training.

Model 4 (M4): Traditional plus Teamwork. The fourth alternative is a combination of the traditional and teamwork approaches. Pairs of individuals are responsible for the completion of one major task and its subtasks. The advantages include minimal training time, increased safety awareness, higher social interaction, and added responsibility.

The complete hierarchical representation of the job design problem is illustrated in FIG. 25-8.

Priority Setting Once the problem has been decomposed (attributes and alternatives have been clearly defined), the following procedure is used to determine the alternatives to be implemented (Canada and Sullivan 1989):

- Determine the relative importance of the attributes
- Determine the relative standing (weight) of each alternative with respect to each attribute
- Determine the overall priority weight (score) of each alternative

Therefore, the next stage involves a series of pairwise comparisons of all the elements. The degree of preference can be quantified on a scale of one to nine as shown in FIG. 25-9 and FIG. 25-10 (Saaty 1982). For a tie as in the case of equal importance, even numbers (2, 4, etc.) are used.

A questionnaire form of the type in FIGS. 25-9 and 25-10 is used for this purpose. In FIG. 25-9, the check marks represent the relative importance of each attribute with respect to the other attributes. For example, job satisfaction is ranked "very strongly more important or preferred" to training in relative importance (3 on Saaty's scale). In FIG. 25-10, the check marks illustrate the relative standing of each alternative (model) with respect to each attribute. For example, the teamwork model is ranked "strongly more important or preferred" to the teamwork/traditional combination design in reference to the job satisfaction criterion.

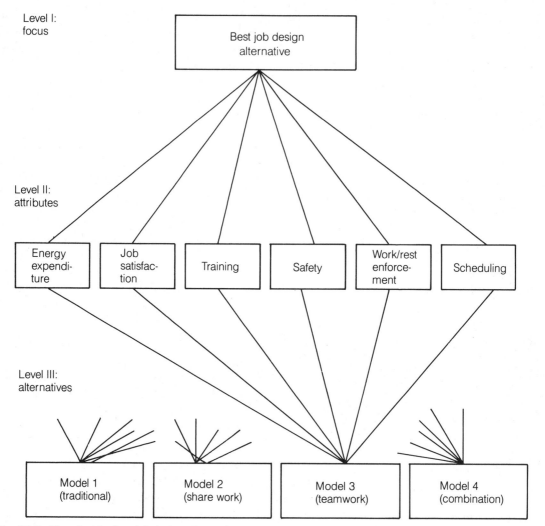

Level I:
focus

Level II:
attributes

Level III:
alternatives

Fig. 25-8. Choosing the best job design alternative.

The priority weights are calculated using matrix algebra as follows:

1. Reconstruct the pairwise comparisons from the questionnaire into matrix form.
2. Convert the matrix elements to the decimal equivalent and total each column.
3. Normalize each column by dividing the elements in each column by the sum of that column.
4. Calculate the priority weight for each attribute by averaging each row (sum of the row divided by the number of elements in the row).
5. Check the results by showing that the sum of the priority weights equals one.

TABLE 25-8 is the preference judgments priority weight computations for the six attributes.

The principal vector calculation resulted in priority weights for each attribute. The weights are listed in TABLE 25-10.

Consistency Check The consistency ratio

Attribute	9	8	7	6	5	4	3	2	1	2	3	4	5	6	7	8	9	Attribute	
Energy expenditure	A													✓					B	Job satisfaction
	A							✓											C	Training
	A							✓											D	Safety
	A							✓											E	Enforcement
	A												✓						F	Scheduling
Job satisfaction	B						✓												C	Training
	B							✓											D	Safety
	B								✓										E	Enforcement
	B								✓										F	Scheduling
Training	C					✓													D	Safety
	C						✓												E	Enforcement
	C											✓							F	Scheduling
Safety	D										✓								E	Enforcement
	D												✓						F	Scheduling
Enforcement	E										✓								F	Scheduling

KEY:

If x is . . . . than y	Then the preference number to assign is:
equally important/preferred	9
weakly more important/preferred	7
strongly more important/preferred	5
very strongly more important/preferred	3
absolutely more important/preferred	1

Fig. 25-9. Checklist for pairwise comparison of attributes.

Energy expenditure (A)	9	8	7	6	5	4	3	2	1	2	3	4	5	6	7	8	9	Energy expenditure (A)	
Model 1	M1								✓										M2	Model 2
Model 1	M1										✓								M3	Model 3
Model 1	M1					✓													M4	Model 4
Model 2	M2										✓								M3	Model 3
Model 2	M2				✓														M4	Model 4
Model 3	M3					✓													M4	Model 4

Job satisfaction (B)	9	8	7	6	5	4	3	2	1	2	3	4	5	6	7	8	9	Job satisfaction (B)	
Model 1	M1													✓					M2	Model 2
Model 1	M1														✓				M3	Model 3
Model 1	M1													✓					M4	Model 4
Model 2	M2									✓									M3	Model 3
Model 2	M2						✓												M4	Model 4

Fig. 25-10. Checklist for pairwise comparison of alternatives.

Attribute		9	8	7	6	5	4	3	2	1	2	3	4	5	6	7	8	9		Attribute
Model 3	M3				✓														M4	Model 4

Training (C)		9	8	7	6	5	4	3	2	1	2	3	4	5	6	7	8	9		Training (C)
Model 1	M1				✓														M2	Model 2
Model 1	M1					✓													M3	Model 3
Model 1	M1							✓											M4	Model 4
Model 2	M2										✓								M3	Model 3
Model 2	M2											✓							M4	Model 4
Model 3	M3												✓						M4	Model 4

Safety (D)		9	8	7	6	5	4	3	2	1	2	3	4	5	6	7	8	9		Safety (D)
Model 1	M1												✓						M2	Model 2
Model 1	M1											✓							M3	Model 3
Model 1	M1											✓							M4	Model 4
Model 2	M2						✓												M3	Model 3
Model 2	M2					✓													M4	Model 4
Model 3	M3					✓													M4	Model 4

Enforcement (E)		9	8	7	6	5	4	3	2	1	2	3	4	5	6	7	8	9		Enforcement (E)
Model 1	M1													✓					M2	Model 2
Model 1	M1												✓						M3	Model 3
Model 1	M1											✓							M4	Model 4
Model 2	M2								✓										M3	Model 3
Model 2	M2							✓											M4	Model 4
Model 3	M3					✓													M4	Model 4

Scheduling (F)		9	8	7	6	5	4	3	2	1	2	3	4	5	6	7	8	9		Scheduling (F)
Model 1	M1				✓														M2	Model 2
Model 1	M1					✓													M3	Model 3
Model 1	M1						✓												M4	Model 4
Model 2	M2											✓							M3	Model 3
Model 2	M2											✓							M4	Model 4
Model 3	M3					✓													M4	Model 4

Key:

If x is . . . . than y	Then the preference number to assign is:
equally important/preferred	9
weakly more important/preferred	7
strongly more important/preferred	5
very strongly more important/preferred	3
absolutely more important/preferred	1

Fig. 25-10. (continued)

Table 25-8. Matrix of Paired Comparisons for Attributes

| | SAATY's 1-9 Scale | | | | | | Decimal Equivalents | | | | | |
	A	B	C	D	E	F	A	B	C	D	E	F
A	1	1/5	1/4	1/4	1/4	1/5	1.00	0.20	0.25	0.25	0.25	0.20
B	5	1	3	2	1	1	5.00	1.00	3.00	2.00	1.00	1.00
C	4	1/3	1	3	2	1/3	4.00	0.33	1.00	3.00	2.00	0.33
D	4	1/2	1/3	1	1/3	1/4	4.00	0.50	0.33	1.00	0.33	0.25
E	4	1	1/2	3	1	1/3	4.00	1.00	0.50	3.00	1.00	0.33
F	5	1	3	4	3	1	5.00	1.00	3.00	4.00	3.00	1.00
						Totals	23.0	4.0	8.1	13.3	7.6	3.1

Normalized Matrix and Priority Weights

	A	B	C	D	E	F	"P" Vector	"C" Vector	Consistency	
A	0.04	0.05	0.03	0.02	0.03	0.06	0.04	0.25	MAX	= 6.475
									CI	= 0.095
B	0.22	0.25	0.37	0.15	0.13	0.32	0.24	1.58	RI	= 1.240
C	0.17	0.08	0.12	0.23	0.26	0.11	0.16	1.09	CR	= 0.077
D	0.17	0.12	0.04	0.09	0.04	0.08	0.09	0.55		
E	0.17	0.25	0.06	0.23	0.13	0.11	1.16	1.01		
F	0.22	0.25	0.37	0.30	0.40	0.32	0.31	2.07		
	1.00	1.00	1.00	1.00	1.00	1.00				

(CR) measures the consistency of the judgments made for each pairwise comparison. If the CR is less than .10, maximum acceptable limit, the priority weighting will be accepted (Saaty 1982). On the other hand, when the calculated CR is significantly greater than .10, the original priority weighting must be reassessed to reduce the number of intransitiveness in judgment as well as the consistency ratio.

Using the procedure detailed by Saaty (1982), the priority weights and consistency ratios are calculated for all the attributes (TABLE 25-9). In each case the consistency ratio is less than the .10 maximum acceptable limit recommended by Saaty

(1982); therefore, it can be concluded that the evaluation ratings for each alternative (model) with respect to each attribute are acceptable.

The weighted evaluation (WE) for each model is computed by multiplying the matrix of evaluation ratings for each alternative by the principal vector of attribute priority weights.

$$WE_k = \sum_{i=1}^{i} \text{Attribute Weight}_i \times \text{Evaluation Rating}_{ik}$$
for all i attributes and k alternatives

TABLE 25-10 shows the results of the calculations for the potroom job restructuring. The four

Table 25-9. Matrix of Paired Comparisons for Alternatives

A. Energy Expenditure

	SAATY's 1–9 Scale				Decimal Equivalents				Normalized Matrix				"P" Vector	"C" Vector	Consistency
	M1	M2	M3	M4	M1	M2	M3	M4	M1	M2	M3	M4			
M1	1	2	1	4	1.00	2.00	1.00	4.00	0.36	0.38	0.36	0.31	0.353	1.445	MAX = 4.061
M2	1/2	1	1/2	4	0.50	1.00	0.50	4.00	0.18	0.19	0.18	0.31	0.215	0.875	CI = 0.020
M3	1	2	1	4	1.00	2.00	1.00	4.00	0.36	0.38	0.36	0.31	0.353	1.445	RI = 0.900
M4	1/4	1/4	1/4	1	0.25	0.25	0.25	1.00	0.09	0.05	0.09	0.08	0.076	0.307	CR = 0.022
Totals					2.75	5.25	2.75	13.00	1.0	1.0	1.0	1.0	1.0		

B. Job Satisfaction

	SAATY's 1–9 Scale				Decimal Equivalents				Normalized Matrix				"P" Vector	"C" Vector	Consistency
	M1	M2	M3	M4	M1	M2	M3	M4	M1	M2	M3	M4			
M1	1	1/5	1/6	1/5	1.00	0.20	0.17	0.20	0.06	0.10	0.05	0.02	0.058	0.235	MAX = 4.262
M2	5	1	2	4	5.00	1.00	2.00	4.00	0.31	0.51	0.59	0.39	0.452	1.990	CI = 0.087
M3	6	1/2	1	5	6.00	0.50	1.00	5.00	0.38	0.26	0.30	0.49	0.354	1.601	RI = 0.900
M4	4	1/4	1/5	1	4.00	0.25	0.20	1.00	0.25	0.13	0.06	0.10	0.133	0.552	CR = 0.097
Totals					16.00	1.95	3.37	10.20	1.0	1.0	1.0	1.0	1.0		

C. Training

	SAATY's 1–9 Scale				Decimal Equivalents				Normalized Matrix				"P" Vector	"C" Vector	Consistency
	M1	M2	M3	M4	M1	M2	M3	M4	M1	M2	M3	M4			
M1	1	5	3	1/2	1.00	5.00	3.00	0.50	0.28	0.33	0.41	0.25	0.319	1.361	MAX = 4.160
M2	1/5	1	1/4	1/5	0.20	1.00	0.25	0.20	0.06	0.07	0.03	0.10	0.064	0.259	CI = 0.053
M3	1/3	4	1	1/3	0.33	4.00	1.00	0.33	0.09	0.27	0.14	0.16	0.165	0.678	RI = 0.900
M4	2	5	3	1	2.00	5.00	3.00	1.00	0.57	0.33	0.41	0.49	0.451	1.906	CR = 0.059
Totals					3.53	15.00	7.25	2.03	1.0	1.0	1.0	1.0	1.0		

	SAATY's 1–9 Scale				Decimal Equivalents				Normalized Matrix				"P" Vector	"C" Vector	Consistency
	M1	M2	M3	M4	M1	M2	M3	M4	M1	M2	M3	M4			
M1	1	1/5	1/4	1/4	1.00	0.20	0.25	0.25	0.07	0.10	0.07	0.03	0.068	0.277	MAX = 4.194
M2	5	1	2	4	5.00	1.00	2.00	4.00	0.36	0.51	0.56	0.48	0.478	2.041	CI = 0.064
M3	4	1/2	1	3	4.00	0.50	1.00	3.00	0.29	0.26	0.28	0.36	0.296	1.280	RI = 0.900
M4	4	1/4	1/3	1	4.00	0.25	0.33	1.00	0.29	0.13	0.09	0.12	0.157	0.649	CR = 0.071
Totals					14.00	1.95	3.58	8.25	1.0	1.0	1.0	1.0	1.0		

E. Work/Rest Cycle Enforcement

	SAATY's 1–9 Scale				Decimal Equivalents				Normalized Matrix				"P" Vector	"C" Vector	Consistency
	M1	M2	M3	M4	M1	M2	M3	M4	M1	M2	M3	M4			
M1	1	1/5	1/4	1/2	1.00	0.20	0.25	0.50	0.08	0.10	0.07	0.05	0.076	0.311	MAX = 4.136
M2	5	1	2	4	5.00	1.00	2.00	4.00	0.42	0.51	0.58	0.38	0.472	1.980	CI = 0.045
M3	4	1/2	1	5	4.00	0.50	1.00	5.00	0.33	0.26	0.29	0.48	0.338	1.441	RI = 0.900
M4	2	1/4	1/5	1	2.00	0.25	0.20	1.00	0.17	0.13	0.06	0.10	0.112	0.450	CR = 0.050
Totals					12.00	1.95	3.45	10.50	1.0	1.0	1.0	1.0	1.0		

F. Scheduling Feasibility

	SAATY's 1–9 Scale				Decimal Equivalents				Normalized Matrix				"P" Vector	"C" Vector	Consistency
	M1	M2	M3	M4	M1	M2	M3	M4	M1	M2	M3	M4			
M1	1	5	2	3	1.00	5.00	2.00	3.00	0.49	0.45	0.56	0.35	0.464	1.924	MAX = 4.127
M2	1/5	1	1/3	1/2	0.20	1.00	0.33	0.50	0.10	0.09	0.09	0.06	0.085	0.350	CI = 0.042
M3	1/2	3	1	4	0.50	3.00	1.00	4.00	0.25	0.27	0.28	0.47	0.317	1.338	RI = 0.900
M4	1/3	2	1/4	1	0.33	2.00	0.25	1.00	0.16	0.18	0.07	0.12	0.133	0.537	CR = 0.047
Totals					2.03	11.00	3.58	8.50	1.0	1.0	1.0	1.0	1.0		

Table 25-10. Weighted Evaluation of Alternatives.

	Attributes						Weighted Evaluation
	A	B	C	D	E	F	
Weight	0.04	0.24	0.16	0.09	0.16	0.31	
Alternatives:							
M1	0.354	0.059	0.319	0.069	0.076	0.464	0.2420
M2	0.215	0.453	0.064	0.478	0.473	0.085	0.2718
M3	0.354	0.355	0.166	0.296	0.339	0.317	0.3045
M4	0.077	0.134	0.451	0.157	0.112	0.133	0.1817

KEY:
A = Energy Expenditure   M1 = Traditional approach
B = Job satisfaction   M2 = Share work equally
C = Training   M3 = Teamwork
D = Safety   M4 = Traditional/teamwork combination
E = Work/rest enforcement
F = Scheduling

alternatives resulted in the following relative weights:

- Traditional approach (M1): 0.2420
- Work shared equally (M2): 0.2718
- Teamwork (M3: 0.3045
- Traditional/teamwork combination (M4): 0.1817

Therefore, since the teamwork approach has the highest relative weighting, it is the best job design for implementation.

SUMMARY

Considering the merit of all the job redesign alternatives examined above, it is obvious that the creation of a new team structure holds the most promise for improvement in the potroom. In concert with this conclusion, we encouraged management to consider a new concept for structuring the potroom teams. Specifically, we recommended the creation of a five person team (crew) for carbon setting tasks: four carbon setters and one crane operator. Having four persons setting carbon will force two consecutive rest breaks on each person; that is, while one person is working on the pot, the other three will be resting in the aisle. When it is

time to go back to the pot, the person who had two successive rest periods will be the next in line. This work/rest pattern will continue until the entire work assignment is carried out.

The team concept as a design for potroom jobs is not new. As the potroom technology has progressed toward full automation, the concept of having job teams and workers handling multiple tasks has become a matter of necessity. Rasmussen and Levin (1984) summarize the findings of a study to assess the impact of changes in job assignments in a Norwegian aluminum smelter over a period of 30 years. Positive as well as negative influences on the quality of working life have been noted. However, in general, the concept of having job teams handling multiple tasks seems to have a positive effect on workers and productivity.

Although implementing any changes (new crew structure or new job/task mix) will increase the time each carbon setter spends in the potroom, the resulting jobs will increase the efficiency and productivity in the potroom, will lower the physiological demands imposed on the work force to acceptable levels, and will enhance the overall safety performance on and off the pot.

A predictive model that categorizes the demands associated with the potroom jobs was developed and validated. This basic model was then used to develop a series of optimal designs (restructure) for the existing jobs. Each of these designs satisfied specific production requirements consistent with established norms for human work capacity. To select from among competing optimum designs, an approach (AHP) that evaluates the impact of various criteria was used. This last analysis selected the optimum model that is likely to come close to satisfying all the requirements for the potroom jobs. The use of this modeling approach to job design yields a *laboratory-on-paper* that can be utilized to evaluate new or emerging requirements or restrictions in the workplace. These evaluations come about without having to actually conduct plant-wide testing or appraisal of any redesign changes or modifications.

REFERENCES

Aberg, U., K. Elgstrand, P. Magnus, and A. Lindholm. "Analysis of Components and Prediction of Energy Expenditure in Manual Tasks." *The International Journal of Production Research* 6:3 (1968): 189-196.

Canada, J. and W. Sullivan. *Economic and Multiattribute Evaluation of Advanced Manufacturing Systems*. Englewood Cliffs, New Jersey: Prentice-Hall, 1989.

Garg, A. "Metabolic Rate Prediction Model for Manual Materials Handling Jobs." Ph.D. diss., The University of Michigan, 1976.

Rasmussen, B. and M. Levin. "Case Study 3 - Technological and Work Design Change Over 26 Years in an Aluminum Plant." In *Automation and Work Design*, edited by F. Butera and J. Thurman, 477. Amsterdam: North Holland, 1984.

Saaty, T. *Decision Making for Leaders: The Analytic Hierarchy Process for Decisions in a Complex World*. Belmont, California: Lifetime Learning Publications, 1982.

26

Artificial Intelligence Applications in Manufacturing

Adedeji B. Badiru[*]

ARTIFICIAL INTELLIGENCE (AI) HAS BEEN CHARAC-
terized by divergent controversial opinions since it
came out of research laboratories several years
ago. Despite the gains that have been achieved by
the technology, many people still argue that AI is
only "hype." The arguments have ranged from the
basic definition of what constitutes intelligence to
questions about the moral, ethical, and economic
aspects of pursuing AI.

DEFINITION AND DEVELOPMENT
OF ARTIFICIAL INTELLIGENCE

While time and advances in research have
answered many of the arguments about AI, others
are yet to be resolved. One of the more intriguing
disagreements in the field of AI is the term *artificial
intelligence* itself. For centuries scholars have
expended much effort trying to determine exactly
what constitutes intelligence and what doesn't. The
debate is still going on. So, if it is not clear what
intelligence is, it becomes even more difficult to
decide what *artificial* intelligence is. Even if these
hurdles are overcome, the burden still exists on
determining a test to check if something is truly

artificial intelligence and not just fancy programming. A definition of natural intelligence might be
"the capability to acquire and use knowledge, to
reason with it, and to solve problems effectively
with it." A formal definition of artificial intelligence
may be stated as follows: artificial intelligence is the
ability of a computer or a computer-based machine
to function autonomously to solve problems that it
is not explicitly programmed to solve.

Artificial intelligence is a strange term for a
technology that promises much potential for
improving human productivity. The phrase seems
to challenge human pride in being the sole creation
capable of possessing real intelligence. All kinds of
anecdotal jokes have been presented at conference
speeches on AI. One conference speaker once
recounted his wife's response when he told her that
he was venturing into the new technology of artificial intelligence. "Thank God, you are finally realizing how dumb I have been saying you were all these
years," was alleged to have been the wife's words
of encouragement to the enterprising husband. One
of my industry associates once remarked that AI
could be better represented by a less unsettling

*Dr. Badiru is an assistant professor of Industrial Engineering at the University of Oklahoma. He has published numerous papers on
project management, expert systems, and microcomputer applications. He is the author of *Project Management in Manufacturing
and High Technology Operations*, John Wiley & Sons, 1988. He is a co-author of *Computer Tools, Models, and Techniques for Project
Management*, TAB BOOKS, 1990. He is the Director of the Expert Systems Laboratory in the School of Industrial Engineering at
the University of Oklahoma. He received his BS degree in Industrial Engineering, MS in Mathematics, and MS in Industrial Engineering from Tennessee Technological University. He received his Ph.D. degree in Industrial Engineering from the University of
Central Florida. He is a member of IIE, SME, ORSA, TIMS, PMI, and AAAI.

by a less unsettling definition such as: "AI is the artificial insemination of knowledge into a machine."

The First AI Conference

The summer of 1956 saw the first attempt to establish artificial intelligence as an organized discipline. The Dartmouth Summer Conference, organized by John McCarthy, Marvin Minsky, Nathaniel Rochester, and Claude Shannon, brought together people whose work and interest founded the field of AI. The conference, held at Dartmouth College in New Hampshire, was funded by a grant from the Rockefeller foundation. It was at that conference that John McCarthy coined the term *artificial intelligence*. In attendance at the meeting, in addition to the organizers, were Herbert Simon, Allen Newell, Arthur Samuel, Trenchard More, Oliver Selfridge, and Ray Solomonoff.

Evolution of Smart Programs

In 1959, a major step in AI software came from Newell and Simon (1961). The product of the joint effort was called General Problem Solver (GPS). GPS was intended to be a program that could solve many types of problems. It was capable of solving theorems, playing chess, and doing various complex puzzles. GPS was a significant step forward in AI and managed to take this step by incorporating several new ideas to facilitate problem solving. The real heart of the system was the use of means-end analysis. Means-end involves comparing a present state with a goal state. This is similar to taking an item from the raw material state to the finished product state in manufacturing. The difference between the two states is determined and then a search is done to find a method to reduce this difference. For example, in manufacturing, this could be a search for the appropriate machining process to achieve a desired product attribute. The means-end process continues until there is no difference between the present state and the desired goal state.

To improve the search procedure, GPS has two important features. The first is that if while trying to reduce the difference using an operator, GPS finds that it has actually complicated the search, it is capable of backtracking to an earlier state and looking for an alternate path or process that could improve on the difference. The second is that sometimes GPS will find an operator that could be used to reduce the difference between the present and goal state if it only had certain conditions satisfied. GPS can then set up a sub-goal state that can ignore these conditions and then continue. In a manufacturing context, the subgoal orientation may relate to the process of substituting one machining process for another based on the current capabilities of the production system.

In 1959, John McCarthy came out with a tool that was to greatly improve the ability of researchers to develop AI programs. He developed a new language called LISP for list processing. It was to become one of the most widely used languages in the field. Of all the major formal programming languages, FORTRAN is said to be the only one older than LISP. This is a fact that seems to surprise many people in view of the relatively recent exposure of LISP.

LISP is distinctive in two areas: memory organization and control structure. The memory organization is done in a tree fashion with interconnections between memory groups. Thus, it enables a programmer to keep track of complex structural relationships. The other distinction is the way the control of the program is done. Instead of working from the prerequisites to a goal, it starts with the goal and works backward to determine what prerequisites there are. This enables a program to be flexible in what prerequisites to satisfy, depending on the goal.

Along a slightly different path of artificial intelligence, there was some work done in 1960 by Frank Rosenblatt in the area of pattern recognition. He devised a mechanism called PERCEPTRON that was supposed to be capable of recognizing letters and other patterns. It consisted of a grid of four hundred photo cells connected with wires to a response unit that would produce a signal only if the light coming off the subject to be recognized crossed a certain threshold.

Unfortunately, Marvin Minsky and Seymour Papert at MIT believed that the concepts of the PERCEPTRON were not sound and published a book in 1968 that demonstrated its limits (Minsky 1968). Their book managed to put a damper on any work in this field for several years. Later it was found that the concepts of PERCEPTRON were not as outrageous as earlier believed. The ability of machines to utilize a method of input similar to the PERCEPTRON is a key element if the machines are to truly imitate humans. In fact, the concept used by PERCEPTRON is similar to the basic approach used in most present generation pattern recognition systems particularly in manufacturing process control.

During the late 1960s, Marvin Minsky and his students at MIT made other significant contributions toward the progress of AI. One student, T.G. Evans, wrote a program that would perform visual analogies. The program was shown two figures that had some relationship to each other and was then asked to find another set of figures from a set that matched the same relationship. The input to the computer was not done by a visual sensor (like the one worked on by Rosenblatt), but instead the figures were described to the system. When completed, the program was said to be capable of performing the task at the level of a high school sophomore. Such process description concept could find application in manufacturing where a *smart machine* could be verbally trained to replicate the steps in a production process.

In an attempt to answer the criticisms about *understanding*, a student at MIT, Terry Winograd, wrote a program named SHRDLU. In setting up his program, he utilized natural language and what is referred to as a micro-world or blocks-world. This limited the scope of the world that the program had to deal with, but the program was set up to actually understand this limited world.

The world of SHRDLU consisted of a set of blocks of varying shapes (cubes, pyramids), sizes, and colors. These blocks were all set on an imaginary table. Upon request, SHRDLU would rearrange the blocks to any requested configuration.

SHRDLU also had the ability to know when a request was unclear or impossible. For instance, if it was requested to ''put the block on top of the pyramid'' it would request from the user to specify more clearly what block and what pyramid. It would also know that the block would not sit on top of the pyramid (a piece of valuable information for design engineers).

Two other things that the program did that were new to programs were the ability to make assumptions and the ability to learn. If asked to pick up a larger block it would assume that you meant a larger block than the one it was currently working on. If you asked it to build a figure that it did not know, it would ask you to explain what it was and, thereafter, it would recognize the object. One major sophistication that SHRDLU added to the science of AI programming was its use of a series of expert modules or specialists. There was one segment of the program that specialized in segmenting sentences into meaningful word groups, a sentence specialist to determine the relationship between nouns and verbs, and a scenario specialist that understood how individual scenes related to one another.

EMERGENCE OF EXPERT SYSTEMS

Beginning in the late 1960s, but really taking shape in the early 1970s, was a special branch of AI that is still growing today: expert systems. Expert systems are the first truly commercial application of work done in the AI field and as such have received considerable publicity. Due to the potential financial rewards, there is currently a heavy concentration in the research and development of expert systems compared to other efforts in AI.

Unlike the attempts to develop general problem solving techniques that had characterized AI before, expert systems seek to solve specific problems. When Edward Feigenbaum undertook setting up the first successful expert system, DENDRAL, he had a specific type of problem that he wanted to be able to solve. In this case it was to figure out which organic compound was being analyzed in a mass spectrograph; it was to simulate the work that an expert chemist would do in analyzing the data, and thus the term *expert system*. The period of time from 1970 to 1980 saw the introduction of numerous expert systems to do everything from diagnosing diseases to analyzing geological exploration information.

Expert Systems Characteristics

By definition, an expert system is a software package designed to mimic the thought process of an expert to solve complex problems in a specific domain. I will now address some of the characteristics of an expert system that make it different from conventional programming of such decision support software packages as Lotus and VisiCalc. These differences are what make an expert system so valuable as a problem solving tool. The general growth of expert systems will significantly increase over the next several years. With this growth of expert systems, many new and exciting characteristics will emerge making the expert system concept even more valuable than conventional programming to solve complex problems. One version of the various definitions of an expert system is presented below:

> An *expert system* is a computerized consultant that uses both facts and heuristics to solve difficult decision problems that are beyond the capability of a nonexpert human. It is akin to a consultant resident in computer memory.

Expert systems are an emerging technology with many possible applications. Past applications range from the expert system MYCIN in the medical field to detect infectious blood diseases, to XCON that is used to configure large computer systems. These expert systems have proven to be quite successful. Other suitable applications for expert systems fall into one of the following categories:

- Interpreting and identifying
- Predicting

- Diagnosing
- Designing
- Planning
- Monitoring
- Debugging and testing
- Instructing and training
- Controlling

Applications that are calculative or deterministic in nature are not good candidates for expert systems. One question that many early critics of expert systems would ask is, "Isn't an expert system a beefed up decision support system?" In fact, decision support systems are much more mechanistic in the manner in which they arrive at a solution. That is, they operate under mathematical and Boolean operators in their execution and arrive at only one static solution. A good example of a decision support system is found in the spreadsheet packages used by businesses everyday. Spreadsheets are used to calculate such things as investment scenarios, capitalization alternatives, and financial budgeting. All of these applications are calculation intensive with very exacting requirements.

Domain Specificity

Expert systems are usually very domain specific. They most likely will cover a specific area of expertise: for example, a diagnostic expert system for troubleshooting computers. The expert system must actually perform all the necessary data manipulation as a human expert would. The knowledge engineer must limit his or her scope of the expert system to just what is needed to solve the target problems.

Special Programming Languages

Expert systems are usually written in a special programming language. The use of languages like LISP, PROLOG, and OPS5 in the development of an expert system simplifies the coding process. The major advantage of these languages, as compared to conventional programming languages, is the simplicity of the addition, elimination, or substitution of new rules. The following is a list of some other advantages of special programming languages for expert systems:

- Mix of integer and real variables
- Extensive virtual memory
- Extensive garbage collection
- Incremental compilation
- Tagged memory architecture
- Optimization of run environment
- Efficient search procedures

Expert Systems Structure

Expert systems are organized in three distinct levels:

- *Knowledge base*—problem solving rules, procedures, and data relevant to the problem domain
- *Working memory*—task specific data for the problem under consideration
- *Inference engine*—generic control mechanism that applies the axiomatic knowledge in the knowledge base to the task-specific data to arrive at some solution or conclusion

These three distinct levels are unique in that the three pieces may very well come from different sources. The inference engine, like EXSYS or VP-Expert, may come from a vendor. The knowledge base may be a specific knowledge base on diagnosing heart problems that comes from a medical consulting firm, and finally, the session data may be supplied by the end user.

The dynamism of the application environment for expert systems is based on the individual dynamism of the components. This can be classified as follows: *most dynamic*, working memory; *moderately dynamic*, knowledge base; and *least dynamic*, inference engine. The most dynamic component, working memory, changes with each problem situation. Consequently, it is the most volatile component of an expert system, assuming, of course, that it is utilized and updated as intended.

The knowledge base, a moderately dynamic component, need not change unless there is a new

piece of information that indicates a change in the problem solution procedure. Changes in the knowledge base should be carefully evaluated before being implemented. In effect, changes should not be based on just one consultation experience. For example, a rule that is found to be irrelevant under one problem situation may turn out to be indispensable in other problem scenarios.

Because of the strict control and coding structure of an inference engine, changes are made only if absolutely necessary to correct a bug or to enhance the inferential process. This is, therefore, the least dynamic component. Commercial inference engines, in particular, change only at the discretion of the developer. Since frequent updates can be disrupting and costly to clients, most commercial software developers try to minimize the frequency of update.

The modularity of an expert system is what distinguishes it from a conventional computer program. Modularity is effected in an expert system by organizing it in three distinct components of knowledge base, working memory, and inference engine as shown in FIG. 26-1.

The knowledge base constitutes the problem-solving rules, facts, or intuition that a human expert might use in solving problems in a given problem domain. The knowledge base is usually stored in terms of *If-Then* rules. The working memory represents relevant data for the current problem being solved. The inference engine is the control mechanism that organizes the problem data and searches through the knowledge base for applicable rules. With the increasing popularity of expert systems, many commercial inference engines are coming into the market. Thus, the development of a functional expert system usually centers around the compilation of the knowledge base. A functional integration of expert systems components in a manufacturing environment is shown in FIG. 26-2.

Benefits of Expert Systems

Following are some of the benefits that are typically associated with expert systems in a manufac-

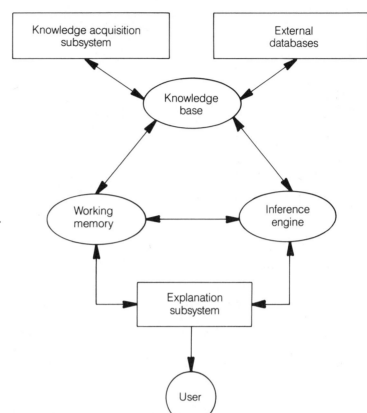

Fig. 26-1. Expert system organization.

turing context:

- Expert systems increase the probability, frequency, and consistency of making good manufacturing process decisions.
- Expert systems help distribute manufacturing expertise.
- Expert systems facilitate real-time, low-cost, expert-level decisions by nonexpert manufacturing personnel.
- Expert systems enhance the utilization of available manufacturing data.
- Expert systems permit manufacturing process objectivity by weighing evidence without bias and without regard for the user's personal and emotional feelings.
- Expert systems permit dynamism in the production system through modularity of structure.

- Expert systems free up the mind and time of the manufacturing expert to enable him or her to concentrate on more creative manufacturing process design activities.

HEURISTIC REASONING

Human experts use a type of problem-solving technique called heuristic reasoning. This reasoning type, commonly called *rules of thumb*, allows the expert to quickly and efficiently arrive at a good solution. Expert systems base their reasoning process on symbolic manipulation and heuristic inference procedures that closely match this human-like thinking process. Conventional programs can only recognize numeric or alphabetic strings and manipulate them only in a programmed predefined manner.

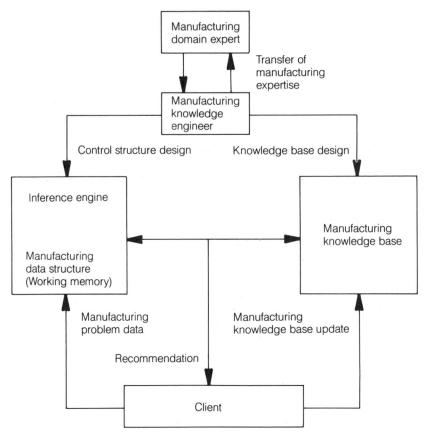

Fig. 26-2. Operational components of an expert system in a manufacturing environment.

Search Control Methods

All expert systems are search intensive. Many techniques have been employed to try to make these intensive searches more efficient. Branch and bound, pruning, depth first search, and breadth first search are just some of the search techniques used to try to efficiently search a knowledge base. Because of the intensity of the search process, it is important that search control strategies be used to handle the accounting aspects of a good search.

Forward Chaining

This method involves the checking of a rule's premise for truth and taking action on the rule's conclusion if the premise proves to be true. This procedure will continue until a solution is found or a dead end is reached. Forward chaining is commonly referred to as data-driven reasoning. An example of data-driven reasoning for manufacturing is a situation where we are given a fixed set of capabilities of a process and we want to determine what kind of products can be generated by the process.

Backward Chaining

Backward chaining is used to backtrack from a goal to the paths that lead to the goal. It is the reverse of forward-chaining. Backward chaining is very good when all outcomes are known and the number of possible outcomes are not large. Backward chaining is also referred to as goal-driven. An example of goal-driven reasoning in manufacturing is a situation where we are given the desired characteristics of a product and we want to determine what kind of process capabilities are needed to achieve the specified characteristics.

USER INTERFACE

The initial development of an expert system is performed by the expert and the knowledge engineer. Unlike most conventional programs in which only programmers can make changes, expert systems changes are discussed and implemented by a group of people. These changes usually are time consuming and costly. Even with the easily changed expert system, strict rules and guidelines need to be established to authorize new or modified rules. A careless user may accidentally introduce some unacceptable rules. Any changes to an expert system should carefully be monitored. Individuals who are fully familiar with the expert system should evaluate and authorize permanent or temporary changes in the system.

Natural Language

The programming languages used for expert systems operate more like how we would talk and answer questions than a cryptic language. We usually state the premise in the form of a question, with actions being stated much like we would verbally answer the question. In the future, some expert systems may even be capable of modifying themselves. If during or after a program run, the expert system determines that a piece of its data or knowledge base is incorrect, or is no longer applicable because the environment has changed, it should be able to update its information accordingly.

Summaries and Explanations

One of the key characteristics of an expert system is that it can explain how it arrived at its recommendation. The expert system is not specifically programmed to do this like a conventional program would have to be, but due to its inherent structure, it can perform the explanation function.

Quantitative and Qualitative Factors

Expert systems not only arrive at solutions or recommendations, but can give the user the level of confidence about the solution. In this manner, the expert system can handle both quantitative and qualitative factors when analyzing problems. This aspect is very important when we consider how inexact most input data is for day to day decision making.

Dynamic Decisions

The problems addressed by expert systems can have more than one solution path or, in some cases, no solution path. This characteristic is quite different from the conventional programs which follow a rigid program path and always arrive at one solution. Expert systems can be designed to solve one or more problems within a given problem domain simultaneously while considering all of the information available in the knowledge base. Sometimes, an expert system is required to solve other problems, possibly not directly related to the specific problem at hand, but whose solution will have an impact on the total problem-solving process.

Multiple Solutions

Because of the dynamic decision process that an expert system is capable of, multiple solutions may be recommended by the system. In other words, the system could be intelligent enough to realize that there may not be one over-all best solution. By recommending more than one solution, the system attempts to mimic the human expert as he would have offered advice about a problem.

Data Characteristics

One of the most unique characteristics of expert systems is that they are capable of working with inexact data. The expert system allows the user to assign probabilities, certainty factors, or confidence levels to any or all input data. This feature more closely represents how most questions are handled in the real world. The computer can take into account all of these factors and make a recommendation based on the best possible solution rather than the only solution. Expert systems available today for handling expert domain problems have been found to be quite superior to conventional programming. The future holds many new characteristics that will even further advance the benefits of expert systems. What information has been to the previous generations of computing, knowledge is to the present generation of computing. Conventional data can now be manipulated to form durable knowledge, which can be processed to generate timely information, which is then used to enhance human decisions. The symbolic processing capabilities of AI technology lead to many potential applications in the manufacturing area.

EXAMPLES IN MANUFACTURING

Expert systems have been developed for solving problems of varying complexities in several problem areas in industry. The potential applications of expert systems to real problems are limited only by the imagination of users. As manufacturers turn more and more to automation to reduce cost and improve productivity, we should begin to witness more aggressive implementation of artificial intelligence capabilities.

Many major applications of expert systems can be found in the manufacturing area. There are current and potential applications of artificial intelligence and expert systems at every stage of the manufacturing process. Expert systems can be utilized in deciding the feasibility of a particular production process given the available resources. It can then be used for assigning resources to specific tasks in the process. The design performance of expert systems in industry has been compared with that obtained from human experts. It has been found that expert system performance was near optimal as far as comparative human performance is concerned. The use of expert systems in manufacturing can be improved considerably with the cooperation from manufacturing experts. Job shops are the most common areas for expert system utilization, probably because of the difficulty involved in

scheduling jobs (Schaffer 1986). I survey several areas of manufacturing below. The survey shows a wide interest in and the potential usefulness of expert systems in the manufacturing environment.

Expert Systems as Industrial Consultants

The primary objective of most expert systems is consultation. An industrial user, who is not an expert, can consult the computer instead of referring to a human expert. Two scenarios can be visualized: consultation to advise a manager in industry and consultation to advise an engineer in industry.

Consultant to the Industrial Manager In this scenario the computer replaces an industrial engineer acting as a consultant to a manager. Consultation involves problem solving in several areas like inventory management, capacity planning, and production scheduling. A typical consultation may involve the following process:

- Discuss with the manager the nature of a problem
- Identify and classify the problem
- Construct a model of the problem
- Solve the model
- Conduct a sensitivity analysis with the model
- Recommend a solution
- Implement the solution

An analyst can develop an expert system that operates as follows. The computer attempts to diagnose the manager's problem by determining the general nature of the problem (e.g., resource allocation, inventory). Once the general nature of the problem has been determined, the characteristics of the situation are analyzed and a model is jointly constructed by the manager and the computer.

For example, if a resource allocation problem is identified, an attempt is made to construct the objective function and the constraints. A quantitative tool such as linear programming, a decision model, or dynamic programming may be suggested and evaluated for suitability. The computer then uses the chosen tool to solve the problem. Finally, a "what-if" analysis may be conducted. The expert system may also act as a nonhuman tutor with the ability to explain terminology, concepts, and computational procedures. In addition, the computer can provide supporting reference materials, examples of typical applications, or any other information as requested by the manager, or explain why a certain model was used and discuss the underlying assumptions.

During consultation, the user may disagree with the logic of why a certain action was undertaken. In such a case the user can change the decision rule(s) that generated the specific action. This type of consultation will probably be limited to simple problems. For more complex problems, a combination of a manager, industrial engineer, and a computer will be required. The availability of such expert systems could relieve the engineer from routine activities, freeing him to deal with complex problems and developmental activities.

Consultant to the Industrial Engineer
An expert system can serve as a consultant and an assistant to the engineer in industry. The engineer can use the computer as a source of information. Also, he or she can use the expert system as a teaching aid to learn the expertise of specialists in certain industrial problem areas where unique expertise is needed. This implies that an engineer, in addition to (or instead of) referring to a printed manual or a book, or a human expert, can consult the expert system. Finally, expert systems can be used as a personal assistant for providing answers to routine questions asked by the engineer.

Moralee (1986) discusses the usefulness of expert system techniques in industrial research. The technology was implemented at the Unilever Research Laboratory in England. The greatest potential for applying expert systems in the laboratory is in the simulation of manufacturing processes. The Unilever expert system research efforts were successfully implemented in the areas of:

- Thin layer chromatograph (analytical chemistry)
- Fault diagnosis on industrial plant
- Identification of components of infrared spectra
- Simulation of manufacturing process

Job Shop Scheduling

Expert systems can be of great help in the domain of scheduling activities in a job shop. The essence of the job shop scheduling problem is the computational effort associated with problems of sufficient size to be useful in the real world (Tou 1987). For example, in the case of five jobs and seven machines, there are $(5!)^7$ or approximately 3.5831×10^{14} sequences; these would require more than eleven years of computer time at the processing rate of a microsecond each. The purpose of using expert systems is to provide a computerized scheduler that has the same knowledge and understanding of qualitative measures as the human scheduler possesses (Kumara, et al. 1986). Fox and Smith (1984) described an Intelligent Scheduling and Information System (ISIS) developed at Carnegie-Mellon University for job shop scheduling. This system contains all the knowledge necessary to plan and schedule production in a job shop environment. It takes into consideration all relevant constraints in the construction of job schedules.

The system selects a sequence of operations needed to complete an order, determines start and end times, and assigns resources to each operation. It can also act as an intelligent assistant, using its expertise to help schedulers maintain schedule consistency and identify decisions that result in unsatisfied constraints. Knowledge in the system includes organizational goals, such as due dates and costs; physical constraints, such as limitations of particular machines; and casual constraints, such as the order in which operations must be performed. ISIS uses a frame-based knowledge representation scheme together with rules for resolving conflicting constraints.

ISIS has additional capabilities of model perusal, reactive plan monitoring, process planning, and resource planning (Bourne and Fox 1984). Townsend (1983) says that ISIS is potentially very useful in the repair shop environment. It can also be used successfully for inventory planning, management control, production scheduling, flexible scheduling, and inventory operations (Smith, et al. 1986).

Engineers at GTE have developed an expert system for thread scheduling. In an environment running over 100 VAX computers, the expert system identifies errors in thread scheduling by interfacing with thousands of lines of ADA code. It determines if an error is caused by software, hardware, or humans.

In addition to scheduling operations on machines, a manager must also schedule personnel. Using an expert system in its tooling division, McDonnell Douglas is developing a scheduling system to monitor current and future work loads. The system will keep track of personnel and job completion dates and give an estimation of future overtime needs. It will also match personnel preferences for overtime work slots and produce a feasible schedule. The system is expected to be capable of handling a work force of up to 150 people.

At Texas Instruments' automated manufacturing center, expert systems have facilitated the required interfaces among robots, vision systems, machine tools, sensors, computer systems, and humans (Herrod 1988). This has resulted in increased flexibility and efficiency of discrete manufacturing. The automated manufacturing center produces high-precision machined metal parts. The center automatically machines, deburrs, washes, and inspects more than 30 different parts. In order to achieve full flexibility, the system must track and synchronize 39 pallets and 250 tools while managing resources for eight machines and an automated guided vehicle.

The expert system that was developed to manage the center includes a planner, a scheduler, and a dispatcher. The planner interacts with the production control staff members who enter monthly part needs. It formulates the monthly part needs into a daily pallet-release plan. This plan is then passed on to the scheduler, which provides the production control staff with the material requirements for the day and a list of tools needed. The scheduler also establishes the sequence in which the jobs should be completed that day. The job sequence is then sent to the dispatcher, which monitors the state of the equipment through a real-time control computer system. As machines become available, the dispatcher indicates the next tasks for the machines.

The expert system also determines and updates the action plan based on the information it receives. It is able to replan to meet changing conditions in the automated manufacturing center. These changes are communicated to the real-time control function. The installation of the system has been completed and it is fully operational.

DCLASS is a comprehensive expert system being marketed by CAM Software, Inc. of Provo, Utah. The system was developed by a research center at Brigham Young University to fill a need for more consistent and efficient decision-making in the manufacturing environment of today. DCLASS installation sites in many parts of the world have reported thousands of dollars worth of savings in areas such as process planning, classification and coding, cost estimating, and design retrieval.

Flexible Manufacturing System Design

The design of a flexible manufacturing system (FMS) is a potential source of challenging expert system application in industry. Fisher (1986) discusses heuristic formulations that can be incorporated into a knowledge base for the design of manufacturing cells. The cells undergo a continuous cycle of design and redesign based on production plans. Such endless need for flexibility complicates the planning and control functions of manufacturing managers. Expert system techniques can be effectively used for designing FMS systems. Mellichamp and Wahab (1987) have developed an expert system capable of analyzing the output from an FMS simulation model. It can also determine whether operational and financial objectives are all met and can identify deficiencies. In addition, it can propose suitable designs for overcoming the deficiencies it had identified earlier. The system uses an analysis-diagnosis-recommendation process and inputs from simulation analysis to analyze an FMS design. Design changes recommended by the system are incorporated into the simulation model and the process repeats until an acceptable design is obtained. When the total capital investment goal of the FMS is not met, the system identifies the replacement for which the cost differential between the specified equipment and the potential substitute is maximum.

Bruno, Elia, and Laface (1986) describe a knowledge based production scheduling system which determines the sequence of part lots to be machined in an FMS and assists in meeting the due dates of lots, while taking into account several related problems such as minimizing machine idle times, machine queues, and work in progress. Blessing and Watford (1987) also report the use of expert system techniques for shop floor control (loading) in the FMS environment. Kusiak (1987) presents two new approaches to designing expert systems for scheduling in a flexible manufacturing system: the goal-based approach and the model-based approach.

In the goal-based approach, the scheduling problem can be formulated as follows. Given the goal schedule, we schedule resources such as parts, machines, tools, fixtures, and pallets in such a way that the deviation between the goal schedule and the current schedule is minimized. In the model-based approach, the scheduling problem is tackled on the basis of known solutions to commonly encountered shop setups. Examples of such scheduling models are presented by French (1982). Kusiak uses the following three rules to illustrate the nature of a scheduling knowledge base:

- Rule 1:
  IF parts p_i and p_j use fixture f_k,
  THEN they should be scheduled at least t units of time apart.
- Rule 2:
  IF part p_i is to be dispatched for machine m_b which is occupied by another part p_j,
  THEN check availability of an alternative machine m_a.
- Rule 3:
  IF a set of tools T is to be loaded into a tool magazine t_m for processing a part p_i on a machine m_b and there is not enough space in t_m,
  THEN remove from the tool magazine t_m as many tools as required by the set of tools T to be loaded.

Operations Planning

Expert systems can be used in manufacturing for detail planning of machine operations. Operations planning is defined as the specification of parameters for the individual operations within a part's process plan. For machining operations, this activity includes selection of the cutting tool, cut sequence, cutting conditions, tool replacement strategy, and so on to produce a single feature such as a slot or hole on a part. The selection of cutting tool, depth of cut, speed, and feed requires machining expertise which is not always available from computerized process planning systems or today's inexperienced process planners and numerical control (NC) programmers.

An expert system, called CUTTECH, is currently in operation in many shops. The system captures metal cutting technology and data for use in recommending productive and economical tools and cutting parameters for machining. The system incorporates expert system techniques but it is not an expert system per se. It acts as both a knowledge source and a knowledge collection point in a machining facility and its functions include selection of cutting tools, cut sequence, speed, and feeds for selective user defined part features to be machined. The rules are stored in decision tables and algorithms and they are applied in descending order of importance in sorting the tools. The system makes it possible for an engineer, who may have little machining experience, to obtain good machining recommendations for a given part feature.

Process Planning

Process planning has been mostly an art that is intuitive and subjective. It is learned after considerable experience in the shop. Today, very few potential process engineers are gaining shop experience while the older generation of process planners are getting to retirement age. Process planning involves the selection of operations and processes needed to produce multiple features on a part and transform the raw material into a finished part. Process planning in the industrial environment is an area requiring considerable amount of human expertise and has been one of the vigorously contested areas of expert system applications. Expert Computer-Aided Process Planning System (EXCAP) developed by Davies and Darbyshire (1984) is an expert system for generating process plans for machining of rotational components. Freedman and Frail (1987) describe an expert system (OPGEN) developed for Hazeltine Corporation (Greenlawn, NY). OPGEN handles the previously manually-implemented process planning for printed circuit boards.

GARI (Kumara, et al. 1986) is another popular knowledge based system for process planning. Its domain is restricted to the metal cutting industry. The knowledge base of GARI is represented by production rules, where the rule antecedents consist of conditions about the part to be manufactured, and the rule actions contain pieces of advice representing technological and economical preferences. The system consists of a planner and a *knowledge box* (Mill and Spraggett 1984). The *box* contains the manufacturing rules used to guide the search for a solution to the process planning problem for a given component. Nau and Chang (1985) present an expert system named SIPP. The system, programmed in PROLOG, uses a frame based knowledge representation scheme. The knowledge base consists of machinable surfaces and capabilities of various machining operations, and a control structure which manipulates the knowledge base in order to construct process plans. SIPP uses best-first strategy based on branch and bound and produces least-cost process plans based on cost criteria that the user desires.

Kumara, et al. (1986) describe another rule based system, named TOM, which has been implemented at the University of Tokyo. The system does not produce complete machine plans but focuses on producing detailed machining plans for some given features (mostly holes). The program is written in PASCAL and implemented on a minicomputer system.

MetCAPP Metcut Research Associates, Inc. of Cincinnati, Ohio, has one of the most comprehensive process planning systems currently on the market (Barkocy and Zdeblick 1987). Their product, MetCAPP, is an integrated planning system consisting of several modules. MetCAPP's first module is CUTDATA, which is equivalent to a library of machining data. CUTDATA's functions are to retrieve machining recommendations and calculate data for planning. This module contains more than 81,000 recommendations for machining several hundred alloys with 40 machining processes.

MetCAPP's second module is CUTTECH. This module provides expert machining operation planning details for part features. The module is built upon the database of CUTDATA, with a generative system which specifies the process to machine part features. CUTTECH provides process planners and/or NC programmers with everything they need except geometry of the tool path.

CUTPLAN, the third component of the process planning system, is a planning document preparation system for merging and storing several CUTTECH sessions to create a variant process plan for a part. CUTPLAN contains a module for estimating processing times from set-up and run-time constants specific to operations not supported in the CUTTECH module. With a database of stored process plans, part characteristics and definitions are grouped using a relational database. This allows the module to take advantage of family-of-parts planning similarities. CUTPLAN also provides an external interface for integrating Metcut's modules with other computer integrated manufacturing (CIM) systems.

According to the developers, MetCAPP is designed to boost industrial productivity by improving planning. This benefit relates to planning accuracy, planning productivity, machining productivity, and tooling standardization.

RIM-PDA Martin Marietta (Bharwani, et al. 1987) has designed a knowledge-based system to assist process engineers and technicians in evaluating the processability and moldability of poly-iso-cyanurate (PIR) formulations for the thermal protection system of the Space Shuttle external tank. The system consists of two segments: one for reaction injection molding and the other for process development. It takes advantage of both symbolic and numeric processing techniques. Its knowledge base includes process knowledge and the knowledge of casual relationships. Process knowledge consists of heuristic knowledge acquired from domain experts, such as case histories of chemical formulations and their moldability in test mold configurations. Process knowledge and the knowledge of casual relationships derived from the empirical data will aid the process engineer in two major ways: (1) identifying a startup set of mold schedules, and (2) refining the mold schedules to remedy specific process problems diagnosed by the system.

The system, named RIM-PDA (Reaction Injection Molding-Process Development Advisor), takes advantage of conventional algorithmic approaches as well as state-of-the-art artificial intelligence methodologies to analyze the identified tasks. Mechanisms for switching between layers of reasoning based on the type of question asked of the system are expected to be incorporated into the system.

Parker Hannifin Corporation An expert system developed by Parker Hannifin Corporation's Tube Fitting Division in Columbus, Ohio, is said to sharply reduce the time required to match the proper tube and fitting connections when designing fluid power systems. The system replaces several pages of the company's Tube Fitting catalog. It can perform the following functions:

- Point out design conflicts automatically
- Note incompatible data immediately
- Refer the user to additional technical data if necessary
- Print out a listing of the properly sized tubing

Process Selection

The task of selecting appropriate processes to produce each of the machined surfaces of a part is a complicated task. Nau and Chang (1983) utilized expert system techniques for automating the process selection activity. In most of the computer-aided process planning systems, process selection works in two steps. First, a group technology code is used to classify a part as being in a family of similar parts. Second, when a process plan for a part is

desired, a human user enters the code for the part into the system and the system retrieves a process plan which was previously used for some part in the family.

In an automated process selection method, expert system techniques are used in accumulating the necessary information about each surface of the part by representing the part as frames. Frames are data structures in which all the knowledge about a particular object or event is stored together. The process selection system gathers information by asking questions and it uses the answers to these questions to make process selection.

Process Control

Expert systems can be used for monitoring thousands of process variables. With such systems, a small crew of operators can regulate the operation of immensely complex industrial processes. Waterman (1987) gives a description of two such systems: FALCON and PDS.

FALCON identifies probable causes of process disturbances in a chemical process plant by interpreting data consisting of numerical values from gauges and the status of alarms and switches. The system interprets the data by using knowledge of the effects induced by fault in a given component and how disturbances in the input of a component will lead to disturbances in the output. Knowledge is represented in the system in two ways: as a set of rules controlled by forward chaining and as a causal model in network form. The system is written in LISP and was developed at the University of Delaware.

PDS, a portable diagnostic system, diagnoses malfunctions in machine processes by interpreting information from sensors attached to the process. The system uses diagnosis methods that relate sensor readings to component malfunctions. PDS uses a forward chaining, rule-based representation scheme implemented in SRL, a frame-based knowledge engineering language. This system was developed at Carnegie-Mellon University in cooperation with Westinghouse Electric Corporation.

Knight, Endersby, and Voller (1984) suggest the feasibility of using expert systems in controlling various processes in an industrial environment. Miller et al. (1986) describes a real-time expert system for process control, called PIPCON (Process Intelligent Control), marketed by LISP Machine, Inc. PIPCON can monitor up to 20,000 measurements and alarms and can assign priorities to alarms to assist an operator in dealing efficiently with a process interruption or fault. Another process control system is PTRANS, which helps control the manufacture and distribution of Digital Equipment Corporation's computer systems. It uses customer order descriptions and information about plant activity to develop a plan for assembling and testing the ordered computer system, including when to build the system. PTRANS monitors the progress of technicians implementing the plan, diagnoses problems, suggests solutions, and predicts possible impending shortages or surpluses of materials.

An expert system to be used as a diagnostic tool for failures in semiconductor fabrication is being developed jointly by the National Bureau of Standards and the Westinghouse Research and Development Center. The tool would help manufacturers pinpoint problems that could cause failures at various stages in the semiconductors fabrication process. The knowledge is based on the collective intelligence and experience of several fabrication experts. Specialists with considerable expertise are usually required to interpret fabrication test data, but such experts are not always readily available. The expert system will allow the semiconductor process personnel to diagnose problems on a personal computer screen in a readily-understood, English language format.

Facility Planning

Industrial facility layout is another candidate area for expert systems and can be used to combine judgmental rules of human experts with quantitative tools in order to develop good facilities design for a variety of situations.

Two such systems are FADES and IFLAPS. FADES is a facilities planning and design system.

The knowledge in this system is represented in the form of rules implemented in logic procedures and first order predicates. The knowledge base comprises the areas of workstation technology, economic investment analysis, development of relationship ratings among workstations, selection of assignment algorithms, input preparation and invocation of algorithm for layout planning, and retrieval of information needed by logic rules from an existing company database. IFLAPS is a multicriteria facilities layout analysis and planning system. This is a rule-based system implemented in PROLOG. The system explains its reasoning through an efficient user interface and acquires new knowledge through rule-based learning.

The Interior Department of the Bureau of Mines has developed an expert system for environmental facility control of coal mines. The system helps in achieving better control of respirable dust and explosive methane gas in underground coal mines. It helps coal mine operators solve problems in dust control for continuous miners, longwall shearers, and methane control. It obtains input about a control problem from the user, analyzes the data, and then suggests approaches to a solution.

Expert Systems in CAD/CAM

Expert systems have been applied to various computer-aided design tasks, such as VLSI and electronic circuits, and have been proposed for CAD/CAM applications. General Electric (Schenectady, NY) is exploring an expert system capable of redesigning an existing design. This system can work on an existing design or it can generate a new one. HICLASS (Hughes Integrated Classification System) is an expert system operating at Hughes Aircraft Company. The areas that are handled by HICLASS are planning methods, processes, standards, cost estimates, scheduling, productivity management, and quality control. This system supports productivity-based automation and integrated design of manufacturing systems. It is capable of deducing the required manufacturing process from engineering design data. The expert system involves three phases:

- Definition: a problem definition phase. The problem associated with an engineering design is presented.
- Reasoning: a problem solving phase. Symbolic processing is done while requirements and constraints are being evaluated until a solution is reached.
- Presentation: a recommendation phase. The recommended solution is graphically presented to the user.

Maintenance and Fault Diagnosis

One area where expert systems have been proven to be quite successful is the area of fault diagnosis and recommendation of repairs. The maintenance of a complex item of equipment involves a diagnostic procedure incorporating many rules as well as judgment decision by the maintenance personnel. Experience is a very important factor in determining the ease with which a mechanic can locate a failure in a component and implement the appropriate correction. Expert systems are now being utilized to assist maintenance personnel in performing complex repairs by presenting menu-driven instruction guides for the diagnostic task. These expert systems incorporate the knowledge of mechanics who are well experienced in the maintenance and repair of that item of equipment. The first maintenance expert system to become commercially available was CATS-1 which was renamed later as DELTA. This expert system was introduced by General Electric Company in 1983. Diesel-Electric Locomotive Troubleshooting Aid or DELTA is now being used in railroad repair shops to assist maintenance personnel in isolating and repairing a large variety of diesel-electric locomotive faults.

Expert systems such as CATS, DART, ACE (Miller et al. 1986), and COMPASS (Waterman 1987) have been used for the purpose of preventive maintenance. Bungers (1986) described an expert system called DEX.C3. The system is used for fault diagnosis in a three gear automatic transmission found in cars produced by Ford Motor Company. DEX.C3 system was primarily developed to demonstrate the principles and potentials of expert systems to the Ford community and also as a means of supporting service stations operated by Ford Company. Piptone (1986) discusses an expert system, Fault Isolation System (FIS), used for providing assistance to a technician in diagnosing faults in electronic parts. Kumara, et al. (1986) also describe an expert system, called FOREST, used for fault isolation and diagnosis in automatic test equipment (ATE). The system attempts to emulate experienced field engineers whose specialty is diagnosing faults undetectable by existing ATE software.

At Hughes Aircraft Company, an expert system has been developed as a feasibility analysis tool. The expert system assists engineers in designing circuit cards by determining the testability of a card for the factory. The system also has links to external databases for direct data inputs. The Oklahoma City plant of AT&T has also developed many expert systems for equipment troubleshooting. One of the systems, named Oklahoma Interactive Expert System or OKIE, was developed to troubleshoot AT&T 3B2 computers (Somby 1987). The system is installed and fully operational. Like many industrial expert systems, most of the operating details of OKIE are proprietary. It is such proprietary constraints that have made it difficult for the public to fully appreciate the contributions that expert systems are making in industry. However, the information restrictions will be alleviated as more aggressive and public domain efforts are reported.

By the end of 1989, many Ford Motor Company dealers across the company no longer had to call Dearborn, Michigan, to talk with company experts every time they ran into difficult engine diagnosis problems. Instead, they simply tap into a new nationwide computer system developed by Ford to duplicate the reasoning that the experts use to solve difficult engine problems.

At Xerox, an expert system named Remote Interactive Communications or RIC is being used for early warning equipment diagnostics. The knowledge base for RIC is based on the reasoning of a special Xerox team of diagnosticians. The system reads data from a copier's internal instruments, senses when something is about to go wrong, and sends a report to a repairman. The repairman can then warn the customer that an imminent breakdown can be avoided by taking appropriate steps. In theory, RIC can prevent a Xerox copier from ever breaking down.

In 1986, IBM installed one of its first expert systems, called Diagnostic Expert Final Test or DEFT. The task of the system is to perform the mundane but critical job of diagnosing problems during the final testing of the giant disk drives that store information for IBM's mainframe computers. DEFT has been adapted as a diagnostic tool for IBM service experts and performs a variety of different tests on many IBM equipment. The system, which costs about $100,000 initially, is said to have generated a payoff of around $12 million in annual savings. It should be mentioned that some of the savings that have been reported by companies are somewhat conservative. This is primarily because companies are cautious about letting competitors find out where their competitive edge lies.

An expert system for troubleshooting blast furnaces went into operation in 1987 at Kawasaki Steel's Mizushima Works in western Japan. The company reports that the system embodies both expert system technology and all the state-of-art technological know-how accumulated in the iron-making area of steel operations over the past decade. Using about 600 *if/then* rules, the system covers all conceivable situations likely to develop inside a blast furnace. The system takes readings on up to 250 process variables.

Texas Instruments, Inc. Applications One diagnostic application developed by Texas Instruments, Inc. involves a highly sophisticated machine used in the production of semiconductors (Herrod 1988). This application illustrates how an expert system can aid in significantly reducing error, avoiding costly waste and downtime. The sophisticated machine, called an epitaxial reactor, is used to deposit thin layers of silicon on silicon wafers. The wafers, a few inches in diameter, are placed in vacuum chambers inside the reactors. The thin film (spitaxial layer) is grown at high temperature by controlling the flow rate and pattern of a mixture of silicon and other reactant gases.

The machine may process several wafers at a time. If it is set up improperly or a failure occurs while in process, thousands of dollars' worth of scrap may result and many hours of reactor time may be wasted. Because the reactors are very complex, only a few experts are skilled in diagnosing and fixing repair problems. Reactors could remain idle for several hours while waiting for a human expert to arrive. To reduce this expensive downtime, a panel of engineers created an expert system, Intelligent Machine Prognosticator (IMP). It consists of seven knowledge bases, including three for faults, one for warnings, another for a hoist that forms part of the system, one for mechanical problems, and one for process problems. The combined knowledge bases contain up to 1000 rules to help the technician in diagnosing the problems. Approximately 90 percent of the potential reactor problems are included in the expert system. It is reported that results with the system have been better than expected. The mean time to repair has decreased by 36 percent.

Another Texas Instruments product is an expert system that troubleshoots a complex electronic device. The device, containing several dozen state-of-the-art analog and digital circuit boards, is tested in an automated test equipment environment. The combination of possible symptoms, uncertainty of failure causes, and the frequent refinement and enhancement of both the product and test environment resulted in an enormous and complex domain. To tackle this large domain, a diagnostic expert system, called Expert Technician, was developed to provide a best-first troubleshooting procedure for junior and senior-level technicians.

A major component of the system is its ability to acquire and update symptom-action associations by which conditions, signs, and symptoms are linked to actions that eliminate the symptoms. These symptom-action links are integrated into the knowledge base as problems are discovered by the automated test equipment and are then strengthened as actions repeatedly result in stopping the symptom. A time-weighting factor is used to reduce the effect of older association events. This way, the likelihoods used by the system to infer the best-first action for a given set of symptoms are based both on frequency of association and recency of the association. This approach is very useful in dynamic domains where the need to identify failure trends is very critical. The final recommendations to the technicians are cost-weighted using standard cost indices for performing the required tasks. The system is presently implemented in the C language on minicomputers that interface with more than 50 computer-based automated test sets via a local area network.

Campbell Soup Expert System One of the most frequently reported diagnostic expert system is the one developed for the Campbell Soup Company of Camden, New Jersey, by Texas Instruments. The expert system project involved solving a diagnostic problem for malfunctions in large soup sterilizers. The large, complex sterilizers are 72 feet high and hold up to 68,000 cans of soup. The soup is raised to a temperature of 250 degrees Centigrade using pressurized steam to kill bacteria. Maintenance of these sterilizers is usually handled routinely by plant personnel. However, some problems could only be solved by an expert knowledgeable in the design and installation of the sterilizers.

Downtime is very expensive because of the large quantity of soup in a sterilizer at any given time and the potential effects of backlog. An expert system was created to capture the knowledge of the human expert who specializes in troubleshooting the sterilizers. The expert was close to retirement. So, the company wanted to retain his expertise and allow him to spend most of his remaining time in designing new equipment. The expert system that came out of the project was developed using the Personal Consultant development shell. The system can troubleshoot about 100 hydrostatic and rotary sterilizers. It also includes all of the start-up and shut-down procedures for the machines.

The system was developed in approximately seven months. It has been installed in about eight of Campbell's U.S. and Canadian plants. It has been found to operate successfully in diagnosing problems. Based on this success, similar systems have been developed to diagnose problems in the equipment that fills cans with soup and those that seal the cans.

Equipment Maintenance Equipment maintenance is another big area for expert system applications. Eagle Technology, Inc. has developed a commercial expert system for maintenance, named Expert Maintenance Management (EMM). Standard modules of the system, designed to run on personal computers, include equipment records, preventive maintenance, work order management, parts inventory, and purchase orders. Users retrieve information and generate work orders using English language words and phrases. An enhancement schedule includes analysis of maintenance costs, maintenance/personnel scheduling, and preventive maintenance.

Material Handling and Supplies

A major challenge facing designers and materials engineers is the selection of engineering materials to satisfy product requirements under existing availability, supply, and production constraints. In an industrial environment, computer control of various material handling activities is a very complex task. The process demands advanced strategic planning, high performance, high reliability, and precise timing. For example, a computer controlling a high-speed conveyor must make the correct decision before the next load reaches its diversion point or it will lose the load. Expert systems can be used for combining advanced logical processes with high speed, multilocation decision making. Expert system techniques have been successfully implemented at the Digital Equipment Corporation facility at Marlboro, Massachusetts, for controlling material handling processes. According to Wynot (1986), the use of expert systems has resulted in increased output, reduced cycle time, reduction of labor, improved equipment utilization, reduction of work-in-process, and improved scheduling.

At Daniel Industries of Houston, Texas, a fluid control and measurement device manufacturer, an expert system running on a personal computer produces dramatic increases in Bill of Material (BOM) and inventory accuracies. The system also enhances design productivity. The company produces some very complex products, consisting of many different parts. Whenever an order is placed, design personnel have to sift through a large number of possible configurations. Since each order is essentially a custom job, the number of possible configurations may be up to trillions. Because of this complexity, the company needs a way to get very accurate bills of material. An accurate bill of material is crucial to their Manufacturing Resource Planning (MRP II) system. They found a solution in an expert system. Since the installation of the system, productivity has increased and inventories have declined.

Selection of Equipment and Operating Conditions

The task of selecting equipment or setting operating conditions to match product and production needs while achieving minimum cost requires extensive knowledge of facts, relationships, and rules that are specific to material handling. In addition, it requires consideration of complex equipment characteristics that can suggest many feasible alternatives. The selection process may have to accommodate multiple conflicting objectives. An expert system can provide the potential for solving this kind of selection problem. Malmborg, et al. (1987) developed a prototype expert system for the truck type selection problem. They define an industrial truck type as a collection of attributes that specify an industrial model in sufficient detail that one or more commercially available truck models could be associated with it.

The engineers at COMSAT Corporation have developed an expert system which selects the correct heater warm-up time for in-orbit operation of the INTELSAT V Spacecraft electrothermal thrusters. When humans performed this task, they were prone to error and required constant cross-checking by an experienced engineer. The expert system provides reliable and quick selection of the correct warm-up time. It avoids potential human error and allows the operations staff to perform higher level tasks.

Chrysler Corporation is developing an expert system to assist engineers and designers in selecting the best fasteners from among the estimated 30,000 types currently available for headlamp assembly. The fastener system is very complex because it must be developed for a large user base and it must incorporate latest developments in fastener technology.

Robotics

The area of robotics is fertile for the application of expert systems. Robots of the past were designed mainly for mechanical functions with preprogrammed instructions. Regardless of its changing environment, the robot would attempt to execute its tasks in the predetermined process. Nowadays, the increasing dynamism of production environments has necessitated the development of intelligent robots that are conscious and adaptable to their changing surroundings. Inagaki (1983) discusses a research effort involving the integration of sensors into assembly robots. Sensors are developed for inner measurements to detect the internal conditions of the industrial robot itself. Sensors are also developed for outer measurements to enable the robot to be responsive to the external conditions of the objects on which it is assigned to work.

Rajaram (1986) contends that it is not sufficient for AI to be integrated into isolated manufacturing systems components such as individual robots. He suggests that intelligence must be distributed at strategic points throughout the manufacturing system. Communication links, policies, and procedures will need to be developed to govern the full integration of robots into the production environment. Bourne (1986), in a related article, comments that past failures in incorporating robots into manufacturing systems have been due to the lack of integrated communication links. Badiru (1988) suggests the use of heuristics in *on-board* knowledge bases to guide the communication functions of industrial robots.

The main envisioned functions of an intelligent robot include processing information, sensing, and motion. Information processing is primarily a brain function. Sensing (seeing and touching) and motion (moving and manipulations) are primarily body functions. The information processing function (thinking) is executed by a computer through an expert system technique. Even though there are no commercially available expert system based robots so far, there are indications that leading robot manufacturers are beginning to incorporate expert systems into their robot designs. Three areas with the potential of using expert systems in robotics include:

- Kinematics and design. For the operation of a robot arm, the kinematic problem must be solved with respect to movement from one cartesian position and orientation to another. An expert system could possibly be implemented to relieve the human expert in the symbolically tedious work of producing such solutions.
- Robot selection. Because of the shortage of experienced applications engineers, an expert system could distribute applications experience among a wider community of users. The knowledge base can be periodically updated to reflect new developments in robot availability and utilization.
- Workplace layout. When robots are to be installed in a new workspace, an expert system can perform the necessary analysis to provide the optimum workspace requirements.

Machine vision, a critical component of robotics, is an area of AI that has been more successful in research laboratories than in actual practice. This is because laboratories operate under controlled conditions while actual practice is subject to all sorts of unanticipated environmental variations. An improvement in practical applications can be achieved by developing expert systems that use heuristics to guide machine vision system operations under various stimuli within a functional loca-

tion. Schreiber (1985) narrates how ZapatA Industries (Frackville, PA), the largest U.S. manufacturer of bottle caps, switched to machine vision for quality control. The result of implementing the vision system was a 33 percent increase in productivity.

Researchers at McMaster University in Hamilton, Ontario, Canada, have designed an expert system task planner to aid in the off-line programming of assembly robots. The system is used for automatic off-line programming of robots by specifying the goal state and the initial state. The robot planner uses a knowledge base for assembly sequences, geometric reasoning, and tooling. Software allows the user to describe the assembly task at a high level. The programmer does not need to specify moves or coordinates because the robot automatically converts its instructions into the detailed steps needed to execute the task.

Machine Tool Applications

Expert system techniques can be used for managing the tool life in an FMS environment. They will limit the occurrence of expensive tool failures (Villa, et al. 1985).

A diagnostic system for a machine tool controller is presently in operation at McDonnell Douglas company. The primary function of this expert system is to allow maintenance people to easily identify problems in the controller. Currently, the system is expected to perform an advisory role for a maintenance staff of about 35 people. Eventually, the system will hook up directly to the controller. It is anticipated that the system will not reduce the number of employees needed in the plant, but will free them up for more creative tasks. The system is expected to help reduce downtime on the plant floor, allowing the company to produce in-house parts that otherwise would have to be contracted from outside manufacturers.

Automation

Most of the functions discussed earlier constitute the main ingredients of factory automation.

The major components in an integrated manufacturing system consist of corporate planning, marketing planning, research and development, engineering design, production planning, manufacturing, warehousing, and product distribution. These components are linked by management information flow, technology information flow, and materials flow.

Tou (1987) presents design concepts of expert systems for engineering design, production planning, and manufacturing. Expert systems are the answer to problems that may be associated with integrated production automation in the future. The broad functional goals for using expert system techniques in the area of factory automation would be to provide expert assistance in the performance of professional and managerial tasks and in integrating and coordinating the management of the factory. Intelligent management systems (IMS) will be a crucial part of the factory of the future.

Process Management

Digital Equipment Corporation is developing the Intelligent Management Assistant for Computer System manufacturing or IMACS. This expert system will assist managers in a computer systems manufacturing environment with paperwork, capacity planning, inventory management, and other tasks related to managing the manufacturing process. IMACS takes a customer's order and generates a rough build plan from which it can estimate the resource requirements for the order. Just before the computer system in the order is built, IMACS generates a detailed build plan and uses it to monitor the computer system's implementation.

The operation of a complex processing plant is a profitable area for the application of expert system technology. Many systems have been developed to assist with the interpretation of the numerous alarm conditions that can occur in large process plants (Nida, et al. 1986). Given the complexity of many industrial processes, reliance on experienced and expert operators is very common. FIGURE 26-3 illustrates a conceptual model of the role of expert sys-

tems in enhancing the management of complex processes. An expert system can provide guidance on the application of control strategies. In cases where the time cycle for operator response can span well over an eight-hour shift, it is important to maintain consistent operating conditions and operator actions. By offering consistent advice around the clock, an expert system could help maintain the required consistency. An example of this application is currently in operation at Broken Hill Proprietary Central Research Laboratories in Shortland, New South Wales.

In another example of the application of expert systems in process management, an expert system (named WELD-SELECTOR) developed by the Colorado School of Mines (Golden, CO) helps engineers make welding decisions. Complexity in welding is growing. There are now hundreds of weldable metals, including specialized alloys. Some of these require highly specific procedures. In most shops, except the specialized ones, the increasing number of welding factors is making decisions about welding more and more difficult. The WELD-SELECTOR expert system helps in reducing the changes for decision errors. The system asks the user a series of questions about the welding to be performed. It searches through its knowledge base to find suitable welding electrodes and narrows down the possibilities to a final recommendation. The system considers chemical and physical properties of the base materials and the intended position of the weld. The expert system is currently being marketed by the American Welding Institute in Knoxville, Tennessee.

Wright-Patterson Air Force Base Aeronautical Systems Division has developed an expert system to greatly reduce the time needed to manufacture composite aircraft parts. The system is used to run an autoclave (oven) that cures the composite parts. The system controls several variables in the curing process to ensure that the finished composite parts will have the desired performance characteristics. Another expert system for the composite industry was developed by ABARIS company of Reno, Nevada, under contract with the U.S. Air Force

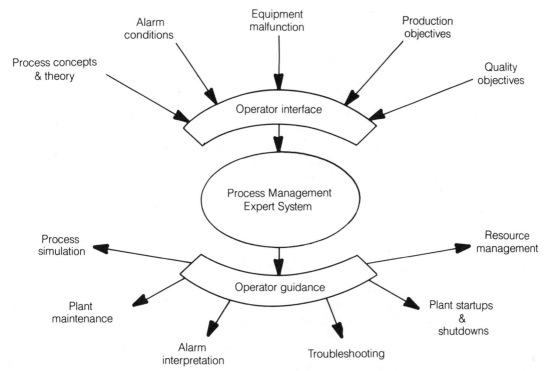

Fig. 26-3. Conceptual model of a process management expert system.

Wright Aeronautical Materials Laboratory in Dayton, Ohio. The system leads users through ultrasound inspection and repair of composite materials.

Composite materials, used increasingly in aircraft parts, have partial failure modes that can cause problems in the field. Because the material is multilaminar and opaque, internal fracture or separation is difficult to identify. So, ultrasound inspection is used to find most of the internal damage. However, each ply of lamination can cause discontinuities of signals that could be interpreted as damage. An expert system helps in analyzing the ultrasound data and obtaining correct interpretations.

Part Programming in Milling Operations

Expert systems can be used for writing complicated part programs for milling operation. Preiss and Kaplansky (1987) discuss the role of an expert system that can automatically write a part program

for a milling process and can act as an assistant to human part programmers. Basically, the input to the program is the graphic representation (a drawing) and user-defined items such as tool details and material type. The program has an initial state—the shape of the raw material—and a goal state—the shape of the final part. The expert system solves the problem of achieving the goal state from the initial state by using machining moves that create the part program needed to generate the desired product.

RESEARCH AGENDA FOR ARTIFICIAL INTELLIGENCE

One potential tool that can enhance the utilization of artificial intelligence in manufacturing is state space modeling. However, some basic research will need to be undertaken in order to determine how best to use this tool and in what areas of the AI/Manufacturing interface. Automated process planning is one area that can benefit from state space modeling techniques.

State Space Representation

A *state* is a set of conditions or values that describes a system at a specified point during processing. The *state space* is the set of all possible states the system could be in during the problem-solving process. State space representation solves problems by moving from an initial state in the space to another state, and eventually to a goal state. This is similar to the *means-end* process discussed earlier in this chapter. The movement from state to state is achieved by the means of operators, typically rules or procedures. A *goal* is a description of an intended state that has not yet been achieved. The process of solving a problem involves finding a sequence of operators that represent a solution path from the initial state to the goal state.

State space techniques have been used extensively to model continuous system problems in engineering applications (Brooks 1983; Walter 1982; Lozano-Perez 1981). The techniques have also been applied to management decision problems (Marshall 1987; Aoki 1981; Szidarovszky 1986; Fox et al. 1987). Pearl (1984) presents several examples of the application of mathematical models to decision and management problems. Two typical examples of state space problem solving are chess-playing and route-finding problems (Shannon 1950). Using an expert system and state space modeling, a manufacturing process can be greatly enhanced.

A state space model consists of definition state variables that describe the internal state or prevailing configuration of the system being represented. The state variables are related to the system inputs by an equation. One other equation relates both the state variables and system inputs to the outputs of the system. Examples of potential state variables in a manufacturing process include product quality level, production cost, due date, resource availability, operator skill level, variable machine tolerance, and productivity level.

In the case of a model described by a system of differential equations, the state-space representation is of the form:

$$z = f(z(t), x(t))$$
$$y(t) = g(z(t), x(t))$$

where f and g are vector-valued functions. In the case of linear systems, the representation is of the form:

$$z = Az(t) + Bx(t)$$
$$y(t) = Cz(t) + Dx(t)$$

where $z(t)$, $x(t)$, and $y(t)$ are vectors and A, B, C, and D are matrices. The variable y is the output vector while the variable x denotes the inputs. The state vector $z(t)$ is an immediate vector relating $x(t)$ to $y(t)$.

The state space representation of a discrete-time linear dynamic system, with respect to a suitable time index, is given by:

$$z(t+1) = Az(t) + Bx(t)$$
$$y(t) = Cz(t) + Dx(t)$$

In generic terms, a process system is transformed from one state to another by a driving function that produces a transitional equation given by:

$$\Psi = f(x|\Theta) + \epsilon$$

where Ψ is the subsequent state, x is the state variable, Θ is the initial state, and ϵ is the error component. The function f is composed of a given action (or a set of actions) applied to objects in the state-modeled process. Each intermediate state may represent a significant milestone in the process. Thus, a descriptive state space model facilitates an analysis of what actions to apply in order to achieve the next desired state or milestone. An example of a simple process is the application of an action to an object which is in a given state or condition.

The application of action constitutes a process activity. The production process involves the planning, coordination, and control of a collection of activities. Process objectives are achieved by state-to-state transformation of successive object abstractions. FIGURE 26-4 shows the transformation of an object from one state to another through the application of action. The simple representation can be expanded to include other components within the process framework. The hierarchical linking of objects provides a detailed description of the process profile as shown in FIG. 26-5.

The process model can further be expanded in accordance with implicit process requirements. These considerations might include grouping of object classes, precedence linking (both technical and procedural), required communication links, and reporting requirements.

The actions to be taken at each state depend on the prevailing conditions. The natures of the subsequent alternate states depend on what actions are actually implemented. Sometimes there are multiple paths (e.g., alternate machining process options) that can lead to the desired end result. At other times, there exists only one unique path to the desired objective. In conventional practice, the characteristics of the future states can only be recognized after the fact, thus making it impossible to develop adaptive plans. In terms of control, deviations are often recognized after the fact, thus mak-

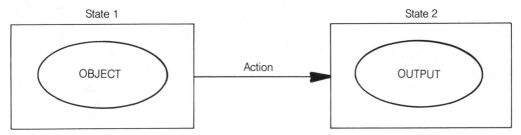

Fig. 26-4. Object transformation.

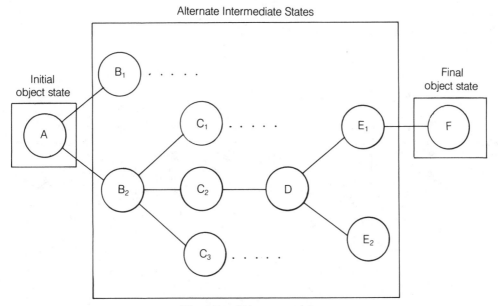

Fig. 26-5. Object state paths.

ing it impossible to develop adaptive plans. In terms of control, deviations are often recognized when it is too late to take effective corrective actions. Both the events occurring within and outside the process state boundaries can be taken into account in the planning function. These internal and external constraints are shown in FIG. 26-6.

Process State Representation

We can describe a manufacturing process by M state variables s_i. The composite state of the system at any given time can then be represented by an M-component vector S.

$$S = \{s_1, s_2, \ldots, s_M\}$$

The components of the state vector could represent either quantitative or qualitative variables (such as voltage, energy, quality level, machining power, surface finish, and tool life). We can visualize every state vector as a point in the M-dimensional state space shown in FIG. 26-7. The representation is unique since every state vector corresponds to one and only one point in the state space.

Process State Transformation

Suppose we have a set of actions (transformation agents) that we can apply to a process so as to change it from one state to another within the state space. The transformation will change a state vector into another state vector. A transformation, in practical terms, may be heat treatment, baking, or a grinding. We can let T_k be the kth type of transformation. If T_k is applied to the process when it is in state S, the new state vector will be $T_k(S)$, which is another point in the state space. The number of transformations (or actions) available for a process may be finite or countably infinite. We can construct trajectories that describe the potential states as we apply successive transformations. Each transformation may be repeated as many times as needed.

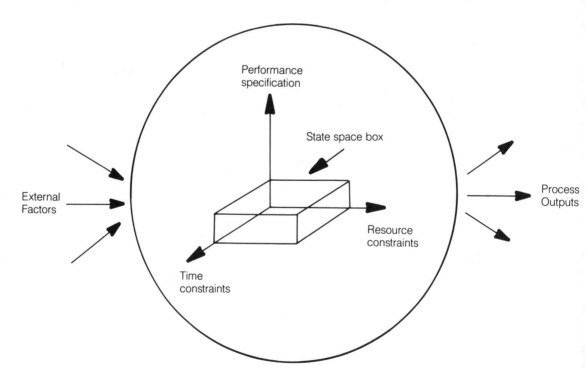

Fig. 26-6. External and internal forces on process.

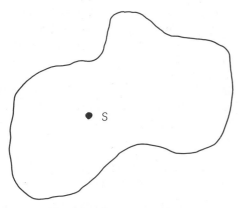

Fig. 26-7. Process state space.

For convenience, we can use the notation T_i to indicate the ith transformation in the sequence of transformations applied. Given an initial state S, the sequence of state vectors is then given by:

$$
\begin{aligned}
S_1 &= T_1(S) \\
S_2 &= T_2(S)_1 \\
S_3 &= T_3(S)_2
\end{aligned}
$$

.
.
.

$$S_n = T_n(S_{n-1})$$

The final state S_n depends on the initial state S and the effects of the transformations applied. The

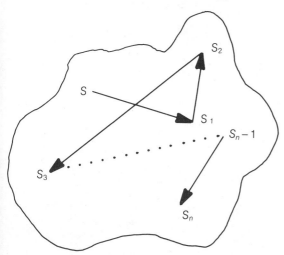

Fig. 26-8. Transformation trajectories in a state space.

sequence is shown graphically within the state space in FIG. 26-8.

State Performance Measurement

A measure of process performance can be obtained at each state of the transformation trajectories. Thus, we can develop a reward function $r^k(S)$ associated with the kth type transformation (Howard 1971). The reward specifies the magnitude of gain (time, quality level, surface finish, hardness, color, equipment utilization, etc.) to be achieved by applying a given transformation. The difference between a reward and a performance specification may be used as a criterion for determining process control actions. The performance deviation may be defined as:

$$\delta = r^k(S) - \varrho$$

where ϱ is the performance specification.

Process Policy Development

Given the number of transformations still available and the current state vector, we can develop a policy, P, to be the rule for determining the next transformation to be applied. The total process reward can then be denoted as:

$$r(S/n,P) = r_1(S) + r_2(S_1) + \ldots + r_n(S_{n-1})$$

where n is the number of transformations applied and $r_i(.)$ is the ith reward in the sequence of transformations. We can now visualize a process environment where the starting state vector and the possible actions (transformations) are specified. We have to decide what transformations to use in what order so as to maximize the total reward. That is, we must develop the best process plan.

If we let υ represent a quantitative measure of the worth of a process plan based on the reward system described above, then the maximum reward is given by:

$$\upsilon(S/n) = \text{Max}\{r(S/n,P)\}$$

The maximization of the reward function is carried out over all possible process policies that can be obtained with n given transformations.

Probabilistic States

In many process situations, the results of applying transformations to the system may not be deterministic. Rather, the new state vector, the reward generated, or both may have to be described by random variables. We can define an expected total reward, $Q(S/n)$, as the sum of the individual expected rewards from all possible states. We let S^p *be a possible new state vector generated by the probabilistic process and let* $P(S^p/S,T^k)$ be the probability that the new state vector will be S^p if the initial state vector is S and the transformation T^k is applied. We can now write a recursive relation for the expected total reward (Howard 1971),

$$Q(_kS/n) = \underset{k}{\mathrm{Max}}\{r^{-k}(S) + \Sigma S^p Q(S^p/n-1)P(S^p/S,T^k)\},$$
$$\text{for } n = 1,2,3,\ldots$$

The notation $r^{-k}(_kS)$ is used to designate the expected reward received by applying the kth type transformation to the system when it is described by state vector S. The above procedure allows the possibility that the terminal reward itself may be a random variable. Thus, the state space model permits a complete analysis of all the ramifications and uncertainties in a manufacturing process.

State Space and Expert Systems Implementation

The *if-then* structure of knowledge representation for expert systems provides a mechanism for evaluating the multiplicity of process states under diversified actions. Expert systems have the advantages of consistency, comprehensive evaluation of all available data, accessibility, infinite retention of information, and lack of bias. An integrated process planning and control system using state space and expert systems may be implemented as shown in FIG. 26-9.

A process manager might interact with the

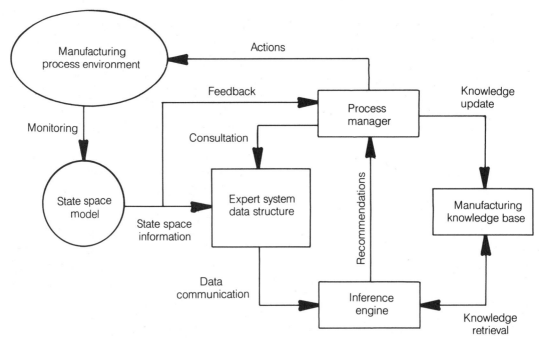

Fig. 26-9. State space/expert system model for manufacturing process.

state space model and the expert system by doing the following:

- Performing the real-time monitoring of the process and then supplying inputs to the state space model
- Getting feedback from the state model
- Consulting the expert system based on the state space information
- Getting recommendations from the expert system
- Taking process actions that eventually generate further inputs to the state model
- Updating the expert system knowledge base as new process knowledge is acquired

The supply of state space information to both the process manager and the expert system in FIG. 26-9 will serve as a control measure. In case the manager does not utilize all available information, the expert system can query him or her for justification.

The previous presentations point out some of the research elements that must be addressed in order to reap the benefits of using state space representation models in the manufacturing environment. Researchers and practitioners will need to investigate the current state of application of artificial intelligence to manufacturing, identify the prevailing shortcomings and problems, and then determine how the existing mathematical and software tools can be utilized to enhance the manufacturing process.

REFERENCES

Aoki, Masana. *Dynamic Analysis of Open Economies*. New York: Academic Press, 1981.

Badiru, Adedeji B. "Successful Initiation of Expert Systems Projects." *IEEE Transactions on Engineering Management* 35: 3 (August 1988a): 186–190.

_____. *Project Management in Manufacturing and High Technology Operations*. John Wiley & Sons, 1988b.

_____. "State Space Modeling for Knowledge Representation in Project Monitoring and Control." Presented at the ORSA/TIMS Conference, Denver, Colorado, October 1988c.

_____. "Cost Integrated Network Planning Using Expert Systems." *Project Management Journal* 19: 2 (April 1988d): 59-62.

_____. "Expert Systems and Industrial Engineers: A Practical Guide to a Successful Partnership." *Computers and Industrial Engineering* 14: 1 (1988e): 1-13.

Barkocy, Brian E. and W. J. Zdeblick. "A Knowledge-Based System for Machining Operation Planning." In *Smart Manufacturing with Artificial Intelligence*, edited by J. Krakauer, 76-88. Computer and Automated Systems Association of SME, Dearborn, Michigan, 1987.

Bergstrom, R. P. "AI: Fad with a Future?" *Manufacturing Engineering* (April 1985): 65.

Bharwani, S. S., J. T. Walls, and M. E. Jackson. "Intelligent Process Development of Foam Molding for the Thermal Protection System (TPS) of the Space Shuttle External Tank." In *Proceedings of Third Conference on Artificial Intelligence for Space Applications: Part I*, 195-202. NASA Conference Publication 2492, Huntsville, Alabama, November 2-3, 1987.

Blessing, J. A. and B. A. Watford. "INFMSS-An Intelligent Scheduling System." In *Proceedings of the IIE Spring Conference*, 476-482, May 1987.

Bourne, D. A. "CML: A Meta-interpreter for Manufacturing." *AI Magazine* 7: 4 (1986): 86-95.

Bourne, D. A. and M. S. Fox. "Autonomous Manufacturing: Automating the Job-Shop." *IEEE Computer* 17: 9 (1984): 76-86.

Brooks, Rodney A. "Solving the Find-Path Problem by Good Representation of Free Space." *IEEE Transactions on Systems, Man, and Cybernetics*, Vol. SCM-13, No. 3, 190-197. March/April 1983.

Bruno, G., A. Elia, and P. Laface. "A Rule-Based System to Schedule Production." *IEEE Computer* 17: 9 (1986): 32-40.

Bullers, William I., Shimon Y. Nof, and Andrew B. Whinston. "Artificial Intelligence in Manufacturing Planning and Control." *AIIE Transactions*, 12: 4 (December 1980): 3351-3363.

Bungers, D. "Using Expert Systems for Customer Service of Ford Europe." In *Expert Systems and Knowledge Engineering: Essential Elements of Advanced Information Technology*. Amsterdam: North Holland, (1986): 215-220.

Davies, B. J. and I. L. Darbyshire. "The Use of Expert Systems in Process-Planning." In *Annals of CIRP*, 33: (1984): 303-306.

DePorter, Elden L., J. M. Sepulveda, and Denise F. Jackson. "The Role of Expert Systems in Cybernetic Systems: An Application to Planning and Control of CIM Systems." Presented at the ORSA/TIMS Conference, St. Louis, Missouri, October 1987.

Dreyfus, Hubert L. *What Computers Can't Do: A Critique of Artificial Reason*. New York: Harper & Row, 1979.

Esogbue, Augustine O. "Dynamic Programming, Fuzzy Sets, and the Modeling of R & D Management Control Systems." *IEEE Transactions on Systems, Man, and Cybernetics*, SCM-13: 1 (January/February 1983): 18-30.

Fisher, E. L. "An AI-based Methodology for Factory Design." *AI Magazine* 7:4 (1986): 72-85.

Fox, M. S. "Callisto—An Intelligent System for Managing Large Projects," Research Report, Intelligent Systems Laboratory, Carnegie-Mellon University, 1987.

Fox, M. S. and S. F. Smith. "ISIS: A Knowledge Based System for Factory Scheduling." *Expert Systems Journal* 1:1 (1984): 25-49.

Freedman, R. S. and R. P. Frail. "OPGEN: The Evolution of an Expert System for Process Planning." *AI Magazine* 7: 5 (1987): 58-70.

French, S. *Scheduling and Sequencing*. New York: John Wiley, 1982.

Gardner, Howard. *The Mind's New Science*. New York: Basic Books, Inc., 1985.

Gieszl, L. R. "The Expert Applicability Question." In *Proceedings of the Conference on AI and Simulation: Simulation Series* 18: 3 (July 1987): 17-20.

Harmon, Paul and David King. *Expert Systems: Artificial Intelligence in Business*. New York: John Wiley & Sons, 1985.

Haugeland, John. *Artificial Intelligence, The Very Idea*. Cambridge, Massachusetts: The MIT Press, 1985.

Herrod, Richard A. "AI: Promises Start to Pay Off." *Manufacturing Engineering* (March 1988): 98-103.

Howard, Ronald. *Dynamic Probabilistic Systems*. New York: John Wiley & Sons, 1971.

Inagaki, S. "Assembly Robot Sensors Designed for Specific Tasks." *Journal of Electronic Engineering*, Tokyo, Japan. 20: 198 (1983): 85-89.

Knight, B., R. Endersby, and V. R. Voller. "The Use of Expert Systems in Industrial Control." *Measurement and Control* 17 (December 1984): 409-413.

Kumara, S. R. T., et al. "Expert Systems in Industrial Engineering." *International Journal of Production Research* 24: 5 (1986): 1107-1125.

Kusiak, Andrew. "Designing Expert Systems for Scheduling of Automated Manufacturing." *Industrial Engineering* 19: 7 (July 1987): 42-46.

Lozano-Perez, Tomas. "Automatic Planning of Manipulator Transfer Movements." *IEEE Transactions on Systems, Man, and Cybernetics*, SCM-11: 10 (October 1981): 681-698.

Malmborg, C. J., et al. "A Prototype Expert System for Industrial Truck Type Selection." *Industrial Engineering* (March 1987): 58-64.

Marshall, G., T. J. Barber, and J. T. Boardman. "Methodology for Modelling a Project Management Control Environment." *IEEE Proceeding-D: Control Theory and Applications*, 134D: 4 (July 1987): 278-285.

Mellichamp, J. M. and A. F. A. Wahab. "An Expert System for FMS Design." *Simulation* 48: 5 (May 1987): 201-208.

Mill, F. and S. Spraggett. "Artificial Intelligence for Production Planning." *Computer-Aided Engineering Journal* (December 1984): 210-213.

Miller, F. D., et al. "ACE: an Expert System for Preventive Maintenance Operations." *Record* (January 1986).

Minsky, M., ed. *Semantic Information Processing.* Cambridge, Massachusetts: The MIT Press, 1968.

Mishkoff, Henry C. *Understanding Artificial Intelligence.* Dallas, Texas: Texas Instruments Publishing Center, 1985.

Moralee, D.S. "The Use of Knowledge Engineering in an Industrial Research Environment—a Retrospect." *Expert System and Knowledge Engineering.* Amsterdam: 101-110, 1986.

Nau, S. D. and Tien-Chien Chang. "A Knowledge Based Approach to Generative Process Planning." Presented at the Symposium of Computer-Aided and Intelligent Process Planning, ASME Winter Meeting, Miami Beach, Florida, 1985.

_____. "Prospects for Process Selection using Artificial Intelligence." *Computers in Industry.* 4 (1983): 253-263.

Newell, Allen and H. A. Simon. "Computer Simulation of Human Thinking." *The RAND Corporation*, (April 20, 1961): 2276.

_____. *Human Problem-Solving.* Englewood Cliffs, New Jersey: Prentice-Hall, 1972.

Nida, K. et al. "Some Expert System Experiments in Process Engineering." *Chemical Engineering Research and Design* 64 (September 1986).

Nof, Shimon Y. "An Expert System for Planning/Replanning Programmable Facilities." *International Journal of Production Research* 22 (1984).

Pearl, Judea. *Heuristics: Intelligent Search Strategies for Computer Problem Solving.* Reading, Massachusetts: Addison-Wesley, 1984.

Pipitone, F. "The FIS Electronics Troubleshooting System." *BYTE* 19: 7 (1986): 68-76.

Preiss, K. and E. Kaplansky. "Automated Part Programming for CNC Milling by Artificial Intelligence Techniques." *Journal of Manufacturing Systems* 4:1 (1987): 51-63.

Rajaram, N. S. "Artificial Intelligence—The Achilles Heel of Robotics and Manufacturing." *Robotics Engineering* (January 1986): 10-15.

Schaffer, G. H. "Artificial Intelligence: a Tool for Smart Manufacturing." *American Machinist & Automated Manufacturing* 130:8 (1986): 83-94.

Schreiber, R. R. "Quality Control with Vision." *Vision* 2:4 (1985): 7-13.

Scown, Susan J. *The Artificial Intelligence Experience: An Introduction.* Digital Equipment Corporation, Maynard, Massachusetts: 1985.

Shannon, Claude E. "Programming a Computer for Playing Chess." *Philosophical Magazine,* Series 7. 41 (1950): 256-275.

Smith, S. F., M. S. Fox, and P. S. Ow. "Knowledge-Based Factory Scheduling Systems." *AI Magazine* 7: 4 (1986): 45-61.

Somby, Tom. "OKIE—Expert System for Trouble Shooting Computer Hardware." Presented at the Symposium on Artificial Intelligence, University of Oklahoma, Norman, November 2-3, 1987.

Szidarovszky, F., M. E. Gershon, and L. Duckstein. *Techniques for Multiobjective Decision Making in Systems Management.* New York: Elsevier, 1986.

Tou, J. T. "Design of Expert Systems for Integrated Production Automation." *Journal of Manufacturing Engineering* 4:2 (1987): 147-155.

Townsend, W. B. "Artificial Intelligence Techniques for Industrial Applications in Shop Scheduling." Master's thesis, Naval Postgraduate School, Monterey, California, June 1983.

Turban, Efraim. "Expert Systems - Another Frontier for Industrial Engineering." *Computers and Industrial Engineering* 10: 3 (1986): 222-235.

Villa, A., et al. "An Expert Control System for Tool Life Management in Flexible Manufacturing Cells." *Annals of CIRP* 34: 1 (1985): 87-90.

Walter, Eric. *Identifiability of State Space Models with Applications to Transformation Systems.* New York: Springer-Verlag, 1982.

Waterman, D. A. *A Guide to Expert Systems.* Reading, Massachusetts: Addison-Wesley, 1987.

Weiss, S. and C. A. Kulikowski. *A Practical Guide to Designing Expert Systems.* Totowa, New Jersey: Rowman & Allanheld, 1984.

Wolfgram, Deborah D., Teresa J. Dear, and Craig S. Galbraith. *Expert Systems for the Technical Professional.* New York: John Wiley and Sons, 1987.

Wynot, M. "Artificial Intelligence Provides Real-Time Control of DEC's Material Handling Process." *Industrial Engineering* (April 1986): 34-44.

Part III

Controlling and Operating the Automated Factory

THIS SECTION DETAILS THE TECHNIQUES USEFUL FOR EFFECTIVELY OPERATING IN AN automated manufacturing environment. The focus of this section is on the technologies that contribute to control and design of automated factories. The list of technologies detailed here is by no means comprehensive due to the diverse and dynamic nature of manufacturing technologies. Because of space constraints, we limited this section to technologies we thought were most relevant. Manufacturing research, however, is growing in momentum. Exciting new technologies and techniques are constantly being developed and thus, this list can only grow.

Guy M. Nicoletti describes networking standards and methodologies used in the implementation of flexible and cellular manufacturing in chapter 27. He emphasizes the hierarchical approach to building these systems. Standard network topologies and protocols are also presented, along with the principles of numerical control. The reader will find the section on fiber optics especially helpful since optical fibers are increasingly being used in the implementation of networks.

One of the major driving forces behind networking, and even behind examining manufacturing as a total system, is the large potential increase in productivity. Johnson A. Edosomwan, in chapter 28 on the meaning and measurement of productivity, describes types of productivity measures at the system or company level. He also details solution methodologies for measuring productivity.

Jayant Rajgopal and Maryanne Frabotta describe manufacturing resources planning as a technique that utilizes a database integrating all functional areas of a manufacturing concern in order to plan and conduct operations efficiently. Chapter 29 provides a valuable overview of the characteristics and operational procedures of a typical MRP-II system, along with implementation guidelines.

Steven Nahmias' chapter 30 presents another perspective on the material requirements problem in his discussion of inventory control models. The focus here is on the control of inventory of items having independent demand. Parameters affecting inventory cost are explained, along with deterministic and stochatic models for single and multiple products and echelons.

A major problem in the use of an MRP-II system is its interface with other components of an automated factory. In chapter 31, Edward A. Bowers emphasizes this important topic and describes the relationship between automated material handling systems and MRP-II. General system requirements are outlined and his contention that an effective automated material handling system must fit into the overall context of CIM environment is both valid and timely.

Thomas A. Mazzuchi and Refik Soyer introduce the concepts of reliability and life testing in chapter 32. Reliability parameters are explained along with the probability distributions used in reliability engineering. The authors also present techniques for assessing and monitoring the reliability of manufacturing software.

Andrew Kusiak's chapter 33 on production scheduling deals with the scheduling of operations on a shop floor that have a short- to mid-term planning horizon. He begins by presenting optimal solutions for scheduling multiple operations on a single machine. Since optimal solutions are not feasible for realistic solutions, a series of heuristic approaches are detailed. One of the most promising new approaches in the field of scheduling is the use of expert systems. Kusiak presents a comprehensive problem formulation, and computational results of a knowledge-based scheduling system.

In chapter 34, J. Bert Keats gives us a description of quality control issues in automated manufacturing. By focusing on specific quality issues and treatments, both statistical and managerial, the author provides a convincing case for repositioning quality as a vital part of the strategy for achieving manufacturing excellence. Only recently, opines the author, has U.S. management responded to off-shore challenges by dramatically changing the way that quality is perceived in manufacturing.

Industrial robots are an important component in automated programmable manufacturing systems. Sheikh Burhanuddin and Bopaya Bidanda detail the more popular geometric configurations of robots used in manufacturing in chapter 35. They explain the selection criteria for selecting industrial robots for specific applications, and describe the design process for developing a robotic workcell.

In chapter 36, Jacob Rubinovitz discusses the implementation and programming aspects of robots. He details roadblocks to flexibility in various application environments with special reference to robotic welding. The author covers issues dealing with flexible part handling, compliance, and programming for changing and partially unstructured environments. Possible solutions and future directions are indicated.

Work measurement not only has a rich tradition in the field of industrial and manufacturing systems engineering, but has also retained its preeminence over the years. Kjell B. Zandin, a pioneer in this field explains the technique he developed—the MOST system. His chapter 37 explains the rationale behind MOST, and principles and procedures for developing time standards based on this technique.

In direct contrast to the rich tradition of work measurement, the field of automatic identification is relatively new. However, during the last few years the use of automatic identification in manufacturing has risen dramatically. Benjamin Nelson's informative chapter 38 describes this new technology with an emphasis on bar codes.

27

Networking for Implementation of Flexible and Cellular Manufacturing Systems

Guy M. Nicoletti*

THIS DISCUSSION OF NETWORKING STANDARDS AND methods used to implement flexible and cellular manufacturing focuses on four main areas. These are as follows: hierarchical control of manufacturing systems, computer and direct numerical control operation, distributed communication systems, and manufacturing automation protocol.

HIERARCHICAL CONTROL OF MANUFACTURING SYSTEMS

The following paragraphs on hierarchical control define three important concepts: pyramid architecture, horizontal architecture, and parallel processing and fault tolerance.

The Pyramid Architecture

Pyramid architecture is computerization of one level of the manufacturing plant at a time. It starts with the MIS department's mainframe, the top of the corporate computing hierarchy. Computeriza-

tion then moves down through lower departments. It will reach the factory level and finally the cell level. An organization has a pyramid approach to computerization when traditional computers such as micro, supermicro, mini, supermini, and mainframes are selected on the basis of software availability.

This selection method leads, of course, to the installation of different—usually incompatible—types of computers and, at the factory level, creates the so-called *Islands of Automation*. The decentralized processing of the pyramid approach does have some positive features:

- Applications are distributed among several systems; failure of a single system does not involve the whole installation
- Response time is fairly adequate for nontime critical operations
- Backing in file transfer and data transmission is reduced to a minimum

*Guy M. Nicoletti is an Associate Professor of Electrical and Mechanical Engineering at the Greensburg Campus of the University of Pittsburgh where he also received pertinent M.S. and Ph.D. degrees. He is the author of several technical publications in the fields of computer integrated manufacturing, industrial communication and network systems, and factory automation; he has appeared as a speaker at related national and international conferences. Dr. Nicoletti is a member of IEEE and of SME; his research interests are in digital control systems and factory automation.

However, the pyramid architecture has several drawbacks:

- Greater cost and complexity
- The use of diverse and incompatible systems, thus thwarting the goals of CIM
- Systems incompatibility among different manufacturing processes, cells, and departments
- Computers run on different operating systems, use different data structure, and support different protocols, thus resulting in very expensive interfacing systems
- Substantial communication overhead
- Limited expansion capabilities, expansion range, and performance

The Horizontal Architecture

Horizontal architecture consists of three operational layers:

- Layer one or top layer—composed of large mainframe computers
- Layer two—a single layer of interconnected fault-tolerant computers; they perform various tasks, from shop floor control and inventory tracking, to engineering changes, control, and drawing management
- Layer three—an interconnection of fault-tolerant, real-time controllers; when a fault occurs, the faulty module is masked from the process; the error is displayed on the front panel as well as at various remote locations; continuity of process control is maintained while the errant module is removed and repaired or replaced.

The multiple processor nature of the horizontal architecture meets most of the goals and requirements of CIM:

- There is data integration, thus permitting a given application of access all of the data
- Multiple tasks can be handled simultaneously
- Multiple processor performance fosters fault-tolerant operation, which in turn guarantees data integrity, an important requirement for the paperless factory automation
- The size issue is removed—power and throughput expandability is attained by simply plugging in extra modules; thus, there is no practical upper limit to performance

Fundamentally then data-integration—the essence of CIM—is much more achievable with horizontal architecture and multiple parallel processors. FIGURES 27-1 AND 27-2 portray the two architectures.

If the automation system already exists in pyramid architecture system, then data integration and protocol translation involve costly and complex interfacing systems. The manufacturing automation protocol (MAP) simplifies interfacing problems.

Parallel Processing and Fault Tolerance

Parallel processing is a computer organization designed to maximize the throughput of computing devices by concurrent, overlapping, or parallel processing of a number of *words*. To parallel process a certain number of words under single instruction control, it is necessary to establish a set of processing elements (PE). A PE may be designed to contain a serial or a parallel arithmetic-logic unit (ALU). In serial design, operations are performed in *bit-slice* sequential manner. In parallel design, the PE performs parallel operations, and the associated processor is called the parallel processor. FIGURE 27-3 shows the basic organization of a parallel processor.

In parallel processing then, instructions and operands are fetched from different memories, while operands undergo certain preexecution manipulations. Accordingly, for each machine instruction there are four classes of operations:

- Instruction fetch
- Decode and address generation
- Operand fetch and data manipulation
- Execution

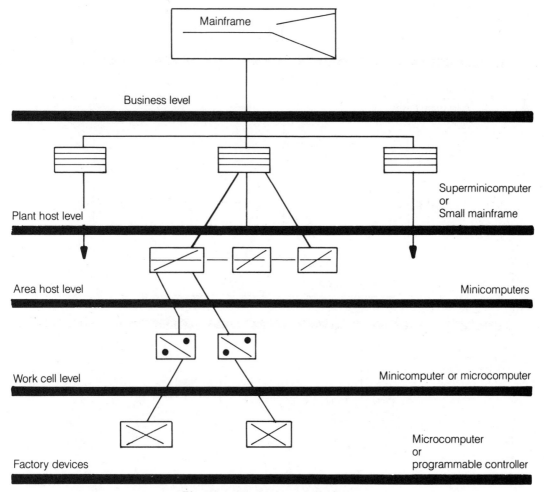

Fig. 27-1. The horizontal architecture.

Data manipulation is implemented via certain data manipulating functions (DMF). Essentially, DMF word manipulations are limited to shifts and masks. Bit-slice manipulating functions involve the following operations:

- Permuting—shift, flip, shuffle, transpose, merge, mix, bit-reverse sort, sort
- Replicating—multiplicate, duplicate
- Spacing—spread, compress, transfer

Characteristic manipulating functions are presented in FIG. 27-4. The DMF can be derived from users' specifications according to the particular application(s) at hand; thus, they are main criteria for parallel processor design.

Other main DMF functions are:

- Bridging between the hardware implementations and the associated language development
- Implementing important mathematical computations such as matrix operations, fast Fourier transform (FFT), and solutions to differential equations
- Executing signal processing, data compression, and multiple responses resolving for real time operation in industrial controls

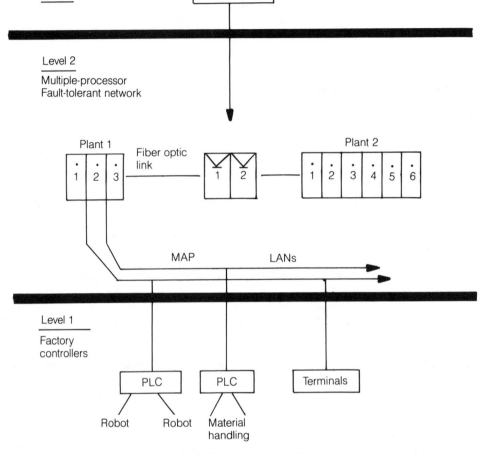

Fig. 27-2. The pyramid architecture.

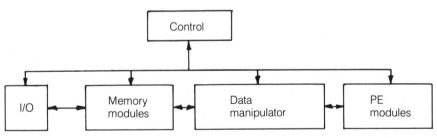

Fig. 27-3. Organization of parallel processor.

The appropriate introduction of data manipulators for parallel processors yields a reduction in the number of sequential operations during processing with subsequent improvement of throughput and hardware utilization, as well as reduced of memory storage space and increased system capability.

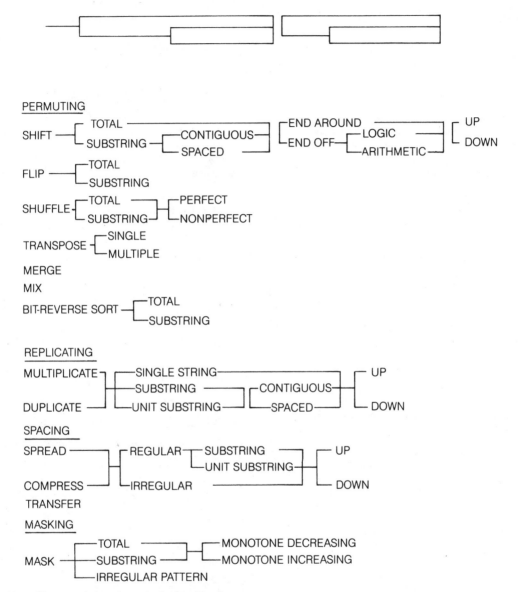

Fig. 27-4. Characteristics of manipulating function.

The most important design parameters for parallel processing are:

- The number of output gates (or communication paths) of each manipulator cell
- The number of control line groups
- The number of manipulator columns (or planes)
- The interconnection paths between cells

The design of a basic data manipulator consists of two fundamental steps: (1) identification of the common characteristics among the bit-slice and word manipulating functions, and (2) design and construction of the associated circuit with a minimum number of hardware components, yet with necessary flexibility for possible alteration according to varying needs.

Two data manipulators designs guarantee the above conditions. The *line manipulator* is a two-dimensional circuit configuration that operates one word or one bit-slice at a time. The *page manipulator* is a three-dimensional extension of the line manipulator and can manipulate a set of words as well as a set of bit-slices.

The design criteria of a data manipulator usually assume a parallel processor module consisting of $N = 2^n$ processing elements and a word width $M = 2^m$ where n is the number of logic cells and m is the number of bits in a word. A parallel multiprocessing system may require a rather large set of PEs and memory modules (MM). This requires multistage interconnection networks (MIN) built with several stages of 2-input 2-output switching elements (SE). The connectivity and the fault tolerance of these interconnections constitute an important problem for the reliable operation of the system. A fault-tolerant interconnection is one that can tolerate faults to some well-defined degree and still provide reliable communication between any input-output pair.

Fault-tolerance can be achieved in the following ways:

- Multiple path between an input/output pair
- Multiple pass routing
- Self-repair switching element
- On-line error correcting

It has been shown that fault tolerance can be achieved only if interconnecting networks of the parallel multiprocessing system can facilitate multiple-path, multiple-pass, and fault-tolerant switching elements.

Evidently then, fault-tolerance must be considered as one of the main factors in choosing a suitable interconnection circuit for the parallel system connection. Since the MINs are the heart of parallel systems, their fault tolerance is extremely impor-

tant. Certain considerations are vital to the design of efficient fault-tolerant systems. To realize a general model of the multistage interconnection network, one proceeds as follows:

- An N-input N-output MIN is constructed in several stages; each stage consists of $N/2$ SEs. Here $N = 2^n$, and n is the number of stages. Thus, an n-stage network will provide a path between each of the N-inputs and the N-outputs.
- The links between successive stages of the network are assigned so that each input can be connected to as many outputs as possible. This is shown in FIG. 27-5. The control lines are omitted for clarity.

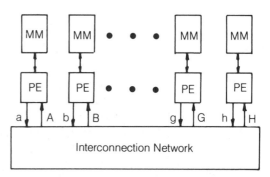

Fig. 27-5. Multistage interconnection network with control lines omitted.

The main objective is to construct a network with *dynamic full access capability* (DFA) so that under a given fault condition, each input of the network is connected to any one of the network outputs in a finite number of passes. The DFA capabilities of MINs are evaluated under stuck-at-faults at the control lines as well as at the inputs/outputs of the SEs.

An efficient fault-tolerant MIN must have DFA capability. The network is designed such that the DFA property is maintained for a maximum number of faults. A valid design procedure based on set theory consists of the following steps:

- The N-inputs N-outputs are partitioned into $N/(2^n)$ sets; each set consisting of 2^n inputs and 2^n outputs.

- The n-stages of the network are designed such that 2^n inputs of one set can be connected to 2^n outputs of another set.

This design scheme yields two important results:

- Each set will consist of n stages, where each stage is formed with 2^{n-1} SEs.
- Each subnetwork becomes a fully connected network of size 2^n input and 2^n output.

In the fault-free partition of $n*2^{n-1}$ SEs connecting 2^n inputs and corresponding outputs, any input can access any one of its outputs in only one pass. If some or all SEs have single faults at the control lines or at the input/output lines, except at the primary input/output lines, then for each partitioned group consisting of $fn*2^{n-1}$ SEs connecting 2^n inputs and corresponding output lines, each rimary input line can be connected to at least one of the primary output lines.

In conclusion, the selection of the connection pattern seems to be the key factor in the minimization process of the path length of the MINs. However, when fault tolerance is considered simultaneously with minimization of path length, the optimization problem of the MINs becomes rather complex.

COMPUTER AND DIRECT NUMERICAL CONTROL OPERATION

Computer numerical control (CNC) is a computerized version of numerical control (NC). A dedicated stored-program computer performs most of the basic NC functions by means of control programs stored in the RAM section of the computer.

The major contribution of CNC machines is an increase of productivity in terms of efficient editing of part programs, faster cycle time, and general programming optimization.

Direct numerical control (DNC) allows NC programs to be downloaded from the memory of a central computer to the memories of a group of interconnected CNC machines. The connection between the central computer and the individual CNCs in the system is maintained only for the time required to transmit NC programs.

Direct numerical control may be integrated with computer aided design systems. When properly designed, DNC yields benefits such as efficient control of manufacturing operations and optimization of production efficiency.

CNC Operation

The microprocessor and the control unit are the nerve center of a CNC operating system. FIGURE 27-6 shows the basic components of a CNC system. Fundamentally, the operation of a CNC system consists of a bidirectional interfacing of the control unit with the human operator and the CNC machine as shown in FIG. 27-7. The control unit performs real time functions related to the implementation of the process at hand such as sequencing and cycle times. The ultimate objective of the controller is to guarantee an orderly and efficient execution of the programmed instructions. There are two main control systems: hard-wired controls and soft-wired controls.

Hard-wired Controls   The hard-wired control system consists of printer circuit boards (PCB), where the particular control logic is wired as a permanent, built-in circuit. The PCB is a plug-in unit implemented in medium-scale integration (MSI);

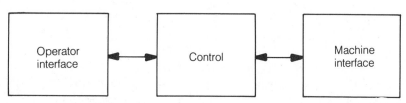

Fig. 27-6. Basic computer numerical control operating system.

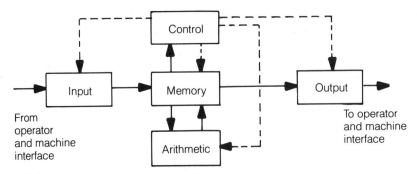

Fig. 27-7. Computer numerical control interfacing system.

the "back-plane" that receives the PCB is also hard-wired. The hard-wired control is designed to accomplish specific operations and, if changes are desired, tedious and costing wiring modifications are necessary. True CNC systems are built with hard-wired controls.

Soft-wired Controls   The soft-wired control system is characterized by the inclusion of a programmable control unit such as a mini or microcomputer with appropriate RAM, and EPROM sections to replace the fixed-logic circuit of the hard-wired PCB. Thus, any required logic, as well as computer instructions, are totally programmable and storable. The combination of storage logic and computer instructions is known as the *application software*. The application software program can be modified or totally changed according to the particular application process at hand.

CNC Programming

Because of the high level of computer sophistication incorporated in the CNC system, relatively complex workpieces can be programmed directly at the machine tool using manual-data-input (MDI) instructions. In advanced cases, operators can input off-line computer-assisted programming instructions by means of special commands at the machine tool using MDI techniques.

When in MDI mode, a part program can be directly entered into the processor using the keyboard on the control. A Cathode-Ray Tube (CRT) displays program entries expressed in compact,

easy-to-use, powerful commands. The entries are displayed on the CRT in an easily read format primarily designed to interactively guide the operator. MDI principal operating modes are:

- Automatic execution of a sequence of programmed machining operations
- Execution of a single program segment at a time
- On site program editing
- Instant display of programs
- Set up procedures
- Entry of offsets such as cutters, and tool length compensation
- Recording of programs on external devices such as tapes and disks
- Loading of programs from external devices
- Automatic tool change
- Loading of CAD generated geometries and automatic translation of coordinates into MDI code

MDI controls have programming capability compatible with typical NC and CNC control functions:

- Part and tool positioning
- Fixing (canned) cycles (drill, counterbore, etc.)
- Linear interpolation
- Circular interpolation
- Rectangular interpolation
- Circular poket milling
- Event programming
- Dwell programming
- Subroutine accessing
- Part surface programming

Part surface programming is also used to simulate the entire machining process. Once the part geometry is entered in the CNC control, operators need only to enter the diameter of the cutter; then the controller automatically generates the tool path for the entire removal of metal as specified by the part program. This part programmed tool path is illustrated in FIG. 27-8.

As mentioned earlier, the functions controlling CNC are part of the MDI operations and are displayed on the CRT in a preset format. A sample format is presented in FIG. 27-9. This programming format is formally known as word address format. It is used as the format for MDI on all CNC machines. The program lines (blocks) may vary in length according to the information contained in them. The block format for word address is as follows:

N...G..X....Y...Z....I...J....K....F....S....T..M..

Only the information needed on a line need be given; the format's flexibility accepts two axis or three axis machining part programming. Each of the letters is called an address (or word). The various words designate the following meanings:

N—The start of a block or "sequence line."

G—Information of a preparatory function. Preparatory functions change the control mode of the machine. Preparatory functions are commonly called G codes.

X—The X-axis coordinate. X can also designate a time interval for a timed dwell.

Y—The Y-axis coordinate.

Z—The Z-axis coordinate.

I—The X-coordinate of an arc centerpoint.

J—The Y-coordinate of an arc centerpoint.

K—The Z-coordinate of an arc centerpoint.

S—Sets the RPM of the spindle.

F—Assigns the feedrate.

T—Specifications of tool data in a tool change operation.

M—Initiation of miscellaneous functions. M functions control auxiliary functions such as turning on and off the spindle and coolant, initiation of tool changes, and signaling of END program.

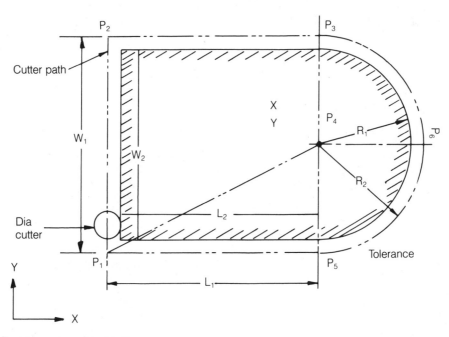

Fig. 27-8. Part programmed tool path.

N	G	X(U)	Z(W)	I	K	F	S,T,M
	I						
0104							
N001	G00	X800	Z2000				
N002		X250	Z100				M41
N003			Z53				S120 M03 M08
N004			Z43				
N005	G01	X205				F0.3	
N006	G00	X250	Z50				
N007			Z40				
N008	G01	X205				F0.25	
N009	G00	X230	Z58				
N010		X192					
N011	G01		Z48			F0.4	
N012		X200					
N013			Z40				
N014	G001	X210	Z49				
N015		X196					
N016	G01						

Fig. 27-9. MDI program format for CNC.

A list of the most commonly used G-codes and M-functions for two-axis CNC turning and three-axis milling are presented in the following lines.

Two-Axis Turning G-Codes.
NOTE: ENGLISH (INCH) FORMAT IS x.xxx FOR X AND xx.xxx FOR Z and xx.x FOR F. METRIC FORMAT IS xx.xx FOR X and xxx.xx FOR Z AND xxx for F.

G CODE PREPARATORY FUNCTION	FORMAT
G00 - RAPID TRAVERSE	N3/G00/Xq4/Za5/F3
G01 - LINEAR INTERPOLATION	N3/g01/XQ4/ZQ5/F3
G02 - CIRCULAR INTERPOLATION CW	N3/G02/Xq4/Zq5/F3
G03 - CIRCULAR INTERPOLATION CCW	N3/G03/Xq4/Zq5/F3
G04 - DWELL	N3/Gp4/X4...DWELL TIME IN 1/100 SECONDS
G21 - EMPTY BLOCK	N3/G21
G24 - RADIUS PROGRAMMING	N000/G24...MUST BE IN BLOCK 0
G25 - SUBROUTINE CALL	N3/G25/L3...L APPEARS IN F COLUMN
G27 - JUMP INSTRUCTION	N3/G27/L3...L APPEARS IN F COLUMN
G33 - THREAD - CONSTANT PITCH	N3/G33/K3...K APPEARS IN F COLUMN
G73 - CHIP BREAK CYCLE	N3/G73/Zq5/F3
G78 - THREAD CYCLE	N3/G78/Xq4/Zq5/K3/H3...K APPEARS IN F COLUMN
G84 - ROUGH TURNING CYCLE	N3/G84/Xq4/Zq5/F3/H3
G85 - REAMING CYCLE	N3/G85/Zq5/F
G86 - GROOVING CYCLE	N3/G86/Xq4/Zq5/F3/H3
G88 - FACING CYCLE	N3/G88/Xq4/Zq5/F3/H3

G89 - REAMING/DRILLING CYCLE	N3/G89/Zq5/F3
G90 - ABSOLUTE PROGRAMMING	N3/G90
G91 - INCREMENTAL PROGRAMMING	N3/G91
G92 - ABSOLUTE PROGRAMMING-SET REGISTERS	N3/G92/Xq4/Zq5
G94 - FEED IN MM/MIN OR IN/MIN	N3/G94
G95 - FEED IN MM/REV OR IN/REV	N3/G95
G64 - FEED MOTORS OFF	
G65 - MAGNETIC TAPE OPERATION	
G66 - RS232 OPERATION	

Two-Axis Turning M Functions.

M00 - PROGRAMMED STOP.....N3/M00
M03 - SPINDLE ON CW.....N3/MO3
M05 - SPINDLE OFF.....N3/MO3
M06 - TOOL CHANGE....N3/M06,Xq4/Zq5/13
M17 - RETURN TO MAIN PROGRAM.....N3/M17
M98 - FOR AXES PLAY COMPENSATION.....N3/M98/X3/Z3
M99 - CIRCULAR INTERPOLATION
(USE wG02,G03 ON PARTIAL ARCS).....N3/M99/I4/K5

SWITCHING EXITS.....N3/M2

M08   M09   M22
M23   M26

Three-Axis Milling G Codes.

NOTE: ENGLISH (INCH) FORMAT IS 4 DIGITS FOR X,Y AND Z (VERTICAL OR HORIZONTAL).

G CODE   PREPARATORY FUNCTION

G00 - RAPID TRAVERSE
      G01 - LINEAR INTERPOLATION
      G02 - CIRCULAR INTERPOLATION CW
      G03 - CIRCULAR INTERPOLATION CCW
      G72 - POCKET CYCLE
      G92 - OFFSET OF REFERENCE POINT
      G04 - DWELL - N3/G04
      G21 - EMPTY BLOCK - N3/G21
      G25 - SUB-ROUTINE CALL - N3/G25/L(F)3
      G27 - JUMP INSTRUCTION - N3/G27/L(F)3
      G81 - FIXED BORING - N3/G81/Zq5/F3
      G82 - FIXED BORING - w/DWELL - N3/G82/Zq5/F3
      G83 - FIXED BORING - w/CHIP REMOVAL - N3/G83/Zq5/F3
      G84 - THREAD CUTTING - N3/G84/K3/Zq5/F3
      G85 - FIXED REAMING - N3/G85/Zq5/F3
      G89 - FIXED REAMING - w/DWELL - N3/G89/zQ5/F3
      G90 - ABSOLUTE PROGRAMMING - N3/G90
      G91 - INCREMENTAL PROGRAMMING - N3/G91
      G74 - THREAD CUTTING (LEFT HAND) - N3/G74/K3/Zq5/F3
      G64 - FEED MOTORS OFF...G65 - MAGNETIC TAPE...G66 - RS232...
           PRESS RETURN
      G40 - TOOL RADIUS COMP. CANCEL - N3/G40
      G45 - ADD TOOL RADIUS - N3/G45
      G46 - SUBTRACT TOOL RADIUS - N3/G46
      G47 - ADD TOOL RADIUS TWICE - N3/G47
      G48 - SUBTRACT TOOL RADIUS TWICE - N3/G48

VERTICAL (METRIC)

N3/G00/Xq5/Yq4/Zq5
N3/G01/Xq5/Yq4/Zq5/F3
N3/G02/Xq5/Yq4/Zq5/F3
N3/G03/Xq5/Yq5/F3
N3/G72/Xq5/Yq4/Zq5/F3
N3/G92/Xq5/Yq4/Zq5

HORIZONTAL (METRIC)

N3/G00/Xq4/Yq4/Yq5/Zq5
N3/G01/Xq4/Yq5/Zq5/F3
N3/G02/Xq4/Yq5/Zq5/F3
N3/GP3/Xq4/Yq5/Zq5/F3
N3/G72/Xq4/Yq5/Zq5/F3
N3/g92/Xq4/Yq5/Zq5

Three-Axis Milling.
M00 - DWELL.....N3/M00
M03 - SPINDLE ON CW.....N3/M03
M05 - SPINDLE OFF.....N3/M05
M06 - TOOL OFFSET (CUTTER RADIUS).....N3/M06/D5/S4/Zq5/T3
M17 - RETURN TO MAIN PROGRAM.....N3/M17
M30 - PROGRAM END.....N3/M30
M99 - CIRCULAR INTERPOLATION
       (USE w/G02,G03 ON PARTIAL ARCS.....N3/M99/J2/K2

SWITCHING EXITS.....N3/M2
M08   M09   M20
M21   M22   M23
M26 - SWITCHING EXIT - IMPULSE.....N3/M26/H3

CNC Functions

The auto-programming function (AP) instructs the CNC to automatically generate a tool path to produce the required part contour. The program comprising the dimension data of the final contour is prepared as the control definition program (CDP). When the CDP is called and specific data for a rough cycle are given, the control automatically generates tool path for rough and finishing cycles respectively. Thus, the programmer can complete the part program simply by entering the dimensions specified in an engineering drawing. APs are possible for two-axis CNC lathes (turning centers), as well as for multiaxis CNC milling (machining centers). The following refer to CNC lathe auto-programming.

G codes to designate cutting mode:

G85—AP Mode I used to call the bar turning rough cut cycle

G86—AP Mode II used to call for copy turning mode

G87—Finish cut cycle

G88—AP Mode III for continuous thread cutting cycle

These codes are used in combination with contour specification. The G codes correlated to the AP modes are:

G81—Starts the longitudinal contour definition

G82—Starts the transverse (on end face) contour definition

G80—End of contour definition

The associated M-functions are:

M32—Straight infeed along thread face in G88
M33—Zigzag infeed in G88
M73—Infeed pattern 1 in G88
M74—Infeed pattern 2 in G88
M73—Infeed pattern 3 in G88

The tool paths generated by the three principal AP modes are portrayed by FIG. 27-10.

Interactive graphics MDI functions (IGF) facilitate the generation of the part program of a workpiece having any contour in which straight lines, tapers, and arcs are combined in the field. The con-

trol automatically determines cutting conditions. CNC data can be created from IGF data. Actual cutting of the part is performed with the generated CNC data, which is also used for checking tool paths. The data entry process for graphic editing functions is performed via CRT interaction as follows:

1. IGF mode is first activated.
2. The material type is selected from a displayed material table. The material table is called from the material data.
3. Length and diameter of the blank together with

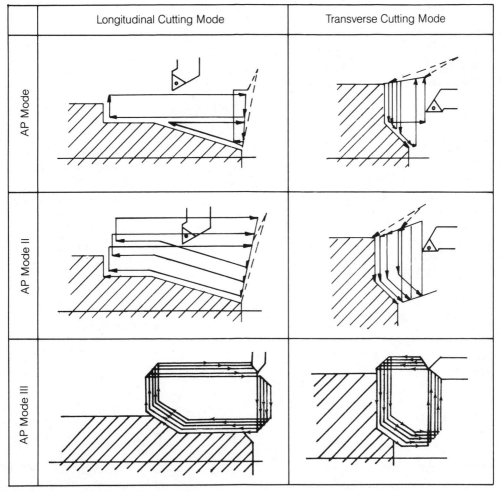

Fig. 27-10. Auto programming tool path modes.

the coordinates of the programming zero are entered.

4. Data defining part contour for respective cutting processes are entered next.

The MDI process is completed and the CRT shows the final contour of the part to be machined. The operator subsequently enters tool data. Corresponding G-codes and F-functions are automatically generated for machining operation. Specific IGF structure and MDI interaction sequence are characteristics of the particular CNC machine at hand.

Economic Justification of CNC

Justification of CNC installations is best compiled in terms of economics and technical and production efficiency. Typical benefits can be attained in the following areas:

- Direct labor
- Tool and fixture cost
- Consumable tool cost
- Inventory carrying cost
- Tool setting cost
- Programming cost
- Maintenance cost
- Planning, flexibility, and scheduling
- Machine utilization
- Tool standardization
- Interchangeability of work, tools, etc.

Direct Numerical Control Operations

Data transmission and the system adopted for data transmission are the heart of DNC installations. A major operating goal of DNC systems is to optimize the operating performance of the communication network. The principal optimization parameters are as follows:

- Minimize the number of idle machines during data transmission cycles
- Minimize operator idle time due to DNC computer response cycle

- Ensure efficient interface of all CNC machines in the DNC system

The operating parameters of a DNC system are:

- Production schedule
- Running time of CNC programs
- Tool requirement for part machining
- Tool replacement after tool failure or wear
- Data on the logistics of program distribution
- Meantime between failures
- Diagnostics of downtime duration and causes
- Analysis of machine utilization
- Diagnostic of machine loading and unloading sequences

Essentially, the operation of a DNC system is characterized in terms of machine design interface, software features, control design specifications, and distributive network efficiency.

DNC Applications

DNC systems are most suitable where significantly large amounts of control data must be managed, stored, and distributed according to well-defined logistic patterns. The DNC concept is effectively employed as the controlling center for flexible manufacturing systems and flexible manufacturing cells, where a number of CNC machining centers are linked by means of electronic data transmission and mechanical automation.

Direct numerical control can also serve as the control and data distribution center for manufacturing systems configured according to group technology criteria for manufacturing parts or families of machines.

Computer vs. Direct Numerical Control

Computer numerical controls are separate and yet correlated manufacturing entities. CNC fits well into manufacturing systems characterized by mid-volume production. CNC machines attain highest productivity when the spindles turning period is such that chip making time is maximized. DNC can play a significant role to achieve this objective through its capability to sense the operating conditions of the various CNC machines through feedback, error diagnostics, and corrective actions.

CNC is a dedicated, localized, automated production. DNC is distributed automated production; it is capable of creating versatile systems that can produce diverse parts, and adapt to different mixes, variations or part types, and lot size.

DISTRIBUTED COMMUNICATION SYSTEMS

Data communication is the orderly transfer of information between two points positioned at any arbitrary distance from one another. Information is transferred via a communication network system. There are two types of networks to transfer information, local area networks (LAN) and wide area networks (WAN).

Local denotes networks limited to a few kilometers in length. *Wide* refers to networks for interconnection of points between very distant geographical areas such as cities and regions, and also to satellite communication between continental stations.

Protocols

The orderly transfer of information is accomplished by a network protocol; a *protocol* is a set of rules to which both endpoints adhere during the transmission and reception of the information. Several types of network protocols are available. The most fundamental and their characteristics will be discussed here.

Data Link Layer Protocols The portion of the network entrusted with the reliability, activation, and maintenance of the physical links is called the data link layer. The protocol can be classified as either bit oriented or byte oriented. In turn, there are many variations within each of these classifications, each defined by standards organizations such as the International Telegraph and Telephone Consultative Committee (CCITT), the Institute of Electrical and Electronics Engineers (IEEE) 802 Committees, and the American National Standards

Institute (ANSI). Other variations are proprietary protocols defined by data communications enterprises or computer manufacturers.

Byte Oriented Protocols In byte oriented protocols, messages or frames are transmitted in blocks or packets. Each block includes a header field, an information field, and a trailer field. Well-defined control characters are used as field delimiters, and they occur as a two character sequence, the first of which is the ASCII control character DLE. Important types of byte oriented protocols are IBM's Binary Synchronous Communications (BiSinc) and DEC's Digital Data Communication Message Protocol (DDCMP). FIGURE 27-11 shows the format of a byte oriented protocol.

Byte oriented protocols are inherently simple, and are suitable for simple man-machine interactions such as terminal data entry, and are implemented over half-duplex type channels.

Bit Oriented Protocols Bit oriented protocol frames are characterized by the format shown in FIG. 27-12. Bit oriented protocols are very suitable for high-speed computer-to-computer interconnections inherent in distributed processing such as real time data transmission for industrial communications.

The ISO OSI Protocol Model

Effective data communications between end nodes in a network can be established only if each end node can understand and apply a consistent set of services (protocols) to the data to be exchanged between them. The framework for the development of such a nonproprietary protocol is found in the International Standard Organization (ISO) Open System Interconnection (OSI) Model.

The ISO OSI model consists of seven layers of well-defined services. Each layer is responsible for providing specific services to the layer above it while requesting necessary services from the layer below it. Since the services at each layer are well defined, they can be applied consistently by each station (node) in the network. This layered structure of protocolled services allows for the interconnection of equipment from different vendors.

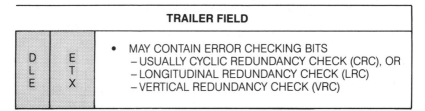

HEADER FIELD									
S Y N C	S Y N C	D L E	S O H	ADDRESSES	BLOCK SEQUENCE NUMBER	FRAME CONTROL	ACK/ NACK/ WACK	D L X	S T X

INFORMATION FIELD

- VARIABLE LENGTH
- CONTAINS DATA TRANSMITTED IN NORMAL OR TRANSPARENT MODES
- MAY NOT BE CONTAINED IN CONTROL MESSAGES

TRAILER FIELD

D L E	E T X	• MAY CONTAIN ERROR CHECKING BITS
		  – USUALLY CYCLIC REDUNDANCY CHECK (CRC), OR
		  – LONGITUDINAL REDUNDANCY CHECK (LRC)
		  – VERTICAL REDUNDANCY CHECK (VRC)

Fig. 27-11. Byte oriented protocol message format.

FLAG	ADDRESS	CONTROL	INFORMATION	FCS	FLAG
ONE OCTET	ONE OR MORE OCTETS	ONE OR MORE OCTETS	0 OR MORE BITS (OR OCTETS IF ALIGNED)	TWO OR FOUR OCTETS	ONE OCTET

Fig. 27-12. Bit oriented protocol message format (Frame Format).

TABLE 27-1 presents the general peer-to-peer services provided by each station in the ISO model.

Operationally, the delivery of data to a particular application program takes place as follows: the OSI protocol acts upon the data at each level to provide frames to the network. Headers applied at each OSI level build up the frames. These frames are then made available to the physical medium as a set of bits so that they can be transmitted through the medium. A reverse process takes place in order to provide the application data to the application program at the receiving station. FIGURE 27-13 shows the OSI data delivery process.

The Department of Defense Protocol

The Department of Defense (DOD) has chosen to develop its own protocol so that it can secure efficient, cost-effective communications among its many heterogeneous computers. The system is commonly referred to as the *DOD Protocol Architecture* (DPA). Fundamental differences between the DPA and the OSI model include the concept of hierarchy versus layering, the importance of internetworking, the utilization of connectionless services, and the approach to management functions. DPA's protocol is organized into four layers:

Table 27-1. The ISO/OSI Protocol Model

Layer	Layer Functions
Application	Provides the service elements to process the exchanged information. Services include resource sharing, file transfer, and database management
Presentation	Provides services necessary to format exchanged data and manage session dialog
Session	Establishes and terminates connections; arbitrates user rights to services; synchronizes data transfers
Transport	Provides functions for error-free delivery of messages such as flow control, error recovery, and acknowledgment
Network	Provides transparent routing of messages between two transport entities
Datalink	Provides rules for transmission on the physical medium such as: packet formats, access rights, errror detection and correction
Physical	Provides mechanical and electrical level interconnection for stations

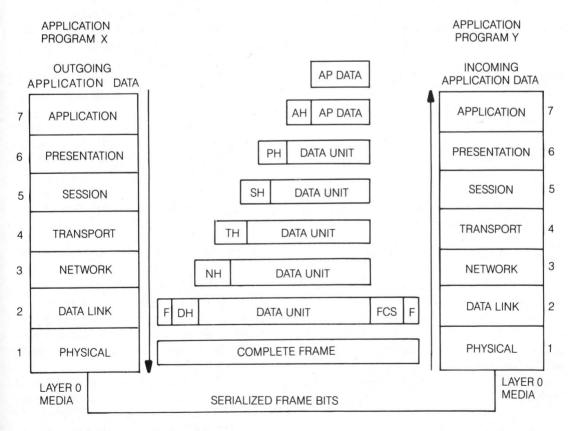

Fig. 27-13. The OSI data delivery process.

the network access, internet, host-host, and process/application layers.

Integrated Services Digital Networking

ISDN is based on all-digital networks. ISDN is a projected worldwide public telecommunications network intended to service a wide variety of user needs. The ISDN will be defined by standardization of user interfaces, and will be implemented as a set of digital switches and paths capable of supporting a wide range of traffic types.

The key objectives of ISDN are:

- Standardization, to permit universal access to the network with a variety of cost-effective equipment
- Transparency, to give users the freedom to develop application protocols within the ISDN concept
- Separation of competitive functions
- Leased and switched services
- Cost-related tariffs
- Smooth migration; the graceful migration toward ISDN of evolving networks with existing equipment and services
- Multiplexed support

The services of ISDN are:

- Facsimile, for transmission and reproduction of graphics, hand-written, and printed material
- Teletex, to exchange correspondence
- Videotex, to offer the capability to transmit a page of data in one second at 9.6 kbps

The transmission structure of any access link will be derived from the following types of channels: *B channel*, 64 kbps; *D channel*, 16 kbps; *C channel*, 8 or 16 kbps; and *A channel*, 4 kHz analog. Of special significance is the inclusion of the B channel. This channel will be designated as the standard user's channel and will carry the following types of traffic:

- PCM-encoded digital voice

- Digital data for circuit-switched or packet-switched applications
- A mix of digital data and digitized voice encoded at a fraction of 64 kbps

ISDN is rapidly approaching reality; there is already an every increasing number and variety of interfacing ICs on the market to facilitate ISDN compatible circuit boards, and off-the-shelf equipment.

Local Area Networks

A local area network is a communications medium that allows computers, terminals, and other intelligent digital devices located in a limited geographic area to be interconnected for the purpose of sharing data and other common resources.

The Institute of Electrical and Electronic Engineers (IEEE) formed the 802 working committee with the charter to formulate standards for local area networks. Standard approved by the committee are forwarded to the International Standards Organization (ISO) through the American National Standards Institute (ANSI) and the U.S. Department of Commerce.

The IEEE 802 committee consists of several working subgroups entrusted with the formulation of distinct but interrelated requirements for local area networks. These subcommittees are identified with the code 802.X, where X assumes values from 1 to 9. A brief description of the subcommittees follows.

- IEEE 802.1 For LAN management and networking.
- IEEE 802.2 For logical link control (LLC) and media access control (MAC) sublayers. The MAC sublayer of the data link layer is typically implemented in silicon. The MAC sublayer interfaces with the Physical Layer and itself consists of various sublayers.
- IEEE 802.3 For the MAC sublayer known as carrier sense multiple access with collision detection (CSMA/CD)
- IEEE 802.4 For token bus control

- IEEE 802.5 For token ring control
- IEEE 802.7 Broadband technical advisory group
- IEEE 802.8 Fiber optic technical advisory group
- IEEE 802.9 For integrated voice/data

The heart of a local area network is the data link layer. This layer consists of two sublayers: the logical link control (LLC) sublayer, and the media access control (MAC) sublayer. These sublayers will be analyzed next.

The Logical Link Control Sublayer The logical link control sublayer provides a common set of services to the network layers of the OSI model. Three types of services exist:

Type 1—Unacknowledged connectionless (or Datagram). Type 1 is a set of services that allows peer entities to transmit data to each other in a connectionless mode. The connection oriented services are provided by the upper layers of the OSI model.

Type 2—Connection oriented. Type 2 consists of a set of services that permit peer entities to establish, use and terminate connection at the data link layer in order to transmit information. In this mode, the data link layer provides services for the transmission and reception of frames.

Type 3—Acknowledged Connectionless (or single frame). Type 3 is a set of services which gives a peer entity the ability to send data and to request data from another peer entity and then to receive acknowledgment and data (if requested). LLCs are usually implemented in software or firmware, often with the aid of features provided in MAC silicon implementation.

The Media Access Control Sublayers The various MAC sublayers and physical layers provide the mechanisms which allow users to share the various networks. These mechanisms are governed by the following protocols.

IEEE 802.3 CSMA/CD. This protocol is a derivative of the original Ethernet specification developed by Xerox; it is presently supported by Digital Equipment Corporation. CSMA/CD allows any end station to access the network when needed in order to transmit a frame. This freedom of network access is offset by the ever present probability of collision between data from various stations attempting to transmit simultaneously. Thus, CSMA/CD is primarily a probabilistic system. For this reason, the system includes a collision detector (CD) mechanism. However, CD causes a roundtrip propagation delay; this is minimized by limiting the physical size of the network.

For these reasons, CSMA/CD is not suitable for networks which service real time operations. It is possible to link several 10 megabits per second (mbps) baseband CSMA/CD 500 meters LAN segments using baseband repeaters in order to extend the size of the network; however, cost-effectiveness is somewhat questionable. A broadband modulation option is also available for CSMA/CD.

In broadband networks, all stations transmit on allocated coaxial cable TV-channels using 6 MHz bandwidth, and receive on another set of channels. The frequency translation and retransmission from the transmission channel (upchannel) to the reception channel (downchannel) is handled by the headend remodulator. A separate collision channel

Table 27-2. Physical Layer Characteristics of IEEE 802.3

IEEE 802.3 Version	Referred to as	Signalling Rate	Segment Length	Media
1Base5	Starlan	1 Mbps	500 meters	Telephone twisted pair
10Base2	Cheapernet	10 Mbps	200 meters	Thin coaxial cable
10Base5	Ethernet (incorrectly)	10 Mbps	500 meters	High grade coaxial cable
10Base36	Broadband CSMA/CD	10 Mbps	3750 meters	Cable television cable

is required in broadband CSMA/CD to ensure fairness of the protocol with the characteristics of broadband modulation. TABLE 27-2 summarizes the technical characteristics of various systems of the Ethernet family of LANs.

IEEE 802.4 Token Passing Bus General Motors Corporation, and the Manufacturing Automation Protocol (MAP) User Group have sponsored and adopted the Token Passing Bus protocol as the primary protocol for industrial automation. The IEEE 802.4 protocol is based on the token passing network access method applied to a bus network topology. The protocol is designed to interface with both broadband and carrierband physical layers. The token consists of a unique MAC frame that is circulated from station to station in descending order based on station address, with the lowest order addressed station on the LAN sending the token to the highest order addressed station on the LAN.

The cyclical passing of the token forms a logical ring in which each station knows both its previous station and its next station. Stations are assigned parameters which control their mode of access to the network. The principal parameters are:

- Slot time, used to set access arbitration parameters
- Station token holding time, to enable control of the worst case time for any station to gain access to the network

The system can implement these parameters at all times and for every station. The access method of the token passing bus is characterized as deterministic. The deterministic performance of the access control can be further enhanced by implementing four levels of priority at the MAC level.

The token passing algorithm is as follows:

1. An end station received the token (an enabling word).
2. If the end station wishes to transmit, it starts transmission from the highest priority queue

first (if that option is implemented), and continues to transmit data frames until the station has no more data to transmit or until it has held the token for a maximum allotted programmed token time.
3. The station then transmits (passes) the token to the next station in the logical ring.
4. All stations perform maintenance functions such as ring initialization, station addition to the logical ring, station deletion from the logical ring, and error recovery.

The physical layer of the IEEE 802.4 token passing bus uses two main transmission rates: 10 Mbps broadband and 5 Mbps carrierband. Broadband token bus channels require a 12 MHz upchannel and a 12 MHz downchannel bandwidths employing ordinary modulation. Carrierband token bus channel uses phase-coherent (FSK) modulation. Actually, carrierband is baseband with modulation where modulation is employed to maximize noise immunity over the standard coaxial cable. Both broadband and carrierband can use various forms of standard 75 Ohm coaxial cables.

IEEE 802.5 Token Passing Ring. The token ring access method has been promoted by IBM for connectivity into IBM networks. Basically, IEEE 802.5 has the following characteristics.

An end station gains access to the network when it acquires control of the token that is circulating on the ring. The token consists of a unique 24-bit control signal that circulates on the ring following each message transfer. There is only one token on the ring at a time. Possession of the token gives a station exclusive use of the network for transmission of data. The token ring passing ring is deterministic; it supports priority access with seven user priority levels that can be assigned to the token.

The physical layer of the token ring method uses a 4 Mbps baseband channel with Manchester encoded data. The physical layout adopts star-wired ring topology, where stations are wired to a central wiring closet but are still connected to each other in a ring structure.

Network Topologies

There are five most commonly used network topologies. These will be described next.

In the *star topology*, each node is directly connected to the central node of the network. All communications between remote nodes must pass through the central node. Star networks are commonly adopted for implementation of point-to-point protocols such as X.25. See FIG. 27-14.

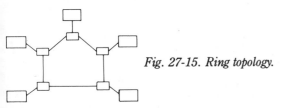

Fig. 27-14. Star topology.

In the *ring topology*, each node is connected only to its two adjacent neighbors. Thus any data transmission between two stations not directly connected to each other, must be routed through the intermediate stations. The IEEE 802.5 token ring protocol and the ANDI X3T9.5 Fiber Distributed Data (FDDI) protocol are ring topology connections. See FIG. 27-15.

Fig. 27-15. Ring topology.

Bus topology consists of a linear run of cable, where each station is connected directly to the main cable. Bus topologies are characterized by important operational features:

- Bidirectional transmission of data from any station on the bus
- Flexible configuration for almost any physical environment
- Easy expansion of the transmission system
- Easy installation for workgroup type settings; this makes the bus topology particularly useful

for industrial as well as office networking where a central cable system is a design requirement

The IEEE 802.3 Carrier Sense Multiple Access with Collision Detection (CSMA/CD), and the IEEE 802.4 Token Bus protocols are bus topology systems. FIGURE 27-16 shows this configuration.

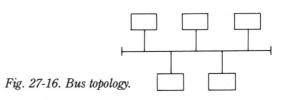

Fig. 27-16. Bus topology.

Hierarchical topology is known also as tree topology. Its configuration utilizes several layers with multiple nodes at a lower level connected to a single node at the next higher level. These nodes are then linked to upper hierarchical nodes. The main operational features are: (1) combination of the tasks of lower nodes in the hierarchy into an integrated functional system, and (2) suitability to order entry systems where local data processing precedes transmission of results to a corporate central computer.

Hierarchical topology design is particularly suitable to LAN bus implementation of factory networks. FIGURE 27-17 illustrates this topology.

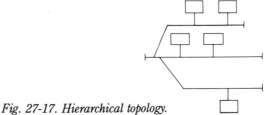

Fig. 27-17. Hierarchical topology.

Unconstrained topology exhibits multiple path combinations between nodes. The transmission criteria rests in the network's ability to route messages from a node to another node in the network in any one of the possible paths available. A typical application of this topology is found in paket switched and circuit switched wide area networks. FIGURE 27-18 shows this topology.

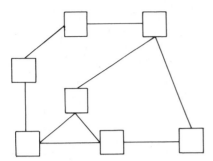

Fig. 27-18. Unconstrained topology.

TABLE 27-3 summarizes the five topologies just described in terms of their advantages and limitations.

Network Interconnections

Network branches or subnetworks in both local area networks and wide area networks may have to be interconnected with each other as well as with the central network. When this is the case, the interconnection, depending on the type and purpose, is implemented with certain intelligent electronic devices. The most commonly used interconnecting devices will be described next. The type of interconnection is defined in terms of the OSI model.

Repeaters perform interconnection of subnetworks at the physical level only. The interconnected subnetworks appear transparent at the media access control level as shown in FIG. 27-19.

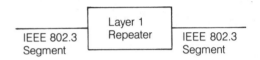

Fig. 27-19. Repeater.

Bridges interconnect subnetworks characterized by consistent addressing schemes, frame sizes, and data rates. This type of interconnection is performed between subnetworks that are physically distinct at the media access sublayer of the Data Link Layer. In other words, the interconnection bridges the limitations of two separate data link layers. This is illustrated in FIG. 27-20.

When two subnetworks exhibit functionally different layers one and two, then functions such as

Table 27-3. Summary of Network Topologies

Topology	Advantages	Disadvantages
Star	Every node connected directly to the central node. Immediate updates at a central point.	Higher cabling costs. Greater communications load on the central node. Single point of failure.
Ring	Potentially lowest overhead and highest throughput of available bandwidth.	Must break ring to add stations. Single point of failure unless implemented by dual rings.
Bus	Lowest cabling cost. Easy to add nodes. Applicable to broadband media. No single point of failure.	Access method may add overhead through contention or granting of access rights, thereby limiting available throughput.
Hierarchical	May mix differing performance requirements of nodes more efficiently. Can offload bandwidth requirements for each level.	Potentiablly higher cabling costs. More complex messages. Routing may be more complex at each level. Longer time for peer-to-peer message transfer.
Unconstrained	Require less network planning. Potential for bandwidth and routing flexibility.	More difficult to manage network. Required routing mechanism at each node.

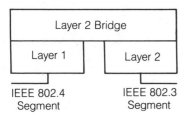

Fig. 27-20. Bridge model.

data path selection and message relaying must be *routed*. The *router* accomplishes this task by creating, among other things, a single address for each node on the network that is recognizable by all other nodes on the network. FIGURE 27-21 illustrates this interconnection.

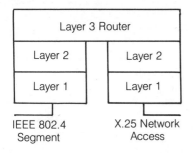

Fig. 27-21. Router model.

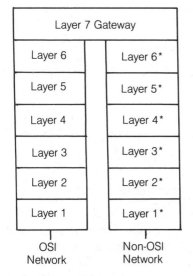

Fig. 27-22. Gateway model.

The *gateway* is a protocol converter; it is designed to interconnect two subnetworks which operate with two different protocols, as would be the case with the IEEE 802.3 carrier sense multiple access with collision detection CSMA/CD and IEEE 802.4 token bus subnetworks. These subnetworks typically have different address structures. The interconnection must take place at the seventh layer of the two network; for this reason, interconnecting with gateways often results in costly and inefficient systems. The manufacturing automation protocol concept is designed to avoid this method. FIGURE 27-22 portrays the gateway interconnection.

THE MANUFACTURING AUTOMATION PROTOCOL

The manufacturing automation protocol (MAP) is a communication scheme based on the IEEE 802.4 token bus protocol over broadband media at the lower layers of the OSI model. The MAP specifications seek to attain two major objectives:

- Standardization of communication equipment designed primarily for industrial automation environment
- Provision of a guaranteed maximum waiting time at each station before channel access is provided; the MAP is designed for this setting

The applications software provides file transfer and manufacturing messaging services; version 3.0 of the MAP specifications also include options for carrierband media and data link options that extend the applicability of MAP into lower levels of factory control. The full implementation of MAP version 3.0 with these options is referred to as the enhanced performance architecture (EPA). A limited subset of EPA is used for manufacturing messaging services and is referred to as mini-MAP. A summary of the principal operations of the MAP layers is shown in FIG. 27-23.

Technical and Office Protocol

The technical and office protocol (TOP) specifications are designed specifically to serve the needs

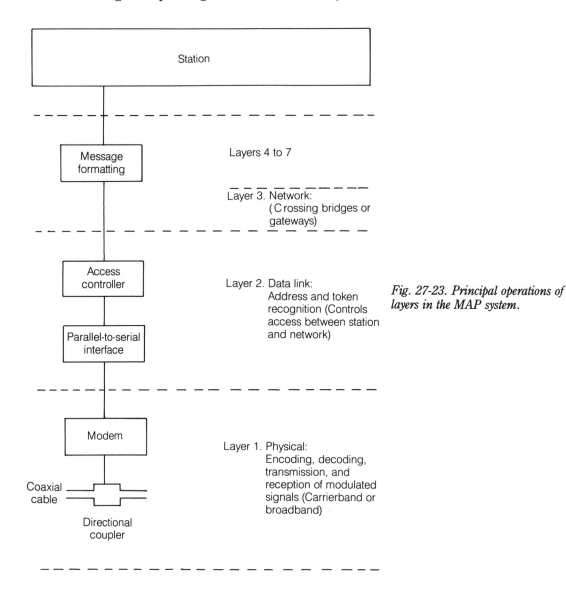

Fig. 27-23. *Principal operations of layers in the MAP system.*

of office automation. Layers one and two use the probabilistic CSMA/CD protocol, which gives adequate performance for most office automation tasks. The application software is targeted at file transfer capability as well as at capabilities for such requirements as electronic mail and graphics interchange. MAP and TOP keep ISO layers three through six exactly the same in both specifications; this feature facilitates the interface of MAP and TOP throughout an industrial complex. FIGURE 27-24 shows the relationship between MAP and TOP specifications.

Fiber Optic Communication

The introduction of fiber optics transmission in LANs is a new as well as everchanging undertaking. Fiber optics data transmission occurs via an optical fiber which consists of a thin (50 to 100 micrometers) flexible medium cable capable of conducting

LAYERS	TOP V1.0 PROTOCOLS	MAP V2.1 PROTOCOLS
Layer 7 Application	ISO FTAM (DP) 8571 File transfer protocol	ISO FTAM (DP) 8571 File transfer protocol, manufacturing messaging format standard (MMFS), and common application service elements (CASE)
Layer 6 Presentation	NULL (ASCII and Binary Encoding)	
Layer 5 Session	ISO Session (IS) 8327 Basic combined subset and session kernel, Full duplex	
Layer 4 Transport	ISO Transport (IS) 8073 Class 4	
Layer 3 Network	ISO Internet (DIS) 8473 Connectionless and for X.25 - Subnetwork dependent convergence protocol (SNDCP)	
Layer 2 Data link	ISO logical link control (DIS) 8802/2 (IEEE 802.2) Type 1, Class 1	
Layer 1* Physical	ISO CSMA/CD (DIS) 8802/3 (IEEE 802.3) CSMA/CD Media access control, 10Base5	ISO token passing bus (DIS) 8802/4 (IEEE 802.4) Token passing bus media access control

Fig. 27-24. Relationship between MAP and TOP.

an optical ray. Fiber optics transmission uses an encoded-signal beam of light by means of total internal reflection. Operationally, an optical fiber guides light waves for frequencies in the range 10^{14} to 10^{15} Hz, which spans the visible portion of the spectrum and part of the infrared spectrum. FIGURE 27-25 shows this concept.

Fiber optic cable consists of a bundle of fibers, at times with a steel core for stability (multistrand); or, it may consist of a single fiber (single strand). FIGURE 27-26 illustrates a multistrand optical fiber.

Optical fibers are made of various glasses and plastics; they offer losses of various degrees. The lowest losses can be obtained with fibers of ultrapure fused silica; ultrapure fibers are very difficult to manufacture and hence are very expensive. Higher-loss multicomponent glass fibers are more affordable at a very good performance. Still more economical are plastic fibers, provided that moderately high losses are acceptable. A typical fiber optic link is illustrated by FIG. 27-27.

A light emitting diode (LED) or an injection

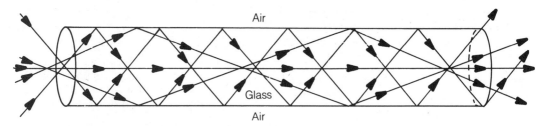

Fig. 27-25. Typical fiber optic light transmission.

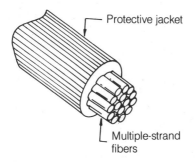

Fig. 27-26. Multistrand optical fiber.

Fiber Optics Transmission   The transmission process consists of the encoding of two binary digits such that the digits represent the presence or absence of light at a certain frequency. Both the LED and the ILD can be modulated according to this encoding. Current practical data rates are in the range of a few hundred Mbps over a few kilometers.

Fiber optics has a great potential for improving the real time transmission requirements of the factory floor. Specifically, a fiber optic broadband LAN for the implementation of a MAP system would significantly enhance the execution of the OSI model.

Fiber Optics Broadband LAN   A fiber optic broadband LAN can support broadband LAN as well as other related broadband services. A fiber optic MAP system can be implemented with the following basic modular components.

Fiber Optic Translator. The fiber optic MAP translator is a device designed to interface a fiber optic network with a conventional head-end remodulator on an existing coaxial MAP network. The translator can be placed at any location on the coaxial network and can support from 8 to 16 fiber optic

laser diode (ILD) is used as a light source. The LED is less costly, operates over a greater temperature range, and has longer operating life. The ILD is more efficient and faster; it can handle greater data rates. At the receiving end of the link is an optical detector such as photodiode; this is a solid-state device which converts light into electrical energy. The optical fiber coupler is a mechanical device that physically links two optical fibers. Modulation of the light carrier is performed as a form of amplitude-shift keying (ASK); the modulation is *intensity* modulation.

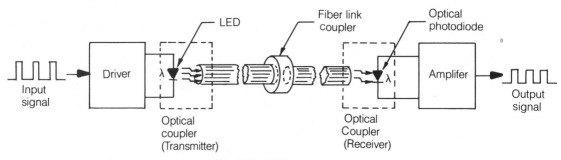

Fig. 27-27. Fiber optic link.

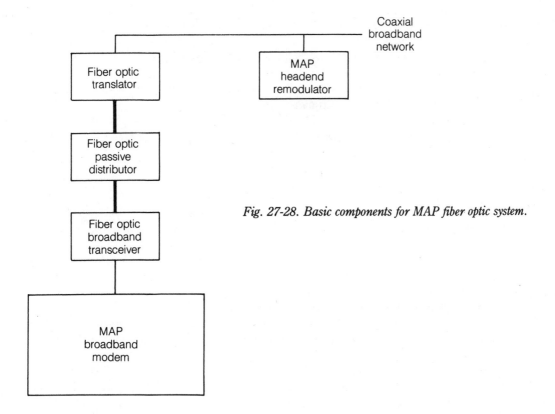

Fig. 27-28. Basic components for MAP fiber optic system.

MAP passive distributors. It has a built-in total redundancy capable of ensuring maximum network reliability and availability. A translator may connect linearly with other translators in the network.

Fiber Optic MAP Passive Distributor. The passive distributor is a network distributive device. Specific functions are:

- Support for up to eight fiber optic MAP transceivers
- Reduction of the overall length requirements for the fiber optic cable

Fiber Optic MAP Broadband Transceiver. The broadband transceiver interfaces with conventional MAP nodes by means of a coaxial cable. FIGURE 27-28 illustrates the modular interconnections. Even though optical fibers are more expensive than usual twisted pair and coaxial cables, they offer important technical advantages such as greater bandwidth, smaller size and lighter weight, lower attenuation, electromagnetic isolation, and greater repeater spacing.

REFERENCES

Control of Manufacturing Systems

Dembold, U., M. B. Seth, and J. S. Weinstein. *Computers in Manufacturing.* New York: Marcel Dekker, Inc., 1977.

Rembold, U., K. Armbruster, and W. Ulzmann. *Interface Technology for Computer-Controlled Manufacturing Processes*. New York: Marcel Dekker, Inc., 1983.

Savas, E. S. *Computer Control of Industrial Processes*. New York: McGraw-Hill Book Company, 1965.

Schmitt, N. M. and R. F. Farwell. *Understanding Electric Control of Automation Systems*. Dallas, Texas: Texas Instruments, Inc., 1983.

Takahashi, Y., M. J. Rabins, and D. M. Auslander. *Control and Dynamic Systems*. Reading, Massachusetts: Addison-Wesley Publishing Company, Inc., 1972.

Parallel Processing and Fault Tolerance

Adams, George B. III and H. J. Siegel. "A Multistage Network with an Additional Stage for Fault Tolerance." *Fifteenth Hawaii International Conference on System Sciences*, January 1982.

Batcher, K. E., "Flexible Parallel Processing and STARAN." In 1972 *Westcon Tech. Papers, Session 1—Parallel Processing Systems*, September 1972.

Lawrie, Duncan H. "Access and Alignment of Data in an Array Processor." *IEEE Transactions on Computers*. C-24 (December 1975).

Falavarjani, K. M. and D. K. Pradhan. "A Design of Fault-Tolerant Interconnection Networks." Silver Spring, Maryland: Computer Society Press, submitted for publication, 1981.

Feng, T. "An Overview of Parallel Processing Systems." In *1972 Westcon Tech. Papers, Session 1—Parallel Processing Systems*, September 1972.

_____. "Some Characteristics of Associative/Parallel Processing." In 1972 *Proc. Sagamore Computer Conference*, August 1972.

_____. "Parallel Processor Characteristics and Implementation of Data Manipulating Functions." Syracuse, New York: Syracuse University, Department of Elec. Computer Engineering, Tech. Rep. TR-72-1 (April 1973).

Feng, T. and C. Wu. "Fault-diagnosis for a Class of Multistage Interconnection Networks." *IEEE Transactions on Computers*. C-30 (October 1981).

CNC and DNC

Aggen, R. O. "Economic Analysis and Justification of A DNC System." Presented at SME Harbor College Seminar, Harbor City, California, October 4, 1975. (Reprinted by Industry Systems Division, Westinghouse Electric Corp., Pittsburgh, Pennsylvania.)

Groover, M. P. and E. W. Zimmers, Jr. *CAD/CAM: Computer-Aided Design and Manufacturing*. Englewood Cliffs, New Jersey: Prentice-Hall, Inc., 1984.

Koren, Y. *Computer Control of Manufacturing Systems*. New York: McGraw-Hill Book Company, 1983.

Nastali, W. F. "Machine Controls: Smarter Than Ever." *Manufacturing Engineering* (January 1986).

Ogorek, M. "Interactive Graphics and Conversion Programming." *Manufacturing Engineering* (January 1985).

Ogorek, J. "CNC Standard Formats." *Manufacturing Engineering* (January 1985).

Pressman, R. S. and J. E. Williams. *Numerical Control and Computer-Aided Manufacturing*. New York: John Wiley & Sons, Inc., 1977.

_____. *Numerical Control and Computer-Aided Manufacturing*. New York: John Wiley & Sons, Inc., Chapter 10, 1977.

Schaffer, G. H. "Getting the Most Out of DNC." *American Machinist* (July 1985).

Industrial Networks, Communications, and Protocols

MAP Specification V2.1A and V2.2, General Motors Manufacturing Automation Protocol, A Communicatoin Network Protocol for Open Systems Interconnection (1986.8.1).

ISA DS72.03, Process Control Architecture, Draft 1 (1986.11.3).

ISO/DIS 8802/4, Information Processing Systems—Local Area Networks—Part 4, Token-passing Bus Access Method and Physical Layer Specifications (1985.5.16).

ISO/DIS 8802/2, Information Processing Systems—Local Area Networks—Part 2, Logical Link Control (1985.5.16).

ISA DS72.02, Process Messaging Service, Draft 3 (1986.10.31).

ISO/TC184/SC5 N66, Industrial Automation Systems—Systems Integration and Communications, Manufacturing Message Specification—Part 1, Service Definition (1987.5.21).

ISO/TC184/SC5 N66, Industrial Automation Systems—Systems Integration and Communications, Manufacturing Message Specifications—Part 2, Protocol Specification (1987.5.21).

Crowder, R. "The MAP Specification." *Control Engineering* (October 1985).

Jones, J. R. "Consider Fiber Optics for Local Area Network Designs." *EDN* (March 3, 1983).

Heyman, D. P. "An Analysis of the Carrier-Sense Multiple-Access Protocol." *Bell System Technical Journal* (October 1982).

Stallings, W. *Local Networks: An Introduction*. New York: Macmillan Publishing Co., Inc., 1984.

_____. *Data and Computer Communications*. New York: Macmillan Publishing Co., Inc., 1985.

Tanenbaum, A. S. *Computer Networks*. Englewood Cliffs, New Jersey: Prentice-Hall, Inc., 1981.

28

The Meaning and Measurement of Productivity

Johnson A. Edosomwan[*]

THIS CHAPTER PRESENTS VARIOUS TYPES OF PRO-ductivity measures at the company level. I discuss the benefits of measuring and managing productivity, and present the universal total productivity measurement model (UTPMM) as well as a step-by-step approach for implementing it. The chapter also reports on the sources of company differences in productivity gains. I discuss the major problem involved in measuring productivity and present strategies for overcoming these problems.

THE MEANING OF PRODUCTIVITY

Productivity is a measure of how well resources are utilized to produce output. It relates output to input and also integrates performance aspects of quality, efficiency, and effectiveness. Productivity does not mean that people should work harder, but work smarter with better tools, techniques, processes, resources, and implementation of new ideas. Productivity technologies are essential for the optimization of production and service processes. The management of productivity can provide the following benefits to companies:

- Productivity management provides the basis for higher real earnings for employees. The reduction in cost of production of goods and services can allow increases in wages without offsetting gains in overall productivity.
- Productivity management results in lower consumer prices for goods and services because the cost of production is reduced due to reduced rework and increased productivity.
- Productivity management enables the effective utilization of resources. More goods and services are produced for reasonable amounts of expended resources. The public also realizes greater social benefits through increased public revenues derived from productivity gains.
- Productivity management can integrate performance aspects of quality to achieve improvement in reduced rework, reduction in scrap, better utilization of tools and equipment, and less work in process inventory, all of which in turn lead to higher productivity.

*Johnson A. Edosomwan is Senior Manager, Production Planning and Industrial Engineering, at IBM's General Products Division in San Jose, California. He is widely recognized as an international expert and consultant in technology, productivity, and quality management. A recipient of the 1988 IIE Outstanding Young Industrial Engineer Award, he has authored or edited eight books. Dr. Edosomwan is listed in Who is Who of Intellectuals, Men of Achievement in the World, Who is Who in Distinguished Leadership, Who is Who in Technology and Innovation, and several other international bibliographies. He is a senior member of IIE and director of IIE for Integrated Manufacturing. He has taught at Polytechnic University, New York and the University of Miami, Florida.

There must be strong awareness that productivity technologies and the level of productivity growth can make a difference in a competitive world economy. The output/input ratio obtained from two similar tasks, processes, and firms can vary significantly depending on how well productivity technologies are properly utilized. The following paragraphs discuss factors that could have potential impact on the level of productivity growth.

Changes result from new breakthroughs in technology and research and development advancement. Most company research is applied to the discovery of new knowledge and know-how that would be of value to the firm in developing new products or cost-reducing technology. Portions of the research and development efforts also focus on engineering and logistics work needed to translate useful inventions into commercially feasible production processes or prototypes of new products. According to J. W. Kendrick (in his 1984 handbook *Improving Company Productivity*), productivity advances are obviously related to the relative volume spent for research and development in various industries, but this is not the whole story. Some of the R&D expenditures made by other industries—those supplying capital goods and intermediate products to a given industry—likewise contribute to the productivity advance. Also, R&D financed by government and universities helps particular industries and companies as well. Despite the interdependence, however, the companies that spend above average on R&D tend to have higher rates of productivity advance.

The education level of workers (professional and nonprofessional) has a reciprocal relationship. The technologically progressive companies offer more opportunities, more skilled and professional occupations, and the workers with higher levels of education and training tend to make a larger contribution to advancing technology.

Many other factors can contribute to company differences in productivity. These include: quality of management; degree of unionization; technologies employed; the culture and organization structure operative in industry; the amount of control and privilege given to workers for innovation and cost reduction activities; and the quality of retraining programs offered to managers and nonmanagers. Additional factors are: the impact of environmental and other government regulations on productive ventures and ideas; and the degree too which individuals within organizations are willing to accept new challenges and take risks in designing and implementing new methods and techniques that improve productivity and technological progress. Changes in labor input through redeployment, reallocation, retraining, and education all contribute to company differences in productivity, as do the following: the level of capacity utilization and volume of real product and services generated; the rate of changes in energy consumption; the degree in which capital and labor are substituted at the firm level; and how well new productivity and quality technologies are put to use.

MEASURING PRODUCTIVITY AT THE COMPANY LEVEL

I have documented elsewhere how a formal productivity measurement system at the company level can have the following benefits:

- Productivity measurement facilitates better resource planning both in the short and long run. It also simplifies communication by providing common measures, language, and concepts with which to think, talk, and evaluate business in quantitative terms.
- Productivity measurement creates a basis for effective supervision of necessary actions to be taken and improves decision making through better understanding of the effect of actions already taken to address a given problem.
- Productivity measurement provides an important motivation for better performance, since it helps to identify on what basis the individual task, product, or operational unit is to be measured.

- Productivity measurement provides the basis for planning the production and service parameters, as well as the profit levels in a company.
- Productivity measurement highlights through indexes areas within the company that have potential improvement opportunities. Productivity values and indexes also provide a way of detecting deviations from established standards so that something is done about such deviations.[1,2,3]

The three types of productivity measures commonly used at the company level are partial productivity, total factor productivity, and total productivity. *Partial productivity* is the ratio of total output to one class of input. Output per man-hour is the best example of partial productivity. Most productivity indexes published by the U.S. Department of Labor have used such measures.[4] Mundel, Melman, and Turner have also used such measures.[5,6,7] According to Edosomwan, Kendrick, Sumanth, Craig and Harris, and Siegel, partial measures of productivity cannot be interpreted as an overall productivity measure since they do not take into account all input costs.[8,9,10,11,12] The danger in using partial productivity measures lies in the emphasis on one input, which may not necessarily have reasonable impact on the total output obtained. Partial productivity measures are useful when used in conjunction with total factor and total productivity measures.

Total factor productivity is the ratio of total output to the sum of associated labor and capital inputs. Sink, Kendrick and Creamer, Taylor and Davis, and Mali have recommended and used the total factor productivity measure.[13,14,15,16] The total factor productivity measure omits the cost of materials, which is one of the vital inputs in business. This measure can be very useful in an environment that is highly labor and capital intensive. However, it is more appropriate when used in conjunction with the partial and total productivity measure.

Total productivity is the ratio of total output to all input factors. Edosomwan, Sumanth, the American Productivity Center, Kendrick, and Craig and Harris have recommended and used this mea-

sure.[17,18,19,20,9,11] The total productivity measure is widely recommended at the company level. It is the most effective measure, especially when used in conjunction with financial measures, partial, and total factor productivities.

OBSTACLES TO MEASURING PRODUCTIVITY AT THE COMPANY LEVEL

The following problems do exist in measuring productivity at the company level:

- Lack of trained professional personnel on productivity management and economic analysis. Companies without personnel trained in productivity measurement techniques are forced to rely solely on financial measures.
- Adequate data are not available for many companies and firms. Where the input and output are available, they are inaccurate or sometimes represent a mixed bag of several quantities that cannot be identified with any particular source, process, operation, or location.
- In some companies, record keeping and management information systems rely heavily on the manual method of computation, which tends to make productivity tracking difficult.
- Appropriate weights for various input and output factors by operational unit are often not available at the company level.
- Detailed data on input and output elements for new and existing processes and product are often fragmented and difficult to gather by cell, operation, or at the individual level.
- Tracking mechanisms may be lacking for monitoring changes that result from the development and introduction of new processes and products.
- Direct quantifiable measures of output and input could be difficult to obtain even if adequate systems exist for proper tracking and compilation.
- Difficulty in measuring output whose characteristics may change over time and how to aggregate heterogeneous units of output and input.
- Difficulty in defining and measuring technological content, capital stocks, group technology cell

contributions, and other inputs, as well as output diversification when the characteristics of all factors are changing.

- Lack of centralized productivity database and measurement system.

UNIVERSAL TOTAL PRODUCTIVITY MEASUREMENT MODEL

The UTPMM was developed using some of the earlier works of Edosomwan, Kendrick, the Bureau of Labor Statistics, Sumanth, Craig and Harris, and the American Productivity Center.[1,2,3,17;18,9,4,19,11,20] The following paragraphs discuss the unique features and properties of UTPMM.

The three types of productivity values and indexes recommended (total, total factor, and partial) provide a more complete picture in assessing the level of productivity gains. The past emphasis on partial measures such as labor productivity could be misleading. Labor input represents only a minute fraction of the total resources utilized to produce the final goods and services of a company. The gains in total productivity are affected by other input such as: material, capital, energy, technology, training, quality of processes, administrative expenses, and research and development expenses.

The input and output components of UTPMM are defined to be consistent with other productivity models, and include the broadest possible components. This provides a model that is useful in measuring productivity at the firm, product, task, and operations unit levels.

Productivity indexes derived using the UTPMM vary with changes in task and process parameters, resources utilized, and output obtained from the transformation of resources. Productivity indexes derived using the UTPMM are comparable over time and can objectively be used to measure the productivity of the firm, tasks, customers, products, work cells, work groups, department, and projects.

UTPMM lends itself to a comprehensive sensitivity analysis of relationships between total, total factor, and partial productivities. For example, by looking at both total and partial productivity indexes

of a nation, specific resources or areas of concern can be identified and improved. Finally, UTPMM provides valuable information for economic analysis, strategic planning, operations improvement, and developing and implementing process improvement plans.

Quantification of UTPMM Inputs and Outputs

The input and output components of UTPMM are shown schematically in FIG. 28-1. The following are relevant essentials involved in understanding the inputs and outputs component required for productivity computations:

INPUTS

- Inputs to be considered are labor, material, capital, energy, technology (robotics, computers, etc.), research and development expenses, administrative expenses, training expenses, and cost of quality.
- Inputs are combined by a specific monetary measure on the basis of relative total contribution to the output produced.
- Quantification of relevant input may vary from one firm to another.
- Input values should be unadjusted for changes in levels of education and training, technology, and quality. These changes are explainable by the total, total factor, and partial productivity values and indexes generated.
- To avoid double counting, the cost of quality should include only the effort required to detect and correct defective units produced during a specific time period.

OUTPUTS

- Outputs used for UTPMM are measured in physical volumes and are thus unaffected by price changes.
- Constant prices as of one period should be used to multiply the units of outputs in order to combine them into aggregate measures.
- The value of the final output should include: finished units produced, partial units produced, and other income associated with units produced.

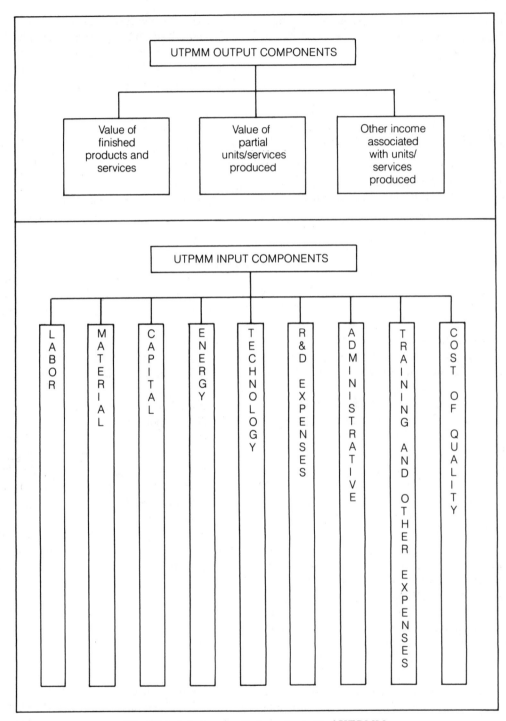

Fig. 28-1. Input and output components of UTPMM.

- Constant prices are used to avoid distortion from inflation and cyclic economic factors.
- Outputs should be based on what is produced and not from inventory. Including physical units from inventory as part of the output is double counting.

Both the input and output components are to be reduced to a common base period. (*Base period* is a reference period to which the input and output in monetary terms is reduced.) The selection of a base period depends on: whether the productivity measurement system is implemented for the first time; the variation pattern for product produced; the normal period of production and service; and the use of managerial judgments. Periods of layoffs and abnormal strikes should not be selected as a base period. A base period should reflect a normal period of production and service when nothing unusual or extraordinary has happened that has an impact on performance.

Derivation of Productivity Values and Indexes

Notations

FU_{ijt} = Value of finished units produced in operational unit i, in site j, in period t.

PU_{ijt} = Value of partial units produced in operational unit i, site j, in period t.

PC_{ijt} = Percent completion of partial units produced in operational unit i, site j, in period t.

SP_{ijt} = Base period selling price per unit produced in operational unit i, site j, in period t.

OI_{ijt} = Value of other income associated with units produced in operational unit i, in site j, in period t.

LI_{ijt} = Labor input utilized to produce output in operational unit i, in site j, in period t.

MI_{ijt} = Material input utilized to produce output in operational unit i, in site j, in period t.

CI_{ijt} = Capital related expense input used to produce output in operational unit i, in site j, in period t. (Includes fixed and working capital such as cash, accounts receivable, tools, plant, buildings, and amortization.)

EI_{ijt} = Energy related expense input (includes electricity, solar energy, water, coal, gas, etc.) utilized to produce output in operational unit i, in site j, in period t.

TI_{ijt} = Variable technology expense input (robotics, computers, etc.) utilized to produce output in operational unit i, in site j, in period t.

RD_{ijt} = Research and development expense utilized to produce output in operational unit i, in site j, in period t.

AE_{ijt} = Administrative expenses associated with units produced in operational unit i, in site j, in period t.

TO_{ijt} = Training and other expenses utilized to produce output in operational unit i, in site j, in period t.

CQ_{ijt} = Cost of quality involved in producing useful output in operational unit i, in site j, in period t.

TP_{ijt} = Total productivity of operational unit i, in site j, in period t.

TF_{ijt} = Total factor productivity of operational unit i, in site j, in period t.

PP_{ijt} = Partial productivity of operational unit i, in site j, in period t.

The total, total factor, and partial productivities are expressed as follows:

TOTAL PRODUCTIVITY

$$TP_{ijt} = \frac{\text{Total measurable output of operational unit } i, \text{ in site } j, \text{ in period } t.}{\text{Total measurable input of operational unit } i, \text{ in site } j, \text{ in period } t.}$$

$$TP_{ijt} = \frac{(FU_{ijt})(SP_{ijt}) + (PU_{ijt})(PC_{ijt})(SP_{ijt}) + OI_{ijt}}{LI_{ijt} + MI_{ijt} + CI_{ijt} + EI_{ijt} + TI_{ijt} + RD_{ijt} + AE_{ijt} + TO_{ijt} + CQ_{ijt}}$$

TOTAL FACTOR PRODUCTIVITY

$$\text{TF}ijt = \frac{\text{Total measurable output of operational unit } i, \text{ in site } j, \text{ in period } t.}{\text{Measurable labor and capital input of operational unit}}$$

$$\text{TP}ijt = \frac{(\text{FU}ijt)\ (\text{SP}ijt)\ +\ (\text{PU}ijt)\ (\text{PC}ijt)\ (\text{SP}ijt)\ +\ \text{OI}ijt}{\text{LI}ijt\ +\ \text{CI}ijt}$$

PARTIAL PRODUCTIVITY

$$\text{PP}ijt = \frac{\text{Total measurable output of operational unit } i, \textit{ in site } j, \text{ in period } t.}{\text{Measurable one class of input (such as labor) of operational unit} i, \text{ in site } j, \text{ in period } t.}$$

UTPMM IMPLEMENTATION METHODOLOGY

The following steps are recommended for implementing UTPMM at the company level:

Step One: Understand the personnel, processes, and sources of all input and output elements by operational unit.

Step Two: Classify the input and output components by operational unit.

Step Three: Understand the input and output for each operational unit. Perform input and output analysis using flow diagrams and variable mapping techniques.

Step Four: Develop appropriate allocation criteria for input and output components. Recommended allocation criteria include proportional contribution to total quantity produced, machine insertion rates, direct hours utilized, energy utilization rates, and ratio of indirect to direct hours utilized are recommended allocation criteria.

Step Five: Design a data collection and information system and centralize the system at the company level.

Step Six: Train company representatives on how to use UTPMM and data collection instruments. Both productivity analysts and other personnel concerned with productivity measurement must be trained.

Step Seven: Test selected productivity measures and data collection systems in selected operational unit. Revise the productivity measurement system based on feedback from the various work units. Document specific aggregate approximation techniques for input and output components for each operational unit.

Step Eight: Implement UTPMM. Collect data periodically and computer productivity values and indexes by operational units and for the firm as a whole. Select a specific base period for productivity comparison and analysis.

Step Nine: Perform productivity trend analysis and interpret measurement findings. Use the productivity indexes and basis for understanding problem areas for improvement opportunities.

Step Ten: Implement an effective organization for ongoing maintenance and improvement of the productivity measurement system.

STRATEGY FOR OVERCOMING COMMON IMPLEMENTATION PROBLEMS

I recommend the following strategies for implementing UTPMM in the work environment:

- Obtain the total support of the entire organization. Management and nonmanagement personnel involved in using UTPMM should know its benefit and have a thorough understanding of the key requirements.
- Set realistic implementation procedures and start implementation after providing adequate education and training on productivity measurement.
- Plan implementation activities ahead of time. Use computer package to ease computation burden.
- Provide adequate focus on cost avoidance, communication among project participants, and encourage cooperation and teamwork.
- Motivate productivity analyst and other personnel involved in the project to do their best. Sell the benefits of the productivity measures and potential impact in improving the effectiveness, quality, and productivity of each operation, unit, and for the firm as a whole.

CONCLUSION

This chapter has presented a universal total productivity measurement model that takes into account total measurable input and output elements. Companies interested in implementing this model should start with detailed analysis of the key input and output and historical data for at least three years. New companies have the advantage of proceeding immediately to appropriate tracking of the operational unit input and output elements. The UTPMM has strong potential for application in measuring productivity of work groups, products, customers, and projects. Successful application of UTPMM requires ongoing maintenance of the productivity measurement program. The maintenance tasks include periodic data collection and periodic computation of productivity values and indexes—using productivity values and indexes to improve both the production and service processes and planning.

ENDNOTES

1. J. A. Edosomwan, "How to Measure Productivity in Electronics Printed Circuit Board Assembly," in (Industrial Engineering and Management Press in collaboration with McGraw-Hill), 1988.

2. J. A. Edosomwan, "A Technology-Oriented Total Productivity Measurement Model," in *Productivity Management Frontiers - I* (B.V. Amsterdam: Elsevier Science Publishers, 1987).

3. J. A. Edosomwan, *Integrating Productivity and Quality Management* (New York: Marcel Dekker Inc., 1987).

4. U. S. Department of Labor Bureau of Labor Statistics, *Monthly Labor Review* (January 1980): 40-43.

5. M. E. Mundel, "Measures of Productivity," *Industrial Engineering* 8: 5 (1976): 32-36.

6. Seymour Melman, *Dynamic Factors in Industrial Productivity* (New York: John Wiley and Sons, 1956).

7. Jon A. Turner, *Computers in Bank Clerical Functions: Implication for Productivity and Quality of Working Life*. 1980.

8. J. A. Edosomwan, *Productivity and Quality Improvement* (England: IFS Publications, 1988).

9. J. W. Kendrick, *Improving Company Productivity: Handbook with Case Studies* (Baltimore, Maryland: The Johns Hopkins University Press, 1984).

10. D. J. Sumanth, *Productivity Engineering and Management* (New York: McGraw-Hill Book Company, 1984).

11. C. E. Craig and C. R. Harris, "Total Productivity Measurement at the Firm Level," *Sloan Management Review* 14: 3 (1973): 13-29.

12. I. H. Siegel, "Measurement of Company Productivity," in *Improving Productivity through Industray and Company Measurement* (Washington, D.C.: National Center for Productivity and Quality of Working Life, Series 2: 15-25).

13. D. S. Sink, *Productivity Measurement, Improvement, Evaluation, and Control* (New York: John Wiley Publishers, 1985).

14. J. W. Kendrick and D. Creamer, *Measuring Company Productivity: Handbook with Case Studies* (Studies in Business Economics, No. 89, New York: National Industrial Conference Board, 1965).

15. B. W. Taylor III and R. K. Davis, "Corporate Productivity—Getting it All Together," *Industrial Engineering* 9: 3 (1977): 32-36.

16. P. Mali, *Improving Total Productivity MBO Strategies for Business, Government and Non-profit Organizations* (New York: John Wiley and Sons, 1978).

17. J. A. Edosomwan, "A Program for Managing Productivity and Quality," *Industrial Engineering* (January 1987).

18. J. A. Edosomwan, "Understanding Computer-Aided Manufacturing Impact on Total Productivity," *Computers and Industrial Engineering* 12:4 (1987): 283-290.

19. D. J. Sumanth, "Productivity Measurement and Evaluation Models for Manufacturing Companies," (Ph.D. dissertation, Department of Industrial Engineering, I. I. T. Chicago, 1979).

20. American Productivity Center, "Productivity and the Industrial Engineer," presented at Region VIII AIIE Conference, Chicago, October 27, 1978.

29

Manufacturing Resources Planning: MRP-II

Jayant Rajgopal[*]
Maryanne Frabotta[**]

MANUFACTURING RESOURCES PLANNING, OR MRP-II as it is more commonly known, is a general framework for planning and controlling the day to day operations of a manufacturing concern. MRP-II may also be viewed as a comprehensive information system that integrates manufacturing and financial data for the entire system into a single database. This common database provides the means to efficiently utilize the resources of the concern in order to meet its overall business objectives.

The term *manufacturing resources planning* is a relatively recent one and stems from the integrative nature of MRP-II systems. The early versions of these systems were referred to as *material requirements planning*, or MRP. As the name implies, these systems were restricted to planning the requirements and timing of materials (raw materials, components, subassemblies, etc.), without specific consideration of the interactions of these plans with other functional areas within the facility.

In the context of the systems in operation today the term MRP would be considered too limited in its scope, even though it is true that material requirements planning still constitutes the heart of any MRP-II system. Another term that is commonly heard is *closed loop MRP*. Systems referenced by this term may be viewed as MRP-II systems without the financial database and may be thought of as the evolutionary link between MRP and MRP-II. Other terms that are in use include manufacturing control systems and factory planning systems. The terminology is, however, becoming increasingly irrelevant as more and more of these systems enter the market.

The basic logic behind MRP-II is quite simple. The objective is to draw up a production plan that will produce the requisite quantities of product at the proper time by planning the timing and requirements of materials and resources. Additionally, these plans must be evaluated in light of their impact on other areas of the manufacturing con-

[*]Jayant Rajgopal is Assistant Professor of Industrial Engineering at the University of Pittsburgh. He teaches courses and conducts research in the planning and control of production systems, and has been involved with the implementation of MRP-II. He is a member of the Society of Manufacturing Engineers, the Institute of Industrial Engineers, the Operations Research Society of America, and The Institute of Management Science.

[**]Maryanne Frabotta is a graduate student in the Department of Industrial Engineering at the University of Pittsburgh. She has ten years of work experience with ALCOA in process control and software development, and is currently conducting research on MRP-II systems for her doctoral dissertation.

cern, such as marketing and order-entry, accounting, purchasing, inventory, payroll, and engineering. Finally, all records that track the operational status of these different areas must be constantly monitored and updated.

The material requirements planning process can become tremendously complicated for anything more than a small concern with a very simple product structure. This is especially true in multistage manufacturing systems where there are several subassemblies and purchased parts; some of these are common to more than one product. Data requirements for planning in such environments are tremendous and the advent of the computer considerably eased this planning procedure. Today, with the widespread use of small, powerful computers and workstations, implementation of the MRP logic and its extension to MRP-II have become reasonably straightforward.

MATERIAL REQUIREMENTS PLANNING

At the heart of all MRP-II systems is the basic material requirements planning (MRP) module. This section is devoted to a detailed study of this module.

The driving force behind MRP is the *master production schedule* or MPS. The MPS is a statement of the end product manufacturing schedule. It is a listing of the requirements of all end products during each time period in some prespecified interval of time (referred to as the *planning horizon*). The MPS serves as the starting point for planning the requirements and timings of all the components that make up the end products. There are a number of excellent references on MPS that detail procedures for arriving at a good MPS (see for example Vollman et al. 1988). The MPS depends on customer orders or anticipated external demand and is usually made up within the constraints of some larger aggregate plan. In this section we shall assume that a preliminary MPS has been decided upon in advance and will concentrate on how a material requirements planning system would go about implementing this plan.

In order to understand the mechanism of material requirements planning, we need to first define and understand the basic building blocks of an MRP system, along with the prerequisites for its application. MRP is best applied to systems where there are relatively few end products or independent demand items—as compared to items whose demand is directly dependent upon these end products. Complex manufacturing and assembly systems such as computers, household appliances, automobiles, and scientific instruments are the most common examples. In such cases there are production requirements for a large number of items; these requirements also tend to be highly intermittent since most end products are manufactured in lots or batches. MRP enables these requirements to be satisfied at the proper time.

Bill of Materials

The critical element of any MRP system is the *bill of materials* or the BOM. Quite simply put, a bill of materials is a detailed description of the composition of every end product and every subcomponent in the system. It may be viewed as an ingredients list that is examined each time plans are made for manufacturing something. A BOM could follow several different forms such as a *modular* BOM, an *indented* BOM, a *summarized* BOM, or a *matrix* BOM. All of these serve the same purpose of listing out the needs of the various subcomponents making up an item.

Consider item EX1 with the structure shown in FIG. 29-1. In practice it would be quite inconvenient to depict the structure of a product in this disorganized fashion, especially for one that involves complex assemblies of parts and subcomponents.

Perhaps the easiest BOM to understand is the so-called *modular* form, which shows only the immediate subcomponents for an item along with their requisite numbers. Modular bills of materials for this item, subassembly S1, subassembly S2, and component C1 are shown in FIG. 29-2. Parts P1 and P2 are purchased from an external vendor and

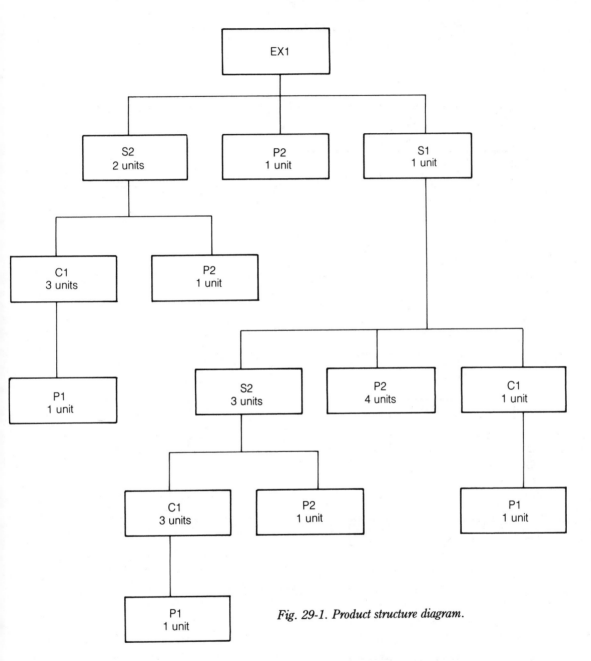

Fig. 29-1. Product structure diagram.

do not have bills of materials of their own. It may be noted that given the requirements for an item, the exact requirements for all components or subassemblies making up the item are easily obtained from the BOM.

Level Coding

In order to use the bills of materials for constructing a time-phased production schedule, the next important concept is that of *level coding*. Each

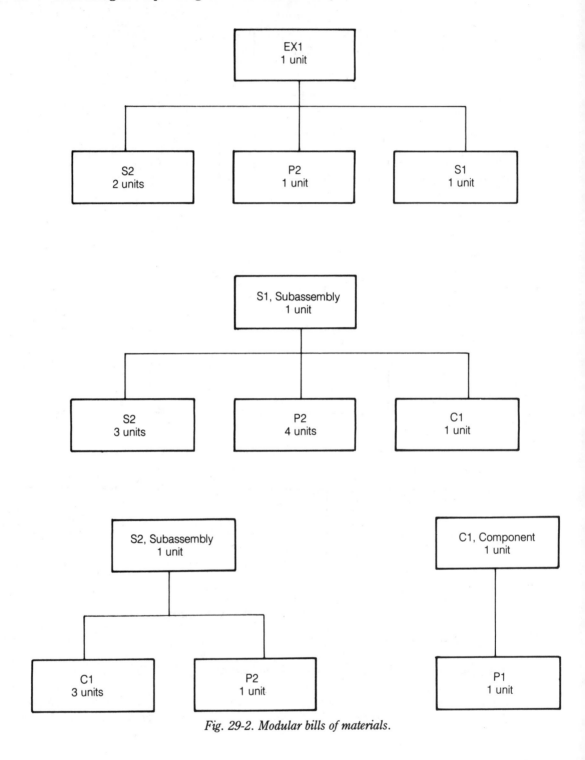

Fig. 29-2. Modular bills of materials.

component or subassembly is assigned a level code depending on its usage. A level *0* item is one which is an end product and is not used as part of any other item. A level *1* item is one which is either used as a subcomponent of a level *0* item, or as an end item by itself. (An example would be an item that is used in the end product and also sold as a spare part.) A level *2* item is either an end product, or used either in a level *1* or a level *0* item. In general, a level *n* item is one that is either an end item or is used only in items possessing level codes lower than *n*. The notion of level coding is very important because it allows the MRP system to decide on the sequence in which it will plan the production (or ordering) of the various items to be made (or ordered). Essentially, orders are first released for the level *0* items based on the MPS, and orders are then sequentially planned and released for all level *1* items, followed by all level *2* items, and so on. The mechanism for this will become obvious as we examine our example.

FIGURE 29-3 gives an *indented* BOM along with the level codes for the various items comprising our example part EX1, which is assumed to be the only level *0* item here. Note that subassembly S2 is directly used in item EX1 (a level *0* item); however, S2 is also directly used to make subassembly S1 (which has a level code of *1*). Therefore the proper level code for subassembly S2 is *2*, and its production should be planned only after that of subassembly S1.

Time Phasing

When an MRP system plans production it specifies not just the quantities but also the exact timing of the production order releases. In order to do this we first introduce the notion of a *time bucket*. A time bucket is some small interval of time that forms the basic unit within the planning horizon (the length of time for which plans are to be made). Production is to be planned for each time bucket in the planning horizon. The choice of an appropriate time bucket depends on the batch sizes used for the end items. In general, smaller time buckets are appropriate if smaller batches are used. In our example we have chosen the time bucket as one week, which is fairly typical, although time buckets as small as one day may be used.

Once the time bucket has been specified, the

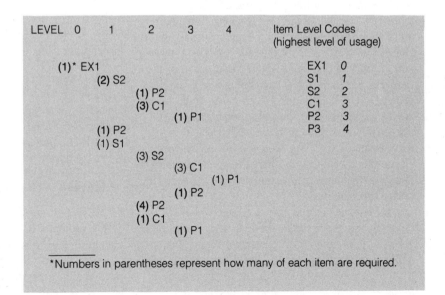

Fig. 29-3. Indented bill of materials.

LEVEL 0	1	2	3	4	Item Level Codes (highest level of usage)	
(1)* EX1					EX1	0
	(2) S2				S1	1
		(1) P2			S2	2
		(3) C1			C1	3
			(1) P1		P2	3
	(1) P2				P3	4
	(1) S1					
		(3) S2				
			(3) C1			
				(1) P1		
			(1) P2			
		(4) P2				
		(1) C1				
			(1) P1			

*Numbers in parentheses represent how many of each item are required.

next important piece of information required by the MRP system is manufacturing or purchasing *lead time*. This information is critical for properly offsetting the order release times of the various manufactured (or purchased) components. For instance, in the case of item EX1, the process of assembling subassemblies S1 and S2 and part P2 to form the item might take two weeks for a batch of 100. For purchased parts, estimation of the lead time is usually straightforward since most often it is independent of the size of the order itself. On the other hand, for manufactured parts this may be somewhat more complicated since the size of the lot being scheduled might have a significant effect on the lead time.

Normally the lead time is expressed in units that are the same as those used to define a time bucket. Given the standard setup and operation times along with the batch size to be used, the MRP system will be able to compute the lead time in time bucket units. The appropriate order releases are then offset by this time.

The MRP Record

We now examine the basic MRP record along with the information contained therein. The MRP record might be viewed as a detailed status report for every time bucket in the planning horizon and for all items in the plant such as raw materials, purchased components, subassemblies, and end products. TABLE 29-1 shows a set of MRP records; the numbers in the table may be ignored for the present. The MRP record contains four basic pieces of information: the gross requirements, the scheduled receipts, the projected available inventory balance, and the planned order releases. These four pieces of information completely describe the status of the item under consideration during the time bucket.

Examining each of these terms, we start by defining the *gross requirement* of an item as the total amount of the item required during the time bucket under consideration. These requirements include those that are directly attributable to usage in other items as well as any independent demand (such as for safety stocks or spares). The requirements

must be satisfied either from inventory or through the receipt of an order. By convention, the demand should usually be satisfied at the beginning of the time bucket.

Scheduled receipts represent existing replenishment orders for the item that are due at the beginning of the time bucket. These represent a definite commitment of the necessary resources and exist as a result of ordering decision that were made in the past. They are recorded only after the production plan has been made and the order actually released. The time bucket in which the receipt is scheduled is obtained by adding the production (or purchasing) lead time to the time bucket where the order for the item was actually released.

The *projected inventory balance* refers to the inventory status of the item that is expected at the end of the time bucket after all transactions (order receipts and satisfaction of all requirements) scheduled for that period have been completed. The calculation of this figure allows the MRP system to decide on whether sufficient stock is available in a given period to satisfy the requirements in that period, or whether an order needs to be scheduled so that it arrives in time to satisfy these requirements.

Finally, the *planned order release* for a time bucket is the size of the replenishment order that is placed at the beginning of the time period. This is obtained by first determining the time period in which the projected inventory balance will become negative, and then moving backward from that time period by an amount equal to the lead time. The planned order is then released after the above time-phasing. As a result, the order will be scheduled for receipt in the time period when the inventory would otherwise have become negative.

Evolution of Schedules

MRP is often referred to as a pull type system. By this we mean that items with demands that are dependent on the demand for some parent product(s) are pulled through the system in the appropriate amounts as and when they are required by their parent items. The independent demand items at the end have the role of initiating this pulling

Table 29-1. Partial MRP Schedule

			WEEK									
			1	2	3	4	5	6	7	8	9	10
LEVEL 0	Gross requirements							100				80
	Scheduled receipts				20							
EX1	Projected inventory balance	10	10	10	30	30	30					
	Planned order releases					70				80		
LEVEL 1	Gross requirements					70				80		
	Scheduled receipts											
S1	Projected inventory balance											
	Planned order releases				70				80			
LEVEL 2	Gross requirements				210	140			240	160		
	Scheduled receipts											
S2	Projected inventory balance	50	50	50	40	100	100	100	60	100	100	100
	Planned order releases			200	200			200	200			
LEVEL 3	Gross requirements				70				80			
	Scheduled receipts											
C1	Projected inventory balance											
	Planned order releases											
LEVEL 3	Gross requirements				280	70			320	80		
	Scheduled receipts											
P2	Projected inventory balance	50										
	Planned order releases											
LEVEL 4	Gross requirements											
	Scheduled receipts											
P1	Projected inventory balance	820										
	Planned order releases											

process. This is in contrast to a push system where items are simply produced and pushed forward according to a schedule that need not be directly dependent on the demand for the products in which these items will eventually be used.

In this section we will examine how the MRP system would go about constructing a production schedule for our example part. To reiterate, the system needs to know how much of a given item is required (the gross requirements); the expected availability of the item (data on the inventory status including scheduled receipts); how something is to be put together (the bills of materials); and the time required for the above activity (the lead times). The important notion here is that of net requirements. To compute the latter, computations are first made for the gross requirement for an item and, by using the BOM, for its immediate subcomponents. The projected inventory and scheduled receipts are then taken into account to calculate the net requirements for all items (these being less than or equal to the gross requirements). Once the net requirements are known, the appropriate lead times are then used to decide on when orders are to be released to meet these net requirements.

To understand this procedure consider item EX1 in FIG. 29-1. The appropriate data on manufacturing and procurement lead times, current inventory status, and lot-sizing policies (these are described in detail a little later) are given in TABLE 29-2. Furthermore, scheduled receipts from previous orders are for 20 units of item EX1 in week 3, and 1000 units of part P1 in week 1. For the development of the MRP schedule, reader refer to TABLE 29-1.

First consider the level *0* items (EX1 in this case). Suppose that over the planning horizon constituted by the next 10 weeks, the master production schedule specifies gross requirements for item EX1 of 100 units in Week 6 and 80 units in Week 10. Noting that 20 units are already due to arrive in Week 3, and that there are 10 units currently in stock, the *net* requirements in Week 6 are for 70 units of EX1. Since the manufacturing lead time is two weeks, an order to meet this net requirement should be released in Week 4. The projected inventory goes to zero at the end of Week 6. The net requirement for EX1 in Week 10 is thus the same as the gross requirement and equal to 80. Offsetting the order by the lead time of two weeks, an order is released for this amount in Week 8.

The next step is to use the BOM (FIG. 29-2) to compute the gross requirements for all immediate subcomponents of EX1. Thus in Week 4 we now have gross requirements of 70 units for subassembly S1, 140 units for subassembly S2, and 70 units for part P2. Similarly in Week 8 the gross requirements are 80 units for S1, 160 units for S2, and 80 units for P2.

Having exhausted the list of level *0* items, we now proceed to level *1* items (S1 in our example). There are no scheduled receipts for subassembly S1; neither is there any existing inventory of the same. Therefore the net requirements are the same as the gross requirements and, based upon the one week manufacturing lead time, orders are released for 70 units in Week 3 and 80 units in Week 7 so that the net requirements in Weeks 4 and 8 respectively may be met.

If we examine the BOM for this S1 subassembly (FIG. 29-2) we see that these order releases translate into the following gross requirements for S1 immediate subcomponents, subassembly S2, component C1, and part P2:

Week No.	S2	C1	P2
3	210	70	280
7	240	80	320

Having exhausted level *1* items, we now move on to the level *2* items, namely S2. The initial inventory of 50 units of S1 implies a net requirement of 160 units in Week 3. However, the economics of the manufacturing process call for a minimum batch size of 200 (as specified in TABLE 29-2). Hence, the order release in Week 2 (the lead time being one week) is for 200 units. The projected inventory balance at the end of Week 3 is 40 units, which implies net requirements of 100 units in Week 4. Therefore, another order in the amount of 200 units is planned for release in Week 3. By the same logic, planned order releases are for 200 units in Weeks 6 and 7 also. The MRP schedule thus far is shown in TABLE 29-1.

The planned order releases for S2 translate into requirements of 600 units for C1 and 200 units for P2 in each of Weeks 2, 3, 6, and 7. It should be noted that with this information, the requirements in Weeks 3 and 7 for component C1 and part P2

Table 29-2. Production Data

Part	Leadtime [Weeks]	Initial Inventory	Lotsizing Policies
EX1	2	10	Lot-for-lot
S1	1	0	Lot-for-lot
S2	1	50	200
C1	1	0	Lot-for-lot
P1	4	820	1000
P2	1	50	Rules of thumb

have to now be revised upwards to 670 and 680 respectively for C1, and 480 and 520 for P2.

Proceeding now to level *3*, we plan the schedule for part P2 and component C1. Note that the batch sizes to be used for P2 are based on rules of thumb and come out to 700 and 800 respectively. Finally, we go to level *4* and plan the production schedule for part P1. We encourage you to work through these two levels yourself and verify the numbers obtained in the final plan, which is displayed in TABLE 29-3.

OTHER ISSUES RELATING TO MRP

In this section we examine some further issues that are relevant to scheduling production by means of the MRP approach.

Accounting for Uncertainties

Classical inventory control systems cope with uncertainties in demand and production by the use of safety stocks or by padding lead times by some safety factor when planning production. MRP sys-

Table 29-3. Complete MRP Schedule

			WEEK									
			1	2	3	4	5	6	7	8	9	10
LEVEL 0	Gross requirements							100				80
	Scheduled receipts				20							
EX1	Projected inventory balance	10	10	10	30	30	30					
	Planned order releases					70				80		
LEVEL 1	Gross requirements					70				80		
	Scheduled receipts											
S1	Projected inventory balance											
	Planned order releases				70				80			
LEVEL 2	Gross requirements				210	140			240	160		
	Scheduled receipts											
S2	Projected inventory balance	50	50	50	40	100	100	100	60	100	100	100
	Planned order releases			200	200			200	200			
LEVEL 3	Gross requirements			600	670			600	680			
	Scheduled receipts											
C1	Projected inventory balance											
	Planned order releases		600	670			600	680				
LEVEL 3	Gross requirements			200	480	70		200	520	80		
	Scheduled receipts											
P2	Projected inventory balance	50	50	550	70			600	80			
	Planned order releases		700				800					
LEVEL 4	Gross requirements		600	670			600	680				
	Scheduled receipts			1000								
P1	Projected inventory balance	820	220	550	550	550	950	270	270	270	270	270
	Planned order releases		1000									

tems tend to favor the latter approach. This is fairly easy to do, but requires some analysis of the lead times for production of various items. While some quantitative analysis is possible, subjective factors tend to dominate the choice of an appropriate safety time for a given operation. Very often these safety margins are automatically accounted for by virtue of the time buckets selected.

For example, if the time bucket is a week of five working days and the actual production time is eight days, then using a two week lead time while planning automatically builds in a safety time of two days. In other instances it may be necessary to actually plan order releases in an appropriately early time bucket, as opposed to an inflation of the lead times as above. In such cases the order receipt will be scheduled for a time bucket earlier than the one in which it is actually required (by an amount equal to the safety time), and the projected inventory balance is updated in an appropriate fashion.

As far as safety stocks are concerned, it is inappropriate to completely eliminate them, but it is also inappropriate to carry safety stocks for every item at every level. Items for which it is common to carry some buffer stock include some finished goods that have relatively high demand, items made at bottleneck operations, subassemblies and components that find wide use in several different end products, and items that are made at work centers with relatively low manufacturing reliabilities. Safety stocks are also used to account for production of scrap. In order to maintain safety stocks, the procedure is to generate an order when the projected inventory balance drops below the safety value, rather than when it drops below zero. In general, safety stocks are carried where there is uncertainty associated with production quantities, as opposed to uncertainty with respect to timing (where safety lead times are appropriate).

It is important to first examine the source of the uncertainty, determine whether it is associated with quantity or timing, and study its effect on the planned schedule. This analysis should be both qualitative and quantitative; after such an analysis a suitable combination of safety stocks and times can be chosen. Once these decisions have been made,

their actual incorporation into the MRP system is a fairly straightforward matter.

Lot Sizing

As we mentioned at the outset, the MPS will normally schedule production for level 0 items in batches. Even if the batches are fairly uniform in their sizes and scheduled at fairly regular intervals, the requirements tend to become highly erratic and lumpy as we move to dependent items at a higher level. This is especially true if we have several level 0 items and many subcomponents that are common to more than one end product. As an illustration of this fact consider the schedule in TABLE 29-3. The gross requirements for EX1 are 100 and 80 in Weeks 6 and 10 respectively. However the requirements for P2 are quite irregular and lumpy (ranging from 70 to 520 units).

Determination of appropriate lot sizes for subassemblies and components is a production planning problem where the demand is deterministic but usually very dynamic. There are a number of approaches described in the literature to solve this problem. Most of these trade off the cost of setups against the cost of carrying inventory. If setup procedures are quick and inexpensive, the easiest approach is to use lot-for-lot batching where the batch sizes are exactly equal to requirements. This is also a sensible approach where products tend to have a relatively large number of levels. In such situations, consolidation of requirements for lower level items into larger batches could result in a very rapid growth in requirements for items at higher levels, and timely satisfaction of the latter could become infeasible with the resources at hand.

In other instances the setup costs may be large enough to necessitate some minimum batch size, and in such situations an attempt could be made to optimize the lot sizes over the planning horizon for a given item. Several procedures exist for this, including approximating the variable demand by some constant value and using the well-known EOQ approach, the exact dynamic programming algorithm of Wagner and Whitin, the Silver-Meal heuristic, and the part-period balancing heuristic.

The interested reader is referred to any good book on quantitative methods in production and inventory control for a discussion of these procedures. However, the use of an optimal approach at one level that does not account for its effect on other levels in the product structure is suboptimal for the entire system. Furthermore, trying to derive an optimal policy for the entire multilevel problem is a formidable undertaking. Therefore, in practice the above-listed procedures are rarely if ever incorporated into an MRP system. If any batching is done, it is usually based on very simple economic analyses or rules of thumb. Thus MRP is not an optimal production scheduling system; however, it is an excellent tool for generating good, feasible schedules without excessive effort.

It is probably also worth mentioning at this point that for very low value items that have an extremely high usage—such as nails, screws, washers, nuts, and bolts—it doesn't make too much sense to assign them level codes or to plan their purchase through MRP on an as required basis. Rather it is better to simply treat them as independent demand items and order based upon historical usage records.

Pegging

Pegging is the process of associating subassemblies or components with specific end-products or customer order. This is a procedure that usually applies to parts that are common to several different products or parts that are used in satisfying orders from several different customers. It is often advantageous to look at the requirements for such parts and determine the relative proportions of these requirements generated by different products. If a shortage of these parts is unavoidable, this process provides a way to determine the specific products whose production is going to be delayed (or orders that may not be satisfied on time). The drawback of course is the effort required to actually do the tracking on the computer. Most modern MRP-II systems have this capability, but it is probably a good idea to use this capability only when the information obtained is critically required.

Updating Records

How much time should elapse between successive updates of MRP records for the various items in use? This time is not to be confused with the planning horizon. Planning horizons must at a minimum be long enough to accommodate the cumulative lead time for the production of the level *0* item with the earliest net requirements as dictated by the MPS. This is the total time required, from the acquisition time of the highest level-coded item, through the times required to obtain the various intermediate items, all the way to the level *0* item. It could, of course, be longer to the extent that the MPS is firm for the future.

Record updates, on the other hand, are a function of the changes in operating conditions (such as machine breakdowns, changes in the product structure, changes in manufacturing lead times, and increased production of scrap) and of new information that may have been received (such as discrepancies in stock status, delays in some part of the schedule, or changes in requirements or in the MPS). Updates are necessary so that plans can be altered to account for these changes. There are two basic options available here: schedule regeneration and net change updates.

In schedule regeneration the entire schedule for all items is regenerated from scratch in a single computer run. In other words, the MRP records are updated for every single item, regardless of whether the item is affected by the new information or not. In contrast a net change approach alters the MRP records only for those items that are directly affected by the changes in the system or the new information received.

The frequency of the updates depends to a large extent upon the updating approach in use. With the first approach, there is usually some fixed time interval such as a week or a month between successive schedule regenerations. This is akin to a periodic review inventory system. With the net change approach, updates are much more frequent and take place each time some event occurs to render inaccurate the MRP records for an item. This is similar to continuous review inventory systems with transaction reporting.

The tradeoffs involved in updating frequencies are obvious. Frequent updates take up a lot of computer time for large systems and are more expensive. On the other hand, they result in vast improvements in accuracy of the information contained in the MRP system with respect to both requirements and inventory status. This accuracy is especially critical in large systems with a number of levels since changes could cascade downward and dramatically alter the accuracy of information about items lower down in the product structure.

The net change approach is in general a better one since the high frequency of updates improves accuracy. At the same time, it is not unduly expensive since only some of the records are processed. However, if the updating is overly frequent it may cause the system to become unstable and introduce error in the updating procedure. We recommend net change updates, supplemented with an occasional regeneration to purge the system and clean up all the records.

CLOSING THE LOOP: MRP-II

So far we have only looked at the planning of timing and quantity of material within the manufacturing system. We have not examined the feasibility of the MRP schedule or its implications for the other functional areas within the system. Early MRP systems were called *infinite capacity* systems since they assumed that sufficient capacity and resources existed to carry out the schedule. Furthermore, there were no real feedback loops to examine the behavior of other areas in the plant in relation to material requirements planning. Neither was there any attempt to really integrate other functional areas such as marketing, accounting, and finance into the planning process. MRP systems gradually evolved into the more comprehensive MRP-II systems precisely in response to these shortcomings. This evolution is often referred to by many practitioners as the process of closing the loop (presumably between different areas of a manufacturing concern). In this section we examine the broader concept of MRP-II.

Capacity Requirements Planning

The first step in this extension from MRP to MRP-II is capacity requirements planning or CRP. CRP is a procedure for ensuring the feasibility of the MRP-generated schedule with respect to available production capacity.

CRP works in an iterative fashion. It starts by taking the schedule generated from the specified master production schedule and calculating the capacity requirements at the various work centers in order to see if the schedule is feasible with the available capacity. The first requirement for this process is the routing for the various parts and components that are manufactured in the plant. The routing for an item is the sequence of work centers that will be visited by the part in the course of its manufacture. The next requirement is the specification of the number of units of resource (typically standard production hours) needed for each operation at each work center. Knowing this, and the information from the MRP module such as net requirements, planned order releases and scheduled receipts (along with their respective timings), the capacity requirements planning module estimates the total number of hours required at each work center for each time period in the planning horizon.

Once this estimate is in hand, the actual resource availability for each time period is estimated. This estimate will take into account factors such as breakdowns, scheduled maintenance, and current work in process at the work centers. A comparison is then made between the resource units required and the number that are actually available to see if the overall production plan is feasible. If the resources are insufficient to meet the requirements of the plan, then there are several options available.

For instance, the excess capacity required may be purchased from an outside source: the excess work at a work center may be subcontracted. Alternatively, overtime may be used to make up the capacity shortage. In some instances a part may have alternate routings, in which case it may be possible to move its processing from the bottleneck work center to one that is less busy. This last option is often feasible with flexible manufacturing systems. Sometimes it may also be possible to temporarily transfer resources (such as personnel or machines) from relatively less busy work centers to the bottleneck one.

Another option that is desirable and often built into the MRP-II system itself is the ability to take the existing schedule and "tweak" it in an attempt to make it become feasible. This is usually not very difficult to do. Assuming that the original master production schedule is a good one, deviations from existing capacity tend to be relatively small. In order to overcome this shortage it may be possible to simply move the production of an item to a nearby earlier time bucket where the capacity is relatively underutilized.

Other than a minor increase in work-in-process inventory, the only problem with this approach is that it could cause the change in the schedule to cascade up the line and alter the schedule of subcomponents with higher level codes. It may then happen that the new schedule now becomes infeasible with respect to some other work center. It is therefore preferable in general to make changes in the production schedule for items with a higher level code whenever there is a choice. In this respect computerized MRP-II systems are quite efficient since they can easily reevaluate alternative schedules in an iterative fashion.

Finally, there is the option of actually altering the MPS itself. This may be necessary if some of the options outlined above are unavailable or too expensive, or if it is not possible to find a feasible alternative schedule by minor modifications to the existing one. This option should be exercised only as a last resort, since a considerable amount of effort usually goes into preparing a master production schedule that is feasible with respect to the larger, aggregate plans of the company and is also efficient at the same time.

As an illustration of the principles enunciated above, we return to our example part of the previous section. Let us examine capacity at a particular work center, say WCX, where two distinct operations take place: the processing of purchased part P1 into component C1 (say Operation One), and the assembly of three units of C1 with one unit of part P2 to form subassembly S2 (say Operation Two). Looking at the MRP table (TABLE 29-3), we note that order releases are planned for 600, 670, 600, and 680 units of C1 in Weeks 1, 2, 5, and 6 respectively, and for 200 units of S2 in each of Weeks 2, 3, 6, and 7. All of these order releases have a lead time of one week—they are due one week after order release.

In order to compute the capacity requirements at work center WCX, the CRP module requires information on standard manufacturing times. These times are often specified (along with details of the appropriate work center) in the bills of materials. Suppose that for our example the standard setup time for Operation One is one hour and that the standard runtime is three minutes per part. Similarly, suppose that the standard setup hours for Operation Two is 15 hours and that the standard runtime per part is nine minutes. The capacity requirements may then be estimated as follows:

Week		hours
1	$1 + 600 \times 0.05$	$= 31$
2	$(1 + 670 \times 0.05)$	$= 79.5$
	$+ (15 + 200 \times 0.15)$	
3	$15 + 200 \times 0.15$	$= 45$
5	$(1 + 600 \times 0.05)$	$= 31$
	$+ (15 + 200 \times 0.15)$	
6	$(1 + 680 \times 0.05)$	$= 80$
	$+ (15 + 200 \times 0.15)$	
7	$15 + 200 \times 0.15$	$= 45$

Having completed the computation of capacity requirements for WCX in each week, the CRP module will then proceed to compute the actual availability of capacity at WCX. Suppose that the company works five days a week with each day consisting of two eight-hour shifts. This yields a gross capacity of 80 hours in each time bucket. Suppose further that the operating efficiency of work center WCX is (a rather optimistic!) 90 percent, thus yielding a total availability of 72 hours of actual production time per week (with the remaining eight hours accounting for breakdowns, scheduled maintenance, and other delays).

When we compare the availability with the requirements, we see that the current schedule is infeasible with respect to work center WCX, since the requirements exceed the availability by 7.5 hours in Week 2 and by eight hours in Week 6. Note that this excess could be reduced by one hour in both cases if Operation One is scheduled before Operation Two in both these weeks. This rescheduling would make use of the previous week's setup and save its one hour setup time. Even so, the capacity requirements are still well in excess of the availability.

A simple way to overcome this problem is to note that WCX is not utilized to its full capacity in Weeks 1 and 5. Some of the production scheduled for Weeks 2 and 6 can, therefore, be moved back by a week. Between the two items scheduled at WCX it is preferable to move the production for C1 back, first because it is a part with a higher level code (which implies that the ripple effect associated with this change will tend to be of a smaller magnitude), and second because its production is already scheduled for Weeks 1 and 5.

In our example we could, for instance, increase the planned order release for C1 in Week 1 from 600 to 770 and decrease it from 670 to 500 in Week 2. This would mean that the capacity requirement at WCX rises to 39.5 hours in Week 1 and falls to 71 hours in Week 2. By a similar logic the order releases for C1 in Weeks 5 and 6 could also be changed from 600 and 680 to (say) 770 and 510 respectively, thus giving rise to new requirements of 39.5 hours in Week 5 and 71.5 hours in Week 6. Since C1 was a level *3* item, the current schedule (TABLE 29-3) has to be readjusted for all items with a higher level code (only P1 in our example). The feasibility of this new schedule must be evaluated by the CRP module for any further adjustments; assuming that none are necessary, the final schedule is displayed in TABLE 29-4.

It is worthwhile mentioning at this point that a good MPS is probably the main prerequisite for any

efficient production control system, since it is the MPS that drives the entire production or manufacturing system. It is therefore worth making the effort to draw up a good master schedule. Normally, the MPS is prepared within the constraints of a larger aggregate production plan by disaggregating the latter into plans for individual end items. One of the primary advantages of closed loop systems lies in their ability to build and evaluate master production schedules quickly. While the MRP-II system can help with this process by evaluating MPS feasibility, the actual construction of these schedules depends to a large extent upon the scheduler and his or her knowledge of the operating environment. It should be emphasized that the time spent on drawing up a good MPS will more than pay for itself in the long run.

Dispatching and Shop Floor Control

Once a feasible production schedule is obtained, the next step is to carry it out. The schedule must be transmitted to the shop floor and detailed plans must be made on how the total workload for each time bucket is to be allocated to the various work centers, on how the work allocated to a given work center is to be sequenced, and on what specific tasks are to be executed on a given day.

As an illustration of these points, refer to the final schedule displayed in TABLE 29-4. Assume that it is now the beginning of Week 1 and that the orders planned for the week (770 units of C1, 700 units of P2, and 1000 units of P1) have all been released to the shop floor and the vendors. The MRP-II databases will now show that these orders will be scheduled for receipt after the appropriate purchasing or manufacturing lead times. For the items ordered from vendors (P1 and P2 in our example), the inventory records will be updated only after the items are actually received.

For items to be made in the plant, namely C1, the MRP-II system will now prepare a dispatch list for the daily production at each work center. In order to do this the routings for the part will be

Table 29-4. MRP Schedule Adjusted for Capacity

Level	Item	Measure	(on hand)	WEEK 1	2	3	4	5	6	7	8	9	10
LEVEL 0	EX1	Gross requirements							100				80
		Scheduled receipts				20							
		Projected inventory balance	10	10	10	30	30	30					
		Planned order releases					70				80		
LEVEL 1	S1	Gross requirements					70				80		
		Scheduled receipts											
		Projected inventory balance											
		Planned order releases				70				80			
LEVEL 2	S2	Gross requirements				210	140			240	160		
		Scheduled receipts											
		Projected inventory balance	50	50	50	40	100	100	100	60	100	100	100
		Planned order releases			200	200			200	200			
LEVEL 3	C1	Gross requirements			600	670			600	680			
		Scheduled receipts											
		Projected inventory balance			170				170				
		Planned order releases		770	500			770	510				
LEVEL 3	P2	Gross requirements			200	480	70		200	520	80		
		Scheduled receipts											
		Projected inventory balance	50		550	70			600	80			
		Planned order releases		700				800					
LEVEL 4	P1	Gross requirements		770	500			770	510				
		Scheduled receipts			1000								
		Projected inventory balance	820	50	550	550	550	780	270	270	270	270	
		Planned order releases		1000									

examined and the various manufacturing operations will be assigned to appropriate work centers. Based upon the time standards data and the sequence of the operations, the standard time required for each operation can then be computed along with its due date so that the entire work order is ready by its date of scheduled receipt.

In our example, suppose that there are two operations to be performed on C1, with the first operation taking 39.5 standard hours at work center WCX (as computed in the previous section) and the second taking 20.5 standard hours at work-center WCY (1.25 hours for setup, and $770 \times 0.025 = 19.25$ hours runtime). At work-center WCX the operation time would then be 39.5 hours and the due date might be specified as the end of the first shift on Day 3 (40 hours into the week). Similarly, at WCY the operation time could be specified as 20.5 hours with the due date specified as the end of Day 4 (64 hours into the week).

By a similar logic all other operations scheduled for the week are also assigned a work center and a due date. Based upon the operation times and due dates, the dispatch list for each work center will then contain the sequence of operations to be performed at that work center. This list will then be prioritized according to the due dates for the operations. The foreman or the shop floor supervisor can then actually start to execute the various operations. At this point, several creative sequencing and scheduling rules (that are not based upon due dates alone) could be employed, especially if there is some flexibility with respect to the due dates. These include criteria such as shortest processing time, available slack time, machine utilization, critical ratio, and slack per operation. The interested reader should refer to any book on quantitative approaches to sequencing and scheduling for a further discussion of these topics.

In addition to scheduling there should also be mechanisms for monitoring the progress of the production plan, and reacting to changes in the system status, such as altered due dates or machine breakdowns. If schedule regeneration is in use, then the requirement is for a rescheduling mechanism until the next regeneration point. Where net change updates are in use, this calls for a means to update the system database in real time.

Typically, MRP-II systems track the work being done at the various work centers by means of input/output reports. This is done by computing the actual standard hours of work that is input to each work center and the standard hours of output coming out of the work center, and then comparing these with the standard hours that are planned for the work center. Any discrepancy between the planned and actual workloads is an indication that the work center is not performing at a satisfactory rate, and orders can then be appropriately expedited. If this is not possible, then the schedule might have to be altered. In addition, MRP-II systems also track and update other miscellaneous databases relating to manufacturing activities such as tooling and scheduled maintenance for machines.

The shop floor control module performs a variety of tasks. These include creating and maintaining shop floor data, recording bar-coded data, collecting feedback data for input/output reports, generating shop floor paperwork (such as workorders), and generating status and exception reports.

MRP-II and other Functional Areas

So far we have been concentrating on how closed-loop MRP-II systems plan and control activities that relate to manufacturing. The primary modules are those that are responsible for material and capacity requirements planning, and for the actual execution of these plans on the shop floor. In this section we examine MRP-II in a broader context by looking at this relationship with various other functional areas in a manufacturing facility. Separate modules are normally built into the MRP-II system to handle these areas and these modules are all interlinked with each other and with the modules that have already been described.

Among the other functional areas, the strongest impact of MRP-II has been in finance and accounting. Typically the dollar is still the bottom line for people who manage complex manufacturing systems, and MRP-II helps in financial planning by maintaining and presenting cost data on a number of different things. A costing module maintains and updates standard costs of purchased parts, standard labor rates, and standard material and overhead rates. It also establishes and maintains costs of work orders, values work-in-process and inventory, and generates costs for manufactured parts. Other capabilities include calculation of sales prices, reporting of cost trends, and generation of reports for on-line review of standard costs.

A second important module is one for handling accounts receivable and accounts payable. This module maintains and updates information on vendors and their accounts, and schedules, approves, processes, and generates documents for payments to vendors. It also posts sales ledger transactions, maintains individual customer ledger balances, and generates overall audit and analysis reports.

A third module commonly found is the payroll support modules. This typically maintains employee information, updates time and attendance data, and generates payroll information for each employee. It usually has several options for consolidating payroll information based on departments or preassigned labor codes, and for generating a variety of reports.

Another area where MRP-II plays an important

role is purchasing. A major problem that people in purchasing very often have is with respect to vendor backlogs and delivery lead times. As backlogs increase, vendors also increase the delivery time, which in turn increases the backlog further. A big advantage that users of MRP-II systems have is that, very often, they can give their vendors a fairly accurate six month to one year schedule. Some initial portion of the schedule may be firm (corresponding to the portion of the planning horizon which is frozen), and this translates into firm orders to the vendor. The rest of the schedule gives the vendors a good idea of what they can expect in the near future, so that they can plan accordingly.

Typically most MRP-II systems have a purchasing information management module. This module creates a master list of vendors, plans and places orders and requisitions, manages inspection of purchased material, expedites late orders, records vendor responses, and tracks vendor performance.

MRP-II also has an important role in marketing. Recall that the master production schedule is the starting point for all MRP activities. Marketing should play a big part in the evolution of the MPS, since in reality the latter may be viewed as a specification of what will be made for sale to the customer. Most MRP-II systems have a forecasting module built in for use by people in marketing. Typically, the benefits to marketing accrue after MRP-II systems have been in operation for some time. These benefits are attributable to the MRP-II system's role as an information system that provides reliable data on realistic and achievable marketing goals.

Another area where MRP-II systems have proved useful is engineering. This is mainly because of the detailed engineering related information, such as manufacturing lead times, tooling, bills of materials, and routings that such systems force a manufacturing concern to hold. These data are invaluable when it comes to design of new products, updating of existing designs, and product standardization.

In summary, MRP-II is more than a mere scheduling mechanism. It is a comprehensive integrative tool that interfaces with every aspect of a manufacturing concern. It promotes the smooth, flexible, and efficient operation of the entire organization by coordinating the functioning of all of its subsystems.

IMPLEMENTATION OF MRP-II SYSTEMS

In this section, we examine some of the issues that relate to the successful implementation of an MRP-II system. One of the foremost proponents of these systems has been Oliver Wight, and much of the material presented in this section is directly attributable to him and his excellent book listed in the references at the end of this chapter. Wight states that the critical elements in implementing an MRP system belong to one of three categories: (1) *people*, (2) *data*, and (3) *technical competence*. These three are ranked in order of significance; a computer system is of course considered a prerequisite.

With respect to the first category, it is critical to remember that people are the key to success. An MRP-II system (or any other system for that matter) does not guarantee a successful business; people do. The people must understand and be sold on MRP-II or it is not very likely to work. It is therefore important to remember that people are the most important resource in implementing an MRP-II system.

With respect to data, the primary areas where a very high level of data accuracy is critical for the closed-loop MRP system to work are (1) the master production schedule, (2) the bills-of-materials, (3) inventory records, (4) routings, and (5) work centers.

Finally, the third area relates to technical competence. This is a direct function of the effort spent in training and education. It is best to start with a detailed implementation plan.

Preliminary Activities

Before beginning the actual conversion to an MRP-II system, it is important to put together a comprehensive plan of action for the implementation project. Some highlights of a typical implementation plan as outlined by Wight are as follows.

First-cut Education Before starting a justification, the following people in top management should be educated with an MRP-II course aimed at top management:

- Chief Executive Officer
- VP Manufacturing
- VP Finance
- VP Engineering
- VP Marketing
- VP Administration

The following managers should attend a course designed for middle management (and preferably offered by the vendor):

- Plant Manager
- Materials Manager
- Purchasing Manager
- Data Processing Systems Manager

As the education program progresses, it should spread out from key users to others in peripheral areas such as the foremen and shop floor supervisors. The programs should be tailored to the needs of the individual groups. Several companies and institutes offer such programs.

Justification Implementation of a comprehensive MRP-II system involve a substantial amount of time and money; whether it is worth the required effort is a matter for each company to decide on its own. Justification should therefore be based upon individual circumstances and not on average figures. The areas where potential for benefits exists are:

- Inventory costs
- Service levels
- Quality
- Cost of purchased goods
- Engineering costs
- Overtime and subcontracting
- Quality of life
- Obsolescence

Potential cost savings in the above areas should

be contrasted against the cost of implementing and maintaining the MRP-II system. In most cases, substantial savings are practically guaranteed as long as the systems are effectively utilized.

Project Leader The next step is the appointment of a project leader. The project leader should be a full-time user of the system. He or she should have been with the company for several years and should be completely familiar with the products, the processes, the problems, and the people. A plant manager would be a good choice.

Professional Guidance While it is critical for the project team to have representatives from all functional areas that will be making use of the MRP-II system, it is also useful to obtain some professional outside help from a consultant of other persons familiar with MRP-II systems and their implementation. The most important quality to consider in hiring a consultant is experience. The best kind of consultant is one who will come in on a regular basis and provide progressive assistance, rather than one who will react to mistakes. Even in dealing with established consulting firms, it is better to have someone who has actually installed a successful MRP-II system elsewhere than a person who comes in occasionally to supervise a group of people who install the system.

Project Plan—with Accountability The next step is to come up with a detailed project plan with a list of activities. Next to each of the activities on the project plan, put a deadline for its completion and the names of the people who will be accountable for attaining results.

Education This is without any doubt the most critical component of the entire implementation process. Once the decision has been made to implement MRP-II, there is no such thing as too much education. The education task is indeed a formidable one, especially when one considers the number of people who need to be familiar with and sold on the system. However, it is worth spending as much time as required on this task. It is possible to achieve this goal of complete education on MRP-II through the use of a variety of live outside classes and video education courses that are available today.

Regular Management Review Finally, there should be regular meetings (at least once in two weeks) involving management in order to review progress of the project plan and ensure that schedules are being met. The project manager and people accountable for various activities in the implementation project should report on the status of the project and discuss any problems with the other members of the project team and top managers in each of the major functional areas.

Conversion to the New System

Once the seven requirements listed in the previous section are met, the company can begin the task of actually converting to the new system. Wight discusses three methods commonly used for this conversion.

The Cold Turkey Approach In the cold turkey approach, the system is installed all at once; the theoretical justification for this being that this is strongly motivational and forces the people to make it work. In practice, however, the people usually end up being overwhelmed by the sheer magnitude of the task and the conversion ends in failure. In general, it is highly inadvisable for any company to ever put an MRP-II system on-line cold turkey.

The Parallel System Approach The parallel method is based on the premise that as long as the new system isn't working yet, it is better to also run the old (existing) system in parallel and stick with the policies dictated by the latter when the old system breaks down.

There are two serious problems with this approach. First, this is very inefficient with respect to the human resources that are available, and places an excessive strain on the workforce. Most often there simply won't be enough people to run both systems and it is far more advisable to use the available personnel to implement the new system. Second, MRP is a computer-based system for doing things that the existing manual planning system could not possibly do. Consequently, there will always be conflicting policies if both systems are run in parallel and the overall situation may become a lot worse.

The Pilot Approach The "pilot" approach is the one that is recommended most because it has the highest probability of success. In this approach a single product (or product-line) is picked and the MRP system is implemented just for this one product. The pilot is used to ensure that the databases for the MRP system are reliable and that the system can correctly determine what material is required and when it is required for the pilot product line. Furthermore, the pilot is useful to check and see if the planner whose product line is being used in the pilot actually understands how the system works. If the system works on the pilot product and the people running the system have demonstrable understanding of its logic, it can then be extended in a modular fashion to other product lines until the entire MRP-II system is installed. This extension is discussed further in the next section.

Modular Implementation

At the outset of this chapter we stated that MRP-II may be viewed as a comprehensive information system that integrates all data concerning the company into a common database accessible to all functional areas within the company. The entire basis for MRP-II is the establishment of this common database. With a modular approach, this is done by putting together the various pieces of the database in a step-wise fashion.

The starting point is the establishment of the engineering data bases. These include things such as part numbers, product structures, routings, operations with lead times, work centers, scrap rates, and tooling. The establishment of the engineering database considerably eases the implementation of individual modules of the MRP-II system and (through the part numbers) also provides a common basis for all other operating units to communicate with each other.

Once the engineering database is established, other modules may be considered for implementation. Usually the first modules for implementation are those that relate directly to manufacturing such as bills-of-materials and low-level codes, master scheduling, material and capacity requirements planning, shopfloor control, work-in-process, and inventory modules. The other modules such as costing, manufacturing accounting, purchasing, payroll, and sales order management can then be added.

The primary advantage of using the modular approach is that the modules can fit into the operating environment and, once the engineering database has been established, top priority can be given to any of the modules without affecting the total MRP-II concept. Furthermore this approach helps to isolate system-related errors from people-related errors and implementation problems can be kept in their proper perspective. In the event of a problem with the implementation, effort can therefore be concentrated more efficiently in a smaller area. Another advantage to this modular approach is that after the basic functions of each module are established, further enhancements to its capabilities can be gradually added on as the users become more comfortable with the system and appreciate its benefits. To reiterate an important principle, the integrity of data is crucial if the full benefits from MRP-II are to be realized; it is worth remembering this point during the entire course of the implementation.

Time Schedules

Wight suggests implementing an MRP-II system on an 18 to 24 month schedule. The elements that are most likely to be crucial during the implementation are those that relate directly to the establishment of the engineering database such as the bills-of-material and the routings. Additionally, the development of the computer software, the establishment of proper inventory status records, and—last but not least—the task of continuously educating people may all be expected to take longer than anticipated.

In the event of a delay in the implementation schedule, the item that is causing the delay should be promptly identified and fixed since a delay in implementation could have important ramifications on the financial justification of the entire project and

the payback period for the investment. Further justification for quick implementation lies in the fact that projects such as these are comprehensive in nature with many different people working on them. It often becomes difficult to maintain momentum and enthusiastic support for the project from all quarters for more than a couple of years. In this regard it may be mentioned that the modular approach to implementation outlined in the previous section is very effective because successful implementation of a module and the consequent increase in productivity helps people become more accepting of the MRP-II system. A small amount of success on a regular basis will sustain enthusiasm and momentum.

LIMITATIONS AND ALTERNATIVES

While MRP-II is a very useful tool in helping manufacturing concerns run efficiently, it is not a cure-all and does have its limitations. First, it can generate schedules only when the MPS is feasible. If the CRP module detects a situation where there is insufficient capacity, the MRP-II system does not, on its own, suggest or implement the best option to overcome the problem.

Second, as we emphasized at the beginning, MRP only searches for feasible schedules. It does not attempt to optimize the schedule in any way. Some systems do have built-in techniques for finding optimal lot sizes (based upon setup and inventory carrying costs) for the dynamic requirements at the various levels. These lot-sizing techniques are applied to one item at a time. However, the product requirements are not independent of each other; they are related through the bills-of-materials. Therefore, even when they do exist such techniques can at best result in some suboptimization.

Third, MRP-II systems do not properly address situations where setup times are sequence dependent, where the setup time for a job is dependent on the job that was previously run on the equipment. (A simplified example of this was given in the section on capacity requirements planning.) This sequencing has to be performed outside of the system.

Finally, MRP-II cannot handle systems where parts have alternate routings in the process plan for their manufacture. An example of this is with a flexible manufacturing system where several different machines might be capable of a specific operation. In this case, MRP-II would not be able to trace and generate these alternate paths within the FMS. However, the entire FMS could be treated as a single resource and MRP could be applied at a broader level of detail.

The above limitations are not really crucial, as long as the user understands their practical implications. MRP-II software packages are in general somewhat ahead of the level of sophistication of most of the users of the system. Experts seem to agree that both the functional level of the software and the functional level demanded by users will continue to increase.

As far as alternatives go, there appear to be two other methodologies that are promising. However, these are only for planning production, and in general are nowhere near as comprehensive or integrative as MRP-II. Nevertheless, one could under some circumstances foresee these options replacing the MRP and CRP modules of an MRP-II system. These options are just-in-time manufacturing (JIT) and optimized production technology (or OPT).

The JIT technique originated in Japan. It is sometimes mistakenly referred to as Kanban; Kanban is only one component of just-in-time manufacturing. The main philosophy here is similar to MRP: to produce only *what* is required *when* it is required. However, JIT goes a little further by attempting to produce in small lots (ideally of size one) so as to minimize inventory. In order to apply JIT successfully, there are very stringent prerequisites. These include stable demand, smooth production, small setup times, highly reliable equipment and 100 percent quality. If it is not possible for one reason or another to meet all these requirements, then JIT should not be attempted. Even though several companies in the U.S. have successfully incorporated just-in-time manufacturing techniques, there are also a number of examples where JIT implementation has been attempted with disastrous results.

OPT is based upon the analysis of bottleneck stages in sequential manufacturing and assembly systems, and upon the use of smart scheduling techniques based upon operations research methodologies. OPT is based on the precept that there is more complexity to manufacturing than MRP-II can handle, and OPT attempts to built more intelligence into MRP-II to deal with the complexity. The application of OPT, however, has not been as widespread as MRP-II. All the same it would appear that we can expect to see more smart scheduling rules and techniques complementing MRP-II systems of the future.

REFERENCES

The literature on MRP and MRP-II is very large and growing as more companies adopt these systems; we do not propose to give a comprehensive literature survey here. Rather, what follows is a short list of excellent references on MRP-II, a starting point for a more extensive research.

Capacity Planning Reprints. Falls Church, Virginia: American Production and Inventory Control Society, 1986.

Material Requirements Planning Reprints. Falls Church, Virginia: American Production and Inventory Control Society, 1986.

Orlicky, J. *Material Requirements Planning*. New York: McGraw-Hill, 1975.

Plossl, G. W. *Production and Inventory Control*. Englewood Cliffs, New Jersey: Prentice-Hall, Inc., 1985.

Vollman, T. E., W. L. Berry, and D. C. Whybark. *Manufacturing Planning and Control Systems*. Homewood, Illinois: Richard D. Irwin, Inc., 1988.

Wight, Oliver W. *Manufacturing Resource Planning: MRPII*. Essex Junction, Vermont: Oliver Wight Limited Publications, Inc., 1981.

_____. *Production and Inventory Management in the Computer Age*. New York: Van Nostrand Reinhold Company, Inc., 1984.

30

Inventory Control Models

Steven Nahmias[*]

MATHEMATICAL MODELING HAS HAD A SIGNIFICANT impact on inventory control. Inventory models form the basis for the logic behind computerized systems marketed both nationally and internationally. The purpose of this chapter is to acquaint the novice with the basics of inventory control modeling and its most significant results to date.

In the United States alone the value of inventories is near one trillion dollars (survey of Current Business 1989). Firms with scientific inventory control techniques have had a substantial advantage in the marketplace. Traditionally, such systems ran on mainframe computers and were reserved for large firms only. However, in recent years inventory control systems are being marketed successfully to small firms. The advent of the personal computer has opened the door for small businesses to reap the benefits of scientific management as well. As the technology of personal computing continues to evolve, we will see increasingly more complex software ported to personal computers.

Operations research has had perhaps its greatest impact in inventory control. It is true that only a very small percentage of the mathematical models that have appeared in the literature have ever been implemented. However, that small percentage has resulted in the control of billions of dollars of inven-

tories. Also, it is not only the simple models that have been implemented. For example, the military has employed very sophisticated multiechelon mathematical models in controlling millions of dollars of repairable inventories and inventories of spares in general.

HISTORICAL NOTES

The first inventory analysis predates formal operations research activities by almost 30 years. Ford Harris (1915) is generally credited with the discovery of the simple EOQ model which formed the basis for later developments. Except for the work of Wilson (1934), virtually no inventory papers appeared before 1950. In the early 1950s, however, several important papers on the mathematical theory of inventory control appeared. These included the studies of Arrow, Harris, and Marshak (1951) and Dvoretzky, Kiefer, and Wolfowitz (1952a and 1952b). Whitin's (1957) monograph was important in linking classical economic theory to inventory control and discussed in detail the (Q,R) model, which became the basis for many commercial control systems. The book by Arrow, Karlin, and Scarf (1958) included a collection of highly technical papers which served as the cornerstone of the mathematical theory of inventories.

*Steven Nahmias is Professor and Chairman of the Department of Decision and Information Sciences at Santa Clara University. He holds a BA in Mathematics and Physics from Queens College, a BS in Industrial Engineering from Columbia University, and MS and PhD degrees in Operations Research from Northwestern University. He also served on the Faculties of the University of Pittsburgh and Stanford University. He has authored or coauthored approximately fifty technical articles which have appeared in a variety of national and international journals. He is the author of *Production and Operations Analysis*, published by Richard D. Irwin in 1989. He is a member of TIMS and ORSA and is an associate editor for both *Management Science* and *Naval Research Logistics*.

Today, inventory models are a mainstay of the literature on operations research. Both national and international journals such as *Management Science, American Institute of Industrial Engineers Transactions, Naval Research Logistics Quarterly, Operations Research*, and the *International Journal of Production Research*, just to name a few, publish articles regularly on inventory problems.

MOTIVATION

Arrow (1958) reviews the motivations for holding inventories in light of the motivations that Keynes proposed for holding cash. In many ways one could consider inventories and cash to be equivalent. At any given point in time one could, presumably, convert inventories to cash and vice versa. Arrow claims that the three motives for holding inventories are the transactionary, precautionary, and the speculative.

These motives may be translated into the following practical terms. Due to economies of scale, it is often economical to produce, to order, or to ship in large lots and store items for later use. This is the transactionary motive. The precautionary motive means that inventories can be a hedge against uncertainty. Uncertainties take many forms and each can be significant. There are uncertainties in supply, in demand, and in lead time. Finally, the speculative motive means that the value of the inventory might rise because of shortages in supply or demand.

TYPES OF MODELS:
Real World or Ivory Tower?

Much of the literature in operations research has come under fire in recent years as ivory tower research. It seems that academics create mathematical models of inventory control with little regard for their relationship to reality. One might argue that academics are wasting their time publishing such esoterica. However, those who espouse this point of view forget one important fact. In any research endeavor the percentage of projects resulting in a concrete product is very small. This is true whether the research is done

with or without government support in universities or is funded by a company interested in realizing a profit from the results.

Inventory research has had a significant impact. Firms often quote inventory as an area in which analytical models have made important inroads. Often it may not necessarily be the results of a particular model that are important, but the approach or method used in its development.

The complexity of an inventory model results from the assumptions made about the systems key characteristics. These include (but are not limited to):

- Demand
- Costs
- Lead time
- Backordering
- Review
- Changes over time
- Multiple echelons
- Interactions

I briefly discuss each.

Demand. The fundamental breakdown is between deterministic demand and random demand. Another distinction is between stationary (constant) or time varying demand. The assumptions about demand are often the most important in determining the complexity of the resulting model.

Costs. All inventory models have as their goal the minimization of costs. (Some models may be defined in terms of maximizing profit, but these two objectives can usually be shown to be equivalent.) Costs may be averaged or discounted. The presence of a fixed order cost will make the model more complex. Furthermore, cost functions are generally assumed to be linear, convex, or concave.

Lead time. The lead time is the amount of time that elapses from the point that an order is placed until it arrives. (Equivalently, it can be thought of as the time from the initiation of production to the completion of production.) The simplest assumption is that the lead time is known and fixed. Although lead time uncertainty is common in practice, it is difficult to incorporate into the analysis.

Backordering. Several assumptions may be made about how the system reacts when demand exceeds supply. The most common and easiest to analyze is that all excess demand is backordered. Backordered demand is reflected by a negative level of on hand inventory. Alternatively, excess demand may be lost. This case, known as lost sales, is common in retailing. Other alternatives exist as well. Part of the excess demand may be lost and part may be backordered, or there may be a fixed impatience time after which customers will cancel their orders.

Review. The two most common review systems are periodic review and continuous review. Periodic review means that inventory levels are known only at discrete points in time, such as when physical stock taking occurs. Continuous review, also known as transactions reporting, means that inventory levels are always known. Point of sale inventory systems in which sales are recorded as they occur would be one example of a true continuous review system.

Changes over time. Some inventories do not retain a uniform utility over time. Electronic components and other types of spare parts may become obsolete. Other types of inventories may deteriorate or decay and must be discarded before satisfying demand. Examples are radioactive materials, food, drugs, photographic film, and human blood. Decay and perishability are difficult processes to model.

Multiple echelons. Multiechelon inventory models have become a topic of considerable interest in recent years. Multiple echelons are common in military depot-base repair systems, warehouse-retailer systems, and multilevel production or distribution systems.

Interactions. Most of the literature concerns single product systems, while most real problems involve multiple products. As long as significant interactions among the individual products are not present, treating each product independently will give adequate results. However, in some systems the interactions among the products cannot be ignored. Examples are products that are economic complements or economic substitutes. Pork and

beef are examples of substitutes and frankfurters and buns are examples of complements.

DETERMINISTIC MODELS FOR SINGLE PRODUCT SYSTEMS

The EOQ model underlines virtually all inventory control models. It considers the basic economic trade-offs present in many real systems and is a valuable means of controlling inventories in many firms even today.

The Basic EOQ Model

The EOQ model requires the following assumptions:

- Demand is known with certainty and fixed at λ units per unit time.
- Shortages are not permitted.
- Lead time for delivery is instantaneous. (As it turns out, this assumption may be relaxed with no additional complexity added to the analysis.)
- There is no time discounting of money. The goal is to minimize average costs per unit time over an infinite planning horizon.
- Only fixed order costs, at K per positive order, and holding costs, as h per unit held per unit time, are present. (One can also include a proportional ordering cost, but it will not appear explicitly in the formula for the optimal order quantity.)

The holding cost is generally written $h = Ic$, where I is an annual interest rate and c is the proportional order cost. The interest rate includes the opportunity cost of alternative investment and costs of physical storage, insurance, theft, and taxes, expressed as a percentage of the dollar value of the inventory.

It is easy to show that optimal policy orders an amount Q each time the on-hand inventory level hits zero. The changes over time of the inventory level appear in FIG. 30-1.

The goal is to find the value of Q that minimizes the average cost per unit time. Since the inventory

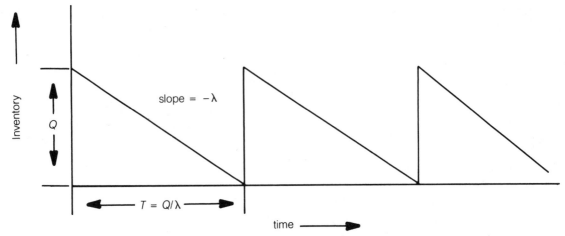

Fig. 30-1. The inventory level for the EOQ Model as a function of time.

level varies linearly between Q and 0 each cycle, the average inventory level is $Q/2$, so that the average annual holding cost is $hQ/2$. Since the demand rate is λ, the time between placement of orders is $T = Q/\lambda$. Furthermore, since there is exactly one setup each cycle, the average annual setup cost is K/T or $K\lambda/Q$.

The optimal value of Q minimizes $hQ/2 + K\lambda/Q$. Taking the first derivative and setting the result equal to zero gives the well known formula

$$Q = \sqrt{\frac{2K\lambda}{h}}$$

which is known as the EOQ formula. This formula provides the correct balance between economies of scale represented by the setup cost and the opportunity costs of alternative investment plus storage costs represented by the holding cost.

Extension to a Finite Production Rate
One straightforward extension of the EOQ model is to the case where a firm produces internally rather than orders from an outside supplier. When this is the case and the rate of production is comparable to the rate of demand, one must modify the EOQ formula. Assume that the rate of production is $\phi > \lambda$. Then we define $h' = h(1 - \lambda/\phi)$ and substitute h' for

h in the EOQ formula above to obtain the optimal production lot size. If ϕ is much larger than λ ($\phi > 10\lambda$), this modification is unnecessary.

Quantity Discounts   Often producers provide an incentive to the consumer to buy in larger lots by reducing the unit cost on large orders. We are all familiar with quantity discounts in the supermarket. In fact, quantity discounting is the basis of the so-called *warehouse* concept of merchandising that has become so popular in recent years.

Many different types of quantity discounts exist, but the most prevalent appears to be the all units discount. Here one receives a discount on all units of an order as long as the order quantity exceeds some minimal level, known as the break point. Multiple break points may also exist so that the unit discount increases as one attains higher break points. For example, one usually pays more per can of beer when the cans are purchased one at a time than when they are purchased in a six pack, and one usually pays more per can for a six pack than for a case.

Let the break points be denoted by $0 = b_0 < b_1 < ... < b_m$. Then we assume that if $b_{i-1} \le Q < b_i$ the unit cost is c_i where $c_i > c_2 > ... > c_m$. Hence the average annual cost of ordering a value of Q between b_{i-1} and b_i is

$$C_i(Q) = c_i \lambda + K \lambda/Q + Ic_iQ/2$$

One can show that the optimal value of Q is either the value of Q minimizing $C_i(Q)$ for some i or one of the break points. Hadley and Whitin (1963) present a systematic means of finding the optimal value of Q for this problem.

An alternative discount schedule is incremental. For an incremental discount schedule, the discount applies only to the units ordered beyond the break point. Here the incentive to move up to the next break point is not as great as it is in the all units case. The optimal order quantity is almost *never* equal to a break point in the all units case. The form of the expected cost function and the computing requirements are more complex than for all unit discounts, however. Hadley and Whitin discuss this case in detail as well.

Additional Extensions

Several other extensions of the EOQ are possible. We only mention these here and refer the interested reader elsewhere for a more comprehensive discussion. One extension is to the case where learning effects are incorporated into the analysis. In this context learning means that the cost or time required for production declines as the cumulative production volume increases. Another extension is to the case where one assumes that price, as well as order size, is a decision variable. A variant of this problem occurs when price increases are announced beforehand. One can also incorporate inflation effects into the analysis. Finally, EOQ models can be generalized to include the effects of an increasing trend in the pattern of demands. The interested reader should refer to the review by Lee and Nahmias (1991) for a more comprehensive treatment of these extensions.

PRODUCTION PLANNING MODELS

The simple EOQ model discussed in the previous section has been generalized in several ways. One of the most important was due to Wagner and Whitin (1958). They considered relaxing the assumption that the demand is constant. Hence, the Wagner-Whitin (WW) model replaces the first assumption above with

- (1') There are known demands for a single item in each n planning periods $r_1, r_2, \ldots, r_n$.

Wagner and Whitin assumed a finite planning horizon, while the EOQ model assumes an infinite planning horizon. The basis of the algorithm is the observation that an optimal policy will only order in periods in which the starting inventory is zero. This means that the order quantity in each period must be the sum of a set of future demands. That is,

$$y_1 = r_1$$

or

$$y_1 = r_1 + r_2$$

or

.
.
.

or

$$y_1 = r_1 + r_2 + \ldots + r_n$$

In general,

$$y_i = 0 \text{ or} \sum_{j=i}^{k} r_j \text{ for } i \leq k \leq n \text{ and } 2 \leq i \leq n$$

A policy that only orders some set of future requirements is known as an exact requirements policy. The observation that an optimal policy is an exact requirements policy cuts down enormously on the number of policies that are candidates for optimality. With this observation, the problem of finding the optimal policy reduces to finding the minimum length path through a one way network, which can be solved by dynamic programming. Although somewhat tedious to solve by hand, problems with long planning horizons can be solved quickly on a computer.

If one replaces the linear holding cost and the setup cost with arbitrary concave cost function, the form of the optimal policy remains the same and the algorithm is essentially unchanged. Zangwill (1966) discovered the structure of the optimal policy and an efficient algorithm for solving the concave production planning problem when excess demand is backordered.

Approximations

Because the concave cost production planning problem arises so often in practice, considerable effort has been expended to obtain efficient approximations. The two approximation methods we will discuss are the Silver-Meal heuristic (Silver and Meal 1973) and the part period balancing heuristic (DeMatteis 1968). Although researchers have proposed several other methods, these two appear to be the most popular and the most efficient.

The Silver-Meal heuristic computes the average cost per period as a function of the number of periods scanned by an order and stops when this function first increases. Let $C(T)$ be the average holding and setup cost for a horizon consisting of T periods. Then

$$C(1) = K$$
$$C(2) = (K + hr_2)/2$$

In general,

$$C(j) = (K + hr_2 + 2hr_3 + \ldots + (j-1)hr_j)/j$$

Once $C(j) > C(j-1)$, we stop and set $y_1 = r_1 + r_2 + \ldots + r_j$ and repeat the process starting again in period j.

Part period balancing is a simpler method (and hence the reason for its apparent greater popularity among users). The idea is to choose the order horizon to most closely balance the total holding cost over the horizon with the setup cost. The total holding cost over j periods commencing with period 1 is $H_j = hr_2 + 2hr_3 + \ldots + (j-1)hr_j$. One finds the value of j so that $H_{j-1} < K < H_j$. The horizon length is chosen as $j-1$ or j depending on whether K is closer to H_{j-1} or H_j.

Several other heuristics for unconstrained production lot sizing exist as well. These include least unit cost, lot for lot, and period order quantity (see McLeavey and Narasimhan 1985 for a discussion of these methods). The literature suggests that the Silver-Meal method is the most accurate of these approximations. However, since most applications in which one would use these algorithms require a computer and one can quickly solve the WW algorithm on a computer, these heuristics are of questionable value.

Capacitated Lot Sizing

The production planning models discussed in the previous sections assumed that there was no limit on the production lot size in any period. However, in most environments there are bounds on the quantities that can be produced. This is known as capacitated lot sizing. The capacitated lot sizing problem is far more difficult to solve than the uncapacitated problem. The fundamental result for the unconstrained problem—that the optimal policy only orders when starting inventory is zero—no longer holds. The capacitated lot sizing problem is known as an NP hard problem. Practically speaking, that means that finding optimal policies is very difficult. Several researchers have suggested optimal policy algorithms for solving this problem (Florian and Klein 1971; Love 1973; and Baker et al. 1978), but these methods are impractical for large scale applications. Heuristic methods have been explored by Karni (1981) and Dixon and Silver (1981). Nahmias (1989) discusses a heuristic method for capacitated lot sizing in the context of materials requirements planning systems. I will not review these heuristics here but only note that they seem to provide reasonably cost effective solutions to the capacitated lot sizing problem.

Other Cost Structures

The WW model assumes only a setup cost and a linear holding cost. However, their results also hold when the ordering and holding costs are general concave functions. A production planning problem whose structure is fundamentally different from WW occurs when costs are convex. Convexity might occur in practice when production costs are linear but there is an upper bound on the amount produced in any period. Veinott ("Production Planning" 1964) developed an algorithm for solving the production planning problem with convex costs. His method requires starting with a requirements schedule of 0 in every period and successively increasing the requirements by one unit until one achieves the desired schedule. He proves that his process will always result in an optimal production schedule. Because most real problems include setup costs, however, a concave cost structure is more common.

Multiple Levels and Multiple Products

Most of the models for multilevel and multiproduct optimization assuming deterministic demand seek optimal lot sizes for MRP systems. One generally formulates such problems as mathematical programs. Because of the presence of setup costs, the resulting formulation is an integer rather than a continuous linear program. Unfortunately, for realistically sized problems the resulting integer program could be too large to solve. A typical formulation of this type is due to McLaren (1976). It is:

$$\text{Minimize} \sum_{i=1}^{N} \sum_{i=1}^{T} K_i \delta_{it} + h_i I_{it}$$

subject to

$$I_{1,t-1} + y_{1t} - I_{1t} = r_t \quad \text{for } 1 \le t \le T$$
$$I_{i,t-1} + y_{it} - I_{it} - m_{i,s(i)} y_{s(i),t} = 0$$
$$\text{for } 1 \le t \le T, 2 \le i \le N$$

$$y_{it} \le \delta_{it} M \quad \text{for } 1 \le t \le T, 2 \le i \le N;$$
$$y_{it} I_{it} \ge 0, \ \delta_{it} = 0 \text{ or } 1$$

In this formulation the objective function is the total handling and setup cost for all items over all time periods in the planning horizon. Item 1 is the end item and is assumed to be unique. The first constraint is the inventory balance constraint for the end item. The second set of constraints are the inventory balance constraints for the subassemblies below the end item level. Interpret m_i, $s(i)$ as the *number of units of component i* required to produce one unit of subassembly $s(i)$ at the next higher level. Note that δ_{it} is the Kronnecker delta function whose value is either 0 or 1 as determined by the final constraint. Taking M to be a large number, the last constraint will result in $\delta_{it} = 1$ if $y_{it} > 0$ and $\delta_{it} = 0$ if $y_{it} = 0$.

A computationally more efficient formulation of this problem using the concept of echelon stock is due to Afentakis, Gavish, and Karmarkar (1984). However, the size of the resulting integer programming problem would probably make this formulation computationally infeasible for most real problems.

STOCHASTIC MODELS FOR SINGLE PRODUCT SYSTEMS

In this section we explore models for controlling a single product inventory system when the demand for the product is random. Most research in this area requires that the distribution of demand be known. Practically, this means that there has been some history of demand from which the probability distribution can be estimated. A common approach is to assume that the form of the distribution is normal and that one uses exponential smoothing to track the mean and standard deviation of periodic demand.

Stochastic models are generally more complex than their deterministic counterparts. However, demand uncertainty can rarely be ignored. Much of the research on stochastic inventory models focuses on finding the form of an optimal policy rather than necessarily developing an efficient computing algorithm. Nonetheless, efficient algorithms do exist. Few commercial inventory systems fail to include some provision for demand uncertainty.

The Newsboy Model

The newsboy model is probably the first stochastic inventory model, but its exact origins are unclear. It is probably safe to say that it was developed sometime in the 1940s. The model is appropriate for a product that perishes quickly; that is after one planning period. One example is newspapers that have a value to the consumer only for a single day. Another is Christmas trees whose utility to the consumer does not extend beyond the Christmas season.

Let y be the number of units purchased at the beginning of the period. Assume that the demand during the period, D, is a random variable with a known probability distribution. Assume that the CDF of demand is $F(t)$ and the PDF of demand is $f(t)$ where t is a realization of the demand. There are several ways one could model the cost structure. One is to use the notion of overage and overage costs, which has advantages for problem solving. Silver and Peterson (1985) used this approach. Another is to adopt the cost structure of Arrow, Karlin, and Scarf (1958). I present the latter approach.

Assume the following cost structure:

- There is a proportional order cost of c per unit.
- There is a holding cost of h per unit remaining at the end of the period.
- There is a penalty cost of p per unit of unsatisfied demand.

We also assume that $p > c$. If D represents the demand in the period then the cost of ordering y when demand is D is

$$G(y,D) = cy + h \max(y - D, 0) + p \max(D - y, 0)$$

The expected cost, say $G(y)$, is

$$G(y) = E[G(y,D)]$$
$$= cy + h \int_0^y (y - t)f(t)dt + p \int_y^\infty (t - y)f(t)dt$$

It is easy to show that $G(y)$ is convex in y. The assumption that $p > c$ guarantees that the minimizing value of y is positive. The optimal order quantity is the value of y where the first derivative of G with respect to y is zero.

$$G'(y) = c + h(F(y)) - p(1 - F(y)) = 0$$

results in

$$F(y^*) = \frac{p - c}{p + h}$$

The ratio $(p - c)/(p + h)$ is known as the critical ratio. As long as F is strictly increasing the optimal

order quantity, y^*, will be unique. The solution is essentially unchanged if there is starting inventory. Let x be the starting inventory. Then the optimal policy calls for ordering $\max(y^* - x, 0)$.

An important generalization of the newsboy model is to the case where there is a fixed cost of placing an order. Suppose that the fixed order cost is K, the starting inventory is x, and one orders to a level y (y is the order up to point and *not* the order quantity). If one doesn't order, the expected cost is $G(x)$, while if one orders to y the expected cost is $K + G(y)$. This system appears in FIG. 30-2.

The optimal policy in this case is characterized by two numbers s and S. S is the same as y^* or the minimizing point on the expected cost curve. s satisfies $s < S$ and $G(S) + K = G(s)$. These points are shown on FIG. 30-2. If x is less than s, then by placing an order to S the expected cost is reduced from $G(x)$ to $G(S) + K$. However, if the starting inventory $x > s$, then it is better not to order since the minimum expected cost that could be achieved by placing a positive order is $G(S) + K > G(x)$. The optimal policy is known as an (s,S) policy and is

If $x < s$ order to S.
If $x \geq s$ don't order.

Multiperiod Analysis

The structural results for the newsboy model above have been extended to the case of multiple planning periods. Dynamic programming is the traditional means for analyzing multiperiod stochastic inventory models. The first such analysis appears to be due to Bellman, Glicksberg, and Gross (1955) who proved that the simple base stock or order up to policy is optimal when no setup cost is present. Assume costs are discounted and the discount factor is $0 < \alpha < 1$. Define $C_n(x)$ as the minimum expected discounted cost for an n period problem (that is, when n periods remain) and the starting inventory is x. When excess demand is backordered, the functional equations defining an optimal

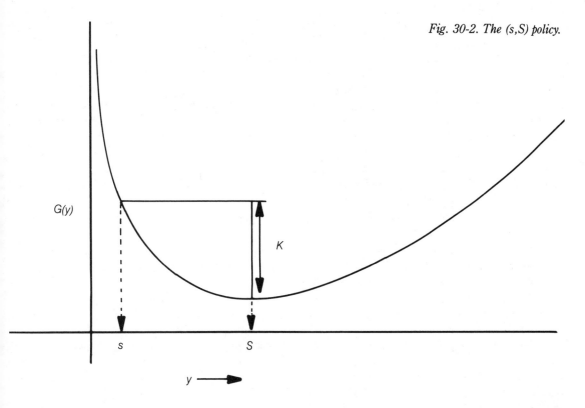

Fig. 30-2. The (s,S) policy.

policy takes the form

$$C_n(x) = \min \left\{ c(y - x) + h\int_0^y (y - x)f(t)dt \right.$$
$$\left. + p\int_y^\infty (x - y)f(t)dt + \int_0^\infty C_{n-1}(y - t)f(t)dt \right\}$$

The analysis proceeds by proving inductively that the bracketed term is convex in y. One could define $C_0(x) = 0$ or $C_0(x) = -cx$. The latter assumption has an important advantage: it results in a stationary optimal policy. That is, if one assumes that inventory left at the end of the planning horizon is salvaged for the original marginal purchase cost, the optimal policy is to order to the same critical number y^* each period solving

$$F(y^*) = \frac{p - (1 - \alpha)c}{p + h}$$

Without the salvage value assumption, the optimal critical numbers decrease as one approaches the end of the horizon. Since stock unused at the end of the planning horizon has no value, the optimal strategy calls for reducing on-hand inventory.

Multiperiod analysis is considerably more complex when there is a positive setup cost for ordering. The problem is that the appropriate function to be minimized in this case is no longer convex. Scarf (1960) defined a new property called K-convexity. He proved that the appropriate functions inherited this property from period to period and furthermore that an (s,S) policy was optimal for K convex cost functions. Many consider Scarf's proof of the optimality of (s,S) policies to be one of the most innovative in inventory analysis.

Approximations for (s, S) Policies

Although Scarf developed an elegant proof of the optimality of (s,S) policies for the general finite horizon dynamic inventory problem, his analysis did not address computational issues. Optimal policies may be found by successive approximations (Wagner, O'Hagen, and Lundh 1965), by policy iteration (Federgruen and Zipkin 1984a), or by utilizing the underlying Markov chain of periodic inventory levels (Karlin in Arrow, Karlin, and Scarf 1958). However, the computation of an optimal policy is complex and time consuming. In many real inventory systems in which policy parameters must be updated on a regular basis for a large number of items, optimal (s,S) policies are not practical. For this reason, approximations are of considerable interest.

Several researchers have suggested methods for computing approximate (s,S) policies. One, known as the power approximation, uses regression analysis to fit a set of parameters to optimal policies (Ehrhardt 1979). Another popular approximation technique recommends using (Q,R) policies obtained from solving the continuous review analogue. (I will discuss continuous review policies below.) Porteus (1985a) provides a comprehensive computational comparison of 17 methods. I refer the interested reader to his study.

Lead Times

When there is a positive lead time for placing an order and excess demand is backordered, the essential structure of the optimal policy remains the same, but the definition of the state variable must be changed. In the models discussed above the state variable is the level of on-hand inventory. When a lead time is present, one defines the state variable as the inventory on hand and on order (known as the inventory position). One implements the policy in the same way as the zero lead time case except that one compares the inventory position rather than the inventory level to the policy parameters.

The extension is not as straightforward when there is a positive lead time and the excess demand is lost rather than backordered (lost sales). In the lead time lost sales case, the optimal policy is a complex nonlinear function of the current inventory

and the vector of all past orders. Karlin and Scarf (in Arrow, Karlin, and Scarf 1958) were the first to see that the optimal policy in this case is not simply a function of the sum of the on hand and on order inventories. Morton (1969) suggested an approximation for this problem which is easy to compute. He suggested ordering to the $\min(y_1, y_2, ..., y_{\tau+1})$ where:

$$F^{(i)}(y_i) = \frac{p - \alpha^{\cdot r}c}{p + h - \alpha^{\tau+1}c}$$

Interpret $F^{(i)}$ as the i-fold convolution of the one period demand distribution F, and τ as the lead time in periods. Nahmias "Simple Approximations" 1979, using entirely different methods, generalized Morton's results to include a positive setup cost for placing an order, uncertainty in the lead time, and partial backordering of demand.

An interesting generalization is to the case where lead times are uncertain. Uncertainty in the lead time is common in practice, so this extension is extremely important. The trouble, as discussed in detail in Hadley and Whitin (1963), is order crossing. If one assumes that successive lead times are independent random variables, then it is possible that orders will cross. That is, an order placed in period k may arrive before an order placed in period $k-1$. If one orders from different suppliers, this is certainly possible. However, if one places all orders with the same vendor, then order crossing makes no sense. The difficulty is that if lead times are random and orders are not permitted to cross, successive lead times are *dependent* random variables. Kaplan (1970) discovered an ingenious solution for this problem. Define

$P_i = P$ {All orders placed i or more periods ago arrive in the current period}

This formulation guarantees that orders will not cross. The arrival of an order requires that all orders placed in earlier periods arrive as well. The unconditional probability that the lead time is i periods is not P_i. However, Kaplan shows how one would compute the P_i from these unconditional probabilities. The form of the optimal policy when the problem is formulated in this fashion is essentially the same as the deterministic lead time case.

Another interesting problem is the so-called multimodel problem. Assume that there are two sources of supply. One has a long lead time and might correspond to rail while the other, which is more expensive, has a shorter lead time which might correspond to air. Whittmore and Saunders (1977) showed that the problem could be formulated as a dynamic program but that the optimal policy is a complex function of a multidimensional state variable. More recently Moinzadeh and Nahmias (1988) show how to construct an efficient heuristic for this problem.

A Forward Formulation

Veinott (1965a) and (1965b) discovered a forward formulation of the dynamic inventory problem that offers several advantages over the traditional backward formulation of the functional equations above. The essence of the method is to write the expected discounted cost for an N period problem in the form

$$f_N = E \left\{ \sum_{n=1}^{N} \alpha^{n-1}[c(y_n - x_n) + L(y_n)] \right\} - \alpha^N cx_{N+1}$$

Interpret $L(y_n)$ as the expected holding and penalty cost in one period. (It is the sum of the holding and penalty cost terms of the function $G(y)$ defined in the discussion of the newsboy model.) Two assumptions are made. One is that excess demand is backordered so that the transfer function is of the form: $x_{n+1} = y_n - D_n$. Another is that the inventory left over at the end of the horizon can be salvaged at a return of c per unit. With these two assumptions one can rearrange the terms in the expression for f_N to obtain

$$f_N = \sum_{n=1}^{N} \alpha^{n-1} W(y_n) - cx_1 - \sum_{n=1}^{N} \alpha_n c\mu$$

where

$$W(y_n) = E[cy_n(1 - \alpha) + L(y_n)]$$

If it is possible to order to the minimum of W in every period than that must be the optimal policy. The essence of the method is to reduce a multiperiod dynamic problem into a series of one period problems. Since one period problems are much easier to analyze than are multiperiod problems, this approach can be useful for gaining insight into the nature of an optimal policy for complex problems. Veinott (1965a) shows how this formulation leads to a simple policy for the batch ordering problem, as when the minimum order size is some constant M. Essentially the same approach can be used to analyze the multiproduct inventory problem which is done in Veinott (1965b).

Unfortunately, this technique does not work when there is a positive setup cost for placing an order. However, it can provide insights into the nature of an optimal policy when fixed costs can be ignored.

Lot Size Reorder Point Models

The most popular method of dealing with uncertainty in inventory models is an adaptation of the EOQ model. The model assumes continuous review. That means that the inventory level is known at all times as opposed to periodic review where the inventory level is known only at discrete points in time. Continuous review was assumed initially for convenience rather than for accuracy. However, with the advent of point of sale scanners, continuous review may actually be a more accurate model of many inventory systems than is periodic review.

The particular continuous review model we present below appears to be due to Whitin (1957), although its exact origins are unclear. Our presentation follows that of Hadley and Whitin (1963). Variants of this particular model form the basis for many commercial inventory control systems (see

Brown 1967, for example). Assume that

- Demands are generated according to a stationary random process whose expectation is λ units per unit time
- Each time the inventory position hits a level R, an order for Q units is placed. This is known as a (Q,R) policy
- There is a positive lead time τ for placing an order
- There is never more than a single outstanding order
- The reorder level, R, is positive
- The demand during the lead time, D, is a random variable with known CDF $F(t)$ and PDF $f(t)$
- Costs are changed against proportional ordering at c per unit, setup at K per positive order, holding at h per unit held per unit of time, and p per unit of excess demand

A sample path for the lot size reorder point system is pictured in FIG. 30-3.

The method of analysis is to obtain an expression for the expected average cost per unit time as a function of the decision variables Q and R and minimize this expected cost with choice of Q and R.

Let a cycle, T, be the time between arrival of successive orders of size Q. Since Q units enter inventory each cycle and the expected demand rate is fixed at λ, it follows that the expected cycle length must be Q/λ. Since there is exactly one order placed each cycle the average cost of setup per unit time is K/T or $K\lambda/Q$. Because units enter and exit the system at the same rate overall, and units leave the system at the rate of the demand, λ, it follows that the proportional ordering cost per unit time is simply $c\lambda$.

The expression for the holding cost used in this model is an approximation. The expected inventory level will vary linearly from s to $Q+s$, where s is the safety stock and is equal to $R - \lambda\tau$. The average of the expected inventory level curve is $s + Q/2$. The holding cost is approximated by $h(s + Q/2)$ or $h(R + Q/2 - \lambda\tau)$. This is only an approximation since

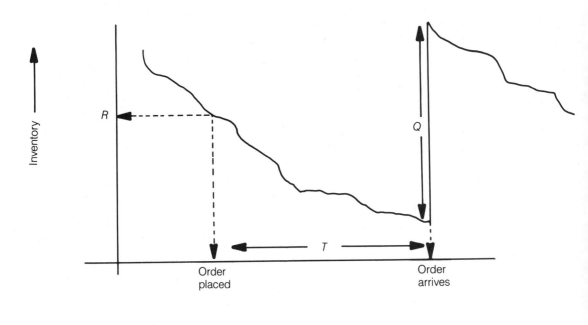

Fig. 30-3. *Changes in inventory levels over time for lot size Reorder Point Model.*

the expectation and averaging operations are done in the wrong order (that is, one should compute the expected average holding cost rather than the average expected holding cost.)

Finally, the expected number of units short at the end of a cycle is max $(D - R, 0)$. It follows that

$$E\left\{\max(D - R, 0)\right\} = \int_R^\infty (t - R)f(t)dt$$

which we define as $n(R)$ for convenience. Since $n(R)$ is the expected number of stockouts in a cycle, the expected number of stockouts per unit time is $n(R)/T$ or $\lambda n(R)/Q$. It follows that the expected cost per unit time, say $G(Q,R)$, is given by

$$G(Q,R) = c\lambda + \frac{K\lambda}{Q} + h\left(\frac{Q}{2} + R - \lambda r\right) + \frac{p\lambda n(R)}{Q}$$

The optimal policy is found by taking the partial derivatives of $G(Q,R)$ with respect to Q and R and setting the result equal to zero. The resultant solution is

$$Q = \sqrt{\frac{2\lambda[K + pn(R)]}{h}}$$

$$1 - F(R) = \frac{Qh}{p\lambda}$$

These two nonlinear equations must be solved simultaneously for Q and R. One iterates between these two equations starting with $Q = $ EOQ until convergence is reached. When the lead time demand is assumed normal, tables are available for the standardized version of $n(R)$. (See Brown 1967.)

We present this model in detail because it, or some variant of it, appears to be the basis for many commercial inventory systems. A slight variant of this model was developed by Wagner (1969). It is also similar to the approach suggested by Brown (1967), which apparently was the basis for IBM's IMPACT inventory control system. Nahmias ("On

the Equivalence" 1976) showed that these models were not only very similar, but yielded identical policies when a constraint on service levels was included. Note that the (Q,R) model could be used to obtain approximate (s,S) policies by setting $s = R$ and $S = R + Q$, although there are more efficient approximations for optimal (s,S) policies.

Inventory Subject to Change

Most inventory models assume that once items enter stock they retain a constant utility until they are consumed. However, many types of inventories change while being stored and their utility may decline. Typical examples are items subject to perishability, decay, or obsolescence. For the sake of our discussion we define perishability to mean that the inventory retains full utility until it reaches its expiration data at which time it must be discarded. Typical examples of perishable items are blood, drugs, photographic film, and certain foodstuffs. Decay occurs when the utility declines as a function of time. Inventories subject to exponential decay are radioactive fuels and drugs and volatile liquids such as gasoline and alcohol. Obsolescence means that the item lifetime cannot be predicted in advance.

There has been considerable interest in the fixed life problem. The models are quite complex owing to the need to keep track of the age distribution of the stock. In general, if the lifetime is m periods the state variable is of the form $x = (x_{m-1}, x_{m-2}, \ldots, x_1)$ where x_i is the amount of stock on hand scheduled to perish in i periods. If y is the amount of the new order of fresh stock and t is the realization of demand then the transfer function giving the amount on hand one period hence is given by

$$s_i(y,x,t) = \left[x_{i+1} - \left(t - \sum_{j=1}^i x_j\right)^+\right]^+$$

for $1 \le i \le m - 1$

Interpret x_m as y. The complexity of the transfer function along with the multidimensional state variable makes the analysis of this problem very difficult. Note that this particular form of the transfer function assumes that the issuing policy is oldest first (FIFO). Clearly, this is the most efficient. When the issuing policy is newest first (LIFO), which occurs in a supermarket when patrons choose to buy milk which has been on the shelves the shortest amount of time, the problem is even more complex. This case was considered by Cohen and Pekelman (1978).

However, most research on ordering policies for perishables assumed a FIFO issuing policy. The structure of optimal policies for lifetimes of two periods was discovered by Van Zyl (1964) and Nahmias and Pierskalla (1973). Finite horizon analysis of optimal policies for arbitrary lifetimes appears in Fries (1975) and Nahmias (1975). Nahmias (1977) compares and contrasts these two models. Several extensions were considered by Nahmias and others in later work. I refer the interested reader to the review, Nahmias (1982). More recent work on this problem considered $(S-1, S)$ policies under continuous review (Schmidt and Nahmias (1985a), and the structure of an optimal policy assuming discrete rather than continuous demand (Nahmias and Schmidt 1986).

The decaying problem is somewhat different in character. It is considerably simpler than the fixed life problem in that one only needs to keep track of the total amount of inventory on hand since the amount that decays is simply a fraction of the amount on hand. Ghare and Schrader (1963) were the first to consider this problem and generalized the simple EOQ formula to account for decay. As it turns out, the decay problem is quite straightforward except when an order lead time is present. The problem is that the decay can only be applied to the inventory on hand and not the inventory on order. Nahmias and Wang (1979) developed a heuristic for this case which is easy to compute and is cost efficient as well. One way that obsolescence has been modeled has been to assume that the planning horizon is a random variable. This approach was the one taken by Pierskalla (1969).

Inventory Depletion Management

A problem related to that of ordering policies for perishable inventory is that of determining the optimal form of the issuing policy. As noted above, the optimal issuing policy for perishable inventory whose utility is constant up until the expiration date is oldest first, or FIFO. However, in some cases the so-called field life function may not be so simple. Derman and Klein (1958) were the first to formulate the issuing problem mathematically (although the issuing problem was discussed prior to the work of Derman and Klein by Greenwood (1955). One assumes that there is a stockpile of n items of varying ages, say $0 < s_1 < s_2 < ... < s_n$, and that an item issued to the field of age s has a lifetime of $L(s)$, where L is known function. The goal of the analysis is to discover conditions under which either a LIFO or a FIFO policy is optimal.

Derman and Klein discovered a clever approach for solving this problem. They used an induction argument on the number of items and were able to show that under certain conditions when either LIFO or FIFO was optimal for $n=2$ items, it was also optimal for $n2$ items as well. Hence the problem was reduced to determining whether LIFO or FIFO was optimal for two items. Several extensions of their results were obtained by Lieberman (1958), Zehna (in Arrow, Karlin, and Scarf 1962), and Pierskalla (1967). Extensions to the case of random field lives were considered by Nahmias ("Inventory Depletion" 1974), Brown and Solomon (1973), and Albright (1976).

STOCHASTIC MODELS FOR MULTIPLE PRODUCTS AND ECHELONS

The models discussed in the previous section assumed a single inventory item. Of course, they can be used to control multiple product systems, except that they do not account for possible interactions among the products. In most systems these interactions are sufficiently small that they can be ignored. Even when this is not the case, incorporating the interactions of many items into a single comprehensive model is probably infeasible. With one notable exception (which I discuss below), few models of multiple products or multiple echelons have ever been implemented. However, as computing becomes cheaper and more powerful, these complex models may be considered more seriously in years to come.

Multiproduct Systems

One approach to analyzing multiproduct systems involves formulating the problem as a multidimensional dynamic program. That is, the functional equations defining an optimal policy would be of the form

$$C_n(\mathbf{x}) = \min \Big\{ \mathbf{c}(\mathbf{y} - \mathbf{x}) + L(\mathbf{y}) \\ + \int C_{n-1}[\mathbf{s}(\mathbf{y},t)]_f(t)dt \Big\} \\ y \geq x$$

where the boldface should be interpreted as a vector quantity. This type of formulation was considered by Evans (1967) in his analysis of a two product system with a resource constraint, and Iglehart (1965) in which there are two products whereby inventories of product two are maintained in order to provide capability for production of product one. Johnson (1969) used a multidimensional dynamic program to analyze the structure of multiproduct systems with a setup cost.

An alternative approach to the analysis of multiproduct systems is based on the myopic approach of Veinott discussed in the section on a Forward Formulation above. Veinott (1965b) determines conditions under which the multiperiod multiproduct inventory problem can be decomposed into *n* single period problems. Although this approach does not work if setup costs are present, it is the most promising method of analyzing many complex multiproduct systems. This approach was used by Veinott (1965c) to analyze a model in which customers are separated by demand classes, and by Bessler and Vienott (1966) to analyze a multiechelon inventory system.

In some cases the structure of a particular multiproduct problem dictates the mode of analysis. One example of such a case is the study reported by Nahmias and Pierskalla (1976) in which two partially substitutable products could be used to satisfy the same demand. One of the products was assumed to have a fixed lifetime while the other was assumed to have an infinite lifetime. The model was suggested by the operation of a blood bank that has the facility to freeze red blood cells.

Multiechelon Models

When inventory is moved from one level of a production or distribution system to another before finally being consumed, we refer to this case as a multiechelon inventory system. A typical multiechelon inventory system is one in which stock is produced at a single factory, stored at regional warehouses, and finally shipped to retail outlets for consumption. This would be a three echelon distribution system.

The first formal analysis of a multiechelon inventory system was due to Clark and Scarf (1960) who considered a system of *N* installations arranged in a pure series system. Transshipments are made to the next echelon only and external demand occurs at the final installation only. The paper assumes *N* = 2 installations, but the results obtained clearly apply to *N* > 2 as well. The fundamental result that they obtained was that the problem could be solved one echelon at a time by incorporating the penalty at one echelon for not being able to meet the demand at the next echelon. This particular study assumed only linear ordering and transshipment costs. A later paper (Clark and Scarf (in Arrow, Karlin, and Scarf, 1962) considered approximations when there was a fixed cost of transshipment. Extensions of Clark and Scarf's model have been considered more recently by Federgruen and Zipkin (1984b).

A multiechelon model which has received considerable attention is METRIC described by Sherbrooke (1968). METRIC was actually developed over a number of years by joint efforts of the

RAND corporation and the Air Force Logistics Command. It is a model of the two echelon base-depot repair system pictures in FIG. 30-4. External demand originates at the base level only as a result of failures in the field. Routine repairs are made at the base level. However, complex repairs must be made at the central depot. The key computation is that the expected number of backorders of item i at base j given spares levels at both the base and depots. This expression forms the basis of an optimization used to establish the optimal spares levels subject to a constraint on the budget. The importance of METRIC and its successors is that models of this type have reached the level of implementation in the United States military forces. Expenditures for spares in the military amount to billions of dollars each year, so this problem has considerable impact. The interested reader should refer to the review by Nahmias (in Schwarz 1981) and the papers referenced there for a more in-depth review of models directed at managing repairable item inventories.

Several researchers have considered the problem of one warehouse supplying N depots. In this case it is generally assumed that there is a lead time from the depot to the warehouses and another lead time from the warehouses to the retailer. The model of Eppen and Schrage (in Schwarz 1981) is essentially an extension of the newsboy model to this setting and the model of Deuermeyer and Schwarz (in Schwarz 1981) is an extension of the (Q,R) model discussed above to this setting.

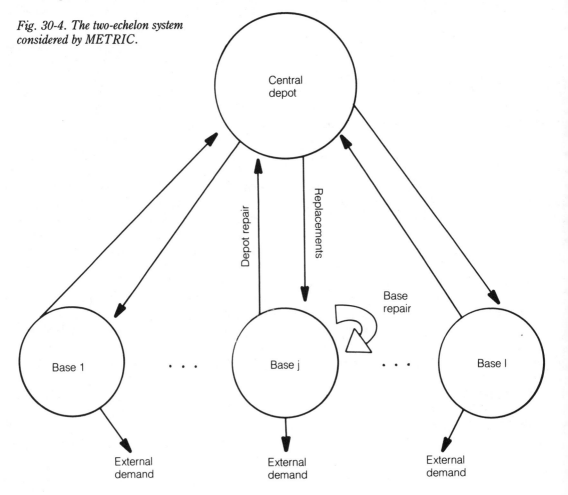

Fig. 30-4. The two-echelon system considered by METRIC.

Little research has been done on the type of multilevel production system that arises in MRP systems when the demand for the end product is a random variable. One exception is the study of Schmidt and Nahmias (1985b) in which the authors considered a production system in which a final product is produced from two components. The components are ordered from an outside supplier with known lead times and there is a lead time for assembly of the end product. Final demand is for the end product only. The authors characterized the form of the optimal order and build policies. To my knowledge this is the only study of this kind that characterizes the form of optimal policies for a multilevel MRP type system with stochastic demand.

JUST-IN-TIME INVENTORY SYSTEMS

With the enormous success of the Japanese economic recovery and their later domination of certain key industries, the world has taken notice of the successful efforts of the Japanese in applying scientific methods to production problems. The so called *just-in-time* inventory system was an outgrowth of the kanban system developed by Toyota Motors. The word *kanban* means ticket in Japanese. It refers to the tickets that are used to effect a transfer of goods from one level of the system to another.

The basic philosophy behind just-in-time is to reduce work in process inventory to a bare minimum. To achieve this goal, items are moved through the system in very small lots and movement is by request only. That is, production at one level is initiated only when a request arrives from the next level. More sophisticated information systems than kanban are possible when using just-in-time. Please see Schonberger (1983) for a more detailed description of the kanban system.

Essentially, just-in-time is a pull system as opposed to MRP which is a push system. Demand originates at the end item level and units are pulled to that level from earlier levels. One might ask how just-in-time relates to EOQ, the basis of inventory models discussed in this review. Recall the EOQ formula:

$$Q = \sqrt{\frac{2K\lambda}{h}}$$

Part of the just-in-time philosophy is to reduce the setup time and hence the setup cost to its bare minimum. This is the reasoning behind the SMED (single minute exchange of dies) due to Shingo (1981). He reports reducing die changing operations that originally took as much as four hours down to less than five minutes. In terms of the original EOQ formula this means reducing the setup cost K. If K is reduced, then according to the EOQ formula above, the value of the optimal lot size Q will be reduced as well. This means that the concepts of just-in-time and classical inventory analysis are not different at all. The difference is that the just-in-time approach does not assume that the setup cost is a fixed constant.

The notion that the setup cost can be treated as a decision variable was explored by Porteus (1985b). He assumed that a one-time charge $a(K)$ would be levied if the setup cost was reduced from its original value of K_0 to a lower value of K. Assuming both linear and logarithmic forms for $a(K)$, he derived the optimal decrease in setup cost using essentially the EOQ model. Zangwill (1987) considered setup reduction in the context of the production planning models discussed early in the section on Production Planning Models. He showed in this context a reduction in the setup cost is not always accompanied by a reduction in inventory levels.

CONCLUSION

Inventory models are an important part of the research effort on production problems in general. Outlets for theoretical papers on inventory include journals such as *Management Science, Operations Research, Naval Research Logistics Quarterly,* and *Mathematics of Operations Research*. More applied papers can be found in *International Journal of Production Research, Interfaces, Decision Sciences,* and *Transactions of the AIIE*. Interestingly, many fewer books are published on inventory models than on queuing models, even though it appears to me that inventory analysis has had a more significant impact in the real world.

Several high quality books and collections of papers were published in the area in the 1960s. They include Hadley and Whitin (1963) (still considered to be the best account of the theory up to that time by many today); Arrow, Karlin and Scarf (1962); Scarf, Gilford, and Shelley (1963); Naddor (1966); and Brown (1967). Johnson and Montgomery's (1974) text was largely devoted to inventory analysis, although scheduling and production planning topics were considered as well. Unfortunately, most, if not all, of these excellent books are out of print today.

Few books published recently are devoted to inventory. One I recommend, if still available, is Love (1979). Silver and Peterson (1985) provide a comprehensive discussion of heuristic methods in their work — probably the most complete coverage of the area in print today. Nahmias (1989) devotes a significant portion of his text, which treats production topics in general, to inventory control.

I feel that inventory theory has been a rich area of research and an important application of operations research methodology in general. Research on inventory models has had a significant impact on the management of inventories in many sectors of the economy. Only recently has the importance of scientific production control methods become apparent as competition from efficient industrial powers overseas has eaten away at the economic domination enjoyed by the United States for so long. This review only touches the surface of this important area and I hope that it will encourage the reader to pursue further study.

REFERENCES

Afentakis, P., B. Gavish, and U. Karmarkar. "Computationally Efficient Optimal Solutions to the Lot-Sizing Problem in Multistage Assembly Systems." *Management Science* 30 (1984): 222-239.

Albright, S. C. "Optimal Stock Depletion Policies with Stochastic Lives." *Management Science* 22 (1976): 852-857.

Arrow, K. A., T. E. Harris, and J. Marschak. "Optimal Inventory Policy." *Econometrica* 19 (1951): 250-272.

Arrow, K. A., S. Karlin, and H. Scarf, eds. *Studies in the Mathematical Theory of Inventory and Production*. Standford, CA: Stanford University Press, 1958.

_____. *Studies in Applied Probability and Management Science*. Stanford, California: Stanford University Press, 1962.

Baker, K. R., P. R. Dixon, M. J. Magazine, and E. A. Silver. "Algorithm for the Dynamic Lot-Size Problems with Time Varying Production Capacity Constraints." *Management Science* 16 (1978): 1710-1720.

Bellman, R. E., I. Glicksberg, and O. Gross. "On the Optimal Inventory Equation." *Management Science* 2 (1955): 83-104.

Bessler, S. A., and A. F. Veinott, Jr. "Optimal Policy for a Dynamic Multi-echelon Inventory Model." *Naval Research Logistics Quarterly* 13 (1966): 355-389.

Brown, M., and H. Solomon. "Optimal Issuing Policies under Stochastic Field Lives." *Journal of Applied Probability* 10 (1973): 761-768.

Brown, R. G. *Decision Rules for Inventory Management*. Hinsdale, Illinois: Dryden, 1967.

Clark, A. J., and H. E. Scarf. "Optimal Policies for a Multi-echelon Inventory Problem." *Management Science* 6 (1960): 475-490.

Cohen, M. A. and D. Pekelman. "LIFO Inventory Systems." *Management Science* 24 (1978): 1150-1162.

DeMatteis, J. J. "An Economic Lot Sizing Technique: The Part Period Algorithm." *IBM Systems Journal* 7 (1968): 30-38.

Derman, C., and M. Klein. "Inventory Depletion Management." *Management Science* 4 (1958): 450-456.

Deuermeyer, B. L., and L. B. Schwarz. "A Model for the Analysis of System Service Level in Warehouse-Retailer Distribution Systems: The Identical Retailer Case," 163-193. In *Multilevel Production/Inventory Control Systems: Theory and Practice*, edited by L.B. Schwarz. North Holland: TIMS 16, 1981.

Dixon, P. S., and E. A. Silver. "A Heuristic Solution Procedure for the Multi-Item, Single-Level, Limited Capacity, Lot Sizing Problem." *Journal of Operations Management* 2 (1981): 23-39.

Dvoretzky, A., J. Kiefer, and J. Wolfowitz. "The Inventory Problem: I. Case of Known Distributions of Demand." *Econometrica* 20 (1952a): 187-222.

————. "The Inventory Problem: II. Case of Unknown Distributions of Demand." *Econometrica* 20 (1952b): 450-466.

Ehrhardt, R. "The Power Approximation for Computing (s,S) Inventory Policies." *Management Science* 25 (1979): 777-786.

Eppen, G. and L. Schrage. "Centralized Ordering Policies in a Multi-Warehouse system with Lead Times and Random Demands," 51-67. In *Multilevel Production/Inventory Control Systems: Theory and Practice*, edited by L.B. Schwarz. North Holland: TIMS 16, 1981.

Evans, R. V. "Inventory Control of a Multiproduct Systems with a Limited Production Resource." *Naval Research Logistics Quarterly* 14 (1967): 173-184.

Federgruen, A. and P. Zipkin "An Efficient Algorithm for Computing Optimal (s,S) Policies." *Operations Research* 32 (1984a): 1268-1285.

————. "Approximation of Dynamic Multilocation Production and Inventory Problems." *Management Science* 30 (1984b): 69-84.

Florian, M. and M. Klein. "Deterministic Production Planning with Concave Costs and Capacity Constraints." *Management Science* 18 (1971): 12-20.

Fries, B. "Optimal Order Policy for a Perishable Commodity with Fixed Lifetime." *Operations Research* 23 (1975): 46-61.

Ghare, P., and G. Schrader. "A Model for Exponentially Decaying Inventories." *Journal of Industrial Engineering* 14 (1963): 238-243.

Greenwood, J. A. "Issue Priority: LIFO vs. FIFO as a Method of Issuing Items from Supply Storage." *Naval Research Logistics Quarterly* 2 (1955): 251-268.

Hadley, G. J. and T. M. Whitin. *Analysis of Inventory Systems*. Englewood Cliffs, New Jersey: Prentice-Hall, 1963.

Harris, F. W. *Operations and Cost* (Factory Management Series). Chicago: Shaw, 1915.

Iglehart, D. L. "Capital Accumulation and Production for the Firm: Optimal Dynamic Policies." *Management Science* 12 (1965): 193-205.

Johnson, E. "On (s,S) Policies." *Management Science* 15 (1969): 80-91.

Johnson, L. A., and D. C. Montgomery. *Operations Research, Production Planning, Scheduling and Inventory Control*. New York: Wiley, 1974.

Kaplan, R. "A Dynamic Inventory Model with Stochastic Lead Times." *Management Science* 16 (1970): 491-507.

Karni, R. "Maximum Part Period Gain (MPG) - A Lot Sizing Procedure for Unconstrained and Constrained Requirements Planning Systems." *Production and Inventory Management* 22 (1981): 91-98.

Lee, H. and S. Nahmias. "Single Product, Single Location Models." In *Handbooks in Operations Research and Management Science, Volume 4, Logistics of Production and Inventory*, chapter 2. Edited by S. C. Graves, A.H.G. Rinnooy-Kan, and P. Zipkin. Amsterdam: North Holland, scheduled for publication 1989.

Lieberman, G. J. "LIFO vs. FIFO in Inventory Depletion Management." *Management Science* 5 (1958): 102-105.

Love, S. F. "Bounded Production and Inventory Models with Piecewise Concave Costs." *Management Science* 20 (1973): 313-318.

Love, S. *Inventory Control* New York: McGraw-Hill, 1979.

McClaren, B. J. "A Study of Multiple Level Lot Sizing Techniques for Material Requirements Planning Systems." Ph.D. dissertation, Purdue University, 1976.

McLeavey, D. W., and S. L. Narasimhan. *Production Planning and Inventory Control*. Boston: Allyn and Bacon, 1985.

Moinzadeh, K. and S. Nahmias. "Operating Policies for an Inventory System with Two Modes of Supply." *Management Science* 34 (1988): 761-773.

Morton, T. E. "Bounds on the Solution of the Lagged Optimal Inventory Equation with No Demand Backlogging and Proportional Costs." *SIAM Review* 11 (1969): 527-596.

_____. "The Near Myopic Nature of the Lagged Proportional Cost Inventory Problem with Lost Sales." *Operations Research* 19 (1971): 1708-1716.

Naddor, E. *Inventory Systems*. New York: Wiley, 1966.

Nahmias, S. "Inventory Depletion Management When the Field Life is Random." *Management Science* 20 (1974): 1276-1283.

_____. "Optimal Ordering Policies for Perishable Inventory-II." *Operations Research* 23 (1975): 735-749.

_____. "On the Equivalence of Three Approximate Continuous Review Inventory Models." *Naval Research Logistics Quarterly* 23, (1976): 31-36.

_____. "Comparison Between Two Dynamic Perishable Inventory Models." *Operations Research* 25 (1977): 168-172.

_____. "Managing Reparable Item Inventory Systems: A Review." In *Multilevel Production/Inventory Control Systems*, edited by L.B. Schwarz, 253-277. North Holland, TIMS 16, 1981.

_____. "Simple Approximations for a Variety of Dynamic Leadtime Lost-Sales Inventory Models." *Operations Research*. 27 (1979): 904-924.

_____. "Perishable Inventory Theory: A Review." *Operations Research* 30 (1982): 680-708.

_____. *Production and Operations Analysis*. Homewood, Illinois: Richard D. Irwin, 1989.

Nahmias, S., and W. P. Pierskalla. "Optimal Ordering Policies for a Product that Perishes in Two Periods Subject to Stochastic Demand." *Naval Research Logistics Quarterly* 20 (1973): 207-229.

Nahmias, S., and W. P. Pierskalla. "A Two Product Perishable/Nonperishable Inventory Problem." *SIAM Journal of Applied Mathematics* 30 (1976): 483-500.

Nahmias, S. and C. P. Schmidt. "An Application of Theory of Weak Convergence to the Dynamic Perishable Inventory Problem with Discrete Demand." *Mathematics of Operations Research* 11 (1986): 62-69.

Nahmias, S., and S. Wang. "A Heuristic Lot-size Reorder Point Model for Decaying Inventories." *Management Science* 25 (1979): 90-97.

Pierskalla, W. P. "Optimal Issuing Policies in Inventory Management-I." *Management Science* 13 (1967): 395-412.

———. "An Inventory Problem with Obsolescence." *Naval Research Logistics Quarterly* 16 (1969) 217-228.

Porteus, E. L. "Numerical Comparisons of Inventory Policies for Periodic Review Systems." *Operations Research* 33 (1985a): 134-152.

Porteus, E. "Investing In Reduced Set-ups in the EOQ Model." *Management Science* 31 (1985b): 998-1010.

Scarf, H. E. "The Optimality of (s,S) Policies in the Dynamic Inventory Problem." In *Mathematical Methods in the Social Sciences*, edited by K. J. Arrow, S. Karlin, and P. Suppes. Stanford, California: Stanford University Press, 1960.

Scarf, H. E., D. M. Gilford, and M. W. Shelly. *Multistage Inventory Models and Techniques*. Stanford, California: Stanford University Press, 1963.

Schmidt, C. P. and S. Nahmias. "(S-1,S) Policies for Perishable Inventories," with C. Schmidt. *Management Science* 31 (1985a): 719-728.

———. "Optimal Policy for a Single Stage Assembly System with Stochastic Demand." *Operations Research* 33 (1985b): 1130-1145.

Schonberger, R. "Applications of Single Card and Dual Card Kanban." *Interfaces* 13 (1983): 56-67.

Schwarz, L. B., ed. *Multilevel Production/Inventory Control Systems: Theory and Practice*. North Holland: TIMS Studies in the Management Sciences, 16, 1981.

Sherbrooke, C. C. "METRIC: A Multi-echelon Technique for Recoverable Item Control." *Operations Research* 16 (1968): 122-141.

Shingo, S. *Study of Toyota Production System from Industrial Engineering Viewpoint*. Japan Management Association, 1981.

Silver, E. A., and H. C. Meal. "A Heuristic for Selecting Lot Size Quantitites for the Case of a Deterministic Time-Varying Demand Rate and Discrete Opportunities for Replenishment." *Production and Inventory Management* 14 (1973): 64-74.

Silver, E. A., and R. Peterson. *Decision Systems for Inventory Management and Production Planning*. 2nd ed. New York: John A. Wiley, 1985.

Survey of Current Business, U.S. Department of Commerce, Bureau of Economic Analysis, Vol. 69, #8, August 1989.

Van Zyl, G. J. J. "Inventory Control for Perishable Commoditites." Ph.D. dissertation, University of North Carolina, 1964.

Veinott, A. F., Jr. "Production Planning with Convex Costs: A Parametric Study." *Management Science* 10 (1964): 441-460.

———. "The Optimal Inventory Policy for Batch Ordering." *Operations Research* 13 (1965a): 424-432.

———. "Optimal Policy for a Multi-product Dynamic Nonstationary Inventory Problem." *Management Science* 12 (1965b): 206-222.

Veinott, A. F., Jr. "Optimal Policy in a Dynamic, Single Product Nonstationary Model with Several Demand Classes." *Operations Research* 13 (1965c): 761-778.

Wagner, H. M. *Principles of Operations Research*. Englewood Cliffs, New Jersey: Prentice-Hall, 1969.

Wagner, H. M., M. O'Hagan, and B. Lundh. "An Empirical Study of Exactly and Approximately Optimal Inventory Policies." *Management Science* 11 (1965): 690-723.

Wagner, H. M., and T. M. Whitin. "Dynamic Version of the Economic Lot Size Formula." *Management Science* 5 (1958): 89-96.

Whitin, T. M. *The Theory of Inventory Management*. Revised Edition. Princeton, New Jersey: Princeton University Press, 1957.

Whittmore, A. S. and S. Saunders. "Optimal Inventory Under Stochastic Demand with Two Supply Options." *SIAM Journal on Applied Mathematics* 32 (1977) 293-305.

Wilson, R. H. "Scientific Routine for Stock Control." *Harvard Business Review* 13 (1934).

Zangwill, W. I. "A Deterministic Multi-period Production Scheduling Model with Backlogging." *Management Science* 13 (1966): 105-119.

Zangwill, W. "From EOQ Towards ZI." *Management Science* 33 (1987): 1209-1223.

31

System Control: Relationship between Automated Material Handling Systems and MRP-II

Edward A. Bowers*

THERE IS MUCH AT STAKE FOR THE MANUFACTURER who is considering a broad based system to integrate a total automated manufacturing systems (AMS) environment with automation, Computer Integrated Manufacturing (CIM), and its ramifications for a MRP-II system. The systems implementer must understand both the capabilities and the limitations of the equipment, processes, and applications software involved. Purchasers and system implementers tend to seek specific software without an overview of the total system design. They tend to focus on software for the control of the machining cells, automated material handling systems (AMHS), and material control functions, all of which are developed and written by different teams, at different times in the cycle. Most times these systems employ mis-matches in file sizes, data collected, or in different languages. The only way these systems will come on line is with a band-aid approach. Band-aids are expensive and time consuming.

Most people are familiar with materials requirement planning systems. However, there are many who do not seek the larger approach of MRP-II, but who should do so, so as to better utilize all of their manufacturing capabilities. The best definition of MRP-II can be traced back to Ollie Wight:

> Technically, MRP-II includes the financial planning as well as planning in units; it also includes a simulation capability. From a management point of view, MRP-II means that the tools are being used for planning the activities of all functions of a manufacturing company.

COMPUTER INTEGRATED MANUFACTURING

Computer integrated manufacturing, or CIM, is a rapidly maturing set of technologies being implemented by a growing number of manufacturers. Although applications differ widely, CIM usu-

*Edward Bowers received his undergraduate education at Parsons College, Fairfield, Iowa, and did his graduate studies at Northern Illinois University, and Michigan State University. He has certifications in Materials Management and Materials Handling from the International Materials Management Society. Mr. Bowers was in charge of the design, specifications, cost estimating, and installation of many flexible material handling systems, in food, automotive, pharmaceutical, and textile industries. He has been instrumental in the installation of MRP-II systems at Carling-O'Keefe, Royal Business Machines, Allis-Chalmers, and North American Philips. He has also provided articles on automation techniques for the ''American Institute of Industrial Engineering.'' His firm is Custom Concepts.

ally involves a combination of the following disciplines.

- Automated manufacturing cells, which consist of a group of computer controlled devices such as CNC machining centers, robotics, and gauges
- Automated material handling systems, such as automated guided vehicles (AGVs), and automated storage/retrieval systems (AS/RS)
- Factory control systems, which allocate and track resources throughout the factory, coordinate the various computer devices, and monitor ever changing factory conditions
- Highly trained factory personnel who play a key role in decision making, and problem-solving roles in support of the automated systems

There are great benefits to CIM and MRP-II, and the two approaches can complement each other well, if the required effort is taken to marry them together at the start of a project. Corporate expertise and full fledged training in MRP-II is a prerequisite to factory automation. A good MRP-II system is required to provide the basic information, such as time phased demand, which drives the automated factory. Deficiencies in planning systems always need to be corrected prior to the factory automation project. Even to the most experienced practitioners of MRP-II, the processes for implementation of CIM can yield significant results.

CIM requires significant improvement in the accuracy of engineering and manufacturing data, which in turn will generate more accurate data for the MRP-II systems. An automated factory is driven by computerized databases, and as a result inaccurate information has a direct effect on the manufacturing operation. If a bad bill of material (BOM) and manufacturing routing is used to move materials to work centers, without manual intervention, the incorrect bill will generate a bad batch of product. Likewise, if their CIM reports incorrect information, the MRP-II shop floor control system will move the wrong materials.

CIM will significantly improve the accuracy and timeliness of inventory data. Work in process inventory data can be obtained directly from the manu-facturing cells, which provide the data as a by-product of computerized control. This benefit can be especially significant in areas where process yields are very variable. AMHS also necessitates an extremely high degree of accuracy. In short, if inventory data are not correct, the automated factory will not work.

CIM requires the formulation of explicit scheduling policies within MRP-II. Informal systems are not understood by CIM. Although this formulation was important without CIM, automation projects force the issue. Once defined, these scheduling policies can then be reflected in the corporate planning systems. The implementation of a CIM and MRP-II project tie-in requires the swift resolution of many difficult business and technological problems which will involve the total manufacturing organization. The efforts of the CIM project team can make the organization better able to handle the ongoing efforts of the MRP-II project.

There are three main areas of interface which must be addressed: communication, scheduling, and manufacturing database. The automation projects must interface with a variety of corporate MRP-II systems. As we have seen these have been installed at different times, or may be concurrent with the efforts of the automation project. The automation and MRP-II systems do utilize different database and communication technology.

Communications

The cost and complexity of computer interfaces are normally underestimated and can be a major factor in the success or failure of the project. The engineers in the automation project tend to get involved in the technology of the equipment, while ignoring the corporate interfaces until too far into the project. Playing catch up later is costly in terms of dollars, lost production, and time schedule.

One of the major problems with MRP-II implementation is the interfacing of the MRP-II system (which is normally a manual data entry system) with people and computers. Within the automated factory there are few users to enter the inventory data at the terminal. Rather, these automated systems interact with process controllers to perform specific tasks. The MRP-II inventory data must be obtained from factory level systems designed to operate using the manufacturing automation protocol. This gap in data collection must be closed.

There are two approaches to this data collection. In the first approach, a file of transactions can be accumulated and transmitted to the MRP-II system at regular intervals in small batches. If errors occur, the transmission can be repeated. The same holds true for information that needs to be transmitted for data from MRP-II to the factory level controllers, like customer orders. However, this approach sacrifices the timeliness of the data so essential to the automation operation.

In the second approach data travels from the automation area to MRP-II by terminal emulation. Terminal emulation makes it close to impossible to prevent the loss of the data in case of controller failure. If the system crashes, it is easy to verify whether or not the transaction was processed when the system comes back on line. Even with its advantages, it is difficult to design or program this method of data error handling in the automated systems.

Developers must strive to patch this information gap, and to provide the best method for their operation to preserve the data integrity, and also to provide instant data on the system performance and operation attributes. This data exchange is critical to the operations being designed with automation in mind. Whatever system is developed by the automation team and/or the MRP-II project team they must adhere to the credo of *timeliness and accuracy*. If this fails, the total system will be a failure from inception.

Scheduling

Scheduling of the operation and shop floor control tie the automated cells and the MRP-II systems together, hand in hand. Some of the older components of MRP-II have by tradition been employed to produce and to maintain realistic shop schedules, MRP, MPS, and CRP. Recently, systems have proceeded to the level of finite scheduling systems,

including systems using artificial intelligence. FIG-URE 31-1 illustrates MRP-II system logistics architecture.

The automated factory today introduces new elements to the scheduling algorithm, making the scheduling project more difficult, but more reliable if done correctly. The precision required to operate the factory now must include such elements as system start and stop times, and order queue. The newer systems can aggregate the data into time buckets such as weeks or days.

The system also needs to provide to the users a fast and effective method to analyze the causes for schedule drift and specify when the system must reschedule the operation. The processing speed of the data is one of the most critical elements in the equation. The scheduling system must be able to be run in minutes rather than hours. This system must be available to consider equipment failures, which are more prevalent in the automated factory environment. More *what ifs* have to be considered.

The total scheduling system must be synchronized to the ever-changing environment on the floor. Once a schedule is developed using the old snapshot data, the system has changed. Methods must be available to place a new schedule in operation, and determine whether changed conditions have made this new freshly generated schedule infeasible due to the changing environments.

The integration of these systems is one of the most trying problems for the automation and MRP-II project team members. Integration is the first item to be considered and by far one of the most crucial. No matter how sophisticated the scheduling system, it is useless if it cannot be easily integrated with both the MRP-II systems and the automated factory operations.

Manufacturing Database

As the MRP-II systems have evolved, the proper overview of the interrelationships of the major elements of the manufacturing databases has been neglected by the user. Normally, users do not understand the data inputs, nor what effect bad or

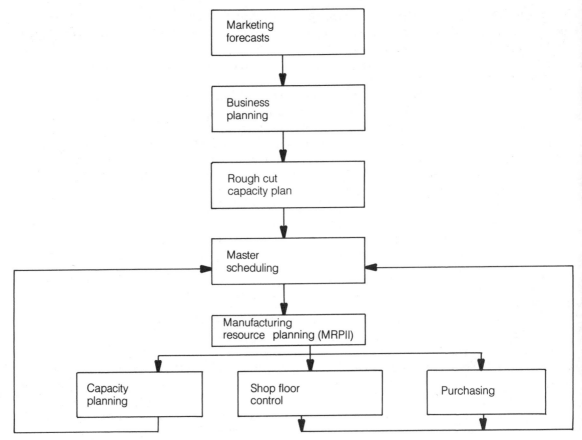

Fig. 31-1. MRP-II system logistics architecture.

missing data have to the system. The prime area of rethinking has been in bills of materials and routings. Each of these data sources must be at least 98 percent accurate in order to maintain proper control. A good portion of the current manufacturing software has been designed using very minor variations of this basic data source. A proper CIM to MRP-II project should include new requirements for the manufacturing database.

New types of data are required to describe the automated manufacturing facilities and equipment. The bill of material may need to include a handling method used to deliver the component. Many items in the CIM environment may not be included such as tools, fixtures, and CNC tapes. With the routing system, there must be the inclusion of the setup and changeover requirements. This area is very

crucial in the overview of the operation, and is many times not fully documented within the routings. These elements will also effect the overall capacity plan for the operation.

There may arise the requirement of special subprograms to provide adequate response times to the control system. As CIM is normally implemented on a dedicated factory level computer, there is no distributed access to the corporate database, nor may it be feasible. A data bridge must be provided for this information.

In many projects, the task of the development of an integrated manufacturing database never gets done because no one includes it in the project scope—often because it would be over the capital budget. Technical and organizational problems are among the most difficult a project must face. Both

CIM and MRP-II software must be designed to simplify the inclusion of all CIM system data into the manufacturing database.

RESTUDY RELATIONSHIPS

The relationship between CIM systems and MRP-II needs to be reexamined. These systems must operate in unison, and be able to communicate with each other. There are integration problems involved, which can normally be handled by software and systems. Nevertheless, there has to be an understanding of the interrelationships on the part of all of those within the organization.

The MRP-II module is the core of the main frame based material control system. The MRP-II module is usually purchased, as opposed to being developed in-house, and the availability of mainframe systems is a dynamic situation with vendors constantly upgrading both the capabilities of their software products and the nature of the support services provided. Since most of the products are modular, a manufacturer can purchase only the required core modules and develop other specialized modules in-house. The standard modules available from most vendors are MRP, bill of materials, inventory control, item master, master production scheduling, rough cut capacity planning, purchasing, and shop floor control.

The ease of acquiring this software and expertise belies the fact that the mainframe system will not work for every organization. Various conditions must exist within the environment to ensure success, commitment, stability, understanding, system disciplines, compatibility, and complexity.

The organizational commitment to the system must be strong, and visible to those who are designing the system and placing the system into service. They must provide the springboard to finance the system, and also to ensure that the management organization is set in place to guarantee success.

It is easier for a mainframe system to operate with stable bills of materials, large batch runs, and relatively short lead times, but these are by no means prerequisites. Initially the system would start with several small databases manually interfaced with different software packages. Over time, as a firm evolves to a full MRP-II system, the databases would be formally integrated into one centralized database to support the entire system.

The system implementers should understand the environment into which they are placing a system. Without this understanding, a large number of unknowns present themselves later in the design and preclude success. A good game plan must be established first.

The management of even a small scale system should not be taken lightly. Numerous practitioners have stressed the importance of using formal project management techniques and have highlighted the requirement for proper systems implementation, effective communication, top management support, training, and user participation. The success of the manufacturer in implementing the controls system and MRP-II will depend on its ability to overcome the disadvantages of being underequipped, and the lack of commonality between the various systems available.

The organization and product lines should not be overly complex. If the proposed system is to be placed within a framework of a broad based and highly variable assembly cycle, the impact of a successful installation would be greatly diminished. A small product-line based company would have the easier time of a total integration of systems and MRP-II.

Experience shows an inherent mismatch among the manufacturer, the mainframe systems, and the control systems available from industry. Many of the systems are based upon general purpose software, providing manufacturers an affordable first step toward formalized systems. Furthermore, most if not all of the basic functions can be implemented on the computer. However, these applications are tools, and to be used correctly they must be carefully tailored to the firm, and have thorough implementation planning, and receive organization commitment. With the proper effort, support, and applications, the result can be a comprehensive mainframe based MRP-II system.

MRP-II evolved from an ordering system into a

planning solution based only upon priorities. This arose out of the old *hot list*. This material shortage list was based on looking at a production schedule, extending it by the bill of materials, checking the inventory availability, and then itemizing what was not there. Normally the planner did not examine delayed orders and did not consider that the materials could be better allocated. The manual system seldom considered items in oversupply situations, so this did not impede production. The fallacy is that the committed expense to oversupply prevented users from obtaining requested materials. This situation is prevalent in smaller or cash-strapped companies.

The main areas not covered in this equation are the capacity, where the rest of the production is (WIP), what parts are due in (purchases), what are they really planning to sell in the future (forecast), and the true manufacturing priorities (having WIP equal demand). Without this total overview, there cannot be a closed loop within the system.

Interfaces

One aggravator of the system control problem is the fact that every computer application has its own user interface, each with its own quirks and rules. This is because the systems typically include modules from different vendors, each with its own interface. In addition, the system includes a number of internally developed interfaces, which also look different from each other. Again this points out a fundamental problem with the interfaces; the different sources would be much less important if each interface was naturally intuitive.

Ineffective interfaces make the systems even more unwieldy than the old paper intensive systems they were meant to replace. Data entry where the workers must enter data from a keyboard indicates ineffective translation of data to another system. These interfaces must be true data translators, and provide the users with the data they require, when they need it. The interfaces should reflect upon the task at hand, rather than reflecting the needs of the software. An effective interface should be able to accept information from many sources, from manufacturing cells, databases, or support modules and pass it without manual modification or data entry.

SYSTEM GOALS

The main goals of a good system should be to:

* Establish the objective
* Assign system accountability
* Create understanding in the company
* Provide the tools to do the job
* Provide for growth
* Measure performance

The main goal for the systems in the automated environment should be aimed at the paperless factory concept. All reports and data required should be able to be retrieved, viewed, or entered on video display terminals or passive systems such as bar code readers. Requests for data should be obtained through the employment of pull down menus, or direct system commands. If required, a hard copy of the data could be obtained through the remote printers tied into the local area network or LAN. Many times, just a screen dump of the information will suffice.

The factory management control systems should provide for the flow of production information through the integration of data from engineering, warehousing, and assembly functions. Tied into this program should be the production plans for the various subvendors. The planning and control function should include production planning for product families, master production scheduling for customer order promising, shipping scheduling, master requirements planning for component scheduling, purchasing plans, production activity control for assembly operations scheduling, capacity requirements planning for shop loading, priority planning for daily dispatch, and inventory planning for material control. These systems should address the need for production queries of "when," "how many," and "where." This will facilitate the solution of production problems including machine utilization, control techniques, planning capabilities, quality control, and excess work in process.

Production Planning

In order to be effective in the area of production planning, certain requirements must be met in the areas of planning, facility loading, and dispatching. Production planning translates the unit goals expressed in the master plan into levels of assembly for the product groups. This aggregate level plan will be tested against the available resources through the process of resource requirement planning (RRP) and represents top management's key "control knob" on the master plan.

Scheduling Systems

A master production and assembly schedule represents a desegregation of product family production plans into individual end items, or into major components when planning bills are used. Master production scheduling must also simulate the resources, including machine types, personnel, and inventory levels, required to accommodate the proposed production schedule or product mix. The simulation capability uses workload profiles for each product and projected resource loads for the existing master schedule. The system identifies net changes in each type of resource as well as under loads and overload of existing resource capabilities. This process is referred to as rough cut capacity planning; it occurs at the higher level planning process.

Operations scheduling establishes projected start and completion dates for all activities on released or planned work orders and automatically verifies availability of tools and materials for the generation of shortage lists. It calls for the delivery of required tools and materials when a selected production load is released, generates initial shop floor load, and identifies potential bottleneck conditions. This function has interactive intervention to undo bottlenecks and simulation capability for use in interactive intervention.

Production activity control also includes the dispatch function, which releases work to specific work centers. While the dispatch function is automatic, a simulation and optimization capability to assist in assigning jobs to equipment is required.

Furthermore, if a manual system is used, it should have the capability to provide detailed recommendations upon request.

The information produced in the capacity requirements planning phase (CRP) is used by assembly management, quality assurance, shop floor supervisors, purchasing, accounting, engineering, and personnel departments. At a minimum, CRP should address and access inventory files and process planning files, convert production requirements for personnel, tools, equipment, and fixtures, identify overload conditions, and provide the capability to evaluate alternative course of action.

Inventory Control

The activities and techniques for maintaining the stock of items at desired levels, whether raw materials, assembled subcomponents, WIP, or finished product is generally referred to as inventory control. These activities include control of the stocking levels, safety stocks, lot sizes for production and purchasing, and lead times, and focuses on management of the numerous resources available.

In addition, the systems used for the inventory control must be designed to interface with the AS/RS systems, miniloads, and product queue at the various automated work cells. These areas must be optimized for efficient flow, and also to allow for the effective utilization of the areas. Overstock of materials at queue areas should be kept at a minimum. In addition, the software employed in the automated storage systems should be examined in order to provide the proper storage slots in the systems and improve the throughput of the systems, based upon the utilization of the stackers and bins. This may require that as the production level varies, or the product lines shift, many of the loads be assigned a different storage slot. Some loads may be brought to the front of the system, whereas others may be reassigned to the rear.

Purchasing systems should be merged into the overall system to aid them in working with vendors placing and expediting orders. For those companies considering JIT concepts, these interfaces among requirements, vendors, storage, and production should be improved. The overall systems should interface with MRP to provide the required feedback of actual delivery schedules, order quantities, and lead times. Needless to say, this information must be timely and accurate; the user of these systems should also be aware that the total data change on a daily basis.

The scheduling of the preventative maintenance of all systems should be considered in the overall design picture. This scheduling must be computerized in order to collect and process equipment statistics. This allows the maintenance department to monitor and act on the machine's productivity, work orders, and requirements for parts and special tools. These systems will also allow CRP modules to include scheduled downtime in their calculations, and to adjust work center loads accordingly.

Control of Engineering Relationships

The engineering database should also be considered in the overall design of the automated factory; it too must interact with the MRP-II modules. This interaction allows engineers to maintain their product engineering information on the computer in terms of parts lists, specifications, and process requirements. This module is most effective when it is fully integrated with the assembly bill of materials special tools, etc., to facilitate engineering changes and reconciliation of product information.

The engineering change control capability enhances efficiency by maintaining the history of product changes as they occur. This database must be available to pick up the changes as they occur. The incorporation of these changes into the assembly bill of materials should reflect in the capability to manage inventory and effectivity dates.

Control of Tools

The relationship between planning and production should be coordinated with the tooling requirements of the automated facility. Time phased requirements for specific tools and test fixtures should be generated on production schedules. This information will then be provided to the scheduling department to help them identify the tool requirement dates and capacity necessary to support the product schedules. Most systems do not schedule tools as a resource. When this element is not included, a product is scheduled, and the tools many times are not available due to repair, conflicting use, or not having been received.

Control of Overhead Items

One crucial item most systems overlook is the inventory and proper use of utilities. Systems are available to monitor energy consumption, turn lights on and off, and adjust heating, ventilation, fume recovery, and air conditioning, and to provide management with reports on utility usage.

Properly implemented, this integrated planning and control system will eliminate the problem of missing resources. It will ensure that all resources required to perform a given job are identified, coordinated, and available when the assembly arrives at a work center. FIGURE 31-2 shows all the functions working together in an integrated MRP-II system within the manufacturing environment. Each of these elements is crucial within the MRP-II equation. If an item is left out, an improper load and capacity figures will be presented to the production department.

AMHS HARDWARE

Some of the main items which must be considered within the overview of a total manufacturing control system are automated storage / retrieval systems (AS/RS), miniload systems, AGVS, robotics, cell controllers, carousels, and conveyors. Each of these systems has been developed over the past decade with a ''head in the sand'' attitude from engineering. The developer of the project scope many times only sought how to handle the material within the system, rather than to examine the total flow of information which would make the system operation viably.

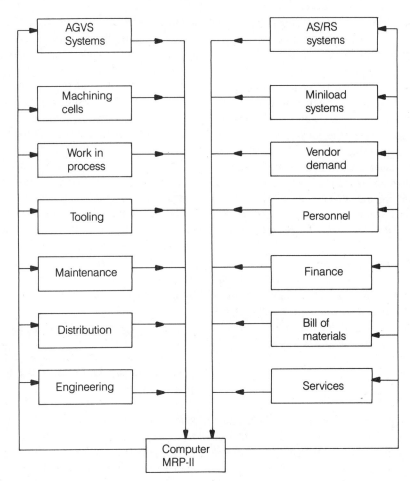

Fig. 31-2. CIM and automated relationships for integrated MRP-II systems within manufacturing environment.

Control of User Interface

To the developer, the user interface is just one part of the application specification; not only is it the most conspicuous part of the system, but it is also the worst defined. Again and again the developer works with specifications that clearly and thoroughly define the desired functionality, but totally disregard the user interface. This comes from the developer's inability to adequately visualize how they will interact with other systems. Once the AMHS system is installed, there will be changes; in fact, many of them.

Historically, more than half the development overruns in time and cost are related to changes in the user interface. Shamefully, the tools developers are using to build these interfaces rarely allow quick changes, even though these changes are inevitable. Developers normally end up requiring additional months, and many dollars to program user interface changes to an application. Due to the length of time and the efforts required for this process, developers do not receive direct feedback from the users about the new changes being developed.

This whole process generates a great deal of frustration in the user and the developer, in addition to a great amount of skepticism and resentment. As this builds, there is a great dependency on the old system, and less desire to make the new system work in a timely manner. It is the old adage of *your* system and *my* system. If the users consider it *your* system they will not work to make it better and will buck the installation the whole way.

The reality of this points to criteria for effective user interfaces. There must be protocols to obtain direct feedback from users. The system should be adaptable to the environment and to the existing systems and procedures. The developers must be able to provide a workable front-end to these modular, multivendor systems without having to change existing hardware and software. Recent technological advances in the manufacturing arena such as graphic terminals, laser readers, bar codes, optical sensors, and OCR make these interfaces possible, and economical.

As the developers increase the employment of interfaces, the more progressive manufacturing companies are seeing a dramatic improvement in cost and productivity. These user interfaces are crucial for system communication, and will finally reflect that there is true integration of systems and equipment.

SYSTEM CONTROL

The data must be entered in a timely manner. The relationship in data input via automatic devices should be integrated to a degree that data is passed when required, in proper form, reliably.

System control can be on a scale from a simple programmable logic controller used to meter the flow of bulk materials to an operation, to a series of interlocking systems employed to meter the proper flow of material through a set grouping of equipment. Without a good overview of what you desire to control, and how it relates to the overall system, it will be impossible to marry the operations together.

It is a prime requirement that whatever control system is developed, all the pieces within the control system must be able to communicate with each other on a timely basis and with a high degree of accuracy and error checking, and that the data required by the system are the data actually required at that time.

If the control system installed reports that an operation was completed long after the next one or two operations, the data are not germaine, and the system will not provide your database with information it can use. Likewise, installation of data collectors which keep reporting the same static environment with unchanging data for hours on end only will increase your processing time. Immediate, accurate information is the key to success.

Too much data is as dangerous as not having the right data. One of the key items to look at is the collection of the data when an operation stops, starts, or when an exception occurs within the operation. These three points will cut down the reporting requirements and a great deal of the extra data. When the system is running fine, it does not require much input. Look at your car dashboard. Most of the gauges there are exception reporting gauges, such as oil pressure and temperature.

Control System Requirements

The control system design must be able to work within boundaries set by the answers to these questions:

- What do I require?
- When do I need it?
- What operations are the critical ones?
- What do I do with the information after it is collected?
- What signals are to be sent back to the reporting area?

When all of these questions are answered, your control schematic will look something like FIG. 31-3.

As indicated in FIG. 31-3, the various levels of the control hierarchy are displayed. The top level shown is the redundant processor sharing the disk storage. Either of the processors can run dependent upon which will be used as the system control and which will be utilized as the backup unit during a session. Groups of disks can be shared in this manner. For instance in a four disk group, one can hold the system software, two can be utilized for data storage, and the last would be utilized as backup, sharing either function of the two.

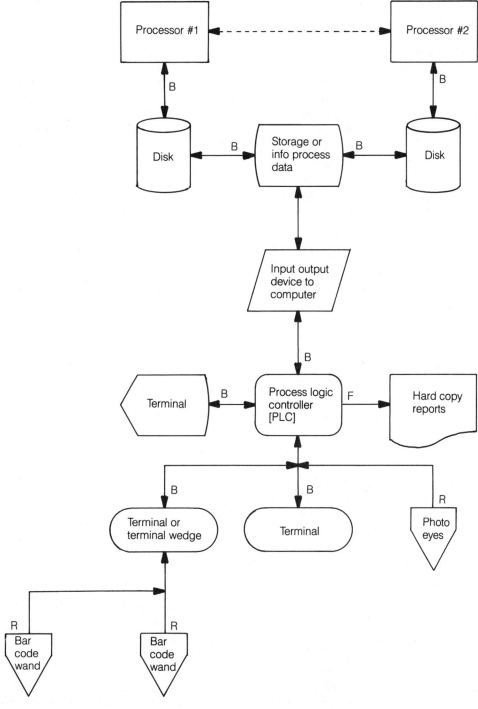

Fig. 31-3. Control schematic for the automated factory.

Below the computer CPU level lie the Programmable Logic Controllers (PLC). The PLC's are utilized to control AS/RS systems, AGVS systems, conveyor systems, robots, etc. The PLC's can be obtained in a wide variety of memory sizes, board configurations, and Input/Output (I/O) arrangements. Thus the PLC can be sized properly for the designed application. As always design in at least 30 percent growth potential.

PLC's can produce reports on throughput, downtime, or WIP. Running through the PLC can be terminals for remote data entry, or retrieval. PLC's have been utilized to download system control from the central CPU for short periods of time during planned CPU switchover. For large systems it is best to maintain a hot backup PLC.

The larger units can have a terminal tied to them to display maps of AGVS routes, AS/RS systems, or conveyor configurations. The activity of the system can be shown with such detail as AGVS vehicle destination, load carried, downtime, awaiting work, battery function, etc. This data can be utilized to produce system status reports, developed at the PLC level, and printed on a printer tied to the PLC.

The PLC's are also utilized as data entry points for photocells on conveyors, traffic cops in an AGVS system, etc. Lower level units can act as interactive data entry points for bar code scanners, or be tied into a data wedge for batch input. PLC's can also be shifted to provide various program changes to system controls. The larger PLC can be utilized to reprogram other PLC's within the system.

The design of this system is crucial to maintaining control, growth potential, reliability, and redundancy.

Features of Control Systems

While most system capabilities, range, communications, protocols, and features vary with the manufacturer, all systems employ base stations to effect communications with the remote device. In some applications these devices are employed at both ends of the communication line to allow standard terminals to communicate with the host. Some of the types of terminals available for automatic identification are bar code, magnetic strip readers, radio frequency, voice, radio frequency data communication (RFRC), and optical code recognition.

There are two basic types of terminals, fixed location or portable. Fixed location terminals generally receive their power from an external source. They are employed at workstations or access points where hard wiring cannot be done easily or in situations where the floor design changes often enough that the wiring locations cannot be planned ahead of time. They can be used on automatic guided vehicle systems or lift trucks, where the power is provided by the vehicle.

Portable terminals are battery powered devices small enough to be carried by the worker and are designed to be either hand held or belt mounted. They are often employed at the receiving area to spot and enter the receipts, or in an environment where a manual inventory is still being performed.

Applications for Terminals

There are many applications for various types of terminals. These applications can tie the on-line control system for material handling directly into the database for MRP-II.

Often the material at receiving cannot be scanned by a hard wired scanner. A portable scanner allows receiving dock workers to go to the material rather than move the material to the fixed scanner. Because these terminals allow on-line reporting, material that is needed immediately can be logged into the host as soon as it arrives, eliminating the delays of batch data processing.

In the pick/put away environment, portable or lift truck mounted terminals are commonly employed to log activity and to guide workers or vehicles to pick/put away locations. With the proper software, the host can determine the most logical picking sequence for multiple orders and can guide the picker to the next location. This will increase the throughput of the system, and allow the system to respond to requirements as they occur. On-line capability also allows the system to identify a secondary pick location if insufficient stock exists at the first identified location. This is very useful in many controlled situations.

The put away mode allows for the host to direct the worker or equipment to the assigned location or allow the operative to select and record the location thus making it available for immediate use. This capability will allow the MRP-II to know the exact location and lot number of all materials.

The area of most benefit to the systems user will be inventory control. As inventory is counted on a real time basis, no interference with other warehouse activities needs to take place. With the properly configured system, a location can be counted and information updated as the transaction takes place. Subsequent activities are then based on the actual count even if another transaction occurs a moment later. Variance reports can be generated for this new input for finance and inventory control. This will also provide for lot controls, first in first out, inventory aging, obsolescence, and true usage activity. Cycle counting can be planned during the stock periods. This keeps the operator busy, provides true randomness, and verifies inventory data "on the fly."

COMPUTERS

The host hardware system should be designed to execute many kinds of jobs concurrently. Jobs consist of one or more processes, each of which can execute a program image that interacts with on-line users, controls peripheral equipment, and communicates with other jobs in the same system or in remote computer systems. Jobs include:

- Customer written interactive, batch, and real time applications
- Interactive and batch development jobs
- System management and control jobs

System Design Criteria

Typically, users interact with applications or system jobs via on-line terminals or benefit from batch or real time applications and manage and control system resources, the proper system design should allow four basic functions. First, the system should enable the application programmer to write, compile, and test programs interactively or in the batch mode, taking advantage of source code, object code, and program image libraries. Second, the programmer must be able to design application systems that require a high degree of job and process interaction, data sharing, response time, and system and device independence. Third, the system manager should authorize users, limit resource usage, and grant or restrict privileges individually. Last, the system operator will be able to monitor operations, service requests, and control batch production.

Program Control

The users should be able to directly control the operation through the operating systems command language. In general, the command language is used by the programmers to develop applications software, by operators to monitor the system, and by systems managers to assign user privileges. Application programmers can also employ the command language to execute their applications programs. The command language should easily extend to provide custom tailored commands defined by the user. Custom written application programs can provide their own command interfaces for people using the system. Transaction processing applications can require several terminals to be slave terminals, meaning that they are tied only to particular application programs that handle requests entered by the user.

The system manager should be able to assign user names and passwords to users who log on the system at a command terminal and can determine their privileges for obtaining services and limits for using resources. Users who access the system through an application terminal interface have the resources and privileges granted to the application programs run on their behalf. An application program itself determines who can request its services.

System Design

The main concerns for system design is to properly control the system operation, process the data, tie-in the users, and design the relationships for the hardware. The equipment selected should be of current technology, so the system is not obsolete before it is installed. The design should be flexible, expandable, and "user-friendly." All facets of the operation should be considered during the design stage. A few of the other main concerns are the processor, operating system, topology, and management of system.

Processor

The processor should be able to execute variable length instructions in the native mode and non-privileged instructions in a compatibility mode. The processor includes integral memory management, a 32-bit interface register, interrupt priority levels, an intelligent console, a programmable real time clock, and a time-of-day and data clock. These will be handy in monitoring the total interaction with MRP-II.

Instruction Sets

The native instruction set provides 32-bit addressing, enabling the processor to address up to four million bytes of virtual address space. The processor memory management hardware should include mapping registers used by the operating system, page protection by access mode, and an address translation buffer that eliminates excessive memory accesses during virtual to physical address translation.

The processor also should provide 32-bit general registers that can be used for temporary storage or as accumulators, index registers, and base registers. The processor offers a variety of addressing modes that use the general registers to identify instruction operand locations, including an indexed addressing mode that can provide a true post-indexing capability.

The native instruction set should be highly bit efficient, and should include integral decimal, char-

acter string, and floating point instructions, as well as integer, logical, and bit field instructions. Instructions and data are of variable length and can start at any arbitrary bit in memory. Floating point instruction execution can be enhanced by a floating point accelerator.

Operating System Design

The I/O subsystem normally consists of the processor's internal bus and the standard mass storage interfaces. The general purpose operating system should provide a highly reliable high performance environment for the concurrent execution of multi-user timesharing, batch, and real time applications. These include:

- Virtual memory management for the execution of large programs
- Event driven priority scheduling
- Shared memory, file, and interprocess communication data protection, based on ownership and application groups
- Programmed system services for process and subprocess control and interprocess communication

Memory management features should be employed to provide swapping, paging, and protection and sharing of both code and data. Memory must be allocated dynamically. Applications should be able to control the amount of physical memory allocated to executing processes, the protection pages, and swapping. These controls should be considered when the system is designed, not after the application is implemented.

Central processing unit time and memory residency are scheduled on a preemptive priority basis. Thus, real time processes do not have to compete with lower priority processes for scheduling services. Scheduling rotates among processes of the same priority.

Application Control

Real time applications control their virtual memory paging and execution priority. Real time applications can eliminate services not required to reduce system overhead. Processes granted the privilege to execute at real time scheduling levels, however, do not necessarily have the privilege to access protected memory and/or data structures.

System services should be included to control processes and process execution, control real time response, control scheduling, and obtain information. Process control services allow the creation of subprocess as well as independent detached processes. Processes can communicate and synchronize using mailboxes, shared files, or multiple common event flag clusters. A group of processes can also communicate using multiported memory.

Applications designers can use the protection and privilege mechanisms to implement system security and privacy. Memory access protection is provided both between and within processes. Each process should have its own independent virtual address space that can be mapped to private pages or shared pages. A process cannot access the private pages of any other process. The four processor access modes to read and/or write protect individual pages within a process. Protection of shared pages of memory, files, and interprocess communication facilities, such as mailboxes and event flags, is based on user identification codes individually assigned to accessions and data.

System Network

The host network should ideally consist of a cluster, which itself consists of two computers connected via a star coupler. Since most systems will be on-line for 24 hours a day, one computer must always be up and running. One will be a primary computer while the other computer will be used as hot backup. (The two computers can be swapped to either function, as operations require.) The hot backup will contain a mirrored image of the operating system and the application software.

System Backup Modes

In the event of the primary computer failure, the system will be able to automatically switch control to the secondary computer in order to resume normal operation. The switch over of control can be accomplished within 10 minutes.

The benefits of a star topology in an MRP-II environment interfacing with advanced automation are the following:

- Within the cluster, a user can upgrade the system by attaching another processor to the star cluster
- A user can upgrade the system by replacing his existing unit with another, larger processor

The two computers will each contain a mirrored image of each other's operating system and the application software. The advantage of this method is that if one goes off-line, the other will be able to take over executing tasks without having the entire system go off-line. FIGURE 31-4 shows a workable computer system configuration.

Data Retention

The information management system includes a file system that will provide volume structuring and protection and record management services that provide device independent access to the peripherals. The system also will support a structure of layered products that are used to organize, maintain, retrieve, and manipulate data quickly, easily, and cost effectively.

The on-disk feature provides a multilevel hierarchy of named directories and subdirectories. Files can extend across multiple volumes; they can be as large as the volume set on which they reside. Volumes are mounted to identify them to the system. The operating system also supports multivolume ANSI-format magnetic tape file with transparent volume switching.

Record/Data Management

The record management system input/output system (RMS) provides device independent access to the disks, tapes, unit record equipment, terminals, and mailboxes. RMS allows user and application programs to create, access, and maintain data

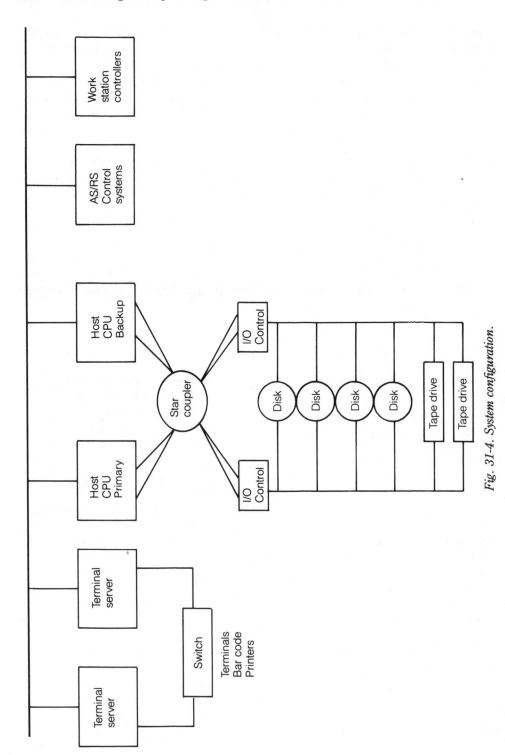

Fig. 31-4. System configuration.

files with efficiency and economy. Under RMS, records are regarded by the user program as logical data units that are structured and accessed in accordance with application requirements. RMS provides sequential record access to sequential file organizations; sequential random, or combined record access to relative file organizations; and sequential, random, or a combination using index keys access to multikey indexed files. Multikey indexed file processing should include incremental reorganization.

Programming

The system should include a complete program development environment for a broad range of languages. In addition to the native assembly language, the system should offer many other optional high-level programming languages commonly used in developing both scientific and commercial applications: FORTRAN, COBOL, BASIC, C, PL/I, and PASCAL. It should provide the tools necessary to write, assemble, or compile and link programs, as well as build libraries of source, object, and image modules.

Programmers must be able to use the system for development while production and MRP-II is in progress. They can interact with the system on-line, execute command procedures, or submit command procedures as batch jobs. Novice programmers should be able to learn the system quickly because the command language accepts standard defaults for invoking the editors, compilers, and the linker. Experienced programmers will appreciate the flexibility and control each tool offers.

Processor Architecture

This processor architecture is specifically designed to support high-level programming. Because the instruction set is extremely bit-efficient, compilation of high-level language user programs is also very efficient. Among the features of the processor that serve to reduce program size and increase execution are:

- Variable length instruction format
- Indexed, short displacement, and program counter relative addressing modes
- Small, constant short literals

Much of the processor architecture also ensures that the operating system incurs minimal overhead for real time multiprogramming. For example, the operating system should employ the context switching instructions and queue instructions to schedule processes. It also uses the asynchronous system trap (AST) delivery mechanism, to speed returns from system service calls. Careful design, coding, and performance measurements can ensure that the flow within the system is as rapid as possible.

Data Integrity

One additional item to be considered is the CPU data integrity. The unit provides memory access protection both between and within processes. Each process has its own independent virtual address space that can be mapped to private pages of any other process. The operating system should use the processor access modes to read and/or write-protect individual pages within a process. Protection of shared pages of memory, files, and interprocess communication facilities, such as mailboxes and event flags, will be used on file ownership and application group identification.

The file system detects bad blocks dynamically and prevents reuse once the files to which they are allocated have been deleted. Integral fault detection hardware should include at least:

- Memory error correcting code that detects all double bit errors and corrects all single bit errors
- Disk error correcting code that detects all errors up to 11 bits and corrects errors in a single burst of 11 bits
- Extensive parity checking
- Peripheral write/verify checking that checks all

input and output disk and tape operations and ensures data reliability

- Track offset retry hardware that enables the operating system to recover from many disk transfer errors

Operating System

The operating system should allow continued running, even if some of its hardware components may have failed. The system automatically determines the presence of peripherals on the processor bootstrap time. If the usual system device is unavailable, the system can be bootstraped from any disk. If memory units are defective, memory is configured so that defective modules are not referenced. Software spooling allows output to be generated, even if the normal output devices are not available. Also, additional devices can be added while on-line.

The system operator can perform software maintenance activities without bringing the system down for stand alone use. The operator can perform disk backup for both full volume backup/restore, concurrent with normal activities. The operating system should be able to support on-line peripheral diagnostics. The system performs on-line error logging of CPU errors, memory errors, peripheral errors, and software errors. The operator or field service engineer can examine and analyze the error log file while the system is in operation.

System Backup

Automatic system restart facilities are required for a smooth transition in the real time MRP-II environment. This allows for the system to come back up without operator interference after a system failure caused by a power interruption, a machine check malfunction, or a fatal software error. The operating system automatically performs machine checks and internal software consistently checks during system operation. If the checks fail, the operating system performs a system dump and reboots the system.

Memory battery backup or uninterruptable power supply (UPS) can be employed to preserve the contents of memory during a power outage. A special memory configuration register indicates to the recovery software whether data in memory has been lost. Following power failure, the recovery software restarts all possible I/O that has been in progress before the failure occurred. Programs can use the powerful asynchronous system trap facility to initiate user specific powerful recovery processing. If memory backup is used, the time-of-year clock allows the recovery software to calculate elapsed time of the outage.

Shadow recording is recommended for redundant database capture, backup, and recovery. Shadow recording will provide simultaneous redundant data capture for all database transactions to physically separate disk devices. In the case of primary disk failure, the secondary disk shall continue to function while the primary disk is off-line for maintenance or repair. When the primary disk is reactivated, the system automatically copies the entire contents of the secondary disk to the primary disk. This will eliminate any data loss and provide greater reliability while ensuring system performance.

The remote diagnostics allow the hardware vendor to run diagnostics, examine memory locations, and diagnose hardware and software problems from a remote diagnosis center. The engineer who goes to the site will be prepared in advance to correct any problems that may have occurred.

System Networking

The networking of the systems and terminals in the automated environment can share resources and exchange information, files, and programs. Furthermore, it will allow the smaller computers in the network to have access to the powerful capabilities of the larger computers, while the larger computers can take advantage of the smaller dedicated systems chosen for specific applications environments.

Some of the points the user should consider in this integration of the total systems environment should be the equipment and functions affected by the manufacturing systems. These range from the collection of the data, to the selection of automated equipment, and the hierarchy of the organization.

BAR CODE SYSTEMS AND SCANNERS

One of the best methods for importing the required data from the manufacturing centers or receiving to the mainframe computer systems would be by the employment of bar codes and scanners. These scanners can be a simple hand held unit that collects a mass of information, and then feeds these data by batch into a *wedge block* attached to a terminal. The scanners can also be a more complex, fixed, mounted unit at a central point where most material has to pass, such as conveyor interfaces, or AGV pickup or drop positions. Again this information can be sent directly to the computer system. As these are fixed in their locations, most of the information garnered can be live.

For larger units, large remote scanners can read a bar code from at least 48 inches away, and in any orientation. Digitized groups of letter, numbers, or bar codes can be collected via television, with the data converted for the use by the MRP-II system.

One of the newer developments is the collection of labor operations, attendance, scrap, and material tied into a real time shop floor control system. These systems are valuable aids to the project team and will provide the mechanisms to collect and interface the data required to make the automated factory work in the MRP-II environment.

AUTOMATED MATERIAL HANDLING SYSTEMS

An automated material handling system involves use of dedicated controllers, tied to a certain type of materials handling equipment that can place, retrieve, and store materials with little external manual interface. Handling systems can be directed from master computers, with commands passed down to these controllers, and the information as to what has been moved can be uploaded to the master computer through the same controller subsystem.

AS/RS

The AS/RS as we normally know it is a multi-aisle storage system consisting of two rows of shelves, parallel to a central aisle. At one end of the system there is an interface between the storage machine and the plant operating environment. The materials are self contained within the system; inventory systems can be developed that report back to a central computer. The workings of the system are totally automatic, with the minimum manual interface being the placing of the loads on the interface, or the directions to the stacker to pick or place a load. AS/RS systems range from miniloads holding many bins of 20 to 30 pounds of materials each, to systems storing large assemblies weighing over 15,000 pounds.

Control Systems for AS/RS   Each of the control systems should have the input as to what is due at the beginning, when it is coming, and where and when it is required. As for the AS/RS system, this system control software should be meshed with purchasing, materials control, manufacturing, scheduling, and shipping. Many systems are designed to store materials, but not the materials that are required now, and have the ability to dispense the materials in a pick list manner. These systems should incorporate the employment of bar code technology to identify and account for the materials without human intervention. There should be a constant relay of material flow back to the master computer to provide a true image of WIP, and enable the material control personnel to redirect the material as need be. In a just in time environment this capability is crucial.

Flexible Manufacturing Systems

Flexible manufacturing systems normally utilize group technology and cellular manufacturing. The approach to the equipment layout is aided by conveyors, robots, AGV, and local area networks to improve material flow. As a rule, many of these systems do not report back to the MRP-II system what material is in queue, what quantity is in process and the expected receipt of material at the next staging area. The control systems are normally islands of integration, and rather than bridges between them, the users must rely on "airplanes" to bridge the gap.

Automated Guided Vehicles

Automated guided vehicles and their control systems are many times designed to direct an AGV to a pickup point to receive material and to move it to the next point; but during the move, the material is lost to the system as to where it is, and exactly what was actually picked up at the interface position. A method must be developed to provide a WIP report as to what is on the AGV system. Without this data, the "lost material" may generate additional demands to manufacture. The next time the system knows where the material is, is when the vehicle completes its move. Again the WIP is understated, or hidden from view.

MRP-II TIE-INS

Areas outside of manufacturing and materials handling also need to be linked with the MRP-II system. These areas include marketing, shop floor control, purchasing, finance, and distribution.

Marketing

One of the main areas to get tied into the integrated system is marketing. The company needs to tie into the system marketing forecasts, product line mixes, game plan, new products, design changes, changes in distribution plans, sales efforts, promotions, and order promise dates. There is no sense planning to manufacture and design the production area for what will not be sold in the future! We can all point to companies who manufacture a broad line of products very well, but yet there is no future market for them: just think of the hula hoop fad when manufacturing was going great guns, yet the market dried up. Communication is critical from the field, through marketing, back to the planning function.

Shop Floor Control

One of the crucial issues involved in the design of a system for control of the operation from order to shipment is the information from the shop. Normally this information is lost to the operation. Once the production control department has issued the order, and the materials are picked for the operating area, the top level system only is aware that the materials are being built, and hopefully the materials will be constructed on time and in the right quantities to supply the open order, or for stock replenishment. The solution for this "lost" information is a good shop floor control system.

A good shop floor system should be able to provide timely and complete answers to a series of questions:

- What is being built?
- Where is it in the operation?
- How much is left in the order after scrap is removed for the operation?
- Do we have to produce more?
- When will the completed materials be available for shipping?
- Can I delay the order; am I ahead of schedule?
- What scrap is being reported? Where? Cause?

Most control systems that are designed without a centralized plan for the interface between CIM, FMS, and AMHS do not provide an information bridge to the MRP-II system. In such systems the main functional areas of the operation lack the information required to carry on the business.

Purchasing

The MRP-II system provides better schedules and better priorities, and lets the purchasing department know where the problems are going to be. Many times, it will provide to the purchasing department an opportunity to push out some delivery dates. The computer system can produce a wide variety of reports for the purchasing areas such as how many dollars are spent with each vendor, the dollar split in items to a group of vendors, and commodity purchasing. The list is endless. The best sign of a good MRP-II and its tie-in to the full automated factory is that the purchasing department has more time to do its job, spend less time firefighting, and more time buying the right items. The data retrieved can also be forwarded to vendors to show how they perform with delivery dates, promised quantities, future demand, etc.

Finance

Accounting systems must be tied into the overall system design. The numbers are essential to running the business. We can see that if all aspects of the numbers are not correct, then finance must reconstruct numbers, or back into financial figures. Some items which must be considered are annual physical inventories, shrinkage, monitoring backlog, price variances, and general ledger entries, etc.

MRP-II integrates all of the included operating systems and financial systems. These include accounts payable, payroll, inventory transactions, stock status, cost systems, billing systems, and accounts receivable.

Distribution

The distribution system of the company requires knowing such basics as where the material is to be shipped; if we have enough in stock, and if not when it is due; when it is due to be shipped; and to whom do we ship it. Many times a receipt of material arrives from the manufacturing area and the distribution group is not aware that it is due. If the distribution area involves the employment of an AS/RS system, the extra or unexpected materials may not have an assignable location. There have been many cases when dedicated systems have been overloaded with unexpected materials.

SUMMARY

As we can see, if the total organization from marketing through procurement, manufacturing, distribution, and support functions are not tied together into one comprehensive system, there is a great potential for failure. Any one area that is left out of the equation can raise havoc within the organization. No system should be designed as an island unto itself. A total integrated system must be designed, and the design must provide room for growth. Nowhere is it more critical than in today's manufacturing environment, where more and more of our technology, production capability, and suppliers are off shore. The American economy can no longer accept a piecemeal approach to systems design.

REFERENCES

Childers, Chester N. "Production Planning on a Microcomputer - Productivity Booster for the Small Manufacturer." *APICS Small Manufacturer Conference Proceedings* (1985), 109-117.

Gallagher, G. R. "The MRP Crusade Meets CAD/CAM." *APICS Conference Proceedings* (1983).

Howard, J. and E. Sommerlad. "The Future Direction of Packaged Software." *APICS Reading in Computers and Software* (1984).

Hurwitz, David R. "Data Capture for MRP-II Systems." *AUTOFACT Conference Proceedings* (1985).

Lewis, P. J. "Integrating the Computer Based Engineering Systems and MRP." *APICS Conference Proceedings* (1983).

Saxe, K. "MRP-II Into CIM: The Interface Phase." *AUTOFACT Conference Proceedings* (1985).

Wight, Oliver W. *Production and Inventory Control in the Computer Age*. New York: Van Nostrand Reinhold Company Inc., 1984.

Wight, Oliver W. "Manufacturing Resource Planning: MRP-II, Unlocking America's Productivity Potential." Essex Junction, Vermont: Oliver Wight Publications, 1981.

32

Reliability Engineering

Thomas A. Mazzuchi[*]
Refik Soyer[**]

IN THIS CHAPTER WE PRESENT AN INTRODUCTION TO the theory of reliability and life testing. We begin with an overview and interpretation of reliability parameters such as mean time to failure, reliable life, residual life, the reliability function, and the failure rate function. We then discuss the notion of aging and give an introduction to some of the more common probability distributions used in reliability. We also give an overview of modeling dependency in reliability analysis. We next conduct some notions concerning life testing procedures such as censoring, accelerated testing, and sequential testing, and discuss statistical procedures for making inference. We proceed with a discussion of reliability at the system level including an introduction to properties of coherent systems, and the construction of system structure functions, and bounds on system reliability functions. Finally we give a brief introduction to some of the more modern topics in reliability such as monitoring reliability growth, inference from accelerated life testing, assessment of the reliability of computer software, use of Bayesian methods, and incorporation of expert opinion in reliability analysis.

NOTATION AND PRELIMINARIES

In this section we introduce notation and preliminaries that will be used in the rest of the chapter. A *failure distribution*, or failure model, represents an attempt to describe mathematically the length of life of a component or a structure. Let the continuous random variable T denote the lifetime of a new component (or unit) and let t be a realization of T. We denote the life distribution of the unit by F defined as

$$F(t) = Pr\{T \le t\}$$

where $t \, \varepsilon \, (0, \infty)$. The *cumulative distribution function* F is referred to as the *failure model* and it represents the probability of failure before a specified time t. We define the probability density (or *failure density*) function of T as

$$f(t) = \frac{d}{dt} F(t)$$

which represents the probability of failure in the

[*]Thomas Mazzuchi received his B.A. in mathematics from Gettysburg College, Gettysburg, Pennsylvania, in 1978 and his M.S. and D.Sc. in operations research from George Washington University, Washington, D.C. in 1979 and 1982 respectively. Currently he is a research mathematician at the Shell Research Labs in Amsterdam. Dr. Mazzuchi's research interests are in software reliability, accelerated life testing, failure rate estimation, reliability demonstration, and reliability estimation with covariate information.

[**]Refik Soyer received his B.A. in economics from Bogazici University, Turkey, in 1978, his M.Sc. in operations research from Sussex University, England, in 1979, and D.Sc. in operations research from George Washington University in 1985. Currently he is an assistant professor in the Department of Management Science at George Washington University and a member of the Institute for Reliability and Risk Analysis at the same university. Dr. Soyer's research interests are in applications of the Kalman filtering, software reliability, accelerated life testing, and Bayesian statistics.

interval $(t, t + dt)$ as

$$f(t) \approx Pr\{t < T < t + dt\} \, dt \text{ for } t \geq 0 \text{ and } dt > 0$$

It follows from the above that

$$F(t) = \int_0^t f(u) du$$

For a specified mission time t, the failure-free performance of the unit is given by the *reliability function*

$$R(t) = Pr\{T \geq t\} \text{ for } t \geq 0$$

that is, reliability represents the probability that the item in question performs its function adequately for a specified time period t. Thus, we can also write

$$R(t) = 1 - F(t) = \int_t^\infty f(u) du$$

and

$$f(t) = -\frac{d}{dt} R(t)$$

Another important concept is the *failure rate* of the random variable T; it is also referred to as the *hazard function*. The failure rate is a function of time. At time t, the failure rate is defined as

$$h(t) = \frac{f(t)}{R(t)} \quad \text{for } t > 0$$

The probabilistic interpretation of the above is that it represents the conditional probability that an item of age t will fail in the interval $(t, t + dt)$; that is,

$$h(t) \approx Pr\{t < T < t + dt \,|\, T \geq t\} \, dt \quad \text{for } dt > 0$$

where the $|$ is read as "given" and is used to denote conditional probability. Using the conditional probability argument, we can write

$$h(t) \approx \frac{Pr\{t < T < t + dt\} dt}{Pr\{T \geq t\}} \quad \text{for } dt > 0$$

As noted in Mann, et al. (1974), the appealing feature of the failure rate is that it enables us to distinguish between different failure models on the basis of physical consideration of the aging properties of the item. Indeed, specification of the failure rate determines the failure model through the well-known result:

$$R(t) = \exp \left\{ -\int_0^t h(u) \, du \right\}$$

Thus all the above functions are related and equally suitable to describe the failure model.

An alternative measure for the reliability of an item is the *reliable life*, defined as the time t_R* for which the reliability will be R^*; that is, t_R* satisfies

$$R(t_R*) = R^*$$

Note that the specification of the complete relationship between t_R* and R^* for all $0 \leq R^* \leq 1$ determines the reliability function.

Another measure widely used in reliability is the *mean life* (or *mean time to failure*) of a component

$$E(T) = \int_0^\infty t \, f(t) \, dt$$

Often denoted as MTTF, this is interpreted as the expected (or long run average) time during which the item is expected to perform in a satisfactory manner. When it is true that $\lim_{t \to \infty} tR(t) = 0$, an alternative expression for MTTF is given by

$$E(T) = \int_0^\infty R(t) \, dt$$

A concept associated with notion of aging is the *mean residual life* of a component of age t. Given by,

$$\frac{\int_t^\infty R(u)\ du}{R(t)}$$

the value represents the conditional remaining time during which the item is expected to perform in a satisfactory manner.

FAILURE RATE CHARACTERISTICS

A device that does not age over time is said to have a *constant failure rate*; that is, its reliability over an additional period of duration dt is the same regardless of its current age. In other words, if the device has not failed up to time t then

$$R(t+dt|t) = R(dt)\ \text{for all } t \text{ and } dt \geq 0,$$

or equivalently

$$R(t+dt) = R(t)\ R(dt)\ \text{for all } dt \text{ and } t \geq 0.$$

This property is also known as the *memoriless* property and the exponential distribution is the only continuous distribution with this property (Barlow and Proschan 1965).

If the unit deteriorates or ages with time, then the failure rate, $h(t)$, is said to be increasing with time. The conditional reliability is a decreasing function of usage; that is,

$$R(t+dt\,|t) = \frac{R(t+dt)}{R(t)}$$

is decreasing in $t \geq 0$ for $dt \geq 0$, and the failure distribution is known as an *increasing failure rate* (IFR) distribution.

Similarly, if the unit improves with usage, then the failure rate is said to be decreasing by time; that is, the conditional reliability, $R(t+dt\,|t)$, is increasing in $t \geq 0$ for $dt \geq 0$. Thus, F is called a *decreasing failure rate* (DFR) distribution.

As noted in Barlow and Proschan (1981), additional classes of failure models can be developed from aging characteristics. A distribution F has *increasing failure rate average* (IFRA) if

$$\frac{\int_0^t h(u)\ du}{t}$$

is increasing in $t \geq 0$ or equivalently if $-(1/t) \times \log[R(t)]$ is increasing in t. Similarly, the failure model F is said to have a *decreasing failure rate average* (DFRA) if $-(1/t)\log[R(t)]$ is decreasing in t. It can be shown that if F is IFR (DFR), then F is also IFRA (DFRA) but the reverse is not true. A complete development of such classes and their properties are given in Barlow and Proschan (1981).

Another class of failure models can be constructed by assuming a failure rate initially decreasing, then staying constant and finally increasing. Such failure rate functions can be represented by what is known as a *bathtub curve* which describes the initial, chance, and wear-out phases over the entire lifetime of an item.

FAILURE MODELS—
Parametric Distributions

In this section we discuss failure models, which are most commonly used in reliability applications.

Poisson Process and
Exponential Distribution

As discussed above, the exponential model is the only distribution having a constant failure rate. (See Theorem 2.3 in Barlow and Proschan 1965.) The exponential failure model can also be characterized by a stochastic process known as Poisson process.

Consider a system (or device) subjected to random events (random shocks) during $[0,t]$. The system will fail only if a shock occurs and will not fail otherwise. Let $N(t)$ denote the number of events during $[0,t]$; then the counting process $\{N(t), t \geq 0\}$ is called a Poisson process with rate $\lambda > 0$ (Ross 1980), if

- $N(0) = 0$.
- The process has independent increments, that is, the number of events occurring in disjoint time intervals are independent.
- The number of events in any interval of length t is Poisson distributed with mean λt; that is for all t and $dt \geq 0$

$$Pr\{N(t+dt) - N(dt) = k\} = \frac{(\lambda t)^k}{k!} e^{-\lambda t}, k = 0, 1, \ldots$$

Alternate definitions of Poisson process can be found in Ross (1980) or in any other introductory text in probability theory. It can be shown that the time intervals between events are independent random variables, identically distributed according to an exponential distribution. Thus, lifetime, T, of the system is described by the exponential model

$$F(t) = 1 - e^{-\lambda t}$$

with density function

$$f(t) = \lambda e^{-\lambda t}$$

and constant failure rate function $h(t) = \lambda$. The mean time to failure under the exponential model is equal to the reciprocal of the constant failure rate; that is $E(T) = 1/\lambda$. A more general form for the exponential model is obtained by introducing a threshold parameter ϕ as

$$f(t) = \lambda e^{-\lambda(t-\phi)}, t \geq 0$$

The threshold parameter ϕ is the minimum value that the random variable T can take. It is also referred to as *guarantee time* and represents the largest time before which failure is impossible.

Due to its constant failure rate, the applicability of exponential distribution is limited. It is applicable to situations where component failure occurs as a result of random shocks rather than aging. It is often used to model the lifetimes of electronic components.

Gamma Distribution

The gamma distribution can be derived as the distribution of time to the kth event in a Poisson process and therefore is an extension of the exponential distribution. The gamma random variable can be obtained as the sum of k independent exponentially distributed random variables each with failure rate λ; that is, it is a k-fold convolution of an exponential distribution.

The probability density function of a gamma random variable T is given by

$$f(t) = \frac{\lambda^k t^{k-1}}{\Gamma(k)} e^{-\lambda t}, \qquad k > 0, \lambda > 0$$

where $\Gamma(.)$ is the gamma function and λ and k are scale and shape parameters. The mean of the gamma distribution is k/λ. When the shape parameter k takes integer values, the gamma distribution is known as the Erlang distribution. When k is an integer, the distribution function of gamma random variable T can be obtained in closed form (Barlow and Proschan 1981) as

$$F(t) = 1 - \sum_{i=0}^{k-1} \frac{(\lambda t)^i}{i!} e^{-\lambda t}$$

If k is noninteger, then the distribution function cannot be evaluated in closed form but can be expressed as

$$F(t) = \frac{\Gamma(k, \lambda t)}{\Gamma(k)}$$

where $\Gamma(k, \lambda t)$ is the *incomplete gamma function* given by

$$\Gamma(k, \lambda t) = \int_0^{\lambda t} u^{k-1} e^{-u} du \qquad (32\text{-}1)$$

The failure rate function also has no closed form expression but may be expressed in terms of equation 32-1.

We note that when $k = 1$, the gamma distribution reduces to an exponential distribution and thus displays a constant failure rate. It can be shown that the gamma distribution is DFR for values of $0 < k < 1$ and IFR for values $k > 1$. Thus, the gamma distribution is more flexible than the exponential model in describing different failure scenarios.

Weibull Distribution

The Weibull distribution combines the mathematical tractability of the exponential distribution with the flexibility of the gamma distribution. The distribution function of the Weibull model is expressed in closed form by

$$F(t) = 1 - \exp\left\{-\left(\frac{t}{\alpha}\right)^{\beta}\right\}, \quad t > 0,$$

where β and α are the shape and scale parameters respectively. The density function is given by

$$f(t) = \frac{\beta}{\alpha}\left(\frac{t}{\alpha}\right)^{\beta-1} \exp\left\{-\left(\frac{t}{\alpha}\right)^{\beta}\right\}, \quad t > 0.$$

and the failure rate by

$$h(t) = \frac{\beta}{\alpha}\left(\frac{t}{\alpha}\right)^{\beta-1}, \quad \beta, \alpha > 0; t > 0.$$

The failure rate of the Weibull distribution is increasing in t for values of $\beta > 1$, decreasing in t for $\beta < 1$ and the failure rate is constant when $\beta = 1$. Thus, the exponential distribution is a special Weibull distribution with $\beta = 1$.

Unlike the exponential model, the Weibull distribution is applicable to a variety of failure scenarios. Because of the monotonicity of its failure rate function, it can be used to model situations where a component is either deteriorating or improving with usage. Weibull (1951) suggested an empirical expression for the failure rate and dis-cussed a variety of actual failure situations that can be represented by the expression. The Weibull distribution can also be motivated as the limiting distribution of the minimum order statistic of independent random variables (Mann, et al. 1974).

A three-parameter Weibull distribution can be obtained by introducing a threshold parameter ϕ to the density function as

$$f(t) = \frac{\beta}{\alpha}\left(\frac{t-\phi}{\alpha}\right)^{\beta-1} \exp\left\{-\left(\frac{t-\phi}{\alpha}\right)^{\beta}\right\}, \quad t > \phi.$$

The mean life under the three-parameter Weibull distribution is given by

$$E(T) = \phi + \alpha \, \Gamma(1 + 1/\beta)$$

For the two parameter Weibull distribution we may obtain the mean using the above expression with $\phi = 0$.

The flexible form of the failure rate function has made Weibull distribution one of the most popular failure models in reliability. The distribution has been used to model fatigue failure, vacuum tube life, ball bearing life, and semiconductor devices failure as well as to model breaking strength and fatigue in textiles.

Truncated Normal Distribution

Although the normal, or Gaussian, distribution is regarded as the most important distribution in statistics, its applicability in reliability is limited since its support is on $(-\infty, \infty)$ and components or systems cannot have negative lifetimes. It is used, however, for representing material properties rather than modeling lifetimes; for example modeling failure as a function of stress rather than time.

The truncated normal distribution is a special form of normal distribution, defined only for positive values; thus it can be used for modeling lifetimes. As mentioned in Barlow and Proschan (1981), empirical investigations have shown that items manufactured and tested under close control may be fitted by truncated normal distribution.

The probability density function for a truncated

normal random variable T is given by

$$f(t) = \frac{1}{\sqrt{2\pi}\ \sigma k}\ \exp\left\{-\frac{1}{2}\left(\frac{t-\mu}{\sigma}\right)^2\right\}, \qquad t > 0,$$

(32-2)

where $\sigma > 0$, $-\infty < \mu < \infty$ and k is a constant defined as

$$k = \int_0^\infty \frac{1}{\sqrt{2\pi}\ \sigma}\ \exp\left\{-\frac{1}{2}\left(\frac{u-\mu}{\sigma}\right)^2\right\}\ du$$

$$= \Phi\left(\frac{\mu}{\sigma}\right)$$

where $\Phi(.)$ is the standard normal distribution function

$$\Phi(z) = \int_{-\infty}^z \frac{1}{\sqrt{2\pi}}\ \exp\left\{-\frac{1}{2}\ u^2\right\}\ du$$

We note that the introduction of k insures that $f(.)$ is a proper density function for nonnegative random variables and that when $\mu >> 3\sigma$, then $k \approx 1$ and equation 32-2 can be treated as the regular normal density. The implication is that the probability that $T < 0$ is so small, that it is negligible. When $k \approx 1$, the mean life is given by (approximately) μ.

Though neither the distribution function nor the failure rate of the truncated (and regular) normal failure model can be expressed in closed form, both may be expressed in terms of $\Phi(.)$. Tables for the standard normal distribution function are found in any introductory text in probability and statistics. The distribution function of the truncated normal failure model is expressed as

$$F(t) = 1 - \frac{1 - \Phi\left(\dfrac{t-\mu}{\sigma}\right)}{\Phi\left(\dfrac{\mu}{\sigma}\right)}$$

Barlow and Proschan (1981) show that the trun-

cated normal distribution has an increasing failure rate.

Lognormal Distribution

If T, the time to failure of a device, is a lognormal random variable, then the natural logarithm of T is a normally distributed random variable. In other words, the lognormal model implies that the logarithm of the lifetime is normally distributed. The density function for this model can be derived by a simple logarithmic transformation of the normal density. As Carter (1986) notes, the lognormal distribution is important in modeling proportional effect phenomena, where a change in a variable at any point in a process is a random proportion of the previous value of the variable; thus it has found many applications in maintenance. A derivation of lognormal distribution using the proportional effect phenomena and other applications of the distribution are discussed in Mann, et al. (1974).

The probability density function of the lognormal distribution is given by

$$f(t) = \frac{1}{\sqrt{2\pi}\ \sigma t}\ \exp\left\{-\frac{1}{2}\left(\frac{\log t - \mu}{\sigma}\right)^2\right\}, \ t > 0,$$

where $\sigma > 0$, $-\infty < \mu < \infty$ are the parameters of the distribution. It can be shown that μ and σ^2 are the mean and variance of the random variable log (T) which is normally distributed. The mean life for T is $\exp(\mu + \frac{1}{2}\sigma^2)$. Neither the distribution function nor the failure rate for the lognormal model can be obtained in closed form; the distribution function may be expressed in terms of the standard normal distribution function as

$$F(t) = \Phi\left(\frac{\log t - \mu}{\sigma}\right)$$

As a function of time, the failure rate first increases to a maximum point and then decreases to zero; it can be shown that the failure rate approaches zero for large lifetimes and at the initial time. The shape of the failure rate is specified by the parameters μ and σ. Depending on the values of σ, the failure rate can be indistinguishable from that of a decreasing or an increasing function of time. Unlike the Weibull model, the lognormal distribution does not contain the exponential distribution as a special case. Goldthwaite (1961) gives a detailed study of the failure rate of the lognormal distribution.

Birnbaum-Saunders Distribution

The Birnbaum-Saunders distribution (Birnbaum and Saunders 1969), also referred to as the fatigue-life model, has been derived using the physical characteristics of the fatigue process. The distribution also offers a probabilistic interpretation of Miner's rule, a deterministic rule that attempts to predict fatigue life under repeated cyclic loading. A derivation of the distribution based on the physical considerations is given in Mann, et al. (1974).

The Birnbaum-Saunders distribution is a two-parameter distribution to model fatigue life T with the distribution function

$$F(t) = \Phi\left[\frac{1}{\alpha}\left\{ \left(\frac{t}{\beta}\right)^{1/2} - \left(\frac{t}{\beta}\right)^{-1/2} \right\}\right]$$

where $\alpha > 0$ and $\beta > 0$ are the shape and scale parameters and $\Phi(.)$ is the standard normal distribution function. The expected lifelength is given by

$$E(T) = \beta\left(1 + \frac{\alpha^2}{2}\right)$$

The probability density function and the properties of the failure rate are discussed in Mann, et al. (1974).

Models Based on Forms of the Failure Rate

Other parametric models have been derived based on the assumption of parametric forms for the failure rate function. Some of the more familiar models of this type are the Gompertz distribution ($h(t) = \exp\{\alpha + \beta t\}$) and the Rayleigh distribution ($h(t) = \alpha + \beta t$). In addition, there are models capable of yielding nonmonotone and even bathtub shape failure rates. These models are often complex and more difficult to handle statistically. A discussion of the use of such models can be found in Glaser (1980) and Hjorth (1980).

MODELING DEPENDENT COMPONENTS

In most reliability analyses, components are assumed to have independent lifetimes. However, in many applications such an assumption is not realistic. It is more reasonable to assume some type of dependence among components. As Barlow and Proschan noted in 1981, such dependence arises out of the common environment in which the components are operating; that is, common environmental stresses or common shocks induce dependence among components. A detailed study of various notions of dependence that arise in reliability and some multivariate distributions that are used to model such dependence can be found in Barlow and Proschan (1981). A more general approach to families of multivariate distributions and how they can be derived are discussed in Marshall and Olkin (1988) and some new distributions are presented.

In this section we give an overview of some well-known multivariate distributions in reliability. Our development will be limited to bivariate distributions and specifically to bivariate exponential distributions common to many reliability analyses.

Let random variables T_1 and T_2 denote the lifetimes of two components. We assume that T_1 and T_2 jointly have a bivariate distribution $F(t_1, t_2)$ with marginals $F_1(t_1)$ and $F_2(t_2)$. The bivariate distribution is said to have a density

$$f(t_1, t_2) = \frac{\partial^2}{\partial t_1 \partial t_2} F(t_1, t_2)$$

if the partial derivative exists everywhere. Other properties of the bivariate distribution function F and the marginal distribution functions F_1 and F_2 are given in Barlow and Proschan (1981).

Bivariate Exponential Distribution of Marshall and Olkin

Marshall and Olkin (1967) derived a bivariate exponential distribution by considering the occurrence of random shocks in a Poisson process. They considered three independent Poisson processes that govern the occurrence of shocks with rates λ_1, λ_2, and λ_{12}. It is assumed that the shocks from the first process are applicable only to the first component and cause it to fail with probability p_1. Similarly, shocks from the second process affect only the second component and cause it to fail with probability p_2. The third type of shocks may cause the failure of both components.

It can be shown that the joint survival probability is given by

$$R(t_1,t_2) = Pr\{T_1>t_1, T_2>t_2\}$$
$$= \exp\{-[\lambda_1 t_1 + \lambda_2 t_2 + \lambda_{12}\ \max(t_1,t_2)]\},$$

and the marginal reliability functions are exponentials given by

$$R_i(t_i) = \exp\{-(\lambda_i + \lambda_{12})t_i\}, \qquad i = 1, 2.$$

The Marshall-Olkin bivariate distribution is the only bivariate exponential distribution with exponential margins (Barlow and Proschan 1981). A generalization of this bivariate exponential distribution to the multivariate case is discussed in Mann, et al. (1974).

Bivariate Exponential Distribution of Freund

Freund (1961) considered a two-component system that can operate even when only one component is functioning. Let T_1 and T_2 be the life lengths of components A and B which are assumed to be operating independently. The random variables T_1 and T_2 are independent having exponential distributions with parameters α and β, respectively. Furthermore, we assume that the failure of A (B) changes the parameter of B (A) from β to β' (α to α'); that is, the failure of A (B) changes the

failure rate of B (A) and thus induces dependence between T_1 and T_2. Simulataneous failures are not allowed in the model.

Freund (1961) obtained the joint density function of T_1 and T_2 as

$$f(t_1,t_2) = \beta\ \alpha'\ \exp\{-\alpha't_1 - (\alpha+\beta-\alpha')t_2\}$$
$$\text{for } 0<t_2<t_1$$

and

$$f(t_1,t_2) = \alpha\ \beta'\ \exp\{-\beta't_2 - (\alpha+\beta-\beta')t_1\}$$
$$\text{for } 0<t_1<t_2$$

where $f(t_1,t_2) = 0$ when $t_1 = t_2$ since both components can not fail at the same time. The marginal distributions of T_1 and T_2 can be obtained as a mixture of exponential densities.

Other bivariate distributions and extensions to multivariate distributions are discussed in Barlow and Proschan (1981). Mardia (1970) also gives a complete discussion of bivariate distributions.

LIFE TESTING

In practice, it is often impossible to completely specify the failure model for the item of interest, yet at the same time it may be desirable to model the failure process or even required to do so to demonstrate the quality of the item for contractual, regulatory, or safety requirements. In order to demonstrate or test this quality, several sample items are tested and conclusions are based on the test results. The term *life testing* is used to describe the designing of experiments to collect life-length data. In designing a life test, three main questions must be answered:

- How many items should be tested?
- Under what conditions should the items be tested?
- When should the test be considered finished?

In the most standard example of life testing, a random sample of a predetermined number of items is tested (*fixed-sample* test) in an environment as close as possible to the operating environment (*ordinary life* test) and the test concludes when every item in the sample has failed (*complete-sample test*). This type of test can prove to be long and expensive when the test items have high reliability. There are, however, several methods for decreasing the required time and/or cost of the life test.

When using the life test to make a decision as to whether the item satisfies or fails to satisfy some specified life requirement, it is often possible to test items one at a time until a decision can be made. Such tests are called *sequential life tests* and have the advantage that the expected number of items tested is usually smaller than the number required for a fixed sample test. Sequential life testing when the underlying failure distribution is the exponential distribution was first described by Epstein and Sobel in 1955 and is explored further by Schafer and Singpurwalla (1970). The procedure is so frequently used by agencies of the U.S. government that is has been incorporated into a series of documents known as the Military Standards. Harter and Moore (1976) and Montagne and Singpurwalla (1985) discuss the consequence of using such procedures when the underlying failure distribution is not exponential. Sequential life tests for other life distributions are not available.

The items may be subjected to an environment more severe than the actual operating environment in order to induce failures more quickly. Such tests are called *accelerated life tests, overstress tests,* or *environmental tests*. The main difficulty with this type of test is in drawing conclusions about the failure characteristics of the item under usual environmental conditions based on failure data obtained under the accelerated conditions. This problem is discussed further later in this chapter, in the section titled "Important Topics in Reliability."

Another method is to use a *censored-sample life test*. For example, it is possible to place *n* items on test but stop the test at a predetermined time t_0 (*type I censoring*) or when $r < n$ items have failed (*type II censoring*). The advantage of type I censoring is that the length of the test is known in advance whereas the disadvantage is that it is possible to terminate the test without observing any failures and this may pose problems in statitiscal inference. These and other difficulties with type I censoring

are discussed by Bartholomew (1963) and Yang and Sirvanci (1977). Data from type II censoring are more easily analyzed with the advantage of decreasing test time and the destruction of less items. The disadvantage of type II censoring is that the length of the test is still not fixed in advance.

Additional censoring methods include using a mixture of type I and type II censoring (Fertig and Mann 1980), or modifications involving censoring at predetermined times (Mann 1969 and Mann 1972). It may also be possible for unplanned censoring to occur. Such is the case when an item on test fails for reasons other than wearout or cannot be tested to failure due to the malfunction of the testing equipment. This is called *random censoring* and is most frequent when life testing is conducted on biological units.

Formation of the Likelihood Function from Life Tests

Even though it may be impossible to completely specify the failure model, it is possible to specify the model as a function of a set of unknown parameters. For instance, it is often the case that based on the physics of the failure process or on an initial guess, the specific parametric form of the model (i.e. exponential, Weibull, etc.) is specified but values of the parameters are not known. Once the life test has been conducted, inference concerning the underlying failure characteristics reduces to inference on the unknown parameters. This may be achieved through the use of the *likelihood function*. The likelihood function is a function of the set of unknown parameters, say $\underset{\sim}{\theta}$ and is formed as the probabilistic expression for the observed life test results. Below we state some common likelihood forms for fixed-sample, ordinary life tests.

Given *n* items placed on test with underlying failure density $f(t | \underset{\sim}{\theta})$ ($\underset{\sim}{\theta}$ unknown) and with failure times $t_1, \ldots , t_n$, the definition of likelihood function most often given in introductory statistics texts is

$$\pounds(\underset{\sim}{t} | \underset{\sim}{\theta}) = \prod_{i=1}^{n} f(t_i | \underset{\sim}{\theta})$$

Yet the above is not for the general life testing situation but rather for the fixed and complete sample ordinary life test case where the parametric form of the failure model is specified. For the type I censoring case the likelihood may be formed as

$$\pounds(\underline{t}|\ \theta, \underline{\delta}) = \prod_{i=1}^{n} f(t_i|\ \underline{\theta})^{\delta_i} R(t_i|\ \underline{\theta})^{1-\delta_i}$$

where

$$\delta_i = \begin{cases} 1, \text{ if } t_i \leq t_0, \text{ for } i = 1, ..., n \\ 0, \text{ otherwise} \end{cases}$$

For the case of type II censoring the likelihood function may be expressed as

$$\pounds(\underline{t}|\ \underline{\theta}) = \frac{n!}{(n-r)!} \left\{ \prod_{i=1}^{r} f(t_{(i)}|\ \underline{\theta}) \right\} R(t_{(r)}|\ \underline{\theta})^{n-r}$$

where $t_{(i)}$ denotes the ith smallest observed failure time.

Even when no parametric form can be specified, it still may be possible to specify the likelihood of the life test. Consider an experiment consisting of independent trials which have only two outcomes. Such trials are known as Bernoulli trials and they often arise in life testing in reliability. For example, the first outcome can be identified with the successful operation (or survival) of an item for a specified mission t^* and the second outcome with the failure of the item before time t^*.

Let n items be placed on test for a time t^* and let random variable Z_i denote the outcome of the ith test item; that is

$$Z_i = \begin{cases} 1, \text{ if } T_i \geq t^* \\ 0, \text{ if } T_i < t^* \end{cases}$$

where T_i denotes the lifetime of the ith test item. Thus, Z_i will take value 1 with probability $p = R(t^*)$ and value 0 with probability $(1-p)$. The random variable Z_i is known as a Bernoulli random variable. Independently testing the n items constitutes a series of n independent Bernoulli trials where each

trial has the same value of p. Then, defining X as the total number of items that have survived to t^*, the likelihood takes the form of the binomial distribution, with parameters p and n, given by

$$\pounds(x|\ n,p) = \frac{n!}{(n-x)!\ x!} p^x (1-p)^{n-x}$$

where p denotes the reliability of the test items. This idea can be expanded by partitioning the test interval further say $(0, t_1^*], (t_1^*, t_2^*], ..., (t_{k-1}^*, \infty)$ and defining the unknown parameters as the probabilities of a test item falling in each subinterval, $p_i = R(t_{i-1}^*) - R(t_i^*) = 1, ...k$, where $t_k^* = \infty$. This approach is often called the *life table approach* and is used in actuarial and biomedical fields. In addition, there are other approaches that do not require specification of the form of the failure model. These approaches are called *nonparametric* methods or *distribution free* methods. Further explanation of these methods can be found in Kalbfleisch and Prentice (1980) and Lawless (1982).

Inference from Life Testing

There are two main methods of inference from life testing: *Bayesian* and *non-Bayesian* (sometimes referred to as *classical*). The non-Bayesian approach centers around obtaining the values of the parameters which maximize the likelihood function. Thus, these are called *maximum likelihood estimates* (MLEs). In some cases the MLEs can be expressed in closed form while in others the use of a nonlinear programming routine may be necessary. The MLEs provide point estimates for the parameters but interval estimates and confidence statements concerning the parameters are more difficult to obtain. These must be derived from the distribution of a function of MLEs. One must often resort to the use of large sample theory where the joint distribution of the MLEs is approximated by a multivariate normal distribution.

In the Bayesian approach, uncertainty concerning the unknown parameters is expressed via a probability distribution called the *prior distribution*. Once data are obtained, this distribution is updated in a natural way using probability theory, namely, using Bayes Law. An overview of Bayesian methods in reliability is given later in this chapter in the section titled "Important Topics in Reliability."

SYSTEM RELIABILITY

Let X_i denote the performance of the ith component of a system over a specified period $[0, t^*]$ then

$$X_i = \begin{cases} 1 \text{ if component } i \text{ survives to } t^* \\ 0 \text{ if component } i \text{ survives to } t^* \end{cases}$$

Note that the dependence of X_i on t^* is dropped, but X_i is indeed dependent on t^*, in particular, X_i is a Bernoulli random variable with parameter

$$p_i = P\{X_i = 1\} = R_i(t^*)$$

where $R_i(t^*)$ is the reliability of component i for time t^*.

Let a system be made up of n components and let X_i, $i = 1, ..., n$ denote the performance of the components over a specified period $[0, t^*]$. Furthermore, let $\phi(X_1, ..., X_n)$ denote the performance of the system over $[0, t^*]$, then,

$$\phi(X_1, ..., X_n) = \begin{cases} 1 \text{ if the system survives to } t^* \\ 0 \text{ if the system fails before } t^*. \end{cases}$$

The function $\phi(X_1, ..., X_n)$ is called the structure function of the system. Again the dependence of $\phi(X_1, ..., X_n)$ on t^* is dropped; in particular, $\phi(X_1, ..., X_n)$ is a Bernoulli random variable with parameter

$$p_s = P\{\phi(X_1, ..., X_n) = 1\} = R_s(t^*)$$

where $R_s(t^*)$ is the system reliability for time t^*. Note that ϕ is a function with 2^n elements in its domain and 2 elements, 0 and 1, in its range. A system is called a *coherent system* if each element of the system is relevant and its structure function is an increasing function of its arguments, that is, if $X_i \leq Y_i$ for all i, then $\phi(X_1, ..., X_n) \leq \phi(Y_1, ..., Y_n)$.

Structure Functions

A *series system* is a system that functions only if all of its components function. This structure function may be represented by

$$\phi(X_1, ..., X_n) = \min\{X_1, ..., X_n\} = \prod_{i=1}^{n} X_i$$

In a *parallel system* only one component must function for the system to survive. The structure function can thus be represented by

$$\phi(X_1, ..., X_n) = \max\{X_1, ..., X_n\} = 1 - \prod_{i=1}^{n}(1 - X_i)$$

In a *k-out-of-n system* at least k-out-of-n components must function for the system to function. Thus the structure function is given by

$$\phi(X_1, ..., X_n) = \begin{cases} 1 \text{ if } \sum_{i=1}^{n} X_l \geq k \\ 0 \text{ if } \sum_{i=1}^{n} X_i < k \end{cases}$$

General structure functions for coherent systems can usually be obtained by representing the system as a network and using the following concepts from network theory:

- *Minimum Path*—The smallest collection of arcs in a network (components in a system), which, when open, will connect a source node to a sink node (whose survival will cause system survival).
- *Minimum Path Set*—The indices of arcs in a network (components in a system) from the minimum path.
- *Minimum Cut*—The smallest collection of arcs in a network (components in a system), which, when closed, will disconnect a source node from a sink node (whose failure will cause system failure).
- *Minimum Cut Set*—The indices of arcs in a network (components in a system) from the minimum cut.

A system will operate if all components in at least one minimum path set operate. Let J_i be the index set of the ith minimum path and let Y_i denote the status of the ith path set; that is,

$$Y_i = \begin{cases} 1 \text{ if all elements of minimum path functioning} \\ 0 \text{ otherwise} \end{cases}$$

thus,

$$Y_i = \prod_{j \in J_i} X_j$$

since all the elements of the minimum path must function for Y_i to equal 1. If there are r minimum path sets then

$$\phi(X_1, \dots, X_n) = 1 - \prod_{i=1}^{r} (1 - Y_i)$$

$$= 1 - \prod_{i=1}^{r} \left(1 - \prod_{j \in J_i} X_j \right)$$

This is called the min path representation of the system.

A system will also operate if at least one component in each minimum cut set operates. Let K_i be the index set of the ith minimum cut and let Z_i denote the status of the ith minimum cut set; that is,

$$Z_i = \begin{cases} 1 \text{ if at least one element functions} \\ 0 \text{ if none of the elements function.} \end{cases}$$

Thus,

$$Z_i = 1 - \prod_{j \in K_i} (1 - X_j)$$

since all elements of the min cut must fail for Z_i to equal 0. If there are s minimum cut sets then

$$\phi(X_1, \dots, x_n) = \prod_{i=1}^{s} Z_i$$

$$= \prod_{i=1}^{s} \left[1 - \prod_{j \in K_i} (1 - X_j) \right]$$

This is called the min cut representation of the system. The determination of which representation to use is a function of the values of r and s.

System Reliability

System reliability is obtained as

$$R_S(t^*) = P\{\phi(X_1, \dots, X_n) = 1\}$$

and is a function of $p_i = P\{X_i = 1\}$, $i = 1, \dots, n$. Usually it is assumed that the components function independently and the system reliability may be obtained using probabilistic arguments or by calculating the expected value of the structure function. The latter is true since for any Bernoulli random variable X we have $E[X] = P\{X = 1\}$. The complexity of the expected value is reduced somewhat by noting that for Bernoulli random variables it is also true that $E[X^m] = E[X]$ for $m \geq 1$.

Both of the above methods require a significant amount of algebraic manipulation. Simple bounds on the system reliability may be obtained using the notions of min paths and min cuts with the assumption of independent components as

$$\prod_{i=1}^{s} \left[1 - \prod_{j \in K_i} (1 - p_j) \right] \leq R_S(t^*) \leq 1 - \prod_{i=1}^{r} \left[1 - \prod_{j \in J_i} p_j \right].$$

For a more detailed discussion of structure functions and system reliability see Barlow and Proschan (1981).

IMPORTANT TOPICS IN RELIABILITY

In this section we give a brief introduction and literature review of some important topics in reliability. The topics discussed by no means provide an exhaustive list but serve as an illustration of areas of current interest in reliability.

Reliability Growth

A complex, newly developed system undergoes several stages of testing before it is put into operation. After each stage of testing, corrections and modifications are made to the system with the hope of increasing its reliability. This procedure is termed *reliability growth*, and is important enough to be codified as MIL-HDBK-189 by the U.S. Department of Defense (1981). It is important to recognize that the term reliability growth is a misnomer and it might not be an appropriate description of what may actually be happening to the system. It is possible that a particular modification, or series of modifications, could lead to a deterioration in the performance of the system. However, the intent of the modifications is to improve performance, and thus the term in question continues to be used. The mathematical models that describe this phenomenon are called reliability growth models. Craw (1972) gives an overview of reliability growth modeling while a review of the more recent results can be found in Ascher and Feingold (1984).

Most of these models assume a mathematical relationship for reliability, which is a function of time sometimes referred to as a reliability growth curve (Crow 1972). One of the most classical reliability growth models is Duane's model (1964), which considers a deterministic approach. Based on some empirical observations on mechanical and electrical devices, Duane assumed a linear relationship between the logarithm of the cumulative failure rate and the logarithm of the total operation time. Mathematically Duane's model may be expressed as

$$h(t) = (1 - \alpha)\lambda t^{-\alpha}, \lambda > 0, 0 \leq \alpha \leq 1$$

where $h(t)$ is the failure rate at time t, and λ and α are parameters. As noted by Crow (1972), if we let $\beta = 1 - \alpha$, then $h(t)$ becomes

$$h(t) = \beta \lambda t^{\beta-1}$$

which is the Weibull failure rate; that is, the values of $\beta < 1$ implying reliability growth. Thus, the Duane model can be stochastically represented as a

nonhomogeneous Poisson process with intensity function λt^{β}. We note that if $\beta = 1$, then the above reduces to a regular Poisson process; in this case there is no reliability growth.

In 1962, Lloyd and Lipow considered a reliability growth model for a system with only one failure mode. For each testing stage it is assumed that the probability of system failure is constant if the failure mode has not been previously eliminated. If the system does not fail, no corrective action is taken before the next stage. If the system fails, then an attempt is made to remove the failure mode from the system. The probability of successfully removing the failure is also assumed to be a constant for each attempt. The authors have shown that the system reliability at the nth stage is

$$R_n = 1 - A \exp\{-C(n - 1)\}$$

where A and C are parameters.

Barlow and Scheuer (1966) considered a nonparametric model for estimating the reliability of a system during the development phase. The authors made no assumptions regarding the functional form to describe reliability growth but did assume that the design and engineering changes would not decrease the system's reliability (Crow 1972). A Bayesian approach to the Barlow-Scheuer model reported by these authors in 1966 was considered by Smith (1977).

Singpurwalla (1982) proposed a Bayesian scheme involving notions of isotonic regression for estimating reliability growth under exponentially distributed lifetimes.

Other approaches for modeling reliability growth involve use of time series methods. The reliability growth process can be viewed as a time series with various stages of testing serving as indices of time. A Box-Jenkins method for analyzing reliability growth data was proposed by Singpurwalla (1978). More recently, in 1985, Horigome, Singpurwalla, and Soyer used a random coefficient autoregressive process for modeling reliability growth process and presented a Bayes empirical Bayes approach for inference. Ramifications of this class of models including adaptive Kalman filter models have been considered by Singpurwalla and Soyer (1985).

Accelerated Life Testing

When inference concerning the life length of a highly reliable item is required, often the life test is conducted under a more severe environment than the operating environment in use. Such a test is called an overstress or accelerated life test and is usually undertaken to save the time and cost of testing. The more severe environment is achieved by increasing one or more of the stress levels which constitute the environment either for the entire test (*fixed-stress accelerated life testing*) of by increasing the stress at predetermined times during the test (*step-stress accelerated life testing*). The statistical problem then, is making inference about the life length at the usual stress conditions, based on failure data obtained under more severe conditions.

There is a large body of literature on this topic but most authors have proceeded by making assumptions about the distribution of the failure times at the different stress conditions and/or the functional relationship between the parameters of the failure distribution and the applied stress. A common assumption is that at all stress levels, the failure times are governed by the members of the same parametric family of distributions such as exponential or Weibull. The functional relationship referred to above is known as an *acceleration* or *time transformation function* and is used to induce a functional relationship between the failure rate and the applied stress conditions. Commonly employed models for describing this relationship are the Arrhenius Law, the Eyring Law, and the Power Law (Mann, et al. 1974: 421). The use of any of these laws is based on the physics of failure of the test item and calls for collaborative efforts with physical scientists.

An overview of the non-Bayesian approaches for analyzing data from accelerated life tests is provided by Meeker and Hahn (1985) and Nelson (1989). Bayesian methods are reviewed in Mazzuchi and Singpurwalla (1988). The step-stress

procedure is discussed in works by DeGroot and Goel (1979), Nelson (1980), and Shaked and Singpurwalla (1983).

Software Reliability

In the past decade, there has been considerable effort in the area of software reliability modeling. Software reliability is a measure of the quality of a piece of software. Specifically, it is "the probability of failure free operation of a computer program in a specified environment for a specified period of time," (Musa and Okumoto 1982). Of interest are issues pertaining to the measurement and quantification of software reliability, the assessment of changes in the software reliability over time (reliability growth), the analysis of software failure data, and the decision process used in software testing (Barlow and Singpurwalla 1985).

The problem of software reliability is different from that of hardware reliability for several reasons. The cause of the software failure is human error rather than mechanical or electrical imperfections or the wearing of components. Once all errors are removed, the software is 100 percent reliable and will continue to be so. Finally, unlike hardware failures, there is no underlying wear process involved but rather the random exposure of software bugs by certain program input types. The input types themselves are generated as part of the operating environment of the software.

During the design phase, the software undergoes several stages of testing. Software reliability modeling centers around the description of the stochastic behavior of the life length of the software at a particular stage of testing following a modification due to an attempted removal of a software fault. Most of the models proposed in the literature allow the failure rate of the software to vary from stage to stage. Models differ in their treatment of the programming environment, the operating environment, and the detection and debugging process.

A formal discussion of the software failure process is given in Musa and Okumoto (1982). Reviews of software models are provided in references by Mazzuchi and Singpurwalla (1988), Musa and Okumoto (1982), Ramamoorthy and Bastani (1982), and Shanthikumar (1983). A unification of software models via the Bayesian perspective is presented in Langberg and Singpurwalla (1985).

Bayesian Methods in Reliability

Bayesian statistics is based on the idea that the only satisfactory means of describing uncertainty is via probability. This means that every uncertainty statement must be in the form of a probability; that several uncertainties must be combined using the rules of probability; and that the calculus of probabilities is adequate to handle all situations involving uncertainty (Lindley 1982). An excellent review of Bayesian statistics can be found in Lindley (1978).

An earlier overview of Bayesian methods in life testing can be found in Mann, et al. (1974). A Bayesian reliability analysis of coherent structures is given in Mastran and Singpurwalla (1978). The recent book by Martz and Waller (1982) on Bayesian reliability analysis is an indication of the increasing importance of Bayesian statistics in reliability. Singpurwalla (1988a) reviews the foundational issues in reliability from a Bayesian point of view.

Let T denote the life length of a fresh component. We assume that uncertainty about T can be described by a failure model with unknown vector of m parameters $\underline{\theta}$; for example, $\underline{\theta}$ will reduce to the failure rate in the case of exponential model. The reliability function of the unit then is given by $R(t|\underline{\theta})$ for $t>0$. The notation $R(t|r)$ denotes the reliability function of T at t, given a parameter r.

Since $\underline{\theta}$ is a vector of unknown quantities, in Bayesian paradigm uncertainty about $\underline{\theta}$ is described by a joint *prior density*, say, $\Pi(\underline{\theta}|\underline{\omega})$, where $\underline{\omega}$ denotes a vector of specified parameters.

Reliability of the unit for a mission time of t can be obtained by the *predictive reliability function*

$$R(t|\underline{\omega}) = \int_{\theta} R(t|\underline{\theta}) \Pi(\underline{\theta}|\underline{\omega}) \, d\underline{\theta}$$

When life data $\underline{d}$, is obtained on the unit, the prior opinion is updated to obtain the posterior density $\Pi(\underline{\theta}|\underline{d}, \underline{\omega})$. The updating is done via Bayes'

Law, specifically,

$$\Pi(\underline{\theta}|\underline{d}, \underline{\omega}) \propto \pounds(\underline{d}|\underline{\theta}) \Pi(\underline{\theta}|\underline{\omega})$$

where $\pounds(\underline{d}|\underline{\theta})$ is the *likelihood function* of $\underline{\theta}$ given $\underline{d}$. If $t_1, \ldots, t_{n_1}$ $(s_1, \ldots, s_{n_2})$, then the likelihood function is

$$\pounds(\underline{d}|\underline{\theta}) = \left\{ \prod_{i=1}^{n_1} f(t_i|\underline{\theta}) \right\} \left\{ \prod_{j=1}^{n_2} R(s_j|\underline{\theta}) \right\}$$

where $f(t|\underline{\theta})$ is the probability density function of T.

Given $\underline{d}$ the assessment about the reliability is also updated from $R(t|\underline{\omega})$ to

$$R(t|\underline{d}, \underline{\omega}) = \int_{\theta} R(t|\underline{\theta}) \Pi(\underline{\theta}|\underline{\omega}, d) \, d\underline{\theta}$$

which is the predictive reliability function after observing data.

Expert Opinion in Reliability Analysis

The use of expert opinion or informed judgment is becoming prevalent in practical applications of reliability and risk analysis. The issue is aggravated by the fact that modern day components and systems are designed for high reliability and so even a small amount of failure data are difficult to obtain in many situations.

As noted by Lindley and Singpurwalla (1986), in current practice, the treatment of expert opinion is undertaken in an ad hoc manner, usually with the experts sitting around a table and reaching a consensus through discussion. Although their results are described quantitatively, the approach does not take into account the experts' biases and differing degrees of uncertainty regarding the numbers given. Also, the method of combining differences of opinion is not formalized. Martz and his colleagues (1984) have pointed out the consequences of using ad hoc procedures in two major reliability studies and emphasized the importance of proper approaches for incorporation and reconciliation of expert opinions in reliability analysis.

A survey of some recent results on formal

treatment of expert opinions in reliability and life data analysis is given by Singpurwalla and Soyer (1988). The key feature of thee approaches is the elicitation, codification, and modulation of expert opinion in a formal manner. The overall methodology is Bayesian and is based on a theme described by Lindley (1983).

A formal treatment of expert opinion for system reliability analysis is given in Lindley and Singpurwalla (1986) where a coherent system of n components is considered. The lifetimes of the components are assumed independent with distributions that have a constant but unknown failure rate. It is assumed that k experts provided an analyst with information on the failure rates of the components. Each expert's opinion of the failure rate was expressed by two numbers that are measures of location and scale. The authors assumed that the uncertainty about failure rate was described by a lognormal distribution and a Gaussian framework was used to model expert opinion. The attractive feature of this approach is the provision to incorporate the analyst's view of the expertise of the experts and this is achieved through the analyst's

likelihood function of the failure rate. The analyst incorporates his/her opinion of the experts' biases and precision as well as the correlations of the experts' inputs. The approach also allows the analyst to model the experts' opinions about the correlation among the components.

Singpurwalla (1988b) considered the use of expert opinion for reliability analysis of components whose lifelengths were described by Weibull distribution; he also introduced an interactive procedure that had been implemented on a personal computer (Aboura and Soyer 1986). In recognizing the fact that experts do not conceptualize in terms of abstract parameters, but rather think in terms of measures of central tendency Singpurwalla (1988b) presented an approach based on the elicitation of expert opinion on median life. The approach uses an Gaussian framework for modeling expert opinion and also allows codification of expert opinion on aging characteristics of the component. An approach which uses Chi-Square distribution for elicitation of expert opinion on median life was introduced by Singpurwalla and Song (1988) for analysis of Weibull distribution.

REFERENCES

Aboura, K. and R. Soyer (1986). A User's Manual for an Interactive PC-Based Procedure for Reliability Assessment, GWU/IRRA/Serial TR-86/14, George Washington University, Institute for Reliability and Risk Analysis.

Ascher, H. and H. Feingold (1984). *Repairable Systems Reliability*. Marcel Dekker.

Barlow, R. E. and F. Proschan (1965). *Mathematical Theory of Reliability*. New York: John Wiley.

——————. (1981). *Statistical Theory of Reliability and Life Testing*.

Barlow, R. E. and E. M. Scheuer (1966). "Reliability Growth During a Development Testing Program." *Technometrics* 8: 53-60.

Barlow, R. and N. D. Singpurwalla (1985). "Assessing the Reliability of Computer Software and Computer Networks: An Opportunity for Partnership with Computer Scientists." *The American Statistician* 39: 88-94.

Bartholomew, D. (1963). "The Sampling Distribution of an Estimate Arising in Life Testing." *Technometrics* 5: 361-374.

Birnbaum, Z. W. and S. C. Saunders (1969). "A New Family of Life Distributions." *Journal of Applied Probability* 6: 319-327.

Carter, A. D. S. (1986). *Mechanical Reliability*. MacMillan.

Crow, L. H. (1972). "Reliability Growth Modeling." Technical Report No. 55, U.S. Army Material Systems Analysis Agency, Aberdeen, Maryland.

Duane, J. T. (1964). "Learning Curve Approach to Reliability Monitoring." *IEEE Transactions on Aerospace* 2: 563-566.

Epstein, B. and M. Sobel (1955). "Sequential Life Tests in the Exponential Distribution." *The Ann. of Math. Statist.* 26: 82-93.

Fertig, K. and N. Mann (1980). "Life-test Sampling Plans for Two-parameter Weibull Populations." *Technometrics* 22: 165-177.

Freund, J. E. (1961). "A Bivariate Extension of the Exponential Distribution." *J. Amer. Stat. Assoc.* 56: 971-977.

Glaser, R. E. (1980). "Bathtub and Related Failure Rate Characterizations." *J. Amer. Stat. Assoc.* 75: 667-672.

Goldthwaite, L. (1961). "Failure Rate Study for the Lognormal Lifetime Model." In *Proceedings of the Seventh National Symposium on Reliability and Quality Control*: 208-213.

DeGroot, M. and P. K. Goel (1979). "Bayesian Estimation and Optimal Designs in Partially Accelerated Life Testing." *Naval Research Logistics Quarterly* 26: 223-235.

Harter, H. and A. Moore (1976). "An evaluation of Exponential and Weibull Test Plans." *IEEE Transactions on Reliability* 26: 100-104.

Hjorth, J. (1980). "A Reliability Distribution with Increasing, Decreasing, Constant, and Bathtub-shaped Failure Rates." *Technometrics* 22: 99-108.

Horigome, M., N. D. Singpurwalla, and R. Soyer, (1985). "A Bayes Empirical Bayes Approach for (Software) Reliability Growth." In *Computer Science and Statistics: The Interface*, edited by L. Billard, 47-55.

Kalbfleisch, J. and R. Prentice (1980). *The Statistical Analysis Failure Time Data*. New York: John Wiley.

Langberg, N. and N. D. Singpurwalla (1985). "Unification of Some Software Reliability Models via the Bayesian Approach." *SIAM J. Sci. and Stat. Comp.* 6: 781-790.

Lawless, J. (1982). *Statistical Models and Method for Lifetime Data*. New York: John Wiley.

Lindley, D. V. (1978). "The Bayesian Approach." *Scandinavian Journal of Statistics* 5: 1-26.

_____. (1982). "The Bayesian Approach to Statistics." In *Some Research Advances in Statistics*, edited by J. Tiago de Oliveira and B. Epstein, 65-87.

_____. (1983). "Reconciliation of Probability Distributions." *Operations Research* 31: 866-880.

Lindley, D. V. and N. D. Singpurwalla (1986). Reliability (and Fault Tree) Analysis using Expert Opinions." *J. Amer. Stat. Assoc.* 81: 87-90.

Lloyd, D. K. and M. Lipow (1962). *Reliability: Management, Methods and Mathematics*. Englewood Cliffs, New Jersey: Prentice-Hall.

Mann, N. (1969). "Three-order-statistic Confidence Bounds for a Weibull Model with Progressive Sampling." *J. Amer. Stat. Assoc.* 64: 306-315.

Mann, N. (1972). "Best Linear Invariant Estimation of Weibull Parameters Under Progressive Sampling." *Technometrics* 13: 521-533.

Mann, N. R., R. E. Schafer, and N. D. Singpurwalla (1974). *Methods for Statistical Analysis of Reliability and Life Data*. New York: John Wiley.

Mardia, K. V. (1970). *Families of Bivariate Distributions*. London: Charles W. Griffin.

Marshall, A. W. and I. Olkin (1967). "A Multivariate Exponential Distribution." *J. Amer. Stat. Assoc.* 62: 516-522.

_____. (1988). "Families of Multivariate Distributions." *J. Amer. Stat. Assoc.* 83: 834-841.

Martz, H. F. and R. A. Waller (1982). *Bayesian Reliability Analysis*. New York: John Wiley.

Martz, H. F., M. C. Bryson, and R. A. Waller (1984). "Eliciting and Aggregating Subjective Judgments—Some Exponential Results." In *Proceedings of the 1984 Statistical Symposium on National Energy Issues*: 63-82.

Mastran, D. V. and N. D. Singpurwalla (1978). "A Bayesian Estimation of the Reliability of Coherent Structures." *Operations Research* 26: 663-672.

MIL-HDBK-189 (1981). "Reliability Growth Management." Headquarters, U.S. Army Communications Research and Development Command.

Mazzuchi, T. A. and N. D. Singpurwalla (1988). "Inference from Accelerated Life Tests: Some Recent Results." In *Accelerated Life Testing and Experts' Opinion in Reliability*, edited by D.V. Lindley and A. Clariaotti, 181-192. Amsterdam: North-Holland Publishing Co.

_____. (1988). "Software Reliability Models." In *Handbook of Statistics, 7: Quality Control and Reliability*, edited by P.R. Krishnaiah and C.R. Rao, 73-96.

Meeker, W. and G. Hahn (1985). *How to Plan an Accelerated Life Test—Some Practical Guidelines*. Volume 10, *The ASQC Basic References in Quality Control: Statistical Techniques*, edited by J.A. Carroll and S. S. Shapiro. American Society for Quality Control.

Montagne, E. R. and N. D. Singpurwalla (1985). "Robustness of the Exponential Sequential Life Testing Procedures." *J. Amer. Stat. Assoc.* 80: 715-719.

Musa, J. and Okumoto, K. (1982). "Software Reliability Models: Concepts, Classification, Comparisons and Practice." In *Electronic Systems Effectiveness and Life Cycle Costing*, edited by J. K. Skwirzynski, 395-423. Springer-Verlag.

Nelson, W. (1980). "Accelerated Life Testing—Step-stress Models and Data Analysis." *IEEE Transactions on Reliability* 29: 103-108.

_____. (1989). *Accelerated Life Testing: Statistical Models, Data Analysis, and Test Plans*. New York: John Wiley.

Ramamoorthy, C. and F. Bastani (1982). "Software Reliability: Status and Perspective." *IEEE Transactions on Software Engineering* 8: 354-371.

Ross, S. M. (1980). *Introduction to Probability Models*. Academic Press.

Schafer, R. and N. D. Singpurwalla (1970). "A Sequential Bayes Procedure for Reliability Demonstration." *Naval Research Logistics Quarterly* 17: 55-67.

Shaked, M. and N. D. Singpurwalla (1983). "Inference for Step-stress Accelerated Tests." *J. Stat. Plan. and Inf.*: 295-306.

Shanthikumar, J. (1983). "Software Reliability Models: A Review." *Microelec. Reliab.* 23: 902-923.

Singpurwalla, N. D. (1978). "Estimating Reliability Growth (or Deterioration) Using Time Series Analysis." *Naval Research Logistics Quarterly* 25: 1-14.

_____. (1982). "A Bayesian Scheme for Estimating Reliability Growth under Exponential Failures." *TIMS Studies in the Management Sciences 19*, 281-296.

_____ . (1988a). "Foundational Issues in Reliability and Risk Analysis." *SIAM Review* 30: 264-282.

_____ . (1988b). "An Interactive PC-Based Procedure for Reliability Assessment." *J. Amer. Stat. Assoc.* 83: 43-51.

Singpurwalla, N. D. and M. S. Song (1988). "Reliability Analysis Using Weibull Lifetime Data and Expert Opinion." *IEEE Transactions on Reliability* 37: 340-347.

Singpurwalla, N. D. and R. Soyer (1985). "Assessing (Software) Reliability Growth Using a Random Coefficient Autoregressive Process and its Ramifications." *IEEE Transactions on Software Engineering* 11: 1456-1464.

_____ . (1988). "The Use of Expert Opinion in Reliability: A Survey." In *Accelerated Life Testing and Expert's Opinions in Reliability*, edited by C. A. Clariotti and D. V. Lindley, 106-115.

Smith, A. F. M. (1977). "A Bayesian Note on Reliability Growth During a Development Testing Program." *IEEE Transactions on Reliability* 26: 346-347.

Weibull, W. (1951). A Statistical Distribution Function of Wide Applicability." *Journal of Applied Mechanics* 18: 293-297.

Yang, G. and M. Sirvanci (1977). "Estimation of a Time-truncated Exponential Parameter used in Life Testing." *J. Amer. Stat. Assoc* 72: 444-447.

33

Production Scheduling:

Classical and Knowledge-Based Approach

Andrew Kusiak[*]

IN THE THEORY OF DETERMINISTIC MACHINE SCHEDuling, a set of parts is to be processed on a set of machines (processors) in order to either minimize or maximize a certain performance measure. A job (part) may consist of a number of operations. All machining parameters are assumed to be known in advance. Each operation is to be processed by at most one machine at a time.

INTRODUCTION TO PRODUCTION SCHEDULING

Depending on the way the parts visit machines there are two modes of processing, flow shop and job shop. Please refer to FIG. 33-1. In the figure, the sketch of the flow shop (a) shows that all parts flow in one direction, while in the job shop (b) the parts may flow in different directions. In both cases a part does not have to visit all machines.

Operation o_i can be characterized by the following data:

- t_{ij} = processing time of operation o_i on machine j
- r_i = readiness of operations o_i for processing

- d_i = due date, the promised delivery time of operation o_i
- w_i = weight (priority); expresses the relative urgency of operation o_i

The mode of processing is called preemptive if an operation may be preempted at any time and restarted later at no cost, perhaps on another machine.

In a set of operations, precedence constraints among them may be defined. The $o_i < o_j$ means that the processing of o_i must be completed before o_j can be started. In other words, the set of operations is partially ordered by $<$, a precedence relation. A set of operations ordered by the precedence relation is usually represented as a directed graph, or *diagraph*, in which nodes correspond to operations and arcs correspond to precedence constraints. For each operation o_i, $i = 1, \ldots, n$, in a given schedule, the following parameters are defined:

- C_i = Completion time of operations o_i
- F_i = Flow time; the sum of waiting and processing times $F_i = C_i - r_i$

*Dr. Andrew Kusiak is a Professor and Chairman of the Department of Industrial and Management Engineering at the University of Iowa in Iowa City, Iowa. He holds the Ph.D. degree in Operations Research, M.Sc. degree in Mechanical Engineering, and a B.Sc. degree in Precision Engineering. Andrew Kusiak is interested in applications of artificial intelligence and optimization in modern manufacturing systems. He is the Editor-in-Chief of the *Journal of Intelligent Manufacturing* (Chapman and Hall) and the author of the *Intelligent Manufacturing Systems* (Prentice-Hall).

(a) Flow shop

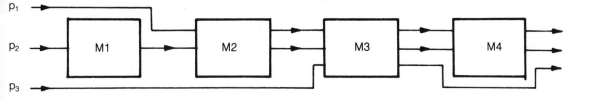

(b) Job shop

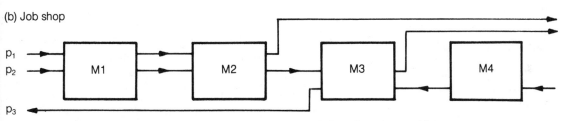

Fig. 33-1. Illustration of two modes of processing, flow shop and job shop.

- L_i = Lateness $L_i = C_i - d_i$
- T_i = Tardiness $T_i = \max \{C_i - d_i, 0\}$

- Maximum lateness: $L_{max} = \max \{L_i\}$
- Mean tardiness:

A schedule for which the value of a particular performance measure attains minimum is called an optimal schedule. To evaluate schedules the following basic performance measures as used:

$$T = \frac{1}{n}\sum_{i=1}^{n} T_i$$

- Mean weighted tardiness:

- Schedule length (makespan): $C_{max} = \max \{C_i\}$
- Mean flow time:

$$T_w = \frac{\displaystyle\sum_{i=1}^{n} T_i}{\displaystyle\sum_{i=1}^{n} w_i}$$

$$F = \frac{1}{n}\sum_{i=1}^{n} f_i$$

- Number of tardy jobs:

- Mean weighted flow time:

$$U_T = \sum_{i=1}^{n} u_i$$

$$F_w = \frac{\displaystyle\sum_{i=1}^{n} w_i F_i}{\displaystyle\sum_{i=1}^{n} w_i}$$

$$\text{where } u_i = \begin{cases} 1, & \text{if } C_i > d_i. \\ 0, & \text{otherwise} \end{cases}$$

SCHEDULING *n* OPERATIONS ON A SINGLE MACHINE

One of the simplest scheduling problems is to schedule *n* operations on a single machine. Let us consider two cases of this problem:

- Case 1: no constraints are imposed
- Case 2: due dates are imposed for all or some operations

Suppose that one attempts to minimize the mean flow time $\overline{F}$ in the one machine scheduling problem without any constraints.

Theorem One

For a one machine scheduling problem, the mean flow time is minimized by the following sequence:

$$t_{(1)} \le t_{(2)} \le \ldots \le t_{(i)} \le \ldots \le t_{(n)}$$

where $t_{(i)}$ is the processing time of the operation that is processed i^{th}. The schedule obtained is optimal and is called the *shortest processing time* (SPT) schedule.

Example One   Given the following data

Operation Number	1	2	3	4	5	6
Processing Time	4	7	1	6	2	3

the SPT schedule is: (3,5,6,1,4,2).

Theorem Two

Suppose that one attempts to minimize the maximum lateness $L_{\max}$ in the one machine scheduling problem with due dates. For the one machine scheduling problem with due dates, the maximum lateness is minimized by sequencing such that:

$$d_{(1)} \le d_{(2)} \le \ldots d_{(i)} \le \ldots \le d_{(n)}$$

where $d_{(i)}$ is the due date of the job that is processed i^{th}.

The schedule obtained is optimal and is called the *earliest due date* (EDD) schedule.

Example Two   Determine the EDD schedule for a problem with six operations for the following data:

Operation Number	1	2	3	4	5	6
Processing Time	1	1	2	5	1	3
Due Date	6	3	8	14	9	3

The EDD sequence is: (6,2,1,3,5,4).

The values of lateness and tardiness for each operation in the sequence are shown in TABLE 33-1. Note in the table that operation number 2 is late ($L_2 = 1$).

Table 33-1. Lateness and Tardiness Data for Example Two

Operation Number	Completion Time	Lateness	Tardiness
6	3	0	0
2	4	1	1
1	5	−1	0
3	7	−1	0
5	8	−1	0
4	13	−1	0

SCHEDULING FLEXIBLE FORGING MACHINE

In this section, I discuss machine scheduling problem with changeover costs and precedence constraints. The problem uses the example of a flexible forging machine.

One of the most frequently emphasized aspects of a flexible manufacturing system (FMS) deals with changeover costs. (For an introduction to the FMS, please refer to Kusiak 1986a, 1986b.) Very often, an FMS is modeled as a system with virtually no changeover costs. In the following paragraphs I attempt to show that changeover costs exist in a FMS, and their reduction is a matter of a planning methodology. An FMS, if not properly planned, may in fact result in unnecessarily large changeover costs. I consider a flexible forging machine (FFM), rather than a large-scale FMS. FIGURE 33-2 shows a schematic top down view, and FIG. 33-3 shows a photograph of an FFM.

The FFM is computer controlled and has the following four automatic options:

1. Part loading
2. Chucks rotation and horizontal movement
3. Tool magazine rotation and oscillation
4. Part loading/unloading

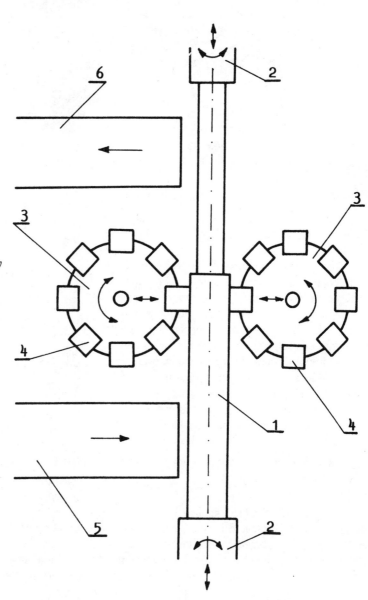

Fig. 33-2. A schematic top-down view of a flexible forging machine.

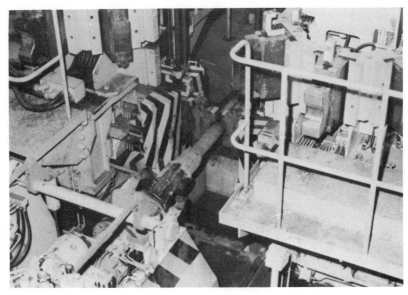

Fig. 33-3. A photograph of the flexible forging machine.
(Courtesy of Ishikawajima-Harima Heavy Industries Co., Japan).

Features of the FFM Scheduling Problem

The FFM scheduling problem has two main features: changeover costs and precedence constraints.

Changeover Costs The idea behind the FMS concept is to reduce or preferably eliminate changeover costs. Due to the progress in FMS hardware and advancement in the planning methodology, it has been possible to reduce these costs, but not to eliminate them entirely. We will see that, in the FFM discussed here, changeover costs occur. Reduction of these costs is a matter of the FFM scheduling.

There are the following four sources of changeover costs in the FFM we are considering:

1. Parts
2. Numerical control programs
3. Chucks holding parts
4. Tools

The changeover cost imposed by loading and unloading parts is dictated by the hardware design and its reduction is beyond operational control. The NC-program is being changed during the loading of a new part and the unloading of the already forged part. The NC-program changeover time is only a small fraction of the loading and unloading time. The chucks are capable of holding many different parts and they are very seldom changed. Tool changeover imposes significant costs, and this issue is of main concern for the optimization model presented later in this section. Moreover, these costs are sequence-dependent. Before a new part (or a batch of parts) is forged, it is usually necessary to change some tools stored in the tool magazines.

Precedence Constraints Classical scheduling problems might be formulated with two types of constraints: (1) due dates, and (2) precedences. The precedence constraints are more appropriate than the due date constraints in modeling the FFM scheduling problem. The FFM is to be integrated with the machining and assembling systems. Often, final products are assembled in a sequence imposed by the market demand. In this case, in order to reduce a volume of in-process inventory, it is desirable to perform the machining and forging process in a sequence imposed by the assembly process. If this sequence is not preserved, a delay in product delivery may occur.

Modeling the FFM Scheduling Problem

Based on previous considerations, one can identify the underlying FFM scheduling problem as the single machining scheduling problem with sequence-dependent changeover costs and precedence constraints. It is known from scheduling theory (see Baker, 1974, p. 94) that the single machine scheduling problem with sequence-dependent changeover costs is equivalent to the *traveling salesman problem* (TSP).

One of the most frequently encountered formulations of the TSP is a mixed integer programming formulation presented below.

Denote:

- n = number of cities (operations in the FFM scheduling problem)
- c_{ij} = traveling (setup) cost from city (operation) i to city (operation) j
- u_i = nonnegative variable
- $x_{ij} = \begin{cases} 1 \text{ if city (operation) } i \text{ immediately precedes city (operation) } j \\ 0 \text{ otherwise} \end{cases}$

The objective function of the traveling salesman problem minimizes the total travel (setup) cost.

$$\min \sum_{i=1}^{n} \sum_{j=1}^{n} c_{ij} x_{ij} \tag{1}$$

$$\text{s.t.} \sum_{i=1}^{n} x_{ij} = 1, \, j = 1,\ldots,n \tag{2}$$

$$\sum_{j=1}^{n} x_{ij} = 1, \, i = 1,\ldots,n \tag{3}$$

$$u_i - u_j + n x_{ij} \leq n-1, \\ i=2,\ldots,n; \, j=2,\ldots,n; \, i \neq j \tag{4}$$

$$x_{ij} = 0,1; \, i,j = 1, \ldots n \tag{5}$$

$$u_i \geq 0 \tag{6}$$

Constraint (2) ensures that in a given tour only one city immediately precedes city j. Constraint (3) imposes that city i is followed by exactly one city. The formulation (1), (2), (3), and (5) is known in the operations research literature as the *assignment problem*. Constraint (4) eliminates subtours generated by solving the assignment problem (1)-(3). Integrality is imposed by constraint (5). Constraint (6) ensures nonnegativity. To illustrate application of the formulation (1)-(6) for solving the forging machine scheduling problem, consider the following example.

Example Three Find the optimal schedule for six parts. Each part is to visit a flexible forging machine only once. The matrix of sequence dependent changeover costs is as follows:

		Part Number				
		1	2	3	4	5	6
	1	∞	7	3	12	5	8
	2	4	∞	2	10	9	3
Part	3	6	7	∞	11	1	7
Number	4	7	3	1	∞	8	8
	5	2	10	2	7	∞	3
	6	4	11	7	6	3	∞

Solving the formulation (1)-(6) by a standard computer code suitable for solving linear 0-1 programming problems (for example LINDO, Schrage 1984) or a specialized algorithm (see for example Lawler et al. 1985) the following optimal solution obtained is:

$$x_{12} = x_{26} = x_{64} = x_{43} = x_{35} = x_{51} = 1$$

which can be also expressed as (1,2,6,4,3,5,1). The cost of the optimal solution is 20.

The flexible forging machine scheduling problem can be described as the TSP problem with precedence constraints. So far, not too many operations research models have been applied to manufacturing systems. In my view there are two basic obstacles (1) model formulations have been too complex, and (2) algorithms for solving these models have been difficult to implement.

The approach presented in this section avoids these obstacles. First of all, I do not consider the standard formulation of the TSP—for example (1)-(6)—because this becomes very cumbersome if the precedence constraints are added. Instead, I present a network formulation. In this formulation the precedence constraints are expressed very easily. In addition, a good feasible solution to the network formulation can be generated by a standard linear programming (LP) code. To obtain the optimal solution, a branch and bound search will be applied.

Two Commodity Network Formulation
As mentioned earlier, the sequence-dependent changeover costs lead to a traveling salesman problem with n cities. In our model, the cities $1,2, ..., n$ correspond to parts (or batches of parts) $p_1, p_2, ..., p_n$ to be scheduled. The distance between cities i and j are to be replaced by the changeover costs c_{ij} = $c(p_i, p_j)$ from part p_i to p_j. The traveling salesman tour, which is simply a permutation of $1,2, ..., n$, indicates directly the order of processing the parts. The precedence constraints are of the form: part p_u before part p_v or, symbolically $p_u \longrightarrow p_v$, for certain combinations of parts p_u and p_v.

To model the scheduling problem, I follow the approach given in Finke et al. (1984). The network flow of two distinct commodities is used to characterize the traveling salesman tours. Consider the TSP with $n=6$ cities and the tour $(1,4,2,3,6,5)$. There are two commodities, P and Q, given in the network. At a selected starting point s (here 1), $(n-1)$ units of the commodity P are available, one unit for each i, $i \neq s$. Complementary to P, Commodity Q has one unit at each i, $i \neq s$, and $(n-1)$ units are required at s. FIGURE 33-4 displays the feasible flow for the tour in our example (positive numbers are supplies and negative numbers are demands).

In general, we require a feasible flow x^P with respect to commodity P:

$$\sum_j x_{ij}^P - \sum_j x_{ji}^P = \begin{cases} n - 1 \text{ for } i = s \\ -1 \text{ elsewhere} \end{cases} \quad (7)$$

$$x_{ij}^P \geq 0 \qquad \text{for all } (i, j)$$

Similarly, we have for commodity Q:

$$\sum_j x_{ij}^Q - \sum_j x_{ji}^Q = \begin{cases} -(n - 1) \text{ for } i = s \\ +1 \text{ elsewhere} \end{cases} \quad (8)$$

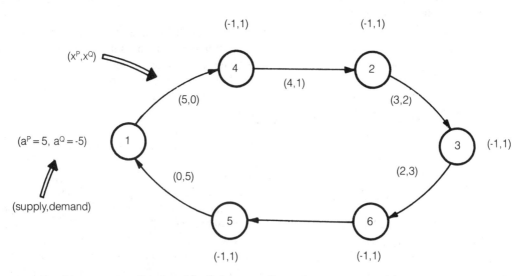

Fig. 33-4. Feasible two commodity flow (x^P, x^Q) in a traveling salesman tour (positive numbers are supplies and negative numbers are demands).

A look at FIG. 33-4 shows that the combined total x_{ij}^P + x_{ij}^Q, is equal to $(n-1)$ for each arc of the tour. This may be expressed as follows:

$$\sum_j (x_{ij}^P + x_{ij}^Q) = n-1 \qquad \text{for all } i \qquad (9)$$

$$x_{ij}^P + x_{ij}^Q = 0 \text{ or } (n-1) \text{ for all } i,j \qquad (10)$$

The constraints (7) to (10) characterize precisely all Hamiltonian tours. A Hamiltonian tour is a loop including all the vertices of a network. In fact, (9) and (10) imply that there is exactly one arc leaving each node i and carrying a combined total flow of $(n-1)$ units. On the other hand, there must be a flow-carrying path from s to every other node (following the commodity P) and a path from an arbitrary point i to s (following Q). It is easily seen that the only possible configuration is a tour.

Since

$$\left(x_{ij}^P + x_{ij}^Q\right)/\left(n-1\right) = 0 \text{ or } 1$$

we obtain a linear expression for the total cost which has to be minimized:

$$\min \frac{1}{n-1}\sum_{ij} c_{ij}\left(x_{ij}^P + x_{ij}^Q\right) \qquad (11)$$

Let us now turn to the precedence constraints. Choose the part p_s so that there are no preceding parts and consider only the commodity P. The total amount of commodity P leaving a point is decreasing along the tour (see FIG. 33-4). Therefore, it is required that:

$$\sum_j x_{uj}^P - \sum_j x_{vj}^P \geq 1 \qquad \text{for } p_u \to p_v \ (v \neq s) \qquad (12)$$

Replacing (10) by:

$$x_{ij}^P + x_{ij}^Q = (n-1)x_{ij} \text{ with } x_{ij} = 0 \text{ or } 1, \text{ for all } ij \ (13)$$

yields a mixed-integer programming formulation.

Example Four   For a given time horizon,

Table 33-2. Tools Required for Forging Five Parts

Tool Number	Part Number				
	1	2	3	4	5
1				1	
2	1		1	1	1
3		1			
4	1		1	1	1
5		1			
6	1		1		
7			1		
8	1		1		1
9		1			1
10				1	
11	1		1		1
12				1	
13	1				
14	1			1	
15		1			1
16			1	1	
17		1			
18			1		1
19	1	1			
20		1			
21		1			
22		1		1	

assume that five parts are to be forged on the flexible forging machine shown in FIG. 33-3. Each part requires a set of eight tools as indicated in TABLE 33-2. For $i = 1,2,\ldots,5$ and $k = 1,2,\ldots,22$, set

$$x_{ik} = \begin{cases} 1 \text{ if tool } k \text{ is used for part } i \\ 0 \text{ otherwise} \end{cases}$$

For any two parts i and j, define the Hamming distance

$$d_{ij} = \sum_{k=1}^{22}\delta(x_{ik},x_{jk}), \qquad (14)$$

where: $\delta(x_{ik},x_{jk}) = \begin{cases} 1 \text{ if } x_{ik} \neq x_{jk} \\ 0 \text{ otherwise} \end{cases}$

The following matrix D of Hamming distances is obtained for the data in TABLE 33-1.

$$D = [d_{ij}] = \begin{array}{c} \\ 1 \\ 2 \\ 3 \\ 4 \\ 5 \end{array} \begin{array}{ccccc} 1 & 2 & 3 & 4 & 5 \\ \left[\begin{array}{ccccc} \infty & 14 & 6 & 10 & 8 \\ 14 & \infty & 16 & 16 & 10 \\ 6 & 16 & \infty & 10 & 6 \\ 10 & 16 & 10 & \infty & 12 \\ 8 & 10 & 6 & 12 & \infty \end{array}\right] \end{array} \quad (15)$$

We set the costs c_{ij} in the objective function (11) equal to the distances d_{ij}.

For the convenience of modeling we introduce a dummy batch (number $s = 0$) and a row and column vector of zero changeover costs. The dummy batch indicates the initial and final state of the tool magazine.

$$D = [d_{ij}] = \begin{array}{c} \\ 0 \\ 1 \\ 2 \\ 3 \\ 4 \\ 5 \end{array} \begin{array}{cccccc} 0 & 1 & 2 & 3 & 4 & 5 \\ \left[\begin{array}{cccccc} \infty & 0 & 0 & 0 & 0 & 0 \\ 0 & \infty & 14 & 6 & 10 & 8 \\ 0 & 14 & \infty & 16 & 16 & 10 \\ 0 & 6 & 16 & \infty & 10 & 6 \\ 0 & 10 & 16 & 10 & \infty & 12 \\ 0 & 8 & 10 & 6 & 12 & \infty \end{array}\right] \end{array} \quad (16)$$

Let us impose the following precedence constraints, sketched in FIG. 33-5. The mixed integer programming problem with objective function (11) and constraints (7), (8), (8), (9), (12), and (13) can be solved by any commercial computer code. Solving the problem with LINDO (Schrage 1984) for the data in matrix (16) and the precedence constraints in FIG. 33-5 produces the following solution:

$$x_{02} = 1, \; x_{25} = 1, \; x_{51} = 1, \; x_{13} = 1, \; x_{34} = 1, \; x_{40} = 1$$

which can be expressed as the schedule: (0,2,5,1,3,4,0).

Algorithm One Alternatively the problem (7)-(12) can be solved by the following branch and bound algorithm (Kusiak and Finke, 1987).

Step 1. Relax constraint (10) and consider the relaxed problem P. See expressions (7), (8), (9), (11), and (12).

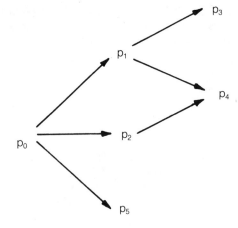

Fig. 33-5. Precedence constraints.

Step 2. Solve the linear problem P. The optimal value L is a lower bound for the optimal feasible tour (feasible with respect to the precedence constraints). Concentrate on the flow graph F, characterized by the pairs of parts or batches (p_i, p_j) for which the optimal values x_{ij}^P and x_{ij}^Q are strictly positive. If the size $|F|$ is n, then a tour and hence the solution is found. If $|F| > n$, try to detect a feasible tour in F by means of the heuristic proposed by Martello (1983). This yields an upper bound U ($U = \infty$ whenever no feasible tour exists).

Step 3. Establish a branch and bound tree and perform Steps 1 and 2 at every node. The branching strategy is as follows: Select a part p_i with the maximum number of leaving arcs in the corresponding flow graph F. Branch on the arc (i,j) with the smallest cost; the left branch uses (i, j) as the only arc leaving p_i and the right branch disallows this arc, denoted by (i,j). These conditions are easily implemented using appropriate penalty costs.

The complete branch and bound tree for the data in matrix (16) and precedence constraints in FIG. 33-5 consists only of three nodes and is shown

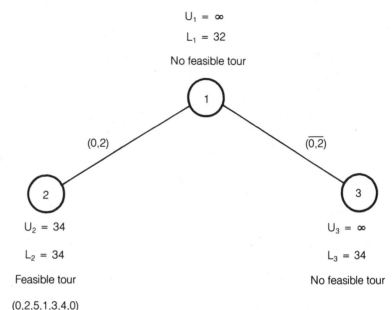

$U_1 = \infty$

$L_1 = 32$

No feasible tour

(0,2)   (0̅,2̅)

2   3

$U_2 = 34$ $U_3 = \infty$

$L_2 = 34$ $L_3 = 34$

Feasible tour   No feasible tour

(0,2,5,1,3,4,0)

Fig. 33-6. Branch and bound tree of example tour.

in FIG. 33-6. The optimal sequence is given by (0,2,5,1,3,4,0) with the corresponding cost 34.

TWO MACHINE FLOW SHOP PROBLEM

Consider scheduling n operations on two machines, each operation in the order of machine M1, machine M2, so that the maximum flow time F_{max} is minimized. To optimally solve this problem, Johnson's (1954) algorithm can be used.

Algorithm Two Kusiak (1986) developed the following efficient implementation of the Johnson's algorithm:

Step 1. Set $k=1$, $l=n$.
Step 2. For each operation, store the shortest processing time and corresponding machine number.
Step 3. Sort the resulting list including the triplets "operation number/time/machine number" in increasing value of processing time.
Step 4. For each entry in the sorted list:
IF machine number is 1, then
(i) set the corresponding operation number in position k,
(ii) set $k = k+1$.

ELSE
(i) set the corresponding operation number in position l,
(ii) set $l = l-1$.

END-IF.
Step 5. Stop, if the entire list of operations has been exhausted.

Example Five The algorithm is illustrated with the following numerical example. Solve the two machine flow shop scheduling problem for the following set of data. The columns i, $j=1$, and $j=2$ represent operation number and processing time t_{ij} of operation i on machine j.

i	$j = 1$	$j = 2$
1	6	3
2	2	9
3	4	3
4	1	8
5	7	1
6	4	5
7	7	6

The result of Step 2 is the following set of triplets.

Operation Number	min $\{t_{i1}, t_{i2}\}$	Machine Number
1	3	2
2	2	1
3	3	2
4	1	1
5	1	2
6	4	1
7	6	2

Step 3 results in the sorted set of triples:

$$
\begin{array}{ccc}
4, & 1, & 1 \\
5, & 1, & 2 \\
2, & 2, & 1 \\
3, & 3, & 2 \\
1, & 3, & 2 \\
6, & 4, & 1 \\
7, & 6, & 2
\end{array}
$$

Step 4 produces the following optimal schedule: (4,2,6,7,1,3,5).

Algorithm Two can also be applied for solving the special case of the two machine shop problem and three machine flow shop problem discussed below.

Two Machine Job Shop Problem

Partition a set of n operations into the following types:

- Type A: those to be processed on machine M1 only
- Type B: those to be processed on machine M2 only
- Type C: those to be processed on both machines in the order M1 then M2
- Type D: those to be processed on both machines in the order M2 then M1

Algorithm Three   Based on the above, an optimal schedule can be constructed.

Step 1.   Schedule the operations of Type A in any order to obtain the sequence S_A.

Step 2.   Schedule the operations of Type B in any order to obtain the sequence S_B.

Step 3.   Scheduling the operations of Type C according to Algorithm Two produces the sequence S_C.

Step 4.   Scheduling the operations of Type D according to Algorithm Two produces the sequence S_D (Note that M2 is the first machine while M1 is the second one).

An optimal schedule, then, for machine M1 is (S_C, S_A, S_D) and for machine M2 is (S_D, S_B, S_C).

To see that this schedule is optimal remember that no time is wasted and hence F_{max} increases, if either M2 is kept idle waiting for operation of Type C to be completed on M1 or M1 is kept idle waiting for jobs of Type D to be completed on M2. This schedule clearly minimizes such idle time.

Example Six   Consider the problem of scheduling nine operations on two machines for the data shown in TABLE 33-3. To find an optimal schedule separate the operations listed in TABLE 33-3 into four types:

- Type A operations—operations 7 and 8 are to be processed on M1 alone. An arbitrary order $S_A = (7,8)$ is selected.
- Type B operations—operations 9 and 10 require M2 alone. Select an arbitrary order $S_B = (9,10)$.
- Type C operations—operations 1, 2, 3, and 4 require M1 first and then M2. Algorithm Three for the four operations problem gives the sequence $S_C = (4,3,2,1)$.
- Type D operations—operations 5 and 6 require M2 first and then M1. Algorithm Two for the two operation problem produces the sequence $S_D = (5,6)$. Note that M1 is now the second machine.

The optimal solution to the problem in Example Six is as follows. The processing sequence for machine M1 is (4,3,2,1,7,8,5,6). For machine M2, the sequence is (5,6,9,10,4,3,2,1). The resulting Gantt diagram is given in FIG. 33-7. From this we see that $F_{max} = 46$ for an optimal schedule.

Table 33-3. Processing Order and Time Data for Example Six

Operation	First Machine		Second Machine	
1	M1	7	M2	1
2	M1	6	M2	5
3	M1	9	M2	7
4	M1	4	M2	6
5	M2	6	M1	4
6	M2	5	M1	5
7	M1	4	-	
8	M1	5	-	
9	M2	1	-	
10	M2	5	-	

Special Case of the Three Machine Flow Shop Problem

Algorithm Two for the two machine flow shop problem can be extended to a special case of three machine flow-shop problem. A condition is needed, that:

$$\text{either } \min_{i=1}^{n} \{t_{i1}\} \geq \max_{i=1}^{n} \{t_{i2}\} \qquad (17)$$

$$\text{or } \min_{i=1}^{n} \{t_{i3}\} \geq \max_{i=1}^{n} \{t_{i2}\}$$

The conditions state that the maximum processing time on the second machine is no greater than the minimum time on either the first or the third one (French 1982). If (17) holds, an optimal schedule for the problem may be found by letting:

$$a_i = t_{i1} + t_{i2}$$
$$b_i = t_{i2} + t_{i3}$$

and scheduling the operations as if they were to be processed on two machines only, but with the processing time of each operation being a_i and b_i on the first and second machines respectively.

Example Seven Solve the three machine flow shop scheduling problem with data listed in TABLE 33-4. First we check whether (17) holds for this problem. Here we have

$$\min_{i=1}^{6} \{t_{i1}\} = 3; \max_{i=1}^{6} \{t_{i2}\} = 3; \text{ and } \min_{i=1}^{6} \{t_{i3}\} =$$

It is easy to note that

$$\min_{i=1}^{6} \{t_{i1}\} = 3 \geq 3 = \max_{i=1}^{6} \{t_{i2}\}$$

and therefore (17) holds. Only one of the inequalities needs to hold. The constructed a_i and b_i times are given in TABLE 33-4. Applying Algorithm Three produces the sequence (2,4,5,1,3,6), the Gantt chart in FIG. 33-8.

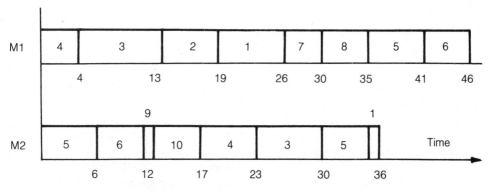

Fig. 33-7. Gantt chart of the optimal solution for the problem in example six.

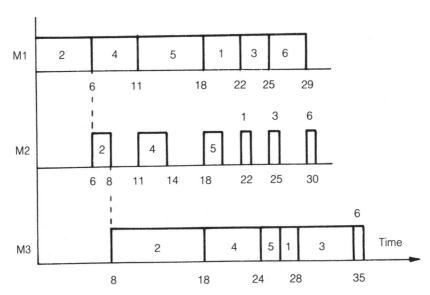

**Table 33-4. Actual and Constructed
Processing Time Data for Example Seven**

| Operation | Actual Processing Times | | | Constructed Processing Times | |
| | t_{i1} | t_{i2} | t_{i3} | a_i | b_i |
	M1	M2	M3	First Machine	Second Machine
1	4	1	2	5	3
2	6	2	10	8	12
3	3	1	6	4	3
4	5	3	6	8	9
5	7	2	2	9	8
6	4	1	1	5	2

Fig. 33-8. Gantt chart for the optimal solution to the problem in example seven.

MODELING THE PROBLEM OF SCHEDULING *n* OPERATIONS ON *m* MACHINES

One of the approaches to scheduling is to model the scheduling problem and then solve it using a commercial computer code or specialized algorithm. This section discusses a new mixed integer programming model for the problem of scheduling *n* operations with precedence constraints on *m* machines.

To present the scheduling model, let me introduce the following notation.

- n: number of parts
- m: number of machines
- (i): the root operation of part i, $i = 1,...,n$
- P_i: set of pairs of operations (k,l) for part i, where k precedes l, $i = 1,...,n$
- Q_i: set of pairs of operations (k,l) for part i, where k and l can be performed in any order, $i = 1,...,n$
- I_i: set of operations without precedence constraints, $i=1,...,n$
- N_p: set of operations to be performed on machine p, $p = 1,...,m$
- n_i: number of operations in part i, $i = 1,...,n$

- t_{ik}: processing time of operation k of part i, k = 1,...,n_i, i = 1,...,n
- x_{ik}: completion time of operation k of part i, k = 1,...,n_i, i = 1,...,n
- M: an arbitrary large positive number

$$y_{kl} = \begin{cases} 1, \text{ if operation } k \text{ precedes operation } l, \\ 0, \text{ otherwise}, \\ k = 1,...,n_i,\ l = 1,...,n_i,\ i = 1,...,n \end{cases}$$

The objective of the scheduling model is to minimize the total completion time of all parts.

$$\min \sum_{i=1}^{n} x_{(i)} \qquad (18)$$

$$\text{s.t. } x_{il} - x_{ik} \geq t_{il} \qquad \begin{matrix} \text{for all } [k,l] \in P_i, \\ \text{for all } i \end{matrix} \qquad (19)$$

$$x_{il} - {}_{ik} + M(1-y_{kl}) \geq t_{il} \qquad \begin{matrix} \text{for all } [k,l] \in Q_i, \\ \text{for all } i \end{matrix} \qquad (20)$$

$$x_{ik} - x_{il} + My_{kl} \geq t_{ik} \qquad (21)$$

$$x_{jl} - x_{ik} + M(1-y_{kl}) \geq t_{jl} \qquad \begin{matrix} \text{for all } k,l \in N_p, \\ \text{for all } p \end{matrix} \qquad (22)$$

$$x_{ik} - x_{jl} + My_{kl} \geq t_{ik} \qquad i \neq j \qquad (23)$$

$$\text{for } [i,k] \in I_i,\ i=1,...,n$$

$$x_{ik} \geq \begin{matrix} t_{ik} \\ 0 \end{matrix} \qquad \text{for all other } i,k \qquad (24)$$

$$y_{kl} = 0,1 \qquad \text{for all } k,l \qquad (25)$$

Constraint (19) imposes that the operations of each part are processed according to the precedences required. Constraints (20) and (21) ensure that any two operations belonging to the same part cannot be processed at the same time. Constraints (22) and (23) ensure that a machine cannot process more than one part at the same time. Constraints (24) and (25) impose nonnegativity and integrality, respectively.

Part 1

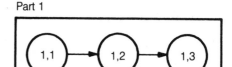

Part 2

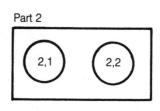

Part 3

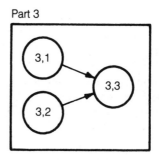

Fig. 33-9. Structure of three parts discussed in example eight.

Example Eight The following example illustrates the application of the scheduling model above. Schedule eight operations belonging to three parts, the structure of which are shown in FIG. 33-9 on two machines. The data required are given in TABLE 33-5. Using scheduling model (18)-(25) to

Table 33-5. Scheduling Data for Example Eight

Part Number	1			2		3		
Operation Number	1	2	3	1	2	1	2	3
Machine Number	1	1	2	1	2	2	1	2
Processing Time	3	5	6	8	4	9	2	7

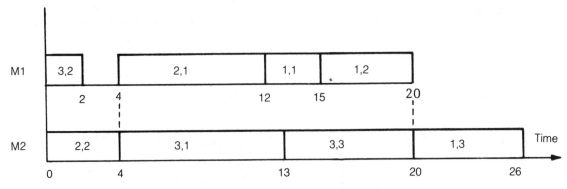

Fig. 33-10. The optimal schedule for example eight.

solve this problem, the optimal schedule $x_{13}=26$, $x_{21}=12$, and $x_{33}=20$, is generated. The schedule appears in FIG. 33-10. The makespan $F_{\max}$ of the schedule in FIG. 33-10 is 26.

The formulation (18)-(25) involves machines and operations only. In order to incorporate other resources such as tools and fixtures as well as due dates the formulation (18)-(25) needs to be extended.

Define:
- m : number of types of resources
- r_s : number of resources of type s, $s = 1, \ldots, m$
- d_i : due date of part i
- N_p: set of operations using resource p, $p = 1, \ldots, r_s$, $s = 1, \ldots, m$.

The extended formulation of the n operation m machine scheduling problem with precedence constraints, limited resources and due dates is presented below:

$$\min \sum_{i=1}^{n} x_{(i)} \qquad (26)$$

s.t. $x_{il} - x_{ik} \geq t_{il}$ $\qquad$ for all $[k,l] \in P_i$, for all i $\qquad (27)$

$x_{il} - x_{ik} + M(1-y_{kl}) \geq t_{il}$ $\qquad$ for all $[k,l] \in Q_i$, for all i $\qquad (28)$

$x_{ik} - x_{il} + My_{kl} \geq t_{ik} \qquad (29)$

$x_{jl} - x_{ik} + M(1-y_{kl}) \geq t_{jl}$ $\qquad$ for all $k,l \in N_p$, for all p, $\qquad (30)$

$x_{ik} - x_{jl} + My_{kl} \geq t_{ik}$ $\qquad$ $i \neq j$ $\qquad (31)$

$x_{(i)} \leq d_i \qquad (32)$

$x_{ik} \geq \genfrac{}{}{0pt}{}{t_{ik}}{0}$ $\qquad$ for $[i,k] \in I_i,\ i=1,\ldots,n$ for all other i,k $\qquad (33)$

$y_{kl} = 0,1$ $\qquad$ for all k,l $\qquad (34)$

Constraint (27) imposes that the operations of each part are processed according to the precedences required. Constraints (28) and (29) ensure that any two operations belonging to the same part cannot be processed at the same time. Constraints (30) and (31) ensure that any resource cannot process more than one part at the same time. Constraint (32) imposes due dates. Constraints (33) and (34) impose nonnegativity and integrality, respectively.

Example Nine The integrality of the scheduling model (26) through (34) is illustrated in the following example. Schedule seven operations belonging to three parts shown in FIG. 33-11 on two machines. The data required are given in TABLE 33-6.

Solving the scheduling model for the above data generates the optimal schedule $x_{12}=5$, $x_{22}=4$, and

Table 33-6. Scheduling Data for Example Nine

Part Number	1		2		3		
Operation Number	1	2	1	2	1	2	3
Machine Number	1	2	2	1	1	2	1
Processing Time	2	3	1	2	3	2	1
Tool Number	1	1	2	2	2	1	2

Part 1

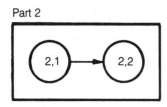

Part 2

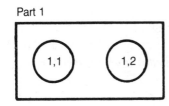

Part 3

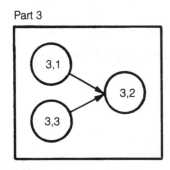

Fig. 33-11. Structure of three parts discussed in example nine.

$x_{33} = 10$ (see FIG. 33-12). This schedule was generated under the assumption that only one copy of each tool was available. Relaxing this assumption results in the schedule $x_{12} = 6$, $x_{22} = 4$, and $x_{33} = 8$ presented in FIG. 33-13. The completion time of part 3 is $C_2 = 8$ rather than $C_1 = 10$ for the solution in FIG. 33-12. As FIG. 33-13 shows, identical tools (1) were used for performing operations (1,1) and (3,2).

A KNOWLEDGE-BASED SYSTEM FOR SCHEDULING IN AUTOMATED MANUFACTURING

Numerical algorithms have traditionally been used for solving scheduling problems. The approach presented in this chapter involves not only algorithms but also declarative and procedural knowledge and an inference engine, all implemented as a knowledge-based system. Readers interested in alternative approaches to scheduling in manufacturing systems may refer to Kusiak (1988, 1989, and 1990).

System Structure

This section discusses the knowledge-based scheduling system (KBSS). KBSS is built using the tandem architecture proposed in Kusiak (1987). FIGURE 33-14 shows the structure of the KBSS.

Knowledge Base   The knowledge in KBSS has been acquired from two experts as well as the literature. Frames represent the declarative knowledge related to scheduling problems, parts and operations, and the schedules generated. Four sample frames for a scheduling problem, part, operation, and the schedule generated are presented below.

Frame 1

```
(Problem_number (Problem_type (e.g. flow-shop))
(Problem_features
        (Number_of_parts,
         Number_of_operations,
         Number_of_precedence_constraints)))
```

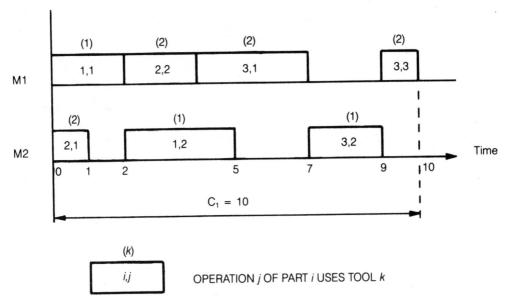

 OPERATION *j* OF PART *i* USES TOOL *k*

Fig. 33-12. The optimal schedule for example nine with limited number of identical tools.

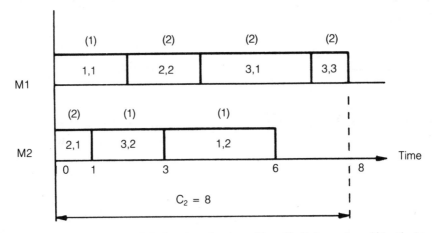

Fig. 33-13. The optimal schedule for example nine with unlimited number of identical tools.

Frame 2

```
(Part_number (Due_date (value))
            (Number_of_operations (value))
            (Number_of_process_plans (value))
            (Process_plan_0 (operation_number,
                            processing_time.,
                            machine_number,
                            tool_number,
```

```
                    pallet_fixture_number,
                    material_handling_carrier_number))

              .
              .
              .

(Process_plan_p (operation_number,
                    processing_time,
                    machine_number,
                    tool_number,
                    pallet_fixture_number,
                    material_handling_carrier_number)))
```

Frame 3

```
(Operation_number (Belongs_to (part_number))
      ((Preceding_op (op_1, op_2, ..., op_a))
       (Successive_op (op_a + 1, op_a + 2, ..., op_b))))
```

Frame 4

```
(Schedule_of_problem (problem_number)
                (Generated_by (algorithm_number))
                (Idle_time (machine_1, machine_2, ..., machine_m))
                (Completion_time (part_1, part_2, ..., part_n))
                (Average_utilization_rate (machine,
                                  tool,
                                  pallet_fixture,
                                  material_handling_carrier))
```

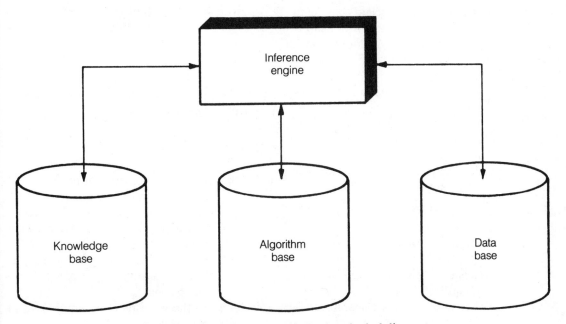

Fig. 33-14. Structure of the knowledge-based scheduling system.

Frame 1 characterizes a scheduling problem and allows the user to select an appropriate scheduling algorithm. Knowledge represented by frames 2 and 3 is used to generate schedules and select alternative process plans. Frame 4 representing the schedules generated is used for rescheduling.

The procedural knowledge of the knowledge-based system is in the form of production rules and is stored in the knowledge base. To handle different problems the production rules are divided into the following three classes:

- Class 1 selects an appropriate algorithm to solve the problem considered
- Class 2 controls the procedure of selecting alternative process plans and modifying the sequence of the priority rules in the heuristic algorithm
- Class 3 evaluates the schedules obtained and performs rescheduling.

Several sample production rules in each class are presented below.

- Class 1

Rule R11. IF the scheduling problem considered is a two machine flow shop problem
THEN solve it using Algorithm Two

Rule R12. IF the scheduling problem has the following features:
○ number of resources involved is less than five
○ number of operations is less than 60
○ alternative process plans are not available
THEN use the mixed integer linear programming formulation (26)-(34)

Rule R13. IF the scheduling problem has the following features:
○ number of resources involved is greater than or equal to five
○ number of operations is greater than or equal to 60
○ alternative process plans are available

THEN use the heuristic algorithm (presented later in this section)

- Class 2

Rule R24. IF the heuristic algorithm is used
AND an alternative process plan is available for some nonschedulable operations due to unavailability of resources
AND the required alternative resources for the operations are available
AND the sum of the waiting and processing time for the operation in the basic process plan is longer than one in the alternative process plan
THEN replace the basic process plan with the corresponding alternative process plan
AND add the corresponding operations to the set of schedulable operations

Rule R25. IF more than one operation has been added to the set of schedulable operations using production rule R24
THEN select an operation with the alternative processing time closest to the value of the corresponding basic processing time

Kusiak and Finke have explored the concept of alternative process plans mentioned in the above production rules (1988).

- Class 3

Rule R36. IF a part in a partial (or final) schedule generated by the heuristic algorithm does not meet the required due date
THEN schedule the part ensuring that the due date is satisfied
AND reschedule other parts using the heuristic algorithm (presented later in this section)

Rule R37. IF the heuristic algorithm is used for rescheduling

AND the starting time of an operation has been fixed for a machine

AND there is idle time between the first operation and the rescheduled operation

THEN attempt to reduce the idle time by using production rule R39

Rule R38. IF all due dates have been met in the final schedule

THEN accept the schedule

Inference Engine The inference engine in the KBSS controls the procedure of triggering rules in the knowledge base and the procedure of schedule generation of the algorithm. One of the greatest advantages of the tandem system architecture is the simplicity of the inference engine. The inference engine in KBSS employs a forward chaining control strategy. In a given class of rules it attempts to fire all the rules related to the context considered. If a rule is triggered, i.e., the conditions are true, then the actions of the rule triggered are carried out. Some rules stop the search of the inference engine for an applicable rule and switch the control process to the algorithm.

The inference engine maintains a list of the rules that have been fired. This list is called *explain*. The rules in *explain* are placed in the order that they were fired. The list forms a basis for building an explanation facility.

A number of algorithms have been incorporated into the KBSS. A *heuristic algorithm* is most likely to be used while solving large scale industrial problems. The next section discusses this heuristic algorithm.

The Scheduling Algorithm

This section presents a heuristic algorithm for manufacturing scheduling. Consider a part to be machined consisting of a number of operations. Each operation is processed on one machine and may require other resources such as tools, pallets, and fixtures. Precedence constraints between operations may also exist. A definition of schedulable operations is introduced.

An operation is *schedulable* at a time t if all of the following conditions are satisfied:

- No other operation that belongs to the same part is being processed at the time t
- All operations preceding the operation considered have been completed before the time t
- All resources required are available at the time t

Algorithm Four (Kusiak and Chen 1988)

Step 1. Initialize current time, set of schedulable operations, and set of completed operations

Step 2. From the set of schedulable operations select an operation using the following priority rules (the sequence of these rules depends on the characteristics of the problem considered):
- P1: with the largest number of successive operations
- P2: belonging to a part with the minimum number of schedulable operations
- P3: with the largest number of immediate successive operations
- P4: belonging to a part with the largest number of unprocessed operations
- P5: with the shortest processing time
- P6: belonging to a part with the shortest slack time

Step 3. Schedule the operation selected in Step 2. Update the resource status and the set of schedulable operations. If the set of schedulable operations is not empty, go to Step 2; otherwise, refer to the inference engine in order to consider an alternative process plan. If an operation becomes schedulable due to availability of the alternative process plan, add the operation to the set of schedulable operations and go to Step 2; otherwise, go to Step 4.

Step 4. Calculate the completion time of each operation scheduled but not completed at the current time. Set the current time equal to the completion time of the operation with the least remaining processing time. Add the operation (or operations in case of a tie) to the set of completed operations. Update the resource status and the set of schedulable operations. If there are no unprocessed operations, stop; otherwise, go to Step 5.

Step 5.   If the set of schedulable operations is not empty, go to Step 2; otherwise, refer to the inference engine in order to consider an alternative process plan. If an operation becomes schedulable due to availability of the alternative process plan, add the operation to the set of schedulable operations and go to Step 2; otherwise, go to Step 4.

It might be useful to discuss priority rules P3 and P6 in Step 2 of the above algorithm. An immediate successive operation used in the priority rule P3 is defined as an operation directly linked by a precedence constraint with the operation considered. A slack time used in the priority rule P6 is defined as a remaining processing time associated with the part considered.

Example Ten   The following example illus-

Part 1

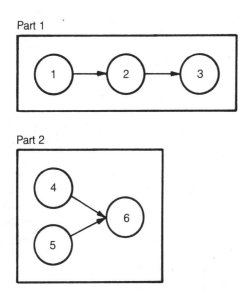

Part 2

Part 3

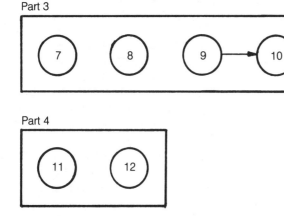

Part 4

Fig. 33-15. Parts with operations and precedence constraints discussed in example ten.

trates the heuristic algorithm. Schedule twelve operations shown in FIG. 33-15 on three machines assume that:

- Three different tools are available to process the operations
- All other resources (pallets/fixtures, material handling carriers, and processing time) are unlimited
- Due dates are not imposed

A process plan PP_k for a part p_k can be defined as follows:

$$PP_k: [(1,t_1,m_1,l_1),...,(i,t_i,m_i,l_i),...,(a,t_a,m_a,l_a)]$$

where: i, t_i, m_i, l_i are operation number, processing time, machine number, and tool number, respectively.

Using the above notation, the basic process plans of the four parts are shown below:

PP_1: [(1,4,2,2),(2,5,1,3),(3,2,3,2)]
PP_2: [(4,6,1,3),(5,3,2,2),(6,3,3,1)]
PP_3: [(7,3,3,1),(8,3,1,2),(9,6,3,1),(10,2,1,3)]
PP_4: [(11,4,3,2),(12,3,2,3)]

The alternative process plans for the four parts are:

PP_1: [(1,6,3,1),(2,6,2,2),(3,4,1,1)];
     [(1,7,1,3),(2,7,1,2),(3,5,1,3)]
PP_2: [(4,6,2,2),(5,4,3,1),(6,5,1,2)];
     [(4,8,3,1),(5,8,1,3),(6,5,2,3)]
PP_3: [(7,4,3,2),(8,5,3,3),(9,7,2,1),(10,2,3,2)];
     [(7,4,2,2),(8,5,2,1),(9,9,1,3),(10,4,1,2)]
PP_4: [(11,4,1,3),(12,5,1,2)];
     [(11,4,3,1),(12,6,3,3)].

The solution procedure is as follows:

Step 1. Initialize
   ○ Current time $t = 0$
   ○ Set of schedulable operations $S = \{1,4,5,7,8,9,11,12\}$
   ○ Set of completed operations $f = \Phi$.

Step 2. Using priority rule P1, operation 1 is selected.

Step 3. Operation 1 that requires tool 2 is scheduled on machine 2. The set of schedulable operations is updated to $S = \{4,7,9\}$. Go to Step 2.

Step 2. Using priority rules P1 and P2, operation 4 is selected.

Step 3. Operation 4 that requires tool 3 is scheduled on machine 1. The set of schedulable operations is updated to $S = \{7,9\}$. Go to Step 2.

Step 2. Using priority rule P1, operation 9 is selected.

Step 3. Operation 9 that requires tool 1 is scheduled on machine 3. The set of schedulable operations is updated to $S = \Phi$. Refer to the inference engine in order to consider an alternative process plan. Since no operation becomes schedulable, go to Step 4.

Step 4. Completion time of operations 1, 4, and 9 are 4, 6, and 6 respectively, and current time is set to 4. Operation 1 is added to the set of completed operations F, $F = \{1\}$. Machine 2 and tool 2 become available after the resource status is updated. The set of schedulable operations is updated to $S = \Phi$. Since not all of the operations have been processed, go to Step 5.

Step 5. Since the set of schedulable operations is empty, refer to the inference engine in order to consider an alternative process plan.

The inference engine activates production rule R24 in Class 2 to select an operation and replaces the basic process plan with alternative one.

Rule R24. SINCE the alternative process plans are available for operations 2, 11, and 12
     AND the alternative resources for operation 2 (machine 2 and tool 2)

have been specified in the alternative process plan

AND the sum of the waiting and processing time for operation 2 in the basic process plan (2 + 5 = 7) is longer than one in alternative process plan (6) THEN operation 2 is added to the set of schedulable operations

AND the basic process plan of operation 2 is replaced with the corresponding alternative process plan (2,6,2,2)

After the basic process plan has been replaced with the alternative process plan, the inference engine transfers the information to the heuristic algorithm and operation 2 is scheduled by the algorithm. The Gantt chart of the final schedule obtained after seven iterations is shown in FIG. 33-16.

Computational Results

This section presents computational results with KBSS. The heuristic algorithm presented is the most likely algorithm to be used while solving industrial scheduling problems in automated manufacturing systems. The results generated by the knowledge-based scheduling system can be improved by using other production rules. The degree of improvement depends upon the quality of knowledge collected.

In order to evaluate the quality of solutions generated by the KBSS, sample problems have been solved. Three measures of performance were used:

- Maximum flow time (F_{max})

$$F_{max} = \max_{j} \{ F_j \} , j = 1,...,N$$

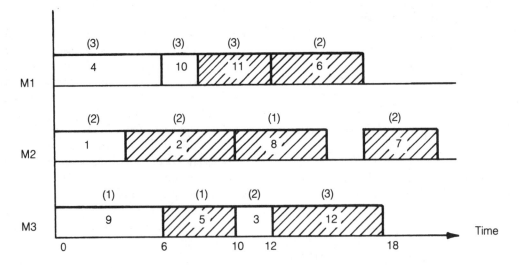

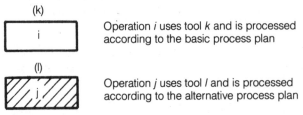

Fig. 33-16. The final schedule for the problem in example ten.

Table 33-7. Computational Results for Scheduling Problems without Machine Breakdowns

Problem 1   14 Machines 20 Parts 160 Operations   Minimum Maximum Flow Time: 24.0

Sequence of Priority Rules	F_{max}	$\bar{F}$	U_m	CPU Time	F_{max}	$\bar{F}$	U_m	CPU Time	F_{max}	$\bar{F}$	U_m	CPU Time
p1-p2-p3-p4-p5-p6	26.5	24.0	0.99	9.32	26.5	24.1	0.99	8.70	26.5	24.8	0.96	7.22
p2-p1-p3-p4-p5-p6	26.5	24.0	0.99	9.23	26.5	24.1	0.99	8.46	29.0	25.3	0.95	7.81
p3-p2-p1-p4-p5-p6	26.5	24.0	0.99	9.25	26.5	24.2	0.99	8.69	29.0	25.3	0.95	8.19
p4-p2-p3-p1-p5-p6	26.5	24.2	0.99	9.81	26.5	24.2	0.99	8.45	26.5	24.4	0.99	8.43
p3-p1-p4-p2-p5-p6	26.5	24.2	0.99	10.1	27.5	24.0	0.99	8.82	26.0	24.5	0.98	8.17
Number of Precedence Constraints	0				48				140			

Problem 2   12 Machines 18 Parts 132 Operations   Minimum Maximum Flow Time: 27.0

Sequence of Priority Rules	F_{max}	$\bar{F}$	U_m	CPU Time	F_{max}	$\bar{F}$	U_m	CPU Time	F_{max}	$\bar{F}$	U_m	CPU Time
p1-p2-p3-p4-p5-p6	30.0	27.2	0.99	6.71	30.0	27.1	0.99	6.06	31.0	27.8	0.98	5.50
p2-p1-p3-p4-p5-p6	30.0	27.2	0.99	6.62	30.0	27.3	0.99	6.16	32.5	28.2	0.99	5.21
p3-p2-p1-p4-p5-p6	30.0	27.1	0.99	6.63	30.0	27.0	0.99	6.03	32.5	28.2	0.96	5.46
p4-p2-p3-p1-p5-p6	30.0	27.2	0.99	6.66	29.5	27.0	0.99	6.07	30.0	27.5	0.98	5.83
p3-p1-p4-p2-p5-p6	30.0	27.0	0.99	7.06	30.0	27.3	0.99	6.58	30.5	27.8	0.97	5.53
Number of Precedence Constraints	0				36				114			

Problem 3   10 Machines 16 Parts 116 Operations   Minimum Maximum Flow Time: 24.0

Sequence of Priority Rules	F_{max}	$\bar{F}$	U_m	CPU Time	F_{max}	$\bar{F}$	U_m	CPU Time	F_{max}	$\bar{F}$	U_m	CPU Time
p1-p2-p3-p4-p5-p6	26.5	24.1	0.99	5.49	24.5	24.1	0.99	4.92	27.5	24.5	0.98	4.27
p2-p1-p3-p4-p5-p6	26.5	24.1	0.99	5.33	26.5	24.1	0.99	4.96	26.5	24.2	0.99	4.60
p3-p2-p1-p4-p5-p6	26.5	24.1	0.99	5.36	24.5	24.1	0.99	4.93	26.5	24.2	0.99	4.75
p4-p2-p3-p1-p5-p6	26.5	24.1	0.99	5.29	26.5	24.0	1.00	4.87	25.5	24.3	0.99	4.56
p3-p1-p4-p2-p5-p6	26.5	24.1	0.99	5.44	26.5	24.0	1.00	4.97	26.5	24.5	0.98	4.51
Number of Precedence Constraints	0				28				100			

Table 33-8. Computational Results for Problems with Machine Breakdowns

	Number of Machines	Number of Parts	Number of Operations	Number of Machine Breakdowns	Number of Preced. Constr.	Duration of Machine Breakdown	Number of Alternative Process Plans for Each Part	KBSS Solution			
								F_{max}	F	U_m	CPU Time
Problem 1	14	20	160	7	0	1.70 5.81 1.31 5.13 2.28 4.69 5.07	0	30.0	26.4	0.92	11.7
							1	27.0	26.1	0.92	12.0
					48	2.31 2.40 1.00 4.56 2.75 1.16 0.09	0	29.0	25.5	0.95	10.1
							1	27.3	25.1	0.96	11.2
					140	3.86 1.09 3.67 4.42 2.02 1.56 1.32	0	31.1	27.3	0.88	9.07
							1	28.6	25.8	0.93	10.8

Minimum Maximum Flow Time:

$F_{max} = 24.0^*$

Problem 2

		0	1
	0.64	32.3	31.0
	3.61	28.9	28.4
12	2.22	0.94	0.95
	3.29	8.01	8.44
	5.27		
	0.13		
		0	1
	1.58	33.3	31.5
	3.49	29.5	29.2
18	6.30	0.92	0.93
	2.60	7.07	7.36
	3.50		
	4.98		
		0	1
	2.41	34.0	32.0
	4.29	30.9	29.2
132	1.14	0.88	0.93
	0.55	6.08	7.45
	0.04		
	5.68		

Minimum Maximum Flow Time: 6

36   114

$F_{max} = 27.0^*$

Problem 3

		0	1
	1.69	30.4	28.0
	5.88	26.5	26.2
10	6.36	0.91	0.92
	1.13	6.58	6.86
	5.98		
		0	1
	3.39	29.9	27.0
	3.92	26.0	25.7
16	1.01	0.93	0.93
	5.89	5.79	5.89
	2.74		
		0	1
	4.27	30.8	27.8
	0.76	27.9	26.5
116	1.47	0.86	0.90
	3.02	5.20	5.61
	6.7		

Minimum Maximum Flow Time: 5

28   100

$F_{max} = 24.0^*$

---

* Values of F_{max} in this column do not include machine breakdowns

• Average flow time (F)

$$F = \sum_{j=1}^{N} F_j/N$$

where: F_j is flow time for machine j and N is the number of machines

• Machine utilization (U_m)

$$U_m = \sum_{j=1}^{N} U_j/N$$

where:

$$U_j = \sum_{i \in M(j)} t_i^{(v)}/F_j$$

$t_i^{(v)}$ = the processing time of operation i using process plan v, and $M(j)$ is the set of operations processed on machine j.

In order to evaluate the effect of different sequences of the priority rules on the solution quality, a number of scheduling problems have been solved for five different sequences of priority rules. Computational results for three sample problems are presented in TABLE 33-7. Problems in TABLE 33-7 include basic and alternative process plans; the processing time of basic and alternative process plans were assumed identical for a given operation.

To compare the impact of alternative process plans on solution quality in a case when machine breakdowns occur, the three problems in TABLE 33-7 were resolved under the assumption that half of the total machines considered breakdown for a random time interval. The duration of the machine breakdowns is uniformly distributed in the interval (0.0,7.0). For comparison the range of the processing times is (0.5,5.0). The results are presented in TABLE 33-8. Since the computational results in TABLE 33-7 suggest that there is no sequence of priority rules which would be dominant to other sequences, the sequence of priority rules is the same as presented in Algorithm Four. All computations reported in TABLES 33-7 and 33-8 were performed on an AMDAHL-5870 computer. In all the sample problems presented in TABLES 33-7 and 33-8 the number of resources, except machines, was assumed unlimited.

The computational results presented in the tables allow us to draw the following conclusions.

1. Schedules generated by the knowledge-based system are of good quality.
2. The results in TABLE 33-7 show that with the increase in the number of precedence constraints, maximum flow time and average flow time increase, and machine utilization decreases.
3. The results in TABLE 33-7 indicate that there is no sequence of priority rules which would be dominant in terms of solution quality.
4. The results in TABLE 33-8 show that incorporation of alternative process plans in a case when machine breakdowns occur provided solutions of better quality, in terms of all the three performance measures, than for the case with basic process plans only.
5. The results in the two tables indicate that CPU time increases with the increase of problem size and decreases with the increase of the number of precedence constraints. CPU time is also slightly affected by the sequence of priority rules.

REFERENCES

Baker, K. R. (1974). *Introduction to Sequencing and Scheduling*. New York: Wiley.

Finke, G., A. Claus, and E. Gunn. (1984) ''A Two-Commodity Network Flow Approach to the Traveling Salesman Problem.'' *Congressus Numerantium* 41: 167-178.

French, S. (1982) *Sequencing and Scheduling: An Introduction to the Mathematics of the Job Shop*. New York: Wiley.

Johnson, S. M. (1954) ''Optimal Two- and Three-stage Production Schedules with Setup Times Included.'' *Naval Research Logistics Quarterly* 1: 61-68.

Kusiak, A. (1986). "Efficient Implementation of Johnson's Scheduling Algorithm." *IIE Transactions* 18: 2: 215-216.

_____. (1990). *Intelligent Manufacturing Systems* Englewood Cliffs, New Jersey: Prentice-Hall.

_____. (1987). "Artificial Intelligence and Operations Research in Flexible Manufacturing Systems." *Information Systems and Operational Research (INFOR)*, 25: 1: 2-12.

Kusiak, A., ed. (1986a). *Flexible Manufacturing Systems: Methods and Studies*. Amsterdam: North-Holland.

_____. (1986b). *Modelling and Design of Flexible Manufacturing System*. New York, NY: Elsevier.

_____. (1988). *Artificial Intelligence: Implications for Computer Integrated Manufacturing*. New York, NY: Springer-Verlag.

_____. (1989a). *Knowledge Based Systems in Manufacturing*. London, U. K.: Taylor and Francis.

Kusiak, A. and M. Chen (1988). "Knowledge-Based System for Scheduling Manufacturing Systems (KBSS)." In *Proceedings of the Symposium on Manufacturing Applications Languages*. National Research Council of Canada, June 20-21: 161-174.

Kusiak, A. and G. Finke (1988). "Selection of Process Plans in Automated Manufacturing Systems." *IEEE Transactions on Robotics and Automation* 4: 4: 397-402.

Kusiak, A. and G. Finke (1987). "Modeling and Solving the Flexible Forging Module Scheduling Problem." *Engineering Optimization* 12: 1: 1-12.

Lawler, E. L., J. K. Lenstra, A. H. G. Rinnooy Kan, and D. B. Shmoys, eds. (1985). *The Traveling Salesman Problem: A Guided Tour of Combinatorial Optimization*. New York: Wiley.

Martello, S. (1983). "An Enumerative Algorithm for Finding Hamiltonian Circuits in a Directed Graph." *ACM Transactions on Math Software* 14: 256-268.

Schrage, L. (1984). *Linear, Integer, and Quadratic Programming with LINDO*. Palo Alto, California: Scientific Press.

34

Quality Control Issues in Automated Manufacturing

J. Bert Keats[*]

IT WOULD BE DIFFICULT TO DISPUTE THE ARGUMENT that the decade of the 1980s saw more changes in virtually all aspects of the quality function than all the changes that transpired in the previous six decades. Some changes were precipitated by events of the 1970s, such as Japan's emergence as a producer of very high quality manufactured goods. However, only recently has U.S. management responded to off-shore challenges by changing dramatically the way that quality is regarded in manufacturing.

This chapter focuses on specific quality issues and treatments—both statistical and managerial—which are uniquely related to today's automated manufacturing environment. Before we explore these issues, it is important to first recognize how and why quality has been repositioned as a vital part of the strategy for achieving manufacturing excellence.

A BRIEF HISTORY OF QUALITY'S ROLE IN MANUFACTURING

The bulk of quality activities from the dawn of the era of interchangeable parts and assembly lines has been those actions associated with inspection and test. While uncertainty exists today about the role of inspection and testing equipment in quality, it is clear that this role has been severely lessened. W. Edwards Deming (1982) has made inspection the topic of one of his 14 points for achieving quality. He calls for manufacturing to "cease dependence on mass inspection" and instead to require statistical evidence of built-in quality in manufacturing and purchasing. Inspection adds no value to the product—it merely separates good from bad, and in some sectors where inspection errors are common, it does not do this very well. Testing also contributes no value added, but it can be argued that some testing is necessary.

Statistical Process Control as a quality tool began in the 1920s with the control charts of Walter Shewhart (1925). Yet, companies using SPC were a very small minority until the 1970s. Today, largely as a result of the successes of Genichi Taguchi (1986), statistical design of experiments in the early stages of product and process development is regarded as the most effective and economical approach to the achievement of quality. While certain aspects of Taguchi's methodology have been subjected to criticism, even the severest critics

*J. Bert Keats is Associate Professor of Industrial and Management Systems Engineering and Director of the Statistical and Engineering Applications for Quality Laboratory (SEAQL), CIM Systems Research Center at Arizona State University. The coauthor of *Engineering: An Introduction to a Creative Profession* (Macmillan), now in its 5th edition, he also served as a coeditor of the 1989 Marcel Dekker volume, *Statistical Process Control in Automated Manufacturing*. He has authored over 30 technical papers, primarily on quality and reliability engineering topics. He holds the Ph.D. degree in Industrial Engineering from Oklahoma State University, M.S. degree in Mathematics from Florida State University, and a B.S.I.E. from Lehigh University.

acknowledge the value of doing statistical experimentation while the product/process is being developed and introducing "noise" variables in the experimentation. The result is a product/process design that is robust in the sense that design parameter levels allow the product/process to function well in the presence of noise and to tolerate shifts in certain process parameters.

Prior to 1970, it was not unusual to examine a company's organization chart and observe that the quality group reported to manufacturing. This scheme placed quality in an adversarial position with manufacturing—a group that was measured on the ability to meet production schedules and to comply with budgetary constraints. Equally devastating were remedies which placed the quality function at headquarters level to act as the policeman or the undercover agent creating what were perceived as roadblocks to timely and cost-effective completions of production orders. Now, in most competitive manufacturing organizations, quality is both *everyone's job* and the means to achieve and retain a viable market share.

It has long been a common practice to randomly inspect a portion of the raw materials or subassemblies purchased from vendors upon delivery and prior to being released to manufacturing. Likewise, random sampling of product to make inferences about quality between stages of manufacturing, such as before a costly operation, was a routine event. A third area where sampling commonly took place was just prior to shipment as a means of control of the outgoing product.

Just-In-Time (JIT) means timely delivery of materials and parts from the vendor to the point of production or assembly, often in small lots. The notion of holding materials or parts for sampling inspection has no place in a JIT environment. Hence, the vendors themselves must take whatever steps are necessary to ensure that the quality of their delivered product is essentially defect-free. In-process and final inspection sampling are not being performed as frequently as in the past as a result of emphasis on smooth, continuous flows and the elimination of bottleneck and "no value-added" operations.

The Zero Defects (ZD) concept makes no concessions to goals or standards other than perfect product. Time-honored plans such as MIL-STD 105D are being eliminated from the procedures of most of the organizations practicing ZD as these plans are AQL-based and the AQL is a nonzero fraction defective value. Sampling will have a role in tomorrow's manufacturing. For example, it will be used to monitor the performance of manufacturing and measuring equipment, and it will be used to determine which of many possible tests will be performed on a product whenever performing all of the tests will have a negative effect on throughput.

The last major historical change to be mentioned here is the effect of the Total Quality Control (TQC) philosophy. The fundamental principles of TQC were established in 1961 by an American, Dr. Armand Feigenbaum, in his book *Total Quality Control*. Like SPC and the statistical design of experiments, it was practiced by few until the impact of off-shore competition was acknowledged. Now, many companies claim to be TQC companies and buttons and posters abound, much in the fashion of the ZD movement of the 1960s. TQC is more than buttons, certificates, and posters; it is and must be a way of conducting everyday business practices by everyone in the organization.

The following TQC concepts are based on a book by Dr. Kaoru Ishikawa (1985), who cites Feigenbaum as the originator of TQC but criticizes Feigenbaum's thoughts that QC specialists are needed to make TQC work. TQC is total involvement and commitment to quality practices by all functions, departments, and individuals in the organization. It uses the customer definition of *quality*. TQC people treat every step in manufacturing as if "the next process is your customer."

Quality is everyone's job—it is not the responsibility of a particular group. Cross function management is practiced. This means that on a regular basis at regularly scheduled meetings, the engineers (designers) talk to the manufacturing people who talk to the quality people who talk to the accountants who talk to marketing and sales, etc. There is now a *respect for humanity* rather than Taylorism or Theory X management.

The respect for humanity aspects place a subset of the time-honored Taylor Principles of Scientific Management in jeopardy. Taylor pioneered work measurement and separated those who plan the work from those who actually do the work. TQC advocates present convincing arguments for parsimonious use of work measurement and the widespread formation of volunteer employee groups with quality and productivity goals in mind.

In participative action teams (based on the quality circle notions), front-line workers assist management in finding the best way to do their jobs, while improving quality and increasing productivity. Vendors must be nurtured, often by training them at your expense. Vendors are regarded as partners. They are informed very early in the development process, are certified to produce high-quality parts, and in turn, must practice TQC. SPC is also practiced. Everyone understands the nature of spread and recognizes that variability must be controlled.

A TQC organization uses seven tools—histograms, pareto analysis, cause and effect diagrams, checklists, stratification, scatter diagrams, and graphs/control charts—for problem identification, definition, and characterization. There is a quest for continuous improvement—we don't stop when goals are reached. The ZD concept is practiced. The *go-straight* percentage is tracked on a regular basis with improvement-oriented goals. This percentage, also known as *first time yield*, is the proportion of product that goes all the way through the manufacturing stages without rework, repair, or replacement.

Training for everyone at all levels is practiced regularly. Training must be part of the strategic plan. Training in statistics, listening, and other people skills, for example, is a regular part of company operations. Finally, all quality practices extend beyond manufacturing to purchasing, marketing, distribution, and service. TABLE 34-1 summarizes some of the changes.

Table 34-1. Quality Then and as It Should Be Now

	Then	Now
Quality Defined	"Conformance to specifications"	"Conformance to customer requirements"
Quality Achieved	Through inspection and later SPC	Through design of experiments and some SPC
People Involvement	Taylorism; Theory X	"Respect of humanity"; Participative action teams
Organization for Quality	Reports to mfg. or as a headquarters "policeman"	"Quality is everyone's job"; No quality specialists
Data for SPC	Scarce; costly to obtain, hence, sampling; high volume runs	We often have all of the data and the ability to quickly analyze it, but in small batches
Acceptance Sampling	Widely used—predominately AQL type	Use is declining—due to JIT and ZD concepts
Quality Information Systems	Managerial—weekly defect and yield reports, tracking vendor performance and quality costs	Real-time for shop floor control at setup and in production

QUALITY IN DESIGN

Let us turn now to a discussion of TQC concepts as they affect design. We will explore quality function deployment, statistical design of experiments, design goals, and statistical aspects of design.

Quality Function Deployment

Consistent with use of customer requirements to define quality is the concept of *quality function deployment* (QFD). Developed in 1972 by Mitsubishi Heavy Industries at the Kobe (Japan) shipyard, it begins by obtaining from the customers their specific needs and desires with respect to the product being designed or redesigned. These needs and wants are not specifically related to the customer's product, but to the entire market.

Next, current or projected design features for the customer's product are compared with the list of market requirements (see FIG. 34-1). The comparison may be on the basis of ratings indicating how well the design feature meets the market requirement or on the basis of degree of correlation (strong, medium, or weak) between what the customer wants and what this feature does for that want. The product features are then related to themselves in the "roof" of the diagram, typically using strength of correlation symbols. As a result of this activity, it may become apparent that two or more features have conflicting design requirements (negative correlation). For example, size or weight may negatively correlate with power output. This implies that a trade-off may be necessary and the QFD exercise has identified it very early in the design process.

The next step is to benchmark the customer's product with that of selected competitors with respect to meeting customer needs and wants using a scale of *same, better,* or *worse.* Enhancements to the QFD process include adding importance measures to the customer needs and wants, including target values for product design features and relating product design features to part and mechanism characteristics. Those companies employing the QFD concept have recognized that

product quality is a function of the way that product design attends to customer needs. The process is simple to review and allows for more interaction from sales and marketing. It also provides for rapid and reasonable comparison of alternatives. More information on QFD may be found in DeVera, et al. 1988; Fortuna 1988; and Morrell 1988.

Statistical Design of Experiments

As a result of the efforts of Genichi Taguchi, statistical design of experiments has been transformed from an analysis after the product has failed or the process has become unstable to a procedure that has been made an integral part of designing that product or process. Taguchi has given the designer a tool to reduce variability. Heretofore, experimentation during design, when it was done at all, consisted in changing one factor at a time with predictable erroneous results. Must of what Dr. Taguchi recommends has intuitive appeal—i.e., do things right up front and find variable levels relatively insensitive to noise (or certain environmental effects) rather than perform costly operations to reduce or eliminate the sources of noise after production has begun.

Statistical design of experiments during the early stages of product or process development has captured the attention of nearly every manufacturing organization. Since Dr. Taguchi's methodologies are specifically identified for statistical experimentation during development, he has justifiably been given credit for creating a thought revolution in design. However, this recognition has been accompanied by much controversy. Most quality engineers and statisticians applaud Taguchi for getting designers involved in statistical experimentation, selecting design parameters robust in the sense that they are relatively insensitive to noise (environmental effects such as temperature, vibration, and humidity), and focusing on the nominal dimension through loss functions rather than treating all observations within specifications alike.

Taguchi has his critics, as well. The following topics have been subject to severe criticism. First, Taguchi experimentation appears to be a "one-

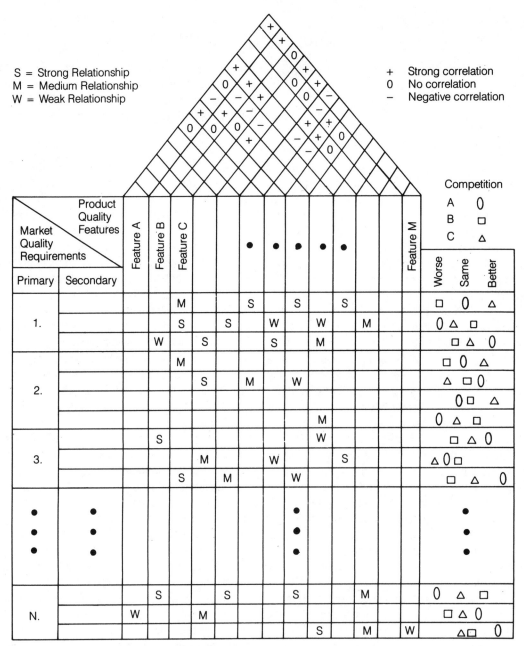

Fig. 34-1. Quality function development matrix structure.

shot'' or ''two-shot'' methodology (parameter and tolerance design followed by a verification experiment), rather than an iterative sequence of small experiments wherein the next experiment is designed on the basis of what was learned from the previous experiment. Second, Taguchi favors orthogonal arrays as the vehicle for fractional factorial experiments and they are such that interactions to be tested must be specified in advance. Third, Taguchi prefers three-level designs, presumably to test for quadratic effects. Critics call such fractional designs overly complex. Fourth, Taguchi favors *signal to noise ratio* as the dependent variable in the absence of loss function data. This ratio combines location and dispersion information, but critics say that the set of variables and associated levels optimal for location are seldom optimal for dispersion; one metric and one analysis are not sufficient. Fifth, Taguchi uses marginal averages to set design levels, but some argue that the effects of interaction are ignored by this process. These are but a few of the problems identified with the Taguchi methodology. Please refer to Box (1988) and Ryan (1988) for more details on some of the points made above.

Those interested in the statistical design of experiments should study the area thoroughly with the idea of understanding how the techniques work and when and why they are appropriate. Such a study should not be limited to the Analysis of Variance (ANOVA) with factorial designs, but should include other ANOVA designs, regression analysis, evolutionary operations (EVOP), response surface methodology, and operations research. As a result of these studies, any individual can then select designs with confidence and with understanding. Such an individual would also be positioned to select or adapt what is right or justifiable about Taguchi methods and ignore the rest.

Design Goals:
Reliability and Maintainability

Many of the activities associated with efforts to achieve quality during the early stages of product and process development now involve reliability and maintainability as well. It is most unfortunate that when reliability and maintainability goals are set and when metrics are defined for both the product and the equipment used in the processes associated with product manufacture, such goals and metrics are often expressed in terms of means: mean time to failure must exceed 1000 hours or mean time to repair must not exceed 30 minutes. Inputs to shop floor scheduling algorithms and software that predicts yields and cycle times likewise are often based on reliability and maintainability means. What is ignored by those who focus on the mean in these activities is intelligent use of the properties of the underlying distribution.

Consider the use of the exponential distribution for time between failures. It is an easy task to show that 63.2 percent of the failures will occur before the mean. Surely we do not want to design a device or a system or specify cycle times based on an event (failure at the mean) for which most of the activities will have already occurred. What is meaningful is to specify a time (or number of cycles) such that a specified large percentage of devices will still be operating at that time—for example, design for an exponential failure distribution so that 95 percent reliability is achieved at 1000 hours. For the Weibull distribution, which also enjoys much use in reliability studies, goals and metrics set for the mean also have little meaning. With a two parameter Weibull distribution, and a shape parameter greater than or equal to one (which is almost always true), the mean will be always less than or equal to the 63.2 percentage point. TABLE 34-2 gives the Weibull density, cumulative density, and reliability followed by log transformations, which make the characteristic value, θ, a linear function of the inverse of the shape parameter, β. These two parameters completely define the distribution and they can be estimated by specifying a pair of reliability goals.

Table 34-2. Reliability: Weibull Case

$$f(t) = \frac{\beta t^{\beta-1}}{\theta} e^{-(t/\theta)^{\beta}} \ , t > 0$$

$$F(t) = 1 - e^{-(t/\theta)^{\beta}}$$

$$R(t) = e^{-(t/\theta)^{\beta}}$$

$$-\ln R(t) = (t/\theta)^{\beta}$$

$$\ln(-\ln R(t)) = \beta \ln t - \beta \ln \theta$$

$$\boxed{\ln \theta = \ln t - \ln(-1n\,R(t))\,1/\beta}$$

Design for X_1% survivability at t_1 hours and X_2% survivability at t_2 hours.

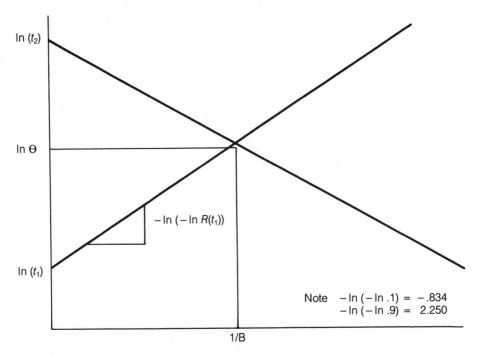

Fig. 34-2. Suggested Weibull reliability goal.

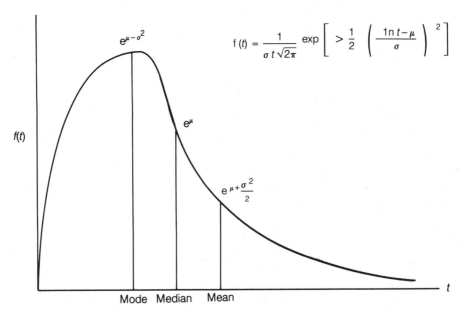

Fig. 34-3. Maintainability: lognormal case.

Suppose that one were to specify that we desire 90 percent survivability for t_1 hours and ten percent survivability for t_2 hours, where t_2 is much larger than t_1 (see FIG. 34-2). Either graphically or analytically, the intersection point of the two lines with slopes -0.834 and $+2.250$ can be determined. The result is the *theta* and *beta* values specifying the appropriate Weibull distribution for the design goal or shop floor metric.

For the maintainability case, the most popular distribution to describe both repair time and down time is the lognormal. FIGURE 34-3 presents a typical lognormal distribution. The median is always greater than the mode and the mean is always greater than the median.

Information associated with cumulative areas of the lognormal is easily obtained using the normal distribution (since the lognormal variate is one whose natural logarithm has the normal distribution). The calculations in TABLE 34-3 indicate that the cumulative value of the lognormal evaluated at

its mean is a function only of *sigma*. Incidentally, *sigma* is not the standard deviation of the lognormal variate but rather the standard deviation of its natural logarithm. If *sigma* is estimated to be one (a rather typical value in actual studies), TABLE 34-3 shows that only 69 percent of the maintenance activities will be completed by the target time, if the target is chosen to be the mean.

If, in a manner similar to what was done for the Weibull reliability case, we were to specify two desirable events, such as "We desire that the maintenance action be completed within 75 minutes with 95 percent certainty" and "We desire that the maintenance action be completed in 10 minutes with 25 percent certainty," then the two parameters of the lognormal, *mu* and *sigma*, which completely specify the distribution, may be estimated either graphically or analytically. FIGURE 34-4 illustrates the graphical results.

The point of these examples is not specifically to use the methodology illustrated above to specify

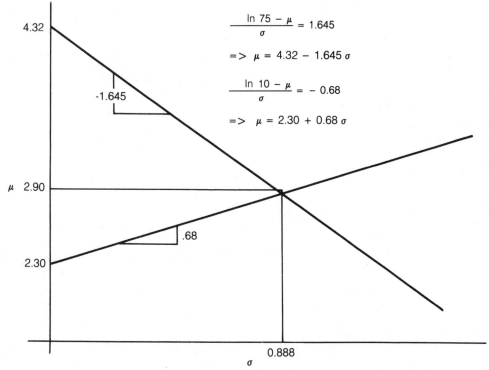

Fig. 34-4. Estimation of lognormal parameters.

Table 34-3. Lognormal CDF Evaluated at the Mean

$$F(x) = \Phi\left(\frac{\ln x - \mu}{\sigma}\right)$$

$$F(e^{\mu + \sigma^2/2}) = \Phi\left(\frac{\ln(e^{\mu + \sigma^2/2}) - \mu}{\sigma}\right)$$

$$= \Phi\left(\frac{\sigma}{2}\right)$$

$$\text{If } \sigma = 1, \Phi\left(\frac{1}{2}\right) = 69\%$$

parameters of the appropriate reliability or maintainability distribution. Indeed there are probably much better ways of doing this. The point is that those associated with design goals and those doing shop floor scheduling and predicting cycle times, where reliability and maintainability have such vital roles, should *not* use means in their specifications.

Statistical Aspects of Design for Manufacturability

Design for manufacturability (DFM) is a must for implementation in product and process development (Boothroyd and Dewhurst 1988). Many modern manufacturing firms have made DFM a part of their technological plans and strategies. While much of what DFM connotes relates to neither statistics nor quality control (DFM includes rules such as *design for z-axis assembly*, *minimize parts count*, and *avoid belt-driven rotary power*), there are several quality issues which must be emphasized. Only *Use of Statistical Tolerances in Design* will be discussed here. Suppose that a function of n variables, $f(x_1, x_2, \ldots, x_n)$, can be expanded with a Taylor series about a particular point, $(x_1^*, x_2^*, \ldots, x_n^*)$:

$$f(x_1, x_2, \ldots, x_n) = f(x_1^*, x_2^{2*}, \ldots, x_n^*)$$

$$+ \quad (x_1 - x_1^*)\frac{\partial f}{\partial x_1}\Big|_{x_1^*, x_2^*, \ldots, x_n^*}$$

$$+ \ldots$$

$$+ \quad (x_n - x_n^*)\frac{\partial f}{\partial x_n}\Big|_{x_1^*, x_2^*, \ldots, x_n^*}$$

+ terms of higher order.

If terms of higher order are neglected, and we assume that the *x*s are independent with means at $x_1^*, x_2^*, \ldots, x_n^*$, respectively, the expected value of the function is approximately given by $f(x_1^*, x_2^*, \ldots, x_n^*)$, and the variance of the function is given approximately by

$$\text{VAR}(X_1)\left[\frac{\partial f}{\partial x_1}\Big|_{x_1^*, x_2^*, \ldots, x_n^*}\right]^2$$

$$+ \quad \text{VAR}(X_2)\left[\frac{\partial f}{\partial x_2}\Big|_{x_1^*, x_2^*, \ldots, x_n^*}\right]^2$$

$$+ \ldots$$

$$+ \quad \text{VAR}(X_n)\left[\frac{\partial f}{\partial x_n}\Big|_{x_1^*, x_2^*, \ldots, x_n^*}\right]^2$$

These properties may be applied to DFM whenever a functional relationship exists between the output (target) and the input (adjustable) variables. Consider the circuit shown in FIG. 34-5, first illustrated by Johnson (1953) and later used by Bowker and Lieberman (1959) in their text. In FIG. 34-5, a phase-shifting synchro is installed between the amplifier and the output voltage. The output voltage is given by $E_0 = E_2 \cos \Theta + E_1 N K \sin \Theta$, where Θ is the phase angle of the synchro inputs. Suppose, initially, that the following specifications have been given for the components: $E_1 = 40 \pm 0.5$ volts; N = 2 to 1 $\pm$ 1%; $K = 3 \pm 2\%$; $\Theta = 60 \pm 1/4$ degrees; $E_2 = 40 \pm 0.4$ volts.

Applying the results of the Taylor series expansion about the nominal values above, the expected output voltage is

$$E(E_0) = 40 \times 1/2 + 40 \times 1/2 \times 3 \times \sqrt{3/2}$$
$$= 72 \text{ volts}$$

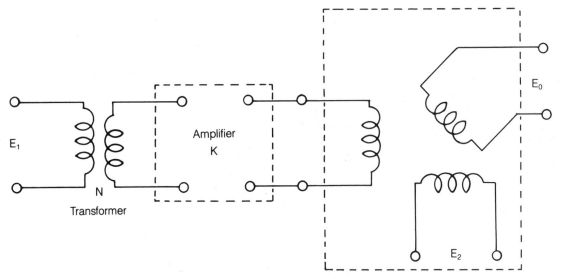

Fig. 34-5. Electrical circuit parameter relationships.

and the variance is

$$\text{VAR}(E_0) = \text{VAR}(E_1)\,(N^* K^* \sin \Theta^*)^2$$
$$+ \text{VAR}(E_2)\,(\cos \Theta^*)^2$$
$$+ \text{VAR}(N)\,(E_1^* K^* \sin \Theta^*)^2$$
$$+ \text{VAR}(K)\,(E_1^* N^* \sin \Theta^*)^2$$
$$+ \text{VAR}(\Theta)\,(E_1^* N^* K^* \cos \Theta^*$$
$$- E_2^* \sin \Theta^*)^2$$

since $\partial E_0/\partial E_1 = N K \sin \Theta,$
$\quad \partial E_0/\partial E_2 = \cos \Theta,$
$\quad \partial E_0/\partial N = E_1 K \sin \Theta,$
$\quad \partial E_0/\partial K = E_1 N \sin \Theta,$
$\quad \partial E_0/\partial \Theta = - E_2 \sin \Theta + E_1 N K \cos \Theta,$

Substituting the numerical values,
$$\text{VAR}(E_0) = \text{VAR}(E_1)\,(1/2 \times 3 \sqrt{3/2})^2$$
$$+ \text{VAR}(E_2)\,(1/2)^2$$
$$+ \text{VAR}(N)\,(40 \times 3 \sqrt{3/2})^2$$
$$+ \text{VAR}(K)\,(40 \times 1/2 \times \sqrt{3/2})^2$$
$$+ \text{VAR}(\Theta)\,(40 \times 1/2 \times 3 \times 1/2 - 40$$
$$\sqrt{3/2})^2$$
$$= (27/16)\text{VAR}(E_1) + (1/4)\text{VAR}(E_2)$$
$$+ (10,800)\text{VAR}(N)$$
$$+ (300)\text{VAR}(K) + (21.54)\text{VAR}(\Theta)$$

In the past, the next step would be to estimate

each of the standard deviations by assuming that a normal distribution is appropriate and then dividing the half-tolerances by the Z-statistic value which leaves alpha/2 in each tail (this assumes that alpha $\times$ 100 percent defectives are allowed or tolerated for each component—e.g., if $Z = 3$ then 0.27 percent defectives will occur with each component). Then, the variance of the output voltage would be determined by substituting the square of these values in the above equation.

In today's manufacturing environment with a zero defect philosophy and the notion of robust product design, this procedure is inappropriate. A more realistic problem would be: "Given that customer requirements dictate that the output voltage, E_0, have a tolerance not to exceed 3 volts, to what specifications shall we select the input parameters?" Suppose that the variances of the input parameters are known from previous experience. Suppose that the standard deviations are estimated to be: S.D.$(E_1) = 0.10$, S.D.$(N) = .001$, S.D.$(K) = 0.01$, S.D.$(\Theta) = .001$, and S.D.$(E_2) = 0.1$. We will first check to see if the customer requirements on the output voltage are met. Substituting the square of these values in the above equation, VAR$(E_0) = 0.060$ or S.D.$(E_0) = 0.24535$. Assume Normality.

With a robust design, we will require a C_p ratio of 2. This implies that the mean of the output voltage may shift $1\frac{1}{2}$ standard deviations in either direction from the nominal value of 72 volts and still only result in 3.4 parts per million defective. A C_p of 2 implies that the tolerance is 12 times the standard deviation. $12 \times 0.24535 = 2.944$. Thus, we can meet the customer's specifications with a probability near 1 while allowing our E_0 mean to shift by 1.5 standard deviations or 0.368 volts. Applying this idea to each input parameter, we would set the specifications at the nominal value ± 6 standard deviations. This allows for the same $1\frac{1}{2}$ standard deviation shift for each mean without measurable effects.

The Taylor series analysis calls attention to those variances with a crucial effect on the variance of the output variance. For example, referring to the equation for the variance of the output voltage. The multipliers of each of the control variable variances coupled with rough estimates of their order of magnitude are meaningful. They identify the variances which must be reduced or controlled if the output variance is to remain within tolerable limits or, better yet, be such that a certain C_p ratio is maintained.

Taguchi uses design of experiments to identify optimal parameters and tolerances for problems such as that above where there is a functional relationship between output and input. He illustrates parameter and tolerance design with the use of the well-known Wheatstone Bridge example (Taguchi 1986, pp. 98-110). It is surprising that Taguchi would recommend a fractional factorial design when no physical experimentation is being performed. With functional relationships, experimentation is really a process of repeated computer simulations. Today's high-speed computers yield the results of all combinations of all factors in a relatively short time frame. It is difficult to understand why any design less than a full factorial would be used in this situation. Box and Fung (1986) show that Taguchi's solution is not optimal and they solve the Wheatstone Bridge problem using nonlinear programming. Whatever the tool—analysis of variance, response surface methodology, or operations re-

search—it is important to recognize that whenever a functional relationship between output and control variables can be established, the designer may take advantage of the use of high-speed computers and examine the effects on output of all of the meaningful combinations of levels of the input variables in a statistical experimental design.

IMPACT OF AUTOMATED MANUFACTURING ON STATISTICAL PROCESS CONTROL

Computer integrated manufacturing (CIM) means both high volume/small variety of parts and low volume/large variety of parts. Groover and Zimmers (1984) categorize CIM as representing volumes of 15 to 15,000 and parts variety from 2 to 800. Such delineations are quite arbitrary, but it should be recognized that automated manufacturing and CIM encompass much more than small batch manufacturing with frequent setups.

For the high-volume case, the problem becomes one of dealing with the avalanche of correlated data accompanying automated shop-floor data acquisition systems. For small batch processing, statistical process control (SPC) is hindered by a lack of data available from current short production runs. Each of these problems is addressed here.

Large Volume Production Processes

Sophisticated data acquisition systems (DAS) can obtain one or more measurements on each and every item, virtually at the point of manufacture. Robots and other numerically controlled equipment have tactile end-effectors, laser vision systems, and voice-recognition circuitry. Thus, we have machines with the ability to "touch," "see," and "hear" and report to computers for control purposes. The volume of data which can be or is being collected is staggering—in many operations, two megabytes per day is not unusual.

For SPC purposes it is clear that data must be available for analysis immediately and that such analysis cannot depend on accessing large databases. Ghosh (1984) suggests data compression with the use of moments of the distribution. Sample moments may be compared with those calculated from a large history of "in-control" conditions. Sturm, Feltz, and Yousry (1988) have used recursive formulations for estimating means and variances in a Bayesian application with higher weights assigned to more recent observations. With recursive formulations, the current data entry is combined with the previous parameter estimate to yield a new parameter estimate using a computationally simple updating equation.

When there are a large number of statistical tests to be performed so that waiting for all the results may affect throughput, Ghosh suggests a test sequencing scheme in which each test is *not* performed on each unit of production. The extent of testing is determined by considering two factors: the cost of rework or scrap needed as a result of failing to detect a defect due to skipping tests, versus savings as a result of increasing throughput. Test sequencing may be systematic or based on the principle of continuous sampling. In systematic test sequencing, if n is the total number of different tests available for each unit and m is an integer constant known as the test compression factor, then the tests to be performed on unit k are $t_{(k-1)mod(m)+jm+1}$ where $j = 0,1,2,\ldots$ and j stops at the largest integer less than m/n. Whenever k is a multiple of m, i.e., $k \bmod(m) = 0$, then tests t_m, t_{2m}, $t_{3m},\ldots$ are performed $(im \leq n)$.

Suppose, there are $n = 23$ tests and $m = 6$ is the test compression factor. Then $j = 0,1,2,3$ since 3 is the largest integer strictly less than 23/6. Consider unit $k = 1$. $(k-1)mod(6)+j\times 6+1 = 1,7,13$, and 19 when $j = 0,1,2$ and 3, respectively. Hence the tests to be performed on unit 1 are t_1, t_7, t_{13}, and t_{19}. Unit 2 will have tests t_2, t_8, t_{14}, and t_{20}. Unit 216 will have tests t_6, t_{12}, and t_{18} since 216 is a multiple of $m = 6$.

Ghosh also presents expressions for the costs mentioned above as a function of the test compression factor. In testing with a scheme analogous to continuous sampling, if test t_j results in conformance (acceptability) for n_j consecutive units then subsequent tests of type t_j are administered on the basis of random sampling at a rate of $1/f_j$. If, during

sampling testing, the unit fails, then consecutive testing is resumed until n_j consecutive units pass test t_j. Factors to be considered in the selection of n_j and f_j include test time; material flow rate; Type I and Type II risks; average outgoing quality (AOQ); and costs associated with testing, false alarms, and defective product downstream.

The practice of test sequencing calls attention to the fact that although the capability of obtaining one or more measurements on each and every item may exist, it is not always feasible to use each measurement for decision making with regard to quality. Measurements not used may or may not be stored in memory for subsequent (off-line) use, depending on the ratio of cost to benefit of having this information available. A crucial issue associated with consecutive measurements is that of a strong likelihood of nonindependence. Many of the traditional tools for SPC such as the Shewhart and CUSUM procedures do not function well (nor were they intended to) with such data. Yet, dependent data is the rule, not the exception, with consecutive observations taken at very close time intervals (less than one second apart for some discrete manufacturing applications). Dealing with dependent data is addressed in the "Time Series Approaches" and "Cumulative Distribution Function Approach" sections of this chapter.

SPC for Small Batch Manufacturing

The requirements of today's dynamic global marketplace dictate a diverse product mix and small batch sizes. Companies following the JIT concept and using manufacturing cells are beginning to achieve a diverse mix and small production lots while containing costs and increasing productivity. The problems associated with small batches with respect to SPC are a lack of data to properly estimate process characteristics, the inability to form logical homogeneous subgroups, and problems in identifying the root cause of quality problems due to an absence of production history.

A meaningful approach to this situation is to study the process, not the product. Koons and Luner (1988) reported on studies at McDonnell

Aircraft Company in which dimensions associated with product produced by each of six different processes (drilling, counter-sinking, reaming, slotting, end-milling, and side milling) were monitored. All parts in all lots were measured. During the production run the company used the Shewhart Chart for individuals accompanied by a moving range chart. At the end of each production lot, the XBAR and variance charts were used to identify departures from chance causes during the study period. Out-of-control points were associated with certain setup problems and tool wear. A procedure for dealing with these problems was initiated. At the end of a two-month study period, processes were found to be in a state of statistical control. The small batch control scheme was then initiated. It consisted of measuring departures from nominal for the product, while ensuring statistical control for the process by continuing the use of the chart for individuals with moving ranges during the lot production and the XBAR and variance charts at the end of a run.

Cheng (1989) has introduced an ANOVA approach with the use of GT codes. The purpose of a GT code is to classify parts in families having similar attributes—both part design attributes such as material type and length/diameter ratio, and surface finish and part manufacturing attributes such as operation sequence, machine tool, and fixtures needed.

Cheng's research suggests that GT code (coupled with ANOVA) may be used to identify SPC families—that is, lists of parts sharing significant ANOVA effects (attributes). Factors in the ANOVA study were attributes (code fields). The three fundamental types of GT codes are monocode, where the interpretation of each succeeding symbol depends on the value of the preceding symbols; polycode, where the interpretation of each symbol in the sequence is fixed; and hybrid, where the features of monocode and polycode are combined. The design of the ANOVA model is based on the GT code: a nested design for monocode, a factorial design for polycode, and a nested-factorial design for hybrid. The purpose of the ANOVA is to identify the code attributes associated with the performance of the quality characteristic, which is the

dependent variable used in the ANOVA. The results of the analysis include an estimate of the process variability associated with significant levels of the attributes.

Parts whose measurements are associated with significance of a GT attribute become members of the same SPC family. For example, consider a three factor design with polycode. If only Attribute A (material) is significant and A has 3 levels—say titanium, aluminum, and beryllium alloy—and titanium and aluminum are not significantly different from each other in the multiple contrasts analysis but do differ from beryllium alloy, then titanium and aluminum are judged to be members of the same SPC part family, while beryllium alloy is a member of another part family. SPC is then performed on small (or large) batches of parts from the same SPC family, regardless of whether or not these family members were processed contiguously in a manufacturing cell as members of a GT family. The ANOVA has provided variance estimates to be used for SPC purposes.

Lill, Chu, and Chung (1988) have focused on SPC at setup for small batches. Indeed, in a JIT/small batch environment, setup is critical. There will be more setups and more reliance on turning out good parts with minimal adjustments during setup. At setup, what has been typically done is to produce the first few parts slowly while measuring quality characteristics and adjusting until two or three or some other number of consecutive parts are satisfactory. Then setup is ''locked in'' and production begins.

With small batches and the necessity of timely delivery to the next process, we no longer have the luxury of ''tweaking'' the process until *process prove-in* is achieved. Statistical setup adjustment (SSA) recommends adjustments as soon as possible for each dimension-producing operation so the chance of producing a part out-of-limits is as low as possible. SSA also provides statistical information about the operation that can be recorded and used in planning similar operations on the same machine or in decisions about maintenance or process changes.

The thrust of SSA is to recommend a setup

adjustment after the first piece with the greatest likelihood of being correct. With knowledge of machine and setup capabilities (from past performance, previous SSA, or expert opinion) the recommended adjustment is a function of the desired or target dimension, machine variability, setup variability (if available), and the first piece measurement. If setup variability (variance) cannot be estimated, Lill, Chu, and Chung recommend the use of an empirical constant related to difficulty of setup. They also discuss how to avoid false adjustments, and how to transition from startup to continuous production, and anticipate the effects of a known trend.

Use of Automated Testing and Inspection Equipment

The data from automated processes is the result of sophisticated inspection, testing, and in-process measurement devices. Automated inspection offers the advantages of low cost, lack of human bias, rapid feedback, and an increased sampling ratio (100 percent in many instances).

Testing differs from inspection in that testing performs a functional evaluation on a device or assembly rather than ascertaining whether or not a part has been manufactured to the accuracy desired in the detailed design. Automated testing is performed by providing a test apparatus at all input and output points of the device being tested. The test apparatus can simulate effects such as load on the device, environmental factors, material effects, and power. Performance is measured under these conditions. Once the test apparatus is in place, desired combinations of circumstances are simulated automatically in cycles. Both steady-state and transient analyses are performed. Measuring sensors provide direct links to a computer for either immediate feedback or later study. Often, particularly with electronic systems, compensating adjustments such as changes in resistances or capacitances may be made to selected devices during testing to qualify a part that otherwise may not have had acceptable parameter values.

In-process measurement occurs after each operation to ensure that the operation was performed correctly. If the in-process measurement reveals a problem with the immediate past operation, a second pass is made with the same part, or if the error resulted in a defective part, another part is substituted before the operation is repeated.

Despite all of these benefits, a great dilemma faces quality practitioners with regard to the extent to which such equipment should be used in manufacturing. As mentioned earlier in this chapter, the role of inspection to achieve quality has been greatly diminished. Shop floor goals include reducing and even eliminating all nonvalue-added operations. However, if high-speed, very accurate inspection devices could be used to measure a part at one stage and provide information to the next stage where compensating adjustments could be made to save an otherwise defective part then indeed this type of inspection could be considered a value-added operation. If the accurate, high-speed inspection device could provide information concerning the root cause of the defective part or information about how to adjust the process to prevent a defective part from being produced, then this device would certainly be more than equipment that separates good from bad. The implications associated with these statements are that inspection can be justifiable and cost-effective if it represents a value-added operation, where value is defined as *cost-saving*.

Valisys Corporation has developed software which among other functions automates the complete cycle of quality inspection, not just the measurement portion (Garcia and St. Charles 1988). It incorporates in software the geometric dimensioning and tolerancing (GD&T) standards in the American National Standards Institute (ANSI) Y14.5 specification. This standard is a precise way of assessing the fit and function of parts. With Valisys software, tooling designers and machinists receive tolerance information in the form of symbolic callouts to each critical feature from the designer.

Other software performs *soft-gaging*. A soft-gage is an electronic model of the worst-case fitting part for a particular feature. An electronic model of the actual part (constructed from points measured by a coordinate measuring machine or CMM) is compared with the soft-gage version so that it becomes obvious whether or not the part deviates from specifications, and if so, where the deviation occurs. Soft-gaging simplifies fixturing and placement. The software also coordinates interfaces between machines so that compensating adjustments (mentioned above) may be made. The software removes much of the ambiguity from design specifications, responsible by some estimates for as much as 80 percent of manufacturing problems. Software such as this may be thought of as part of a Design for Metrology program.

System designers in companies practicing DFM are taught to exercises judgment in specifying test and inspection stations through participation in scenarios representing material flow through such stations. FIGURE 34-6 presents a typical flow diagram used with inspection and test scenarios. In the figure, "I" is an inspection station (perfect inspection assumed), "O" is a manufacturing operation, "T_1" and "T_2" are test stations with less than 100 percent effectiveness, "A" is an analysis or diagnosis station, and "R" represents rework or repair. The designers know that first time yield (FTY), the percentage of product assembled and shipped without rework or scrap, is the product of the Poisson probabilities of no defects (zero defects per unit or zero d/u) in each of the manufacturing

operations with opportunities for defects.

$$\text{First Time Yield} = \exp\left(-\sum_i d_i/u_i\right)$$

Yield at any operation is $\exp(-d/u)$. Other relevant calculations include: manufacturing starts at any operation = 1/Yield; total test time per unit = starts × test time per unit for nonrepairable units; total test time per unit = $(1 + d/u)$ × test time per unit for repairable units; capacity = 1/total test time per unit; and total inspection time per unit = 1 + (1 − yield) = $2 - \exp(-d/u)$.

Exercises with scenarios such as that depicted in FIG. 34-6 involve specifying an input d/u and a test effectiveness (probability of detecting a defect) as well as providing estimates of the cost of inspection, cost of test, cost of analysis, and cost of rework. The system designer then performs calculations for scenarios with various configurations of test and inspection equipment to ascertain the effect on yield, cycle time, capacity, and cost. It soon becomes apparent that with more inspection and test, the d/u at output decreases (yield increases), but cycle time and cost are driven upward and capacity decreases. The lesson to be learned is that achieving better yields by extensive use of test and inspection equipment is both time

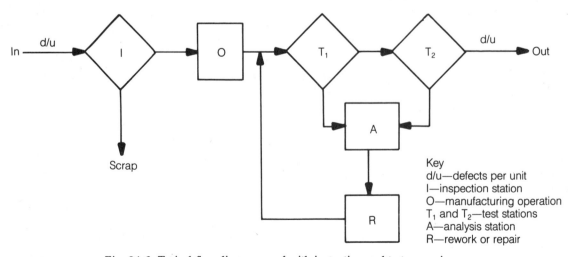

Fig. 34-6. Typical flow diagram used with inspection and test scenarios.

consuming and expensive. The obvious and optimal alternative is to design and manufacture better parts so that the need for test and inspection is greatly reduced.

SHOP FLOOR QUALITY INFORMATION SYSTEMS

Traditional quality information systems (QIS) have been developed primarily for managerial use—tracking defect rates and yields, monitoring the performance of suppliers, and collecting quality cost data. The QIS has been a prime source of information for the traditional "Monday Morning Quality Report," which presents information about last week's quality activities. Such information systems satisfy an important need and should continue to be used. However, what we should see more of and what is extremely crucial in automated manufacturing is a quality information system that collects and delivers knowledge to the shop floor at the precise point needed and in a timely manner.

Jung (1987) proposed such a system, consisting of four data exchange points—at setup, in-process, at inspection and test, and with the corrective action report file. At setup, attributes associated with setup such as operator, machine, and materials and tools used are captured so that traceability exists. Other information in this file includes setup instructions displayed in pictorial form and specific do's and don'ts including warnings about problems associated with improper setups. In-process information for each operation within a batch is gathered for those quality variables needed in SPC. Aggregate statistics as well as defect or failure data with the order of occurrence preserved are used. Data representing prior runs with the same part or part family are combined with current information for SPC purposes.

At inspection or test stations, failure data are collected with specific location, part, and other codes accompanied by a "probable cause" if the equipment and associated software has diagnosis capability. Information supplied to these stations includes intelligence about root causes of similar or identical failures in the past using confidence statements based on historical results. When defects or failures are analyzed for probable cause and corrective action is initiated to remove the cause, information from the corrective action procedure is stored. When this part is made again, information from this file will be transferred to the setup file and the in-process file and to the test and inspection stations.

THE ROLE OF EXPERT SYSTEMS

Must has been written about the use of an expert system in diagnosing a fault and recommending corrective action. Often such suggestions for the use of this type of artificial intelligence are accompanied by reports of successful implementations. However, as of this writing, there have been virtually no citations in either the expert systems or the statistical literature which focus on the application of an expert system to a statistical test or on the data being used for such a test. It is clear from conversations with several statisticians and quality engineers that research and implementations in this area have been done; the lack of published accounts is probably due to the advantage to be gained by keeping such developments proprietary.

In the majority of instances, the operator of a process station lacks both the time and expertise to define and reason with the procedures, the data, and the statistics calculated from the data. This highlights the potential need for a knowledge-based system to be integrated with the procedures to provide reasoning capabilities in a timely manner. The following five suggestions were made by Keats, Date, and Kim (1988) in a report to Digital Equipment Corporation.

1. The expert system is used to select parameters for the statistical tests. It combines history, analysis, and intuition and uses trade-offs (e.g. false alarms vs. misses) to select parameters such as the magnitude of the shift to be detected, the head start (such as the FIR in the CUSUM), and the margin of error.

2. When two or more statistical tests are applied to the same set of data, the expert system is used to decide whether or not an undesirable

shift has occurred—not by applying voting rules, but rather by allowing the tests to work in concert with each other. For example, suppose that one test has generated an *out-of-control* signal. The expert system could use information about how far along the other appropriate tests are in yielding the same result and base its conclusion accordingly.

3. The expert system applies deep and heuristic knowledge for making decisions concerning: (a) the extent to which past data should be used in current decisions, (b) the weights or values to be used when past and present data are combined for decision-making purposes, and (c) the form (detail or summary) in which data is to be stored for future use.

4. The expert system compares current process data with past data to determine if target values should be changed in order to reflect process improvements.

5. The expert system may dictate certain warm-up periods for tests known to take time before any decision can be made (such as Wald's sequential probability ratio test or SPRT).

Cheng and Hubele (1989) have developed an automatic process deviation reasoning system which includes a deviation recognition mechanism and a knowledge-based system. The system is intended to emulate the human expert in interpreting and troubleshooting process deviations. Its functions include recognizing process deviation, identifying sources of variation, determining controllable variation, and suggesting the direction of actions. The proposed deviation recognition system includes a domain-independent pattern recognition algorithm and a domain-dependent set of decision rules to identify and signal out-of-control situations.

INTERFACES WITH TRADITIONAL PROCESS CONTROL

When we speak of traditional process control, we refer to the methodologies practiced for more than half a century by control engineers—methodologies which focus on the use of the error signal to identify when and how to adjust the input variables

so that the output remains on target. Much of this work has been confined to the process industries and only recently has discrete manufacturing taken advantage of the benefits offered. Coupled with these developments is the introduction of statistical techniques. A few will be reported here.

The standard control algorithm is the proportional-integral (PI) algorithm in which the manipulated variable, M, is changed in proportion to the error, E, between the target, R, and the controlled (output) variable, C, and changed in proportion to the change in the error:

$$\Delta M_i = IhE_i + P\Delta E_i$$

where
$$E_i = R_i - C_i$$
$$\Delta M_i = M_i - M_{i-1}$$
$$h = \text{control interval}$$

P and I, the proportional control gain and the integral control gain, respectively, are related to the dynamics of the process. The dynamics involve the Gain, G, which is the change in the manipulated variable as a result of the control action; the dead time, D, which represents the time delay before the controlled variable changes as a result of a change to M; and the time constant, T_d. T_d represents the desired response of the controlled variable to a step change in the target.

Koenig (1988) compared the use of this algorithm applied at regular time intervals independent of the nature of disturbances to the system with SPC/integral only control where the Shewhart control chart, coupled with the "Western Electric Company Rules," was applied to the controllable variable values in the presence of both autocorrelated disturbances and white noise. Results indicated that SPC/integral control performed well when the disturbance was white noise and a small time constant prevailed, but PI-only control was superior with larger time constants and in the presence of autocorrelated noise, regardless of the time constant. The problem with the Shewhart control chart is that signals for control appear only after the process has changed. What is needed is an SPC tool which predicts controllable variable values such as a time-series model.

Hunter (1986) has suggested the use of a proportional, integral differential (PID) model fashioned after another traditional control algorithm. Hunter based his model on the exponentially weighted moving average (EWMA), which is a predictive time-series model equivalent to the autoregressive integrated moving average (ARIMA) model differenced once with a single moving average term. Hunter's model is given by

$$\hat{y}_{t+1} = \hat{y}_t + \lambda_1 e_t + \lambda_2 \Sigma\ e_t + \lambda_3 \nabla e_t.$$

∇ represents the first difference in errors. No investigations of the use of this model with industrial data have been reported, but it does present some interesting possibilities.

Box and Jenkins (1976) describe two approaches for process control using transfer functions. Transfer functions have long been a part of the procedures used by control engineers. A transfer function describes the relationship between the output and the input of any element in the process control loop. In a feedforward control situation, appropriate when disturbances (noise) are measurable, two transfer functions are employed. One connects the observed disturbances to the output, while the other connects the compensating variable and the output. The latter function indicates a change to be made in the compensating variable to minimize the mean square error. The effect of time delays must be considered. Feedback control may be applied when the source of disturbance is either not known or cannot be measured. This approach uses the error signal to determine the compensating effect to the input. The transfer function links the input (controllable variable) to the output (manipulated variable).

The contribution made by Box and Jenkins to these two models is one of introducing a statistical treatment. Sum of squared error is considered and time series analysis is a part of the procedure in that ARIMA or spectral functions are used in the transfer function control. MacGregor and Wong (1980) describe a multivariate transfer function control model for use with a chemical reactor. Transfer function/time series used in discrete manufacturing have not been reported to date, but applications are expected in the near future.

APPLICATIONS WITH CORRELATED DATA

Let us look at two applications: a time-series approach, and use of the cumulative distribution function.

A Time-Series Approach

When automated data collection systems obtain consecutive measurements from a high-volume manufacturing process, traditional statistical process control procedures are not appropriate for use with the individual measurements; such data are usually dependent and may be nonnormal as well.

Montgomery and Friedman (1989) report the use of time series methodology to filter the correlated data (see FIG. 34-7). Industrial data were used in their investigation. During a period of stability, an ARMA model is fit to the data. Typically, a maximum of two terms of either type is required. After the appropriate model is identified, the error values (which should be normally distributed and independent) are tracked with either a CUSUM or geometric moving average (GMA) chart. The GMA is the same as the EWMA. When out-of-control signals are given, the implication is that the model no longer fits the data and the most likely cause is a shift in the process mean (a change in process variance may also cause such signals). Yourstone (1988) has automated the procedure with software which fits the ARMA model and then tracks the error signal.

Use of the Cumulative Distribution Function

Coleman (1989) has developed a statistic that is most appropriate for consecutive observations. He proposes charting the product of a transformation of cumulative distribution values. It is well known that the cumulative distribution function (cdf) has the uniform distribution on the unit interval. Furthermore, it is an easy task to show that $-2\ln(u)$,

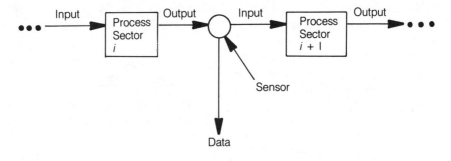

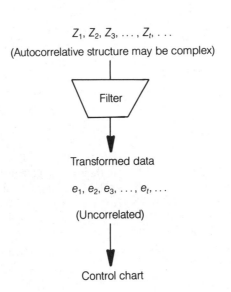

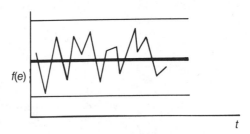

Fig. 34-7. Use of time-series filter to obtain uncorrelated data for SPC use.

where u is a uniform variate, is distributed exponentially with parameter $1/2$(mean = 2). This exponential variate is also a chi-square variate with two degrees of freedom. Because of the self-reproduc-

ing property of the chi-square distribution,

$$\sum_{i=1}^{K} -2\ln(u_i) = -2\sum_{i=1}^{K}\ln(u_i) = -2\ln\prod_{i=1}^{K}u_i$$

has the chi-square distribution with $2k$ degrees of freedom. If the distribution of x is known so that $f(x)$ may be obtained for any x, then -2 times the log of the product of k independent observations may be compared with the tail values of a chi-square distribution to make inferences about a shift in the process.

STATISTICAL TREATMENTS— Small Fraction Defective

A Scheme for Monitoring Small Process Fraction Defective

Many companies are now setting goals or targets for fraction defective. As technology and quality practices improve, the target values are getting smaller and smaller. One hundred parts per million defective (100 ppm) is a common goal in many industries, whereas ppm levels below 50 are said to exist in a few others. It makes no sense to set such lofty goals without sound procedures for identifying whether or not such targets are being achieved and identifying shifts or changes (either up or down) in the small fraction defective rate.

It is obvious that when defect levels are of the order of magnitude mentioned above, sampling is of no use as sample sizes large enough to allow the possibility of a single defective would approximate 100 percent inspection. Lucas (1985) has provided the methodology for dealing with small fraction defectives. Suppose that it is possible to obtain a rough count of the number of nondefective items produced between defectives. These counts might be obtained by combining information about defectives found during manufacturing with those items found to be defective in the field. It is obvious that record-keeping must be such that time order of production is roughly preserved so that counts of good items occurring between defectives are reasonably accurate. The Time Between Events CUSUM (increasing rate case) is given by

$$S_i = \text{MAX} \ (0, \ k - y_i + S_{i-1})$$

where S_i is the CUSUM value after the ith defective item is found, k is a constant based on the design of the plan, y_i is the number of good units between defectives, and S_{i-1} is the previous CUSUM value (value after the i-1st defective was found). To find k, one must first specify acceptable and detectable defective rates, u_a and u_d, respectively. Suppose, for example, that the target value was 50 ppm and 100 ppm is deemed unacceptable. Then $u_a = 50$ and $u_d = 100$.

We next compute

$$k_b = (\ln u_d - \ln u_a)/(u_d - u_a)$$

and then $k_t = k_b \times u_a$. In our example, $k_t = \ln 2/(u_d - u_a) \times u_a = \ln 2 = 0.693$ since $u_d - u_a = 2u_a - u_a = u_a$. In fact, any ratio $u_d/u_a = 2$ will produce a k_t ratio of 0.693. Next, we use the average run length table provided by Lucas, a portion of which is shown in TABLE 34-4 (Lucas 1985). The purpose of the table is to select h_t, which will determine the control limit for the plan.

The basis for selection is the *average run length* (ARL), which is defined as the average number of observations that have occurred after the shift but before an out-of-control signal is given. Two columns of the ARL table are used: the column that indicates no shift (count rate $\times u_a = 1$) and the column representing the shift to be detected (count rate $\times u_a = 2$, in this case).

Table 34-4. Portion of ARL Table— Time between Events CUSUM

h_t	k_t	h_t/k_t	Count Rate* μ_a	
			1.0	*2.0*
2.1	.7	3	49.9	9.56
2.8	.7	4	110.	12.9
3.5	.7	5	230.	16.4
4.2	.7	6	468.	19.9
4.9	.7	7	948.	23.4
5.6	.7	8	1870.	26.9

*Data above from Table 7: TBE CUSUM ARL's; Inc. rate; No FIR.

Source: J.M. Lucas, "Counted Data Cusum's," *Technometrics* 27:2 (May 1985): 129-144.

Clearly, we desire a large ARL when no change has taken place and a small ARL when the detectable change occurs. The choice of h_t is thus very subjective and is strictly a function of the decision-maker's perceptions of large and small. Obviously these perceptions are related to the cost of searching for a false alarm and the cost of allowing defects to escape.

For our purposes, suppose that $h_t = 2.8$ is selected. To complete the plan, we now consider the magnitude of u_a: $k = k_t/u_a = 0.7/50/10^6 = 14,000$ and h, the upper control limit $= h_t/u_a = 2.8/50/10^6 = 560,000$. Note that k provides a buffer around the observed good items between defectives. When the process is meeting the target, the expected value of y_i is 20,000, the reciprocal of u_a. The CUSUM will not increase until the observed value exceeds 14,000. We will conclude that the fraction defective rate has shifted to 100 ppm if and when the CUSUM value exceeds 560,000. The k_t value is appropriate for any detectable to acceptable mean defective ratio of 2. Likewise for h_t. One has only to change the k and h values. For example if $u_a = 2$ ppm and $u_d = 4$ ppm, then $k = .7/2/10^6 = 350,000$ and $h = 2.8/2/10^6 = 1,400,000$.

When the u_d/u_a ratio is 1.5, k_t is approximately 0.8. The increasing rate case has been illustrated here. When a test for a decreasing fraction defective rate is desired a similar procedure described by Lucas is used (Lucas 1985).

The Time Between Events CUSUM assumes a Poisson process that implies that the number of good items between defectives is distributed exponentially. However, this test is extremely robust. Keats (1988) has conducted extensive simulations with data from non-Poisson processes and found that the test works very well in detecting shifts under these conditions. The test is reasonably accurate. In over 13,000 simulation runs with varying defective rates and three types of shifts in the mean rate (sudden, gradual, and step), Keats reported that the test averaged 91 percent correct decisions (found the shift when it occurred), five percent false alarms (reported a shift when none

was present), and four percent misses (failed to detect the shift).

Reporting and Comparing Small Fraction Defective Levels

Care must be exercised in comparing yields and other statistics based on ppm levels. Consider three different types of printed circuit boards. Each has the same fraction defective level, expressed in ppm, due to problems with vendors, automation insertion of parts, and the wave solder process. The defective rates for each type of problem are presented in TABLE 34-5. A yield (e^{-d/u_a}) calculation is performed for each type of board as seen in TABLE 34-6. Note from TABLE 34-6 that the only difference among the three types of boards is in the number of components on each. Yet the yields are vastly different. When comparisons like this are made, a penalty is imposed on the boards with more components. To avoid this situation, yield should not be computed for comparison purposes.

When comparing two or more units calculate ppm/part which is given by ppm/part = defects/board $\times 10^6$/parts/unit. For each of the three boards, this figure would be 3500 ppm/part and each type of board would be judged to have the same defective problem, as they should be. Some companies use defects per million opportunities (dpmo) or parts defective per million opportunities (ppmo) as the metric for standards and comparisons. An opportunity is an occasion for a defect to occur. For example, on a printed circuit board with 200 components there may be 1700 opportunities for a defect to occur: each solder joint is an opportunity, each insertion is an opportunity, etc.

**Table 34-5. Defect Rates for
Three Problems on Printed Circuit Boards***

	Vendor Problem (V)	Machine Insertion (M)	Wave Solder (W)
PPM	200	900	800
d/u	.0002	.0009	.0008

*Each board averages 3 solder joints per part.

Board	Number of Parts	Defects per unit				Yield (%)
		V*	M*	W*	Total	
1	100	.02	.09	.24	.35	70.5
2	500	.10	.45	1.2	1.75	17.4
3	1000	.20	.90	2.4	3.5	3.0

Table 34-6. Yield Calculations for Three Circuit Boards

*V = Vendor problem, M = Machine Insertion, W = Wave solder.
Note: Each board averages three solder joints per part.

OPTIMAL INTERVALS FOR MONITORING AUTOMATED PROCESSES

Taguchi, Elsayed, and Hsiang (1989) present several economically based models that are well suited for use in an automated manufacturing environment. The models help identify the optimal production interval for monitoring or examining equipment to determine whether or not an adjustment, overhaul, or recalibration is necessary. The intervals are expressed in terms of units produced. First, a model is developed representing a loss, based on several costs and other conditions to be discussed below. Then the optimal interval, n^* is determined by differentiating the loss function with respect to n. To illustrate this procedure, we present one of the Taguchi, Elsayed, Hsiang models intended for use with variables data, which include control limits. The loss per unit, L, is given by

$$L = B/n + C/u + A/\Delta^2[D^2/3 + ((n+1)/2 + l)D^2/u]$$

where B is the cost associated with measurement or inspection. C is the cost associated with making an adjustment, and u is the average adjustment interval of the process—u is based on past records concerning how often the process actually had to be adjusted, both as a result of problems found during monitoring and as a result of unscheduled adjustments. To continue, A is the loss per unit for product not meeting specifications, Δ is the half-tolerance of the process (half the difference between specification limits), D is the current control limit, and l is the lag of measurement which repre-sents the number of units produced between the time that measurement or inspection begins and the process (or equipment) is stopped for an adjustment. Optimal values for n and D are found taking partial derivatives of the loss function and equating them to zero. These equations can be solved one at a time since neither has the other factor in it. For the formulation above,

$$n^* = [2uB/A]^{1/2} \times \Delta/D$$

and

$$D^* = [3C/A \times D^2/u \times \Delta^2]^{1/4}.$$

Taguchi, Elsayed, and Hsiang discuss a number of other situations for which similar loss function models are appropriate. There are many interesting applications of such economically based models such as in monitoring the performance of automated testing equipment, scheduling maintenance, and performing overhauls or change-outs.

A BAYES APPROACH

Sturm, Feltz, and Yousry have developed and tested a procedure most useful in a data intensive manufacturing environment. The procedure uses recursive formulations to avoid having to access large databases. The procedure assumes that an observation at time t is a sample of one from a normal distribution whose mean also has a normal distribution with a fixed mean. Using weights, which determine the extent to which past data are used to obtain posterior parameter estimates, such estimates are used with each new observation to compare the short-term estimate of the mean with the long-term estimate. The long-term estimate is centered graphically in a box and whisker plot. Shifts in the process mean, estimates of product meeting specifications, and test set comparisons are possible. The procedure works in real time to control the voltage level of a power supply from a test set. No sampling takes place—each and every voltage reading is used to produce Bayes estimates of long- and short-term means and variances and such estimates are used for control.

A BRIEF SUMMARY

Quality control for manufacturing in the 1990s emphasizes the Total Quality Control concept. Quality and reliability must be made a part of the design process. Statistical design of experiments plays a vital role. Statistical process control must adapt to keep pace with automated manufacturing—adapt to the requirements of a small batch/JIT system and adapt to meet the needs of a data intensive-high volume transfer line. Intelligence in the form of expert systems is beginning to be used to precondition the data for SPC analysis and is being used with the statistical tests as well. Quality information systems are being developed for shop-floor control as well as for management reports. SPC is now being used in combination with traditional engineering control methods. Small defect rates (ppm level) can be tracked and tested for changes. New SPC techniques have been designed to handle the correlated data associated with consecutive observations resulting from the ability to have all the data. Economically based approaches are being used to identify optimal production intervals for monitoring a process to determine whether or not a need exists to recalibrate, adjust, or change out parts. The summaries and references presented here will, I hope, assist you in identifying the proper approach for solving quality problems.

REFERENCES

Boothroyd, G. and P. Dewhurst. "Product Design and Manufacture for Assembly." *Manufacturing Engineering* (April 1988): 42-46.

Bowker, A. H. and G. J. Lieberman. *Engineering Statistics*. Englewood Cliffs, New Jersey: Prentice-Hall, 1959.

Box, G. "Signal-to-Noise Ratios, Performance Criteria and Transformations." *Technometrics* 30: 1 (February 1988): 1-17.

Box, G. and C. Fung. "Studies in Quality Improvement: Minimizing Transmitted Variation by Parameter Design." *Report No. 8, Center for Quality and Productivity Improvement*. University of Wisconsin, Madison, February 1986.

Box, G. E. and G. M. Jenkins. *Time Series Analysis: Forecasting and Control*, rev. ed. San Francisco: Holden-Day, 1976.

Cheng, C. S. "Group Technology and Expert System Concepts Applied to Statistical Process Control in Small-Batch Manufacturing." Ph.D. dissertation, Department of Industrial and Management Systems Engineering, Arizona State University, 1989.

Cheng, C. S. and N. F. Hubele. "A Framework for a Rule-Based Deviation Recognition System in Statistical Process Control." In *Proceedings, 1989 Annual International Industrial Engineering Conference*. Toronto, 1989.

Coleman, D. E. "Generalized Control Charting." In *Statistical Process Control in Automated Manufacturing*, edited by J. B. Keats and N. F. Hubele, 155-191. New York: Marcel Dekker, 1989.

Deming, W. E. *Quality, Productivity and Competitive Position*. Massachusetts Institute of Technology Center for Advanced Engineering Study, Cambridge, Massachusetts, 1982.

DeVera, D., T. Glennon, A. A. Kenny, M. A. H. Khan, and M. Mayer. "An Automotive Case Study." *Quality Progress* (June 1988): 35-38.

Feigenbaum, A.V. *Total Quality Control: Engineering and Management.* New York: McGraw-Hill, 1963.

Fortuna, R. M. "Beyond Quality: Taking SPC Upstream." *Quality Progress* (June 1988): 23-28.

Garcia, C. J. and D. P. St. Charles. "Automating GD & T." *Quality* (June 1988): 56-58.

Ghosh, S. P. "An Application of Statistical Databases in Manufacturing Testing." In *Proceedings, International Conference on Data Engineering.* Los Angeles, Sponsored by the IEEE Computer Society, IEEE Catalog Number 84CH2031-3, 1984.

Groover, M. P. and E. W. Zimmers, Jr. *CAD/CAM Computer-Aided Design and Manufacturing.* Englewood Cliffs, New Jersey: Prentice-Hall, 1984.

Hunter, J. S. "The Exponentially Weighted Moving Average." *Journal of Quality Technology* 18: 4 (October 1986): 203-210.

Isikiwa, K. *What is Total Quality Control? The Japanese Way.* Englewood Cliffs, New Jersey: Prentice-Hall, 1985.

Johnson, R. H. "How to Evaluate Assembly Tolerances." *Product Engineering* (January 1953).

Jung, D. "Information Systems Design for Pre-Process Quality Assurance." Master's Thesis, Department of Industrial and Management Systems Engineering, Arizona State University, 1987.

Keats, J. B. "Design Goals: Mathematical and Statistical Implications." *Third National Symposium, Statistics in Design and Process Control: Keeping Pace with Automated Manufacturing,* Arizona State University, 1988.

Keats, J. B., S. C. Date, and D. Y. Kim. "Development of a Statistical Process Control Procedure and a Knowledge-Based System for Use with Attributes Data." Final Report, Digital Equipment Corporation, Phoenix, Arizona and Marlboro, Massachusetts, 1988.

Koenig, D. M. "Control of Noisy Processes by SPC/Integral-Only and Conventional Methods." Corning Glass Technical Paper, 1988.

Koons, G. F. and J. J. Luner. "SPC: Use in Low-Volume Manufacturing Environment." *1988 ASQC Quality Transactions* Dallas: 1988.

Lill, M. H., Y. Chu, and K. Chung. "Statistical Setup Adjustment (SPC for Small Batch Machining)." In *Proceedings, 1988 Annual Industrial Engineering Conference,* Orlando, Florida: 1988.

Lucas, J. M. "Counted Data CUSUM's." *Technometrics* 27: 2 (May 1985): 129-144.

McGregor, J. F. and A. K. L. Wong. "Multivariate Model Identification and Stochastic Control of a Chemical Reactor." *Technometrics* 22: 4 (November 1980): 453-464.

Montgomery, D. C. and D. J. Friedman. "Statistical Process Control in a Computer Integrated Manufacturing Environment." In *Statistical Process Control in Automated Manufacturing,* edited by J. B. Keats and N. F. Hubele, 67-87. New York: Marcel Dekker, 1989.

Morell, N. E. and the Editors of *Automotive Engineering.* "Quality Function Deployment; Disciplined Quality Control." *Automotive Engineering* (February 1988): 122-128.

Ryan, T. P. "Taguchi's Approach to Experimental Design: Some Concerns." *Quality Progress* (May 1988): 34-36.

Shewhart, W. A. "The Application of Statistics as an Aid in Maintaining Quality of a Manufactured Product." *Journal of the American Statistical Association* (1925): 546-548.

Sturm, G. W., C. J. Feltz, and M. A. Yousry. "A Strategy for Analyzing Manufacturing Data in Real-Time Continuous Variable or Process Parameter Analysis." *AT&T Engineering Research Center*, Princeton, New Jersey: 1988.

Taguchi, G. *Introduction to Quality Engineering*. Tokyo: Asian Productivity Organization, 1986.

Taguchi, G., E. A. Elsayed, and T. C. Hsiang. *Quality Engineering in Production Systems*. New York: McGraw-Hill, 1989.

Yourstone, S. A. "Real-Time Process Quality Control in a CIM Environment." *Third National Symposium, Statistics in Design and Process Control: Keeping Pace with Automated Manufacturing*, Arizona State University, 1988.

35

The Industrial Robot:
Applications in Discrete Manufacturing

Sheikh Burhanuddin[*]
Bopaya Bidanda[**]

AN INDUSTRIAL ROBOT IS A GENERAL PURPOSE, reprogrammable manipulator capable of performing a variety of useful tasks in industry. Typical robot applications include spot welding, spray painting, loading and unloading of machines, assembly, and inspection.

The term *robot* is derived from Czech and means *forced labor*. The modern robot is based on a combination of teleoperator and numerical control (NC) technologies. Teleoperators were developed in early 1940s for handling radioactive materials. Numerical control was developed for machine tools in the late 1940s and early 1950s. As its name suggests, numerical control involves the control of the actions of a machine tool by means of coded numerical information. Robots require more degrees of freedom and more effective and powerful control software than NC machines.

Although several patents for robots were issued in the U.S. and U.K. in the early 1950s, the first commercial robot was installed in 1961 by Unimate. Robots started playing a major role in manufacturing in the late 1970s.

ROBOT ANATOMY

Industrial robots are available in a variety of shapes and configurations. Most industrial robots consist of a manipulator attached to a base. The base is fastened to the floor. The manipulator consists of a body, an arm, and a wrist. Relative movements between the various components of a robot are provided by a series of prismatic (linear) and/or angular (revolute) joints.

Industrial robots are available in a wide variety of shapes and physical configurations. The selection

[*]S. Burhanuddin holds a master's degree in Mechanical Engineering from the University of Manitoba, Canada and a Ph.D. in Industrial Engineering from West Virginia University. His areas of interest include manufacturing systems and production planning. His publications have appeared in AACE and AFS transactions. He is affiliated with the Department of Industrial and Manufacturing Engineering at Oregon State University.

[**]Bopaya Bidanda is an Assistant Professor of Industrial Engineering at the University of Pittsburgh. His teaching and research interests include computer integrated manufacturing systems, computer graphics, and machine vision. He completed his doctoral degree at the Department of Industrial & Management Systems Engineering at Pennsylvania State University. In addition, he has worked for a number of years in the aerospace industry in the areas of manufacturing and production planning, and control. He is a senior member of the Institute of Industrial Engineers and the Society of Manufacturing Engineers.

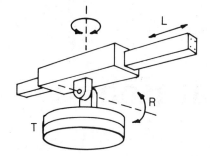

Polar Coordinate Body-and-Arm Assembly

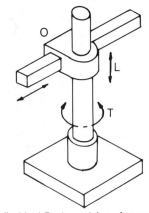

Cylindrical Body-and-Arm Assembly

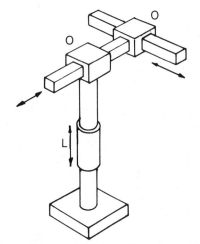

Cartesian Coordinate Body-and-Arm Assembly

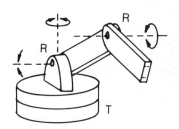

Jointed-Arm Body-and-Arm Assembly

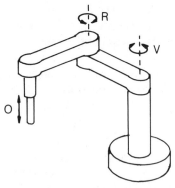

SCARA Body-and-Arm Assembly

Source: Mikell Groover, AUTOMATION, PRODUCTION SYSTEMS, AND COMPUTER INTEGRATED MANUFACTURING, © 1987, pp. 305-307. Reprinted by permission of Prentice-Hall, Inc., Englewood Cliffs, NJ.

Fig. 35-1. Common robot configurations.

of the physical configuration of a robot depends upon its intended application. Most commercial industrial robots are designed on the basis of one of five basic configurations. These configurations are

- Polar (or spherical)
- Cylindrical
- Cartesian
- Jointed-Arm
- SCARA

Each configuration has its advantages and disadvantages with regard to strength, maneuverability, and speed. FIGURE 35-1 (Groover 1987) shows two types of prismatic joints and three types of revolute joints. Prismatic joints include a linear joint (L) and an orthogonal joint (O). Revolute joints include a rotational joint (R), a twisting joint (T), and a revolving joint (V).

DEGREES OF FREEDOM

A *degree of freedom* in robotics is the ability of the end effector to move in an independent direction. It should not be confused with an axis of motion. Any solid object has a maximum of six degrees of freedom, as shown in FIG. 35-2. A robot with a fixed end effector may have up to three degrees of freedom. Adding additional axis of motion to the structure does not increase degrees of freedom but may improve maneuverability. Three

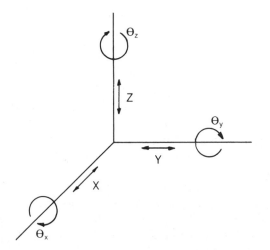

Fig. 35-2. The six degrees of freedom.

degrees of freedom are enough to place the end effector as a whole in any position—but not at any angle. Three additional degrees of freedom may be added to the structure by attaching a wrist to the end of the manipulator. A robot's wrist can swivel (roll), bend upwards or downwards (pitch), and bend from side to side (yaw). For some applications, six degrees of freedom are not necessary, and a wrist having one or two degrees of freedom can be used instead.

ROBOT GEOMETRY

The five basic configurations mentioned earlier provide five robot structure geometries. A *polar geometry* robotic arm has two rotary joints for rotation in a horizontal and vertical plane, and a prismatic joint for arm extension and retraction. This type of arm can move fast in the vertical direction.

The *cylindrical geometry* robot consists of a vertical column, relative to which an arm assembly can be moved up and down. The arm can rotate in a horizontal plane, and extend and retract as well. This type of arm can move much faster than the cartesian type.

The *Cartesian geometry* robot consists of three perpendicular slides along x, y, and z axes. Cartesian robots are generally large and posses the appearance of a gantry-type crane. These robots are suitable for applications where a large area has to be covered.

The *jointed-arm geometry* robot is also called anthropomorphic because of its likeness to a human arm. Its arm has a shoulder joint and an elbow joint, and the arm can be swiveled about the base. The jointed-arm robot is the most maneuverable and is often used for spray painting. It is slow moving and cannot cover a large area.

The acronym *SCARA* in a SCARA geometry robot stands for Selective Compliant Assembly Robot Arm. All the revolute joints in the arm rotate about vertical axes. This robot is very rigid in the vertical direction, but compliant in the horizontal direction. The robot is suitable for performing insertion tasks for assembly in a vertical direction where some side-to-side adjustment is needed to mate the two parts properly.

Most industrial robots are fixed on a pedestal base. Fixed robots are cheaper and easier to control. Mobility in robots provides additional degrees of freedom and more flexibility. Availability of low-cost computers has simplified the control problem in mobile robots. Depending upon the type of mobility, robots can be classified as follows:

- Robots mounted on a pedestal base; the standard robot mounting.
- Robots supported from top or side; from a ceiling or wall to save floor space.
- Robots on a track; used to do welding and painting on moving or fixed workpieces.
- Robots mounted on an overhead gantry; move in a horizontal rectangular plane and are used for heavy industrial work.
- Robots mounted on vehicles with wheels or tracks; expected to become available within few years for industrial and military applications.
- Robots with multiple (four to six) legs are under development. This design provides robot mobility in difficult terrain.

THE WORK ENVELOPE

The work envelope or work volume is space within which a robot can manipulate its wrist end. The shape and size of the work envelope is determined by the robot's physical configuration, the sizes of the components of the manipulator, and the limits of the robot's joint movements. FIGURE 35-3 shows work envelopes for cylindrical, polar, and jointed-arm robots. Polar and jointed-arm robots have partial spheric work envelopes, a cartesian robot has a rectangular cubic work envelope, and a cylindrical robot has cylindrical work envelope. The size and shape of the work envelope of a robot is important in work cell design and safety considerations.

End Effectors

End effectors are gripping and holding devices and tools mounted on the end of the robot wrist. The end effector adapts the general purpose robot to a particular task. End effectors are often designed for a particular application but can also be bought off the shelf for a variety of tasks. Most robot manufacturers design and fabricate end effectors for their customers. End effectors are particularly suitable for handling heavy and sharp objects, hot and cold materials, and corrosive substances. They are not as good as human hands in handling complex shapes and fragile parts. Tactile sensors can make end effectors more sensitive.

End effector holding devices are mounted at the end of the robot wrist. These devices include plates with mounting holes and bayonet pin mounts. Solenoids can be used to release the clamping pin used to hold the end effector. End effectors can be classified into two categories: gripping devices and tools.

Gripping Devices as End Effectors Gripping devices are end effectors used to grasp and hold parts, raw materials, and tools. These devices include mechanical grippers, vacuum cups, magnetic grippers, and adhesive grippers. (Hooks, scoops, ladles, and inflatable bladders are also used as end effectors.)

Mechanical grippers use mechanical fingers to grasp objects. The fingers can either be detachable or an integral part of the gripper. Detachable fingers of various sizes and shapes can be attached to the same gripper (FIG. 35-4A Groover et al. 1986). Fingers can also be designed to grasp an object from outside as well as from inside. Mechanical linkages, cams, gears, and screws are used to actuate grippers (FIG. 35-4 C, D, E, and F Groover et al. 1986). Parts are held in grippers either by physical constriction of the part within the fingers as shown in FIG. 35-4B or by the friction between the fingers and the object. The friction force is equal to the product of the normal gripping force applied by the fingers on the object and the coefficient of friction between the fingers and the object. The friction force must at least be equal to the weight of the object. Allowance must be made for the force of acceleration, particularly if it is in the same direction as the force of gravity. A friction force two to three times the weight of the object is considered to be adequate.

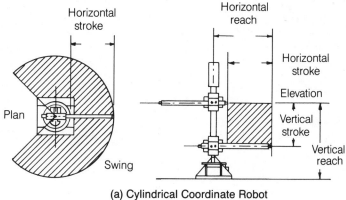

(a) Cylindrical Coordinate Robot

Fig. 35-3. Work envelopes for cylindrical, polar, and jointed-arm robots.

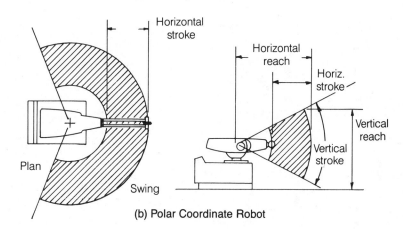

(b) Polar Coordinate Robot

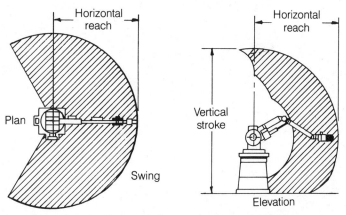

(c) Revolute or Jointed Coordinate Robot

Source: A.J. Critchlow, *Introduction to Robotics* (Macmillan Publishing Company, 1985) 12-13, 60-61.

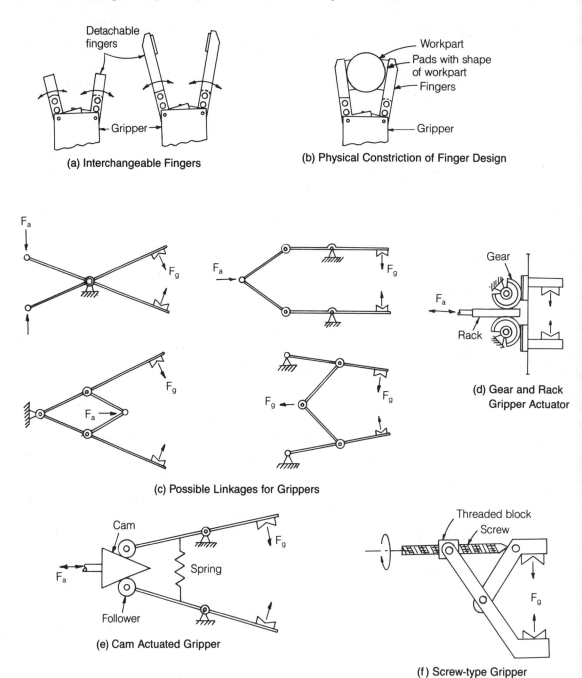

(a) Interchangeable Fingers

(b) Physical Constriction of Finger Design

(c) Possible Linkages for Grippers

(d) Gear and Rack Gripper Actuator

(e) Cam Actuated Gripper

(f) Screw-type Gripper

Source: Mikell Groover, *Automation, Production Systems, and Computer Integrated Manufacturing,* © 1987, pp. 305-307. Reprinted with permission of Prentice-Hall, Inc., Englewood Cliffs, NJ.

Fig. 35-4. Gripper mechanisms.

Vacuum cups, also called suction cups, can be used for handling objects with flat, smooth, and clean surfaces such as sheets of metal, glass, and plastic. Multiple cups are used for handling large objects. Vacuum cups are usually made of elastic materials such as rubber and soft plastic. Vacuum is created by pumps or venturi tubes. Venturi tubes require a reliable supply of shop air. The lift capacity of a vacuum cup can be determined by multiplying the area of the vacuum cup and the negative air pressure between the cup and the object. A safety factor of two is adequate. If the object is to be turned vertically during the handling then the coefficient of friction between the cup and the object must be considered. The object will slide unless the friction force is greater than the weight of the object.

Magnetic grippers are useful in handling ferrous materials in sheet form. These grippers have very fast pickup times, can accommodate variations in part size, and can handle metal parts with holes (not possible with vacuum grippers). Disadvantages of magnetic grippers include limited precision due to the possible side slippage, residual magnetism remaining in the workpiece, and the difficulty in picking one part at a time. Magnetic grippers can be made of electromagnets and permanent magnets. The magnetism in electromagnetic grippers can be easily turned off when a part is to be released at the end of the handling cycle. Electromagnetic grippers require a direct current power supply. Permanent magnets do not require a power supply but a stripping device is needed to separate the part from the magnet at the end of the handling cycle. Permanent magnet grippers are suitable for use in explosive environments.

Adhesive grippers are used for handling fabrics and other light weight material. The adhesive material is loaded in the form of a continuous ribbon into a feeding mechanism attached to the robot wrist.

Tools as End Effectors In many industrial applications, robots are required to manipulate tools rather than handle objects. If the work cycle requires only one tool, the tool can be attached to the wrist. For work cycles requiring multiple tools, a gripper is attached to the wrist. The gripper manipulates and exchanges tools during the cycle. The controller provides the signals to actuate the gripper. Tool changing can also be accomplished by using cradles and snap-in tools. The cradle retains the snap-in tool when the robot lowers the tool into the cradle and pulls its wrist away. The process is reversed to pick up tools from cradles. Some of the examples of tools used as end effectors include spray painting nozzles, spot welding electrodes, arc welding torches, heating torches, adhesive applicators, screwing devices, and rotating spindles for drilling and grinding.

ROBOT DRIVE SYSTEMS

The capability of a robot to perform a task is provided by the drive system used to power the robot. Power is applied at the joints either directly or through gears, chains, belts, and cables. Common drive systems used in robots are electrical, hydraulic, and pneumatic.

Electrical Drives

Electrical drive systems are used to power small to medium robots and are particularly suitable for precise work such as assembly. Electrical drive systems include stepper motors and DC servomotors.

Stepper Motors Stepper motors are used in small robots where torque requirement is low. Stepper motors are built to rotate through a specified number of steps in one revolution. Steps typically range from 1.8 to 30 degrees apart, depending upon the number of poles in the rotor and the stator. The rotor is made up of permanent magnets. When a drive current is applied to a selected set of stator windings, dissimilar poles on the stator and the rotor line up. Thus the motor holds its torque and position. When the polarity of the stator poles is reversed, the rotor is forced to step from one position to another. An incrementally rotating electric field on stator windings causes the rotor to rotate in a stepping fashion.

The rotational speed depends on how fast the magnetic field is incremented. Stepper motors are capable of providing precise motion without closed loop circuits. An excessive load on a stepper motor can cause a loss of steps. The precision of stepper motor drives can be further improved by using encoders and potentiometers for feedback control.

Stepper motors are cheaper than other drives and lend themselves to direct digital control. A limitation of stepper motors is that the available torque is inversely proportional to speed. Stepper motors are noisy and do not have a smooth drive.

DC Servomotors A dc motor is based on the principle that a current carrying wire experiences tangential force when placed in a stationary magnetic field. The stationary magnetic field is provided by field windings or permanent magnets mounted on a stator. The rotating rotor (armature) windings are connected to a commutator, which is a cylinder of insulated copper segments mounted on the rotor shaft. The armature windings receive current through brushes rubbing against the commutator. The commutator and brushes keep the current flowing in the correct direction to provide continuous one direction rotational torque.

DC motors allow precise control of the speed over a wide operating range by manipulation of the voltage applied to the motor. DC motors have smooth and continuous motion. There is no inherent control of position in a dc motor. Position control is accomplished by a control system called a servo loop. The servo loop receives speed and position feedback from sensors. The control system continuously monitors the position of the motor and compares it with the desired position. By using a feedback loop the controller can deliver to the motor dc voltage that is proportional to the observed error. When the error is reduced to zero the voltage goes to zero and the motor stops. The dc motor holds its torque when it comes to rest under power. The ability to hold axis positions between commands to change positions makes dc servomotors suitable for automation equipment such as numerical control (NC) machines and robots.

Hydraulic Drives

Hydraulic drives use hydraulic motors driven by high pressure oil to provide linear or rotary motion to a robot's axes. A hydraulic system consists of a hydraulic power supply, an electrohydraulic servovalve, a sump, and a hydraulic motor. The hydraulic power supply provides high pressure oil as the working fluid. It consists of a pump, a motor for driving the pump, and a filter. The electrohydraulic servovalve controls the flow of high pressure oil to the hydraulic motor. It is a component of the closed-loop servo system that provides control over the positions of axes. Open-loop drives go from point to point but cannot be controlled to stop at points in between. The sump or accumulator receives used oil from the hydraulic motor and makes it available to the hydraulic power supply. The hydraulic motor is driven by high pressure oil. It is either a hydraulic cylinder for linear motion or a rotary type motor for angular motion.

Hydraulic drives are faster and more powerful than electric drives. These drives provide smooth sliding motion and high acceleration. Hydraulic robots are suitable for handling heavy loads. They are almost exclusively used in explosive environments such as spray painting. Hydraulic systems are prone to oil leakage. The oil must be kept clean and protected against contamination.

Pneumatic Drives

The working fluid used in pneumatic drives is compressed air at approximately 90 psi which is piped through most factories. Both linear cylinders and rotary actuators are used to provide the motion required at the axes of a robot. Pneumatic robots usually operate at mechanically fixed end points for each axis. Programmable controllers are frequently used to control the timing and sequence of motions in a cycle. Cushions are used to slow the pneumatic cylinder at the end of its motion to prevent damage to the robot or parts being handled. Pneumatic drives are lighter, cleaner, and cheaper than hydraulic and electric drives. Pneumatic robots can be very practical if they can be made to work with high accuracy and repeatability. Pick and place, machine loading and unloading, and other simple operations with high cycle rates are the applications reserved for these robots.

ACCURACY AND REPEATABILITY

Accuracy and repeatability are two aspects of a robot's precision. *Accuracy* relates to how closely the robot can be taught to move to a target position. The accuracy of a robot depends upon its control resolution, and mechanical inaccuracies. In the absence of mechanical inaccuracies, the accuracy may be considered as one-half of the control resolution. Mechanical inaccuracies include backlash in gear mechanisms, in leadscrews and actuators, and the deflection in joints caused by arm extension and workload.

Repeatability is the ability of a robot to return, time after time, to the taught position. The robot does not always return to the taught position on subsequent repetitions of the motion cycle. Instead, it forms a cluster of points resembling a sphere around the taught point. The radius of the idealized sphere is often quoted as the repeatability by robot manufacturers. The repeatability improves with lower speed. For most purposes it is sensible to choose good repeatability over good accuracy if there is a trade-off. Small assembly robots have repeatability as low as ± 0.002 inches, whereas hydraulic robots used in automotive industry are rated at ± 0.050 inches. Major factors affecting the accuracy and repeatability of the robot include deflection due to gravity, deflection due to acceleration, backlash in gears and belt drives, and thermal effects.

Deflection Due to Gravity

The deflection caused by the force of gravity on robot arm members and the object being carried effects the accuracy of the robot if the robot is taught a point by defining the cartesian coordinates of the point. However, if a teach pendant is used for programming the robot, then the effect of deflec-

tion is compensated in the process. The downward deflection, D, of a robot arm caused by the weight of an object is given by

$$D = PL^3/3EI$$

where P is the weight of an object carried at the end of an arm of length L, E is the modulus of elasticity of the arm material, and I is the moment of inertia of the arm. It is difficult to determine analytically the overall deflection at the end effector because robots consist of several members and the effective horizontal distance changes continuously while the arm is in motion.

Deflection due to Acceleration

The radial force of angular acceleration causes deflection of the arm given by the equation,

$$D = maL^4/3EI$$

where m is the mass of the object and a is the angular acceleration. The deflection due to angular acceleration becomes significant if angular moves are carried in a sequence with quick starts and stops. Enough time should be allowed between moves to settle the whipping motion to zero.

Backlash in Gears and Belt Drives

Backlash is the slack in gears and belt drives that causes errors in positioning. Backlash can be compensated in two ways; first, by using very precise gearing or antibacklash gearing, and second, by compensating for backlash through control software. In this second method of backlash compensation, the controller sends additional pulses equivalent to the amount of backlash to the drive whenever the direction of motion is reversed. The amount of backlash has to be measured and entered into the control software.

Thermal Effects

The accuracy and repeatability specifications change when the temperature of the environment surrounding the robot changes. It is difficult to estimate the changes in overall accuracy and repeatability due to change in temperature without taking actual measurements. The change in length, ΔL, of an arm of length L is given by:

$$\Delta L = L\alpha\Delta T$$

where α is the coefficient of linear expansion per degree and ΔT is the change in temperature.

PARAMETERS USED IN ROBOT SELECTION

The selection process for choosing a robot starts with the recognition of a dominant robot characteristic needed for a particular task. For example, load carrying capacity is a dominant characteristic in material handling and loading applications; speed and precision are dominant features in assembly applications. The next step is to collect information on various robot models with the dominant characteristic. Then, one must evaluate the other essential characteristics to narrow down the number of candidate robots. At the end of this process only a few robots remain. Finally, an economic analysis is performed to make the final decision about the most appropriate robot.

Some of the important robot characteristics are

- Physical configuration
- Load carrying capacity
- Drive systems
- Speed
- Control systems
- Shape and size of work envelope
- Precision

A large number of physical configurations are available. Five basic types have already been mentioned (see FIG. 35-1). The selection of a particular physical configuration depends upon various factors such as the type of motions preferred in an application (straight line motions are desirable in assembly applications), degrees of freedom, and the type of programming language available.

The load carrying capacity of a robot depends upon its physical size and drive mechanism. The net load carrying capacity is determined by subtracting the weight of the end effector from the rated load capacity of a robot.

Electric and hydraulic drives are used on sophisticated robots. A pneumatic drive is used on small robots with limited motion sequence.

The work cycle time of an industrial robot depends upon the speed of movement. Different portions of the work cycle can be programmed at different speeds. Heavier objects should be moved at slower speeds to improve the precision with which the object must be located at the end of a given move.

A robot controller coordinates the combined movements of the joints and sequences the motions according to a program. Most robot controllers are microprocessor-based systems. They may be classified according to the level of sophistication: limited-sequence, point-to-point, and continuous-path. Limited-sequence control is used on simple pneumatic robots that are capable of a limited sequence of motions. The extent of motion on each joint is controlled by limit switches. Point-to-point control is more sophisticated than limited-sequence control. Here, the controller is programmed to learn and playback the individual positions of the robot arm. Continuous-path is the most sophisticated control. The path taken by the arm to reach a destination point is controlled and played back during the work cycle.

The shape and the size of the work envelope of a robot is important in work cell design and safety considerations. The coordinate system of a robot's structure and its size determine the size and shape of the work envelope.

Accuracy and repeatability determine the precision with which a robot locates an object at a desired position.

ROBOT SELECTION AND JUSTIFICATION

The feasibility study for a robot project involves operational, technical, and economic considerations. Operational and technical feasibility includes evaluation of all the requirements and limitations of the robot application as well as the technical capabilities of several potential robot candidates. As with any new equipment purchase, a robot represents a substantial initial investment in return for a future annual cost savings. All relevant economic factors must be included in the economic justification for the investment in a robot project. The following two case studies describe the robot selection and justification process.

A CASE STUDY IN SELECTION AND ECONOMIC JUSTIFICATION

Koren provides the following case study in robot selection and justification (1985), quoted verbatim. A high-volume automotive parts manufacturer decided to introduce robots into the plant. The plant was modern with different degrees of automation levels utilized to increase productivity. However, at the time of the study, robots were not operating in the plant. The objective of the study was to help the manufacturer to introduce the first robot into the plant. This included selecting the most suitable operation for the first robot and choosing a commercially available robot for this application.

Based upon preliminary discussions with the plant management personnel, several possible manufacturing operations for robotizing were suggested, and the following criteria were set:

- Sufficient volume, with production on a two-shift basis each day
- Ease of introduction to the plant from acceptance, maintenance, and engineering points of view
- Payback period must be less than two years based upon two-shift operation
- Selection of the robot must be based on its performance as well as on the availability of other models of robots from the same vendor (for the purpose of future standardization of robots in the plant)
- An adequate amount of space around the selected machine for the robot without major rearrangements
- Safety as a primary goal

The study included an initial walk through the plant to search for more possible operations to robotize, followed by a thorough survey. All together about a dozen operations were found to be good candidates for introducing the first robot into the plant, and many others that could be robotized in the far future. A project team inspected these operations and a workstation information sheet was filled out for each of them (FIG. 35-5; Koren 1985). Drawings of parts, fixtures, machine layouts, and a plant layout were obtained for all of these operations, and each application was discussed.

The operation found to be most suitable for the first robot installation was a machine-loading task, in which an operator picked up four parts at a time and loaded them onto the machine by a twist-and-press motion. The parts were brought in in a tub that was set next to the operator. During the year, the machine handled three types of parts. However, the shape and weight of these parts varied only slightly, with the weight of the heaviest part being about 1.1 pounds (0.5 kg).

The reasons for selecting this operation were

- Low occurrence of irregular parts
- All parts could be handled with one feeder and one gripper
- Volume of parts was high enough to keep operation going two shifts per day, year-round
- The payback period was found to be 1.2 years (see analysis at the end of this section)
- Projected productivity increase of 30 percent; the cost-benefit ratio associated with it was not included in the economic analysis, since the shorter machine time does not contribute at present to the productivity of the entire line. However, it does have future benefits

The next step was the selection of the robot for the loading operation. The initial criteria were a noncartesian coordinate robot with at least four controlled axes and payload between 11 and 50 pounds (5 to 23 kg). The minimum payload required was estimated as follows:

- Weight of the heaviest part is 1.1 pounds; a

WORK STATION INFORMATION SHEET

Client: _____   Plant: _____   Date: __/__/__

Operation: _____   Machine #: _____   Bay: _____

	ITEM				ITEM	
1	Number of different parts processed on machine			24	Can parts be loaded in same way as previous operation?	
2	Part name			25	Can parts be loaded in same way into next operation?	
3	Part number			26	Is operator judgement required?	
4	Part weight (range)			27	Is vision required?	
5	Part size (range)			28	What is line speed?	
6	Part material			29	What is line spacing?	
7	Part temperature			30	Are parts prints available (including tolerances)?	
8	Cycle time			31	Is work station layout available?	
9	Number of elements per cycle			32	Is fixture print (including tolerances available)?	
10	Load/unload time			33	What is ambient temperature range?	
11	Hourly production rate			34	Is environment dirty?	
12	What is the recorded efficiency?			35	Is environment corrosive?	
13	Number of shifts			36	Is environment dry/humid?	
14	Number of operators/shift			37	Is environment dangerous or unsuitable for human operator?	
15	Is the standard measured or negotiated?			38	Any sand, chip, liquid discharged in process?	
16	Are there any irregular operations?			39		
17	Are photographs of work stations available?			40		
18	Is operator using one or two hands?					
19	How is part presented (are drawings available)?					
20	How is part removed (are drawings available)?					
21	What is required tolerance for handling?					
22	What is handling height above floor?					
23	What is the required part orientation?					

USE THIS AREA FOR ADDITIONAL NOTES

_____

_____

_____

_____

Fig. 35-5. A work station information sheet used in plant survey.

potential simultaneous loading of four parts is required

• Estimated weight of a gripper with several sets of jaws is 6.5 pounds

In selecting the robot, a computerized robot data bank was used. The six robots listed in TABLE 35-1 were found as appropriate candidates. All four vendors in the table had a record of hundreds of robot installations and provided service and spare parts on short notice. The breakdown of the robot system prices in TABLE 35-1 is given in TABLE 35-2. The additional costs in TABLE 35-2 are $3500 for a riser (stand), and $9500 and $10,000 for engineering and riser.

The next point to be considered was the loading-cycle time. There are three possible methods of loading the parts:

- Loading the four parts simultaneously by a gripper with four sets of jaws; the maximum required loading-cycle time was 24 seconds. Only one programmed motion was required at the loading stage
- Loading two parts at a time by a double-jawed gripper; a pitch motion of the wrist was a necessity; the required cycle time was 12 seconds
- Loading one part by a simple gripper; the four parts were loaded by four separate programmed motions of the robot. The maximum cycle time of the robot was 6 seconds.

The price of the appropriate gripper depended on the loading method. The costs of grippers in TABLE 35-2 are given for a two-part gripper. Vendor C provided a one-part gripper for $3500, a two-part gripper for $5500, and a four-part gripper for $11,000. These numbers were used for comparison. Since the parts were supplied to the job site in a tub, the adding of a feeder to provide oriented parts was a necessity. The prices of the feeders also depended on the loading method as follows: one-path feeder, $33,000; two-path feeder, $38,000; and four-path feeder, $51,500. Therefore, the extra cost for installation of a two-part gripper and feeder was $7000, and for a four-part gripper and feeder was $26,000.

The programming capability and the cycle time of the six robots were checked, and the following conclusions were drawn:

- Robot 1 can load only four parts at a time because of its programming capability (limited-

Table 35-1. Suitable Robots for the Case Study

Model	Vendor	Drive	Axes	Payload, lb	Price, $
1	A	Pneumatic	4	20	35,500
2	B	Pneumatic	5	33	47,500
3	C	Hydraulic	5	50	48,000
4	C	Electric	6	22	82,000
5	B	Electric	6	13	75,500
6	D	Electric	6	14	75,500

Table 35-2. Breakdown of Robot System Cost (in Dollars)

Model	Robot Price	Sensor Cost	Two-part Gripper Cost	Additional Cost	Total Robot Cost
1	22,000	2000	8,000	3,500	35,500
2	32,000	2000	10,000	3,500	47,500
3	31,000	2000	5,500	9,500	48,000
4	65,000	2000	5,500	9,500	82,000
5	60,000	2000	10,000	3,500	75,500
6	56,000	2000	7,500	10,000	75,500

sequence type); this requires the most expensive gripper and feeder
- Robots 2 and 3 cannot operate in a cycle time of 6 seconds; therefore they can load simultaneously either two or four parts
- The electric-driven robots can operate in any loading method; note, however, that the price difference between robots in this group and the previous group (robots 2 and 3) is $30,000 on the average

Based on these considerations and the robot cost, the following conclusions were made. First, the application does not justify the use of electric-driven robots, which are much more expensive. This leaves the slower robots (1, 2, and 3) and dictates that parts must be loaded either in pairs or four at a time. Therefore, the price of the feeder and gripper is increased by $7000 (for pairs) or $26,000 (for quadruplet loading). This price difference, however, is still smaller than the incremental cost (approximately $30,000) paid for the electric robots.

Second, simultaneous loading of two rather than four parts is recommended, since it reduces the complexity and cost of both the feeder and the gripper.

Third, the cheapest robot, robot 1, is not recommended for this application. Its programming method requires the use of a four-part loading. However, the basic price difference between robot 1, and robots 2 and 3 (i.e., $12,000 or $12,500) is smaller than the cost difference between a four-part and a two-part feeder-gripper system ($19,000), meaning that if the cost of the whole system is considered, then the use of robot 1 rather than robots 2 or 3 is not justified.

Fourth, the two remaining robots, 2 and 3, have the required capabilities to perform the task, and their price is comparable. Robot 3 is more sophisticated than robot 2, and three of its five axes are fully programmable. Robot 3, however, is large in size, and because of space restrictions in the machine neighborhood, there is not enough room for it. Therefore robot 2 is the best choice for the application.

Table 35-3. Cost Analysis of Robot System in Case Study

Robot (basic price)	$32,000
Accessories:	
Gripper (for two parts)	10,000
Riser	3,500
Sensors	2,000
	$47,500
Feeder (2-path)	38,000
Installation and shipping	2,500
Total capital investment	$88,000

The next step was to conduct a cost analysis. The total cost of the robot system used in this study is shown in TABLE 35-3. Note that the price of the system is almost three times the basic price of the robot. In addition to this investment, there is an annual maintenance cost estimated at 10 percent of the cost of the robot and accessories: $4750.

The robot was to eliminate the cost of two operators paid $20.4 per hour (including fringe benefits). Based upon 16 hours per day and 240 days per year, the total annual savings are $78,336. The payback period (in years) is the total investment divided by the net annual savings (total annual savings less annual maintenance).

$$\text{Payback period} = \frac{88,000}{78,336 - 4750} = 1.2 \text{ years}$$

which is a typical number for a two-shift operation.

Besides studying the systematic approach to achieve the goals of this robotic project, you might notice the following:

- The basic price of the robot is $32,000, but the total installation price (excluding the feeder) is estimated as $50,000, namely 1.6 times higher. As a rule of thumb, multiply the basic price of the robot by 2 to obtain the total installation price in the plant.
- If the application requires a special gripper, the vendor should be asked to design and build the gripper. The vendor has more experience, and having the vendor design the gripper also means that responsibility would not be split.

- Based on two-shift operation the payback period for most robot installations is between one and two years.
- During the installation phase, safety measures must be studied and solved. Safety devices will add extra cost to the project, but safety must be a primary goal in each robot installation.

A CASE STUDY IN SETTING UP A WORK CELL

Sharon, Harstein, and Yantian provide the following case study, quoted verbatim (1987). It will be useful if we consider some of the problems that can occur and the decisions that have to be made during the setting up of a work cell. For our example we will take a work cell that involves the processing of two die-cast items produced together. The casting is placed into a press that separates and deflashes them prior to their subsequent machining.

Before we start to physically set up the manufacturing cell we must know what we want to achieve technically and what economic criteria have to be applied. The technical processes are as follows:

- Remove the items from the die-casting machine
- Separate the individual items from each other and deflash them
- Machine one face of the component flat
- Drill and tap two holes
- Inspect the items
- Place the finished items into a magazine ready for dispatch

Once we determine the technical needs of the product, our next stage is to quantify the economic criteria. To do this we ask:

- What is the maximum acceptable manufacturing cost?
- What are economic batch sizes?
- How quickly must the item be made in order to satisfy predicted or known demand?

Task Analysis

The time occupied by the item within the cell is known as the throughput time; the time spent in adding value to the item is known as the cycle time. In functional machine layouts there is a considerable difference between these two values; however, in work cells the difference is minor.

The cycle time is governed by the slowest operation within the cell. This does not necessarily mean the slowest machine. If for example a machine had a cycle time of 20 seconds, a product cycle time of ten seconds could be achieved merely by installing a second machine to run in parallel with the first.

Let us now consider the operation times for each activity within the diecasting cell:

- Casting, 60 seconds
- Separation, 2 seconds
- Machining face, 15 seconds
- Drilling and tapping, 20 seconds
- Inspection, 10 seconds

The robot servicing this cell has to perform all of the transfer operations within the cycle time of the die-casting machine. If it does not, then the die-casting machine will have to wait until the robot is free before the unloading can continue. This will result in underutilization of the machine. Some process problems may also arise because the machine is not functioning continuously.

We must also not forget that the other processes must be accommodated within the 60-second process time of the die-casting machine. We can work out the available time for robot transfer by taking the difference between the cycle time of the die-casting machine and the sum of the cycle times of the other processes. Using the times given above, the available time for robot transfers is therefore

$$60 - (2 + 15 + 20) = 23 \text{ seconds}$$

The inspection operation will be conducted using a vision system at the dispatch magazine. This means that the components only have to be placed in the inspection machine and that after processing they will be palletized by a device controlled entirely by that machine. The information on quality will be fed back to the other units of the cell, as and when adjustments are needed.

FIGURE 35-6 shows the desired physical arrangement of the cell and we must now select the robot that can service this arrangement. The robot's work envelope must be capable of enclosing all of the elements within the cell. The robot must also have the speed and repeatability such that the work is completed within the time allowance and that items are picked up, transferred, and placed with the desired precision. Let us assume that, for various reasons, the robot shown in FIG. 35-7 was selected as being suitable. The quoted velocities of the robot are:

- Slew, 120 degrees per second
- Horizontal extension of arm, 1.2 meters per second
- Vertical lift of arm, 0.5 meters per second

The arc of approximately 270 degrees (shown in FIG. 35-6) has to be covered twice in the available robot transfer time. This is because the robot has to reverse in order to return to its starting position. Since the various pick-and-place stations cannot usually be arranged to lie on a single arc, the robot must extend and contract its arm. It must also move vertically so that objects can be lifted or lowered. In terms of tasks, it must go to five separate places in the cell: the die-casting machine, the press, the mill, the drill, and the inspection/magazine station. The robot cycle includes four pickup operations: those at the die-casting machine, the press, the mill, and the drill; and four placement operations, one each at the press, the mill, the drill, and the inspection/magazine station. The robot cycle assuming it is ready to enter the die-casting platen with its gripper open is shown in TABLE 35-4.

In total there are 47 actions to the cycle with very few, if any, that can be performed simultaneously, because of the problems of collision with the

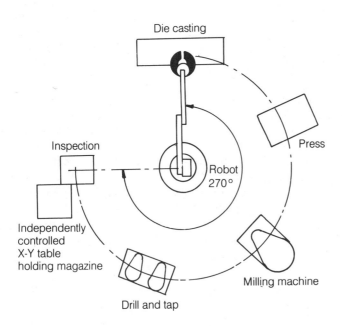

Fig. 35-6. The desired physical arrangement of the cell.

Source: D. Sharon, et al., *Robotics and Automated Manufacturing* (Pitman Publishing, 1987)
        151-154. Reprinted with permission.

Table 35-4. The Robot Cycle

1. Extend arm	25. Extend arm
2. Lower to grasp casting	26. Lower arm to pick up processed parts
3. Close gripper	27. Lift arm
4. Lift arm and casting from platen	28. Contract arm
5. Contract arm out of die-casting machine	29. Rotate to drilling and tapping machine
6. Rotate arm to press	30. Extend arm
7. Extend arm into press	31. Lower arm to place components into jig
8. Lower arm so that casting enters trimming tool	32. Release gripper
9. Open gripper	33. Lift arm
10. Lift arm	34. Contract arm
11. Contract arm out of press	35. Wait for drilling and tapping operation to finish
12. Wait for trim cycle to finish	36. Extend arm
13. Extend arm into press	37. Lower arm to pick up processed parts
14. Lower arm onto the two items	38. Activate gripper
15. Activate gripper	39. Lift arm
16. Lift arm and components out of die	40. Contract arm
17. Contract arm out of press	41. Rotate to inspection station
18. Rotate to milling machine	42. Extend arm
19. Extend arm into milling machine work space	43. Lower arm and components into jigs on inspection machine
20. Lower arm and components into jig	44. Release part
21. Release gripper	45. Lift arm
22. Lift arm	46. Retract arm
23. Contract arm	47. Rotate arm back to start position
24. Wait for milling cycle to finish	

different machines within the cell. We conclude that the robot will not be able to service the cell in the time available. If you consider some of the motions you will understand why this is so. The velocities quoted for the robot are maximum and since we do not know the robot's acceleration capacity, we cannot compute the actual arm velocities that would be realized. However, even if we assume that the stated velocities are valid for all of the motions, then the return motion of the arm will require 2.25 seconds and, assuming that all in/out motions are 0.8 meters, we have:

$$(16 \times 0.8)/1.2 = 10.7 \text{ seconds}$$

We also have sixteen up/down motions of 0.25 meters that equal:

$$(16 \times 0.25)/0.5 = 8.0 \text{ seconds}$$

and eight gripper operations of say a quarter of a second each, giving a time of two seconds. Finally, we have the four intermachine angular motions,

which if they are equal come to 67.5 degrees each. Therefore the minimum traverse time is:

$$(4 \times 67.5)/120 = 2.25 \text{ seconds}$$

The total time by the above computations is 25.2 seconds or almost ten percent over that allowed.

So what can we do? One approach would be to have a double-armed robot with an angle of 135 degrees between the arms; this would mean that the output of two cycles of the die-casting machine would be in the process at the same time. In practice this would mean picking up components from the die-casting machine and the mill and transferring them to the press and the drill; after these operations are complete, the double-armed robot would move them from the press and the drill to the mill and inspection. The cycle then starts from the beginning again.

In every manufacturing cell it is of prime importance that the jigs into which the components are placed are designed such that any minor placement errors are automatically corrected. If both the jig

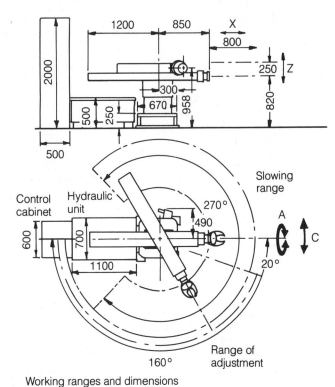

Fig. 35-7. The robot selected for the cell.

Working ranges and dimensions
(in millimetres)

Source: D. Sharon, et al., *Robotics and Automated Manufacturing* (Pitman Publishing, 1987)
        151-154. Reprinted with permission.

and component are designed with this in mind, then there should be few problems. Other considerations are for the jigs and machines to be cleaned every cycle such that swarf and other debris do not contaminate either the component or the jigs and so cause setting errors that could scrap the components.

REFERENCES

Critchlow, A. J. *Introduction to Robotics*. Macmillan Publishing Company, 1985, 60-61.

Groover, M. P. *Automation, Production System, and Computer Integrated Manufacturing*. Prentice-Hall, Inc., 1987, 305-307.

Groover, M. P., M. Weiss, R. Nagel, and N. G. Odrey. *Industrial Robots*. New York: McGraw-Hill Book Company, 1986, 118-124.

Koren, Y. *Robotics for Engineers*. New York: McGraw-Hill Book Company, 1985, 276-281.

Sharon, D., J. Harstein, and G. Yantian. *Robotics and Automated Manufacturing*. Pitman Publishing, 1987, 151-154.

36

Industrial Robot Applications:
Planning, Implementation, and Programming

Jacob Rubinovitz[*]

BY DEFINITION, INDUSTRIAL ROBOTS ARE THE ULTI-mate flexible manufacturing devices. The Robot Institute of America (RIA) defines an industrial robot as ''a reprogrammable multifunctional manipulator designed to move material, parts, tools, or other specialized devices through variable programmed motions for the performance of a variety of tasks.'' However, when we take a closer look at the reality of robot implementations in industry a different picture emerges. Most robots are employed in a single, repetitive task, such as spot-welding, painting along an automotive assembly line, or loading and unloading parts into manufacturing equipment. Robotic assembly lines are typically set up for an assembly of a specific product, manufactured in large quantities in a mass-production type of environment.

There are serious limitations to the flexibility of currently available industrial robots and their ability to perform a variety of tasks. Representative of these limitations is the limited implementation of robots in arc-welding operations. The arc welding application itself can benefit considerably from the use of robots. The work environment is hostile and potentially dangerous to human workers. Both the welders and people working around the welding area are exposed to a variety of hazards such as toxic fumes, eye damage, electrical shock, and burns. High positioning accuracy and consistent welding speeds are required for production of quality welds. These requirements demand a high degree of skill and effort from a human operator. A robot can perform the welding task with high repetitive accuracy, and remove the human operator from the unhealthy environment.

However, in spite of being the ''Dangerous, Dirty, Difficult, and Dull'' type of task for which robots were meant, introduction of robots into arc-welding has been relatively slow. The main reason for this situation is not technological, but economi-

*Jacob Rubinovitz has recently joined the Faculty of Industrial Engineering and Management of the Technion-Israel Institute of Technology, as a Senior Lecturer. His research interests are in the areas of Manufacturing Planning and Control, CAD/CAM integration, and automated manufacturing. Dr. Rubinovitz received his Ph.D. in Industrial Engineering from The Pennsylvania State University. He also holds a B.Sc. in Industrial Engineering and Management, and a M.Sc. in Industrial Engineering, both from The Technion-Israel Institute of Technology.

cal. The major portion of arc-welded products is manufactured in small and medium batch sizes, for which the expensive setup related to the need of special fixtures and robot reprogramming cannot be justified.

In this chapter, we will first analyze the limiting factors to robot flexibility, as well as the technologies which allow flexibility within a variety of tasks confined to a specific application area. Knowledge of the limiting factors, along with the technologies and solutions which enable flexibility, is essential for realistic and successful planning of a robotic application. Then, we will review robot programming, which is the key to the promised robot flexibility. Finally, some recent research and development results of a task-level programming system for robotic arc-welding will be presented, as a representative example of the trends and efforts to increase robot flexibility through advanced programming systems.

LIMITING FACTORS TO ROBOT FLEXIBILITY

In general, industrial robot flexibility is limited to factors related to the robot's physical configuration, and the physical attributes of accessory devices the robot needs to complete its task.

The first such limiting factor is the basic kinematic configuration of the arm of an industrial robot. The vast majority of commercially available robots have one of the following five basic configurations:

- Cartesian coordinates (rectangular) configuration
- Cylindrical configuration
- Polar coordinates (spherical) configuration
- Jointed-arm (articulated) configuration
- SCARA (Selective Compliance Assembly Robot Arm)

Each configuration has advantages and disadvantages that limit the scope and variety of applications fit for it. In machine loading and unloading applications, the ability of the robot to reach into narrow and deep openings without interference with the sides of the opening is important. The cylindrical configuration has a natural geometric advantage for such an application, while a jointed-arm robot would be completely inadequate for such a task. On the other hand, the jointed-arm configuration has the dexterity needed to reach above and around obstacles in a welding or painting task, an ability which is not available with the other configurations.

The SCARA configuration is specifically designed for vertical insertion and assembly tasks. It has a stiff and rigid structure in the vertical direction, which allows it to exert a high force during insertion, and bear higher payloads. It also can use passive compliance in the horizontal plane, which makes assembly with tight tolerances possible. A large cartesian coordinates gantry-type robot has the high rigidity required for carrying heavy loads, but may be unfit for other applications. In general, the payload that a given robot will be able to carry will be affected by its basic configuration much more than by its drive systems.

The extent and shape of the robot work space is determined by its basic configuration, physical dimensions of the links, and the limits on motion around each of its joints. Most industrial robots are bolted to the floor in one predetermined location, although mobility can be increased in some applications by mounting the robot on a track or an overhead gantry. With this limited mobility of most industrial robots, the application and layout is planned around the robot work space. If a cylindrical robot is selected to load parts into machines in a flexible manufacturing cell, the machines would be configured around the robot, within its work envelope. The flexibility of the robot would be limited within the machine-tending application, to load a variety of parts into the machines in the cell.

Another major factor limiting the scope of applications in a given industrial robot is the control system of the robot. The two main types of control used in industrial robots are point-to-point (PTP) control, and continuous path (CP) control.

Point-to-point controllers lack the computational ability to perform trajectory interpolation, such that the path and velocity of motion of the robot end effector tool center point can be controlled. These PTP controllers, which are typically cheaper, can control the robot to reach a desired sequence of discrete points, and perform operations at these points, but do not control the path taken by the robot to get from one point to the next, nor the velocity along that path. Robots with point-to-point control are limited to applications such as machine loading and unloading, palletizing, and spot welding. In programming the robot, care must be taken to avoid collisions since the path between any two programmed points cannot be easily predicted by the operator.

Continuous-path controlled robots are required for applications such as spray-painting, grinding, deburring, or arc-welding, in which both the path and velocity of the tool must be closely controlled. Robotic assembly may also require continuous path control to successfully complete insertion operations. However, in carefully planned assembly applications, where only vertical insertion is used and compliant devices are employed, point-to-point control would suffice.

The limitations of a given robot configuration, work space, and control system are the main factors to consider when selecting an industrial robot for a specific type of application. Industrial robots are not really the general-purpose machines capable of being used for almost any task, as the inexperienced user may be misled to believe from their definition. In planning a robotic application, the scope of such application has to be carefully defined. Only then is it possible to proceed to a selection of a robot with configuration, work space, control system, and all the other technical specifications such as payload, power system, speed and accuracy, most fit and cost-effective for the application extent.

Even within a carefully defined application area robot flexibility is limited by the capabilities of its end-effector, the variety of tools that can be mounted on its wrist, and the need for feeders and fixtures as accessory devices helping the robot to locate parts.

Robot end-effectors are either grippers designed to allow the robot to pick up objects, or specialized tools designed to perform a certain process such as spot-welding, arc-welding, or deburring. Specialized tools and grippers can represent more than 10 percent of the robot cost, and their flexibility is low. In a manufacturing process that requires a specific tool and additional auxiliary equipment, such as in arc-welding or spot-welding, the robot will be typically limited to the single process defined by its tool. In certain other processes, such as deburring, grinding, or other metal removal operations, a common interface for tool-mounting can be designed, and a tool-changing rack with multiple tools can be used to increase the flexibility of the robotic application.

Gripper flexibility is also limited due to conflicting requirements for gripper design resulting from various part sizes and geometry, part material and surface, or temperature of the parts to be manipulated. If parts of different shapes and characteristics have to be handled in a manufacturing cell by a single robot, or assembled in a robotic assembly cell, a single gripper of simple design would not provide the flexibility required. A change-over system, similar to a tool-changing rack, can be used to replace the entire gripper, or select different gripper fingers. Such systems are expensive, but they may be adequate for machine loading and unloading operations in which the robot can change tools during an otherwise idle time, while waiting for a machine to complete its manufacturing cycle.

However, in assembly tasks, such tool-changing activity will cause a major increase in the cycle time required for assembly by the robot. This problem could be resolved by a design of a universal gripper, and research and development work in this area is still ongoing. One research direction is patterned after the human hand, which has the required versatility. The mechanical and control complexity of such device resulted in most designs (such as the Stanford/JPL hand or the HITACHI Ltd. hand) being limited to three fingers. Another approach of passive adaptation to the form of the object grasped uses a conventional gripper in which elastic fingers can conform to the shape of the object, either by pneumatic pressure or by fixing packed granular powder around the part using magnetic forces or vacuum. The main problem with both designs is the difficulty to control the exact position and orientation of the grasped part.

Sensory capabilities of most industrial robots are relatively limited. Research in computer-vision is still far from practical solutions to problems such as picking an item from a bin of unordered parts. Technologies for seam-tracking, such as may be needed for robotic arc-welding, are available but expensive. As a result, most robotic applications have to rely on consistent placing and location of the work-pieces within the robot work space. Part feeders can be used to deliver parts to the robot in a known position and orientation. Fixtures have to be designed to consistently locate parts, so that a robotic job can be repeated without reprogramming and without expensive sensory devices. Both feeders and fixtures limit the flexibility of the robotic installation. Most feeders are designed to handle, deliver, and orient a single part, or a limited range of geometrically similar parts. Vibratory bowl-feeders are more versatile, and are capable of handling a larger variety of parts by mechanical changes and adjustments of the sorting and orienting tooling at the end of the bowl track. However, the specific tooling is expensive, and requires considerable setup time for adjustment and change, limiting the flexibility to change over from one part to another for small production lots.

Recently, special programmable bowl-feeders have appeared, increasing the flexibility of feeding. One type, developed by Westinghouse, allows automatic adjustment of tooling under computer control, in order to accommodate different parts. Another, even more flexible programmable feeder, developed by Programmable Orienting Systems, Inc. (POSI), uses a matrix of photosensors coupled through a fiberoptics cable to a computer controller. The controller software is programmed to recognize whether a part in the required orientation is present at the end of the bowl-feeder track, and reject any other parts back to the bowl by activating a stream of compressed air.

Fixtures present yet another roadblock to achievement of flexibility in robotic applications. Due to the stringent requirement for consistent and accurate part positioning in robotic applications, fix-

tures for applications such as robotic welding are much more expensive than fixtures for manual welding, which only need to hold the part in place. In addition, in certain applications, multiple fixtures or pallet fixtures are required, so that the robot may work continuously, while parts are loaded into a fixture in another station.

In some instances, a policy using an appropriate part type mix and a single fixture for each part type is possible, thus reducing the setup cost related to tooling, and increasing the probability that smaller lot sizes would be acceptable and cost-effective in the robotic application. One such analysis of the savings in robotic arc-welding was performed by Knott, Bidanda, and Pennebaker (1988). The analysis used a single fixture policy and an appropriate part type mix, such that one part type is welded by the robot, while another part type is loaded into a fixture at the loading station. The analysis showed that due to the savings in tooling costs, the probability of the acceptance of a candidate job for robotic welding increased by a factor between 1.6 and 2.0, when based upon ROI criteria.

The limits to flexibility of robots within a certain application group, which are posed by the physical limitations of grippers, tooling, feeding devices, and fixtures, can be reduced by technological solutions and developments. However, the real promise for increased robot flexibility depends on better sensory capabilities for robots, coupled with more powerful and "intelligent" programming systems. Such systems would allow relaxation of some of the stringent positioning and orientation requirements, which make feeders and expensive fixtures a necessity in robotic applications.

ROBOT PROGRAMMING SYSTEMS

Most robots used in industry today are programmed by an on-line programming method. This method is known as teaching by showing or guiding. The robot is moved through a sequence of desired positions, either by moving the end-effector manually or by the use of a teach pendant. The joint coordinates corresponding to each position are recorded by the robot controller. The main advantage of this method is ease of use. Programming may be performed relatively easily by shop floor workers, and does not require special computer programming skills. This programming method is sufficient for a wide variety of repetitive tasks for long production runs, and when modifications to the preprogrammed sequence are not required. However, there are severe limitations to on-line programming, when applied to more advanced, flexible manufacturing (mostly in low and medium batch production).

The main disadvantage of on-line programming is the limited ability to use sensory inputs as a guide for different program alternatives. When using most on-line teach-and-repeat programming methods, one cannot program sensory inputs and conditional branching, which is based on these inputs. In the most advanced on-line programming systems, such as the teach-pendant programming unit for the second generation of ASEA Industrial Robots, limited conditional branching based on sensory inputs is allowed (ASEA 1984). Such advanced on-line programming capabilities are only starting to appear in commercial systems, and are in fact a combination of the teaching-by-guiding method and a full robot-level programming language.

Another disadvantage of on-line programming is that it has to be performed using the actual robot, an expense of time which could be otherwise used for actual production. Since in many robotic applications the robot is only a part of a larger manufacturing cell, on-line programming actually wastes the useful production time of several production resources. In addition, on-line generated programs can seldom be moved from the robot on which they were programmed to another robot, even if it is of the same type. These limitations increase the need for off-line robot programming systems. Such systems may offer additional advantages in programming tasks where computation rather than teaching is more effective (such as palletizing), and can benefit from integration of information about the task environment from a CAD system.

Two main levels may be distinguished between the existing off-line programming methods: robot-level programming and task-level programming (Lozano-Perez and Brooks 1984). Robot-level programming combines three elements:

- The capability of a general-purpose computer programming language
- The ability to use sensors
- The capability of specifying robot motions in terms of either world or tool-center-point (TCP) coordinates

The key advantage of robot-level programming is the ability to use input from external sensors, such as force or vision, to modify the robot motion. This allows for implementation of an adaptive, or actively compliant system. However, robot-level programming systems are much more difficult to program than on-line teach-by-guiding systems, and require considerable expertise in computer programming and in the design of sensor-based motion strategies.

Task-level programming systems attempt to simplify the robot off-line programming process by a user interface through which only a specification of the robot task goals and the relationships of objects in the robot environment is required. Such task-level specification is completely robot-independent. It is not necessary to specify paths or positions that depend on robot geometry or kinematics. The task-level system uses a task planning module, which converts a user specification of a task into a robot-level program. Complete geometric models of the robot and its task environment are required as input for the task planner. Task-level robot programming systems, while carrying the promise of robot-independence and ease of programming, are still an area of research and development. Several basic issues must be resolved if such systems are to become a shop-floor reality. These would include interface standardization with the surrounding manufacturing equipment and geometric CAD modelers, finding efficient algorithms for robot collision-free path planning, and designing a proper human-robot interface for ease-of-use of such a system.

Robot-Level Off-Line Programming Systems

The need for an off-line programming language for industrial robots, motivated by the need for sensor-based control, was first realized in 1960 and 1961, with the development of Mechanical Hand Interpreter (MHI) at MIT by H. A. Ernst. The first textual robotic language was limited to specification of movement and grasping commands, and sensor-based branching (Critchlow 1985). The first general-purpose robot programming system was WAVE, developed at Stanford University (Paul 1977). The input to WAVE is a description of end-effector positions in Cartesian coordinates. The system coordinates joint motions for controlled velocities and accelerations through the end-effector trajectory, and integrates multiple sensors, including a vision system, to provide programmed compliance. The algorithms used by WAVE for robot control are computationally intensive, and have to run off-line to generate the robot program.

These pioneering research efforts led the way to development of multiple robot programming languages, either by university researchers or industrial robot manufacturers. At present, about 200 different robot programming languages exist, most of them robot specific (Rembold and Dillmann 1985). Several survey articles review and evaluate some of these languages and discuss current trends (Bonner and Shin 1982, Gruver et al. 1983, Soroka 1983, Ranky 1984).

Several attributes may be defined to classify and evaluate this large number of robot programming languages. The first such attribute is the type of programming language used. Two mainstreams of robot programming systems development are: systems based on existing data processing languages, and systems based on existing numerical control languages.

Systems based on existing data processing languages include: PAL (developed by Richard Paul), RAIL (developed by AUTOMATIX), HELP (developed by General Electric), JARS (developed by NASA Jet Propulsion Lab)—all based on PASCAL; VAL (developed by UNIMATION) and MAL (developed at the Milan Polytechnic for Olivetti Sigma robots)—both based on a BASIC-like syntax; and RPL (developed by SRI International), which is a structured programming language using a FORTRAN-like syntax with LISP-like features. AML, a well structured interactive language and control system for robots developed by IBM, may also be classified in this group, as it combines qualities of APL, Pascal and LISP with special constructs, which add flexibility and power in development of robot applications.

Robot programming systems that are based on numerical control languages include: RAPT or Robot APT, developed at the University of Edinburgh as a programming language for assembly purposes; ROBEX or ROBoter EXapt, developed at the Laboratory of Machine Tools and Production Engineering in Aachen and based on the EXAPT NC programming system; and MCL or Machine Control Language developed by McDonnell Douglas Corporation under the ICAM program and based on the APT NC language. The NC-based programming languages aim to control different robots by using different post-processors for specific robots, using the approach of CLDATA file interpretation.

The current robot programming languages scene clearly resembles the Tower of Babel. Most of the languages are tailored to support a single manufacturer's robot, and each has its own way of handling sensory input and robot programming functions. Portability of software from one robot to another is virtually nonexistent. This situation can be partly attributed to the continuously and rapidly developing technologies of robot controllers, microcomputers, and smart sensor devices. It is difficult to establish standards when a fast developing technology is constantly changing the capabilities and possible architecture of a robotic system.

Most of the algorithms for robot control that were handled off-line by languages such as WAVE, are accomplished in today's advanced robotic systems in real time, by firmware embedded in a few special-purpose microprocessor chips in the robot controller. It seems that the robot related technology is mature enough for definition of system architecture and establishment of language and interface standards. One pioneering effort in this direction has been initiated by a working group of the German Engineering Association VDI, which has suggested a standard for robot-level programming interface called IRDATA, which is based on the CLDATA standard interface for controlling NC-machines.

Task-Level Off-Line Programming Systems

Considerable research work has been done on different aspects of task-level programming (Lozano-Perez and Brooks 1984, D'Souza et al. 1983, Pickett et al. 1984, Sjolund and Donath 1983, Rembold and Dillmann 1985). Although more research and development is needed before complete and general task-level systems will become an industrial reality, the work that has been done so far provides guidelines for the required architecture and the main elements of such systems.

RoboTeach, an off-line robot programming system developed by General Motors Research laboratories and based on GMSolid solid modeling package (Pickett et al. 1984), is built around a world modeling subsystem, which contains the geometric representation of robots, robot tools, workpieces, and other objects in the robot work-cell environment. This world model is designed to support subsystems for: robot workcell layout design, program generation and editing, program simulation, and program translation and downloading. Research still continues on the main elements of this task-level off-line programming system: program generation and editing, program simulation, and program translation and downloading. Some of the issues that need to be resolved are:

- The degree to which the task specification and program generation system is dependent on any given application domain
- Method of selecting geometric or textual programming for specifying robot task
- The degree to which the program generation and editing functions incorporate simulation
- Methods for interference checking in the simulation subsystem

- The selection of standards for the program translation and downloading subsystem

An architecture for a task-level off-line robot programming system that is similar to that of RoboTeach is proposed for ATLAS, the Automatic Task Level Assembly Synthesizer (Lozano-Perez and Brooks 1984). ATLAS is an architecture for a task-level system, which integrates previous research in the area of task planning, and provides a framework for future research. It has not been implemented yet in a working system. ATLAS includes the following three main elements:

- The world model, which contains all the information on objects in the task environment, and on the kinematic structure of the robot; this information defines the constraints on the motions to be planned by the task-planner
- The task model, which describes the sequence of states or operations necessary to complete the task
- The task planner, which converts the user specification contained in the task model, within the constraints described by the world model, into a robot-level program to carry out the task. The task-planner itself contains several modules, which deal with planning subproblems such as: gross motion planning, fine motion planning, and grasping

Another task-oriented robot programming system is being developed for an autonomous robot at the University of Karlsruhe (Rembold and Dillmann 1985). The suggested structure for this system consists of eight basic parts. These are a CAD module, a world model, a planning module, an interactive programming and teach-in module, a robotic language compiler (SRL), an interpreter, a monitor, and a simulator.

An analysis of all the suggested structures for task-level robot programming systems reveals three major common elements: the task level user interface, the task planner, and the robot interface. The task-level user interface enables the user to create a world-model and describe the task, using either an interactive CAD system or a textual language. The world-model is a geometric model of the workpiece, the robot, and the work environment (tools, fixtures, etc.). The user specifies the required robot task using this world model.

The task planner element of the system converts the user specification of a task into a robot-level program. It may use local and global planning and optimization algorithms to convert the task specification, within the constraints of the world-model, into a detailed sequence of robot motion commands. The robot interface element of the system creates the link between the robot-level program and the robot controller.

Although there is yet no evidence of practical implementation of a complete task-level system on the shop-floor or in a research lab, considerable research and development work has been done on each of the three major elements of such a system. The following sections include a detailed discussion of each of these elements, and a review of the related research.

Task-Level User Interface Task-level user interface is the set of tools or the language by which the task is specified. The task specification is goal-oriented—it specifies what should be done to accomplish the task at hand. It should be independent of the specific robot that accomplishes the task, and need not consider paths or positions which are dependent on the robot geometry and kinematic constraints.

The design of such a task-level language must answer several questions, outlined in the following paragraphs. First, would the task specification be independent of the application or would it be limited to a well-defined application domain? Research work on task-level, application independent, robot programming systems have not yet culminated in a working system (Lozano-Perez and Brooks 1984). Partial automatic robot programming systems for well-defined task domains are much easier to achieve (Latombe 1983, Bourez et al. 1983).

Second, what should be the level of task specification? Task specification for the application domain of arc-welding could be anything between a higher-level task description command, for example:

WELD SPIDER_WEB_ASSEMBLY

and a lower-level command sequence, for example:

MOVE TO A1 ON WELD_A
WELD WELD_A BACKHAND SPEED 20
MOVE TO B1 ON WELD_B
etc...

Decisions concerning the level of task specification are in fact decisions partitioning the task knowledge between the system user and the system. If the system has more task-related knowledge and "intelligence" (a larger database of facts and rules), the programmer needs less skill and can specify more easily complex and detailed tasks, working with higher-level task-description commands. In the Automatic Programming System for a Spray Robot, developed for the Citroen-Meudon FMS, the task specification consists of the part geometry described in a wire-frame model in a CAD system (Bourez et al. 1983). The detailed path planning of the robot, including collision detection, is performed manually by the robot programmer. The schemes suggested for the ATLAS programming system (Lozano-Perez and Brooks 1984) and the task-oriented programming system being developed at the University of Karlsruhe (Rembold and Dillmann 1985) include expert modules that achieve highly automatic robot programming from the task-level specification.

Third, what form will be used for the task specification? A manufacturing task can be specified in many forms: process plans, machine routes, process and part drawings, or even by presenting as an example a sample part or a part model. In the same way, task specification for a robot may be done by a textual language, by a model based on a CAD system, or by some special-purpose data structure.

When deciding what form to use for task specification, the criteria should be effectiveness and ease of use. Based on these criteria, the selection of specification form need not be the same for different tasks. When specifying an assembly task, textual language might be the most effective form for specification, as in the following example using AUTOPASS (Koren 1985):

```
PLACE BRACKET IN FIXTURE SUCH THAT
    BRACKET.BASE CONTACTS FIXTURE.TOP
PLACE INTERLOCK ON BRACKET SUCH THAT
    INTERLOCK.BASE CONTACTS BRACKET.TOP
    AND INTERLOCK.HOLE IS ALIGNED WITH
    BRACKET.HOLE
```

However, such a textual specification will not necessarily be the most effective way of specifying an arc-welding task. A form of "show and tell" in which the task programmer indicates the weld seams on a CAD model of the part and is prompted to supply the required welding parameters would be a more efficient and easy to use form in order to specify an arc-welding task. Most weld seams are part of the geometry that was already defined when the welded item was designed using the CAD system. The user needs only to indicate these seams and their starting and ending points on the CAD system monitor, and then define the required welding parameters.

This approach to task-level specification, directly using a CAD system geometric model, was used for automatic programming of a robot used for spray-washing at Citroen-Meudon FMS (Bourez et al. 1983), and in an experimental robot task-planning system developed at the University of Minnesota (Sjolund and Donath 1983). Yet another approach, representing task sequences by a network data structure, was used in the GM Robo-Teach project, using the network data structure provided by GMSolid (Pickett et al. 1984).

The Task Planner and Task Planning Algorithms   The task planner provides the link in a task-level robot programming system between the task description and the manipulator level program. The degree of difficulty related to this translation from the task level to the manipulator level depends on the level of the task specification and the degree of independence from the specific task domains. However, even for a limited and well-defined task domain this translation poses a very difficult problem, involving geometric and strategic ramifications. As a result, the research trend in this area has been to solve subproblems of the task-planning problem—subproblems that relate to well-defined task domains.

One set of subproblems deals with path finding, grasping, and part mating. Path finding methods and algorithms will be reviewed in detail here, since this problem applies to several robotic task domains, and its solution is needed for task-level programming of assembly robots, material handling robots, autonomous vehicles, and welding robots. Grasping and part mating problems are mainly related to the task domains of robotic assembly and material handling and will not be reviewed here.

Another set of task-planning problems deals with the global task plan and its optimization. This set of problems is closely related to a specific task domain for which a solution is sought, since the problem formulation and required solution differ for different task domains. Some of the work in this area, which can be related to this research work of task-planning for arc-welding, will also be reviewed.

Path Finding   The path finding problem can be stated as follows: "Given an object with an initial position, a goal position, and a set of obstacles located in space, the problem is to find a continuous path for the object from the initial position to the goal position, which avoids collision with obstacles" (Latombe 1983).

One class of algorithms used to solve this problem belongs to the "generate and test" paradigm (Lozano-Perez and Wesley 1979). These algorithms operate by iterating three general steps until a solution is found:

- Hypothesize a simple candidate path from initial position to goal position
- Test the candidate path for potential collisions
- If collisions are detected, modify the path, and repeat until no collisions are detected

Testing for possible collisions involves use of algorithms for computing collision among solids. The techniques used for such collision testing include two-dimensional projections (Boyse 1979), decomposition of volumes into cells (Ahuja et al. 1980), parallelepipedic and spherical approximations (Powell 1982), and set membership classification based on constructive solid geometry representation (Tilove 1980).

Another approach for solving the find-path problem avoids the computational complexity associated with the collision testing algorithms by explicitly representing the collision-free space (Udupa 1977, Lozano-Perez and Wesley 1979, Brooks 1982). This method is known as the *configuration space method*. The method, first reported by S. M. Udupa, consists of shrinking the moving object to a point while expanding the obstacles based on the shape and orientation of the moving object. These grown obstacles define forbidden regions, and the space outside these regions constitutes collision-free space.

To find a path in the collision free space, a visibility graph is constructed. This is an undirected graph VG(N,L) which is defined by the node set N = V U {S,G}, where V is the set of all vertices of the grown obstacles and S and G are the start and goal points of the planned path, and by a link set L which is the set of all links (n_i, n_j) which can connect the N nodes by a straight line that does not overlap any obstacle (FIG. 36-1). The shortest collision-free path from S to G can be found by search of the shortest path in this visibility graph. The algorithms based on the configuration space approach are computationally intensive, both in the configuration space mapping calculation and in the shortest path search stages.

Computational acceleration strategies based on bounding all workspace and manipulator polyhedra by either spheres or cylinders have been suggested by W. E. Red (Red 1984). Another method to reduce the computational complexity of the shortest path search in the visibility graph is through the use of heuristics. In particular, the *A** algorithm developed by Hart, Nilsson, and Raphael (1968) has been used for path determination by several authors (Davis and Camacho 1984, Lozano-Perez and Wesley 1979). The *A** algorithm allows the use of heuristic information in the form of cost esti-

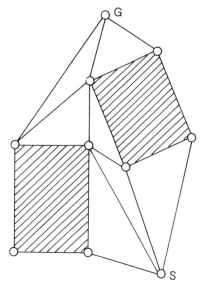

Fig. 36-1. Visibility graph.

mates of the cost to travel from each node to the goal. Initially, the start node is placed on a list of candidate nodes for examination (the OPEN list). At each step, the node with minimum total path cost estimate is moved onto a CLOSE list, and its minimum cost estimate visible successor nodes are placed on the OPEN list. Hart et al. have shown that the algorithm finds an optimum path when the cost estimate is a lower bound estimate of the true cost of travel to the goal node. The effectiveness of the algorithm increases and the number of trial paths is reduced when good estimates of the travel cost are available.

An approximation scheme for the shortest path finding problem in three dimensions which is fully polynomial (as opposed to the exact solution for which the fastest known algorithm is doubly exponential) has been suggested by C. H. Papadimitriou (1985). This approach allows the user to control how far the achieved solution would be from the optimum. The algorithm is still computationally intensive: about 10^{10} steps are required to find solutions to a scene with 50 lines and three decimal places of precision that are at most 10 percent of the optimum. Nevertheless, the author argues that since the algorithm lends itself easily to parallel processing, its practicality will increase with advances in parallel processing.

Global Task Planning and Optimization The methods and problem formulation for global planning and optimization of a robotic task are dependent on the specific task domain. In most of the work related to task-level programming systems, it is either assumed that the global task plan is defined by the user as part of the task specification, or a global task-planning module is included in the system architecture, but no details are given about how such a module works.

Lozano-Perez and Brooks, in their proposed architecture for the automatic task level assembly synthesizer (ATLAS) assume that the input description of the task completely specifies the sequence of assembly (Lozano-Perez and Brooks 1984). The task-oriented programming system being developed at the University of Karlsruhe will include a global planning module for planning the assembly sequence. However, details on how this module will work are not given in the research reported to date (Rembold and Dillmann 1985). The architecture suggested for an adaptive flexible robotic welding system for the U.S. Space Shuttle main engine includes a weld path programming station and acknowledges the need for highly automated procedures for generation of path programs for multipass weldments, but details of such procedures are not given (Martin and Ruokangas 1985).

A task-level off-line programming system for robotic arc-welding was developed recently in the Robotics Welding Lab at the Pennsylvania State University (Rubinovitz and Wysk 1988a). This system includes a global task-planning module that employs algorithms aimed to minimize the nonproductive time during travel between welds while selecting a welding sequence that minimizes thermal distortions in the welded area. The path planned for torch travel between the weld seams must not collide with the work environment. The task planning algorithms use a model of the robot motion capabilities to assign optimal motion velocities to different travel segments, and to estimate time of motion. The final welding sequence is planned using a Traveling Salesman Algorithm (TSA).

A method for optimizing bin picking and insertion plans for assembly robots was developed by Drezner and Nof (1984). The assembly plan problem is divided into the bin assignment problem and the pick-insert sequencing problem. The bin assignment problem is formulated and solved as a Minimax assignment problem, and the pick-insert sequencing problem is formulated and solved as a traveling salesman problem.

CAD-based Programming and Robotic Cell Design

Robot simulation, robotic cell design, and off-line robot programming using computer graphics and specialized CAD systems represent powerful tools for planning robotic applications. Simulation models that accurately represent proposed robotic cells in a visual and animated model are valuable tools for evaluating design alternatives, verifying feasibility, designing work-cell layout, verifying robot programs, and evaluating cell performance. Some of these systems allow off-line programming of the robot by leading it in the model environment rather than in an on-line teaching mode.

Some of these systems have been developed at university and research institutions laboratories. These include IGRIP, SAMMIE, and GRASP developed at the University of Nottingham; STAR developed at the University of Wisconsin; and ROBOCELL from the Centre for Flexible Manufacturing Research and Development of McMaster University. Commercial systems include ADJUST, developed at McDonnell Douglas Automation Company; ROBOCAM developed by SILMA Inc.; ROBOT-SIM of GE-Calma; ROBCAD from Tecnomatix, Inc.; ROBOGRAPHIX from ComputerVision; and a robot simulation module which is part of the CATIA system of Dassault Systemes. FIGURE 36-2A, B, and C shows a model and simulation of a robotic cell for electronic assembly developed using the ROBCAD system, and a photograph of the actual cell based on this design.

The Robotic Welding Lab of the Pennsylvania State University took a combined approach to CAD-

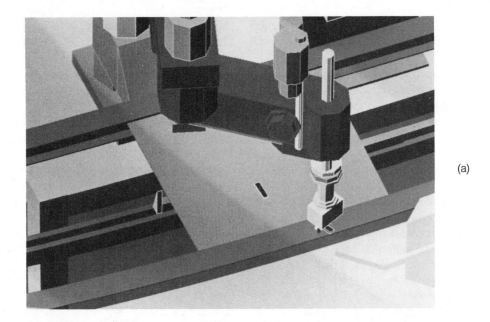

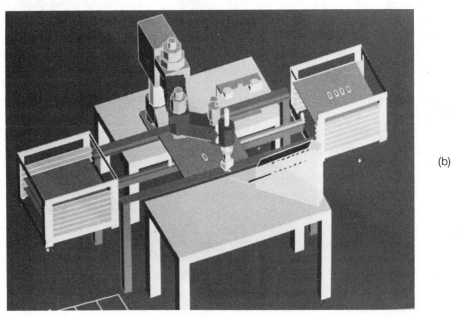

Fig. 36-2. Model (a) and simulation (b) of a robotic cell for electronic assembly. (courtesy of Technomatix, Inc.).

based programming and cell design (Rubinovitz and Wysk 1988a,b). In this system, the commercial robot simulation module of the CATIA CAD system served as the user interface for task description

and modeling to a task-level robot programming system. This system goes a step beyond existing simulation systems in automatically generating an optimized robot-level program from the task

(c)

Fig. 36-2c. The actual implementation of a robotic cell for electronic assembly. (Courtesy of Technomatix, Inc.).

description created in the CAD system. FIGURE 36-3a and b shows the model of the arc-welding cell and a welding task created using the CATIA robotic module for the task-planning system. The illustration also shows a photograph of the actual welding cell and task. This programming system for robotic arc-welding will be presented in the next section, as an example of the trends and efforts to increase robot flexibility through advanced programming systems.

TASK-LEVEL PROGRAMMING SYSTEM FOR ROBOTIC ARC-WELDING

Task planning for robotic welding consists of two major planning functions:

- Planning the sequence for welding the different weld seams, and planning the welding torch path

of travel between the seam ends. The main objective of this function is to minimize the non-productive (not arc-welding) time during travel between welds, while selecting a welding sequence that minimizes thermal distortions in the welded area. The path planned for torch travel between the weld seams must not collide with the work environment.

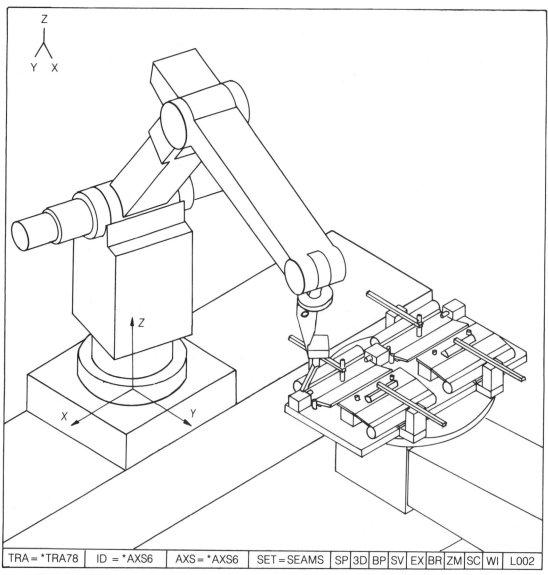

| TRA = *TRA78 | ID = *AXS6 | AXS = *AXS6 | SET = SEAMS | SP | 3D | BP | SV | EX | BR | ZM | SC | WI | L002 |

Fig. 36-3a. Solid model visualization of the ASEA IRB/L6 robot during task simulation.

Fig. 36-3b. The actual welding cell.

- Planning the motion along the welds. This function includes specification of welding parameters such as welding gun orientation, travel speed, wire feeding speed, current, and voltage. It also deals with the correct tracing of the weld seam, and taking corrective actions for problems of fit and gap variations in the weldments. The main objective is to maintain good and consistent weld quality.

I will describe in some detail here a system concerned with the first function, which is that of global task planning and optimization. This is a complex planning problem since the sequence of weld in the assembly must be established so that both the weld distortion and the cycle time are minimized and the operation is collision free.

The second function, which deals with specification and control of local weld parameters, is typically accomplished by a welding expert. Such weld parameters as current, voltage, and welding speed are specified by the weld designer, and are controlled during execution by adaptive control techniques. Novel research and development work to provide expert systems as an aid for design of weld-parameters has been conducted by Tonkay and Knott (1987). Joint tracking and adaptive control of welding parameters is also an active area of research and development, with prototype systems being used for actual shop-floor operation (Richardson 1986, Agapakis et al. 1986). Integration of such work with the global task planning system will result in a complete automated system for robotic arc-welding planning, programming, and control.

The global welding task-planning and optimization system includes three main subtasks:

- Mapping the robot capabilities; this is needed both to select the optimum motion conditions, and to estimate times for motion; motion time estimates along each suggested travel-path segment are required to evaluate different travel alternatives

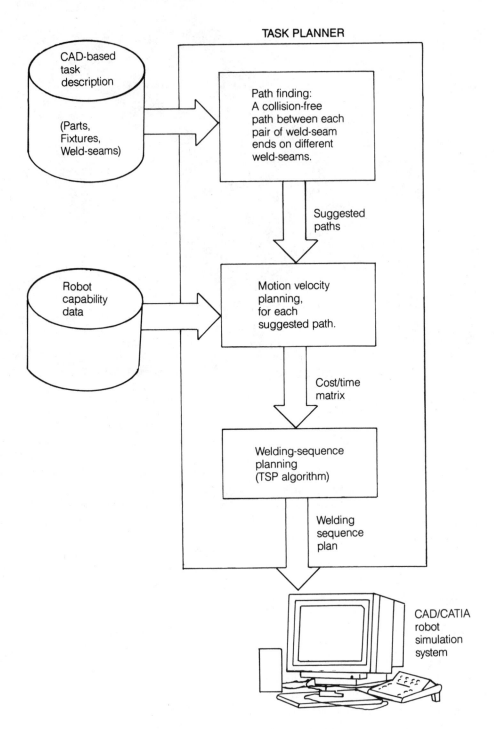

Fig. 36-4. Structure of the task planner.

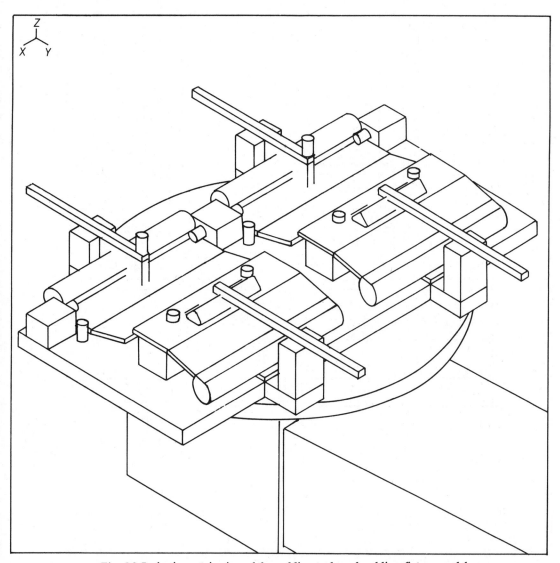

Fig. 36-5. An isometric view of the welding task and welding fixture model.

- Generating collision-free paths between each pair of weld seams, and calculating the total time required for motion along each such candidate path
- Finding the shortest time travel sequence between the weld seams, based on the data and travel alternatives provided by the first two steps

The structure of the task-planning and optimization system is shown in FIG. 36-4.

The input to the path planning system is a task level specification of the welding activity, in the form of the geometry of the required weld seams, and the geometry of the part and related tooling and fixtures. The welding task is specified by using an existing part geometry, as defined in a CAD system. Since the path planner helps in automatic generation of a robot level program from a task level specification, it helps to reduce the setup involved in manual programming of a robot. The path-plan-

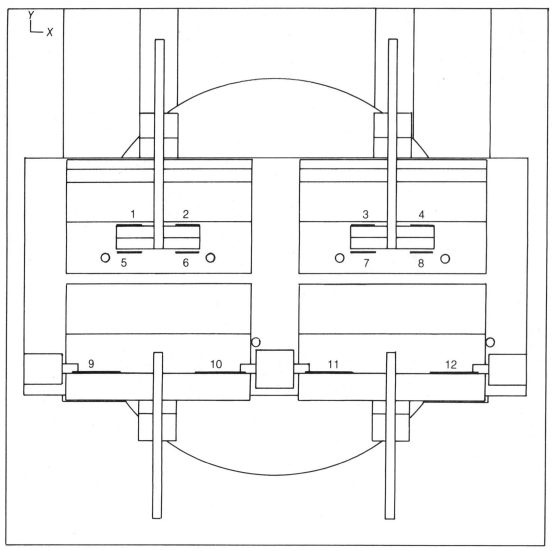

Fig. 36-6. Top view of the sample welding task. The weld seams are labeled 1 to 12, and drawn as thick black lines.

ning algorithms also increase the productivity of the arc-welding process by increasing the arc time/non-arc time ratio. Thus, the system can help in the justification of robotic arc-welding for both low and high batch production. A sample welding task, as defined in the CAD system, is shown in FIG. 36-5 and 36-6.

The Task Planner

The task planner module creates the link between the task level robot program specification and the complete robot level welding program. To accomplish this end, the task planner module must solve two related problems. First, in which order should the welding of the different weld seams be performed? This problem is the welding sequence problem. The main objective of weld sequence planning is to minimize the robot tool-center-point travel time between the weld seams, and hence maximize the arc-on time and the welding productivity. An additional objective while solving the welding sequence problem is to reduce thermal distortions in the welded product by allowing the area in which welding was completed to cool down before further welding in close vicinity.

The second problem to be solved asks the question, what path should the welding torch follow in going from the end of one weld seam to the beginning of the next weld seam? This problem is the path-finding problem. The planned path should avoid collisions between the robot tool-center-point, the part itself, and the part fixtures.

The solutions to the path-finding problem and the welding sequence problem are part of the task-planner algorithm, which is composed of three major steps:

- For each pair of weld seams, find a collision-free path between the weld seam ends
- Plan the required travel velocity for each path, and estimate the travel time along each path, taking into account the shape of the path, the travel velocity, and acceleration and deceleration along the path
- Using the travel time estimates, solve the welding-sequence problem. This problem is formulated and solved as a modified Traveling Salesmen Problem. The solution defines the complete path for the welding task.

The methods and algorithms employed in each of the three major steps of task planning are described in the following sections.

Planning Collision-Free Paths Between Weld Seam Ends

The first problem that the task planner has to solve is the planning of a collision-free path between

an end of one weld seam and the start of next weld seam, for all the possible paths of travel between the weld seams defined in the welding task. The solution of this problem provides data about distances between each and every pair of weld seam ends to the third step of the task-planner, which solves the welding sequence problem. The notion of distance between the weld seam ends can be used to represent different measures, such as actual Euclidean distance, travel time, and cost.

The problem of finding the shortest path between two points in an environment with three-dimensional obstacles is a difficult combinatorial problem. Different solution methods for this problem have been proposed (Latombe 1983, Lozano-Perez and Wesley 1979, Red 1984, Davis and Camacho 1984). Some of these methods reduce the computational complexity of the search for solution by using heuristics. This approach was adopted for the welding task path planning.

In order to supply the necessary data for the welding sequence planning step, the path-finding problem has to be solved for each and every pair of weld-ends not on the same weld seam. The problem can be represented by a nondirected network.

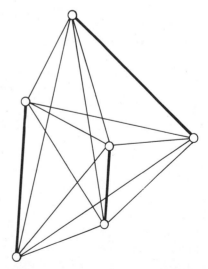

Fig. 36-7. Nondirected network for a welding sequence problem with three weld seams.

A nondirected network for a problem with three weld seams is shown in FIG. 36-7.

There are $2n$ nodes in such a network. Nodes that belong to the same weld seam are connected by a single arc, represented in FIG. 36-7 by a heavy line. There is also an arc from each node to any one of the other nodes in the network that are not on the same weld seam. The distances between the nodes on different seams are not predetermined by the weld seam geometry. These distances must be determined by solving the path finding problem.

For n weld seams, there are $2(n^2 - n)$ arcs between different weld seams, in addition to the n arcs representing the weld seams. The path finding problem has to be solved $2(n^2 - n)$ times, for each of these arcs.

In a task planning problem with 30 different weld seams, 1740 possible arcs must be examined. It should be noted that in practice, most welded parts have less than 30 different weld seams. Even for smaller problems, efficient algorithms are needed to make the path-finding solution computationally feasible.

In order to resolve this problem, it was subdivided into two major portions:

- Classification of the travel arcs into two groups:
  ○ Arcs along which travel in a straight line without colliding with objects in the environment is possible
  ○ Arcs for which path-finding around obstacles is needed, as they will cause collisions if traversed in a straight line
- Solution of the path-finding problem for each of the arcs in the second group

The first step is accomplished using an efficient collision detection procedure based on a three dimensional clipping algorithm developed by Cyrus and Beck (1978). The procedure reduces the size of the path-finding problem that must be solved in the second step. However, it can be quite a large problem even if relatively few obstacles exist, as demonstrated by the example in FIG. 36-8 through 36-10. This example consists of an environment with five objects and 14 welding seams, which are marked in the figures by heavy lines. The collision detection procedure executed for this environment identified 68 arcs along which travel in a straight line without collisions is possible, and 296 colliding arcs for which path-finding is required.

Efficient algorithms are thus needed to solve the path-finding step for each one of the colliding arcs. Such efficiency is achieved by using a heuristic that exploits knowledge of the welding-task domain and of the capabilities of the welding robot.

The first step of the solution method reduces the three-dimensional problem into a two-dimensional problem, by creating a plane of motion for the robot tool-center-point, and planning the path of travel in this plane. This plane contains the two weld seam end points between which the travel path is planned. The primary plane of motion selected and created between two weld seam ends is parallel to the Z-axis. This heuristic is motivated by two assumptions:

1. The weld design has to allow access to the weld seams from above the part. As a result, motion in a plane parallel to the Z-axis is not likely to encounter additional obstacles during retraction and approach.
2. By withdrawing the welding gun in the Z-direction, it will be possible to reach a collision-free plane above the part, in which straight line motion above all the obstacles is possible. The resulting path of motion around the obstacles will be composed of only three straight line segments: withdrawal to the collision-free plane, travel in a straight line, and approach to the target point.

The path-planning algorithm plans the path around obstacles using the following steps:

1. Generate a plane of motion which passes through the pair of weld-seam ends for which the path is planned, and is parallel to the Z-axis.
2. Intersect this plane with all polyhedral volumes in the task environment for which collisions with a straight line between the two weld-seam ends were detected.

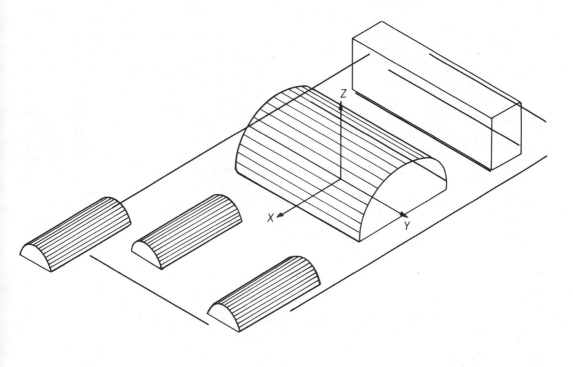

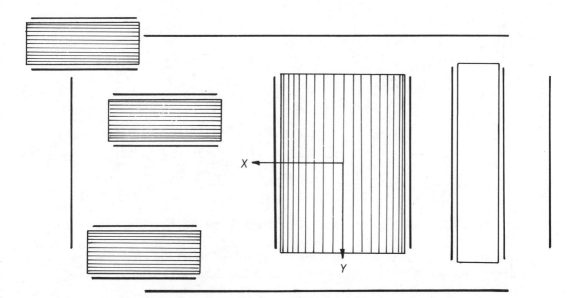

Fig. 36-8. Sample welding task with five objects and 14 weld seams.

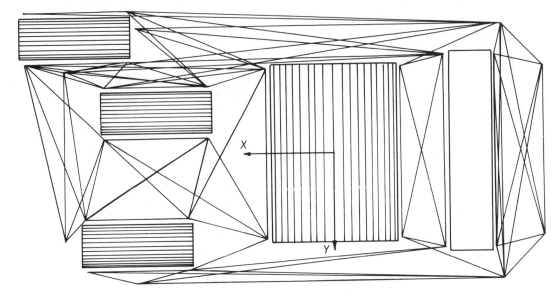

Fig. 36-9. All the collision-free arcs in a sample welding.

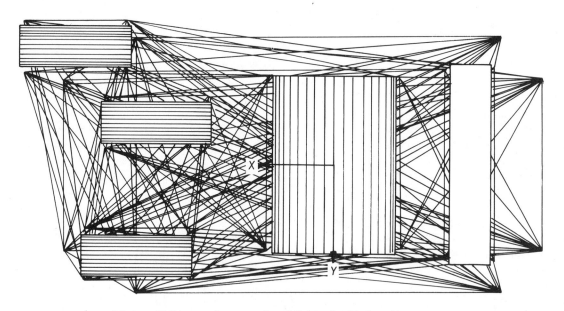

Fig. 36-10. All the colliding arcs in a sample welding task with five objects and 14 weld seams.

3. Use the set of polygon vertices resulting from the intersection to compute a three-segment path passing above all the volumes.
4. Estimate the time of travel along this path, based on robot capability data.

Planning Travel Velocity and Estimating Time of Travel

The Path Planner aims to minimize the time of travel between weld seams, which is nonproductive time. In order to establish the welding sequence which minimizes the time of travel between weld seams, estimates of the travel time along each of the possible travel paths are needed.

Four elements contribute to the time of travel along a suggested path:

1. The time needed to accelerate from zero velocity at the end of a weld seam to the programmed travel velocity along the path
2. The time of travel along the path at the constant programmed travel velocity
3. The time needed to decelerate from the constant travel velocity along the path to zero velocity at the beginning of a new weld seam
4. The time delay caused when traveling at a reduced velocity through via points around obstacles. A *via point* is a point near which the robot tool-center-point must pass in order to avoid collisions, without stopping.

In order to estimate the time of travel for each one of the four time elements above, the programmed travel velocity of the robot when traveling between weld seams has to be established. During the travel between weld seams, the travel velocity is restricted only by the dynamic capability of the robot, and it is desirable to traverse this distance as fast as possible. However, at high velocities deviations may occur from the straight-line motion trajectory due to controller errors and the high inertial and centripetal forces acting at the robot arm. It is undesirable to program the robot to move at velocities which cause a large deviation from the controlled straight line trajectory. Study of the performance limits of the robot is thus needed in order to establish the highest feasible velocity for motion between the weld seams. Programming the robot to move at such velocity during task planning will result in a minimum travel time along any given segment.

The need to establish the abilities and limitations of robots as part of job and skills analysis for effective utilization of industrial robots has been indicated by Nof et al. (1980). Performance measurement to establish robot time and motion

(RTM) data has also been reported (Nof and Lechtman 1982). The RTM work, however, does not investigate the limits of robot capability.

To develop a complete mapping of robot capabilities for off-line task planning, time and motion data were collected to establish the performance capabilities of the ASEA IRB/L6 welding robot. This welding robot served as the test environment for the task planning system developed. The time and motion study results were analyzed to create a model for travel velocity planning and time estimation. A table of trajectory errors at maximum attainable velocities for specific travel segments was developed and used for task planning.

Solving the Weld Sequence Problem

The welding sequence problem can be formulated as a modified traveling salesman problem. The symmetric traveling salesman problem is: "Given an n by n symmetric matrix of distances between n cities, find a minumum-length tour that visits each city exactly once" (Lin and Kernighan 1973).

In the welding sequence problem there are n weld seams, all of which must be completed by the robot torch. We may look upon the $2n$ weld seams ending points as $2n$ cities in the traveling salesman problem. The welding sequence problem can now be stated as follows: Given n weld seams and a $2n$ by $2n$ matrix of distances between the $2n$ weld seam end, find a minimum-length tour that visits each of the n weld seams exactly once, entering a weld seam through one end and leaving through the other. The planning of these visits is basically a traveling salesman problem, with the additional constraint that the weld seam arcs must all be included in the solution tour. The notion of distance between the weld seam ends can be used to represent different measures, such as actual Euclidean distance, travel time, and cost. In this research, the objective is to minimize the nonproductive travel time between the weld seams, thus increasing the welding-arc on to welding-arc off time ratio. Hence the travel time estimates for the travel along each possible travel-arc are used in the distance-matrix to find the minimum-time tour.

The solution of large traveling salesman problems using efficient and effective heuristic methods have been treated extensively in the literature (Lin and Kernighan 1973, Anderson et al. 1982, Crowder and Padberg 1980). Some of these procedures can provide solutions within two to three percent of optimality (Golden et al. 1980). Based on this observation, a heuristic based on the nearest neighbor tour construction procedure generates several tours which describe a welding sequence. The shortest of these tours is selected and compared to a lower bound of the solution for the traveling salesman problem. Such a lower bound can be derived from the minimum spanning tree of the TSP problem graph (Christofides 1975). If considerable improvement to the initial solution can be expected, additional iterations are performed, using a branch and bound type of algorithm.

The Robot Interface

The outcome of the task-planning module must be a complete robot-level welding program. This complete program should contain an exact specification of all the data needed for execution of the welding task, as follows:

- A complete description of the geometry of the robot tool-center-point trajectory along the weld paths and between the welds
- Information on the orientation of the welding torch at each segment of travel
- Information on the velocity of torch travel when welding and when traveling between welds
- Welding parameters for the welded seams, such as welding current and voltage, wire feed rate, and weld start and end conditions.

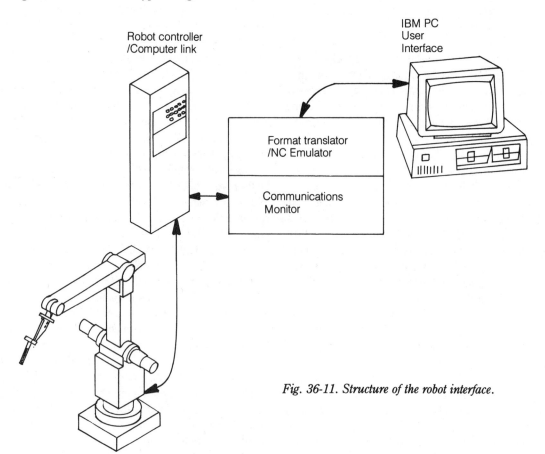

Fig. 36-11. Structure of the robot interface.

The purpose of the robot interface is to transfer this robot-level program to a specific robot controller for execution. Such a robot interface was developed and implemented for the ASEA IRB/L6 welding robot controller.

The first issue to be resolved when designing the robot-level interface is the format and language of the robot-level program. Many different languages are currently used for robot-level programming (Soroka 1983), Rembold and Dillmann 1985). No single language or format can be identified as an accepted standard. Existence of such an accepted standard could facilitate the development of a common interface to the controllers of different robots.

The robot interface developed for the ASEA IRB/L6 S2 controller can accept the robot-level program generated by the task-planning module in two different formats. The first format is a CATIA robotic task file. A file in this format can be created directly by the CATIA task simulation function. The second format is a standard NC file in word-address format, based on EIA standard RS-273-A. A file in this format can be created directly from different CAD systems by using the numerical control capabilities of these systems and a post-processing program. Translators that post-process both formats to the internal format of the ASEA IRB/L6 S2 controller are used.

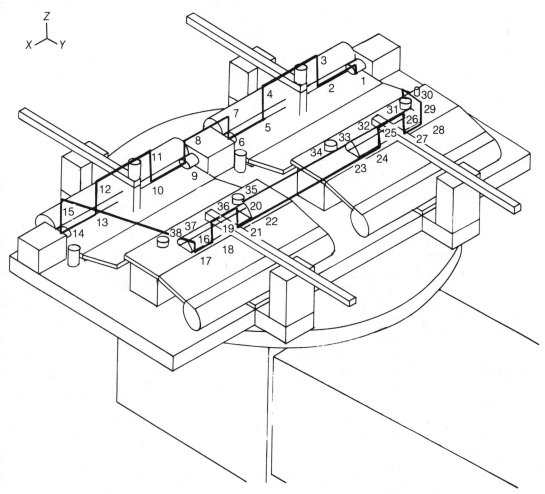

Fig. 36-12. Planned path for a welding task.

```
N1G01X0Y0Z0F100M20
N2G01X1000Y0Z0F500M21
N3G01X0Y0Z832F400
N4G01X1616Y0Z0F700
N5G01X0Y0Z-832F400M20
N6G01X1000Y0Z0F500M21
N7G01X0Y0Z576F300
N8G01X1296Y0Z0F600
N9G01X0Y0Z-576F300M20
N10G01X1000Y0Z0F500M21
N11G01X0Y0Z832F400
N12G01X1616Y0Z0F700
N13G01X0Y0Z-832F400M20
N14G01X1000Y0Z0F500M21
N15G01X0Y0Z896F400
N16G01X-944Y3024Z0F1100
N17G01X0Y0Z-256F200M20
N18G01X-500Y0Z0F300M21
N19G01X0Y0Z512F300
N20G01X-728Y0Z0F400
N21G01X0Y0Z-512F300M20
N22G01X-500Y0Z0F300M21
N23G01X-3184Y0Z0F1100M20
N24G01X-500Y0Z0F300M21
N25G01X0Y0Z512F300
N26G01X-728Y0Z0F400
N27G01X0Y0Z-512F300M20
N28G01X-500Y0Z0F300M21
N29G01X0Y0Z552F300
N30G01X0Y-560Z0F300
N31G01X0Y0Z-552F300M20
N32G01X500Y0Z0F300M21
N33G01X728Y0Z0F400M20
N34G01X500Y0Z0F300M21
N35G01X3184Y0Z0F1100M20
N36G01X500Y0Z0F300M21
N37G01X728Y0Z0F400M20
N38G01X500Y0Z0F300M21
```

Fig. 36-13. The NC file generated by the task planning system for a welding task.

The robot-interface consists of three main elements:

- A communication monitor resident in a personal computer
- ASEA computer link option
- Translators from the two robot-level program formats to the internal ASEA robot controller format

FIGURE 36-11 depicts the structure of the robot interface. A robot-level program which was generated by the system for a sample part is shown in FIG. 36-12 and FIG. 36-13, as represented in the CATIA CAD system where it can be used for task verification and simulation, and in the NC word-address format.

SUMMARY

This chapter started by questioning the myth of robot flexibility, which has its roots in the definition of industrial robots. We have reviewed the physical limitations to flexibility of robots, and concluded that flexibility may be possible within a specific application group, provided that better sensory systems and programming systems are available and technological solutions are used to increase flexibility of grippers, feeders, and robotic fixtures.

A comprehensive review of robot programming systems was presented, starting with the on-line programming systems prevalent in industrial applications, and ending with off-line, CAD-based systems, which can help in design of the robotic cell, selection of robots best fit for the task, and can increase both the productivity and flexibility of robotic programming.

Finally, an advanced CAD-based off-line programming system for robotic arc-welding was presented, to demonstrate the difficulty related to realization of such systems, along with the promise they carry for increased productivity of robot applications.

REFERENCES

Agapakis, J. E., J. M. Katz, M. Koifman, G. N. Epstein, J. M. Friedman, D. O. Eyring, and H. J. Rutishauser. (1986). "Joint Tracking and Adaptive Robotic Welding Using Vision Sensing of the Weld Joint Geometry." *Welding Journal* 65: 11 (November 1986).

Ahuja, R. T. Chien and N. Bridwell. (1980). "Interference Detection and Collision Avoidance among Three Dimensional Objects." Paper presented at First AAAI Conference, Stanford, August 1980.

Anderson, D. R., D. J. Sweeney, and T. A. Williams. (1982) *An Introduction to Management Science* 3rd edition. St. Paul, Minnesota: West Publishing Company, 1982.

ASEA Robotics. "Programming Manual - IRB 6/2,IRB 60/2,IRB 90S/2." Publication no. CK 09-1401E, ASEA Robotics, June 1984.

Bonner, Susan, and Kang G. Shin. (1982). "A Comparative Study of Robot Languages." *Computer* 15: 12 (December 1982): 82-96.

Bourez, Marc, Francoise Legre, Michel Parent, Jean-Guy Queromes, and Alex Renault. (1983). "Automatic Programming of a Spray Robot." In *AUTOFACT Europe Conference Proceedings*, 2/126-2/134, September 1983.

Boyse, J. W. (1979). "Interference Detection among Solids and Surfaces." *Comm. ACM* 22: 1 (January 1979), 3-9.

Boyse, J. W. and J. E. Gilchrist. (1982). "GMSolid: Interactive Modeling for Design and Analysis of Solids." *IEEE Computer Graphics and Applications* 2: 2 (March 1982), 27-40.

Brooks, Rodney A. (1982). "Symbolic Error Analysis and Robot Planning." *The International Journal of Robotics Research.* 1: 4 (Winter 1982): 29-68.

Brown, C. M. (1982). "PADL-2: A Technical Summary." *IEEE Computer Graphics and Applications* 2: 2 (March 1982): 69-84.

Burgam, Patrick M. (1984). "Programmable Robots Accelerate Arc Welding Automation." *Manufacturing Engineering* (December 1984): 64-65.

CATIA User Manual. (1986). Program Number: 5668-760, IBM Corporation and Dassault Systemes, July 1986.

Christofides, Nicos. (1970). "The Shortest Hamiltonian Chain of a Graph." *Journal of SIAM (Appl. Math.)* 19: 689.

————. (1975). *Graph Theory, an Algorithmic Approach.* Academic Press, 1975.

Conigliaro, Laura. (1981). "Robotics Presentation, Institutional Investors Conference: May 28, 1981." *Bache Robotics Newsletter 81-249.* Bache Halsey Stuart Shields, Inc., New York, October 28, 1981.

Critchlow, Arthur J. (1985). *Introduction to Robotics.* Macmillan Publishing Company, 1985.

Crowder, H. and M. W. Padberg. (1980). "Solving Large-Scale Symmetric Travelling Salesman Problems to Optimality." *Management Science* 26 (1980): 495-509.

Cyrus, Mike and Jay Beck. (1978). "Generalized Two- and Three-Dimensional Clipping." *Computer and Graphics* 3: 23-28.

D'Souza, Chris, Detlef Zuhlke, and Ch. Blume. (1983). "Aspects to Achieve Standardized Programming Interfaces for Industrial Robots." In *Proceedings of the 13th International Symposium on Industrial Robots*, 7/110-7/121. Chicago, Illinois, April 1983.

Davis, R. H. and M. Camacho. (1984). ''The Application of Logic Programming to the Generation of Paths for Robots.'' *Robotica* 2 (1984): 93-103.

de Pennington, Alan, M. Susan Bloor, and Mazin Balila. (1983). ''Geometric Modeling: A Contribution Towards Intelligent Robots.'' In *Proceedings of the 13th International Symposium on Industrial Robots*, 7/35-7/54. Chicago, Illinois, April 1983.

Derby, S. J. (1982). ''Computer Graphics Robot Simulation Programs: A Comparison.'' In *ASME Robotics and Advanced Applications Conf. Proc.*, 203-212. Winter Annual Meeting, November 1982.

Dillmann, Ruediger. (1983). ''A Graphical Emulation System for Robot Design and Program Testing.'' In *Proceedings of the 13th International Symposium on Industrial Robots*, 7/1-7/15. Chicago, Illinois, April 1983.

Drezner, Zvi and Shimon Y. Nof. (1984). ''On Optimizing Bin Picking and Insertion Plans for Assembly Robots.'' *IIE Transactions* 16: 3 (September 1984): 262-270.

ElMaraghy, H. A., L. Hamid, and W. E. ElMaraghy. (1987). ''Robocell: A Computer-Aided Robots Modelling and Workstation Layout System.'' *The International Journal of Advanced Manufacturing Technology.* 2: 2 (1987): 43-59.

Fougere, T. J. and J. J. Kanerva. (1986). ''RobotSim-A CAD Based Workcell Design and Off-Line Programming System.'' In *SME Robots 10 Conference Proceedings*, 7.1-7.12. Chicago, Illinois: April 1986.

Forland, E. Christopher. (1983). ''Taking Advantage of the Industrial Robot as a Welder.'' In *FABTECH International Conference Proceedings*, 9/1-9/11. September 26-29, 1983.

Golden, B., L. Bodin, T. Doyle, and W. Stewart Jr. (1980). ''Approximate Traveling Salesman Algorithms.'' *Operations Research* 28: 694-711.

Gruver, William A., Barry I. Soroka, John J. Craig, and Timothy L. Turner. (1983). ''Evaluation of Commercially Available Robot Programming Languages.'' In *Proceedings of the 13th International Symposium on Industrial Robots*, 12/58-12/68. Chicago, Illinois, April 1983.

Hart, P., N. J. Nilsson, and B. Raphael. (1968). ''A Formal Basis for the Heuristic Determination of Minimum Cost Paths.'' *IEEE Trans. Syst. Sci. Cybernetics* SSC-4: 2 (July 1986): 100-107.

Hemzacek, Raymond T. (1983). ''Gas Metal Arc Welding - Process and Application.'' In *FABTECH International Conference Proceedings*, 5/16-5/24. September 26-29, 1983.

Held, M. and Karp, R. M. (1970). ''The Travelling Salesman Problem and Minimum Spanning Trees.'' *Operations Research* 18: 1138-1162.

———. (1970b). ''The Travelling Salesman Problem and Minimum Spanning Trees—Part II.'' *Math. Prog* 1: 6-25.

Hoffman, James A. (1983). ''An Introduction to Arc Welding Machine Tools.'' In *FABTECH International Conference Proceedings*, 5/1-5/15. September 26-29, 1983.

Jablonowski, J. (1983). ''Robots That Weld.'' *American Machinist.* ''Special Report 753,'' 127: 4 (April 1983): 113-128.

Knott, K., B. Bidanda, and D. Pennebaker. (1988). ''Economic Analysis of Robotic Arc Welding Operations.'' *Int. J. Prod. Res.* 26: 1 (1988): 107-117.

Koren, Yoram. (1985) *Robotics for Engineers.* McGraw-Hill Book Company, 1985.

Latombe, Jean-Claude. (1983). ''Toward Automatic Robot Programming.'' In *Proceed-

ings of '83 International Conference on Advanced Robotics, 203-212, September 12-13, 1983: Tokyo, Japan

Lin, S. and B.W. Kernighan. (1973). "An Effective Heuristic Algorithm for the Travelling-Salesman Problem." *Operations Research* 21 (1973): 498-516.

Lozano-Perez, Tomas and Michael A. Wesley. (1979). "An Algorithm for Planning Collision-Free Paths Among Polyhedral Obstacles." *Communications of ACM* 22: 10 (October 1979): 560-570.

Lozano-Perez, Tomas and Rodney A. Brooks. (1984). "An Approach to Automatic Robot Programming." In *Solid Modeling by Computers: From Theory to Applications*, edited by Mary S. Pickett and John W. Boyse, 293-327. Plenum Press, 1984.

Martin, Jim F. and Corinne C. Ruokangas. (1985). "An Architecture for an Adaptive Flexible Robotic Welding System." *SAMPE Journal* 21: 1 (January-February 1985): 20-24.

Nitzan, D., C. Barrouil, P. Cheeseman, and R. Smith. (1983). "Use of Sensors in Robot Systems." In *Proceedings of '83 International Conference on Advanced Robotics*, 123-132. Tokyo, Japan: September 12-13, 1983.

Nof, Shimon Y., James L. Knight, and Gavriel Salvendy. (1980). "Effective Utilization of Industrial Robots - A Job and Skills Analysis Approach." *AIIE Transactions* 12 (1980): 216-225.

Nof, Shimon Y. and Hannan Lechtman. (1982). "Robot Time and Motion System Provides Means of Evaluating Alternate Robot Work Methods." *Industrial Engineering* (April 1982): 38-48.

Ogorek, Michael. (1985). "CNC Standard Formats." *Manufacturing Engineering* (January 1984): 43-45.

Papadimitriou, Christos H. (1985). "An Algorithm for Shortest-Path Motion in Three Dimensions." *Information Processing Letters* 20 (June 12, 1985): 259-263.

Paul, Richard P. (1977). "WAVE: A Model-based Language for Manipulator Control." *Industrial Robot* 4 (1977): 10-17.

_____. (1983). "Sensors and the Off-Line Programming of Robots." In *Proceedings of '83 International Conference on Advanced Robotics*, 307-312. Tokyo, Japan: September 12-13, 1983.

Pickett, Mary S., Robert B. Tilove, and Vadim Shapiro. (1984). "Roboteach: An Off-Line Robot Programming System Based on GMSolid." In *Solid Modeling by Computers: From Theory to Applications*, edited by Mary S. Pickett and John W. Boyse, 159-184. Plenum Press, 1984.

Powell. (1982). "An Efficient Collision Warning Algorithm for Robot Arms." Paper presented at Second AAI Conference, Carnegie-Mellon, August 1982.

Ranky, Paul G. (1984). "Programming Industrial Robots in FMS (A survey with particular reference to off-line, high-level robot program generation using VAL, VAL-II, AML and MARTI)." *Robotica* 2 (1984): 87-92.

Ranky, Paul and C. Y. Ho. (1985). *Robot Modelling - Control and Applications with Software*. IFS (Publications) Ltd. UK and Springer-Verlag, 1985.

Red, W. Edward. (1984). "Minimum Distances for Robot Task Simulation." *Robotica* 2 (1984): 230-238.

Rembold, U. and R. Dillmann. (1985). "Artificial Intelligence in Robotics." Report of Institute for Informatik III, Robotics Research Group, University of Karlsruhe, West Germany, 1985.

Richardson, R. W. (1986). "Robotic Weld Joint Tracking Systems—Theory and Implementation Methods." *Welding Journal* 65: 11 (November 1986).

Rubinovitz, J. and R. A. Wysk. (1988a). "Task-Level Off-Line Programming System for Robotic Arc Welding—An Overview." *Journal of Manufacturing Systems* 7: 4 (December 1988a): 293-306.

———. (1988b). "Task Planning and Optimization for Robotic Arc Welding—An Algorithmic Approach." *Manufacturing Review* 1: 3 (November 1988b).

Sjolund, Paul and Max Donath. (1983). "Robot Task Planning: Programming Using Interactive Computer Graphics." In *Proceedings of the 13th International Symposium on Industrial Robots*, 7/122-7/135. Chicago, Illinois, April 1983.

Soroka, Barry I. (1983). "What Can't Robot Languages Do?" In *Proceedings of the 13th International Symposium on Industrial Robots*, 12/1-12/8. Chicago, Illinois, April 1983.

Tilove, Robert Bruce. (1980). "Set Membership Classification: A Unified Approach to Geometric Intersection Problems." *IEEE Transactions on Computers* C-29: 10 (October 1980): 874-883.

Tonkay, G. L. and K. Knott. (1987). "Process Specification Using an Expert System." IMSE Working Paper 87-113, *Industrial and Management Systems Engineering Working Paper Series*. The Pennsylvania State University, 1987.

Udupa, Shriram M. (1977). "Collision Detection and Avoidance in Computer Controlled Manipulators." In *Proceedings of the 5th International Joint Conference on Artificial Intelligence*, 737-748. Cambridge, Massachusetts, August 1977.

Wadsworth, P. K., R. G. Thorne, and J. E. Middle. (1983). "Feasibility Studies for Small Batch Robotic Arc Welding." In *Proceedings of the 13th International Symposium on Industrial Robots*, 6/1-6/12. Chicago, Illinois, April 1983.

Welzl, Emo. (1985). "Constructing the Visibility Graph for n-Line Segments in $O(n^2)$ Time." *Information Processing Letters* 20 (May 1985): 167-171.

Wood, Brian O. and Mark Fugelso. (1983). "MCL: Manufacturing Control Language." In *Proceedings of the 13th International Symposium on Industrial Robots*, 12/84-12/96. Chicago, Illinois, April 1983.

37

Development of Engineered Time Standards Using the MOST Work Measurement Technique

Kjell B. Zandin*

BECAUSE INDUSTRIAL ENGINEERS ARE TRAINED that with sufficient study any method can be improved, many efforts have been made to simplify the analyst's work measurement task. This has, for instance, led to a variety of work measurement systems now in use. These achievements also led us to examine the whole concept of work measurement to find a better way for analysts to accomplish their mission. This induced the formation of a new approach later to be known as *MOST*—Maynard Operation Sequence Technique.

THE *MOST* CONCEPT

Work to most of us means exerting energy, but we should add, to accomplish some task or to perform some useful activity. In the study of physics, we learn that work is defined as the product of force times distance (W = $f \times d$) or, more simply, work is the displacement of a mass or object. This defini-

tion applies quite well to the largest portion of the work accomplished every day including pushing a pencil, lifting a heavy box, or moving the controls on a machine. Thought processes or thinking time is an exception to this concept, as no objects are being displaced. For the overwhelming majority of work, however, there is a common denominator from which work can be studied: the displacement of objects. All basic units of work are organized (or should be) for the purpose of accomplishing some useful result by simply moving objects. That is what work is. *MOST* is a system to measure work; therefore, MOST concentrates on the movement of objects.

Work, then, is the movement of objects following a tactical production outline. Efficient, smooth, productive work is performed when the basic motion patterns are tactically arranged and smoothly choreographed (methods engineering). The move-

*Kjell B. Zandin is Senior Vice President of H.B. Maynard and Company, Inc., Pittsburgh, Pennsylvania. In the late 1960s, he developed the new concept of work measurement which subsequently became Maynard Operation Sequence Technique, MOST® Systems. Mr. Zandin introduced manual MOST systems to U.S. industry and supervised the development of MOST® Computer Systems, considered to be the state-of-the-art in work measurement today. Mr. Zandin holds a master's degree in mechanical engineering (1962) from Chalmers University of Technology in Gothenburg, Sweden. He has written numerous articles on work measurement, work management, and worker participation published by technical and management publications in the U.S. and Sweden. Mr. Zandin is a senior member of the Institute of Industrial Engineers and the Society of Manufacturing Engineers. Mr. Zandin received the first "Technical Innovation in Industrial Engineering Award" presented by the Institute of Industrial Engineers in 1986.

Parts of this chapter were extracted from the textbook *MOST® Work Measurement System* by Kjell B. Zandin with the permission and courtesy of the publisher, Marcel Dekker, Inc., New York, New York.

movement of objects follows certain consistently repeating patterns such as reach, grasp, move, and position the object. As the MOST concept began to take shape, these patterns were identified and arranged as a sequence of events or subactivities manifesting the movement of an object. A model of this sequence acts as a standard guide in analyzing the movement of an object. The actual motion content of the subactivities in the studied sequence of events vary independently of one another. These concepts provides the basis for the MOST Sequence Models.

The primary elements in the sequency models are no longer basic motions, as they are in MTM (Methods Time Measurement), but are instead fundamental activities (collections of basic motions) dealing with moving objects. These activities are described in terms of subactivities fixed in sequence. In other words, to move an object, a standard sequence of events occurs. Consequently, the basic pattern of an object's movement is described by a universal sequence model instead of an aggregate of detailed basic motions synthesized at random.

Objects can be moved in only one of two ways: either they are picked up and moved freely through space, or they are moved while in contact with another object. For example, a box can be picked up and carried from one end of a workbench to the other or it can be pushed across the top of the workbench. For each type of move, a different sequence of events occurs; therefore, a separate MOST activity sequence model applies. The use of tools is analyzed through a separate activity sequence model, which allows the analyst the opportunity to follow the movement of a hand tool through a standard sequence of events, which in fact is a combination of the two basic sequence models.

Consequently, only a few activity sequences are needed for describing manual work. The basic MOST Work Measurement Technique includes the following sequence models:

- The General Move Sequence for the spatial movement of an object freely through the air

- The Controlled Move Sequence for the movement of an object when it remains in contact with a surface or is attached to another object during the movement
- The Tool Use Sequence for the use of common hand tools
- The Manual Crane Sequence for the measurement of moving heavy objects by using, for instance a jib crane, is also part of the Basic MOST System, although used less frequently than the three first sequence models

THE BASIC MOST® WORK MEASUREMENT TECHNIQUE: Sequence Models

General Move is defined as moving objects manually from one location to another freely through the air. To account for the various ways in which a General Move can occur, the activity sequence is made up of four subactivities:

- **A**—Action distance (mainly horizontal)
- **B**—Body motion (mainly vertical)
- **G**—Gain control
- **P**—Placement

These subactivities are arranged in a *sequence model* consisting of a series of logically organized parameters. The sequence model defines the events or actions that always take place in a preset order when an object is being moved from one location to another. The General Move sequence model, which is the most commonly used of all available sequence models, is defined as follows:

- **A**—Action distance
- **B**—Body motion
- **G**—Grasp
- **A**—Action distance
- **B**—Body motion
- **P**—Placement
- **A**—Action distance

These subactivities, or sequence model parameters as they are called, are then assigned time-related index numbers based on the motion content of the subactivity. This approach provides complete analysis flexibility within the overall control of the sequence model. For each object moved, any combination of motions could occur, and, using MOST, any combination could be analyzed. For the General Move sequence, these index values are easily memorized from a brief data card like the one shown in FIG. 37-1. A fully indexed General Move sequence, for example, might appear as follows:

$$\mathbf{A_6\,B_6\,G_1\,A_1\,B_0\,P_3\,A_0}$$

where:

- $\mathbf{A_6}$ = Walk three to four steps to object location
- $\mathbf{B_6}$ = Bend and arise
- $\mathbf{G_1}$ = Gain control of one light object
- $\mathbf{A_1}$ = Move object a distance within reach
- $\mathbf{B_0}$ = No body motion
- $\mathbf{P_3}$ = Place and adjust object
- $\mathbf{A_0}$ = No return

This example could, for instance, represent the following activity: "Walk three steps to pick up a bolt from floor level, arise, and place the bolt in a hole."

	BASIC MOST® SYSTEMS			GENERAL MOVE	A/B/G/P
Index	A Action distance	B Body motion	G Gain control	P Placement	Index
0	≤ 2 in ≤ 5 cm			Hold Toss	0
1	Within reach		Light object Light objects SIMO	Lay aside Loose	1
3	1-2 steps	Bend and arise 50% occ	Non SIMO Heavy/bulky Blind/obstructed Disengage Interlocked Collect	Adjustments Light pressure Double	3
6	3-4 steps	Bend and arise		Care/precision Heavy pressure Blind/obstructed Intermediate moves	6
10	5-7 steps	Sit/ stand			10
16	8-10 steps	Through door On/off Platform			16

Fig. 37-1. Basic MOST General Move data card.

General Move is by far the most frequently used of the three sequence models. Roughly 50 percent of all manual work occurs as a General Move, with the percentage running higher for assembly and material handling work, and lower for machine shop operations.

The second type of move is described by the *Controlled Move* sequence. This sequence is used to cover such activities as operating a lever or crank, activating a button or switch, or simply sliding an object over a surface. In addition to the A, B, and G parameters from the General Move sequence, the sequence model for Controlled Move contains the following subactivities:

- **M**—Move controlled
- **X**—Process time
- **I**—Align

As many as one-third of the activities occurring in machine shop operations may involve Controlled Move sequences. A typical activity covered by the Controlled Move sequence is the engaging of the feed lever on a milling machine. The sequence model for this activity might be indexed as follows:

$$A_1 B_0 G_1 M_1 X_{10} I_0 A_0$$

where:

- A_1 = Reach to the lever a distance within reach
- B_0 = No body motion
- G_1 = Get hold of lever
- M_1 = Move lever up to 12 in. (30 cm) to engage feed
- X_{10} = Process time of approximately 3.5 seconds
- I_0 = No alignment
- A_0 = No return

The third sequence model comprising the basic MOST technique is the *Tool Use* sequence model. This sequence model covers the use of hand tools for such activities as fasten or loosen, cutting, cleaning, gauging, and recording. Certain activities requiring the use of the brain for mental processes can be also classified as Tool Use: reading and inspection, for example. As indicated above, the Tool Use sequence model is a combination of General Move and Controlled Move activities. It was developed as a part of the basic MOST systems, merely to simplify the analysis of activities related to the use of hand tools. It will later become obvious to the reader that any hand tool activity is made up of General and Controlled Moves.

The use of a wrench might be described by the following sequence:

$$A_1 B_0 G_1 A_1 B_0 P_3 F_{10} A_1 B_0 P_1 A_0$$

where:

- A_1 = Reach to wrench
- B_0 = No body motion
- G_1 = Get hold of wrench
- A_1 = Move wrench to fastener a distance within reach
- B_0 = No body motion
- P_3 = Place wrench on fastener
- F_{10} = Tighten fastener with wrench
- A_1 = Move wrench a distance within reach
- B_0 = No body motion
- P_1 = Lay wrench aside
- A_0 = No return

Time Units

The time units used in MOST are identical to those used in the basic Methods Time Measurement system (MTM), and are based on hours and parts of hours called Time Measurement Units (TMU). One TMU is equivalent to 0.00001 hour. The time value in TMU for each sequence model is calculated by adding the index numbers and multiplying the sum by 10. In our previous General Move sequence example, the time would be

$$(6 + 6 + 1 + 1 + 0 + 3 + 0) \times 10 = 170 \text{ TMU}$$

corresponding to approximately 0.1 minute. The time values for the other two examples are computed in the same way. The Controlled Move totals up to

$$(1 + 0 + 1 + 1 + 10 + 0 + 0) \times 10 = 130 \text{ TMU}$$

and the Tool Use

$$(1 + 0 + 1 + 1 + 0 + 3 + 10 + 1 + 0 + 1 + 0) \\ \times 10 = 180 \text{ TMU}.$$

All time values established by MOST reflect the pace of an average skilled operator working at an average performance rate. This is often referred to as the 100 percent performance level that in time study is achieved by using leveling factors to adjust time to defined levels of skill and effort. Therefore, when using MOST, it is not necessary to adjust the time values unless they must conform with particular high or low task plans used by some companies. This also means that if a time standard for an operation is properly established by using either MOST, MTM, or stopwatch time study, the TMU values should be identical or almost identical for the three techniques.

The analysis of an operation consists of a series of sequence models describing the movement of objects to perform the operation. FIGURE 37-2 shows a basic analysis using the example of electronic assembly. Total time for the complete MOST analysis is arrived at by adding the computed sequence times. The operation time may be left in TMU or converted to minutes or hours. Again, this time would reflect pure work content (no allowances) at the 100 percent performance level. The final time standard will include the allowance factor consisting of P (personal time), R or F (rest or fatigue factor), and D for unavoidable delays (often determined by a work sampling study).

Application Speed

MOST was designed to be considerably faster than other work measurement techniques. Because of its simpler construction, under ideal conditions basic MOST requires only ten applicator hours per measured hour.

Accuracy

The accuracy principles that apply to MOST are the same as those used in statistical tolerance control. That is, the accuracy to which a part is manufactured depends on its role in the final assembly. Likewise, with MOST, time values are based on calculations that guarantee the overall accuracy of the final time standard. Based on these principles, MOST provides the means for covering a high volume of manual work with an accuracy that can be determined and controlled.

Method Sensitivity

MOST is a method-sensitive technique; it is sensitive to the variations in time required by different methods. This feature is very effective in evaluating alternative methods of performing operations with regard to time and cost. The MOST analysis will clearly indicate the more economical and less fatiguing method.

The fact that MOST is method sensitive greatly increases its worth as a work measurement tool. Not only does it indicate the time needed to perform various activities, it also provides the analyst with an instant clue that a method should be reviewed. The results are clear, concise, easily understood time calculations that indicate the opportunities for saving time, money, and energy.

Documentation

One of the most burdensome problems in the standards development process is the volume of paperwork required by widely used predetermined work measurement systems. Where the more detailed systems require between 40 and 100 pages of documentation, MOST requires as few as five. The substantially reduced amount of paperwork enables the analysts to complete studies faster and to update standards more easily. It is interesting to note that the reduction of paper generated by MOST does not lead to a lack of definition of the method used to perform the task. On the contrary, the method description produced with MOST Systems is a clear, concise, plain-language description

	MOST-calculation	Code: 1	00	60,4,8	20,1
		Date: 3-19-85
	ELECTRONIC ASSEMBLY	Sign: KZ
		Page: 1/1

Activity: ASSEMBLE RESISTOR OR DIOD ON PC BOARD

Conditions:

No.	Method	No.	Sequence Model	Fr	TMU
		2	$A_1 B_0 G_3 A_1 B_0 P_1 A_0$	1/4	15
1	PUSH CARROUSEL TO	5	$A_1 B_0 G_1 A_1 B_0 P_6 A_0$		90
	POSITION COMPONENT		A B G A B P A		
			A B G A B P A		
	TRAY		A B G A B P A		
			A B G A B P A		
2	MOVE 4 COMPONENTS		A B G A B P A		
	TO BENCH		A B G A B P A		
			A B G A B P A		
3	BEND COMPONENT		A B G A B P A		
	LEGS WITH TOOL		A B G A B P A		
			A B G A B P A		
4	READ DRAWING TO		A B G A B P A		
	LOCATE RESISTOR/DIOD		A B G A B P A		
	POSITION	1	$A_1 B_0 G_1 M_3 X_0 I_3 A_0$	1/8	10
			A B G M X I A		
5	POSITION RESISTOR OR		A B G M X I A		
	DIOD ON BOARD		A B G M X I A		
			A B G M X I A		
6	FASTEN COMPONENT		A B G M X I A		
	WITH PLIERS	3	$A_1 B_0 G_1 A_1 B_0 P_3 M_1 (A_1 B_0 P_1 A_0)$	(1/8)	73
		4	$A_0 B_0 G_1 A_1 B_0 P_0 T_{10} A_0 B_0 P_0 A_0$		100
7	CUTOFF EXCESS WIRE	6	$A_1 B_0 G_1 A_1 B_0 P_0 (F_5) A_1 B_0 P_1 A_0$	(2)	110
	WITH CUTTER	7	$A_1 B_0 G_1 A_1 B_0 P_0 (C_3) A_1 B_0 P_1 A_0$	(2)	110
			A B G A B P A B P A		
			A B G A B P A B P A		
			A B G A B P A B P A		
			A B G A B P A B P A		
			A B G A B P A B P A		
			A B G A B P A B P A		
			A B G A B P A B P A		
			A B G A B P A B P A		
			A B G A B P A B P A		

TIME = .305 ~~millihours (mh.)~~/minutes (min.) 508

Fig. 37-2. Basic MOST analysis example (electronic assembly).

of the activity. These method descriptions can very well be used for operator training and instruction.

Applicability

In what situations can MOST be used? Because manual work normally includes some variation from one cycle to the next, MOST, with its statistically established time ranges and time values, can produce times comparable to more detailed systems for the majority of manual operations. Therefore, MOST is appropriate for any manual work that contains variation from one cycle to another irrespective of cycle length. Basic MOST should not be used in situations in which a short cycle (usually up to 10 seconds long) is repeated identically over an extended period of time. In these situations, which, by the way, do not occur very often, the more detailed Mini MOST version should be chosen as the proper work measurement tool. In fact, Mini MOST was developed to cover highly repetitive, short cycled work measurement tasks. At the other end of the spectrum, Maxi MOST was developed to measure long cycle (two minutes or more), nonrepetitive operations such as heavy assembly, maintenance, and machine setups.

THE GENERAL MOVE SEQUENCE MODEL

The General Move sequence deals with the spatial displacement of one or more objects. Under manual control, the object follows an unrestricted path through the air. If the object is in contact with, or restrained in any way by another object during the move, the General Move sequence is not applicable.

Characteristically, General Move follows a fixed sequence of subactivities identified by the following steps:

1. Reach with one or two hands a distance to the object(s), either directly or in conjunction with body motions.

2. Gain manual control of the object(s).
3. Move the object(s) a distance to the point of placement, either directly or in conjunction with body motions.
4. Place the object(s) in a temporary or final position.
5. Return to workplace.

These five subactivities form the basis for the activity sequence describing the manual displacement of the object(s) freely through space. This sequence describes the manual events that can occur when moving an object freely through the air and is therefore known as a *sequence model*. The major function of the sequence model is to guide the analyst through an operation by adding the dimension of a preprinted and standardized analysis format. The existence of the sequence model provides for increased analyst consistency and reduced subactivity omission.

Parameter Definitions

A; Action Distance   The action distance parameter covers all spatial movement or actions of the fingers, hands, and/or feet, either loaded or unloaded. Any control of these actions by the surroundings requires the use of other parameters.

B; Body Motion   The body motion parameter refers to either vertical up and down motions of the body or the actions necessary to overcome an obstruction or impairment to body movement.

G; Gain Control   The gain control parameter covers all manual motions (mainly finger, hand, and foot) employed to obtain complete manual control of an object and to subsequently relinquish that control. The G parameter can include one or several short-move motions whose objective is to gain full control of the object before it is to be moved to another location.

P; Placement   The placement parameter refers to actions at the final stage of an object's displacement to align, orient, and/or engage the object with another object before control of the object is relinquished.

Parameter Indexing

Index values for the above four parameters included in the General Move sequence model can be found in FIG. 37-1. Definitions of all available index values for the four General Move parameters can be found in the MOST textbook (published in 1980). The definitions for action distance have been included below as an example.

Action Distance (A) Action distance covers all spatial movement or actions of the fingers, hands, and/or feet, either loaded or unloaded. Any control of these actions by the surroundings requires the use of other parameters.

$A_0 <2$ **in (5 cm)** Any displacement of the fingers, hands, and/or feet a distance less than or equal to 2 inches (5 cm) will carry a zero index value. The time for performing these short distances is included in the Gain Control and Placement parameters. An example activity is reaching between the number keys on a pocket calculator or placing nuts or washers on bolts located less than 2 inches (5 cm) apart.

A_1 **within Reach** Actions *within reach* are confined to an area described by the arc of the outstretched arm pivoted about the shoulder. With body assistance—a short bending or turning of the body from the waist—this *within reach* area is extended somewhat. However, taking a step for further extension of the area exceeds the limits of an A_1 and must be analyzed with an A_3 (one to two steps). Here is an example of a within reach activity: with the operator seated in front of a well laid out workbench, all parts and tools can be reached without displacing the body by taking a step.

The parameter value A_1 also applies to the actions of the leg or foot reaching to an object, lever, or pedal. If the trunk of the body is shifted, however, the action must be considered a step A_3.

A_3 **One to Two Steps** In taking steps, the trunk of the body is shifted or displaced by walking, stepping to the side, or turning the body around

using one or two steps. Steps refers to the total number of times each foot hits the floor.

Index values for longer-action distances involving walking on flat surfaces as well as up or down ladders can be found in FIG. 37-1 for up to ten steps. This will satisfy the need for action distance values for most work areas in a manufacturing plant. Should, however, longer walking distance occur, the table can be extended. All index values for walking are based on an average step length of 2.5 feet (0.75 m).

General Move Examples

1. A man walks four steps to a small suitcase, picks it up from the floor, and without moving further places it on a table located within reach:

$$A_6 B_6 G_1 A_1 B_0 P_1 A_0 \quad \textbf{150 TMU}$$

2. An operator standing in front of a lathe walks six steps to a heavy part lying on the floor, picks up the part, walks six steps back to the machine, and places it in a three-jaw chuck with several adjusting actions. The part must be inserted 4 inches (10 cm) into the chuck jaws:

$$A_{10} B_6 G_3 A_{10} B_0 P_3 A_1 \quad \textbf{330 TMU}$$

3. From a stack located 10 feet (3 m) away, a heavy object must be picked up and moved 5 feet (2 m) and placed on top of a workbench with some adjustments. The height of this stack will vary from waist to floor level. Following the placement of the object on the workbench, the operator returns to the original location, which is 11 feet (3.5 m) away:

$$A_6 B_3 G_3 A_3 B_0 P_3 A_{10} \quad \textbf{280 TMU}$$

THE CONTROLLED MOVE SEQUENCE MODEL

The Controlled Move sequence describes the manual displacement of an object over a controlled path. That is, movement of the object is restricted in at least one direction by contact with or an attachment to another object.

The Sequence Model

The sequence model takes the form of a series of letters representing each of the various subactivities (called parameters) of the Controlled Move activity sequence:

$$A\ B\ G\ M\ X\ I\ A$$

where:

- **A**—Action distance
- **B**—Body motion
- **G**—Gain control
- **M**—Move controlled
- **X**—Process time
- **I**—Align

Parameter Definitions

Only three new parameters are introduced; the **A**, **B**, and **G** parameters were discussed with the General Move sequence and remain unchanged.

M; Move Controlled The move controlled covers all manually guided movements or actions of an object over a controlled path.

X; Process Time The process time parameter occurs as that portion of work controlled by processes or machines and not by manual actions.

I; Align The align parameter refers to manual actions following the controlled move or at the conclusion of process time to achieve the alignment of objects.

The index value definitions for the above parameters (M, X, and I) can be found in the MOST textbook (Zandin 1980).

Controlled Move Examples

1. From a position in front of a lathe, the operator takes two steps to the side, turns the crank two revolutions, and sets the machining tool against a scale mark:

$$A_3\ B_0\ G_1\ M_6\ X_0\ I_6\ A_0 \quad \textbf{160 TMU}$$

2. A milling cutter operator walks four steps to the quick-feeding cross lever and engages the feed. The machine time following the 4 inch (10 cm) lever action is 2.5 seconds:

$$A_6\ B_0\ G_1\ M_1\ X_6\ I_0\ A_0 \quad \textbf{140 TMU}$$

3. A material handler takes hold of a heavy carton with both hands and pushes it 18 inches (45 cm) across conveyor rollers:

$$A_1\ B_0\ G_3\ M_3\ X_0\ I_0\ A_0 \quad \textbf{70 TMU}$$

4. Using the foot pedal to activate the machine, a sewing machine operator makes a stitch requiring 3.5 seconds process time (the operator must reach the pedal with the foot):

$$A_1\ B_0\ G_1\ M_1\ X_{10}\ I_0\ A_0 \quad \textbf{130 TMU}$$

THE TOOL USE SEQUENCE MODEL

The Tool Use sequence is composed of subactivities from the General Move sequence, along with specially designed parameters describing the actions performed with hand tools or, in some cases, the use of certain mental processes. Tool Use follows a fixed sequence of subactivities occurring in five main activity phases:

1. Get object or tool
2. Place object or tool in working position
3. Use tool
4. Put aside object or tool
5. Return to workplace

The Sequence Model

These five activity phases form the basis for the activity sequence describing the handling and use of hand tools. The sequence model takes the form of a series of letters representing each of the various subactivities of the Tool Use activity sequence:

- ABG; get object or tool
- ABP; place object or tool
- Use tool
- ABP; aside object or tool
- A; return

where:

- **A**—Action distance
- **B**—Body motion
- **G**—Gain control
- **P**—Placement

The space in the sequence model, "Use Tool," is provided for the insertion of one of the following Tool Use parameters. These parameters refer to the specifications of using the tool and are:

- **F**—Fasten
- **L**—Loosen
- **C**—Cut
- **S**—Surface treat
- **M**—Measure
- **R**—Record
- **T**—Think

Tool Use Examples for Fasten and Loosen

1. Obtain a nut from a parts bin located within reach, place it on a bolt, and run it down with seven finger actions:

$$A_1 B_0 G_1 A_1 B_0 P_3 F_{10} A_0 B_0 P_0 A_0 \quad \textbf{160 TMU}$$

2. Obtain a power wrench from within reach, run down four 3/8 inch (10 mm) bolts located 6 inches (15 cm) apart, and set aside wrench:

$$A_1 B_0 G_1 A_0 B_0 (P_3 A_1 F_6) A_1 B_0 P_1 A_{0 (4)} \quad \textbf{440 TMU}$$

3. From a position in front of an engine lathe, obtain a large T-wrench located five steps away and loosen one bolt on a chuck on the engine lathe with both hands using five arm actions. Set aside the T-wrench from the machine (within reach):

$$A_{10} B_0 G_1 A_{10} B_0 P_3 L_{24} A_1 B_0 P_1 A_0 \quad \textbf{500 TMU}$$

THE MOST SYSTEMS FAMILY

In addition to the basic MOST systems, several application oriented versions of MOST are now members of the MOST Systems family: Mini MOST, Maxi MOST, and Clerical MOST. A new version, Mega MOST, is under development for future applications.

The Mini MOST System

Basic MOST was not designed to measure short cycled operations, although the original MOST version can be applied to nonidentical operations of ten seconds or less and still meet the accuracy criteria.

Therefore, the Mini MOST version of MOST Work Measurement Systems was developed to satisfy higher accuracy requirements that apply to very short cycled, highly repetitive, identical operations. Such operations may only be from two to ten seconds long and are being performed over long periods of time.

Mini MOST consists of two sequence models:

- General move; A B G A B P A
- Controlled move; A B G M X I A

These sequence models are identical to the two basic sequence models in the Basic MOST version. There is one major difference, however. The multiplier for the index value total is one (1) for Mini MOST. Therefore, if the sum of the applied index values is 64, this is also the total TMU value for the sequence model. Another difference compared to Basic MOST is that distances in Mini MOST will be measured in inches. The application speed of Mini MOST is about 25:1 under ideal conditions compared to about 10:1 for Basic MOST.

The definitions and descriptions of the parameters and elements in Mini MOST have been excluded because of space considerations. The second edition of *MOST Work Measurement Systems* includes a complete review of Mini MOST Work Measurement Systems (Zandin 1989).

The Maxi MOST System

In order to satisfy the need for a fast, less detailed but still accurate and consistent system for the measurement of long cycled, nonrepetitive, nonidentical operations, Maxi MOST was developed.

Maxi MOST consists of five sequence models with a multiplier of 100. The sequence models are:

- Part handling
- Tool/Equipment use
- Machine handling
- Transport with powered crane
- Transport with wheeled truck

For a complete listing of Maxi MOST sequence models and parameters, see FIG. 37-3. An example of a typical Maxi MOST analysis, this one for truck assembly, has been included as FIG. 37-4. Maxi MOST has a measurement factor of three to five analyst hours per measured hour and is therefore a very cost-effective technique to use in a large number of cases where minute details are unnecessary or even detrimental to proper work instructions. The recommendation is to use Maxi MOST for nonidentical cycles that are two minutes or longer.

The definitions and descriptions of the parameters and elements in the Maxi MOST System have been excluded because of space considerations. The second edition of *MOST Work Measurement*

Activity	Sequence model	Sub-activity
Part handling	A B P	A = Action walking distance
		B = Body motion
Tool/Equipment use	A B T	P = Get and place part(s)
		T = Tool/equipment use
Machine handling	A B M	M = Operate machine or fixed equipment
Transport with crane	A T K T P T A	A = Action walking distance
		T = Transport
		K = Hook up and unhook
		P = Place object
Transport with wheeled truck	A S T L T L T A	A = Action walking distance
		S = Start and stop
		T = Transport
		L = Load and unload

Fig. 37-3. Maxi MOST systems sequence models.

No.	Method Description	Sequence	Fr	mh
	Maxi MOST® CALCULATION 100X			
	Area *735 ENGINE LINE*	Date *4·2·80*	Sign. *TWF*	Page *1/1*
	Operation *POWER STEERING PUMP*			
	Title *ASSEMBLE POWER STEERING COMPRESSOR TO ENGINE*		Time mh/min *3.0*	
	Conditions *CUMMINS ENGINE*		Per *ENGINE*	
1	*MOVE COUPLING ¿ RETAINING RING AT BENCH*	$A_0 B_0 P_1$		1
2	*POSITION RETAINING RING TO COUPLING USING PLIERS*	$A_0 B_0 T_3$		3
3	*MOVE BOLT INTO COUPLING*	$A_0 B_0 P_1$		1
4	*5 STRIKES TO KNOCK RETAINING RING INTO COUPLING - HAMMER*	$A_0 B_0 T_1$		1
5	*MOVE COUPLING ¿ POWER STEERING PUMP TO ENG. DOLLY 6 STEPS 1 BEND*	$A_1 B_1 P_1$		3
6	*LOOSEN 2 BOLTS FROM COVER PLATE USING IMPACT-SOCKET CHANGE - 8 STEPS 3 BENDS*	$A_1 B_3 T_3$		7
7	*MOVE 2 BOLTS W/WASHERS, COVER PLATE ¿ GASKET FROM ENGINE TO BINS - RETURN TO TABLE 20 STEPS*	$A_3 B_0 P_1$		4
8	*MOVE 2 BOLTS W/LW, GASKET ¿ TUBE OF LOCTITE TO DOLLY - 4 STEPS - 1 BEND*	$A_1 B_1 P_1$		3
9	*APPLY LOCTITE TO ENGINE IN TWO LOCATIONS*	$A_0 B_0 T_3$		3
10	*POSITION GASKET TO COMPRESSOR - POSITION COMPRESSOR TO ENGINE*	$A_0 B_0 P_3$		3
11	*INSTALL 2 BOLTS TO ENGINE, 1 BEND*	$A_0 B_1 T_{10}$		11
12	*TIGHTEN 2 BOLTS USING WRENCH - AVG. 15 turns 10 STEPS - 1 BEND*	$A_3 B_1 T_6$		10
	PART HANDLING A B P	TOOL/EQUIP USE A B T	MACHINE HANDLING A B M	TRANSPORT WITH CRANE A T K T P T A	TRANSPORT WITH TRUCK A S T L T L T A	Total mh *5.0*

© HBMCo. 1980

Fig. 37-4. Maxi MOST example (truck assembly).

Systems (see Reference #2) includes a complete explanation of the Maxi MOST work measurement system.

Clerical MOST

MOST Clerical systems is based on three sequence models identical to those in Basic MOST:

- General move
- Controlled move
- Tool/Equipment use (two data cards)

The parameters for these sequence models are shown in FIG. 37-5.

Mega MOST

The main purpose of adding a version of MOST on the 1000 multiplier level is to simplify and accelerate the standard setting for long (over 20 minutes) nonrepetitive operations in areas such as assembly and maintenance.

While Mini MOST is totally generic and Basic MOST about 60 to 80 percent generic, Maxi MOST is primarily tool oriented, and Mega MOST is part and operations-oriented. Mega MOST will be adopted for automated calculation of standards.

PRINCIPLES AND PROCEDURES FOR DEVELOPING TIME STANDARDS

A standard MOST calculation form should be used for all analysis work using Basic MOST. (Similar forms have been designed for use with Mini MOST and Maxi MOST.) As can be seen from the included example in FIG. 37-2, this form consists of four sections: (1) a header identifying the activity to be measured and the work center (area) in which it is being performed; (2) a method description step-by-step (left half); (3) preprinted sequence models in three groups—general move, controlled move, and tool use; and (4) a field for the time value or time standard for the activity (bottom part). Please note that the activity time or standard does not include any allowances at this stage. Prior to applying this time standard, the time value on the form should be multiplied by the appropriate allowance factor thereby constituting the standard time for the operation. A frequency factor (Fr) for each sequence model can be specified in the column next to the TMU value column for the sequence model. Normally, the space provided on one page of the MOST calculation form will allow for analyses up to approximately one minute.

MOST can be applied either for direct work measurement of defined operations or be used as a

Activity	Sequence model	Sub-activities
General move	*A B G A B P A*	A - Action distance B - Body motion G - Gain control P - Placement
Controlled move	*A B G M X I A*	M - Move controlled X - Process time I - Alignment
Equipment use	*A B G A B P A B P A*	H - Letter/paper handling T - Think R - Record K - Calculate W - Type
Tool use	*A B G A B P A B P A*	F - Fasten L - Loosen C - Cut M - Measure

Fig. 37-5. MOST clerical systems sequence models.

basis for standard data. In the case of short-cycled unique operations (for example, assemblies), the direct approach is better. On the other hand, if a great variety of the operations are being performed at one work center (such as a lathe or drill press) method, the standard data approach is the most efficient and economical method. A work sheet including standard data units, each one backed up by a MOST analysis, will provide a fast and simple way to calculate standards. Initially, the desired accuracy level for the resulting standards should be determined and the work sheet designed accordingly. This means that the tighter the accuracy requirements are, the more elements and the more decisions have to be made in order to set a standard. A multipage detailed work sheet will take more time and cost more to use than a single-page work sheet with few elements designed for a lower accuracy level. Consequently, the economics of setting standards is a direct function of the required accuracy of the output.

For instance, if the required accuracy is ± 5 percent with 95 percent confidence over an eight hour period, the work sheet may consist of 75 different elements while a ± 10 percent accuracy with 90 percent confidence over a 40 hour period may produce a work sheet with only 10 to 15 elements. The difference in application time will be substantial, and since standard setting normally is an ongoing activity, the cost saving potential is considerable.

In all situations where MOST is being used, the top-down approach should be followed. A two-step decision model can be put to use; the first step asks: Is it appropriate and practical to do direct measurement? If "yes," the work should be measured by using the MOST calculation form. If the answer is "no," a sample of the typical operations or activities for the work center should be broken down into logical suboperations. Each such suboperation will then be measured using MOST and placed on a work sheet for the calculation of time standards. In some instances, suboperations may have to be broken down still one more level and later combined into combined suboperations before assigning them onto the work sheet.

By following the top-down approach, the database with standard data (suboperation data) will remain compact and more manageable than if the conventional bottom-up procedure is applied.

MOST is an application oriented or user friendly system that will require some unlearning and rethinking by its users experienced in conventional work measurement. It is a new concept not only with regard to work measurement but also in the standards application area.

MOST COMPUTER SYSTEMS

The logical sequence model approach lends itself very well to a computerized application. Therefore, in 1976 the first lines of code were written in an effort to develop a software program that would advance the state-of-the-art of work measurement. While other computerized systems use element symbols or numerical data as input, MOST computer systems use method descriptions expressed in plain English. In other words, MOST computer systems are a language based system. Today the computerized MOST program reminds you of an expert system although this term was not generally known when the development started.

Computerized MOST Analysis

The input for a computer MOST analysis consists of work area data and a method description. Based on this information, the computer will produce a MOST analysis as output; the computer actually completes the work measurement task automatically. A simple but representative work area layout sketch is also part of the output. A typical example of a work area description is shown in FIG. 37-6 and the MOST analysis for an operation performed in that work area is shown in FIG. 37-7.

In designing the program, the MOST system architects followed the basic philosophy of establishing a time standard as a direct function of the work conditions. The computer was therefore programmed to produce a time standard based on clearly defined and complete work conditions. The computer was also programmed not to allow the

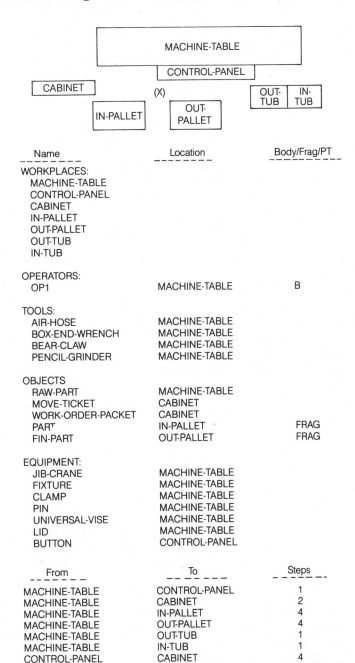

Fig. 37-6. Computerized work area data example (Machining).

Name	Location	Body/Frag/PT
WORKPLACES:		
MACHINE-TABLE		
CONTROL-PANEL		
CABINET		
IN-PALLET		
OUT-PALLET		
OUT-TUB		
IN-TUB		
OPERATORS:		
OP1	MACHINE-TABLE	B
TOOLS:		
AIR-HOSE	MACHINE-TABLE	
BOX-END-WRENCH	MACHINE-TABLE	
BEAR-CLAW	MACHINE-TABLE	
PENCIL-GRINDER	MACHINE-TABLE	
OBJECTS		
RAW-PART	MACHINE-TABLE	
MOVE-TICKET	CABINET	
WORK-ORDER-PACKET	CABINET	
PART	IN-PALLET	FRAG
FIN-PART	OUT-PALLET	FRAG
EQUIPMENT:		
JIB-CRANE	MACHINE-TABLE	
FIXTURE	MACHINE-TABLE	
CLAMP	MACHINE-TABLE	
PIN	MACHINE-TABLE	
UNIVERSAL-VISE	MACHINE-TABLE	
LID	MACHINE-TABLE	
BUTTON	CONTROL-PANEL	

From	To	Steps
MACHINE-TABLE	CONTROL-PANEL	1
MACHINE-TABLE	CABINET	2
MACHINE-TABLE	IN-PALLET	4
MACHINE-TABLE	OUT-PALLET	4
MACHINE-TABLE	OUT-TUB	1
MACHINE-TABLE	IN-TUB	1
CONTROL-PANEL	CABINET	4

change of a time value without a change of the underlying work conditions. A change of, for instance a distance, or a gain control or a placement of an object or a body motion, results in a different standard. This discipline has proven to increase the uniformity and consistency of the method descriptions and analyses. Equally important is the fact that one does not have to read both the method description and the MOST index values to interpret an analysis. A review of the method is adequate:

```
LOAD PART IN FIXTURE WITH BOX END WRENCH AT MULTI SPINDLE VERTICAL DRILL 2000
PER  PART                                      OFG: 2   02-Jan-89

      OP1 BEGINS AT MACHINE-TABLE

   1  PLACE PART FROM IN-TUB TO FIXTURE
                    A3   B0   G1   A3   B0   P3   A0                  1.00   100.
   2  PUSH SLIDE CLAMP AT FIXTURE
                    A1   B0   G1   M1   X0   I0   A0                  1.00    30.
   3  FASTEN 2 NUTS AT FIXTURE WITH 4 ARM-TURNS USING
BOX-END-WRENCH AND ASIDE
          A1   B0   G1   A0   B0   (P3   A1   F10)   A1   B0   P1   A0    (2)  1.00   320.
   4  FASTEN SCREW FASTENER AT FIXTURE 1 SPIN USING FINGERS
          A1   B0   G1   A1   B0   P1   F1   A0   B0   P0   A0             1.00    50.
                                                   TOTAL TMU    500.
```

Fig. 37-7. Computerized MOST analysis example (Machining).

the index values and the time standard are a by-product and a direct function of the method.

How is it possible for the computer to generate a MOST analysis from the input of only work area data and a method description? How does the computer select the right sequence model and the correct index values? As has been explained above and also can be seen from the example in FIG. 37-6, all action distances and body motions are specified as part of the work area data. Therefore, the A and B parameters in the sequence models will be assigned an index value from the work area information.

Three additional variables remain to be determined: (1) sequence model selection, (2) index value for the G-parameter, and (3) index value for the P-parameter. This required information has been compounded into one word: a keyword. This keyword, always found in the beginning of each method step, has been chosen from a list of commonly used English activity words such as MOVE, PLACE, and POSITION. For instance, the keyword PLACE will mean the General Move sequence model and a combination of G_1 and P_3 to the computer. MOVE indicates the same sequence model with a $G_1 P_1$ combination and Position, a $G_1 P_6$ combination. A GET preceding MOVE, PLACE, and POSITION will render a $G_3 P_1$; $G_3 P_3$; and $G_3 P_6$ respectively.

Similar keywords are available for all sequence models in the MOST Computer Systems. The memorizing of approximately 30 to 50 keywords for

Basic MOST will provide the analyst with a sufficient vocabulary to be able to perform most of the analysis work.

Since both the work area data and the method description are entered within a well structured format, it would obviously be possible to dictate this information using a hand-held tape recorder. A person can, in most situations, talk as fast as or faster than an operator can perform an assembly or a machining operation. Therefore, the data collection becomes much more efficient. The conventional handwriting of methods is usually cumbersome and inefficient. While the dictation of a method in principle will require the observation of just one cycle, the writing of the same method will require observation of several cycles. The information on the tape will then be transcribed by the analyst or a typist on a CRT terminal as input to the program. In the future, when a voice recognition system becomes available for practical applications, this intermediate step can be eliminated.

Data Management

The major advantage of a computerized application of MOST lies in the databases (suboperations and standards). These are accumulated as a result of the MOST analysis work and calculation of standards. The filing, searching, retrieving, and updating of the data becomes extremely efficient and fast compared to a manual system. Some functions requiring manipulations of data such as mass updating, simulations, and history of standards are very impractical or impossible to execute manually; the computer can perform them routinely and quickly.

A complete database system for filing and retrieving suboperations and time standards is the backbone of MOST Computer Systems. The database has been designed to handle up to 2 million standards and suboperations.

The filing system for the database is also using the *word* concept. All suboperation data are filed and retrieved under well-defined words in five categories: activity, object/component, equipment/product, tool, and work area origin. The filing system for standards is in all cases being customized to fit the user's requirements and includes such conventional header items as part number, operation number, and work center number.

MOST Computer System— A Complete System

A MOST Computer System is a complete program for measuring work and calculating time standards as well as documenting and updating these standards. It consists of a basic program and a set of supplementary modules; FIG. 37-8 shows a system overview. The basic program includes the following features:

- Work measurement
- Suboperation database
- Time standards calculation
- Standards database
- Mass update
- Documentation of work conditions (Work Management Manual)

Supplementary modules are:

- Machining data (feeds, speeds, and process times)
- Welding data
- Line balancing

- Process planning (can be expanded to include generative process planning)
- Cost estimating
- Performance reporting

The objective with MOST Computer Systems is to adapt the system to cover all possible aspects of establishing time standards in a wide range of situations. Another objective is to make the updating and maintenance of standards efficient and simple. Our intention is also to stimulate the industrial engineer both in industry and in universities and colleges to adopt a positive attitude toward a fundamental and widely used discipline: the measurement of work.

SUMMARY AND FUTURE TRENDS

During the 1950s and 1960s, the work measurement market started to become inflated with conventional derivatives of the original MTM system (MTM-1). That trend has continued with one exception: MOST. In the mid 1960s, my company, H.B. Maynard and Company Inc., felt that a new approach, a more practical and user friendly method, and more importantly a faster and simpler technique was necessary to maintain a reasonably high level of interest in work measurement. MOST seems to have been the answer. Over 17,000 persons representing more than 4,000 organizations have become certified MOST users. MOST has been translated into at least 15 languages and is in use in more than 30 countries around the world. MOST satisfied all the criteria of simplicity, speed, accuracy, consistency, applicability, integrity, and universality that can be put on a modern work measurement technique and system. MOST computer systems represent the state-of-art in the areas of work measurement and time standards. The users enthusiastically endorse and support MOST.

A renaissance in work measurement has been noticeable during the past few years, perhaps because of a military standard (MIL-STD-1567A) issued by the Department of Defense in 1983. Since then, defense contractors have been obligated to comply with this standard on major con-

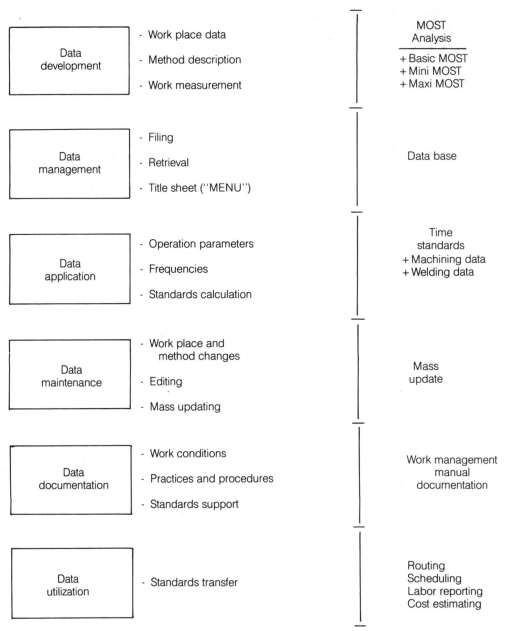

Fig. 37-8. MOST computer systems overview.

tracts. Compliance includes fully documented time standards (80 percent coverage) based on a recognized predetermined motion time system. MOST systems has very successfully been used by a large number of defense contractors to satisfy the re-

quirements of MIL-STD-1567A. Service industries have also shown an increased interest in work standards for staffing, manpower planning, and budgeting.

Despite the efforts by industry to increasingly

automate manufacturing operations, I believe that the measurement of work done by people is here to stay for many more years. The advantages of knowing and being able to plan from realistic and consistent standards are just too great to dismiss.

The work measurement and standard setting disciplines have to become simpler, faster, and more integrated with other functions to attract the attention they deserve. MOST Systems and MOST Computer Systems have proven to meet those requirements to a great extent. Nevertheless, more can be done and more will be done. Today's computer technology has reached a level that can-

not be ignored by wo̶ rement specialists. If they take advantage ̶chnology, time standards could and shoul̶e a logical and integral part of any busine̶m as is the case in many companies alread̶

The general trend ̶stry is automation. Therefore, we will see f̶mated procedures for calculating and updati̶ standards based on data developed and mai̶ by industrial engineers. A direct link to a CA̶tem with the purpose of producing process p̶d cost estimates based on these standards wi̶ become a reality within the next few years.

REFERENCES

Zandin, Kjell B. *MOST Work Measurement Systems.* New York: Marcel Dekk̶ 1980.
———. *MOST Work Measurement Systems, Basic MOST, Mini MOST, Ma̶ OST.* 2nd ed. New York: Marcel Dekker, 1990.
Industrial Engineering Handbook. 3rd ed. New York: McGraw-Hill, 1971.

38

Automatic Identification: An Efficient Data Collection Tool for Manufacturing Control Systems

Benjamin Nelson*

BAR CODES ARE EVERYWHERE: IN THE GROCERY store, on magazines, under the hoods of cars, in the hospital, and on cartons, cases, and paperwork worldwide. Even the smallest store or business can realize the advantage of bar codes and automatic identification. With increasing frequency, bar codes are saving money, controlling and reducing inventory, and providing timely, accurate data to management and sales. Certainly you need to know how you can put bar codes to practical use, but you also should have an understanding of the basics.

INTRODUCTION

There is nothing new about codes and symbols. The ancient Sumerians used a code called cuneiform to identify wine jugs and keep track of business dealings. Much later the Arabs, Greeks,

and Romans developed codes we call alphabets that allow us to express sounds and ideas. Right now your eyes are scanning one of those codes, and your brain is decoding the data, and storing it for future use.

Bar codes are exactly the same as the alphabet. A series of wide and narrow lines can be scanned with an electronic "eye" (scanner), decoded by an electronic "brain" (computer), and the data stored to provide information or to cause something to happen.

Although automatic identification was proposed in the early 1930s, it took until World War II and the development of microelectronics to make the first bar code system practical. When the microprocessor came along in the 1970s the industry took off and has been expanding at an ever-increasing rate.

This chapter will give you a better understand-

*Benjamin Nelson is responsible for Industrial Market Relations for MARKEM CORPORATION of Keene, New Hampshire. He has been with MARKEM for 37 years in Manufacturing, Engineering, Sales, Scanmark, and Marketing Communications. Mr. Nelson has been involved in the bar code industry since 1969 and has made bar code presentations to over 170 organizations in the United States, Canada, Australia, and Europe. He is the author of numerous articles dealing with and helping educate users about bar coding. He has chaired numerous AIM committees and was the 1985 recipient of the Richard Dilling Award given annually for outstanding contributions to the Automatic Identification Industry.

All drawings furnished by Markem Corporation, Keene, NH 03431. For more information on codes and systems, contact AIM USA, 1326 Freeport Rd., Pittsburgh, PA 15238.

ing of how bar codes work. We'll dissect a bar code symbol, discuss the most common bar code schemes, and along the way look at some real life applications.

The data in this chapter were correct as of early 1990. The automatic identification industry is changing rapidly. Equipment prices are dropping, print speeds are increasing, and scanners and printers are getting more versatile. Thus prices, print speeds, and related information included here are guides only, indicating comparative data of one system to another.

SYMBOLOGY

Webster defines symbology as "the art of expression by symbols, a study of symbols, or a system of symbols." Here's a symbol: water. We recognize this symbol, scan it with our eyes, decode it with our brain, and visualize a liquid. The code used is the modern Roman alphabet. If we use the Spanish language, we get agua; the chemical language, H_2O. Bar codes also use symbols to express thoughts. A number expressed in Code 39 uses a different arrangement of bars and spaces as the same number symbolized in UPC (Universal Product Code) or Interleaved Two of Five code.

Scanners are getting smarter. Like our eyes, they are able to recognize a variety of symbols and, through a process called autodiscrimination, interpret these codes and symbols and provide us with meaningful information, information we get in real time to make things happen now.

Each bar code has certain characteristics that make it different from all others. At the same time there are characteristics that are common to all.

Encodation

Each code uses a series of bars and spaces (modules) to represent characters. Each code has a character assignment chart and each symbol consists of at least five required parts: (1) quiet zone, (2) start character, (3) data characters, (4) stop character, and (5) quiet zone (see FIG. 38-1). Some codes may have a sixth part, the check character,

Fig. 38-1. A USS-Codabar symbol encoding "A378-59B."

which appears after the data characters and before the stop character.

All symbols have stop and start characters. FIGURE 38-2 shows the makeup for the Interleaved Two of Five code. Note that the two left-hand bars are *narrow, narrow* while the two right-hand bars are *wide, narrow*. These start and stop characters serve three purposes. First they uniquely identify the code, for each different code has a different arrangement of start and stop characters. It is this feature that allows one scanner to read several different codes (autodiscrimination). Second, it tells the scanner if the code is being read left to right or right to left. If the scanner is reading the symbol backwards, all the data are stored and then displayed or transmitted in the proper order. Third, they tell the scanner to start reading the symbol and to stop looking for additional data when all data bars have been scanned. There is also a clear area on each end of the symbol to allow the scanner to get ready to read the next symbol.

All the common codes use a series of wide and narrow bars and spaces to encode data: a wide bar or space equals binary one; a narrow bar or space, binary zero. As only ones and zeros are used, most codes can be expressed in binary form, the language used by computers. Each code has a chart showing the arrangement of these ones and zeros.

Fig. 38-2. Start stop bars in the Interleaved Two of Five code.

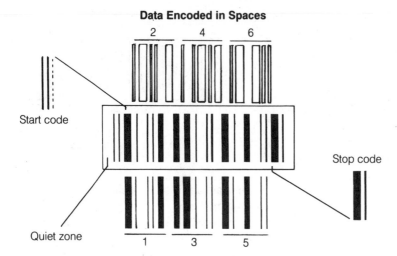

Data Encoded in Spaces

Start code

Stop code

Quiet zone

Data Encoded in Bars

Fig. 38-3. Six-digit Interleaved Two of Five example.

Data Character	Bar and Space Position Weight				
	1	2	4	7	P
-1-	1	0	0	0	1
-2-	0	1	0	0	1
-3-	1	1	0	0	0
-4-	0	0	1	0	1
-5-	1	0	1	0	0
-6-	0	1	1	0	0
-7-	0	0	0	1	1
-8-	1	0	0	1	0
-9-	0	1	0	1	0
-0-	0	0	1	1	0

FIGURE 38-3 is the chart for the Interleaved Two of Five code.

Bar codes are either *continuous* or *discrete* depending on the way a symbol is assembled and measured. The UPC Code found in the grocery store is a *continuous* code. That is, the total width of the wide and narrow bars making up each character is measured from the beginning of one character to the beginning of the next character, as FIG. 38-4 illustrates. The intercharacter gap, the space between the end of one character and the beginning of the next character, is significant. Each character is dependent on the adjacent characters.

Code 39, illustrated in FIG. 38-5, is an example of a *discrete* code. A discrete code is character independent. The width of the intercharacter gap has no bearing on the width of the symbol or on adja-

cent characters. Discrete codes are normally easier to print and scan.

A common mistake is to try to put too much data in the symbol. Treat the symbol as a license plate or part number and keep the bulk of the data in the computer. Unless absolutely necessary, it is unwise to exceed about 20 characters in a part number. Too long a symbol is unwieldy to print, more difficult to scan, and can take up too much space on a small product.

Security

How secure are the various codes? How accurate? What are the chances of the code and scanner giving wrong information? Hand written data will typically average one error in 300 bits of informa-

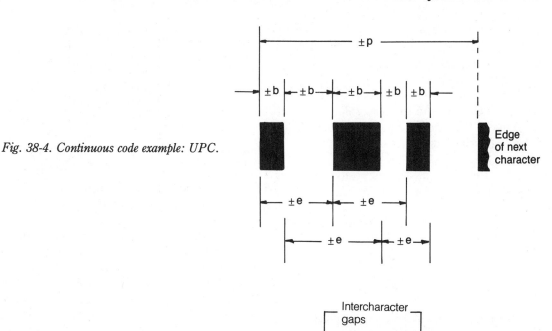

Fig. 38-4. Continuous code example: UPC.

Fig. 38-5. Discrete code example: Code 39.

tion. A good bar code may give one error in three to four million bits.

When the Department of Defense ran the Logmars tests of Code 39 they experienced four errors in 563,243 bar code labels that averaged 24 characters in length. In the UPC tests at Kroger Stores in Cincinnati, shoppers were offered 100 free green stamps for any error they could find. No stamps were ever given. Even poorly printed symbols will not give more than one error in several million characters scanned. You may get a *no read*, where the scanner cannot read the symbol, but you won't get an *error read*. An *error read* is when a scanner reads the symbol and reports different data from that which you encoded. The use of a check

digit can increase the accuracy to one in many millions.

Check Digits

Some codes (Code 39, Codabar) are secure enough to not need a check digit except under special circumstances. Others like UPC and Code 93 require them every time. There are times when it may be necessary to add a check digit because extra security is needed as for a controlled drug.

Check digit schemes, designed to catch various types of errors, are mathematical computations involving the characters in the symbol and are appended to the end of the symbol. When the symbol is decoded, the scanner does the same computation and if the answer equals the printed check digit, it is accepted as a valid read. This is not as complicated as it sounds.

Typical is the *modulo ten* check digit scheme for the UPC Code. An example follows. FIGURE 38-6 is the UPC symbol for a popular hand lotion. To compute the check digit:

1. Add all numbers in the odd positions starting with the number system number:

$$0 + 2 + 4 + 7 + 1 + 9 + 0 = 23$$

2. Multiply the answer by three:

$$23 \times 3 = 69$$

3. Sum the numbers in the even positions:

$$8 + 3 + 7 + 0 + 8 = 26$$

4. Add steps two and three together:

$$69 + 26 = 95$$

5. Add a number to 95 that makes it evenly divisible by 10:

$$95 + 5 = 100$$

6. The check digit is five and is added to the symbol after the last data character.

This calculation is done automatically by the printers and scanners used to produce and read symbols. As with start and stop bars, check digits can be transmitted and displayed, or used and suppressed depending on scanner programming and the user's desire.

Density

Density refers to the number of data characters that can be placed in a given area. For example, assuming a bar/space width of .0075 (standard

Fig. 38-6. UPC symbol of a popular hand lotion.

for several codes) you can place 9.4 Code 39, 17.8 Interleaved Two of Five, or 15 Code 11 characters on a label one inch long.

Density can be high, medium, or low with several variations within each category. While many densities are available, nominal high density is 9.4 CPI (characters per inch), medium density 5.4 CPI, and low 3.5. With labels produced by photo composition it is possible to make narrow bars, .004 inch wide, providing around 15 CPI with good definition, but not all scanners can read them. At the other end of the scale, bars .250 inch wide with a density of less than one CPI are sometimes used when the product must be read at a great distance or at extreme speeds. Density is important for two reasons. First, density determines the type of scanner you will use, the scanning dot diameter of that scanner, and the size of the symbol. Where a high density symbol must be read at very close range, a similar but low density symbol may be read at a distance of several feet.

Density also determines the size of the label required or the amount of space needed on the product to print the symbol. FIGURE 38-7 shows the relative density of typical symbols.

Standards and Specifications

There are many benefits from working with recognized industry standards and specifications. Let me define the word *standard* as it applies to automatic identification. A standard is like the three-legged stool in FIG. 38-8: remove one leg and the stool is unstable and won't work very well.

The first leg to support the standard is the *technical specification* for the code. The specification

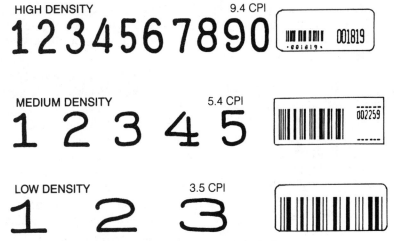

Fig. 38-7. Typical characters per inch.

describes bar width and height, the ratio of wide to narrow bars, and all those things needed to allow the manufacturers of printers and scanners to produce and read the symbols. This technical specification is needed by the engineers, but not typically by most users.

The second leg of the stool is the *industry specification* describing how such members of that industry as the manufacturer, distributor, and end user can all use the same symbol. The industry specification describes symbol size, format, where to place the symbol on the product, the data to be encoded and captured, fields of information, and any options to personalize the symbol while leaving it useful to the rest of the industry.

Our final stool leg is the *application specification*. How are *you* going to print this label and apply it to *your* product. At what point do you plan to scan the label and what are you going to do with the information you capture. This is your part of the standard and here you can do anything you want. By department, activity, warehouse, or sales group—you decide as long as you stick to the technical and industry specifications.

By using a recognized standard, you have the widest choice of printers, scanners, systems, and assistance. If you call any vendor of automatic identification equipment and say "I need to meet XYZ standard," the vendor will know exactly what you mean and what equipment he can provide for you.

Types of Standards

There are three other kinds of standards to consider. First, there are *industry standards* put together by an industry committee working together for the benefit of all. Examples are the UPC Standard developed primarily for the grocery

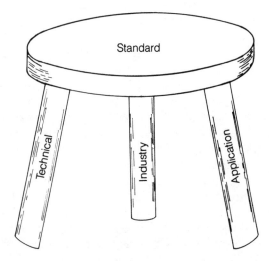

Fig. 38-8. A standard is like a three-legged stool.

industry but now being used by others, and the UPCC Shipping Container Standard used by the meat industry. The Health Industry has a standard that uses Code 39. All these are voluntary standards that allow the manufacturer, distributor, and end user to all take advantage of the same symbol. Each group took a recognized standard and adapted it to its own needs. Nearly 30 industries now have printed standards.

Next, there are *customer standards* that require the manufacturer to bar code his product before he ships it to his customer. An example is the standard for the automotive industry action group (AIAG) that must be followed if one plans to sell in that industry. This industry standard is based on the technical specification for the Code 39 and the application needs of the automotive industry. Logmars with Code 39 for the Federal Government is another example of a customer standard.

Last is your own *internal standard* perhaps for production tracking, order picking, job entry, or some other specialized application. Two examples include a quality control operation on blood samples in a hospital using Code 39 as described in the HIBCC Standard, and following a circuit board or a skid of parts through production. An internal standard and specification describes the code to use, the label material, where the label will be located on the product, label layout, data to be recovered, the industry or customer standard being referenced, and any other information needed to make the system work.

If possible, adopt an industry standard for internal use. If you are required by your customer to bar code, turn this requirement into an advantage to create additional savings and increase profits. Another good reason for adopting an existing standard is that it might be possible to have vendors do the bar coding. That is what UPC, AIAG, and Logmars did. They insisted that vendors bar code products in accordance with their standards.

Specifications may also include information on how the label will be scanned. For example, with some scanners label width is fixed at a maximum of about two inches; with others there is virtually no limit on symbol size. The scanner used may determine code density and the amount of data to be encoded. Here are some other considerations:

- What environment must the label withstand? Is a paper label adequate or is a ceramic print on steel needed to survive very high temperatures? Or a photo lithographed aluminum label designed for harsh environments?
- How large can the label be? The label should not overwhelm the product and yet should be correct for the scanner and system.
- Mil Std 1189 describes Code 39 and the format one would use for the information the U.S. Government (Logmars) wants to recover. Its companion, Mil Std 129J, shows where the label must be placed on inner and outer cartons. These might serve as a guide for an internal standard.

With a known standard scanners, conveyors, and handling systems can be designed more efficiently to provide information on what is happening, where it is happening, and when it is happening.

The Automatic Identification Manufacturers Association (AIM) is involved with writing standards. AIM Universal Symbol Descriptions (USD) are a recognized source for those wishing to adopt or develop a standard for their own industry. AIM's new Uniform Symbology Standards clearly define—technically—how a symbol is put together. The AIM Technical Committee has worked with many groups offering advice and guidance on the development of application standards specific to individual industries.

Common Codes

One can choose from over 50 different codes. Each was developed to meet a specific need for an industry or activity. However, only a few are in common use. The following is a brief description of seven of the most popular codes. Examples of each are illustrated. Note that they all use wide and narrow bars, but the space out, start, and stop

Fig. 38-9. Universal Product Code (UPC).

arrangement and width of the bars is different in each.

Universal Product Code The universal product code was adopted by the grocery industry in 1973 after two and a half years of study. This is the symbol one sees on all grocery products, magazines, and many over the counter medical items. The UPC is actually two codes in one. In FIG. 38-9, note the two longer narrow bars in the center of the symbol. The left five characters and the right five characters each have a different arrangement of bars and serve different purposes. FIGURE 38-10 is a closeup of the two sides of the UPC.

The left five characters are assigned by the Uniform Code Council and identify the manufacturer of the product. The right five characters are assigned by the manufacturer to identify each of his products. There are always 12 characters in a UPC symbol. In addition to the ten mentioned, a number system character appears in the left hand side and a check digit on the right. The number system character is unique to UPC. It tells the computer what type of product the symbol represents; for example, zero (0) is a grocery product, three (3) is a pharmaceutical item, and five (5) is for coupons.

UPC was designed specifically for the retail industry. It is rarely used in industrial applications because it is not a versatile code. There are four different widths of bars and spaces, and very specific rules to follow on changing the size of the symbol. Length is fixed at 12 characters.

Code 39 By far the world's most popular industrial code, Code 39 is full alphanumeric and is supported by more standards, software, printers, scanners, and industries than any other code. With the addition of four control characters, Code 39 can be expanded to encode the entire ASCII set of 128 characters. Code 39 can be used for numbers only, letters only, or any combination of alphanumeric plus six punctuation characters and a space. An example appears in FIG. 38-11.

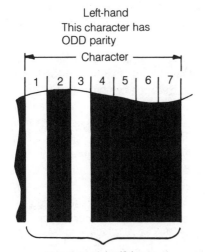

Left-hand
This character has
ODD parity

5 dark modules/2 bars

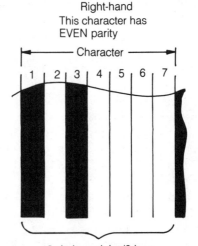

Right-hand
This character has
EVEN parity

2 dark modules/2 bars

Fig. 38-10. Two sides of the UPC code; each serves a specific purpose.

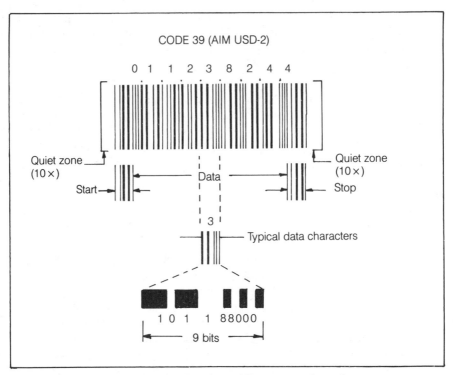

Fig. 38-11. Code 39, the world's most popular code.

Code 39 is discrete, self checking, and character independent. No check digit is required. However, a modulo 43 check digit scheme is available. Code 39 can be any length and any density and is accurate to one misread in several million characters (the Federal Government says one in thirteen million).

Logmars (the Federal Government), HIBCC (Health Industry Bar Code Council), AIAG (Automotive Industry Action Group), and NATO (North Atlantic Treaty Organization) are a few of the organizations that have adopted Code 39. All have printed standards available.

Interleaved Two of Five Interleaved Two of Five is unique in that both bars and spaces carry data. It is called Two of Five because each character contains five modules, two of which are wide.

The Interleaved Two of Five Code (I 2/5) is widely used in warehouse and distribution activities. The Automotive Industry Action Group (AIAG) and the Meat Industry are the prime movers behind this code.

I 2/5 was developed to meet the need of a low density code that would not occupy too much space. By using the bars for the characters in the odd numbered position and the spaces for the even numbered, the symbol is compressed by nearly one half. FIGURE 38-12 is an example of this code.

There must always be an even number of digits in the code and the scanner is programmed to receive a specific number of characters. The start code is *narrow narrow* and the stop *wide narrow*.

If only an odd number of digits will be significant, a leading zero must be added because I 2/5 must always consist of an even number of digits. Although a check digit is not normally required, there is a standard scheme available. Should the addition of a check digit result in an odd number of digits, a leading zero must again be added.

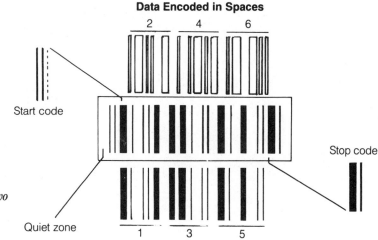

Data Encoded in Spaces

Start code

Stop code

Quiet zone

Fig. 38-12. Six-digit Interleaved Two of Five example.

Data Encoded in Bars

Data Character	Bar and Space Position Weight				
	1	2	4	7	P
-1-	1	0	0	0	1
-2-	0	1	0	0	1
-3-	1	1	0	0	0
-4-	0	0	1	0	1
-5-	1	0	1	0	0
-6-	0	1	1	0	0
-7-	0	0	0	1	1
-8-	1	0	0	1	0
-9-	0	1	0	1	0
-0-	0	0	1	1	0

Codabar Codabar was developed for retail applications but was never widely accepted. The 17 different widths of bars made it too difficult to print (it has since been modified to 4 different widths).

Codabar was the first code whose accuracy was proven in computer tests. The Committee for Commonality in Blood Banking in America (CCBBA) chose Codabar for identifying blood bags and samples for two reasons. At the time, it was the only code computer checked for accuracy. It is unique in that it can have a large intercharacter gap in the code and still be read. A label can be placed on the blood bag, then later another label identifying donor or blood bank added, and both labels read as one. Another common Codabar application is the paper envelope from photo finishers. The two Codabar symbols designating dealer and price are put on the envelope at different times, yet read as one. Codabar is also used in library systems, and by Federal Express on all its air way bills.

Codabar is pictured in FIG. 38-13. This code is numeric only with a choice of four different alpha start and stop characters. Although not required, a check digit is available. Codabar is a very secure code.

Code 128 Code 128 can encode the entire ASCII set. When used for numbers only, Code 128 can have a density of over 24 characters per inch. However, as there are three bar widths versus two for most other codes, printing of Code 128 can be more difficult. An example is in FIG. 38-14. Code 128 is not as well supported by the printer/scanner industry as some of the other codes.

Code 128 has been adopted by three industry

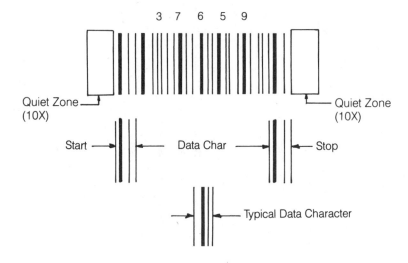

Fig. 38-13. Codabar code.

Fig. 38-14. Code 128 symbol structure.

groups. The Uniform Code Council and the International Article Numbering Association (EAN) are specifying Code 128 for serialized shipping containers. This type container is widely used in the apparel industry and in distribution. VICS (Voluntary Industrial Communication Standard), a committee of the American Apparel Manufacturers Association (AAMA), has suggested Code 128 for all containers in distribution.

Code 49 Stacked codes are the latest entries in the *highest density* race. Code 49 was invented by Dr. David Allais of Intermec Corporation. (Dr. Allais also invented Code 11, Code 93,

and was the coinventor of Code 39 and Interleaved Two of Five.)

Code 49 can contain two to eight rows of data and can encode the entire ASCII set of 128 characters. A check digit appears at the end of each row. No human readable interpretation is specified. Further information is available from Intermec or from AIM.

An example format is illustrated in FIG. 38-15. (It is encoded according to the October 1987 feasibility version of Code 49.) In this example, the bars in each row are eight modules ("X" dimensions) high. Rows are separated by a one-module-wide

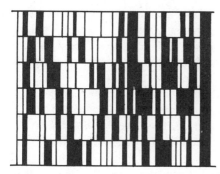

Fig. 38-15. Code 49 format example.

black line. The top and bottom of the symbol are also delineated by one-module-wide black borders.

If an eight-row symbol were constructed in the fashion of the above example, then the overall symbol height would be 73 modules.

The lines at the top and bottom of the symbol in the example extend two modules beyond the start and stop patterns. This suggests a two-module quiet zone at either end. Overall width becomes 74 modules, making an eight-row symbol essentially square.

Following is an example of Code 49 reduced to one quarter inch for use on electronic components. This symbol contains 74 modules identical to the larger example. This code requires a 16-bit processor.

Code 16K   Another stacked code for ultra-high density is Code 16K designed by Ted Williams of Laserlite Systems. The code requires only an 8-bit processor to decode.

Code 16K uses the character set of Code 128 and the edge-decodable UPC-A Subset and can contain 90 percent more data than a same-sized square symbol of Code 49.

The symbol consists of 2 to 16 rows. Each row has a two-bar/two-space start pattern, a 1-X bar separator, five three-space/three-bar internal characters, followed by a two-space/two-bar stop pattern for a 70-X width or 81-X with quiet zones.

Start and stop patterns are standard seven-element UPC-A patterns, with even parity on the left and odd parity on the right. Digits 7 and 8 are not

used in order to keep 100 percent edge-to-edge decodability.

Each row has five internal characters. The first character in the first row is the S character, which defines the number of rows in the symbol and the start code. The last two characters in the last row are check characters. The remaining characters are data characters. The number of data characters varies from 7 in a double row to 77 in a 16-row symbol.

Internal characters are the same as Code 128 11-module characters, except bars are spaces and spaces are bars. Code 16K uses the standard Code 128 code sets of A, B, and C. In addition, the Code 128 start and stop character patterns are used to increase the data character set to 107.

Like Code 49, Code 16K is read with hand laser scanners. Rows can be scanned in any order and are assembled automatically by the scanner decoding device. Both the electronic and pharmaceutical industries are very interested in Code 16K.

Note: As this was written, a new family of codes called "matrix codes" have been offered to the industry for comment. Matrix codes look like a checker board and are reported to have higher density than stacked codes. Both the electronic industry and the government have expressed interest, but not enough details are available to give definitive information.

Selection Criteria

Bar code symbols range from bars .0625 inch high by .005 inch wide on the edge of a printed circuit board to a two foot square series of bars .500 inch or wider on railroad box cars. Select a symbol that fits the product as long as it does not violate the rules of bar ratios and a scanner can be found to read them.

A symbol should do the job intended; it should uniquely identify the product and provide the data needed. This leads us into some of the rules. One needs to know a little bit about density, the rule of X, and Standards available to help meet these rules and all the others that govern the Automatic Identification Industry.

The Rule of X

The rule of X is simple. The width of the narrow bar is X and all the narrow bars and narrow spaces must equal X. The wide bars and spaces must all equal some multiple of X. Even simpler, if all the bars and spaces are not of a consistent width throughout the symbol, the scanner cannot read them. If printing will be done in-house, the specification for each code must be followed for problem free use. The rules are explained in detail in the Uniform Symbol Descriptions available from AIM.

The symbol chosen will also affect the type of scanner to be used or, conversely, the type of scanner used will determine the bar width, density, and size of the labels. A label on a printed circuit board that will be read with a pen scanner may have a narrow bar .0075 inch wide. The same data on a carton on a conveyor, moving at 200 feet per minute and scanned from two feet away, may require a narrow bar .040 inch wide. The final authority on bar code and label size will normally be the scanner supplier.

PRINTING THE BAR CODE SYMBOL

Once the decision is made to use bar codes, a choice must be made to either buy labels from an outside source, or make them in-house. What are the advantages and disadvantages of the make vs. buy decision? The kind of data to be captured, the environment, time constraints, customers' needs, and industry standards must all be considered. Following are descriptions of the most common printing methods, along with various label stocks and costs, to help make this important choice.

We are all familiar with the UPC bar code symbology at the local supermarket. These symbols are normally printed with the package graphics on high speed flexographic presses by converters. Tolerances, plates, film masters, and scanners are all designed specifically for this market. The method to accomplish this is described in the UPC manual.

Industrial uses of bar code symbols require more specialized and, perhaps, more sophisticated printing methods. The UPC symbol identifies only fixed data about manufacturer and product. Industrial symbols must also be able to identify random information such as lot numbers, weight, shift, operator, route, and date. The need for random specific data limited the use of industrial bar codes until the advent of the microprocessor.

Let us look at this premicroprocessor technology and the ways one could generate bar code symbols in-house. There were really only two methods: wet ink with rubber plates or mats, and hot stamping with metal plates. Both had strengths and weaknesses.

Printing Symbols
In-House in the "Old Days"

Wet ink required a rubber or plastic mat (printing plate) for each legend (see FIG. 38-16). These plates were molded from metal or plastic masters. Narrow bars below about .010 inch for high density codes could not be molded into plates for in-house use. Print pressure, ink film, and viscosity were crucial—too crucial in fact for practical production line applications. Letterpress ink printing did not produce consistently good quality. Scan rates tended to be low and the entire system was labor intensive.

Hot stamping used a dry ribbon with a predetermined ink thickness (see FIG. 38-17). This eliminated the wet ink problems, but one still needed a separate metal plate for every legend. Because these plates were etched from photographic masters, they were very accurate. Bar widths down to about .010 inch were possible with consistent quality. Print quality was superb. The scan rate was typically high. Label cost was higher than by most other methods.

The latest developments in hot stamping combine hot stamping to print logos and fixed information, and thermal transfer for the variables. Now one can have the high quality of hot stamped labels along with the advantage of random information. Data input to the printer is by keyboard, computer or other on-line device.

Wet ink is not suitable for high density random information. Hot stamping is marginal cost wise. Its main use is for very high quality multicolor labels

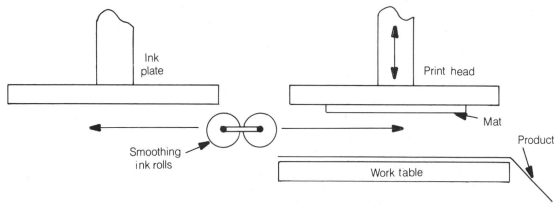

Fig. 38-16. Wet ink technique.

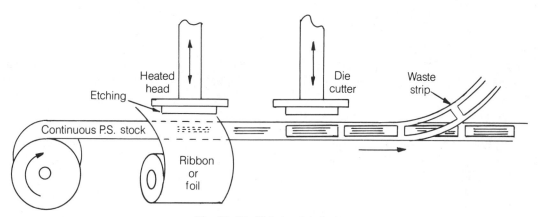

Fig. 38-17. Hot stamp technique.

but it can be used for medium and low density symbols.

In-House Printing with Microprocessors

With the introduction of the microprocessor some great new techniques have been developed. Just as hand held calculators, digital watches, and cameras have benefited, so has industrial printing equipment. There are some excellent new systems available. Choices include electrostatic, full-formed character, dot matrix, ink jet, thermal, thermal transfer, and laser.

Electrostatic Printing Electrostatic (also called ion deposition) is a noncontact, multistep process. It typically uses a dielectric transfer drum and specially coated paper. Patterns of electrical images are charged either onto the paper or the drum. Particles of dry ink called toner are attracted to the charged areas and are then fixed permanently by pressure rollers or by heat. This system is similar to your office copier except no master is required. See FIG. 38-18.

Instead of a master, several label formats are preprogrammed into the printer's memory. Variable data for each label field is chosen by the operator. First the format, then variable data are entered via keyboard or host computer. Label length and width are variable as are bar widths and character size.

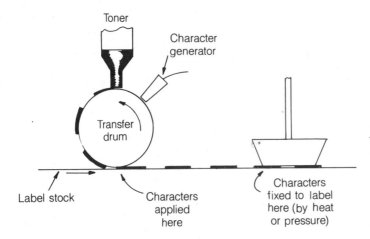

Fig. 38-18. Electrostatic printing process.

These printers are fast, operating at 400 to 800 inches per minute regardless of the amount of printing on the label. As they are a noncontact form of printing, they are quiet and suited to the office or computer room as well as in production areas. They are expensive, with a typical price of around $50,000.

Dot Matrix Printing   Dot matrix is another popular method of impact printing. This system produces a series of dots in a pattern to form characters or bars. On some printers the head is fixed and the label stock moves; on others the head moves and the stock is fixed. The label stock is usually moved by tractor feed using a sprocket or pins to engage holes in the edges of the stock. See FIG. 38-19.

The typical print head consists of a series of pins arranged in lines to form a five-by-seven or

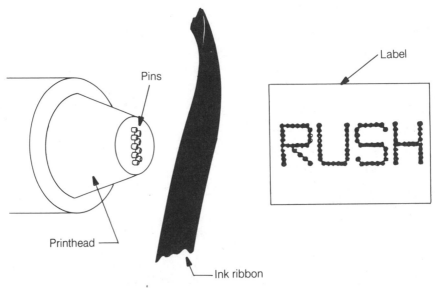

Fig. 38-19. Dot matrix impact printing process.

seven-by-nine matrix. A microprocessor activates solenoids causing the pins to move forward in the correct sequence to form characters. The basic unit of printing is the dot. Since these dots are .015 inch or larger, it can take 250 or more pin movements to make a single two-to-one bar code symbol with a narrow bar .015 inch by .250 inch long. Thus, print speed will vary according to the printed area.

Dot matrix will *crash print* multiple part forms, although normally only the top copy will be 100 percent scannable. Dot size prevents the printing of high density codes or odd ratios (like 2.2:1). Label size is limited only by the size of paper you can feed through the machine. Formats are infinitely variable and simple graphics can be printed, depending on the skill of the programmer. Prices range from $5,000 to $20,000.

Preformed Character Impact Printers Preformed character impact printers work very much like your office typewriter. The bars and characters are engraved or etched in reverse on a rotating drum. Paper, vinyl, or polyester label stock and a dry carbon ribbon pass between the drum and a hammer operated by an electromagnet. The hammer forces the paper and ribbon against the drum, causing the image to be transferred from the ribbon to the label. Each hammer stroke forms a complete character or bar. See FIG. 38-20.

The hammers are controlled by a microprocessor from data input via keyboard or computer. Label format is limited to what can be engraved or etched

on the drum so these printers are normally dedicated to a single application. Print quality is very high. Label production varies depending on the length of the label and the amount of data. Typically, 40 to 100 labels per minute can be printed.

This system can also produce a laminated label by laying a clear polyester or similar film over the label as printing takes place. A printer/applicator version is available that produces bar code labels from blank, die-cut stock and applies the label just printed to items moving on a conveyor. Label sizes range from one-quarter-inch-by-one inch to three-by-five inches. Up to 12 lines of type are possible on a variety of plain or preprinted pressure sensitive label stocks. Prices range from $9,000 to $19,000.

Thermal Printing Thermal printing has been used in office equipment for some time but is new to the bar code industry. Thermal printers use a heated print head and special heat-activated paper. The print head typically consists of square "dots" in a five-by-seven to 16-by-20 matrix that are selectively heated and cooled under microprocessor control. The heated dot causes chemicals in the paper to turn brown or black creating the image. Data is entered by CRT and keyboards or computer. See FIG. 38-21.

There are few moving parts so the printers are inexpensive, quiet, and are ideally suited to offices, libraries, and hospitals. Production is ten to 45 labels per minute. Some label stocks may not scan in the B900 nanometer range due to the chemical

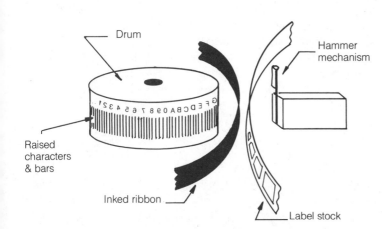

Fig. 38-20. Preformed character impact printing process.

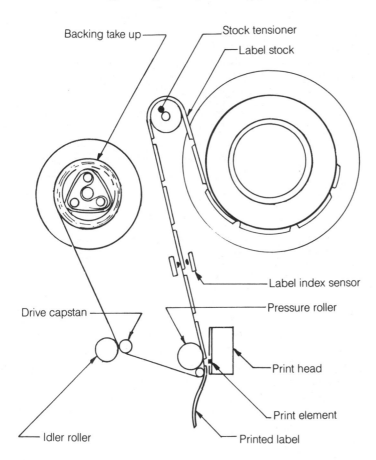

Fig. 38-21. Thermal printing process.

color of the stock, restricting scanning to visible light scanners. Simple graphics can be printed and at least one printer produces three color labels. Prices range from $2,000 to $20,000.

Thermal labels are printed with heat that causes the paper to change color. Thus, an environment where there is excessive heat can cause thermal labels to turn black. Bright sunlight also destroys the labels in a short time. So, for permanence, thermal would not typically be a first choice. Recent advances in paper design suggest that thermal labels will last up to 18 months indoors without excessive fading.

Thermal Transfer Printing Thermal transfer printing uses a one time printing ribbon and a variety of standard paper stocks. The heated "dots" cause the print ribbon to release its color and adhere it to the label media. The printing is of

better quality than thermal and the symbols scan in both the B633 and B900 bands. Prices are in the $10,000 to $20,000 area.

Thermal transfer solves the fading problem and, in addition, allows you a wider choice of label stocks and preprinting. This method is rapidly replacing thermal printing.

Ink Jet Printing Ink jet printing has been used on high speed filling lines by the beverage industry for several years. It is fast, up to 2,000 ten-digit codes per minute using a five-by-seven dot matrix format.

Most ink jets use a dyestuff ink that flows and spreads in the fibers or paper stocks, causing the dots to vary in size and shape depending on the substrate, dot density, and amount of ink. Because there is no carbon in the ink, some scanners are unable to read some ink jet prints. See FIG. 38-22.

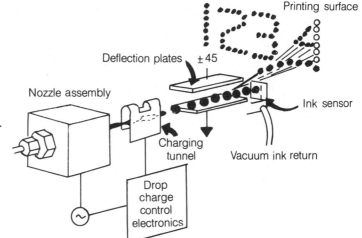

Fig. 38-22. Ink jet printing process.

Ink jet is ideal for date codes but does not lend itself to other than very low density symbols. Dot control is not precise; there is some ink splatter and line widths and shapes may vary.

A recent development has resulted in a family of drop on demand ink jet printers that use a hot melt ink that dries instantly on contact and eliminates ink spread. High-quality bars as narrow as .005 inch can be printed on some media and read by all scanners with a suitable dot size. The price range for ink jets is from $10,000 to $40,000.

Laser Printing Laser: a magic word describing a new science used in medicine, engineering, space, communications, and the printing industry. Two laser printing systems are available. One requires a high power laser that actually etches the print into the surface. The other system, most common to the printing industry, uses a low power laser that burns off a top coating allowing the substrate to show through.

Print speed is high, but print area is small. Thus, the laser is most useful for applying date codes or printing on very small areas such as on electronic components. Resolution directly on products is low; it is fine for human readable, but print contrast tends to be too low for consistent scanning.

A new series of laser office printers are used to print pages of data or sheets of labels. A laser

beam, microprocessor controlled, activates areas on a photoreceptor drum; toner is then attracted to the activated areas. The system is similar to electrostatic printing, described earlier. Print quality and contrast are superior with up to a 300 by 300 dots per inch matrix. Prices range from $5,000 to $250,000. See FIG. 38-23.

Purchased Labels

If random information is not required and it is known in advance what labels are needed, it may be more practical to purchase them from an outside vendor than to set up an in-house printing system. Labels purchased from a commercial label house will most likely be made by one of three methods. All three can meet any industry standards specified and will normally be checked for quality before shipment.

Photo composition can provide any density required. Since they are made by computer and a photo process, each label is actually a photograph and is the highest quality label obtainable.

Flexographic labels are the most common and are produced on high speed presses using wet ink and photographically produced printing plates. Quality is determined by the skill and attention of the pressman, and is normally in the mid-range.

Lithography is an offset process using a metal

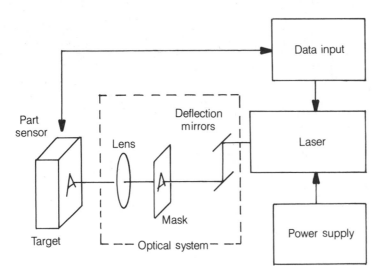

Fig. 38-23. Laser printing process.

plate and blanket. Quality is equal to flexographic. The label source will decide which method is most cost effective.

In choosing a process, one must consider the color of the reflected light from the printed label. Many standards and specifications require that the symbols scan in the B633-B900 nanometer range. The type of label stock and the ink or ribbon used affect this scanning range. Generally if a good quality EDP paper (not recycled stock), and an ink or ribbon containing carbon is used, there shouldn't be any problems. Some electrostatic and thermal labels can cause scanning problems in the infrared range due to chemicals in the paper.

How to Choose a Label Printing Process

The microprocessor has resulted in a tremendous improvement in printing technology. From a simple, stand-alone unit producing one label at a time by keyboard entry to computer control, each system has its own features, advantages, and benefits. We can classify these into four areas.

The first is *volume*. How many labels are needed per minute, shift, day, product, or run? How many character lines or documents are required? Next is *flexibility*. This is the ability of the printer to produce the format needed to meet the specification. Third is *resolution*. Does the density

of the code and the print quality meet the required standards? Last is *cost*. Which system is most cost efficient for the label intended?

TABLE 38-1 puts all the selection criteria and key operating characteristics in chart form for each of the in-house systems we have discussed. TABLE 38-2 lays out the pros and cons of each system.

High flexibility, volume, or resolution equal high cost. As volume, flexibility, and resolution drop, so too does the capital expense.

Labels, Adhesives, and Application

Once the system is chosen, there are three more things to consider: label stock, adhesive, and applying the label to the product. Labels are no longer just paper but vinyl, polyester, acetate, and other special materials. Adhesives can be permanent, removable, heat activated, or formulated to withstand extreme cold. As you consider label stock, adhesives, and application method, you have many possibilities. For example, the tire industry needed a label to go on a green (uncured) casing and withstand the vulcanizing process. A combination of special adhesive and polyester laminate solved the problem. Additional options include:

• Property management labels that self destruct if someone tries to remove them

Table 38-1. Selection Criteria and Characteristics of In-House Printing Techniques

	Impact Formed	Dot Matrix	Ink Jet	Ink jet Hot Melt	Thermal Transfer	Electrostatic	Laser
Bar Edge Definition	Excellent	Fair/Low	Low	Excellent	Excellent	Excellent	Excellent
Minimum Bar Width	.005	.015	.014	.005	.0075	.0075	.0075
High Density	Yes	No	No	Yes	Yes	Yes	Yes
Medium Density	Yes	Yes	Yes	Yes	Yes	Yes	Yes
Low Density	Yes	Yes	Yes	Yes	Yes	Yes	Yes
Scans-B633 Band	Yes	Yes	Yes	Yes	Yes	Yes	Yes
Scans-B900 Band	Yes	Yes	Maybe	Yes	Maybe	Yes	Yes
Dispense One Label	Yes	No	No	No	Yes	No	No
Prints Documents	No	Yes	No	Yes	No	No	No
Print Speed/Min.	40-100	30-50	2000	High	10-50	200-300	Up to 3000
Volume	Med	Low/Med	High	High	Low	High	High
Flexibility	Low	High	Med	High	Low	Med	High
Resolution	High	Med	Low	High	High	High	High
Cost-Printer	Med	Med	High	High	Low	High	High
Relative Label Cost	Low	Med	Low	Low	Med	Med	Low

- Laminated labels to withstand oil, dirt, chemicals, humidity, or other harsh environments
- Invisible (to the eye or office copier) labels for sensitive documents; scannable only with an infrared wand
- Circuit board labels that go through fluxing, wave soldering, and cleaning baths
- Colored labels for specialized applications

The list goes on and on. A label supplier can usually supply the correct stock and adhesive for the intended environment and life expectancy.

Labels are applied to products by machine or by hand. If hand application is employed, an adequate supply of preprinted labels must always be available. If labels are printed ahead of time, the addition of variables such as weight or lot number must be considered. If scanning with a fixed-beam scanner, the operator must place the labels in exactly the same spot each time. With moving-beam scanners, placement is not so critical.

A variety of automatic applicators are available. Some take a roll of labels, sense each product, strip a label from its backing, and apply the label with a jet of air or a pressure arm. Some incorporate a simple printer to add dates, lot numbers, or other variable data as the labels are applied. Type has to be manually changed each day or shift. No bar codes are possible.

Both the thermal printer and the fully formed impact printer offer a system that allows complete variable data, including random bar codes, and presents a label for hand application. As random data, from a scale for example, reaches the printer, a label is produced, stripped from its backing, and presented to the operator. The label is then applied. This system eliminates the need to stock preprinted labels. Some of these same printers can also print a label and automatically apply it in a predetermined position on a moving product. These systems combine the best in label printing and basic robotics under microprocessor control.

SUMMARY

The quality of the print is more important than the type of printer used. Quality is affected by ink spread, spots, voids, bar edge roughness, paper quality, and reflectance. Labels must be printed to the specifications of the code.

The current state of the art offers systems from small stand-alone units to full computer opera-

System	Pro	Con
Electrostatic	Large labels, high speed, prints horizontal and vertical bars on same label; intermix codes	No preprinting (if electrostatic paper is used); physically very large, no high density, special paper required
Impact	High quality print, high-med-or low density, preprinted stock, many accessories and options	Dedicated to one code; cannot rearrange format; noisy
Dot Matrix	Prints multi part forms, infinitely variable formats	Fair print quality, no high density, will not print to all specifications
Thermal	Quiet, inexpensive	Labels will fade in bright light or heat; special paper required
Thermal Transfer	Permanent high quality print, quiet, many stocks	Expensive label, print scratches off some stocks easily
Ink Jet (liquid ink)	Fast, silent	No high density, poor quality
Ink Jet (hot melt)	Fast, silent high density, excellent quality	Limited ink selection for substrates
Laser on products	Prints most surfaces	Expensive, slow, low contrast
Laser on Labels	Fast, superior quality	Very expensive printers
Wet Ink	Inexpensive	No consistent quality, labor intensive, no random data possible
Hot Stamp	Excellent quality, multicolor prints	No high density, plates expensive, no random data possible unless combined with thermal transfer

Table 38-2. Pros and Cons of Each Printing System

tion. Prices of systems are reasonable, considering what each can do, and more importantly, what each is required to do. Without a correctly printed symbol, the entire system fails. Remember the important rule in bar coding:

"It makes no difference how it looks to you; it is how it looks to the scanner and computer that is important."

AIM GLOSSARY OF TERMS

active tag   Active Tags are radio frequency identification devices which require batteries for their operation.

AIM   Automatic Identification Manufacturers, Inc. The publishers of this document.

alignment   In an automatic identification system, the relative position and orientation of a scanner to the symbol.

alphanumeric   The character set which contains letters, numbers, and usually other characters such as punctuation marks.

ANSI   The American National Standards Institute—nee United States of America Standards Institute (USASI)—is a non-governmental organization responsible for the development of voluntary industry standards.

antenna   In a radio frequency identification system, the antenna is the device which radiates and/or receives the RF energy.

aperture   The opening in an optical system implemented by a physical baffle that establishes the field of view.

ASCII   The character set and code described in American National Standard Code for Information Interchange, ANSI X3.4-1977. Each ASCII character is encoded with 7-bits (8 bits included parity check). The ASCII character set is used for information interchange between data processing systems, communication systems, and associated equipment. The ASCII set consists of both control and printing characters.

aspect ratio   In a bar code symbol, the ratio of bar height to symbol length.

autodiscrimination   The ability of bar code reading equipment to recognize and correctly decode more than one symbology.

average background reflectance   Expressed as a percent; the simple arithmetic average of the background reflectance from at least five different points on a sheet.

background   The spaces, quiet zones and area surrounding a printed symbol.

bar   The darker element of a printed bar code symbol.

bar code   An automatic identification technology which encodes information into an array of varying width parallel rectangular bars and spaces.

bar code character   A single group of bars and spaces which represent an individual number, letter, punctuation mark, or other symbol.

bar code density   The number of data characters which can be represented in a linear unit of measure. Bar code density is often expressed in characters per inch.

bar code label   A label which carries a bar code symbol and is suitable to be affixed to an article.

bar code reader   A device used to read a bar code symbol.

bar code symbol   (See "symbol".)

bar height   (See "bar length.")

bar length   The bar dimension perpendicular to the bar width. Also called height.

bar width   The thickness of a bar measured from the edge closest to the symbol start character to the trailing edge of the same bar.

bar width reduction   Reduction of the nominal bar width dimension on film masters or printing plates to compensate for systematic errors in some printing processes.

base line   A reference line used to specify the desired vertical position of characters printed on the same line.

BCD   Binary Coded Decimal. (See "Decimal, Binary Coded".)

bidirectional   A bar code symbol capable of being read successfully independent of scanning direction.

bidirectional read   (See "bidirectional".)

binary   The number system that uses only 1's and 0's.

bit   An abbreviation for "binary digit." A single element (0 or 1) in a binary number.

capture window   In an automatic identification system employing RF, that volume which defines the active portion of the radio frequency antenna pattern.

centerline   The vertical axis around which character elements are located for letters, numerals, or symbols.

character   1. A single group of bars and spaces which represent an individual number, letter, punctuation mark, or other symbol. 2. A graphic shape representing a letter, numeral, or symbol. 3. A letter, digit, or other symbol that is used as part of the organization, control, or representation of data.

character alignment   The vertical or horizontal position of characters with respect to a given set of reference lines.

character set   Those characters available for encodation in a particular automatic identification technology.

check character   A character included within a message whose value is used to perform a mathematical check to ensure the accuracy of that message.

check digit   (See "check character.")

clear area   (See "quiet zone.")

code   (See "bar code.")

code reader   (See "bar code reader.")

continuous code   A bar code symbology where all spaces within the symbol are parts of characters, e.g. USS-I 2/5. There is no intercharacter gap in a continuous code.

data rate   In an automatic identification system employing RF, the rate at which data are communicated between the identification tag and interrogator. Typical units are bits per second or bytes per second.

data capacity   The amount of memory in an RF tag.

Decimal, Binary Coded (BCD)   A numbering system using base 2, that represents each decimal digit by four binary bits, with the place values equal to 8, 4, 2, and 1, reading from left to right.

decoder   As part of a bar code reading system, the electronic package which receives the signals from the scanner, performs the algorithm to interpret the signals into meaningful data and provides the interface to other devices.

density   (See "character density.")

depth of field   The distance between the maximum and minimum plane in which a code reader is capable of reading symbols.

diffuse reflection   The component of reflected light which emanates in all directions from the reflecting surface.

discrete code   A bar code symbology in which the spaces between characters (intercharacter gap) are not part of the code, e.g., USS-39.

DSSG   Distribution Symbology Study Group.

EAN   European Article Numbering System, the international standard bar code for retail food packages.

element   In a bar code symbol, a single bar or space.

film master   A photographic film representation of a specific bar code or OCR symbol from which a printing plate is produced.

first read rate   (See "read rate.")

font   A specific size and style of printer's type.

guard bars   The bars which are at both ends and center of a UPC and EAN symbol. They provide reference points for scanning.

helium neon laser   A type of laser commonly used in bar code scanners. It emits coherent red light at a wavelength of 633 nm.

horizontal bar code   A bar code or symbol presented in such a manner that its overall length dimension is parallel to the horizon. The bars are presented in an array which look like a picket fence.

intercharacter gap   The space between two adjacent bar code characters in a discrete code. For example, the space between two characters in USS-39.

interleaved bar code   A bar code in which characters are paired together using bars to represent the first character and spaces to represent the second, i.e., USS-I 2/5. (See also "continuous code.")

interrogator   In an automatic identification system employing RF, the device which triggers the identifying tags to respond with a modulated RF message.

ladder code   (See "vertical bar code.")

laser scanner   An optical bar code reading device using a low energy laser light beam as its source of illumination.

LED   Light emitting diode. A semiconductor that produces light at a wavelength determined by its chemical composition. The light source often used in bar code readers.

LF   Low frequency. 30 – 300 kHz.

light pen   In a bar code system, a hand held scanning wand which is used as a contact bar code reader held in the hand. (See "wand scanner.")

MF   Medium frequency. 300 kHz to 3 MHz.

MHI   The Material Handling Institute, Inc.

microwave   A radio wave between 0.1 and 100 centimeters in wavelength or 1 to 100 GHz. Several automatic RF identification systems use this frequency band.

misread   A condition which occurs when the data output of a reader does not agree with the data encoded in the bar code symbol.

module   The narrowest nominal width unit of measure in a bar code.

modulo check digit or character   (See "check character.")

moving beam bar code reader   A scanning device where scanning motion is achieved by mechanically moving the optical geometry.

nanometer   A unit of measure used to define the wavelength of light. Equal to 10^{-9} meter.

nominal   The exact (or ideal) intended value for a specified parameter. Tolerances are specified as positive and negative deviations from this value.

nonread   In a bar code system, the absence of data at the scanner output after an attempted scan due to no code, defective code, scanner failure, or operator error.

numeric   A character set that includes only numbers.

OCR-A   An abbreviation commonly applied to the character set contained in ANSI Std. X3.17-1981. (ISO 1073 Part 1)

OCR-B   An abbreviation commonly applied to the character set contained in ANSI Std. X3.49-1975. (ISO 1073 Part II)

opacity   The optical property of a substrate material that minimizes show-through from the back side or the next sheet. The ratio of the reflectance with a black backing to the reflectance with a white backing. Ink opacity is the property of an ink that prevents the substrate from showing through.

orientation   The alignment of a bar code symbol with respect to horizontal. Two possible orientations are horizontal with vertical bars and spaces (picket fence) and vertical with horizontal bars and spaces (ladder).

overhead   In a bar code system, the fixed number of characters required for start, stop, and checking in a given symbol. For example, a symbol requiring a start/stop and two check characters contains four characters of overhead. Thus, to encode three characters, seven characters are required to be printed.

PCS   Print contrast signal—A measurement of the ratio of the reflectivities between the bars and spaces of a symbol, commonly expressed in percent. PCS is calculated as:

$$PCS = \frac{R_1 - R_d}{R_1}$$

where: R_1 is the reflectance of the light background
R_d is the reflectance of the dark bars.

passive tag   Passive tags are radio frequency identification devices that do not have any internal power source. Their energy source is the power emitted from adjacent antennas.

picket fence code   (See "horizontal bar code.")

pitch   Rotation of a bar code symbol about an axis parallel to the direction of the bars.

preprinted symbol   A symbol which is printed in advance of application either on a label or on the article to be identified.

print contrast   (See "PCS.")

print quality   The measure of compliance of a bar code symbol to the requirements of dimensional tolerance, edge roughness, spots, voids, reflectance, PCS, quiet zone, and encodation.

quiet zone   A clear space, containing no machine readable marks, which precedes the start character of a bar code symbol and follows the stop characters. Sometimes called the "Clear Area."

RF   (See "radio frequency.")

radio frequency   An electromagnetic wave.

radio frequency tag   An electronic tag capable of receiving/storing and/or transmitting digital information by means of, and in response to, RF energy.

range   In radio frequency system range is defined as the maximum allowable distance between the antenna and the tag.

read/only   Read/only identification systems employ radio frequency tags which contain preprogrammed data.

read/only tag   An RF tag that is capable of only being read.

read/write   In an RF automatic identification system, the capability of the RF tags to have their stored data changed by an external RF signal.

read/write tag   In an automatic identification system employing RF, an electronic tag capable of receiving, storing, and transmitting digital information.

read rate   The ratio of the number of successful reads on the first attempt to the number of attempts.

reflectance   The ratio of the amount of light of a specified wavelength or series of wavelengths reflected from a test surface to the amount of light reflected from a barium oxide or magnesium oxide standard under similar illumination conditions.

resolution   In a bar code system, the narrowest element dimension which can be distinguished by a particular reading device or printed with a particular device or method.

SAW   Surface acoustic wave. A technology by which radio frequency signals are converted to acoustic signals and confined within a small substrate made from lithium niobate or other crystalline materials. SAW waves propagate at relatively low speed with reference to radio waves and, as such, a small substrate may produce relatively long time delays.

scanner   An electronic device that electro-optically converts optical information into electrical signals. For RF systems see "interrogator."

self-checking   A bar code or symbol using a checking algorithm which can be independently applied to each character to guard against undetected errors.

show-through   The generally undesirable property of a substrate that permits underlying markings to be seen.

skew   Rotation of a bar code symbol about an axis parallel to the symbol's length.

sniff mode   The mode in which some radio frequency based systems search for a radio frequency tag. The interrogator continually emits trace amounts of radio waves until a tag is detected. Upon detection, interrogation is made at the maximum power.

space The lighter element of a bar code usually formed by the background between bars.

space width The thickness of a space measured from the edge closest to the symbol start character to the trailing edge of the same space.

spectral response The variation in sensitivity of a reading device to light of different wavelengths.

specular reflection The mirrorlike reflection of light from a surface.

spot The undesirable presence of ink or dirt in a space.

STAC Symbol Technical Advisory Committee to the Uniform Code Council, Inc. (See "Uniform Code Council.")

start-stop character or pattern A special bar code character that provides the scanner with start and stop reading instructions as well as scanning direction indicator. On a horizontally oriented symbol, the start character is normally at the left-hand end of and the stop character is normally at the right-hand end.

substitution error A misencodation, misread, or human key entry error where a character that was to be entered is substituted with erroneous information. Example: Correct information—1, 2, 3, 4; substitution—1, 2, 3, 5.

substrate The surface on which a bar code symbol is printed.

symbol A combination of bar code characters including start/stop characters, quiet zones, data characters, and check characters required by a particular symbology, which form a complete, scannable entity.

symbol density The number of data characters per unit length.

symbol length The distance between the outside edges of the quiet zones.

TCS Transport Case Symbol.

tilt Rotation of a bar code symbol about an axis perpendicular to the substrate.

UCS Uniform container symbol.

UHF Ultrahigh frequency. 300 to 3000 MHz.

ULF (See "VLF.")

UCC Uniform Code Council, Uniform product code Council, the organization which administers the UPC and other retail standards.

UPC Universal product code. The standard bar code symbol for retail food packages in the United States.

USS Uniform symbol specification. The current series of symbology specifications published by AIM; replace the USD series and currently include USS-I 2/5, USS-39, USS-93, USS-Codabar, and USS-128.

verifier A device that makes measurements of the bars, spaces, quiet zones, and optical characteristics of a symbol to determine if the symbol meets the requirements of a specification or standard.

vertical bar code A code pattern presented in such orientation that the axis of the symbol from start to stop is perpendicular to the horizon. The individual bars are in an array appearing as rungs of a ladder.

VLF Very low frequency. Frequency less than 30 KHz.

void The undesirable absence of ink in a bar.

wand (See "wand scanner.")

wand scanner A hand-held scanning device used as a contact bar code or OCR reader.

"X" dimension The nominal dimension of the narrow bars and spaces in a bar code symbol.

BIBLIOGRAPHY

Article on Factory Data Collection, Page 59, courtesy of Helmers Publishing Corporation, Peterborough, New Hampshire.

Chart, Page 63, courtesy of Intermec Corporation, Lynnwood, Washington.

Glossary courtesy of Automatic Identification Manufacturers, Inc., Pittsburgh, Pennsylvania.

Index

A

A.T. Kearney, 263
Abbott Laboratory, 20
accelerated life testing, 646
accounting, manufacturing resources
  planning for, 582-583
ACE expert system, 511
acquisition management, 207
activity-based costing, 260-263
adhocracy, 12
ADJUST robot programming system,
  733
aerospace industry, automated technologies in, 235-236
affirmative action, 24
Amalgamated Clothing and Textile Workers Union, 148
*American Institute of Industrial Engi-
  neers Transactions,* 590, 605, 606
*American Machinist and Automated
  Manufacturing,* 97
American National Standards Institute
  (ANSI), 276, 543
American Society for Quality Control
  (ASQC), 45
AML robot programming system, 728
analytic hierarchy process (AHP), job
  design and, 485-494
analytic solid modeling, 287
andon concept, 101
animation, 234, 409, 414, 422-423
anthropometry, 119, 120
  job design and, 461
  predictive job design modeling using,
  472-478
antialiasing, terminals, 273
APPAS process planning software, 376
appraisals, product, 42-43
Array Technologies, 253
Arthur D. Little Inc., 5
artificial intelligence (*see also* expert
  systems), 234, 378, 395, 496-525
  conferences held on, 497
  definition and development of, 496
  expert systems and, 498-501, 522-523
  FORTRAN, 497
  general problem solver (GPS) program, 497
  heuristic reasoning, 501-503
  languages for, 503

LISP, 497
  ongoing research in, 517-523
  pattern recognition, PERCEPTRON,
  497, 498
  probalistic states, 522
  process policy development, 521-522
  process state representation/transfor-
  mation, 520
  SHRDLU program for, 498
  simulation and, 423
  smart machines, 498
  smart program evolution, 497-498
  state performance measurement, 521
  state space representation, 518-520,
  522-523
  user interface for, 503
Askin, Ronald G., group technology,
  234, 317-366
assembly, automated (*see also* product
  design), 174
  physical simulation model for, 442-443
assembly, manual, 178
AT&T, 50, 276
ATLAS robot programming system, 729,
  730
attitudinal bargaining, unions, 144
audits, 43
AUTAP system, coding systems, process
  planning, 376
AutoCAD, 383
automated guided vehicles (AGVs),
  system control and, 630
automated layout design program
  (ALDEP), 453
automated material handling (AMH),
  528, 629, 631
automated technologies, 158-161, 235-
  249
  assembly, 174
  automatically programmed tools
  (APTs), 240
  batch production principles, 244
  CAD/CAM, 159, 174
  capacity requirements planning (CRP),
  240
  computer aided process planning
  (CAPP), 241
  computer integrated manufacturing
  (CIM), 241, 611-614
  computer numerical control (CNC),
  240, 535-542

costing, 237
  direct numerical control (DNC), 240,
  542-543
  distributed numerical control (DNC),
  240
  expert systems and, 515-517
  fixed vs. flexible automation, 238-239
  flexible manufacturing system (FMS),
  159, 174, 244
  global economy, effect of, 161
  group technology, 239-240, 247-248
  human engineering for, 237
  industrialized nation restructing, 161-
  162, 161
  industry breakdown for, 235-237
  information systems, 162-163, 198-
  219, 240-241
  job shop production principles, 243
  just-in-time (JIT) manufacturing, 240,
  244
  lead time reductions, 238, 244
  machining centers, 159
  manufacturing resources planning,
  567-588
  mass production principles, 243
  materials requirements planning
  (MRP), 240
  numerical control systems, 158, 240
  product redesign for, 189-190
  productivity vs., 237, 238
  programmable automation, 239
  quality control and, 237, 238
  responsible autonomy management,
  165, 166
  robots, 158-159
  safety engineering for, 237
  selection criteria for, 241
  social values vs., 160, 163-164
  strategic planning for, 132-138
  work-in-progress reductions, 237-238,
  244
Automatic Identification Manufacturers
  Association (AIM), 778
automatic identification systems (*see* bar
  coding; coding systems)
automatic test equipment (ATE), expert
  systems and, 511
automatically programmed tools (APTs),
  240
automotive industry, automated technologies in, 236

Other Bestsellers of Related Interest

CONFIGURATION MANAGEMENT HANDBOOK—W.V. Eggerman

Now, for the first time under one cover, the *Configuration Management Handbook* lays out field-tested plans that will help your firm achieve high performance on government-contracted jobs without struggling through years ot trial-and-error experience. Here's in-depth information on the scope and application of all DoD and military standards and specifications for the management, change control, and status reporting of contractor specifications, engineering drawings, and related technical documentaion. 210 pages, Illustrated. Book No. 3375, $29.95 hardcover only.

NETWORKING WITH NOVELL® NETWARE® : A LAN Manager's Handbook—Paul Christiansen, Steve King and Mark Munger

From the fundamentals of local area network terminology and processing to the basic components of NetWare, you're sure to find this book incisive as you investigate, set up, and use NetWare. Providing authoritative descriptions of network management and control features, the authors discuss: hardware, login script commands and shell functions, accounting and security, menuing systems and more. 232 pages, Illustrated. Book No. 3283, $18.95 paperback, $28.95 hardcover.

DESIGN GUIDELINES FOR SURFACE MOUNT TECHNOLOGY—Vern Solberg

Increased production volumes . . . more efficient, cost effective products . . . improved manufacturing efficiency . . . reduced size of electronic products—these are just a few of the advantages surface mount technology (SMT) can bring to your manufacturing process. This new guide offers the most detailed coverage available of the design, manufacture, and testing of substrate assemblies using SMT. 192 pages, 166 illustrations. Book No. 3199, $52.00 hardcover only.

GALLIUM ARSENIDE IC TECHNOLOGY: Principles and Practice—Neil Sclater

Now you can explore this decade's most exciting breakthrough in integrated circuit fabrication technology! With this book, Neil Sclater offers you the key to being on the cutting edge of the fastest growing field in semiconductor technology. Here is an excellent, non-mathematical overview of gallium arsenide (GaAs) ICs: how they are manufactured and packaged, what benefits they provide, and what the future holds for these innovative devices. 272 pages, 153 illustrations. Book No. 3089, $26.95 hardcover only.

THE LINEAR IC HANDBOOK—Michael S. Morley

Far more than a replacement for manufacturers' data books, *The Linear IC Handbook* covers linear IC offerings from all the major manufacturers—complete with specifications, data sheet parameters, and price information—along with technological background on linear ICs. It gives you instant access to data on how linear ICs are fabricated, how they work, what types are available, and techniques for designing them. 624 pages, 366 illustrations. Book No. 2672, $49.50 hardcover only.

ALGORITHMS ON GRAPHS—H.T. Lau

Algorithms on Graphs provides a ready source of plug-in FORTRAN code for some of the most useful algorithms yet developed. You can use these efficient algorithms to solve almost any graphing problem dealing with the principles of: connectivity, shortest paths, minimum spanning tree, traversability, and node coloring. For each topic, you will find a description of the problem, an outline of the solution, an example, and a listing of the code used. You can use the programs just as they are—no problem-solving is required. 238 pages, Illustrated. Book No. 3429, $29.95 hardcover only.

Other Bestsellers of Related Interest

TIPS AND TECHNIQUES FOR ELECTRONICS EXPERIMENTERS—2nd Edition—Don Tuite and Delton T. Horn

Packed with practical circuit-building tips and techniques, this completely revised and updated edition of a classic experimenter's guide also provides you with ten complete projects. These include a random number generator, an electronic organ, and a deluxe logic probe. Covering such basics as soldering and mounting components, finding and correcting malfunctions and making practical component substitutions, this book also covers: the use of breadboards and techniques for finishing your projects. 160 pages, 83 illustrations. Book No. 3145, $12.95 paperback, $19.95 hardcover.

PRACTICAL ANTENNA HANDBOOK
Joseph J. Carr

This is the most comprehensive guide available on designing, installing, testing, and using communications antennas. Carr provides a unique combination of theoretical engineering concepts and the kind of practical antenna know-how that comes only from hands-on experience in building and using antennas. He offers extensive information on a variety of antenna types (with construction plans for 16 different types), including high-frequency dipole antennas, microwave antennas, directional beam antennas, and more. 416 pages, 351 illustrations. Book No. 3270, $21.95 paperback, $31.95 hardcover.

Prices Subject to Change Without Notice.

Look for These and Other TAB Books at Your Local Bookstore

To Order Call Toll Free 1-800-822-8158
(in PA, AK, and Canada call 717-794-2191)

or write to TAB BOOKS, Blue Ridge Summit, PA 17294-0840.

Title	Product No.	Quantity	Price

☐ Check or money order made payable to TAB BOOKS

Charge my ☐ VISA ☐ MasterCard ☐ American Express

Acct. No. _____ Exp. _____

Signature: _____

Name: _____

Address: _____

City: _____

State: _____ Zip: _____

Subtotal $ _____

Postage and Handling
($3.00 in U.S., $5.00 outside U.S.) $ _____

Add applicable state
and local sales tax $ _____

TOTAL $ _____

TAB BOOKS catalog free with purchase; otherwise send $1.00 in check or money order and receive a $1.00 credit on your next purchase.

Orders outside U.S. must pay with international money order in U.S. dollars.

TAB Guarantee: If for any reason you are not satisfied with the book(s) you order, simply return it (them) within 15 days and receive a full refund. BC